MW01405620

Leo Strauss on Maimonides

Leo Strauss on Maimonides

The Complete Writings

EDITED WITH AN INTRODUCTION BY

Kenneth Hart Green

THE UNIVERSITY OF CHICAGO PRESS
Chicago and London

Leo Strauss (1899–1973) was one of the preeminent political philosophers of the twentieth century. He is the author of many books, among them *The Political Philosophy of Hobbes*, *Natural Right and History*, and *Spinoza's Critique of Religion*, all published by the University of Chicago Press. **Kenneth Hart Green** is associate professor in the Department for the Study of Religion at the University of Toronto. He is the author of *Jew and Philosopher: The Return to Maimonides in the Jewish Thought of Leo Strauss.*

The University of Chicago Press, Chicago 60637
The University of Chicago Press, Ltd., London
© 2013 by The University of Chicago
All rights reserved. Published 2013.
Printed in the United States of America
22 21 20 19 18 17 16 15 14 13   1 2 3 4 5

ISBN-13: 978-0-226-77677-4 (cloth)
ISBN-13: 978-0-226-77679-8 (e-book)
ISBN-10: 0-226-77677-8 (cloth)
ISBN-10: 0-226-77679-4 (e-book)

Library of Congress Cataloging-in-Publication Data

Strauss, Leo.
 Leo Strauss on Maimonides : the complete writings / edited with an introduction by Kenneth Hart Green.
   pages cm.
 Includes bibliographical references and index.
 ISBN-13: 978-0-226-77677-4 (cloth : alk. paper)
 ISBN-10: 0-226-77677-8 (cloth : alk. paper)
 ISBN-13: 978-0-226-77679-8 (e-book)
 ISBN-10: 0-226-77679-4 (e-book)   1. Maimonides, Moses, 1135–1204.
2. Jewish philosophy.   I. Green, Kenneth Hart, 1953–   II. Title.
 B759.M34S76 2013
 181′.06—dc23
                                                                2012022900

♾ This paper meets the requirements of ANSI/NISO Z39.48-1992 (Permanence of Paper).

In memory of four great teachers:

EMIL FACKENHEIM

ALLAN BLOOM

MARVIN FOX

ALEXANDER ALTMANN

"There is no honor higher than that which is due to a teacher, and no reverence deeper than that which should be paid to him."
MAIMONIDES, "HILKHOT TALMUD TORAH," CHAPTER 5, PARAGRAPH 1, IN *SEFER HA-MADDA, MISHNEH TORAH*

"One repays a teacher badly if one always remains only a pupil."
NIETZSCHE, "THE BESTOWING VIRTUE," PART 1, CHAPTER 22, SECTION 3, IN *THUS SPOKE ZARATHUSTRA*

Contents

Editor's Preface xi
Acknowledgments xxxiii

Editor's Introduction:
Leo Strauss's Essays and Lectures on Maimonides 1

I. Point of Departure: Why Study Medieval Thinkers?

1. How to Study Medieval Philosophy (1944) 91

II. On Maimonides

2. Spinoza's Critique of Maimonides (1930) 119

3. Cohen and Maimonides (1931) 173

4. The Philosophic Foundation of the Law: Maimonides' Doctrine of Prophecy and Its Sources (1935) 223
   Appendix 4A: Introduction to *Philosophy and Law* [the First Two and the Last Three Paragraphs] 266
   Appendix 4B: Chapter 2 of *Philosophy and Law*, "The Legal Foundation of Philosophy: The Commandment to Philosophize and the Freedom of Philosophizing" [the Introductory Section and Section B, "Maimonides"] 269

5. Some Remarks on the Political Science of Maimonides and Farabi (1936) 275

6. The Place of the Doctrine of Providence according to Maimonides (1937) 314

7. Review of *The Mishneh Torah*, Book 1, by Moses Maimonides, Edited according to the Bodleian Codex with Introduction, Biblical and Talmudical References, Notes, and English Translation by Moses Hyamson (1939) 329

8. The Literary Character of *The Guide of the Perplexed* (1941) 341

9. Maimonides' Statement on Political Science (1953) 399

10. Introduction to Maimonides' *The Guide of the Perplexed* (1960) 417

11. How To Begin To Study *The Guide of the Perplexed* (1963).. 491

12. Notes on Maimonides' *Book of Knowledge* (1967)............ 550

13. Note on Maimonides' *Treatise on the Art of Logic* (1968) 569

14. Note on Maimonides' *Letter on Astrology* (1968)............ 572

III. On Isaac Abravanel, the Last Medieval Maimonidean

15. On Abravanel's Philosophical Tendency and Political Teaching (1937) 579

Appendix: The Secret Teaching of Maimonides (c. 1937–40) 615
Abbreviations: Editions to Which Leo Strauss Frequently Refers, or Recent Editions and Translated Versions of Works to Which the Editor Frequently Refers 619
Sources and History of the Texts 627
Bibliography: Selected Works on Leo Strauss and Medieval Thought Related to Maimonides 633
Index 647

Editor's Preface

The present volume is dedicated to offering in as complete a form as possible the chief essays and lectures of Leo Strauss on Moses Maimonides. It consists mainly of those essays that appeared in print entirely at Strauss's direction during his own life (1899–1973), but also those that were disseminated as lectures which he composed and delivered, and which remained unfinished as literary works.[1] Thus, this volume embraces sixteen works by Strauss; in

---

1. The six exceptions to works published by Strauss himself during his life are as follows, with the essential details presented insofar as they are known to the present editor. (1) The lecture "How to Study Medieval Philosophy" Strauss did not publish himself; he apparently delivered it as a lecture at the Fourth Institute of Biblical and Post-biblical Studies, held on 16 May 1944. However, this seems (as the evidence suggests) to have been delivered on several occasions, which might seem to make it closer to being a publishable piece—although it is no doubt still an unfinished lecture, as the notes to it will attest. (2) The lecture "Cohen and Maimonides" (originally "Cohen und Maimuni") was apparently delivered, in some form, on 4 May 1931 at the Academy for the Science of Judaism in Berlin. However, due to the shape of the manuscript, in what form it was delivered can no longer be determined with certainty; it seems unlikely to have been in the precise form of the manuscript, which in length alone (never mind its unfinished quality) seems impossible for the span of a single lecture. Thanks to the pioneering research and valiant deciphering labors of Heinrich Meier, yielding consistent and completed works based on both Strauss's handwritten manuscripts and his marginal notes to typed works, we currently possess Strauss's first nonhistoricist historical treatment of Maimonides' thought. In the lecture, Strauss criticizes the defense of Maimonides on modern, neo-Kantian grounds by Hermann Cohen; i.e., the former is considered, in principle, wiser than the latter, and hence the former is the superior of the latter with regard to philosophic thinking. But "Cohen and Maimonides" also assumes a very different sort of approach to how best to read Maimonides than the one derived from Cohen, never mind Spinoza. If this is the case, then perhaps it is better to say that in this lecture there is available the first prolonged "Straussian" reflection, which anticipates the approach of *Philosophy and Law*. That is to say, he uses a premodern thinker (Maimonides) as a standard against which a modern thinker (Cohen) is measured, which vastly surpasses the elements of such an approach as they started to embryonically manifest themselves in "Spinoza's Critique of Maimonides." This is a lecture that did not appear in print during Strauss's own life, but had to wait until Heinrich Meier made it accessible in *Philosophie und Gesetz: Frühe Schriften*, vol. 2 of *Gesammelte Schriften*, pp. 393-429. Meier published it, of course, in its German original; the version of it made available to readers in the present volume is its first English translation. Although it too is evidently not a completely finished piece, as a quick perusal of the text and the text-critical notes by the editor makes plain (pp. 429-36), it is certainly worthy of most careful consideration. Items (3) and (4) are the two brief "Notes": the first is on Maimonides' *Treatise on the Art of Logic*, and the second is on Maimonides' *Letter on Astrology*. All indications available to me are that the "Notes" were more or less finished, carefully composed pieces, and hence as close as possible to being publication ready. He planned for the two "Notes" to appear in print in his

twelve, what we see are finished essays, of widely varying length, which are mostly works of literary art, and which encompass topics as assorted in Maimonides' oeuvre as prophecy, providence, law, logic, theology, political science, astrology, codifying of law, numerology, hermeneutics, and imaginative or artistic style as it issues in cognitive purpose. And what we encounter in the three lectures (chronologically listed), "Cohen and Maimonides," "How to Study Medieval Philosophy," and "Introduction to Maimonides' *The Guide of the Perplexed*," are works originally designed for speaking, and yet very unevenly presented with regard to how finished they are, but since they were addressed to very different audiences and in very different times and places (as well as phases of his own life), also of unusually divergent character in terms of approach, style, and substance. At the end is an appendix, "The Secret Teaching of Maimonides." It consists of a brief fragment, formally a two-page academic proposal, which in content is mostly supplementary to Strauss's main corpus of works on Maimonides. However, the piece is still quite revealing for its reflection of the major turn in his thought about Maimonides as it was then just in process. This fragment shows the first signs of his detection that there is an esoteric literary dimension in Maimonides' *The Guide of the Perplexed*.

---

last volume, whose contents and arrangement were of his own design—see *Studies in Platonic Political Philosophy*, with the comment by Joseph Cropsey, p. vii—but which he was not permitted to complete by his own hand. (5) "Introduction to Maimonides' *The Guide of the Perplexed*" is a lecture that Strauss delivered at the Hillel House of the University of Chicago in two sessions, on Sunday 7 February 1960 and on Sunday 14 February 1960. He neither published this lecture by himself nor even preserved it in written form, so as to allow for the use of a manuscript. Instead, the lecture has been transcribed by the present editor from five tapes which do survive (although the tapes have since been technically remastered to ensure greater accuracy); that makes this the first appearance in print of the lecture. (6) The fragment appearing as an appendix, "The Secret Teaching of Maimonides," was recently discovered in the Leo Strauss Archive in the library of the University of Chicago. No doubt numerous advantages accrue to us, helping advance our comprehension of Strauss's thought, from the fortunate survival of these materials, and especially as concentrated in the three lectures. Yet even with this advance, it is also fair to say that Strauss's published works by themselves represent perhaps his major legacy thus far and have already transformed Maimonidean studies in the 20th century. Indeed, it looks most likely that this revolutionary scholarly work, which appeared in print during Strauss's life, will continue to make a major impact on Maimonidean studies at the very least in the 21st century and perhaps beyond. Hence, it was thought best that these be brought together in one volume of their own, based on what was actually published through Strauss's efforts, and on what has become known about the lectures edited through the efforts of others. Besides the impressive essays of Strauss's (forming the bulk of the present volume), which so far have not diminished in their impact, it remains to be seen what force the previously unpublished or unfinished works will carry (just appearing in print in the present volume for the benefit of English-speaking readers): whether they will exercise an equivalently significant influence on future views of Maimonides, not to mention whether they will reshape our view of Strauss's own philosophic achievement and scholarly enterprise. And since a good deal of Strauss's youthful oeuvre remains untranslated (much with bearing on Maimonides), it is to be hoped that some serious and venturesome scholar will set it as his special task to translate this supplementary work, and thus make it better known in the future.

Of the three spoken lectures by Strauss, the first is relatively youthful and is a trial-run attempt to differentiate Maimonides from his modern neo-Kantian admirer Hermann Cohen, in which he shows how Maimonides' wisdom perplexingly combined an astonishingly "modern" with a startlingly "unmodern" sensibility. Once Strauss had recognized this peculiar but compelling mixture of Maimonides, he was constrained to pry the medieval writer away from the smothering embrace of his modern admirer, for Cohen's was a blinding esteem that led him to distort Maimonides' true views and prevented him from reaching a sober assessment. The second (chronologically, although it appears first in the present book) is a rhetorically skilled and even polemical presentation of the proper manner of approach to historical and philosophical study of medieval texts, ideas, and thinkers, in which Maimonides is virtually the main focus, and by which Strauss attempts to show how we can move beyond the historicist approach to history, which thus can free us to read these authors as they wished to be read and not as modern prejudice tends to cause us to misread them. It also contains Strauss's very enlightening response to Gershom Scholem's famous blast in *Major Trends in Jewish Mysticism* against the medieval Jewish philosophers, whom he criticized for the absence of a persuasive, compelling, and efficacious popular religious teaching, and whom he contrasted—much to the disfavor of the Jewish philosophers—with the Jewish mystics. And in the third, Strauss was concerned with leading students toward an accurate overview of Maimonides' thought and teaching, grounded in the mature understanding that Strauss had reached of *The Guide of the Perplexed*, which rather than mellowing with age had become radicalized. This is true even though it is also the case that the lecture is much clearer on the surface—and much gentler in presentation—than the parallel essay (i.e., number 11 in this book), which is the most carefully composed in its every detail, the deepest in its consideration of Maimonides' thinking, and yet undoubtedly the most difficult to penetrate of his works on Maimonides. This last lecture was delivered in 1960 at the Hillel House of the University of Chicago, and it shows Strauss's impressive ability to elegantly and articulately encapsulate his essential insights about Maimonides, while expressing those perceptions in a well-ordered and vividly dramatic fashion. Transcribed from tape recordings (almost complete, but still unfortunately fractional and imperfect), which have not previously been published, this introductory lecture focuses directly on Maimonides' *Guide* by addressing itself to the book's dialectical literary style and unfolding structure, as well as by awakening a needful uncertainty about its purpose. But it also limns in broad contours Strauss's deepest insight about Maimonides, i.e., that *how* he expressed himself in his greatest book is the key to *what* he taught and thought. For Strauss indicates in this lecture that however much Maimonides may have allowed his thinking to be shaped and guided by his philosophic teachers (especially Plato, Aristotle, and Farabi), he always remained his own man as a thinker, and he never forgot to use what they taught him for his own original ends, which were fully in accord with the exigencies of the Jewish spiritual situation (such as the relation between reason and revelation, as it impinges on individual searchers and on the collective political entity) and its historical imperatives.[2] In doing so, Strauss also shows us in oblique fashion how surprisingly relevant Maimonides' seemingly "medieval" mode of thought as writer, thinker, and teacher is to our most modern concerns and issues, and hence how very much he still has to teach us, even while with our very different historical experience we should never merely imitate or blindly follow his instruction.

These works in their entirety span an almost fifty-year period, allowing us to observe Strauss as a highly resourceful, bold, free, and vigorous intellect while he excavates the lost treasure of a great mind, in the process of which he reaches ever-deeper levels in the penetration of his thought. In other words, these essays and lectures record Strauss's long way toward and deepening reflection on Maimonides. In them, we are also able to discern how Strauss's efforts moved him from what has been previously designated by the present writer as his first through his third stages of development with respect to his own thinking about Maimonides. These, combined as a totality, do not surpass one another so much as each obtains a further level of profundity in the ability to encompass Maimonidean thought as to what preceded it, forming a completed unity. To simplify these levels as each may be reduced to a single word, I believe that they may be summarized as follows: the theological; the political; and the esoteric.[3]

In the middle section of the present volume, entitled "On Maimonides," the essays appear in chronological order of publication (or if lectures, in order of composition and delivery). The first and the last items in the continuously numbered table of contents, because they are not devoted directly to Mai-

---

2. See "Introduction to Maimonides' *Guide*," chap. 10 below, i.e., his very last comment at the end of the discussion period.

3. The notion of Strauss's thought as passing through three distinguishable stages of development in his approach to Maimonides (and on which basis Strauss's entire thought may be analyzed) has been elaborated in Green, *Jew and Philosopher*.

monides per se, are presented in separate sections. The first item (number 1) is a lecture on studying medieval philosophy in general, although specific issues with respect to Maimonides are a constant point of reference. The last item (number 15) is an essay on rethinking Isaac Abravanel with regard to his philosophical and political orientation, although it emerges from this serious reconsideration that Abravanel is Maimonides' faithful student as well as antagonist. These first and last numbers not only do not address Maimonides directly, but also do not follow the chronological order of Strauss's essays as in the middle section. What they do both demonstrate, however, is how much Strauss's powerful thinking about the medievals was galvanized by his often-unpredicted sightings of a previously unseen Maimonides, which set much of the direction and agenda for his study of medieval philosophy, even though he elaborates on themes only obliquely related to his designedly Maimonidean essays.

The aspiration to completeness could not be achieved perfectly. First, all of *Philosophy and Law* (1935) has as it ostensible purpose a leading focus on Maimonides (and his "predecessors," i.e., Alfarabi and Avicenna), but it is already in print twice as an English-language book. As a result, only the chapter expressly dedicated to Maimonides, and several other paragraphs in which he is directly discussed by name, were selected for the present volume. Second, numerous mentions of, references to, or passages (occasionally substantial) on Maimonides dispersed through Strauss's other works could obviously not all be gathered or contained in the present volume if it was to achieve its intended aim of focusing mainly on Strauss's most impressive and transformative essays on Maimonides while confined to the limitations of a single book.[4] Third, Heinrich Meier, in the remarkable edition of Strauss's

---

4. The most striking of such mentions, which also in my opinion shows the direction in which Strauss's mind moved, is contained in the opening three paragraphs and the single closing paragraph of his first great essay on the "Second Teacher" (following Aristotle), i.e., Abu Nasr al-Farabi (c. 872–951): "Farabi's *Plato*," in *Louis Ginzberg Jubilee Volume*, ed. Saul Lieberman et al. (New York: American Academy for Jewish Research, 1945), pp. 357–93, especially pp. 357–58 and 392–93. For readers lacking ready access to Strauss's key Farabi essay, those essential paragraphs read as follows (shorn of the technical notes in the first three paragraphs):

> It is generally admitted that one cannot understand the teaching of Maimonides' *Guide of the Perplexed* before one has understood the teaching of "the philosophers"; for the former presents itself as a Jewish correction of the latter. To begin with, one can identify "the philosophers" with the Islamic Aristotelians, and one may describe their teaching as a blend of genuine Aristotelianism with neo-Platonism and, of course, Islamic tenets. If, however, one wants to grasp the principle transforming that mixture of heterogeneous elements into a consistent, or intelligible, whole, one does well to follow the signposts erected by Maimonides himself.
>
> In his letter to Samuel ibn Tibbon, he makes it abundantly clear that he considered the greatest authority in philosophy, apart from Aristotle himself, not Avicenna or Averroes, nor even

complete writings that he has so far produced and continues to work on, has managed to discover, decipher, and edit several manuscripts (some not smaller than the essays in the present volume) of youthful works related to Maimonides, even if not directly on him. This is not even to mention numer-

---

Avempace [i.e., Abu Bakr ibn Bajja], but Farabi. Of Farabi's works, he mentions in that context only one by its title, and he recommends it to Ibn Tibbon in the strongest terms. Thus we may assume to begin with that he considered it Farabi's most important book. He calls that book *The principles of the beings*. Its original title is *The political governments*.

There can be no doubt as to the proper beginning, i.e., the only beginning which is not arbitrary, of the understanding of Maimonides' philosophic background: one has to start from an analysis of Farabi's *political governments*. It would be unwise to attempt such an analysis now. In the first place, we lack a satisfactory edition. Above all, the full understanding of the book presupposes the study of two parallel works of Farabi's, *The principles of the opinions of the people of the virtuous city* and *The virtuous religious community*, the second of which has not yet been edited at all. Maimonides presumably preferred *The political governments* to these parallel presentations. To discover the reason for that preference, or, at any rate, to understand *The political governments* fully, one has to compare the doctrines contained in that book with the doctrines contained in the parallel works, and thus to lay bare the teaching characteristic of *The political governments*. For that teaching consists, to some extent, of the silent rejection of certain tenets which are adhered to in the other two works.

* * *

It would be rash to maintain that the foregoing observations suffice for establishing what Farabi believed as regards the *substantiae separatae*. They do suffice however for justifying the assertion that his philosophy does not stand and fall with the acceptance of such substances. For him, philosophy is the attempt to know the essence of each of all beings: his concept of philosophy is not based on any preconceived opinion as to what allegedly real things are truly real things. He has infinitely more in common with a philosophic materialist than with any nonphilosophic believer however well-intentioned. For him, philosophy is essentially and purely theoretical. It is the way leading to the science of the beings as distinguished from the science of the ways of life. It is the way leading to that science rather than that science itself: the investigation rather than the result. [*Strauss's note*: Not without good reason does he introduce philosophy as the art which supplies the science of the beings, and not as that science itself. Consider also § 26.] Philosophy thus understood is identical with the scientific spirit "in action," with *skepsis* in the original sense of the term, i.e., with the actual quest for truth which is animated by the conviction that that quest alone makes life worth living, and which is fortified by the distrust of man's natural propensity to rest satisfied with satisfying, if unevident or unproven, convictions. A man such as Farabi doubtless had definite convictions concerning a number of important points, although it is not as easy to say what these convictions were as the compilers of textbooks and of most monographs seem to think. But what made him a philosopher, according to his own view of philosophy, were not those convictions, but the spirit in which they were acquired, in which they were maintained, and in which they were intimated rather than preached from the housetops. Only by reading Maimonides' *Guide* against the background of philosophy thus understood, can we hope eventually to fathom its unexplored depths.

As for Strauss's peculiar, ironic, and provocative comments in his letters, consider what he writes to his friend Gershom Scholem on 2 October 1935: "Provisionally I will publish an introduction to the *Moreh* with the title: 'Hobbes' Political Science in Its Development,' which should come out next year with Oxford Press." See *Hobbes Politische Wissenschaft und zugehörige Schriften—Briefe*, vol. 3 of *Gesammelte Schriften*, p. 716. If he is referring to *The Political Philosophy of Hobbes* (Oxford: Clarendon, 1936), how precisely is it an "introduction" to the *Guide*? For further comments on Rambam in letters to Scholem, cf. also pp. 714, 715–16, and 742–44, for letters of 14 December 1934, 2 October 1935, and 22 November 1960.

ous enlightening passages in his letters (at least those which Meier has so far edited) that present moments of breakthrough to discovery. It was not possible to contain all of these youthful unfinished works or portions of unrelated mature works in a single volume; as for the letters, a separate volume dedicated to a selection of these is currently being worked on and will in due course appear in print.[5] However, the letters are referred to often and at length in the notes of the "Editor's Introduction," which can guide readers to the passages relevant to Strauss's thought on and rediscovery of Maimonides.

Hence, readers of Strauss's work and searchers in Strauss's thought should have no doubt in their minds that the impact made by Maimonides on Strauss as thinker and writer passes beyond the limits of the sixteen essays and lectures contained in this book. This larger impact is reflected by comments and thoughts that appear in numerous other works (as well as several key moments in which ideas of or passages in Maimonides are alluded to),[6] which is especially—although not only—the case in his analyses of the great Islamic philosophers. However, I do not hesitate to assert that this volume contains, to state my view unambiguously, the most significant, the deepest, and the most powerful contributions that Strauss made, in a bold and venturesome scholarly career, devoted to the rediscovery of a lost Maimonides, and to the recovery of his genuine thought and teaching (at least with regard to its essential insights) as in substantial measure expressing a still valid and still useful wisdom.[7] And this is not to obscure the fact that this "contribu-

---

5. It is to be edited and translated by Werner Dannhauser. One hopes that this will contain a goodly portion of the letters in which Maimonides is discussed.

6. It is difficult to know for certain (but, I would venture to say, highly unlikely) whether Strauss's revolutionary approach to Plato (from which most of the best of recent Platonic studies have derived, even if these are not "Straussian") would have been possible if it had not been preceded by his great discovery of the "esoteric-exoteric" divide in Maimonides' *Guide*. This is the once-ignored fact that Plato was deliberately a writer of dialogues (and not treatises), in which a hidden dimension—and perhaps ultimately the most significant dimension—resides beneath or beyond the literary surface of the characters, speeches, actions, etc., as defined by the author, who controls the story told as a work of art. To know the teaching and thought of Plato requires a double awareness of what occurs on the surface and what is being conveyed (and concealed) in a subtler sense beneath the surface. See Laurence Lampert, "Strauss's Recovery of Esotericism," in *Cambridge Companion to Leo Strauss*, especially pp. 63–69. He notices and traces, in Strauss's letters of 1938–39 to his friend Jacob Klein, the phases in Strauss's process of "recovering" esotericism as he moves almost directly from Maimonides to Plato.

7. With regard to the title of this book, *Leo Strauss on Maimonides: The Complete Writings*, it is entirely the decision of the present editor. I assume full responsibility for the title, although it is only proper to acknowledge that it was arrived at in consultation with Professor Nathan Tarcov, administrator of the Leo Strauss Literary Estate, and with John Tryneski of the University of Chicago Press. However, for any who might be surprised by "The Complete Writings" because it might seem to imply that the present works were all equally finished writings, I have already discussed the need to keep in mind the literary

tion" (as Strauss also chose for the subtitle of the four still-noteworthy essays in *Philosophy and Law*) remains highly controversial, almost fifty years since the last of Strauss's major works on Maimonides were produced. Indeed, it is no exaggeration to suggest that this may have been one of the four great scholarly rediscoveries of the 20th century in the field of Jewish studies (to which field, besides philosophy and political science, he formally contributed his study of Maimonides), on par with his friend Gershom Scholem's recovery and presentation of Kabbalah, with the rescue, retrieval, and editing of the treasure trove of medieval materials stored in the Genizah of the Ben Ezra Synagogue in Cairo, and with the accidental uncovering in the modern state of Israel and the gradual editing by scholars around the world of the ancient Dead Sea Scrolls of Second Temple–era Judea.

This points to one of the key tools of investigation that enabled Strauss to make his revolutionary rediscovery: though not a historicist, he was keenly conscious of history and historical context. He insisted that Maimonides' achievement, as teacher, writer, and thinker, must be considered in the proper historical context of medieval Jewish philosophic thought primarily as it emerged from and related itself to Muslim philosophic, political, and theological thought. This is to be contrasted with the Christian philosophic, theological, and political thought on which Maimonides would subsequently exercise an enormous influence, especially but not solely through Thomas Aquinas, and in which light Maimonides' achievement tended to be seen by most 18th-, 19th-, and 20th-century Western scholars. It is not that this historical impact, which he may well have made, is to be slighted, and it is not to dismiss the possibility that considering on whom Maimonides' teaching made its greatest impact may even reveal something significant about this teaching itself; it is only to maintain that it is a distorting lens through which to view Maimonides himself in his own right, and not as one who merely prepared subsequent trends. Indeed, this had been the tendency of most scholarly work on Maimonides until Strauss appeared on the scene and forced a

---

dissimilarity between the two types of works in this book, i.e., the need to read the essays and the lectures according to a different standard. But it should at least be noted that the lectures in this book were originally delivered by Strauss in written form; and since two of the three of them have previously appeared in print, they have already entered the world as separate, essay-like written works. With regard to titles, and especially that of the companion volume, Kenneth Hart Green, *Leo Strauss and the Rediscovery of Maimonides* (Chicago: University of Chicago Press, 2013), I refer readers to Strauss's frequent use of the word "rediscovery" in the essays and lectures of this book: see especially "Cohen and Maimonides," "The Literary Character of *The Guide of the Perplexed*," and "Notes on Maimonides' *Book of Knowledge*," chaps. 3, 8, and 12 below.

radical transformation in understanding (whose unfolding has not yet been fully completed), overturning several centuries of entrenched conventional scholarly wisdom, for he also insisted on a thoroughly revised view of what the Islamic philosophers expressed in their books.[8] Strauss also maintained that Maimonides must be compared with the very greatest thinkers in the history of philosophy, from Plato on the one end to Machiavelli on the other. Further, this requires the consideration of his thought as much in relation to political science, to philosophy, and to literary art as to theology, Judaica, and the study of religion in its historical aspect. Last but not least, while it may be true that Strauss's writings encompass several stages in the development of his thought as it spanned almost fifty years,[9] even so and in the spite of these significant changes, this body of work evinces greater impressiveness for the unity of his thought in its essential contours. For almost from the beginning to the end of his life he perceived the heart and soul of Maimonides' thought in his capacity to make greater cognitive and moral sense of the conflict between reason and revelation, and hence to reconcile these two forces better, than any modern thinker with whom he was acquainted.[10] At the very least we can suggest about this rediscovery that, if not for his transformative and even electrifying relation to Maimonides established during his 1920s spiritual struggles and his 1930s wanderings around Europe and eventually to America, Strauss would likely not have "become Strauss," i.e., the Leo Strauss who is known to us from his fully mature American achievements.[11]

---

8. See Georges Tamer, *Islamische Philosophie und die Krise der Moderne: Das Verhältnis von Leo Strauss zu Alfarabi, Avicenna, und Averroes* (Leiden: E. J. Brill, 2001). See also "Introduction to Maimonides' *Guide*," chap. 10 below: "A more adequate understanding of Maimonides may be said to have started when people began to take seriously what Maimonides said himself about his [own] background. . . . It compels us to make an entirely new beginning, which is in fact identical with Maimonides' own beginning."

9. For a differently oriented study from the analysis mentioned in n. 3 above, one which lays greater stress on the connection with Farabi as most vital to Strauss's thought, see Daniel Tanguay, *Leo Strauss: An Intellectual Biography*, trans. Christopher Nadon (New Haven: Yale University Press, 2007).

10. Shlomo Pines, a friend of Strauss's since his youth in Germany, made the following, rather astonishing statement: According to Pines, recalling Strauss in 1920s Berlin, he "was in this period already familiar with Plato's *Laws*, and had begun to discover the medieval Jewish philosophers and their Islamic predecessors. As a result, he came to the conclusion that Maimonides was a deeper thinker than Spinoza. Many of the opinions that he held until the end of his life crystallized already in those days, and I remember things that he said then which [I] find in writings that he wrote some thirty years later." See "On Leo Strauss," trans. Aryeh Leo Motzkin, *The Independent Journal of Philosophy* 5, no. 6 (1988): 169-71.

11. See Heinrich Meier, "How Strauss Became Strauss," in *Enlightening Revolutions: Essays in Honor of Ralph Lerner*, ed. Svetozar Minkov (Lanham, MD: Lexington Books, 2006), pp. 368-70; "Vorwort des Herausgebers," in *Philosophie und Gesetz: Frühe Schriften*, vol. 2 of *Gesammelte Schriften*, pp. XX-XXVIII; *Reorientation: Leo Strauss in the 1930s*, ed. Martin D. Yaffe and Richard S. Ruderman (New York: Palgrave Macmillan, forthcoming). See also Green, *Jew and Philosopher*, pp. 93-109.

It is unusual, if not altogether rare, for a great scholar to also be a great thinker or philosopher: Strauss was one. (To be sure, he modestly referred to himself only as a scholar, albeit among those who "can try to philosophize.")[12] Is this concurrence of scholar and thinker then an accident, or are there aspects of his purposes as a thinker that are manifested or fulfilled in his scholarly work and action, and vice versa? His rediscovery of Maimonides' literary artfulness, political genius, depth of thought, and rootedness in esotericism is not only one of the great moments in modern historical scholarship of the 20th century in the history of philosophy and Jewish thought, but it also continues to bear fruit, first, in the amount of impassioned debate about Maimonides it still manages to generate; and second, especially in its effort to revive Maimonides as a "contemporary" philosopher and Jewish thinker, with regard to which endeavor Strauss seems to have been triumphant. As for the passionate scholarly efforts to refute Strauss's rediscovery, these show no signs that they have abated or are likely to subside; this is undoubtedly another indication of the excellence and vigor of Strauss's scholarly work as a challenge which continues to provoke and so vivify contemporary thought, and which cannot be so readily disposed of, because it is grounded in obstinate facts. But however factual, Strauss knew that this rediscovery was revolutionary: in a letter to a friend about his first reading, he speaks of what he will write as if equal to "dropping a bomb."[13] Nahum Glatzer warned Strauss that this claim about Maimonides, if misconstrued or wrongly presented, might threaten the very future of Judaism.[14] Indeed, Glatzer's warning seems to have acutely alerted

---

12. See "What Is Liberal Education," in *Liberalism Ancient and Modern*, p. 7. The full sentence is "We cannot be philosophers, but we can love philosophy; we can try to philosophize."

13. See letter to Jacob Klein of 16 February 1938, in *Hobbes Politische Wissenschaft und zugehörige Schriften—Briefe*, vol. 3 of *Gesammelte Schriften*, pp. 549–50.

14. Nahum Glatzer (1903–90) was an eminent Jewish scholar who wrote about rabbinic literature, the history of Jewish philosophy, Franz Rosenzweig, and Franz Kafka. He was born in Lemberg, Austria-Hungary, and died in Tucson, Arizona. Glatzer followed Martin Buber as professor of Jewish religious history at the University of Frankfurt. On the advent of Hitler he fled Germany and immigrated to Palestine. Eventually he moved to the United States, in the late 1930s. Starting in the early 1950s, Glatzer taught for several decades in the Department of Near Eastern and Judaic Studies at Brandeis University, and from the mid-1970s at Boston University in a postretirement career of teaching in Jewish studies. He was responsible for editing numerous distinguished anthologies: ancient, medieval, and modern sources of Judaism; the book of Job as viewed in its commentary tradition; Kafka's complete stories; Buber's essays *On the Bible*; and selected stories of Israeli Hebrew writer S. Y. Agnon. He also edited *Judaism: A Quarterly Journal of Jewish Life and Thought*. And perhaps most famously, Glatzer was the chief disciple of Franz Rosenzweig, whose monumental spiritual biography (*Life and Thought*) first brought Rosenzweig to the attention of, and forever made his name in, the English-speaking world. The book was unique for its ability to speak both to the scholars and to the faithful. Strauss had likely been acquainted with Glatzer ever since their common days of teaching together during the 1920s at Rosenzweig's "Lehrhaus" in Frankfurt.

Strauss to a dilemma or quandary and directed him to rethink how to present the results of his great rediscovery, which, once begun, produced in him an almost unquenchable fascination with the study of Maimonides, seemingly lasting until the very end of his life. Certainly a second reading seems to have taught Strauss, awakened by Glatzer, to temper what he judged the quality of dynamite in what he was conveying. This issued in a presentation of Maimonides' teaching that manifested the artful care, intellectual precision, moral purpose, and skillful literary restraint which Maimonides himself had exercised, and which he expressly intended his readers to imitate.[15]

The efforts to refute and reverse Strauss's rediscovery of Maimonides (encompassing esotericism and beyond), which do not seem likely to cease in the immediate future, may also represent a sign of Strauss's compositions on Maimonides as an unyielding challenge to the contemporary self-image. This is perhaps because the contemporary mind (often called "postmodern") is bothered by the notion that the specific conflict between reason and revelation may not have been settled (even if the preference of "postmodernism" in general is for unsettled issues). It is also bothered by the possibility that Maimonides may have thought this conflict through better than the leading modern philosophers, and especially than the principal "postmodern" thinkers like Martin Heidegger. Besides that, Maimonides is further faulted (as this must be laid beside his concern with revelation) for his criticism of reason because it is put together with his (almost unconditional) defense of reason. It is also likely a motive for some, in wishing to get rid of Strauss's goad, that esotericism presents something embarrassing about Maimonides, as this brings to light his "free mind," which some (both religious and secular) might wish to bury beneath traditional notions of what is allowed to be contained in the (medieval) religious mind, and certainly in an authoritative Jewish mind who was one of the greatest teachers ever of the divinely revealed law.

It may also be the case that this forces the confrontation with Strauss as the main blockage to long-established (but certainly respectable, and perhaps even noble) efforts to duly subordinate both Judaism and philosophy to Hermann Cohen, to neo-Kantianism, and to the modern moral interpreta-

---

15. See especially "Literary Character," chap. 8 below. See Heinrich Meier, *Leo Strauss and the Theologico-Political Problem*, trans. Marcus Brainard (New York: Cambridge University Press, 2006), p. 23, n. 32, for Strauss's first response to Glatzer's remark, in a letter of 16 February 1938 to Jacob Klein, and for his fascinating letter of 20 May 1949 to Julius Guttmann, in which he mentions his "hunch" that "Maimonides was a 'philosopher' in a far more radical sense than is usually assumed today." If this is true, as he continues, esotericism imposes a responsibility on the writer, and makes it, "as one says these days, an 'existential' concern."

tion of human experience, which cuts across and harmonizes any differences between modern religious and secular standpoints. Besides this, the philosophic thought of Hermann Cohen represents perhaps the predominant trend in modern Jewish thought, even if often unacknowledged, and even if often disguised as a "purified" Spinozism, a "corrected" Kantianism, or an "advanced" existentialism (whether of the Rosenzweig or of the Heidegger or of the Levinas versions). Cohen's philosophic thought was the first form of modern thinking in which the need to legitimate itself in terms of Maimonides manifested itself as well as pointing to how to do so. That thought must, according to these same protagonists, alone be shown to encompass and fulfill the Maimonidean legacy; this is apparently required, according to those same protagonists, in order to establish continuity with and authority in the Jewish past if the modern Jewish project is to prevail and be vindicated. It may well be the case that, on this level, the debate is not so readily resolved. Strauss himself remained a great admirer of Cohen, even as he rejected his fundamental position and, in the wake of it, preferred a revived Maimonides (more or less adapted to modern circumstances).[16] But he certainly seems to have believed that this sort of debate—Maimonides versus Cohen—can only be helpful to modern Judaism if it is conducted on the high plane on which the great issues it raises deserve to be discussed.

As for the question of what impact Strauss's thought, especially as aided by Maimonides, may make on thinking human beings of the future, it may need something like Zhou Enlai's 20th-century answer to a query made to him about the impact of the 18th-century French Revolution: "Too early to say." His work is mostly very difficult, almost deliberately so (albeit with a certain irresistible charm, and even enchanting quality, for those who make the effort), and it is still a surprise if it is somehow capable of making substantial numbers of people think. Yet most of his essays and books manifest great rhetorical power and show themselves able to move readers to fresh thinking, if those readers are willing to do the work that his essays and books also require. Not much evidence for this on an ample scale is yet discernible, beyond specialized circles, for it is clear that his works so far are rarely taught in their own name, but mostly are used as scholarly commentary, if not as grist for his opponents' mills. The quality of thought in his critics and opponents has most often not risen to the level in clarifying enlightenment,

---

16. See "Jerusalem and Athens," in *Jewish Philosophy and the Crisis of Modernity*, pp. 398–99, as well as numerous other references to Cohen in the same book. For Maimonides dealt with in the context of Strauss's own modern Jewish thought, see the "Editor's Introduction" to the same book, pp. 36–45.

and even criticism, of his own friends, students, and admirers. This paradox is perhaps another reason to seriously consider the suggestion, which we have heard made, that perhaps the most interesting philosophic debates, and the most exhilarating theological-political discussions, in our era are those between Straussian factions.[17] Yet Strauss has made a progressively greater impact since his demise, and some of his ideas have gradually penetrated to an ever-greater number of minds; certainly one very key element of his impact has been his astonishing essays and lectures on Maimonides and his thought's issue in Maimonideanism.

This is not even to mention the supposedly direct political influence that he and his ideas are asserted to have exercised on some political leaders: did he act as posthumous guide for two US presidents, Ronald Reagan and George W. Bush, both of whom apparently neither had knowledge of him nor were his students? (I shall leave aside the claim that high advisers of these presidents were in the grip of "Straussianism," for this is to enter the realm of disorders of the mind.) Are his views on philosophic and scholarly matters somehow able to generate a political ideology? Intellectual honesty compels me not to evade, even in a book dedicated to his study of Maimonides, the disconcerting attacks on the value and meaning of Strauss's work. For to take seriously his argument for the excellence of Maimonides' mind and the modern worth of studying his books assumes that readers must *not* give credence to the charge of his political and academic opponents that this is an argument which somehow also claims to revive the medieval world in which Maimonides lived, a charge which I am tempted to dismiss as absurd, if it is not at bottom calculated to make Strauss's thought seem averse to the modern. So I must briefly consider the issues that have been raised even on this diminished level of argument.

Mainly these are matters for speculative historians or political psychologists, since Strauss did not compose any ideological tracts, from which his views may be isolated and traced to his students. Whatever may be attributed—in the heat of political or academic battle—to him as a teacher or even writer, we are probably not yet competent to judge whether it is precisely correct, never mind whether it is even possible, to trace to him any of

---

17. See Michael Zuckert, "Straussians," in *Cambridge Companion to Leo Strauss*, pp. 263–86. It was not he who made the suggestion to which I refer, and so he is not to be blamed for it or credited with it. However, his absorbing article might be judged to illustrate the truth of this suggestion in action, insofar as it touches on much bigger philosophic themes than those that can be dismissed as limited somehow to parochial disputes and quarrels among fellow Straussians.

the political things attributed to his teaching, or perhaps to his obiter dicta. What is supposedly traced to him most often seems a highly doubtful, if not suspiciously motivated, etiology. But then, to speak in favor of the influence he may have exercised on his students by his personal political convictions, there is no doubt (at least for those who bear him no animus, and who consider his words with equitable judgment) that, first, he was stalwartly loyal to the modern West, to constitutional liberal democracy, and to the United States of America. Second, seen in light of modern Jewish history, in which hatred for the Jews and their vulnerability to the very worst evildoers seem impossible to remove, he was an ardent supporter of the State of Israel. Third, he tenaciously opposed tyranny; this was especially his attitude toward the communist tyranny in the Soviet Union; it only followed his zealous hatred of the Nazi tyranny in Germany, to which he was vehemently opposed, and which made Winston Churchill, the man who led the fight against Nazi tyranny (not to mention the man who defined the "iron curtain"), one of his enduring personal heroes.[18]

To carry this logic one step further—and insofar as these facts of his animosity to tyranny, his keen favorableness to the West, and his unconditional rejection of those who hate the Jews may be considered, in all fairness, firmly established—it is highly probable that he would have been opposed to Islamism. I can only speculate, but I believe that he would have regarded this as an ideology which make makes use of an unconscionable terrorism, which aspires to tyranny on the scale of domineering world-empire, which remains implacable in its loathing for and aggression against the West, and which makes fully apparent its hatred for the Jews, whom it wishes to destroy in conscious continuity of Nazi goals. However, we cannot say on this general basis that he would have accepted the need to follow any specific provisions, strategy, or tactics to defeat Islamism or its terrorism on behalf of tyranny, which requires prudential judgment of statesmen about the relevant forces in the field and the needs in the circumstances. But even if the facts as I stated them are true about his past ascertainable political convictions, and even if everything I suggested about what he might think in the present or the future were proven to be most probable (it being almost forty years since his

---

18. See Leo Strauss, "Churchill's Greatness," *Weekly Standard* 6, no. 16 (January 3, 2000), or http://www.weeklystandard.com/author/leo-strauss. Strauss delivered these remarks, apparently "spontaneously," in class on 25 January 1965 in the wake of Churchill's death. Even Strauss's calculated appearance of "spontaneity" in these remarks was itself an eminently Churchillian thing to do. In the quip of his good friend Lord Birkenhead, "Winston has devoted the best years of his life to preparing his impromptu speeches."

demise), one still cannot be certain about the impact of his personal political opinions on others in the unfolding of history.

So bracketing for the moment everything speculated about Strauss's opinions on the present and the future, the most that can be said about the knowable past is that this may have amounted, in the immediate wake of his own life and teaching career, to an impact made by his political opinions on some of his students. But even if he did make such an impact on some of his immediate students as has earned him both praise and blame, only the unfolding of history will tell if something in the depths of his thought, adorned as it may be with a moral rhetoric, will continue to guide political men beyond the generation of his own students, or whether it was the ephemeral consequence of a pedagogical presence perhaps peculiarly charismatic or perhaps uncommonly wise. Saying anything other than this is to leave what can be known and to surrender to a virtual paranoia that is beyond reason, although to be sure for me to call it "paranoid" as motive is to claim knowledge of private chambers in the minds of his opponents, to which of course I do not have access. It is quite likely simple baseness in which partisan motives dominate all fair-mindedness, while to say paranoia may almost be to mitigate the accusers. If base, it seems motivated by political concerns which mostly preoccupy political and academic partisans, who are concerned with smearing, and thus disarming, a perceived enemy in the court of public opinion.

Since Strauss's known opinions which he held during his life are nothing to be ashamed of and seem in some respects peculiarly unsympathetic to the actual regimes of the medieval or the ancient worlds, they are no bar to a serious study of Maimonides as potentially relevant in the present. Nor need any fair-minded person fear being convinced of his claim for Maimonides, which in no sense evident to reason makes it possible to somehow claim that this conflicts with being a good citizen in a modern Western liberal democracy, or with being a faithful member of a respectable and decent religious community.

In any case, if one may dare a prediction, it is not impossible that his thought may emerge as the equal in the 21st century to what Nietzsche's and Heidegger's was in the 20th century. However, this parallel is not meant to obscure the role that Strauss actually wished to play as the anti-Nietzsche, and especially as the anti-Heidegger. Indeed, on a certain level, Strauss was the greatest anti-Heideggerian of the 20th century. At the very least, he hoped to tentatively explore premodern thought (both medieval and ancient) and investigate its forgotten reserves and resources in search of the antidote to their combined poison, for through those two thinkers modern thought, according to Strauss, had shown itself to be potentially toxic and thus latently destructive. But this absolutely required him, and those who are taught by him about turning in a certain direction of greater rationality, to make a most careful and open-minded study of their philosophic toxins first, if the noxious elements are to be isolated and used for discovering the antidote. For he is at his deepest and most powerful, as a philosophic "healer" and guide, in his emphasis on the beneficial lessons in thinking which we can derive from studying the medievals and the ancients. This, to be sure, is not in any sense to counsel use of their past wisdom as a simple prescription.[19] Nor did he ever reject modern thought root and branch (his most vehement critics to the contrary notwithstanding), for he recognized that this thought alone determines our present situation and must predominantly guide us; and he also acknowledged how much this thought still contains of the wise, the good, and the true in it, which we must study carefully and use judiciously, by drawing on its best teachings and its legacy of helpful knowledge in our march toward the unknown future. Instead, what concerned him about the Nietzsche-Heidegger trend of contemporary thought was its tendency toward nihilism, which may well have been a (but not the) legacy of modern thought, insofar as in its radicalized tendency, it wants to remake the world with man as its total owner and master—a fantastic, futile, megalomaniacal, and self-defeating hope. Strauss seems to have believed that he had caught sight of definite contours, or at least certain elements, of a cure to the nihilism brought on by Nietzsche and Heidegger in the medievals and the ancients, which is still available for us to recover as moderns. He suggested that this premodern wisdom might potentially help us to deal with, better apprehend, and even surpass those current trends of thought that bedevil us, *if* we use what we uncover and recover of this complex lost legacy judiciously and prudently.

It should be mentioned that a proper approach to Strauss on the medievals would encompass several other thinkers and philosophers on whom he wrote very significant essays, and whose original thought he helped to bring to contemporary attention (often by interpreting them as unconventionally as he did Maimonides). One must hope that some day this work on the me-

19. See Leo Strauss, *The City and Man* (Chicago: University of Chicago Press, 1977), p. 11. Strauss would himself anticipate and warn against the threat to the "free mind" (or freedom of thought) located in an academic ideology, which he perceived could potentially arise or follow even from his own scholarly program. This has been most astutely and cleverly elucidated by Nathan Tarcov, "On a Certain Critique of 'Straussianism,'" in *Leo Strauss: Political Philosopher and Jewish Thinker*, ed. Kenneth L. Deutsch and Walter Nicgorski (Lanham, MD: Rowman and Littlefield, 1994), pp. 259–74.

dieval thinkers beyond Maimonides will be assembled, edited, and appear in print together—to mention only perhaps the most interesting examples, the sections on Alfarabi, Avicenna, Averroes, and Gersonides in *Philosophy and Law* (1935);[20] his groundbreaking essay on Marsilius of Padua (1963) as a powerful Christian political thinker of the Averroist school, who prior to Strauss was remembered mostly by scholars who specialized in obscure aspects of medieval history and theology;[21] the last section of the chapter "Classical Natural Right" in *Natural Right and History* (1953), which forms almost a separate and stand-alone essay, as it were, contrasting the Averroist with the Thomist medieval approaches to Aristotelian natural right;[22] the three essays on Farabi, which are absolutely essential for comprehending his view of Maimonides, and which appeared at three different phases in his unfolding thought ([1] "On a Lost Writing of Farabi" [1936],[23] [2] "Farabi's *Plato*" [1945],[24] [3] "How Farabi Read Plato's *Laws*" [1957]);[25] and a complex, finely crafted, and strangely compelling interpretation of Yehudah Halevi's *Kuzari* (1943), in which he presents a deep excavation of Halevi's hidden and multilayered approach to morality, religion, and philosophy.[26] Anyone who wishes to seriously probe the complete views of Strauss on the medievals must consider these additional essays and portions of books. These works are essential for comprehending Strauss's subtle and never simple views of medieval philosophy in its Jewish, Christian, Muslim contexts, and how the views of their great thinkers emerged from and pertained to ultimate premises about certain fundamental dualisms: philosophy and prophecy, philoso-

---

20. Leo Strauss, *Philosophie und Gesetz: Beiträge zum Verständnis Maimunis und seiner Vorlaüfer* (Berlin: Schocken Verlag, 1935); *Philosophie und Gesetz: Frühe Schriften*, vol. 2 of *Gesammelte Schriften*, pp. 3–123; *Philosophy and Law*.

21. See Leo Strauss, "Marsilius of Padua," in *History of Political Philosophy*, ed. Strauss and Cropsey, 2nd ed., pp. 251–70; 3rd ed., pp. 276–95. It was reprinted in *Liberalism Ancient and Modern*, pp. 185–202; by its title this might seem like a curious location for Strauss to choose for his essay on a medieval political thinker; it is at least to be noted that his introductory essay to the English translation of Maimonides' *Guide*, "How To Begin," is also reprinted in the same book.

22. See Leo Strauss, *Natural Right and History* (Chicago: University of Chicago Press, 1953), pp. 157–64.

23. See *Monatsschrift für Geschichte und Wissenschaft des Judentums* 80, no. 1 (1936): 96–106; *Philosophie und Gesetz: Frühe Schriften*, vol. 2 of *Gesammelte Schriften*, pp. 167–76, with marginal handwritten additions by the author, p. 177. A translation by Martin D. Yaffe and Gabriel Bartlett is to appear in Yaffe and Ruderman, *Reorientation: Leo Strauss in the 1930s*.

24. See Strauss, "Farabi's *Plato*" (see n. 4 above).

25. See Leo Strauss, "How Farabi Read Plato's *Laws*," in *Mélanges Louis Massignon* (Damascus: L'Institut français de Damas, 1957), vol. 3, pp. 319–44; reprinted in *What Is Political Philosophy?*, pp. 134–54.

26. See Leo Strauss, "The Law of Reason in the *Kuzari*," *Proceedings of the American Academy for Jewish Research* 13 (1943): 47–96; reprinted in *Persecution and the Art of Writing*, pp. 95–141.

phy and politics, philosophy and theology, or philosophy and law. And then there is also the relation between the dualism Plato and Aristotle especially in the matter of the seeming accident of which primary sources were available to which traditions, i.e., Plato's *Republic* among the Muslims, Aristotle's *Politics* among the Christians. As Strauss was the first to query, did the accident of which books were circulated in each tradition determine the political views they pursued, or did the political views they pursued determine which books were circulated? Strauss never ignored what could be genuinely known about this sort of matter on the historical level, but he would also often ask unconventional questions about history that led him to original and unusual (some might say eccentric) answers.

To reiterate: Strauss was an astounding scholar, as these essays no doubt prove, but it is not this alone that makes him great; it was his genuine recovery of the philosophic thought of Maimonides, and his vast and ambitious effort to wrestle with what it would signify to speak of an authenticated, if critical, recovery of the possibility of philosophy in the manner in which Maimonides grasped such a possibility. His way was to never let his own thought reach a stasis, but he kept it in motion, as it were; not only do these essays testify to great progress in the unfolding of his own thought, often by a will to criticize the results he had reached in his own previous effort. This is also made evident by the marginal notes added to his own essays (transcribed by Heinrich Meier), which show not just scholarly refinements, advances, or corrections, but also often his genuine and almost constant rethinking of the positions which he had himself just recently maintained, as a challenge to any complacency of mind. That he often light-heartedly indicated these things, and at his own expense, shows a certain detachment toward the honor due to scholarly achievement.

Besides gathering together and reprinting as carefully as possible Strauss's major essays and lectures on Maimonides, my subsidiary aim, though only fragmentarily achieved, has been to make Strauss's often forbidding scholarly apparatus friendlier to scholars, students, and other readers who are not trained on his level and who might wish to pursue some of his sources in modern English and Hebrew editions, i.e., who are willing to make the effort, not just to think through his thought, but also to let Strauss educate them. For this forbidding scholarly apparatus reflects—setting aside for the moment his always penetrating thought—his vast and deep learning, which he shares generously with his readers, and which he utilizes to direct them to significant but often forgotten sources for the enlightenment of the mind. To make the essays and lectures completely accessible is beyond my scholarly attainments, but I have done what I was able to do to the best of my ability.

This has been substantially aided by several scholars who first walked some of these same trails; it is in their well-worn paths that I follow, i.e., those who have previously edited Strauss's as well as Maimonides' works, and who have issued critical editions in several languages. The versions that they have produced, often carefully annotated, have been most helpful for doing what I could to make this book as useful as possible to students, scholars, and other readers; they have made it possible for me to borrow liberally from their achievements. To them all I owe a substantial debt. I especially wish to acknowledge Rémi Brague for his French translation and edition of Strauss's Maimonides essays,[27] and Heinrich Meier for his editing of the complete works of Strauss (of which so far three volumes have appeared in print) in which some of these essays have been helpfully reproduced with notes.[28] I am also in the debt of Joseph Cropsey, for his edition of Strauss's *Studies in Platonic Political Philosophy*, in which "Notes on Maimonides' *Book of Knowledge*" was reproduced, and in which "Note on Maimonides' *Letter on Astrology*" and "Note on Maimonides' *Treatise on the Art of Logic*" first appeared in print. I also wish to acknowledge the previous editors of "How to Study Medieval Philosophy": David Bolotin, Christopher Bruell, and Thomas L. Pangle. I am grateful to the following translators for letting me use their work: Robert Bartlett, who translated "Some Remarks on the Political Science of Maimonides and Farabi" from the French original; and Gabriel Bartlett and Svetozar Minkov, who translated "The Place of the Doctrine of Providence according to Maimonides" from the original German. As for the Literary Estate of Leo Strauss, with whose permission the present volume has been put together and is being published, my sincerest thanks to Joseph Cropsey, with whose gracious help this project was started; and to Nathan Tarcov, by whose generous help and wise counsel it is that the project is being finished. It is only appropriate that I make mention of my colleagues who worked on the original series in which the present book took its first shape, and who gave advice which assisted even in the forming of this book: thanks to Michael Zank and to the late Eve Adler. In that connection, I would especially like to acknowledge the friendship, assistance, advice, and munificent labors of Martin D. Yaffe, from whom I have received so much and to whom so much

---

27. *Maïmonide*.
28. Leo Strauss, *Gesammelte Schriften*, ed. Heinrich Meier, 3 vols. (thus far) (Stuttgart: J. B. Metzler, 1996, 1997, 2001).

is due for his help with this book and with so much else. I am most grateful to Martin D. Yaffe and Ian Alexander Moore for their splendid translation from the German of "Cohen and Maimonides," which they graciously consented to do specially for the present volume. I would like to sincerely thank Sara Kathleen Alvis for her English translations from the Latin of several passages in Strauss's article on Abravanel, and of a passage in a note in his "The Place of the Doctrine of Providence." And I would also like to acknowledge Professors Steven Harvey, Eric Lawee, Avraham Melamed, and Elliot R. Wolfson, who most generously shared their knowledge with me and so helped greatly in the editing of, and the notes on, specific essays by Strauss. I very much appreciate Dr. Hillel Fradkin and Professor Libby Garshowitz for their gracious willingness to lend assistance with their erudite linguistic skills in order to ensure the accuracy of foreign-language transliterations, the former with Arabic and Judeo-Arabic, and the latter with Hebrew. And I owe a debt to the anonymous readers of the University of Chicago Press, whose careful and conscientious reading of a long manuscript pointed me toward several definite improvements and saved me from several potentially embarrassing errors. I also owe a great debt to Mr. Erik Carlson of the University of Chicago Press for his superb job of copyediting the manuscript. Not only did his intelligence, precision, and exceptional skill make the work vastly better, but also his wit and good humor made him a pleasure to work with. Martin D. Yaffe and Evan M. Lowe of the University of North Texas deserve full credit for their committed and serious efforts in the preparation of the index.

I would like to acknowledge and sincerely thank the Social Sciences and Humanities Research Council of Canada for its generous support during the years in which I did research on Strauss's works on Maimonides and prepared the manuscript. It is also my pleasure to convey my great appreciation to the Tikvah Fund for its most helpful and generous financial support during the period of readying the manuscript for publication, which subvention to the University of Chicago Press will enhance the book's accessibility to students.

A word on the dedication: this is to acknowledge four great teachers with whom I had the privilege to study, listed in the order in which I encountered them as their student. I hope it is enough, for the debt I owe them, to say that each of them in their own way opened my eyes to the challenges and the delights of studying the thought of Maimonides and of Leo Strauss. This obligation toward them remains the case even if it is also true that I did not always follow their way, which I am confident was to follow their way.

I have discussed aspects of this book with such a great number of people that to mention them all would make for an utterly unwieldy list. Though the pages available do not permit me to acknowledge them all by name, it would be ungrateful of me not to say that this volume would never have attained whatever achievement it may represent if not for conversations with an abundant number of friends and colleagues. But three good friends I must mention by name: Clifford Orwin, Arthur Fish, and Norman Doidge. Our freewheeling, rollicking discussions have been one of the great pleasures of life for too great a number of years to count. This is also the fitting occasion on which to recognize the extraordinary efforts of those intrepid students (graduate and undergraduate) who have engaged in the study of the *Guide* with me in a seminar that I have been teaching for the past twenty years or so. They know who they are, and I only regret that this is not adequate acknowledgment. I am grateful to all of them.

And finally, I am deeply beholden to Sharon, who helped in myriad ways, and who smoothed the path of the book and its editor at every turn: she is my sine qua non.

Acknowledgments

All of these writings are published with the permission of the Literary Estate of Leo Strauss. The editor gratefully acknowledges the assistance and cooperation of the administrators of the Literary Estate, Joseph Cropsey and Nathan Tarcov.

The editor gratefully acknowledges the permissions to reprint the writings of Leo Strauss from the following sources:

"How to Study Medieval Philosophy" is reprinted by permission of the University of Chicago Press from *The Rebirth of Classical Political Rationalism: An Introduction to the Thought of Leo Strauss; Essays and Lectures*, by Leo Strauss, edited with an introduction by Thomas L. Pangle. This is approximately the same lecture which appears in that volume by the title of "How to Begin to Study Medieval Philosophy." Copyright © 1989 by The University of Chicago.

"Spinoza's Critique of Maimonides" is reprinted from *Spinoza's Critique of Religion*, by Leo Strauss, translated by Elsa M. Sinclair. Copyright © 1965 by Schocken Books, Inc. Reprinted by permission of Schocken Books, published by Pantheon Books, a division of Random House, Inc.

"Cohen and Maimonides" is a 1931 lecture in German that was transcribed, with notes, from a manuscript by Heinrich Meier and first published as Leo Strauss, „Cohen und Maimoni", in: *Gesammelte Schriften*, Band 2: *Philosophie und Gesetz—frühe Schriften*. S. 393–436 (ISBN: 978-3-476-01212-8) © 1997 J.B. Metzlersche Verlagsbuchhandlung und Carl Ernst Poeschel Verlag GmbH in Stuttgart. Martin D. Yaffe and Ian Alexander Moore prepared the English translation for the present volume. The translated lecture appears in print by permission of the Literary Estate of Leo Strauss.

"The Philosophic Foundation of the Law: Maimonides' Doctrine of Prophecy and Its Sources," the first two paragraphs and the last three paragraphs of the "Introduction" to *Philosophy and Law*, and the introductory section and section B, "Maimonides," of "The Legal Foundation of Philosophy," are reprinted from *Philosophy and Law: Contributions to the Understanding of Maimonides and His Predecessors*, by Leo Strauss, translated by Eve Adler. Reprinted by permission of the State University of New York Press. Copyright © 1995.

"Some Remarks on the Political Science of Maimonides and Farabi" originally appeared in print in *Interpretation: A Journal of Political Philosophy* 18, no. 1 (Fall 1990): 3–30. It was translated by Robert Bartlett. It is reprinted by permission of the Literary Estate of Leo Strauss, of the translator, and of *Interpretation: A Journal of Political Philosophy*.

"The Place of the Doctrine of Providence according to Maimonides" is reprinted from *Review of Metaphysics* 57 (March 2004): 537–49. It was translated by Gabriel Bartlett and Svetozar Minkov. It appears with the permission of the Literary Estate of Leo Strauss, of the translators, and of the *Review of Metaphysics*.

"Review of *The Mishneh Torah*, Book 1, by Moses Maimonides, Edited according to the Bodleian Codex with Introduction, Biblical and Talmudical References, Notes, and English Translation by Moses Hyamson" originally appeared in *Review of Religion* 3, no. 4 (May 1937): 448–56. It is reprinted by permission of the *Review of Religion*.

"The Literary Character of *The Guide of the Perplexed*" first appeared in *Essays on Maimonides*, edited by Salo W. Baron (New York: Columbia University Press, 1941), pp. 37–91. It was reprinted by the author in Leo Strauss, *Persecution and the Art of Writing* (New York: Free Press, 1952; Chicago: University of Chicago Press, 1988), pp. 38–94. It is reprinted by permission of The University of Chicago Press.

"Maimonides' Statement on Political Science" is reprinted by permission of The Free Press, a division of Macmillan, Inc., from *What Is Political Philosophy? And Other Studies*, by Leo Strauss. Copyright © 1959 The Free Press. It originally appeared in print in *Proceedings of the American Academy for Jewish Research* 22 (1953): 115–30.

"Introduction to Maimonides' *The Guide of the Perplexed*" is a tape-recorded lecture (delivered in two sessions) that has been transcribed by the editor for the present volume and hence is previously unpublished. This lecture appears in print by permission of the Literary Estate of Leo Strauss.

"How To Begin To Study *The Guide of the Perplexed*" is reprinted by permission of the University of Chicago Press from *The Guide of the Perplexed*, by Moses Maimonides, translated by Shlomo Pines. Copyright © 1963 by The University of Chicago. It is reprinted by permission of The University of Chicago Press.

"Notes on Maimonides' *Book of Knowledge*" (1967) is reprinted with permission from *Studies in Mysticism and Religion Presented to Gershom G. Scholem*, edited by Efraim E. Urbach, R. J. Zwi Werblowsky, and Chaim Wirszubski (Jerusalem: Magnes Press, 1967), pp. 269-83. Copyright © 1967 by Magnes Press. Reprinted by permission of the publisher.

"Note on Maimonides' *Letter on Astrology*" and "Note on Maimonides' *Treatise on the Art of Logic*" are reprinted by permission of the University of Chicago Press from *Studies in Platonic Political Philosophy*, by Leo Strauss. Copyright © 1983 by The University of Chicago. They are both reprinted by permission of The University of Chicago Press.

"On Abravanel's Philosophical Tendency and Political Teaching" is reprinted from *Isaac Abravanel: Six Lectures*, edited by J. B. Trend and H. Loewe (Cambridge: Cambridge University Press, 1937). Reprinted by permission of the publisher.

"The Secret Teaching of Maimonides" is a written fragment that was discovered in the Leo Strauss Archive of the University of Chicago, and hence is previously unpublished. This fragment appears in print by permission of the Literary Estate of Leo Strauss.

Editor's Introduction
LEO STRAUSS'S ESSAYS AND LECTURES ON MAIMONIDES

The sixteen essays and lectures of Leo Strauss on Moses Maimonides, which are brought together for the first time in the present book, were composed at various points during Strauss's scholarly career and cover almost the full length of his life as a thinker. They reflect not only significant changes in his thought, but also an astonishing consistency, which in a certain measure may be considered of even greater impressiveness than the changes. Indeed, it seems that early on Strauss reached a single, distinctive conviction about Maimonides, which placed him in position to view Maimonides' thought from a unique angle, and which received expression in virtually his first essay on Maimonides. I refer to Strauss's audacious conviction—tentative at first as a working hypothesis—that Maimonides was cognitively superior in the realm of Jewish thought to not only all of his predecessors and contemporaries, but also to his later heirs and disciples.[1]

To be sure, when Strauss arrived at what was then an utterly unconventional conviction (between 1925 and 1928), it mainly pertained to Jewish thought, and there was no reason to suspect that it was his intention to imply anything beyond this realm. Likewise, his reasons for thinking this about Maimonides changed substantially during the next decade and a half, so it is astounding that the conviction persisted even where the grounds for it must

---

1. At the height of his scholarly career, Strauss unambiguously expressed the insight which he had reached, and which he was to hold (in spite of significant changes in his thought) to the end of his life. He articulated it vis-à-vis Maimonides' fiercest critic, Spinoza, who is also regarded as one of *the* most powerful modern philosophers. It was a judgment which was surely calculated to shock his modern readers: "Maimonides . . . was a deeper thinker than Spinoza." See "On a Forgotten Kind of Writing" (1954), in *What Is Political Philosophy?*, p. 230. But almost twenty-five years prior, at the very beginning of his lecture "Cohen and Maimonides" (1931), chap. 3 below, Strauss enunciates the purpose of his study of the two thinkers, in which they are contrasted as much as juxtaposed. He pursued this study only so that he could "gain access to Rambam by starting with Cohen: Cohen is to open up [for him] the access to Rambam." At this juncture close to his point of departure in thinking and research, he is already tacitly suggesting that for him Maimonides was the superior, if not the deeper, thinker.

have shifted dramatically. What seems to have been a transformative moment for Strauss was when he recognized not only that this conviction was defensible in Jewish thought, but that it also startlingly held an equal weight and force in most philosophic thought. As Strauss brings to light, Maimonides' strength as a thinker was at least in a considerable measure due to the fact that he had the unusual ability to comprehend with profundity as well as to present fair-mindedly both sides in the essential debate between "Jerusalem and Athens." As such, he was able to dispassionately judge the contending claims of revelation and reason, or the Bible and philosophy, each of which claims against its challenger to represent the highest truth. Indeed, Strauss goes so far as to call Maimonides "the greatest analyst" ever of these two rival claimants to the truth, and of their "fundamental difference."[2]

If, as Strauss conjectured, Maimonides was to be claimed as a cognitively superior thinker, then his position must have about it a perennial quality, which to Strauss seemed to be manifest in the ability of his thought to survive an array of antagonists who strove to weaken and even destroy his authority as a thinker, never mind those who from friendly motives attempted to assimilate him to their thought even if it diverged from his own. It was able to withstand the vehement assaults of powerful critics like Benedict Spinoza, his most serious early modern philosophic opponent. It was also able to survive the smothering embrace of thoughtful admirers like his greatly appreciative late modern philosophic devotee Hermann Cohen. And it was even able to prevail against the obstinate ambivalence maintained by supposed continuators, mostly unsympathetic though also deferential, like the medieval theologian and biblical commentator Isaac Abravanel.

Paradoxes abounded in the wake of Strauss's study of Maimonides, and everything suggests that this fact already struck him quite forcefully. One need only see these things in light of Maimonides' fate among the modern philosophers to immediately grasp some of the paradoxes inherent in the Maimonides uncovered by Strauss. Thus, what Spinoza rejected, Leibniz held dear, even though both are counted as great modern rationalists who on fundamental issues are almost equivalent to one another. Likewise, Solomon Maimon vigorously assisted in the post-Kantian deconstruction of Aristotle's

---

2. See "Progress or Return?," in *Jewish Philosophy and the Crisis of Modernity*, p. 110. Strauss stresses that he thinks this is especially the case about Maimonides in *The Guide of the Perplexed*. For other remarks on Maimonides in the same book, see pp. 111–12, 125, 151–53, 163–66, 176, n. 58, 209–10, 214, 250–53, 270, 278–79, 418–20, 426–27, 462–63, 468–70. The passage on p. 119 may also contain references to *Guide* 3.5 and 20, although he makes no mention of Maimonides by name.

psychology and epistemology, yet the same man revered Maimonides, who had been a firm adherent of Aristotle's views on knowledge and the human mind. As for the fate of Maimonides in modern Judaism, his legal thought somehow managed to inspire the unyielding loyalty of traditionalists who simultaneously suspected modernity and along with it his philosophic thought as a threat to Judaism; his medieval philosophic thought excited the zeal of partisans of the modern Jewish Enlightenment who simultaneously criticized his legal thought as a relic of a benighted, authoritarian past. Yet something about the "medieval" Maimonides paradoxically acted as a spur for Strauss himself and helped him to confront the dilemmas and contradictions with which he was faced as a modern Jew.

However, Strauss was also fascinated by the way in which Maimonides' thought somehow had the capacity both to encompass philosophic contradictions and to transcend historical limitations, elements which routed most other thinkers. As Strauss stated in a lecture to a modern audience for whom Maimonides was viewed as an unapproachable and even acutely problematic figure: "Only if [the modern premises] are questionable can we become seriously interested in Maimonides."[3] It is beyond dispute that this statement reflects the course of Strauss's own thought in his turn to ancient and medieval thinkers as a source of wisdom. At the same time, it does not diminish the challenge that Maimonides continues to represent for modern thought even at its most decidedly modern. For as Strauss knew, even the staunchest defenders of "the modern premises" (like the philosopher and Jewish thinker Hermann Cohen) are well aware that these have been radically called into doubt by the failure of modern rationalism to offer adequate solutions to certain fundamental problems. This has made them too wonder whether Maimonides might not be useful to them in helping to mount their defense of the modern. And so along with admitting the paradoxes, Strauss also continued to adhere to his notion of a Maimonides who not only cannot be dispensed with, but whose thought is somehow requisite for modern man if he is to succeed against his most formidable challenges. This is the point where one can at least begin to make sense of Strauss's strange and seemingly paradoxical counsel: in order to "resolve our perplexity"—precisely as moderns, and not by resorting to "ultra-modern thoughts"—he suggests that we "apply for aid to the medieval Enlightenment . . . of Maimonides."[4]

3. "Introduction to Maimonides' *Guide*," chap. 10 below.
4. "Appendix 4A: Introduction to *Philosophy and Law*," chap. 4 below

While Strauss's reverence for Maimonides did not vary much during almost fifty years of studying his work (not to mention his reading and researching of Maimonides' critics and students), it is curious that the grounds for this high regard did change in significant respects. Indeed, it is among the most absorbing things that careful readers of this book will have the chance to observe and to reflect on. For example, how did Strauss in his relative youth arrive at his original conviction about Maimonides as cognitively superior? Moreover, how did Strauss continue to adhere to his original assessment of Maimonides as one of the deepest of thinkers, while seeming to radically modify the grounds on which he based this conviction? What is the proper place we should assign to Maimonides in the history of Western thought, and is he a guide who can still point us in the right way with regard to our spiritual dilemmas? Although the answers to such questions are not so simple to obtain, I believe that the evidence for Strauss's ever-deepening views on Maimonides' thought along with some of the answers to the aforementioned questions are made clear in these essays and lectures, spanning the course of his scholarly career and representing the most salient elements of his own thought on the most pressing issues which we face in the modern era.

Strauss was also aware that the heirs of Maimonides' thought cover a broad spectrum in the realm of Jewish thought, never mind in the sphere of philosophy, which makes it difficult for some to believe they were all conscientious "students" of his thought, and especially of *The Guide of the Perplexed*, as Strauss seems to suggest. To be sure, Strauss certainly never denied the great divergences in thought from Maimonides among most of these heirs in subsequent history. Yet he also traced much of what was most interesting in these legatees precisely to the cognitive excellence that Maimonides taught them to cultivate and the dialectical resourcefulness that he taught them to emulate: this was perhaps his greatest legacy to posterity. According to this unusual angle of approach, Strauss's Maimonides bequeathed *both* an incisive way of thinking *and* an artful manner of writing, rather than a set of fixed Maimonidean doctrines uniformly passed on to his heirs, since what they did with this legacy often seemed to carry them very far indeed from his actual teachings.

Perhaps most illustrative of the point is the massive impact, both direct and oblique, that Maimonides made on the Kabbalists. This showed Strauss how deeply, and at what a distance, his powerful thought could impress itself even on his harshest opponents and severest critics. Strauss's casual remarks in these essays and lectures often highlight or at least allude to this multifaceted and formative character of Maimonides' thought. Consider the "venturesome hypothesis" which Strauss withdraws almost as quickly as he asserts it: "Indeed, as it seems that there had existed no Kabbalah, strictly speaking before the completion of the *Guide*, one might suggest that Maimonides was the first Kabbalist."[5] This may be more of an instance of Straussian irony than is usually admitted, but it is not a less serious assertion about Maimonides for that reason. As Strauss observed, his achievement was so great and so exemplary—and in this, he was like other giants of philosophic thought, such as Plato or Hegel—that he guided even those who wished to reject him. In this sense, one might suggest that Strauss's almost continuous work on Maimonides is a prolonged study of how to bring about a philosophic revolution.

Yet in the end, Strauss's modern rediscovery of Maimonides as one of the deepest of thinkers—not only relative to his own historical period—depended on certain decisive insights which Strauss himself managed to extract from Maimonides' thought, teachings, and writings through his own careful and close readings, which certainly did not follow conventional signposts. Every so often these seem to have arisen from insights occasioned by repeated readings (occurring in "lightning flashes," to employ the language of Maimonides), in which he suddenly perceived something hidden flash by in Maimonides' audacious "thought moves." It is noteworthy that Strauss seems to have believed it was necessary to expose Maimonides' often-courageous cognitive breaks with and criticisms of tradition, despite the fact that Maimonides frequently made the effort to conceal this strain in his thought, and despite Strauss's own accustomed defense of Maimonides' discreetness and reticence.[6] Strauss may have felt obliged to shout Maimonides' radicalism from the rooftops (or so this might seem to some), thinking that otherwise the enormous subtlety and concealed depths of Maimonides' thought were sure to have been lost on modern obtuseness, which was produced by the belief in modern superiority and the assumption of historical progress. These things, in Strauss's telling, show the true nature of Maimonides, who, though always a loyal Jewish thinker and defender of the Jewish faith, was also a truly intrepid explorer and searcher for enlightenment in the realm of thought, allowing truth and not dogma or prejudice to guide him. This was a discovery—or as he eventually recognized, a rediscovery—which brought Strauss

---

5. "Literary Character," chap. 8 below.
6. Ibid., section IV, entitled "A Moral Dilemma."

to a completely novel level of comprehension, unprecedented for modern thought, of what was occurring in the Maimonidean texts, which allowed him to break with the entire contemporary, if not centuries-long, scholarly and philosophic consensus. Strauss arrived at the startling recognition that Maimonides deliberately contradicted himself in his writings. Indeed, this was a rediscovery that challenged what Strauss himself originally had anticipated or been prepared to acknowledge, and so must at first have required some surmounting of resistance in himself. Yet Strauss came firmly to believe that Maimonides intentionally used contradictions as a mode of expression consistent with the truth, in order to preserve the rights of the free mind as well as to hint at truths he held which stood against conventional opinion or pious belief, in a period in which speaking the truth was both dangerous and unwise. As we know from Strauss's letters, the Maimonides he rediscovered surprised and thrilled him at least as much as it astounded those who first read Strauss's essays or heard his lectures.[7]

Among those who were transformed by reading Strauss's essays on Maimonides was the American political thinker and essayist Irving Kristol. In an introduction to a recently issued, posthumous book of Kristol's essays, Gertrude Himmelfarb brings to prominence the definite influence exercised by Strauss:

> Strauss's *Persecution and the Art of Writing*, in 1952, produced [in Kristol, as he reports,] "the kind of intellectual shock that is a once-in-a-lifetime experience." . . . What impressed him was not so much [Strauss's] political views (which were more implicit than overt) but the mindset that informed [his] discourses upon culture, religion, society, philosophy, and politics alike. [Kristol's] review of *Persecution and the Art of Writing* focuses on Maimonides as the exemplar of Strauss's major themes: the relation of the esoteric to the exoteric, of reason and revelation, of philosophy and the polity. It concludes

---

7. See "A Giving of Accounts," in *Jewish Philosophy and the Crisis of Modernity*, pp. 462–63: "Maimonides was, to begin with, wholly unintelligible to me. I got the first glimmer of light when I concentrated on his prophetology and, therefore, the prophetology of the Islamic philosophers who preceded him. One day when reading in a Latin translation Avicenna's treatise, *On the Division of the Sciences*, I came across this sentence (I quote from memory): the standard work on prophecy and revelation is Plato's *Laws*. Then I began to begin to understand Maimonides's prophetology and eventually, as I believe, the whole *Guide of the Perplexed*. Maimonides never calls himself a philosopher; he presents himself as an opponent of the philosophers. He used a kind of writing which is in the precise sense of the term, exoteric. When Klein had read the manuscript of my essay on the literary character of the *Guide of the Perplexed*, he said, 'We have rediscovered exotericism.' To this extent we completely agreed."

by commending Strauss for accomplishing "nothing less than a revolution in intellectual history" by recalling us to the "wisdom of the past."[8]

What Kristol voiced, more than half a century ago while he was still a convinced liberal (since it was to be fifteen years until he emerged as a Neoconservative), anticipated the major impact that Strauss's works on Maimonides were to make on several generations of scholars, thinkers, and students. This is not to take for granted that Strauss himself would have given credence to the specific political uses to which any of his readers (Kristol among them) drew from his rediscovered Maimonides. However, as I believe it is not unreasonable to predict, these works of Strauss's are likely to continue to make this same sort of major impact on present and future generations of thinking men and women.

To be sure, Strauss's essays and lectures on Maimonides were able to make this impact only very gradually, working their magic on readers at first with less than dramatic fanfare. Nevertheless, they also decidedly hit their target. And however paradoxically it may have been manifested, they advanced and enlarged their impact by their peculiar mixture of scholarly precision, literary flare, and intellectual excitement. I would suggest that they were able to do this (at least in substantial measure) because of Strauss's decision to take Maimonides with the utmost seriousness, as a "perennial" thinker of greater profundity than most, as well as a classical literary artist of remarkable verve, subtlety, and originality—at the time all highly unconventional assertions. This was both in spite of his "medieval" character but also because of it, since Strauss perceived in Maimonides a unique exemplar capable of (as Kristol put it) "recalling us to the 'wisdom of the past,'" something that Strauss recognized modern man was desperately in need of. Or rather, to make this point with the appropriate reserve, and to place it in the proper context: the wisdom of the future is in need of aid from the wisdom of the past, whose vital elements can be recovered while not abandoning or denying our modernity. As a scholar and teacher, Strauss regarded it as his duty to try to instruct modern man about such lost wisdom, thus helping him

8. See Gertrude Himmelfarb, "Irving Kristol's Neoconservative Persuasion," *Commentary* 131, no. 2 (February 2011): 27. The original review by Kristol of Strauss's *Persecution and the Art of Writing* (1952), to which Himmelfarb refers, appeared in the still-liberal *Commentary* 14 (1952): 392–97. Kristol's report on the enormous impact made on him by Strauss's writings, teaching, and thought is presented in "An Autobiographical Memoir," in *Neoconservatism: The Autobiography of an Idea* (New York: Free Press, 1995), pp. 7–9.

to recover it for his own uses, as Strauss had progressively recovered it for himself. As Strauss concluded, we are unlikely to receive its like from any modern source, and yet we are urgently in need of this Maimonidean wisdom precisely as moderns: his is an essential fund and font of a forgotten wisdom which, it emerges, is vital for us and can still speak to us, especially because like him we are similarly compelled to spiritually wrestle with the still vigorous challenges of "Jerusalem and Athens." And as Strauss seems to have viewed it, Maimonides' wisdom is still capable of being employed by us for our own prudent use in the present, *if and only if* we judiciously adapt it to our own situation. To be sure, Strauss knew that this opportunity afforded by Maimonidean thought depends on whether we can, like Maimonides, recover access to the "wisdom of the past" as it actually was, with a historically accurate and philosophically adequate account, which requires the utmost scholarly care, precision, and thoughtfulness. In that case, this wisdom may yet paradoxically prove to be of great helpfulness to us in dealing with our own most pressing modern, and even postmodern, dilemmas.

"How to Study Medieval Philosophy" (1944) is Strauss's mature effort to consider what it means to engage in the serious study of medieval philosophy, especially as it relates to the thought of Maimonides. Yet simultaneously he wonders whether it is even possible for modern readers to comprehend medieval thought and not to distort it in the process of modern study. Strauss suggests that in order to avoid this hazard, modern readers must adopt a fresh approach to the matter: if they are to be truly open minded, they must begin with the premise that they may in fact have something to *learn* from the medievals, rather than seeing them only in the light of what they may have contributed in advance to the establishment of modern thought. In addition to this, Strauss counsels modern readers to avoid merely tallying the record of errors which the medieval philosophers are presumed to have committed as compared with what has been attained in the ostensibly superior realm of modern philosophy and science. Although it was not Strauss's aim to dismiss or to disparage modern thought, his intention was to show how to aver its limits so as to be fully alert to the dilemmas in which modern philosophic thought remains entangled. In fact, he goes so far as to question whether the moderns have so benefited from the medievals as to have advanced beyond them, at least on certain fundamental issues. Accordingly, he points to the medievals who produced the first true debate between the rival claims of faith and reason inasmuch as they contended with one another about the truth. As Strauss puts it, "The Middle Ages witnessed the first, and certainly the first *adequate*, discussion between these two most important forces of the Western world: the religion of the Bible and the science or philosophy of the Greeks. It was a discussion, not between ethical monotheism and paganism, i.e., between two religions, but between religion as such and science or philosophy as such."

In order to grasp what is still alive in this medieval discussion, Strauss assembles the pieces of his well-known argument by maintaining that what is needed to penetrate medieval thought is a strictly "historical" (rather than "historicist") approach to studying past, and especially premodern, thinkers. This imposes a duty on modern scholars and students to try to comprehend the thinkers of the past just as they comprehended themselves—which is no simple task—rather than to try to comprehend them better than they comprehended themselves.[9] This is the reverse of what had been previously assumed by almost everyone: that modern thought is self-evidently and unconditionally superior to the thought of the past, which rests on the prior belief in the progressive character of modern thought. However, as Strauss observes, we can no longer be so confident in this belief, faced as we are with the historical facts reminding us of our chastened modern condition, in that we have witnessed "catastrophes and horrors of a magnitude hitherto unknown."[10] This suggests that the past (although it is not to be romanticized) may not, as compared with the present, have represented the depths of barbarism and benightedness we once might have supposed, calling at the very least for a reconsideration of past thought and philosophy as not necessarily grounded in depravity, ignorance, unfairness, or superficiality.

For Strauss, one must instead make the effort at the very beginning to examine what it is to be modern, and to wonder afresh about the belief in the superiority of modern thought as supposedly a product of progress in history. One must try to discern as precisely as possible what genuine progress is, in what spheres genuine progress may have been made, and what aspects of progress are only ostensible and hence illusory. (His most serious effort in this regard, which cuts across any differences between his study of Jewish thought and his study of philosophy or political thought, appeared astoundingly in "How To Begin To Study *The Guide of the Perplexed*.") Next one

---

9. See "How to Study Medieval Philosophy," chap. 1 below.
10. See "Jerusalem and Athens," in *Jewish Philosophy and the Crisis of Modernity*, p. 399.

must suspend such a belief tentatively, at least while one is in the act or process of interpreting thinkers of the past. Otherwise, we cannot hope to even potentially learn anything *from* them, other than to confirm the superiority of the way we live and think now, which is to ignore the things here that are deficient for us in our modern world, and so to discount the possibility of our being in dire need of better advice and direction from a perhaps deeper premodern wisdom. Or as Strauss puts this in the most radical terms, based on what his argument must imply, "Therefore, if we are interested in an adequate understanding of medieval philosophy, we must be willing to consider the possibility that medieval philosophy is simply true, or, to speak less paradoxically, that it is superior, in the most important respect, to all that we can learn from any of the contemporary philosophers."

Besides certain methodological concerns (such as the duty to pay meticulous attention to precise terminological differences, and his explanation of why the "utmost literalness" in translations is to be prized), Strauss also advocates for an authentically historical approach to medieval philosophy. This leads to a momentous statement by Strauss that needs to be reflected on, although I can only highlight it: "The historian of philosophy must then undergo a transformation into a philosopher or a conversion to philosophy, if he wants to do his job properly, if he wants to be a competent historian of philosophy." If the historical approach is to be properly pursued, Strauss also stresses the need to carefully assess the differences between the life conditions of philosophy in the medieval Islamic world (which contributed to Maimonides' thinking) and the life conditions of philosophy in the medieval Christian world, as such differences exercised a great influence on medieval Jewish thought. This is not because Strauss thinks one is essentially superior to the other on any religious or political grounds, but rather because the greatest medieval Islamic philosophers—due to their self-consciousness about the theological-political context in which philosophy arose, and how this aided their further self-reflective consideration of the conditions which enable it to survive—made a much greater effort to think through what Strauss viewed as perhaps the "most fundamental question of philosophy, [i.e.,] the question of its own legitimacy and necessity." Indeed, it was Maimonides' full awareness of this elementary problem that likewise impelled him to approach the challenges to Jewish thought with "a philosophic radicalism which is absent from modern philosophy."

This radical thinking about the necessary conditions of philosophic thought and the philosophic life is a notion that perhaps cannot be stressed too much or too often for comprehending Strauss's own thought and its bold originality. Almost from the beginning Strauss recognized a certain limited though not negligible superiority of medieval philosophic thought to its modern equivalent, which transcended the obvious difference between them, i.e., they were superior because of how much they sensed the need to justify philosophy, and also because of how they did this. Despite the greater political freedom of modern thought, and its consequent triumphs in modern science, which we are entitled and even duty bound to cherish, Strauss concluded that modern thinking suffers from a sort of forgetfulness about why philosophy is necessary. As a consequence, Strauss believed the specific differences between the moderns and the medievals must always be kept in mind, especially by those who are tempted to precipitately judge modern thought to be definitively superior to medieval thought. Whatever may be the continued problems with assessing the relative merits of modern and medieval thought, Strauss came already at this point to the firm conviction that it is absolutely not sufficient to view the latter as, at most, a "mere" predecessor of the former.

"Spinoza's Critique of Maimonides" (1930) reproduces a core chapter from Strauss's first major book, *Spinoza's Critique of Religion*. It represents Strauss's original endeavor to penetrate the thought of Maimonides, but as seen in the light of and contrasted with Spinoza and modern philosophy. Though this was a critical and reflective effort to wrestle with Maimonides as a thinker who was capable of presenting a serious challenge to Spinoza and his claim to the sufficiency of modern thought, Strauss was subsequently to judge this chapter (and the book of which it was a key constituent) fatally flawed in terms of its main presupposition. He had assumed as his starting point that modern philosophy and science had definitively superseded, and perhaps also refuted, the medieval philosophy in which the thought of Maimonides is rooted.[11] As he was to put it from a mature perspective, "The present study was based on the premise, sanctioned by powerful prejudice, that a return to premodern philosophy is impossible." And yet even in this early work based on the premise of the necessity of modern thought, which he will later go so far as to characterize as a "powerful prejudice," he perceived

---

11. See "Preface to *Spinoza's Critique of Religion*," in *Jewish Philosophy and the Crisis of Modernity*, p. 173.

that Spinoza did not manage to vanquish and surpass Maimonides on every ground. This point, one may confidently assert, is cogently demonstrated by him in "Spinoza's Critique of Maimonides."

Even then, as becomes evident through a careful reading of this chapter, it seems there was a nagging doubt that plagued Strauss about what it was that compelled Spinoza to attack Maimonides so vehemently: was it perhaps because he was not able to subdue him quite as efficiently as he claimed? It is thus clear even from the beginning that Strauss was moved by an uncertainty (nurtured by Hermann Cohen) as to whether Spinoza was a decidedly superior thinker to Maimonides. If this was so, it is likely Strauss was also wondering about the usefulness of the scholarly project on which he was about to embark. He surely knew how much had already been written by historians of modern thought on Spinoza's "sources" and on who had exercised what philosophic influences on him. Why did he want to study Spinoza's criticisms, which had supposedly devastated Maimonides' thought, if it was only to make one last tally of Maimonides' defeated forces on the battlefield of philosophic history? The walking again of well-trod paths certainly was unlikely to yield an impressive prize for a bold voyager like Strauss: his hope was to discover an unknown continent of thought. As an ambitious scholar at the onset of his career, Strauss was searching for a worthier challenge, especially since, although he respected Spinoza, he did not view him with the same awe in which most modern Jewish thinkers held him. Even so, why did he write a long chapter dedicated to Maimonides, who, as Strauss entered the field, was of interest mainly to antiquarian historians as an example of medieval Jewish high culture? And why write on him as the direct target of Spinoza's criticism, especially since Spinoza's *Theologico-Political Treatise* only deals with Maimonides briefly, almost tangentially, and certainly dismissively?

In a significant measure, it may have been the combined spur of Strauss's two immediate predecessors—Hermann Cohen and Franz Rosenzweig—that impelled him to consider whether it is feasible to champion Maimonides against Spinoza. It is possible to clarify how this came to be by seeing it in light of the following: Cohen set a tough-minded if wrongheaded (according to Strauss) course against Spinoza, whom he faulted for numerous errors, while he also made forthright philosophic assertions in defense of Maimonides' ethics as still relevant to modern philosophy and hence to Jewish thought, implying Maimonides was not a completely obsolete thinker. Rosenzweig launched a bold modern theological counteroffensive against Spinoza and in favor of Maimonides by suggesting that revelation (formulated on the "personal" level) is the key to unlocking the religious secrets concealed in the Jewish tradition, which somehow modern Judaism had forgotten. This combined spur somehow helped Strauss to conceive of a way of uncovering a certain "primordial element" in Maimonides' thought, which had been able to withstand the destructive criticism directed against it by Spinoza. Spinoza had mounted his attack on Maimonides with great resourcefulness of rhetoric and in a supremely disdainful mode, but if his choice of weapons evoked shock and awe among his readers for the skillfulness of his dismissal, it had merely obscured his critique's flimsy substance vis-à-vis the primordial element in Maimonides, to which reference has previously been made.

This primordial element, which became the main issue for Strauss, turned on the status of revelation, at least as it had been defended by Maimonides in the form of prophecy. Maimonides mounted his defense of revelation in a meticulously cognitive manner, fully consistent with philosophy and science, so as not to base it on faith alone. Further, according to Strauss he merely safeguarded its *possibility* in accord with the properly designated limits of reason and nature, and not on arbitrary dogmatic assertions. Strauss discovered that this trenchant understanding had made Maimonides' position on prophecy impervious to Spinoza's effort to debunk it. This was because his debunking effort had been based on a mere presupposition, derived from overreaching modern reason. It had acted on the imperial assumption that it could decisively refute revelation: it claimed to do so by showing it as superfluous through the potential ability of science to explain quite adequately on its own everything in the world, even though—as Strauss clearly indicated—this had never actually been achieved, and indeed was almost certain never to be accomplished.

To show that Maimonides' thought was able to withstand Spinoza's attack required Strauss to proceed with a rare theological discernment and dialectical verve, even if he did not share the traditional belief in the *textual* aspect of revelation on which Maimonides' defense had seemed to depend. This means to say, Strauss was willing to grant to Spinoza his argument for biblical criticism as a "new science" that, once established, cannot be so readily removed. Insofar as Maimonides' view depended on belief in the divine mind and will manifesting itself in the form and contents of a book and revealed at a certain moment in history, Maimonides' position was seriously vulnerable. Yet even if Spinoza's critical-historical method of reading the Hebrew Bible represented in certain measure a decisive victory with regard to revelation actualized as book, Strauss was not quite so convinced that the fundamental element in this argument, i.e., revelation qua revelation, had ever been settled in a rationally satisfying way. To be sure, the various and sundry modern (and even orthodox) endeavors to vindicate revelation by rooting it in text and tradition as these are alleged to rise to divine status through a mere assertion of faith was unknown to the medieval Maimonides, who instead accepted it as an uncontested historical fact, even though he knew that the miracles surrounding it were always philosophically challengeable.

Even so, what is for Strauss the "primordial element" of Maimonides' thought, i.e., the unassailable belief in the *possibility* of revelation, is not dependent on history but rather rests on the fundamental religious ground of belief in the omnipotent God, this belief being something that it is impossible to refute rationally. Moreover, Strauss views this belief as possessing a greater depth than those attempts to reduce it to an aspect of medieval thought, which can itself be readily dismissed as scientifically obsolete. Instead, he conceives it as protected by the limits of philosophy *as such* in any era. Yet Strauss did not conclude that Maimonides' basic position on revelation is rooted pure and simple in general religious grounds, since the asserted teaching of faith in the omnipotent God is something that merely supports it. Instead, he emphasized the solidly rational, defensive stance of the Maimonidean position, which has cognitive validity of a permanent nature since it is built on the integrity of its reasoning process—and hence which is primarily philosophical, and only secondarily theological. Thus, theology (based on faith) appears only once the limits of reason have been established and demonstrated by reason, i.e., once man's lack of ability to know everything essential in the universe has been definitively established in terms of science. Only if man did possess the complete ability to know everything essential in the universe would it perhaps be possible to disprove the existence of an omnipotent God, and thus to render Him superfluous. But even man's utmost accomplishments in science will never allow him knowledge of everything essential, since the powers of the human mind cannot comprehend with certainty what is contained in the entire universe.

Hence, if philosophy or science as Spinoza conceived of them has never been able to refute revelation as a *possibility*, so Maimonides' basic position—such as whether the written text was once historically revealed as is—is still sustainable, and can be defended as valid, just as much now as then. The *possibility* of revelation has been and is still assured. That, for Strauss at this point in his thinking, was the decisive issue. Based on this reasoning, Strauss highlighted why Spinoza may well have considered Maimonides not so much the best champion of the medieval worldview as perhaps the most formidable rationalist representative of religious thought that is capable of being defended by a philosophic mind. This made Maimonides' way of thinking and of reading scripture not only a key exegetical obstacle, but also the major intellectual challenge that had to be removed if modern thought was to be victorious in its effort to build a different type of human world. This differently configured world is to be based on secular-rational science and will promulgate an altered (i.e., demythologized) view of man, God, nature, and scripture, not to mention one which will obviously also be immune to any supernatural messages that revelation might claim to bring.

At this beginning point of Strauss's voyage of discovery, he allowed that Spinoza had quite rightly relegated Maimonides to the ranks of those who employed a Jewish version of medieval Christian "scholastic philosophy" merely in order to defend the "pregiven Jewish position." As it happens, this is a phrase that Strauss never precisely defines, although it will have to be surmised that this refers to revelation. With regard to his recurring to medieval Christian "scholastic philosophy" in order to make sense of Maimonides, it will also be perceived by Strauss as a wrong turn he made, prepared first by Spinoza and next by almost the entire modern scholarly consensus. As Strauss observed, this made philosophy for Maimonides not so much an essential challenge to faith as merely a means to a theological end: once its threat had been neutralized, it was merely a highly useful tool in the perennial defense of revelation. To use such a tool as philosophy for such a purpose apparently did not—according to Strauss at this point—strike Maimonides as problematic. And as a result, Strauss did not regard Maimonides as needing to question philosophy as something that might not be so simple for religion to deploy for its own uses. Instead, he was most impressed with Maimonides' apparent certainty that philosophy or science is a legitimate tool for religion and poses no threat to it, because it *cannot* refute revelation. This lent Maimonides' thought a fully "modern" cast of mind in a neoorthodox spirit, a spirit that he also associated with the theology of Franz Rosenzweig, to whose memory he dedicated the book in which this study originally appeared. As his language reflects, Strauss followed in a clear manner the conventional modern scholarly view (distinctly traceable to Spinoza) that tended to see Maimonides' thought in light of Christian medieval philosophy rather than Muslim medieval philosophy, which at this point he did not think of as two significantly different things, at least insofar as he had to consider how to apply the difference to Maimonides. No doubt he recognized Maimonides as a sort of radical rationalist in some sense, but solely in the realm of theology: "Maimonides defines his position by two frontiers. In the face of orthodoxy he defends the right of reason, in the face of philosophy he directs attention to the bounds of reason.... The contest between belief and unbelief takes place on the plane of Aristotelian science."[12]

This perhaps prompted Strauss to conclude his study by wondering whether Maimonides possessed "some reasoning" that accounts for why he adhered even to the "pregiven Jewish position": for a man so close to philosophy, how is he able to justify his resort to revealed (as opposed to natural) theology other than by elementary loyalty to the "pregiven Jewish position"? As already noted, at this juncture Strauss seems to identify Maimonides' "pregiven Jewish position" more or less with revelation. But is it revelation pure and simple that he is calling the pregiven position? Strauss speaks of Maimonides' need for *something* beyond a mere "historical proof for the fact of revelation," which he knew already was not the sort of reasoning in which Maimonides usually rooted his most serious arguments. He sensed enough about Maimonides even then to "assume" that there had to be some "more radical significance"—and hence some less dogmatic implication—even to his adherence to what he calls the "pregiven Jewish position," i.e., conceived as revelation. So far as he was able to perceive at this point, "Maimonides himself casts no light" on that "radical significance."

Strauss did not believe that it was possible to uncover the full grounds for comprehending in what deepest reasoning this "radical" thinking was grounded, at least on the basis of what Maimonides himself wrote as he currently read it. He will subsequently articulate his impasse at this point by implying, with a paradox, that as he did with Spinoza, so too he did with Maimonides, reading him "too literally because he did not read him literally enough." ("Too literally" because "not literally enough" is the leitmotif of Strauss's 1965 "Preface" to *Spinoza's Critique of Religion*.) This "radical significance" will only emerge plainly to sight for him (although he may have been at work on it for quite a while) with the essay "The Philosophic Foundation of the Law: Maimonides' Doctrine of Prophecy and Its Sources" (hereafter "Maimonides' Doctrine of Prophecy"), which reflects his great rediscovery of Islamic medieval philosophy. He will uncover it as *the* source that helped him trace a vital, and not merely antiquarian, path toward classical political philosophy. This also proved to be the necessary framework and

---

12. "Spinoza's Critique of Maimonides," chap. 2 below.

entry point that enabled him to penetrate the obscure edifice of Maimonides' theological reflections. What was to be discovered by Strauss is dubbed by him "prophetology": he located through it the only adequate approach to Maimonides' view on revelation. If prophetology made Maimonides' prospect on revelation accessible, it also did not distort it by filtering it through modern presuppositions. Ultimately this will also bring Strauss to perceive in the *Guide* the labyrinthine logic of Maimonides' literary art, which helped him to unfold an entirely fresh vista on Maimonides' thought.

The next leg of Strauss's journey in search of Maimonides is represented by a lecture he delivered during the last days of his scholarly apprenticeship in Germany: "Cohen and Maimonides" (1931).[13] It is evident from this lecture that he was beginning to accurately comprehend Maimonides, although in certain aspects of his thought it is clear that Maimonides continued to perplex him. Even though Strauss had early on separated himself from the philosophic as well as Jewish legacy of Hermann Cohen,[14] this lecture epitomizes his first direct confrontation with Cohen's unprecedented modern reverence for Maimonides. To be sure, this reverence seems to have been mostly about

13. Evidently Strauss did deliver the lecture to the audience for which it was prepared, i.e., the Academy for the Science of Judaism in Berlin, the institute that had employed him as a researcher since 1925. However, it seems doubtful that he delivered this lecture precisely as written, or at least as actually preserved; this is made unlikely by its length alone. See the letter to Gerhard Krüger of 7 May 1931 in *Hobbes Politische Wissenschaft und zugehörige Schriften—Briefe*, vol. 3 of *Gesammelte Schriften*, pp. 384–85.

14. See "Introductory Essay to Herman Cohen, *Religion of Reason out of the Sources of Judaism*," in *Jewish Philosophy and the Crisis of Modernity*, pp. 267 as well as 281–82. Cf. also "A Giving of Accounts," ibid., p. 460; "Jerusalem and Athens," ibid., pp. 398–99; *What Is Political Philosophy?*, p. 242. For his allegiance to and yet break from Cohen's school, see especially *Studies in Platonic Political Philosophy*, p. 31: "At that time [I] was a doubting and dubious adherent of the Marburg school of neo-Kantianism." The "time" to which this refers, insofar as it represents the beginning of his study with Edmund Husserl, was in 1922. His view of Cohen in this period is perhaps best stated in his letter to Dr. Gottschalk of December 28, 1931, a letter that wavers ambivalently between steadfast reverence and sharp criticism, in Alan Udoff, "On Leo Strauss: An Introductory Account," in *Leo Strauss's Thought: Toward a Critical Engagement*, ed. Alan Udoff (Boulder, CO: Lynne Rienner, 1991), p. 22, n. 3. (Just who "Dr. Gottschalk" was, the person to whom Strauss addressed the letter drawn from the Leo Strauss Archive, remains so far unknown; nothing besides the name is stated on the letter itself.) Occurring in Strauss's letter to Gerhard Krüger (see n. 13 above) are his comments on the lecture's significance for the progress of his own thinking: "I attempted to show that Cohen had been, *in spite of everything*, right in his assertion that Maimonides was *fundamentally* a Platonist, and *not* an Aristotelian; to be sure, one cannot show this quite as *directly* as Cohen had done. In this lecture I made public for the first time my thesis about Islamic-Jewish scholasticism, that it understands revelation within the political and legal framework laid out by Plato." The emphases are Strauss's own. Strauss perhaps only first fully elaborated his thinking on how Socrates was substantively prior to even Plato and Aristotle in "The Origins of Political Science and the Problem of Socrates" (1958), ed. David Bolotin, Christopher Bruell, and Thomas L. Pangle, *Interpretation* 23, no. 2 (Winter 1996): 127–207.

Cohen's justifying his own late turn to Jewish philosophy rather than about any effort to precisely grasp Maimonides as he actually was. As a result, Cohen's depiction of Maimonides presented him as if he had anticipated Cohen's own thought. Yet simultaneously—if not also paradoxically—Cohen almost unwittingly pointed Strauss toward a more authentic Maimonides. As his voyage of discovery unfolded, this emerged as a fateful moment for him, since in the wake of the encounter that Strauss had staged between Spinoza and Maimonides, and additionally urged on by Cohen, he continued his endeavor—though less determined by modern premises—to search for greater clarity about reason and revelation in the thought of Maimonides. This thought, if definitely medieval, only further fascinated Strauss since it was, as he uncovered, peculiarly rooted in philosophy at its ancient origins, i.e., in the way of Socrates, as Cohen himself had almost naively brought this to light.

This eventually yielded the principal debt that Strauss owed to Cohen, although what he gave him was no simple gift but a seemingly eccentric contention which he had to rethink for himself: Maimonides was fundamentally and at the deepest level a Platonist rather than an Aristotelian. To be sure, Cohen's contention about Maimonides stood against the consensus that had been declared by most modern scholars and philosophers, and that was consecrated as fact in all of the textbooks, which made Cohen seem not only eccentric but also badly misguided. Yet Strauss recognized an essential truth in it, even if he also became convinced that Cohen had maintained this contention for the wrong reason, namely, his assertion of Plato's belief in the primacy of the good as rooted solely in the *moral* good. Of course, Strauss acknowledged Cohen's attempt to think through the history of philosophy for himself in an effort to establish his own philosophy on a solid ground, which allowed him to conceptualize afresh such great thinkers as Plato and Maimonides. Almost no other modern philosopher (with a couple of interesting exceptions, such as Gottfried Wilhelm Leibniz and Solomon Maimon) had, like Cohen, shown such a high regard for Maimonides as a thinker who is still vital, and not merely a historical relic: Cohen alone took Maimonides seriously as a thinker who, even though medieval, still had much to teach modern thinkers, whether or not they fully accepted his teachings. What Cohen had unwittingly helped to clarify for Strauss was that Maimonides' thought was peculiarly rooted in philosophy at its archaic and yet still somehow compelling origins, this being in the ancient mode of Socrates rather than in the modern mode of Immanuel Kant.

What had impelled Strauss to move beyond Cohen as a guide to Maimonides? Strauss believed that although Cohen was capable of powerful insights, he tended to be misguided about how to accurately read Maimonides. Already in 1931 Strauss took a hermeneutical stand on the side of the "historical" explication of texts rather than the "idealizing" interpretation, viewing the historical approach as better able to bring the careful reader closer to the reality of a past thinker's actual thought. To do this, he was compelled to raise the question of why Cohen had first turned to Maimonides, which may at least also imply that Strauss was questioning why he himself was turning for help in the same direction. Cohen focused on Maimonides as a portion of his effort to produce a modern Jewish philosophy that, through an interpretation of the Jewish tradition, proved this tradition to be fully consonant with the truths of modern rationalism and the Enlightenment. We may summarize this justifying motive by saying that, in essence, Cohen was trying to prove that moral rather than intellectual perfection is the highest excellence for human beings, which seemed better harmonized with the moral egalitarianism of the modern Enlightenment.[15] He claimed to show that this was especially evident in the major works of Maimonides, which could only be proved by the explication of his texts in the Cohenian manner. Ultimately, according to Cohen, Maimonides best represented the cause of rationalism and enlightenment not only in Judaism, but also in modern Western religion per se as it relates to morality. Since Strauss did not reject this rationale given by Cohen as at least a respectable motive for studying Maimonides, it seems clear that he too was in search of an answer to whether there can be an enlightened Judaism, and if so, then what shape it will need to assume.

Although Strauss persevered with Cohen on Maimonides as the model of rationalism and enlightenment rooted in religious tradition, he gradually became convinced that this medieval form of rationalism (though loosely linked with the modern form) was not strictly speaking the same sort of enlightenment. That is to say, a break had occurred at some point along the way as this rationalism marched toward the modern. And it only follows from this that if these were not the same, this would radically challenge the claims that Cohen made for Maimonides. Likewise, Strauss started to entertain severe doubts about the exegetical method used by Cohen to prove his case. Maimonides postulated his "allegorical" interpretation as the correct method for

---

15. See "Cohen and Maimonides," chap. 3 below. Cf. also Martin D. Yaffe, "Leo Strauss on Hermann Cohen's 'Idealizing' Appropriation of Maimonides as a Platonist," in *Reorientation: Leo Strauss in the 1930s*, ed. Martin D. Yaffe and Richard Ruderman (New York: Palgrave Macmillan, forthcoming).

reading the Hebrew Bible, since this aimed to uncover the original thinking of the biblical authors as made evident in scripture. Cohen claimed his "idealizing" interpretation was merely a revised version of the same thing, in which modern ideas were supposedly adapted to a method by which one was made able to enter ancient thinking. However, Strauss perceived that Cohen presumed to grasp these authors *better* than they grasped themselves, not *as* they grasped themselves, putting modern thought automatically on the superior level. This made the past relevant only insofar as it is an advance version of modern wisdom, rather than containing potential guides, capable of being uncovered in past sources, which the present might not possess, or to which it might not otherwise obtain ready access, whatever the reason may be as to why it lost touch with these truths. As Strauss recognized, Maimonides asserted the potential value of the past because he was able to rediscover in the sources the original mind beneath their surface meaning, so allowing his era to be potentially guided, or at least informed, by ancient wisdom. Hence, even if one might judge both Maimonides and Cohen as rationalists, and even if both expressed themselves in favor of enlightenment, this is not enlightenment in precisely the same sense or of the same type. In fact, Strauss discovered that each construed the terms of rationalism and enlightenment quite differently, which henceforth would make it imperative for him to identify these divergences in order to recognize their ramifications.

Once Strauss uncovered the ancient philosophic realism concealed beneath Maimonides' medieval thought, it was difficult for Strauss to conceive of him as a piously moralistic thinker enveloped in quasi-modern rationalism. As a result of this critical insight, Strauss was also able to offer an explanation for Cohen's motive for thinking as he did, and that was to become decisive for Strauss's own mature thought. If Cohen helped Strauss to perceive the Platonic basis of Maimonides' thought, Strauss's version did not imply the radical opposition between Plato and Aristotle to which Cohen subscribed, and which he also ascribed to Maimonides, because both Plato and Maimonides (according to Cohen) criticized Aristotle for a faulty reasoning which supposedly caused him to demote morality. Yet Strauss lucidly perceived, contrary to Cohen, that Aristotle certainly did not lack a serious and even primary focus on ethics. In Cohen's misreading, Aristotle had been charged with this lack merely because he rated the life of the mind ultimately higher than the moral life, which stood against the intellectual egalitarianism of the modern Enlightenment. However, it was plain to Strauss that Maimonides, in his own assessment of the highest purpose toward which human life naturally tends, had maintained precisely the same position on this essential issue as had Aristotle and Plato: he believed in the primacy of intellectual perfection rather than in any merely moral good as the very highest potential excellence of human beings. Further, Maimonides judged this notion entirely consistent with the most authoritative notions about the good life and human excellence that have always been promulgated in the Jewish tradition.

Similarly, Cohen comprehended Plato's thought so as to elevate the precedence of morality in it, and Strauss acknowledged a sort of truth in Cohen's contention. However, Strauss also believed that Cohen missed or misconstrued the priority and value of *politics* (to which ethics is subordinated) in relation to philosophy for Plato. To Strauss, even revelation and hence religion has to be seen in light of the political, at least as this was Platonically conceived. Likewise, Strauss was prompted by Cohen to comprehend the significance of Socrates in Plato's written dialogues. This turn to Socrates (his life, fate, and teaching) had somehow been appreciated by Cohen as what Maimonidean thought seems to imply. But what he had not appreciated was that this focus on Socrates, who had been closely linked with Plato and Aristotle, was first raised to prominence by the great Islamic philosophers who had exercised a major influence on Maimonides. Rather than allotting to Socrates the primarily moral core that Aristotle occasionally seemed to assign to him, Maimonides and the Islamic philosophers helped Strauss to discover a deeper understanding of what philosophy is, and how high its value is in human life, by considering Socrates on his own as opposed to how he was envisaged by Cohen (never mind Aristotle). Strauss perceived that Socrates had been responsible for launching a fresh start for philosophy, based on the priority of the eternal questions, and the pursuit of philosophy as a way of life. This makes its one essential (if two-sided) truth—i.e., our need to know what the right or best life for man is, and the difficulty of our ever being certain about it—something that is never to be surpassed or submerged by the discovery of any other truths. Philosophy is almost unavoidable, and it certainly cannot be readily overturned, because the very basis of philosophy remains a problem for itself as much as for its critics and opponents.

Strauss was not, in the final analysis, as persuaded by the moral and political protections of modern individualism in the form espoused by Cohen. This was a belief that distinctively accompanied Cohen's faith in historical progress, but Strauss regarded them both as flawed in their conception of human nature, and of what it is possible to make of humanity as a totality. And if Cohen explicitly faulted Plato—and implicitly faulted Maimonides, whose basic views clearly accorded with those of Plato—for neglecting to adhere to modern notions about individualism, Strauss started to become aware of something deeper in the conception of man envisioned by Plato and Maimonides. It could perhaps even be suggested that Strauss was drawn to them precisely for their tacitly critical attitude toward what were to become the modern notions. Strauss's attraction to what he viewed as the freer thinking by premodern philosophers seemed to show him that the modern notions do not contain the whole truth about man, even if for him they constitute a significant part of it, i.e., natural equality, and (as Maimonides puts it) "the differences among the individuals belonging to the human species."[16] Meanwhile, in spite of the tacitly critical attitude assumed by Plato and Maimonides toward ancient and medieval ideas that approximated the modern notions, Strauss also allowed them to teach him to vigorously resist the temptation (unlike some contemporary "conservative" European thinkers with whom he was acquainted) to abandon or diminish reason and enlightenment in the process of thinking through such criticism. In this sense it was possible to vindicate Cohen and Maimonides together: they were no doubt united by a common, unyielding commitment to both reason and enlightenment, and to the Jewish tradition, whatever their differences. However, there is no doubt that the most significant result of Strauss's critical research into the legacy of Cohen was his recognition that Maimonides, in surveying human nature, had presented him with a deeper version of rationalism and enlightenment, because of what these taught him about the contemplative life as this shapes our view of what man is. This is indeed ironic, considering that Cohen had declared these as his special jurisdiction, claiming that modern philosophy possessed a greater profundity about man than any attained by its ancient and medieval predecessors.

As Strauss ends this lecture, it is evident that he was critically aware of the looming crisis which modern philosophic thought faces, especially in the wake of Heidegger's radical historicism. According to the belief which it is evident he was already going toward and which did not have to await the

---

16. See *Guide* 2.40, p. 382, in which Maimonides definitely affirms human individuality as a good, while he also assumes a balanced and dialectical attitude toward it; see also 3.12, pp. 447–48, in which Maimonides definitely affirms natural equality among human beings as a good (indeed, as "established" by God), while he also assumes a balanced and dialectical attitude toward it. As for the tacit and dialectical teaching on progress that Maimonides elaborates, consider *Guide* 3.29 and 32, in conjunction with Strauss's treatment of this theme in "Introduction to Maimonides' *Guide*," and "How To Begin," chaps. 10 and 11 below.

later unfolding of his thought, what modern philosophy is most in need of is a reconsideration of the natural perspective which he calls—in the joint spirit of Plato, Aristotle, and Maimonides—the "*eternal* good" and the "*eternal* order*.*" This somehow enduring perception of human things as they present themselves in their unchanged, essential manifestation contrasts with the radically historical (and hence constantly varying) one that has come to dominate modern thought. Even as early as 1931, Strauss hints in this lecture that this is *the* most significant issue which modern thought will have to consider in the immediate historical future. Much is concealed beneath these provocative and unconventional remarks, which Strauss was only to bring fully to light in his subsequent teaching. As Strauss's lecture "Cohen and Maimonides" assuredly concludes, it is this lost, forgotten, or rejected dimension of philosophy which still contains a wisdom about man once self-evident to most Western philosophers in the tradition of Socrates. Strauss observed that only this wisdom can help to remedy the contemporary collapse of seriousness about moral issues which even in Cohen's mind was of such essential concern.[17] To be sure, this did not prevent Strauss from remaining impressed by Cohen for his original thought about what philosophy is. However, in trying to defend the noble cause of enlightenment and rationalism against its "postmodern" philosophic critics, sophisticated detractors, and cultured despisers, Strauss reckoned that Cohen could not repel their attacks by an unavailing philosophical endeavor to unconditionally defend progressive morality as the absolute truth.

Here Strauss seems to have already reached the conviction that even

17. Although written much subsequent to 1931, Strauss's comments on the debate between Martin Heidegger and Ernst Cassirer at the Davos philosophy conference of 1929 reflect the same attitudes toward the fate of the philosophic and political project of Cohen as are already contained in the lecture: see "Kurt Riezler" (1956), in *What Is Political Philosophy?*, pp. 246, as well as the almost identically similar views in his review of Cassirer's *The Myth of the State* (1947) in the same book, p. 295. Indeed, its historical fate was summarized by Strauss in viewing Cassirer's project as contrasted with Heidegger's project: "Having been a disciple of Hermann Cohen [Cassirer] had transformed Cohen's philosophic system, the very center of which was ethics, into a philosophy of symbolic forms in which ethics had silently disappeared. Heidegger on the other hand explicitly denies the possibility of ethics because he feels that there is a revolting disproportion between the idea of ethics and those phenomena which ethics pretended to articulate." Likewise: "if Cassirer were right in his appraisal of the rights-of-man thesis of the enlightenment [i.e., as no longer encountering serious difficulties], an adequate answer to the challenge raised by the doctrines favoring the political myth of our time—for example, those of Spengler and Heidegger—would have been not an inconclusive discussion of the myth of the state, but a radical transformation of the philosophy of symbolic forms into a teaching whose center is moral philosophy, that is, something like a return to Cassirer's teacher Hermann Cohen, if not to Kant himself. Considering the criticism to which Kantian ethics is open, this demand is not met by Cassirer's occasional restatements of Kantian moral principles."

Cohen's morality—which was a form of "rationally commanded" neo-Kantianism, as this culminated in philosophy and Judaism reconciled at their peak as a true expression of the modern-historical synthesis—must *somehow* prove itself to be eternally true beyond its merely progressive-historical character. And as this led Strauss to further surmise, Cohen's flawed scholarly-historical effort to rehabilitate Maimonides as a firm support for his own philosophical and political project could not help but progressively disintegrate due to the fact that this did not capture Maimonides as he truly was; such a historically artificial Maimonides could not bear the historical weight of carrying Cohen's project. The suddenly recognized reality of Maimonides—which ran contrary to Cohen's attempt to "idealize" him as a modern paragon, while distorting in historical-scholarly terms his authentic achievement—actually made him of greater interest to Strauss. This is because Strauss now viewed Maimonides' thought as a resilient standpoint in philosophy, from which it is possible for a valid, balanced, and friendly criticism of the moderns to emerge.

"Maimonides' Doctrine of Prophecy and Its Sources" (1935) offers a trenchant and pioneering treatment of Maimonidean "prophetology." This is a term that Strauss himself apparently devised in order to highlight a unique feature of medieval thinkers like Maimonides and his "predecessors" Alfarabi and Avicenna: they cogitated on the nature of prophecy and elaborated their speculations in a specialized yet synoptic science. This unusual term "prophetology" not only highlights their applying themselves to revelation per se reconfigured as a philosophic or scientific study of the prophet, but also emphasizes that they concentrated their focus on the careful analysis of human nature (psychology) and how it is to be best fulfilled in the well-ordered human society (political science), which they based on Platonic and Aristotelian notions. (As an aside, it is possible that Strauss's invention of this term may also have been his way of expressing a contrast between Maimonides and Spinoza, bringing to light through this coinage that both of them originated "new sciences": critical reasoning about the Bible versus critical reasoning about the prophet.) Maimonides' prophetology, which in principle approximated that of his medieval Islamic predecessors, is premised on an acceptance of the divine Law conveyed by the prophet, in which the revelation of God crystallizes itself. According to this conception, the prophet is the superlative or most perfect human being, defined according to the specifications of Platonic-Aristotelian-Farabian thought. This rational acceptance of the Law is established on the prior view that not only is the prophetic Law able to justify the life devoted to reason or enlightenment, but it actually commands such a life, at least for those who by nature are equipped for it. Thus, the Law issued by such a prophet, humanly perfected by nature, complements the religiously sanctioned search for rational "enlightenment" with the unresolved debate between reason and revelation. As such, the unique character of revelation qua revelation is preserved, according to Maimonides, in the Law's containing a *very* limited number of "suprarational" teachings irreducible to reason. At least as Strauss brings it to light, the prophetic Law preserves the tension between these two spiritual forces (if one may so put it), while it also allows for their continued fruitful dialogue with one another.

As should be noted, this essay is a chapter drawn from a book, which was the next major work produced by Strauss: *Philosophy and Law: Contributions to the Understanding of Maimonides and His Predecessors* (1935). The subtitle, however, is slightly misleading, since—as the monumental introduction makes much clearer—the book as an entirety is concerned not just with comprehending Maimonides' and his predecessors' thought, but also with its possible usefulness as a helpful corrective to modern thought. In terms of its unspoken historical context, Strauss wrote it in the shadow of four appallingly grim occurrences: Adolf Hitler's rise to power in Germany; the deprivation of the civil rights of the Jews in Germany by the Nazi government acceptable to the majority; the frailty of the enlightened West's resistance to the Nazi regime, and its unwillingness to defend or assist the Jews; and the shocking betrayal by Martin Heidegger of the Western tradition of philosophy (which he dismissed as discredited rationalism), in his swearing fealty to the tyrant Hitler and his Nazi ideology and regime. Seen in this light, the book exemplifies Strauss's search for an adequate defense of rationalism in the face of its modern collapse as well as his tacit investigation of the causes of the collapse, which he predicated on the historical victory both of the Bolsheviks in Russia and especially of the Nazis in Germany. This was also one of the last Jewish books that Schocken Press was allowed to release in Nazi Germany. As such, it represents a passionate effort by a relatively youthful German Jew to somehow come to terms with the spiritual dilemma provoked by the unprecedentedly dire political situation in which he and his fellow German Jews had been cast for almost three years since 1933. It attempted to go to the heart of the spiritual dilemma concealed in these events by discerning the signs of an unparalleled crisis befalling modern Judaism and the West. The book is definitely a turning point in Strauss's own thought as well.

In this chapter (also appearing in print as a separate article),[18] we witness Strauss's first direct confrontation with the thought of Maimonides. Previously, he had mostly contrasted Maimonides with his early modern critic Spinoza, and with his late modern defender Cohen. What is also noteworthy about this essay is that he deals with an array of subjects that were to henceforth preoccupy him and be the objects of his subsequent thought, i.e., Plato and Aristotle, revelation and reason, ancients and moderns, political philosophy in history, the relevance of medieval thought, etc. These topics were closely aligned with his ever-deepening study of Maimonides's works, since it was in his efforts to break through the seemingly impenetrable edifice of Maimonides's thought that these issues first rose to the surface. Maimonidean thought, as he was to recognize, somehow managed to uniquely balance the vital conflict between reason and revelation as that conflict was framed by the divergent claims of politics, theology, philosophy, morality, and education conceived in a scriptural context. Indeed, it is in order to pursue this unique balance that Strauss concentrates on what he dubs the prophetology of Maimonides, since he discovered that this was made a specialized medieval science for the sake of highlighting the nature of prophecy and revelation as compatible with philosophy or science. As such, it was capable of being rendered the focus of systematic study, since he regards it as being rooted in the natural human context. It is perhaps no surprise, then, that although there are seventeen chapters of his *Guide* (2.32–48)—roughly in the center of the book—dedicated to the careful elaboration of prophecy or revelation, Maimonides puts his discussion of this theme precisely in the context of the science of human nature in society.[19]

It is to be observed that Strauss emphasized the "rationalist" approach

18. In fact, the article by Strauss appeared in print almost simultaneously with the chapter in the book, although it is clear that the former was written first, and the latter is a subsequently edited version of it. The circumstances surrounding the vicissitudes of this article are discussed by Strauss in a note to the chapter. Although their contents are highly similar in most respects, the chapter contains many curious if slight changes, as well as a few occasionally remarkable differences. The present editor has offered in the notes to "Maimonides' Doctrine of Prophecy," chap. 4 below, details on how the later chapter differs from the earlier article.

19. Concerning matters which will rise to prominence in subsequent essays of the present book, the Maimonidean prophetology may perhaps be located in the middle of the book: roughly between the center as to chapter numbers (2.13 or 2.15) and the center as to structure (3.1–7). For the ambiguity about what the central chapter is, and a discussion of what the proper middle chapter of the *Guide* is, see "Introduction to Maimonides' *Guide*," chap. 10 below, with n. 57.

to prophecy and revelation typical of Maimonides and his Islamic predecessors even though they aimed not to contravene a parallel commitment to religion, just so long as this is conceived in a properly enlightened form. Hence the rational study of religion (especially encompassing prophecy and revelation) must be rightly coordinated—and perhaps subordinated—to the rational study of politics and ethics, by which it has to be cognitively delimited. According to Strauss, this works for Maimonides as an approach to revealed truth because as a Jew he first accepts and obeys the *Law* (a political actuality) that is allowed to personify revelation as prior fact. Thus, for those like Maimonides who first accept the order of the Law and proceed from its authority, the life devoted to reason or enlightenment is not only legitimated by the Law, but is actually commanded by it, at least for those who are equipped by nature for such a strenuous and challenging but infinitely mind-stimulating life, so that this *seems* to resolve the conflict between reason and revelation. This is a conviction that Maimonides shares with the Islamic philosophers whose teaching he has adapted, although as brought to light by Strauss perhaps he stresses in greater measure than they do the complete conformity of the Law with reason, while he likewise requires it to contain a certain, very limited number of suprarational teachings.[20]

At the present juncture, it is not clear how Strauss interprets this "divergence" in Maimonides' thought.[21] It is worth considering an example relevant to that divergence: is viewing the Law as being completely permeable to reason a mere "myth" promulgated by Maimonides, or is this an actual fact that he believes he can genuinely prove, as he claims? Strauss makes plain that Maimonides had allowed himself to be taught by the two previous Islamic philosophers, Alfarabi and Avicenna, from whom he acquired the essential contours of his science, although perhaps they were not sufficient to provide him with its entire contents in every case. In other words, Maimonides followed them on most points—or rather, he held certain key points in common with them—while he also joined some of their ideas together and produced an original synthesis of their admittedly not-always-parallel thought, thus determinedly maintaining his autonomy as a thinker. Indeed, Strauss actually claims that it was Maimonides who best thought through this shared

---

20. See "Appendix 4B: The Legal Foundation of Philosophy," chap. 4 below. See also *Philosophy and Law*, p. 77; *Philosophie und Gesetz: Frühe Schriften*, vol. 2 of *Gesammelte Schriften*, p. 64.

21. See Marvin Fox, *Interpreting Maimonides: Studies in Methodology, Metaphysics, and Moral Philosophy* (Chicago: University of Chicago Press, 1990), pp. 67–90, who stresses (apparently against Strauss) the significance of the logical difference between the two terms, "contradictions" and "divergences," which are seemingly highlighted in *Guide* 1.Intro., p. 20.

tradition, carrying it to the furthest point possible.[22] Yet Maimonides also diverged from his predecessors on several related points, probed by Strauss for their unusual reasoning, whose remarkable character he sheds light on. This resulted in Strauss's effort to trace the origins of their shared prophetology—received, appropriated, and revamped by Maimonides—and to uncover its roots in Roman-Hellenistic philosophy, and ultimately in the classical philosophers, Plato and Aristotle. And what he uncovered among these ancient philosophers was that, countermanding Cohen and supporting Spinoza, the medieval position was composed of a common philosophy, although it was not necessarily guilty of the crimes with which Spinoza charged it, i.e., with justifying the medieval "priestly regime" and its manifest corruptions. Likewise contrary to the image of Plato and Aristotle as deeply opposed philosophers, which Cohen had vigorously promoted for his own reasons impelled by modern philosophy, this common philosophy—certainly with numerous, significantly variant strains—formed an essential unity in which it was possible to adhere to *both* Plato *and* Aristotle. This is because their common philosophy was grounded in the unifying figure of Socrates, who stood at its origin. To be fair, Strauss acknowledges that revisiting Socrates was something to which Cohen had actually pointed him. But Strauss's own study of Maimonides was able to carry this point much further: it proved to him that "Socrates" as a revolutionary figure in the history of philosophy led as much to Aristotle as it did to Plato, and certainly also showed the way eventually to Maimonides.

But why is any of this history ultimately significant? How much can any of these historical issues help us now? Here Strauss, never succumbing to the temptation of historicism as antiquarianism, always raises the spiritual dilemmas of the present moment as the context in which even the study of the medievals must be set. His epic introduction to *Philosophy and Law* wrestles with the current state of modern Judaism, which Strauss construes as caught in an almost irresolvable predicament, because the rule of reason, in which modern Judaism had rooted itself, has collapsed. Decidedly not wanting himself to say farewell to reason, Strauss begins and ends with an argument for the need to reconsider Maimonides and his approach to "enlightenment," however seemingly obsolete it had been declared because it

---

22. Strauss impressively characterizes Maimonides' version as follows: "Maimonides' prophetology . . . in general is the most fully elaborated form of the medieval prophetology" (die Prophetologie Maimunis . . . die ausgeführteste Form der mittelalterlichen Prophetologie überhaupt ist). See *Philosophy and Law*, p. 77; *Philosophie und Gesetz: Frühe Schriften*, vol. 2 of *Gesammelte Schriften*, p. 64.

had been assigned to the medieval past and conceived as its mere "product." In the less closely interpretive and more synthetically exhilarating line of reasoning in the introduction as it stands on its own, Strauss makes a compelling and thoroughly original argument to show the continued pertinence of the "Maimonidean" approach for those whose minds remain open to the unresolved debate between reason and revelation, and yet who will not abandon their commitment to reason in favor of just retreating from modern irrationalism to revelation, whether "fundamentalist" or "progressive."[23]

Essentially Strauss endorses Hermann Cohen's phrase that Maimonides is "the 'classic of rationalism' in Judaism." However, contrary to Cohen, for Strauss this is because his "rationalism" is *not* entirely of the modern type, but rather of an ancient-medieval type, which he claims can avoid the degradation and collapse of modern rationalism, as he witnessed it occurring around him in Germany of the 1920s and 1930s. Indeed, this is one of Strauss's most radical claims in the book: he maintains that the flowering of irrationalism is of a sort which can ironically be traced to modern rationalism itself. A footnote makes the point with the utmost acuteness: "[Modern] 'irrationalism' is just a variety of modern rationalism, which in itself is already 'irrationalistic' enough." If Strauss may have moderated somewhat this harsh judgment in his subsequent works, it remained true for him that Maimonides' classical (as opposed to "merely" medieval) rationalism and enlightenment endures for him as the standard against which any present and future rationalism is still to be measured.

According to how Strauss formulates the modern dilemma, he regards it as a choice between two untenable alternatives: on the one hand, liberal faith in the necessary rational progress of history, and on the other hand, Nietzschean-Heideggerian existentialism as adapted to its manifold left and right versions. At this point, he also defines the aforementioned unsustainable choice as being between orthodoxy and atheism:

> If finally there is in the modern world only the alternative "orthodoxy or atheism," and if on the other hand the need for an enlightened Judaism is urgent, then one sees oneself compelled to ask whether enlightenment is necessarily modern enlightenment. Thus one sees oneself induced—provided one does

---

23. For a better comprehension of Strauss's contentions advanced in favor of the "Maimonidean" approach as still current, readers are especially urged to consult the entire "Introduction" of *Philosophy and Law*, only selectively reproduced in the present book as appendix 4A to "Maimonides' Doctrine of Prophecy."

not know from the outset, as one cannot know from the outset, that only new, unheard-of, ultra-modern thoughts can resolve our perplexity—to apply for aid to the medieval Enlightenment, the Enlightenment of Maimonides.

The only genuine escape from this dilemma is to "apply for aid" to Maimonides, in such a manner as to make his position intellectually and morally compelling again, so much so that it might paradoxically save modern reason and the Enlightenment. No doubt this was a far-reaching claim, and he knew that thinking men and women would entertain serious doubts. At the same time, Strauss warned that one must acquaint oneself with the objections to his argument on behalf of Maimonides, so that this "escape" from our impossible choice is to be done by rational people acting rationally, and not merely as an extravagant gesture or act of will, bespeaking despair, muddleheadedness, distress, or loss of nerve. One must probe in such a thorough fashion as to know, and not merely believe or assert, the answers to such questions as What are Maimonides' most essential teachings, especially as can endure beyond the medieval context? What may be the genuinely obsolete elements of his teachings, and can they be legitimately separated from the historical context in which they arose, or from related elements critical to his thought? Moreover, is it genuinely possible to accept on rational grounds the Maimonidean position even as adapted to the modern circumstances, or is it just a subjective preference or wish?

Strauss is careful to enumerate the main demurrals against the Maimonidean position, perhaps because he knows that most modern thinkers will be disposed to automatically reject Maimonides' thought. Indeed, he anticipated their response, in which this position will automatically be considered morally regressive, scientifically antiquated, and made obsolete by history and progress. Hence, I believe Strauss conceals beneath his historical presentation the fitting "Maimonidean" reply to each of these demurrals, rather than directly addressing the matter of his continued relevance. Strauss appeared to understand that however much contemporary thinkers may rationally doubt the premises of modern thought, this doubt is not enough for most of them to seriously consider looking to the past for guidance, for fear of throwing away what is still good and true in modern thought as benefits the modern individual, and for worry about seeming to try to overturn modernity as in recent massively destructive fits of collective irrationalism. In fact, he shows himself to accept these as perfectly reasonable qualms by presenting the questions himself as sound concerns, which he himself can see just as well:

> Is [the Maimonidean position] not the precursor and model of just that moderate Enlightenment of the seventeenth and eighteenth centuries that was least able to stand its ground? Is it not even altogether more "radical" in many respects, more dangerous to the spirit of Judaism, than the modern Enlightenment? Is it not based on the irretrievable Aristotelian cosmology? Does it not stand or fall with the allegorical method of interpretation? Is not the modern Enlightenment therefore, with all its questionableness, still preferable to the medieval?

It seems that Strauss cannily aims to get his readers to explore these doubts *while* he brings them through the process of comprehending the subtleties of Maimonidean thought. By proceeding in this way, he suggests that the answers to these reasonable questions will arise in the midst of this presentation and hence tacitly indicates that these "old" ideas can be fittingly adapted to a new historical situation, i.e., the contemporary world, while not abandoning the best aspects of modern thought and simultaneously also addressing the failures of modern thought. The assumption of this procedure seems to be that modern readers are entitled to ask whether Maimonides successfully managed to reconcile revealed religious tradition, based on scripture and guided by Law, with the political philosophy descended from Plato and Aristotle. Did he do this in such an inventive and expeditious fashion so as to prove that Maimonidean thought might also be accommodated to modern thought?

If I am correct in my assessment of Strauss's response to these critical challenges, he was especially thrilled to make his first discovery of the powerful medieval Muslim philosophic thinkers, Alfarabi and Avicenna, with whom Maimonides was closely connected. This is because it not only helped him to clarify Maimonides' thinking, but it also seems to have occurred to him that it allowed him to restore a broken link with the ancients. This had hitherto not been sufficiently appreciated by modern scholars (even by the likes of the great 19th-century scholar Salomon Munk, who was familiar with these Maimonidean "predecessors"), since these scholars tended to see the medieval Islamic philosophers in light of the tradition of medieval Christian philosophy and its modern heirs. But that perspective tends to obscure or distort the Platonic-political point of origin in which thinkers like Alfarabi, Avicenna, and Maimonides grounded their thought. This made it necessary for Strauss to determine as precisely as possible what Maimonides' close connection with them had been, and specifically why and at what points he had diverged from them. But in the end the vital element in Strauss's rediscovery of medieval Islamic philosophy was the focus on political philosophy, and especially on Platonic political philosophy, drawing as they did on both the *Republic* and the *Laws* as the keys to unlocking how to apprehend revelation and how to define its proper purpose in the life of human beings. Strauss noticed that Maimonides' and the Muslim philosophers' approach stressed the place of divine Law in revelation, a focus peculiar to Judaism and Islam that distinguished it from Christianity, even if the differences among the three revealed religions are ultimately not quite so simple. According to the Platonic-Farabian view adopted by Maimonides, the divine intention was to guide human beings toward perfection, and this required that at the same time the emphasis be put on society, ergo law: revealed or prophetic law orders well the affairs of most human beings in their common life together, while it also simultaneously prompts the select types with the potential for it toward the ultimate human perfection. As Strauss recognized, this view is a philosophic expression of a concern with the unavoidable and irreducible character of human nature as twofold, i.e., those able and those unable to be fully enlightened, which Plato first articulated as a required awareness in properly defending philosophy itself. As Plato and Farabi also taught him, it is a divide that man cannot make disappear, although he may moderate it somewhat by political and pedagogical enlightening measures, and hence philosophers must think through the consequences of the limits of that which can be changed in human nature.

Thus, the vital element in Strauss's rediscovery of the leading medieval Islamic philosophers, as they provided the model or prototype for Maimonides, was constituted by their focus on Platonic political philosophy. Indeed, as Strauss observed, perhaps the crucial turning point in their recovery of the principles of Platonic political philosophy was its helpful grounding for their prophetology, which was itself based on Plato's more or less predicting the type of the prophet needed in order to actualize the best state. Plato had already discovered the principles that were vital to advance the freedom of philosophic thinking in its theological-political context. Or as Strauss restates the Maimonidean point, the unconditional requirement for establishing the best human society is the perfection of the human being in the prophet, who is seen in light of Plato's notion of the philosopher-king. To be sure, Strauss was aware that this Platonic prescription for grounding the best human society—which makes true happiness, virtue, and perfection possible—had been adapted to medieval conditions by Alfarabi and Avicenna. It was precisely this adaptation that allowed Maimonides to make a similar adjustment of enlightenment to Judaism, thus rendering Plato's principles susceptible to being equated with the exact biblical description of the prophet, and especially with Moses the lawgiver. This insight permitted Strauss to perceive clearly why the prophet is so necessary for Maimonides, and why his prophet must conform to the list of requirements that is distinctive of Maimonides's crucial chapters on prophecy, and especially of the central chapter (*Guide* 2.40). And that for Strauss bore perspicuous implications as to what makes for the type of the model leader in any time and place.

To be sure, Maimonides did not follow his "predecessors" slavishly, and in fact he suggested quite a number of changes to the Jewish tradition, paralleling some of those which his Islamic predecessors had devised. He was well aware that this combined approach to revelation and politics did not begin with the medieval Islamic philosophers, for even they had their predecessors, and the roots of this doctrine are traceable to Hellenistic thought from the era of the Roman empire, i.e., Cicero and those who followed in the same line. Similarly it was no longer evident to Strauss that this doctrine has to be laid to rest with the onset and unfolding of modernity, since it curiously reappears (however distorted its form) in the middle of the 19th century.[24] Thus, this Platonic form of thought about prophetic statesmen becomes relevant again in the era of Nietzsche: he advocated for the rather vaguely defined "superman" as what was needed to resolve the general flatness or superficiality of modern thinking about human nature, and the resulting crisis of modern Western civilization. Yet as Strauss's revival of Maimonides should begin to make transparent, Nietzsche's "superman" might be contrasted very much

24. Harry V. Jaffa, in "Straussian Geography: A Memoir and Commentary" (2011), states the following about the relevance of Strauss's approach to Maimonides in his own work: "My conception of Lincoln was influenced from the outset by Strauss's exposition—especially in the long [Saturday] afternoons in Riverdale[, New York, in personal conversations at his home during 1944-49]—of the meaning of prophecy in Maimonides, and of the relationship of prophecy to philosophic kingship. The epigraph for Strauss's *The Argument and Action of Plato's 'Laws'* was from Avicenna, and was as follows: '[T]he treatment of prophecy and the Divine law is contained in . . . the *Laws*.' The cross-fertilization of inspiration, between Plato, Avicenna, and Strauss, which implies the mutual influence (or confluence) of Reason and Revelation, is mind-boggling, but it is not improbable, if one grants that the conversation of great minds is not confined to time and place. And, like the proverbial fly on the wall, one need not be a great mind to profit greatly from such conversations." See *Crisis of the Strauss Divided: Essays on Leo Strauss and Straussianism, East and West* (Lanham, MD: Rowman and Littlefield, 2012).

to his disadvantage with Maimonides' precisely defined prophetic lawgiver, who manifests classical virtues such as reasonableness and humanity that are still virtues essential to the superlative human being. This reconsideration seems to have further suggested to Strauss the need to philosophically reconceptualize the ancient theological-political grounding of Western civilization.[25] In doing so, Strauss shows the first signs of a breaking awareness of the momentous difference between esoteric and exoteric teaching vis-à-vis philosophic writers in the medieval and modern enlightenments. This awareness, although at this point only nascent, was to eventually grow and transform his entire conception of the history of philosophy and its relations with religion.

"Some Remarks on the Political Science of Maimonides and Farabi" (1936)[26] signals a realignment in Strauss's understanding of Maimonides. With it, he began his excavation, as a sort of philosophic archaeologist, of one of the crucial influences on Maimonides' thought: the work of the Muslim philosopher Farabi. It was in the work of this thinker that ancient philosophic thought had obtained perhaps its most authentic medieval analyst and reviver. (As Strauss was of course also aware, Maimonides had other key formative shapers of his thought, such as Alexander of Aphrodisias, one of the ancient commentators on Aristotle, not to mention Avicenna, another Muslim philosopher.)[27] But once Strauss decided, as shown by this essay, to concentrate on Farabi as a key to Maimonides, it was a sign that he had set his mind on standing against, if not overturning, the modern scholarly consensus. As a rule, 19th- and 20th-century scholars had almost uniformly declared an undifferentiated "Aristotle" to have been the major stimulus to his thought, even though they admitted that this was in some sense filtered through the lens of Muslim philosophers (and also the great Greek commentators on Aristotle). But Strauss asked, in just what sense was he a student of Aristotle? And whose Aristotle was it? True, he had already broken with convention by uncovering the

---

25. For an example of Strauss's own subsequent efforts in this direction that might suggest at least a Maimonidean inspiration, see "On the Interpretation of Genesis," in *Jewish Philosophy and the Crisis of Modernity*, pp. 359–76.

26. Referring to this article, Shlomo Pines suggests that Strauss provided "the first adequate recognition of the relation between al-Farabi's and Maimonides' political theory." See "Translator's Introduction: The Philosophic Sources of *The Guide of the Perplexed*," in *Guide*, p. lxxxix, n. 56. Worth studying as a complement to Strauss is the entire section on Farabi in Pines's introduction, pp. lxxviii–xcii.

27. For Alexander of Aphrodisias, see also "Introduction to Maimonides' *Guide*," chap. 10 below, with n. 76.

connection with Plato, but he was uncertain about the "type" of Plato who had made an impact on Maimonides: how, or in what form of thought, had Plato been transmitted to Maimonides? Even in the somewhat concealed or elusive form in which he appears by name in the *Guide*, it seemed evident that this is not as the paragon of political philosophy, i.e., as the author of the *Republic* and the *Laws*.[28] He seemed closer to the Plato of medieval Christian tradition, the Plato of the *Timaeus*, who speculated on cosmology and cosmogony. Yet Strauss sensed the presence of a Plato pointing in a different direction, even if he did not play a great role by name in the *Guide*.

To be sure, Strauss knew that among the medieval thinkers, Farabi was known as "the second teacher," this implying the one who followed Aristotle (and who subsumed Plato) in preeminence of thought, since Aristotle was regarded by the medievals as "the first teacher" of philosophy. Yet Farabi, as he discovered, also wrote several works on Plato as a philosopher, as well as on Plato's connection with Aristotle; moreover, Farabi also wrote a work reviewing each one of Plato's dialogues, in a sequence which he considered most rational. As for Maimonides' attitude toward Farabi, he had plainly affirmed his utmost respect for him, commending him fulsomely in a famous letter to his Hebrew translator Samuel ibn Tibbon. So Strauss began to wonder: precisely what sort a role had he played in forming the thought of Maimonides?[29] Strauss attempted to pinpoint those critical ideas, topics, and angles of approach by which Farabi had, as it were, guided Maimonides, touching especially on his Platonic political science, in which Farabi had been the first to efficaciously adapt the *Republic* and the *Laws* to the era of revealed religions. Indeed, as Strauss started to perceive, he had distinctively made

---

28. See *Guide* 1.17, p. 43; 2.6, p. 263; 2.13, pp. 283–84; 2.15, p. 290; 2.25, pp. 328–30; 2.26, p. 331; 3.18, p. 476. Besides the first and last items, all of the other references in the *Guide* are to Plato's views on creation or cosmology. As it happens, the first and last items do refer to aspects of his political philosophy. Maimonides mentions by name only one work by Plato: the *Timaeus*.

29. In Maimonides' famous letter to Ibn Tibbon, he more or less reports directly on the formative impact made by Farabi on him. In it he praises the thought of Farabi most highly and pays tribute to some of his works as free of fault. To be sure, prior to Strauss's uncovering these things, almost no one among the scholars knew a great deal about what was unique or original in Farabi's thought. Thus, Strauss is no doubt also responsible for "rediscovering" Farabi, which chapter in the history of his achievement has yet to be fully written. Strauss did possess some useful sources from which he struggled his way toward Farabi: Moritz Steinschneider's thorough bibliographic study; Salomon Munk's impressive scholarly notes in his Judeo-Arabic edition and French translation of the *Guide*; Leon Gauthier's pioneering 19th-century studies of medieval Islamic philosophy; Ernest Renan's provocative book on Averroes and Averroism, which contains comments on Farabi; and and the fresh study of and approach to medieval Islamic philosophic thinkers begun by his brother-in-law, Paul Kraus. Besides the present work, Strauss produced a youthful article on Farabi, "Eine Vermisste Schrift Farabis" (1936), and two mature articles, "Farabi's *Plato*" (1945), and "How Farabi Read Plato's *Laws*" (1957).

Platonic political science the framework in which the entirety of philosophy is to be viewed. But beyond this Strauss also ventured to determine the specific relation between the different philosophic stances of each thinker. He discovered that Maimonides, while following Farabi on some major themes, also diverged from him on several significant issues, awakening Strauss to wonder: what aspects of Farabi's thought were not adequate for Maimonides' purposes?

But prior to trying to discern the limits of Maimonides' Farabianism, Strauss makes his searching move toward Farabi of even greater moment by asserting the following claim: "It is only in their political doctrine that the medieval philosophers [like Farabi and Maimonides] discuss the [fundamental] basis of their thought." This is especially the case insofar as it connects their thought with "their belief in Revelation" as that which makes it unique vis-à-vis ancient and modern thought. Indeed, as a result of this claim Strauss wanted to know why politics is judged by Maimonides to be the master science, which encompasses even "theology" or "divine matters," since Maimonides expresses this contention only obliquely, although Strauss interpreted this elusiveness as intended.[30] Strauss explained that Maimonides proceeded so circumspectly in order to avoid the result which would likely follow from it: the offense caused to some if the Torah is explicated in the light of political science or philosophy. It would especially link Maimonides' views on the Torah with the politics of Plato as read by Farabi, who in offering commentary on the *Republic* and the *Laws* renders the superlative human achievement dependent on an actualized society which has been legislated by a prophet, who is conceived on the model of Plato's philosopher-king. In the divine Law proclaimed by such a prophet is contained the secret of teaching in which it is possible to form the character and mind of those who are fitted by nature to be philosophers as well as virtuous kings or legislators in the future. This is a Platonic notion of divine Law, reshaped by Farabi, so that revelation serves, in the language of Nietzsche, as "a prelude to the philosophy of the future."

If, as Strauss's article helps to clarify, Maimonides maintains certain divergences from Farabi, it is either because he sticks closer to Aristotle on some points or because he adapts Plato slightly differently to the theological-political needs of the Jewish situation. Or to put it metaphorically, Maimonides appreciates that although Farabi may have been aiming right, even so in shooting his arrows he slightly missed the center of the target. In other

---

30. See *Guide* 2.40 and 3.27–28.

words, Maimonides diverged from Farabi neither because he deviated from him on the political goal nor because he rejected the supremacy of philosophy in favor of the supremacy of faith for knowing the truth. He continued in the tradition of Farabi to conceive of revealed religion (i.e., divine Law) as being a natural facet of man's life in society with his fellow men, which allows him to achieve his ultimate perfection, a notion which is more or less equal to Platonic (or that which Strauss also prefers to call in this essay "Platonizing") politics. Thus, Strauss first concentrates on Maimonides' *Treatise on the Art of Logic*, chapter 14, in which he enumerates and delineates the elements of philosophy as branches of knowledge or divisions of science. Strauss notes that Maimonides focuses most of his attention in this same chapter on the discussion of "political science" as a chief component of what philosophy is, asking why in his logical statement Maimonides differs from Farabi on three key notions: (1) why Maimonides discusses happiness only as a facet of politics and in a political context, while he maintains ethics as a therapeutic art or science separate from, or at most preliminary and supportively helpful to, politics; (2) why he first presents political philosophy in terms of a whole composed of four parts, while as he proceeds he only differentiates and discusses three subdivisions, with the issue turning on governance of the city (third subdivision) versus governance of the great nation or of the nations (fourth subdivision); (3) why the task of dealing with "theology" or "divine matters" is assigned by Maimonides to politics, although he could readily have located it in the division of philosophy which deals with "metaphysics."

Strauss continues by turning to the *Guide* and traces how this is a virtual reworking, via Farabi, of fundamental doctrines of Plato in his *Republic* and *Laws*, whether on esotericism (which Strauss first broaches, although he probes it only in the most limited fashion), on prophecy, or on providence. By the end of this assessment Strauss is moved to ask perhaps his most radical question, to which an answer had to be deferred by him to a future study. He so proceeds precisely as he completes or rather suspends his discussion of Farabi, since he makes sure to imply that Maimonides continued his connection with the great medieval Muslim thinker, whatever divergences this study may have uncovered. Strauss's radical query is to ask whether Maimonides is not (apparently unlike Farabi) indeed *entirely* joined to Plato, and hence to ancient philosophic thought? This brings him to further ask whether Maimonides truly diverges from Plato on *the* two most fundamental issues, namely, on the nature of God in His unity, and on His creation of the world. Although Strauss refrains from hazarding any definite answers (much as some might like to consider the mere questions as already tacit answers), these questions are controversial merely by his asking them.

Strauss's audacious mode of thinking about Maimonides in "Some Remarks on the Political Science of Maimonides and Farabi" undoubtedly makes a statement that he had asserted his complete autonomy from conventional modern scholarly wisdom. It clearly reflects his choice to freely follow the logic of Maimonides' thought wherever it might lead him, however radical and shocking to some. It seems to have further ensued that for Strauss at this phase in his career, he accepted only a single duty imposed on the scholar if he is to be conceived of as an honest searcher: the right of the modern scholar to consider and judge Maimonides' thought entirely free of what might be designated the dictates of piety or the pressures of tradition. He already called attention to the fact that Maimonides at least in the *Guide* had himself supported these dictates or pressures only inasmuch as they can be made to conform with reason, and at the present juncture this seemed to him a quite sufficient limit. Inspired by this intrepid example, the true modern scholar (who adheres to the free critical sense as his governing principle) is for Strauss apparently required to declare only those results to which the honest confrontation with the truth might seem to yield, even if they break with piety or tradition. However, this unfettered audacity of Strauss's is not something that he maintained. In a very little while he appeared to decide that it is better to present the thought of Maimonides in a less imprudent and more responsible way than that which he verges on in this essay. As he will conclude, a conscientious commitment to the truth is not such that it makes it necessary to blatantly disclose everything one observes in an author. When he was ready to write "Literary Character," and whatever experience may have produced this change, Strauss had already withdrawn from such unhesitant daring and resolved in favor of something closer to a modern version of Maimonides' own studied reticence, in which flashes of boldness are speedily covered by a more or less conventional scholarly veneer. This novel position, which he will quickly adopt, is based on the assumption that one can trust the intelligence of careful readers to discover an author's true meaning so long as an occasional, if arresting, word to the wise is provided by the adept scholar.

"The Place of the Doctrine of Providence according to Maimonides" (1937) indicates on the surface only a slight change of Strauss's trajectory with regard to Maimonides, but at a deeper level it appears to exemplify his turn in quite a different direction. During the next several years it will carry Strauss ever closer to his unscheduled destination: his arrival at the "literary character" of the *Guide*, in which things of much greater profundity and mysteriousness will be uncovered. Thus, what is perhaps most noteworthy about this essay is that in it Strauss begins to espy and delineate the contours of the hidden table of contents of the *Guide*, which Maimonides had managed to bury just beneath the surface, as it were, concealed in plain sight. He reached this juncture by discerning that the order in which the key topics are arranged and treated, and so the undeclared but tacit logic by which they are elaborated, are not accidental, traditional, or merely convenient, but highly significant.

A certain tone of mastery in presenting his views on the *Guide* also starts to make itself evident. At last fully liberated from Cohen's scientifically ethical Maimonides and from Spinoza's theologically dogmatic Maimonides, Strauss starts to perceive the political as precisely the manner by which the rational is rendered supreme for Maimonides, and by which for him a man who holds to the way of philosophy can also be a vigorous defender and adherent of revealed Law. This is because he can regard such a Law as the paramount product of the prophet conceived in Platonic-Farabian style. In that conception, the prophet represents the unique human figure who subordinates the Law, and so also providence, to the best possible actualization of the perfect political order relative to the historical circumstances in which he is cast or which are at his disposal. Indeed, such is the ultimate purpose of what the true prophet and his Law primarily aims to achieve: to bring about a political regime that is as well ordered as possible, considering the human material which the prophet has to work with. To be sure, the prophetic lawgiver knows that he must do this didactically as well as with an eye toward the future, an insight that Strauss drew from the logic of Maimonides' argument. This strategy would maximize the chances that the greatest number of human beings would perfect themselves, and hence minimize the chances that the greatest number of human beings would corrupt themselves, in conformity with the permanent economy of souls normally distributed in human nature. These purposes, fully in accord with the teachings of Plato and Farabi, amount to an admission that even this most divine of laws, which the "perfect" prophetic lawgiver can only bring relative to his circumstances, will not likely—although it is always a possibility!—ever achieve complete, fully actualized, permanent enlightenment of all human beings in history. For Maimonides, as Strauss perceived, the Torah and divine Law of this type will always be progressively if haltingly marching toward perfection. But by its continued advancement, that almost alone demonstrates its "divinely" providential character, since what this law aims for as "divine" is human life at its peak for as great a number of adherents as it is possible in its current state to attain. This also offers a lesson to wise modern thinkers, teachers, and leaders: aim high, but do not let this ideal aim obscure from the manifest impossibility of most people attaining the goal. Even prophetic statesmanlike "perfection" always requires adjusting one's "divine" sights to human reality.

Thus, on the issue of divine watchfulness or supervision of man in the world, Strauss shows that Maimonides transmits a twofold teaching of providence, which is subdivided as follows: that which merely conforms with the Law in its ordinary sense, following what is right for the collective order; and that which conforms with the Law in its true sense, by augmenting what is good for the selected or exceptional individuals, and hence fulfilling the Law's highest divine purpose. This teaching about providence for those who are intellectually excellent is truly particular or "personal." As for providence for those ordinary human beings who have not made (or who, for one reason or another, cannot make) the requisite effort to perfect themselves, this is essentially universal or not truly "personal," i.e., it is closer to what Maimonides styles "governance," although for them it is always at least a potential if they choose to pursue it. In this way, Strauss traces the truly philosophic—and hence also political—logic of Maimonides on providence, which manages simultaneously to remain obedient to the Law even if not obeying its conventional self-image as entirely egalitarian, and to offer a hope for a personalized benevolent fate for those with whom it is most concerned, i.e., those whom Maimonides calls "the single virtuous ones." As he tacitly contends, their intellectual excellence is of the greatest benefit to themselves, but also it is of the greatest benefit to their society. This is because the Law helps to endow "the single virtuous ones" with the potential for bringing into being further superlative rulers and legislators, since the Law aims to produce their perfection for themselves and for itself. The Law conveys its twofold message to them such that, properly educated, they will help to shape and maintain the well-ordered society of the future, while in the present this likewise ensures their complete freedom to think and to obtain knowledge.

Hence, Maimonides' views on providence—aided by the pointer of their assigned location in the *Guide* as a significant hint—are for Strauss determined by philosophically political notions of providence already evident in Plato. Providence is *not* mainly a theological notion, as it is for Christian philosophic thought, but rather it is predominantly a political notion, as it is for Muslim philosophic thought: it helps to regulate the well-ordered society, and especially the souls of those human beings it produces in the process of fulfilling its twofold mandate. Strauss started to perceive that like Plato, Maimonides holds the "the single virtuous ones" responsible for their fellow citizens, since it *both* helps them to escape the cave *and* renders them duty bound to return to the cave, teaching them why they must do so, once they have climbed to the surface and seen the true light of the sun, which the Law itself assists them to do. In sum, Strauss shows himself to have attained a completely mature and confident comprehension of Maimonides as a medieval political Platonist, with a growing literary sensitivity to accompany it, which is also guided by Plato, the master of the art by which philosophic truths are communicated in dialogue form. At least with respect to politics philosophically comprehended, which apparently transcends the ancient-medieval divide, Maimonides' treatment of providence proves that revelation in the pure and simple sense of the term is not *the* decisive and all-encompassing issue Strauss had once believed it was, since revelation for Maimonides as a literal *textual* authority is not adequate to unqualifiedly determine how the biblical form of providence is to be religiously defined. This too, for Maimonides, is to be put in the context of building and maintaining the best political order.

With the "Review of *The Mishneh Torah*, Book 1" (1939), i.e., with his turn to the *Book of Knowledge*, Strauss as a scholar and thinker steps beyond the boundaries of the *Guide*. Here he starts to consider critically the larger Maimonidean corpus, especially the work that in its contents (although not in its style) is most closely connected with the *Guide*. His review tacitly asks how the same man who was author of the *Guide* also managed to have been the author of the *Mishneh Torah*: what are the unifying, or at least binding, threads stitching the two works together in the mind of the original author? Rather than trying to answer this big question directly, Strauss proceeds almost immediately to the scholarly details. His first move is to appreciate Hyamson's edition for its academic merit, which allowed modern scholars to correct those serious textual errors that had appeared in the manuscripts due to scribes who had made either lax renderings or self-appointed additions and omissions. This is especially noteworthy because the revisions in Hyamson's edition are shown by Strauss to make a serious impact much beyond the merely scholarly dimension. In other words, Strauss wants his readers to sense the substantial weight that these "mere" textual variants and revised readings carry in the proper comprehension of Maimonides' thought. Thus, this is not a review for scholars alone and is no sense concerned only with the examination of recondite and abstruse matters.

Strauss addresses himself to the following seven topics, each of which may well impinge on the correct understanding of Maimonides as thinker if seen in light of the variants occurring in Hyamson's edition: the composition of the fourteen-volume *Mishneh Torah* as a single book (although focusing on the *Sefer ha-Madda*, or *Book of Knowledge*), and especially its overarching literary plan as a totality, which Strauss was perhaps the first to judiciously reason about and emphasize, as a factor which has to be deliberated on in order to make sense of the book as a work of art; theology; angelology; ethics; the Law; eschatology; and words of special significance. The pattern that may be discerned in this list emerges from Strauss's tendency to stress the subtle, if concealed, continuity between the *Guide* and the *Sefer ha-Madda*, since both books are addressed, even if in a different fashion, to the same type, i.e., those who are careful readers, whether actually or only potentially so. To choose such readers as the highest addressees of his *Mishneh Torah* reflects something far greater than a mere literary skill which Maimonides appreciates: it is a comment on how well and how deeply the reader thinks, or at least is capable of thinking.

All the same, Strauss also presents pointed criticism of Hyamson's edition. He notes that Hyamson neglected to specify whether, how much, and how precisely the numbered paragraphs, familiar from the printed versions, concur with the manuscript, since according to Strauss—who assumes it was done deliberately by Maimonides, and not accidentally or casually—this sort of information is a vital clue to his intentions as an author. It is especially the case with this specific manuscript, since it bears Maimonides' signature, attesting to the fact that he personally checked it himself. Strauss, calling the *Sefer ha-Madda* "a book full of mystery," also raises the issue of its "literary character" in general as a whole of five parts, which are further subdivided. To be sure, Strauss curiously calls for applying the same literary approach not just to the *Sefer ha-Madda*, but also to the *Mishneh Torah* as an entirety, a method that he will shortly apply to the *Guide*. To Strauss, each of these works form a unity determined by the author, which can be evidenced in its very careful literary construction. Thus, he faults Hyamson for the imprecise rule he chose to follow with regard to rendering Maimonides' key terms: for Strauss, in the case of any work by Maimonides, one must translate as consistently as possible the regularity of terms, on the one hand, and their significant divergences, on the other hand. This is because Strauss was convinced that these are meticulously selected pointers that Maimonides deliberately plants in the text, which function as directional hints for the benefit of his most careful readers. Strauss discerned that these were not adequately differentiated by Hyamson as translator, who should have been thinking of readers whose Hebrew is not sufficient to enable them to check such words in the original, but who may be wondering whether they are used consistently, and if not, why not. Strauss also highlights that Hyamson, for some inexplicable reason, neglected to use the better Hebrew text, which he had just edited, from which to translate this English version.

In the middle of the review, Strauss makes a statement which may be designated a turning point, if not a revelatory moment, in which he makes known (as if for the future) the astonishingly rigorous standard necessary for any serious reading of Maimonides: "The question may be raised whether a translation meeting all the conditions which excellent translations of most philosophic or halakhic books have to fulfill, would be an adequate translation of a work of Maimonides. The answer . . . naturally depends on which view we hold of the character of Maimonides' writings."[31] He holds "an adequate translation" of any work by Maimonides to a very rigorous standard—indeed, to the most rigorous standard possible in assessing any book and how to translate it. This is "revelatory" because it will, as things unfold, be Strauss's unyielding view about "the character of Maimonides' writings": that Maimonides wrote them with a style which is as careful, precise, artful, deliberate, and thoughtful as it is possible for a human author to achieve. Thus, with this statement Strauss announces his view, which will henceforth be determinative for him, that Maimonides ranks among the very greatest minds as well as the very greatest writers in the history of Western thought.[32] And by this Strauss also declares the purpose of the *Mishneh Torah* to be entirely consistent with the purpose of the *Guide*, since both are the work of the same consummate writer.

Strauss's words of high esteem for Maimonides, even if only tacitly spoken, putting him alongside some of the greatest thinkers in the history of Western

---

31. See "Review of *The Mishneh Torah*, Book 1," chap. 7 below.
32. For Strauss on the "great minds," and their connection with the "great books," see "What Is Liberal Education?," in *Liberalism Ancient and Modern*, pp. 3–8.

philosophy, is a fitting passageway to the next essay: "The Literary Character of *The Guide of the Perplexed*" (1941). This is perhaps the most significant of all the provocative essays and lectures that appear in the present book. It represents a major breakthrough, because in it Strauss—by a sudden and huge leap—penetrates to a depth of perception for which nothing in the previous essays or lectures, however brilliant, quite prepares the reader. As it happens, it is also the midpoint in Strauss's rediscovery of Maimonides, perhaps not chronologically but certainly conceptually: it is the core, even the heart and soul, of that rediscovery. Strauss brought about a revolution in comprehending the thought of Maimonides, which helped him also to bring about a related revolution in the history of Western thought, by fathoming three remarkable things about the *Guide*: it is utterly unconventional as to its purpose; its "literary character" proves to be a key to its true meaning and shows how valuable it is to consider its structure; it is candid in its claim that it is deliberately written in such a manner as to be comprehended on two levels. This rediscovery made by Strauss occurred following centuries of what can only be designated as a sort of forgetfulness, setting in at least since medieval scholars ceased to write on the *Guide* in the mode of commentary and since modern scholars commenced the study of the book in the historical mode. This endowed Strauss with the means to uncover the deliberately hidden logic by which its author had composed the *Guide* as a book sui generis, and by which he had also concealed the end he was aiming at: full enlightenment for those who need it. This hidden logic had not merely been forgotten but, as Strauss rather boldly suggests, perhaps had never been penetrated to the full depth that Maimonides had determined at its origin. As this led Strauss to further conclude, if there is a quite different *Guide* concealed beneath the *Guide* that is encountered on the surface, then perhaps that surface also conceals the directions as to how to get to the hidden depth. For these too may have been surreptitiously hidden by the author, who did not want every reader to probe its depths. Strauss embarked on a search for those directions.

To be sure, Strauss reminds readers that, while Maimonides hid some things and made some things astoundingly difficult, not everything is quite so concealed. Maimonides himself had unambiguously declared that his book had been composed on two levels, even if this announcement had been ignored by most modern scholars: one for the few selected (i.e., attentive) readers, and the other for the many ordinary (i.e., neglectful) readers. The author had also plainly revealed that he employed a "method of contradictions" in transmitting his teachings, and he offered rudimentary guidelines as to how this method works. As this would seem to imply, some of its teachings had not merely been deliberately hidden, but also virtually encoded or encrypted. Strauss also reminds students of the *Guide* about Maimonides' warning, quite candidly proclaimed, that readers must pay *meticulous* attention to every single word in his book, since each and every word was carefully and deliberately selected—however apparently disordered, unsuitable, or even muddled they might appear. This is no doubt an enormous and audacious assertion by an author; are modern critical readers obligated to accept such an assertion? Strauss argued that we must at least tentatively accept this assertion, until we know whether it is defensible.

As Strauss brings to light, Maimonides claimed to have been able to master an ancient art of writing, one mastered not just by the biblical authors but also by philosophic authors like Plato (*Guide* 1.17). This is a rare literary art that is only capable of being practiced by a few great minds, and as Strauss elucidates, Maimonides was able to perfect this art in a certain measure because he had achieved the highest measure of intellectual excellence. A philosophic writer of "genius," as he might be termed, not only is possessed of an exceptional depth of knowledge and has not only engaged in a profundity of theorizing, but is also one who is in complete control of his imaginative faculty to dispose of as he wills in his art. This twofold supreme capacity is manifested in the very greatest thinkers who become artists, and ultimately in the unique human type that Maimonides defines as the prophet. It is a capacity needed both to convey useful teachings to the many who are not in the habit of thinking and also to communicate hints to the "single virtuous ones" who passionately wish to investigate the truth. Thus, Strauss perceived that in essence Maimonides was copying a "divine" capacity, which he was able to perfect as much as humanly possible, while halting at the limit of proclaiming himself a prophet. Or as Strauss makes bold to say, Maimonides wrote his deepest book in a unique sort of style which often seems to lack style, and which as such aimed to imitate the original book of secrets in its utmost concealed profundity, i.e., the Hebrew Bible. However, Strauss also never ignored the primary strategy of Maimonides, which was to present his first concern as solidly grounded in the duty to follow "not the ambiguous advice of the philosophers but the unequivocal command of the law": hence his highest purpose as a leader and teacher of his community was to serve and protect the divine Law, in which as it happens a concern for the truth is mandated.

Thus, as Strauss also discloses, Maimonides did not leave his selected readers on their own in their effort to uncover his secrets: he provided the key to his own "code"—which, ironically, was itself not so readily deciphered! To obtain the key, the careful reader was already required to make a heroic effort to untangle knots, which, once completed, allowed him to open a series of otherwise closed doors. If the *Guide* is, as Strauss puts it, "a book [sealed by its author] with seven seals," it is designed to be unsealed only by him who has made his own not only Maimonides' cognitive orientation but also his moral concern. Thus, the reader for whom Maimonides ultimately wrote, and in whose talents and virtues he trusted, was to be closer to the type of searcher who can locate the mysterious way to the center of a multifaceted and obscure labyrinth. Such a searcher will also know how to avoid all manner of false paths, roadblocks, and pitfalls. The search itself is a labor of love, but even so it is still a labor—a labor of thought—in which only the worthy who pass his tests will conceive its truths properly and so ultimately be admitted access to the sanctum, as with the true lover who must pass through trials to secure the heart of his beloved. According to Strauss, Maimonides certainly followed the ancient Socratic maxim, which trusted in the coincidence of moral excellence and superlative intelligence;[33] but he also believed in and anticipated a diplomatic maxim of Ronald Reagan: "Trust but verify." As Strauss makes known, Maimonides trusted in the best souls because he wrote for them a book which revealed the secrets of the Torah. But as Strauss perceived, Maimonides also required the truly virtuous searcher to pass through a series of literary tests, running a thinking man's obstacle course, in which it is possible to verify his traits as an honest lover of the truth with the requisite quality of soul. Passing the test shows him that he is worthy in both senses of the term, i.e., cognitively and morally, to have the truth revealed to him; this is done gradually but surely in the persistent and repeated study of his book. The results of the test are affirmed by the book itself, as it were, revealing its secrets to fit readers.

This leads Strauss to make a statement that is most unusual, if not perplexing: "Contradictions are the axis of the *Guide*." Strauss's point seems to be not only that Maimonides deliberately contradicts himself in the artful

---

33. Strauss characterizes the category of literature to which the *Guide* belongs and the class of people for which it is designed, even if his depiction might seem to subordinate the truth of logic to a paradox, in the following terms: "This [book] would be impossible if the Socratic dictum that virtue is knowledge, and therefore that thoughtful men as such are trustworthy and not cruel, were entirely wrong." See *Persecution and the Art of Writing*, p. 25.

construction of his book, as he admits to doing, but also that this "method" is his preferred mode of concealment in conveying truths. But why did Maimonides conceive of this most peculiar procedure as essential for him as an author? Even to try to answer this question as Strauss presents it, it is first needful that Maimonides' elaborate techniques of concealment, as Strauss most originally illuminates them, be considered, tacitly asking why these concurrent techniques (though still employed) were not chosen as the "axis." Only once these have been briefly surveyed in their enormous compass will it be possible for me to venture a brief suggestion as to how Strauss's answered the aforementioned question. Strauss rather startlingly dispersed through the essay an enormous list of techniques used by Maimonides in artfully concealing his own true opinions vis-à-vis the Torah, or rather, the true opinions of the Torah hidden in the Torah. Some might even be tempted to think that in the complex construction of this essay, Strauss is actually instructing by example, and so is attempting to imitate Maimonides, offering a hint about his own views. However that may be, this is a sample list of those numerous Maimonidean techniques as Strauss enunciates them: ambiguous words; mottoes, epigraphs, or apostrophes; unfinished sentences and jumbled statements; inexact or fragmentary quotations; citations of texts which he requires the reader to check and often complete, rework, or connect with related passages; words or phrases at the beginning of chapters; repetitions which are not the same; omissions; chapter headings both regular and irregular; "intentional perplexities"; exaggerations; obscurity; briefness of speech; hidden motives; clumsy transitions; abrupt changes of topic; inappropriate expressions; little words; relative clauses; conditional sentences; long sentences with multiple or complex parentheses; carefully scattered topics, the parts of which, once they are reconstructed in their premeditated unity, form a coherent whole; the appearance of surface disorder rooted in a subtle but concealed order; secret words; obscured reasons; logical contradictions; irregular references to books, whether his own or those of others; dual logical entailments of assertions which are divergent if not considered in their proper contexts or traced to their proper linkages. Indeed, Strauss lengthens this astounding list and augments its provocative argument by contending that, for Maimonides, things implicitly hinted at are often of greater significance than things dealt with or asserted in explicit fashion.

To be sure, this list of techniques will seem to some readers a strangely immoderate, if not unnecessary, amount of reticence in Maimonides. Some readers may demur that it makes it almost impossible to determine with sufficient certainty the true views which Maimonides himself held. Yet Strauss proceeds precisely as a modern historical scholar and not as a traditional defender of the law: he only reports on what he observes; he is not passing judgment. As a result, he will only concede this much to such doubts or protests: Maimonides had conceived of it as his duty to obey the law in full; the law commands the keeping of secrets (never mind its special ban on their written transmission); and, as Strauss also notes, it has to be admitted that this is the first book in the history of Judaism, as is indeed asserted by Maimonides himself, in which the secrets of the Torah are fully recorded in a book. The task required the utmost reticence of Maimonides in order to balance the needs of the few (which must be met if the society formed by the law is to reach its highest potential) with the needs of the many (who must be protected, a major concern in which the command of the law is grounded). This is not even to mention that those with the potential quality in their souls to enter the sanctum of the secrets will always have to be tested in advance *by the book itself* (so to speak) in order to winnow the worthy from the unworthy. Thus did Strauss venture his answer to the question of why Maimonides conceived this most peculiar authorial procedure of deliberately contradicting himself in his own book as the best possible "method" of concealment: he decided that it is most useful for a writer who must both defend the law by protecting the secrets of the Torah and simultaneously reveal them in a book to those of his readers who like to think. To employ contradictions is to utilize a "method" which hides the truth from the ill equipped with the utmost efficacy, since the many unwise and uneducated are unlikely to be able to actually identify a logical contradiction, to disentangle it from the covered recess to which it has been consigned, to separate it from poetical or rhetorical modes of speech, or to be disconcerted by the mere fact of a logical contradiction in matters pertaining to religion. But it is well suited for the expression of truths to the few logically adept thinkers, especially once they have been trained by Maimonides in the proper art of interpretation, since their virtue (as trained and tested by Maimonides) will guard them against revealing the secrets to those who are not fit for them.[34]

---

34. For those who wish to further pursue Strauss's unique approach to Maimonides' method of contradictions, consider the following passages. First, refer to his discussion of how to decide between two contradictory statements: how is one to know which contradictory statement avers the truth in the view of Maimonides, and which hides it beneath something else? See "Literary Character," chap. 8 below, and *Persecution and the Art of Writing*, pp. 69–70. Second, what is the significance of Strauss's assertion that contradictions offer the truth in one of two contradictory statements; is this not to offer the truth frankly rather than to conceal it? See "Literary Character," chap. 8 below, and *Persecution and the Art of Writing*,

Strauss resourcefully raises to the surface not only the brilliant literary devices devised by Maimonides in order to remain technically loyal to the law in his fashion, but also how Maimonides on a certain level had to break the law precisely in order to obey or to preserve it, which itself followed legal precedent for dealing with emergency situations. The law commanded Maimonides to guard the secrets of the Torah and to keep them oral, which he conceived both literally and not so literally: they were kept secret but they also had to be written in a book, because those who have need of them deserve to know them, and possess the right to know them precisely in their being adherents of the law. "Orality," as Strauss discovered, was preserved in the legal and literary fiction of how Maimonides composed his book, i.e., it was not a book in the usual sense of the word, but instead a series of personal letters sent in logical sequence by a single teacher to a single student. Also the student's ability, aptitude, and skills, which meet the requirements stipulated by the law, are presented by Maimonides in the beginning: he is a well-trained student of the law, is well versed in philosophical literature, and remains a loyal Jew of sound mind, even if spiritually tormented. Thus Maimonides' book also proves itself to meet the technical requirements of the law, not just by how it is written, but also by whom it is written for. His conscientious self-defense to any who might criticize and even condemn his entire endeavor is also presented, as Strauss notes: to do otherwise than reveal the wisdom about the Torah which he has acquired is, as Maimonides puts it, as if he were to deprive a beneficiary of his legitimate legacy, thus "robbing one who deserves the truth of the truth" (*Guide*, introduction to pt. 3, p. 416). His love of the truth, because he is committed to the Torah, remains uncompromised.

But as Strauss asked, doing so irrespective of the fact that this might seem to have been obvious, even with this fiduciary rectitude toward his student "and toward those like him" (*Guide*, "Epistle Dedicatory") with respect to the truth, did Maimonides need to justify his high level of concealment because the Torah has something to hide that is peculiarly threatening to the uneducated, unworthy, or unprepared? Strauss seems to think so. Thus, Strauss speaks of certain explanations even "of a single word" containing, for Maimonides, a "high explosive" which, if handled by the vicious, is incendiary to unenlightened faith, and "which can destroy all beliefs not firmly grounded

---

p. 74. Third, how is it possible to know precisely the thing to which something hidden refers? See "Literary Character," chap. 8 below, and *Persecution and the Art of Writing*, p. 57.

in reason." Strauss also takes seriously a "moral dilemma," which manifests itself in the will of the modern historical scholar not so much to penetrate the secrets as especially to reveal them: if Maimonides had not believed in his right to freely give away the secrets, was the modern historical scholar entitled to disregard his qualms—and hence can he truly comprehend Maimonides and the secrets which he teaches if such qualms are disregarded?

Proceeding from such reflections on Maimonides' fundamental premises as a writer, Strauss shapes an approach to the *Guide* which diverges from most modern scholarly assumptions. This issues in a subtle "method" of reading that became his trademark. His first approach is to see the *Guide* in light of how its author presents himself, and not how modern readers tended to perceive it in view of modern thought. This led him to stress that it is a book primarily defined by its Jewish character. Based on a careful reading of what Maimonides himself both posits and negates about his own book, he believes it is best to classify it not in any sense as a "philosophic book" (a point he curiously repeats thrice in five paragraphs), but rather as a Jewish book, and regards it as such in at least two senses. First, it is a book concerned almost solely with how to properly educate a certain sort of Jew in the correct interpretation of scripture. For the sort of Jew to which Strauss refers, he points to how Maimonides succinctly characterizes him in the "Epistle Dedicatory" and the "Introduction" to the *Guide*: he is both a thinking and loyal Jew, but perplexed precisely because he is trying to be both thoughtful and faithful, impulses which seem to conflict. His perplexity is a form of spiritual suffering, derived from his belief in the wrong (i.e., unreasonable) readings as somehow mandated by tradition, and so engendering what Maimonides calls "heartache and great perplexity" in the best souls, which will cripple them in their attempts to fulfill their potential for human greatness. Second, this is also a Jewish book because it focuses on those accurate readings that give expression to the deepest original intentions of the Torah, while of course simultaneously also correcting wrong readings. Those right readings, if taken seriously and comprehended properly by the designated reader, will not only guide his mind and heart toward healing the worst spiritual wounds produced by the aforementioned conflict, but on a deeper plane will also educate and enlighten him, and so bring him closer to what Maimonides considers human perfection. As Strauss reads Maimonides, this is the true purpose of the Torah, even if it is only fulfilled in rare human beings, as must be limited by what human nature (or the "created order") makes possible. Hence, if Strauss defines the *Guide* as a Jewish book in the sense of "a book devoted to the explanation of the secret teaching of the Bible," then this is not only an indication that there is, for Maimonides, such a secret teaching, but also that this teaching is aimed to produce a certain type of "perfected" human being.

At the same time, Strauss also disallows the conventional idea that this is a "philosophic book" in any modern sense of the term. Thus, Strauss compels the modern reader who is engaged in studying his essay to repeat Maimonides' cure of the soul, if on a slightly different level: the modern reader is supposed to grasp mainly *how* Maimonides approached the Torah; he is to think through for himself the *reasoning* which is concealed beneath Maimonides' teaching; the reasoning will clarify the *necessity* for the strange logic which Maimonides employed in his book; he is to imitate the thinking of the philosopher while he is not to become one. To be sure, whether Strauss's own argument is ultimately so simple as to make a Jewish book so completely irreconcilable with a philosophic book is a question which he also asked himself and which he causes his readers to ask. Is it possible to think like a philosopher, and yet not to truly be one? Strauss's "method" of subtle hints and strategic use of paradox to foster deeper reflection in his readers might seem as it if it is as contorting of the mind as Maimonides' own method, but he has his reasons for proceeding as such which he believes are in Maimonides' spirit. Hence, Strauss also leaves it for his reader to answer these questions in his own way, depending on the human type to which that reader belongs and whether he has the fortitude and resilience to follow Strauss's Maimonidean logic and the strenuous life of thinking this seems to require.

Strauss appears to be teaching his best readers at the highest level to appreciate Maimonides as a free mind, whose thinking is as bold, deep, and original as any modern thinker's, despite his seemingly "unmodern" purpose. He perceives that Maimonides is not aiming to "liberate" even his best readers from the life of Torah and tradition, but he is helping such readers to reconcile themselves to them, and elevates them to a place that transcends the usual conflicts by its allowing room for freedom of thought while keeping in the bounds of the law. The unusual model which Maimonides promotes and which he stands for in his legacy of books may seem, according to Strauss's presentation, paradoxical, but instead it is dialectical, and hence it is not self-contradictory: he counsels his best readers to be orthodox in morality and in public life, but to be as unorthodox, or even heterodox, as needed in the private realm of the mind and in the company of like-minded searchers, whose life is legitimated by the Torah itself. As such, this dialectical approach persuades his best readers to think untraditionally, and he supports them in their efforts to keep doing so, since he views such freedom of mind as a key facet of the Torah itself.

With "Maimonides' Statement on Political Science" (1953) Strauss seemingly takes a step away from the *Guide* again. In this essay he looks at Maimonides' youthful *Treatise on the Art of Logic*, and he gives an especially careful scrutiny to its last, or fourteenth, chapter, which he had already considered, if very differently, in "Some Remarks on the Political Science of Maimonides and Farabi." Strauss concludes that the *Logic* is not in any sense "a Jewish book, i.e., a book written by a Jew as a Jew for Jews as Jews." However, along with this apparently unconditional avowal (which itself seems convolutedly stated), Strauss's judicious reading also brings him to perceive a subtle message conveyed by Maimonides (carefully crafted "between the lines," as it were) concerning the relation of logic to Judaism. The *Logic* concerns itself with philosophy as a discipline which is of immediate relevance and usefulness to all human beings in all times and places, insofar as man has a dual nature and is both a rational and a political being. Indeed, he apparently needs it for both sides of his being, even if it fulfills a different purpose in each. In this way, Maimonides manages to legitimate logic for *anyone* concerned with human beings and their dual nature, while avoiding the need to address directly whether it is legitimate for Jews in terms of their specific divine Law.

In the same last chapter of the *Logic* (and subordinate to the limited passage in it which Strauss dubs a "statement on political science"), he also discovers Maimonides offering a dialectical interpretation of morality in its political context. In Maimonides' brief discussion of what Strauss designates "common-sense morality," his presentation establishes it as "the most impressive expression of man's dual nature." Or to state it otherwise, according to Strauss Maimonides never forgets the fundamental dualism in human nature as a permanent challenge. That is to say, man is actually divided between his rational and political sides, and this divide is not as readily harmonized as might at first appear, even by logic. This is a reflection of how seriously Maimonides approaches political science—even in his treatment of logic—as the leading or master science, and not just among the human sciences, since it better than logic comprehends the human soul. Indeed, Strauss seems to suggest that, for Maimonides, this is the science in which philosophy is perhaps most comprehensively encompassed as well as best protected. This is the case because through it one conceives of philosophy primarily as a way of life, as the life led by the thinker who must confront how to preserve his life with regard to those human beings who choose not to think, who may even be hostile to thinking, and who must be reconciled to those who love to think. And so philosophy, even in the simplest form of logic, is through political science able to address the needs, the meaning, and the value of that thinking way of life and the potential threats to it in the manner of life of most human beings, who reject thought but who fill and bring to life the human society that the thinker needs and depends on.

Indeed, this leads Strauss to venture the assessment "that the *Logic* is the only philosophic book which Maimonides ever wrote." Yet the consequence of this is that one must not read his *Logic* as addressed mainly to Jews as Jews, even if no doubt it is additionally addressed to them. In his *Logic* Maimonides attempts to delineate the whole of philosophy in its articulated parts, divided as it is by theoretical and practical halves, even though these are not necessarily equal halves, never mind whether it is possible to speak of them as equal in dignity. In his analysis of Maimonides' effort to define the essential contours of philosophy, Strauss especially focuses on a peculiar aspect of the way in which Maimonides defines political philosophy. This is the strangest feature of the demarcation highlighted by Strauss, namely, the claim that "we" no longer need the books of the philosophers on politics. Strauss proceeds to reflect carefully on to whom, for Maimonides, this "we" is referring; he concludes that, for Maimonides, the "we" is humanity in the era of man ruled by divine laws. But as he discovers by an intricate explication, it is not that "we" no longer need those books *altogether*; instead, this need very much continues. True, we no longer need them for their practical political recommendations as to specific actions that fulfill general directives or teachings, but we do still very much need them for their theoretical wisdom or comprehension about what revealed religions signify at their highest, or what they ultimately point us toward as to our human purposes. This follows, as Strauss demonstrates contrary to first impressions, precisely if "the function of revealed religion is emphatically political." These philosophic books help to elucidate for "us" explicitly, even if the divine laws also do so implicitly, such essential notions as imaginary and true happiness, and the proper ends of human life which make for true happiness; the divergences between the means to both; and how the "adequate knowledge of the rules of justice" which the philosophers' books contain may be helpful for us with regard to uncovering how these things are made operative in the divine law. Thus, according to Strauss, the one big thing which Maimonides wishes to imply, even if he never quite asserts it directly, is that the Jews are additionally in need of political philosophy as much as any other political entity, although this is not to deny the element which claims to transcend the political in Judaism, and which he fully acknowledges.

What this curiously proves, Strauss believes, is that Maimonides' prophetology—especially, although not only, in the *Guide*—is "a branch of political science." But precisely because this is saying something that some will not want to hear, as Maimonides himself well knew, much had to be concealed by him. Hence, Strauss also believes it is needful to emphasize the technique of obscurity and hints which Maimonides utilized even in the *Logic*; indeed, it is absolutely essential to grasp what is conveyed in these hints in order to comprehend the true contents of Maimonides' thought even on logic. Thus, Strauss focuses—rather bizarrely to some—on the number seven as one of the key "principles" around which the *Guide* (not to mention his other works) is organized. Indeed, in "Maimonides' Statement on Political Science" Strauss also makes his first rudimentary effort to articulate the complete concealed structure of the *Guide*, and why it is grounded in the number seven. According to Strauss, Maimonides makes use (which some contest) of a philosophic numerology as an element of his literary art: the number seven seems to be connected with Maimonides' orientation toward the priority of the human (and the natural) in his theology. So much is this the case as a self-conscious device that Strauss is willing to designate "seven" and its multiples as a decisive hint employed even in his first youthful work, i.e., his *Logic*. To be sure, Strauss admits that this is not an *entirely* serious technique for Maimonides (or for any deep-thinking writer), but he adds that this is also perhaps never *entirely* playful. Thus, Strauss leaves his readers with an unresolved perplexity: how precisely is numerology related to logic for Maimonides? To most reasonable readers, they might seem antithetical, but Strauss suggests that this is not the case for Maimonides.

Such paradoxes abound, for reasons which are not entirely pellucid: Strauss seems as if he is starting to make the work of the readers of his essays almost as difficult as Maimonides did in his books. He puts challenges and obstructions in their course, but refuses to clarify what his reasons may have been. Was it only a desire to test their mettle? For example, Strauss focuses (especially in n. 25) on what Maimonides regarded as the requirement that proper readers—of the *Guide*, but implying also of the *Logic*—be sufficiently skilled in knowing how to write for both the simple-minded multitude and for the educated elite. Why must this be so? It seems as though Strauss provides no reason. Similarly, Strauss leads readers to think, according to a certain counting of key terms, that perhaps "the science of God and the angels" is precisely in the middle, and hence in the heart, of philosophy, as defined by how its separate sciences are to be divided. But this also brings him to doubt whether "the account of the chariot," contrary to its appearance as the fundamental metaphysical or theological teaching of the *Guide* (located in 3.1–7), is not actually even dealing with this same metaphysical or theological "science," but is concerned with something else, although what that is, he does not say.

He recognized that serious difficulty thanks to a criticism first made by the critical medieval commentator Isaac Abravanel, and repeated by the modern historical scholar Salomon Munk. They unwittingly noticed a contradiction, but they did not know what to do with it, other than to judge Maimonides wanting as a thinker and writer. Strauss, by contrast, considers such contradictions to be clues lying on the surface, which with the aid of the author himself should teach us instead to dig beneath the surface and to search for something deeper. According to Strauss, a superbly artful author like Maimonides deliberately puts such contradictions in our path as an obstacle to make us halt or if need be to trip us, and so to make us think. Thus Strauss used even the *Logic*, seemingly the most forthright and unequivocal of his writings, to illustrate specifically how Maimonides, at every point, used hints and even contradictions as artful conveyances in every work to indicate his deepest thought.

Toward the end of his discussion on the status of political philosophy in Maimonides' thought, Strauss seems to raise doubts about what he had previously concluded. Indeed, his last word is bewildering and even mysterious, and yet it seems to me likely that this was done deliberately—even if it is not so clear as to just *why* he did so. Strauss finishes by offering a peculiar explanation of what he has been calling Maimonides' "statement on political science": he characterizes it as "a masterful epitome of the problem of revelation as it presents itself from the point of view of the philosophers." What can he mean by this description? Is he saying that Maimonides' consideration of political science in the context of logic reflects a concern with revelation as viewed solely by philosophy? If Maimonides in his *Logic* writes as a philosopher who conceives of revelation as a question in need of answer (and not as an obvious and authoritative truth), what is this saying about the Maimonides who wrote the *Guide*, not to mention the *Mishneh Torah*? He seems to imply that this one insight somehow contains the solution to other "riddles" and anomalies of the *Logic* in its entirety. What is *the* "problem of revelation" to which Strauss refers? Is it somehow political? And how is a solution to it achieved by seeing it in the light of philosophy, which Strauss says that Maimonides employed in order to comprehend revelation, yet which he did fairly rather than by filtering it through a distorting lens?

Whatever one may make of how Strauss characterizes the achievement of Maimonides' "statement on political science," Strauss concludes by acclaiming Maimonides as "the great eagle," a title by which he was most famously praised by medieval Jews. Strauss writes as if he has forgotten his previous remarks about Maimonides in his *Logic* as seemingly concerned solely with philosophy, even as it addresses revelation. Yet Strauss brings his essay to a true close by crafting a peculiar comment about "the greatest sacrifice" which Maimonides had to make in order to defend the Torah against the philosophers, and tacitly links this with his observation about Maimonides' keen-eyed perception and his concern for his fledglings. On this point I shall offer a tentative idea as to what it is that Strauss may be saying: he suggests that this "greatest sacrifice" concerns the manner in which the completely free mind of Maimonides operated, maintaining itself as such even with its unconditional fidelity to the Torah. If this is the case, Strauss is saying that Maimonides courageously risked walking the tightrope between Torah and philosophy: one has to go as far as possible with philosophy, whatever the risks, if one is to come to an adequate defense of the Torah. It is for this that he wished to serve as a model for his students or readers. In other words, he did not have to be known or famed as a philosopher in order to think like one. Moreover, it was in this fashion that Maimonides was able to appropriate philosophic truth in the context of the Torah, as this might otherwise have been closed to him as a Jew.

"Introduction to Maimonides' *The Guide of the Perplexed*" (1960) is a lecture reflecting Strauss's fully mature approach to Maimonides and his *Guide*. Being a lecture, it has the advantage of showing Strauss in a relaxed frame of mind not so much evident in his closely argued essays. As such, it makes evident the virtues of Strauss's teaching style in the classroom. It not only summarizes most of his major ideas on Maimonides, but also advances some of them in novel directions. In terms of what is most fresh relative to what has so far been discussed by Strauss, it raises the issue of precisely how Maimonides composed his great book. Moreover, it addresses itself in a preliminary but scarcely rudimentary fashion to uncovering the unapparent, if not deliberately concealed, structure of the *Guide*. It emerges that Maimonides not only probed the "secrets" of the Torah, but also adopted its method of "secretive" transmission, not only in the construction of his book but also in its plan, which, according to Strauss, made a formative impact on its argument. This allowed Strauss to obliquely raise the unavoidable issue of how the Torah itself was composed, if Maimonides was able to imitate it: he hints at, but never answers, the question of whether the Torah is a book written as the *Guide* was written. Notwithstanding this, Strauss elicits from Maimonides that since the "secrets" are most emphatically the secrets of the Torah *as a book*, and hence of a humanly readable book, one has to be trained in the art of carefully reading artfully written books if one is to advance in comprehending at least the *Guide* (if not also the Torah) as an authored, masterfully constructed book.

Strauss determines that Maimonides' book was designed, as much as anything, to be an instruction manual on how to properly read the Bible. Strauss argues that this makes the book primarily an exegetical work, concerned with teaching the correct forms of biblical interpretation, especially dwelling on the distinction between the literal and the figurative as the key to attaining an adequate explication of the text. Maimonides so limited himself, as Strauss perceives, because it is through this aperture that he was best able to sharpen his focus on the big questions of philosophy, religion, politics, and history. He views these as a Jew in the framework of Judaism, which communicates and passes on in literature its approach to the deepest problems of human life. Ever keeping in mind the limits of the written word as a truth both the ancient rabbis and Socrates held dear, Maimonides' view of what the Torah and his books are designed for helps the Jewish approach to remain vital. This is because he attempts, via tradition, to raise commentary on the book to a higher cognitive level, doing so through the form that Judaism prefers, i.e., unending oral discussion, even if this is based on the written word as a starting point.[35]

Of course, Strauss notes that Maimonides' book also combines training

---

35. For Strauss on Socrates' use of books, which he employed in the company of his friends, even if he did not himself write any, see "What Is Liberal Education?," in *Liberalism Ancient and Modern*, p. 6; "The Problem of Socrates," in *Rebirth of Classical Political Rationalism*, p. 140. For Strauss on the Jewish preference for the oral, and for the limits of discursive truth articulated in language whether written or oral, see "Perspectives on the Good Society," in *Jewish Philosophy and the Crisis of Modernity*, p. 444.

in interpretation with what he calls schooling in "speculation," which is instruction in thinking, excogitation not linked to specific biblical texts. Strauss emphasizes how Maimonides carefully divides this dual teaching by sections and subsections, which organize the argument dialectically so as to alternate these two approaches with one another—first exegesis and next speculation, back and forth—at least in the first part of the *Guide*. This dialectical procedure seems to have been mainly oriented to what Strauss calls the "typical addressee" of the *Guide*. Who Maimonides' "typical addressee" is, and why he chose this unusual procedure in order to educate him, is only briefly addressed by Strauss in his lecture. However, Strauss discusses this directly and in much greater detail—as well as at least dropping hints about an "atypical" addressee, and hence a deeper logic of the book, which transcends the surface and hence the "typical"—in the thought-provoking but difficult essay that is to follow, namely, "How To Begin."

The lecture in which Strauss introduced the *Guide* to students at the University of Chicago in 1960 is unique among the works of Strauss on Maimonides for its beginning with a candidly exoteric presentation of Maimonides' views in the *Guide*. It is true that this is next called into doubt for its adequacy. Yet there then follows the start of an account tentatively suggesting what may have been communicated on the esoteric level, even if it is also the case that this is not fully elaborated by Strauss in what he chooses to present. To be sure, this is not so unprecedented: Strauss is often elusive about his own views and speaks mostly as a commentator;[36] and indeed, he only *alludes* to what Maimonides' true views on crucial matters *may* have been. Limiting himself to suggestiveness about Maimonides' true views means that whatever Strauss says, he will not make the true views plainly evident. However, since he acknowledges the great debates through history that have been generated by this lack of clarity about those views, one might say that there is in this subtle pointing to history a hint about what might constitute his *own* notions of Maimonides' true views. As Strauss makes readers notice, disputes among commentators about what Maimonides' true views on crucial matters were have tended to accumulate around the fundamental issue of what his deepest concern was: was it the challenges and puzzles of philosophy (defined at

---

36. Cf. Strauss's remarks on the true commentator, who is not necessarily lacking in a free mind, and hence who possesses the capacity to think not only freely of the truth but also deeply for himself; see "Introduction" to *Persecution and the Art of Writing*, pp. 14–17. The introduction is of course an abbreviated version of Strauss's "Farabi's *Plato*," which is worth consulting for the original context in which the argument occurs: *Louis Ginzberg Jubilee Volume*, ed. Saul Lieberman et al. (New York: American Academy for Jewish Research, 1945), pp. 357–93.

least since Socrates as truth, human nature, the best regime, the governing mind, etc.), or was it the authoritative issues of medieval theology (that which is common to the three monotheistic religious traditions: the divine nature, creation, prophecy, providence, scripture, etc.)? To put this point otherwise, which for him was the subordinate, and which the leading, concern?

In point of fact, Strauss's lecture on the *Guide* proceeds on the premise (which he had already firmly established in "Literary Character") that this book is most emphatically a Jewish book, written by a Jew for Jews. Hence the *Guide* is not merely a philosophic book in any sense of the word, insofar as one tends to think of such books, whether medieval or modern, as treatises or dialogues dedicated to direct discussion of theoretical questions and practical problems as cultivated in philosophic tradition. And yet it is likewise not merely a theological book, which as conventionally formulated would generally be a faith-based elucidation concerned with the common legacy of the three monotheistic religious traditions, as well as with their historical differences, and hence with a defense of the specifically Jewish beliefs as truer or better. Instead, as Strauss notes, Maimonides tends to pay special attention to the essential human grounds and general state of nature in which the vitality and usefulness of the religious traditions derived from the Hebrew Bible are rooted: Strauss points particularly to its political relevance to the modern person inasmuch as it concerns itself with the common life of man in society, something which (as corresponds to the modern desire for the universal) transcends Maimonides' era. Thus, Strauss shows that Maimonides' book is at least at first focused solely on the thinking Jew: well educated in Jewish and philosophic sources, resiliently if waveringly loyal, and yet suffering from a sort of critical perplexity which brings on almost a perpetual anxiety.

That is to say, Strauss indicates that this book is philosophical but in its own fashion and not bound by historical restraints, since it addresses itself to the life and dilemmas of the thinker. Further, the specific "spiritual" dilemma of this sort of addressee is utilized as representative of a general crisis in the Jewish society for which Maimonides regards himself (as well as his addressee) as responsible. Following from this, Strauss explains how the book is political, calling on the addressee not only to think but also to act in a certain fashion, while he ever keeps in mind the permanent imperatives of philosophic pedagogy. Strauss introduces his own students to the book by obliquely awakening them to its parallel relevance to them and their concerns with regard to meaning, value, the future of modern civilization, and its relation to religious piety. Since religion, as Maimonides shows, is unavoidable,

Strauss wants his "typical" student to perceive through this lecture that the "spiritual" dilemmas which their great medieval predecessor had faced were in fact not all that different from the similar "spiritual" dilemmas which they must confront. As he teaches them to appreciate, this great book is not just a monument, but is still eminently useful to them for thinking through their own most immediate predicament, which amounts to confronting the rival and contending claims of reason or science and religion in the modern era.

The *Guide*, insofar as it is a "Jewish book" and concentrated on the "spiritual" dimension, is according to Strauss primarily concerned with *agada* rather than with *halakha*. For as "the true science of the Torah" teaches, the secrets of the Torah concern the fundamental principles which lie beneath the Torah as Law, and hence cannot be conceived ultimately as mere Law. Strauss locates the nub and nexus of Maimonides' book as focused on the Hebrew Bible, for it is in this that the tradition originated and remains rooted. The *agada* is a sort of deepening reflection through which biblical terms and parables are properly elucidated or seen in their proper light. It emerges that this is the main cause of perplexity and confusion among those select souls for whom Maimonides wrote his book: they tend to misread the Torah, if not the Hebrew Bible as an entirety, and hence to be led to miscomprehend its purpose, meaning, and value. To Maimonides, the Torah is not only the primary and original book of revelation, but also engenders the conception of revelation itself, which is the cause of so much perplexity, since what it is for a book to be shaped by God's word is so often misconstrued. What strikes Maimonides as most remarkable about the revealed book is its capacity to educate its best readers—through its carefully constructed and layered multivalent terminology—about human beings in full, and about the highest purposes of human life in society. To be sure, Maimonides knew that it achieves this pedagogical purpose supported by its teachings about divine and natural matters, but Strauss was most astonished by Maimonides' emphatic focus on revelation as a teaching about human beings. Hence, in Strauss's "introductory" lecture on the *Guide*, he seems to suggest that Maimonides' approach to the Hebrew Bible is at its best for its capacity to capture this idea of the nature of revelation per se, which as Maimonides believes (and Strauss seems to concur) is merely reproduced with apposite variations in the parallel religious traditions. And true revelation in the Torah emerges as an impressive form of human reasoning in its own right about man and the world, which can compete with philosophy (although based on different fundamental premises) concerning which is the wisest.

Strauss also raises the issue of why at the beginning Maimonides assiduously avoids dealing directly with the topic of natural science, as if it is some sort of threat to religion. As Strauss notes, Maimonides makes multiple and unambiguous statements dismissing the notion that this science is somehow antithetical to the Law. Instead what interests and drives Maimonides, as Strauss discerns, is that this science may be misapprehended so as to obstruct and debilitate how one comprehends the *purpose* of the Law. He helps to show his addressee how natural science is philosophy's perennial and necessary ground. Once the addressee has been fully educated about it (through a reading of scripture in which passion is to be moderated), Maimonides is able to explain how knowledge of natural science is not a destroyer of the Law, but merely changes "the grounds on which it is to be obeyed." Of course, the "merely" is not to be slighted, but is a major point.

Consequent to Maimonides's roundabout approach to natural science, Strauss devotes himself to accounting for some features of the *Guide* which prove to follow from it: brief remarks on who the main or typical addressee of the *Guide* is, and on what his principal characteristics are; why Maimonides began the *Guide* as he did, with the focus on clarifying misleading terms; and why he chose the specific terms he did, and which he focuses on in the first forty-nine chapters of the *Guide*. Strauss brings to light that this selection and arrangement of issues is determined by the imperative to reject the corporeality of God, which is fundamental to him. As Strauss observes, it is of even greater weight than the rejection of idolatry, because corporeality (as Strauss shockingly claims on Maimonides' behalf) is the true basis of idolatry, and hence is even worse than idolatry, which idolatry is hence merely a symptom. As Strauss elucidates, Maimonides' first concern is to cure the diseases of the mind, which will next alleviate the sufferings of the heart.

This lecture finishes with a question and answer period that is almost as interesting as the two-part lecture that preceded it. Strauss expresses his conviction that, however much Maimonides made use of Greek philosophy, what he presents as his definitive teaching is affirmatively Jewish. This is not merely Greek philosophy with a Jewish veneer, but is an attempt to wrestle with the challenge of ancient Greek thought, and with what the best Greek thinkers taught about God, man, and the world in order to, if possible, make it consistent with Jewish teachings. Strauss is convinced that Maimonides' finished doctrine, though it makes abundant use of Greek philosophy as is sufficient for "philosophically" clarifying Jewish teaching, nonetheless is able to bring to light "what the Bible fundamentally means." Thus, the Maimonidean doctrine of attributes (as well as his related doctrines) is *not* a mere explication of Greek philosophy (whether Platonic, Aristotelian, or neo-Platonic) in Jewish terms, but rather is an authentic interpretation of the biblical teaching: It "is surely not an Aristotelian teaching. And it is not even, in the way in which Maimonides presents it at any rate, what one could ascribe to neo-Platonism. In the end one must realize, I think, that it is so crucial to distinguish it from these Greek teachings."

In the process of clarifying Maimonides' highly peculiar positions for skeptical students, Strauss seems to reveal and articulate his own vital conviction: Maimonides' teaching is fully consistent with the Jewish tradition and the classical Jewish sources, despite the fact that he harmonizes them with philosophy or science. This appears to be something greater than a mere cover for doubts which Strauss himself entertains about the validity of Maimonides' project: Strauss seems genuinely impressed by Maimonides' elementary and steadfast loyalty to the Jewish teaching, albeit of course as he construes it. This continues to be relevant to us, as Strauss confirms toward the end of the discussion period and as he forcefully presents it at the beginning of the first lecture. Indeed, his preliminary argument in the lecture, prior to dealing with Maimonides' *Guide* itself, amounts to a prolonged explanation of why we should still be interested in Maimonides, due to the evident deficiencies, dilemmas, and impasses of modern thought. Even if Maimonides labored as rigorously as it was possible for him to do to defend Jewish teachings in terms of Socratically based ancient and medieval philosophy and science, he also based his argument for science as authentically Jewish on the permanent, transhistorical character of philosophy. Only by such an acutely thoughtful argument, according to Strauss, was Maimonides able to make the Jewish teachings coherent and in harmony with the truly rational contents of philosophy and science and prove them to be a genuinely Jewish heritage, and hence beyond its merely Greek-ethnic and -linguistic character. This is the case even if it is correct, as also Strauss admits, that a simple, traditional Jew who has been raised and educated *only* "in the biblical-talmudic tradition" may well be "greatly surprised" by Maimonides' ultimate doctrine. Yet Strauss maintains that this is not the last word. For at the end as at the beginning, Maimonides proceeded from his unyielding fidelity to Judaism, as Strauss contends. Indeed, Strauss in the lecture seems determined to imply that it was because of this fidelity that Maimonides was careful to make sure that this series of philosophic, political, and scientific doctrines, superbly probed and appropriated by him, remained consistent with the most authentically Jewish teachings.

"How To Begin To Study *The Guide of the Perplexed*" (1963) made its debut as the "Introductory Essay" to the superlative English-language translation of the *Guide*, completed by Shlomo Pines, Strauss's friend and colleague in the study of Maimonides. ("It may even be the best translation ever made," is Strauss's high praise indeed for Pines's work.) His essay begins with what it is not unwarranted to deem the most impressive effort ever made to map the plan and structure of Maimonides' great book. In doing so, Strauss was able to discern an astonishing regularity and order in the book, even though the *Guide* was previously regarded by most modern scholars as scrambled, haphazard, disorganized, and even random. Strauss notes, however, that some distinctive sections—e.g., the doctrine of attributes in *Guide* 1.50–60, or the "prophetology" in *Guide* 2.32–48—were always clearly recognized. But how and why this clustering of parts made for a whole seems never to have actually been fathomed by any prior scholars, who did not view structure as mattering very much, and who appreciated it more for the trajectory of the book as a less orderly Jewish version of a common medieval theology.[37]

There is no doubt that one of the crucial aspects of the *Guide* discovered (or rediscovered) by Strauss is its "esoteric" dimension, which appears to provide a key to unlocking its "secrets." To be sure, some medieval readers had been so impressed by the "esoteric imperative" articulated by Maimonides in the *Guide* that they actually composed their own esoteric commentaries on the book, although modern scholars had generally dismissed these as belonging to an obsolete past. Indeed, contrary to such commentaries, they believed this specific dimension of the *Guide* itself may be disregarded with no loss of understanding of the book's contents, since whatever may perhaps be contained in its overarching plan and structure are merely accidental features. Unlike other modern scholars, Strauss approached the book with fresh eyes, seeing that Maimonides planted a system of pointers, avail-

---

37. Its "disordered" appearance would make it epitomize Jewish books, which are typically judged by most modern scholars to have been written in an "associative" or "organic," rather than a logical, style. Strauss did not dismiss this judgment; he only deemed that it is superficial. To be sure, Maimonides embraced this style, but he used it for his own literary purposes that did not eschew a rigorous logic of its own.

able to be uncovered only by thoroughly studying the surface of the book itself, since this system was hidden in plain sight. By following this system of pointers to the deeper plane deliberately obscured from most hasty and neglectful readers, Strauss was then able to perceive what was in fact quite visible with regard to the book's essential if concealed contours.

To be sure, Strauss's rediscovery of the esoteric teaching in the *Guide* is still disputed by some; and even those who are willing to reluctantly concede the point, often deny its scope as well as what it might seem to imply about the character of Maimonides as a thinker, i.e., whether Strauss is right to identify him as in the select company of the "free minds," a type no different among the ancients as among the moderns. Whatever one may conclude about full-scale esotericism and how it is to be related to the mind of Maimonides, this essay undoubtedly represents not just a fresh beginning but also an advanced deepening in Strauss's own reading of the *Guide*. Indeed, Strauss boldly ventured to suggest as a possibility that so far no one has yet been able to completely probe its furthermost depths, and Strauss was clearly determined to make a single-minded and unprecedented effort to do so. In this process, he seems to have judged it requisite that he himself write about this book in such a fashion that his analysis becomes a sort of esoteric commentary on an esoteric book. Despite the fact that Strauss was a modern scholar, this essay seems to represent his growing belief that the only adequate method of uncovering the actual intention of Maimonides is to attempt to present the true views of Maimonides in a somewhat hidden or at least diversionary fashion. This is because the author of the book himself contended that his own views could not be articulated correctly in direct expression, and this contention, according to Strauss, cannot be discounted.

As a result, "How To Begin" is an immensely difficult and deliberately elusive analysis, the fruit of twenty-five years of study, according to Strauss himself. (In fact, it was probably closer to forty years, if one counts his pre-"Literary Character" works, though Strauss would probably dismiss these fifteen years as wasted, due to what he would likely consider his previously flawed perspective on the *Guide*.) Beneath its obscure, if not calculatedly bland, surface Strauss issues a radical challenge to most conventional images of Maimonides as a conservative thinker: it calls for readers to recognize him as one of the truly "free minds," a term which he seems to have borrowed from Nietzsche (even if it is often mistranslated as "free spirits"), and which differentiates among other traits the rare type known as the philosopher. In a certain respect, Strauss also decided to imitate the *Guide* by his choice to write the introductory essay in a virtually stream-of-consciousness style: it is characterized by unduly complicated sentences, lengthy paragraphs, and lack of any section breaks, headings, or subheadings. In spite of its apparent disjointedness, it may possess a greater logic than appears on the surface. Yet it certainly requires of its readers an enormous effort in studying two works simultaneously, calling them to make sense of both Strauss's carefully written text itself and Maimonides' *Guide* on its own by frequent references to chapters which have to be checked and compared.

As a consequence, it is essential to isolate a number of key components in this perhaps most complex essay by Strauss in order to guide readers through its problematic workings, and to stimulate questions about it. First, Strauss uncovers a concealed plan of the book; he further observes that this plan is divided by sections and subsections, with the number seven as its operative key or crucial organizer. Strauss tacitly provokes readers to ask: why seven, and yet why not always seven? Why is it ordered as an ascent followed by a descent with *ma'aseh merkavah* (i.e., Ezekiel's vision of the chariot) at the peak? And what is Maimonides saying about *ma'aseh merkavah*, the most secret teaching of the Torah, that it is located at just this juncture, occurring in just such a form? Is *ma'aseh merkavah* what it seems to be, i.e., "metaphysics" in the simplest sense of Aristotle's book by the same name, or is it actually directing the minds of his best readers to a different orientation, such as a political one that revolves around the word "governance"?

Second, as Strauss delineates it, the book is written in two "literary" styles, each apparently with a very different purpose: the exegetical component and the speculative component, which are unevenly distributed through the book. If Strauss is correct about that, why conceptually would Maimonides decide to compose his book in this fashion, employing two distinctly different literary styles? Certainly if the book is chiefly about how best to interpret the Hebrew Bible, one might think that it should be entirely exegetical, but this is obviously not the case in any simple sense. And if it possesses a seriously speculative facet that is not tied to scripture, does this change the intention of the book from what Maimonides states at the beginning of his own "Introduction," and even according to the notion of the book presented by Strauss at the start of his essay, not to mention in other works?

Third, Strauss lays much stress on the private versus the public dimensions of Maimonides' teaching. Is this merely Maimonides' way of reflecting the secret teaching of the Torah? Or is that rather Maimonides' subtle manner of adding his own original teaching in between the lines? Did his presenting the book as a series of letters to his student allow him to obliquely reveal the secrets of the Torah as he conceives, reconstructs, and even advances them?

Fourth, Strauss attempts to classify the *Guide* in order to grasp Maimonides' fundamental premises. He asks: is it a "Jewish book," or is it a "philosophic book"? And while Strauss unambiguously declares it a "Jewish book," which echoes Maimonides' own claims for it, is it possible that contained in this pronouncement is Strauss's own hint that he believes it somehow to also be simultaneously a "philosophic book," however this term may be conceived?

Fifth, the *Guide* is not written for a single type of addressee, but rather, as Strauss discloses, for three separate types or even classes: two of the "atypical" sort (i.e., the "critical and competent" on the one hand, and the vulgar on the other hand), and one of the "typical" sort (i.e., Rabbi Joseph and scholars or students like him). Regarding the main set of "typical" addressees to which Rabbi Joseph belongs, Strauss highlights two main issues: doubts about the "typical" addressee's knowledge of natural science, and the consequences of such a lack; and his adherence to authority, whether religious, philosophic, pedagogical, or political. Strauss suggests that there is a peculiar interlinking in the contents of the book; this interlinking enables the author to speak simultaneously to these three classes of addressees. Yet one is concurrently forced to ask: is it even possible that Maimonides could have hoped to achieve this almost unfeasible feat of authorial literary virtuosity?

Sixth, Strauss provocatively confronts Maimonides' conception of "progress" in the Jewish tradition. One might at first be surprised that this was a concern of Maimonides, since it had long been a truism among modern scholars that Maimonides did not judge history to be a serious matter, besides one's entrenched tendency to consider this a quintessentially modern notion. Strauss makes several clear statements about the notion of progress in Maimonides that might shock his readers by their confident boldness. For example, Strauss states: "Once one has granted that there is an intrabiblical progress beyond the teaching of Moses," then "one will not be compelled to deny the possibility of a postbiblical progress." In another instance he affirms: "The progress of incorporealism is accompanied by a progress of asceticism." How is it possible to explain this idea of progress in Strauss's treatment, which as a historical notion seems to contradict the image of Maimonides as one who believes in the eternality of biblical truth? Likewise, how does Strauss arrive at the definite result that progress, as he indicates, is a distinctly implicit theme present in this book as well as in Maimonides' other works, although it is never made materially explicit by him?

Seventh, among the odd features of Strauss's introductory essay, it is to be noted that it covers the *Guide* only from 1.1 to 2.24 at the furthest; it finishes close to the middle of the book in page numbers, but not in chapter numbers. According to Strauss's own version of the plan of the book, 2.24 is the point at which the "defense of the belief in creation out of nothing against the philosophers" concludes. It is also at this point that his essay reaches a virtual climax with Maimonides' strange but striking statement about "*the* true perplexity," which Strauss was the first to highlight. As enhances Strauss's point, Maimonides only once uses this obviously significant phrase in his book. Whatever this may mean, it is certainly the case that Strauss concentrates most of his attention on part 1 of the *Guide* only (which makes it somewhat resemble the 18th-century commentary by Solomon Maimon). Why did Strauss produce an introduction so weighted, and seemingly so limited, even if it is also true that dispersed through this essay are numerous references to the subsequent chapters and topics of the book?

Eighth, Strauss is determined to show that Maimonides puts tremendous emphasis, by his chosen beginning of the book, on his fierce antagonism to "corporealism," the belief in the corporeality of God. Indeed, Strauss is willing to carry it so far as to say on Maimonides' behalf: "Not idolatry but the belief in God's corporeality is a fundamental sin." Also: "Corporealism [is] the hidden premise of idolatry." Is there a deeper point that Strauss is trying to prove about the *Guide* by drawing this much attention to the stress which Maimonides lays on anticorporealism, and if so, then what is Strauss trying to expose? And from this what does he want his readers to infer?

Ninth, a pattern of statements as enigmatic as Strauss's seemingly undue stress on corporealism can further be observed in the introductory essay as a whole. It can only be concluded that this pattern reflects a deliberate effort made by Strauss to puzzle and provoke thought in his readers by the sudden occurrence of these arresting statements, which break through an apparently lackluster prose. There are several such statements that help to illustrate this point, which it is then requisite to connect with numerous others occurring in the essay in order to make sense of the pattern. As an example, Strauss states: "Maimonides does not discuss the implication which was stated, for it is one of the secrets of the Torah and we are only at the beginning of our training." What is the "implication"? And was it actually ever "stated" previously? As another instance, consider the following: "By this irregularity our attention is drawn to a certain numerical symbolism that is of assistance to the serious reader of the *Guide*: 14 stands for man or the human things and 17 stands for nature." On what basis is he assigning to Maimonides the use of numerical symbolism in the *Guide*? And why are just those numbers associated with just those things? For a further case: "'Governance' [is] as it were the translation of *Merkavah* ('Chariot'), as appears from 1.70." Is it so evident from 1.70 that this generic notion identifying *Merkavah* with "governance"—which he is careful not to qualify by limiting it to God—appears quite so manifest in the chapter to which he refers? Finally: the unanticipated and certainly peculiar political-historical analogy concerning post–World War II Germany, in order to reflect on the two possible proofs (philosophical and theological) for the existence of God! Besides uncertainty about its meaning and value in the context of the argument in his presentation, what is one to make of this strangest of parallels that appears unrelated to everything else occurring in the essay?

Tenth, Strauss clearly maintains that lexicography plays an enormous role in the *Guide*, implying that there is a system of terms which it is essential to know if Maimonides' readers are to penetrate the true contents, teaching, and purpose of the Hebrew Bible. Strauss puts emphasis on how these distinctly lexicographic chapters function, in both their regular and irregular forms; and he obliquely suggests why they vary as they do. He also focuses a substantial amount of his complex analysis on the role these chapters play in the book's structure. At the same time as admitting that this is undoubtedly a brilliant discovery, one is also compelled to ask whether Strauss is right about the significance of lexicography, and about the place in which most parts of it occur in the *Guide*? Even if these things are just as Strauss presents them, then why did he need to be obscure about this matter specifically? And by applying himself so assiduously to the study of lexicography, what is he implying by this about Maimonides' concealment techniques and the reasons for them?

Eleventh, Strauss makes a point of stressing that Maimonides employed a most blatant contradiction about Moses. (To be sure, this must also be connected with Strauss's claims about Maimonides' "method of contradictions" in the book.) As Strauss states, "Undoubtedly Maimonides contradicts himself regarding Moses' prophecy." This is so blatant because, as Strauss observes, Maimonides declares that he will not speak explicitly or implicitly about Moses, and yet it is obvious that he breaks this rule, speaking about him often and almost emphatically. Yet Strauss is almost never so direct in proclaiming Maimonides' contradictions on a number of other issues dealt with in the book (even if he hints at one or two), which he was certainly free to do. Why would this issue be treated so differently from all other issues that Strauss could have addressed on Maimonides' contradictions?

Twelfth, Strauss notes that regarding the structure of the book, "The *Guide* consists then of seven sections or of thirty-eight subsections. Wherever feasible, each section is divided into seven subsections." Let us notice how Strauss proceeds when considering the seventh section alone, which is entitled "Man's perfection and God's providence (3.51–54)": it is the only section in which God and man are combined, and indeed it is the only section which makes "man" the evident thematic focus; it is the last section of the book; and it is the end of the last half, which Strauss dubs "Actions," inasmuch as the book is partitioned in unequal halves. Why solely in the seventh section is it not "feasible" to divide it by seven subsections, but only in this case by two subsections?[38]

These are several suggested questions that address some of the most obvious difficulties in Strauss's "How To Begin." They may be helpful as signposts to some readers who wish to begin trying to disentangle the evident perplexities which Strauss himself leaves for readers of the *Guide*, insofar as he must divide the "serious" and the unserious readers. One may regard them as strange but useful guides, lodged in the problematic features of Strauss's own essay, which are supposed to be advantageous for untying the literary knots and philosophic perplexities which attend Maimonides' *Guide*, while not betraying Maimonides', or even the Torah's own, secrets. Yet even with this attempt at clarifying Strauss's presentation through highlighting the obvious difficulties, Strauss still leaves us with a conundrum which it is not so simple to resolve: is it appropriate for a modern scholar to imitate the procedure of a medieval writer and thinker? And if Strauss thinks that it is appropriate, how is he able to justify this approach?

"Notes on Maimonides' *Book of Knowledge*" (1967) is Strauss's first literary effort to deal directly with the *Mishneh Torah* since his review of Moses Hyamson's edition of the Bodleian manuscript of *Sefer ha-Madda* (*Book of*

---

38. Strauss offers a sort of clue, almost in passing, toward the end of "Introduction to Maimonides' *Guide*," chap. 10 below: "Seven is in a way—but not completely—the key number for this mysterious work." Yet why only "in a way" and "not completely"? The significance of the number seven is most directly addressed in "Maimonides' Statement on Political Science," chap. 9 below.

Knowledge) in the 1930s. In this work of the 1960s, written for a book of essays in honor of his friend Gershom Scholem, he proceeds from his essential insight that Maimonides mostly wrote "Jewish books." Yet he is also fully aware that this entire book, *Mishneh Torah*, and especially the *Book of Knowledge*, conveys a different sort of Jewish sensibility from that which received expression in the *Guide*. He encapsulates this difference in the following terms: "the purposes of the *Guide* and the *Mishneh Torah* differ so greatly" with "the most important substantive difference" between them being that they belong to the two different "kinds of science of the Law"—the *Guide* to the science "in the true sense," and the *Mishneh Torah* to the science "in the ordinary sense." He attempts to clarify this even further by ascertaining that the "roots" of the Law, its deepest truths, are dealt with most fully in the *Guide*, while those same "roots" are either merely stated or discussed with "much greater brevity" in the *Mishneh Torah*. In other words, these two books—contrary to the impression he might have created in "Literary Character"—are aimed at the same truths, but they bring them to light for another sort of reader who is pedagogically and cognitively at a different stage of philosophic development.

What the two books have in common is that they both address the fundamental difference between the adherents of the Law and the philosophers, namely, belief in the creation of the world versus the eternity of the world. Yet as Strauss notes with some obvious surprise, the *Mishneh Torah* (and especially its *Book of Knowledge*) "establishes the existence of God on the basis of the view, which he rejects in the *Guide*, that the world is eternal." As Strauss paradoxically concludes from this, the *Mishneh Torah* is "in an important respect . . . more 'philosophic' than the *Guide*," because this book of law "in the ordinary sense" has, for whatever reason, less concern with defending the "roots" of the Law apologetically, but rather is bold enough to put them fully in the context of science. This is no doubt a most astonishing statement about the two books. If what Strauss highlights is correct, this is most perplexing as to what Maimonides is thinking, and what he is doing.

"Yesodei ha-Torah" ("Laws of the Basic Principles of the Torah," which is the first of the five sections of the *Book of Knowledge*) "stands or falls," according to Strauss, by the distinction between what are the *true* roots of the Law and what are not. It is for this reason that Strauss perceives Maimonides to have focused on the most significant roots—the "secrets" of the Torah, which are comprised in *ma'aseh bereshit* and *ma'aseh merkavah*—at the very start of "Yesodei ha-Torah," and hence of the *Book of Knowledge*, and hence in the most augmented sense of the entire *Mishneh Torah*. Yet curiously, as Strauss also observes, Maimonides treats them in reverse order. As Strauss contends, Maimonides assigns them their true order of rank: first *ma'aseh merkavah*, and only next *ma'aseh bereshit*, directly contrary to the *Guide*'s presentation. Why Maimonides does so in this context alone is not entirely clear, even from Strauss's enigmatic presentation. However, it is in a passing comment in *Guide* 1.70, noticed by Strauss through his usual careful reading, that this perception appears to be confirmed: the first four chapters of "Yesodei ha-Torah" (dedicated in reverse order to *ma'aseh merkavah* and *ma'aseh bereshit*), as Maimonides seems to imply, are *the* "Book of Knowledge." Strauss thinks that perhaps precisely because this four-chapter unit lacks the definite article in *Guide* 1.70, it is differentiated and highlighted by Maimonides as the most fundamental knowledge.

Strauss suggests that in the different sections of the *Sefer ha-Madda* "the tension" between philosophy and the Torah becomes "thematic," and even though at least at several points it verges on a contradiction, at only one point does Strauss say that this actually "proves . . . to be a contradiction." This makes it probable that, according to Strauss, at most points Maimonides seems to do his best to reduce or resolve this "tension." Thus, in considering "De'ot" (i.e., "Laws of Character Traits"), Strauss brings to light Maimonides' endeavor to explore the conflict of the two fundamental moral teachings, inasmuch as this seems to involve an unavoidable confrontation. Strauss observes that Maimonides actually "juxtaposes philosophic morality and the morality of the Torah" and at least at the beginning (or on the surface) makes no effort to diminish their conflict. Likewise, with regard to "human goodness" Strauss indicates that Maimonides separates "wisdom and piety," depicting this difference as an essential and irremovable human divide. And yet Strauss also explains that subsequently Maimonides shows that the Law can bridge this divide (even if this divide cannot be obliterated), once the Law's subtle and dialectical teaching has been properly apprehended. This is a possibility which had hitherto—until Maimonides elaborated it—been unappreciated.

As Strauss presents it, this is a book concerned with the defense of the Torah, which is why it is designated a "Jewish book." Yet Maimonides' procedure for doing so, as Strauss states the issue with uncustomary audacity, is "to "introduce philosophy into the Holy of Holies by as it were rediscovering it there." Strauss elaborates on his own radical statement as follows: since "philosophy requires the greatest possible awareness of what one is doing," and since he suggests that Maimonides was self-consciously working with philosophy in order to bring about a "fundamental change" in the comprehension and function of the Law, he must have been aware that what he was doing via this fundamental change as a philosophic reformer amounted to a "conscious . . . criticism of the way in which the Torah was commonly understood." Strauss highlights for readers the critical dimension in Maimonides' thought that he is willing to boldly apply to Judaism, and hence he shows by this subtle emphasis on Jewish self-criticism that the thrust of Maimonides' project is not just a criticism of certain unproven philosophic tenets. Yet precisely if this suggestion of conscious criticism in Maimonides is correct, then Strauss suggests that Maimonides is merely implementing the fundamental change in accord with the overarching "philosophic" principle that he believed has always truly governed the Torah. Perhaps the best explanation of what Strauss had come to think about Maimonides' historic project is provided by a couple of lines in "How To Begin": "Maimonides' link with the Torah is, to begin with, an iron bond; it gradually becomes a fine thread. But however far what one may call his intellectualization may go, it always remains the intellectualization of the Torah."[39]

Although Strauss lays stress on the plan by which Maimonides constructed the *Mishneh Torah*, and especially the *Book of Knowledge* (identifying which was itself most original), he did not get the chance to expatiate on the details, which would have been an enormous enterprise. However, he did make an incisive though controversial remark about Maimonides' leading procedure, which bears consequences for his plan. In several cases highlighted by Strauss, the literary procedure Maimonides abides by is as follows: to begin with the philosophic position (even if not with philosophy by name), and next to proceed to the religious-traditional position. As such, theology is first consistently subordinated to philosophy and receives its due only subsequently. Or as Strauss also enunciates the same point with a slightly different emphasis: repetitions—a technique, as Strauss stresses, which is a favorite in the *Guide*, and which is used most frequently as a form of concealment—often serves in the *Book of Knowledge* the purpose of "correcting" philosophy in favor of religious tradition.

---

39. See "How To Begin," chap. 11 below. Cf. also "Introduction to Maimonides' *Guide*," chap. 10 below, which states the same point slightly differently: "If I may summarize this development: Maimonides' link with the Torah is, to begin with, an iron bond; it gradually turns [and] becomes a fine thread. But however far the conscious spiritualization of the Torah may go, that spiritualization always remains a spiritualization of the Torah."

As an instance which may exemplify this point, Strauss notices that Maimonides avoids the use of the word "to create" with respect to God in the first chapter of the the *Book of Knowledge*; it enters his purview only once his discussion has turned to the creatures in the second chapter. Similarly, the word "belief" is only introduced once he talks about prophecy (chapter VII); it is not used in *ma'aseh merkavah* or *ma'aseh bereshit*. A divergent approach is employed for the theme of "nature," which is crucial for his effort to allow the establishment of philosophy or science as a legitimate authority in Judaism. It is treated at three separate points in the essay; he demonstrates how for Maimonides it gradually emerges from "custom" or "way" and becomes definitive; yet he also shows how Maimonides is silent about "nature" in "De'ot," if it impedes the purposes of his moral teaching. Last but not least, Strauss perceives how the passion for knowledge and science, which Maimonides wishes to arouse, runs like a leitmotif through the entire book. It reappears as a dominant theme even at the end of "Teshuvah" ("Laws of Repentance"), which might seem far removed from a connection to his aim of cognitive advancement in his society. Yet that proves not to be the case. In this matter, he emphasizes that the love of God is the antidote to any temptation to act morally for mercenary motives. But in order to love God, one must know Him; and in order to know Him properly and fully, Maimonides refers his readers not to *Sefer ha-Madda*, but again to *Sefer Madda*, i.e., the four chapters with which the book commenced. Apparently he has not departed even slightly from the goal he set, and toward which he oriented his entire book from the very first line, this being "to *know* that God exists." In other words, he directs his most attentive students to the serious study of *Sefer Madda*, i.e., "Yesodei ha-Torah," chapters I–IV, which contains only *ma'aseh merkavah* and *ma'aseh bereshit*, and which also happens to be the gateway to what Strauss calls (in "How To Begin") the "enchanted [and enchanting] forest" of the *Guide*.

One may say, in order to conclude, that "Notes on Maimonides' *Book of Knowledge*" is the first noteworthy, major effort to see the *Sefer ha-Madda* (if not the entire *Mishneh Torah*) in light of the *Guide*, especially as it was viewed from the standpoint reached by Strauss in his previous, mature work. Strauss's prior work had paid scrupulous attention to minute details as significant, be they Maimonides' uses of language, the variations of his terminology, or his conveying of meaning through structure. It had allowed Strauss to construct a novel perspective on Maimonides as a radical thinker, a Jewish theologian acutely attuned to the challenges of philosophy, an almost revolutionary legislator, and a statesmanlike figure of great historical impact on his society, a perspective that in this essay showed its great value for the original study of Maimonides' oeuvre much beyond the *Guide*.

"Note on Maimonides' *Treatise on the Art of Logic*" (1968) continues Strauss's seasoned effort to apply the results of his study of the *Guide* and its author to his other major works. Most noteworthy is that this is reiterated to have been the sole work composed by Maimonides that Strauss can state unequivocally "is not a Jewish book."[40] As Strauss emphasizes, this is not only because Maimonides wrote it at the request of "a master of the legal (religious) sciences" who seems not to have been Jewish, or because he uses no specifically Jewish cases to illustrate his points in logic. It is also because Maimonides speaks in his treatise as a pure logician: when he freely uses the first-person plural, according to Strauss, the "we" he is speaking for is "we logicians." Strauss also shows that in the treatise Maimonides maintains no preference for Judaism or favoritism for Torah by referring (in chap. 4), absent of any judgment, to Ishaq the Sabian as a legitimate authority or at least a legitimate case in point. This approach to reasoning differs greatly from Maimonides' references to Sabianism in the *Guide*, where he presents it as almost the diametrical opposite of Judaism. However, so long as logic alone is his concern, such a thing as the religious difference between "Sabianism" and "Judaism" is of no interest to him. Indeed, one could say that by Maimonides' doing logic in this way, he expresses his respect for the independence of the mind; it exemplifies his commitment to the freedom in which the life of the mind has to be conducted. One might even go so far as to conclude that the fact that Maimonides wrote this book is a significant proof of Strauss's interpretation of Maimonides in and of itself.[41] This also demonstrates to contemporary readers that Maimonides did not need to be modern in order to staunchly maintain the right of the logician, the philosopher, or the scholar to reach

---

40. For Strauss on the *Logic*, see also "Some Remarks on the Political Science of Maimonides and Farabi," chap. 5 below; and especially "Maimonides' Statement on Political Science," chap. 9 below, which also stressed that this alone "is not a Jewish book."

41. See "Introduction" to *Persecution and the Art of Writing*, p. 20, for a comment on the dubious status of logic in traditional Judaism: "As late as 1765, Moses Mendelssohn felt it necessary to apologize for recommending the study of logic, and to show why the prohibition against the reading of extraneous or profane books does not apply to works on logic." The context of Mendelssohn's apology is, of course, significant for the present purpose: it appeared in the introduction to his commentary on Maimonides' *Treatise on the Art of Logic*. See also *Leo Strauss on Moses Mendelssohn*, trans. and ed. Martin D. Yaffe (Chicago: University of Chicago Press, 2012), pp. 18, 251–59.

judgments based solely on reason, rather than on the edicts of theological dogma or the dictates of political authority.

At the same time Strauss also notices some seeming divergences from the fidelity to logic pure and unalloyed. He wonders why in chapter 3 Maimonides comes to regard such terms as "the noble" and "the base" as a matter of logic. Is it because he himself is "a master of the legal (religious) sciences," or is it rather because he is attentive to the needs of his addressee, in whose request the book had its beginning and to whose type he can perhaps hope to appeal on behalf of logic at least for its usefulness? That this is not what drives him is suggested by his rejection of any syllogistic "proofs" for creation, since he makes clear that the generic flaw in these is their "disregard of the difference between the natural and the artificial things." As this undoubtedly proves to Strauss, Maimonides holds no theological brief for creation while he is engaged in the elucidation of logic, as might tempt him to compromise its rigor and honesty. Strauss also notices that only in chapter 9 are the "philosophers" first mentioned by name. This class is discussed dispassionately: he reports on their view of God as only a remote cause, and their consequent view of "what befalls human beings," in which case they only regard the "proximate cause" as relevant. It will become evident in the next essay that this "philosophic" position on providence is opposed to Maimonides' own view as a Jewish teacher, but in this context Strauss wants readers to observe that as a logician Maimonides reports on the philosophers with the utmost matter-of-factness. Similarly, Strauss notes—concealing any surprise, other than as revealed by the fact that this is noted at all—that as a logician Maimonides accepts only body as "the highest genus of being": this might seem to confirm the truth of Sabianism in its materialism ("the Sabians knew no gods but the stars"). But Strauss is careful to also note that this book by Maimonides is "written for beginners." As Strauss would seem to imply, Maimonides gives Sabianism its due in the realm of logic, but he is not obligated as a result to take it as the last word.

Strauss ends the "Note" on the last (fourteenth) chapter, which is a return to his concern with Maimonides' political science as this is treated in the *Logic*. Until he had devoted an entire essay to it (i.e., "Maimonides' Statement on Political Science"), that was a largely unappreciated element of Maimonidean thought; but beyond what Strauss has already written, he seems to still regard it as crucial even for comprehending Maimonides' thought about logic. Discussing chapter 14 (a favorite Maimonidean number) allows Strauss to make some further comments on points which he seems to think are in need of additional special emphasis. Thus, Maimonides, in considering the division of the sciences, "speaks . . . at greatest length of political science." He especially notices Maimonides' "silence on government of a nation," which he regards as "strange," and he wonders if it shows his doubt as to whether political science has anything special to say about the "small nation." Yet he ends on a different note that might seem to raise serious qualms about this last point: Maimonides speaks of "the great nation or all nations," a form of speech that in context Strauss may be employing as a suggestion that it serves as Maimonides' conscious denial of the world-empire (in which all the nations are encompassed) as a human possibility. If man *cannot* establish a utopian world-empire (dreamed of by Christianity and Islam in his era), it surely restores the feasibility of "the nation" as a necessary and legitimate topic of political science, which seems to imply its sufficiency to encompass the Jews. Strauss conjectures that if this apparent rejection of world-empire as a human possibility is so for Maimonides, this may reflect what is known as "Averroism," and he refers readers to Marsilius of Padua, *Defensor Pacis*, in order to confirm what it is for this to be the case. But Strauss's primary point seems to be that on this issue, as on numerous others, Maimonides is willing to identify (and to communicate it in a subtle form) with philosophical thoughts of the most radical sort, if they seem "logical" to him regarding human nature, despite what the religious traditions might advance as pious imperatives.

"Note on Maimonides' *Letter on Astrology*" (1968), which was composed on July 21–23, 1968, is Strauss's last-known piece of work on Maimonides. To adapt Strauss's own phrase about Maimonides' work, I would deem this piece to be "a masterful epitome" of his thinking on the conflict between revelation and philosophy. In it Strauss uncovers how Maimonides prudently resolves this conflict by highlighting the strategic unity that emerges between the two contenders due to their common opposition to astrology, which they both reject unambiguously as a pseudoscience. In this concise piece, Strauss first brings to light Maimonides' argument by focusing on his subtle effort to get his addressees to distinguish between his own opinions and those of the tradition by the selective and careful use of language, i.e., "my" view versus "our" view. He nudges them to recognize the value of independent thought; indeed, Strauss speaks of Maimonides' effort to foster a "critical posture" in them. Hence, Maimonides quietly but surely urges his readers, as Strauss notices, to reject the authority of books that they are willing accept merely because they are old books, implying that they need to study new books like his own. These new books contain the proper critical perspective on and posture toward idolatrous literature insofar as that literature also embraces (which he is careful to add) all books of astrology. Moreover, this will help to free their minds and allow them to make sense of the laws of Moses inasmuch as these laws are grounded in resistance to idolatry, ergo also to astrology. To be sure, Strauss also perceives Maimonides' strange silence on the subject of "the Sabians." In the *Guide*, knowledge of Sabianism had served as the key to unlocking the secrets of the laws of Moses, but in the present context it is apparently not even worthy of a mention, although Maimonides' reasons for this silence are not given by Strauss. Is Strauss now tacitly suggesting on Maimonides' behalf that this is because the minds of his contemporary addressees are still too much in the grip of residual Sabian ideas?

As with previous works of Strauss on Maimonides, the essential issue at stake is "the relation of the philosophers and the Torah." Strauss notes that Maimonides strangely speaks of "philosophers who teach creation out of nothing," although he names no such philosopher. Yet as he would seem to imply, Maimonides must maintain this position on philosophy because he is aiming to reduce "the difference, as stated in the *Guide*, between philosophy and the Torah" and so to form "a unitary front . . . against astrology." Hence, the *Letter on Astrology* reformulates the divide between the philosophers and the Torah along different lines from those in the *Guide*. This restatement has both sides agree on governance (or what Strauss prefers to render as "government"), which concerns the general rules by which the world operates, but disagree on "providence," which concerns individual human beings and specific societies. Indeed, as Strauss astoundingly suggests, Maimonides ultimately provides a sounder divide than creation versus eternity, this being their differing views on the nature of human freedom. Even if both philosophy and the Torah agree that "men's actions" are not ruled by "compulsion," this still leads them, according to Strauss, to a different result about man. For the philosophers, man's fate is random, like that of the beasts; for the Torah, man's fate is in accord with justice. According to Strauss, the implication of this key difference is that Maimonides is wilily presenting the argument that the true issue which ultimately divides philosophy and revelation is providence, rather than creation.

From here Strauss leads the perplexed reader to ask the crucial question that he otherwise refrains from answering: which version of Maimonides' teaching is his true one? In the *Guide* he regards the concept of providence in the Torah as being "consequent on the intellect" (*Guide* 3.17), which is very close indeed to how some philosophers (and especially his favorite Aristotelian, Alexander of Aphrodisias) have formulated providence. This suggests a fairly high consonance between philosophy and the Torah insofar as it makes the fate of human beings more or less follow from their cognitive excellence rather than their free actions, or the decisions on which those actions are based. Yet Strauss finishes the "Note" with a hint that at least seems to award preference to the different view articulated by Maimonides in the *Letter on Astrology*. However, this may not be the contradiction that it at first appears to be, inasmuch as the *Guide* is usually regarded by Strauss as superior to a popular work like the *Mishneh Torah*, never mind the *Letter on Astrology*. I suggest this is only apparent because Strauss resolves this contradiction by directing attention to Maimonides' "rather casual remark" about the defeat of the ancient Jewish kingdom in the past. Maimonides says that the Jews lost their kingdom due to their preoccupation with astrology (which he calls "sheer nonsense" pretending to be a science) rather than focusing on the study of the proper military arts and sciences. Strauss connects this "rather casual remark" with Maimonides' formal statement about the hope for the restored Jewish kingdom in the messianic future (which significantly transpires in a discussion at almost the very end of the *Mishneh Torah*). There he assures his readers, based on textual "proofs," that this will not happen through any miracle, but will entirely conform to the order of nature as it normally operates in the world.

Strauss first offers a parenthetical explanation on Maimonides' behalf, in which Maimonides' own intention in the original "rather casual remark" is conceived to have been a call to ever keep in mind the difference between proximate and remote causes, and thus to preserve the same causally distant role played by the divine in the projected future event, which mindfulness depends on human knowledge. Thus, it seems that the *Guide* perspective remains supreme. Of course, this cannot account for why Strauss stresses the changed orientation of Maimonides in the *Letter on Astrology* on the basis for distinguishing between philosophy and Torah. In other words, with regard to the loss of the ancient Jewish kingdom, the past event occurred no differently from how the future event will happen: in nature. Both events entirely unfold from normal causes, which ancient Israel attempted to avoid by distracting itself with idolatry and pseudoscience such as astrology. Although

Strauss surmises that Maimonides *ultimately* viewed these historical events as being due to the "will" of God, this is only in the sense that God created the universe and established its permanent order, or "laws." As Strauss conceives Maimonides' view, it is not God's habit to interfere in His own order or to disregard His own "laws"; it is for human beings to know that it is through nature that God almost entirely expresses His will, and to rule themselves accordingly.

Hence, for Maimonides, everything with respect to individual human beings and specific societies ("providence") still depends on the intellect, which he continues to take with the utmost seriousness. This means the proper object of human life is to cultivate the mind toward the achievement of excellence in accordance with nature (and especially human nature), as commanded by God, and as supported by a society in which its citizens are educated in genuine science and philosophy. Thus, the perfection of the intellect is still completely compatible with the Torah as presented in the *Letter on Astrology*, concentrated as it is on providence as exemplifying justice on the individual level. For the future theological-political hope is still a reverse image of the past theological-political sin, since in considering what the hoped-for messianic fulfillment will be like, Maimonides makes excellence of intellect (as in substantial measure formed by science and philosophy), dispersed through society as much as possible, absolutely essential for the restoration and preservation of Jewish freedom.

"On Abravanel's Philosophical Tendency and Political Teaching" (1937) signifies a step away from Strauss's direct confrontation with Maimonides' writings. Instead, it shows Strauss's concern with Maimonideanism, i.e., with the historical impact made by Maimonides' thought, with his "students" as it were, and with what one might call his "spiritual" legacy. Although Strauss makes numerous passing comments through these essays and lectures on Maimonideanism (e.g., on Kabbalah as a paradoxical Maimonidean derivative), it is only in this piece that he composed a full study of a single aspect of it. To be sure, Abravanel was an atypical sort of Maimonidean, since he was both a great admirer and a severe critic of his hero. Even though one might say that Abravanel merely represents a certain aspect of Maimonides' impact, this is still significant for that fact alone. Indeed, Strauss concerned himself with this very issue in this essay: precisely what place did Maimonides' thought occupy in Abravanel's thought? How and why was Maimonides' thought able to make such a great impact on Abravanel and yet at the same time remain limited in the philosophic influence it exercised?

This essay has about it some rather uncharacteristic features for Strauss's oeuvre on Maimonides. In terms of biography, it is one of several works written in the unsettled years of Strauss's wanderings in Europe during the turbulent 1930s, when he briefly sojourned in Great Britain, where the plan for a book of essays on Abravanel arose. But of greater relevance, this essay is the fruit of a brief stage in his development, representing a period of highly concentrated rethinking that followed his writing of "Maimonides' Doctrine of Prophecy." Ultimately this was most productive in that it helped to prepare him to compose "Literary Character." While in the former piece he had already discovered the key role played by Farabi and his Platonic political approach to philosophy and religion, it was only in the latter piece that he made his philosophic breakthrough to Maimonidean literary esotericism, facilitated by what some call his prior "Farabian turn."[42] It was from this transforming position (however named) that he never retreated, although in his subsequent thought he was able to probe its depths much further.

The Abravanel essay shows occasional signs of the movement in thought toward a very different notion of Maimonides from the one Strauss had hitherto conceived, since he realizes that Maimonides must be properly comprehended if Abravanel's break with him is to make any sense. The key to Maimonides, as Strauss stalwartly maintains, is Platonic political philosophy as elaborated by the Islamic *falasifa* like Farabi and Avicenna, who were in need of Plato (rather than Aristotle) because of the emphasis he had put on envisioning the best, even the perfect, regime established by a philosopher-king, which they perceived as directly parallel with the divine Law delimiting and governing their era. If revelation defined the medieval world, its appearing in the crystallized form of the Law made the pursuit of philosophy, as Strauss recognized, something which had to be legitimated in terms of the Law. And if revelation alone (conceptualized chiefly as prophecy) is able to make actual the best political order, which Plato the philosopher had conceived on his own even absent the assistance of prophecy, it must make the rise to philosophy imperative for those human beings who are fit for it, however limited their numbers may be. In other words, the prophet for Maimonides as for

---

42. See Daniel Tanguay, *Leo Strauss: An Intellectual Biography*, trans. Christopher Nadon (New Haven: Yale University Press, 2007), pp. 79–98.

Farabi and Avicenna was virtually the same as the philosopher-king envisaged by Plato, although for the former he had been actualized while for the latter he was only a human potential, perhaps at most to be prayed for.

It is by this method that, to use Strauss's own language, Maimonides made his "attempt to harmonize the Jewish tradition with the philosophical tradition": he follows and even imitates Plato's *Laws* especially as refurbished by Farabi. But according to Strauss, Maimonides acknowledges that there are two essentially different sorts of human beings: the few who like or even need to think and the many who do not. If this is the case, then the Law as supremely wise, as he also acknowledges, is required to provide two different types of belief needed for their common life together. Thus, Maimonides harmonized the fundamental classes of human beings by focusing on two levels of belief: the necessary and the true; one is admixed for the vulgar many, the other is pure for the philosophic few, although doubts whether this harmony is quite so readily achieved will start to make a greater impact on Strauss's thought and become formative for how he will proceed.

Strauss, who had been following this line of thought for several years, curiously diverges in his essay on Abravanel by starting to emphasize that one of these levels of belief is not merely true—but also "secret." For as he began to perceive, the two levels had to be distinguished most quietly in order to protect the rightful authority of Law itself, lest it subvert the acceptance of and obedience to the Law by the great majority. Strauss recognized that Maimonides was able to "make this essential distinction only in a disguised way, partly by allusions, partly by the composition of his whole work, but mainly by the rhetorical character, recognizable only to philosophers, of the arguments by which he defends the necessary beliefs." This led Strauss to discern a key distinction that he will only fully elaborate in "How To Begin": just as he recognized that there have to be two levels of belief in a human society based on revelation, so also must there be two levels in belief the *Guide* itself: the "true" and the "necessary," as Maimonides clearly articulates this distinction in one of his most political chapters concerned with Law (3.28). As a consequence, Strauss pondered what it might imply for Maimonides to assert the imperative of those two levels in his book: the "literal" level, which is aimed at readers barely educated in the knowledge of philosophy and science but with the potential to grow (i.e., those whom Strauss will eventually call Maimonides' "typical addressees"), and the "secret" level, which is "addressed to true philosophers" (i.e., those whom Strauss will eventually call Maimonides' "atypical addressees"). Strauss then even broaches the fascinating suggestion, in advance of his subsequent rediscovery, that the "radical" and the "moderate" readings of the *Guide* (well known in medieval tradition, especially among his commentators) were not idealized reworkings by some of his "students," but fully intended by Maimonides himself! However, he makes no further comment on how Maimonides may have devised a mode of expression which allowed him to achieve this literary feat that enabled him to accommodate and so communicate efficaciously with both types of readers in a single book.

It is precisely this "ambiguous nature of Maimonides' philosophical work," i.e., as a book written on two levels, for two types of readers, that began to lead Strauss to a greater comprehension of the position of Abravanel, and especially of his response to Maimonides. As Strauss contends, Abravanel admired Maimonides and his virtuoso achievement as a Jewish thinker like no one else, while somehow simultaneously rejecting him like no one else. In fact, Abravanel criticized Maimonides almost as thoroughly as he praised him. What Strauss calls the "ambiguity" of Maimonides obviously continues even in his relation to Abravanel. Strauss suggests that the precondition for Abravanel's establishing his own original position was his unwillingness to properly understand Maimonides, whose work *on the philosophic level* he wanted to decisively overturn. Strauss views their confrontation not on the psychological level (i.e., as an Oedipal drama), but as a sort of theological-political quarrel. For Strauss, the key to Abravanel is that he builds everything by proceeding from the "literal" level of Maimonides' book as not just the true teaching of Maimonides, but also as its *only* teaching; hence this "literal" level is allowed to serve as the basis for his own teaching. But Strauss starts to raise some doubts about what is perhaps the most significant "literal" issue, which never seems to have occurred to Abravanel: was Maimonides *philosophically* serious about creation? (To be sure, Strauss is not in any sense suggesting by this that Maimonides was not *theologically-politically* serious about creation, which he most surely was. But these are two different things, as Strauss himself wanted his better readers to comprehend.) Is there any truly persuasive rational or compelling empirical evidence for that doctrine, as Maimonides himself presents it? If not, then this must bring one to acknowledge, however reluctantly, two fundamental points: Maimonides never argues for creation beyond the realm of dogma, which even in terms of dogma is not awarded a coveted position in his Thirteen Principles; and he never argues for creation as knowable in terms of truth, since this for Maimonides would imply something that is *philosophically* knowable, and then he would have to admit that such knowledge is by nature impossible.

In essence, Strauss is contending that Abravanel defended the "literal" teaching of the *Guide*, as elaborated in the *Commentary on the Mishnah* and the *Mishneh Torah*, "against the implications ... of the [secret] teaching of the *Guide*." In other words, Strauss regarded Abravanel's view of Maimonides as being steeped in serious misconceptions, not to say acute misreadings, which it had been a principal aim of the *Guide* to correct, at least as Strauss was starting to perceive this corrective imperative in Maimonides. And of course this "literal" view, elaborated by Abravanel, avoids setting eyes on the "secret" level, since this may have been too radically rationalistic for Abravanel to accept or even countenance. Strauss characterizes Abravanel's view as an "unphilosophic traditionalism" which verges on an "antiphilosophic traditionalism." It is precisely as a result of this that, as Strauss concludes, "for [Abravanel] political philosophy loses the central importance which it had for Maimonides." Or as Strauss also puts it, "Abravanel's depreciation of political philosophy, which is a consequence of his critical attitude towards Maimonides' rationalism, thus implies a decisive limitation on the content of political philosophy." What this "depreciation" or "critical attitude" held by Abravanel is made to signify for Strauss is that Maimonides' political philosophy was erroneously conceived to be a product "of the Aristotelian [rather] than of the Platonic type." Hence, Abravanel neglected to recognize Moses as a Platonic-Farabian prophet, as he was presented to be by Maimonides: leader, statesman, teacher, lawgiver, priest, governor (mundane tasks which, for Abravanel, are performed by Jethro), as well as *philosopher*, who acts as the most practical and theoretical guide to his people. This conception, for Abravanel, provided too much scope for rationalism. As Strauss viewed it, Abravanel's own position is a paradoxical resort to Aristotelianism, but paradoxical mainly because it is of the medieval Christian scholastic-clerical type: his Moses is principally a miracle worker and a high priest (almost instead of Aaron) and, most of all, a communicator of *supernatural* teachings.

Yet curiously, however "antiphilosophic" Strauss ascertains Abravanel to have been, it is interesting that this did not prevent him from also discovering in Abravanel a definite excellence of mind: "For eloquent though he could be, he certainly was no sophist: he had a strong and sincere belief in the one truth." One might say that this is one of the paramount Maimonidean attributes that Strauss uncovers in Abravanel—or perhaps this is even one of the main traits he derived from Maimonides as a teacher who grounded thinking in the one truth.

If Strauss is indeed suggesting that this demonstrates that Maimonides made a certain deep impression on Abravanel's philosophical capability, then he also seems to carry this further by attempting to show *how* Maimonides was able to exercise an influence on those like Abravanel. Yet was there anything decisive in this? In the end, this essay appears to present Abravanel as almost a case study of one who prefers the philosophy of Christian scholasticism to that of the Jewish rationalists like Maimonides (and his Muslim philosophical predecessors). This preference for scholasticism is characterized by doubts, based on supposedly biblical teachings, about whether the city is a natural entity, and whether man in general is political by nature. In contrast, Maimonides (along with his predecessors) curiously seems to have prepared a sort of classical republicanism based on human freedom, which scholars like Abravanel resisted as "unbiblical." Starting from "unpolitical, and even antipolitical premises, . . . [Abravanel] arrived at the political creed of clericalism." Though it seems far removed from the spirit which animates Strauss's essays and lectures devoted solely to Maimonides, the Abravanel essay may offer us instruction in our era (almost seventy-five years in its wake) about how by eschewing Maimonidean rationalism, Abravanel somehow prepares modern "fundamentalism" *avant la lettre*. For instead of granting any legitimacy to the free human mind, from which he recoils in dismay as the cause of Jewish suffering, Abravanel exorcises Maimonidean rationalism, which Strauss thought Abravanel regarded as a threat precisely because it is such a credible exegesis of tradition. As a result, Abravanel argues for relying on the *sources* of tradition rather than on *tradition itself*, since tradition remains too susceptible to succumbing to the appeal of reason. As Strauss presented it, Abravanel believed Judaism is able to save itself only by breaking away completely from autonomous reason, and by reclaiming the true origins and their magical authenticity as its highest authority.

"The Secret Teaching of Maimonides" (c. 1937–40) forms an appendix to Strauss's main corpus of works on Maimonides because in its present form it is not a fully finished work. In terms of period, it was written somewhat prior to "Literary Character," although precisely how much is not known. What it shows is the first sign of a major turn occurring in Strauss's thought. He speaks of needing to "establish the essential content of Maimonides' philosophical teaching," as if what is on the surface and seemingly evident is not adequate. In other words, he has noticed that the obvious is not so obvious, and as a result of this he is already speaking of a Maimonidean "secret teaching." Yet Strauss is also still referring to Maimonides' "philosophical teaching" (as if he presented himself as a philosopher rather than as a Jewish thinker), and to "the philosophic and the non-philosophic" sections of the *Guide* (as if these were clearly distinguished units in the book). Such terms as these he will refrain from employing in the wake of "Literary Character."

Strauss stresses the uniqueness of the *Guide* as a book as well as the category of literature to which it belongs. Indeed, he differentiates how he is about to read the book as contrasted with how it was read by both the medieval commentators and the modern scholars: in this brief work he seems to believe that he is the first to observe that Maimonides as an author is "consciously . . . enigmatic," this leading him to proceed deliberately by a method of "allusions and hints." Strauss tacitly makes an anticipatory claim to novelty in this proposal, though he was not the first to have discovered Maimonides' "secret teaching"; on the other hand, he was undoubtedly the first for several centuries to have become aware again of that hidden dimension in the *Guide*. In any case, he will withdraw that tacit claim once he has reacquainted himself with what some of the medieval commentators knew about the *Guide*'s esoteric (or "secret") teaching. This, however, is not to detract from the originality that he did achieve in the future course of his methodical study of the *Guide*, although at this juncture its scope and magnitude had not yet become fully evident to him.

He also first articulates the principle, which will be crucial for everything he will henceforth produce on the *Guide* (not to mention for the way in which he will approach Spinoza's *Theologico-Political Treatise*): I refer to his principle that the *Guide* must be read just as, or rather in the same manner as, Maimonides himself read the Bible. This is also a principle which, as he may have wished to imply by his silence on the matter, was not evident to *either* medieval commentators *or* modern scholars who preceded him, which is quite correct. Consequently Strauss also emphasizes that Maimonides focused on the Bible as an "enigmatic work," as was his own *Guide*. As this suggests, for Maimonides they are somehow equivalent works, at the very least in terms of the category of literature to which they both deserve to be assigned for alert consideration, i.e., the category of works which are deliberately designed to be enigmatic, and hence which contain a "secret teaching."

Strauss announces his noteworthy plan, which he was never to quite fulfill as avowed, to make a "dictionary of Maimonides' secret terminology." In other words, he is already proceeding as if he knew there is a "secret terminology" in the *Guide*, which can then be reduced to the limited form and perhaps alphabetic order of a dictionary. At the same time what was beginning to strike Strauss forcefully about the *Guide*, as he had already started to notice in "The Place of the Doctrine of Providence," was a notion which he again stresses: the *location* of the treatment of a topic in the book is almost as significant as the treatment itself; how it is placed in the unfolding, if concealed, logical order of the book is a major clue to how Maimonides conceives of such a topic. To be sure, he was not able to enunciate the full implications of this notion in the present context of a brief academic proposal, but it so happens that he will elucidate them quite fully in several of his subsequent works.

In sum, "The Secret Teaching of Maimonides" represents a salient bridge in which Strauss is glimpsed in the act of crossing, as it were, from one side to the other in how he will henceforth most unconventionally view Maimonides and his *Guide*.

In the present introduction I have attempted to focus on selected major themes and issues as they have appeared in Strauss's essays and lectures on Maimonides, especially as those seemed to me of greatest interest. It has been my main concern to emphasize original moments of discovery in Strauss's thought, as they received expression in these essays and lectures. A subsidiary effort has also been made to illuminate how his studying Maimonides through his entire adult life affected his own thinking, even if it is the case that I was mostly only able to allude to this obliquely. Thus, this has also shown itself by occasionally highlighting how significant elements of Strauss's own thought first made their appearance in these works. His thought on its own as it relates to his work on Maimonides certainly deserves serious consideration as a separate matter; but it was not my chief aim in the present context to probe that thought much beyond how it may have helped him to make advances in the study of Maimonides, or how the study of Maimonides may have advanced his own thought.

However, beyond my immediate goals as the editor in this work, I do hope that the project of bringing together these essays and lectures will materially contribute to the future study both of Maimonides' thought, and also of

Strauss's thought. Likewise it is it my hope that they might help to illuminate how much Strauss has actually advanced the study of Maimonides, through which great progress has already been made toward gradually but steadily rediscovering Maimonides' authentic thought. Hence, together with the details provided by the notes to the essays and lectures, it is to be hoped that this book will simultaneously be of substantial use both to students in courses on the thought of Maimonides or of Strauss, and to scholars doing research on the same figures, and will stimulate further study in the future of the works of them both.

I have not been able to fully restate, other than almost perfunctorily, what I think Maimonides' authentic thought represents to Strauss. Certainly Maimonides' perception of a deep tension in human beings—between philosophic life and the life of Torah—resonated very powerfully for Strauss, and may have shaped much of his thinking, insofar as his study of Maimonides contributed to his own growth and progress as a thinker. I believe Strauss followed Maimonides in suggesting that this tension between the two fundamental alternatives raises an unavoidable dilemma about whether they are essentially irreconcilable. Certainly Strauss was ready to affirm, along with Maimonides, that this tension cannot be brought to a complete and total harmony in an unredeemed world, and this it represents as a sort of perennial quarrel in the human heart and mind. The struggle to bring about a greater amount of harmony through a fertile tension, in individual human beings and thus in collective human affairs—whether through pedagogy, dogma, governance, prophecy, constitutions, or law—is what Maimonides and Strauss shared together, however differently this effort may have been performed by each of them.

Let me conclude with a religious thought which is not entirely foreign to either "the great eagle" or to the modern scholar who perhaps most closely watched him in flight. The Messiah is the hope—proclaimed as not unreasonable by Maimonides, and as a matter eminently worthy of serious consideration by Strauss—that some day this harmony may be fully achieved, while not doing away with the very fundamental tension which both acknowledged for so long as history is not yet completely redeemed. If pursued together in actuality, i.e., Maimonides' hope and Strauss's consideration, they promise something—through the very struggle rather than by the fulfillment alone—that enriches human life and that, strengthened by the common search for the one truth, brings it ever closer to this noble goal.

I

Point of Departure: Why Study Medieval Thinkers?

1
How to Study Medieval Philosophy[1]

EDITOR'S NOTE

The first appearance in print of this lecture was in Strauss, *Rebirth of Classical Political Rationalism*, pp. 207–26. That first version appeared with the title "How to Begin to Study Medieval Philosophy," henceforth referred to as "HBSMP" (1989). A subsequent edition appeared in print as "How to Study Medieval Philosophy," edited by David Bolotin, Christopher Bruell, and Thomas L. Pangle, *Interpretation* 23, no. 3 (Spring 1996): 321–38, henceforth referred to as "HSMP" (1996). Those editors acknowledge the help of Heinrich and Wiebke Meier in deciphering handwritten changes made to the manuscript in pencil by Strauss, and of Hillel Fradkin in the translation and transcription of Hebrew and Arabic words. The subsequent edition represented an effort to produce a version as close as possible to the original typescript, which apparently was used by Strauss to deliver his lecture at the Fourth Institute of Biblical and Post-biblical Studies, on 16 May 1944. So far as I am aware, no one knows whether the lecture was actually delivered, or if it was, in what form it was spoken, since no tape recoding survives; hence, no one knows at what point Strauss made the changes of the main text and in the margins. The present editor has carefully consulted and compared both previous versions and has based this version on both of them, but with the greatest effort made to integrate the better readings that appear in the subsequent version. However, not every change made to the 1996 version has been utilized in the present version (e.g., for the sake of readability, some of the brackets have been removed). With regard to the meticulous notes of the 1996 version, only those judged most significant have been reproduced, but any divergences from the 1996 version that might affect the meaning in

---

1. The decision has been made to retain the title from the 1996 version. This is on the assumption that, as the title appearing on the original lecture typescript, this is the one that Strauss himself wanted it to be known by. It has been so decided even if the title as it appears in the edition of *Rebirth of Classical Political Rationalism* has perhaps made the lecture better known by the other name.

91

this version of the lecture have been duly noted. Thus, the notes to "How to Study Medieval Philosophy" in the present volume are entirely the work of the present editor, or of the editors of the same lecture in its 1996 version (from whose work the present editor has greatly benefited), and are not to be attributed to Strauss himself.

[I.]² WE RAISE THE QUESTION OF HOW TO STUDY MEDIEVAL PHILOSOphy. We cannot discuss that question without saying something about how to study earlier philosophy in general, and indeed about how to study intellectual *history* in general.

In a sense, the answer to our question is self-evident. Everyone admits that, if we have to study medieval philosophy at all, we have to study it as exactly and as intelligently as possible. As exactly as possible: we are not permitted to consider any detail, however trifling, unworthy of our most careful observation. As intelligently as possible: in our exact study of all details, we must never lose sight of the whole; we must never, for a moment, overlook the wood for the trees. But these are trivialities, although we have to add that they are trivialities only if stated in general terms, and that they cease to be trivialities if one pays attention to them while engaged in actual work: the temptations to lose oneself in curious and unexplored details on the one hand, and to be generous as regards minutiae on the other, are always with us.

We touch upon a more controversial issue when we say that our under-

---

2. The "HBSMP" version appears with no numbered sections; the "HSMP" version appears with four sections, the last three of which are numbered, with the Roman numerals starting on section "II." (We are entitled to assume that this conforms with the original lecture typescript.) However, the first section is not listed as number "I," as one might perhaps have anticipated. The numbering of sections has been preserved in the present version, but the unnumbered first section has had a Roman numeral "I" added to it in square brackets (to show it has been assigned as a section marker only by the present editor). I do so on the model of "Maimonides' Doctrine of Prophecy," chap. 4 below, in both versions of which Strauss started the numbering with "I," although they do so at different locations in the text. Such consecutive section numbering seems have been the style most frequently chosen by Strauss, but he usually began with "I": see also "Some Remarks on the Political Science of Maimonides and Farabi," and "The Literary Character of *The Guide of the Perplexed*." The present editor has assumed that perhaps this absence may not have been deliberate, but rather may have been due to the fact that Strauss did not submit this lecture to an ultimate, rigorous editing. However, some readers may regard this as an unwarranted assumption: the divergence from any supposed standard procedure may itself have been significant, however much it may seem to produce a certain lack of clarity. It is possible not only that this absence was deliberately chosen, but also that this manuscript may be missing the proper beginning of the lecture, in which section "I" was perhaps marked. For that reason, such readers should be alerted to the fact of the absence of a number on the first section in the original lecture typescript, which is (to say it again) why the addition has been highlighted by the square brackets.

standing of medieval philosophy must be *historical* understanding. Frequently people reject an account of the past, not simply as inexact or unintelligent, but as unhistorical. What *do* they mean by it? What *ought* they to mean by it?

According to a saying of Kant, it is possible to understand a philosopher better than he understood himself.[3] Now, such understanding may have the greatest merits; but it is clearly not historical understanding. If it goes so far as to claim to be *the* true understanding, it is positively unhistorical. The most outstanding example of such unhistorical interpretation, which we have in the field of the study of Jewish medieval philosophy, is Hermann Cohen's essay on Maimonides' ethics.[4] Cohen constantly refers statements of Maimonides, not to *Maimonides'* center of reference, but to his *own* center of reference; he understands them not within *Maimonides'* horizon, but within his *own* horizon. Cohen had a technical term for his procedure: he called it "idealizing" interpretation.[5] It may justly be described as the modern form of allegoric interpretation. At any rate, it is professedly an attempt to understand the old author better than he understood himself.[6] Historical understanding means to understand an earlier philosopher exactly as he understood him-

3. Immanuel Kant, *Critique of Pure Reason*, A314/B370, trans. Paul Guyer and Allen W. Wood (Cambridge: Cambridge University Press, 1998), p. 396:

> I note only that when we compare the thoughts that an author expresses about a subject, in ordinary speech as well as in writings, it is not at all unusual to find that we understand him even better than he understood himself, since he may not have determined his concept sufficiently and hence sometimes spoke, or even thought, contrary to his own intention.

4. Hermann Cohen, "Characteristik der Ethik Maimunis," in *Jüdische Schriften*, ed. Bruno Strauss, intro. Franz Rosenzweig, 3 vols. (Berlin: C. A. Schwetschke und Sohn, 1924), 3.221–89. It first appeared in print in *Moses ben Maimon: Sein Leben, seine Werke, und sein Einfluss*, ed. W. Bacher, M. Brann, D. Simonsen, and J. Guttmann, 2 vols. (Leipzig: G. Fock, 1908–14; reprint, Hildesheim: Olms, 1971), I, pp. 63–134. For an English translation, see Hermann Cohen, *Ethics of Maimonides*, trans. Almut Sh. Bruckstein (Madison: University of Wisconsin Press, 2004). Strauss had already engaged in substantial discussion of Cohen's approach to Maimonides: see "Cohen and Maimonides," chap. 3 below, a lecture delivered (in Germany) thirteen years prior to the present lecture (delivered in the United States), i.e., 1931 versus 1944.

5. "HSMP" (1996): Strauss originally had "procedure," but it has been struck through by pencil, and for it he substitutes "interpretation." Strauss also discusses Cohen's "idealizing interpretation" in "Introduction" to *Philosophy and Law*, pp. 23–30; "Preface to *Spinoza's Critique of Religion*," and "Introductory Essay to Hermann Cohen, *Religion of Reason*," in *Jewish Philosophy and the Crisis of Modernity*, especially pp. 165–66, 271–72, with editor's remarks, pp. 18–21.

6. "HSMP" (1996): a section of this paragraph was put in square brackets in pencil, starting with "The most outstanding example" and ending with "than he understood himself." The editors of the 1996 version observe that an explanatory note appeared in the margin on a corner of the page of the manuscript, but it has been half torn away. What remains of the note is not intelligible. For the sake of readability, the brackets have been removed, since they do not seem essential to Strauss's argument in the context of the paragraph. Readers may judge for themselves.

self.[7] Everyone who has ever tried his hand at such a task will bear me out when I say that this task is an already sufficiently tough assignment in itself.

In the normal and most interesting case, the philosopher studied by the historian of philosophy is a man by far superior to his historian in intelligence, imagination, and subtlety. This historian does well to remind himself of the experience which Gulliver had when he came in contact, through necromancy, with the illustrious dead. "I had a Whisper from a Ghost, who shall be nameless, that the Commentators of Aristotle and other great philosophers always kept in the most distant quarters from their Principals, through a Consciousness of Shame and Guilt, because they had so horribly misrepresented the meaning of those authors to Posterity."[8] The most *sustained* effort of the most *gifted* historian hardly suffices to carry him for a short moment to the height which is the native and perpetual haunt of the philosopher: how can the historian even *dream* of reaching a point from which he can look *down* on a philosopher?[9]

For the attempt to understand a philosopher of the past better than he understood himself, presupposes that the interpreter considers his insight superior to the insight of the old author. Kant made this quite clear when suggesting that one can understand a philosopher better than he understood himself. The average historian is much too modest a fellow to raise such an enormous claim in so many words. But he is in danger of doing so without noticing it. He will not claim that his *personal* insight is superior to that of, e.g., Maimonides. But only with difficulty can he avoid claiming that the *collective* insight available today is superior to the collective insight available in the twelfth century. There is more than one historian who in interpreting, say, Maimonides, tries to assess the *contribution* of Maimonides. His contribution to what? To the treasure of knowledge and insight which has been accu-

---

7. "HSMP" (1996): Strauss originally had "Maimonides e.g.," but it has been struck through by pencil, and for it he substitutes "an earlier philosopher." This is, of course, one of the leitmotifs, and most original tropes, of Strauss as a reader of the great books: he called for "historical interpretation," i.e., that modern readers must strive to understand the great thinkers of the past—who are also the authors of great books—*just as* they understood themselves. See, e.g., "Political Philosophy and History," in *What Is Political Philosophy?*, pp. 56–77.

8. See Jonathan Swift, *Gulliver's Travels*, ed. Robert A. Greenberg (New York: W. W. Norton, 1970), p. 168, pt. III: "A Voyage to Laputa, Balnibarbi, Luggnagg, Glubbdubdrib, and Japan"; chap. VIII: "A further Account of Glubbdubdrib. Ancient and Modern History corrected."

9. This entire paragraph has been added, based on a separate sheet that was attached to the lecture manuscript. It was meant either to continue from the previous paragraph, or to stand as a separate paragraph, which last possibility is how it has been decided to present it. It is reproduced in the text of the present version of the lecture as if the flow of the argument was to have been expressed in it. However, it is not certain that this is what Strauss intended. The present version follows "HSMP" (1996); the paragraph on the separate sheet is not added to "HBSMP" (1989) either as text or as note.

mulated throughout the ages. That treasure appears to be greater today than it was, say, in the year of Maimonides' death. This means that when speaking of Maimonides' "contribution," the historian has in mind the contribution of Maimonides to the treasure of knowledge or insight as it is available *today*. *Hence, he interprets Maimonides' thought in terms of the thought of the present day*. His tacit assumption is that the history of thought is, generally speaking, a progress, and that therefore the philosophic thought of the twentieth century is superior to or nearer *the* truth than the philosophic thought of the twelfth century. I contend that this assumption is irreconcilable with true historical understanding. It necessarily leads to the attempt to understand the thought of the past *better* than it understood itself, and not *as* it understood itself. For it is evident that our understanding of the past will tend to be more *adequate*, the more we are *interested* in the past; but we cannot be seriously interested, i.e., passionately interested, in the past, if we know beforehand that the present is, in the most important respect, superior to the past. It is not a matter of chance that, generally speaking, the historical understanding of the continental romantics, of *the* historical school, was superior to the historical understanding of eighteenth-century rationalism; it is a necessary consequence of the fact that the representatives of the historical school did *not* believe in the superiority of their time to the past, whereas the eighteenth-century rationalist believed in the superiority of the Age of Reason to all former ages. Historians who start from the belief in the superiority of present-day thought to the thought of the past, feel no necessity to understand the past by itself: they understand it as a preparation for the present only. When studying a doctrine of the past, they do not ask primarily: what was the conscious and deliberate intention of its originator? They prefer to ask: what is the contribution of the doctrine to *our* beliefs? What is the meaning, unknown to its originator, of the doctrine from the point of view of the present? What is its meaning in the light of *later* developments? Against this approach, the historical consciousness rightly protested in the name of historical truth, of historical exactness. The task of the historian of thought is to understand the thinkers of the past *exactly* as they understood themselves, or to revitalize their thought according to their *own* interpretation of it. To sum up this point: the belief in the superiority of one's own approach, or of the approach of one's time, to the approach of the past is fatal to historical understanding.

We may express the same thought somewhat differently as follows. The task of the historian of thought is to understand the thought of the past exactly as it understood itself; for to abandon that task is tantamount to abandoning the only practicable criterion of objectivity in the history of thought. It is well known that the same historical phenomenon is interpreted in most different ways by different periods, different generations, and different types of men. The same historical phenomenon appears in different lights at different times. New human experiences shed light on old texts. No one can foresee, e.g., how the Bible will be read one hundred years hence. Observations such as these have led some people to adopt the view that the claim of any one interpretation to be *the* true interpretation is untenable. Yet the observations in question do not justify such a view. For the infinite variety of ways in which a given text can be understood does not do away with the fact that the author of the text, when writing it, understood it in one way only, provided he was not muddle-headed.[10] The light in which, e.g., the history of Samuel and Saul appears on the basis of the Puritan revolution, is not the light in which the author of the biblical history understood that history. And *the* true interpretation of the biblical history in question is the one which restates, and makes intelligible, the biblical history as understood by the biblical author. Ultimately, the infinite variety of interpretations of an author is due to conscious or unconscious attempts to understand the author better than he understood himself; but there is only one way of understanding him *as* he understood himself.[11]

To return to the point where I left off: the belief in the superiority of one's own approach, or of the approach of one's time, to the approach of the past is fatal to historical understanding. This dangerous assumption, which is characteristic of what one may call progressivism, was avoided by what is frequently called historicism. Whereas the progressivist believes that the present is superior to the past, the historicist believes that all periods are equally "immediate to God." The historicist does not want to *judge* the past, e.g., by assessing the contribution of each person, but rather seeks to understand and to relate how things have actually been, *"wie es eigentlich gewesen ist,"*[12] and in

---

10. Strauss has added in pencil, "provided he was not muddle-headed," as recorded by "HSMP" (1996).

11. "HSMP" (1996) notes that Strauss has added to the end of this paragraph a comment in pencil; it is put at the bottom of the page. It runs as follows: "Application to *sociological* interpretation: it is an attempt to understand the past better than it understood itself—it has its merits—but it is not historical understanding in the precise sense of the term."

12. *"Wie es eigentlich gewesen ist"*/"As it actually was." This is the famous remark that was made by one of the great 19th-century German historians, Leopold von Ranke, to encapsulate the proper task of modern historical study. See "Vorrede zur ersten Ausgabe," in *Geschichten der romanischen und germanischen Völker von 1492 bis 1535* (Leipzig: Duncher und Humblot, 1885), pp. V–VIII, and especially p. VII. For a fairly literal English translation, see: "'Introduction' to *History of the Latin and Teutonic Nations*," in Leopold von Ranke, *The Secret of World History: Selected Writings on the Art and Science of*

particular how the *thought* of the past has been. The historicist has at least the *intention* to understand the thought of the past exactly as it understood itself. But he is constitutionally unable to live up to his intention. For he knows, or rather he assumes, that, generally speaking and other things being equal, the thought of all epochs is equally true, because every philosophy is essentially the expression of the spirit of its time. Maimonides, e.g., expressed the spirit of his time as perfectly, as, say, Hermann Cohen expressed the spirit of *his* time. Now, all philosophers of the past claimed to have found *the* truth, and not merely the truth for their *time*. The historicist, however, asserts that they were mistaken in believing so. And he makes this assertion the basis of his interpretation. He knows a priori that the claim of Maimonides, e.g., to teach *the* truth, the truth valid for all times, is unfounded. In this most important respect, the historicist, just as his hostile brother the progressivist, believes that his approach is superior to the approach of the thinkers of old. The historicist is therefore compelled by his principle, if *against* his intention, to try to understand the past better than it understood itself. He merely repeats, if sometimes in a more sophisticated form, the sin for which he blames the progressivist so severely. For, to repeat, to understand a serious teaching, one must be seriously interested in it, one must take it seriously. But one cannot take it seriously if one knows beforehand that it is "dated." To take a serious teaching seriously, one must be willing to consider the possibility that it is simply true. Therefore, if we are interested in an adequate understanding of medieval philosophy, we must be willing to consider the possibility that medieval philosophy is simply true, or, to speak less paradoxically,[13] that it is superior, in the most important respect, to all that we can learn from any of the contemporary philosophers. We can understand medieval philosophy only if we are prepared to learn something, not merely *about* the medieval philosophers, but *from* them.

It remains true, then, that if one wants to understand a philosophy of the past, one must approach it in a *philosophic* spirit, with *philosophic* questions: one's concern must be primarily, not with what other people have thought about the philosophic truth, but with the philosophic truth itself. But if one approaches an earlier thinker with a question which is not *his* central ques-

---

History, ed. and trans. R. Wines (New York: Fordham University Press, 1981), pp. 56–59, and especially p. 58. It is also translated (although not in any sense as literally) in: Leopold von Ranke, *The Theory and Practice of History*, ed. and trans. G. G. Iggers and K. von Moltke (Indianapolis: Bobbs-Merrill, 1973), pp. 135–38, and especially p. 137: "The present attempt [at history] . . . merely wants to show how, essentially, things happened."

13. Strauss has added in pencil, "to speak less paradoxically," as recorded by "HSMP" (1996).

tion, one is bound to misinterpret, to distort, his thought. Therefore, the philosophic question with which one approaches the thought of the past must be so broad, so comprehensive, that it permits of being narrowed down to the specific, precise formulation of the question which the author concerned adopted. It can be no question other than the question of *the* truth about the whole.

The historian of philosophy must then undergo a transformation into a philosopher or a conversion to philosophy, if he wants to do his job properly, if he wants to be a competent historian of philosophy. He must acquire a freedom of mind which is not too frequently met with among the professional philosophers: he must have as perfect a freedom of mind as is humanly possible. No prejudice in favor of contemporary thought, even of modern philosophy, of modern civilization, of modern science itself, must deter him from giving the thinkers of old the *full* benefit of the doubt. When engaging in the study of the philosophy of the past, he must cease to take his bearings by the modern signposts with which he has grown familiar since his earliest childhood; he must try to take his bearings by the signposts which guided the thinkers of old. Those old signposts are not immediately visible: they are concealed by heaps of dust and rubble. The most obnoxious part of the rubble consists of the superficial interpretations by modern writers, of the cheap clichés which are offered in the textbooks and which seem to unlock by one formula the mystery of the past. The signposts which guided the thinkers of the past must be *recovered* before they can be used. Before the historian has succeeded in recovering them, he cannot help being in a condition of utter bewilderment, of universal doubt: he finds himself in a darkness which is illumined exclusively by his knowledge that he knows nothing. When engaging in the study of the philosophy of the past, he must know that he embarks on a journey whose end is completely hidden from him: he is not likely to return to the shore of his time as the same man who left it.

II. True historical understanding of medieval philosophy presupposes that the student is willing to take seriously the claim of the medieval philosophers that they teach *the* truth. Now, it may justifiably be objected, is this demand not most unreasonable? Medieval philosophy is based, generally speaking, on the natural science of Aristotle: has that science not been refuted once and for all by Galileo, Descartes, and Newton? Medieval philosophy is based on practically complete unawareness of the principles of religious toleration, of the representative system, of the rights of man, of democracy as we understand it. It is characterized by an indifference touching on contempt to poetry and history. It seems to be based on a firm belief in the verbal inspiration of the Bible and in the Mosaic origin of the oral Law. It stands and falls with the use of a method of biblical interpretation as unsound as the allegoric interpretation. In brief, medieval philosophy arouses against itself all convictions fostered by the most indubitable results of modern science and modern scholarship.

Nor is this all. Medieval philosophy may have been refuted by modern thought, and yet it could have been an admirable and highly beneficial achievement for its time. But even this may be questioned. A strong case can be made for the view that the influence of philosophy on medieval Judaism was far from being salutary. Most of you will have read the remarkable book by Dr. Gershom Scholem, *Major Trends in Jewish Mysticism*.[14] Dr. Scholem contends that from the point of view of Judaism, i.e., of rabbinical Judaism, the Kabbalah is by far superior to Jewish medieval philosophy. He starts from the observation that

> both the mystics and the philosophers completely transform the structure of ancient Judaism. . . . [But] the philosopher can only proceed with his proper task after having successfully converted the concrete realities of Judaism into a bundle of abstractions. . . . By contrast, the mystic refrains from destroying the living structure of religious narrative by allegorizing it. . . . The difference becomes clear if we consider the attitude of philosophy and Kabbalah respectively to the two outstanding creative manifestations of Rabbinical Jewry:

---

14. Gershom Scholem, *Major Trends in Jewish Mysticism* (New York: Schocken, 1941, 1946, 1954). Strauss and Scholem maintained a five-decades-long friendship (the 1920s through the 1970s), fascinating elements of which are revealed in their surviving letters; for the complete edition of their correspondence, see *Hobbes Politische Wissenschaft und zugehörige Schriften—Briefe*, vol. 3 of *Gesammelte Schriften*, pp. 699–771. A French translation of the complete correspondence has appeared: *Cabale et philosophie: Leo Strauss et Gershom Scholem Correspondance 1933–73*, trans. Olivier Sedeyn (Paris: Eclat, 2006). For a sketch of crucial aspects in the contours of their friendship, see Steven B. Smith, "Gershom Scholem and Leo Strauss: Notes toward a German-Jewish Dialogue," in *Reading Leo Strauss: Politics, Philosophy, Judaism* (Chicago: University of Chicago Press, 2006), pp. 43–64. And for Scholem's testimony to their unique friendship, in his letter to Strauss's widow, Miriam, of December 13, 1973, consider the following:

> In Leo Strauss we have lost a man whose intellectual power I treasured above all others in this generation. Though our life trajectories and intellectual assumptions contrasted greatly, for years we had the secure feeling that we shared a deep fraternity far beyond intellectual differences. In my mind's eye I have the image of a thinker of immense depth, precision, and integrity who made an indelible impression on his pupils, many of whom I have met over the years.

See Gershom Scholem, *A Life in Letters, 1914–1982*, ed. and trans. Anthony David Skinner (Cambridge, MA: Harvard University Press, 2002), p. 455; *Hobbes Politische Wissenschaft und zugehörige Schriften—Briefe*, vol. 3 of *Gesammelte Schriften*, p. 772.

Halakhah and Aggadah, Law and Legend. It is a remarkable fact that the philosophers failed to establish a satisfactory and intimate relation to either.... The whole world of religious law remained outside the orbit of philosophical inquiry, which means of course, too, that it was not subjected to philosophical criticism.... For a purely historical understanding of religion, Maimonides' analysis of the origin of the *mitzwoth*,[15] the religious commandments, is of great importance, but he would be a bold man who would maintain that his theory[16] of the *mitzwoth* was likely to increase the enthusiasm of the faithful for their actual practice.... To the philosopher, the Halakhah either had no significance at all, or one that was calculated to diminish rather than to enhance its prestige in his eyes.... The Aggadah ... represents a method of giving original and concrete expression to the deepest motive-powers of the religious Jew, a quality which helps to make it an excellent and genuine approach to the essentials of our religion. However, it was just this quality which never ceased to baffle the philosophers of Judaism.... Only too frequently their allegorizations are simply ... veiled criticism.[17]

Scholem does not leave it at suggesting that our medieval philosophers were, qua philosophers, blind to the deepest forces of the Jewish soul; he suggests also that they were blind to the deepest forces of the soul of man as man. Philosophy, he says, turned "its back upon the primitive side of life, that all-important region where mortals are afraid of life and in fear of death, and derive scant wisdom from rational philosophy."[18] The Kabbalists, on the other hand, "have a strong sense of the reality of evil and the dark horror that is about everything living. They do *not*, like the philosophers, seek to evade its existence with the aid of a convenient formula."[19]

We ought to be grateful to Dr. Scholem for his sweeping and forceful condemnation of our medieval philosophy. It does not permit us to rest satisfied with that mixture of historical reverence and philosophic indifference which is characteristic of the prevailing mood. For Scholem's criticism, while un-

---

15. "HSMP" (1996): Strauss omits the transliterated Hebrew word "*mitswoth*" as used by Scholem.

16. "HSMP" (1996): Strauss used the word "ideology" instead of the word "theory" used by Scholem. The original has been restored, although readers should consider whether Strauss's change was deliberate, and if so, what his point may have been. Scholem speaks about the "ideology of Judaism" on p. 23: both philosophy and mysticism "tend to produce an ideology of Judaism, an ideology moreover which comes to the rescue of tradition by giving it a new interpretation."

17. See Scholem, op. cit., pp. 23, 26, 28–31.

18. Ibid., p. 35.

19. Ibid., p. 36. "HSMP" (1996) notes that Strauss has underlined the word "*not*" in Scholem's phrase "They do not, like the philosophers," while Scholem himself did not underline this word.

usually ruthless, cannot be said to be paradoxical. In fact, to a certain extent, Scholem merely says quite explicitly what is implied in the more generally accepted opinion on the subject. The central thesis underlying the standard work on the history of Jewish philosophy, Julius Guttmann's *The Philosophy of Judaism*, is that our medieval philosophers abandoned, to a considerable extent, the biblical ideas of God, world, and man in favor of the Greek ideas, and that the modern Jewish philosophers succeed much better than their medieval predecessors in safeguarding the original purport of the central religious beliefs of Judaism.[20] In this connection we might also mention the fact that Franz Rosenzweig considered Hermann Cohen's posthumous work, *Religion of Reason out of the Sources of Judaism*,[21] to be definitely superior to Maimonides' *The Guide of the Perplexed*.[22]

Criticisms such as these cannot be dismissed lightly. Nothing would be more impertinent than to leave things at a merely dialectical or disputative answer. The only convincing answer would be a real *interpretation* of our great medieval philosophers. For it would be a grave mistake to believe that we dispose already of such an interpretation. After all, the historical study of Jewish medieval philosophy is of fairly recent origin. Everyone working in this field is deeply indebted to the great achievements of Salomon Munk, David Kaufmann, and Harry A. Wolfson in particular. But I am sure that these great scholars would be the first to admit that modern scholarship has

20. See Julius Guttmann, *Die Philosophie des Judentums* (Munich: E. Reinhardt, 1933). For an English translation, see *Philosophies of Judaism*, trans. David W. Silverman (Philadelphia: Jewish Publication Society, 1964). See also "Der Streit der Alten und der Neueren in der Philosophie des Judentums (Bemerkungen zu Julius Guttmann, *Die Philosophie des Judentums*)," in *Philosophie und Gesetz: Beiträge zum Verständnis Maimunis und seiner Vorlaüfer* (Berlin: Schocken Verlag, 1935), pp. 30–67; *Philosophie und Gesetz: Frühe Schriften*, vol. 2 of *Gesammelte Schriften*, pp. 29–66; "The Quarrel of the Ancients and the Moderns in the Philosophy of Judaism: Notes on Julius Guttmann, *The Philosophy of Judaism*," in *Philosophy and Law*, pp. 41–79. A recent edition of this same English translation of Guttmann's book has brought at least the title closer to that name by which Guttmann designated it himself, both in its original German form and in the Hebrew translation which represented his own revision of the original work: *Philosophy of Judaism: The History of Jewish Philosophy from Biblical Times to Franz Rosenzweig*, trans. David W. Sliverman (Northvale, NJ: Jason Aronson, 1988); however, while it restores the singular ("*Philosophy*"), it drops the definite article at the beginning of Guttmann's own title ("*The* Philosophy"). For contemporary assessments of the legacy of Guttmann's approach to Jewish philosophic thought, see Jonathan Cohen, *Philosophers and Scholars: Wolfson, Guttmann, and Strauss on the History of Jewish Philosophy*, trans. Rachel Yarden (Lanham, MD: Lexington Books, 2007); Steven Harvey, "The Value of Julius Guttmann's *Die Philosophie des Judentums* for Understanding Medieval Jewish Philosophy Today," in *Studies in Hebrew Literature and Jewish Culture*, ed. Martin F. J. Baasten and Reinier Munk (Dordrecht: Springer, 2007), pp. 297–308.

21. In the lecture manuscript, Strauss has used the original German title, *Religion der Vernunft*.

22. I have not been able to trace, thus far, the source of Franz Rosenzweig's judgment on Hermann Cohen's *Religion of Reason out of the Sources of Judaism* as "definitely superior" to Maimonides' *The Guide of the Perplexed*.

not yet crossed the threshold of such works as Halevi's *Kuzari* and Maimonides' *Guide*: "*Ben Zoma 'adayin baḥuẓ.*"²³ We are still in a truly preliminary stage.

But quite apart from this perhaps decisive consideration, the critical remarks quoted can be answered to a certain extent without raising the gravest issue. Dr. Scholem takes it for granted that our medieval philosophers intended to express, or to interpret, in their philosophic works, the living reality of historical Judaism, or the religious sentiments or experiences of the pious Jew. Their real intention was much more modest, or much more radical. The whole edifice of the Jewish tradition was virtually or even actually under attack from the side of the adherents of Greek philosophy. With all due caution necessitated by our insufficient information about what happened in the Hellenistic period of Jewish history, one may say that the Middle Ages witnessed the first, and certainly the first *adequate*, discussion between these two most important forces of the Western world: the religion of the Bible and the science or philosophy of the Greeks. It was a discussion, not between ethical monotheism and paganism, i.e., between two religions, but between religion as such and science or philosophy as such: between the way of life based on faith and obedience and a way of life based on free insight, on human wisdom, *alone*. What was at stake in that discussion were not so much the religious sentiments or experiences *themselves*, as the elementary and inconspicuous *presuppositions* on the basis of which those sentiments or expe-

---

23. "HSMP" (1996): a Hebrew phrase ("*Ben Zoma 'adayin baḥuẓ*") completes Strauss's sentence. Hillel Fradkin transliterated Strauss's Hebrew for the text of "HSMP" (1996), and also translated the phrase in a note: "Ben Zoma is still outside." As the editors add, the source is a phrase from Babylonian Talmud, Hagigah 15a; most apposite, it is also used by Maimonides in *Guide* 3.51. (The same passage in which the phrase first appeared is also a theme of 1.32 and 2.30.) Maimonides employs it as a proof-text in his parable of "the ruler in his palace," for scholars who "are only engaged in studying the mathematical sciences and the art of logic," and who as a result "walk around the house searching for its gate." They never locate the door and so never enter the ruler's palace. This puts such scholars on par with "the jurists who believe true opinions on the basis of traditional authority and [who] study the law" on matters of practice, but who do not reach the level of theory with regard to "the fundamental principles of religion" and "the rectification of belief." *If* Strauss was thinking of Maimonides in his use of this talmudic phrase, he seems to suggest that "the historical study of Jewish medieval philosophy," whatever the "greatness" of its "achievements" in a "preliminary" sense, has actually (in the words of Maimonides) "not yet crossed the threshold" of "the ruler's habitation." In other words, it is far removed from the core of what the medieval philosophic thinkers actually thought, and has not yet penetrated to that deeper level. Strauss's focus on the *proper* study of medieval philosophy, and especially of the Jewish medieval philosophy on which his lecture primarily concentrates, is thus concerned with directing historical scholars to how to locate "the gate" of "the ruler's palace." It offers the hope that this might ultimately help them at least to begin to "cross the threshold," i.e., to break through to the concealed core, as he tacitly claimed to do with his immensely subtle, often difficult, and yet truly radical readings of precisely "Halevi's *Kuzari* and Maimonides' *Guide*."

riences could be more than beautiful dreams, pious wishes, awe-inspiring delusions, or emotional exaggerations. It was very well for the Kabbalist Moses of Burgos to say that the philosophers end where the Kabbalists begin.[24] But does this not amount to a confession that the Kabbalist as such is not concerned with the *foundations* of belief, i.e., with the only question of interest to the philosopher as philosopher? To deny that this question is of paramount importance is to assert that a conflict between faith and knowledge, between religion and science, is not even thinkable, or that intellectual honesty is nothing to be cared for. And to believe that the specific experiences of the mystic are sufficient to quell the doubts raised by science or philosophy is to forget the fact that such experiences guarantee the absolute truth of the Torah in no other way than that in which they guarantee the absolute truth of the Christian dogma or of the tenets of Islam; it means to minimize the importance of the doctrinal conflicts among[25] the three great monotheist religions. In fact, it was the insoluble character of those doctrinal conflicts which engendered, or at any rate strengthened, the impulse toward philosophic studies. (It is perhaps not altogether insignificant that Jewish philosophy has proved to be much more impervious to the influence of the Christian dogma than the Kabbalah.)[26]

One may say, of course—and this is the implication of the view taken by Guttmann and Rosenzweig in particular—that modern Jewish philosophy has discussed the question of faith and knowledge, of religion and science, in a much more advanced, in a much more mature, way than medieval Jewish philosophy. At the root of all our internal difficulties is, after all, the conflict between the traditional Jewish beliefs and, not Aristotelian metaphysics, but modern natural science and modern historical criticism. And this conflict is being discussed, of course, not by *medieval* Jewish philosophy, but by *modern* Jewish philosophy. Yet there is another side to this picture. Modern Jewish philosophy from Moses Mendelssohn to Franz Rosenzweig stands

---

24. For Moses of Burgos and his statement discussed by Strauss, see Scholem, op. cit., p. 24. Of course, it cannot but remind one of Newton's famous remark (in a letter to Robert Hooke, of February 5, 1676): "If I have seen a little further it is by standing on the shoulders of giants." But Moses of Burgos did not aim to honor his precedessors even while clearly surpassing them, as Newton did: his distinct aim was to reduce the pretensions of the philosophers (like Maimonides), who perhaps do not even look around open-mindedly, as the mystics do; hence they are not aware of, and certainly they cannot discover, the realms in the mind, in the world, and in God imagined by the Kabbalists.

25. The original manuscript has "between"; I follow "HBSMP"(1989) by substituting for it "among."

26. The original manuscript has the last sentence in the paragraph surrounded by square brackets, added in pencil; I follow "HBSMP"(1989) by substituting for them conventional parentheses.

and falls with the basic premises of modern philosophy in general. Now, the superiority of modern philosophy to medieval philosophy is no longer so evident as it seemed to be one or two generations ago. Modern philosophy led to a distinction, alien to medieval philosophy, between philosophy and science. This distinction is fraught with the danger that it paves the way for the admission of an unphilosophic science and of an unscientific philosophy: of a science which is a mere tool, and hence apt to become the tool of any powers, of any interests that be, and of a philosophy in which wishes and prejudices have usurped the place belonging to reason. We have seen modern philosophy resigning the claim to demonstrable truth and degenerating into some form of intellectual autobiography, or else evaporating into methodology by becoming the handmaid of modern science. And we are observing every day that people go so far in debasing the name of philosophy as to speak of the philosophies of vulgar impostors such as Hitler. This regrettable usage is not accidental: it is the necessary outcome of the distinction between philosophy and science, of a distinction which is bound to lead eventually to the *separation* of philosophy from science. Whatever we might have to think of neo-Thomism, its considerable success among non-Catholics is due to the increasing awareness that something is basically wrong with modern philosophy. The old question, discussed in the seventeenth century, of the superiority of the moderns to the ancients, or vice versa, has again become a topical question. It has again become a *question*: only a fool would presume that it has already found a sufficient answer. We are barely beginning to realize its enormous implications. But the mere fact that it has again become a question suffices for making the study of medieval philosophy a philosophic, and not merely a historical, necessity.

I would like to stress one point which is of particular significance for the right approach to medieval philosophy. The development of modern philosophy has led to a point where the meaningfulness of philosophy or science as such has become problematic. To mention only one of its most obvious manifestations: there was a time when it was generally held that philosophy or science is, or can, or ought to be the best guide for social action. The very common present-day talk of the importance and necessity of political *myths* alone suffices to show that, at any rate, the *social* significance of philosophy or science has become doubtful. We are again confronted with the question, Why philosophy? Why science? This question was in the center of discussion in the beginnings of philosophy. One may say that the Platonic dialogues serve no more obvious purpose than precisely this one: to answer the question, Why philosophy? Why science?, by justifying philosophy or science before the tribunal of the city, the political community. In fundamentally the same way, our medieval philosophers are compelled to raise the question, Why philosophy? Why science?, by justifying philosophy or science before the tribunal of the law, of the Torah. This most fundamental question of philosophy, the question of its own legitimacy and necessity, is no longer a question for modern philosophy. Modern philosophy was from its beginning the attempt to replace the allegedly wrong philosophy or science of the Middle Ages by the allegedly true philosophy or science: it did not raise any longer the question of the necessity of philosophy or science *itself*; it took that necessity for granted. This fact alone can assure us from the outset that medieval philosophy is distinguished by a philosophic radicalism which is absent from modern philosophy, or that it is, in the most important respect, superior to modern philosophy.[27] It is then not altogether absurd that we should turn from the modern philosophers to the medieval philosophers with the expectation that we might have to learn something *from* them, and not merely about them.

III. The student of medieval philosophy is a modern man. Whether he knows it or not, he is under the influence of modern philosophy. It is precisely this influence which makes it so difficult and, to begin with, even impossible, really to understand medieval philosophy. It is this influence of modern philosophy on the student of medieval philosophy which makes an *un*historical interpretation of medieval philosophy, to begin with, inevitable. The understanding of medieval philosophy requires, then, a certain *emancipation* from the influence of modern philosophy. And this emancipation is not possible without serious, constant, and relentless *reflection* on the specific character of *modern* philosophy. For knowledge alone can make men free. We modern men understand medieval philosophy only to the extent to which we understand *modern* philosophy in its specific character.

This cannot possibly mean that the student of medieval philosophy must possess a complete knowledge of all important medieval and modern philosophies. The accumulation of such a vast amount of knowledge, of factual information, if at all possible, would reduce *any* man to a condition of mental

---

27. "HSMP" (1996): the major portion of this paragraph in the original manuscript was put in square brackets in pencil, starting with "I would like to stress" and ending with "superior to modern philosophy." For the sake of readability, the brackets have been removed, since they do not seem essential to Strauss's argument in the context of the paragraph. Readers may judge for themselves.

decrepitude. On the other hand, it is impossible for any genuine scholar to rely on those *fables convenues*[28] about the difference between medieval and modern thought which have acquired a sort of immortality by migrating from one textbook to another. For even if those clichés were true, the young scholar could not know that this is the case: he would have to accept them on trust. There is only one way of combining the duty of exactness with the equally compelling duty of comprehensiveness: one must start with detailed observations at strategic points. There are cases, e.g., in which a medieval work has served as a model for a modern work: by a close comparison of the imitation with its model, we may arrive at a clear and lively firsthand impression of the characteristic difference between the medieval approach and the modern approach. As an example one could mention Ibn Tufayl's *Hayy ibn Yaqzan* and Defoe's *Robinson Crusoe*.[29] Defoe's work is based on the Latin translation, made in the seventeenth century, of the work of the Arabic philosopher.[30] Both works deal with the question of what a solitary human being can achieve with his natural powers, without the help of society or civilization. The medieval man succeeds in becoming a perfect philosopher; the modern man lays the foundation of a technical civilization. Another type of strategic point is represented by modern commentaries on medieval texts. A comparison of Mendelssohn's commentary on Maimonides' *Treatise on Logic* with the Maimonidean text itself could well perform the function of an entering wedge into our subject.[31] The third type would be detailed modern

28. "*Fables convenues*" may be translated (or rather defined)—although somewhat unsatisfactorily—as "conventional fables." I suppose their colloquial rendering might be somewhat closer to the contemporary phrase "urban legends."

29. See Abu Bakr Muhammad ibn Tufayl [also Ibn Tufail] (1105–85), *Hayy ibn Yaqzan*, trans. George N. Atiyeh, in *Medieval Political Philosophy*, ed. Lerner and Mahdi, pp. 134–62. The Atiyeh translation, for all of its virtues, is not the work complete in itself, but only selected sections. For a complete translation, see *Ibn Tufayl's Hayy ibn Yaqdan: A Philosophical Tale*, trans. Lenn Evan Goodman (Chicago: University of Chicago Press, 2009). See also *The Journey of the Soul: The Story of Hai bin Yaqzan*, trans. Riad Kocache (London: Octagon, 1982). For the 1719 work by Daniel Dafoe (1660–1731), see *Robinson Crusoe*, ed. Michael Shinagel (New York: Norton, 1994); *Robinson Crusoe*, ed. Thomas Keymer, with notes by Thomas Keymer and James Kelly (Oxford: Oxford University Press, 2007). Although Strauss's original spelling of the title is *Yuqdhân*, I have standardized it as *Yaqzan*, in accord with contemporary scholarly conventions.

30. Edward Pococke, the great English Orientalist and Arabic scholar (and author also of *Porta Mosis*, the first Latin translation of selected portions of Maimonides' Arabic-language *Commentary on the Mishnah*), made the first Latin translation of Ibn Tufayl's *Hayy ibn Yaqzan* in 1660. It appeared in print in 1671. George Ashwell made the first English translation, drawn from the Latin translation of Pococke; it appeared in 1686. And Simon Ockley made the first English translation of *Hayy ibn Yaqzan* based on the Arabic original, which appeared in 1708.

31. For a translation of Strauss's brief introduction to selections from Mendelssohn's commentary on Maimonides' *Treatise on the Art of Logic*, see *Leo Strauss on Moses Mendelssohn*, trans. and ed. Martin D. Yaffe (Chicago: University of Chicago Press, 2012).

polemics against medieval teachings, such as Spinoza's critique of Maimonides' teaching and method in the *Theologico-Political Treatise*. By observing what theses of Maimonides are misunderstood or insufficiently understood by Spinoza, one is enabled to grasp some of the specifically modern prejudices which, to begin with, prevent us, at least as much as they did Spinoza, from understanding Maimonides. Yet all examples of the three types mentioned are open to the objection that they may mislead the unwary student into taking the difference between these specific modern and medieval philosophies for *the* difference between modern philosophy as such and medieval philosophy as such.

To grasp that general difference, there is, I think, no better way than a precise comparison of the most typical divisions of philosophy or science in both the Middle Ages and the modern period. It is easy to compile a list of the philosophic disciplines which are recognized today, from the curricula of present-day universities, or from the title pages of systems of philosophy composed in the nineteenth and twentieth centuries. Compare that list with, say, Alfarabi's or Avicenna's division of philosophy. The differences are so big, they are so appallingly *obvious*, that they cannot be overlooked even by the most shortsighted person; they are so obtrusive that they compel even the most lazy student to *think* about them.[32] One sees at once, e.g., that there do not exist in the Middle Ages such philosophic disciplines as aesthetics or philosophy of history, and one acquires at once an invincible and perfectly justified distrust of the many modern scholars[33] who write articles or even books on medieval aesthetics or on medieval philosophy of history. One becomes interested in the question: when did the very terms "aesthetics" and "philosophy of history" appear for the first time? One learns that they made their first appearance in the eighteenth century; one starts reflecting on the assumptions underlying their appearance—and one is already well on one's way. Or take the absence of a discipline called "philosophy of religion" from medieval philosophy. How many books and pamphlets have been written on Jewish philosophy of religion in the Middle Ages, on something, that is, which strictly speaking does not exist. Something must be basically wrong with all these books and pamphlets. In the place of our modern philoso-

---

32. According to "HSMP" (1996), an entire sentence has been struck through by pencil: "Such a study is even more exciting than the reading in a first-class historical dictionary." It follows "think about them."

33. "HSMP" (1996): the phrase "*nomina sunt odiosa*" has been struck through by pencil, following "modern scholars." The phrase means "Names are odious or hateful." It implies: "I shall not stoop to mentioning (infamous) names." It was used by Cicero, and it became a Latin proverb.

phy of religion, we find in medieval philosophy theology as a philosophic discipline, *natural* theology as it was formerly called. There is a world of difference between natural theology, the philosophic doctrine of *God*,[34] and philosophy of religion, the analysis of the *human attitude* toward God. What is the meaning of that difference? What does it mean that the greatest work of medieval Christianity is entitled "Summa *Theologica*," whereas the greatest work of the Reformation is entitled "Institutio Christianae *Religionis*"? And what does it mean that Maimonides excludes the discussion of *religious* subjects from his *Guide*?[35] This is exactly the type of questions with which one has to *start* in order to arrive eventually at a true, exact, historical understanding of medieval philosophy.

Many scholars consider the type of questions which I have mentioned as pedantic, not to say bureaucratic. They would argue as follows: why should we not describe a medieval philosopher's remarks on poetry, e.g., as his contribution to aesthetics? The medieval philosopher would have considered those remarks as belonging to poetics, or to ethics, or perhaps even to political science. He conceived of poetry as an essentially purposeful activity, as an activity destined to please by instructing or to instruct by pleasing. He conceived of poetics as a technical art destined to teach how to make good poems, etc. He considered poetry essentially subservient to ulterior purposes such as moral improvement. In short, he had a terribly narrow view of poetry. Thanks to our modern philosophers, we know better: we know that poetry is something existing in its own right, and that aesthetics, far from teaching a poet how to make poems, is the analysis of poetic productivity and of aesthetic enjoyment or appreciation or understanding. The modern view being so manifestly superior to the medieval view, why should we hesitate for a moment to refer the medieval philosopher's remarks on poetry to *our* center of reference, and hence to describe them as belonging to aesthetics? Well, this is precisely the mental habit which makes impossible historical understanding of medieval philosophy. If we know from the outset that the medieval view of the matter is wrong or poor, we should not waste our time in studying it; or if someone does not mind wasting his time, he simply will not command the intellectual energy required for truly understanding a view for which he cannot have any real sympathy. Since I mentioned this example of aesthetics versus poetry, I may be permitted to add that the medieval view of poetry

---

34. "HSMP" (1996): the word "philosophic" has been added.
35. See *Guide* 3.8, p. 436; and compare with "Literary Character," chap. 8 below. In the previous sentence, the former work is by Thomas Aquinas, and the latter work is by John Calvin.

ultimately goes back to Plato's *Republic*, i.e., to the work of a man who cannot be accused of having had a monkish lack of sense of beauty.[36]

The implication of the point I have been trying to make is that *terminology* is of paramount importance. Every term designating an important subject implies a whole philosophy. And since, to begin with, one cannot be certain which terms are important and which terms are not, one is under an obligation to pay the utmost attention to any term which one reads, or which one uses in one's presentation. This naturally brings us to the question of *translations*. There is no higher praise for a translation of a philosophic book than that it is of utmost literalness, that it is in *ultimitate literalitatis*, to avail myself of the Latinity of those wonderful medieval translators whose translations from the Arabic into Hebrew or from either language into Latin infinitely surpass most modern translations I know,[37] although their Latin in particular is frequently in *ultimitate turpitudinis*.[38] It is difficult to understand why many modern translators have such a superstitious fear of translating literally. It leads to the consequence that a man who has to rely entirely on modern translations of philosophic works, is unable to reach a precise understanding of the thought of the author. Accordingly, even the poorest linguists (such as the present speaker) are compelled to read the originals. This was not so in the Middle Ages. Medieval students of Aristotle, who did not know a word of Greek, are by far superior as interpreters of Aristotle to modern scholars, who possess a simply overwhelming knowledge of Greek antiquities. This superiority is decisively due to the fact that the medieval commentators disposed of most literal translations of the Aristotelian text and that they stuck to the text and the terminology of the text.

IV. The foregoing remarks apply to the study of medieval philosophy in general. Now let us turn to Jewish medieval philosophy in particular. Medieval Jewish philosophy consists broadly of two types, an earlier type which flour-

---

36. "HSMP" (1996): the entire preceding paragraph in the original manuscript was put in square brackets in pencil, starting with "Many scholars consider" and ending with "a monkish lack of sense of beauty." For the sake of readability, the brackets have been removed, since they do not seem essential to Strauss's argument in the context of the paragraph. Readers may judge for themselves.

37. "HSMP" (1996): the words "with the exception of Schleiermacher and Salomon Munk," following "modern translations I know," have been struck through by pencil. On other occasions Strauss praised their translations, even if not their interpretations.

38. If Strauss translates the Latin phrase "*ultimitate literalitatis*" as "of utmost literalness," so it is perhaps best to translate the Latin phrase *ultimitate turpitudinis* as "of utmost shamefulness." My thanks to Sara Kathleen Alvis for her advice on how best to translate the phrase. In her notes to me she was careful to add: "these phrases do not seem to be classical Latin."

ished in an Islamic environment, and a more recent type which emerged in a Christian environment. I shall limit myself to the older type, which is more interesting from the point of view of our methodological question, to say nothing of other considerations. There are specific difficulties obstructing our understanding of Arabic-Jewish philosophy, as well as of the Islamic philosophy on which it is dependent. History of philosophy, as distinguished from doxography, is an outgrowth of the modern world. Its program was stated for the first time by Francis Bacon.[39] Originally it was considered as something outside of philosophy proper, as a pursuit for antiquarians rather than for philosophers: it became an integral part of philosophy in the nineteenth century only, owing to Hegel in particular. History of philosophy, being an outgrowth of Christian Europe, has a congenital inclination to take its bearings as regards the study of medieval philosophy by the standards of Christian or Latin scholasticism. The student of medieval philosophy, as a modern man, is prevented by the influence of modern philosophy on his thought from understanding medieval philosophy, if he does not coherently reflect on the difference between modern and medieval philosophy. Similarly, the student of Islamic and Jewish philosophy, who as a historian of philosophy participates in a tradition of *Western* origin, is prevented by that tradition from understanding Islamic and Jewish philosophy, if he does not coherently reflect on the difference between Christian scholasticism and Islamic-Jewish philosophy.

One has to start from the difference between Judaism and Islam on the one hand, and Christianity on the other. For the Jew and the Muslim, religion is primarily not, as it is for the Christian, a *faith* formulated in dogmas, but a *law*, a *code* of divine origin. Accordingly, *the* religious science,[40] the *sacra doctrina*, is not dogmatic theology, *theologia revelata*, but the science of the law, *halakha* or *fiqh*. The science of the law thus understood has much less in common with philosophy than has dogmatic theology. Hence the status of philosophy is, as a matter of principle, much more precarious in the Islamic-Jewish world than it is in the Christian world. No one could become a competent Christian theologian without having studied at least a substantial part

---

39. With regard to Francis Bacon as grounding the modern history of philosophy, perhaps Strauss was thinking of the third division of the six divisions planned for his "Great Instauration" of the sciences. It appeared in plan only as a fragment, appended as a sort of addendum to Bacon's *The New Organon*: "Preparative toward Natural and Experimental History." See *The New Organon and Related Writings*, ed. Fulton B. Anderson (Indianapolis: Bobbs-Merrill, 1960), pp. 271–92. See also Fulton B. Anderson, *The Philosophy of Francis Bacon* (Chicago: University of Chicago Press, 1948), pp. 34–35.

40. "HSMP" (1996): "the religious science" has "*the*" underlined.

of philosophy; philosophy was an integral part of the officially authorized and even required training. On the other hand, one could become an absolutely competent halakhist or faqih[41] without having the slightest knowledge of philosophy. This fundamental difference doubtless explains the possibility of the later complete collapse of philosophic studies in the Islamic world, a collapse which has no parallel in the West in spite of Luther. It explains why, as late as 1765, the Ashkenazic Jew Mendelssohn felt compelled to offer a real apology for recommending the study of logic, and to show why the prohibition against the reading of extraneous or profane books does not apply to the study of works of logic. It explains at least partly why Maimonides' *Guide* in particular never acquired the authority enjoyed by Thomas Aquinas's *Summa Theologica*. Nothing is more revealing than the difference between the beginnings of these two most representative works. The first article of Thomas's great *Summa* deals with the question as to whether theology is necessary apart from, and in addition to, the philosophic disciplines: Thomas defends theology before the tribunal of philosophy. Maimonides' *Guide*, on the other hand, is explicitly[42] devoted to the science of the law, if to the *true* science of the law; it opens in the form of[43] a somewhat diffuse commentary[44] on a biblical verse;[45] it opens as a defense of philosophy before the tribunal of traditional Jewish science rather than as a defense of traditional Jewish science before the tribunal of philosophy. Can one even imagine Maimonides opening the *Guide* with a discussion of the question as to whether the *halakha* is necessary in addition to the philosophic disciplines? Maimonides' procedure is illustrated by a treatise of his contemporary Averroes, the explicit purpose of which is the *legal* justification of philosophy: it discusses in *legal* terms, in terms of the Islamic law, the question as to whether the study of philosophy is *permitted* or *forbidden* or *commanded*.[46] Philosophy

41. In both cases, it designates a "scholar of the law" in the sense of one who is both knowledgeable in, and competent to render decisions about, the law.
42. "HSMP" (1996): "is explicitly" has been substituted for "claims to be" in Strauss's original manuscript.
43. "HSMP" (1996): as an alternative on top of the line containing the words "it opens in the form of," Strauss wrote "Its first chapters look like."
44. "HSMP" (1996): as an alternative on top of the line containing the word "commentary," Strauss wrote ("a *midrash*").
45. "HSMP" (1996): added on top of the line containing the word "biblical verse," Strauss wrote "which verse." The verse discussed by Maimonides, to which Strauss refers, is Genesis 1:26. See *Guide* 1.1, pp. 21–23. In this context one must notice that Maimonides is solely addressing himself to correct scriptural exegesis, rather than any legal inferences from the text.
46. See Averroes, *Decisive Treatise*, trans. Charles E. Butterworth (Provo: Brigham Young University Press, 2001), p. 1. As it seems to me, it is of this work that Strauss was almost certainly thinking.

was clearly on the defensive, not so much perhaps in fact, but certainly as far as the legal situation was concerned. There is more than one parallel to Averroes' argument in Jewish literature.

The problematic status of philosophy in the Jewish Middle Ages finds its most telling expression in the use of the terms "philosophy" and "philosopher." We take it for granted that men such as Maimonides and Halevi were philosophers, and we call their respective books without hesitation philosophic books. But do we act in agreement with their view of the matter by doing so? In their usage, philosopher designates normally a man whose beliefs are fundamentally different from those of the adherents of any of the three monotheist religions, whether he belongs nominally to one of these religions or not. The philosophers as such are supposed to form a group, a *sect*, fundamentally distinguished from the group [or sect] of the Jews, that of the Muslims, and that of the Christians.[47] By calling thinkers such as Halevi and Maimonides "philosophers," we implicitly deny that there is a *problem* in the very *idea* of a Jewish philosopher or of Jewish philosophy. But of nothing were these men more deeply convinced than of this, that Jewish philosophy is, as such, something problematic, something precarious.[48]

Now let us consider the other side of the picture. The official recognition of philosophy in the Christian world doubtless had its drawbacks. That recognition was bought at the price of the imposition of strict ecclesiastical supervision. The precarious position of philosophy in the Islamic-Jewish world, on the other hand, guaranteed, or necessitated, its *private* character, and therewith a higher degree of inner *freedom*. The situation of philosophy in the Islamic-Jewish world resembles in this respect its situation in classical Greece. It has often been said that the Greek city was a totalitarian social order: it comprised and regulated, not only political and legal matters proper, but morality, religion, tragedy, and comedy as well. There was, however, one activity which was, in fact and in theory, essentially and radically *private*, transpolitical, and transsocial: philosophy. The philosophic schools were founded, not by authorities civil or ecclesiastical, but by men *without* au-

---

47. "HBSMP" (1989) has "the sect of the Jews, that of the Muslims, and that of the Christians." According to "HSMP" (1996), it should be: "the group of the Jews, that of the Muslims, and that of the Christians." The present version assigns priority to "group," but retains "sect" in qualifying square brackets.

48. For the point at which Strauss became aware of this issue, and or least the point at which he consciously ceased to employ that terminology in his own works, cf. appendix below to the present book, "The Secret Teaching of Maimonides."

thority, by private men. In this respect, I said, the situation of philosophy in the Islamic world resembles the *Greek* situation rather than the situation in Christian Europe. This fact was recognized by the Islamic-Jewish philosophers themselves: elaborating on a remark of Aristotle, they speak of the philosophic life as a radically *private* life: they compare it to the life of a hermit.[49]

Religion is conceived by Muslims and Jews primarily as a law. Accordingly, religion enters the horizon of the philosophers primarily as a *political* fact. Therefore, the philosophic discipline dealing with religion is not philosophy of religion, but political philosophy or political science. The political science in question is a specific one: Platonic political science, the teaching of Plato's *Republic* and of his *Laws*. No difference between Islamic-Jewish philosophy on the one hand and Christian scholasticism on the other is more palpable than this: whereas *the* classic of political science in the Western world was Aristotle's *Politics*, the classics of political science in the Islamic-Jewish world were the *Republic* and the *Laws*. In fact, Aristotle's *Politics* was unknown to the Islamic-Jewish world,[50] and the *Republic* and the *Laws* made their appearance in Christian Europe not before the fifteenth century.

The Islamic law as well as the Jewish law is, of course, considered a divine law, a law given by God to men by the intermediary of a prophet. The prophet is interpreted by Alfarabi, Avicenna, and Maimonides in terms of the Platonic philosopher-king: as the founder of the perfect political community. The doctrine of prophecy as such is considered by these philosophers a part of political science. Avicenna describes Plato's *Laws* as the standard work on prophecy. This view of the essentially political character of prophecy influences the very plan of Maimonides' *Sefer ha-Mitzvot* and of his *Sefer ha-Madda*.[51] Its implications appear from Maimonides' remark that the neglect

---

49. Besides Ibn Tufayl's *Hayy ibn Yaqzan* and Abu Bakr ibn Bajja's *The Regimen of the Solitary* (*Tadbir al-Mutawahhid*), one might also consider the seemingly passing, but actually pointed, comments of Maimonides in *Guide* 2.36, pp. 371–72. See also Pines, "Translator's Introduction," in *Guide*, pp. cvi–cviii.

50. Cf. also "Maimonides Doctrine of Prophecy," chap. 4 below, n. 191; "Some Remarks on the Political Science of Maimonides and Farabi," chap. 5 below, n. 5.

51. Maimonides' *Sefer ha-Mitzvot* [Book of Commandments], as a separate book, is an effort to enumerate and arrange in order the traditional 613 laws of the Torah, the first such effort ever ventured. With regard to his *Sefer ha-Madda* [The Book of Knowledge], it is the first of fourteen volumes of his code of law, the *Mishneh Torah*, in which he discusses not only the practical requirements of the law, but also its theoretical grounds or fundamental principles, which was an unprecedented endeavor, and which produced much controversy. The *Mishneh Torah* as an entirety is an effort to classify, categorize, and assemble the laws in logical order and by rational plan, rather than by the associative or "organic" form of talmudic

of the arts of war and of conquest in favor of astrology led to the destruction of the Jewish state.⁵²

The difference between Islamic-Jewish philosophy and Christian scholasticism shows itself most clearly in the field of practical philosophy. As regards theoretical philosophy, both Islamic-Jewish philosophy and Christian scholasticism build on substantially the same tradition. But in political and moral philosophy, the difference is fundamental. I have mentioned the absence of Aristotle's *Politics* from the Islamic-Jewish world. Equally significant is the absence from it of the Roman literature, of Cicero, and the Roman Law in particular. This leads to the consequence that the doctrine of natural law, so characteristic of Christian scholasticism, and indeed of Western thought up to the end of the eighteenth century, is completely lacking in Islamic-Jewish philosophy: it appears in some later Jewish writers only under the influence of Christian thought. It is true, the Islamic theologians, the *mutakallimūn*, had asserted the existence of rational laws which were practically identical with what were called natural laws in the Occident; but the Islamic-Jewish philosophers reject this view altogether. The rules of conduct which are called by the Christian scholastics natural laws, and by the *mutakallimūn* rational laws, are called by the Islamic-Jewish philosophers generally accepted opinions. This view appears in the Christian Middle Ages only at their fringes, as it were, in the teaching of Marsilius of Padua, the most energetic medieval opponent of clerical claims.⁵³

This leads me to the last point which I would like to make in order to indicate the extent and bearing of the difference separating Islamic-Jewish philosophy from Christian scholasticism, and in order to justify my contention that a genuine understanding of Islamic-Jewish philosophy must be based on constant awareness of that difference. That school of Christian scholasticism, which was most deeply influenced by Islamic philosophy, was Latin Averroism. Latin Averroism is famous for its doctrine of the double truth, for its assertion that a thesis may be true in philosophy but false in theology and vice versa. The doctrine of the double truth does not occur in Averroes himself or in his predecessors. Instead, we find in Islamic philosophy a relatively ample use of the distinction between exoteric teachings, based on rhetorical argu-

---

literature. See "Review of *The Mishneh Torah*, Edited . . . by Moses Hyamson," chap. 7 below; and "Notes on Maimonides' *Book of Knowledge*," chap. 12 below.

52. See "Note on Maimonides' *Letter on Astrology*," chap. 14 below. See also "On Abravanel's Philosophical Tendency and Political Teaching," chap. 15 below.

53. See Leo Strauss, "Marsilius of Padua," in *History of Political Philosophy*, ed. Strauss and Cropsey, 3rd ed., pp. 276–95. It is reprinted in *Liberalism Ancient and Modern*, pp. 185–202.

ments, and esoteric teaching, based on demonstrative or scientific arguments. Up to now, students of Islamic philosophy have not paid sufficient attention to this distinction, which is evidently of absolutely decisive importance. For if the true, scientific teaching is an esoteric, a *secret*, teaching, we have no right to be as[54] certain as we are accustomed to be that the public teaching of the Islamic philosophers is their real teaching. We would have to acquire a special technique of reading not necessary for the understanding of books which set forth the views of their authors directly, without any concealment or circumlocution. It would be wrong to trace the esotericism in question to certain spurious phenomena of dying antiquity: its origin has to be sought in Plato himself, in the doctrine of the *Phaedrus* concerning the superiority of oral teaching to teaching by writings, in the doctrine of the *Republic* and the *Laws* concerning the necessity of noble lies, and, above all, in the literary technique used by Plato himself in all his works. One may safely say that before this *Platonism* of the Islamic philosophers has been duly studied, our understanding of Islamic philosophy rests on extremely shaky foundations. Similar considerations apply to the Jewish philosophy which is dependent on Islamic philosophy. Everyone who has read the *Guide* knows how emphatically Maimonides insists on the secret character of his own teaching: he warns his reader from the outset that he has set forth only the chapter headings of the secret teaching, and not the chapters themselves.[55] In the *Kuzari*, we are confronted with a similar situation: the final conversion of the Kuzari to Judaism is the consequence of his listening to a highly secret interpretation of the secret teaching of the *Sefer Yetzira*.[56] It was with a view to phenomena such as these that I ventured to say that our understanding of medieval philosophy is still in a truly preliminary stage. In making this remark, I do not minimize the debt which we owe to Harry A. Wolfson and Isaac Heinemann in particular, who have spoken on the peculiar literary technique of our medieval philosophers[57] on various occasions. What is required, beyond

54. "HSMP" (1996): as an alternative on top of the line containing the word "as," Strauss wrote "so."
55. See *Guide* 1.Intro., pp. 6–7.
56. See Leo Strauss, "The Law of Reason in the *Kuzari*," in *Persecution and the Art of Writing*, p. 119, n. 70, which makes the same point.
57. "HSMP" (1996): "our medieval" has been bracketed in pencil, with the word "earlier" written on top of the line apparently as an alternative. With respect to the highlighting of Isaac Heinemann and Harry A. Wolfson, it is not clear which works Strauss had in mind by mentioning their names. Heinemann produced much significant scholarly work on medieval Jewish thought, and its relation to Greek and Roman thought; especially impressive and enduring is his work on the "reasons for the commandments" in the history of medieval Jewish thought. See Isaak Heinemann, *Die Lehre von der Zweckbestimmung des Menschen im griechisch-römischen Altertum und im jüdischen Mittelalter* (Breslau: H. & M. Mar-

the general observations, is a coherent and methodic application of those observations to the actual interpretation of the texts. Only after this interpretation has been completed will we be in a position to judge of the *value*, of the *truth*, of our medieval philosophy. For the time being, it is good policy to suspend our judgment and to *learn* from these great teachers. For there are many important lessons which modern man can learn only from premodern, from unmodern, thinkers.

---

cus, 1926). See also Yizḥak Heinemann, *Taʿamei ha-mitzvot be-sifrut Yisraʾel* (1st ed., 1942; reprint, Yerushalayim: Horev, 1993); *The Reasons for the Commandments in Jewish Thought: from the Bible to the Renaissance*, trans. Leonard Levin (Boston: Academic Studies Press, 2008). At least in the section on Maimonides (*Reasons*, trans. Levin, pp. 95–119), Heinemann is acutely aware of the literary subtlety that characterizes this approach. But perhaps most apposite was his *Altjüdische Allegoristik* (Breslau: M. & H. Marcus, 1935); his work in this area was advanced, with greater focus on the medievals, in an article that Strauss would seem not to have been able to know (if the present lecture was finalized during the 1940s): "Die wissenschaftliche Allegoristik des jüdischen Mittelalters," *Hebrew Union College Annual* 23 (1950): 611–43; for Maimonides especially, pp. 628–31. With respect to Wolfson, he produced no major scholarly work dedicated to medieval Jewish philosophy in its aspect as literature; his book on Hasdai Crescas is concerned mainly with medieval criticism of Aristotelian physics: *Crescas's Critique of Aristotle: Problems of Aristotle's Physics in Jewish and Arabic Philosophy* (Cambridge, MA: Harvard University Press, 1929). His articles on such medieval Jewish thinkers as Halevi and Maimonides are usually focused on a specific philosophical or theological topic. But perhaps Strauss was thinking of Wolfson's true historical magnum opus, i.e., *The Philosophy of Spinoza: Unfolding the Latent Processes of His Reasoning* (Cambridge, MA: Harvard University Press, 1934), even though it is not a work on a medieval writer, or on a philosophic writer who emerged from the historical context to which Strauss points. It begins with two chapters which especially deal with literary considerations as needful for uncovering the philosophic thought of Spinoza, whose historical sources are "concealed" in his *Ethics*, even if unconsciously so: "Behind the Geometrical Method," and "The Geometrical Method," pp. 3–60. With regard to the historical and literary method of Wolfson in the aforementioned book, Strauss advanced several substantive criticisms: see "How to Study Spinoza's *Theologico-Political Treatise*," in *Jewish Philosophy and the Crisis of Modernity*, pp. 181–233, especially pp. 214–16; or in *Persecution and the Art of Writing*, pp. 142–201, especially pp. 188–90.

II

On Maimonides

2

Spinoza's Critique of Maimonides

EDITOR'S NOTE

The chapter entitled "Spinoza's Critique of Maimonides" in the present book reproduces Leo Strauss, *Spinoza's Critique of Religion*, trans. Elsa Sinclair (New York: Schocken, 1965; Chicago: University of Chicago Press, 1997), chap. VI, pp. 147–92, with the notes appearing on pp. 293–98. In the original English-language edition of the book, chapter VI is entitled "The Critique of Maimonides." (This chapter title follows the German, although the ten chapters in that original edition are divided not just by numbers but by letters as well.) The German title of the original book is *Die Religionskritik Spinozas als Grundlage seiner Bibelwissenschaft: Untersuchungen zu Spinozas "Theologisch-Politischem Traktat"* (Berlin: Akademie-Verlag, 1930; Hildesheim: Georg Olms, 1981). See also Leo Strauss, *Die Religionskritik Spinozas und zugehörige Schriften*, vol. 1 of *Gesammelte Schriften*, pp. 56–354; and especially "Die Kritik an Maimuni," pp. 195–247 (with Strauss's marginal handwritten additional comments transcribed, pp. 355–61). The notes have been renumbered sequentially for the present edition; for the convenience of those who may wish to refer to the previous versions (German and English), the note numbers as they appear in the original German edition and the English translation (the numbers of both are identical) are shown in square brackets and bold. The manner by which Strauss refers to Spinoza's works is addressed in the first note of the book (trans. Sinclair, p. 274): "The basic text for the references to Spinoza's writings is [Carl] Gebhardt's edition of the *Opera* [4 vols., Heidelberg, 1924–26]. The *Tractatus theologico-politicus* (abbreviated *Tractate*) is cited according to the pagination of the *editio princeps*, [as is] followed by Gebhardt." (I retain Strauss's *Tractate*, although it has become a scholarly convention to abbreviate Spinoza's work as *Treatise* or as *TPT*.) Thus, Strauss's references are to what he calls the "*editio princeps*": C[arl] H[ermann] Bruder, *Spinoza Opera* (Leipzig, 1843–46).

(However, most scholars since the appearance in print of Gebhardt's edition use his page numbers as the standard text for references.) Strauss also very occasionally cites Carl Gebhardt's German translation: *Theologisch-politischer Traktat* (Leipzig: Dürr, 1908); and Manuel Joel's study: *Spinoza's "Theologisch-politischer Traktat," auf seine Quellen geprüft* (Breslau: Schletter [H. Skutsch], 1870). Passages from Spinoza's *Theologico-Political Treatise*, which Strauss quotes in the original Latin, are translated for the benefit of the English-language reader. The translations used are drawn, with permission of the translator, from Spinoza, *Theologico-Political Treatise*, trans. Yaffe, followed by the page numbers of Yaffe's edition enclosed in curly brackets. Since Strauss cites references to the pages numbers of the Bruder edition, these are followed by references to pages numbers in Yaffe's translation in square brackets in the text and the notes. Curly brackets are similarly used to enclose other references to English translations or editions. For those readers who want to review the Latin of Spinoza, Yaffe's translation also contains the page numbers of the Gebhardt edition. Since Spinoza did not use italicized special emphases as a form of literary art, all such (whether in the Latin, or as likewise imitated in Yaffe's English version) are Strauss's own additions. Strauss's number references in parentheses, following references to chapter numbers of the *Guide*, are to the relevant pages of Salomon Munk's French translation; beside them have been added number references in square brackets, which are to the (approximate) equivalent pages in Maimonides, *Guide*, trans. Pines. The supplementary reference material set in square brackets in the notes is entirely the work of the present editor; it attempts to provide additional scholarly data useful for some readers in studying the contents of Strauss's own notes. As for the role that this chapter played in the unfolding of Strauss's thought, it is best summarized in the following statement of a contemporary scholar: "Only in the chapter of *Spinoza's Critique of Religion* devoted to Maimonides does Strauss discuss some of the elements of what later became his distinctive treatment of the relations between reason, science, or philosophy, on the one hand, and dominant political and religious traditions, on the other hand." See Hugh Donald Forbes, *George Grant: A Guide to His Thought* (Toronto: University of Toronto Press, 2007), p. 140.

A. THE DIVERGENCES BETWEEN SPINOZA AND MAIMONIDES

1) According to Spinoza's own view

FOLLOWING SPINOZA'S OWN DISTINCTION BETWEEN THE "SKEPTICAL" and the "dogmatic" conception of the relation between reason and Scripture (*Tractate*, pp. 166f. [Yaffe, pp. 169–70]), we divided his critique of religion into the critique of orthodoxy and the critique of Maimonides. Since Spinoza has not followed this division in constructing the *Tractate*, but has in almost every chapter chosen to discuss or analyze orthodoxy and Maimonides, historical and critical interpretation has no choice but to take responsibility for itself using that division. If it evades this task it will not pass beyond idle repetition of what Spinoza has surely himself stated better. The external structure of the *Tractate* cannot be binding on the interpreter, since it is partially conditioned by the two subsidiary aims that Spinoza is following, apart from his primary and highest aim in composing the *Tractate* (defense against the allegation of atheism, and ensuring freedom for the public expression of opinion). In accord with the primary and highest aim of the *Tractate*, the interpretation must look at each position criticized, as that position presents itself, and thus bring to light the problematic nature of Spinoza's critique of religion as an attempt to liberate "the more prudent sort" from their imprisonment in revealed religion, so that they can philosophize.

For the sake of that liberation, the "prejudice" that reason must subject itself to the supra-rational or contra-rational revelation contained in Scripture is to be eliminated. In the face of "dogmatic" theology, the task is to be differently defined, since this theology does not subject reason to Scripture but Scripture to reason. The most general definition of the task of the *Tractate* reads: radical *separation* of philosophy (reason) from theology (Scripture). Since the "dogmatists" recognize as the meaning of Scripture only what the text means as interpreted in the light of rational truth, argumentation on the ground of the letter of Scripture is not possible. In the case of Maimonides, the plane available from the outset for the criticism is that of reason. On the plane of reason, the compatibility of reason and revelation is to be questioned. However, with this the aim of the critique is not yet fully defined. Maimonides does not merely assert that revelation and reason are mutually compatible, but above all that revelation is necessary for salvation, or that reason is insufficient for such conduct of life as leads to beatitude. These two assertions are brought into union by the contention that only such fulfillment of the Law is pious and assures "a share in the future world" as takes place in obedience to God's revealed will, although the Law be by content in accord with reason (the seven Noachide Laws) and binding on all men (*Tractate*, pp. 65f. [Yaffe, pp. 64-65]).[1] It is at any rate in this way that Spinoza understands Maimonides' position. We must now ask whether, and within what limits, this reading of Maimonides' position corresponds to that position itself. At the same time, the real and ultimate divergence between Spinoza and Maimonides must be established and analyzed.

Maimonides defines his position by two frontiers. In the face of orthodoxy he defends the right of reason, in the face of philosophy he directs attention to the bounds of reason. Under orthodoxy we are to understand in the first place the standpoint of those rabbis who invoke only the authority of the Bible and of the Talmud, without making any effort to find a philosophic basis for their teachings. Maimonides' verdict on these "vulgar" theologians is no less harsh than is Spinoza's corresponding verdict. His reproach against them runs: because of their stupidity and ignorance, they accept the impossible as possible by standing to the letter of the text, when that text is intended as allegory or analogy. They concern themselves exclusively with the outer shell of the "secrets of the Torah," hinted at in certain passages of the Talmud and of the Midrashim, and do not heed that these have a hidden kernel. In the face of this orthodoxy, Maimonides defends the right of reason by taking

---

1. [182] "Hilkhot Melakhim" VIII, 11. The tenor of the passage used as evidence by Spinoza is somewhat softened, but not essentially modified, if we use the reading given in the *editio princeps*. Manuel Joel calls attention to the difference between the readings in his *Spinoza's theologisch-politischer Traktat auf seine Quellen geprüft* (Breslau, 1870): pp. 55f. Joel also refers to Joseph Caro, *Kesef Mishneh*, which characterizes the passage quoted by Spinoza as Maimonides' own opinion, in other words, as not traditional; he omits to note that this commentator continues: "it (i.e., Maimonides' own opinion) is correct." [For an English translation of "Hilkhot Melakhim" VIII, 11, see "Laws concerning Kings and Wars," trans. Hershman, p. 230, with n. 11 on p. 308. Hershman's translation of the critical last phrase in Maimonides' paragraph is still highly controversial; it is certainly not the self-evident view of Maimonides. For a different perspective, advanced in several works, see, e.g., "Preface to *Spinoza's Critique of Religion*," in *Jewish Philosophy and the Crisis of Modernity*, pp. 163-64. On the one hand, a contemporary Hebrew edition, containing the alternate version seemingly preferred by Strauss, is "Mclakhim," ed. Rubenstein, p. 398 with n. 69. On the other hand, a recent Hebrew edition, which is based on Yemenite Jewish manuscripts, and which claims greater "authenticity" (as if the matter has been settled, which is a still-to-be-established proposition), contains the version tacitly rejected by Spinoza: Rabbeinu Moshe ben Maimon, *Sefer Mishneh Torah*, ed. Yohai Makbili, Yehiel Kara, and Hillel Gershuni (Neve Shanan [Haifa], Israel: Or Vishua, 2009), "Hilkhot Melakhim," chap. 8, para. 11, p. 1241; cf. pp. 12 [Hebrew] and xiv [English]. For a history of the dispute which the controversial phrase has engendered, and in which a certain position is also advocated, see Steven Schwarzschild, "Do Noachites Have to Believe in Revelation? (A Passage in Dispute between Maimonides, Spinoza, Mendelssohn, and Hermann Cohen): A Contribution to a Jewish View of Natural Law," in *The Pursuit of the Ideal*, ed. Menachem Kellner (Albany: State University of New York Press, 1990), pp. 29-59.]

as his hermeneutic principle: "All passages which contradict rational insight when taken literally are to be interpreted allegorically."[2] In the second place we must understand by the orthodoxy which Maimonides is contesting, the orthodoxy of the Arabs, the so-called *kalam*, which influenced certain Jews. Maimonides defends the right of reason against the *kalam* in the main by two principles:

(1) What exists does not adapt itself to opinion, but right opinions are those that adapt themselves to the existent. Science must take its bearings not by what *might* be, but by what is real, visible, manifest.

(2) Only on the basis of thorough investigation of what is, as it really is, hence only on the basis of Aristotelian natural science, is theology possible.

This distinction permits delimitation not only from the *kalam* but from philosophy as well. Characteristic of the philosophers is the doctrine of the eternity of the world. Against this, Maimonides sets out to defend the doctrine of faith, that God freely created the world, freely bestowed on the prophets His gifts and His grace, and freely judges mankind. He is aware that in so doing he is at one with the aim of the *kalam*. But Maimonides wishes to prove on the basis of solid science what the *kalam* sought to prove under the actual but unclear assumption of what it intended to prove, and further in total disaccord with the real visible order of the world. Science leads to the complete disjunction: creation of the world or eternity of the world. Science cannot settle which member of this disjunction represents the truth. The question whether the world is eternal or was created stands at the frontier where reason must halt. This frontier must be shown to be such to philosophy. Now on the assumption of the eternity of the world—this was demonstrated by Aristotle—and also on the assumption of the creation of the world, it follows that God exists, that He is one, and that He is incorporeal.

---

2. [183] Maimonides, *Moreh Nevukhim* 1.Intro. (pp. 6–8, 15) [Pines, pp. 5–6, 9–10]; 1.71 (pp. 332–35) [Pines, pp. 175–76]; 2.25 (pp. 195f.) [Pines, pp. 327–28]; 2.27 (pp. 205–6) [Pines, p. 333]; 2.32 (p. 260) [Pines, pp. 360–61]; 3.51 (p. 435) [Pines, p. 619]. The figures in parentheses indicate the pages in Salomon Munk's translation, *Le Guide des égarés*. [See the "Editor's Note" above for an explanation of the figures in square brackets. Henceforth, rather than following Strauss's use of the original Hebrew title, *Moreh ha-Nevukhim* (devised in its well-known Hebrew form by Samuel ibn Tibbon as the first translator of the book during Maimonides' own life, who was able to consult with the author himself by letter), references in the notes have been changed to the standard English title—*The Guide of the Perplexed* instead of *Moreh ha-Nevukhim*, and *Guide* instead of the abbreviated *Moreh*—so as to maintain consistency with the rest of the present book. Strauss mainly refers to Salomon Munk's Judeo-Arabic edition and French translation. The thus-far still definitive critical edition of Issachar Joel of the *Dalalat al-ha'irin* (building on and correcting Munk's edition) only appeared in print in 1931 (Jerusalem), which postdated his book. If he made any use of the German translation—R. Fürstenthal, pt. I (Krotoschin, 1839), M. Stern, pt. II (Vienna, 1864), and S. Scheyer, pt. III (Frankfurt, 1838), all of which, in the text these translators based themselves on, preceded Munk—it is not evident.]

These three basic theologems are thus strictly demonstrable. However, the *kalam*, which set out to support these theologems by the doctrine of creation, makes the theologems questionable, since the creation of the world is not strictly demonstrable. In opposition to the *kalam*, Maimonides intends first—in view of the fact that the creation of the world is not provable—to set the three fundamental theologems beyond all doubt, and then and then only to treat the question to which philosophic thinking is impotent to give a decisive answer—creation of the world versus eternity of the world. In favor of the creation of the world and against the eternity of the world, he sees as a first line of argument, that the doctrine of creation is handed down to us by the prophets, and as a second line of argument, the objective probability.[3]

2) As contrast regarding the central theological assumption

According to Maimonides' exposition, the first two metaphysical assumptions of the *kalam* run:

(1) All bodies are composed of atoms, atoms are the substance of bodies.

(2) The void exists.[4]

The striking agreement between this metaphysics and Epicurean metaphysics facilitates understanding of the meaning to be ascribed to Maimonides' critique of the *kalam*. Epicurean and Lucretian atomism belongs to the context of thought constituted by the intention to free the mind from the fear inspired by religion. "This disturbance of mind and this darkness cannot be dispersed by the rays of the sun, the shining arrows of the day, but only by the contemplation of nature, and by investigation of nature." The principle of this natural science lies in the proposition: never, even by the action of the gods, can something be created out of nothing, for in that case anything and everything could come into being from anything, unneedful of seeds; nothing would then be required to remain within its own order, within the definite and continuous mode of its arising. But it is manifest that reality has a definite and continuous order. Since in the realm of the manifest there is not only definite, continuous order, but also indefiniteness and discontinuity, it is necessary to assume that underlying the manifest order there is another order, atomism, as the real order of things, if we are radically to exclude the

---

3. [184] *Guide* 1.71 [Pines, pp. 175–84]; 1.73 [Pines, pp. 194–214]; 2.16 [Pines, pp. 293–94]. The question whether Maimonides' interpretation of the *kalam* is adequate cannot and need not be answered here.

4. [185] *Guide* 1.73 [Pines, pp. 175–84].

operation of divine powers.[5] At the furthest pole from Epicurean metaphysics is the metaphysics of the *kalam* as the result of faith in the sovereign power of God, who every moment creates all things out of nothing. For the *kalam*, according to the teaching of which the atoms are in each moment of time being created out of nothing, according to the sovereign and arbitrary will of God, atomism is the correlate of a radical denial of the manifest order of nature as an inherent, continuous nexus. Both these forms of atomism deny the solidity of the manifest order. That of Epicurus, so that he may eradicate faith in gods who act; that of the *kalam*, by reason of faith in the acting God. Both diverge from the manifest order in opposite directions. Between these two extremes, which touch one another, stands Aristotelian science. It stays fast within the manifest order. In express adherence to Aristotelian science, Maimonides appeals against the *kalam* to the manifest order. On this ground he sets out to prove that the world is created out of nothing. To achieve this, he cannot but understand the divine creative will as an ordering and rational will. His metaphysics therefore centers on the problem of the relation between reason (understanding) and will in God.

On the basis of the manifest order, on which Maimonides seeks to prove the creation of the world as possible, even probable, the philosophy which Maimonides contests and rejects as incompatible with Judaism, that of the

---

5. [186] Lucretius I, 140ff.

[But it is your excellence and the pleasure of the sweet friendship
I hope to have with you that urges me to undergo hardship
however great and to keep my watch in the quiet of the night
as I try to find the right words and poem with which at last
I might be able to hold a clear light up to your mind
that will allow you to see deeply into obscure matters.
Therefore this fear and darkness of the mind must be shattered
apart not by the rays of the sun and the clear shafts
of the day but by the external appearance and inner law of nature.
Its first principle will take its starting point for us as follows:
nothing ever comes to be from nothing through divine intervention.
The reason that fear so dominates all mortals is
because they see many things happen on earth and in the heavens
the causes of whose activities they are able in no way
to understand, and they imagine they take place through divine power.
For which reason, when we see that nothing can be created from nothing,
then we will more correctly perceive what we are after:
the source from which each thing is created, and the way
each thing happens without divine intervention.

See Lucretius, *On the Nature of Things*, trans. Walter Englert (Newburyport, MA: Focus, 2003), p. 5, I.140-58. See also "Notes on Lucretius," in *Liberalism Ancient and Modern*, pp. 76-139, and especially pp. 76-80.]

Arab Aristotelians, arrives at the opposite conclusion, at the doctrine of the world as eternal. Thus the contest between belief and unbelief takes place on the plane of Aristotelian science. To this extent, we may at the outset ignore the difference between the teleological metaphysics of the twelfth century and the mechanical physics of the seventeenth century. By adopting the doctrine of Ibn Rushd, Spinoza would already overstep the boundary drawn by Maimonides. Spinoza teaches, as do the Arab philosophers, the eternity of the world, in contradiction of the doctrine of creation laid down by revealed religion. That those philosophers considered themselves believers in revelation, and actually were believers in revelation, need not concern us here, when we are investigating only the opposition of Spinoza to revealed religion as understood by Maimonides. The first formulation for this opposition is thus: doctrine of the eternity of the world versus doctrine of the creation of the world.

With the doctrine of the eternity of the world the denial of miracles is given, with the doctrine of the creation of the world the possibility of miracles is admitted.[6] In the context of the *Tractate*, Spinoza justifies his denial of the possibility of miracles by means of the proposition: "Dei voluntas, et Dei intellectus in se revera unum et idem sunt; nec distinguuntur, nisi respectu nostrarum cogitationum, quas de Dei intellectu formamus" (*Tractate*, p. 48). ["God's will and God's understanding are in themselves really one and the same. Nor are they distinguished except with respect to our thoughts that we have formed of God's understanding" {Yaffe, p. 47}.] It follows from this proposition that God wills all things which He knows, that thus the distinction between the possible and the actual has no ontic significance. There is nothing possible except or beside the actual: the actual is of necessity such as it is; the rules of actual events are necessary laws, eternal truths; the modification of nature, the annulling of a law of nature, the miracle is an absurdity (*Tractate*, pp. 68f. [Yaffe, pp. 68–70]). A scholar believes he has shown that the proposition that in God intellect and will are one and the same is to be found in the work of Maimonides also, and therefore that there is a basic agreement between Maimonides and Spinoza;[7] the conclusion was surely agreeable to Spinoza himself, who not unintentionally, and particularly in the *Tractate*, adopted such a formulation for his central assertion as echoes traditional teachings. If one were justified in assuming this agreement, then

---

6. [187] *Guide* 2.25 (pp. 197f. in Munk translation) [Pines, pp. 327–28].
7. [188] Joel [op. cit.], pp. 47f.

Spinoza's doctrine—not despite, but on account of his denial of miracles and of creation—would then be seen as the consistent further development of Maimonides' theology, which is considered to be the culmination of Jewish theology.

Maimonides concludes from the unqualified oneness and simplicity of God that it is impossible that God should have positive attributes. Each positive attribute would posit a manifold in God. Thus it is in particular impossible to attribute intellect and will to God, to distinguish God's intellect and God's will from His essence. For this reason the distinction between intellect and will in God loses the significance it has in precise speech. Were Spinoza to have adopted this assertion of identity in meaning and not merely in words, he would then have been obliged to assert the identity of thought and extension in the same way as the identity of intellect and will. Even by so doing, he would not have achieved a genuine concord. For Maimonides, the proposition means a reality which is higher than all human understanding: since God is indeed one, nothing positive can be said of Him. His being is ineffable, uncompassable. We grasp only the That, not the What of God, if by the What more is to be conveyed to our minds than by the That.[8] So the human comprehension is transcended by the conclusion drawn, namely that the intellect of God and the will of God are not distinguishable from God's essence, and therefore not distinguishable one from the other, for we grasp will and intellect only as clearly different from one another. Spinoza, however, makes the claim of understanding the identity of will and intellect, as in his doctrine the identity of will and intellect indeed holds for man as well as God. Whereas for Maimonides, the identity-proposition cannot but be incomprehensible for the very reason that it negates in regard to God the duality known to us from the observation of ourselves. Spinoza's proposition of identity does not express opposition to the positive attributes, but exclusively opposition to will as distinguished from intellect.

Spinoza can therefore draw from the proposition of identity conclusions for understanding created things only because this proposition is comprehensible to him, and is not merely the limit set to all comprehension. Maimonides on the other hand sees himself compelled by his understanding of the created thing, to attribute to the incomprehensible Creator intellect and will distinguished one from the other, in improper speech. For the analysis of

---

8. [189] *Guide* 1.51 (pp. 183f.) [Pines, pp. 113–14]; 1.53 (pp. 213f.) [Pines, p. 122]; 1.58 (pp. 241f.) [Pines, pp. 135–36].

"things created" provides the probability-proof for the creation of the world. The creation of the world can, however, be asserted only if intellect and will are differentiated in God. One of the "philosophers'" arguments against God's being Creator runs: If an *agens* acts at one time and at another time fails to act, the cause on the one occasion is that there is a stimulus to action, or hindrances are not present, whereas another time that stimulus is lacking or hindrances are present, which one time cause the will to act, another time to refrain from action—in other words, which change the will. Now God is not moved by stimuli to action, nor by hindrances to refrain from acting. Thus it is not possible that on the one occasion He acts, and on another occasion refrains from action. Rather is it the case that He, who is pure actuality, necessarily acts always. Maimonides replies: there are in fact no stimuli and no hindrances which at one time determine God to act, and at the other to refrain from acting. His will determines itself spontaneously now in the one way, now in the other. It is peculiar to the will, now to will and another time to refrain from willing. Since the essence of will is spontaneity, God may on the one occasion will to act and therefore act, and on another occasion will not to act and therefore not act. It is not an imperfection, but the essence of will that it wills and does not will. The matter is obviously very different in the case of the intellect. Nonunderstanding is obviously less perfect than understanding. It is therefore impossible that God should on one occasion know and on another occasion not know.[9] Thus with a view to the creation of the world, will in its peculiar character is attributed to God, and thus, and as a matter of fact, a distinction is drawn between will and intellect in God. Thus there is no basis for saying that Maimonides and Spinoza both assert that will and intellect are one and the same. It must indeed rather be stated, taking into account the immediate connection between the assertion of creation and the attribution to God of will in its peculiar character, that this is the very opposition between Maimonides and Spinoza: identification of intellect and will in God versus distinction between intellect and will in God.

One might think that the contradiction between Maimonides' denial of all positive attributes to God and his attribution of will to God entitles Spinoza to his "development" of the identity-proposition. In fact no contradiction is present. The denial of positive attributes is to be understood from the assertion that God's essence is incomprehensible. The attribution of will to God—

---

9. [190] Ibid., 2.14 (p. 119) [Pines, p. 288]; 2.18 (pp. 141f.) [Pines, pp. 300–301]; 3.20 (p. 153) [Pines, p. 483].

possible only in improper speech, but necessary in such—is the surpassing means of adumbrating the incomprehensibility of God. The very proof that establishes the volitional character of God at the same time establishes the incomprehensibility of God.

The preceding definition of the opposition between Maimonides and Spinoza can suffice to cast light upon the opposition regarding dogma. The connection existing between the judgment passed on miracles as possible or impossible and the central theological assumption has already been mentioned. Spinoza further concludes from the identity of intellect and will in God that revelation of a Law is impossible. A law presupposes the possibility of transgression. If God wills everything which He knows, and if, being omniscient, He fully knows human action, then human action against the will of God is impossible; hence a law revealed by God is impossible. Maimonides on his side—holding fast to the impossibility of attributing to God either intellect or will in proper speech—is obliged by the fact of the revealed Law to make the distinction necessary in improper speech between intellect and will in God; "since the whole sacred legislation, what it commands and what it forbids, rests on this base: that God's foreknowledge does not lead the possible out of its nature" (i.e., make it actual). Not everything which is possible, which God knows, is simultaneously willed or made actual by Him. In particular, God's knowledge of possible human actions does not call forth these actions into actuality, neither those which conform with His will nor those which contradict His will.[10] From the central theological assumption it follows that sin as sin against God is impossible according to Spinoza and possible according to Maimonides. This consequence in its turn is the condition for tolerance in principle on the one hand, or for the persecution of enemies and haters of God on the other. Maimonides expressly holds fast to the assertion that there are inexcusable rebellions against the Torah, carried out "with hand upraised" and blasphemies against God, whereas Spinoza holds that even the devil, and precisely the devil, as the most excellent of all rational creatures, cannot rebel against God.[11]

In his critique of Maimonides' theory of prophecy, Spinoza does not explicitly apply the proposition of the identity of God's intellect and God's

---

10. [191] *Tractate*, pp. 48f. [Yaffe, pp. 47–48]; *Guide* 3.20 (pp. 150–54) [Pines, pp. 481–84].

11. [192] *Guide* 3.41 (pp. 330–32) [Pines, pp. 565–66]; 1.36 (pp. 137f.) [Pines, pp. 84–85]; *Tractatus politicus* II, 6. [See "Editor's Note" above: Strauss refers to Spinoza, *Tractatus Politicus*, as edited by Gebhardt, in *Opera*. See *Political Treatise*, trans. R. H. M. Elwes (New York: Dover, 1951), p. 293: "But they (i.e., the divines) say, that he (i.e., the first man) was deceived by the devil. Who then was it, that deceived the devil himself?"]

will. His express critique, however, presupposes the critique which follows from that proposition. Only a God who is free and unfathomable wisdom can truly reveal Himself. It is an essential character of revelation that it should be a free gift bestowed by God, and that it cannot be acquired by human talent or training. The Islamic philosophers, in whose footsteps Maimonides followed, recognized revelation, and so conceived the natural preconditions of revelation that Maimonides could adhere to their views. Spinoza's critique is linked to these views which Maimonides shares with the philosophers. But Maimonides must in the name "of our Torah and of our religion," make one reservation: that a man endowed to receive prophecy, and properly trained for it according to the philosophers' correct specifications, may nevertheless be restrained from prophesying by the miraculous intervention of God's will. Since God acts with unfathomable freedom, selective revelation is possible. But Spinoza, by reason of his central theological assumption, must deny the possibility of selective revelation.[12]

If God's essence may be sufficiently known by the natural light, particular revelation is deprived of urgency, if not of meaning. For under this condition there is sufficient knowledge of God "common to all men," which cannot be complemented or surpassed by revelation, nor does it require to be vouched for by revelation. If God's essence is hidden and unfathomable, if all human knowledge of God is fragmentary and intermittent, then there cannot but be a genuine interest in revelation; if God is hidden from us by the world and by our preoccupation with that world, if our knowledge of God is comparable to the occasional flash of lightning in a night of profound darkness, if then there may be gradations in the clarity of this vision, from almost unceasing illumination to complete benightedness, and if the zenith of clarity was attained only by Moses *the* prophet, and if all other human knowledge of God remains in varying degree far below that zenith: then acceptance of the unsurpassable teaching of Moses, far transcending the knowledge of all other men, is due and binding. If God is a hidden God, then theology is not a discipline like the other transparent, methodical disciplines; if its object is not open to sight always continuously, but manifests itself only from time to time, then

---

12. [193] *Guide* 2.32 (pp. 262f.) [Pines, pp. 361–62]; *Tractate*, p. 1 [Yaffe, pp. 1–2]. Maimonides makes the further reservation that the prophecy of Moses is different in nature from the prophecies of the other prophets; cf. *Guide* 2.35 [Pines, pp. 367–69], 2.39 [Pines, pp. 378–81], and also *Mishneh Torah*, "Hilkhot Yesodei ha-Torah" VII, 6. [For "Hilkhot Yesodei ha-Torah" VII, 6, see Maimonides, "Laws of the Basic Principles of the Torah," trans. Hyamson, p. 42b.]

the only fitting way in which to speak of God is by recourse to parables and enigmas.[13] Thus the interest in the Torah as both the document of revelation and at the same time the mode of its interpretation (the allegorical), is based on Maimonides' central theological premise, just as Spinoza's central theological premise leads to the consequence that he can set up a theology *more geometrico*, sufficient unto itself, unconcerned with the teachings of others, and especially unconcerned with the opinions of the biblical teachers, is perfectly clear and distinct, and that he sees no reason for speaking in riddles and parables, and therefore tolerates no such form of speaking, and recognizes no other meaning than the literal meaning of the text itself.

3) As contrast regarding the conception of man

From the opposition in regard to the central theological presupposition there necessarily follows adoption of the opposed position toward revelation. Yet is the central presupposition in fact the first presupposition?

From Spinoza's theological presupposition the decision on allegedly actual revelation directly follows: revelation is not actual, because it is not possible. Maimonides on the other hand requires as a justification for revelation, apart from the assumption of the possibility and the urgent need for revelation in general, also the historical justification of the particular revelation made to Moses. The historical justification is by its nature open to historical critique. Thus it is open to Spinoza, independently of any denial of the possibility of revelation itself, to apply historical critique to the allegedly actual revelation. The historical critique does not differ essentially in meaning and limits when directed against Maimonides' position than when directed against orthodoxy. When Spinoza proves, following an allusion made by Ibn Ezra, that Moses could not have written the Torah, he does not strike Maimonides. For "He who says: the Torah is not given by God—he who says, and be it only of a single verse, of a single letter, here Moses spoke only out of his own mind—denies the Torah."[14] In principle, no critique of Scripture can touch Maimonides' position, since such critique is capable of no more than establishing what is *humanly* possible or impossible, whereas his opponent assumes the divine origin of Scripture. But to the extent that this assumption

---

13. [194] *Guide*, 1.Intro. (pp. 10ff.) [Pines, pp. 7–8].
14. [195] Maimonides, "Hilkhot Teshuvah" III, 8. [See "Hilkhot Teshuvah," trans. Hyamson, pp. 84b–85a.]

is historically justified by recourse to allegedly reliable tradition,[15] critique of that tradition is in principle possible. It is only cursorily that Spinoza applies criticism to Jewish tradition as such, to the tradition as distinct from the matter transmitted by that tradition. The only actual instance is his recalling the Sadducee polemics against the Pharisees (*Tractate*, p. 91 [Yaffe, p. 90]). His fundamental critique of the Jewish tradition is contained in his argument against the Catholic Church, which he uses in his answer to Burgh (*Epistle* 76). He inquires of Burgh whether he believes that all the arguments adduced by him—even assuming that all the reasons adduced by Burgh speak for the Catholic Church, and only for that Church—can be *mathematically* proved. No historical legitimation can meet the standard of certainty that Spinoza here sets. But it is equally true that the same applies to any historical refutation. Therefore the concern lies essentially with philosophic critique, which does not—as does historical criticism—stop at undermining belief in revelation, i.e., in a particular revelation, but eradicates this belief altogether, by cutting away any possible interest in revelation.

Yet is not belief in revelation the source from which interest in revelation springs? Is the interest in revelation not grounded in the knowledge conveyed by revelation that God is a hidden God? Or has this interest in revelation a prior reason? The basis of Maimonides' theory is Aristotelian physics, the analysis of the actual order of the world. Stringently pursued, science leads to the question, creation of the world or eternity of the world? But the answer to the question transcends the range of that science. Unguided human reason finds itself exposed to error when faced with the central question on which being or non-being of revelation depends, according to Maimonides' unmistakable declaration. What is truly accessible to man is only his world, the sublunary world. Even Aristotle, *the* philosopher, has himself progressed no further than to knowledge of this world.[16] In the face of this limitation upon all human understanding, Maimonides demands caution and mistrust in regard to the inclination of human thinking, and points to the Jewish tradition founded by Moses' prophecy.[17] Thus according to the inner structure of Maimonides' science the interest in revelation precedes the belief in revelation. The insight into the insufficiency of the human understanding—an insight gained on the basis of Aristotelian science, in principle prior to the in-

---

15. [196] Maimonides rejects in principle the proof through miracles; see "Yesodei ha-Torah," VIII. [See "Hilkhot Yesodei ha-Torah," trans. Hyamson, pp. 43b–44b.]

16. [197] *Guide* 2.22 (p. 179) [Pines, pp. 319–20]; 2.24 (p. 194) [Pines, pp. 326–27].

17. [198] Ibid., 2.23 (p. 182) [Pines, p. 321].

troduction of the central theological presupposition—motivates the recourse to revelation; this insight inclines man to the acceptance of revelation. The difference between Maimonides and "philosophy," and therewith between Maimonides and Spinoza, comes to light first in the assertion that human reason is inadequate for solving the central problem. In the conviction that human *reason* is inadequate lies the reason for concern with revelation. Concern with revelation precedes belief in revelation.

This is evident independently of the preceding reasoning, which took its bearing by the structure of Maimonides' science. If revelation is believed in, without the belief being supported by interest in revelation, the belief in revelation becomes a piece of knowledge alongside other knowledge, from which the most weighty conclusions for knowledge may result, indeed must result. For example, for the philosopher who reasons from the fact of revelation to the attributes of God, revelation is devoid of significance except as fact, like any other fact which in its character of fact is only an object. Spinoza does justice to this state of things by providing for the *Tractate*, which devotes its basic part to critique of revealed religion, a Preface which contains a critique of interest in revelation, i.e., of the assertion of human insufficiency. There he integrates the critique of the belief in revelation and of the content of that belief into the most fundamental critique, that of the interest in revelation.

Since for Maimonides, as for Spinoza, the human perfection predelineated in human nature consists simply in knowledge of God, the assertion "human understanding is inadequate to answer the central theological question" means for Spinoza no less than "man is unable to direct life to its goal, *beatitudo*." To the question "is purely human capacity sufficient for the conduct of life?" the answer given by Maimonides is contradicted and completely opposed by Spinoza: "nihil enim lumen naturale exigit, quod ipsum lumen non attingit, sed id *tantum*, quod nobis clarissime indicare potest, bonum, sive medium ad nostram beatitudinem esse" ["the natural light requires nothing that that same light does not reach, but *only* what it can indicate very clearly to us as being good, or a means to our blessedness" {Yaffe, p. 47}]. It is essentially on this ground that Spinoza denies that fulfillment of Mosaic law is necessary for attaining *beatitudo*; for this law requires observance of "ceremonies, i.e., actions which are in themselves indifferent, and which are binding only by virtue of having been posited" (*Tractate*, p. 48 [Yaffe, p. 47]). Even Maimonides who, be it said, takes the greatest pains to demonstrate the rational character of Mosaic law, admits that the individual regulations of that law are binding only by virtue of having been posited. With reference to certain regulations for sacrifices, he suggests that no one will ever be able to discover a reason for them.[18] Since, however, Maimonides considers Mosaic law as *the* divine law, as *the* way to *beatitudo*, Spinoza is justified in the following view: "At Judaei contra plane sentiunt; statuunt enim veras opiniones, veramque vivendi rationem *nihil prodesse ad beatitudinem* quamdiu homines eas ex solo lumine naturali amplectuntur, et non ut documenta Mosi prophetice revelata: hoc enim Maimonides cap. 8. Regum lege II aperte his verbis audet affirmare" (there follows a quotation from Maimonides—*Tractate*, p. 65 [Yaffe, pp. 64-65]). ["Yet the Jews plainly feel to the contrary. For they state that true opinions and the true plan of living *contribute nothing to blessedness*, so long as human beings embrace them by the natural light alone and not as lessons revealed prophetically to Moses. For Maimonides dares to affirm this openly in these words in *Laws of Kings* 8.11" {Yaffe, p. 64}.]

The whole structure of Maimonides' science corroborates Spinoza's judgment. Revelation beyond all doubt guarantees more than reason can of itself guarantee. Reason needs revelation, reason desires the solution offered by revelation. We may now define the contrast between Maimonides and Spinoza in the formula: Human inadequacy versus human adequacy. One may raise the objection that belief in human inadequacy, distrust of human capacity for reasoning, is in point of fact not characteristic of Maimonides. This objection derives its force from a comparison of Maimonides' position with other positions based on belief in revelation. But this consideration is inappropriate when the question concerns the characteristic difference existing between Spinoza, who denies revealed religion, and Maimonides, who affirms it.

The position which Spinoza is contesting, the compatibility of reason and Scripture, assumes the inadequacy of human intellect for attaining perfect knowledge of God. What is true for Maimonides is true of all believers in revelation who are confronted with the claim raised by independent human reflection developed into philosophy to guide life. If independent human reflection, if man's capacity in his quality as human being, is adequate for the guidance of life, revelation is dethroned; there may perhaps still be belief in revelation, but certainly no longer interest in revelation. Spinoza, convinced as he is of the adequacy of human capacities for the guidance of life, turns not only against Christianity with its doctrine of original sin, but also against Mai-

---

18. **[199]** Ibid., 3.26 (pp. 207-10) [Pines, pp. 508-10]; 3.49 (p. 411) [Pines, pp. 605-6].

monides and against Judaism in general, in so far as this latter fosters, or even merely tolerates, the concern with supernatural guidance of human life.

4) As contrast regarding the attitude toward Jewish life

The definitions so far established in the matter of the divergence between Maimonides and Spinoza are insufficient. The opposition of the central theologems is called into question by the fact that it is not the central theologems, but the assertion of insufficiency which is the first word from Maimonides that distinguishes his view characteristically from that of the "philosophers." In the context of Maimonides' science the declaration of insufficiency precedes the central theologem. If Spinoza's assertion of human sufficiency were the genuine contrary of Maimonides' assertion of insufficiency, then that assertion must precede his central theologem in the context of Spinoza's science. It does not, however. It is impossible that it should do so, since for Spinoza there is no physics preceding theology, so that at the frontier of physics, along with the theological problem, the insufficiency of human intellect comes to sight. Nevertheless, the opposition "insufficiency-sufficiency" is serviceable, and justified at least as provisional description of the prescientific difference. It will become clear that this second definition comes nearer to the root of the opposition than does the first, which was limited to opposition in the field of dogma. We cannot, however, limit ourselves to the dogmatic element, because Spinoza's critique of Maimonides has so wide a range.

Maimonides sees as the indispensable basis of revealed religion, more precisely of Judaism, the doctrine that the world is created, not eternal. In confirmation of this he does not simply refer to passages from Scripture in which the creation of the world is specifically taught. For these passages are, in his opinion, even more easily to be interpreted as in favor of the doctrine of the eternity of the world than are the no less numerous passages which attribute corporeality to God, and which he has already interpreted in the sense that God is incorporeal. Two reasons bring him to his decision to adhere strictly to the literal meaning of the Scriptural passages that tell of creation. In the first place, the eternity of the world is not proved, whereas it is already proved that God is an incorporeal being. In the second place: "To assert that the world is eternal, as does Aristotle, i.e., to assert this as a necessity in the sense that nature does not change and that nothing ever departs from its customary course, would amount to destroying the Torah root and stock, to accounting all miracles as fictions, and to declaring baseless everything for which the Torah makes one hope and of which it makes one fear."[19] This coordination of the two reasons would seem to rob the second of all weight. For assuming that Aristotle had proved the eternity of the world, would Maimonides have let himself be influenced by the second reason? In fact, the two reasons are most closely connected. Maimonides asserts not merely that the eternity of the world has not been proved, but rather that it is unprovable.[20] Contradiction between the two reasons is therefore impossible. Yet this leaves unclear the relation between the two reasons, between the philosophical reason and the conclusions drawn from the presuppositions of Judaism. The relation becomes clear if one assumes that the inference of basic tenets of Judaism is also scientific in character. The part played in the first reason by the fact of the actual world-order is taken in the second reason by the fact of the Torah. The second reason therefore involves no *metabasis eis allo genos* [shift from one genus to another], since it too is based on fact. By the fact of the Torah is meant the fact of the revealed character of the Torah. Even though this fact is not as obvious as is the actual world-order, it can nevertheless be unimpeachably proved by historical tradition and by reflection. Maimonides' context of thought may then be summed up as a nexus of scientific reasoning. Scientific reason shows first of all the limits set to itself (critique of the philosophic proofs adduced for the eternity of the world); that same scientific reason then shows the possibility of revelation; and finally, by arguments taken from history, it demonstrates that the foundation of Judaism was by a genuine revelation, and in so doing shows that the conditions of such revelation are actual.

The inference from the fact of revelation leads up to the condition of possibility of revelation. This condition is, however, fully expressed in those theologems which are recognized even by the "philosophers," the unity and incorporeality of God.[21] As is shown by the circumstance that Maimonides derives his theory of prophecy from the "philosophers," the fact of revelation as such does not, in Maimonides' view, presuppose the creation of the world. It is therefore not inference from the fact of revelation that proves the creation of the world, but inference from miracles, which accompany the period

19. [200] Ibid., 2.25 (pp. 195–97) [Pines, pp. 327–28].
20. [201] Ibid., 2.16 (p. 129) [Pines, pp. 293–94]; 2.17 (p. 137) [Pines, p. 298]; 2.22 (pp. 179f.) [Pines, pp. 319–20]; 2.23 (pp. 185f.). [An error seems to have been made regarding "185f." as a page reference to 2.23 in Munk; 2.23 ends on p. 183; p. 185 refers to 2.24; but to judge by the contents of the *Guide* regarding the point which Strauss made in the text that is addressed by this note, it suggests he meant to write: 2.23, trans. Munk, p. 182f.; and hence Pines, pp. 321–22.]
21. [202] Ibid., 3.45 (pp. 351f.) [Pines, pp. 576–77].

of revelation generally, from the nexus of providence postulated throughout Scripture—providence which includes the miracles, and shows itself most plainly in the miracles. It is not revelation but creation that is vouched for by miracles. Maimonides' corpus of doctrine presupposes the reality of miracles, to the extent that it contains within itself more than doctrines grounded in physics, i.e., the proof for the three fundamental theologems (the existence, the unity, and the incorporeality of God) and the critique of the proofs adduced for the eternity of the world, and to the extent that the theory establishes the doctrine of creation strictly, and not merely as probable. In other words, that part of his doctrine which for Maimonides is most important, is exposed to Spinoza's superior critique of the knowability of miracles and has been discussed before. The source from which that critique draws its strength is the spirit, conscious of itself, of natural science in a stage of high progress. Under the assumptions of the twelfth century Maimonides' body of theory is scientifically possible, to the extent that the science of the twelfth century has the character of an essentially completed discipline, and does not live within a horizon forever receding, in which an infinite series of questions and answers to questions will follow one another. It is possible for Maimonides to defend against the philosophers of his time a view that can no longer be defended over against Spinoza.

Strictly speaking, the inference from the fact of miracles is usable as proof only against the doctrine of the eternity of the world, i.e., of the eternity of the actual order of the world, and not for the biblical teaching on the creation of the world. Maimonides expressly states that from the Platonic doctrine according to which God created the world from matter co-eternal with Himself according to His will, there follows the possibility of miracles. He nevertheless decides in favor of creation out of nothing against the Platonic doctrine since the latter doctrine, he alleges, is not proven.[22] This implies: the literal meaning of Scripture is valid as binding truth, so long as the contrary remains unproved. Scripture is acknowledged as true on the basis of the assumption that Scripture is revealed. This assumption is based on proof from history. As soon as "unprejudiced examination" is begun, controversy breaks out along the whole unsurveyable line of combat. An infinite abundance of instances and counterinstances begins to accumulate. What is to happen in the time before this question is resolved? How meantime, until the matter is settled once and for all, is the Jew to live? Is he justified even in pleading, let

---

22. [203] Ibid., 2.25 (pp. 197–98) [Pines, pp. 328–29].

alone zealously fighting, for the continuance of Judaism, if its title-deed stems from a tradition, the reliability of which is to be tested by historical examination of boundless extent, perhaps never to be decided by a final verdict? To place the burden of proof on him who contests the reliability of that tradition, to take it that it suffices to ward off attack, would mean admitting that one holds one's position not by virtue of historical proof, asserting the preemptive rights of hitherto-accepted opinion as such; it would amount to committing a *petitio principii* [circular reasoning]. But even if the most compelling historical considerations are taken as finally establishing the central event on Sinai, the revelational character of this event is still far from established. On the premises acceptable to the positive mind, the factual character of revelation is as little to be established as the factual character of any other miracle as such. Here too it is the case that what Maimonides could adduce in opposition to the philosophers of his own time can no longer be convincingly adduced against Spinoza.

Were one to leave the matter at this point, one would be failing to do justice to the basis of Maimonides' position, which remains unimpaired by all the changes that have occurred in the time that separates Maimonides from Spinoza. One would, therefore, fail to do justice to the problematic character of Spinoza's critique of religion. The inference leading back to the premises of the Torah is only formally comparable with the ascent from the actual order of the world to the First Cause. What is introduced by an inference is in truth originally familiar, corroborated by daily life as lived. It is not possible for any interpretation of *The Guide of the Perplexed* to disregard the fact that this book is not addressed to philosophers of another faith, nor to unbelieving philosophers, but exclusively to believing Jews, and, be it admitted, particularly to those believing Jews who have, by reason of their training in philosophy, fallen into doubt and perplexity, into a conflict between the views that they have taken over on the basis of the tradition and their philosophic insights. The assumption of the traditional faith is expressly declared: the stage of intellectual formation that necessarily precedes the stage of philosophic knowledge is obedience in act to the Torah; knowledge of the truths embodied in faith on the basis of tradition is necessarily prior to proof of those truths, that is, to philosophy. Maimonides is not setting up a pedagogic program by virtue of sovereign philosophy. He himself had in his own life followed this advice given to the young. He also was brought up as a Jew, before he turned to philosophy. As a Jew, born, living and dying with Jews, he pursued philosophy as a Jewish teacher of Jews. His argumentation takes its course, his disputes take place, within the context of Jewish life, and for that context. He defends the context of Jewish life which is threatened by the philosophers in so far as it is threatened by them. He enlightens Judaism by means of philosophy, to the extent that Judaism can be enlightened. He elevates Judaism by means of philosophy once again to the height it originally attained, so far as Judaism had descended from that height as a result of the disfavor of the times;[23] Maimonides' philosophy is based in principle and throughout on Judaism.

Spinoza also was born and brought up as a Jew. However matters may stand with the cogency of the critique by means of which he justifies his apostasy from Judaism, the result, at the least the result, is the radical and continuing distance from Judaism. The actual distance from Judaism creates an entirely new situation for the critique. It is no longer needful for Spinoza to justify his apostasy from Judaism before the tribunal of Judaism. On the contrary, he requires of Judaism that it should justify itself before the tribunal of reason, of humanity. He casts off the onus of proof from his own shoulders, and sets it on the shoulders of his opponent. The justification which Spinoza can require is not merely defense of Judaism. The best defense of Judaism would be powerless. What is demanded is the positive justification of Judaism on grounds that are external to Judaism, and before a judge who, perhaps devoid of hatred, certainly devoid of love, tests with inexorable severity the arguments advanced—with "a free mind." To take one's bearings by Judaism, as Maimonides had done, seems to him to be remaining imprisoned in *prejudice*; his Jewish upbringing seems to him to have been a process of becoming imbued with prejudices; distance from Judaism seems *freedom from prejudice*.

If, in the polemics of the previous age, and still to some extent in Spinoza's own polemics, the weightiest suspicion that could be cast on an opponent was the reproach of innovation, from now on the *jus primi occupantis* [right of first occupant] is denied. Doctrines or institutions can no longer be defended on the ground that they are prescriptive and generally recognized. All prejudices are questioned. The more radical the doubt, the greater the assurance that one becomes free from prejudices. Innovation, apostasy, arbi-

---

23. [204] Ibid., 1.Intro. (pp. 7f.) [Pines, pp. 5–6]; 1.71 (pp. 332–35) [Pines, pp. 175–76]; 2.25 (p. 198) [Pines, pp. 503–4]; 3.54 (p. 459) [Pines, pp. 633–34]. Cf. the essay by Franz Rosenzweig, "Apologetisches Denken," reprinted in *Kleinere Schriften* (Berlin, 1937), pp. 31–42. [See Franz Rosenzweig, "Apologetic Thinking," in *Philosophical and Theological Writings*, ed. Michael L. Morgan, trans. Paul W. Franks (Indianapolis: Hackett, 2000), pp. 95–108.]

trariness as terms of reproach have finally lost their capacity to strike terror to the heart.

Thus the free mind becomes free. It becomes what it is. It brings its potential into actuality. It presupposes itself, as faith presupposes itself. If faith cannot keep down unbelief, unfaith cannot cast down faith. On what ground is critique to take place, if faith and unfaith have no common ground? Critique of religion such as Spinoza has in mind, radical critique of religion, refutation of religion is possible only if faith and unfaith have some ground in common. Otherwise the critique never reaches the position under criticism.

B. SPINOZA'S CRITIQUE

1) The critique on the basis of Maimonides' science

Spinoza's critique of Maimonides becomes possible only by virtue of the fact that Maimonides trespasses on scientific ground, and endeavors to erect his structure of theory on that ground. Since that theory is presented as a *reconciliation* of reason and revelation, critique becomes possible first as the proof that reason and revelation, understood in the sense in which Maimonides understands them, are irreconcilable. This primary critique does not call Maimonides' assumptions into question at all; it merely questions the consistency of his position. Our first task is to isolate this primary critique.

Maimonides reconciles reason and revelation most fundamentally by identifying the distinctive aim of the Torah, divine law, with the aim of philosophy. The characteristic difference between divine law and human law is that the purpose of the latter is to serve the perfection of the body, whereas divine law is directed to the perfection of the soul as well as to the perfection of the body. Perfection of soul consists in the perfection of theoretical intellect. For the theoretical intellect is peculiar to man, this intellect is his, regardless of all relations with whatever is external to him. Perfect knowledge of being in its actual order, recognition of being as created, the knowledge of God as Creator, thus conveyed, is the precondition and the element of man's whole relation to God, which therefore is predelineated in man, as his proper perfection. Bodily perfection is health; the means necessary for health cannot be secured by man living as single individual. For the sake of his bodily well-being, man seeks life in community with his kind. Life in community presupposes prevention of acts of violence, and moralization on the part of each member of the community. The true perfection of man, the perfection of intellect, is on the other hand essentially non-social. Essentially, it exists and persists not by virtue of life in community, nor for the benefit of the community, in contradistinction to moral perfection. The Torah, the divine law, thus has three objects: (1) the prevention of acts of violence, the external order of life in community; (2) the moral training of mankind; (3) the perfecting of knowledge.[24]

Spinoza's teachings on the legitimate aims of human desire bear a close resemblance to those of Maimonides on the aims of the Torah.[25] There are three aims of human desire: (1) to understand the nature of things by their first causes; (2) to keep the passions in check, or to acquire the habit of virtue; (3) to live in security and with a sound body. In the perfection of our understanding lies our proper perfection. Understanding leads of itself to knowledge of God and to love of God, as the final goal of all human action. Determination of the means that are required for the attainment of that goal is the task of divine law. The distinction made between understanding and virtue falls away on closer scrutiny. In the wise, understanding and virtue are one. The distinction is appropriate only in reference to the multitude, since the multitude can be induced to tame its passions even without understanding. Seen in this light, virtue is nothing more than civilization in Maimonides' sense, social perfection. Social life is essentially founded in the concern with security and health, the means of attaining which are not within the capacity of man as single individual, whereas the proper perfection of man depends only on such means as belong to the individual human being.[26]

Maimonides and Spinoza thus have the same conception of the end peculiar to divine law.[27] Spinoza concludes from this conception that divine law, which brings about the highest and hence non-social perfection in man, has no bearing on society. In the first place, it is not addressed to societies, but to the individual as individual: in other words, to every human being as human being. Therefore it is addressed not only to certain men, to a particular

---

24. [205] *Guide* 2.40 (p. 310) [Pines, p. 383]; 3.27 [Pines, pp. 510–12]; 3.28 [Pines, pp. 512–14]; 3.31 (p. 248) [Pines, p. 524]; 3.51 (pp. 437ff.) [Pines, pp. 620–21]; 3.54 (pp. 460f.) [Pines, pp. 634–35].

25. [206] Joel (pp. 44ff.) has already indicated this concordance. Joel's indications have been used in the present study, and, where necessary, have been completed or amended. [Strauss refers of course to Manuel Joel, not to Issachar Joel: see "Editor's Note," and n. 2, above.]

26. [207] *Tractate*, pp. 32ff. [Yaffe, pp. 33–34]; pp. 45ff. [Yaffe, pp. 44–46]; cf. *Ethics*, IV, 28; V, 25, 38, 40 [see Spinoza, *Ethics*, trans. W. H. White, rev. James Gutmann (New York: Hafner, 1949), pp. 207–8, 269, 276, 278].

27. [208] The divergence of their views on the *origin* of divine law (according to Maimonides it is essentially revealed, according to Spinoza essentially not revealed) is not taken into consideration in the present context.

group, as is Mosaic law, which is plainly addressed only to the Jews. Secondly, it is directed at each man as individual, whether he lives among men or as a hermit. It is obvious that the greater part of the precepts contained in Mosaic law are to be observed not by the individual, but by society in its entirety. So Spinoza deduces from the conception of divine law which he holds in common with Maimonides that Mosaic law is not divine law.[28]

In this argumentation only the critique of the particularist character of Mosaic law is really cogent from Spinoza's point of view. This critique may easily be rejected by referring to the universal function of the particular-Jewish law: to educate mankind in true worship of God through Israel.[29] However, what is very strange, because in direct opposition to Spinoza's own intent, is the critique of the social function of Mosaic law. The realization of the highest aim of man (knowledge of God) is bound up with the realization of the lower aim (security in living), hence with life regulated by law, in society with others (*Tractate*, p. 59 [Yaffe, pp. 58–59]). Now, means are to be determined with regard to the aim, to the final aim; therefore the standards of political life are to be determined with regard to knowledge of God (*Tractate*, p. 46 [Yaffe, p. 46]). From the relation between the realization of the higher and that of the lower aim, Maimonides too concludes that divine law must determine the means which serve the aim of human law with a view to the proper aim of the divine law.[30] How then are we to understand that Spinoza completely severs divine law and human law: ". . . per humanam [legem] intelligo rationem vivendi, quae ad tutandum vitam, et rempublicam *tantum* inservit; per divinam autem, quae *solum* summum bonum, hoc est, Dei veram cognitionem, et amorem spectat" (*Tractate*, p. 45). ["By a human (law), I understand a plan of living, which *only* serves to protect life and the republic. By a divine one,

---

28. [209] "In superiore Capite ostendimus, legem divinam, quae homines vere beatos reddit, et veram vitam docet, omnibus esse hominibus *universalem*; imo eam ex humana natura ita deduximus, ut ipsa humanae menti innata, et quasi inscripta existimanda sit. Cum autem caeremoniae, eae saltem, quae habentur in Vetere Testamento, *Hebraeis tantum* institutae, et eorum imperio ita accomodatae fuerint, ut maxima ex parte ab universa *societate*, non autem ab *unoquoqe* exerceri potuerint, certum est, eas ad legem divinam non pertinere, adeoque nec etiam ad beatitudinem et virtutem aliquid facere" (*Tractate*, p. 55). ["In the previous Chapter, we have shown that the divine law that renders human beings truly blessèd and teaches true life is *universal* for all human beings. Indeed, we have so deduced it from human nature that it is to be figured that it is innate and as it were inscribed in the human mind. Since, however, the ceremonies—those that are found in the Old Testament at least—were instituted *only for the Hebrews*, and moreover were so accommodated to their imperium that for the most part they could not be practiced by *anyone* away from *their society* as such, it is certain that they do not pertain to the divine law; and so they do not do anything for blessedness and virtue either" {Yaffe, p. 55}.] Cf. *Tractate*, p. 47. [Cf. Yaffe, p. 47.]
29. [210] *Guide* 3.41 (p. 333) [Pines, pp. 565–66].
30. [211] Ibid., 3.27 (pp. 211f.) [Pines, pp. 510–11].

however, I understand one that has to do *solely* with the highest good, that is, with the true knowledge and love of God" {Yaffe, pp. 44-45}.][31]

In this part of the *Tractate*, Spinoza's critique of the Law is a critique of the significance of the ceremonial law for salvation. What he is concerned with is the question whether the ceremonies stand in *immediate* relationship to the highest aim of life, to the love of God, as Maimonides had held.[32] Spinoza not only does not contest the political value of ceremonies, in other words, the value which is only mediate in relation to *beatitudo*: he in fact asserts this value polemically with the utmost emphasis (*Tractate*, pp. 59ff. [Yaffe, pp. 58-61]). In this connection, and only in this connection, *lex humana* [human law] and *lex divina* [divine law] must stand opposed. Facing the question of the immediate value for salvation of the ceremonies, Spinoza adopts the Christian position towards Mosaic law as a whole, in comparison with the "new law" (or, as the case may be, with the New Testament) as a whole. The Christian cleavage made between the Old Testament and the New (or the old Law and the new Law) stresses the same characteristics, which are also used in the distinction made between *lex divina* and *lex humana*: the former regulates external actions; it derives its force from fear of punishment; it promises worldly goods.[33] Starting from this point, Spinoza adopts the Christian conception of the relation between the divine law and the human law, which can by no means be reconciled with his own conception of the relation between *beatitudo* and the State.

The discussion between Spinoza and Maimonides thus seems to hinge on the question of what place is to be allocated to ceremonial law: or—since the political interpretation of ceremonial law is not in conflict with Maimonides' fundamental definitions of the divine law—on the question of the political value of this body of law. Meanwhile there is the question of whether it has

---

31. [212] *Tractate*, p. 46 is irreconcilable with this: "Media igitur, quae hic finis omnium humanarum actionum . . . exigit, jussa Dei vocari possunt . . . atque adeo ratio vivendi, quae hunc finem spectat, lex Divina optime vocatur. Quaenam autem haec Media sint, et quaenam ratio vivendi, quam hic finis exigit, et quomodo hunc optimae *reipublicae* fundamenta sequantur, et ratio vivendi inter homines, ad universalem Ethicam pertinet." ["The means that this aim of all human actions requires . . . can therefore be called God's biddings, . . . and so the plan of living which has to do with this aim is best called the Divine Law. What these means are and what plan of living this aim requires, and how the foundations of the best *republic* and plan of living among human beings follow from it, however, pertains to universal Ethics" {Yaffe, p. 45}.]

32. [213] Cf. inter alia *Guide* 3.44 [Pines, p. 574]. For all that, the distinction made (*Guide* 3.52) [Pines, pp. 629-30] between the actions prescribed by the Law, and which have as their aim the *fear of God*, and the views taught by the Law, which have as their aim the *love* of God, come very close to Spinoza's interpretation of ceremonial Law.

33. [214] Thomas Aquinas, *Summa theologica* II, 1, qu. 91, art. 4 and 5; qu. 95, art. 1; qu. 99; qu. 107; Calvin, *Institutes* IV, 20; I, 5; II, 11; cf. *Tractate*, pp. 34, 45, 51, 56 [Yaffe, pp. 34, 44, 50, 55-56].

binding power. In Spinoza's view, law that is binding is set up by the supreme power in a given state at a given time. He does distinguish between the actual state and the best state. For the time being, the possibility remains open that Mosaic law politically interpreted contains the constitution of the best state, especially since Spinoza asserts that his theory of the state contains no element that has not already long been seen by the politicians (*Tractatus politicus*, I, 3-4), and he has every appearance of placing Moses in the first rank of rulers notable for their shrewdness. That Mosaic law is a model to be followed was particularly asserted by orthodox Calvinism, with which Spinoza is compelled to dispute in the *Tractate*. In this debate therefore Spinoza must once more justify his falling away from Judaism.[34] In his rejection of the assertion just made, he shows himself as completely conditioned by regard for the situation in the Netherlands (or, as the case may be, in Europe in general), for the claims of the Christian churches, and for the dangers to peace arising from these. No power on earth seemed at the time less capable than religion of fulfilling the primary need for peace. Thus the difference existing between Maimonides' views and those of Spinoza regarding the value of the Mosaic law would seem to be reducible to the different social and political situations obtaining in the twelfth and in the seventeenth centuries. But before Spinoza could find access to the political stresses weighing on the Netherlands and on the whole of Europe, and therewith to the sovereign secular state entirely independent of both Scripture and tradition, and this in such a fashion that he could then make decisive objections against the value of Mosaic law, it was necessary that he should first have cut himself away from Judaism. In this process, denial of the importance of Mosaic ceremonial law for salvation together with the political interpretation of that law plays a decisive part.[35] That interpretation was not from the first supported by the political interest, and indeed differed but little from the inclination of contemporary *libertins* to place kings and priests in the same category. But what are we to think of the denial of the direct importance of ceremonies for salvation?

For Spinoza as for Maimonides, the significance of *lex divina* is determined without regard to the particular character of Mosaic law, but by reason

---

34. [215] Gebhardt, in the Introduction to his German translation of the *Tractate* (Leipzig, 1922), xvii: Spinoza "seeks to prove that the inevitable result of an independent priesthood and even of the institution of prophecy was the greatest harm to the state. In this matter Spinoza's debate with Judaism is entirely at one with the innermost aim of the *Tractate*."

35. [216] Cf. the report in [Jean Maximilian] Lucas, *La Vie et l'esprit de Monsieur Benoît de Spinosa* (see [Jacob] Freudenthal, *[Die] Lebensgeschichte [Spinoza's in Quellenschriften, Urkunden, und Nichtamtlichen Nachrichten]* (Leipzig: Veit, 1899), p. 7).

of a general reflection on the essence of man. With a view to the aim thus discovered, the ways which lead to that aim, the content of *lex divina*, are to be determined. Assuming that several different means conduce to the same end, that no single one of these means is more highly justified by the end than others, then the choice of the means may be left to the arbitrary decision of the individual. Therefore, from rational insight into divine law, there is no reason to prefer the means laid down in Mosaic law to other equally good means. On the other hand, there is also no reason for preferring these other means to the traditionally accepted ones. The deciding factor therefore is the attitude to revelation, to the Jewish tradition. Spinoza's position is determined by his fundamental alienation from Judaism. Thus it is to this alienation (the "freedom from prejudice") that the rejection of Mosaic law is to be traced. However Spinoza may try to justify this alienation, by proving the impossibility of revelation or by casting doubt on the reality of the revelation made to Moses, our present concern is simply to show that his attempt to prove the incompatibility of the two elements, which according to Maimonides' view are united in the Torah, is indefensible on the basis of his own theory. This attempt reveals itself to historical reflection as belonging to an intermediate stage, in which Spinoza has already freed himself from the social nexus of Judaism but has not yet found his home in the liberal secular state. But if the irreconcilable character of the contrast existing between *lex divina* and *lex humana* has not been demonstrated, it will never be possible to demonstrate from Scripture that Mosaic law is a purely human law. For Spinoza can do no more than assert by an unjustified exaggeration, which he himself cannot continue to sustain,[36] that the ultimate aim of *lex divina* is not revealed also in Mosaic law. The compatibility of *lex divina* and *lex humana*, however, necessarily follows from the relationship between *beatitudo* and the state.

A similar judgment must be passed on Spinoza's attempt to prove that philosophy and theology are irreconcilable by assuming that philosophy is a matter for the wise minority, and that socially intended revealed religion is a matter for the unwise majority. This attempt too belongs to the context of the critique of Maimonides. According to Maimonides, the precepts of Mosaic law convey two groups of articles of faith: first, the fundamental truths as such, and second, propositions that must be believed for the sake of maintaining order in human communities.[37] Similarly Spinoza makes a distinction

---

36. [217] Cf. *Tractate*, pp. 145, 151f., 157 [Yaffe, pp. 147–48, 151–53, 156].
37. [218] *Guide* 3.28 [Pines, pp. 512–14].

between true and pious dogmas (*Tractate*, p. 162 [Yaffe, p. 164]). If *beatitudo* requires living together, and thus demands the state, and therewith general recognition of such pious dogmas, then the comprehensive unity of *lex divina* must be granted, since this law conveys fundamental truths as well as merely pious dogmas. For it is only the wise elite who, by their insight into the fundamental truths, are directly induced to conduct themselves in a manner favorable to social life. The majority, the unwise, need quite other methods of education. They must be brought to believe in God's mercy and punitive justice. But is the general run of men ever concerned with the fundamental truths? Spinoza, at first in opposition to Maimonides, answers with a negative. He takes recourse to the impossibility of a knowledge of *intelligibilia* that is not founded on one's own insight, on demonstration.[38] This reasoning is not far removed from Maimonides, who intimates that the knowledge of God of which the general run of men is capable, and which is sufficient for them, has no cognitive significance whatever.[39] It must be conceded that Maimonides

38. [219] "Quod si quis dicat, non esse quidem opus Dei attributa intelligere, at omnino simpliciter, absque demonstratione credere, is sane nugabitur: Nam res invisibiles, et quae solius mentis sunt objecta, nullis aliis oculis videri possunt, quam per demonstrationes; qui itaque eas non habent, nihil harum rerum plane vident; atque adeo quicquid de similibus auditum referunt, non magis eorum mentem tangit, sive indicat, quam verba Psittaci, vel automati, quae sine mente, et sensu loquuntur" (*Tractate*, p. 156). ["For if someone says that the task is not to understand God's attributes but to believe altogether simply, without demonstration, surely he will be trifling. For invisible things, and those that are objects of the mind alone, can be seen by no other eyes but through demonstrations. Accordingly, those who do not have them, plainly see nothing of these matters. And so, whatever hearsay they report concerning such things does not touch or indicate their mind any more than the words of a parrot or a puppet, which speak without mind or sense" {Yaffe, pp. 157–58}.]

39. [220] This is shown by collating *Guide* 1.35 (pp. 131f.) [Pines, pp. 80–81]: "There is no need to inform the multitude of the fact that God has no positive attributes" with 1.60 (pp. 263–66) [Pines, pp. 145–47]: ". . . whosoever ascribes positive attributes to God has not merely imperfect knowledge of God, but no knowledge of Him whatsoever." [With regard to the passage from 1.35, so far as I have been able to determine, no version or translation of the *Guide* known to me quite matches what Strauss offers in his original German. But the following passage, according to Pines's English translation, p. 80 (which roughly corresponds with Munk's French translation, pp. 131–32), might perhaps have been what he was thinking of:

As for the discussion concerning attributes and the way they have been negated with regard to Him; and as for the meaning of the attributes that may be ascribed to Him, . . . it should be considered that all these are obscure matters. In fact, they are truly *the mysteries of the Torah* and the *secrets* constantly mentioned in the books of the prophets and in the dicta of the Sages, may their memory be blessed. They are the matters that ought not to be spoken of except *in chapter headings*, as we have mentioned, and only with an individual such as has been described.

Regarding the passage from 1.60, as Strauss's original German presents it, it too relates only obliquely to the versions and translations of the *Guide* known to me. But the following passage, according to Pines's English translation, p. 145 (which roughly corresponds with Munk's French translation, pp. 263), might perhaps have been what he was thinking of:

I shall not say that he who affirms that God, may He be exalted, has positive attributes either falls short of apprehending Him or is an associator or has an apprehension of Him that is different

recognizes as an intermediary stage between unmeaning automaton-like speech and genuine philosophic understanding such an understanding of the fundamental truths taken by themselves which indeed remains dependent on trust in the wise men who possess true knowledge.[40] That the multitude should adopt such an attitude to the wise man seems Utopian to Spinoza: the multitude would be more likely to ridicule than to honor the philosopher who ventured to claim authority in matters spiritual (*Tractate*, p. 100 [Yaffe, p. 99]). This critique comes from considering as typical the philosopher living "cautiously" remote from the crowd, whereas Maimonides, by a standard by no means Utopian, has in mind the philosophically enlightened rabbi, who feels himself responsible for the guidance of the multitude and who enjoys the people's confidence. Thus this critique too has already its root in Spinoza's alienation from Judaism. Furthermore, Spinoza himself requires acknowledgment by the multitude of certain fundamental teachings which clearly must be understood if they are to fulfill their function of inculcating piety. To these *pia dogmata* [pious teachings], which are to be believed for the sake of piety and not for their truth, belong some propositions of which the intent is in full accord with the truths which Spinoza himself recognizes (e.g., the oneness, uniqueness, absolute knowledge, absolute right of God).[41] By this the intermediary stage, postulated by Maimonides, between total lack of understanding (or ignorance) and genuine philosophic knowledge is conceded. The difference shows itself only in the fact that Maimonides requires recognition of the fundamental truths (existence, unity, incorporeality, knowledge, power and eternity of God) for their own sake, and expressly distinguished from the socially required articles of faith (the punitive justice and the mercy of God). Recognition of *one* truth is to unite all men, the wise and the foolish. For faith given to untruth is idolatry, *sin*. Those who go astray on matters of faith are inexcusable; for even if they themselves are incapable of independent thinking, there is nothing to prevent them from seeking guidance from the wise.[42]

Spinoza's critique of the law is critique of sin, as sin against God. Does there exist, apart from all humanly constituted law, a law plainly imposed

---

from what He really is, but I shall say that he has abolished his belief in the existence of the deity without being aware of it.]

40. [221] *Guide* 1.50 (p. 180) [Pines, p. 111]; 1.33 (p. 117) [Pines, pp. 71–72]; 1.35 (pp. 132f.) [Pines, p. 81].
41. [222] *Tractate*, pp. 163f.; p. 151 [Yaffe, pp. 163–64; 150–51].
42. [223] *Guide* 1.35 (pp. 131f.) [Pines, pp. 80–81], 1.36 [Pines, pp. 82–85]; 3.28 (p. 214) [Pines, p. 512].

on all men, and of which transgression is sin? Is there human action which contravenes the will of God? For Spinoza, *this* is the question regarding the *lex divina*, and to the question understood in this sense his answer is No. However much he may agree with Maimonides on the purpose of the *lex divina*, according to him the means necessary for the highest aims of human life *may* be called "God's commandments" (*Tractate*, p. 46 [Yaffe, p. 46]); i.e., they are only improperly so called; for it is against reason to consider God as Lawgiver (*Tractate*, pp. 48–51 [Yaffe, pp. 47–50]). On the critique of God as lawgiver depends then the critique of the compatibility of philosophy and theology, of truth and piety, in one body of doctrine on revelation. The attempt made to prove a direct contradiction between the elements which Maimonides treats as united in Mosaic law comes to grief on this issue also. The same is true of Spinoza's critique of Maimonides' theory of prophecy. This doctrine also assumes the compatibility of two heterogeneous elements. For various reasons, Maimonides must distinguish between outer and inner meaning in Scripture, between the literal and the real meaning.[43] He must therefore present the act of prophetic perception in such a way that the co-existence of inner truth and expression by imagery becomes understandable. He therefore teaches that in the act of prophetic perception imagination and understanding work together, that the necessary condition for prophecy is the utmost perfection of both imagination and understanding in the prophet.[44] Spinoza, on the other hand, taking his stand on the unambiguous evidence of experience and of reason, denies the possibility of such cooperation of intelligence and imagination, that is, a cooperation of both in perfection: the stronger the power of understanding, the less the power of the imagination, and vice versa (*Tractate*, p. 15 [Yaffe, p. 17]). Maimonides does not deny that imagination, when it influences understanding, may impair and inhibit it. But he asserts that apart from the pernicious effect of imagination on understand-

43. [224] The basic reason is that in proper speech there is nothing to be said about God, except to state that He is beyond our comprehension. The second reason: if the literal meaning were the true meaning of Scripture, many statements made in Scripture would be contrary to truth, and this would be in conflict with the revealed nature of Scripture. The third reason is that the divine law fulfills its two functions at one and the same time, by regulating man's communal life by its outer meaning, and by communicating fundamental truths by its inner meaning. [See] *Guide* 1.Intro. (pp. 7–19) [Pines, pp. 5–12]. [In a different section of *Spinoza's Critique of Religion* trans. Elsa Sinclair (New York: Schocken, 1965), p. 256, Strauss shows the theme of "God as lawgiver" to have been seen by Spinoza in quite a different light, i.e., not as relates to philosophy, but rather as relates to piety and policy. In the section of the book which discusses Spinoza's conception of the Bible, Strauss emphasizes that Spinoza recognizes this notion as possessed of a much higher, and even permanent, worth: "By the idea of *Deus legislator*, Moses created the enduringly valid basis of piety."]

44. [225] *Guide* 2.32 (pp. 261f.) [Pines, p. 361].

ing, there is the highly beneficial effect of understanding on imagination. If man is entirely dominated by desire for knowledge, his imagination busies itself day and night with the object of his knowledge. So, this cooperation of imagination is far from impairing the dignity and power of prophecy, or robbing prophecy of all cognitive value; it vouches all the more for the prophet's being completely gripped by "active understanding," which is the precondition of all human knowledge.[45] Spinoza's critique thus presupposes the proof that understanding does not influence imagination as imagination influences understanding. This proof is contained in the critique of the conception of imagination shared by Maimonides with others, a critique which is a result of Descartes' revolution of science.

The critique of prophecy has the incontestable advantage over the critique of divine law, that it is immediately given with Spinoza's own doctrine, whereas the critique of divine law contradicts Spinoza's own doctrine. But even for the former the same result holds at which one arrives if one traces the critique of divine law back to its root: it presupposes the constitution of Spinoza's philosophy. The attempt to demonstrate that there is an inherent contradiction in Maimonides' doctrine has failed. This attempt had to be made, if the opponent was to be driven *ad absurdum* as far as possible on his own ground.

Now it might be said in particular of the critique of the doctrine of prophecy—and a corresponding comment might be made on all other parts of the critique of Maimonides: no more is needed than the proof that the opinions of various prophets contradict each other in their assertions on God, and that these opinions are vulgar; for with this proof, independently of all critique of the concepts of understanding and imagination, it is established that the words of the prophets have no cognitive value. In other words, what seems to be immediately available as the plane of the critique is not only Maimonides' philosophy but also Scripture. But Spinoza's critique of Maimonides on the basis of Scripture presupposes that the literal meaning is the true meaning of Scripture. This presupposition is however rejected in principle by Maimonides, since it would lead to conclusions that would contradict the revealed character of Scripture. Therefore, before argument can be taken up against Maimonides on the basis of Scripture, his hermeneutics must be called into question. In his explicit and coherent critique of Maimonides' hermeneutics (*Tractate*, pp. 99–102 [Yaffe, pp. 97–100]), Spinoza ar-

---

45. [226] Ibid., 2.36 (pp. 281–84) [Pines, pp. 369–71].

gues to some extent on the basis of findings from his own Bible science. This line of argument presupposes the critique of Maimonides' hermeneutics, and is therefore circular. For that reason, we shall not consider it. We shall further disregard the argument based on the assumption that the multitude is incapable of directing its life by the precepts of philosophy, and thus, as has already been shown, presupposes the alienation from Judaism. There then remain two arguments which require more precise scrutiny.

Spinoza calls up against Maimonides' principle of interpretation an insight, sharpened by the Reformation and by humanism, into the actual meaning and purport of the Scriptural text, which must be allowed to stand, and which may not be turned or twisted, or highhandedly and arbitrarily interpreted. Spinoza sees as lacking from Maimonides' exegesis the requisite prudence and caution, exclusion of his preconceived opinions. He voices his astonishment over the lack of scruple with which Maimonides disregards the most obvious counterinstances, and the headlong license with which he adapts Scripture to his preconceived opinions. Spinoza's scientifically trained mind forbids the allegorical interpretation of Scripture. The scientific, "unprejudiced" attitude towards Scripture, to which he makes claim, and by virtue of which he has the possibility of rejecting Scripture, is however in itself not so much a presupposition as a consequence of radical critique of revealed religion. Maimonides' interpretation of Scripture, even in its most venturesome moments, and particularly in these—through which the original meaning of Scripture is apparently or in fact put aside in favor of philosophemes, i.e., doctrines totally alien to Scripture—is nevertheless guided by concern with Scripture. This concern springs from concern with the conduct required of man, required of the Jew, by Scripture. On the other hand, Spinoza's scientific approach to Scripture presupposes total absence of any concern with Scripture, of any need for Scripture; in a word, freedom from prejudice, i.e., alienation from Judaism.

The second argument against Maimonides' hermeneutics to be considered here runs: if the true meaning of a passage in Scripture can be brought out only by the interpretation of the passage with a view to the truth of the matter spoken of in the passage, then that objective truth must have been established beyond doubt.[46] Spinoza robs this central objection of some of its

---

46. [227] "... adeoque de verso sensu Scripturae, quantumvis claro, non poterit (i.e., Maimonides) esse certus, quamdiu de rei veritate dubitare poterit, aut quamdiu de eadem ipsi non constet. Nam quamdiu de rei veritate non constat, tamdiu nescimus, an res cum ratione conveniat, an vero eidem repugnet;

substance by the comment which he adds to it, that the objective truth on the matters mentioned in Scripture is never capable of being established by the light of natural reason. This comment does not amount to a great deal. For to Spinoza the fact that "almost everything which is to be found in Scripture cannot be deduced from facts known by the natural light," amounts to nothing less than stating that the greater part of Scripture is indubitably in conflict with objective truth—and in so doing Spinoza implies that objective truth is established and at our disposal. The objection under consideration has a meaning almost entirely hidden by Spinoza's explanation, the same meaning as the critique of the knowability of miracles. This meaning of his objection is, in fact, that Maimonides' interpretation of Scripture in regard to objective truth is essentially interpretation guided by the teaching of Aristotle. For Aristotle is the philosopher par excellence. Admittedly, Aristotle is not infallible: it is to be conceded that in astronomy and mathematics for instance he has been superseded by later investigations. His science applies truly only to the sublunary world.[47] Nevertheless his investigations essentially span the whole realm accessible to human reason. Only on the assumption of such a completion of science is the principle of interpretation adopted by Maimonides capable of application. As long as reason is not yet in full possession of the truth, as long as reason must have doubts and is therefore imperfect, it cannot bring to light the (assumed) perfect truth of Scripture; it would draw Scripture into its own uncertainty and incompleteness. Not until science is completed and perfect can it unlock the mysteries of Scripture. The final interpretation of Scripture, therefore, is an impossible undertaking on the basis of the essentially progressive, hence always imperfect new science. The type of theory with which Maimonides is confronted refuses itself far less to the identification with revelation than does the opposite type which Spinoza has in mind. This holds quite apart from the difference in the substantive assertions. The emergence of positive science living in the limitless horizon of future tasks and discoveries makes Maimonides' principle of interpretation im-

---

et consequenter etiam tamdiu nescimus, an literalis sensus verus sit an falsus" (*Tractate*, p. 100). ["... he (i.e., Maimonides) could not be certain about the true sense of Scripture, however clear, so long as he could doubt the truth of the matter or so long as the truth about it was not established for him. For so long as the truth of the matter is not established, we do not know whether the matter agrees with reason or instead conflicts with it. And consequently we do not know whether the literal sense is true or false either" {Yaffe, p. 98}.]

47. **[228]** *Guide* 2.19 [Pines, pp. 302–12]; 2.22 (p. 179) [Pines, pp. 319–20]; 2.24 (pp. 193f.) [Pines, pp. 326–27].

possible of acceptance. Accepting it would have the absurd consequence, for instance, that the account of creation would have to be interpreted anew with each advance made in geology, paleontology, and other relevant sciences.

Even the critique of Maimonides' hermeneutics is thus not in the first place critique on Maimonides' own ground. It presupposes the constitution of the new, ever developing science—assuming that this critique does not demand scientific reserve in interpretation of Scripture as a matter of course, and that it therefore presupposes the alienation from Judaism. Therefore the constitution of the new science is presupposed also in the critique on the basis of Scripture, a critique rendered possible by the critique of Maimonides' hermeneutics. Critique of hermeneutics is part of that critique which sets out to demonstrate on Maimonides' own ground the incompatibility of the elements, namely, philosophy and revelation, which Maimonides believes to be compatible. This critique becomes possible, as has been shown now regarding all its parts, only because Spinoza takes his conception of philosophy, or even his critique of *Deus legislator* or his alienation from Judaism, for granted. Therefore Spinoza's critique of Maimonides is not to be understood as at bottom an attempt to separate philosophy and theology from one another. It is not worth wasting a word on this separation, if "philosophy" is understood in Spinoza's sense.

2) The critique on the basis of modern metaphysics

Spinoza's critique of Maimonides is carried out on four different planes of argument:

(1) On the basis of Maimonides' science, as critique of the inherent untenability of that science;
(2) On the basis of the literal meaning of Scripture, as critique of Maimonides' conception of revelation;
(3) On the basis of history, as critique of the revealed character of the Torah;
(4) On the basis of philosophy, as critique of the possibility of revelation as such.

The critique on the basis of Maimonides' science, and even more the critique on the basis of Scripture, is to be put aside as untenable. As far as the historical critique is concerned, this is possible against Maimonides only as critique of the Jewish tradition regarding the revealed character of the Torah.

But, as has already been mentioned, Spinoza criticizes the Jewish tradition only casually. From his point of view, the critique of the Jewish tradition is of only slight importance. Thus the main weight of the critique is brought to bear on the possibility of revelation as such. This critique is not exposed to fundamental objections, since Maimonides has attempted to construct his doctrine on scientific grounds.

The question, Is revelation possible at all?, is in the nature of things not the primary question within the philosophic critique, which—with a view to its final and complete result—can be taken as providing the answer to the question posed. That question does not stand out as the primary question if we bear in mind what Maimonides' position was. The basis of this position is the analysis of the actual order of the world. The problem of revelation becomes necessary only when one faces the limiting question: creation of the world or eternity of the world?

Therefore, after eliminating the three other stages of the critique, the first question to be faced on the plane of the philosophic critique is:

Is it possible to ascend from analysis of the actual order of the world to theology and to revelation? This question, which Spinoza treats most clearly in his critique of whether miracles can be known as such, is the central theme of the positive critique, which is to be distinguished from the metaphysical critique by the fact that metaphysical critique casts doubt on the legitimacy of starting from the analysis of the actual order of the world and therefore seems to be more radical than the positive critique. Since the positive critique has already been treated in the analysis of the critique of orthodoxy, we shall here do no more than investigate the metaphysical critique. The essential difference between the two kinds of critique becomes manifest from the clear difference between the two assertions which Spinoza adduces in order to contest the knowability of miracles:

(1) No good reason suggests that we should attribute limited power and force to nature.
(2) The power of nature is infinite, and no event occurs that does not follow from the laws of nature (*Tractate*, pp. 69, 76 [Yaffe, pp. 69, 76]).

The second assertion assumes Spinoza's metaphysics, as appears from all the reasons adduced by Spinoza; the first assertion is independent of this metaphysics, of any metaphysics. It is grounded exclusively in the insight that not all the laws of nature are known to us. It therefore stands clear of the two diametrically opposed "dogmatic" assertions: "the power of nature is limited," "the power of nature is unlimited." Now one may doubt whether positive science, living within a limitless horizon of questioning and questing, could ever have arisen at all, had not the concept of infinity in modern metaphysics opened the way. But on the basis of the development, which found its first completion in Kant's discussion of the antinomies of pure reason, one cannot doubt that the completely open character of positive science is in itself independent of the "dogmatic" assertion of infinity. Indeed, if this assertion otherwise is indeed "dogmatic," then positive science is not only independent of that concept, but actually, as soon as positive science has arrived at a sufficient understanding of itself, is seen to be incompatible with that assertion. In spite of the ultimate opposition between the positive mind and the spirit of modern metaphysics, the content of modern metaphysics is more favorable to positive science than was the content of earlier metaphysics; and, moreover, the positive mind is itself the basis of modern metaphysics.

A) THE CONCEPT OF PREJUDICE AND MODERN METAPHYSICS. The word "prejudice" is the most appropriate expression for the dominant theme of the Enlightenment movement, for the will to free, open-minded investigation: "prejudice" is the unambiguous polemical correlate of the all too ambiguous term "freedom." True, the Enlightenment itself introduced other prejudices, which took the place previously occupied by the prejudices which the new had dislodged. The Enlightenment never in fact completely freed itself from the very prejudices which it set out to eliminate and destroy. But this means no more than that the Enlightenment was itself only imperfectly "enlightenment"; it is no radical objection to the intent of the Enlightenment because the objection is itself made in accordance with that intent, but above all since every age suffers the same fate. Each age can judge only on the basis of its own experiences, and therefore it judges, whether expressly or tacitly, on future experiences, and in so doing also on those past experiences which will themselves become comprehensible only in the light of future experiences. But since every age has its own experiences, and, in principle, the capability of holding strictly to its experiences in its judgments, the admonition to freedom from prejudice is meaningful. The particular character of the Enlightenment is due primarily to the unforgettable insistence with which it first of all proclaimed this admonition.

From the will to pursue knowledge, to see things with one's own eyes, to submit judgment unconditionally to observation and reflection, comes the struggle against prejudice. This struggle is in no need of justification over against the human inclination to take the easy way. Because the Enlightenment understood its struggle against prejudice as a battle against taking the easy way and against inertia, and fought the battle on these terms, it failed to recognize the questionable character of its fight. The justification—and at the same time the questionable character of "prejudice" as a category—does not come to light until revealed religion is taken into consideration. No one denies that the traditions of revealed religion have brought down from past ages many "prejudices," in the common usage of the term, in their train. But this important obvious fact is external or, at the most symptomatic. What is important is that revealed religion essentially appeals to a fact that is prior to all human judgment, to the revelation made by God, the King of the world. However spacious the field in which the judgment of later generations is permitted to range in approaching this event, what counts in the final instance, according to the meaning of revelation itself, is what is written: "Not with our fathers did the Lord make this covenant, but with us, who are all of us here alive this day" [Deut. 5:3]. The present of revelation is quite other than the present of experience, in which the positive mind lives, and this by reason of the fact that the latter experience is and wishes to be immediate experience, to be as close as possible to the experienced, whereas the immediate hearing of revelation quenches the will to immediacy, and calls forth the desire for non-presence, for mediacy. Those who indeed hear revelation cannot will that they hear it immediately: "They said unto Moses: speak thou with us, and we shall hearken: and let not God speak with us, for we shall surely die" [Exod. 20:16]. They cannot summon the *will* to approach so close as to see with their own eyes: "the people saw, then trembled and stayed afar" [Exod. 20:15]. If the will to mediated hearing of revelation is grounded in actual hearing of revelation, then the tradition of revealed religion, and with this the obedience to the tradition and the fidelity to that tradition, is grounded in the actual hearing of the present revelation. Then all critique of prejudice, and even more, all critique of the "rigidity" of the tradition from the point of view of "experience," cannot touch the seriousness and the depth of the *will*, grounded in immediate hearing, to mediacy.[48]

48. [229] The will to mediacy of hearing, not merely the actual mediacy of hearing, is the element of revealed religion. In his polemic against the attempts made to understand Scripture from the "religious experience" of the prophets, Friedrich Gogarten on his side misses the point when he completely denies that (in the Scriptural sense) God is heard by men without mediation. He states in his *Theologische Tra-*

When the prophets call their people to account, they reproach them not only on account of this or that transgression, but they recognize as the root and the meaning of all particular transgressions the fact that the people had deserted their God. It is on account of this falling away that the prophets reproach the people. At one time, in the past, the people was faithful; now it is fallen away; in the future, God will restore it to its original state. The natural, original, pristine is *fidelity*; what has to be accounted for, and what is not accountable for, is the falling away.

If what is required of man in relation to God is fidelity, trust, and obedience, then above all what is required is trust when all human assurance fails, obedience when all human insight fails. In this spirit Abraham ibn Daud, Maimonides' forerunner, justifies the superiority of the revealed commandments, which are beyond human understanding, to the rational commandments. The high example is the obedience of Abraham who made ready to sacrifice his son at the command of God, even though God had promised

---

dition und theologische Arbeit (Leipzig, 1927), p. 12, n. 2, "Man wird vielleicht auf die alttestamentlichen Propheten . . . verweisen, um zu zeigen, dass es auch ein Wort gibt, das Gott dem Menschen unmittelbar sagt. Aber das scheint mir ein Missverständnis zu sein. Denn bei den Propheten ist es ganz klar, dass sie Gottes Wort nur hören in ihrer strengen Gebundenheit an das Volk, und das heisst bei ihnen ja wirklich nicht an eine nationale Idee, sondern an den Nächsten. Es heisst doch, alles vergessen, was die Propheten sagen, sie in dem, was sie sagen, nicht ernst nehmen, wenn man nicht sieht, dass diese Männer kein individuelles, oder wie wir dafür auch gerne sagen, rein religiöses Verhältnis zu Gott gehabt haben, und dass sie gerade als Propheten in der engsten Gebundenheit an ihr Volk und die strengste Verantwortlichkeit ihm gegenüber das Gotteswort hören und sprechen." ["One might perhaps refer to the Old Testament prophets, . . . in order to show that there is also a Word which God communicates unmediated to man. However, it seems to me that this is a misunderstanding. For with the prophets it is entirely clear that they hear God's Word only in close connection with the people; and that really means for them not indeed (connected) with a national idea, but rather with the fellowman. This, however, means—though everyone forgets it—that what the prophets say and the way in which they say it is not taken seriously if one fails to see that these men did not have an individual—or as we instead also like to say, a purely religious—relation to God, but that precisely as prophets they hear and speak God's Word (only) in nearest connection with their people and in strictest responsibility for them" {editor's own translation}.]

Here only this is justified, and it is indeed justified without any reservation whatsoever, that the prophets were not *concerned* with their "direct experience," but with their demands and their announcements; that proper understanding of the prophets is possible to begin with only if we start from what they demand and announce: that therefore the question of what they "experience" is possible only on the basis of radical misunderstanding—or radical critique. Gogarten however himself controverts his important insight by his entirely "metaphysical" assertion that even the prophets do not hear God without mediation. Once Gogarten has taken his stand on a plane which is essentially indifferent, the objection must be put to him on that same level, that the prophets—even if they heard God's word only "by virtue of their close union with their nation"—nevertheless did not receive their message from their nation, but directly from God. The attempt to even out the distinction between prophet and nonprophet, to deny the fact of this difference—a distinction existentially irrelevant but no less factual for that—is symptomatic of a position from which miracles in the strict sense can no longer be asserted, not even accidentally.

him that his son should be his heir, even though Abraham, had he wished to pretend to wisdom, could not but find that command absurd.[49]

The attitude of obedience, if it allows inquiry at all, limits inquiry, not from without, but by permeating inquiry itself. In the beginning was the revelation. Inquiry is nothing other than making the revelation fully one's own, elucidating it. As such, it is limited. At these limits, the living obedience, which is effective throughout, becomes visible. Obedience does not arise at the end of the inquiry as a makeshift but precedes all inquiry.

Defection can be spoken of only if fidelity is primary. The perfection of the origin is the condition that makes sin possible. If sin is actual, the forgiveness and the restoration into the pristine state is of the future, and then there is suffering for the past which is present, and there is hope for the future.

The positive mind, which rebels against revealed religion, is characterized precisely by this: that it looks toward the future, not merely hoping for it, but rather using its own powers to build the future, and that it does not suffer from the past. The positive mind is incapable of suffering from the past, since it has not lost an original perfection by a Fall, but has by its own effort worked itself out of the original imperfection, barbarism, and rudeness. What is felt from within as fidelity, as obedience, appears to the positive mind as stupidity, imprisonment in prejudices. To that mind, "rebellion" is "liberation," "to become an apostate" is "liberty." The contraries prejudice-freedom correspond strictly to the contraries obedience-rebellion, and strictly contradict them.

From the attitude of obedience, rebellion can never arise. Every rebellion presupposes readiness and capacity for rebellion, liberty to reject Scripture, "as we reject the Qur'an and the Talmud," hence rebellion itself. There is no gradual transition in this. Apostasy as such is not to be justified. Therefore

---

49. [230] [Abraham ibn Daud,] *Emunah ramah*, at the end. [See *Ha-Emunah ha-Ramah*, Hebrew trans. Solomon Even Lavi, and German trans. Samson Weil (Frankfurt am Main, 1852; reprint, Berlin, 1919, and Jerusalem, 1967); *The Exalted Faith*, trans. Norbert Samuelson, and ed. Gershon Weiss (Rutherford, NJ: Fairleigh Dickinson University Press, 1986), pp. 265–66 (p. 217a, ll. 1–8; Hebrew edition, p. 298):

> Afterward, He commanded (Abraham) to offer a sacrifice and (Abraham) did not want to become sophistical and debate (the claim by) saying, "Where are the notable assurances and the notable expectations that You promised?" Rather, he risked fulfilling His commandments and he had faith that there is no proportion to his knowledge in relation to the knowledge of God, may He be exalted. This way of (Abraham) was not concealed from God, may He be exalted. Rather, since He intended that his conduct and his character be a model (that) those like him perform who hearken to (and) accept (the will of) God, and (by this) example they set their internal direction to (God's commandment), (thus,) these values are fine notions that improve the way of wisdom, because they are the difference and the distinction between heresy and faith.]

it is of no account which particular grounds Spinoza adduces for his own apostasy. The critique in its entirety is contained in the question: is what is called apostasy indeed apostasy? Is not what is given prior to inquiry in fact prejudice?

With a view to the radical meaning of revealed religion it must be said: there exists *the* prejudice pure and simple. Therefore freedom—falling away from revelation—also exists. Therefore the struggle of the Enlightenment against prejudice has an absolute meaning. For this reason the age of prejudice and the age of freedom can stand opposed to one another. For the age of freedom it is essential that it be preceded by the age of prejudice. "Prejudice" is an historical category. This precisely constitutes the difference between the struggle of the Enlightenment against prejudices and the struggle against appearance and opinion with which philosophy began its secular journey.

What has been said so far is valid for the positive notion of "prejudice," from which the metaphysical conception of "prejudice" is derived, and from which it diverges. The peculiar meaning of the metaphysical concept is expressed in classic style, in its simplest and strongest form, in Descartes' resolve to doubt of everything in order to free himself once and for all from all prejudices. Once in one's life, one must doubt of everything if one desires to liberate oneself from all prejudices—this is what Descartes demands. Once in one's life—the fresh beginning once made, the entirely primary and entirely decisive beginning once found, when the domain of truth has been measured by paces absolutely certain, when the structure of science has been erected on foundations absolutely certain, there is no longer any place left for doubt. One makes a beginning so as to arrive at the end. And the end is reached when in principle all questions, all questions of principle, have been answered. In this way philosophy is intended as completed science, while the positive open science is being founded.

Descartes' metaphysics is connected with the positive mind not only through the fact that his *Meditationes de prima philosophia* [*Meditations on First Philosophy*] expressly excludes everything "which bears on faith or on the conduct of life," and pursues the goal of "finally establishing something fixed and permanent in the sciences," but also by the explicit divergence in the treatment of the very metaphysical problem from scholastic metaphysics. This divergence is an essential moment in Spinoza's critique of Maimonides. When Descartes is asked why he had departed from the way carved out by Thomas Aquinas and by Aristotle, he first adduces these two reasons: (1) the existence of God is far more evident than the existence of any object of sense;

(2) by following the chain of causes I can but come to a knowledge of the imperfection of my understanding, but from such knowledge nothing follows regarding the existence of God; therefore, knowledge of God is not possible on the basis of analysis of the actual order of the world. This result of positive critique is thus the presupposition underlying Descartes' founding that kind of metaphysics which liberates positive investigation of natural causes from all limitations, which replaces the traditional ascent from physics to theology by the descent from theology to physics; knowledge of God is possible only on the basis of my knowledge of myself, not so much by asking myself from what cause I came forth in the past, but rather by what cause am I preserved in the present.[50] The foundation of metaphysics is to be what is present, what is available as present. The "liberation from every sequence of causes" and "liberation from all prejudices" have the same, positive intention as basis.

50. [231] "Primo itaque, non desumpsi meum argumentum ex eo quod viderem in sensibilibus esse ordinem sive successionem quandam causarum efficientium; tum quia Deum existere multo evidentius esse putavi, quam ullas res sensibiles; tum etiam quia per istam causarum successionem non videbar alio posse devenire, quam ad imperfectionem intellectus mei agnoscendam, quod nempe non possim comprehendere quomodo infinitae tales causae sibi mutuo ab aeterno ita successerint, ut nulla fuerit prima. Nam certe, ex eo quod istud non possim comprehendere, non sequitur aliquam primam esse debere, ut neque ex eo quod non possim etiam comprehendere infinitas divisiones in quantitate finita, sequitur aliquam dari ultimam, ita ut ulterius dividi non possit; sed tantum sequitur intellectum meum, qui est finitus, non capere infinitum. Itaque malui uti pro fundamento meae rationis existentia mei ipsius, quae a nulla causarum serie dependet, mihique tam nota est ut nihil notius esse possit; et de me non tam quaesivi a qua causa *olim* essem productus, quam a qua tempore *praesenti* conserver, *ut ita me ab omni causarum successione liberarem*." Descartes, *Meditationes, Primae Responsiones* (ed. princ., pp. 139f.). ["Firstly then, I did not base my arguments on the fact that I observed there to be an order or succession of efficient causes among the objects perceived by the senses. For one thing, I regarded the existence of God as much more evident than the existence of anything that can be perceived by the senses; for another thing, I did not think that such a succession of causes could lead me anywhere except to a recognition of the imperfection of my intellect, since an infinite chain of such successive causes from eternity without any first cause is beyond my grasp. And my inability to grasp it certainly does not entail that there must be a first cause, any more than my inability to grasp the infinite number of divisions in a finite quantity entails that there is an ultimate division beyond which any further division is impossible. All that follows is that my intellect, which is finite, does not encompass the infinite. Hence I preferred to use my own existence as the basis of my argument, since it does not depend on any chain of causes and is better known to me than anything else could possibly be. And the question I asked concerning myself was not the cause that *originally* produced me, but what is the cause that preserves me *at present. In this way I aimed to escape the whole issue of the succession of causes.*" René Descartes, "Author's Replies to the First Set of Objections," in *The Philosophical Writings of Descartes*, trans. John Cottingham, Robert Stoothoff, and Dugald Murdoch (Cambridge: Cambridge University Press, 1984), vol. II, p. 77 (Adam and Tannery, pp. 106–7). The emphases on certain passages have been added by Strauss. Strauss's references to "Adam and Tannery" are to *Oeuvres de Descartes*, ed. Charles Adam and Paul Tannery, 11 vols. (Paris: Vrin, 1983). It has been revised and corrected during the last century, but Strauss probably used the original edition (12 vols.) of 1896–1909.] Cf. Spinoza, *Tractate*, p. 16: "Et proh dolor! res eo iam pervenit, ut, qui aperte fatentur, se Dei ideam non habere et Deum non nisi per res creatas (quarum causae ignorant) cognoscere, non erubescant philosophos atheismi accusare." ["And alas! the matter has by now gone so far that those who openly confess that they have no idea of God and do not know God except through created things (of whose causes they are ignorant) are not ashamed to accuse Philosophers of Atheism" {Yaffe, p. 17}.]

In this sense Spinoza constructs his system. This system does not begin with the analysis of the actual world-order, but with elements that are beyond all doubt, i.e., with "certain very simple concepts" with which what relates to the nature of God is connected. Thus it is proved that God necessarily exists, is omnipresent, that everything that exists has the ground of its being in God, and that all our conceptions involve in themselves the nature of God, and are conceived through it.[51] Thus it is proved that nothing could have been produced by God in any other manner and in any other order than that in which it was in fact produced. Therefore any reasoning based on analysis of the actual order of the world is in principle impossible against Spinoza.

B) THE CRITIQUE OF PROPHECY. With Descartes' fundamental doubt, through which the final liberation from all prejudices, the final foundation of science is to be achieved, the notion of knowledge is posited from which Spinoza's critique of Maimonides' doctrine of prophecy follows. It has already been mentioned that the decisive element in this doctrine is the conception of the imagination. Maimonides presupposes the Aristotelian analysis of imagination (*De anima*, Gamma 3) by which the relation of imagination to sensory perception and to intelligence is thus defined: in the first place, imagination is inferior to sensory perception and to the intellect, in that the latter are as such truthful, whereas imagination is in most cases deceptive. Secondly, imagination is superior to sensory perception in that imagination is capable of functioning without sensory perception, for instance during sleep. Imagination is thus essentially distinguished from sensory perception. Therefore critique of imagination is in no sense critique of sensory perception. Maimonides' critique of sensory perception is exclusively directed against the sensory conception of what is supersensory, against the conception of the incorporeal as corporeal, or necessarily linked to the body. This false conception is however not due to sensory perception, but to imagination.[52] Further, since imagination can function independently of sensory perception, there exists the possibility that the intellect may force imagination into its service for perceiving the supersensory: hence the possibility of prophecy.

---

51. [**232**] Cf. *Tractate*, adnot. vi, in which Spinoza refers to his own presentation of Descartes' theory [Yaffe, pp. 240–41]. ["Adnot." refers to Spinoza's own annotations at the end of the *Theologico-Political Treatise*, trans. Yaffe, pp. 239–52. Annotation 6, Yaffe, pp. 240–41, concerns whether God's existence is self-evident.]

52. [**233**] *Guide* 1.26 (pp. 88ff.) [Pines, pp. 56–57]; 1.49 (pp. 176f.) [Pines, pp. 109–10]; 1.51 (p. 182) [Pines, p. 112]. Cf. *Millot ha-Higayon* VIII. [See "Logic," in *Ethical Writings*, trans. Weiss and Butterworth, pp. 59–104, with a complete translation of "Chapter Eight," pp. 156–58.]

Spinoza's critique of this doctrine of prophecy follows from the conception of knowledge posited by Descartes' radical doubt. Radical doubt is directed as much against whatever is not fully certain and indubitable as against what is manifestly false. What is accepted as true on the evidence of the senses is from the outset liable to come under doubt, and therefore to be rejected. In this step it is taken as decisive ground for dubiety that everything which is perceived by the senses in waking life may equally well be encountered in dream. Anything perceived by the senses might equally well be the work of imagination. Otherwise expressed: the knowledge proved beyond all possibility of doubt must stand beyond the difference between waking and dream, between sensory perception and imagination. Only mathematically certain knowledge fully meets this supreme demand. Judged by this demand, the difference between sensory perception and imagination loses its weight. In our context, it is of no importance that from this point of view the fear of *Deus deceptor* [a God who deceives] besets even mathematical certainty, and that, in order to counter this most radical of all suspicions, the *cogito, sum* [I think, therefore I am] is discovered as fundamental fact. The assessment of imagination is not modified by these considerations. Even after the discovery of the *necessario sum* [I who am certain that I am, or, I who necessarily exist] and of the *sum res cogitans* [I am a thing that thinks] there still remains: *fieri posse ut omnes istae imagines, et generaliter quaecumque ad corporis naturam referentur, nihil sint praeter insomnia* [at the same time that all such images and, in general, everything relating to the nature of the body, could be mere dreams].[53] It is true that certainty of the existence and of the goodness of God guarantees in principle the truth of sensory perception, the difference between waking and dreaming; yet the definition of true knowledge, as not to be impaired by the fact that it may have occurred in dream, is retained: *nam certe, quamvis somniarem, si quid intellectui meo sit evidens, illud omnino est verum* [for even though I might be dreaming, if there is anything which is evident to my intellect, then it is wholly true].[54]

Spinoza draws the conclusion. He no longer distinguishes, in his division

---

53. [234] *Meditations*, ed. princ., pp. 22f. [See René Descartes, "Meditations on First Philosophy: Second Meditation," in *The Philosophical Writings of Descartes*, vol. II, p. 19 (Adam and Tannery, p. 28). For *"necessario sum,"* "(I who) necessarily exist," see ibid., "Second Meditation," p. 17 (Adam and Tannery, p. 25); for *"sum res cogitans"* ("I am a thing that thinks," or, "I am a thinking thing"), see ibid., "Second Meditation," pp. 18 and 19 (Adam and Tannery, pp. 27 and 28), and "Third Meditation," p. 24 (Adam and Tannery, p. 34).]

54. [235] Ibid., pp. 86f. [*The Philosophical Writings of Descartes*, "Fifth Meditation," p. 49 (Adam and Tannery, p. 71).]

of forms of perception, between sensory perception and imagination. The lowest form of knowledge, *opinio vel imaginatio* [opinion or imagination], is in principle liable to error, whereas rational and intuitive knowledge are in truth (*Ethica* II, 40, scholium 2) ["This kind of knowing advances from an adequate idea of the formal essence of certain attributes of God to the adequate knowledge of the essence of things"]. This means indeed immediately that it is sensory perception rather than imagination which falls to a lower rating. But since the distinction between sensory perception and imagination thus loses its importance at the same time, legitimate cooperation between imagination and intellect in an act of perception can as little be conceded any more as previously, on Maimonides' assumptions, cooperation could be conceded between sensory perception and understanding in the knowledge of incorporeal being. Imagination and understanding exclude each other. All the more is the heightened activity of imagination, which is evident in all the prophets (and admitted by Maimonides also) an unmistakable sign that the prophets were particularly poorly endowed for purely intellectual activity (*Tractate*, p. 15 [Yaffe, p. 17]).

The matter does not however rest at this stage, that sensory perception and imagination are rejected together, in such a way that the difference between them becomes in the final issue a matter of indifference. But to the extent that the undeniable difference between perception and imagination, as the difference between *waking* and *dreaming*, is taken into account, the rejection of perception and imagination together reflects the *absolute* preference for waking as against dreaming. Whether and to what extent this preference is not already an essential motive in the Cartesian proposition of philosophic doubt cannot be investigated here. For Spinoza in any case it is a matter of course—so much a matter of course that he mentions it only in passing—that dream-perception is altogether valueless. On the other hand, the evaluation of dream, as in certain respects superior to the waking condition, is characteristic of the position which he is contesting.[55] Thus the outcome for Spinoza

---

55. [236] *Tractate*, pp. 3-6 [Yaffe, pp. 3-6], in particular p. 6 [Yaffe, p. 6], the "clear corroboration" by Num. 12:6-7. On p. 4: "... in somnis, tempore scilicet, quo imaginatio maxime naturaliter apta est, ad res, quae non sunt, imaginandum" ["... in dreams (at the time when the imagination is most capable of imagining things that are not)" {Yaffe, p. 3}]. Maimonides' doctrine of prophecy (and that of the "philosophers" of his age) is based on the traditional doctrine of the veridical dream; cf. for instance, Averroes' Paraphrase to Aristotle's *De somniis* (Venice, 1560), VII, 169: "Dicamus igitur quod istarum comprehensionum quaedam dicuntur somnia, et quaedam divinationes, et quaedam prophetiae. Et quidam homines negant ista, et dicunt ea contingere casu. Sed negare ea est negare sensata. Et maxime negare vera somnia. Nullus enim homo est, qui non viderit somnium, quod non enunciaverit ei aliquod futurum ... sermo de istis omnibus idem est, et sermo de quiditate somnii sufficiet: quia esse eorum non differunt nisi secun-

is that prophetic perception is cognitively inferior to sensory perception—or, at the most, of no greater value.

Midway between the critique of Spinoza the renegade and that of Maimonides the believing Jew, there stands the new founding of science by Descartes the Catholic. In other words, from Descartes' assumptions, Spinoza's radical critique of religion does not inevitably and immediately follow. Nevertheless it must be stated that once Maimonides' position is adopted, once the union of faith and knowledge peculiar to his position is accepted as the point of departure, adoption of Cartesianism cannot but lead to critique of religion. This shows most plainly in Spinoza's critique of Maimonides' theory of prophecy. Maimonides, by not accepting, as do the Christian theologians,[56] an essential

---

dum magis et minus, sed tantum differunt secundum nomina propter hoc quod vulgus dicit. Dicunt enim quod somnia sunt ab Angelis; et divinationes a Daemonibus; et prophetiae a Deo, aut cum medio, aut sine medio. Et Aristoteles non fuit locutus nisi tantum de somniis." [An English translation of Averroes' text is offered in what follows; it is close to but not identical with what Strauss utilizes of the Latin version. What follows is a translation based on the Arabic and Hebrew versions, and not only on the Latin version consulted by Strauss: "We say that of these perceptions there are some that are called dreams, others that are called divination, and still others that are called prophecy. Many people have denied the existence of this class of perceptions and have attributed to chance the existence of any such perceptions as may appear. Other people have affirmed such perceptions, and still others have affirmed some and denied others. To reject their existence is tantamount to rejecting the existence of sense-objects, and especially the existence of true dreams; for there is not a person who has not at times had dreams that warn him of that which will happen in the future.... It will suffice to state concerning these dreams that they differ to a greater or lesser degree, that is to say, their causes do. Indeed the names of these perceptions differ only because of the difference in the opinions of people regarding the causes of these perceptions. The latter is a well-known fact, for people think that dreams come from angels, divination from demons, and prophecy from God.... Of these latter kinds of matters Aristotle treats only in connection with dreams." See Averroes, *Epitome of "Parva Naturalia,"* trans. and ed. Harry Blumberg (Cambridge, MA: Medieval Academy of America, 1961), pp. 39–40.] Scientific insights cannot possibly occur in dreams (p. 171). There is a striking similarity between Spinoza's Epistle 17 and Aristotle's *De divinatione per somnum* 464a27ff. [Aristotle, *On Prophecy in Sleep*, ed. and trans. W. S. Hett (Cambridge, MA: Harvard University Press {Loeb Classical Library}, 1957), 464a27ff., p. 383: "For some cases of vivid dreams there are particular explanations, e.g., the fact that men have special foresight about their friends is because those who are great friends care about each other: for just as they are especially apt to perceive and recognize each other at a distance, so too in the case of impulses; for the impulses of familiar friends are themselves more familiar." Spinoza, *Complete Works*, vol. 2, letter XVII (in the Van Vloten edition), trans. R. H. M. Elwes (London: George Bell, 1901), pp. 325–26, letter to Peter Balling, 20 July 1664: "(The imagination) may, therefore, imagine a future event as forcibly and vividly, as though it were present; for instance, a father (to take an example resembling your own) loves his child so much, that he and the beloved child are, as it were, one and the same. And since (like that which I demonstrated on another occasion) there must necessarily exist in thought the idea of the essence of the child's states and their results, and since the father, through his union with his child, is a part of the said child, the soul of the father must necessarily participate in the ideal essence of the child and his states, and in their results, as I have shown at greater length elsewhere. Again, as the soul of the father participates ideally in the consequences of his child's essence, he may (as I have said) sometimes imagine some of the said consequences as vividly as if they were present with him."]

56. **[237]** Thomas Aquinas, *Summa theologica* III, qu. 172, art. I; Calvin, *In harmoniam ex Matthaeo, Marco, et Luca compositam Commentarii* (ed. Tholuck), I, 51 [John Calvin, *A Harmony of the Gospels, Matthew, Mark, and Luke*, trans. A. W. Morrison, ed. David F. Torrance and Thomas F. Torrance (Grand Rapids, MI: Eerdmans, 1972)], and also the *Commentary on Daniel*, 2:2; 2:4; 4:4f.; [Samuel] Maresius,

difference between the natural dream, and the dream that is bestowed by grace, but by understanding prophecy as potentiality only from what is essential to man as man, binds up his theory of prophecy so closely with his own conception of man, and in particular with the Aristotelian conception of sensory perception and of imagination, that his theory stands or falls according to acceptance or rejection of that Aristotelian conception. Spinoza could therefore all the more easily start from Jewish theology rather than from Christian theology, adopt Maimonides' view rather than the view advanced by Descartes, in order to demolish with Cartesian means the unity which Maimonides had attempted to establish between knowledge and faith.[57]

C) THE CRITIQUE OF MIRACLES. Descartes has before him at least the possibility of discriminating clearly between the sciences and all that relates to faith and the conduct of life. This possibility does not exist for Maimonides, nor for Spinoza, since in their view love of God is the single aim of human life, but science, scientifically founded knowledge of God, is the presupposition and element of love of God.[58] Spinoza's critique of religion in so far as it is more than positive critique can be understood at a deeper level if one starts from this central harmony between Maimonides and Spinoza than if one starts from Cartesian science. That this is the case is seen when one compares Spinoza's critique of miracles with Maimonides' doctrine of miracles.

Videntes sive Dissertatio theologica de prophetia et prophetis (Groningae, 1659), passim (explicitly polemic against Maimonides' theory of prophecy: II, 13).

57. [238] Spinoza's relation to Maimonides on the one hand, and to Descartes on the other, is treated by [Manuel] Joel, *Zur Genesis der Lehre Spinozas* (Breslau, 1871) and by [Leon] Roth, *Spinoza, Descartes, and Maimonides* (Oxford: Clarendon, 1924); Roth overestimates the importance in intellectual history of Spinoza's relationship to Maimonides, which is doubtless important in Spinoza's philosophical development. Roth does not sufficiently take into account that the theories regarding which Spinoza stands with Maimonides against Descartes (and against the *kalam*) are for the most part not peculiar to Maimonides, but are the common property of the "philosophers." Spinoza's agreement with Averroes is certainly of greater objective importance than his agreement with Maimonides. Our interpretation is to be understood within this limitation, and this is justified, since we are considering Spinoza's relationship to Maimonides not in regard to Maimonides' importance in general in the history of philosophy, but as an element in Spinoza's critique of religion. Cf. further the detailed review of Roth's book by T. J. de Boer, "Maimonides en Spinoza" (*Mededeelingen der Koninklijke Akademie van Wetenschappen*, Afdeeling Letterkunde, Deel 63, Serie A, No. 2), Amsterdam, 1927.

58. [239] This is not contradicted by the fact that Maimonides asserts the inadequacy of scientific knowledge of God, for in so doing he does not assert the independence of faith in relation to science, except for "the multitude." Furthermore, we must bear in mind that Maimonides' theology has its roots in the context of Jewish life and faith, and that for him the scientific foundation is entirely secondary. But at this particular moment we are concerned solely with the position which Maimonides exposes to Spinoza's critique and in so far as he exposes it to that critique. See above [fifth and sixth paragraphs of section A, subsection 4].

Exhaustive consideration of Maimonides' theory of miracles is not required for this purpose.[59] It will suffice to indicate the tendencies in Maimonides' theory which, if thought through, lead to Spinoza's critique of miracles.

We have already seen (see above, third paragraph of section A, subsection 4) what importance Maimonides attributes to miracles. The inference drawn from biblical miracles is a highly important argument for the creation of the world, as opposed to the eternity of the world. Given the fact of the creation of the world, the possibility of miracles is posited. The urgency with which recognition of the possibility of miracles is put forward seems out of keeping with Maimonides' tendency to weaken and to limit the bearing of the biblical accounts of miracles. How does it come about that a theologian who enters the lists full of zeal for the assertion of creation is made ill at ease by the actual miracles? Can it be, in the final instance, that we must see the reason for resistance to miracles in the assertion of the creation of the world?

Creation of the world is the precondition of miracles. Thus miracles cannot controvert the assertion that the world is created. Although the creation of the world is not strictly demonstrable, nevertheless, the analysis lays hold on those characteristics of the world that make the doctrine of the world as created more probable. The possibility and the limits of miracles are preindicated by the characteristics which indicate that the world is created. In the first place, the reason why the world has the character that it possesses does not lie in the world itself. The world might be quite other than it in fact is. The world is what it is by virtue of having been determined by the will of a being who wills, and who as such can will that the world can be different. Miracles are therefore possible. In the second place, the actual order of the world, the visible harmony of the world as a whole, shows that the ground which determines that world must be a rational will: God will therefore not undo the order of the world through miracles, the order which He in His wisdom has placed in the world. Miracles are "changes of nature," that is, changes of the particular natures: for instance, of water into blood, of the stave into a snake. These transformations do not imperil the harmony of the whole, they do not endanger the broad character of the universal order, because God foresaw them prior to the creation of the world, but above all

---

59. [240] Jacob Kramer gives a complete presentation in his dissertation, "Das Problem des Wunders im Zusammenhang mit dem der Providenz bei den jüdischen Religionsphilosophen von Saadia bis Maimuni" (Strassburg, 1903). Kramer also offers, as does Joel, textual evidence of the harmony existing between Maimonides and Spinoza in their interpretation of the biblical accounts of miracles.

because they are only transient and not permanent modifications, because they occur only rarely, not frequently.[60]

Maimonides' doctrine of miracles assumes the distinction between the enduring and the transient, between what always occurs and what occurs rarely, as an ontologically relevant distinction. If this distinction is called into question, if the order of the world is also, and in particular, determined with consideration of events that happen rarely and outside the normal course of events, then the possibility that miracles should be spoken of in Maimonides' manner falls to the ground. Even though it happens but rarely, and only transiently, that water changes into blood, in so far as it occurs at all, it belongs in the same sense to the order of the world as those events which occur regularly and which persist. In that case, the rule that water does not change into blood is only provisionally significant, as opposed to the universal law, which embraces within itself the regular and the rare. On the assumptions of the modern conception of nature therefore, miracles, in their character of deviation from rule, are distinguished from the regular occurrences only "in relation to the imperfect character of our understanding." Therefore, a rare and transient change of nature, a change, as Maimonides says, "only in some particularities," is as much a subversion of the natural order as would be the falling of the stars.

How legitimate this critique is from Maimonides' own point of view appears from the fact that Maimonides tends to deny changes of the sempiternal. This reveals the dependence of his doctrine of miracles on certain cosmological assumptions. This doctrine assumes a qualitative difference between heaven and earth.[61] To these assumptions Maimonides links the conception

---

60. [241] *Guide* 2.19 (pp. 148–61) [Pines, pp. 304–9]; 2.27 [Pines, pp. 332–33]; 2.28 (pp. 209f.) [Pines, pp. 335–36]; 2.29 (pp. 224ff.) [Pines, pp. 345–46].

61. [242] It is rewarding to compare the interpretation of Psalm 148:6, given in the same context by Maimonides and by Spinoza, from this point of view. "He hath also established them for ever and ever: He hath made a decree which shall not pass away." Spinoza relates the passage to the eternity and unchangeability of nature, Maimonides uses words which seem to be to the same effect. What they intend is shown in the commentaries by Ibn Ezra and David Kimchi on the passage, which are written in terms of the same cosmological assumptions as Maimonides' own. Ibn Ezra: "They never change, for they are not composed of the four elements." Kimchi: "They are not like those creatures in which the individuals perish, and the species persists, but their individuals persist as does the species." Thus these exegetes consider as exempt from change—and in this they follow the Psalmist—not nature but the heavens. According to Spinoza, Eccles. 3:14 teaches the impossibility of miracles because it teaches the immutable character of the order of nature; according to Maimonides, the eternal duration of the world, after it was created. Maimonides, as though forestalling Spinoza's interpretation, adds the end of the verse, which, as he asserts, contains an allusion to the miracles (*Guide* 2.28 [Pines, pp. 334–36] and *Tractate*, p. 81 [Yaffe, p. 80]). On the passage from Eccles. 1:9, which Spinoza uses for the same purpose, cf. Ibn Ezra who also limits unchangeability here to the heavens and to genera and species. Of further relevance in this connection is Maimonides' at-

of miracles. He does so in order to be able to maintain the assertion of miracles as a scientifically possible assertion. By so doing, he exposes this conception to criticism from a more advanced stage in knowledge of nature.[62] He defines miracle as a change of nature, and he denies changes of the sempiternal. The moment the conception of nature is modified so that the distinction between "always" and "as a rule" (more often than not) loses its meaning, indeed even in the moment when the distinction between heaven and earth loses its significance, denial of miracles in heaven must lead to the denial of miracles altogether. If the attitude to miracles alters on the way from Maimonides to Spinoza, this occurs not in the first place as the result of a change in the attitude to revelation, but already in consequence of change in attitude to Aristotelian physics. Modern science was not needed for evoking skepticism regarding miracles. The reason that induced Maimonides himself to forsake the natural philosophy contained in the *kalam*, induces him to weaken and limit the assertion that miracles occur: consideration of the actual order of the world; the same reason, but adducing the modern conception of nature, leads to Spinoza's critique of miracles.

An essential of miracles is that they occur without human intervention in nonhuman things, for the sake of men. Maimonides denies that the purpose of miracles is to evoke faith in the prophets "for in the heart of the man who believes because of miracles there remains doubt." But the greatest miracles, those granted to Moses, which are distinguished from those of other prophets in essence and not only in degree, happened "according to the need," in relation to the imperilment of the children of Israel.[63] The assertion of miracles therefore includes in itself the more general assertion that God cares for men, and for the well-being of men. What makes miracles possible is not

---

tempt to explain away the miracle accorded to Joshua, by reason of the presupposed unchangeability of celestial events (*Guide* 2.35 [Pines, pp. 367–69]; and also Gersonides on Josh. 10:12).

62. [243] Thomas Aquinas, in his doctrine of miracles (otherwise more radical than Maimonides) does this also, when he considers the miracle accorded to Hezekiah (the recession of the sun) to be a greater miracle than the parting of the Red Sea or the wakening of the dead to life (*Summa contra Gentiles* III, 101). To the best of my knowledge, later Catholic teaching has discarded this view. [Thomas Aquinas, *Summa contra Gentiles*, trans. Vernon J. Bourke et al. (New York: Hanover House, 1957), bk. 3, chap. 101, "On Miracles: . . . [2] Now, there are various degrees and orders of these miracles. Indeed, the highest rank among miracles is held by those events in which something is done by God which nature never could do. For example, that two bodies should be coincident; that the sun reverse its course, or stand still; that the sea open up and offer a way through which people may pass. And even among these an order may be observed. For the greater the things that God does are, and the more they are removed from the capacity of nature, the greater the miracle is. Thus, it is more miraculous for the sun to reverse its course than for the sea to be divided."]

63. [244] "Yesodei ha-Torah" VIII, 1; *Guide* 2.35 [Pines, pp. 367–69]. [See "Laws of the Basic Principles of the Torah," trans. Hyamson, p. 43b.]

only creation but, more immediately, providence. The Jewish conception of providence, which is Maimonides' point of departure, asserts that all good or evil that may happen to men happens justly, as reward or punishment.[64] The miracles, which rarely occur, which occur only in particularities, and do not persist, have their place in the continuous, always equal context of providence. They differ by their miraculous nature from the universal context of providence, but they presuppose it since they presuppose that God does indeed concern Himself with men, and does not leave them to chance.

Maimonides explains the assertion—to each man occurs what he merits by his works—by the closer definition that divine providence follows the emanation of divine intellect, that man partakes of providence in accordance with the participation of the human intellect in the divine intellect. Providence is not equally concerned with all men. Providence protects the individual according to his perfection, according to the degree of his knowledge of God and of his love of God.[65] Thus the reward of virtue is the consequence of virtue, the punishment of vice is the consequence of vice. Maimonides resolves the difficulty that remains—that the just suffer and the unjust live in happiness—in his interpretation of the Book of Job. The happiness with which Job is preoccupied is the happiness which consists in possession of external goods (wealth, children, health). Hence his suffering. He suffers from the loss of these goods. Job, as is clearly to be seen from Scripture, prior to the revelation at the end, through which he attains to true knowledge of God, is not wise, but only morally perfect. The just man suffers—this means that the morally perfect man suffers from the loss of external goods. But moral perfection is not the genuine perfection of man: it is a perfection that exists only in community life, by virtue of community life. Therefore it does not make man immune to external happenings. What is entirely a man's own is perfection of knowledge, which is fulfilled in knowledge of God, which can and must be the only desire of man in order that he may become impregnable to all external happenings.[66] Maimonides expressly states that providence watches over the well-being of the pious, over every step they take. He is far from asserting that the highest perfection of man is a matter of indifference for his external fate, but he asserts that this perfection *makes* for indifference to external fate.

64. [245] *Guide* 3.17 (p. 125) [Pines, pp. 469–70].
65. [246] Ibid., 3.17 (pp. 130, 135) [Pines, pp. 471–72, 474]; 3.18 [Pines, pp. 474–77].
66. [247] Ibid., 3.22 [Pines, pp. 486–90]; 3.23 [Pines, pp. 490–97]; 3.51 [Pines, pp. 618–28]; 3.54 [Pines, pp. 632–38].

But if *interest* in all external things dies away, then the interest in all help from without also dies away, and therewith dies all interest in miracles.

The only interest—which absorbs all other interests into itself or robs them of all value—is to be the desire to draw close to God. Entry into the "inner court of God's house" may be gained only by scientific knowledge of God, and this in its turn is based on natural science. Thus theory is only a means, but an indispensable, immediate, and most important means of attaining *beatitudo*. The final bound set to knowledge is the knowledge of God as Creator, the knowledge of God as unfathomable, a knowledge obtained through recognizing the mysterious character of things created. Contemplation of created things, however, leads directly to lessened interest in miracles, in the modifications made in the existing world-order for the benefit of man. Maimonides finds, as does Spinoza, that given man's insignificance compared with the universe, man's claim to be the end for which the world exists is untenable. Thus we understand Maimonides' effort to weaken and limit the bearing of the biblical reports of miracles. His mind, accustomed to seeing the free, creative divine will of God in the grand, eternally unchanging order of the universe, has no spontaneous interest in direct intervention by God, as exemplified in miracles.

Light is cast on the relation between the assertion of creation and the assertion of miracles by the following argument, typical of the Enlightenment.[67] The world, as created by God, is perfect; by intervention into its order, by miracles, the perfect world becomes of necessity less perfect; it is unthinkable that God should will this. Thus the impossibility of miracles is inferred from the presupposed creation of the world. But by the creation of the world the possibility of miracles is posited beyond doubt. If the possibility of miracles is denied, then the creation of the world is also denied. The line of argument adopted against the possibility of miracles is, then, formally not tenable if the creation of the world is asserted. Maimonides does not attribute any contradiction to the writer of Ecclesiastes, when he finds in one and the same verse of this book (3:14) a denial of change in the order of the world (the purpose of change would be a further approach to ultimate perfection, but the world

---

67. [248] This line of argument is indicated in Spinoza's work (*Tractate*, p. 69 [Yaffe, pp. 68–69]), and developed by Voltaire in the *Dictionnaire philosophique portatif*, in his article on Miracles. [See Voltaire, "Miracles," in *Philosophical Dictionary*, trans. Peter Gay (New York: Basic Books, 1962), pp. 392–98. The original article contains three numbered sections, and an appendix on the miracles of Jesus; Gay's translation contains only the first section; but the argument against miracles, based on the Creator's perfection, occurs in the first section.]

is already perfect, since it is created)—and a justification of miracles.[68] If Maimonides' interpretation is elaborated according to its own tenor, it is plain that no contradiction occurs here. The world is not modified, even in the smallest particular, on account of any imperfection. For the world is perfect, by reason that it is created. God intervenes in the natural order not for the sake of nature[69] but for the sake of man.[70] This amounts to stating that from the assertion of creation, with which, as has been shown, the possibility of miracles is posited—from this assertion as a theoretical assertion, founded on analysis of the world, there is no immediate way to the assertion of miracles, to the assertion of miracles as having actually occurred. In point of fact, the assertion of creation as a theoretical assertion, by its immanent tendency, if one carries it to its conclusion, bars the way to any assertion of miracles. For the theorist who sees his goal, or the last stage before reaching his goal, in the contemplation of the order of the universe, rejects as absurd the claim that man is the final end of the world. He cannot will that the natural order shall be changed for the sake of man. To him it seems petty to assert the interest "only" of man, in the face of the universe. Thus the ground is cut away from any interest in miracles. The conclusion from creation against miracles—an untenable conclusion—has its basis in the genuine clash of interests on which the assertion of creation of the world on the one hand, the assertion of miracles on the other hand, is based.

The decline of interest in miracles does not refute the assertion of miracles. If the assertion of miracles is to be refuted, the assertion of the creation of the world must be refuted. In Spinoza's case, this assertion follows from his system. Prior to the system, prior to the metaphysical critique founded on the system, there is the positive critique which remains on the same plane as did Maimonides' attempted justification. Positive critique is unable to refute the assertion that the world was created. It limits itself to examining the reasoning underlying that assertion. But by finding the reasoning defective

---

68. [249] *Guide* 2.28 (p. 209) [Pines, pp. 335–36].

69. [250] Which the above-mentioned argument, characteristic of the Enlightenment, assumes; cf. Spinoza: "... alias enim [i.e., with the assertion of miracles], quid aliud statuitur, quam quod Deus naturam adeo impotentem creaverit, ejusque leges et regulas adeo steriles statuerit, ut saepe de novo ei subvenire cogatur, si eam conservatam vult..." (*Tractate*, p. 69) ["... for otherwise (i.e., with the assertion of miracles), what else is being stated than that God created a nature so impotent and established such sterile laws and rules for it that He is often compelled to reinforce it anew if He wants it to be preserved..." {Yaffe, p. 69}].

70. [251] According to Maimonides, miracles are intended by the words in Eccles. 3:14: "and God did thus, so that He might be feared." [Strauss seems to refer to *Guide* 2.28 (Pines, p. 336).]

positive critique gains the right to reject the opposed assertion of creation as unfounded. For the assertion was made on allegedly scientific grounds: positive critique rejects it as an unfounded assertion, as an overhasty hypothesis. This critique is scientific critique, and in principle not questionable, since the assertion called in question is itself intended as a scientific assertion.

3) The limitation of this critique

In his controversy with Maimonides, Spinoza can fight on his own ground, on the basis of science. He has no need first to conquer the territory, and establish his right on it. But if Spinoza's critique of Maimonides is in fact not critique of religion at all, but philosophic critique of scholastic philosophy, the term critique of religion, applied as designation of Spinoza's critique of Maimonides, is erroneous in principle. It makes no difference to this finding that Maimonides does not himself from the outset build up his position on the basis of science, but merely defends on that basis his pregiven Jewish position. For the pregivenness may be understood as the outcome of some reasoning, i.e., of a historical proof for the fact of revelation. It was our belief that we could justifiably assume that the pregivenness had a more radical significance, but Maimonides himself casts no light on this more radical significance.

The critique carried out in the *Theologico-Political Tractate* is directed less at Maimonides' "dogmatic" position than against the "skeptical" position of the orthodox, and in point of fact less against Jewish orthodoxy than against the Christian orthodoxy of the Reformation. This latter orthodoxy understands the pregivenness of its position as already vouched for by the doctrine of "the inner witness of the Holy Spirit." If one examines Spinoza's critique of this doctrine, the critique, formally considered, turns out to rest on a *petitio principii*. Nevertheless, Spinoza's critique of orthodoxy has great potentialities—not only as defensive critique of the scientific foundations of the orthodox position, but also as critique for attack on the consequences flowing from the orthodox position. We may assume justification in principle for that critique despite its formally questionable character because this opponent too in principle acknowledges the right of science. For that very reason, the essentially problematic character of Spinoza's critique of religion could not as yet be brought into full light. This problematic character becomes manifest only when the radical critique of religion is brought to bear on a religious position which is as radical as Spinoza's critique. As such a position we must recognize that taken by Calvin. It is highly probable that Spinoza knew this position directly.[71] Whether he did or not, Calvin's position, as the foundation of the orthodox position which Spinoza is contesting, is the predestined object of the critique.

71. [252] A Spanish translation of Calvin's *Institutio Christianae Religionis* [*Institutes of the Christian Religion*] was among the books in Spinoza's library (see Freudenthal's *Lebensgeschichte*, p. 160).

3

Cohen and Maimonides[1]

EDITOR'S NOTE

The first appearance in print of this German lecture, "Cohen und Maimuni" (1931), was in Leo Strauss, *Philosophie und Gesetz: Frühe Schriften*, vol. 2 of *Gesammelte Schriften*, pp. 393–436. The editor, Heinrich Meier, deciphered handwritten changes that were made in pencil to the manuscript by Strauss himself. The resulting edition by Meier represented an effort to produce a version as close as possible to the original typescript, which apparently was used by Strauss as the basis of a lecture he was to deliver in the auditorium of the Academy for the Science of Judaism in Berlin on 4 May 1931. I say, "as the basis for a lecture," since the form in which we possess the manuscript is undoubtedly much too long for any actual lecture; how he adapted it for delivery is not

---

1. Lecture to be given on May 4, 1931. [The wording of the lecture, which Leo Strauss gave on 4 May 1931 in the auditorium of the Academy for the Science of Judaism in Berlin, can no longer be reconstructed with certainty, since Strauss must have shortened the overly long text considerably, and since, among other things, he for this reason replaced the first part of the original manuscript with a new introduction. The new introduction is found on separate numbered pages that were added to the first of the two manuscript notebooks. The beginning in the manuscript notebook is crossed out (nn. 34 and 39), but Strauss evidently had the aim of still making considerably more extensive deletions in the first part (see n. 171). One place at which the older text may join the new introduction is designated in n. 101. Since only assumptions can be made about the final redaction—pages may have been lost, which, like the introduction, were put in the manuscript notebook—the complete text of the two manuscript notebooks is reproduced immediately after the introduction.]

{We have used the text of the lecture "Cohen und Maimuni" and its editorial apparatus as found in Strauss, *Philosophie und Gesetz: Frühe Schriften*, vol. 2 of *Gesammelte Schriften*, ed. Heinrich Meier (Stuttgart: J. B. Metzler, 1997), 393–436. Numbers inside curly brackets { } in boldface in the running text refer to the pages of this edition. In the translated text of the manuscript itself, rounded parentheses ( ) occurring within quotations designate Strauss's interpolations, angle brackets < > designate Strauss's deletions, and square brackets [ ] designate interpolations of Meier's (as explained in the notes) or else those of the translators. In the notes, square brackets enclose Meier's editorial remarks, and curly brackets enclose the remarks of the translators or the present editor; unenclosed remarks are Strauss's own. For the explanation of other signs (angle brackets and asterisks) used in the notes, see nn. 6 and 15–15. Generally, we have tried to retain the look of Strauss's manuscript, except that lengthy quotations in Strauss's text are reformatted as block quotations, abbreviated citations are expanded by means of bracketed interpolations, and Greek (and Hebrew) fonts are transliterated (or translated, as in the Munk page number in parentheses in n. 198, below). See also nn. 2, 4, and 5 below.}

known to anyone. So far as I am aware, the only evidence available that this lecture was actually delivered (in whatever form it may have been spoken) is in Strauss's letter to Gerhard Krüger of 7 May 1931: see *Hobbes Politische Wissenschaft und zugehörige Schriften—Briefe*, vol. 3 of *Gesammelte Schriften*, pp. 384–85. Hence, no one knows at what point Strauss made the changes of the main text and in the margins, as noted by the original editor. The English translation has been specially made for the present edition by Martin D. Yaffe and Ian Alexander Moore, in consultation with the present editor. The detailed notes to "Cohen and Maimonides" offer comments on the state of the text (which was not a finished literary work), provide Strauss's specific scholarly references or translate them, and furnish original editions as well as English translations of the works of which he made use. Thus, the notes combine the work of Heinrich Meier, and of Martin D. Yaffe and Ian A. Moore, with some very slight additional changes made by the present editor. The present editor and the translators wish to acknowledge the scholarly work of Heinrich Meier, to whom we owe a great debt. Most of his notes on the state of the manuscript as well as on decisions made in editing it, as they appear in the original German edition, have been directly translated. The notes not enclosed in brackets are the work of Strauss himself who, although he did not provide the manuscript with proper and detailed notes, did occasionally make (in the text or margins of the lecture manuscript) comments, references, or textual changes; these had already been moved by the German editor from the text or margins (as they appeared in the manuscript) to the notes. The complex layering of the notes in three components (i.e., those of Strauss, of Meier, and of Yaffe and Moore), which it was impossible to completely simplify, requires some clarification; this has been provided by the translators in the section of n. 1 that is enclosed in curly brackets, as well as nn. 5, 6, and 15–15 below.

INTRODUCTION

THE TOPIC "COHEN AND MAIMONIDES" REQUIRES A MORE PRECISE definition; for the "and" is all too undefined. It gives the impression that we, as if sovereign spectators or even judges, wanted to allow both these outstanding men to *pass before* us. If we had had such a comparative-historical interest, then we would have named Rambam,[2] the earlier one, first. But by

---

2. {Instead of *Maimuni* ("Maimonides"), Strauss uses RMbM (pronounced "Rambam"), the traditional acronym in Hebrew for "Rabbi Moshe ben Maimon." Also, instead of *Guide* (sc., *of the Perplexed*), he uses the Hebrew title *Moreh* (sc., *ha-Nevukhim*). In order to standardize references in the present work,

our having named Cohen, the later one, first, we gave it to be understood that we wanted *to gain access to* Rambam by starting with Cohen: Cohen is to open up for us the access to Rambam.

If we put our trust in Cohen's lead,[3] this does not signify that we mean to follow him blindly. Blindly following [him] would lead, *if* we were ever misdirected by particular assertions of Cohen's—and there are particular {394} assertions of Cohen's by which we *would have to* be misdirected—to our rejecting his lead *totally*. And with that, we would be robbing ourselves of important insights. Instead it is a matter of our following the right track of Cohen's and not allowing ourselves to be put off course by his aberrations. We shall therefore have to criticize Cohen. That is why the discussion will be more about Cohen than about Rambam, although for us it is first and last a matter of the understanding of Rambam. One *more* reason for putting Cohen's name first. So much for the justification of the title. Now on to the issue!

Cohen dealt most thoroughly with Rambam in his essay "Characteristics of Maimonides' Ethics," which appeared in 1908 in the collection *Moses ben Maimon*.[4] The title of this essay makes it appear as though *only one part* of

---

Strauss's use of *Moreh* has been changed to *Guide*; but readers should be aware that in this lecture Strauss referred consistently to the Hebrew (translated) title of Maimonides' book. This is the title by which the book has been known to most Jewish readers, especially until the most recent centuries. Its standard use relates to the fact that most of the *Guide*'s Jewish students in the late medieval and early modern eras, until perhaps the nineteenth century, read it in its Hebrew translation; and for many, this is still true. There have then been few readers other than specialized scholars—at least until the appearance of the Salomon Munk–Issachar Joel critical edition of the original Judeo-Arabic text (1930–31)—who have read or been able to study it in its original Judeo-Arabic, which was not readily available, and certainly not in a critical edition. For its first seven centuries, it has lived in, and learning of it has largely been conducted based on, its great Hebrew translation by Samuel ibn Tibbon, at least as a Jewish book and at least until very recently. (One should also mention the other well-regarded, if often criticized, medieval Hebrew version, by Yehuda al-Ḥarizi.) Curiously it is one of the rare classics still known mainly as a translated book (as compared with most classics, other than perhaps the Hebrew Bible), whether it is read in Hebrew (which language has recently been the beneficiary of two fine new modern Hebrew translations, one by Yosef Kafah, and the other by Michael Schwarz), in Latin (by Augustinus Justinianus and Jacob Mantino, of the al-Ḥarizi version, or by Johannes Buxtorf the Younger, of the Ibn Tibbon version), in French (by Salomon Munk), or in English (by Shlomo Pines). Indeed, Ibn Tibbon's medieval Hebrew version, *Moreh ha-Nevukhim*, has curiously, and until very recently, had a status and authority almost equal to, and on occasion seemingly even greater than, the author's own original-language version in Judeo-Arabic. Even Arabic speakers who have used the *Guide* have tended to use Arabic transliterations (which required the numerous Hebrew words and passages to be translated), rather than the original Judeo-Arabic version itself.}

3. {Strauss uses the verbs *führen* ("to lead") and *leiten* ("to guide") and their cognates almost interchangeably. Unless otherwise indicated, *führen* and its cognates will always be rendered as "to lead" and its cognates, and *leiten* and its cognates will always be rendered as "to guide" and its cognates.}

4. {Hermann Cohen, "Charakteristik der Ethik Maimunis," in *Moses ben Maimon: Sein Leben, seine Werke, und sein Einfluss*, ed. W. Bacher, M. Brann, D. Simonsen, and J. Guttmann, 2 vols. (Leipzig: G. Fock, 1908–14; reprint, Hildesheim: Olms, 1971), I, 63–134. Unless otherwise indicated, page numbers in parentheses in Strauss's lecture (by which he cites Cohen's essay in his manuscript) refer to this volume.}

Rambam's doctrine were treated in it, to wit, ethics. This appearance vanishes when one recalls what ethics signifies for Cohen. Ethics, as the doctrine of man, is the *center* of philosophy, according to Cohen's express declaration at the beginning of his *Ethics of the Pure Will*.[5] It needs logic as its preparation and aesthetics as its completion—it is therefore not the *whole* of philosophy; but it is the *central* philosophical discipline. For Cohen, therefore, "Characteristics of Rambam's Ethics" signifies "Characteristics of the Center of Rambam's Philosophy," [or] "Central Characteristics of Rambam's Philosophy." As a matter of fact, the *whole* of Rambam's philosophy[6]—even his logic and metaphysics—is treated in Cohen's essay, treated from the viewpoint of its ethical meaning, which is the same as its *human* [meaning, i.e.], its proper[7] [meaning]. Because for Cohen the center of philosophy lies in ethics, for that reason he is free to look at the[8] human meaning of Rambam's doctrine: "the center of gravity of his thought . . . lies in ethics" (98/99). "In Maimonides . . . despite all the scholastic rigor of the dialectics, his focus is always the contemporary living significance of the concepts. *This contemporariness, however, lies in ethics*"[9] (91/78). "His metaphysics (has) its effective epicenter in his ethics" (73/23). *Cohen, being himself guided by contemporary-ethical or, more exactly, political interest, opens up for us the access to the contemporary-ethical, political meaning of Rambam's philosophy*. We want to put this thesis at the beginning of our considerations. We hope to be able to make it intelligible and to prove it.—

To these the present translation adds, following a slash, the corresponding page numbers of Cohen, *Ethics of Maimonides*, trans. Almut Sh. Bruckstein (Madison: University of Wisconsin Press, 2004). No attempt has been made to harmonize our renderings of Cohenian passages with Bruckstein's considerably freer renderings. "Charakteristik der Ethik Maimunis" is reprinted in Cohen, *Jüdische Schriften*, ed. Bruno Strauss, intro. Franz Rosenzweig, 3 vols. (Berlin: C. A. Schwetschke & Sohn, 1924), 3.221–89; also in Cohen, *Kleinere Schriften* IV, *1907–1912*, ed. Hartwig Wiedebach (Hildesheim: Olms, 2009), 161–269.}

5. {Cohen, *Ethik des reinen Willens* (Berlin: Bruno Cassirer, 1904), 1. Strauss's references to the *Ethik* in the text of his lecture are to this edition, whose pagination differs slightly from the 2nd, revised edition and its subsequent reprints (2nd ed., Berlin: Bruno Cassirer, 1907; 7th ed., Hildesheim: Olms, 2008)—the changes in the reprints have to do with the editorial apparatus only. To the page numbers in the text (and in nn. 104, 114, and 272 below), the present translation therefore adds, following a double slash, the corresponding page numbers of the revised edition(s).}

6. <philosophy completely> {A word or set of words preceding or following text enclosed with angle brackets designates whether the deleted material comes before or after that word or those words in the manuscript, respectively. In the present case, the phrase "philosophy completely" was deleted in favor of "the *whole* of Rambam's philosophy."}

7. {The German is *eigentlich*, whose range of meaning includes both "proper" and "real." This frequently occurring word and its cognates are rendered as either "proper" or "real" and their cognates, according to the immediate context.}

8. <the central position of ethics in the thought> {In the present case, the phrase "the central position of ethics in the thought of" was deleted in favor of "the human meaning of Rambam's doctrine."}

9. {The emphasis is Strauss's.}

Cohen is to lead[10] us to the understanding of Rambam. *How is it that our understanding of Rambam is in need of guidance?* Because *initially* he is *not* {395} accessible to us. He is not accessible to us because we live in a *totally different world*: in the world of "modern culture," as Cohen likes to say.[11] We want to avoid this expression, because it makes a highly vulnerable and contentious issue appear all too invulnerable, all too self-evident. Modern culture has its roots in the Age of Enlightenment, in the seventeenth and eighteenth centuries; what we see around us today is only the will of the seventeenth century executed. The *executed* will shows up differently than the will *before* its realization; but if one wants to *understand* the executed will, one needs to orient oneself initially not by *that* which has come about but by that which was wanted originally. If the roots of modern culture lie in the Enlightenment, then we characterize ourselves aptly in saying: we are *enlightened*. We are enlightened even when with Fichte we have to laugh at Nicolai;[12] even when we are fed up with Voltaire;[13] indeed, *precisely* then: for we are fed up with him because we know him inside and out, because we know him from the inside even if we do not know him from the outside, i.e., from his writings.

If, however, the real obstacle to our understanding of Rambam is our being enlightened—then is Cohen's not the worst lead [to follow]? Is he not *also* enlightened? Is he not even an *enlightener himself*? Precisely *because* he is that, because for him the Enlightenment is not something that defines him without his knowing it—this is the situation in which *we* find ourselves generally—but because he *grasps*[14] it consciously and expressly, [because] it is for him not self-evident, he is in an *original* manner what we are in a *derivative* manner. And only by starting from an original is an [15-]original-[15]

---

10. [Noted as an alternative without definitive reference as to placement in the text:] to guide {Here the German is *anleiten*. Cf. nn. 3 above and 252 below.}

11. {E.g., Cohen, "Das soziale Ideal bei Platon und den Propheten" [The Social Ideal in Plato and the Prophets], in *Jüdische Schriften*, I, 306–30; see 306.}

12. {See Johann Gottlieb Fichte, "Friedrich Nicolai's Leben und sonderbare Meinungen" [Friedrich Nicolai's Life and Peculiar Opinions], in *Sämmtliche Werke*, ed. J. H. Fichte, 8 vols. (Berlin: Veit, 1845-46), VIII, 1–93.}

13. {Cf. n. 67 below.}

14. [Noted as an alternative without definitive reference as to placement in the text:] makes {it} an issue of his

15-15. [Inserted between the lines or added in the margin by Strauss.] {Throughout the text, when two footnote markers are of the same number and when they appear at the beginning and end of a word, phrase, sentence, or paragraph, it indicates that the words enclosed within them are in some exceptional state in the original text, the particulars of which are further elaborated in the notes. In the notes themselves (see nn. 23, 43, 58–58, 65, 87, 94, 171, and 198 below), whereas Strauss's deletions are designated by angle brackets (see nn. 1 and 6 above), his interpolations are designated either by an asterisk following

understanding, is consequently also an original[16] understanding of Rambam, then possible.

Cohen understands the Enlightenment in an original manner.[17] In the originality of his thought, he endeavors to establish the origins of his thought. In the accomplishing of this establishment, he discovers Rambam as the "*classic of rationalism*" (*Religion der Vernunft*).[18] Cohen[19] opens up to us Rambam as an enlightener within the horizon of the Enlightenment.

The expression "rationalism" emerged in the argument[20] with the theological tradition: rationalists are originally those who believe in the adequacy of reason for the guidance of life and who, precisely for that reason, believe that man may confront Scripture freely [and] critically, [21-]that reason may interpret Scripture[-21]. Cohen has in mind this concrete meaning of rationalism {396} in naming Rambam in another passage the "rationalist of Judaism."[22] We therefore say: Cohen as an enlightened Jew opens up to us the understanding of Rambam as an *enlightened Jew*.[23]

---

the interpolation, in the case of a single word, or by two asterisks enclosing it, in the case of more than one word: *...*}

16. <the> {In the present case, "the" was deleted in favor of "an original."}

17. {In the previous paragraph, this phrase has rendered the German phrase "*in* ursprünglicher Weise"; here the same phrase, without emphasis, renders the German adverb *ursprünglich*.}

18. {Hermann Cohen, *Religion der Vernunft aus den Quellen des Judentums*, 2nd ed. (Frankfurt am Main: J. Kauffmann, 1929), 73; *Religion of Reason out of the Sources of Judaism*, trans. Simon Kaplan, intro. Leo Strauss (New York: Ungar, 1972), 63:

Maimonides becomes a classic of rationalism in the monotheistic tradition most decisively, perhaps, through his interpretation of the crucial problem of negative attributes.}

19. <Cohen discovers> Cohen
20. {Or confrontation. The German is *Auseinandersetzung*.}
21-21. [Inserted between the lines or added in the margin by Strauss.]
22. {*Religion der Vernunft*, 410; *Religion of Reason*, 352:

Maimonides is the rationalist of Judaism. He must, therefore, subject the laws to that rationalist criticism which is presupposed by the erection of the positive structure of the teaching.}

23. [Strauss noted to himself here in square brackets:] *Then continue*:—Judaism illuminated in the <horizon> spirit of *Plato*.
[In the manuscript, two completely crossed out paragraphs follow:]

<What is "enlightened Judaism"? What is "enlightenment"?> <*"Enlightened Judaism" is a *program*: it signifies the requirement to understand, to illuminate, Judaism philosophically. It signifies *more*. One should not understand the expression as if, to be sure, in Cohen's opinion Judaism really needed philosophy whereas philosophy in turn did not need Judaism. Rather, Cohen is completely at one with Rambam that philosophy has {something} to learn from Judaism as well. For them both, it has to do with the *compatibility* between Judaism and philosophy, with their *reciprocal penetration*. In order to make clear what this reciprocal penetration signifies, we shall attempt a *provisional* clarification of what "enlightenment" is.*

<Let us recall the classical Age of the Enlightenment, the seventeenth and eighteenth centuries. The Enlightenment is *polemical*. We can attempt to define it by way of that against which it struggled. This was called "*superstition*" at that time. Cohen no longer speaks of superstition, but of

If[24] we reflect on the expression "enlightened Judaism," it shows up as follows: "Enlightenment" is here understood as something that is *added to* Judaism, that when conceived from the point of view of Jewish needs is, to be sure, called on as an aid in the interest of Judaism (87/63) but, even so, is *in itself, from its own point of view*, not Jewish. But of what human type and provenance is the Enlightenment? It has its origin in *Greek* philosophy.

This definition,[25] however, is very easily misunderstood. It seduces one into thinking of the so-called Greek Enlightenment, of *sophistry*.

In one of his last statements ("The Social Ideal in Plato and the Prophets"),[26] Cohen defines the power that Judaism needed for its completion and perfection as *Platonic* philosophy. If for Cohen it is therefore a matter of *enlightened Judaism*, then by this he has in mind: *a Judaism understood within the horizon of Plato*. And if he discovers Rambam as an enlightened Jew, then this means: he discovers Rambam as a Jew who understands his Judaism within the horizon of Plato.

In order to understand this assertion correctly, one must consider that for Cohen Plato is[27] in no way the ancestor of *all* philosophy, but only of the *true* philosophy. But there is at all times alongside the true philosophy a philosophy in quotation marks, which Cohen designates as "eclecticism."[28] The ancestor of this fundamentally erroneous philosophy is, according to Cohen, Aristotle. Plato and Aristotle represent an *eternal opposition*, the eternal opposition not only between *correct* and *false* philosophizing, but between philosophizing in the state of *fidelity* to the most important concern of man and philosophizing in the state of *betrayal* of this concern. Cohen's text testifies that this formulation is no exaggeration: "Aristotle is guided by enmity against the Idea; against the Idea of the Good" [(82/51)]. "Enmity against the Idea" is emphasized in the text.

---

myth, and he understands by this the manner in which humanity *originally* lived, thought, saw, understood itself. But it is the same themes, which were earlier fought against as superstition and which one attempts to understand today by the title "myth." And this is an indication of the originality of Cohenian thought, that he is not content with wanting to *understand* myth, but that for him it has to do with his *fight*: throughout his whole posthumously published work the struggle against myth is still going on. We thus say provisionally: the Enlightenment is the *struggle of science against myth*.>

24. <We have hitherto been content with a quite provisional understanding of "enlightenment."> If we reflect

25. {Cf. the last sentence of Strauss's two completely crossed out paragraphs translated in n. 23 above.}

26. {See n. 11 above.}

27. Plato is <the ancestor>

28. {Cf. 103/105, with Cohen, *Logik der reinen Erkenntnis* (2nd ed., Berlin: Bruno Cassirer, 1914; 4th ed., Hildesheim: Olms, 1977, 2005), 595, 598.}

The proposition "Cohen discovers Rambam as understanding his Judaism within the horizon of Plato" therefore implies: and *not* within the horizon of Aristotle. And *thus,* moreover, Cohen's assertion also reads: "Maimonides was in deeper harmony with Plato[29] than with Aristotle" (105/114).

This assertion can have a simple and unparadoxical meaning. For Rambam, one of the most important problems, perhaps the most important,[30] is the question of whether the world is eternal or created. Against Aristotle's {397} doctrine of the eternity of the world, he asserts [its] createdness. In this context, he remarks that Judaism is, to be sure, inconsistent[31] with the Aristotelian doctrine of the eternity of the world, but [is] very well [consistent] with Plato's doctrine of the formation of the world by the Demiurge.[32] Now Cohen is not thinking about *this* Platonism. As *he* understands Platonism, his assertion that Rambam was a Platonist is at first glance—and not only at first glance—a paradox.

In order to recognize and resolve this paradox, we must first of all clarify how Cohen really understands *the opposition between Plato and Aristotle.*[33]

[*Beginning of the Text in the Version of the Manuscript Notebooks*]

[34]<We characterize Cohen's position vis-à-vis Rambam in general by the proposition: Cohen *venerated* Rambam. This seems to be a matter of self-evidence that says nothing: for what Jew did not venerate Rambam![35] He who is Israel's eternal teacher, as Cohen calls him [(105/113f.)]. Cohen's veneration of Rambam, however, is in truth *not only not self-evident but even paradoxical.* We shall put his paradox and its resolution at the epicenter of our consideration. (Since the framework of a lecture does not permit an exhaustive treatment of our topic, we must limit ourselves to what is central; but what is central about it will surely be judged differently according to the

---

29. {"Plato" is emphasized in the Cohenian text, although not in Strauss's quotation.}
30. most important <for Rambam>
31. {The German is *unverträglich.* Strauss uses various terms having to do with agreement. We have tried to render each so as to keep them distinct: "accord" (*Einverstandnis*), "agreement" (*Verständigung*), "at one" (*einig*), "to coincide" (*zusammenfallen*), "compatibility" (*Vereinbarung*), "concord" (*Einsinnigkeit*), "to concur" (*übereinstimmen*), "concurrence" (*Übereinstimmung*), "harmony" (*Einklang*), "understanding" (*Verständnis*).}
32. {See *Guide* 2.25 (Pines, pp. 328f.).}
33. [Here the newly written introduction ends.]
34. [The text in the manuscript notebook begins with four completely crossed out paragraphs. Strauss had initially noted in the margin, then, after mentioning the title in the newly composed introduction, again crossed out:] <"Characteristics of Maimonides' Ethics" 1908>
35. [Note in the margin:] "Piety"

difference of standpoints; we reach a point of view relieved of a subjective arbitrariness if we inquire into[36] the inner difficulty, into the paradox of Cohen's relation to Rambam.)>

<[37-]Cohen's veneration for Rambam is not simply paradoxical, however. There is a very broad and important area in which it is, in any case, not baffling. This area we shall have to mention, at least. But even in this area it is not self-evident.[-37]>

<Cohen's veneration for Rambam is *not self-evident*. It signifies an express *option* for a thoroughly non-self-evident possibility. The option for Rambam signifies the option for a {398} Judaism philosophically understood, for the philosophical illumination of Judaism, for an *enlightened* Judaism.[38] To be sure, this expression should not be understood as if in Cohen's and Rambam's opinion Judaism needed philosophy whereas philosophy in turn did not need Judaism. Rather, both are at one that philosophy has [something] to learn from the doctrines of Judaism. For them it has to do with the compatibility between philosophy and Judaism, with their reciprocal penetration; *this* is what is meant by the expression "enlightened Judaism." That the will to this compatibility is not self-evident, however, is illuminated when one considers that there were and still are philosophers—the best-known is Spinoza—who were of the opinion that it would only be to philosophy's disadvantage if it were brought into any connection with revelation, and that there were and perhaps still are Jews—the best-known are those men who in the age of Rambam declared themselves against his philosophical writings—who were of the opinion that Judaism would be destroyed by philosophizing.>

<Enlightened Judaism is as little self-evident as enlightenment is self-evident. For there are still other possibilities for being a man and being a Jew than being an enlightened man and an enlightened Jew. The proof of this is that the Enlightenment pits itself *against* a human possibility. In the classical Age of Enlightenment, in the seventeenth and eighteenth centuries, what the Enlightenment had to fight against was called "superstition." If it were really and simply superstition, then the Enlightenment would in fact be a matter of self-evidence. We no longer follow the Enlightenment in that way without further qualification; we no longer speak of superstition, but of *myth*, and understand by this the manner in which humanity *originally* lived,

---

36. {The German expression is *fragen nach*. It occurs frequently and is also rendered as "question about" or "ask about."}
37-37. [Inserted between the lines or added in the margin by Strauss.]
38. [Noted in the margin:] *survey the terrain in advance*, before we arrive at the real *position*.

thought, saw, understood itself; and for us it is altogether a *problem* when we think not mythically but scientifically. Whoever struggles against myth in the name of science, therefore, does something altogether *not* self-evident; he does something distinctive. Cohen and Rambam are at one in this non-self-evidence distinctive of them; and not only in the struggle, but also in *how* they struggle.>[39]

We would say, perhaps: the Bible emerged within a mythical horizon; and the problem that the Bible sets for us is the question: whether what *matters* to the Bible, whether what the Bible {399} *really* wants, is bound to this horizon. The possibility of an enlightened Judaism depends on the fact that what matters to the Bible is *not* bound to the mythical horizon. This[40] can initially be understood *thus*—and just *thus* is it often understood—that the horizon[41] is treated as unreal, as a *quantité négligeable*,[42] such that the mythical horizon can be exchanged as one likes, as it were, for the scientific one. Were[43] this so, [44]then[44] one could speak only of the replacement of myth by science, only of enlightenment, not of an enlightened Judaism; there could be no discussion of a *reciprocal* penetration of science, philosophy, and Judaism. If, however, enlightened Judaism is more than an *application* of the Enlightenment *to* Judaism, if it is supposed to be Jewish *in itself*, then the replacement of myth by science must be *in* Judaism's *sense*; then myth must be fought against in the name of Judaism. The negation of the mythical horizon must occur in the name and at the behest of what Scripture *really* wants. Therefore, it cannot mean that the replacement of myth by science does not touch Judaism, but [rather] that the replacement of myth by science is a Jewish need; a Jew has an obligation to science. Rambam sees this obligation articulated in the commandment of knowledge of God, which he conceives as scientific knowledge. Cohen cannot find this obligation in the Bible so directly; for him the obligation to science could only result from the grounding of the moral function of science. But there is full concurrence in the result: *enlightened Judaism signifies the reception of the enlightenment of philosophical provenance into*[45] *Judaism, accomplished in the name and at the behest of Judaism.*

---

39. [End of the portion of the beginning of the text expressly crossed out in the manuscript notebook.]
40. <It thus depends on the fact that the mere horizon and the real one can be distinguished> This
41. horizon <so to speak>
42. {French: negligible quantity.}
43. <*This expression is too weak, however, for were this simply so,*> Were
44–44. [Inserted between the lines or added in the margin by Strauss.]
45. <*on*>

And as the Jews always remain the apostles of their faith, so it was the regard for religion which drove them into the arms of knowledge. Religion was in a sorry state; they all lament the decline of religion in their day and that they are calling on philosophy to curb it. They zealously repudiated the suspicions of the obscurantists and the mockery of the skeptics in the consciousness that it would have to be helped and that *only philosophy*[46] could help. (86f./63)

The struggle [47-]of science[-47] against myth[48] which is accomplished in the name[49] of the doctrine of the Bible leads to divesting the Bible of mythical elements, to transferring the Bible's real doctrine out of the mythical horizon into the horizon of science, {400} to *divesting* the Bible and Jewish tradition in general of myth. This divesting is accomplished in Rambam['s works] in the form of *allegorizing*: if a biblical passage contradicts scientific insight, then it is supposed that an inner meaning which is in harmony with the scientific insight underlies the outer meaning, the literal meaning of the passage which contradicts the scientific insight. The outer meaning is a figurative presentation of the one really meant. This conception presupposes that the biblical teachers were themselves in possession of science, but that for whatever reasons and for whatever purposes they expressed science in figurative form. [50-]The biblical teachers, especially the prophets, therefore must have been philosophers *also*, though *more* than philosophers, since besides philosophical insight they also had the power to present this insight figuratively, sensuously, effectively.[-50] *Allegorical interpretation wants to understand the author as he understood himself.* [51-]From this point of view, the resistance that the modern age has to allegorizing is self-explanatory. To understand the[-51] author as he understood himself—precisely this is the ambition of the historian; to the historical consciousness, allegorizing appears as a violation of the text. Thus it is no longer possible for us to follow Rambam when, for instance, he draws Aristotelian cosmology from the Bible; and it is not because we no longer believe in this cosmology but in another one; indeed, it also seems comical to us when, for instance, someone [likewise] finds in

---

46. {The emphasis is Strauss's.}
47-47. [Inserted between the lines or added in the margin by Strauss.]
48. myth <is>
49. name <of Judaism>
50-50. [Designated in the margin and provided with a deletion sign.]
51-51. [Noted in the margin as a replacement for the passage not crossed out in the text:] From this point of view, the resistance that one generally has today to allegorizing is understandable. {To understand} An

the Bible the assertions of the present-day natural sciences. The reason for this is the underlying insight,[52] which Spinoza articulated with particular forcefulness—to say nothing of Luther—, that to the Bible science simply does not matter, that "Moses admittedly did not want to teach obedience in conformity with the sciences" (*Jüdische Schriften* III 298f.).[53] From the insight into the profoundly unscientific character of the Bible, Spinoza drew the consequence that science and philosophy, on the one hand, and the Bible, on the other, have nothing to do with each other and belong to totally different worlds: science is the concern of the few wise, the Bible is oriented to the multitude. The Bible is rejected because the manner[54] in which the biblical teachers understood themselves conflicts with scientific insight.

[55-] This critique, which the modern age had applied to allegorizing generally and Spinoza had applied to Rambam's allegorizing in particular, Cohen makes implicitly his own: he grants that[56] it is not allegorizing {401} but historical-critical interpretation which understands the author as he understood himself. However, on the basis of this concession[57] and within the limits demarcated by it, he professes the principle of allegorizing. [-55]

[58-]Allegorizing and the critique of allegorizing concur in that it is the sole

---

52. {More or less literally: insight in principle. The German here is *prinzipiell*. Elsewhere, "in principle" is *grundsätzlich*.}

53. {Strauss quotes from Cohen's "Spinoza über Staat und Religion, Judentum und Christentum" [Spinoza on State and Religion, Judaism and Christianity], loc. cit., 290–372.}

54. {Or mode. The German is *Art*. Elsewhere, except where noted otherwise, "manner" is always *Weise*.}

55–55. [Inserted between the lines or added in the margin by Strauss.]

56. that <allegorizing does *not* understand the author>

57. concession <he turns back to allegorizing insofar as this {i.e., understanding an author as he understood himself} is possible on the basis of it. His>

58–58. [The new paragraph replaces two paragraphs that were removed by several vertical or oblique lines:]

<Allegorizing itself and the critique of allegorizing concur in that interpretation has nothing to do other than to determine <<the>> how the author understood himself. Cohen, on the contrary, starts from the Kantian insight that the possibility exists for understanding an author *better* than he understood himself. <<(And this is for Cohen not merely a possibility or merely a scientifically valuable maxim, <<<but a *duty* that has its basis in <<<<the good will>>>> *the obligation to tradition, in the duty to fidelity.*>>> *but the most radical form of annihilating what ought to be annihilated (*Religion der Vernunft*, 204 and 44 par. 2, 3 {*Religion of Reason*, 175, 37f.})*.)>> This "understanding an author better than he understood himself" Cohen calls *idealizing interpretation*. With this concept Cohen accomplishes a *vindication of allegorizing*, the method of Maimonides. I shall attempt to point out the character of idealizing interpretation by means of a central example.>

<There exists for every honest man the greatest difficulty of submitting himself* to the Bible as it concerns the accounts of *miracles*. I do not mean by this that on the basis of solid knowledge we could say that miracles are impossible, or that this or that miracle is impossible; but only that

task of interpretation to discover how the author understood *himself*. Cohen, on the contrary, starts from the Kantian insight that the possibility exists for understanding an author *better than* he understood himself.[59] This "understanding an author better than he understood himself" Cohen calls *idealizing interpretation*.[60] Idealizing interpretation is therefore distinguished from allegorical interpretation,[61] namely, by the interpreter's consciousness of his *distance* from the author, by his *superiority* to the author; we do not wish to efface this distinction in any case; but the deep commonality must also be emphasized as something no less important: idealizing interpretation—like allegorical [interpretation]—also recognizes a twofold meaning: a literal, non-binding, improper meaning, and an inner, binding, proper one. And the idealizing interpretation of Scripture fulfills the same function as Rambam's allegorizing [interpretation]: divesting Scripture of myth in inner accord with the *real* meaning of Scripture. Idealizing interpretation repeats allegorizing in a more reflective form. Thus Cohen accomplishes a *vindication of allegorizing*: he grants the criticism of allegorizing that allegorizing misconstrues the text inasmuch as it is not a plain-sense understanding of the text but a *reinterpretation* of it. But this reinterpretation is not a violation but a "reshaping":[62] a transformation of the earlier, the mythical, into the later. "And it is a question whether such reshaping is not the best form of annihila-

---

on these bases, whose analysis would lead too far {astray}, there exists a peculiar reluctance, a peculiar discomfort, regarding miracles. In order to be convinced of this, one need only read how, for instance, S. R. Hirsch expresses himself about miracles in his commentary on Exodus. With regard to Cohen, there is no doubt not only that miracles were of little importance for him, but also that he did not believe in them. We shall attempt to show how a position is to be taken toward the problem of miracles in the spirit of Cohen.>

{In the first deleted paragraph, things are complicated by the fact that deletions occurred inside deletions. To make this as clear as possible within the circumstance that this was an unfinished manuscript, one, two, three, and even four angle brackets have been used to show the level of editing at which these deletions occurred. See, e.g., Samson Raphael Hirsch on Exod. 4:1–5. *Der Pentateuch/Chamishey Chumshey Torah*, übersezt und erläutert von Samson Raphael Hirsch 5 vols. (Frankfurt am Main, 1867-78), Heft 2; *The Hirsch Chumash, Sefer Shemos*, trans. Daniel Haberman (New York: Feldheim, 2005), 48–50.}

59. {See Kant, *Critique of Pure Reason*, A314=B370. See "How to Study Medieval Philosophy," chap. 1 above.}

60. {See *Religion der Vernunft*, 78, 89f., 94, 172, 303f., 307; *Religion of Reason*, 68, 77, 81, 148, 260, 263. Cf. Cohen, "Die Bedeutung des Judentums für den religiösen Fortschritt der Menschheit" [The Significance of Judaism for the Religious Progress of Humanity], *Jüdische Schriften*, I, 18f.; reprinted as "Die Bedeutung des Judentums für den religiösen Fortschritt," in *Kleinere Schriften* IV, 429; "The Significance of Judaism for the Progress of Religion," ibid., 456.}

61. [The formulation that is found without reference marks as a note at a different place on the same page of the manuscript notebook should evidently replace the following passage, which was not removed in the running text:] by the consciousness of the *distance* from the author

62. {See the following note.}

tion" (*Religion der Vernunft*, ch. X, §19).[63] Whoever is familiar with Cohen knows that the *question* is only meant rhetorically:

> Against* every routine approach, the insight must prevail that progress in religious knowledge has been accomplished through the revision and reinterpretation of the sources, while these themselves remain preserved in their individual layers and have been at most rearranged or given different emphasis. (*Religion der Vernunft* I 5)[64]

Seen from this point of view,[65] Rambam's allegorizing signifies not an outward assimilation of the Bible to Aristotelian philosophy—this it is in part *also*; *most decisive*, however, is that it is the resumption of the efforts of the prophets, the redactors, and the targumim.[66] Of more particular significance for Cohen in this respect {402} was that he could discover the connection of Maimonides' historical interpretation of the sacrificial legislation with the prophetic critique and reinterpretation of sacrifice.[-58]

Allegorizing and—in the more reflective form—idealizing interpretation give the possibility of *applying a critique to the ancient without making a break with the ancients*. Critique is the element of the Enlightenment, which itself is described by its most famous representative as *esprit de discussion et de critique*.[67] Critique signifies: critique of the given; not resting with the given, [68]-not giving legitimacy to the world from the outset,[-68] [but] asking rather: *why* then is it really so? *The question about the purpose of the commandments* is therefore *critical*. Divesting the commandments of their mythical provenance is accomplished in answering it. For with this, indeed, it must be taken into account that a part of the biblical commandments is of mythical provenance. Now if, however—given the presupposition of the acknowledgment of the

---

63. {I.e., *Religion der Vernunft*, 204; cf. *Religion of Reason*, 175. We have used Strauss's own translation of this sentence in *Spinoza's Critique of Religion*, 24f.; or *Liberalism Ancient and Modern*, 250.}

64. {I.e., *Religion der Vernunft*, 44; *Religion of Reason*, 38, translation modified.}

65. [Noted in the margin as an alternative:]

From this insight, it turns out

***

Thus understood, Rambam's allegorizing in particular does not present [itself] *<chiefly> so much as* an outward assimilation of the Bible to the Aristotelian philosophy foreign to it, but rather as a resumption

66. {I.e., translations of the Hebrew Bible into vernacular languages, especially Aramaic.}

67. {French: "spirit of discussion and criticism (or critique)." See Voltaire, *Dictionnaire philosophique portatif* (London, 1764), 1596, s.v. "*Moïse*," section I, *in princ*.}

68–68. [Inserted between the lines or added in the margin by Strauss.]

Law,[69] given the preservation of historical continuity—the question is asked within an enlightened horizon about the purpose of the laws, then the laws receive an enlightened justification: they group themselves around a non-mythical center. "The reasons that are required for the laws, and *to the extent that they are required*, refer the laws to the tribunal of reason" (80/46).[70] This center, however, is Scripture's *real* doctrine; here Scripture's mythical horizon is dissolved by Scripture's non-mythical center. When Rambam teaches, for instance, that the purpose of the sacrificial legislation is the weaning from idol worship as defined by sacrificing to idols,[71] sacrifice as such becomes something unreal; now it is no longer a matter of sacrifice, but only of pure worship of God, worship of the *one* God. Thus what is mythical according to its origin acquires a non-mythical meaning.—In that the question is asked about the purpose of the laws, the result is that "value distinctions" are made "as regards the content of the Torah."[72] Cohen sees in this the "motivating idea[73] of his (Rambam's) entire life's work." And this idea[74] he makes entirely his own.

The Enlightenment's question as regards the given, *Why* then is it really so?, implies: Is it then *good* as it is? Enlightened critique is essentially practical, ethical; it has the goal of *improvement*. The good concerning which the Enlightenment wants to improve, it calls, ultimately, *humanity*.[75] Our task cannot be the analysis of this *goal*[76] of the Enlightenment and its connection with reason, the *vehicle* of the Enlightenment. We content ourselves with a {403} typical example, well known to all. The heirs of the Enlightenment in our time see the abolition of the death penalty as one of their most important objectives. The impartial observer has to notice that the opponents of capital punishment are argumentatively superior to its partisans, [since] the principle of retribution, [77-]of expiation,[-77] is not presentable as perspicuously

---

69. {Throughout the text, the word "law" (*Gesetz*) is capitalized when it implies in the immediate context revealed Law.}

70. {Cohen's original text emphasizes "reasons," rather than "to the extent," as in Strauss's quotation.}

71. {Maimonides, *Guide* 3.32 (Pines, pp. 529–31).}

72. {80/46. Likewise for the sentence that follows.}

73. {The German expression is *treibenden Gedanken*. We shall call attention to each occasion where, for the sake of English idiom, we have rendered *Gedanke* (literally, "thought") as "idea." Generally, we have saved "thought" or "thinking" for *Denken*. Unless otherwise indicated, *Idee* is always "Idea" (capitalized).}

74. {The German is *Gedanke*. See the previous note.}

75. {The German here is *Humanität*. Elsewhere, "humanity" is always *Menschheit*.}

76. [Noted in the margin as a replacement for the word not crossed out in the text:] concept

77-77. [Inserted between the lines or added in the margin by Strauss.]

in the light of reason as are the principles to which the Left appeals. The interest in retribution appears as an impenetrable, dark, affective principle, which psychology attempts to subvert on all levels ([e.g., as] desire for vengeance [, etc.] . . .). Insofar as we follow reason, we are humane, gentle; insofar as our institutions are constructed according to reason, these institutions are humane—however much something in us may also rebel against them: this is the enduring faith of the Enlightenment, undefeated to the present day, at any rate. Thus we understand what it signifies for Cohen when he can render the guiding idea[78] of Rambam's *Hilkhot Teshuvah*[79] with the words: "All fanaticism of retribution is deprived of its infernal claim by *one* single moment of repentance; repentance cheats Satan out of his directives [for the condemned]" [80-](125/165)[-80]. I pass over everything Cohen believed he was able to find to confirm it in the humane ideas[81] in Rambam's legal code, etc. How pleased he was with Rambam's *critique of asceticism*. The popular concept of the Enlightenment as it is familiar to all of us, as it is—in a certain manner—fulfilled in all of us, gives a rough introduction to the range of subjects [82-]in which Cohen can open up for us the understanding of Rambam.[-82]

[83]<[84-]Cohen links himself to the [line of] succession of Rambam because for him it is a matter of enlightened Judaism;[-84] for Rambam is the classic representative of enlightened Judaism, the "classic of rationalism" (*Religion der Vernunft*).[85] [86-]*The same thing*[-86] that Rambam had attempted with the

---

78. {The German is *Leitgedanken*. See nn. 3 and 73 above.}
79. {See Maimonides, "Hilkhot Teshuvah," trans. Hyamson, 81a–91b.}
80–80. [Inserted between the lines or added in the margin by Strauss.]
81. {The German is *Gedanken*. See n. 73 above.}
82–82. [Noted in the margin to replace the statement not removed in the text:] in which a deep and unparadoxical concurrence exists between Cohen and Rambam. {At the very beginning of this sentence, the phrase has been rendered, "the popular concept of the Enlightenment," i.e., the last word has been capitalized, and the definite article has been used. A possible alternative is to translate the phrase as "the popular concept of enlightenment." In the original German ("*Der populäre Begriff der Aufklärung*"), it is ambiguous whether that to which Strauss refers is *the* Enlightenment as a modern movement, or whether it concerns the idea of enlightenment as a permanent human possibility beyond historical specificity, equally directed to Maimonides as to Cohen. As readers should be aware, this is a difficulty that runs through the translation in general. The decision has been made to so render it in the present case because the entire paragraph which precedes it has been discussing Cohen's relation to *the* Enlightenment as a modern movement.}
83. [Both of the following paragraphs in the manuscript were subsequently enclosed with angle brackets.]
84–84. [Noted in the margin to replace the passage not removed in the text:] In that it was for Cohen a matter of enlightened Judaism, he gave himself over to the heritage of Rambam;
85. {See n. 18 above.}
86–86. [Inserted between the lines or added in the margin by Strauss.]

means of his time, the philosophy of his age, [and] therefore by means of *Aristotelian* philosophy, Cohen in the nineteenth and twentieth centuries had attempted with the means of his time, the philosophy of his age, [and] therefore by means of *Kantian* philosophy. *But it is precisely in this that the paradox of Cohen's veneration for Rambam consists.*[87] For Aristotelian and Kantian philosophy are for Cohen not something like earlier and later, less imperfect and more perfect philosophy, but they represent an *eternal opposition*, the[88] eternal opposition not merely of false and correct philosophizing, but of philosophizing in the state of betrayal of the most important concern of man and philosophizing in the state of fidelity to this {404} concern. Cohen's text testifies that this formulation is no exaggeration: "Aristotle is guided by enmity against the Idea; against the Idea of the Good" [89-](82/51)[-89]. ("Enmity against the Idea" is emphasized in the text.)[90]>

<Let me be understood correctly! Without a doubt, in order to understand Cohen's veneration for Rambam one must start from the fact that Rambam was a Jew and an enlightened Jew, and that there is a very deep and encompassing commonality [between him and] Cohen the passionate Jew and passionately enlightened Jew—despite all difference of philosophical opinions. But even with[91] this cautious formulation, we[92] cannot escape the paradox. For the expression "despite all difference of philosophical opinions" would only be permitted in that case if for Cohen philosophy dealt with mere *opinions*, if philosophical doctrine did not matter to him so *much*, and precisely so unconditionally. However, quite certainly that goes against Cohen's passionate conviction: that [conviction] very much depends, it depends *unconditionally*, on philosophical truth. But then we are [93-]not[-93] dealing with a mere *difference* but, insofar as Rambam follows Aristotle and Cohen follows

---

87. [Noted in the margin as an alternative:] But even <because this is so>, *to the extent that this is the case*, <Maimonides' ability to be a paradigm {is} really> it is impossible for Cohen to recognize Rambam as his paradigm and his teacher.

88. <*den Gegen*> the {It appears that Strauss began to write *den Gegensatz* ("the opposition").}

89-89. [Inserted between the lines or added in the margin by Strauss.]

90. [Noted in the margin:]

If Kantian and Aristotelian philosophy conduct themselves in this way, however, then the {. . .} is

* * *

Under these circumstances, it is impossible for a student of Aristotle to be able to be recognized by Cohen as a teacher.

91. <in>

92. <{there} remains the pa> we {It appears that Strauss began to write *Paradox* ("paradox").}

93-93. [Inserted between the lines or added in the margin by Strauss.]

Kant, with an *opposition*, with *the opposition* between correct and fundamentally erroneous philosophizing. And if Rambam was *really* an Aristotelian and *therefore* philosophized fundamentally erroneously, then Cohen's veneration for Rambam is put to a severe test; indeed, since Cohen was no less a passionate philosopher than he was a passionate Jew, it becomes *impossible*. The opposition between Kant and Aristotle cannot be shaken; the veneration for the great teacher Rambam must be maintained unconditionally; the difficulty can only be removed, then, by demonstrating that Rambam *at bottom* was *no* Aristotelian.[94] This is the road that Cohen in fact took.>[95]

Before we follow Cohen down this road, we must (1) establish[96] the *positive* meaning of the *negative* assertion that Rambam was at bottom no Aristotelian, and (2) *then* elucidate what is important about that *eternal* opposition.

If, in other words, Aristotelian and Kantian philosophizing presents a complete disjunction, so that every man philosophizes [whether] expressly or not as [either] an Aristotelian or a Kantian, then Cohen's assertion appears to imply: Rambam was at bottom a Kantian. From Cohen's viewpoint, that is not quite so absurd as it sounds initially; but since we are dealing with an opposition that {405} is already paradoxical enough in itself, we wish to spare ourselves further paradoxes as much as we can. And we can certainly do that. For indeed [97-]according to Cohen[-97] it [is] not at all the case that Kant was the *first* who philosophized in the correct manner. According to Cohen, the ancient paradigm[98] of correct philosophizing is: *Plato*. And *thus* Cohen's central assertion then also reads: "Maimonides was in deeper harmony with Plato than with Aristotle" (105/114). [99-]And we must therefore say: Cohen guides us to the understanding of Rambam as a Platonist.[-99] We therefore need to ask what the *opposition between Plato and Aristotle* signifies.[100]

---

94. [Note in the margin:]

<Or in other words> Yet that means—since *according to Cohen* Plato (Socrates)* is the initiator of the tradition of correct philosophizing—and is demonstrated, that Rambam was a Platonist

***

Primacy of theory—primacy of practical reason (critique of theory as improper thinking)

95. [End of the paragraphs enclosed with angle brackets.]
96. <make clear> establish
97-97. [Inserted between the lines or added in the margin by Strauss.]
98. <The> ancient <classic> → The ancient paradigm
99-99. [Inserted between the lines or added in the margin by Strauss.]
100. signifies <for Cohen>

PLATO AND ENLIGHTENMENT[101]

Now here is where great difficulties arise. The difficulties are so great that they do not permit us to answer the question in precisely the form in which it was posed. We will instead be able to answer it only in an *essentially more limited* form. We believe, however, that by this limitation not only is our real problem not shortchanged, but one can even begin to do it justice.

If one tries to answer the question of what is important about the opposition between Plato and Aristotle on the basis of Cohen's presentations, one comes up against the great difficulty that Cohen does not discuss this opposition within its original, ancient horizon, but violates this horizon, if not invariably, then nevertheless fundamentally.[102]

As Cohen understands Plato from the point of view of Kant, so he understands Aristotle from the point of view of Hegel. What especially concerns his understanding of Aristotle is that by its orientation to Hegel it is very often misguided. For Cohen, Hegel was the philosopher who had no inner connection with the fundamental science, the mathematical science of nature, who in this sense was a *metaphysician*, a "dogmatist of the absolute,"[103] *and* the philosopher of political *reaction*.[104] Kant, on the other hand, was the founder of the mathematical science of nature, the consummator of the work of Newton {406} *and* that of Rousseau, the father of the *French Revolution*.[105] One[106] should not for a moment lose sight of the *political* side of this opposi-

---

101. [Note in the margin:] *Plato and Enlightenment*. [After having composed the new introduction, Strauss may have intended to continue with his lecture here.]

102. [The manuscript continues at first with the following overview, which was later crossed out:]

<We show
1) that and how Cohen transcends this horizon,
2) how he justifies this transcending,
3) why we cannot follow.
1)> As Cohen

103. {Cohen applies this description to metaphysicians in general, and Aristotle in particular, at 86/62.}

104. {Cf. 85/58 (and Bruckstein's commentary ad loc.) with *Ethik*, 331f.//349f., 393//415f., 458//484f.}

105. {Cohen, *Kants Begründung der Ethik*, 3rd ed., reprint (Hildesheim: Olms, 2001), vif., 32f., 168f., 373, 466, 506 (on Newton); 167ff., 334, 378f., 389, 396f., 407f., 453, 501, 511, 521f. (on Rousseau). Note: the pages of the original 3rd edition have been reduced in size for the reprint edition, which makes references to reprint page numbers, especially in the first half of the volume, differ from those in the original 3rd edition.}

106. <Above all, the *political* side of this opposition adds to it> One

tion if one wants to understand[107] Cohen correctly; for Cohen *himself* did not for a moment lose sight of it. And it[108] truly does not signify any degradation of Cohenian philosophy if this point is emphasized.[109] It is self-evident that one should not thereby think of the paltry dealings of party politics, but that one must think of what Schiller calls[110] the "*great* objects of humanity,"[111] which are as such *political* objects. Politics is the field in which political, moral, [and] inner oppositions come to *decisive expression*,[112] where with respect to these oppositions things go *all out*, where it *becomes manifest* what is important about these oppositions. And this becoming manifest is nothing external or supplementary, but the internal, the philosophic as it presses outward from within toward expression, toward deed, toward realization. This is a fundamental idea[113] precisely of Cohenian ethics.[114] [115-]This is what Cohen means when in the *Ethik* [116-](168//176)[-116] he replaces the point of view of *intention*[117] with that of *action*. "Pure willing fulfills itself, perfects itself in pure action" (169//177). Only so does it become intelligible that he can on one occasion say in his *Ethik* (20//21):

> If today a hateful, sneering resistance ventures forth against (the) innermost vital core of the Kantian spirit, then it has grown along with the malicious, retrograde movements of our time, and is [to be] *characterized and judged by this connection*.[-115]

We find it to be superfluous to polemicize in detail against this interpretation of Aristotle. [118]<Whoever knows nothing at all about Aristotle, may be

---

107. <allow> {Strauss might have had in mind: "if one wants to allow Cohen to be understood correctly."}
108. <that>
109. <articulated>
110. <{for Schiller} are>
111. {Friedrich Schiller, *Wallensteins Lager* [Wallenstein's Camp], "Prologue," l. 65, in *Sämtliche Werke in zehn Bänden*, ed. Hans-Günther Thalheim et al., 10 vols. (Berlin: Aufbau-Verlag, 1980–2005), vol. 4 (1984), *Wallenstein: Ein dramatisches Gedicht*, 9; the emphasis is Strauss's.}
112. [Note in the margin:] <91, §2>
113. {The German is *Grundgedanke*. See n. 73 above.}
114. [Note in the margin:] <*Ethik* 20, par. 4–5//21f.>
115-115. [Inserted between the lines or added in the margin by Strauss.]
116-116. [Inserted between the lines or added in the margin by Strauss.]
117. {The German is *Gesinnung*. In the next paragraph, the German for the Greek *megalopsuchia* ("greatness of soul") is *grosse Gesinnung* (more or less literally, "grand intention," or perhaps "greatness of mind").}
118. [The rest of this paragraph and the following six paragraphs are marked with two large deletion signs, which refer to two full pages of the manuscript.]

reminded that the principle[119] of the mean is familiar to him as a Greek idea[120] by the name of[121] *measure*. Cohen[122] was not the first who completely misunderstood the principle of the mean as a praise of mediocrity; but it remained[123] reserved for him to make fruitful for the interpretation of Aristotle the *political* evaluation of the philistinism that festers in mediocrity, which Young Germany[124] had taken up.>

<In these circumstances, his[125] overall judgment on the *Nicomachean Ethics* does not surprise us: [126-]107f./123f. *Jüdische Schriften* III 263f.[-126]>

[Eudaemonia is the goal of Aristotelian ethics. One has reason to be of the view that without it Aristotle's ethics would not at all have arrived at the great recognition it enjoys; in it is contained the only speculative matter in the whole book; otherwise the book would be very interesting and valuable for anthropologists, {407} psychologists, moral researchers and statesmen, but this loquacious book would not at all have any systematic value, even for Aristotle's system. Eudaemonia alone is the breath that links ethics with the soul of his metaphysics.]

119. <the idea {*Gedanke*}> {See n. 73 above.}
120. {The German is *Gedanke*. See n. 73 above.}
121. <as the idea {*Gedanke*} of> {See n. 73 above.}
122. <He is> Cohen
123. <was>
124. {"Young Germany" ("Das Junge Deutschland") was a group of German writers between 1830 and 1850 who were influenced above all by Ludwig Börne (1786–1837) and Heinrich Heine (1797–1856). Consider the following remark by a well-known literary historian:

> ... Heine was at one and the same time a passionate lover of liberty and an out-and-out aristocrat. He had the freedom-loving nature's thirst for liberty, pined and languished for it, and loved it with his whole soul; but he had also the great nature's admiration for human greatness, and the refined nature's nervous horror of the rule of mediocrity.
>
> In other words, there was not a drop of conservative blood in Heinrich Heine's heart. His blood was revolutionary. But neither was there a drop of democratic blood in his heart. His blood was aristocratic, his desire was to see genius acknowledged as leader and ruler.
>
> ... He does not dread a condition of liberty, to which any liberty we have yet known on earth is child's play; but he does not believe that liberty would result from the realization of the Philistine ideals of the average mind. All mediocrity, Liberal and Republican mediocrity included, he abhors, as inimical to great individuality, to great liberty.

Georg Brandes, *Die Hauptströmungen der Litteratur des neunzehnten Jahrhunderts: Vorlesungen, gehalten an der Kopenhagener Universität von G. Brandes; Uebersetzt und eingeleitet von Adolf Strodtmann, W. Rudow [und] A. v. d. Linden*, 6 vols. (Leipzig: Veit, 1891), vol. 6, *Das Junge Deutschland*, 132f.; *Main Currents in Nineteenth-Century Literature*, trans. from the Danish by Diana White and Mary Morison, 6 vols. (New York: Boni and Liveright, 1923; London: Heinemann, 1923), vol. 6, *Young Germany*, 114f.}

125. his <judgment on>
126-126. [Inserted between the lines or added in the margin by Strauss.] {The Cohenian passage inserted in the square brackets immediately following this citation is Meier's editorial interpolation.}

Thus Cohen judges an immortal work that breathes Aristotle's spirit on every page, the spirit of rigorous analysis and calm description, and an approximate representation of its significance is given when it is said that the last chapter of *Beyond Good and Evil*, which is titled "What Is Noble?,"[127] is a paraphrase of the four pages[128] in which Aristotle analyzes *megalopsuchia*, [129]-"greatness of soul."-[129] The caricature rises to *demonizing* when Cohen [130]-explains the-[130] fact that Aristotle teaches that ethical objects can be set forth only "roughly and in outline"[131] as follows: "It is *enmity against the Idea*—against the Idea of the Good—which guides him there" (82/50). For what is a man who is filled with enmity against the Idea of the Good, who *hates* the Idea of the Good, other than a devil?

<This critique of Cohen is imperative for the sake of justice—for the sake of justice even toward Cohen. For one does [a] terrible injustice to him—as to any man—if one makes him into another man than he was [132]-so as to venerate a *phantom* in his *name*-[132]. If we *truly* venerate Cohen, then our veneration will withstand a just and necessary critique.>

<This critique would be enough if it dealt with a mediocre author. But with a man like Cohen [we] will have to ask ourselves how then such a procedure was possible which seems to mock all [133]-truth,-[133] justice, and tolerance. For with him even aberrations must come from a *depth* not to be found in a mediocre author. "Under the surfaces lie depths . . . ," as Rosenzweig says in the introduction to the *Jüdische Schriften*.[134]>

<We objected to Cohen's treatment of Aristotle in that it seems to mock all justice, all tolerance. We will not be able to avoid the question of whether *this* viewpoint, the viewpoint of {408} *tolerance*, is the ultimate viewpoint. Let us be instructed about this by Cohen himself! Cohen deals with the problem of tolerance in the passage of his posthumously published work ("Religion der Vernunft aus den Quellen des Judentums")[135] in which he brings up the treat-

---

127. {I.e., Nietzsche, *Jenseits von Gut und Böse, Neuntes Hauptstück*, in *Sämtliche Werke*, ed. Giorgio Colli and Mazzino Montinari, rev. ed., 15 vols. (Berlin: De Gruyter, 1999), V, 205–40; *Beyond Good and Evil*, chapter 9, in *Basic Writings of Nietzsche*, trans. Walter Kaufmann (New York: Modern Library, 1967, 2000), 391–427.}

128. {I.e., 1123a34–1125a35.}

129–129. [Inserted between the lines or added in the margin by Strauss.] {See n. 117 above.}

130–130. <states the following to explain the>

131. {1094b20.}

132–132. [Inserted between the lines or added in the margin by Strauss.]

133–133. [Inserted between the lines or added in the margin by Strauss.]

134. [Note in the margin:] "Above the depths lie surfaces, under the surfaces lie depths; they are bound up in the unity of man." *Jüdische Schriften* I, p. XIIIf.

135. {See n. 18 above.}

ment of idol worship in the Bible and especially in the prophets. Here Cohen recovers a ground from which tolerance appears as an *alien, disturbing* point of view. I deliberately draw attention to this passage, as it seems to me that hitherto this appears not to have been adequately appreciated—not even in its significance for Cohen's personality and doctrine. *Religion der Vernunft* 60, [line] 11—61, par. 3[136]> [:

> There can be no other God. There cannot be another Being[137] besides God's unique Being. Therefore, there can only be one unique worship of God, one unique love of God. Monotheism cannot acknowledge any tolerance of polytheism. Idolatry has to be eradicated absolutely. This decision is the precondition of true monotheism, the monotheism of love for God, of worship of God grounded in love.
>
> One has not acquired a true understanding of monotheism, which unites theory and practice, if one has not grasped the eradication of idolatry as an imperative necessity, if one believes one is able to detect even a trace of intolerance, of fanaticism and misanthropy in this holy zeal against the false gods. These suspicions merely disclose that one's own heart is not completely filled with the unique God and with the necessity of his unique Being, with the dual necessity of knowledge and acknowledgment[138] that constitutes man's relation to this unique God. On the other hand, for one who has made the unity of this duality of knowledge and will his own, there is no alternative: the worship of the unique God unavoidably requires the eradication of false worship. In this respect there can be no pity and no regard for men. The love for God uproots quietism. The true worship of God must be established and secured among men. Therefore the worship of false gods has to be annihilated from the earth. There is no alternative in the history of God's spirit. There is no higher spiritual authority that could release men from this fundamental duty. As monotheism and polytheism are absolutely contradictory, so are the worship of God and idol worship.
>
> In these considerations there is no {409} higher authority to which we may appeal. Rather, we must try to understand the *world history of the spirit*

---

136. {I.e., *Religion der Vernunft*, 60f.; *Religion of Reason*, 52f., translation modified. The Cohenian passage inserted as a block quotation in the square brackets immediately following is Meier's editorial interpolation.}

137. {The German is *Sein*. Henceforth, unless noted otherwise, "Being" is *Sein*, "being" or "essence" is *Wesen*, "existing . . ." is *seiend* . . . (though "existence" is either *Dasein* or *Existenz*, and "to exist" is sometimes *bestehen*), "human being" or "man" is *Mensch*, and "living being" is *Lebewesen*.}

138. {Or profession. The German is *Bekenntniss*. The verb "acknowledge" in the previous paragraph, however, is *anerkennen*.}

from its own[139] principles. In this theoretical problem of the history of the spirit, we cannot allow *tolerance* to have any say in the matter, [since tolerance] recognizes [it] as a duty to understand and to condone all views. Tolerance can come into play only for the ethical problem of world history in its practical application to men and peoples, from the viewpoint of the education of humanity. If, however, the *prophets* had to have created[140] the history of the spirit, then for them tolerance had to be an alien, a disturbing point of view. Therefore we need not consider the primitive age and the rudeness of its customs in order to understand the hostile opposition of the prophets to idol worship; the contradiction in principle between monotheism and polytheism sufficiently explains that historical duty of monotheism in its negative conduct toward polytheism.

To be sure, men had to be sacrificed for this purpose, men from their own people no less than from other peoples. However, the prophets did not fail to appreciate the humanity of men as such. "Thou shalt not abhor the Edomite, for he is thy brother" (Deut. 23:8). Only the historical principle, insofar as it was brought to victory, unavoidably requires the destruction of idol worship.]

<Is what we are supposed to say [something] that we cannot really say of ourselves: to say about this that our heart is completely filled with the unique God, or with the Idea of the Good? If despite everything we take for ourselves the freedom to criticize Cohen, to sustain our critique of Cohen even though we now know from what biblical depths the passion of his Aristotle critique derives, then we have no other justification than that Cohen was plainly not *only* a believing Jew and a biblical theologian, but *also* a philosopher. One cannot bow to a philosopher; one must examine his assertions. Even philosophy is in truth not absolutely tolerant; in any case, it is not so in *the* sense that it "recognizes [it] as a duty *to understand* and *to condone* all views."[141] In philosophy's sense it is definitely a duty to disapprove of false views, to reject them. To be sure, one must also do justice to the views that are false and deserve to be rejected. And Cohen has not done justice to Aristotle.>

<No one can with impunity evade the duty to historical justice. Not even

---

139. {Literally: one-sided.}

140. {Less idiomatically: had to have shaped creatively. The German expression is *schöpferisch zu gestalten hatte*.}

141. {Strauss is quoting from the third sentence of the third paragraph in the preceding block citation. The emphases here are Strauss's.}

Cohen. We recall the—by the way, {410} respectful—manner in which Cohen in his *Logic of Pure Knowledge* dismissed Phenomenology, which was then just emerging, as [a form of] scholasticism.[142] This justification for dismissal shows that Cohen surmised the deep connection of Phenomenology with Aristotle, the teacher of scholasticism. If Phenomenology has meanwhile become an all-prescribing power—whoever is not familiar with the *academic* concept of Phenomenology may be reminded that Franz Rosenzweig's concept of the New Thinking[143] is the *popular* concept of this philosophy—then this signifies a decisive step toward the re-establishment of Aristotelianism. The past, Aristotelianism, ostensibly overcome by Cohen, has risen anew and threatens to put seriously into question Cohen's life's work in the form he gave it. And not only that—Aristotelianism, and unidealized, unmodernized Greek philosophy in general, is not only a threat and for that reason already of contemporary interest. Above all, the modern presuppositions that for Cohen were *absolutely binding*, as one of his last statements demonstrates ("The Social Ideal in Plato and in the Prophets"),[144] may well appear to us decayed and brittle one day; perhaps then we will be happy if unidealized, unmodernized Greek philosophy shows us a way out of the modern anarchy.>[145]

In defining the opposition between Plato and Aristotle, therefore, we hold to the *unidealized* opposition and refrain from Cohen's [historical] breachings of the Greek horizon.

What therefore is important about the opposition between Plato and Aristotle? For it is a matter of an *opposition* according to Cohen, who contests[146] the thesis that "Aristotle must have nevertheless understood his teacher *before* all the epigones"[147] [148]-(70/14)-[148] and thereby asserts that Aristotle, [149]-who was in the Academy for twenty years,-[149] did not at bottom understand Plato, his personal teacher. This thesis too is paradoxical. Against it, modern research has shown the deep connection between Plato and Aris-

---

142. {Cohen, *Logik der reinen Erkenntnis*, 55-57.}
143. {Franz Rosenzweig, "Das neue Denken: Einige nachträglich Bermerkungen zum *Stern der Erlösung*" [The New Thinking: A Few Supplementary Remarks to the *Star of Redemption*], in *Kleinere Schriften* (Berlin: Schocken Verlag, 1937), 373-98; reprinted in *Franz Rosenzweig: Der Mensch und sein Werk: Gesammelte Schriften*, vol. 3, *Zweiströmland: Kleinere Schriften zu Glauben und Denken*, ed. Reinhold und Annemarie Mayer (The Hague: Nijhoff, 1984), 139-61; *The New Thinking*, trans. Alan Udoff and Barbara Galli (Syracuse: Syracuse University Press, 1999), 67-102.}
144. {See n. 11 above.}
145. [End of the portion of the text marked with two large deletion signs.]
146. <sets up> contests
147. {Cohen's original text emphasizes "Aristotle," rather than "before," as in Strauss's quotation.}
148-148. [Inserted between the lines or added in the margin by Strauss.]
149-149. [Inserted between the lines or added in the margin by Strauss.]

totle; at the frontier of this research we come across the thesis that Aristotle *completed* Plato's work.[150] We are not required to take a position on this quarrel. The difficulty that shows up in this quarrel, however, forces us into a modification—permitted in Cohen's sense, by the way—of our question. Cohen says (70/14f.):

> Perhaps one should say that he (Aristotle) would have grasped the Idea in general if he had been able to grasp the Idea of the Good. But for this he was missing not merely the Platonic capacity, but *above all* [and] *to begin with* the {411} Socratic one.[151]

The specific essence of Aristotelian philosophy therefore comes to the fore *to begin with* and *above all* and *all the more* in the opposition to Socrates. We therefore leave open the question about Plato's place between Socrates and Aristotle, and ask: *What does the opposition between Socrates and Aristotle signify?*,[152-]whereby we understand by Socrates the Socrates of the Platonic dialogues.[-152]

There is no *doctrine* of Socrates. Indeed, Socrates *could* not teach; he could only *question* and through his questioning help bring out insight in others. At first, [it was] the insight that what they supposed they knew, in truth they did not know. Not that he himself knew what the others did not know. But his wisdom—the famous wisdom of Socrates—consisted precisely in that he knew he knew nothing.

Even this knowing about not-knowing is no *doctrine*: Socrates is also *no skeptic*. A doctrine, a philosophical doctrine at least, is an answer to a question. Socrates, however, answers nothing. The apparent answer that he gives (knowing about not-knowing) is only the most penetrating expression of the question. Socratic philosophizing means: questioning.

But one for whom questioning is not about an answer does not truly question; and for one who like Socrates makes questioning the purpose of his life, it is *unconditionally* about an answer. But why is it that Socrates *remains* with the question? Perhaps because it is impossible to know anything, anything at all? But then did Socrates really know nothing? Yet he knew something;

---

150. {See Werner Jaeger, *Aristoteles: Grundlegung einer Geschichte seiner Entwicklung* (Berlin: Weidmann, 1923); *Aristotle: Fundamentals of the History of his Development* (Oxford: Oxford University Press, 1934).}

151. {The emphases are Strauss's.}

152-152. [Inserted between the lines or added in the margin by Strauss.]

he even knew *very much*; he knew, for example, that Athens' greatest sons, Themistocles and Pericles, had not in truth helped Athens, as all the world believed;[153] he knew that a life like that of Alcibiades was not a life worthy of man;[154] who among us would dare to assert that he knew so much? In these circumstances, how can Socrates say that he knows nothing? How can he *despite* his knowledge *remain* with the question? The answer is that he *wants* to remain with the question. And that is because questioning *matters*; because a life that is not questioning is not a life worthy of man. But why does questioning matter? Or, asked differently: *what* then is being asked *about*? What then is questionable? Many sorts of things are questionable. But if Socrates' questioning is a questioning that *matters*, then it cannot be *any old* questioning. It is not a questioning about the things in Hades, under the earth and in the heaven;[155] but [it is] solely *the* questioning which gets at what is *worthy* of questioning, what is necessary for *living*, at questioning about the manner in which one ought to live, at questioning about the {412} just life. Questioning about the just life, i.e., each individual's searching for and giving of an account of his life, whether he has lived justly, i.e., *taken responsibility* for his life. Socrates' question compels [one to take] responsibility; and whoever comprehends it comprehends that a life which does not consist in [taking] responsibility, which does not consist in constant examination, is not worth living for man. Socrates therefore does give an answer to the question about the just life: *questioning about the just life—that alone is the just life*. "The greatest good for man is this: to converse each day about virtue and the other subjects about which you hear[156] me conversing as I examined myself and others; an unexamined life, however, is not worth living for man" (*Apology* 38A). Questioning about the good, what it itself is really, questioning about the Idea of the Good—this alone is philosophizing Socratically.

Questioning and examining is not the self-questioning and self-examining of the solitary thinker; it is *mutual* self-questioning and *mutual* self-examining; it is *being responsible for oneself* in the original sense: one can be responsible for oneself only before a *person*. Socrates always philosophizes only with others. His questioning about the just life is a questioning *together*. He questions each together with the others not because he wants to convince the others—only a tutor can want that—but because he is after *agreement and*

---

153. {See Plato, *Gorgias* 515C–519B.}
154. {See Plato, *Symposium* 215E–216B.}
155. {Cf. Plato, *Apology of Socrates* 19A–D.}
156. <heard> hear

harmony. He is after agreement and harmony because only with agreement and harmony, with concord of the citizens, can the state truly be a state. The true state—this is truly living together; and human life in its essence is about living together; that is why the just life is living together justly, the true state; that is why all the virtues of the individual are possible and intelligible only by starting with the state. Thus the knowledge sought by Socrates is an accord arising from[157] an agreement about the good, which qua human good is the common good. *Socratic questioning about the just life is a questioning together about the just life together for the sake of the just life together*, for the sake of the true state. Socrates' questioning is essentially *political*.

The word "political" is necessarily ambiguous. We ran into this ambiguity already, when we spoke of Cohen's political passion and his political conception of the history of philosophy, and had to ask not to think of the paltry dealings of party politics. This ambiguity is so fundamental that {413} it cannot be gotten rid of by, for instance, the fact that one distinguishes between spiritual politics and special-interests politics. One need only read Plato's *Protagoras* in order to recognize how much the political art of this sophist [sc., Protagoras] is "spiritual politics"; indeed, it concurs *in content* with what is recommended to us nowadays as "spiritual politics."[158] The ambiguity is not at all to be avoided. It has its basis in [the fact] that human life is as such life together and thus political life. That is why every human action and motivation and thought is in itself political. But it is not always *expressly* so. We speak of men as statesmen when they are oriented to life together in an *express* manner, when that is what they are occupied with. One can be expressly involved in life together *without* responsibility or *in* responsibility[159]—[ergo,] ambiguity.[160] Without responsibility—i.e., without [the] question about the good, i.e., in the opinion that one knew what the good is. If I know what the good is, then I can teach it, teach it publicly; I can therefore also *write*. But if I have no knowledge about the good at my disposal, then I cannot teach, cannot teach publicly, cannot write. Because Socrates knows that he knows nothing, that all understanding can only be accord, for that reason he turns not to the multitude but only to the individual; his conversation with others is

---

157. <on> from

158. {For "spiritual politics" (or the politics of spiritual renewal as opposed to the politics of special interests), cf. *Jahrbücher für geistige Politik* [Yearbooks for Spiritual Politics], vol. I, *Das Ziel: Aufrufe zum tätigem Geist* [The Goal: Calls for the Proactive Spirit], ed. Kurt Hiller (Munich: Georg Müller, 1915), especially 34, 92, 128, 201, with *Protagoras* 318D–328D.}

159. [Noted in the margin and designated as an insertion:] ambiguity

160. [Note in the margin:] cf. *Gorgias*

dialogue. That is why he only *speaks* and does not write. For what is written is *necessarily* misunderstood; it cannot defend itself against misunderstanding; it *always says only one and the same thing*—whereas what matters is always to *say* the One True [Thing] differently. [161-]*Phaedrus* ch. 60.[-161, 162]

The fundamental ideas[163] of Socratic-Platonic philosophizing, thus sketched, are preserved—with certain modifications—in Cohenian philosophizing:

> 1) There is only *one* question: the question about the just life. Cohen (63f./2): there must and can be "nothing higher and nothing more urgent for the human spirit ... than its morality." "Socrates ... speaks of nature like a Nazarene:[164] trees cannot teach me, but only men in the city [can]. . . . Ethics as the doctrine of man becomes the center of philosophy."[165] (*Ethik* 1//1)
> 2) The question about the good must *remain* a question: "The moral is {414} ... a problem that always rejuvenates itself, appearing again in ever new questions, [with] every new solution only raising new questions." (70/15)
> 3) The question and the object of the question are, in themselves, *political*: Cohen interprets the Platonic *Crito* in the following way, [166-]and in this sense he makes it his own[-166] (*Ethik* 250//265): "There is no self-consciousness that is to be acquired without regard for the state and without being guided by the idea of the state."[167]

However, if that is what Socratic or Platonic philosophizing means, then must not each thinking man be a Socratic or a Platonist? Is it then not self-evident that the question about the Good is the highest and most urgent question? Let us ask instead under what conditions the Socratic question would *not* be the highest and most pressing question. Under *two* conditions:

> 1) if the just life were not questionable, if we *knew* what the Good is;
> 2) if man and his life in general were *not so important*.

161-161. [Inserted between the lines or added in the margin by Strauss.]
162. {I.e., Plato, *Phaedrus* 275C-276A.}
163. {The German is *Grundgedanken*. See n. 73 above.}
164. {I.e., a Christian.}
165. {"*Ethics as the doctrine of man becomes the center of philosophy*" is emphasized in the Cohenian original.}
166-166. [Inserted between the lines or added in the margin by Strauss.]
167. {The German is *Staatsgedanken*. See n. 73 above; cf. n. 272 below. Earlier in this sentence, "being guided" is *Leitung*. See n. 3 above.}

The fulfillment of both these conditions characterizes Aristotelian philosophizing.

Ad 1) "The moral is not a problem for him . . ." (70/15): Cf. Aristotle's statement on the aim of ethics: "*ou gar hin[a] eidômen ti estin hê aretê [skeptômetha], all' hin['] agathoi genô[m]e[th]a*"[168] [(*Ethica Nicomachea* 1103b27f.)].[169]

Ad 2) "His metaphysics is directed toward the universe . . ." (72/17): "*atopon gar ei tis tên politikên ê tên phronêsin spoudaiotatên oietai einai, ei mê to ariston tôn en toi kosmoi anthrôpos estin*"[170] (*Eth[ica] Nic[omachea]* 1141a20ff.).

That is how Aristotle recovers the fundamental possibility of the Greeks called into question by Socrates: the life [spent] in pure contemplation and understanding, in *theory* (*theôria*). And if Socratic philosophizing is questioning about the good of human life, about the true state, then Aristotelian philosophizing is pure contemplation of existing [things] and understanding of Being. And if Socratic philosophizing is in itself political, then for Aristotle politics moves into second place.—[171]

---

168. {"for we are inquiring not in order to know what virtue is but in order to become good." Here and in the following, Strauss's quotations from Aristotle, like Cohen's own, are in the original Greek fonts. Corrections to the manuscript text are added in square brackets.}

169. [Noted in the margin:]

decency
psegomen gar {"for we blame"; see *Ethica Nicomachea* 1130a21.}

170. {"for it is absurd for anyone to believe that politics or prudence is the most serious [knowledge] if man is not the best thing in the cosmos"}

171. [Noted in the margin:] *If at this point <1/2 hour> *20 minutes* are still left, interpolate*:

From this point of view, an ambiguity in the concept of enlightenment can be designated, to which Cohen (83 par. 2 / 53) draws attention: quote. ["Could Maimonides assume in his position the formula of Aristotle without any reservation? Were this the case, the entire rationalism of Maimonides, which he retained in the search for the principles of the Law, would then have the significance of a historical and anthropological interest, which Maimonides also manifestly evinces, yet on which his point of emphasis does not lie. Then his rationalism could not have the fundamental tendency of letting his theology culminate in ethics, as also his dogmatics aims at an ethics in each of its steps. Then this ethics would instead consist in an enlightenment borrowed primarily from, for instance, a history of the Sabians. The difference shapes always and in every regard the significance of God for this theology and, as one must presuppose, therefore also for this ethics."]

Then: Enlightenment polemical. Against superstition, against myth. Opposition between myth and science. (Correspondingly: between the concept of enlightened Judaism and the mythical horizon of Scripture.)

{The Cohenian sentences quoted in square brackets are Meier's editorial interpolation.}

[172]<Now what does this opposition have to do with the opposition between myth and enlightenment, by which we informed [ourselves] regarding the question about Cohen's understanding of Rambam? Is it not[173] then also and precisely Aristotle who is *enlightened* in the highest understanding of the word? Indeed, one need only think of his {415} writing on dream and dream interpretation.[174] But this concept of "enlightenment" is not sufficient. Enlightenment's struggle against myth as Cohen understands and conducts it, is carried out at such a depth that it is *likewise* directed against pure theory.>

<"Mythical man is interested only in the question about the *whence* of the world: with religion, this question recedes, [and] is supplanted by the new question: *whither*? *Purpose* steps into the foreground as against causality. It is not the primal cause, not the primal ground, which so much needs to become *the* problem of knowledge which could swallow up all other questions, as it is the question about the purpose of nature that becomes, especially in the purpose of the human world, the main question of human cognition." [175-]*Jüdische Schriften* I 94.[-175]>

<"For the spirit of *knowledge of nature*, all interest is concentrated on the *present*; in *its* existence all Being is enclosed; it has absorbed the past into itself. Thus, under the exclusive influence of this orientation of thinking, man too lives wholly in the present; it constitutes and establishes his reality. Mythical thinking *nevertheless* traces this reality *at most* back into a pre-existence, and where it devises a future for the individual, this is only just a *continuation* of the present or a *repetition* of the past, not however a *new* type of existence." [176-][*Jüdische Schriften*] III 141f.[-176] [177-]Aristotle's manner of thinking is therefore *mythical*, if it can be said of him that ". . . for him all of the future is only a rebirth of the past and its unsurpassable wisdom" (70/15).[-177]>

<It is therefore not only an opposition *within* philosophy, but an opposition that determines the constitution of philosophy itself.—>[178]

The proper perfection of man consists in contemplation and understand-

---

172. [The following four paragraphs are marked with a deletion sign in the margin.]
173. not <Aristotle>
174. {See Aristotle, *Peri enupniôn* [*On Dreams*]; cf. also Aristotle, *Peri tês kath' hupnôn mantikês* [*On Divination during Sleep*].}
175–175. [Inserted between the lines or added in the margin by Strauss.] {Strauss quotes from Cohen's "Einheit oder Einzigkeit Gottes" [Unity or Uniqueness of God], *Jüdische Schriften*, I, 187–99.}
176–176. [Inserted between the lines or added in the margin by Strauss.] {Strauss quotes from Cohen's "Religion und Sittlichkeit" [Religion and Morality], *Jüdische Schriften*, III, 98–168.}
177–177. [Inserted between the lines or added in the margin by Strauss.]
178. [End of the portion of the text marked with a large deletion sign.]

ing; indeed, in contemplation and understanding there is a difference of value[179] about the rank of the *object* of contemplation and understanding: the highest knowledge is knowledge of the highest being. And both Jews and Greeks call the highest being: God. The ideal of *theôrein* becomes the ideal of *knowledge of God*. The highest science is theology. From this point of view it becomes intelligible how the Jews and non-Jews of the Middle Ages could avail themselves of Aristotelian philosophy: what matters for man is designated in *Scripture* too as knowledge of God.

Now, however, because the God the knowledge of whom Scripture enjoins and the God the knowledge of which is Aristotle's goal are different, {416} *for that reason* Rambam can never at bottom be an Aristotelian. "All honor to the God of Aristotle; but truly he is not the God of Israel" (81/50). "The difference exactly constitutes always and in every respect the significance of God[180] for this theology . . ." (83f./53). It is

> non-objective and superficial to derive his (sc., Rambam's) intellectualism in ethics and theology simply from Aristotle. One would then also have to want to recognize his God as Aristotle's. Yet since God, the God of the prophets, . . . becomes for him [the] object of knowledge, whereas this God is no longer the God of Aristotle, then the concept of knowledge of God must also be one that is other than the concept of metaphysical knowledge of God in Aristotle. (91/75)

This signifies *first of all*: if the *biblical* God becomes [the] object of theory, then theory must necessarily be modified. In[181] his discussion of the commandment to love God and to fear Him, Rambam[182] asks about the *way* that leads to love of God and fear of God. This way is knowledge of the *world*. *Physics* here is understood as the way to love of God and fear of God. [183-]*Yesodei ha-Torah* II, 1–2.[-183, 184] Quite without question, the[185] Aristotelian ideal [186-]thus[-186] acquires a meaning that it can never have for Aristotle himself.

---

179. [The text initially read, and was later corrected accordingly:] If the proper perfection of man consists in contemplation and understanding, then there is thus in contemplation and understanding a difference of value

180. {Emphasized in Cohen's original text: *the significance of God*}

181. <I would like to illustrate this with an example that Cohen remarkably does *not* address.> In

182. <he>

183–183. [Inserted between the lines or added in the margin by Strauss.]

184. { *Sefer ha-Madda* (*The Book of Knowledge*), 35b.}

185. <the {. . .} becomes> the

186–186. [Inserted between the lines or added in the margin by Strauss.]

But such modifications should not be overestimated. They need not be more than *nuances*. Cohen, however, asserts more: he asserts that, through the biblical concept of God and the understanding of knowledge of God as knowledge of the biblical God, theory is *uprooted*.

COHEN'S INTERPRETATION OF RAMBAM'S DOCTRINE OF ATTRIBUTES[187]

If knowledge of God as theory is to be man's highest possibility, then God's essence must be knowable; it must be possible to make statements, positive statements about God's essence; it must be possible to ascribe definite attributes to God. But Rambam denies the possibility of positive attributes, because they call God's unity and uniqueness into question. Unity: they involve the distinction between essence and quality (accident). Uniqueness: they make the Creator and the created comparable (as for instance when {417} "existence" is predicated of both).[188] "What content does knowledge of God then have, however, without knowledge of His attributes?" (88/66). "How could Rambam[189] dispute knowledge of attributes and, on the other hand, make knowledge of God at the same time into the fundamental principle of his theology and his ethics?" (88/67f.). It signifies first of all: knowledge of God is possible only by way of *denial*. What is denied are defects, *privations*. The meaning of naïve positive attributes is only the *negation of a privation*. (Thus "God's eternity" signifies that He has not come-into-being; "life," that He is not a dead body; "powerful," that He is not weak; "willing," that He is not idle....) That does not appear to say much: only "to ward off a frivolity" (101/104). Rambam is saying *more*, however; he interprets, e.g., "powerful = not weak" as follows: God's existence is sufficient for bringing forth other things outside of Himself.[190] That implies: the negation of the privation does not merely reinstate the positive attribution,[191] but goes beyond it;[192] it replaces the positive attribute, which is only immanent, only designates the essence of God as an absolute, by a transitive one: it makes a statement about God *only in His correlation with the world. The rejection of positive attributes*

---

187. [Note in the margin:] *Cohen's Interpretation of Rambam's Doctrine of Attributes*
188. {See *Guide* 1.52, 56 (Pines, pp. 117–18, 131).}
189. {The Cohenian original reads "Maimonides."}
190. {See *Guide* 1.53, 58 (Pines, pp. 122, 136).}
191. {Literally: the position.}
192. [Note in the margin:] "God is not idle" = "God is the *origin* of activity."

signifies the rejection of knowledge of God as knowledge of an absolute; in this sense, it implies the rejection of metaphysics.

Knowledge of positive attributes is impossible. However, they can[193]

> not be denied in every sense; for revelation itself establishes such attributes.... Of which sort, however, are the attributes that revelation sets forth? They are those that ... solely and exclusively define Him (God) as a moral being, as a *being of morality*: in the words of Scripture, as merciful and gracious, and abundant in love and fidelity.

I.e., as the *paradigm* of morality, as simply the *Idea* of morality (89/68f.). Rambam calls the attributes of this sort *attributes of action*: they are attributed to God as the paradigms of human action.

Rambam is therefore saying: 1) the positive attributes are in truth negations of privations; 2) the positive attributes are attributes of action. And in a passage in the *Guide* he says: It is to be observed as regards the attributes in the books of the prophets "that they are the attributes of action, or that they indicate the negation of their privations."[194] He thereby *equates* the negation of {418} privations with the attributes of action. Negation of privations, however, signifies that statements about God are possible only as statements about God in His correlation with the world; if, however, the attributes of action are the same as the negation of privations and signify "attribute of action" as much as the paradigm of human action, then it follows that statements about God are possible only as statements about God in His correlation with the human world as the moral paradigm of man; God *is* in the correlation with man as with a moral being.

This interpretation of Rambam concurs completely with Cohen's own theology. He says (*Religion der Vernunft* 39)[195] in explanation of Micah's dictum ("He has told thee, O man, what is good"[196]):

> Thus, with regard to the problem of the good, God and man enter into a necessary community. God has to proclaim *this* and proclaim it to *man*. Does He

---

193. <themselves> can

194. {See *Guide* 1.59 (Pines, p. 142: "that they are attributes of action or that they indicate the negation of their nonexistence in God"). Cf. n. 215 below.}

195. {*Religion der Vernunft*, 39; *Religion of Reason*, 33, with Strauss's italics added.}

196. {Micah 6:8.}

have anything else to say at all? And is there any other being to whom He has anything to say?

Cohen is conscious of the *dubiousness* of this concurrence. He says (100/101):

> Here we come to a point at which I follow the fundamental idea[197] of my own systematic logic. It is thereby declared that the impartiality of the discussion, the objectivity of the historical elucidation, is put to a hard test. Meanwhile the reader, like the author, can first of all rest assured that *all* history of philosophy is beset or, as one should perhaps say, ought to be beset with this danger of an independent interest of speculation and therefore inevitably with the favoring of a single problem. There is, on the other hand, only one remedy against it, which is the thoroughgoing investigation of the literary sources and the rigorous distinction of hypothesis from fact.

Cohen himself thereby exhorts us, as it were, not to trust his assertions blindly, but to verify them carefully.

Cohen's assertion divides into three parts:

a) *equivalence* of attributes of action *and* negation of privations;
b) interpretation of negation of privations as a judgment about origin (correlation);
c) attributes of action define God solely and exclusively as the paradigm of morality.[198]

---

197. {The German is *Grundgedanken*. See nn. 73 and 163 above.}

198. [In two pages that are likewise found in box 8, folder 5, of the *Nachlass*, Strauss made notes in pencil to "Cohen's Interpretation of Maimonides' Doctrine of Attributes," which he used for the text in the manuscript with several changes and rearrangements. The notes read without regard to all of the early and middle stages:]

> Cohen's line of thought */ Argumentation* can be rendered in summary as follows: Since Rambam understands by God not the God of Aristotle, but the God of Israel, the "God of the prophets," "so must the concept of knowledge of God also be one that is other than the concept of metaphysical knowledge of God in Aristotle" (91/75). That this is so is proven, according to Cohen's assertion, by Rambam's doctrine of the attributes of God. According to this doctrine, the attributes of God occurring in Scripture are not actual, i.e., not to be understood as designations of the divine essence, but as negations of defects, of privations, or as descriptions (not of the essence, but) of the actions of God. Cohen's interpretation of this doctrine divides naturally into three parts: (a) interpretation of the negations of privations as "judgments of origin"; (b) interpretation of the attributes of action as attributes of moral action; (c) identification of the negations of privations with the attributes of action.

Ad a) If one compares the passage at *Guide* 1.59 (Munk 258 [Pines 142]) with the parallel in 1.58 ([Munk] 245 [Pines 136]), it follows unambiguously that the attributes of {419} action and the negation of privation are distinguished as the *two* ways in which something can be stated of God.

Ad b) The negations of privations are by no means *all* negations of privations of the sort that correlation is accomplished in them. E.g., "God lives" signifies "God is not without life," [199-]"not ignorant," "not dead" (*Guide* 1.58 [Pines 135f.])[-199]. "God exists" signifies [200-]"his nonbeing[201] is unthinkable,"[-200] "his nonexistence is impossible."

Ad c) Cohen: the attributes[202] that revelation sets forth define God solely and exclusively as a *moral* being. Cohen *is content* with that; not only is he

---

(a) Rambam's interpretation of the positive attributes occurring in Scripture as negations of privations does not appear to say [as] much; if the sentence "God is eternal" signifies "God has not come-into-being," or "God is powerful" signifies "God is not weak," then significations filled with content are transformed into mere defenses against "frivolities" (101/104). Rambam is saying considerably more, however; he interprets, e.g., "powerful = not weak" as follows: God's existence is sufficient for bringing forth other things outside of Himself. That implies: <the negation of privation does not merely posit, in any case> in that the positive attribute is understood as negation of a privation, the positive attribute, which is only "immanent," only designates the essence of God as an absolute, is replaced / is explained by a "transitive" attribute, that statements about God are possible and meaningful only as statements about God in His correlation to the world. The rejection of the positive attributes therefore signifies the rejection of knowledge of God as of an absolute, signifies the rejection of metaphysics.—What, however, now steps into the place of metaphysics for Rambam? In other words: what is the exact sense of each "correlation" of God and world?

(b) Cohen finds the answer to this question in Rambam's doctrine of the "attributes of action." The positive attributes can "not be denied in every sense; for revelation itself sets up such attributes. . . . Of which sort, however, are the attributes that revelation establishes? They are those that . . . solely and exclusively determine him (God) as a moral being, as a being of morality: in the words of Scripture, as merciful and gracious, and abundant in love and faithfulness." The "attributes of action" therefore determine God as the paradigm of morality, as the Idea of morality (89/69).

1 Negation of a privation = establishment of a correlation
2   = establishment of the correlation between God and man as moral being

The perfection stated of God only improperly: 1.26, 1.53 *in fine*

The only positive attributes are attributes of action: 1.52 *in fine*

The only attributes that occur in Scripture are attributes of action *or* indications of perfection 1.53 (sc., {Munk} 106b), 1.59 *in fine*

199-199. [Inserted between the lines or added in the margin by Strauss.]
200-200. [Inserted between the lines or added in the margin by Strauss.]
201. {The German is *Nichtsein*. See n. 137 above.}
202. attributes <of action>

content merely with that, [but] he takes it up with passion; *this* is, indeed, precisely his intention. For Rambam, on the other hand, ²⁰³⁻exactly⁻²⁰³ herein lies a *problem*. This fact is already a proof that he intends something quite different than Cohen does. Namely, after he has shown that the qualities ascribed to God by revelation concern only His effects or actions, Rambam sees himself compelled to explain why Scripture was *satisfied* with, was *limited* to, the mentioning of the moral qualities of God, even though Moses recognized that *all* qualities = God's actions. His answer: this happened because God's moral actions make possible the existence and leadership[204] of human beings; *they* are therefore the paradigm for every leader of human beings; that is why Moses, who had a people to rule, asked about them; they are "*necessary for the leadership of states.*" There is therefore a *specific reason* why Scripture in the passage concerned speaks *only* of moral actions; *it is self-evident that* there are also actions of God which are *not* "attributes of action" in this sense. These are the attributes of God which concern His effects on the extra-human world, on the universe. God says to Moses: "I shall let all My goodness pass before you"—i.e., according to Rambam: God gave him a thorough knowledge of *all* existing things. ²⁰⁵⁻*Guide* 1.54 [Pines 123ff.]; *but* cf. *Guide* 3.54 [Pines 635ff.].⁻²⁰⁵

Cohen's own assertion, which he believes he is able to rediscover in Rambam, namely, that God's Being is Being in correlation with man as with a moral being, says, in other words: man, the morality of man, is the purpose of the world. Precisely here Cohen sees the opposition between Plato and Aristotle: Plato teaches that morality is the purpose of the world, with the idea[206]

203-203. [Inserted between the lines or added in the margin by Strauss.]

204. {Or guidance. The German is *Leitung*. See n. 3 above. Likewise later in this sentence: "leader" is *Leiter*; and "leadership" is, again, *Leitung* (emphasized in Strauss's German)—for the expression "*notwendig für die Leitung von Staaten*," see *Guide* 1.54 (Pines, p. 128: "needed for the governance of cities").}

205-205. [Inserted between the lines or added in the margin by Strauss.]

206. {The German here, as later in the sentence, is *Idee*. See n. 73 above. At the present juncture it may be useful to consider the criticism of Strauss mounted by Benjamin Aldes Wurgaft, "How to Read Maimonides after Heidegger: The Cases of Strauss and Levinas," in *The Cultures of Maimonideanism: New Approaches to the History of Jewish Thought*, ed. James T. Robinson (Leiden: Brill, 2009), p. 377: "It is worth asking, however, whether or not Strauss's criticism of [Cohen's] Maimonides was based on a careful reading of Cohen's 1908 essay, which had in fact been committed to a strict division between the Good and worldly being, and [which] could have yielded precisely the strong critique of Heideggerianism for which Strauss hoped." The passage which follows in the text, discussing Cohen's view of Plato, seems to provide the evidence controverting the charge that Strauss did not read Cohen carefully enough on this point: as is clear from this passage, Strauss was fully aware that the Good is (in an as yet

that the Idea of the Good transcends in dignity and power the true Being of the Idea. As for Aristotle, in contrast:

> Nature accomplishes its good on {420} the basis of *its*[207] principles, and in virtue of these in the *relative purposes* of beings. For what purpose this whole of nature is here, and that this purpose constitutes morality, this question and this answer lie outside the Aristotelian mind. (72/18)

Does Maimonides teach otherwise than Aristotle here? He undoubtedly teaches the same thing. In his discussion of the question about the purpose of the universe, of nature, he first of all presents the Aristotelian view of nature and shows, entirely as Cohen does in the passage just adduced, that on the basis of this view one can *not* ask about the purpose of the universe. However, he continues, there are people [who are of the opinion] that according to *our* view, according to the view of those who believe in the creation of the world therefore, the ultimate purpose of the world can be asked about; accordingly, it is believed that the purpose of the world is: the human race [is] intended for worship of God. This view is rejected by Rambam: the existence of the world has no other purpose than the free will or the wisdom of God. And completely in Aristotle's sense he refers to *how small* man is in comparison with the cosmos (with the spheres and the separate intelligences).[208-] *Guide* 3.13 [Pines 452ff.].[-208]

If therefore man is *not* the purpose of the world, if there is something greater than he in the world, then he cannot be what [ultimately] matters; then politics cannot be the highest and most important science; then the highest thing is: contemplation of existing [things] and understanding of Being.

Aristotle gave expression to this priority of pure contemplation and understanding over all moral action by the distinction between dianoetic and

---

undefined sense) "transcendent" for Cohen, as it was most emphatically for his Plato. Let it be suggested by the present editor, in order to designate the ground on which discussion of this point would have to be further pursued, that such transcendence of the Good remains true for Cohen just so long as humanity has not reached the messianic goal of history in history (showing his "transcendence" is not the same as Plato's "transcendence"), which on principle it can never reach but which asymptotically it must ever and again strive for. As it seems to me, Strauss merely wondered whether Cohen's "transcendence" of the Good is as sustainable or as persuasive in history or in being as the "transcendence" of the Good in Plato or in Maimonides.}

207. {Strauss's emphasis. Later in Cohen's sentence, *relative purposes* is Cohen's own emphasis as well.}

208-208. [Inserted between the lines or added in the margin by Strauss.]

ethical virtues.[209] Rambam makes this distinction entirely his own. He teaches that moral perfection is of a lower rank than intellectual [perfection],[210] because it is *only* in the mutual[211] relations of human beings, whereas the latter pertains to the human being, to the individual *for himself*; moral perfection is useful at bottom only for others, not for oneself; intellectual perfection pertains to one[self] *alone*; it pertains to one[self] *simply.* [212-]*Guide* 1.54[213] [Pines 123ff.] = *Eth[ica] Nic[omachea]* X 7.[214] Distinguishing the wise from the multitude [is] *fundamental*: esotericism. (Cohen 102n/104:[215] in Rambam it goes further; but one should not communicate that to the multitude!)[-212] {421}

The moral is as such the social—but then Rambam's ideal existence is unambiguously trans-moral. Man's highest possibility consists—Rambam's statements on this are unambiguous—not in moral action but in pure understanding.

When knowledge of God becomes knowledge of the God of Israel, it uproots the priority of pure understanding—so runs Cohen's assertion. We have seen that this assertion does not withstand examination. Is[216] Cohen's first and [most] proper assertion, that Rambam is in deeper harmony with Plato than with Aristotle, thereby disposed of? If one has gotten lost in the details, then one must recall Cohen's *guiding*[217] *insight*: "All honor to the God of Aristotle; but he is not the God of Israel."[218] This fundamental fact, thus expressed by Cohen, *can* surely not remain without consequences for Rambam and the understanding of Rambam. Cohen's fundamental insight is so evident that in fact it remains unshaken. But Cohen concludes too quickly. We must deal with the fact that Rambam adopts Aristotle's ideal of life, *theôrein*. We have to start with this fact.

Aristotle says (*Eth[ica] Nic[omachea]* X 7) in his analysis of the philosophical existence: whereas the just man, the courageous man, the prudent

---

209. {See *Ethica Nicomachea* 1103a14ff.}
210. [Note in the margin:] Only in the understanding is *complete autarchy* possible.
211. {Reading *gegenseitigen* for *gegenwärtigen*.}
212-212. [Inserted between the lines or added in the margin by Strauss.]
213. {Conceivably, "1.54" is a transcription error for "3.54"; in any case, see n. 205-205 above.}
214. {See n. 219 below.}
215. {Cohen's note quotes (in Hebrew) *Guide* 1.59: "But regarding the other attributes that occur in the books of the prophets and are recited during the perusal of these books, it is believed, as we have made clear, that they are attributes of action or that they indicate the negation of their nonexistence. . . ." (Pines, p. 142).}
216. Is <therefore Ram>
217. {The German is *führend*. See n. 3 above.}
218. {See *Philosophie und Gesetz: Frühe Schriften*, vol. 2 of *Gesammelte Schriften*, 416. See also the previous section in the present lecture, and "Maimonides' Doctrine of Prophecy," chap. 4 below.}

man et al., in order to act qua just, etc., always needs others with whom and in relation to whom he acts justly, etc., [and] whereas *he* therefore is not simply self-sufficient, the wise man can also live existing for himself in contemplation, and, indeed, he does so all the more, the wiser he is. "Admittedly, it is perhaps better if he has collaborators; but nevertheless"—although in his case an advantageous possibility also exists to being with others—"he is self-sufficient in the highest degree."[219] Although understanding is in itself asocial, *it* can nevertheless *experience* per accidens an advantage in shared understanding.

With this statement of Aristotle, we compare a statement of Rambam. He says: there is superiority and inferiority of understanding in human beings; one man understands only[220] for himself, another—going further—is in a position to help others understand.[221-] *Guide* 2.37 ([Munk] 289f. [Pines 373f.]).[-221] This implies: although understanding is in itself asocial, nevertheless an advantage can *proceed* per accidens from it to another.[222]

Common to both:[223] understanding is self-sufficient, absolutely perfect. But it has to do with others *accidentally* and, to be sure, that in having to do—in a determinate manner—with {422} others, it discloses[224] possibilities of superiority and inferiority.

Perhaps it is *not* accidental that, in the passage in which he recapitulates Aristotle's analysis of the philosophical life, Rambam does not speak of the advantage that understanding *experiences* through collaborators, but that he speaks—although in another passage[225]—of the advantage that *proceeds* to another. Perhaps the difference between Rambam and Aristotle which was surmised by Cohen proclaims itself in this [manner of speaking].

Pure understanding stands higher than moral action—this must be unconditionally maintained as Rambam's doctrine. But is the philosopher for that reason man's highest possibility? According to Rambam's doctrine, the *prophet* stands *higher* than the philosopher. Hence, if there is a limitation, a calling into question, an uprooting of the Aristotelian ideal in Rambam, then it must show up in his *prophetology*.

How does the prophet relate to the philosopher according to Rambam's doc-

---

219. {*Ethica Nicomachea* 1177a34–b1, with 1177a32ff.}
220. <sufficiently>
221–221. [Inserted between the lines or added in the margin by Strauss.]
222. another. <And like Aristotle the>
223. both <statements>:
224. <contains in itself> discloses
225. {See *Guide* 2.11 (Pines, p. 275).}

trine? He is *superior* to him. He has first of all *philosophical* insights to which the philosopher could never attain. He has a faculty of *surmising* that makes it possible for him to see future events[226] as though they were happening in front of him corporeally. This signifies that the prophet is superior to the philosopher as *knower*. In this way, therefore, the priority of understanding is not only not limited, but is even *underscored*. [227]-*Guide* 2.38 [Pines 377f.].[-227]

The prophet is further distinguished from the philosopher, however, in that he is in a position to present philosophical insights *figuratively*: in the act of prophetic knowing not only is the intellect at work, as in the case of the philosopher, but the imagination is grasped and led by the intellect. This capability of figurative presentation enables the prophets to address the multitude who are incapable of philosophical insight, [and] to lead[228] them. This is not the *sole* purpose of figurative presentation; but in any case [it is] an important purpose. From this it follows that the prophet is distinguished from the philosopher in that he has the capability *to lead* the *multitude*.

About the relationship of philosopher and prophet, Rambam expresses himself further: in the case of the philosopher only the intellect is actualized, in the case of the prophet first the intellect and then the imagination. [229]-[*Guide*] 2.37 [Pines 374].[-229] The prophet is therefore *more* than a philosopher. In order to positively determine this "more," we ask which class of men is then characterized by the actualizing of the imaginative faculty alone. This class {423} dazzles in all colors: statesmen, legislators, soothsayers, magicians. Prophecy is therefore a unity of philosophy, on the one hand, and politics, divination, and magic, on the other.

It remains entirely unclear here where the stress lies: whether politics, divination, and magic are equally important, equally distinctive, or whether any one of the three plays a special role. We ask first of all: which is then the *most perfect*, the highest rank of prophecy? The prophecy of Moses. It is distinguished from the prophecy of all other prophets by its alone having had the consequence of calling us to the *Law*. Abraham, e.g., was inspired in the highest degree, but did not do *more* than *to instruct, to teach*,[230] men; he did not call them to *lawful actions*. In the same way, the post-Mosaic prophets do nothing other than exhort regarding the fulfillment of the Law given by

---

226. <things>

227–227. [Inserted between the lines or added in the margin by Strauss.]

228. {Or guide. The German is *leiten*. Likewise in the last sentence of this paragraph. See nn, 3 above, and 233 below.}

229–229. [Inserted between the lines or added in the margin by Strauss.]

230. {Or advise. The German is *belehren*.}

Moses. *The peak of prophecy is therefore legislation.*[231-][*Guide*] 2.39 ([Munk] 301 [Pines 378f.]).[-231]

But Moses *also* towers above the other prophets by the faculty of knowledge and by his miracles. It therefore still remains open what [is] then most distinctive of the prophets: politics, magic, [or] divination. We therefore ask: *what* then really matters *ultimately*? what is the *ultimate purpose* of prophecy? why then does man really need prophecy?

The answer Rambam gives, although [he] does not give it expressly as such, runs [as follows]: man, according to his nature, [and] in contradistinction to the other living beings,[232] needs socialization; on the other hand, in no other species does there exist such great diversity, indeed contrariness, among individuals as exists precisely in the human species. Since therefore socialization is nowhere so necessary and nowhere so difficult as precisely in the case of men, men are thus in need of a *leader*[233] who regulates the actions of individuals such that a concurrence resting on statute replaces the natural contrariness. There are two types[234] of leadership: legislation and governance. The legislator draws up the regulations for actions, the king enforces obedience to them. Governmental leadership, therefore, always presupposes an already [existing] legislation. [235-][*Guide*] 2.40 [Pines 382].[-235] Now, as concerns legislation, it can have as its purpose either the perfection of man's *body* or that of his *soul*. Or rather—since the realization of the higher perfection has the realization of the lower one as its necessary presupposition—legislation can limit itself to the bringing about of the perfection of the body, {424} or it can aim at the perfection of the body in service to the perfection of the soul. The law that has as its goal the perfection of the soul is a *divine* law, and its proclaimer is a *prophet*. The perfection of man's soul is his *proper* perfection. [236-]*Guide* 3.27 [Pines 511f.].[-236] We can therefore say: the prophet is the proclaimer of a law that is directed toward man's proper perfection; or, since the law aims at making life together possible: *the prophet is the founder of a community that is directed toward the proper perfection of man.*

231–231. [Inserted between the lines or added in the margin by Strauss.]
232. <beings> {In the present case, the word "beings" [*Wesen*] was deleted in favor of "living beings" [*Lebewesen*].}
233. {Or *guide*. The German is *Leiter* (emphasized by Strauss). Likewise in the next sentence, "leadership" is *Leitung*; and two sentences later, "governmental leadership" is *regierende Leitung*. See n. 3 above.}
234. {Elsewhere: manners. The German is *Weise* (in the plural). See n. 54 above.}
235–235. [Inserted between the lines or added in the margin by Strauss.]
236–236. [Inserted between the lines or added in the margin by Strauss.]

We saw just now that the prophet was defined as: *philosopher*,[237] *statesman*, *seer*,[238] *and miracle worker in one*. If, however, the founding of a community directed toward man's proper perfection is the *purpose* of prophecy, then we have to conclude: the prophet must be a philosopher, a statesman, a seer, and a miracle worker *in one*, so that he can be the founder of a perfect community, of the *ideal state*.

Our reasoning has a lacuna [in it]. We came to our answer by way of the question: what then is the *purpose* of prophecy according to Rambam? We said that Rambam gives us an answer, but not expressly as such. It must therefore still be shown that the answer is an answer *in* Rambam's *sense*.

An elaborate theory of prophecy preceded Rambam. He makes reference to it expressly and accepts it expressly—to be sure,[239] with a reservation that is, however,[240] not significant in our context.[241] We have a right in principle, therefore, to draw on Rambam's[242] Islamic predecessors, [even] if he himself eludes our grasp.

237. <{a} unity> *philosopher*
238. <sooth> *seer*
239. <admittedly>
240. <admittedly>
241. {See *Guide* 2.32 (Pines, pp. 361–63); but cf. also 2.29 (Pines, pp. 345–46). Concerning Maimonides' "reservation" as regards the prophetology of his predecessors, cf. Strauss, *Philosophie und Gesetz* (Berlin: Schocken Verlag, 1935), 106; *Philosophie und Gesetz: Frühe Schriften*, vol. 2 of *Gesammelte Schriften*, 107; *Philosophy and Law*, 117f.; "Maimonides' Doctrine of Prophecy," chap. 4 below:

> In Islamic philosophy there are two opposing views on miracles. According to the doctrine of the *kalam*, miracles take place through the power of God, not through the activity of the prophet; the prophet's relation to the miraculous event is none other than that of announcing it beforehand; the occurrence of the previously announced miracle is the divine confirmation of the prophet; it is by means of this announcement that miracles proper differ from the miracles worked by holy men and sorcerers. In opposition to the *kalam*, the *falasifa*—on the grounds that whatever occurs does not spring from the unconditioned free will of God but must proceed from other occurrences and under fixed conditions—teach that miracles are performed and not just announced by the prophets. Maimonides is taking the principle of the *falasifa* into account when he teaches that miracles are, in a certain sense, in nature: when God created nature, He put into it the faculty of bringing forth miracles at predetermined times; God lets the prophet know the time for which he should announce the occurrence in question, and this is the "sign" of the prophet. Thus Maimonides, like the *falasifa*, denies that God interferes at His free will in the world created by Him, but, on the basis of the *falasifa*, he adheres to the view of the *kalam* on the role played by the prophet in the miracle: the prophet only announces the miracle, he does not perform it; it is performed by God. But if the miracle is performed by God and not by the prophet, then prophecy itself can depend on God's free miracle-working. This is why Maimonides can teach that prophecy can be miraculously withheld from a man who fulfills all the conditions of prophecy. This teaching is the reservation that he holds against the prophetology of the *falasifa*. This reservation is possible only if the miracle is not really performed by the prophet. Thus, the fact that Maimonides abandons the doctrine of the prophet's miracle-working is the only factor distinguishing his prophetology from the *falasifa*.}

242. Rambam's <Arabic precursors>

THREE / 216

Moreover, in our case we have a still more specific[243] right [to draw on his Islamic predecessors]. An old commentator—Shem Tov ibn Falaquera—in his commentary on the relevant Rambam passage adduces an excerpt from Avicenna which was manifestly the model for the aforementioned chapter from Rambam.[244] It is therefore certain that this *part* of Rambam's prophetology also goes back to Islamic sources. The source itself is available to us: it is in Avicenna's *Metaphysics*, whose doctrine in both its versions (*Najāt* and *Shifā'*)[245] concurs completely with this [passage]. We therefore go back to *Avicenna*.

In his treatise *On the Parts*[246] *of the Sciences*,[247] Avicenna instructs us as

---

243. <peculiar> specific
244. {See Shem Tov ben Joseph ibn Falaquera on *Guide* 2.40, in *Moreh ha-Moreh*, ed. Yair Shiffman (Jerusalem: World Union for Jewish Studies, 2001), 289–90:

> And [thus] Ben [i.e., Ibn] Sina says that insofar as human beings are in need of dealings with one another, they are in need of a fixed [or established] law [*chok yadua*]. For it is not possible that things will be seen in the same way by all of them [i.e., by all human beings]. For how will it be seen that one is worthier [i.e., in a matter of negotiating their dealings] by the other who is violent [by nature]; and hence they are in need of a lawgiver who legislates for them one law [applying] equally to everyone. And therefore they [i.e., human beings] have greater need of a lawgiver than they do for the growing of hair on the eyebrows, [or] for the concave shaping of the arches of the feet, and for other things like this, that are useful but not necessary for the survival of animals [lit.: living beings]. And it is not possible that divine providence [*ha-hashgakha ha-elohit*] would order [or cause] the existence of those useful things [i.e., for the survival of animals], and not order [or cause] the existence of this on which [their survival, i.e., in the case of human beings] rests. It is not possible that there exists the primary providence [i.e., God] and the angels, which know those useful things, and [yet] do not know the usefulness of the lawgiver who gives the laws. Therefore it is necessary that the prophet exists, and it is necessary that he be a human being, and that he possess special attributes which do not exist in other human beings; and this is the prophet sent by God, may He be blessed. And it is required by divine wisdom to send him [i.e., the prophet] and all that he will legislate in the mission from God, may He be blessed. And God, may He be blessed, requires of the prophet that he legislate worship of Him, and that there be useful things in His worship, and that the religion [or law] [*dat*] will confirm that He is the cause of the existence of man. And thus [he further] said: the traditional things are opinions that are justified by those [previous points], because they are things which are supported by their speeches [i.e., of the prophets], and it is believed that they are true speeches, or that they contain fitting things in them, or that one may know fitting thoughts through them, by which human beings achieve happiness, for which reason we believe [those traditional] things which we received from the teachers of the religion [or law] [*dat*]. (Trans. Kenneth Hart Green)

Cf. Avicenna, "Healing: Metaphysics X," trans. Michael Marmura, in *Medieval Political Philosophy*, ed. Lerner and Mahdi, 99–100; or Avicenna, *The Metaphysics*, trans. Marmura, 364–66. Cf. also Strauss, *Philosophie und Gesetz*, 110ff.; *Philosophie und Gesetz: Frühe Schriften*, vol. 2 of *Gesammelte Schriften*, 111ff.; *Philosophy and Law*, 122ff.}

245. {The *Najāt* ("Deliverance") is Avicenna's epitome of his larger work, the *Shifā'* ("Healing"). On the *Najāt*, see Fazlur Rahman, *Avicenna's Psychology: An English Translation of Kitāb al Najāt, Book II, Chapter VI* (London: Oxford University Press, 1952). On the *Shifā'*, see n. 248 below.}

246. <Division>

247. {See Avicenna, "On the Divisions of the Rational Sciences," trans. Muhsin Mahdi, in *Medieval Political Philosophy*, ed. Lerner and Mahdi, 96f.}

follows: that there is prophecy and that the human race in its existence is directed by a law given through a prophet {425} are taught by the science of *politics*. It is *this* science that teaches, further, which characteristics are common to all religious laws and which differ according to nation and time, and how divine prophecy and false prophecy are distinguished. If therefore the necessity of prophecy is to be taught by politics, then the purpose of prophecy is, undoubtedly, *political*. And of the three moments that we had to distinguish in prophecy besides philosophy—politics, magic, and divination—politics has priority.

In conformity with his program, Avicenna has treated prophecy in his politics (at the conclusion of his *Metaphysics*).[248] In this context we encounter the remarkable sentence: "The first purpose of the legislator in legislating is the division of the city into three parts: into *leaders*,[249] *artisans, and guardians*."[250] This means: the legislator divides the city in line with the division prescribed by Plato in his *Republic*.[251] The legislator according to Avicenna, however, is necessarily a prophet. We must therefore say: *the business of the prophet is understood by Avicenna according to the guidance*[252] *that Plato's "Republic" gives*.

This observation is confirmed over and over again. In a special treatise on prophecy,[253] Avicenna makes reference to statements of Plato's in justification of the esoteric character of prophecy.[254] *These* statements are, admittedly, pseudo-Platonic; and [yet] in another respect the fact that this is so is in no way inconsequential. But just as little is it inconsequential that Avicenna in his doctrine of prophecy understands *himself* as a student of Plato.

In the aforementioned treatise *On the Division*[255] *of the Sciences*, Avicenna says expressly: the political writings of Plato and Aristotle dealt with proph-

---

248. {See Avicenna, "Healing: Metaphysics X," in *Medieval Political Philosophy*, ed. Lerner and Mahdi, 98–111; or Avicenna, *The Metaphysics*, trans. Marmura, 364–78.}

249. {The German is *Leiter*. See n. 3 above. Marmura renders Avicenna's Arabic term, *mudabbir*, as "administrators"; see the following note. The translators are indebted to Professor Joshua Parens, University of Dallas, for this and related information.}

250. {Loc. cit., Ch. 4, beginning: *Medieval Political Philosophy*, ed. Lerner and Mahdi, 104; *The Metaphysics*, trans. Marmura, 370.}

251. {Literally: state. The German is *Staat*. Likewise in the remainder of the manuscript except in Strauss's parenthetical citations and in connection with nn. 256 and 257 below, where Strauss uses *Republik*.}

252. {The German is *Anleitung*. Cf. nn. 3, 10, 167, and 228 above.}

253. {Avicenna, "On the Proof of Prophecies," trans. Marmura, 112–19.}

254. {Ibid., 116 (with 119, containing Marmura's nn. 3 and 4 ad loc.).}

255. {See n. 247 above.}

ecy in its political character.[256] These writings appear here as the fundamental books of prophetology, just as the *Nicomachean Ethics* does as the fundamental book of ethics. Aristotle's *Politics*, however, has never been translated into Arabic, so it appears.[257] *That is why Averroes saw himself*, as he himself says, obliged to comment on Plato's *Republic* instead of Aristotle's *Politics*. Even in this commentary, incidentally, we note the tendency to interpret prophecy, i.e., the law of Muhammad, in the light of Plato {426}. Plato's *Republic* therefore had a greater influence *in fact* than Aristotle's *Politics*. Could that have been only *accidental*?

We have attempted to clarify the opposition between Plato and Aristotle as an opposition of questioning about the good and the life [spent] in pure contemplation and understanding. Questioning about the good is questioning about what the good as such is, [i.e.,] is questioning about the *Idea* of the Good. For it to be able to be asked about justly, a *preparation* is necessary. There is need of a *detour*, on which it must be asked, among other things: what the soul is; what its parts are; what science is; what being is; what the One is, etc. It must *also* be asked, therefore, what Aristotle will then ask about later though *no longer* in alignment with the question about the good. This means, however: contemplation and understanding, in the sense and with the tasks that Aristotle sets for them, have already been fully[258] elaborated in Plato; that is why Plato knows, just as exactly as Aristotle does, that man's happiness consists in pure contemplation and understanding. Philosophers, says Plato, live in the belief that they have already been relocated during [their] life to the Islands of the Blessed (*Rep[ublic]* 519C). Understanding is, for Plato just as for Aristotle, man's highest possibility. The *decisive difference* consists in the manner[259] in which they *conduct* themselves toward this pos-

---

256. {See *Medieval Political Philosophy*, ed. Lerner and Mahdi, 97:

> The treatment of kingship is contained in the book by Plato and the book by Aristotle on the regime, and the treatment of prophecy and the Law is contained in their two books on the laws.

(Cf. Marmura's note ad loc.:

> While in the case of Plato the references are unmistakably to the *Republic* and the *Laws*, the references to Aristotle are less certain. Avicenna may be referring to the two books given in the bibliographies of Aristotle's writings, which bear the same titles as the two works by Plato.)}

257. [Moritz] Steinschneider, [*Die*] *Hebräische Übersetzungen* [*des Mittelalters und die Juden als Dolmetscher* (Berlin: Kommissionsverlag des Bibliographischen Bureaus, 1893; reprint, Graz: Akademische Druck-u. Verlagsanstalt, 1956)], p. 219. "Aristotle's *Politics* has never been translated into Arabic." {See also "Some Remarks on the Political Science of Maimonides and Farabi," chap. 5 below, n. 5, as well as the text to which it refers.}

258. [Noted as an alternative between the lines:] fundamentally

259. {Or mode. The German is *Art*. See n. 54 above.}

sibility. Aristotle sets it completely free; [or] rather, he leaves it in its natural freedom. Plato, on the other hand, does *not permit* to philosophers "what is now permitted to them," namely, the life in philosophizing ²⁶⁰⁻as⁻²⁶⁰ *abiding* in philosophizing, in the beholding of the truth. He "*compels*" them "to care for others and to guard them" (*Rep[ublic]* 519D–520A). With this, the state is a state *in actuality, a true state* ([*Republic*] 520C). The philosopher who has elevated himself in the beholding of the truth about the beautiful, just, and good in *purity*, lives and *wants* to live in it, is *bound back* to the state by the harsh command of the legislator, which considers the order of the whole and not the happiness of the parts. The philosopher stands *under* the state, *under* the law. Philosophy has to be responsible *before* the state, before the law: it is not absolutely sovereign.

What was *required* by Plato, philosophy's standing ²⁶¹⁻under⁻²⁶¹ the law, is *fulfilled* in the age of the revealed religions. Despite all the freedom in the pursuit of knowledge, the philosophers of this age are at each moment conscious of their responsibility for the maintenance of the lawful order, their responsibility before the law: they justify the fact of their philosophizing before the tribunal of the {427} law; they derive their *authorization* for philosophizing as a legal *obligation* to philosophize; they conceive their freedom to interpret the document of revelation rationally as an *obligation* to interpretation; they conceive the esoteric character of their philosophy as a *duty* to secrecy: as a *prohibition* against communication. The *Platonism* of these philosophers is given with their *situation*: with their standing under the law as a matter of fact.

Because they stand under the law as a matter of fact, they no longer need to *seek* the law, the state, as Plato does:²⁶² the binding order of life together is for them *given* through a prophet. That is why they are *authorized by the law*, free for understanding in Aristotelian freedom. *That is why* they can aristotelize. Cohen expresses it [thus]: Rambam

> underestimated the danger residing in the depreciation of ethics in Aristotle. And from his standpoint he could overlook this danger more easily, *since he saw the value of ethics kept safe in his religion*. (87/64)²⁶³

260–260. [Inserted between the lines or added in the margin by Strauss.]

261–261. [Inserted between the lines or added in the margin by Strauss.]

262. [The new beginning of the paragraph is noted in the margin, but the old wording was not adapted accordingly:] They no longer need to *seek* the law, the state, as Plato does:

263. {The emphasis is Strauss's. The Cohenian original emphasizes the first rather than the second sentence. We have used the translation of these sentences as found in Strauss, *Philosophy and Law*, 133.}

Since the law is *given* to them, it is not the leading and primary theme of their philosophizing: they do not need to *ask* about it. [264-]That is why metaphysical problems occupy a very[265] much larger space in their writings than the question about the just order of human life together.[-264, 266] But they have to *justify* and *understand* it. And this understanding is accomplished within the horizon of *Plato*.

Let us recall the definition of the prophet that issued to us from Maimonides: the prophet is the founder of a community that is directed to the proper perfection of man. We allowed ourselves to say: the prophet is the founder of the ideal state. We can say *more* if we look back at Avicenna; namely, the prophet is the founder of the *Platonic* state. He *fulfills* what Plato *required*, what he *foretold*. But this means that *revelation, the Law, is understood in the light of Plato*.

Plato had seen the actualization of the true state as dependent on philosophers becoming kings and kings becoming philosophers: political power and philosophy must coincide. With this representation of the philosopher-statesman, the framework within which the prophetology of Rambam and that of the Islamic philosophers move seems to be demarcated. Admittedly, a distinctive change had {428} to be made before the representation of the prophet as philosopher/statesman/seer/miracle-worker *in one* could come about. This change was already accomplished in the age of Hellenism: here we encounter the representation of the wise lawgivers of old who were rulers, philosophers, and seers *in one*. We read in Cicero (*De div*[*inatione*]) I 40.89):

> Omnino apud *veteres*, qui rerum potiebantur,
> *iidem* auguria tenebant. Ut enim *sapere*, sic
> *divinare regale* ducebant, ut testis est *nostra*
> *civitas*. . . .[267]

What this change signifies; how the inclusion of *divination* is dependent on the return to the *past*, i.e., on the *givenness* of the Law; [and] how this further

---

264–264. [Inserted between the lines or added in the margin by Strauss.]
265. <infinitely>
266. [Note in the margin:] Alfarabi, Timaeus (Reinhardt)
267. {"Generally among *the ancients* who were in control of things, *the same men* held the auguries. For both *wisdom* and *divining* alike guided *rulership*, as *our city* is witness. . . ." Cf. Cicero, *De Senectute, De Amicitia, De Divinatione*, ed. and trans. W. A. Falconer (Cambridge, MA: Harvard University Press, 1959), 320/321 (translation modified; the emphases are Strauss's).}

development was [already] laid out by Plato himself: these are questions that we can only *enumerate* here.

I have to content myself with having shown in a rough sketch how I have visualized the rehabilitation of Cohen's thesis that Rambam is in deeper harmony with Plato than with Aristotle. I only point to the fact that Cohen himself has called attention to the connection underscored by us, about which he had however been informed only by the scanty remarks in Munk's *Mélanges de philosophie juive et arabe*. He says: "Averroes translated Plato's *Republic*. Did Maimonides read it?"[268] (132/189). "*Translated*" is probably a slip of the pen; in Munk it says, as is also correct, that Averroës *commented on* Plato's *Republic*.[269] The *Republic* had already been translated in the ninth century; and it is doubtless [the case] that Rambam knew it either directly or indirectly—through Avicenna or Alfarabi.—

I sum up: the Cohenian starting point, "All honor to the God of Aristotle, but He is not the God of Israel," leads no further if one interprets the God of Israel as the God of *morality*. Instead of morality, one must say: *Law*. The idea[270] of law, of *nomos*, is what unifies Jews and Greeks: the idea of the *concrete*, binding order of life, which is covered over for us by the Christian and the natural-right tradition, this idea [is the one] under whose spell at least our philosophical thought moves. By the *Christian* tradition: [I mean the one] that starts out with the Apostle Paul's radical *critique* of law. By the *natural-right* tradition: [I mean the one] that stipulates an *abstract* system of norms which must first be filled in and made serviceable by *positive* right. Cohen himself puts us on the road to the recovery of this basic concept of humanity, by replacing the criterion of intention with that of action, {429} by orienting his ethics in principle to jurisprudence, by teaching that there is no self-consciousness "that is to be acquired without regard for the state and without being guided by the idea of the state,[271]"[272] by being a *political philosopher* filled with political passion.

---

268. {Salomon Munk, *Mélanges de philosophie juive et arabe*, new ed. (Paris: Vrin, 1927), 314.}

269. {See *Averroës on Plato's "Republic,"* trans. Ralph Lerner (Ithaca: Cornell University Press, 1974).}

270. {Here and in the rest of this sentence, "idea" is *Gedanke*, and "thought" is *Denken*. See n. 73 above.}

271. {The German is *Staatsgedanken*. See n. 73 above, as well as the following note. Earlier in this sentence, "being guided" is *Leitung*. See nn. 3 and 167 above.}

272. {Cohen, *Ethik*, 250//265. Strauss's quotation here omits the words *des Gesetzes* immediately following *Staatsgedanken* in Cohen's sentence. Cohen's original sentence reads: "There is no self-consciousness that is to be acquired without regard for the state and without being guided by the political idea [*Staatsgedanken*] of law [*des Gesetzes*]." Cf. n. 167 above.}

Cohen's Platonism opens up for him the understanding of Rambam as a Platonist. The *limit* of his understanding is given with his replacing the idea[273] of *law* with that of *morality*. This is the meaning of his fundamental critique of Plato, which reproaches Plato "for orienting the I, to be sure, toward the point of view of the state, but at the same time dissolving it in the latter as well" (*Ethik* 552//584). Cohen thereby contrasts the modern idea of the individual with Plato; it is this idea which,[274] in its consequences, leads Cohen to his *defining* political position, to his passionate support for the politics of "the great *Left* of humanity," to the politics of progress; this idea sets the limits of his understanding of Plato, and thereby also of his understanding of Rambam. We will not be able to understand Plato, and thereby also not Rambam, until we have acquired a horizon beyond the opposition progress/conservatism, Left/Right, Enlightenment/Romanticism, or however one wants to designate this opposition; not until we again understand the idea of the *eternal* good, [275-]the *eternal* order,[-275] free from all regard for progress or regress.

Finis.

273. {Here and in the rest of this paragraph, "idea" is *Gedanke*. See n. 73 above.}
274. which <Cohen>
275-275. [Inserted between the lines or added in the margin by Strauss.]

4
The Philosophic Foundation of the Law

MAIMONIDES' DOCTRINE OF PROPHECY AND ITS SOURCES[1]

EDITOR'S NOTE

"The Philosophic Foundation of the Law: Maimonides' Doctrine of Prophecy and Its Sources" reproduces the translation which appeared as a chapter by the same title in a book by Leo Strauss, *Philosophy and Law*, trans. Eve Adler, chap. 3, pp. 101–33, with the notes appearing on pp. 145–54. The history of the chapter in its original context as a separate article was traced by Strauss himself in his first note. The present essay was to have appeared in *Korrespondenzblatt der Akademie für des Wissenschaft des Judentums* around 1931, but the journal was forced to cease publication. As a result, it first appeared in print as a separate article in *Le Monde Oriental* (Uppsala) 28 (1934): 99–139, with the shorter, likely original title, "Maimunis Lehre von der Prophetie und ihre Quellen" ("Maimonides' Doctrine of Prophecy and Its Sources"). It next was reprinted as chap. 3

---

1. [1] This essay, written in the summer of 1931, was intended in its original form, from which the present form does not differ in any important point, for publication in the *Korrespondenzblatt der Akademie für die Wissenschaft des Judentums* (Berlin, 1931), and had been accepted for publication by the editors of that journal, which however was no longer able to publish at that time. It appeared in its original form in the journal *Le Monde Oriental* (Uppsala) 28 (1934): 99–139. The essay aims only to clarify the presuppositions of Maimonides' prophetology; it does not aim at a complete presentation of this doctrine elucidating all its obscurities. The most recent attempt at a complete presentation is that of Zevi Diesendruck, "Maimonides' Lehre von der Prophetie," in *Jewish Studies in Memory of Israel Abrahams* (New York: Jewish Institute of Religion, 1927), pp. 74–134. This is not the place for a thorough discussion of his inquiry or of the rest of the literature. [Strauss added the following statement as a sort of preface to his essay in its *Le Monde Oriental* version (henceforth, *MO*), which was removed from its prominent position and relegated (in a revised form) to the first note of the *Philosophie und Gesetz* version (henceforth, *PG*): "The present essay sets itself the task of clarifying the presuppositions of Maimonides' prophetology; it is not a complete presentation of his doctrine, [i.e., it is not] an elucidation of all of its obscurities and contradictions." ("Die vorliegende Aufsatz stellt sich die Aufgabe, die Voraussetzungen der Prophteologie Maimunis aufzuklaren; er beabsichtigt nicht eine vollständige Darstellung dieser Lehre, eine Aufhellung aller ihrer Dunkelheiten und Widerspruche.") A concern with the "obscurities and contradictions" evident in Maimonides' thought henceforth became *the* focus of Strauss's subsequent study of Maimonides, which in fact he was to characterize as the key which unlocks its deepest secrets. See "Literary Character," chap. 8 below. But the key, the lock, the hidden spheres, and the reasons for employing such concealing notions were already shaped in the mold of the discovery made by *Philosophy and Law* (henceforth, *PL*), of which the present essay forms an especially essential component: see n. 262 below.]

of Strauss's book the original German title of which was *Philosophie und Gesetz: Beiträge zum Verständnis Maimunis und Seiner Vorlaüfer* (Berlin: Schocken Verlag, 1935), with the longer chapter title of the present volume. As Heinrich Meier comments in his recent bibliography of Strauss's writings on the website of the Leo Strauss Center at the University of Chicago (http://leostrausscenter.uchicago.edu/pdf/Strauss_Bibliographie_3-5-09.pdf), the original version in *Le Monde Oriental* appeared as the third chapter of *Philosophie und Gesetz* in a "slightly abbreviated and revised" form. (It is of course the translated form of this chapter that appears in the present book.) For the most recent and complete edition of the original German version, see Strauss, *Philosophie und Gesetz: Frühe Schriften*, vol. 2 of *Gesammelte Schriften*, pp. 87–123. The additions of the present editor to Strauss's notes have been put in square brackets. Likewise, Strauss's "slight abbreviations and revisions" (i.e., the *Le Monde Oriental* version reworked as the *Philosophie und Gesetz* version) been also been duly recorded in the notes, in case they may show some significantly shifting features of his thought. With reference to the major differences between the two versions of the article (which was, of course, Strauss's first study of Maimonides' thought in its own right), I would direct readers especially to nn. 2, 8, 43, 147, 232, 243, and 262 below. For the convenience of those who may wish to refer to the previous versions, the note numbers as they appear in the original edition, in the reprinted German edition (ed. H. Meier), and in the English translation (ed. E. Adler), are shown in square brackets and bold; the note numbers of these three versions are identical. This essay appeared as a chapter in one of the last Jewish books that Schocken Press was allowed to release in Nazi Germany, signifying perhaps a spiritual effort to come to grips with the unprecedented situation in which the German Jews had found themselves since 1933, and meanwhile it seeks to go to its heart in order to diagnose the crisis of modern Judaism which their situation represented to Strauss in 1935.

I[2]

PROPHETOLOGY IS A CENTRAL PART OF THE DOCTRINE OF *THE GUIDE of the Perplexed*. Some conception of its difficulties[3] is given by the list of

2. [In *MO*, the first section has no number; in *PG*, the first section is number I. As a result, *MO* has an unnumbered introductory paragraph and four sections headed by Roman numerals; *PG* has five sections headed by Roman numerals, and hence no unnumbered introductory paragraph. *MO* begins with a sentence presented in the note above.]

3. [2] The central position and the difficulties of his prophetology are fully and emphatically discussed by Diesendruck (loc. cit., 74–79).

conditions which, according to Maimonides' doctrine, the prophet must satisfy. The prophet must have at his disposal: (1) a perfect intellect; (2) perfect morals; (3) a perfect imagination; (4) the faculty of courage; (5) the faculty of divination; and (6) the faculty of government (of men). What do these various[4] conditions of prophecy have in common with one another? What gives this rhapsody a unified, lucid order? Our orientation must take its departure from a correct understanding of the fact that prophetology is a central part of the doctrine of the *Guide*. This fact, correctly understood, means that the position for whose clarification and defense the *Guide* was written is possible only if prophecy exists in the sense explicated[5] by Maimonides' prophetology. Hence the understanding of his prophetology is entirely dependent on understanding the position associated[6] with it. Starting from a provisional understanding of this position, we develop the part of his prophetology that can be understood on that[7] basis (Part II). The other part of Maimonides' prophetology cannot be elucidated, either in itself or in relation to the first part, from Maimonides' own statements; this is because Maimonides in his prophetology follows a centuries-old reigning philosophic tradition whose premises he no longer even mentions.[8] He does not follow this tradition slavishly: on the one hand he restricts its doctrines, and on the other hand he extends them;[9] but he remains within a circle of question and possible answer already marked out before him. It is therefore necessary to return to his sources. We must ask therefore about the relation of his prophetology to the prophetology of Alfarabi and Avicenna.[10] In the light of these sources we

    4. [*MO*: "fundamentally various" or "fundamentally diverse" ("grundverschiedenen"); *PG*: "various" or "diverse" ("verschiedenen").]
    5. [*MO*: "asserted" or "contended" ("behaupteten"); *PG*: "explicated" ("explizierten").]
    6. [*MO*: "corresponding" ("entsprechenden"); *PG*: "associated" ("zugeordneten").]
    7. [*MO*: "its" ("seiner"); *PG*: "that" ("desselben").]
    8. [*MO*: "for Maimonides in his prophetology follows a centuries-old reigning philosophic tradition under whose influence he stood, [and] whose premises he no longer even discusses" ("denn Maimuni folgt in seiner Prophetologie einer seit Jahrhunderten herrschenden philosophischen Tradition, in deren Bann er derart steht, dass er deren Voraussetzungen gar nicht mehr diskutiert"); *PG*: "this is because Maimonides in his prophetology follows a centuries-old reigning philosophic tradition whose premises he no longer even mentions" ("schuld daran ist, dass Maimuni in seiner Prophetologie einer seit Jahrhunderten herrschenden philosophischen Tradition folgt, deren Voraussetzungen er gar nicht mehr zur Sprache bringt"). The phrase which Strauss removed—"under whose influence he stood" ("in deren Bann er derart steht")—might be designated a historicism: he seems to have originally presumed that this position was not chosen by Maimonides for good reasons, but was an influence almost unconsciously exercised on him by his historical situation. Strauss seems to have corrected the faulty impression he created.]
    9. [*PG* adds the words "on the one hand" ("einerseits") and "on the other hand" ("andererseits").]
    10. [*MO*: "Ibn Sina (Avicenna)"; *PG*: "Ibn Sina." It is Eve Adler, the English translator, who has made it only "Avicenna."]

interpret first (Part III) the part of his prophetology not discussed in Part II, and finally the entire system of his prophetology (Part IV). The complete interpretation of the prophetology will, for its part, contribute to a deeper understanding of Maimonides' position (Part V).

II

One can with a certain right call Maimonides' position "medieval religious Enlightenment." With a certain right: namely, if one accepts the view that not only for the modern Enlightenment—and thus for the Age of Enlightenment *proper*,[11] from which the expression "Enlightenment" is customarily *transferred*[12] to certain phenomena of the Middle Ages (and of antiquity)—but also for Maimonides and his predecessors and successors in the Middle Ages,[13] it is a matter of the freedom of human thought, the "freedom of philosophizing." But one must not for a moment leave any doubt that these medieval philosophers were precisely *not* Enlighteners in the proper sense; for them it was *not*[14] a question of *spreading*[15] light, of educating the *multitude*[16] to rational knowledge, of *enlightening*;[17] again and again they enjoin upon the philosophers the duty of *keeping secret*[18] from the unqualified multitude the rationally known truth; for them—in contrast to the Enlightenment proper, i.e., the modern Enlightenment—the *esoteric*[19] character of philosophy was unconditionally established. To be sure, even in the seventeenth and eighteenth centuries there were men who, to quote Voltaire, claimed: "Quand la populace se mêle â raisonner, tout est perdu"; and on the other hand, even men like Maimonides had in mind a *certain*[20] enlightenment of all men.[21] But

11. [Emphasis on "proper" ("eigentlichen") added to *PG*.]
12. [Emphasis on "transferred" ("übertragen") added to *PG*.]
13. [3] The following observations about the "medieval Enlightenment" are oriented exclusively to the representative Islamic and Jewish *philosophers*.
14. [Emphasis on "not" ("nicht") added to *PG*.]
15. [Emphasis on "spreading" ("verbreiten") added to *PG*.]
16. [Emphasis on "multitude" ("Menge") added to *PG*.]
17. [Emphasis on "enlightening" ("aufzuklären") added to *PG*.]
18. [Emphasis on "keeping secret" ("geheimzuhalten") added to *PG*.]
19. [Emphasis on "esoteric" ("esoterische") added to *PG*.]
20. [Emphasis on "certain" ("gewisse") added to *PG*.]
21. [4] Cf. *Guide* 1.35 in the beginning. Cf. also Gersonides' polemic against esotericism, referred to above. [*MO*: The note (p. 101, n. 1) provides the reference to Gersonides, *Milḥamot Ha-Shem* [*Wars of the Lord*] (Leipzig: C. B. Lorck, 1866; reprint, Berlin, 1923), p. 8, ll. 6–30; *PG*, p. 89, n. 4, points to the same reference on p. 82, n. 37, and the discussion on pp. 82–83. (In *PL*, trans. Adler, it appears on p. 145, n. 4, with references to discussion on pp. 92–93; cf. also p. 144, nn. 37 and 38.) For Strauss on Gersonides' polemic against Maimonides' view of esotericism, see *PG*, pp. 82–83, as well as 64–66 ("der Zersetzung des Platonismus"), 68, 79–86; *PL*, trans. Adler, pp. 95–96, as well as 77–78 ("the decay of Platonism"), 82,

if one considers[22] that the modern Enlightenment, as opposed to the medieval, generally *publicizes*[23] its teachings, one will not object to the assertion that the medieval Enlightenment was essentially esoteric, while the modern Enlightenment was essentially exoteric. Even the most provisional characterization of Maimonides' position must not leave out of account this specific difference from the modern Enlightenment.

The esoteric character of the "medieval religious Enlightenment" is based on the prevailing ideal of the *theoretical*[24] life, just as the exoteric character of the modern Enlightenment is based on the conviction—prevalent long before its formulation, foundation, and radicalization by Kant—of the primacy of *practical*[25] reason. Hence one can provisionally characterize Maimonides' position as follows: it maintains the Greek ideal of the life of *theory*,[26] as classically explicated by Aristotle at the end of the *Nicomachean Ethics*, on the assumption of the *revelation*.[27] Two things accordingly are established for

---

92–100. For Gersonides' "polemic against esotericism," see *The Wars of the Lord*, trans. Seymour Feldman (Philadelphia: Jewish Publication Society, 1984), vol. 1, pp. 93–98, 100–101, 102–3: "Those authors ... who do not follow this procedure but increase obscurity either because of poor organization or opacity of language so that the easy becomes difficult, defeat the purpose for which they have written their books. They have actually increased the perplexity of their readers as well as not having given them anything worthwhile; unless it was the intention of the author to conceal [his ideas] from the masses so that only a few would understand [his words], because such ideas would, if understood, cause harm to the masses. . . . But this is not our intention in this book! We wish that the amplitude of our language, as well as its explanation and proper order, make our intentions, together with their profundity, explicit to the reader." The complicated topic of Gersonides and esotericism has recently been reconsidered; while he is not a Maimonidean pure and simple, this is not a factor that he unconditionally dismisses; however, he certainly treats it quite differently, and hence he writes very differently. See Robert Eisen, "The Torah and Esoteric Discourse," in *Gersonides on Providence, Covenant, and the Chosen People: A Study in Medieval Jewish Philosophy and Biblical Commentary* (Albany: State University of New York Press, 1995), pp. 99–113. Eisen especially highlights Gersonides' remarks in the introduction to his commentary on the Song of Songs: see Levi ben Gershom (Gersonides), *Commentary on Song of Songs*, trans. Menachem Kellner (New Haven: Yale University Press, 1998), pp. 3–4, 7–8, 12, 14, as well as Kellner's "Translator's Introduction," pp. xxiii–xxix. For the famous remark of Voltaire ("When the masses [start to] occupy themselves with reasoning, all is lost."), it appears in a letter to Étienne Noël Damillaville, of April 1, 1766. An English translation of the relevant section of the letter, with an interesting "defense" of the view expressed by Voltaire in it, is offered in Peter Gay, *Voltaire's Politics* (Princeton: Princeton University Press, 1959), pp. 265–66, n. 70.]

22. [*MO*: "If one bears in mind" ("Aber wenn man sich vor Augen hält"); *PG*: "If one considers" ("Aber wenn man bedenkt").]

23. [Emphasis on "publicizes" ("propagiert") added to *PG*.]

24. [Emphasis on "theoretical" ("theoretischen") added to *PG*.]

25. [Emphasis on "practical" ("praktischen") added to *PG*.]

26. [Emphasis on "theory" ("Theorie") added to *PG*.]

27. [Emphasis on "revelation" ("Offenbarung") added to *PG*. In the present essay, Strauss chooses to articulate the view of Maimonides (as well as of Alfarabi and Avicenna) by speaking most often of "die Offenbarung" ("the revelation"), i.e., with the German definite article, even though he is usually referring to (prophetic) revelation as a general idea rather than as a specific law or event. Eve Adler, the translator, believed that this was a significant and deliberate choice by Strauss (carrying a slightly strange, although not erroneous, sound even in German), and hence preserved the use of the definite article in her translation,

Maimonides: first, that the revelation is *simply*[28] binding, and second, that for a man to be a perfect man is *simply*[29] a matter of living the life of theory. These heterogeneous convictions are unified by the fact that the summons and education to the theoretical life is considered the highest (though not the only) end of the revelation. After all, Scripture commands men "to know God," and the highest subject of theory is the highest being, i.e., God. Hence[30] Maimonides teaches that the specific property of the revelation, of the divine law, as opposed to all merely human laws, is concern for the improvement of belief, i.e., for the dissemination of correct opinions about "God and the angels," the education of men to true knowledge of all that is.[31]

The revelation itself, then, summons to philosophizing the men suited to it; the divine law itself commands philosophizing. Philosophy, *free on the basis of this authorization*,[32] takes for its subject matter all that is. Thus the revelation itself, like all that is, becomes its subject matter. It is in prophetology that the revelation, as the *law*[33] given by God through a *prophet*,[34] becomes a subject matter of philosophy.

If the revelation were *merely*[35] the miraculous deed of God, it would be simply beyond all human understanding. The revelation is intelligible only insofar as God's deed of revelation is carried out through secondary causes, is worked out in the creation, in created *nature*.[36] If it is to be *wholly*[37] intelligible, it must be simply a *natural*[38] fact. The means through which God carries out the deed of revelation is the prophet, i.e., an extraordinary man, pre-eminent above all, but in any case a *man*.[39] Therefore the philosophic

---

even though it is not a common literary style or form of speech in English. Her position on Strauss's intention in employing such a mode of expression seems to have been that he aimed to highlight the emphasis put by Maimonides (and his Islamic predecessors) on the *uniqueness* of every authoritative revelation as something specific and singular, i.e., it is always *"the* revelation," whether construed as prophetic law or as miraculous event. The present editor has accepted the translator's decision.]

28. [Emphasis on "simply" ("schlechthin") added to *PG*.]
29. [Emphasis on "simply" ("schlechthin") added to *PG*.]
30. [*MO*: "In this sense" ("In diesem Sinn"); *PG*: "Hence" ("Daher").]
31. [5] *Guide* 2.40 and 3.27–28.
32. [Emphasis on "free on the basis of this authorization" ("auf Grund dieser Ermächtigung freie") added to *PG*.]
33. [Emphasis on "law" ("Gesetz") added to *PG*.]
34. [Emphasis on "prophet" ("Propheten") added to *PG*.]
35. [Emphasis on "merely" ("bloss") added to *PG*.]
36. [Emphasis on "nature" ("Natur") added to *PG*.]
37. [Emphasis on "wholly" ("ganz") added to *PG*.]
38. [Emphasis on "natural" ("natürliche") added to *PG*.]
39. [Emphasis on "man" ("Mensch") added to *PG*.]

understanding of the revelation, the philosophic foundation of the law, means the explanation of prophecy from the *nature of man*.[40]

Maimonides was able to presuppose such an explanation of prophecy. The Islamic Aristotelians—the *falasifa*[41]—had taught that prophecy is a certain perfection of human nature that the suitably endowed man necessarily achieves through suitable practice. Maimonides accepts this teaching with the single reservation that the suitably endowed and suitably prepared man does not *necessarily*[42] become a prophet: God can, at his discretion, deny prophecy to such a man. This miraculous denial[43] of prophecy, however, has essentially the same character as the miraculous denial of the exercise of the faculty of vision or the faculty of moving one's hand.[44] But this means that it is only the denial[45] of prophecy that is miraculous, not prophecy as such; prophecy as such is natural.[46] Therefore, although the suitably endowed and prepared man does not necessarily become a prophet, still it is necessary that the prophet be a suitably endowed and prepared man. Prophecy is bound to certain conditions. These conditions, as Maimonides teaches in agreement with the *falasifa*, are: perfection of the intellect, of the morals, and of the imaginative faculty.[47] One understands[48] why precisely these conditions are necessary if one asks: how must prophecy be constituted such that, under the

---

40. [Emphasis on "nature of man" ("Natur des Menschen") added to *PG*.]

41. [*MO* had a note affixed to it (p. 102, n. 2), which was removed from *PG*: "Arabic for *philosophoi* [Strauss's original with the Greek letters]; the Aristotelians were designated by Islamic and Jewish writers as simply 'philosophers.'" ("Das arabisierte *philosophoi* [Strauss's original with the Greek letters]; als 'Philosophen' schlechthin werden von den islamischen und jüdischen Autoren die Aristotelicker bezeichnet.")]

42. [Emphasis on "necessarily" ("notwendig") added to *PG*.]

43. [In the present sentence, one of the key words has been changed: what was "Prevention" ("Verhindern") in *MO* has become "Denial" ("Versagen") in *PG*. Also, the structure has been changed very slightly. *MO*: "However, the miraculous prevention of prophecy has to be seen as essentially the same as the miraculous prevention of . . ." ("Mit der wunderbaren Verhindern der Prophetie verhält es sich nun aber gründsatzlich ebenso wie mit dem wunderbaren Verhindern an . . . zu sehen"); *PG*: "This miraculous denial of prophecy, however, has essentially the same character as the miraculous denial . . ." ("Dieses wunderbare Versagen der Prophetie hat nun aber gründsatzlich denselben Charakter was die wunderbare Versagen . . ."). Curiously, in the English translation of the *Guide* by Shlomo Pines, 2.32 (pp. 361–62), he prefers to render Maimonides' term as God's miraculous "prevention," Strauss's original choice.]

44. [6] *Guide* 2.32 (261f.). [*MO* had added to the present note, which was removed from *PG*, a reference to Salomon Munk's Judeo-Arabic edition of and notes on the *Guide*, with French translation: "Munk translation, 261f."]

45. [*MO*: "prevention" ("Verhindern"); *PG*: "denial" ("Versagen"). See also n. 43 above.]

46. [7] Thus Maimonides can say that the Emanation (see below [seventh, eighth, ninth, and thirteenth paragraphs of section II]) in dream differs from that in prophecy not in kind, but only in degree.

47. [8] 2.32 (261f.) and 36 (287).

48. [*MO*: "It emerges" or "It ensues" ("dies ergibt sich"); *PG*: "One understands" ("dies versteht man").]

revelation communicated by prophets, the theoretical life as the specific perfection of man is possible, or, such that the specific property of the revelation as opposed to all merely human laws can be concern for the dissemination of correct opinions about "God and the angels."

If the revelation is to communicate the fundamental theoretical truths, then the bringer of the revelation, the prophet, must have at his disposal the knowledge of these truths. He must at least be *also*[49] a philosopher, an actual knower; the perfection of the intellect, acquired through practice and instruction, is a condition of prophecy.[50]

The simply binding revelation is addressed to all, but only some, only few have the capacity for the theoretical life. Hence the truths to which, or on the basis of which, the revelation is simply binding must be communicated to the multitude in proportion to their power of comprehension. These truths must therefore—at least in part—be presented figuratively. The prophet must therefore be a man who, while having philosophic knowledge at his disposal, is at the same time capable of presenting it figuratively; besides perfection of the intellect, perfection of the imaginative faculty is also a condition of prophecy.[51]

The process of acquiring knowledge is understood by Maimonides, as by the *falasifa*, in accordance with the then prevalent view of the Aristotelian doctrine, as an actualization of the human intellectual capacity (the "hylic intellect") by the extrahuman, superhuman "active intellect," which is the lowest of the immaterial intelligences. The active intellect is in turn conditioned, in its being and activity, by God. But in the case of prophetic knowledge, the influence of the active intellect on the human intellect is not sufficient. Because the prophet must make himself intelligible[52] also and precisely to the multitude, and therefore must speak figuratively, the active intellect must in his case influence also the imaginative faculty. We have now collected the elements united in Maimonides' definition of prophecy. This definition runs: "Prophecy in its essence is an emanation emanating from God through the active intellect first to the intellectual faculty and then to the imaginative faculty."[53]

Therefore, since in the case of prophecy not only the intellect (as in the

---

49. [Emphasis on "also" ("auch") added to *PG*.]
50. [9] 2.36 (284).
51. [10] 1.34 (end), 2.47 (356), 3.27 (210f.).
52. [*MO*: "must be intelligible" ("verständlich ... muss"); *PG*: "must make himself intelligible" ("sich ... verständlich machen ... muss").]
53. [11] 2.36 (281).

case of philosophic knowledge), but also the imaginative faculty is influenced by the active intellect, prophecy is, as Maimonides explains immediately following his definition of prophecy, "the highest rank of man and the uttermost perfection that can be found in the human race." This in itself makes the prophet unconditionally *superior*[54] to the philosopher, and a fortiori to all other men. But he is superior to the philosopher even in the philosopher's own sphere, as a knower: he can know *immediately*,[55] without "premises and conclusions," what all other men can know only mediately; consequently he can have at his disposal insights that could not be attained by the man whose knowledge is merely philosophic.[56] So it is understandable that, with regard to the central question that man is incapable of answering scientifically (the question whether the world is eternal or created),[57] Maimonides can instruct the philosopher to follow the prophet.[58] The philosopher in his philosophizing can take his bearings by the prophet, since the prophet has at his disposal insights that are not accessible to merely philosophic knowledge.

But the prophet's superiority over the philosopher is called into question by the very fact in which his superiority first emerged: the collaboration of the imaginative faculty in the act by which he acquires knowledge. It is not much of an exaggeration to say that the entire *Guide*[59] is devoted to a critique of the imaginative faculty. Above all, the arguments of the first part, whose purpose[60] is to protect the purity of the concept of God and to combat all conceptions that call God's absolute unity into question, are directed against an imaginative understanding of Scripture.[61] The imaginative faculty is[62] flatly *opposed*[63] to the intellect; it grasps only the particular, not the general; in its activity it cannot in any way free itself from matter, and therefore can never come to know a form; for this reason one must not pay it any attention at all. It necessarily impairs the activity of the intellect; liberation from

54. [Emphasis on "superior" ("überlegen") added to *PG*.]
55. [Emphasis on "immediately" ("unmittelbar") added to *PG*.]
56. [**12**] 2.38 (297f.).
57. [*PG* added the parentheses around ("bezüglich der Frage: ob die Welt ewig oder erschaffen sei"). These parentheses were judged redundant by Eve Adler for her English translation, which has the phrase appear as: "the question, whether the world is eternal or created."]
58. [**13**] 2.23 (182).
59. [Both *MO* and *PG* have the transliterated Hebrew title, "*Moreh Nevukhim*" (*Guide of the Perplexed*), although the system used to transliterate the Hebrew is slightly different in each case.]
60. [*MO*: "end" or "goal" ("Ziel"); *PG*: "purpose" ("Zweck").]
61. [*PG* has deleted a phrase from the end of this sentence that in *MO* was added to it: "that is opposed to the intellectual [understanding] of it [i.e., Scripture]" ("das dem intellektuellen entgegengesetzt ist").]
62. [*MO*: "as such" ("als solche"); it is missing in *PG*.]
63. [Emphasis on "opposed" ("entgegengesetzt") added to *PG*.]

its influence is an indispensable condition of true knowledge.[64] Under these circumstances Spinoza appears to be merely drawing a consequence when, in a polemic against Maimonides, he says that anyone distinguished by an especially strong imaginative faculty—as are the prophets, in Maimonides' and Spinoza's view—is especially ill qualified for pure knowledge, and when he therefore denies that the prophets had anything more than vulgar knowledge.[65] But this "consequence" is so obvious[66] that it would not have escaped Maimonides if it had actually been the consequence of his doctrine.

First of all it must be observed that the distrust of the imaginative faculty, the depreciation of the imaginative faculty, is maintained in Maimonides' prophetology; according to this doctrine, what distinguishes the highest rank of prophecy, the prophecy of Moses, is precisely the fact that the imaginative faculty does *not*[67] collaborate in it.[68] But with this observation not much appears to have been gained, since in any case the "ordinary" prophets—all the prophets except Moses—must be superior to the philosophers in spite of the collaboration of the imaginative faculty in their knowledge and even because of this collaboration. There remains therefore the problem of how the collaboration of the imaginative faculty can be the basis of a superiority. But this much follows in any case: the ordinary prophets' knowledge stands between Moses' knowledge, which is free of the collaboration of the imaginative faculty, and the philosophers' knowledge, which is likewise free of the collaboration of the imaginative faculty; hence the difference between the greatest prophet and the philosophers can be ascertained without any consideration of the imaginative faculty; this difference includes both the difference between Moses and the ordinary prophets and the difference between the ordinary prophets and the philosophers; thus the difference between the ordinary prophets and the philosophers, and therewith the initially paradoxical possibility that the collaboration of the imaginative faculty is the basis of the prophets' superiority over the philosophers, becomes intelligible from the deeper difference. We must therefore ask how, according to

---

64. [14] Cf. especially 1.73 (407f.).
65. [15] [Spinoza,] *Tractatus theologico-politicus*, II. ["In keeping with piety, the Prophets could have been ignorant, and really were ignorant, not only about such matters, but also about others of greater importance. For they taught nothing specific about the divine attributes, but had quite vulgar opinions about God. Their revelations were also accommodated to these as well ... so that you may easily see that they are to be praised and diligently commended not so much for grandeur and preëminence of intellect, as for piety and a steadfastness of spirit." Spinoza, *Theologico-Political Treatise*, trans. Yaffe, p. 24.]
66. [*MO*: "evident" ("liegt so zutage"); *PG*: "obvious" ("naheliegend").]
67. [Emphasis on "not" ("nicht") added to *PG*.]
68. [16] 2.36 (288) and 45 (348).

Maimonides' teaching, Moses' knowledge differs from the knowledge of the philosophers.[69]

The natural representative of the philosophers is *the*[70] Philosopher, Aristotle. Now of Aristotle it is the case that everything he says about the world below the lunar sphere is undoubtedly true, while his views about the upper world, especially about the separate intelligences, are in part only probable, and in part actually false.[71] What is true of Aristotle is all the more true of all other nonprophetic men: man can know only the world below the lunar sphere, the world that surrounds him, lies before his eyes and is familiar to him, the world to which he belongs, *his* world; only this lower world is directly accessible to him; his knowledge of the upper world necessarily remains fragmentary and doubtful. The terms "upper" and "lower" world express not only a spatial relationship but also a difference of rank: the upper world is the world higher in rank; it is inaccessible to human knowledge not only because of its spatial distance but also because of its high rank. The lower world is the world of becoming and passing away; the ground of all becoming and passing away—of all imperfection in general—is matter; matter, our limitation by it and our dependence on it, is the reason why we can only inadequately fulfill our proper and highest destiny, the knowledge of the upper world, of "God and the angels."[72] The highest objects of knowledge are secrets from us; only occasionally does the truth shine on us so that we suppose it is day, but it is at once withdrawn again from our view by matter and our matter-bound life. We live in a deep dark night, only occasionally lit up by flashes of lightning. The rank-ordering of men can be represented by this image. One man is illuminated by flash after flash with only brief intermissions, so that for him night almost turns into day; this rank of almost continuous life in the light is the rank of Moses. For others the flashes occur only at great intervals; this is the rank of the other prophets.[73] And finally there are men whom only one

---

69. [*PG* has added the entire last sentence: "We must therefore ask how, according to Maimonides' teaching, Moses' knowledge differs from the knowledge of the philosophers." ("Wir haben also zu fragen, wie sich nach der Lehre Maimunis die Erkenntnis Mosches von der Erkenntnis der Philosophen unterscheidet.")]

70. [Emphasis on "the" ("der") added to *PG*.]

71. [**17**] 2.22 (179).

72. [**18**] 2.24 (194) and 3.8–9.

73. [**19**] To be sure, the observation about the rank of the prophets other than Moses is found only in Ibn Tibbon's Hebrew translation (cf. Munk, *Guide* 1.11, n. 2); but it is required by the whole context. [In *MO*, the note at the end has several additional words: "but it is legitimated, indeed required, by the whole context" ("sie ist aber durch den ganzen Zusammenhang legitimiert, ja geradezu erfordert"); *PG* has only "but it is required by the whole context" ("sie ist aber durch den ganzen Zusammenhang erfordert"). As for the sentence in the text of Strauss's essay to which footnote marker 73 is affixed, it is

flash illumines once in the whole night; to this rank belong those of whom it is said, "They prophesied, but they did so no more."[74] Then there is a class of men whose darkness has never been illumined by a lightning flash, but only by polished bodies of the kind of certain stones that shine at night; and even this small light does not shine on us (!) continuously, but appears and vanishes again immediately. Finally there are men who see no light at all. This last class is the multitude of the ignorant. The first three classes comprise all prophets, from the highest to the lowest prophet. Thus the class whose darkness is illuminated only by a small and indeed a borrowed, indirect light must be the class of the philosophers. Hence it is by the indirectness of their knowledge of the upper world that the philosophers differ from the prophets, who have at their disposal a direct knowledge, greater or lesser, of the upper world.[75] The ordinary prophets differ from Moses in that they do not live, like him, continuously in the light, but are illuminated by lightning flashes only at greater intervals. In the *Mishneh Torah* ("Yesodei ha-Torah" VII, 6)

---

based as he acknowledges only on Ibn Tibbon's Hebrew version of the *Guide*. Thus, Strauss writes: "For others the flashes occur only at great intervals; this is the rank of the other prophets." Munk's note on the corresponding passsage in Ibn Tibbon reads as follows: "The Hebrew version of Ibn Tibbon adds here the following passage," which same passage Munk next puts in Hebrew: "'There are those for whom, between the flashes, great intervals occur, and this is the rank of the other prophets.' This passage is not found in any of the Judeo-Arabic manuscripts; likewise, one neither finds it in the Hebrew version of Al-Ḥarizi, nor in the extracts of R. Shem Tov ibn Falaquera. See his *Moreh ha-Moreh* (Pressburg, 1837), p. 9." See in *Shelosha Kadmonei Mefarshei ha-Moreh* [*Three Early Commentators on the "Guide"*] (Jerusalem: Ortsel, 1961), which reprints the following: Falaquera, ed. M. L. Bisseliches (Pressburg, 1837); Joseph ibn Kaspi, ed. S. Z. Werbluner (Frankfurt on Main, 1848); Moses Narboni, ed. J. Goldenthal (Vienna, 1852). "However, this passage also exists in the manuscripts of the Ibn Tibbon version, and it is reproduced by the commentators on this version, as likewise by Samuel Zarza, in his *Mekor Ḥayyim*, where in commenting on the Pentateuch he deals with Numbers 11:25. In sum, this passage is superfluous; for what follows these words, 'they prophesied, and they did so no more,' says more or less the same thing." Strauss (in the present essay) obviously differs with Munk about the fittingness or the necessity of the sentence added by Ibn Tibbon. Yet by way of contrast, it is not added in *Guide*, trans. Pines: cf. p. 7. Cf. also Shem Tov ibn Falaquera, *Moreh ha-Moreh*, ed. Yair Shiffman (Jerusalem: World Union for Jewish Studies, 2001), pp. 121–22, for the passage to which Strauss refers.]

74. [*Guide* 1.Intro., p. 7; Maimonides refers to Numbers 11:25. *PG* changed and lengthened slightly the content and structure of this sentence: "And finally there are men whom only one flash illumines once in the whole night; to this rank belong those of whom it is said, 'They prophesied, but they did so no more.'" ("Und endlich gibt es Menschen, denen in der ganzen Nacht nur einmal ein Blitz aufleuchtet; dieser Stufe gehören die an, von denen es heisst: 'Sie prophezeiten und fuhren nicht fort.'") The form that it assumed in *MO* is as follows: "Others only one flash illumines in the whole night; to this rank belong those of whom it is said, 'They prophesied, but they did so no more.'" ("Anderen leuchtet in der ganzen Nacht nur ein Blitze auf; dieser Stufe gehören die an, von denen es heisst: 'Sie prophezeiten und fuhren nicht fort.'")]

75. [20] *Guide* 1.Intro., pp. 10–12. In interpreting the passage we follow the Hebrew commentators; cf., e.g., Narboni: "The pure stone, i.e., demonstration and especially speculation." Cf. also *Guide* 2.38 (297f.). [For the Narboni passage, see *Shelosha Kadmonei Mefarshei ha-Moreh*, p. 2a, l. 9.]

Maimonides expresses this difference as follows: the ordinary prophets do not have prophetic knowledge at their disposal whenever they wish, whereas prophecy does rest upon Moses whenever he wishes; Moses does not have to prepare himself for prophecy like the other prophets, he *is*[76] always prepared. In the passage[77] cited it is mentioned as a further difference that in the course of their prophetic knowledge the ordinary prophets are in fear, bewilderment, and agitation, while Moses receives his prophecy in repose and steadiness. If we think back to the simile of the deep dark night and the lightning flashes that illuminate it, we understand what Maimonides is alluding to with his talk of the ordinary prophets' bewilderment: the all-too-dazzling, unfamiliar light of direct knowledge of the upper world bewilders and terrifies the ordinary prophets.[78] And if the philosophers differ from the prophets in not knowing this bewilderment and terror, they owe this "superiority" solely to the circumstance that on them only the "small light" of indirect knowledge shines: it is *because*[79] the prophet sees more and more directly than the philosopher that he is bewildered. From this it can also be understood how the collaboration of the imaginative faculty in prophetic knowledge can be the basis of the prophet's superiority over the philosopher: it is *because*[80] the prophet knows more and more directly than the philosopher, because he is blinded by the all-too-dazzling, unfamiliar light, that he presents the known figuratively; the known fills him *completely*,[81] seizes him completely, thus including his imaginative faculty as well. Since the imaginative faculty is completely seized, put completely into service, "from above," it certainly cannot *derange*, as it deranges philosophic knowledge in the case of other men. The prophet represents "God and the angels"[82] figuratively and thus corporeally not because he *holds* them to be corporeal—only the ignorant do this[83]—but because he has come to know them directly in their incorporeality, and thus more clearly than the philosopher has; his understanding of the upper world is precisely

76. [Emphasis on "is" ("ist") added to *PG*.]
77. [*MO*: "above" ("oben"); *PG* removed it.]
78. [*PG* added as a finishing phrase: "the ordinary prophets" ("die gewöhnlichen Propheten"); it is missing from *MO*, which pointed only to "them" ("sie").]
79. [Emphasis on "because" ("weil") added to *PG*.]
80. [Emphasis on "because" ("weil") added to *PG*.]
81. [Emphasis on "completely" ("ganz") added to *PG*.]
82. [*MO*: "the known" ("das Erkannte"); *PG*: "'God and the angels'" ("'Gott und die Engel'"). In the previous sentence, Strauss seems to mean "derange" (*stören* or *stört*) in the sense of "disturbs," "disorders," or "confuses."]
83. [*MO* (in parentheses): "as the ignorant hold them to be corporeal" ("wie es die Unwissenden für körperlich halten"); *PG*: "only the ignorant do this" ("dies tun nur die Unwissenden").]

not[84] an imaginative *understanding*;[85] the figurative *representation*[86] of the known results from his superabundant[87] knowledge. The collaboration of the imaginative faculty in the prophet really rests not upon an inferiority of his knowledge to philosophic knowledge, but upon an infinite superiority to it: the prophet stands in *direct*[88] union with the upper world.

Now it is possible for us to understand the third condition of prophecy—perfection of morals. The express emphasis on this condition might at first appear superfluous, for moral perfection appears to be an indispensable condition of intellectual perfection. Yet experience shows that there are men of intellectual perfection who are still ruled by the desire for sensual pleasures and thus[89] far removed from moral perfection. How is this fact to be understood? An intellectually perfect man who is not a prophet is undoubtedly filled *also*[90] with desire for knowledge, and he can satisfy this desire only insofar as he frees himself from desire for the lower pleasures; but he is not *completely*[91] filled with desire for knowledge. Man is barred from knowledge of the upper world by his bondage to *his*[92] world, by his corporeality and sensuality. Usually he is completely engrossed in his inclinations and endeavors in this world. That this is so is shown in his dreams: when dreaming, man has in a certain sense detached himself from the world around him; but what he dreams is completely determined by his worldly inclinations and endeavors. Hence a man may well have a strong desire for knowledge and accordingly, if he is suitably endowed and trained, may achieve intellectual perfection; but it is not necessary on that account that his most private inclinations and endeavors, as revealed in dream, be directed to knowledge. Thus it is not enough for man to free himself from sensual perception; he must free himself from all sensual appetite, from all dependence on the world; in the hidden depths of his heart he must want nothing but knowledge of "God and the angels." If he does so, if *therefore*[93] he "*dreams*"[94] of nothing but this knowledge, then, provided he is a man of perfect imaginative faculty and perfect

---

84. [Emphasis on "not" ("nicht") added to *PG*.]
85. [Emphasis on "understanding" ("Verständnis") added to *PG*.]
86. [Emphasis on "representation" ("Darstellung") added to *PG*.]
87. [*MO* had what, one must assume, was the erroneous "exuberant" ("überschwänglichen"); *PG* corrected it to "superabundant" ("überschwenglichen").]
88. [Emphasis on "direct" ("unmittelbarer") added to *PG*.]
89. [*PG* removed the emphasis on "thus" ("also"), which *MO* put on it.]
90. [Emphasis on "also" ("auch") added to *PG*.]
91. [Emphasis on "completely" ("ganz") added to *PG*.]
92. [Emphasis on "his" ("seine") added to *PG*.]
93. [Emphasis on "therefore" ("also") added to *PG*.]
94. [Emphasis on "'dreams'" ("'träumt'") added to *PG*.]

intellect, he will perceive, in the condition of detachment from the material world—in dream and vision—only divine things, he will *see*[95] only God and His angels.[96]

To summarize, the prophet is a man of perfect intellect and perfect imaginative faculty, who is completely ruled by desire for knowledge of the upper world. Only such a man can be in *direct*[97] union with the upper world, can directly know "God and the angels." This knowledge, superior to all other human knowledge, qualifies him to be a *teacher* of men, a teacher *even*[98] of the *philosophers*; in particular, the fact that even his imaginative faculty is wholly seized by knowledge of the upper world qualifies him for the figurative presentation of his knowledge and hence for the instruction of the *multitude*.

III

The part of Maimonides' prophetology discussed up to this point is intelligible entirely within itself. The real difficulties affect the part to be discussed now, and not only in itself[99] but also in its relation to the first part.[100] We begin with a preliminary orientation in the subject matter of the part of Maimonides' prophetology[101] that has not yet been discussed.

Up to this point we have encountered the imaginative faculty only in its function of representing the insights of the intellect figuratively; the actualization of the intellect is the necessary condition of this function of the imaginative faculty. But in addition to this imitative activity of the imaginative faculty in prophetic knowledge, it also has an independent activity of its own, or at least an activity whose dependence on the activity of the intellect is not apparent from the outset; this activity is the basis of *knowledge of the future*.[102] The future is known not only by prophets but also—though in an inferior way—by ordinary men, and by these it is known in the veridical dream. In

---

95. [Emphasis on "see" ("sehen") added to *PG*.]
96. [**21**] 2.36 (284–87); cf. 1.34 (125–27) and 50 (181).
97. [Emphasis on "direct" ("unmittelbarer") added to *PG*.]
98. [Emphasis on "even" ("also") added to *PG*.]
99. [*MO*: "and not only [this part] in itself" ("und zwar sowohl diesen Teil in sich selbst"); *PG*: "and not only [this part taken] in itself" ("und zwar sowohl diesen Teil für sich genommen").]
100. [*MO* has a sentence following next that is missing from *PG*; this is almost certainly due to Strauss's own editing: "In order to remove these [difficulties], we must consider *the sources* of Maimonides." ("Um sie zu beseitigen, werden wir *die Quellen* Maimunis berücksichtigen müssen.") A more or less similar sentence appeared in both *MO* and *PG*, toward the bottom of the next paragraph.]
101. [*MO*: "the prophetology" ("der prophetologie"); *PG*: "Maimonides' prophetology" ("der prophetologie Maimunis").]
102. [Emphasis on "knowledge of the future" ("Erkenntnis der Zukunft") added to *PG*.]

sleep, when the senses are at rest, the imaginative faculty is free to receive the emanation of the active intellect; in this way[103] the future becomes known to man. The activity of the imaginative faculty in veridical dream differs only in degree from its activity in prophetic knowledge of the future; the imaginative faculty of the prophet is of the greatest possible perfection, but it is the same faculty in him as in all men. The veridical dream arises through the influence of the active intellect on the imaginative faculty, just as philosophy is actualized through the influence of the active intellect on the (human) intellect. If the active intellect affects both the intellect *and*[104] the imaginative faculty, then prophecy occurs.[105] The question is whether Maimonides means that the intellect and the imaginative faculty collaborate in the prophet's knowledge of the future[106] in the same way as they collaborate in the figurative representation of theoretical insights. And this is not the only question that remains unanswered in Maimonides.[107] He also does not answer the more fundamental question: how is it to be understood that such essentially different activities as the figurative representation of theoretical insights and knowledge of the future are both characteristic of the prophet? We shall attempt to answer this question through a consideration of Maimonides' *sources*.[108] In order to justify this procedure we must explain the general relationship of Maimonides' prophetology to the prophetology of the *falasifa*.

Maimonides himself says that his doctrine is completely in accord with the doctrine of the *falasifa*—with the exception of *one*[109] point. This one

---

103. [*MO*: "by this means" ("auf diesem Weise"); *PG*: "in this way" ("auf diesem Wege").]
104. [Emphasis on "and" ("und") added to *PG*.]
105. [**22**] *Guide* 2.36 (281–83) and 37 (290f.).
106. [**23**] Maimonides says explicitly that the prophet's knowledge of the future (his ability to see the future before him as an embodied present) belongs to the imaginative faculty. This perfection of the imaginative faculty corresponds to that [*MO*: "the" ("die"); *PG*: "that" ("diejenige")] perfection of the intellect in accordance with which the prophet attains theoretical insights directly, without premises and conclusions. Now this further actualization of the imaginative faculty by the active intellect—and thus not only that actualization which enables it to present theoretical insights figuratively—must have as its necessary condition the influence of the active intellect on the intellect of the prophet: the active intellect acts only on the intellect, and only through the medium of the intellect does it act on the imaginative faculty (*Guide* 2.38 [298]). This assertion stands in open conflict with the earlier assertion that the active intellect acts, in the case of veridical dreams, only on the imaginative faculty; the conflict is sharpened if one understands Maimonides' further assertion that veridical dreams and prophecy differ only in degree to mean that even in the prophet's knowledge of the future, only the imaginative faculty is influenced by the active intellect. Cf. below, note [**34**].
107. [*MO*: "Maimonides leaves us in the dark not only with regard to this question" ("Nicht nur hinsichtlich dieser Frage lässt uns Maimuni im dunkel"); *PG*: "And this is not the only question that remains unanswered in Maimonides" ("Nicht nur diese Frage bleibt bei Maimuni beantwortet").]
108. [Emphasis on "sources" ("Quellen") added to *PG*.]
109. [Emphasis on "one" ("einem") added to *PG*.]

point is the reservation that prophecy, which occurs under fixed conditions, does not, as the *falasifa* hold, occur necessarily, but can be denied by God at His discretion in spite of the fulfillment of all the conditions. Maimonides' reservation, then, does not affect the essence and the natural conditions of prophecy. According to the doctrine of the *falasifa*, the conditions of prophecy are perfection of the intellect, the morals, and the imaginative faculty; this is what Maimonides teaches too. According to Maimonides, prophecy in its essence is an emanation from God, issuing through the medium of the active intellect first to the intellect and then to the imaginative faculty; the *falasifa* had already taught the same thing before him. Thus, in the decisive accounts of prophecy, Maimonides is, according to his own express assurance, in agreement with the *falasifa*.[110]

The writings of Alfarabi and Avicenna come into account as the foremost sources of Maimonides. The most comprehensive and detailed presentation of *Alfarabi*'s[111] prophetology is found in his work *The Ideal State*.[112] We shall consider only this presentation in the following. Alfarabi speaks of prophecy in two different passages of the *Ideal State*. In each of these passages he treats a different kind of prophecy, although without expressly saying so: the first kind he treats is based on the imaginative faculty alone, the second on both the intellect and the imaginative faculty. The imaginative faculty has three functions: it preserves the impressions of sensibilia; it combines these

---

110. [24] *Guide* 2.32 (261–63), 36 (281 and 287), 37 (290f.). [*MO*: "Thus, in the crucial analyses of prophecy, Maimonides is, according to his own express declaration, in agreement with the *falasifa*." ("In den entscheidenden Bestimmungen der Prophetie stimmt also Maimuni seiner ausdrücklichen Erklärung nach mit den *falasifa* überein."); *PG*: "Thus, in the decisive accounts of prophecy, Maimonides is, according to his own express assurance, in agreement with the *falasifa*." ("In den massgebenden Erklärungen der Prophetie stimmt also Maimuni seiner ausdrücklichen Versicherung nach mit den *falasifa* überein.")]

111. [Emphasis on "Alfarabi's" ("Alfarabis") added to *PG*.]

112. [25] Fr[iedrich] Dieterici has edited (Leiden, 1895) and translated (Leiden, 1900) this text. Our citations will follow the page and line numbers of Dieterici's edition. [See the two volumes that now are reprinted together as one: *Alfarabi's Abhandlung Der Musterstaat*, edited in the Arabic and translated into German by Friedrich Heinrich Dieterici (Hildesheim: Olms, 1985). For Strauss's notes, the title will be rendered here in English as *The Ideal State*. This follows the decision made by Eve Adler, English translator of the volume *Philosophy and Law* (1995), in which the present essay of Strauss's originally appeared, as to how to translate the title of the German edition of Farabi's work, rendered by Dieterici as *Der Musterstaat*. (To be sure, the German might also have been rendered in English as *The Model State*.) However, in the only complete English translation of the work, also containing an Arabic edition, the title is translated by its editor, Richard Walzer, as *The Perfect State*. It is to be noted that these miscellaneous versions (in German and English) tend to obscure the original Arabic title of the work, which in full is actually *Mabadi Ara Ahl al-Madina al-Fadila*, i.e., *The Opinions of the People of the Virtuous City*. Hence I believe it would have been better to abbreviate the title as *The Virtuous City*, as Strauss himself will do as of "Some Remarks on the Political Science of Maimonides and Farabi" and henceforth. See chap. 5 below.]

impressions; finally and preeminently, it reproduces the sensibilia.[113] In general, and thus also for its reproductive function in particular, it is dependent on receiving material from elsewhere. In the waking state it receives material especially from sense perception. But since in this state it is entirely in the service of the other faculties of the soul, its own independent activity cannot develop; this development occurs in sleep, when the senses and the intellect are at rest. It then reproduces what the senses have perceived; sometimes it elaborates by analogy what the intellect presents to it; by analogy—namely, since it is not capable of receiving the intelligibles as such, it imitates them by representing them sensibly. Thus it represents the intelligibles of the highest perfection (such as the first cause, the immaterial existences, the heaven) by means of the most perfect sensibles (things of beautiful appearance). In the same way it elaborates analogically what is presented to it by the other faculties of the soul (the nutritive faculty, etc.).[114] The imaginative faculty can also receive content from the active intellect. In this case it takes over the functions of the (human) intellect. There are two kinds of intellect: the theoretical, which knows the intelligibles, and the practical, which has to do with the particulars (*particularia*). If the active intellect works on the imaginative faculty, the latter receives *either*[115] intelligibles *or*[116] particulars—and especially future particulars. It necessarily represents the intelligibles as sensibles; but as for the particulars, it sometimes presents them as they actually are, while in other cases it represents them by other particulars that are more or less similar to them.[117] Thus, knowledge of the future arises in the same way as sensible apprehension of intelligibles: through the influence of the active intellect on the imaginative faculty. There are various ranks of imaginative comprehension. At the lowest rank and occurring most frequently is knowledge of the future in sleep, the veridical dream; higher than the dreamer of veridical dreams is he who grasps intelligibles in figurative form while asleep; highest is he who is capable of receiving in the waking state both (future) particulars and the

---

113. [26] *Ideal State* 48, 3–5; cf. *Guide* 2.36 (282). [See Alfarabi, *Perfect State*, trans. Walzer, chap. 14, para. 2, pp. 210–11.]

114. [27] *Ideal State* 47, 17–48, 9; 49, 8–10; 50, 9–13. [See *Perfect State*, trans. Walzer, chap. 14, paras. 1–2, pp. 210–11; para. 4, pp. 214–15; para. 6, pp. 218–19. *MO*: "what is presented to it by the nutritive faculty, etc." ("was ihr dargeboten wird von der Ernährenden Kraft usw."); *PG*: "what is presented to it by the other faculties of the soul (the nutritive faculty, etc.)" ("was ihr von den anderen Seelenkräften (der Ernährenden Kraft usw.) dargeboten wird").]

115. [Emphasis on "either" ("entweder") added to *PG*.]

116. [Emphasis on "or" ("oder") added to *PG*.]

117. [28] Loc. cit., 50, 21–51, 4; 51, 14–20. [See *Perfect State*, trans. Walzer, chap. 14, para. 7, pp. 218–21; para. 8, pp. 222–23.]

figures of intelligibles; this rank is the highest that the imaginative faculty can attain, and altogether the highest that man can reach by means of the imaginative faculty. The condition of this (the first) kind of prophecy is then the highest perfection of the imaginative faculty.[118] The second kind of prophecy differs from the first in that its condition is not only the highest perfection of the imaginative faculty but also the actualization of the intellect. To the man who fulfills these conditions, God grants revelations through the mediation of the active intellect: what emanates from God to the active intellect, the active intellect then allows to emanate first[119] to the intellect of the appropriately disposed man and then[120] to his imaginative faculty.[121] Through what emanates from the active intellect to the prophet's intellect, he becomes a philosopher, and through what emanates from the active intellect to his imaginative faculty, he becomes a prophet, i.e., one who warns about the future. His imaginative faculty must be so perfect that it can receive from the active intellect not only the particulars but also the intelligibles in sensible form.[122] The man who fulfills the stated conditions is capable of communicating what he has received from the active intellect in a manner adapted to the multitude.[123] This man stands at the simply highest rank of humanity[124]—in contradistinction to the first kind of prophet, who achieves only the highest rank of humanity attainable through the imaginative faculty alone.

Comparison of Maimonides' prophetology with that of Alfarabi shows[125]

---

118. [29] Loc. cit., 52, 7–23; 51, 10–12. The superiority of waking knowledge over that in dreams is decisive also for Maimonides' rank-ordering of the prophets; cf. *Guide* 2.45 with 41 (313f.). [See *Perfect State*, trans. Walzer, chap. 14, para. 9, pp. 224–25; para. 8, pp. 220–21.]

119. [*PG* adds "first" ("zuerst").]

120. [*MO*: "dann" ("then"); *PG*: "then" or "after that" ("danach")]

121. [30] Maimonides too [likewise] defines prophecy in this way; cf. *Guide* 2.36 (281).

122. [31] *Ideal State* 57, 17–58, 1; 58, 18–59, 1. [See *Perfect State*, trans. Walzer, chap. 15, para. 8, pp. 240–43; para. 10, pp. 244–45.]

123. [32] Cf. loc. cit., 59, 6 and 69, 19–70, 3 with 52, 15–16. [See *Perfect State*, trans. Walzer, chap. 15, para. 11, pp. 246–47, and chap. 17, para. 2, pp. 278–79, with chap. 14, para. 10, pp. 224–25.]

124. [33] Loc. cit., 59, 2–3. Cf. *Guide* 2.36 (281). [See *Perfect State*, trans. Walzer, chap. 15, para. 11, pp. 244–45.]

125. [34] In Maimonides' prophetology it remained particularly unclear whether and in what sense Maimonides claims that the active intellect directly influences the imaginative faculty (see above, note [23]). We now attempt to show what emerges from a consideration of Alfarabi's prophetology towards answering this question. Like Alfarabi, Maimonides teaches that in the case of prophetic knowledge, the active intellect influences first the intellect of the prophet and *"then"* [*PG* adds emphasis on "'then'" ("'danach'")] his imaginative faculty (*Ideal State* 58, 22 and *Guide* 2.35 [281]) [*Perfect State*, trans. Walzer, chap. 15, para. 10, pp. 244–45]; like Alfarabi, he attributes the prophet's knowledge of the future to his imaginative faculty (59, 1 and 2.38 [298]) [*Perfect State*, trans. Walzer, chap. 15, para. 10, pp. 244–45]. In prophetic knowledge, then—regardless of whether it is an imaginative grasp of the intelligibles or knowledge of the future—there occurs, according to both Alfarabi and Maimonides, no direct influence of the active intellect on the imaginative faculty. But how does it stand with nonprophetic knowledge? Maimo-

that Maimonides denies the lower, exclusively imaginative prophecy, which Alfarabi had recognized. For Maimonides, therefore, the highest rank of humanity and the highest rank of the imaginative faculty coincide in prophecy *per se*,[126] while Alfarabi could distinguish the highest rank of the imaginative faculty as such from the simply highest rank of humanity.[127] Maimonides, then, recognizes as prophecy only the higher kind of prophecy. With regard to the latter, he is largely in agreement with Alfarabi. It is only an apparent difference that Alfarabi does not mention moral perfection as a condition of prophecy; that full agreement actually reigns between Maimonides and Alfarabi is shown by Alfarabi's statements about happiness: happiness consists in freedom from matter; it is attained directly through the actualization of the intellect; but moral virtue is an indirect condition.[128] A real difference may lie in the fact that Alfarabi denies the possibility of superphilosophical [*über-philosophischen*] knowledge of the upper world through prophecy: through the influence of the active intellect on his intellect the prophet be-

---

nides immediately follows his unconditional denial of direct influence with a remarkable polemic: he denies that people who lack intellectual perfection can receive theoretical insights in sleep (2.38 [299f.]). This possibility had been recognized by Alfarabi; he teaches that in the veridical dream and in the lower rank of prophecy the active intellect even imparts intelligibles to the imaginative faculty. Perhaps Maimonides intends his denial of the direct influence of the active intellect on the imaginative faculty strictly with reference to prophecy as such—thus not with reference to the veridical dream—and [*PG* adds emphasis on "and" ("und")] in anticipation of his denying the possibility that a man whose intellect is not perfect could receive theoretical insights in dream; perhaps he does not deny any more than Alfarabi does that, in knowledge of the future through veridical dream, the active intellect acts directly on the imaginative faculty. In fact he even expressly asserts direct influence in the case of the (future-knowing) veridical dream (2.37 [291]). Speaking against the attempt to harmonize Maimonides' contradictory assertions in this way, by reference to his relationship to Alfarabi, is the following consideration, which also has reference to this relationship. It is striking that Maimonides says, in the passage where he speaks about the activity of the imaginative faculty in general, that it is at its strongest when the senses are at rest (2.36 [282]), while Alfarabi, whom he otherwise follows throughout (see above [third and fourth paragraphs of section III]), says in the same connection that it is when the senses *and the intellect* [*PG* adds emphasis on "and the intellect" ("und der Verstand")] are at rest (47, 21f. and 51, 15-17) [*Perfect State*, trans. Walzer, chap. 14, para. 1, pp. 210–11, and chap. 14, para. 8, pp. 220–21]. Is this a case of Maimonides' looseness of expression, or a case of conscious correction? If the latter, he appears to be saying that even in knowledge of the future through the veridical dream, there is collaboration by the intellect; in this case his statement that in the veridical dream the active intellect influences only the imaginative faculty, and not the intellect, would have to be understood as follows: in the veridical dream too, the influence of the active intellect on the imaginative faculty takes place only by way of the intellect; but if the intellect is not perfect, that influence passes over it almost without leaving a trace (cf. 2.37 [291]).

126. [Emphasis on "prophecy" ("der Prophetie") added to *PG*. Eve Adler, the English translator, conveyed this sense by the phrase "prophecy *per se*," since in proper English it makes no sense to say that the highest ranks of human beings and of the imaginative faculty "coincide in *the* prophecy," especially because he is not referring to the prophecy of a specific man, but to prophecy in general.]

127. [35] *Guide* 2.36 (281). *Ideal State* 52, 11–12 and 59, 2–3. [See *Perfect State*, trans. Walzer, chap. 14, para. 9, pp. 224–25, and chap. 15, para. 11, pp. 244–45.]

128. [36] *Ideal State* 46, 7–47, 3. [See *Perfect State*, trans. Walzer, chap. 13, paras. 5–7, pp. 204–9.]

comes a philosopher[129]—nothing other and nothing higher than a philosopher.[130] Even if Maimonides' teaching on this important point differs from Alfarabi's, Maimonides does not thereby come into conflict with *the falasifa*: he found in *Avicenna*,[131] at any rate, the doctrine of the prophet's direct knowledge. According to Avicenna the highest capacity distinguishing the prophets is the capacity for direct knowledge, not based on[132] syllogisms and proofs.[133]

Avicenna teaches[134] that the highest rank among men is held by those who have attained intellectual and moral perfection; among these in turn—and thus among all men—he who is disposed to the rank of prophecy is the most excellent.[135] The prophet is characterized by the following three capacities

129. [37] Loc. cit., 58, 23. [See *Perfect State*, trans. Walzer, chap. 15, para. 10, pp. 244–45.]

130. [38] Perhaps Ibn Tufayl's polemic against Alfarabi's prophetology (*Hayy ibn Yaqzan*, ed. [Léon] Gauthier [Beirut, 1936], p. 12) also supports this interpretation; a passage in Alfarabi's *Philosophical Treatises* (ed. Dieterici, Leiden 1895, p. 75) would be a counter-example, if this passage and its whole context actually comes from Alfarabi, and not, as seems to me more likely, from Avicenna. Cf. however the passage from Alfarabi cited above [ninth and tenth paragraphs of section IV]. [See Ibn Tufayl, "Hayy ibn Yaqzan," trans. George N. Atiyeh, in *Medieval Political Philosophy*, ed. Lerner and Mahdi, pp. 135–62, and especially p. 139, for Gauthier, p. 12.]

131. [Emphasis on "Avicenna" ("Ibn Sina") added to *PG*.]

132. [*MO*: "relying on" ("fussender"); *PG*: "based on" ("beruhender").]

133. [39] *De anima* V, 6 (*Opera Avicennae*, Venice, 1508, fol. 26b); *Tis' rasa'il* (Constantinople 1298), 84; [Samuel] Landauer, "Die Psychologie des Ibn Sina," in *Zeitschrift der deutschen morgenlandischen Gesellschaft* 29 (1875): [339–72, and especially] 410f. [It is a German translation of Avicenna's *Compendium on the Soul* (*Maqala fi 'l-nafs*). See also *Psychologie d'Ibn Sina (Avicenne) d'après son oeuvre As-Sifa*, Arabic text and French translation by Jan Bakos (Prague: Éditions de l'Académie Tchécoslovaque des Sciences, 1956). For *Tis' rasa'il*, 84, see Avicenna, "On the Proof of Prophecies," trans. Marmura, p. 115.]

134. [40] *Avicennae Metaphysices Compendium*, ex arabica latine reddidit [Nematallah] Carame (Roma 1927), 243s; cf. especially the translator's notes p. 244. The Latin translation of the parallel passage in Avicenna's *Greater Metaphysics* (X, 1 [Venice 1508], fol. 107b3) is simply unintelligible. I have consulted the original of the *Greater Metaphysics* in a Berlin manuscript (Minutoli 229, fol. 165b–166a). Cf. also the presentation of Avicenna's prophetology in Ghazali's *Tahafut [al-Falasifa]* (ed. [Maurice] Bouyges [Beirut 1927], pp. 272–75). [See now Averroes, *Tahafut al-Tahafut*, trans. Simon van den Bergh (London: Luzac, 1954), containing the work by Ghazali against which Averroes contended. For the pages to which Strauss refers, see vol. I, pp. 313–14. See also: Fazlur Rahman, *Avicenna's Psychology: An English Translation of Kitab al-Najat, Book II, Chapter VI with Historico-Philosophical Notes and Textual Improvements on the Cairo Edition* (London: Oxford University Press, 1952); Avicenna, *The Metaphysics of "The Healing*," ed. and trans. Michael Marmura (Provo: Brigham Young University Press, 2005); Al-Ghazali, *The Incoherence of the Philosophers*, trans. (with parallel Arabic text) Michael E. Marmura (Provo: Brigham Young University Press, 2000).]

135. [41] Avicenna says also in the *Risala fi 'ithbat an-nubuwa* (*Tis' rasa'il* 84) that the prophet occupies the highest rank among the earthly existences; cf. *Guide* 2.36 (281). [For *Tis' rasa'il*, 84, see Avicenna, "On the Proof of Prophecies," trans. Marmura, p. 115. One of the anonymous reviewers for the University of Chicago Press made known to me that the title, *Risala fi 'ithbat an-nubuwa*, had been misstated by Strauss: he had it as "fi 'itbat," but this should have been "fi 'ithbat." Readers will notice that this title has been corrected.]

of his soul: (1.) perfection of the imaginative faculty; (2.) capacity to perform miracles; (3.) direct knowledge. The man who has at his disposal, in addition to intellectual and moral perfection, these three capabilities, receives revelations: he hears the word of God, and he sees God's angels in visible form. There is an order of rank among the three capacities characteristic of the prophets: imaginative prophecy occupies the lowest rank; higher than this is prophecy that has the power to alter matter, to work miracles; the highest rank is occupied by the prophecy consisting in the simply highest perfection of the theoretical intellect.[136] This must not be understood as if the prophet of the highest rank does not have at his disposal also the capabilities of the prophets of both other ranks. That Avicenna specifically accepts[137] the collaboration of the imaginative faculty in prophecy as such, and therefore also in prophecy of the highest rank, is shown by his definition of prophecy as such:[138] prophecy is[139] hearing the word of God and seeing the angels of God in *visible*[140] form.[141]

We may therefore say that the decisive factors of Maimonides' prophetology are also found, in the same context, either in Alfarabi or in Avicenna or in both.[142]

---

136. [42] *De anima* IV, 4 (Venice 1508, fol. 20b) and V, 6 (fol. 26b).

137. [*MO*: "As concerns specifically the collaboration" ("Was inbesondere das Mitwirken . . . angeht"); *PG*: "That Avicenna specifically accepts the collaboration" ("Dass Ibn Sina inbesondere das Mitwirken . . . annimmt").]

138. [*MO*: "it follows clearly from the fact that he defines prophecy *per se* as" ("so ergibt es sich klar daraus, dass die Prophetie als solche bestimmt wird als"); *PG*: "is shown by his definition of prophecy as such" ("zeigt seine Definition der Prophetie als solcher").]

139. [*PG* adds: "prophecy is" ("Prophetie ist").]

140. [Emphasis on "visible" ("sichtbarer") added to *PG*.]

141. [43] Diesendruck claims (loc. cit., 83ff.) that the imaginative faculty is not constitutive for prophecy according to either Alfarabi or Avicenna. He arrives at this assertion with regard to Alfarabi merely because he does not take *The Ideal State* into consideration. [In *MO*, Strauss has: "acquainted with" ("kennt"); in *PG*, it is: "taken into consideration" ("berücksichtigt").] With regard to Avicenna he relies exclusively on Shahrastani. [See Shahrastani, *Struggling with the Philosopher: A Refutation of Avicenna's Metaphysics (Musara'at al-Falasifa)*, ed. and trans. Wilferd Madelung and Toby Mayer (London: I. B. Tauris, 2001), pp. 55–56, 71–72, 97–98.]

142. [44] Two characteristic teachings of Maimonides should be mentioned, although they do not affect the foundation laid by the *falasifa*. Maimonides emphatically stresses that one of the conditions of prophecy is perfection of the intellect acquired through instruction and study (2.32 [263]; 36 [284 and 287]; 38 [300]; 42 [323]). With this teaching he enters into opposition against Avicenna, who understands the prophet's capacity for direct knowledge in the sense that the prophet does not depend upon instruction at all (*De anima* V, 6; *Rasa'il* 44f.). We find this view even more sharply formulated in Averroes: "... it is known that the Prophet (namely, Muhammad) was an illiterate man among an illiterate, vulgar, nomadic people, which had never concerned itself with sciences and to which knowledge had never been attributed, which had never concerned itself with investigations about the beings, as did the Greeks and other peoples among whom philosophy had been perfected over long ages" (*Philosophie und Theologie von Averroes*, trans. M[arcus] J[oseph] Müller [Munich: G. Franz, 1875], p. 94). [For an English translation of the work by Averroes edited by Müller, see: *The Philosophy and Theology of Averroes*, trans. Mohammad Jamil-ur-Rehman (Baroda: Widgery, 1921), p. 254.] Compare with this the altogether different judgment

of Maimonides about *his* people, *Guide* 1.71 in the beginning. To corroborate his view, Averroes cites three Qur'an passages. This view is in fact the orthodox doctrine of Islam; cf. Ali ibn Rabban at-Tabari, *Kitab ad-din wad-daula* (Cairo 1923), 48–50, and Ali ibn Muhammad al-Mawardi, *A'lam an-nubuwwa* (Cairo 1315) (as per the obliging information of Mr. Abd-ul-alim). Maimonides' emphatic insistence on the prophets' need of instruction could be understood therefore as a polemic against Islam: he accepts the Islamic assertion of the fact that Muhammad had had no instruction at all, but he considers it already admitted in this assertion that Muhammad's claim to be a prophet is unjustified. [The phrase "to be a prophet" ("Prophet zu sein") is missing from *MO*, and has been added to *PG*.] At first glance it appears to be of fundamental importance that Maimonides excludes the prophecy of Moses from his prophetology on principle. He explains that in the *Guide* he will say not a single word, not even by allusion, about the prophecy of Moses; that it differs fundamentally from the prophecy of the other prophets; that it is incomprehensible to man (2.35 [277f. and 281]). He thereby gives the impression that, besides his explicit reservation against the prophetology of the *falasifa* (2.32 [262f.]), he wishes to make yet a further reservation. Is this really his intention? Despite his above-mentioned statement, he gives us some information on how he understands the uniqueness of Moses' prophecy: Moses heard the word of God without the mediation of the imaginative faculty (2.45 [348]); he defines this uniqueness even more sharply by saying that Moses prophesied without images (2.36 [288]). This assertion cannot possibly hold without limitation; for Maimonides not only does not doubt, but emphasizes time and again, the figurative character of many expressions of the Torah. Almost every page of the *Guide* can serve as evidence of this; here let it suffice to mention the fact that Maimonides, in the part of his prophetology where he discusses thematically the figurative character of prophetic speech, promiscuously adduces passages from both the Torah and the prophetic books; at the beginning of the relevant chapter (2.47) it is expressly stated that the instrument of prophecy, the imaginative faculty, leads to the figurative character of prophetic speech. Since Moses speaks in images no less than the other prophets, he must have the capacity to express his insights in the form of images; that is, he must have a perfect imaginative faculty at his disposal and he must employ this faculty. One realizes how Maimonides' apparently contradictory assertion is to be understood if one follows a clue that Maimonides himself gives. In the passage where he says that Moses did not prophesy in images like the other prophets (2.36 [288]), he refers to his previous remarks on this subject. By these he probably means first of all his observations in "Yesodei ha-Torah" (VII, 6). [See Maimonides, "Laws of the Basic Principles of the Torah," trans. Hyamson, p. 43a.] There the "non-imaginative" character of Moses' prophecy is defined as follows: he heard the word of God in the waking state, not in a dream or a vision; he saw the things themselves without enigma and image; he was not terrified and bewildered. What this means is that he was simply *not under the influence* [the emphasis on "not under the influence" ("nicht im Bann") has been added by Strauss to *PG*] of the imaginative faculty when he was in the condition of prophetic comprehension; he was not bewildered like the other prophets by direct contemplation of the upper world; it does not mean, and cannot mean, that he did not have the imaginative faculty *at his disposal* [the emphasis on "at his disposal" ("verfugte") has been added by Strauss to *PG*] in the manner of the prophets [the phrase "in the manner of the prophets" ("in der Weise der Propheten") is missing from *MO* and has been added to *PG*], since he *must* [the emphasis on "must" ("müsste") has been added by Strauss to *PG*] have had it at his disposal when, under other circumstances, he wished to guide the multitude through speeches that would be intelligible to them.—That Maimonides does not deviate from the prophetology of the *falasifa* with his doctrine of Moses' prophecy follows also from the observation of Narboni, in his commentary on Ibn Tufayl's *Hayy ibn Yaqzan*, that Maimonides adopted this teaching from Alfarabi and Ibn Bajja; cf. Steinschneider, *Al-Farabi (Alpharabius)[: Des Arabischen Philosophen Leben und Schriften mit besonderer Rücksicht auf die Geschichte der Griechischen Wissenschaft unter den Arabern, nebst Anhängen Johannes Philoponus bei den Arabern, Leben, und Testament des Aristoteles von Ptolemaeus, Darstellung der Philosophie Plato's; Grösstentheils nach handschriftlichen Quellen* (St. Petersburg 1869; reprint, Amsterdam 1966)], p. 65 n. 11. [Steinschneider's remark may be translated as follows: "In his commentary on Ibn Tufayl's *Hayy ibn Yaqzan*, Narboni says expressly that he cannot conceal (the fact) that Maimonides' distinction between the prophecy of Moses and that of the other prophets was influenced by Ibn Bajja and Alfarabi."] Cf. also the observation of Efodi cited by Munk (II, 288 n. 1). ["According to Efodi, the author had wished to make it understood here, without being so bold as to say it clearly, that Moses himself had need, up to a certain point, of the imaginative faculty, in order to predict the future. Abravanel (loc. cit., fol. 35a) considered this opinion of Efodi's as a genuine heresy." Translated by Kenneth Hart Green.]

The only essential[143] factor, at least in Avicenna's doctrine, that is lacking in Maimonides' prophetology is the doctrine of the prophets' miracle-working faculty. Admittedly there can be found in his writings several scattered statements in the sense of this doctrine,[144] but it emerges that they cannot be decisive if one recognizes the overall tendency of his doctrine of miracles. Here too his sources must be considered. In Islamic philosophy there are two opposing views on miracles.[145] According to the doctrine of the *kalam*, miracles take place through the power of God, not through the activity of the prophet; the prophet's relation to the miraculous event is none other than that of announcing it beforehand; the occurrence of the previously announced miracle is the divine confirmation of the prophet; it is by means of this announcement that miracles proper differ from the miracles worked by holy men and sorcerers. In opposition to the *kalam*, the *falasifa*—on the grounds that whatever occurs does not spring from the unconditioned free will of God but must proceed from other occurrences and under fixed conditions—teach that miracles are performed and not just announced by the prophets. Maimonides is taking the principle of the *falasifa* into account when he teaches that miracles are, in a certain sense, in nature: when God created nature, He put into it the faculty of bringing forth miracles at predetermined times; God lets the prophet know the time for which he should announce the occurrence in question, and this is the "sign" of the prophet.[146] Thus Maimonides, like the *falasifa*, denies that God interferes at His free will in the world created by Him, but, on the basis of the *falasifa*, he adheres to the view of the *kalam* on the role played by the prophet in the miracle: the prophet only announces the miracle, he does not perform it; it is performed by God. But if the miracle is performed by God and not by the prophet, then prophecy itself can depend on God's free miracle-working. This is why Maimonides can teach that prophecy can be miraculously withheld from a man who fulfills all the conditions of prophecy. This teaching is *the* reservation that he holds against the prophetology of the *falasifa*. This reservation is possible

143. [*MO*: "substantial" ("massgebende"); *PG*: "essential" ("wesentliche").]
144. [45] *Guide* 2.35 (279), 37 (291), 46 (354f.); "Yesodei ha-Torah" VIII, 1. [See Maimonides, "Laws of the Basic Principles of the Torah," trans. Hyamson, p. 43b.]
145. [46] The following is based on the account of Ibn Khaldun: *Prolégomènes d'Ebn-Khaldoun*, ed. [Étienne] Quatremère (Paris 1858), I 168–70. [See Ibn Khaldun, *The Muqaddimah: An Introduction to History*, trans. Franz Rosenthal, 3 vols.{corrected and augmented edition} (Princeton: Princeton University Press, 1967), vol. 1, pp. 187–90. It is also available as Ibn Khaldun, *The Muqaddimah: An Introduction to History*, trans. Franz Rosenthal, ed. and abridged by N. J. Dawood (Princeton: Princeton University Press, 1967), pp. 71–74.]
146. [47] *Guide* 2.29 (224).

only if the miracle is not really performed by the prophet. Thus, the fact that Maimonides abandons the doctrine of the prophet's miracle-working is the only factor distinguishing his prophetology from that of the *falasifa*. This confirms his own statement that his prophetology differs in only one point—namely, in the reservation mentioned—from that of the *falasifa*. Thus, in light of the fundamental agreement between Maimonides and the *falasifa*, we have a fundamental right, whenever Maimonides' own statements leave us in uncertainty, to interpret the obscurities of his prophetology by recourse to the relevant doctrines of the *falasifa*.[147] Having established this right for ourselves, we return to the question left unanswered by Maimonides. This question runs: how is it to be understood that such fundamentally different activities as figurative representation of theoretical insights and knowledge of the future are both characteristic of the prophet?

If one returns to Alfarabi's doctrine, this obscurity is explained as follows. Knowledge of the future is knowledge of the particulars (*particularia*); knowledge of the particulars belongs to the *practical*[148] intellect; when future things become known in veridical dream or in prophecy, the imaginative faculty is acting on behalf of the practical intellect. Knowledge of the intelligibles, whose sensible representation is the mark of prophecy, belongs to the *theoretical*[149] intellect; when intelligibles become known in veridical dream or in prophecy, the imaginative faculty, which to be sure cannot apprehend the intelligibles as such, but must necessarily represent them figuratively, is acting on behalf of the theoretical intellect.[150] The fact that the prophet—the prophet simply, according to Maimonides, or the prophet of the higher kind, according to Alfarabi—has at his disposal both knowledge of the intelligibles and knowledge of the future means, therefore, that the prophet has at his disposal (perfect) theoretical and practical knowledge. But theoretical knowledge consists in unclouded, pure intellectual apprehension of the intelligibles; the sensible representation of intelligibles has nothing to do with theoretical knowledge; the point of it is only to communicate to the multitude certain doctrines without which the existence of the community is not possible. While the purely intellectual "inner sense" of prophetic speeches transmits theoretical truths, the imaginative "outer sense" of these speeches

---

147. [*MO*: "by a consideration of his sources" ("unter Berücksichtigung seiner Quellen"); *PG*: "by recourse to the relevant doctrines of the *falasifa*" ("durch Rekurs auf die entsprechenden Lehren der *falasifa*").]
148. [Emphasis on "practical" ("praktischen") added to *PG*.]
149. [Emphasis on "theoretical" ("theoretischen") added to *PG*.]
150. [**48**] *Ideal State* 50, 18–51, 2. [See *Perfect State*, trans. Walzer, chap. 14, para. 7, pp. 218–21.]

transmits doctrines that are useful specifically for improving the condition of human communities.[151] Thus the collaboration of the imaginative faculty in prophetic knowledge—both in knowledge of the future and in sensible representation of the intelligibles, which occurs only for the sake of guiding the multitude—has in any case a practical purpose. It is, then, understandable how Maimonides can say that if the active intellect influences only man's imaginative faculty, he becomes a statesman and legislator or a dreamer of veridical dreams or a soothsayer or a sorcerer. All these activities, springing from influence on the imaginative faculty alone, and apparently having nothing[152] in common with each other, do have in common with each other the essential factor[153] that they are *practical*.[154] On the other hand, if his intellect alone is influenced by the active intellect, a man becomes a philosopher, a *theoretical*[155] man; and if both his intellect and his imaginative faculty are influenced by the active intellect, he becomes a prophet.[156] Prophecy is therefore a union of theoretical and practical perfection (and also a heightening of each of these perfections beyond the measure attainable by nonprophets). As the active intellect must influence the prophet's intellect if the prophet is to be able to communicate theoretical truths to men, if he is to be able to be men's *teacher*,[157] so must the active intellect influence the prophet's imaginative faculty if he is to be able to fulfill his *practical*[158] task. Prophecy is both theoretical and practical; the prophet is *teacher and governor in one*.

IV

If the necessary condition of prophecy is that the active intellect influences both the intellect and the imaginative faculty, and if its influence on the intellect alone makes a man a philosopher, while its influence on the imaginative faculty alone makes a man a statesman, a dreamer of veridical dreams, a soothsayer, or sorcerer, then this means that *the prophet is philosopher/statesman/*

---

151. [49] *Guide* 1.Intro. (19).
152. [*MO*: "potentialities" or "possibilitities" ("Möglichkeiten"); *PG*: "facts" ("Tätigkeiten"). Eve Adler, the English translator, has not rendered the word literally, in order to make for correct English: "apparently having nothing in common with each other," rather than "apparently having no facts in common with each other."]
153. [*MO*: "essence" ("Wesentliche"); *PG*: "essential factor" ("wesentliche Moment").]
154. [Emphasis on "practical" ("praktisch") added to *PG*.]
155. [Emphasis on "theoretical" ("Theoretiker") added to *PG*.]
156. [50] *Guide* 2.37 (290f.).
157. [Emphasis on "teacher" ("Lehrer") added to *PG*.]
158. [Emphasis on "practical" ("praktische") added to *PG*.]

seer/(miracle-worker) in one. Now, are the practical abilities[159] that are "gathered up" in prophecy equivalent to one another? If one recalls the parallel in Alfarabi's *Ideal State*, where the prophet appears as philosopher and seer in one,[160] one might be inclined to see mantics as the supreme practical function of the prophet. Even the miracle-working of the prophet derives from mantics, in that the prophet's only contribution to a miracle is that he announces it beforehand. We must therefore ask: is mantics or politics the supreme function of the prophet? We sharpen the question: what[161] is the final end of prophecy? Why does the human race[162] depend on prophets?

The answer that Maimonides gives to this question, though he certainly does not give it expressly as such, runs: man is by nature a political being, and,[163] in contradistinction to the other living beings, he is by nature in need of association; on the other hand, in no other species is there so great a variety, even an opposition, in the character of the individuals as there is in the human species. Since, therefore, association is nowhere so necessary and nowhere so difficult as precisely among men, men need a *governor*[164] to regulate the affairs of individuals in such a way that a concord based on statute replaces the natural opposition. The existence of the human race therefore depends on the existence of human individuals who have the capacity of governing; hence the divine wisdom that willed the existence of the human race had to give it this capacity. There are two kinds of government: legislation and rule. The legislator lays down the norms for affairs, the sovereign en-

---

159. [*MO*: "potentialities" or "possibilities" ("Möglichkeiten"); *PG*: "Vermögen" ("abilities").]
160. [51] *Ideal State* 58, 23–59, 1. [See *Perfect State*, trans. Walzer, chap. 15, para. 10, pp. 244–45.]
161. [*MO* had "then" ("denn"); in *PG*, it is removed.]
162. [*MO*: "humanity" ("Menschheit"); *PG*: "human race" ("Menschengeschlecht"). See also n. 210 below.]
163. [52] For the understanding of this "and," reference should be made to Aristotle, *Politics* III, 6 (1278b, 19ff.). ["Now it has been said in our first discourses, in which we determined the principles concerning household management and the control of slaves, that man is by nature a political animal; and so even when men have no need of assistance from each other they none the less desire to live together by common interest, so far as each achieves a share of the good life. The good life then is the chief aim of society, both collectively for all its members and individually; but they also come together and maintain the political partnership for the sake of life merely, for doubtless there is some element of value contained in the mere state of being alive, provided that there is not too great an excess on the side of the hardships of life, and it is clear that the mass of mankind cling to life at the cost of enduring much suffering, which shows that life contains some measure of well-being and of sweetness in its essential nature." See Aristotle, *Politics*, trans. Harris Rackham (Cambridge, MA: Harvard University Press, 1944), pp. 200–203.]
164. [Emphasis on "governor" ("Leiters") added to *PG*. It could have been translated as "leader." Brague translates it into French as "guide." See *Maïmonide*, p. 127. Even if this may not determine how best to translate the term, which obviously has a certain flexibility, it is at least to be noted that in the two chapters from the *Guide* to which Strauss refers, for the one Shlomo Pines has rendered what seems to be the relevant passage as "ruler" (*Guide* 2.40, p. 382), and for the other he translates it by "to govern" (*Guide* 3.27, p. 510).]

forces compliance with them; the ruling government already assumes therefore the legislating government; the primary kind of government is *legislation*.[165] Now legislation can have as its end either the bodily or the spiritual perfection of man; or rather—since the realization of the higher perfection necessarily assumes the realization of the lower—legislation can limit itself to the establishment of the means that serve bodily perfection, or it can strive for bodily perfection in the service of spiritual perfection. Spiritual perfection—more precisely, the perfection of the intellect—is the specific perfection of man.[166] The law directed to the specific perfection of man is a *divine law*,[167] and its proclaimer is a *prophet*.[168] The prophet is therefore the proclaimer of a law directed to the specific perfection of man. But the law aims at making it possible to live together. Hence the prophet is the founder of a community directed to the specific perfection of man.

Maimonides' teaching has proved to be that the prophet is philosopher/statesman/seer/(miracle-worker) in one. Now since the end of prophecy is the founding of the community directed to the specific perfection of man, we may conclude that the prophet must be philosopher/statesman/seer/(miracle-worker) in one *in order that*[169] he may be the founder of the community directed to the specific perfection of man, the perfect community. If the founder of the perfect community must be a prophet, but the prophet is more than a philosopher, this means that the founding of the perfect community is not possible for a man who is only a philosopher. Hence the philosopher too is dependent on a law given by a prophet; the philosopher too must obey the prophet; he would have to obey him even if his theoretical insight were no less than the prophet's; for this theoretical insight would not make him capable of legislation; and man, as a political being, can live only under a law.

On the way to the definition of the prophet, "the prophet as philosopher/statesman/seer/(miracle-worker) in one is the founder of the perfect community," we came upon the question, "what is the end of prophecy?" We said that Maimonides certainly gives us an answer to this question, but not expressly as such. It must therefore still be shown that the doctrine of Maimonides to which we have made reference is, in his view, to be considered the answer to our question. To show this, we must go back again to the sources.

---

165. [Emphasis on "legislation" ("Gesetzgebung") added to *PG*.]
166. [53] *Guide* 3.54 (461f.).
167. [Emphasis on "divine law" ("göttliches Gesetz") added to *PG*.]
168. [54] *Guide* 2.40 and 3.27. [Emphasis on "prophet" ("Prophet") added to *PG*.]
169. [Emphasis on "in order that" ("damit") added to *PG*.]

Shem Tov [ibn] Falaquera, in his interpretation of the chapter of Maimonides' *Guide* that deals implicitly with the end of prophecy (2.40), cites a parallel from the *Metaphysics* of Avicenna, which evidently must be considered the closest source for Maimonides' exposition. This parallel becomes intelligible in its full bearing only if one considers it in the light of Avicenna's almost programmatic explanation of the place of prophetology in the whole of the sciences. From his treatise "On the Parts of the Sciences" it emerges that the science treating thematically of prophecy is, in his view, *politics*.[170] This already means that the end of prophecy is political, that the supreme practical role of the prophet is not mantics but political government.[171]

In the previously-mentioned treatise, Avicenna first enumerates the subjects of politics: the kinds of regimes and political associations; the kind and manner of their maintenance and the cause of their decline; the way in which the various forms of state change into one another. Then he proceeds: "Of this, what has to do with kingship is contained in the book[172] of Plato and of Aristotle on the state, and what has to do with *prophecy* and the *religious law* is contained in both of their books on the *laws*[173] ... this part of practical philosophy (namely, politics)[174] has as its subject matter the existence of prophecy and the dependence of the human race, for its existence, stability, and propagation, on the religious law. Politics deals both with all the religious laws collectively and with the specific characters of the individual religious laws by nation and epoch; it deals with the difference between divine prophecy and all invalid pretensions."[175] In accordance with his classification of the

---

170. [Emphasis on "politics" ("Politik") added to *PG*.]

171. [55] That the end of prophecy is legislation and not knowledge of the future is asserted with particular emphasis—in a polemic against Gersonides—by Joseph Albo, *Iqqarim* III, 12. [See Albo, *Ikkarim (Roots)*, trans. Husik, vol. III, chap. 12, pp. 107–11: "The principal purpose of the prophetic institution existing in the human race is not to foretell the future or to regulate particular matters that interest individuals, such as are communicated by diviners and star-gazers, but to enable a whole nation or the entire human race to attain human perfection.... The necessity of prophecy is that men may be guided toward eternal happiness, that they may know through it what is agreeable to God and what is not, and that they may attain to the destiny intended for mankind by doing those things which are agreeable to God.... Since the purpose of prophecy is that the human race may be guided by God, (this) means revelation of the Torah."] The extensive agreement of this chapter with *Guide* 2.39 is further evidence for the interpretation of Maimonides' prophetology developed above.

172. [The singular is Avicenna's, not Strauss's.]

173. [Emphasis on "laws" ("Gesetze") added to *PG*.]

174. [56] Practical philosophy, as Avicenna has explained just before this, consists of three parts: ethics, economics, and politics.

175. [57] The Arabic text was published in *Tis' rasa'il* (Constantinople 1928), pp. 73f. For the establishment of the text I have used, besides that edition, a Gotha manuscript (A 1158, fol. 159). A Latin translation, apparently based on a somewhat fuller text, is located in the collection of Andreas Alpagus (Venice 1546), 140b–141a; there is a Hebrew translation which considerably abridges the text in Falaquera's *Reshit*

sciences, Avicenna treats prophecy in the concluding portion of his *Metaphysics*, which is devoted to practical philosophy. To be sure, he speaks of prophecy also in his psychology, but in this context he discusses only the characteristic capacities of the prophets, and hence only the means, not the end and significance, of prophecy. That prophecy as such is not a theme of psychology is shown especially by the fact that, in his psychology, he treats the prophetic capacities not systematically but in quite disparate passages—wherever, that is, he is discussing[176] a faculty of the soul whose highest perfection is characteristic of the prophet.

The dependence of the human race on prophecy is portrayed by Avicenna in essentially the same way as by Maimonides. Man differs from the animals in that his life cannot be perfect if he lives for himself alone; man can live properly as man only if he lives in community; the existence and the welfare of the human race depends on men's living in community; community presupposes reciprocal intercourse; this intercourse is not possible without regimen and justice; regimen is not possible without a lawgiver; the lawgiver must be able to address men and to bind them to the regimen given by him; he must therefore be a man. He must not let men abide in their opinions about justice and injustice; for each considers just what is advantageous to himself and unjust what is disadvantageous to himself; consequently the human race is dependent for its existence on such a man; but such a man is a *prophet*. It is therefore impossible that divine providence should not exercise care for this necessity. It is therefore necessary that there actually is (or was) a prophet. He must have characteristics that are lacking in other men, so that these may surmise his superiority and he may be distinguished from them.[177]

If one approaches this account of prophecy from the parallel statements of the *Guide*,[178] one misses at first glance the sharp distinction between the

---

Ḥokhmah, ed. Moritz David (Berlin 1902), pp. 58f. [For the statement on the division of the sciences and on the purport of Plato's two main works (*Tis' rasa'il*, 73f.), see Avicenna, "On the Division of the Rational Sciences," trans. Mahdi, pp. 96–97.]

176. [*MO*: "treating" ("behandelt"); *PG*: "discussing" ("erörtert").]

177. [58] *Avicennae Opera* (Venice 1508), Metaphysics X, 2, and *Avicennae Metaphysices Compendium*, ed. Caramel, pp. 253–55. The Arabic text of the *Greater Metaphysics* was available to me in the Berlin manuscript of Minutoli 229 (fol. 168b–169a), and the Arabic text of the *Compendium* in the Rome edition, 1593. Cf. also Avicenna's *Isharat wa-tanbihat* in *Le livre des théorèmes et des avertissements*, ed. J. Forget (Leiden 1892), p. 200. [For a French translation, see: *Livre des Directives et remarques* (*Kitab al-Isharat wa-'l-Tanbihat*), trans. A.-M. Goichon (Paris: Vrin, 1951), pp. 487–88. For Avicenna's *Metaphysics* X, 2 of *The Healing* (*Al-Shifa*), see Avicenna, *The Metaphysics*, trans. Marmura, pp. 364–66.]

178. [*MO*: "from the account which historically conditioned it, as presented in the *Guide*" ("von der durch sie geschichtlich bedingten Begründung, die im *More nebukim* vorliegt"); *PG*: "from the parallel statements of the *Guide*" ("von den durch entsprechenden Darlegungen des *More newuchim*").]

divine law, whose end is the specific perfection of man and whose proclaimer is a prophet, *and*[179] the merely human law, whose end is only the perfection of the body and whose proclaimer is a statesman. Nonetheless, this distinction already proclaims itself in the passage cited (see above [fourth and fifth paragraphs of section IV]) from the treatise "On the Parts of Science"; Avicenna distinguishes there between the part of politics dealing with *kingship*[180] and the part dealing with *prophecy and religious law*.[181] In a related context he says: the use of *politics*[182] consists in coming to know how the communal relation among human individuals must be fashioned in order that they may mutually help one another towards the well-being of the *bodies*[183] and the maintenance of the human race.[184] This statement compels us to ask: how, then, does prophecy differ from all that is merely political? We allow this question to be answered by Avicenna himself. In a treatise devoted specifically to the account of prophecy he says: the (prophetic) mission is the inspiration whose end is "the welfare of *both*[185] worlds, that of (eternal) existence and that of passing-away, through science *and*[186] political government. The commissioned one (the prophet) is he who proclaims what he has learned ... through inspiration, in order that, through his views, *the welfare of the sensible world* may be achieved *through political government and (the welfare) of the intelligible world through science.*"[187] Thus prophecy differs from merely political government in having as its end not only, like the latter, the well-being of the body, the welfare of the sensible world, but also the perfection of the intellect, the specific perfection of man. Thus Maimonides' teaching on the end of prophecy is completely in agreement with the teaching of Avicenna.

Comparison of Maimonides' teaching with the teaching of Avicenna confirms the view that according to Maimonides' teaching the prophet as philosopher/statesman/seer/(miracle-worker) in one is the founder of the perfect

---

179. [Emphasis on "and" ("und") added to *PG*.]
180. [Emphasis on "kingship" ("Königtum") added to *PG*.]
181. [Emphasis on "prophecy and religious law" ("Prophetie und religiösem Gesetz") added to *PG*.]
182. [Emphasis on "politics" ("Politik") added to *PG*.]
183. [Emphasis on "bodies" ("Körper") added to *PG*.]
184. [59] *Tis' rasa'il*, p. 2f.
185. [Emphasis on "both" ("beiden") added to *PG*.]
186. [Emphasis on "and" ("und") added to *PG*.]
187. [60] Ibid., p. 85. [See Avicenna, "On the Proof of Prophecies," trans. Marmura, p. 115f. Emphasis on "the welfare of the sensible world ... through political government and (the welfare) of the intelligible world through science" ("das Heil der sinnlichen Welt mittels der politischen Leitung und [das Heil] der intelligiblen Welt mittels der Wissenschaft") added to *PG*.]

community. Avicenna calls the perfect community "the excellent city" or "the city of beautiful conduct";[188] we may say rather "the ideal state." *The prophet is the founder of the ideal state.* The classic model of the ideal state is the *Platonic* state. Avicenna refers to Plato's works on the state, the *Republic* and the *Laws*, as the classic presentations of politics, just as he refers to Aristotle's *Ethics* as the classic presentation of ethics; in particular, the *Laws* is for him the authoritative presentation[189] of the philosophic teaching on prophecy.[190] To be sure, he mentions in this connection also Aristotle's *Politics*; but it can have been known to him only by title, since it was never translated into Arabic.[191] The following passage from Avicenna's *Greater Metaphysics* shows how very decisive is the orientation precisely towards the Platonic state: "The first purpose of the legislator in legislating must be the articulation of the city into three parts: the rulers, the craftsmen, and the guardians."[192] Thus the prophet must divide the state according to the division prescribed by Plato in the *Republic*. The prophet is the founder of the Platonic state; the prophet carries out what Plato called for.[193]

188. [61] *Metaphysics* X, 5 (Berlin manuscript, Minutoli 229, fol. 174b–175a). [See Avicenna, *The Metaphysics*, trans. Marmura, pp. 374–78.]

189. *MO*: "standard-work" (Strauss's original is in English); *PG*: "authoritative presentation" ("massgebende Darstellung").

190. [62] *Tis' rasa'il*, p. 73f. [See Avicenna, "On the Proof of Prophecies," trans. Mahdi, p. 97]; see above [fourth and fifth paragraphs of section IV].

191. [63] [Moritz] Steinschneider, *[Die] Hebräische Übersetzungen des Mittelalters und die Juden als Dolmetscher* (Berlin: Kommissionsverlag des Bibliographischen Bureaus, 1893; reprinted, Graz: Akademische Druck-u. Verlagsanstalt, 1956), p. 219. [Cf. also "How to Study Medieval Philosophy," chap. 1 above, text at n. 50; "Some Remarks on the Political Science of Maimonides and Farabi," chap. 5 below, n. 5.]

192. [64] *Metaphysics* X, 4 in the beginning. (Minutoli 229 fol. 171b). [See Avicenna, *The Metaphysics*, trans. Marmura, p. 370: "The legislator's first objective in laying down the laws and organizing the city must be (to divide) it into three (groups): administrators, artisans, and guardians."]

193. [65] The statements about the laws to be proclaimed by the prophet (Avicenna, *Metaphysics* X, 2–5) [Avicenna, *The Metaphysics*, trans. Marmura, pp. 364–78] are of course governed in their particulars by Islamic law. Further investigation is needed of whether and to what extent Avicenna was influenced here by Plato even in details. For the time being, let me refer only to the following parallels. Avicenna: ". . . the first thing that must be determined by law in the city is the matter of marriage, as that which leads to propagation; the legislator must summon to it and arouse the desire for it; for through it the species endure . . ." (*Metaphysics* X, 4) [Avicenna, *The Metaphysics*, trans. Marmura, p. 372]. Plato: "What law must the legislator establish first? Will he not, in accordance with nature, first regulate by his orders the beginning of generation for the cities? . . . Is not the beginning of generation for all cities the marital union and partnership? . . . If the marriage laws are given first, this would be, as it seems, the proper thing with regard to the right ordering of the city" (*Laws* 720e–721a). Avicenna also refers to Plato as an authority for the statement that speech in enigmas and images is a condition of prophecy: "It is imposed on the prophet as a condition that his speech be intimation and his words hints; and as Plato says in the book of the *Laws*, he who does not understand the meaning of the prophet's intimations does not attain the kingdom of God. Thus in their writings the most renowned philosophers of the Greeks, and their prophets, employed images and figures in which they concealed their secrets, e.g., Pythagoras, Socrates, and Plato" (*Tis' rasa'il* 85). [For *Tis' rasa'il* 85, see Avicenna, "On the Proof of Prophecies," trans. Marmura, p. 116.]

The author of this view of prophecy appears to be *Alfarabi*.[194] His engagement with Platonic politics is attested most manifestly by the fact that he composed an "epitome" or "summa" of Plato's *Laws*.[195] We have already mentioned that Alfarabi distinguishes two species of prophecy (see above [fourth and fifth paragraphs of section III]). Now it is very important to observe in what context he treats each of the species. He speaks of the lower[196] prophecy in the context of psychology; the higher prophecy he discusses— essentially as in Avicenna and Maimonides—only after he has treated "man's need for association and for mutual aid." He thus gives us to understand that the higher prophecy, prophecy proper, differs from vulgar mantics of all ranks in its *political*[197] mission; the only context in which prophecy proper can be understood radically is that of politics. Here "politics" and "political" are to be understood in the Platonic sense: for Alfarabi it is not a matter of a state in general, but of the state directed to the specific perfection of man, the "excellent state," the ideal state. The sovereign of the ideal state, according to Alfarabi, must be a man of perfect intellect and a perfect imaginative faculty; he must be a man to whom God imparts revelation through the medium of the active intellect.[198] In other words, the sovereign of the ideal state must be a prophet—a philosopher and seer in one.[199] He must have at his disposal

---

194. [Emphasis on "Alfarabi" ("al-Farabi") added to *PG*. Also, a note added to *MO* (p. 129, n. 1) has been removed from *PG*: "Paul Kraus subsequently called to my attention that even prior to Alfarabi, Platonic politics had exercised a considerable influence on Islamic thought. Kraus will treat this influence in his studies on the history of early Islamic sects and heretics." ("Nachträglich Paul Kraus darauf hingewiesen, dass die Platonische Politik schon vor al-Farabi einen erheblichen Einfluss auf das Islamische Denken augeübt hat. Kraus wird diesen Einfluss in seinen Studien über die frühislamischen Sekten- und Ketzergeschichte behandeln.") The book to which Strauss refers only appeared in print posthumously thanks to the efforts of Rémi Brague, who gathered together a series of Krauss's studies in book-form: *Alchemie, Ketzerei, Apokryphen in frühen Islam: Gesammelte Aufsätze*, ed. Rémi Brague (Hildesheim: Georg Olms Verlag, 1994). It contains Kraus's eleven studies on Islamic sects and heresies, as well as a brief biography by the editor. For a further comment on the debt Strauss owed to Paul Kraus, see "Some Remarks on the Political Science of Maimonides and Farabi," chap. 5 below, n. 7.]

195. [**66**] Steinschneider, *Alfarabi*, p. 61. Cf. generally Steinschneider's chapter on Alfarabi's ethical and political writings (loc. cit., pp. 60–73). [See n. 44 above for full details on Steinschneider's book. A study by Strauss himself of the same work will subsequently appear in print: "How Farabi Read Plato's *Laws*," in *Mélanges Louis Massignon* (Damascus: L'Institut français de Damas, 1956), vol. 3, pp. 319–44; reprinted in *What Is Political Philosophy?*, pp. 134–54. The first half of the sentence has been changed very slightly. *MO*: "His engagement with Platonic politics is given most manifest proof by the fact that" ("Von seiner Beschäftigung mit der platonischen Politik legt am handgreiflichsten die Tatsache Zeugnis ab"); *PG*: "His engagement with Platonic politics is attested most manifestly by the fact that" ("Seiner Beschäftigung mit der Platonischen Politik wird am handgreiflichsten die Tatsache bezeugt").]

196. *MO*: "niederen" ("lower"); *PG*: "niedrigen" ("lower").]

197. [Emphasis on "political" ("politische") added to *PG*.]

198. [**67**] *Ideal State* 57, 13–59, 13. [See *Perfect State*, trans. Walzer, chap. 15, paras. 7–11, pp. 240–47.]

199. [**68**] Ibid., 58, 23–59, 1. [See *Perfect State*, trans. Walzer, chap. 15, para. 10, pp. 244–45.]

by nature the following properties, *inter alia*:[200] he must love learning and learn easily; he must have a strong memory; he must not be eager for sensual pleasures; he must love the truth and hate deception; he must not be a money-lover; finally, he must be "firmly resolved upon the object whose accomplishment he considers necessary, courageous about it, brave,[201] fearless, and not faint-hearted." That is, the sovereign of the ideal state—and only a *prophet*[202] can be the sovereign of the ideal state—must have by nature the qualities which, according to Plato's requirement, the *philosopher-kings*[203] must have by nature.[204]

The prophetology of Maimonides and the *falasifa* refers to Plato not only in assuming the union of philosophy and politics as a condition of the perfect state, whose founder can only be a prophet; also of Platonic origin is the way in which the prophet's being-a-philosopher is understood. The prophet is a man who, after receiving the *revelation*[205] (*wachj*), is capable of bringing to men the *message*[206] (*risala*) which leads to the welfare of the sensible world by means of political government and to the welfare of the intelligible world by means of science (see above [seventh paragraph of section IV]). The revelation is an emanation from God which bestows upon the prophet, through the medium of the active intellect, direct knowledge of the upper world. Only direct knowledge of the upper world, it appears, makes the prophet capable of the government of men that is proper to him, namely, politics and science united in one. Maimonides illustrates the character of this direct knowledge through the following image. All men live from the outset in a deep dark night; for only a few men is this night ever illuminated at all; for most of these—the philosophers—by a borrowed, earthly light, and for a very few— the prophets—by lightning flashes from on high (see above [twelfth paragraph of section II]). In his commentary on the passage in the *Guide* where this image occurs, Shem Tov [ibn] Falaquera refers to his explanation of a re-

---

200. [69] Ibid., 59, 10–60, 11. [See *Perfect State*, trans. Walzer, chap. 15, para. 12, pp. 246–49.]

201. [70] From this it can be understood why Maimonides emphasizes bravery as a condition of prophecy in the *Guide* (2.38). The talmudic statement that "prophecy rests only upon one who is wise, *strong (courageous)*, and rich" does not come into question as a source for this assertion of Maimonides, as follows also from the fact that Maimonides takes that statement as his basis in an entirely different exposition of his prophetology; cf. *Guide* 2.32 (263 and Munk's n. 2 there).

202. [Emphasis on "prophet" ("Prophet") added to *PG*. In *PG* (ed. Meier), note a printing error: it means to say "kann nur ein *Prophet* sein," and not "kann nur ein *Prophet* ein."]

203. [Emphasis on "philosopher-kings" ("Philosophen-Könige") added to *PG*.]

204. [71] Plato, *Republic* [bk. 6] 485a–487a; cf. also ibid. [bk. 2], 374e–376c and *Laws* [bk. 4] 709e–710c.

205. [Emphasis on "revelation" ("Offenbarung") added to *PG*.]

206. [Emphasis on "message" ("Botschaft") added to *PG*.]

lated passage in the same work (3.51). There he cites a parallel from Alfarabi which says the following:[207] there are three ranks of men; the first is the rank of the *multitude*; the multitude know the intelligible things only in material forms; they are like those who live in a cave and on whom the sun has never shone; they see, as it were, only the shadows of things, never the light itself; the second rank is the rank of the *philosophers*; these know the intelligible things, but only indirectly, as one sees the sun in the water; what one sees in the water is only the image of the sun, not the sun itself; the philosophers are like men who have left the cave and beheld the light; the third rank is the rank of the *blessed*;[208] the men of this rank see the thing in itself, they see as it were the light itself, in their seeing there is absolutely nothing of seeming, they themselves become the thing which they see. The relation, confirmed by Falaquera's allusion, between the *Platonic cave-image*[209] and Maimonides' image of the deep dark night illuminated by lightning flashes, warrants this view: just as, according to Plato, the perfect state can be actualized only by the philosopher who has ascended out of the cave into the light and has beheld the idea of the good, so, according to Maimonides and the *falasifa*, the perfect state can be actualized only by the prophet, for whom the night in which the human race[210] is stumbling about is illuminated by lightning flashes from on high, by direct knowledge of the upper world.

V

The prophet as philosopher/statesman/seer/(miracle-worker) in one is the founder of the ideal state. The ideal state is understood according to Plato's guidance: the prophet is the founder of the Platonic state. Plato's requirement that philosophy and political power must coincide if the true state is to become actual, Plato's concept of the philosopher-king, furnishes the outline whose filling-in in the light of the actual revelation yields the concept of

---

207. [72] *Moreh ha-Moreh* (Pressburg 1837), p. 132; the reference on p. 9 of this edition is marred by a misprint ("31" instead of "51"). [See *Shelosha Kadmonei Mefarshei ha-Moreh*, op. cit., for the passage in Falaquera's *Moreh ha-Moreh* to which he refers; see also *PL*, trans. Adler, p. 140, n. 16, for further discussion on Falaquera's view of Maimonides' Farabian, and ultimately Platonic, source. Cf. also Shem Tov ibn Falaquera, *Moreh ha-Moreh*, ed. Yair Shiffman (Jerusalem: World Union for Jewish Studies, 2001), pp. 121–22.]

208. [Emphasis on "blessed" ("Glückseligen") has been missed by Eve Adler's English translation, *PL* (1995), p. 127, l. 11.]

209. [Emphasis on "Platonic cave-image" ("Platonischen Höhlengleichnis") added to *PG*.]

210. [*MO*: "humanity" ("Menschheit"); *PG*: "human race" ("Menschengeschlecht"). See also n. 162 above.]

prophecy held by the *falasifa* and Maimonides. An understanding of this prophetology depends therefore on illuminating the relation between the concept of the prophet and the Platonic concept of the philosopher-king; it depends ultimately on illuminating the relation of the *falasifa*'s position to the position of Plato.

The relation of the *falasifa* and Maimonides to Plato is characterized in the first place by the fact that the former proceed from[211] an un-Platonic premise. For them the *fact*[212] of the revelation is certain; for them therefore it is also certain that a simply binding law, a divine law, a law proclaimed by a prophet with the force of law, is actual. This law authorizes them to philosophize. In philosophizing, they inquire into the possibility of the actual law; they answer this inquiry within the horizon of Platonic politics; they understand the revelation in the light of Platonic politics. They derive Platonic politics from an un-Platonic premise—the premise of the revelation.

The attempt to understand the actual revelation within the horizon of Platonic politics compels modifications of the Platonic framework in the light of the actual revelation. It suffices to recall the significance[213] of the prophet's knowledge of the future (and miracle-working) for Maimonides and the *falasifa*. In this way the Platonic framework is only modified, stretched as it were, but not exploded; it remains the spiritual bond that unites philosophy and politics. The modification in question implies, as such, a *critique*[214] of Plato. This critique gets its whole weight from being able to appeal to the fact of the revelation. From the *factual*[215] answering of the Platonic inquiry into the true state there follows a modification of the Platonic sketch, i.e., a critique of the Platonic answer. If the founder of the perfect community can only be a prophet, this implies that the founding of the perfect community is not possible for the man who is only a philosopher. It is not the case that, as Plato holds, the coincidence of philosophy and political power suffices for the realization of the true state; the ruler-philosopher must be *more*[216] than a philosopher. In sketching the true state, Plato predicted the revelation; but just as, in general, it is only the fulfillment that teaches a full understanding of the prediction, so the Platonic sketch must be modified on the basis of the actual revelation, the actual ideal state.

211. [*MO*: "have" ("haben"); *PG*: "proceed from" ("ausgehen von").]
212. [Emphasis on "fact" ("Faktum") added to *PG*.]
213. [*MO*: "role played" ("Rolle ... spielt"); *PG*: "significance {had}" ("Bedeutung ... hat").]
214. [Emphasis on "critique" ("Kritik") added to *PG*.]
215. [Emphasis on "factual" ("faktischen") added to *PG*.]
216. [Emphasis on "more" ("mehr") added to *PG*.]

The way to the modification of the Platonic outline proposed by the *falasifa* and Maimonides had already been opened in the Hellenistic age.[217] In this age we encounter the teaching that in primeval times ruler, philosopher, and seer coincided in one.[218] This teaching differs from the Platonic concept of the philosopher-ruler in two factors apparently—but only apparently[219]— having nothing in common with one another: (1) its high estimation of mantics; and (2) the conviction that the perfect condition of humanity actually existed in antiquity;[220] in this teaching too the ideal rulership is a fact, not merely a desideratum.[221] Another factor distinguishing the *falasifa*'s prophetology from Plato's doctrine of the philosopher-ruler, the doctrine of the prophet's miracle-working, is anticipated by neo-Pythagorean views.[222] The doctrine of the prophet's direct knowledge, by which he differs from the philosopher, is anticipated especially by Philo.[223]

---

217. [*MO*: "had already been opened in the age in which all the fundamental principles of medieval philosophy had in general been established: the Hellenistic age" ("in dem Zeitalter angebahnt worden, in dem überhaupt alle Grundlagen der mittelalterichen Philosophie festgestellt worden sind: im Zeitalter des Hellenismus"); *PG*: "had already been opened in the Hellenistic age" ("war bereits in dem Zeitalter angebahnt worden").]

218. [73] Cf., e.g., Cicero, *De divinatione* [*On Divination*] I, 41, 89. Karl Reinhardt has given a detailed interpretation of this doctrine and seeks to trace it back to Poseidonius as its originator: *Poseidonius* (Munich: Beck, 1921), esp. pp. 429ff. [With regard to paragraph 41, Wardle comments on the lost Latin epic poem, *Annals*, by Ennius the Vestal, which Cicero makes much use of in his approach to divination: "Ennius [as presented by Cicero] achieves a Hellenistic remodeling of the Homeric tale of Tyro's rape by Poseidon (*Odyssey* 11.235–59), transforming a concealing sleep into a revelatory dream." As for paragraph 89, he translates it as follows:

> Furthermore, did not Priam, the king of Asia, have a son Helenus and a daughter Cassandra who were diviners, the one by auguries and the other by mental agitation and divine stimulation? We see it written that certain brothers Marcii, born of a noble family, were prophets of this kind in the time of our ancestors. And does not Homer record that Polyidus of Corinth prophesied many things to others and death for his son as the latter set off for Troy. Certainly among the ancients, those who held power were also masters of augury, for they considered wisdom and divination to be equal marks of kingship. Witness to this is our state, in which kings were augurs and, later, private citizens who had been granted that priesthood governed the state by the authority of their religious beliefs.

See Cicero, *On Divination*, bk. 1, trans. David Wardle (Oxford: Clarendon Press, 2006), pp. 74, 213. For the character in the dialogue who is the speaker of these lines, see the editor's note to "Maimonides' Statement on Political Science," chap. 9 below.]

219. [*MO*: "but actually only apparently" ("aber wirklich nur scheinbar"); *PG*: "but only apparently" ("nur scheinbar").]

220. [*MO*: "previously" ("bereits"); *PG*: "in antiquity" ("in der Vorzeit").]

221. [*MO*: "requirement" ("Forderung"); *PG*: "desideratum" ("Desiderat").]

222. [74] Cf. Tor Andrae, *Die Person Muhammeds [in Lehre und Glauben seiner Gemeinde]* (Stockholm: Vorstedt, 1918), p. 360. [See also (although not the same work, even with the similar title): Tor Andrae, *Mohammed: The Man and His Faith*, trans. Theophil Menzel (New York: Charles Scribner's Sons, 1936).]

223. [75] Cf. the statements on Philo's doctrine of enthusiasm in Hans Lewy, *Sobria ebrietas: Untersuchungen zur Geschichte der antiken Mystik* (Giessen: Alfred Töpelmann, 1929), pp. 56ff. The *pneuma*

But what must it mean that the prophetology anticipated in the Hellenistic age is conditioned ultimately and decisively by Platonic politics? Is this fact a mere curiosity? Is it solely based on or due to the circumstance that Plato just happened to be considered "the divine Plato," and that besides this the politics of the other great man, Aristotle, remained unknown as a result of a remarkable accident? The dependence[224] of the prophetology of Maimonides and the *falasifa* on Platonic politics would be more than a curiosity and an accident if these men were, after all—Platonists, if their un-Platonic premise—the fact of the revelation—were at bottom not so un-Platonic as it seems at first glance. Hermann *Cohen*[225] claimed that Maimonides, at least, was a Platonist.[226] We adopt this claim as our own, but on the basis of a consideration which completely diverges in detail from Cohen's[227] grounds, and which compels us to include the *falasifa* in this claim as well.

The claim that the *falasifa* and Maimonides are, after all, to be classed as Platonists has, at first, everything against it; or, insofar as anything does speak for it at first, even what speaks for it robs it of all certainty and all significance. For the *doctrine*[228] of the *falasifa*—and of course one must first of all keep to the doctrine—is much more Aristotelian on the one hand, and neo-Platonic on the other, than properly Platonic; hence they appear to be Platonists in no other sense than that every Aristotelian and every neo-Platonist is a pupil of Plato. But this is not the sense in which Cohen[229] meant[230] his claim; indeed it was one of the most important concerns of his philosophical-historical endeavors to conceive the relation of Aristotle to Plato as an irreconcil-

---

has the same function for Philo as the active intellect has for the *falasifa* and Maimonides. ["Philo can then declare axiomatically that the prophet must be a sage just as likewise the perfect sage must be a prophet, for the knowledge possessed by both of them is identically provided by the *pnuema* of divine wisdom." Translated by the present editor, p. 58.]

224. [*MO*: "conditionedness by" ("Bedingtheit durch"); *PG*: "dependence on" ("Abhängigkeit von").]

225. [Emphasis on "Hermann" removed from *PG*.]

226. [76] To bring forward the evidence for this claim is the most important task of his essay "Charakteristik der Ethik Maimunis" (first appeared in the collection *Moses ben Maimon* (Leipzig, 1908), I, pp. 63-134; reprinted in the *Jüdische Schriften*[, ed. Bruno Strauss, intro. Franz Rosenzweig, 3 vols. (Berlin: C. A. Schwetschke und Sohn, 1924), 3:221-89]. Our citations below are by the page numbers of the first edition. [See *Moses ben Maimon: Sein Leben, seine Werke, und sein Einfluss*, ed. W. Bacher, M. Brann, D. Simonsen, and J. Guttmann, 2 vols. (Leipzig: G. Fock, 1908-14; reprint, Hildesheim: Olms, 1971), I, 63-134. Cf. also "Cohen and Maimonides," chap. 3 above.]

227. [Emphasis on "Cohen's" removed from *PG*.]

228. [Emphasis on "doctrine" ("Lehre") added to *PG*.]

229. [Emphasis on "Cohen" removed from *PG*.]

230. [*MO*: "however, did not mean" ("aber nicht gemeint"); *PG*: "not . . . meant" ("nicht gemeint").]

able *opposition*.²³¹ Guided by this view of the relation between Aristotle and Plato, he arrived at a claim that is meaningful only on this premise, while this same premise—not to mention the express Aristotelianism of Maimonides—admittedly makes it paradoxical: the claim that "Maimonides was in deeper harmony with Plato than with Aristotle" (105).²³²

231. [Emphasis on "opposition" ("Gegensatz") added to *PG*.]
232. [Strauss finishes the equivalent paragraph of *MO* with a sentence he decided to cut from *PG*. Then there follow two full paragraphs in *MO* (pp. 134-36), which were also cut from *PG*. Also, a third paragraph in *MO* closely resembles the *PG* paragraph which begins "Cohen versteht den Gegensatz" (p. 119); but what would have been the parallel in *PG* has had its first and last sentences cut as compared with how it appeared in *MO*. Since the essay in its *Le Monde Oriental* version is not readily available, and since the deleted material—one sentence at the end of the middle paragraph (p. 134), two full paragraphs which follow, and a sentence at the beginning of the next paragraph and another again at the end of the same paragraph—has not yet been conveyed in Meier's edition of Strauss's *Gesammelte Schriften*, I believe that the best course of action is to translate the entire deleted section, as well as to transcribe the original alongside it, for those who may wish at present to consider this material as it was.]

"In order to understand this claim, we shall present Cohen's view of the opposition between Platonic and Aristotelian philosophizing; in order to do that, we shall leave out of account that part of Cohen's formulation which is not in keeping with the facts at issue.

"Platonic philosophy is the implementation of 'the Socratic program' (63). Socratic is the conviction 'that there is nothing higher and of more urgent concern to the human spirit than a morality' (63f.). 'Socrates . . . speaks as a Nazarene of nature: the trees cannot teach me, but only men in the city. . . . Ethics as the doctrine of man becomes the center of philosophy.' (*Ethics of the Pure Will*, p. 1) Socratic is the conviction that there is only *one* question which matters, the question of the right life. Socratic is the conviction that morality is without habit and without dogma, but 'a problem which has to be ever and again renewed, occurring in ever new questions, bringing out in every new solution only new questions' (70). In this way Cohen adopts the Socratic conviction that the right life comes to be in the inquiry into the right life, that the inquiry into the right life must remain, in a certain way, a question (cf. *Apology* 38a). Cohen interprets Plato's *Crito* in the following manner, and in this interpretation he makes it his own: 'There is no self-consciousness which can be acquired without consideration of the state, and without guidance from political thought.' (*Ethics of the Pure Will*, p. 250) The Socratic inquiry into the right life asks about the right common life, about the right order of the common life, about the true state; the Socratic inquiry is political. Since Plato always philosophized in the sense of the 'Socratic program,' so one can say: Platonic philosophizing means, inquiry into the good, into the idea of the good.

"The Socratic inquiry is not the most urgent inquiry under two conditions: {1} if the right life is not questionable, if we know what the good is; {2} if man and his life, and his right life, is in general not important. According to Cohen, the fulfillment of these two conditions is characteristic of Aristotelian philosophizing: {1} 'the moral is for him (i.e., Aristotle) not a problem' (70); his ethics is 'empiricist' (108); {2} 'his metaphysics is focused on the universe,' not on human morality (72); or, as Aristotle himself says: it is absurd to be of the opinion that politics or moral insight is the most important thing, since surely man is not the most excellent being in the cosmos. (*Nicomachean Ethics* 1141a20ff.) Therefore, the Aristotelian ideal of life is the life of pure contemplation and understanding, the life of theory. And if Platonic philosophizing means inquiry into the good of human life, into the true state, then Aristotelian philosophizing means pure contemplation of beings and pure understanding of Being. And if Platonic philosophizing is essentially political, so for Aristotle politics necessarily moves to second place.

"If one proceeds from this conception of the relation between Plato and Aristotle, so it appears one must, without any doubt, call Maimonides and the *falasifa* Aristotelians. . . . Under these circumstances, the assertion—Maimonides was in deeper harmony with Plato than with Aristotle—is a paradox."

["Um diese Behauptung zu verstehen, vergenenwärtigen wir uns Cohen Ansicht über den Gegensatz des platonischen und des aristotelischen Philosophierens; dabei sehen wir ab von dem Teil der Formulierungen Cohens, der dem geschichtlichen Tatbestand nicht angemessen ist."

Cohen understands the opposition between Platonic (Socratic) and Aristotelian philosophizing as the opposition between the primacy of inquiry about the good, about the right life, about the true state, and the primacy of interest in the contemplation of that which is and in knowledge of being.[233] But precisely if one views the relation of Plato and Aristotle in this way, one seems bound to identify the *falasifa* and Maimonides unconditionally as Aristotelians. In Cohen's words, "That which Maimonides did not simply learn from Aristotle, but in which Aristotle was and remained for him, with all the depths of their difference, a model and guide, is the enthusiasm for pure theory, for scientific knowledge for its own sake and as the final, absolute end of human existence."[234]

Cohen most forcibly establishes his paradoxical doubt of Maimonides'

["Die platonische Philosophie ist die Ausführung 'des Sokratischen Programme' (63). Sokratisch ist die Überzeugung, 'dass es nichts Höheres und nichts Angelegentlicheres für den menschlichen Geist geben dürfe, als seine Sittlichkeit' (63f.). 'Sokrates . . . redet wie ein Nazarener von der nature: die Bäume können mich nicht belehren, wohl aber die Menschen in der Stadt . . . Die Ethik, als Lehre vom Menschen, wird das Centrum der Philosophie.' (*Ethik des reinen Willens* S. 1) Sokratisch ist die Überzeugung, dass es nur *eine* Frage gebe, auf die es ankommt, die Frage nach dem rechten Leben.—Sokratisch ist die Überzeugung, dass die Sittlichkeit keine Sitte und kein Dogma ist, sondern 'ein Problem, das immer wieder sich zu verjüngen hat, in immer neuen Fragen auftritt, in jeder neuen Lösung nur neue Fragen heraufbrigt' (70). In dieser Weise eignet sich Cohen die sokratische Überzeugung an, dass sich das rechte Leben im Fragen nach dem rechten Leben vollzieht, dass die Frage nach dem rechten Leben in gewisser Weise Frage bleiben muss (vgl. Apol. 38 A).—Cohen interpretiert Platons "Kriton" folgendermassen, und er macht ihn sich in dieser Interpretation zu eigen: 'Es gibt kein Selbstbewusstein, welches ohne Rücksicht auf den Staat und ohne Leitung durch den Staatsgedanken zu winnen wäre.' (l.c. S. 20) Die sokratische Frage nach dem rechten Leben fragt nach dem rechten Zusammenleben, nach der rechten Ordnung des Zusammenlebens, nach der wahrhaften Staat; die sokratische Frage is politisch. Da Platon immer im Sinn des 'Sokratischen Programms' philosophiert hat, so kann man sagen: platonisch philosophieren heisst fragen nach dem Guten, nach der Idee des Guten.

["Die sokratische Frage wäre unter zwei Bedingungen nicht die dringlichste Frage: {1} wenn das rechte Leben nicht fraglich wäre, wenn wir wüssten, was das Gute ist; und {2} wenn der Mensch und sein Leben und sein rechtes Leben überhaupt nicht so wichtig wäre. Der Erfülltheit dieser Bedingungen kennzeichnet nach Cohen das aristotelische Philosophieren: {1} 'Das Sittliche ist für ihn (Aristoteles) nicht ein Problem' (70); seine Ethik is 'empiristisch' (108); {2} 'Seine Metaphysik ist auf das Universum eingestellt,' nicht auf die menschliche Sittlichkeit (72); oder, wie Aristoteles selbst sagt: es wäre widersinnig, wenn einer meinte, die Politik oder die sittliche Einsicht wäre am wichtigsten, da doch der Mensch nicht das vorzüglichste Wesen im Kosmos ist. (*Ethica Nicomachea* 1141a20ff.) Daher ist das aristotelische Lebensideal das Leben im reinen Betrachten und Verstehen, die Theorie. Und wenn platonisch philosophieren heisst: fragen nach den Guten des menschlichen Lebens, nach dem wahrhaften Staat, so heisst aristotelisch philosophieren: reines Betrachten des Seienden und Verstehen des Seins. Und wenn das platonische Philosophieren wesentlich politisch ist, so rückt für Aristoteles die Politik notwendig an die zweite Stelle.

["Geht man von dieser Auffassung des Verhältnisses von Platon und Aristoteles aus, so scheint man das *falasifa* und Maimuni ohne jades Bedenken als Aristoteliker bezeichnen zu mussen. . . . Unter diesem Umständen ist die Behauptung: Maimuni war in tieferem Einklang mit Platon als mit Aristoteles, paradox."]

233. [77] Cf. esp. pp. 63f., 70, 72 and 108.
234. [78] Cohen italicized the sentence.

Aristotelianism with the lapidary sentence, "All honor to the God of Aristotle; but truly he is not the God of Israel" (81).[235] We cannot discuss here how Cohen seeks to show positively that Maimonides was a Platonist; still less can we discuss the fact that and the reason why Cohen's statements about this are untenable in detail, and depend on a misconstruction of the historical evidence. We limit ourselves to emphasizing that Cohen's way of demonstrating his view in detail, and thus the untenability of this demonstration, leaves unaffected the insight that precedes this demonstration and guides it: the God of Aristotle is not the God of Israel; for this reason a Jew as Jew cannot be an Aristotelian; for him it can never at any time be left at a matter of the primacy of theory; he cannot assert this primacy unconditionally and unreservedly; if he asserts it, he must restrict it in some way, so that ultimately he calls it into question through this restriction.

Maimonides undoubtedly asserts the primacy of theory. But—and this[236] is decisive—for him the philosopher does not occupy the highest rank in the human race: higher than the philosopher stands the prophet. If, therefore, there is anything that can call Maimonides' Aristotelianism into doubt, it is surely his prophetology. The precedence of the prophet over the philosopher lies partly, to be sure, in the superiority of prophetic, direct knowledge over philosophic, indirect knowledge, but also, at the same time, in the capacity for governing that distinguishes him from the philosopher: the prophet, in contradistinction to the philosopher who merely knows, is teacher and governor in one. In light of the fact that Maimonides and the *falasifa* assert the precedence of prophecy over philosophy, and in such a way that they see the end of prophecy in the founding of the ideal state, they can be called Platonists in Cohen's sense.[237] It has been shown above that, and in what sense, the prophetology of these philosophers[238] must be characterized[239] as Platonic in respect of its historical origin as well.

But under these circumstances, how is it to be understood that, apart from their prophetology, the *falasifa* and Maimonides follow Aristotle more than

---

235. [79] Similar expressions are to be found also on pp. 83f. and 91.
236. [*MO*: "and this 'but' is decisive" ("und dieses Aber ist entscheidend"); *PG*: "and this is decisive" ("und dies ist entscheidend"), i.e., the "but" ("Aber") has been removed.]
237. [*MO*: "can Maimonides and the *falasifa* be called Platonists" ("dürfen wir Maimuni und die *falasifa* als Platoniker bezeichnen"); *PG*: "they can be called Platonists in Cohen's sense" ("dürfen sie als Platoniker im Sinne Cohens angesprochen wirden").]
238. [*MO*: "their prophetology" ("ihrer Prophetologie"); *PG*: "the prophetology of these philosophers" ("die Prophetologie dieser Philosophen").]
239. [*MO*: "can be regarded" ("angesprochen werden kann"); *PG*: "must be characterized" ("charakterisiert werden muss").]

Plato?[240] The Platonic inquiry[241] into the ideal state, into the good, compels one to make a detour (cf. *Rep.* 435d and 504b)[242] along which one must ask, *inter alia*, what the soul is, what its parts are, what science is, what that-which-is is. Hence in Plato's intentions, too, one must inquire into everything into which Aristotle, though no longer with a view to the one question about the good, inquires. And not only this.[243] Plato teaches no less decisively than Aristotle that happiness and the specific perfection of man consists in pure contemplation and understanding. The essential difference between Plato and Aristotle is revealed only[244] in the way in which they *conduct* themselves towards theory as the highest perfection[245] of man. Aristotle sets it completely free; or rather, he leaves it in its natural freedom. Plato, on the other hand, *does not permit*[246] the philosophers "what is now permitted them," namely, the life of philosophizing as an abiding in the contemplation of the truth. He "*compels*"[247] them to care for the others and to guard them, in order that the state may really be a state, a true state (*Rep.* 519–520c). The philosopher, who has *raised*[248] himself above the sensible world in the contemplation of the beautiful, the just, and the good as such, and who lives in

240. [*MO*: "the primacy of theory? To put the question otherwise: How is it possible that, in spite of their Platonism, they aristotelize?" ("den Primat der Theorie behaupten? Anders gefragt: wieso haben sie trotz ihres Platonismus die Möglichkeit zu aristotelisieren"); *PG*: "apart from their prophetology, . . . follow Aristotle more than Plato?" ("abgesehen von ihrer Prophetologie, mehr Aristoteles als Plato folgen?"). Also, *MO* has the following sentence at the beginning of the next paragraph, which was removed from *PG*: "We have attempted to clarify for ourselves, in connection with Cohen, the opposition between Plato and Aristotle as an opposition on inquiries into the true state and the true way of life in pure contemplation and understanding." ("Wir haben uns in Anschluss an Cohen den Gegensatz Plato-Aristoteles als Gegensatz von Fragen nach wahrhaften Staat und Leben im reinen Betrachten und Verstehen klarzumachen versucht.")]
241. [*MO*: "the inquiry" ("Die Frage"); *PG*: "the Platonic inquiry" ("Die Platonische Frage").]
242. [The two references to Plato's *Republic* were added to *PG*.]
243. [*MO*: "However, that is to say: theory is, for Plato, fully developed; Plato knows as thoroughly as Aristotle that the happiness of man consists in pure contemplation and understanding. The philosopher, he says, lives in the belief that he has been removed, even while he is still alive, to the Isles of the Blessed (*Rep.* 519c)." ("Dass heisst aber: die Theorie ist bei Platon völlig ausgebildet; Platon weiss daher genau so wie Aristoteles, dass die Glückseligkeit des Menschen im reinen Betrachten und Verstehen besteht. Die Philosophen, sagt er, leben in dem Glauben, sie seien schon während ihres Lebens auf die Inseln der Seligen versetzt (*Rep.* 519c)."); *PG*: "And not only this. Plato teaches no less decisively than Aristotle that happiness and the specific perfection of man consists in pure contemplation and understanding." ("Und nicht nur dies: Platon lehrt nicht weniger entschieden als Aristoteles, dass die Gluckseligkeit und die eigentliche Vollkommenheit des Menschen in reinen Betrachten und Verstehen besteht.")]
244. [*PG* added "only" ("allein"), which *MO* lacked.]
245. [*MO*: "possibility" or "potentiality" ("Möglichkeit"); *PG*: "perfection" ("Vollkommenheit").]
246. [Emphasis on "does not permit" ("gestattet . . . nicht") added to *PG*.]
247. [Emphasis on "'compels'" ("'zwingt'") added to *PG*.]
248. [Emphasis on "raised" ("erhoben") added to *PG*.]

that contemplation and *wants*[249] to live in it, is called *back*[250] to the state,[251] *bound*[252] back to the state, by the command of the founder of the state, a command which considers first the ordering of the whole and not the happiness of the part. Even the philosopher as such[253] stands under the state, is answerable for himself before the state; he is not simply sovereign. What Plato *called for*[254]—that philosophy stand under a higher authority [*Instanz*], under the state, under the *law*[255]—is *fulfilled*[256] in the age of belief in revelation.[257] With all their freedom in the pursuit of knowledge, the philosophers of this era are conscious at every moment of their answerability for the law[258] and before the law:[259] they justify their philosophizing before the bar of the law; they derive from the law their *authorization*[260] to philosophize as a legal *duty*[261] to philosophize.[262] The Platonism of these philosophers is given with their *situation*,[263] with their standing in fact under the law. Since they stand in fact under the law, they admittedly no longer need,[264] like Plato, to *seek*[265] the law, the state, to *inquire* into it:[266] the binding and[267] absolutely perfect regimen of

249. [Emphasis on "wants" ("will") added to *PG*.]
250. [Emphasis on "back" ("zurück") added to *PG*.]
251. [*PG* added "is called *back* to the state," which *MO* lacked.]
252. [Emphasis on "bound" ("gebunden") added to *PG*.]
253. [*PG* added "Even . . . as such" ("auch als solcher"), which *MO* lacked.]
254. [Emphasis on "called for" ("gefordert") added to *PG*.]
255. [Emphasis on "law" ("Gesetz") added to *PG*.]
256. [Emphasis on "fulfilled" ("erfüllt") added to *PG*.]
257. [*MO*: "in the age of religious revelations" or "in the age of revealed religions" ("im offenbarungsreligiösen Zeitalter"); *PG*: "in the age of belief in revelation" ("im offenbarungsgläubigen Zeitalter").]
258. [80] "Hence, like Maimonides and Averroes especially, they are no less jurists" than philosophers.
259. *MO*: "are conscious . . . of their responsibility for the continuance of the legal order, their responsibility before the law" ("ihrer Verantwortung für den Bestand der gesetzlichen Ordnung, ihrer Verantwortung vor das Gesetz bewusst"); *PG*: "are conscious . . . of their answerability for the law and before the law" ("ihrer Verantwortlichkeit für das Gesetz und vor das Gesetz bewusst").]
260. [Emphasis on "authorization" ("Ermächtigung") added to *PG*.]
261. [Emphasis on "duty" ("Verpflichtgung") added to *PG*.]
262. [81] Cf. [*Philosophy and Law*, pp. 82–85; *Philosophie und Gesetz: Frühe Schriften*, vol. 2 of *Gesammelte Schriften*, pp. 69–71. In *MO*, two clauses, separated by semicolons (almost amounting to full sentences of their own), follow this phrase. Note that these have both been removed from *PG*: "they conceive of their freedom to rationally interpret the document of revelation as a duty of this interpretation; they justify the esoteric character of philosophy from the obligation of keeping secret, from the prohibition of public communication" ("sie begreifen ihre Freiheit, die Offenbarungsurkunde vernunftgemäss zu interpretieren, als Verpflichtung zu dieser Interpretation; sie rechtfertigen den esoterischen Charakter der Philosophie aus der Pflicht zur Geheimhaltung , aus dem Verbot der offentlichen Mitteilung").]
263. [Emphasis on "situation" ("Situation") added to *PG*.]
264. [The word "admittedly" ("freilich") was added to *PG* in the phrase "they no longer need, like Plato" ("brauchen sie nicht mehr wie Platon"), as *MO* had it.]
265. [Emphasis on "seek" ("suchen") added to *PG*.]
266. [The phrase "to *inquire* into it" ("nach ihm zu *fragen*") has been added to *PG*.]
267. [*PG* added the "and" ("und").]

human life[268] is *given*[269] to them by a prophet. Hence they are, as authorized by the law, free to philosophize in Aristotelian freedom: they can *therefore* aristotelize. Cohen expresses it thus: Maimonides "underestimated the danger residing in the depreciation of ethics in Aristotle. And from his standpoint he could overlook this danger all the more easily, since he saw the value of ethics kept safe in his religion" (87). Since the law is *given*[270] for Maimonides and the *falasifa*,[271] it is not the leading and first theme of their philosophizing.[272] It is for this reason that the metaphysical themes[273] occupy so much more space in their writings than the moral-political.[274] But as philosophers, of course, they must attempt to *understand*[275] the given law; this understanding is made possible for them by Plato, and only by Plato.

Appendix 4A | INTRODUCTION TO *PHILOSOPHY AND LAW* [THE FIRST TWO AND THE LAST THREE PARAGRAPHS]

EDITOR'S NOTE

As an aid to readers who wish to precisely follow the stages in Strauss's developing views on Maimonides and its unfolding logic, the first two and the last three paragraphs of Strauss's monumental introduction to *Philosophy and Law*, pp. 21–22, and 38–39, are reproduced as appendix 4A. The introduction as a whole wrestles with the current state of modern Judaism (not to mention the modern world per se), which Strauss construes as caught in an irresolvable predicament. He begins and ends with an argument for the need

---

268. [*MO*: "common life" or "life together" ("Zusammenlebens"); *PG*: "human life" ("Menschlichen Lebens").]
269. [Emphasis on "given" ("gegeben") added to *PG*.]
270. [Emphasis on "given" ("gegeben") added to *PG*.]
271. [*MO*: "them" ("ihnen"); *PG*: "Maimonides and the *falasifa*" ("Maimuni and the *falasifa*").]
272. [*MO* had the phrase at the end of the sentence "they do not need to inquire into it" ("sie brauchen nicht nach ihm zu fragen"), which is removed in *PG*.]
273. [*MO*: "problems" ("Probleme"); *PG*: "themes" ("Themen").]
274. [*MO*: "the inquiry into the true state" ("die Frage nach dem wahren Staat"); *PG*: "than the moral-political" ("als die moralisch-politischen").]
275. [Emphasis on "understand" ("verstehen") added to *PG*.]

to reconsider Maimonides and his approach to "enlightenment," however seemingly obsolete it was declared to be, because it has been assigned to the "medieval" past. In the less closely interpretive and more synthetically exciting argument of the introduction as it stands on its own (not to mention the sustained flow of the book as an entirety), a compelling and thoroughly original argument is made to show the continued pertinence of the "Maimonidean" approach for anyone whose mind remains open to the unresolved debate between reason and revelation, which persists even in modernity. Thus, for a better comprehension even of the contentions that Strauss advances in favor of this "Maimonidean" approach, it is needful to consider the book as a whole, and readers are urged to consult the parts of the book which are not reproduced in the present book. The single note is Strauss's own. See also Leo Strauss, *Philosophie und Gesetz: Frühe Schriften*, vol. 2 of *Gesammelte Schriften*, pp. 9–10, 26–27. One of the anonymous reviewers of the University of Chicago Press has suggested that this reading needs to be supplemented by another section, which highlights the core issue for Strauss, namely, the opposition between orthodoxy and Enlightenment: see *Philosophy and Law*, pp. 32–34; and *Philosophie und Gesetz: Frühe Schriften*, vol. 2 of *Gesammelte Schriften*, pp. 21–23.

IN THE PHRASE OF HERMANN COHEN, MAIMONIDES IS THE "CLASSIC OF rationalism" in Judaism. This phrase appears to us to be correct in a stricter sense than Cohen may have intended: Maimonides' rationalism is the true natural model, the standard to be carefully protected from any distortion, and thus the stumbling-block on which modern rationalism falls. To awaken a prejudice in favor of this view of Maimonides and, even more, to arouse a suspicion against the powerful opposing prejudice, is the aim of the present work.

Even if one is free of all natural inclination towards the past, even if one believes that the present, as the age in which man has attained the highest rung yet of his self-consciousness, can really learn nothing from the past, one still encounters Maimonides' teaching as soon as one seriously attempts to make up one's mind about the present so assessed. For such an attempt can succeed only if one continually confronts modern rationalism, as the source of the present, with medieval rationalism. But if one undertakes a confrontation of this kind seriously, and thus in the freedom of the question which of the two opposed rationalisms is the true rationalism, then medieval rationalism, whose "classic" for us is Maimonides, changes in the course of the investigation from a mere means of discerning more sharply the specific character of modern rationalism into the standard measured against which the latter proves to be only a semblance of rationalism. And thus the self-evident starting-point, that self-knowledge is a necessary and meaningful undertaking for the present, acquires an unself-evident justification: the critique of the present, the critique of modern rationalism as the critique of modern sophistry, is the necessary beginning, the constant companion, and the unerring sign of that search for truth which is possible in our time.[1]

. . .

Thus at last the "truth" of the alternative, "orthodoxy or Enlightenment" is revealed as the alternative, "orthodoxy or atheism." Orthodoxy, with its hostile eye, recognized from early on, from the beginning, that this is the case. Now it is no longer contested even by the enemies of orthodoxy. The situation thus formed, the present situation, appears to be insoluble for the Jew who cannot be orthodox and who must consider purely political Zionism, the only "solution of the Jewish problem" possible on the basis of atheism, as a resolution that is indeed highly honorable but not, in earnest and in the long run, adequate. This situation not only appears insoluble but actually is so, as long as one clings to the modern premises. If finally there is in the modern world only the alternative "orthodoxy or atheism," and if on the other hand the need for an enlightened Judaism is urgent, then one sees oneself compelled to ask whether enlightenment is necessarily modern enlightenment. Thus one sees oneself induced—provided one does not know from the outset, as one cannot know from the outset, that only new, unheard-of, ultramodern thoughts can resolve our perplexity—to apply for aid to the medieval Enlightenment, the Enlightenment of Maimonides.

But has not the Enlightenment of Maimonides long since been overcome? Is it not the precursor and model of just that moderate Enlightenment of the seventeenth and eighteenth centuries that was least able to stand its ground? Is it not even altogether more "radical" in many respects, more dangerous to the spirit of Judaism, than the modern Enlightenment? Is it not based on the irretrievable Aristotelian cosmology? Does it not stand or fall with the allegorical method of interpretation? Is not the modern Enlightenment therefore, with all its questionableness, still preferable to the medieval?

It would be unpardonable to ignore these or similar doubts. Rather than

---

1. "Irrationalism" is just a variety of modern rationalism, which in itself is already "irrationalistic" enough.

discuss them thoroughly point by point, which would be possible only in the framework of an interpretation of Maimonides' *Guide of the Perplexed*, we shall attempt in what follows to point out the leading idea of the medieval Enlightenment that has become lost to the modern Enlightenment and its heirs, and through an understanding of which many modern certainties and doubts lose their force: the idea of Law.

Appendix 4B

CHAPTER 2 OF *PHILOSOPHY AND LAW*, "THE LEGAL FOUNDATION OF PHILOSOPHY: THE COMMANDMENT TO PHILOSOPHIZE AND THE FREEDOM OF PHILOSOPHIZING" [THE INTRODUCTORY SECTION AND SECTION B, "MAIMONIDES"]

EDITOR'S NOTE

As an aid to readers who wish to precisely follow the stages in Strauss's developing views on Maimonides and its unfolding logic, the central section of the chapter entitled "The Legal Foundation of Philosophy: The Commandment to Philosophize and the Freedom of Philosophizing" (*Philosophy and Law*, trans. Eve Adler, pp. 89–92), is reproduced as appendix 4B. It is dedicated to Maimonides' validation of philosophy in terms of religious law and theology, which in the fuller version of the complete book is compared with similar and divergent arguments elaborated by both Averroes and Gersonides. However, for a better comprehension of the deeper issues and persistent dilemmas which Strauss raises, and in order even to make proper sense of the reproduced section, readers are urged to consult the other parts of the chapter, as well as Strauss's book as a whole. The notes are Strauss's own, with the present editor's additions in square brackets. However, the numbers in bold and square brackets, immediately following each note number, are the note numbers in the chapter of Strauss's original German edition, *Philosophie und Gesetz*, and in the English translation, *Philosophy and Law*.

They are added to aid the reference to that book for readers who may wish to recur from this selection to the fuller context of Strauss's argument. For the full original text and notes, see *Philosophie und Gesetz: Frühe Schriften*, vol. 2 of *Gesammelte Schriften*, pp. 67–68, 75–78. The only change made has been to transliterate five brief passages presented by Strauss in their original Hebrew, Judeo-Arabic, and Arabic script (notes **[12]**, **[15]**, and **[17]**).

THE MEN WHOSE TEACHINGS OFFER THE READIEST ACCESS TO THE philosophic and hence unbelieving basis of medieval Jewish (and Islamic) philosophy, the medieval rationalists, developed in greater or lesser detail and coherence a legal foundation of philosophy, that is, a defense of philosophizing before the bar of revelation. This fact—even if it happens that one rationalist or another did not intend the legal foundation of philosophy straightforwardly, but wrote only to allay the suspicion *of others*—is already sufficient proof that the reality of the revelation, of the revealed law, is the decisive prephilosophic premise of these philosophers. Even if, after assuring themselves of the permittedness or commandedness of philosophizing as such, they can explain the possibility of the revelation philosophically, and can ultimately regard reason as the sole judge of the truth or falsehood of revelation, nevertheless *before* all endeavors and convictions of this kind, before *all* philosophizing, the fact of the revelation stands firm. It makes no difference whether this fact is acknowledged on the basis of a direct insight into the superhuman origin of the document of revelation or on the basis of an indirect, historical proof; because both the direct insight and the proof are independent of all specifically philosophic consideration, and particularly of all reflection on the necessary conditions of revelation, they are in fact prior to the legal foundation of philosophy and thus prior to philosophizing itself.

On this prephilosophic premise of the fact of revelation, and *only* on it, but necessarily on it, there arises the need for a legal foundation of philosophy. For at first the revealed law makes philosophizing questionable from the ground up. A God-given and therefore perfect law necessarily suffices to guide life to its true goal. What then is the sense of philosophizing? Does it necessarily lose its seriousness? Or if it retains this, does it necessarily lead away from the *one* duty and task of man, of the Jew? What has the Jew to do with Plato or Aristotle, that he should keep watch at their door to learn wisdom from them? Are not the works of these philosophers profane books, which seduce the heart with fictitious views and erroneous opinions?[1] To put it in basic terms, is philosophizing forbidden or permitted or actually commanded?

In what follows, we will consider how Averroes, Maimonides, and Gersonides answered this question. We begin with Averroes, since he treats the legal foundation of philosophy thematically in a treatise devoted specifically to this end, the *Decisive Treatise (Fasl-al-Maqal)*.[2] Our primary interest is in Maimonides, the "classic of rationalism" in Judaism. In order to understand better the "moderate" rationalism of Maimonides, one must look ahead to the far more "radical" view of Gersonides in an explicit polemic against Maimonides. One can see more sharply in the "radical" teaching of Gersonides than in the "moderate" teaching of Maimonides what is meant by "rationalism" in medieval Judaism.

...

B. MAIMONIDES

Since the legal foundation of philosophy is not the theme of the *Guide*, one will not find in this book so coherent a discussion of it as presented in Averroes' *Decisive Treatise*. Hence one must collect the pertinent statements of Maimonides from the various parts of his work.[3]

The law summons to belief in the most important truths (God's existence, unity, etc.). Belief, though, is not just lip-service, but understanding of what is believed; belief is perfect only if a man has seen that the opposite of what is believed is in no way possible. Hence the law summons to the understanding and to the demonstration of the truths it imparts. Therewith it implicitly commands knowledge of the world; for God can be known only from His works. Of course the law has not imparted this knowledge explicitly, but only insofar as it commands one to love God and to fear God, it commands knowl-

---

1. [1] Cf. Mendelssohn's Preface to his commentary on Maimonides' *Millot ha-Higgayon* [Treatise on the Art of Logic] (*Gesammelte Schriften* II, 205). [For the critically edited Hebrew original, see: *Hebraïsche Schriften*, I, ed. Haim Borodianski (Bar-Dayan), in *Gesammelte Schriften Jubiläumsausgabe*, vol. 14 (Breslau: Akademie-Verlag, 1938; reprint, Stuttgart–Bad Cannstatt: Frommann-Holzboog, 1972), pp. 29f. See for a recent edition Maimonides, *Be'ur Melekhet ha-Higayon*, ed. Kafah, pp. 5–10.]

2. [2] Edited (*Philosophie und Theologie von Averroës*, Munich 1859) and translated (*Philosophie und Theologie von Averroës*. Translated from the Arabic, Munich 1875[, reprinted, Weinheim, 1991]) by M[arcus] J[oseph] Müller. Our citations follow the page and line numbers of Müller's edition; these page numbers are given also in Müller's translation. [For English translations, see Averroes, "The Decisive Treatise," trans. George F. Hourani, in *Medieval Political Philosophy*, ed. Lerner and Mahdi, pp. 164–86; Averroes, *Decisive Treatise*, trans. Butterworth, pp. 1–33.]

3. [9] With the following cf. also "Yesodei ha-Torah" IIff.

edge of the world as *the* way to the love of God and the fear of God. The acquisition of the truths prescribed by the law presupposes various preliminary studies: mathematics, logic, and physics.[4]

Scripture and tradition show that as God's activity in general is perfect, so also is the law given by Him. This law—the law as a whole and each individual commandment—necessarily has a reason, a rational end. Divine law differs from human laws in that it serves the highest end, the specific perfection of man; the specific perfection of man is knowledge, the knowledge of God.[5] Thus the end of the law is identical with the end of philosophy.

If philosophy as authorized by the law leads to a result that conflicts with the literal sense of the law, if the literal sense is *therefore* impossible, then we must interpret the literal sense, i.e., treat it as figuratively meant.[6] To be interpreted are preeminently all scriptural passages that attribute corporeality and mutability to God. In this case it is a duty to convey to the multitude, too, that the passages in question must not be understood literally: no man must be left to believe in the corporeality of God, just as no man must be left to believe in the nonexistence of God or in the existence of other gods.[7] But of the other subjects of metaphysics, of "the secrets of the Torah," one may impart only the elements, and then only to suitable persons. The multitude must be prevented from occupation with these subjects: it is *legally prohibited* to teach them openly.[8]

Maimonides is thus in agreement with Averroes that the law commands: (1) to philosophize; (2) in case of a conflict between philosophy and the literal sense of the law, to interpret the literal sense; (3) to keep the interpretation secret from all the unqualified.[9] Thus to Maimonides, as previously to Averroes, the question must be posed: does the right of interpretation hold with-

---

4. [10] *Guide* 1.34 (120f.); 1.50; 3.28 (214f.); 3.51 (435ff.). (The numbers in parentheses refer to the pages of Munk's translation.)

5. [11] *Guide* 2.40; 3.25-27; 3.52; 3.54.

6. [12] *Guide* 1.28 (96) and 2.25. *Ma'amar tehiyyat ha-metim: niztarekh le-faresh ha-davar she-peshuto nimna'* ["We must interpret a speech whose literal meaning is impossible."] (*Kovetz*, ed. Lichtenberg, II, 10b). [See Maimonides, *Kovetz*. Strauss refers to a passage in Maimonides' "Treatise on Resurrection," which was written in Arabic and received its original medieval Hebrew translation from Samuel ibn Tibbon, the first Hebrew translator of the *Guide*. It appears in its most recent critical edition: Maimonides, *Igrot ha-Rambam*, ed. Shailat, I, pp. 315-74, and especially p. 367. For an English translation from the original Arabic, see "Treatise on Resurrection," trans. Fradkin, in Lerner, *Maimonides' Empire of Light*, pp. 154-77, and especially p. 172: "We are only compelled to interpret a speech whose literal meaning is impossible." See also "Essay on Resurrection," in *Crisis and Leadership*, trans. Halkin, pp. 211-45, and especially p. 228.]

7. [13] *Guide* 1.35 (132f.).

8. [14] *Guide* 1.Intro. (9f.); 1.33; 1.34; 1.50 (182); 3.Intro. (3f.); 3.7 (44).

out any restriction? The question has been sharpened: is the revelation (the law) superior to reason in such a way that revelation conveys truths that reason cannot contradict because these truths are not accessible to reason? The answer of Maimonides is beyond doubt: human intellect has a limit which it cannot cross; for this reason man is obliged, for the glory of his Lord, to halt at this limit and not to reject the teachings of revelation that he cannot comprehend and demonstrate.[10] Philosophy is free—in its own sphere. Its sphere is nature, not super-nature; more precisely, the world below the heaven, not the heaven; its sphere is the world of man.[11]

It is above all in connection with his discussions of the problem of creation that Maimonides speaks of the inferiority of the human intellect in comparison with revelation. He concludes that it is impossible for man to reach by way of science the answer to the question, "Is the world eternal or created?" Science can indeed weaken the arguments of the "philosophers" for the eternity of the world; beyond that, it can make the creation of the world probable; but it cannot demonstrate it; it must finally leave the question unanswered

---

9. [15] The agreement actually extends considerably further. It holds especially with regard to the philosophic foundation of the law. Here we shall mention only two particular agreements belonging to the legal foundation of philosophy. Maimonides (*Guide* 1.35, 132f.) teaches that one must say to him who cannot understand the interpretation of the text, *hadha al-nas yafhom tawiluhu ahl al-ilm* ("the interpretation of this text is understood by the men of knowledge"); Averroes refers in the same connection to the Qur'an verse: *wa ma y'alim t'awiluhu 'ila 'allah wa 'ahl al-burhan* ("only God and the men of demonstration know its interpretation") (M. J. Müller, loc. cit., p. 16, l. 13). ["The Decisive Treatise," trans. Hourani, p. 177; *Decisive Treatise*, trans. Butterworth, p. 20, l. 15, with n. 39.] To be sure, Maimonides requires that one impart to the layman in question that the passages may in no case be understood literally (this concerns passages whose literal meaning attributes corporeality to God). Maimonides explains (*Guide* 1.33, 116) that Scripture presents the metaphysical *'ala ma yusadid 'al-dhahan nahwa wujuduhu la 'ala haqiqat mahiyatiha* ("[in such a manner that the mind is led] toward the existence of the objects of these opinions and representations but not toward grasping their essence as it truly is." Pines, p. 71); cf. Averroes, loc. cit., p. 17, ll. 7–9: the interpretation must refer only to quality, not to existence; for it is implicit in this assertion of Averroes that the law's teaching is obligatory only about existence, not about the What or the How. [See "The Decisive Treatise," trans. Hourani, p. 178; *Decisive Treatise*, trans. Butterworth, p. 21, ll. 12–14.]

10. [16] *Guide* 1.31 (104f.); 1.32 (114).

11. [17] *Guide* 2.24 (194); letter of Maimonides to R. Chisdai (*Kovetz* II, 23a): *va-'ani 'omer she-da'at ha-'adam yesh la qez, ve-khol zeman she-ha-nefesh ba-guf 'eina yekhola le-yeda' ma le-ma'ala me'en ha-teva'... 'aval kol ma she-be- teva', yekhola hi la-da'at u-le-histakkel* ["Now I say that human knowledge has a limit, and so long as the soul is in the body it is not able to comprehend what is above nature... but it is able to know and to contemplate everything that is in nature." Strauss refers to a passage in Maimonides' "Letter to Rabbi Hisdai ha-Levi of Alexandria" (Maimonides, *Kovetz*, II, 23a). This letter—ten answers to a series of (ten?) questions put to Maimonides—is preserved only in a report of a student, who apparently read the original letter and who reports on its gist to an unknown correspondent in language deliberately other than that used by Maimonides himself. This report survives in Hebrew; and it is possible that the original letter was also written in Hebrew. What is closest to being a critical version of this Maimonidean "letter" (although, to be sure, it represents his known views from other sources) is that which appears in the following edition: Maimonides, *Igrot ha-Rambam*, ed. Shailat, II, pp. 677–86, and especially p. 678. For an English translation, see "Maimonides' Letter to Hasdai ha-Levi," in Maimonides, *Letters*, trans. Stitskin, pp. 102–12, and especially p. 103.]

and accept the solution presented by revelation. Thus Maimonides acknowledges a supernatural truth as such.[12]

From here we glance back at the teaching of Averroes. We have left open the question of whether Averroes acknowledges supernatural truths or not. Against the affirmative answer it has been contended that there could not be supernatural truths for Averroes precisely because Islam has no official spiritual doctrine.[13] But we see that in any case this argument has no demonstrative force; for Judaism too has no official spiritual doctrine, and yet there is for Maimonides a supernatural truth. But though comparison with Maimonides' teaching does nullify the argument in question, it confirms the view which this argument was meant to support. Maimonides' assertion of the insufficiency of human intellect takes its concrete meaning as an assertion of the insufficiency of human intellect to answer the question, "created world or eternal world?" Indeed for Maimonides it is known that Scripture teaches the creation of the world and—what is even more important for him—that Judaism forfeits its foundation if the assertion of creation is abandoned. Averroes on the contrary considers the question "creation or eternity of the world?" irrelevant to dogma (13, 17-14, 5). Thus he lacks the most important reason that brings Maimonides to assert the insufficiency of human intellect and its dependence on revelation. From this we conclude that Averroes basically acknowledges the sufficiency of human intellect, and thus that the passages in which he speaks of a superiority of the theoretical teaching of revelation over that of reason are in need of "interpretation."

The question whether human intellect is sufficient or insufficient, whether it needs or does not need guidance by revelation, whether it is in this sense free or bound, proves to be secondary if one considers that for Averroes no less than for Maimonides the primacy of the law is firmly established: philosophizing is commanded by the law, philosophy is authorized by the law. The freedom of philosophy depends upon its bondage. On this assumption philosophy as authorized by the law is nothing other than the understanding or the demonstration of the truth already imparted by the law, nothing other than the *appropriation of the law*.

---

12. [18] See *Philosophie und Gesetz*, pp. 52–56; *Philosophy and Law*, pp. 64–67; *Philosophie und Gesetz: Frühe Schriften*, vol. 2 of *Gesammelte Schriften*, pp. 51–55.

13. [19] [Léon] Gauthier, "Scolastique musulmane et scolastique chrétienne" (*Revue d'Histoire de Philosophie* 2 [1928], pp. 251ff.) and [G. M.] Manser, *Das Verhältnis von Glauben und Wissen bei Averroës* (Paderborn, 1911), p. 77.

5

Some Remarks on the Political Science of Maimonides and Farabi

EDITOR'S NOTE

"Some Remarks on the Political Science of Maimonides and Farabi" basically reproduces the translation made by Robert Bartlett, which appeared in *Interpretation* 18, no. 1 (Fall 1990): 3–30. The original French version by Strauss from which it was translated, "Quelques Remarques sur la Science Politique de Maïmonide et de Farabi," first appeared in print in *Revue des Études Juives* 100 (1936): 1–37. Bartlett added a version of the following note of acknowledgement to his English translation: "The translator wishes to thank Professor Christopher Bruell and Dr. Hillel Fradkin for their help, and to acknowledge the Social Science and Humanities Research Council of Canada for its support. All square bracketed additions to the notes are the responsibility either of the translator or of the editor [i.e., of *Interpretation*, Dr. Hilail Gildin]. Dr. Fradkin and Professor Aryeh Motzkin kindly provided the translations and transliterations of the Hebrew and Judeo-Arabic notes. The editors thank M. Rémi Brague, and the editor of *Revue des Études Juives*, M. Gérard Nahon, for their assistance." The present editor has made some slight editorial changes to the original translation, and especially to the notes. Also, the number (amounting to 120) and division of the notes are rearranged from the English translation, in order to make them conform with how they appeared in Strauss's original French version. For the expediency of reading Strauss's text, and so as not to impede such reading by undue editorial pedantry, the differences in this edition between the original translator's comments and additions, and those of the present editor, will not be indicated, since all are put in the same square brackets. Professor Bartlett has recently (2010) been able to thoroughly review the translation in consultation with the present editor; as a result, further changes have been made in order to improve linguistic accuracy and stylistic felicity. Insofar as these goals may not have been achieved,

I assume full responsibility as final editor for the differences between the two versions. I have also greatly benefited from, and acknowledge gratefully, the edition in French of Rémi Brague: Leo Strauss, "Quelques Remarques sur la Science Politique de Maïmonide et de Farabi," in *Maïmonide*, trans. and ed. Rémi Brague (Paris: Presses Universitaires de France, 1988). Even though their origins are not always shown, I owe a sizable debt to his work, especially for numerous scholarly comments, references, and translations in the notes. See also *Philosophie und Gesetz: Frühe Schriften*, vol. 2 of *Gesammelte Schriften*, pp. 125-58. For marginal handwritten comments subsequently added by Strauss to his own copy of the essay, which have been helpfully transcribed by Heinrich Meier, see pp. 159-65. These are eminently and even imperatively worthy of consulting for Strauss's additional thought and research on numerous topics treated in or related to his own article.

THERE IS, IN THE PHILOSOPHY OF MAIMONIDES AS WELL AS IN THAT OF his Muslim masters and his Jewish disciples, a political science. The principal teaching of this science is summarized in the following theses: men need, in order to live, guidance [*direction*] and, as a result, a law; they need, in order to live well, [or] in order to attain happiness, a divine law that guides them not only, like the human law, toward peace and moral perfection, but further toward the understanding [*l'intelligence*] of the supreme truths and thereby toward supreme perfection; the divine law is given to men by a man (as intermediary) who is a "prophet," i.e., one who combines in his person all the essential qualities of the philosopher as well as those of the legislator and king; the activity proper to the prophet is legislation.[1]

The importance of this political science is, at first sight, rather slight. Maimonides, for example, does not appear to have devoted more than four or five chapters of his *Guide of the Perplexed* to it. But given the position religion occupies in medieval thought—i.e., revealed religion, more precisely

---

1. Cf. *Philosophie und Theologie von Averroes*, ed. M[arcus] J[oseph] Müller (Munich, 1859 [edited texts]; Munich 1875 [with German translation]), p. 98, 15-18 ["just as it is evident to him that the work of the physician is healing, and that that which produces healing emanates from the one who is a physician, so it is equally evident to him that the work of the prophets, peace be on them, is to establish the religious laws (*wad' ash-shara'i'*) thanks to an inspiration (*waḥy*) coming from God, and that one who engages in the aforesaid work is a prophet (*nabiy*)"] and p. 102, 2-3 ["if the work of the prophets, on account of which they are prophets, is nothing other than to establish the religious laws as a result of an inspiration coming from God, may He be exalted"]. [These two Averroean passages, to which Strauss only refers, have been translated by the present editor from the French translation of the Arabic by Rémi Brague, in "Quelques Remarques sur la Science Politique de Maïmonide et de Farabi," in *Maïmonide*, p. 143, n. 1.]

the revealed *law*, the Torah or the *shari'a*—it must be inferred that political science, which is the only philosophical discipline treating this law as such, is of capital importance. It is only in their political doctrine that the medieval philosophers discuss the basis of their thought, the most profound presupposition by which they distinguish themselves from ancient thinkers on the one hand, and from modern thinkers on the other: their belief in Revelation.

The medieval character of the politics of Maimonides and the *falasifa* is not contradicted by the fact that it is nothing other than a modification, however considerable, of an ancient conception. For there is a profound agreement between Jewish and Muslim thought on the one hand, and ancient thought on the other: it is not the Bible and the Qur'an, but perhaps the New Testament, and certainly the Reformation and modern philosophy, that brought about the break with ancient thought. The guiding idea upon which the Greeks and the Jews agree is exactly the idea of the divine law as a single and total law that is at the same time religious law, civil law, and moral law. And it is indeed a Greek philosophy of the divine law that is the basis of the Jewish and Muslim philosophy of the Torah or the *shari'a*; according to Avicenna, Plato's *Laws* is the classic work on prophecy and the *shari'a*.[2] The prophet occupies in this medieval politics the same place the philosopher-kings occupy in Platonic politics: by fulfilling the essential conditions of the philosopher-kings, enumerated by Plato, he founds the perfect city, i.e., the ideal Platonic city.

The facts just sketched and studied more closely in a previous study have

---

2. Cf. *Philosophie und Gesetz*, pp. 113 and 64-65. [See *Philosophy and Law*, pp. 124-25 and 75-76; chap. 4 above, seventh through ninth paragraphs of section IV. See also "Introduction" to *Persecution and the Art of Writing*, p. 10; "A Giving of Accounts," in *Jewish Philosophy and the Crisis of Modernity*, p. 463; Strauss, *The Argument and the Action of Plato's "Laws"* (Chicago: University of Chicago Press, 1975), p. 1.] In R. Sheshet ha-Nasi's letter, published by Alexander Marx ["Texts By and About Maimonides"], *Jewish Quarterly Review*, N.S., 25 (1935): [pp. 371-428, and especially] 406ff., one finds the following note concerning Plato's *Laws*, certainly based not on a direct knowledge of it, but on a tradition whose history is not yet elucidated. R. Sheshet says [p. 424, ll. 299-304]:

> Va-'od ra'iti ba-sefer nimusei ha-sekhel 'asher ḥibber 'Aplaton ve-a'sar bo ha-devarim she-ne'esru be-torahtenu ha-qadosha. Kegon lo tirẓaḥ ve-lo' tin'af ve-lo' tignov ve-lo' ta'ane ve-re'akha 'ed sheqer va-lo' taḥmod u-she'ar ha-devarim 'asher ha-sekhel more le-himmana' mehem. Gam ba-miẓvot 'ase ẓiva la-'asot ẓedaka va-mishpat. Ve-rav ha-devarim 'asher middat ha-sekhel melammedet la-'asitam min ha-devarim ha-ketuvim be-torahtenu ha-'amitit ha-qedosha.

> [I have also seen in the Book of the Laws of the Intellect (i.e., the *Laws*) which Plato composed, that he forbids in it the things which are forbidden in our holy Torah. For example: thou shalt not murder, and thou shalt not commit adultery, and thou shalt not steal, and thou shalt not bear false witness against thy neighbor, and thou shalt not covet, and the rest of the things which the intellect teaches to refrain from. Also, with respect to the positive commandments, he (i.e., Plato) commanded to perform justice and righteousness. And many of the things which the virtue of the intellect teaches to do are among the things which are written in our true and holy Torah. Translated by the present editor.]

not always received the attention they deserve.³ Let us note only that Salomon Munk mentions in the table of contents to his edition and translation of *The Guide of the Perplexed* neither "city," "politics," "government," "governance," "legislator," "economics," nor even "ethics" or "morality," i.e., those words which are encountered rather frequently and, what is more, are of considerable importance in the *Guide*.⁴ For Munk and for those others who have followed him, the doctrine of Maimonides and the *falasifa* is an Aristotelianism contaminated or corrected by neo-Platonic conceptions. This opinion is not false, but it is superficial. As soon as it has been uttered, one is obliged to give an account of the relation between the Aristotelian elements and those of a neo-Platonic origin, and to pose this question: why does the Aristotelianism of Maimonides and the *falasifa* admit of such a great influence from neo-Platonism (or vice versa)? It does not suffice to reply that this amalgam was something brought about before the advent of Muslim and Jewish philosophy—at least not until one proves in advance (as no one has yet done) that the *falasifa* were conquering barbarians who took what they found and not philosophers who were *searching*. But for what were they searching? Let us take as an example a phenomenon apparently as independent of any choice and, above all, as far removed from theologico-political presuppositions, as the activity of Averroes as a commentator. Now, if one compares the commentaries of Averroes with the works of Aristotle himself, one immediately sees that two of Aristotle's treatises have not been commented on by the Commentator: the *Politics* on the one hand,⁵ and the treatise on dreams

---

3. See the preceding note [i.e., referring to *Philosophie und Gesetz/Philosophy and Law*]. Cf. also Erwin I. J. Rosenthal, "Maimonides' Conception of State and Society," in *Moses Maimonides*, ed. Isadore Epstein (London: Soncino, 1935), pp. 189-206.

4. Let us note further that Munk tends to level the political character of the respective passages of *Le Guide des égarés*, 3 vols. (Paris, 1856-66), by translating, for example, *madani* as "social" ["*social*"] (cf. especially 3.31, p. 68b, *'al-imal 'al-siyasiyah 'al-madaniyah*, which Munk translates as "the practice of the social duties" ["la pratique des devoirs sociaux," p. 248]). Let us add that the translation of *madinah* as "state" ["*état*"] instead of "city" ["*cité*"] is all the more erroneous. In philosophical texts, one often ought to translate even the Hebrew word *medinah*, not as "province" ["*département*"] or "district" ["*region*"], but as "city" ["*cité*"].

5. Averroes himself declares that he does not know it [i.e., the *Politics*]. According to [Moritz] Steinschneider, [*Die*] *Hebräischen Übersetzungen* [*des Mittelalters und die Juden als Dolmetscher* (Berlin: Kommissionsverlag des Bibliographischen Bureaus, 1893; reprint ed. Graz: Akademischen Druck-u., Verlaganstalt, 1956)], p. 219, it was never translated into Arabic. It may be, however, that Farabi knew it through the intermediary of those of his friends who knew Greek. Averroes reports: "Apparet autem ex sermone Abyn arrim [Abi nazr] Alfarabii, quod inventus est (i.e., liber Politicorum Aristotelis) in illis villis." (*Aristotelis Opera*, Venetiis 1550, Vol. III, fol. 79a, col. 1, ll. 36-38). ["It is clear, moreover, from Alfarabi's report, that it (Aristotle's *Politics*) was found in those cities."] Also *Averrois Paraphrasis in Platonis Rempublica* (loc. cit., fol. 175b, col. 1, ll. 38-39). [Cf. Averroes, *On Plato's "Republic,"* trans. Lerner, "First Treatise," p. 4 (22, ll. 2-6): "The first part of this art is in Aristotle's book known as the *Nicomachea* (i.e.,

and divination by dreams on the other.⁶ This choice is not due to chance: Averroes was unable to comment on these treatises of Aristotle because their reception would have made impossible the philosophical explication of the *shari'a*. For this explication, which is rather a justification, is based on the supposition that the prophet, whose prognostic faculty is conjoined [*apparentée*] to "veridical dreams," is the founder of the ideal city in the sense of the *Republic* or the *Laws*. It was to justify the *shari'a* against the objections of heretics or skeptics, or rather to give a reasonable, truly philosophical guidance to Shi'ite hopes concerning the *imam*,⁷ that, at the beginning of Muslim philosophy, Farabi opted for Platonic politics, perhaps moved by philosophical convictions not very different from those Plato had in going to Syracuse; and this is the reason that, at the end of the epoch in question, Averroes came to comment on Plato's *Republic* instead of Aristotle's *Politics* and to give an explication of "veridical dreams" that accords better with such passages of Plato than with the treatise—so matter-of-fact—of Aristotle.

It is only by beginning from the Platonizing politics of Farabi—and not at all by beginning either from modern conceptions or from the analogies, however remarkable, which scholasticism properly speaking provides—that one can hope to arrive at a true comprehension of the Muslim and Jewish philosophies

---

the *Ethics*), and the second in his book known as the *Governance* (i.e., *Politics*) and also in this book of Plato's (i.e., *Republic*) that we intend to explain since Aristotle's book on governance has not yet fallen into our hands." See also Shlomo Pines, "Aristotle's *Politics* in Arabic Philosophy," *Israel Oriental Studies* 5 (1975): 150–60. Cf. also "How to Study Medieval Philosophy," chap. 1 above, text at n. 50; "Maimonides' Doctrine of Prophecy," chap. 4 above, n. 191.

6. Averroes believed that he commented on this treatise [i.e., *On Dreams* and *On Divination in Dreams*, which are treated as a single work because of their both being contained in the *Parva Naturalia*]; but it is easy to see that his paraphrase is not based on Aristotle's treatise. One must judge in the same way regarding the few words with which Farabi claims to summarize the subject of Aristotle's treatise (see Falaquera, *Reshit Ḥokhmah*, ed. [Moritz] David (Berlin, 1902), p. 87, 1.27–32). (It remains to show on another occasion that the third part of the *Reshit Ḥokhmah* is the translation of Farabi's book on the philosophy of Plato and Aristotle.) [See Leo Strauss, "Eine vermisste Schrift Farabis," *Monatsschrift für Geschichte und Wissenschaft des Judentums* 80, no. 1 (January 1936): 96–106. An English version will appear shortly, translated by Martin D. Yaffe and Gabriel Bartlett, as "A Lost Writing of Farabi," in *Reorientation: Leo Strauss in the 1930s*, ed. Martin D. Yaffe and Richard S. Ruderman (New York: Palgrave Macmillan, forthcoming). On Aristotle's treatises on dreams, cf. also Alfarabi, *Plato and Aristotle*, trans. Mahdi, p. 121.] Cf. also the remarks concerning the *De Somno et Visione* of Kindi in A. Nagy, *Die philosophischen Abhandlungen des Kindi* (Münster, 1897), pp. XXII–XXIII. As regards the defective knowledge of the *Parva Naturalia* among the Muslims in general, cf. Max Meyerhof, *Von Alexandrien nach Bagdad* (Berlin: Abhandlungen der Preussischen Akademie der Wissenschaften, 1930), p. 27. [See also Averroes, *Epitome of "Parva Naturalia,"* trans. and ed. Harry Blumberg (Cambridge, MA: Medieval Academy of America, 1961), pp. 39–53.]

7. I owe the invaluable information on this and such other points as bear on the intellectual atmosphere in which Farabi lived and thought, to my friend Paul Kraus. Cf., while awaiting his subsequent publications, his "Beiträge zur islamischen Ketzergeschichte," in *Revista degli Studi Orientalia* 14 (1934): 94–129 and 335–79. [For Strauss's further comments on Paul Kraus, see "Maimonides' Doctrine of Prophecy," chap. 4 above, n. 194.]

of the Middle Ages. It is difficult to believe that no one has profited, so far as we know, from the testimony given by Maimonides himself.[8] He writes to Samuel ibn Tibbon: "Do not concern yourself with logic books except those composed by the wise Abu Nasr al-Farabi; for what he has composed in general, and in particular his book *The Principles of the Beings*—all of this is of the purest flour." And he adds immediately that the books of Avicenna, though of merit, are not comparable to Farabi's. This testimony, sufficiently precise in itself, gains a decisive importance if one recalls that the authentic title of the book of Farabi's particularly praised by Maimonides is *The Political Governments*; that this book contains metaphysics (theology) as well as politics; that the politics therein is based directly on the politics of Plato, whose *Laws* were commented on by Farabi; and that his metaphysics is inseparable from Platonizing politics: true metaphysics is the collection of the "opinions of the people of the perfect city."[9] In a century which was not considerably less "enlightened" than that of the sophists and Socrates, where the very bases of human life, i.e., political life, had been shaken by chiliastic convulsions on the one hand and, on the other, by a critique of religion the radicalism of which recalls the freethinkers of the seventeenth and eighteenth centuries,[10] Farabi had rediscovered in the politics of Plato the golden mean equally removed from a naturalism that aims only at sanctioning the savage and destructive instincts of "natural" man, the instincts of the master and the conqueror; and from a supernaturalism that tends to become the basis of a slave morality—a golden mean that is neither a compromise nor a synthesis, that is hence not based on the two opposed positions, but that suppresses them both, uproots them by a prior, more profound question, by raising a more fundamental problem, the work of a truly critical philosophy.

8. Cf. now Rosenthal, loc. cit. [See n. 3 above. Maimonides' direction to Ibn Tibbon, recommending the most careful study of Farabi, occurs in the single letter from the author to the translator which has survived: see *Igrot ha-Rambam*, ed. Shailat, II, pp. 511–24. For an edition of two versions rendered in Hebrew (obviously not yet based on Shailat's critical edition), see Alexander Marx, "Texts by and about Maimonides," *Jewish Quarterly Review*, N.S., 25 (1935): 374–81. For an English translation, see *Letters*, trans. Stitskin, pp. 130–36.]

9. This [i.e., *Opinions of the People of the Perfect City*, otherwise known as *Opinions of the People of the Virtuous City*] is the title of Farabi's other major work. [The most recent edition appeared under the title Alfarabi, *Perfect State*, trans. Walzer. In subsequent essays Strauss will mainly employ the alternative title of the work, whose significant difference may be shown by added emphasis: "Opinions of the People of the *Virtuous* City" (al-Madina *al-Fadila*). For the alternate Farabian title of *The Principles of the Beings*, as used by Strauss in the present essay, i.e., *The Political Governments*, see n. 24 below.]

10. Cf. the studies on Razi that Kraus has begun to publish in *Orientalia* of Rome under the title of "Raziana." [See *Orientalia*, N.S., 4 (1935): 300–334; 5 (1936): 35–56, 358–78. One of the fundamental works by Razi, which was critically edited as well as discussed by Paul Kraus in the first article from *Orientalia* (1935) to which Strauss points (*k. al-sira al-falsafiyya*), has since been translated into English: see Razi, "The Book of the Philosophic Life," trans. Charles E. Butterworth, *Interpretation* 20, no. 3 (Spring 1993): 227–36.]

The Platonizing politics of Farabi is the point of departure for anyone who wishes to understand (and not merely to note [*constater*]) the neo-Platonism of the *falasifa* and Maimonides that in the last analysis is—like the neo-Platonism of Plotinus himself—a modification of authentic Platonism, i.e., of a philosophy the primordial intention of which is the search for the perfect city. And it is again by beginning from the exigencies of Farabi's Platonizing politics that one can and must understand the reception of Aristotle's physics: Platonism did not give (or appeared not to give) sufficient guarantees against the superstitions of dying antiquity; the rebirth, threatened by hybrid speculations, of Platonic politics was not possible without the aid of Aristotle's physics, which preserved the basis of Socrates' and Plato's inquiry, the world of common sense.

The motives that guided Farabi in his work of restoration are not more clearly visible in the thinkers who followed him: they maintained only his results. In these circumstances, one cannot hope for a satisfactory analysis of any phenomenon of Jewish[11] and Muslim philosophy before the reconstitution of the philosophy of Farabi. This reconstitution can only be successful through a close collaboration between Arabists, Hebraists, and historians of philosophy. One can only hope to initiate [*amorcer*] this work in the following pages by showing the influence exercised on Maimonides by the Platonizing politics of Farabi.

I

Maimonides treats of political science as such in what one may call his encyclopedia of the sciences, which is found in the last chapter of his summary of logic, entitled *Millot ha-Higgayon*, written in his early youth.[12] This is what

11. For even the doctrines formed in a Christian setting are constituted only in opposition to Maimonides: they thus cannot be interpreted without the preliminary interpretation of the *Guide*, which presupposes the reconstitution of the Farabian doctrine. [For the sort of view to which Strauss opposes his own approach—a view which seems unaware of the impact made by the Islamic philosophers, and especially Farabi, on Maimonides' thought—consider J. L. Teicher, "Christian Theology and the Jewish Opposition to Maimonides," *Journal of Theological Studies* 43, no. 169–70 (1942): 168–76.]

12. The Arabic original of the last part of the *Millot* seems to be lost; see Steinschneider, *Hebräische Übersetzungen*, p. 434. [The Arabic text has since been recovered. See Israel Efros, "Maimonides' Arabic Treatise on Logic," *Proceedings of the American Academy for Jewish Research* 34 (1966): 155–60; Hebrew (and Arabic) section, pp. 9–34. The rediscovered full Arabic text was edited by Mubahat Turker, "Musa Ibn-i Meymun'in *Al-Makala fi Sina'at al-Mantik*: Inin Arabca Asli," *Ankara Universitesi Dil ve Tarih Cografiya Fakultesi Dergisi* 18, no. 1–2 (1961): 40–64. For the passage to which Strauss refers, see "Logic," in *Ethical Writings*, trans. Weiss and Butterworth, pp. 158–61; they render the key Arabic term (in French, *moeurs*) as "moral habits" (p. 160); see also "Logic," trans. Efros, pp. 61–65; he renders the key Arabic term as "the subject of virtues" (p. 64).]

he says: philosophy is divided into two parts, speculative philosophy and practical philosophy, which is also called human philosophy or again political wisdom. Political wisdom is divided into four parts: (1) governance of man by himself, (2) governance of the household, (3) governance of the city, (4) governance of the great nation or of the nations. The first fosters virtues as much moral as intellectual, and with regard to it, "the philosophers have many books on mores [*moeurs*]." The three other parts of political science form a unity in opposition to the first: while the one (ethics) is concerned with the governance of man by himself, the others treat of prescriptions (*ḥukim*), i.e., the regimes by which man governs other men. The second part (economics) conduces to the proper ordering of domestic affairs. The third part (the governance of the city) makes known happiness [*félicité*] and its acquisition; it is this that teaches one to distinguish between true happiness and true evil, and imaginary happiness and imaginary evil; it is this that establishes the rules of justice by which human societies are well ordered; it is by this that the wise of the perfect nations establish the laws (*nimusim*); by these laws, the nations subject to the wise are governed; "the philosophers have many books, accessible in Arabic, on all these matters . . . , but we have no need, in these times, of all that, i.e., of the prescriptions (*ḥukim*), the ordinances (*datot*), the laws (*nimusim*), the governance of those men[13] in divine matters."

Despite the difficulties in the text, one thing is beyond doubt: Maimonides distinctly declares that "we have no need, in these times, of all that," i.e., of politics properly speaking, and even of economics. The final words indicate rather clearly the reason why they are not needed: politics contains rules concerning "the divine matters." Now, we—we Jews—we have the Torah that governs us in a perfect manner in all political matters, and especially in the divine matters related to them: it is the Torah that renders superfluous politics properly speaking and economics.[14]

13. We read, following the manuscript Mm. 6. 24. (fol. 29a) of the Cambridge University Library, *ha-'anashim ha-hem* ["those people"] instead of *ha-'anashim* ["the people"] of the [printed] editions. [As Brague comments (*Maïmonide*, p. 150, n. 13), Efros does not indicate this variant reading in any of the manuscripts of the translations that he examined: in Ibn Tibbon (63, 9); in Aḥitub (99, 17); in Vivas (129, 2). Brague also notes that the Arabic original of Maimonides, *Treatise on Logic*, as presented by Efros—*PAAJR* 34 (1966): 33, l. 16—has *"an-nas,"* i.e., "the people"; this would also be *ha-'anashim* in Hebrew.]

14. It is, moreover, in this way that the passage in question is understood by the commentators we have been able to consult (an anonymous commentator in the edition of Cremona, Comtino, and Mendelssohn). One finds some interesting parallels which confirm our interpretation in the *Emunah Ramah* of Abraham Ibn Daud [ed. Samson Weil (pt. III, Frankfurt am Main, 1852; reprinted, Berlin, 1919, and Jerusalem, 1967)] (pp. 98 and 101) and in the fragments, published by Richard Gottheil, of an encyclopedia of the sciences composed by an unknown Muslim author (["A Genizah Fragment of a Treatise on the Sciences in General," in] *JQR*, N.S., 23 (1932): [pp. 163–80, and especially p.] 178[, fol. 3a, l. 19; En-

To understand better this important declaration, it must be noted that Maimonides does not make a similar remark concerning ethics (he says simply that the philosophers have many books on it), logic, or speculative philosophy. That he did not judge as useless or superfluous the books of the philosophers on all these sciences, that he recommended the study of these books many times, is too well known to require proof. It suffices to remark that the judgment in question concerning politics is found in a summary of logic, based on the "books of the philosophers." Here, then, is the complete meaning of Maimonides' declaration: of all the philosophical disciplines, it is only politics properly speaking and economics that are rendered superfluous by the Torah.

On this point, the teaching of *The Guide of the Perplexed* scarcely differs from that of the *Millot ha-Higgayon*. Maimonides says there that the Torah gives only some summary indications concerning speculative matters, whereas, regarding political matters, "everything has been done to render it (what concerns the governance of the city) precise in all its details."[15] One needs, then, the "books of the philosophers" on the speculative sciences; but one may do without their books on politics, since all the necessary information regarding politics and economics[16] is found in the Torah.[17] Here is the

---

glish translation, p. 170]). [See also *Ha-Emunah ha-Ramah*, ed. (Hebrew trans. Solomon Ibn Labi) and (German) trans. Samson Weil (Frankfurt am Main, 1852; reprint, Berlin, 1919, and Jerusalem, 1967); *The Exalted Faith*, trans. Norbert Samuelson, and ed. Gershon Weiss (Rutherford, NJ: Fairleigh Dickinson University Press, 1986), p. 257 (208b, l. 16–209a, l. 3; Hebrew edition, pp. 303–302): "We will explain in this chapter that the end that is realized by practical philosophy is the achievement of happiness, and that this (end) is perfected by improvement of the virtues first, governance of the household second, and laws of the city third. We will explain that this (state of affairs) is found in our Torah in the most perfect way possible." The translation has been amended. See also p. 263 (213b, l. 13–214a, l. 1; Hebrew edition, p. 300): "When an examiner examines (this topic) in detail he will find everything that the conclusions of the science of the philosopher reach. (The reason for) this is that practical philosophy exists in the Torah in a more perfect way. It is taken from the Torah and (the Torah) proceeds with it to its end."] We do not dispute that the words "in these times" may be taken in the sense "during captivity." Understood in this way, the final phrase implies: political science was needed when the Jewish state existed, and it will be needed again after the coming of the Messiah. According to this interpretation, the practical importance of political science would be greater than it is according to the interpretation we have preferred as being better in accord with the whole of Maimonides' doctrine. [Strauss will (in about two decades) interpret this passage and explore the implications of that entire fourteenth chapter, with a greater depth of analysis: see "Maimonides' Statement on Political Science," chap. 9 below. For medieval Hebrew encyclopedias, often leaning much on Arabic originals or models, see *The Medieval Hebrew Encyclopedias of Science and Philosophy*, ed. Steven Harvey (Dordrecht: Kluwer, 2000).]

15. *Guide* 3.27. Cf. 3.54 (p. 132a), and 1.33 (p. 37a). [See *Guide*, trans. Pines, 3.27, p. 510; 3.54, p. 633; and 1.33, pp. 71–72.]

16. Cf. *Guide* 3.28 (p. 61b), and 3.51 (p. 127a). As regards the relation between the household and the city, see *Guide* 3.41 (p. 90b). [See *Guide*, trans. Pines, 3.28, p. 513; 3.51, p. 625; and 3.41, pp. 561–62.]

17. Cf. the remark on the guiding interest of the rabbis in *Guide* 1.Intro. (p. 11a). [See *Guide*, trans. Pines, 1.Intro., p. 19.]

reason why Maimonides, when speaking of the studies that must precede the study of metaphysics, does not mention politics, or even ethics, although the "perfection concerning political governments" is according to him one of the essential conditions to be fulfilled by him who wants to be initiated into metaphysics.[18] The first stage [*degré*] of the studies is the study of the Torah:[19] it replaces the study of politics (and perhaps also that of ethics) because the Torah has rendered politics superfluous.

Whether or not this is Maimonides' last word on political science, we must draw all the information on the matter from the few phrases he devotes in the *Millot* to this science of doubtful utility. That he divides philosophy into speculative philosophy and practical philosophy, that he calls the latter political or human philosophy, that he divides it into ethics, economics, and politics properly speaking, all this is well explained by the Aristotelian tradition, whose influence on his thought is known. But here are the facts which strike the present-day reader: (1) Maimonides does not mention happiness [*félicité*] when speaking of ethics, [but] he does so only when speaking of politics properly so-called; (2) he begins by dividing practical or political philosophy into four parts but, later on, he distinguishes among only three: the distinction between the governance of the city on the one hand, and the governance of the great nation or of the nations on the other, made with such clarity at first, appears to be of no consequence; why then is it made?; (3) without any prior justification, Maimonides attributes to politics strictly speaking the treatment of the "divine matters."

(1) It would not be possible to resolve these difficulties without recourse to Maimonides' immediate source, the political works [*oeuvre*] of Farabi. Farabi also sometimes divides practical or political (*madaniyya*) philosophy into ethics (*kholqiyya*) and philosophy of government (*siyasiyya*).[20] But

---

18. *Guide* 1.34 (p. 41a). [See *Guide*, trans. Pines, 1.34, p. 78.]
19. *Guide* 3.54 (p. 132b). [See *Guide*, trans. Pines, 3.54, pp. 633-34).]
20. [For Farabi's divisions of philosophy, see] *Kitab al-tanbih 'ala sabil al-sa'ada* (Hyderabad, 1346 A.H.), pp. 20-21. The division of practical philosophy into ethics, economics, and politics is found in one of *[Alfarabi's] philosophische Abhandlungen [aus Londoner, Leidener, und Berliner Handschriften herausgegeben* (Leiden: Brill, 1890) for Arabic edition]; *[Alfarabi's] philosophische Abhandlungen [aus der Arabischen übersetzt* (Leiden: Brill, 1892) for German translation], published by Friederich Dieterici, p. 51, ll. 19-21. [The Farabian work to which Strauss refers is "The Preliminary Studies Necessary to Philosophy," chap. 2. I follow the title of Farabi's work provided in *Maïmonide*, p. 152, n. 20. The passage to which Strauss seems to refer occurs in Dieterici (1892), p. 86, ll. 9-12, which may be translated from the German as follows: "The books of Aristotle teach about the practical application of philosophy, for the most part (concerning themselves with) the proper production (*gute Herstellung*) of morals. One learns (*kennenlernt*) about this for the sake of the governing (*Verwaltung*) of the city on the one hand, and for that of the household on the other."]

this division does not correspond to his guiding idea. Ethics is concerned with the distinction between good and bad actions, and between the virtues and the vices; now, this distinction is made in relation to the final end of man, happiness [*félicité*]: the virtues are good only to the extent that they are means to acquire happiness;[21] as a result, the search for happiness, the distinction between true and imaginary happiness, must precede the distinction between the virtues and vices, between good actions and bad.[22] But there is happiness only in and through political communities.[23] This is why Farabi, in his composition [*dissertation*] on political governments, only speaks of happiness and, with all the more reason, of the virtues, after having explained the necessity and general structure of political communities; and this is also why he teaches there that happy men are those who are governed by the ideal leader [*chef*] of the ideal community;[24] the leader [*chef*] of the ideal commu-

21. *Alfarabi's Abhandlung der Musterstaat*, ed. F[riedrich] Dieterici (Leiden: Brill, 1895; reprinted, Hildesheim: Olms, 1985), pp. 46, ll. 18–19. [See Alfarabi, *Perfect State*, trans. Walzer, para. 6, pp. 206–7.]

22. "Political science examines the types of actions and ways of life which depend on the will, and the habits . . . from which these actions and ways of life derive, and the ends for which these actions are performed. And it distinguishes between the ends for which the actions are performed and the ways of life are followed; and it explains that there is an end which is true happiness . . . and it distinguishes between the actions and the ways of life, and explains that those by which one attains true happiness are the praiseworthy goods and virtues . . . and that the condition of their existence in man is that the perfect actions and perfect ways of life be determined in the cities and nations in a hierarchical manner and that they be practiced in common." Alfarabi, *Ihsa al-ulum* [*The Enumeration of the Sciences*] (Cairo, 1931), p. 64. Compare the parallels in *Musterstaat*, p. 46, ll. 7–21 and in the *Kitab tahsil al-sa'ada* (Hyderabad, 1345 A.H.), pp. 15–16. [The *Ihsa* has been partially translated by Fauzi M. Najjar, in *Medieval Political Philosophy*, ed. Lerner and Mahdi, pp. 24–30; he translated a section of chap. V, "On Political Science, Jurisprudence, and Dialectical Theology." For a new and complete version of the same chap. V, see Alfarabi, *Political Writings*, trans. Butterworth, pp. 76–84. For the passage referred to in the *Musterstaat*, see Alfarabi, *Perfect State*, trans. Walzer, see pp. 204–7. A translation of the *Kitab tahsil al-sa'ada* ("The Attainment of Happiness") is available in Alfarabi, *Plato and Aristotle*, trans. Mahdi, pp. 13–50; the passage to which he refers is para. 20, p. 24.]

23. *Kitab tahsil al-sa'ada*, p. 14. [See also] *Musterstaat*, pp. 53–54. [See Alfarabi, *Plato and Aristotle*, trans. Mahdi, para. 18, p. 23; see also *Perfect State*, trans. Walzer, pp. 204–7.] Cf. the preceding note.

24. *Kitab al-siyasat al-madaniyya* (Hyderabad, 1346 A.H.), pp. 42 and 50. [The text has been edited: *Al-Farabi's The Political Regime*, ed. Fauzi M. Najjar (Beyrouth: Imprimerie Catholique, 1964). A partial translation, also by Najjar, appears in *Medieval Political Philosophy*, ed. Lerner and Mahdi, pp. 32–57, and especially pp. 34 and 37. A complete translation of *The Political Regime* (also known as *The Principles of the Beings*) by Muhsin Mahdi is forthcoming in the Cornell University Press series of Alfarabi's writings, and specifically of *The Political Writings*, ed. Charles Butterworth. The title of Farabi's work that Strauss, in this essay, refers to as *The Political Governments* is regarded by most present-day scholars as better rendered by *The Political Regime*. It is requisite to add a further note on what has been rendered as "first leader." In some translated works of Farabi, and of Maimonides (on which Strauss will comment in n. 65 below), it is offered instead as "first chief," due to a desire to retain utmost closeness to the original Arabic term. (Cf. also n. 59 below, with regard to a passage in Averroes, *On Plato's "Republic,"* trans. Lerner, who uses "chief" to render the same term.) Hence, Strauss's original uses the French term, "*chef*," as was noted in square brackets. However, for the sake of greater clarity in English, and to maintain as much consistency as was possible with the other essays and lectures in this volume, readers should know that the decision was made jointly by the translator and the present editor to render it with the one

nity establishes the ordering of the actions by means of which men are able to attain happiness. Since happiness depends on the political community, it is no longer necessary, it is no longer even possible, to distinguish between ethics and politics; in his encyclopedia of the sciences,[25] Farabi does not even mention ethics.[26] And—what is perhaps weightier still—in his enumeration of the opinions which each member of the perfect community must have, Farabi immediately passes from the opinions concerning God and the world to opinions concerning the perfect community and happiness without saying a word about the virtues in the entire enumeration in question.[27] In the final analysis,[28] there is not in Farabi an ethics which precedes politics or which is separable from it. In any case, it is in following Farabi that Maimonides attributes the discussion of happiness to politics strictly speaking. Compared to the corresponding doctrine of Farabi, the order of the practical sciences in Maimonides—an order according to which the discussion of happiness is connected with politics strictly speaking, and the discussion of the virtues with ethics—presents itself as a compromise between the conception of Farabi and that of Aristotle:[29] Maimonides, it seems, while accepting Farabi's

---

term, "first leader," although with the French accompanying it as [*chef*], to make clearer what "leader" translates.]

25. *Ihsa al-ulum*. This small treatise, whose singular importance is noted by Ibn al-Qifti, is more a critique of the sciences, a note distinguishing between the sciences on the basis of their value, than an encyclopedia properly speaking. [Brague, in *Maïmonide*, p. 154, n. 25, translates the Arabic text, which I translate from his French rendering: "Al-Qifti's text is reproduced by Dieterici in his edition of *Alfarabi's Philosophische Abhandlungen*, Arabic, p. 115, and German, p. 188: 'Next there came from him a remarkable book, the *Enumeration of the Sciences*, with the doctrine of the ends of each of these (i.e., the sciences); this is to say that his encyclopedia is arranged in steps. In this work, he is original, for no one before him had followed this path; those who study the sciences, whoever they may be, cannot avoid being guided by this book and beginning by studying that which is in it.'"]

26. Cf. also *Kitab tahsil al-sa'ada*, pp. 14 and 16. [See Alfarabi, *Plato and Aristotle*, trans. Mahdi, para. 18, p. 23, and para. 21, p. 25.]

27. [As regards Farabi on the virtues, see] *Musterstaat*, p. 69 [*Perfect State*, trans. Walzer, para. 1, p. 276]. In the parallel text (*Kitab al-siyasat al-madaniyya*, p. 55) [*Medieval Political Philosophy*, ed. Lerner and Mahdi, p. 40], the actions which conduce to happiness are mentioned at the end of the enumeration.

28. [Ethics and politics are not separable,] that is, if one bases the interpretation of Farabi on his principal writings. At present, it suffices to note that even the titles, for example, of *Kitab tahsil al-sa'ada* ("The Attainment of Happiness") on the one hand, and of *Kitab al-tanbih'ala sabil al-sa'ada* ("Note Concerning the Path toward Happiness") on the other, indicate rather clearly that the first is most important; this judgment is confirmed by the analysis of the two writings themselves: the first is the introduction to a book on the philosophy of Plato and Aristotle, the second is the introduction to a grammatical work; and only the first is mentioned by Ibn al-Qifti as one of the most important writings of Farabi. Now the distinction between ethics and politics is found only in the second.

29. Compare the attempt, similar to Maimonides, to reconcile the Farabian point of view with that of Aristotle, which is found in the fragment of an encyclopedia of the sciences published by Gottheil (see n. 14 above); according to the unknown author who, moreover, cites Farabi's treatise on the perfect city as one of the classic books on politics, the order of the practical sciences would be the following: (1) politics;

point of view, is intent on preserving a certain independence of ethics as a *medicina mentis* [spiritual medicine];[30] this is why the books of the philosophers on ethics retain their value for him; but, as regards happiness, he too judges that it is the object only of politics properly speaking.

(2) According to Farabi, there are three classes of complete communities: the small, which is the city; the intermediate, which is the nation; the large, which is the union of many nations (or "the nations").[31] The difference between the complete (*kamila*) communities regarding their size does not imply a difference regarding their internal structure: the city may be as perfect (*fadila*), i.e., directed by an ideal leader [*chef*] toward happiness, as the nation[32] or the nations.[33] Yet there is at least a theoretical preference for the city: it is not by chance that Farabi entitled his most complete political treatise [*traité*] "the perfect city" and not "the perfect nation."[34] One might say that the perfect city is the ancient core, borrowed from Plato's *Republic*, that Farabi tries to guard and leave intact; however, he may be compelled by the theologico-political presuppositions of his time to enlarge the Platonic framework, to acknowledge the political units [*unités*] larger than the city: the nation or nations. It is equally then in following Farabi that Maimonides distinguishes between the governance of the city on the one hand and the

---

(2) ethics; (3) economics. [See Gottheil, op. cit. (n. 14 above): fol. 2a, l. 1–2b, l. 13; English translation, pp. 168–72.]

30. Cf. *Shemonah Perakim*, III. [See "Eight Chapters," in *Ethical Writings*, trans. Weiss and Butterworth, pp. 65–67. The phrase might also be translated as "medicine or healing of the mind." For a recent treatment of Maimonides' "spiritual medicine" (or moral psychology) as a separate science, consider David Bakan, Dan Merkur, and David S. Weiss, *Maimonides' Cure of Souls: Medieval Precursor of Psychoanalysis* (Albany: State University of New York Press, 2009). With regard to the phrase "*medicina mentis*," Strauss may perhaps have borrowed it from the title of a book by Ehrenfried Walter von Tschirnhaus, *Medicina Mentis* (1687, 1695). As the phrase was originally conceived, the "medicine of the mind" recommended and elaborated by Tschirnhaus was mathematical logic.]

31. *Musterstaat*, p. 53, 17–19. [See *Perfect State*, trans. Walzer, para. 2, pp. 228–31. See also] *Siyasat*, p. 39. [See *Medieval Political Philosophy*, ed. Lerner and Mahdi, p. 32.] Cf. *Kitab tahsil*, beginning, and pp. 21–23. [See *Plato and Aristotle*, trans. Mahdi, pp. 13, 28–30.]

32. Let us recall that Maimonides himself speaks of "perfect nations." [See also "Maimonides' Statement on Political Science," chap. 9 below. However, the passage to which Strauss referred, apparently if seen in light of the better Arabic original discovered only subsequent to Strauss's article (see n. 12 above), has led its most recent translator to render the passage quite differently, so as to make "perfect" modify not the "nation" (or "religious community"), but rather those "learned men" who legislate for it. The passage concerned occurs in chap. 14 of Maimonides, *Treatise on Logic*, which Charles Butterworth translates as follows: "The learned men of past communities, each according to his perfection, used to fashion regimes and laws by which their kings would govern the subjects." See "Logic," in *Ethical Writings*, ed. Weiss and Butterworth, pp. 158–61, and especially p. 161.]

33. *Musterstaat*, p. 54, 5–10. [See *Perfect State*, trans. Walzer, para. 3, pp. 230–31.] [See also] *Siyasat*, p. 50. [See *Medieval Political Philosophy*, ed. Lerner and Mahdi, pp. 36–37.]

34. Cf. also *Musterstaat*, p. 69, 17–19; this passage could be the direct source of the respective passage of Maimonides. [See *Perfect State*, trans. Walzer, para. 1, pp. 278–79.]

governance of the great nation or of the nations on the other,[35] a distinction he neglects later on in order to speak of a preference for the governance of the city.

(3) If it is political science that makes happiness known, and if there is no true happiness in this life, but only in the next,[36] in other words, if there is no true beatitude without the knowledge of the beings separated from matter,[37] of God and the angels, political science must be concerned with the "divine things." This is why the most important of Farabi's political books, *The Perfect City*[38] and *The Political Governments*, are at the same time metaphysical treatises. There is still another connection between the politics of Farabi and "divine things." Farabi teaches that the "first leader" [*"chef premier"*] of the perfect city must be a "prophet" and "*imam*."[39] "First leader," "*imam*," and "legislator" are identical terms;[40] the "first leader" is as such founder of a religion.[41] As a result, it is not possible to separate the political things from the

---

35. According to the *Thesaurus philosophicus linguae hebraicae et veteris et recentioris* of Jacob Klatzkin (Berlin: Eshkol, 1928–33) (s.v. *hanhagah*) *hanhagat ha-medinah* would correspond to internal politics, *hanhagat ha-'ummot* to external or world politics ("Weltpolitik") [i.e., "international politics"]. The origin of this misunderstanding seems to be the explication of the words in question given by Mendelssohn in his commentary on the *Millot*. Mendelssohn, a student of Christian Wolff and other theoreticians of modern natural right, translates *hanhagat ha-medinah* as "Polizei" ["police"]. Another error also caused by insufficient knowledge of the politics of Farabi is the translation of *medinah mequbbeẓet* by "Republik" instead of "Demokratie" (see op. cit., s.v. *medinah*). [The Arabic term of Farabi, *al-madina al-jama'iya*, was rendered by his Hebrew translator, Moses ibn Tibbon, quite literally as *medinah mequbbeẓet* in Hebrew; he also translates it as both *ha-medinah ha-mequbbeẓet* and *ha-medinah ha-qibbuẓit*. Muhsin Mahdi, *Alfarabi and the Foundations of Islamic Political Philosophy* (Chicago: University of Chicago Press, 2001), p. 131, restates Farabi's definition of democracy as follows: "(6) the regime of corporate association (democracy), the main purpose of which is being free to do what they wish." No single English word or phrase quite conveys the precise, literal sense of the original Arabic term or its translated Hebrew equivalent. Fauzi Najjar translates these same Arabic passages of Farabi in the *Political Regime*, as they are referred to by Strauss, as "free association in the democratic city and the city of the free," and "the democratic city." See *Medieval Political Philosophy*, ed. Lerner and Mahdi, p. 42, 50–53. My thanks to Professor Steven Harvey for his help with the Arabic terminology in the works of Farabi, and with how those original terms are rendered in the various Hebrew and English translations. See also, on related matters concerning Hebrew terminology (i.e., "political association"), Menachem Lorberbaum, *Politics and the Limits of Law: Secularizing the Political in Medieval Jewish Thought* (Stanford: Stanford University Press, 2001), pp. 28–29.]

36. *Ihsa al-ulum*, p. 64. [See "Enumeration of the Sciences," trans. Najjar, in *Medieval Political Philosophy*, ed. Lerner and Mahdi, p. 24; *Political Writings*, trans. Butterworth, p. 76.]

37. *Kitab tahsil*, pp. 2 and 16 [*Plato and Aristotle*, trans. Mahdi, para. 21, p. 25]; *tanbih*, p. 22.

38. This book [*The Perfect City* or *The Virtuous City*] is classified as a "political book" in the manuscripts of the British Museum and the Bodleian Library.

39. *Musterstaat*, p. 58, 18–59, 11 [*Perfect State*, trans. Walzer, paras. 10–11, pp. 244–47]; cf. ibid., p. 69, 15: "The first leader [i.e., "*premier chef*"] and how revelation is brought about" [*Perfect State*, trans. Walzer, para. 1, pp. 278–79].

40. *Kitab tahsil*, p. 43. [See *Plato and Aristotle*, trans. Mahdi, para. 58, p. 47.]

41. See *Musterstaat*, p. 70, 10, and the context. [See *Perfect State*, trans. Walzer, para. 2, pp. 280–81.]

divine things. By subordinating the religious sciences, jurisprudence (*fiqh*), and apologetics (*kalam*) to politics, Farabi drew this consequence.[42]

It is, then, Farabi's doctrine that Maimonides has in mind when he speaks, in the *Millot*, of politics. Now the politics of Farabi, for its part, is a modification of the politics of Plato: the "first leader" ["*chef premier*"] is, according to Farabi, not only *imam*, prophet, legislator, and king, he is also and above all a philosopher;[43] he must by nature have at his disposal all the qualities which characterize, according to Plato, the governors of the ideal city;[44] he is Plato's king-philosopher. As a result, the judgment passed by Maimonides on political science accords with Platonic politics, or at least with a Platonizing politics. And this judgment means: philosophical politics, which is the search for the ideal city governed by the philosophers, or for the ideal law, is now superfluous, because the Torah, given by a prophet (as intermediary) whose faculties surpass those of the greatest philosopher, leads men toward happiness in a manner infinitely more certain and perfect than the political regimes imagined by the philosophers.

But it is one thing to search for the ideal law when it is not yet known, quite another to understand the ideal law once it is given. It may well be that political science, while being superfluous for the former, is indispensable for the latter. Two things are certain before any subsequent examination of the texts. First, Maimonides' judgment that politics, and only politics, and especially Platonizing politics, is rendered superfluous by the Torah implies: the Torah is first and foremost a political fact, a political order, a law; it is the ideal law, the perfect *nomos*, of which all other laws are more or less imitations.[45] And second: being a philosopher, Maimonides must pose for himself

---

42. This is the title of the last chapter of his encyclopedia of the sciences (*Ihsa al-ulum*): "On political science and the science of the *fiqh* and the science of the *kalam*." ["On Political Science, Jurisprudence, and Dialectical Theology," trans. Najjar, in *Medieval Political Philosophy*, ed. Lerner and Mahdi, p. 24; "On Political Science, the Science of Jurisprudence, and the Science of Dialectical Theology," trans. Butterworth, in *Political Writings*, p. 76.]

43. *Musterstaat*, p. 58, 18–59, 5 [*Perfect State*, trans. Walzer, paras. 10–11, pp. 244–47]; *Kitab tahsil*, pp. 42–43 [*Plato and Aristotle*, trans. Mahdi, para. 57, pp. 46–47].

44. *Musterstaat*, p. 59, 11ff. [*Perfect State*, trans. Walzer, para. 12, pp. 246–47]; *Kitab tahsil*, pp. 44–45 [*Plato and Aristotle*, trans. Mahdi, para. 60, p. 48]. This passage is found almost word for word in the text of the *Rasa'il Ikhwan al-Safa* (Cairo, 1928), vol. IV, pp. 182–83. [Cf. also *Rasa'il Ikhwan al-Safa* [*Epistles or Encyclopedia of the Brethren of Purity*], ed. Butrus Bustani (Beirut, 1957), vol. IV, p. 129f.]

45. This is what Falaquera says in his *Sefer ha-Mevakesh* [Book of the Seeker], ed. Traklin (Warsaw, 1924), p. 90. ["With regard to the laws (*nimus*) of the rest of the nations, these their wise men and their rulers establish according to their interests, and according to the era, and (according to) their opinions; they strengthen them by making them resemble the laws of our Torah, and bring the practices which they enjoin nearer to the practices which the Torah enjoins."] Cf. Maimonides, *Responsa* [*Teshuvot ha-*

the question of knowing what the *raison d'être* of the Torah is, what its reasonable end and its natural conditions are. He needs, then, a philosophical discipline the subject of which will be the Torah, the divine law as such; as the Torah is a law and hence a political fact, this discipline must be political science. And as the political science known to and judged by Maimonides to merit some attention is a Platonizing politics, it will be, in the final analysis, the doctrines of the *Republic* and the *Laws* that will determine the manner in which Maimonides understands the Torah.

II

Before interpreting any passage of *The Guide of the Perplexed*, one must remember that this work is an esoteric book. Maimonides has concealed his thought, so his book must be read with particular attention; its subtle allusions are perhaps more important than the doctrines developed in an explicit manner.

The divine law occupies the last place among the main subjects discussed in *The Guide of the Perplexed*. Maimonides takes up the subject only after having finished the discussion of the purely speculative themes—whose conclusion is clearly marked by the interpretation of the *ma'aseh merkavah* [account of the chariot], which sums up, to a certain extent, all of metaphysics[46]—and of the problems of providence and of evil that, being the conditions closest to practical problems, mark the passage from the speculative to the practical domain. The part of the *Guide* treating of the divine law is therefore (if one abstracts from the last chapters—3.51–54—which contain more of a conclusion to the work in general than the discussion of a new subject) the only practical part of the work: there is no treatise on morality included in it. It will perhaps be said that it is not possible to draw any conclusion from this, the *Guide* being neither a "system of philosophy" nor even a "summa

---

Rambam] ed. A. Freimann (Jerusalem, 1934), p. 337 [no. 369, letter to Ovadia the Proselyte; see also *Igrot ha-Rambam*, ed. Shailat, no. 12, pp. 231–41, especially p. 240: "all the religions steal from their religion (i.e., the religion of the Jews); one adds something here, another removes something there, one alters something here, another lies about something there and slanderously ascribes to YHVH speeches which are not true, one ruins the fundamental principles, another attributes perverse things [to God]"). See also "The Response of Maimonides to Joseph ibn Gabir," in *Letters*, trans. Stitskin, pp. 86–94.]

46. Cf. *Guide* 3.7 beginning. Compare also the analogous interpretation of the *ma'aseh bereshit* [account of the beginning] in *Guide* 2.30, which marks the conclusion of the discourses on physics. [See *Guide*, trans. Pines, 3.7, p. 428; 2.30, pp. 348–59. Strauss refrains in this context from clarifying just why he says that *ma'aseh merkavah* "sums up" only "*to a certain extent*, all of metaphysics."]

theologica," but simply a "guide of the perplexed," i.e., it does not contain a complete exposition of Maimonides' opinions. But precisely because Maimonides' philosophical work is a "guide of the perplexed," because it treats among the philosophical questions only those that have a decisive importance for the philosophizing Jew, the fact that it does not contain a treatise on morality, but, in its place, an analysis of divine law, merits noting: morality, as distinguished from the divine law, is not of capital importance for Maimonides.[47]

The discussion of the divine law (*Guide* 2.25–50) contains nothing other than, first, the proof that a divine law insofar as it is a divine law must be reasonable, having a manifest utility, and, second, the search for the reasonable ends of the given divine law, that of Moses. The fundamental questions—why is a (divine) law necessary?, and how is a divine law distinguished from a human law?—are almost not taken up. The reason for this is that they have been treated sufficiently in a preceding part of the *Guide*, in the theory of prophecy (*Guide* 2.32ff.). The foundations of the theory of the law are hence not found anywhere else than in the doctrine of prophecy. It could not be otherwise: "It is known that the belief in prophecy precedes the belief in the law; for if there is no prophet, there is no law."[48]

It is difficult to understand the exact meaning of Maimonides' prophetology if one does not know first the philosophical place of this doctrine. By treating prophecy before formally finishing the metaphysical discussions by the interpretation of the *ma'aseh merkavah*, Maimonides seems to indicate that prophetology is connected with metaphysics, and this conclusion seems to be confirmed by the fact that Avicenna expressly attributes the theory of prophecy to metaphysics. However, Avicenna does not count prophetology as an integral part of metaphysics; according to him, the doctrine of prophecy as well as that of life after death are but "branches" of metaphysics.[49] Further, he clearly declares that it is politics which explains the necessity of prophecy and the law, as well as the difference between true prophets and pseudo-prophets.[50] But, to understand Maimonides, Farabi's view is much more im-

---

47. As regards the similar attitude of Farabi concerning morality, cf. above [sixth paragraph of section I].

48. *Guide* 3.45 (p. 98b). [See *Guide*, trans. Pines, 3.45, pp. 576–77.]

49. See the Latin translation of his "Division of the Sciences," in *Avicennae compendium de anima* etc., *ab Andrea Alpago . . . ex arabico in latinum versa* (Venice, 1546): pp. 143b–44b.

50. Loc. cit., pp. 138b–39a; cf. *Philosophie und Gesetz*, pp. 110–14. [See *Philosophy and Law*, pp. 120–25; see also chap. 4 above, first through ninth paragraphs of section IV.]

portant than Avicenna's. Now Farabi mentions belief in revelation only after the belief in the "first leader" ["*chef premier*"].[51] Let us add that Averroes himself sees prophecy as an essentially political fact: the action proper to the prophet is legislation.[52] There is then a perfect agreement among the most important *falasifa* regarding the essentially political character of prophecy and, as a result, regarding the connection between prophetology and political science. Maimonides did not have the slightest reason to separate himself here from the *falasifa*, of whose principal theses concerning prophecy he approves. There is a direct proof of this: in the summary of the philosophical principles found at the beginning of the *Mishneh Torah*, Maimonides speaks of prophecy and of the law only after having formally finished the summary of metaphysics (*ma'aseh merkavah*) and physics (*ma'aseh bereshit*).[53] In so doing, he expresses the opinion that prophecy is not a subject of speculative philosophy, but of practical or political philosophy. In the *Guide*, it is true, this opinion does not reveal itself by the composition; in this work, prophetology is treated before [the discussion of] metaphysics is formally finished; but this alteration of the usual order is, as will be seen, the necessary order, easily explained by the end, peculiar to the prophetology of the *Guide*, of establishing the foundation of the philosophical exegesis of Scripture.[54]

---

51. *Musterstaat*, p. 69, 15. [See *Perfect State*, trans. Walzer, para. 1, pp. 278–79.]

52. See [first paragraph of the present chapter above].

53. The discussion of prophecy and law is found in "Hilkhot Yesodei ha-Torah" VII–X; cf. the conclusion of the metaphysics and physics, loc. cit., II, 11 and IV, 10–13. [See "Laws of the Basic Principles of the Torah," trans. Hyamson, pp. 42a–46a; 36b; 39b–40a; cf. for chapters and paragraphs II, 11, and IV, 10–13 especially, "Book of Knowledge," trans. Lerner, in *Maimonides' Empire of Light*, pp. 146, 152–53.]

54. This is why Maimonides attaches the greatest importance to the final chapter of the prophetology (*Guide* 2.48 beginning). [See *Guide*, trans. Pines, 2.48, pp. 409–10.] In order to understand the composition of the *Guide*, one must take note of the order of the dogmas presented in the *Commentary on the Mishnah* (Sanhedrin X), which is found, though somewhat modified, in "Hilkhot Teshuvah" III, 6–8. [See: Maimonides, "Hilkhot Teshuvah" ("Laws of Repentance"), trans. Hyamson, pp. 84b–85a; *Commentary on the Mishnah (Sanhedrin)*, trans. Rosner, pp. 151–58; *Commentary on the Mishnah*, Sanhedrin X, in *Reader*, ed. Twersky, pp. 401–23.] According to this order, the dogmas concerning the existence, unity, and incorporeality of God and the eternity of God alone, occupy the first place; immediately following are the dogmas concerning prophecy in general and the prophecy of Moses and the Torah in particular; and only after this the dogmas concerning providence and eschatology. The source of this order seems to be the Mu'tazilite doctrine of the *usul* [roots], which determines the composition of the *Emunot ve-Deot* of Saadia Gaon. [See Saadia ben Joseph ha-Gaon, *Beliefs and Opinions*, trans. Samuel Rosenblatt (New Haven: Yale University Press, 1948); *Doctrines and Beliefs*, trans. Alexander Altmann, in *Three Jewish Philosophers* (New York: Atheneum, 1969).] (Cf. the interesting remark of Shlomo Pines in *Orientalistische Literaturzeitung*, 1935, col. 623.) The order in question can be found again in the *Guide* inasmuch as the first class of dogmas is treated in the greatest portion [*la plus grande partie*] of 1.1–2.31, the second in 2.32–48, and the third in 3.8–24. Maimonides departs from this order for different reasons, among others

Maimonides takes up the theory of prophecy by discussing the different opinions concerning it, and by establishing, against the vulgar opinion, the principle that prophecy is linked to certain natural conditions, especially to the perfection, acquired by studies, of the intellect (*Guide* 2.32–34). He then explains that there is an essential difference between the prophecy of Moses and that of the other prophets: the whole doctrine of prophecy, developed in the following chapters, does not address the prophecy of Moses (2.35). It is only after these preliminary clarifications that Maimonides defines prophecy; "the essence of prophecy," he says, "is an overflow [*émanation*] from God, which pours out [*se répand*] of the Active Intellect (as intermediary), first to the rational faculty and then to the imaginative faculty" (2.36). To understand better this far too "scholastic" definition, one must pose the following question: what does this overflow [*émanation*] produce if it pours out [*se répand*], not to the two faculties together, but only to one of them? Here is Maimonides' answer: "If this intellectual overflow [*émanation*][55] pours out [*se répand*] only to the rational faculty, without having poured out [*se répande*] to the imaginative faculty ... it is this (that constitutes) the class of knowers, of the men of speculation.... If the overflow [*émanation*] pours out [*se répand*] only to the imaginative faculty ... the class thereby constituted are the governors of the cities and the legislators and the diviners and the augurs and those who have veridical dreams, and similarly those who effect miracles by extraordinary artifices and the occult arts without being knowers..." (2.37).[56] Now the prophecy that results from the overflow [*émanation*] pouring out

---

when adopting, to a certain extent, the following order drawn up by Farabi of the "opinions of the people of the perfect city": (1) the first cause and its attributes (*Guide* 1.1–70); (2) angels and celestial bodies (2.3–9); (3) physical bodies, justice and wisdom as seen in their government (2.10–12); (4) the human soul and the way in which the active intellect inspires it, the first leader [*le premier chef*] and revelation (2.37–40). This order is followed more strictly in "Hilkhot Yesodei ha-Torah." [See n. 53 above for full reference, and especially chaps. I–IV, VII–X: Hyamson, pp. 34a–40a, and 42a–46a; cf. Lerner, pp. 141–53.]

55. One must note that Maimonides uses as synonyms "divine overflow" ["*émanation divine*"] and "intellectual overflow" ["*émanation intellectuelle*"]. In so doing, he acknowledges that prophecy is a natural phenomenon. Compare *Guide* 2.48 beginning, a passage whose singular importance is noted by Maimonides himself. ["After this introduction, listen to what I shall explain in this chapter and consider it with particular attention, with an attention exceeding the attention with which you consider the other chapters of this Treatise." *Guide*, trans. Pines, 2.48, p. 410.]

56. Regarding this passage, Munk (*Le Guide des égarés* II, p. 373) makes the following remark:

It may seem strange that the author places legislators beside diviners and counts them among those whose imagination rules over reason. But one sees later (chapter XL, pp. 310–11) that the author does not mean to speak here of purely political legislation which, as he himself says, is the work of reflection; he has only had in mind those of the ancient legislators who believed themselves inspired, claimed to be prophets, and presented their laws as dictated by a divinity....

[*se répandant*] to the two faculties together must unite in itself the effects produced if the overflow [*émanation*] pours out [*se répand*] to only one of them. As a result, the prophet is a philosopher and statesman (governor or legislator), and at the same time a diviner and magician. As for the magical faculty of the prophet—a theme dear to Avicenna—Maimonides has little interest in it. What characterizes the prophet, according to him, is the union (which is at the same time a considerable augmentation) of the faculties of the philosopher, statesman, and diviner: the prophet is a philosopher-statesman-diviner.

That this is Maimonides' opinion is proved, moreover, by the fact that he adds to the two chapters treating the essence and the conditions of prophecy a third (2.38), in which he explains that the prophet necessarily possesses the following three faculties: the faculty of courage, the faculty of divination, and the immediate knowledge of speculative truths without knowledge of the premises. Now this last, while being an essential expansion of philosophical knowledge, nonetheless remains a speculative faculty: we have then only to show that the faculty of courage, which characterizes the prophet, represents or indicates his political function. Maimonides would not speak of extraordinary courage as an essential condition of prophecy if he did not believe that the prophet as such is exposed to the gravest dangers. Now if the prophet received his inspiration, whether of a speculative order (concerning God and the angels) or a practical order (concerning future matters), only for his own perfection, he would not be exposed to dangers as a prophet. It is then of the essence of the prophet that he receive inspiration, that he "ascend" precisely so as to "descend," in order to guide and instruct men;[57] for, as a result of this social function that necessarily displeases unjust men, he is in perpetual danger.[58] Although this danger is inevitable even if the prophet restricts himself to instructing men, it is much more threatening when the prophet opposes,

---

This remark is not right. In the passage mentioned by Munk, in *Guide* 2.40, Maimonides expressly says that a purely political law, i.e., a law which has no other end than the ordering of social relations and the prevention of injustice and violence, is necessarily the work of a man who has no other perfection than that of the imagination. On the other hand, when speaking of legislation which is the work of reflection, Maimonides does not only have in mind purely political laws, but also and above all laws whose end is the intellectual perfection of men, projected by philosophers. Let us add that Maimonides uses the word "imagination" in a very broad sense: by attributing the purely political laws to the imagination, he follows Farabi's opinion according to which these laws are the work of a "sensual aptitude." (See [in the present essay above, ninth and tenth paragraphs of section II; see also *Guide*, trans. Pines, 2.40, pp. 383–84].)

57. *Guide* 1.15. [See *Guide*, trans. Pines, 1.15, p. 41.]

58. Maimonides immediately passes from the exposition of the social function of the prophet (2.37, last part) to that of prophetic courage (2.38, beginning). [See *Guide*, trans. Pines, 2.37–38, pp. 375–77.]

as a guide of just men, the injustices of tyrants or the multitude. This is why the first example of prophetic courage cited by Maimonides is the example of Moses, who, "a lone man, presented himself courageously, with his staff, before a great king *to deliver a nation from the slavery* imposed by him."[59]

59. *Guide* 2.38 (p. 82b). Cf. also 2.45 (pp. 93a–94a). [See *Guide*, trans. Pines, 2.38, pp. 376–77; 2.45, pp. 395–97.] The Arabic word Maimonides uses to designate the courage (*iqdam*) of the prophets recalls the passage of the *Perfect City* (p. 60, 9–11) [*Perfect State*, trans. Walzer, para. 12, pp. 248–49], where Farabi, in enumerating the conditions of the "first leader" ["*premier chef*"], also speaks of this faculty. Let us remark in passing that this enumeration only reproduces the enumeration of the conditions of the philosopher-kings in Plato's *Republic*. Moreover, Farabi, in a parallel (*Kitab tahsil*, p. 44) [*Plato and Aristotle*, trans. Mahdi, para. 60, p. 48], cites Plato expressly. Averroes himself speaks of the courage of the prophets when paraphrasing Plato's discourse on the courage of the guardians; "ideoque neque Prophetis, neque magistratibus formido, aut metus conveniens." *Averrois Paraphrasis in Platonis Rempublica* Tr. I (*Opera Aristotelis*, Venetiis, 1550, Vol. III, fol. 176b, col. I, 1.64–65). [Cf. Averroes, *On Plato's "Republic*," trans. Lerner, p. 23: "Hence prophets and chiefs ought not to be characterized as being fearful."] The *falasifa* attribute greater value to courage than did Plato and Aristotle (cf. above all *Laws* [bk. I], 630e–631c, a passage from which one must begin in order to understand the tendency which determines the composition of the *Nicomachean Ethics*). ["Now the good things are twofold, some human, some divine. The former depends on the divine goods, and if a city receives the greater it will also acquire the lesser. If not, it will lack both. Health leads the lesser goods; in the second place is beauty; third is strength, both in running and in all the other motions of the body; and fourth is wealth—not blind but sharp-sighted, insofar as it follows prudence. Prudence, in turn, is first and leader among divine goods. Second after intelligence comes a moderate disposition of the soul, and from these two mixed with courage comes justice in the third place. Courage is fourth. All of these last goods are by nature placed prior in rank to the first, and this is the rank they should be placed in by the legislator." Plato, *The Laws*, trans. Thomas L. Pangle (New York: Basic Books, 1980), 631b–d, p. 10.] The increased prestige accorded courage is explained by two characteristics of Islam: (1) the missionary tendency which is inherent in a universal religion; and (2) the polemic against "superstitious" menaces which are inherent in a universal religion that is thereby popular.

(1) As the *falasifa* were Muslims, they recognized the commandment of the holy war, understood by them as a civilizing war, or rather, they were guided by the idea of a civilization realizable only through civilizing wars: this idea is absent from the thought of Plato. Averroes, in his paraphrase of the *Republic*, speaks of this in the following manner: "(Dicimus) Platonem, cum de virtutibus tractare instituit, de fortitudine primo initium sumpsisse, enimvero, ratio ipsa, modusque sciendi, quibus eam perfectissimam cives adipiscantur, et servent, ea est, ut quod primum sil operum huius virtutis propositum in civitate observemus. Dicendum ergo est duplicem omnino viam esse, ex qua virtutes in animis civium reperiantur. Alteram, si illorum animis, seu Rhetoricis, seu Poeticis orationibus altius opiniones imprimentur . . . hoc autem disciplinae genus in eos ut plurimum convenit cives, qui a teneris similibus rebus assueverint, atque ex his duabus disciplinae viis prior illa naturae magis consentanea est. Posterior etenim ea est, cuius usus in adversarios potissimum, ac odiosos nobis est, eosque qui virtutibus illis debitis adhaerere recusant, quam quidem viam quis nuncuparit . . . castigatricem. Neminem autem latere debet huic posteriori viae, inter cives huius Reip. praestantissimae locum non esse. . . . Atqui nonnullae aliae gentes improbae adeo existunt, minimeque virtuti parentes, quarumque mores inhumani sunt, ut nulla alia ratione institui possint, nisi cum illis confligatur, ut virtutibus obsequantur. . . . Similisque ratio est in legibus, quae ab humanis legibus non discrepant. Quemadmodum nostra haec lex divina, cum via ipsa, quae ad Deum gloriosum ducit, sit duplex: altera quidem, quae sermone, atque oratione nititur: altera, quae armis. Sed cum haec particularis ars (i.e., bellica) non nisi morali via tuto perficiatur . . . , haec certe ipsa virtus fortitudo est . . . estque quod Aristoteles sensit de praestantissimae Reipub. bellis, ut Alpharabius memorat: *quod tamen a Platone hoc in libro dictum videtur non in eum sensum, ut haec ars ad eum finem adinventa sit, verum ob necessitatem* . . . quae sane sententia probabilis est, si hominum genus quoddam daretur, quod proclive ad humanas perfectiones, contemplativas praesertim, esset" (loc. cit., fol. 175a, col. 2, l. 36–175b, col. 1, l. 50). [Averroes, *On Plato's "Republic*," trans. Lerner, pp. 10–13: "And we say that the virtue of cour-

The triad philosopher-statesman-diviner immediately calls to mind the politics of Farabi, according to which the "first leader" ["*premier chef*"] of the perfect city must be a philosopher and diviner ("prophet"). It remains to be seen whether Maimonides also regards the founding of the perfect city as the *raison d'être* of revelation. It has been thought that the principal end

---

age is that with which Plato began to introduce the discussion of the bringing-about of these virtues. As we have said, the way of understanding how it is attained by the citizens and preserved with respect to them in the most perfect manner [requires that] we consider what is primarily intended by the actions of this virtue in the city. We say that there are two ways by which the virtues in general are brought about in the souls of political human beings. One of them is to establish the opinions in their souls through rhetorical and poetical arguments. . . . This first way of teaching will mostly be possible only for whichever of the citizens grew up with these things from the time of his youth. Of the two ways of teaching, this one is natural. The second way [of teaching], however, is the way applied to enemies, foes, and him whose way it is not to be aroused to the virtues that are desired of him. This is the way of . . . chastisement by blows. It is evident that this way . . . will not be applied to the members of the virtuous city. . . . As for the other nations, which are not good and whose conduct is not human, why there is no way of teaching them other than this way, namely, to coerce them through war to adopt the virtues. This is the way in which matters are arranged in those Laws belonging to this our divine Law that proceed like the human Laws, for the ways in it that lead to God (may He be exalted!) are two: one of them is through speech, and the other through war. Since this art of war is not completed other than by a moral virtue by which it draws near to what is appropriate and in the appropriate time and measure—i.e., the virtue of courage . . . This is what Aristotle asserts about the wars of the virtuous city, according to what Abu Nasr [al-Farabi] reports. *But from what we find concerning this in this book of Plato's, why according to him this part [of the soul, i.e., courage] is not prepared for this end [i.e., war] but rather is on account of necessity . . . This opinion would only be correct if there were but one class of human beings disposed to the human perfections and especially to the theoretical ones."*] Compare Farabi, *Kitab tahsil*, pp. 31–32. [See Alfarabi, *Plato and Aristotle*, trans. Mahdi, pp. 36–37.]

(2) When paraphrasing the passage of the *Republic* where Plato demands that the philosophers be brave (486b), Averroes says: "Ad haec Fortitudo quoque in hoc octavum obtinebit locum, nam sine fortitudine rationes illas debiles, non demonstrativas, in quibus eum (i.e., philosophum) educari contigit, nec contemneret, neque refelleret, quod quidem magis etiam perspicuum est in his, qui in nostris civitatibus educati sunt." (Loc. cit., fol. 182b, col. 1, ll. 40–45) [Averroes, *On Plato's "Republic*,*"* trans. Lerner, p. 73: "The eighth [condition is] that he be courageous. For one who has no courage will be unable to despise the non-demonstrative arguments on which he [i.e., the philosopher] has grown up, and especially if he has grown up in these cities"]. These phrases imply a certain critique of Plato's point of view, as one sees by comparing them with the passage of Plato paraphrased by Averroes. This critique is carried out in an explicit manner in the paraphrase of the tenth book of the *Republic*: "decimus Platonis liber huic civili, quam tractamus disciplinae, nihil admodum (confert) . . . (Plato) suasorias inductiones, ac rationes locis quibusdam depromptas subdidit, quibus animam immortalem esse probaret. Et infert deinde fabulam . . . Enimvero iam nos antea saepius prae diximus, istiusmodi fabulas non esse alicuius momenti. . . . Etenim Platonem videri eam fictam, fabulosamque rationem ingerere, quae tamen nihil ad humanam probitatem necessaria sit. . . . Quippe quod homines non paucos cognoscimus, qui suis ipsi legibus, atque moribus freti expertes plane, et rudes istarum fictionum, nihil virtute, nihil vitae instituto professoribus talium historiarum concesserint" (fol. 191b, col. 2, ll. 11–39). [Averroes, *On Plato's Republic*, trans. Lerner, pp. 148–49: "What the tenth treatise encompasses is not necessary for this science. . . . Then he mentions thereafter a rhetorical or dialectical argument by which he explains that the soul does not die. Then there is a story. . . . We have made it known more than once that these stories are of no account. . . . It is this that has brought us to an untruth such as this. It is not something necessary to a man's becoming virtuous. . . . For we see here many people who, in adhering to their *nomoi* and their Laws, albeit devoid of these stories, are not less well off than those possessing [these] stories."]

As regards another difference in principle between the *falasifa* and Plato, see n. 81 below. [See also Averroes, *Jihad in Medieval and Modern Islam: The Chapter on Jihad from Averroes' Legal Handbook*, "*Bidayat al-Mudjtahid*," trans. and ed. Rudolph Peters (Leiden: E. J. Brill, 1977).]

of revelation according to him was the proclamation of the most important truths, above all those not accessible to human reason. But if this is the exact meaning of Maimonides' opinion, why does he say that the divine law is limited to teaching these truths in a summary and enigmatic manner, while in political matters, "every effort has been made to render precise what concerns the governance of the cities in all its details"?[60] And, above all, why do these truths form a part—certainly the most noble part, but all the same [only] a part—of a *law*? Not only the proclamation and the propagation of the most important truths but also and above all the founding of a perfect nation is "the end of the efforts of the patriarchs and Moses during their whole lives."[61] The founding of a perfect nation, and consequently the proclamation of a perfect law which must serve as a constitution to the perfect nation, is according to Maimonides the *raison d'être* of prophecy. The proof of this is the fact that even seems to render doubtful all of our argumentation: the distinction between the prophecy of Moses and that of the other prophets. Indeed, if the prophetology of Maimonides has as its object only the latter [i.e., this being to distinguish between the prophecy of Moses and that of the other prophets], as he expressly intends, what reason has one to suppose that precisely the political character of "ordinary" prophecy is in any way found in the prophecy of Moses? To this question, which any attentive reader of *Guide* 2.35–38 would not be able to avoid, Maimonides responds in the following chapter (2.39). He says: "After having spoken of the essence of prophecy, made known its true state, and shown that the prophecy of Moses our master is distinguished from the prophecy of the other (prophets), we will say that it is this (prophetic) perception [*perception*] (of Moses) alone which has had the necessary consequence of calling us to the law." The rest of the chapter in question may be summarized by saying that the prophets prior to Moses prepared, and those who followed him protected or confirmed, the divine legislation accomplished by Moses (as intermediary),[62] which is

60. *Guide* 3.27–28. Cf. 1.33 (p. 37a); "Hilkhot Yesodei ha-Torah" IV, 13. [See *Guide*, trans. Pines, 3.27–28, pp. 510–14; 1.33, pp. 71–72; "Laws of the Basic Principles of the Torah," trans. Hyamson, pp. 39b–40a; "Book of Knowledge," trans. Lerner, pp. 152–53.] See also [Shem Tov ben Joseph ibn] Falaquera, *Sefer ha-ma'alot* [chap. 2], ed. Ludwig Venetianer (Berlin, 1894; reprint, Jerusalem, 1970/5730): p. 48, 7–9 ["in order to become perfect in the intellectual virtues, whose general principles are mentioned in our holy Law and whose details are explained in the books of the wise (*be-sifrei ha-ḥakhamot*) composed according to the way of demonstration (*al derekh ha-mofeit*), and in order to become perfect in the ethical virtues (*be-ma'alot ha-yeẓiriot*) whose general principles and whose details are explained in our holy Law . . ."].
61. *Guide* 3.51 (p. 127a). [See *Guide*, trans. Pines, 3.51, p. 624.]
62. Cf. also "Hilkhot Yesodei ha-Torah" IX, 2. [See "Laws of the Basic Principles of the Torah," trans. Hyamson, p. 44b.]

the most perfect legislation there is. Moses, chief [*chef*] of the prophets, is hence not less but more a statesman than the other prophets: he alone is the founder of the perfect political community. This is the reason why Maimonides affirms so clearly and repeatedly that the prophecy of Moses is superior to that of the other prophets, even to that of the patriarchs. This affirmation is not the repetition of something commonplace: it betrays a specific tendency. The passage of the *Mishneh Torah* that treats of the difference between the prophecy of Moses and that of the other prophets is based on a similar passage of the *Mishnat R. Eliezer*.[63] Now in this source of Maimonides, it is affirmed in an immediately preceding passage that the prophecy of the patriarchs is superior to that of Moses and the other prophets. And from this passage Maimonides has borrowed nothing. On the contrary, his prophetology implies a critique of the principle of the point of view that dominates the prophetology of the *Mishnat R. Eliezer*: he affirms expressly that the prophecy of Moses is superior to that of the patriarchs.[64] As regards the efficient cause of the superiority of the prophecy of Moses over that of the patriarchs, he expresses himself only by allusions; but he shows without any reserve the "consequence" of this superiority, or rather its final cause: only the prophecy of Moses is legislative.

This means that only Moses is the philosopher-legislator in Plato's sense or the "first leader" ["*premier chef*"][65] in Farabi's sense. But Maimonides does not say this expressly:[66] he limits himself to indicating the signs which suffice for "the intelligent one who will understand," for an attentive and duly

---

63. Cf. the remarks of M[oritz M.] Guttmann, *Monatsschrift für Geschichte und Wissenschaft des Judentums* (1935): pp. 150–51.

64. Cf. above all the contrary interpretation of Exodus 6:3 in Maimonides' source (*Mishnat R. Eliezer*, ed. H. G. Enelow [New York: Bloch, 1933; reprint, Jerusalem: Makor, 1970], p. 112, 20–23) ["The patriarchs had no need of having the Tetragrammaton explained to them, but the other prophets had to have the Tetragrammaton explained to them, because the people of their generation had need of it. The proof for this is in that which happened to Moses our master, to whom it was spoken, 'God said to Moses, "I am that which I am,"' but about the Holy Name spoken to him He also said, 'I appeared to Abraham, etc., but My name YHVH I did not make known to them'"], and in Maimonides himself: *Guide* 2.35 (p. 77a). [See *Guide*, trans. Pines, 2.35, p. 367.]

65. One finds the expression "first chief" ["*premier chef*"] (*al-ra'is al-awwal*) used figuratively in the *Guide* 1.72 (p. 103a), and the expression "chief of the law" (*ra'is al-shari'a*) twice in 2.40 (p. 86b). [See *Guide*, trans. Pines, 1.72, p. 191, "first principal part"; 2.40 (p. 383), "the whole purpose of the chief thereof," and "in accordance with the opinion of that chief."]

66. Cf., however, with the definition of "*imam*" in Farabi (*Kitab tahsil*, p. 43 [*Plato and Aristotle*, trans. Mahdi, pp. 46–47]), the following words of Maimonides concerning Moses: *liana harakatuhu kulha wa kalamatuhu biha yaqtadi wabiha yatma' 'al-wusul lisa'adah 'al-dunya wal-akhra* "... because they would [imitate] his [Moses'] every movement and speech and would wish thereby to attain happiness in this world and the other (world)." *Shemoneh Perakim*, ed. Wolff (Leiden: Brill, 1903), p. 15. [See "Eight Chapters," in *Ethical Writings*, ed. Weiss and Butterworth, chap. IV, p. 74.]

instructed reader; and let us never forget that Maimonides would not have considered sufficiently instructed to understand the *Guide* anyone who did not know Farabi, and especially his treatise [*traité*] on political governments. He had reasons, not only apologetic, but also and above all philosophic, to be reserved when speaking of the prophecy of Moses, i.e., of the legislative prophecy: he neither wished, nor was able, nor had any need, to lift the veil which conceals the origins of the Torah, the foundation of the perfect nation. Whether the revelation of the Torah is a miracle or a natural fact, whether the Torah came from heaven or not—as soon as it is given, it is "not in heaven" but "very nigh unto thee, in your mouth and in your heart, that thou mayest do it" [Deuteronomy 30:12, 14]. Not the mystery of its origin, the search for which leads either to theosophy or to "Epicureanism," but its end, the comprehension of which guarantees obedience to the Torah, is accessible to human reason. Guided by this conception, Maimonides, after having explained that the prophecy of Moses, qua legislative prophecy, is distinguished from that of all the other prophets, takes up in the following chapter (2.40) the fundamental question concerning the end, the reason of the law.

Why is the law—the law in general, and the divine law in particular—necessary? Man is naturally a political being, and he can live only when united with other men.[67] But man is at the same time much less naturally capable of political life than any other animal; the differences between the individuals of the human species being much greater than those between the individuals of other species, one does not see how a community of men would be possible. Farabi had responded to this question by showing that it is precisely as a result of the natural inequality among men that political life becomes possible: inequality is only the reverse side of what is, properly speaking, a graduated order.[68] Maimonides follows a somewhat different path. From the extraordinary variation between human individuals, he draws the consequence that men who are so unequal, so different from one another, can live together only if they have a guide who corrects the vicious extremes, either by supplying what is lacking or by moderating what is in excess. This guide prescribes the actions and morals [*moeurs*] all must perpetually practice, in accord with the same rule; he establishes, in opposition to the natural variety of

---

67. *Guide* 1.72 (p. 103a). [See *Guide*, trans. Pines, 1.72, pp. 190–91.]
68. *Kitab al-siyasat*, pp. 45–48. [No complete English translation of Alfarabi, *The Political Regime*, is yet available; the sections rendered as "The Political Regime," trans. Najjar, in *Medieval Political Philosophy*, ed. Lerner and Mahdi, do not comprise these pages. The omitted section of pp. 45–48 would have been put in the break marked on p. 35.]

vicious extremes, the conventional accord [*harmonie*] of a reasonable mean [or equibalance] [*milieu*]; he establishes an "equal" law, as equally removed from excess as from deficiency.[69] The task of the legislator, then, is to establish accord [*harmonie*] between men of opposed dispositions by reducing the extremes to a just and identical mean [or equibalance] [*milieu*] by means of a single and identical law, which will never be changed. Of these opposed dispositions, Maimonides cites as an example the opposition between hardness and softness: "[For you may find among us two individuals who seem, with regard to every moral habit, to belong to two different species.] Thus you may find in an individual cruelty that reaches a point at which he kills the youngest of his sons in his great anger, whereas another individual is full of pity at the killing of a bug or any other insect, his soul being too tender for this."[70] Although this is but an example, it merits some attention as being the only one adduced by Maimonides. Now, it is precisely the opposition between hardness or ferocity on the one hand, and tameness [*mollesse*] or softness on the other, that is of decisive importance in the politics of Plato: it is the end of the true legislator to make a "fabric" out of the opposed dispositions of the naturally brave man and the naturally moderate [*modéré*] man, dispositions that would degenerate into ferocity or hardness and tameness [*mollesse*] or cowardice, if they were not disciplined. The city, then, is in need of a guardian [*surveillant*] who forges a harmonious alliance out of these two disharmonious dispositions:[71] this end may be achieved either in a city governed by philosophers, or in a city governed by reasonable laws; in the latter

---

69. *Guide* 2.40 (p. 85a-b), and 2.39 (p. 84b). [See *Guide*, trans. Pines, 2.40, pp. 381–82; and 2.39, p. 380. The Maimonidean term translated as "morals" in Strauss's essay ("*moeurs*" of the French original, following Munk) is rendered by Pines as "moral habits" (p. 382).]

70. *Guide* 2.40 (p. 85b). [See *Guide*, trans. Pines, 2.40, p. 282. Strauss's original essay conveyed the sentence of Maimonides as it appeared in Munk's French translation (Deuxième Partie, Chapitre XL, p. 307); the translator and editor have decided to substitute for it Pines's better English translation. However, to translate the French version of Munk for those readers who may want to know precisely how the sentence is presented in Strauss's original essay: "the hardness of an individual who will go so far as to cut the throat of his young son on account of the violence of his anger, while another feels pity for the violent death of a gnat or a reptile, having a soul too tender for that." In our version, the first Maimonidean sentence is put in square brackets not because it appears as such in the *Guide*, but rather because (although not a feature of Strauss's original) it was judged helpful for readers who wish to consider the fuller context of the sentence highlighted by Strauss. With regard to the "equibalance" of the perfect law, see *Guide*, trans. Pines, 2.39, p. 280.]

71. *Republic* 375c and 410d–412a; *Statesman* 306 ff.; *Laws* [bk. VI], 773. Cf. Hans-Georg Gadamer, *Plato und die Dichter* (Frankfurt am Main: Vittorio Klostermann, 1934), pp. 18–19. [Reprinted in *Platos dialektische Ethik und andere Studien zur platonischen Philosophie* (Hamburg: Meiner, 1968). For an English translation, see also "Plato and the Poets," in *Dialogue and Dialectic: Eight Hermeneutical Studies on Plato*, trans. P. Christopher Smith (New Haven: Yale University Press, 1980), pp. 39–72, and especially pp. 55–58.]

case, the laws must always remain the same in opposition to the unregulated pleasures that are never the same and that are never in relation to the same things.[72]

A law, to be truly "equal," must not be purely human. By human law is meant a law that aims only at the welfare [*bien-être*] of the body or, in other words, a law which "has no other end than putting in good order the city and its affairs, and keeping injustice and rivalry from it" so that "men may obtain some sort of imaginary happiness, which corresponds to the view of the respective legislator." The author of a law of this sort possesses only the perfection of the "imagination";[73] he is not and cannot be a philosopher (and still less a prophet), he is "ignorant": he does not know true happiness, which is always one and the same; he searches for, and causes others to search for, one of the different forms of imaginary happiness. Farabi also had spoken of the "ignorant" governors who do not need philosophy, who can achieve their purposes [*fins*] by means of the "experimental faculty" alone, by means of a "sensual aptitude";[74] and their purpose—the purpose of the "ignorant city"—is an imaginary happiness: either what is necessary for the preservation of the body, or wealth, pleasures, glory, victory, or liberty.[75] True happiness consists in the welfare [*bien-être*] of the soul, i.e., in the knowledge, as perfect as possible, of all that exists, and above all of the most perfect beings, of God and the angels; it is at this that the perfect city aims according to Farabi, the divine law according to Maimonides. But as true happiness can only be obtained after man has achieved the "welfare [*bien-être*] of the body, which consists in the city's being well governed," "the divine law has as an end two things, namely, the welfare [*bien-être*] of the soul and that of the body."[76] That Maimonides characterizes a law that aims at the perfection of the intelligence as a "divine law" appears, at first glance, surprising: cannot a law of this sort be the work of a philosopher? Was knowledge not the purpose in relation to which the Platonic legislator established his laws? Let us recall, however, that Plato began his dialogue on the laws with the word "God"—this dialogue, and no other work—and that according to him the true law aims not only at

72. *Laws* [bk. II], 660b-c.
73. *Guide* 2.40 (p. 86b), and 3.27 (p. 59b). [See *Guide*, trans. Pines, 2.40, p. 384; and 3.27, p. 510.]
74. "*Qowwa qarihiyya hissiyya.*" We follow here the text of the Palencia edition, which is confirmed by the Latin translation of Gerard of Cremona.
75. Cf. *Musterstaat*, p. 61, 19-62, 20, and *Ihsa al-ulum*, pp. 64-65 and 68-69. [See *Perfect State*, trans. Walzer, paras. 16-18, pp. 254-57. See "Enumeration of the Sciences," trans. Najjar, in *Medieval Political Philosophy*, ed. Lerner and Mahdi, pp. 24-25, 26-27; *Political Writings*, trans. Butterworth, pp. 76-77, 80.]
76. *Guide* 2.40 (p. 86b), and 3.27. [See *Guide*, trans. Pines, 2.40, p. 384; and 3.27, pp. 510-12.]

"human" goods, i.e., at the goods of the body, but also and above all at "divine" goods, the first of which is knowledge.[77] Maimonides is then in perfect accord with Plato in seeing as the trait characteristic of the divine law the fact that it aims at the perfection of knowledge.

The perfect law,[78] given by the prophet-legislator who unites in his person all the essential qualities of the philosopher and of the statesman while surpassing them in a miraculous manner, can only be understood and transmitted by men who also have at their disposal the qualities of the philosopher and of the statesman, although in a much more imperfect manner: the "secrets of the Torah" ought to be confided only to a man who is perfect "regarding political governments and the speculative sciences (and who possesses) with this a natural penetration, intelligence, and eloquence in order to present the subjects in such a way that they may be glimpsed." These "conditions" to be fulfilled by the rabbi-philosopher recall the "conditions"[79] enumerated by Farabi to be fulfilled by the "first leader" ["*premier chef*"],[80] which, for their part, are derived from the conditions required by Plato of the philosopher-kings. The rabbi-philosopher must fulfill at least some of the conditions of the king-philosopher, since he is the authentic interpreter of the work of the

---

77. *Laws* [bk. I], 631b–d. Cf. 624a and 630d–e.
78. "*al-shari'a al-kamila.*" [See also] *Guide* 3.46 (p. 104a). [See *Guide*, trans. Pines, 3.46, p. 586.]
79. *Musterstaat*, p. 60, 14 and 18, and 59, 5; *Kitab tahsil*, p. 44. [See *Perfect State*, trans. Walzer, para. 13, pp. 248–51, and para. 11, pp. 244–47; *Plato and Aristotle*, trans. Mahdi, para. 60, p. 48.]
80. *Guide* 1.34 (p. 41a) [*Guide*, trans. Pines, 1.34, p. 78]:

fatamal kayf ishtaratu binas kitab kamal 'al-shakhs fi 'al-siyasat 'al-madinah wafi 'al-'ulum al-natariya ma'a dhaka tab'a wafahm wahsan 'ibarah fi 'isal 'al-ma'ani bitalwih wahiniah mosrin lo siterei torah.
[Consider how, by means of a text of a book, they laid down as conditions of the perfection of the individual, his being perfect in the varieties of political regimes as well as in the speculative sciences and withal his possessing natural perspicacity and understanding and the gift of finely expressing himself in communicating notions in a flash. If all this is realized in someone, then the mysteries of the Torah may be transmitted to him.]

Cf. again *Guide* 1.33 (p. 37b) [*Guide*, trans. Pines, 1.33, p. 72]:

'an yakun fahman fatnan dhaki 'al-taba'i'a yash'aru bi'al-ma'ani bi'isar talwih
[that he be full of understanding, intelligent, sagacious by nature, that he divine a notion even if it is only very slightly suggested to him in a flash.]

Farabi mentions among others the following conditions to be fulfilled by the "first chief":

an yakouna bi'l-tab'i jayyida'l-fahmi . . . thomma an yakouna jayyida'l-fitnati dhakiyyan idha ra'a 'l-say'a bi 'adna dalilin fatana lahou 'ala'l-jihati 'llati dalla 'alayhi'l-dalil, thomma an yakouna hasana l-'ibara
[He should be by nature excellent at understanding. . . . He should possess natural perspicacity; when he sees the slightest indication of a thing, he should grasp what the indication points to. He should have the gift of finely expressing himself.]

See *Musterstaat*, p. 59, 16–21. [Cf. *Perfect State*, trans. Walzer, para. 12, pp. 246–49.]

legislator (prophet)-philosopher who, for his part, has actualized [*réalisé*] what the philosopher Plato could only call for [*postuler*]: the divine legislation. It is the rabbi-philosopher who must guide, as representative [*vicaire*] of the legislator-philosopher, those who are not capable of understanding the esoteric teaching of the legislator; if these refuse to submit to his direction, they render themselves without excuse.[81] As regards the "political governments" that the rabbi-philosopher must know, there can be no doubt that they are the juridical norms contained in the written and oral Torah: it is then by beginning from the Platonic conception of the philosopher-king that Maimonides arrives at the philosophical justification of the study of the *halakha* [sacred Law].

In his treatise on the philosophy of Plato and Aristotle, Farabi, when summarizing Plato's *Republic*, had said: "Insofar as man lives in association with men of this (i.e., corrupt) nation, his life will not be a human life; but if he separates himself from them and distances himself from their way of living by striving to attain perfection, his life will be miserable and he will never attain what he wishes, for one of two things will happen to him: either he will be killed, or he will be deprived of perfection. This is why he needs another nation, different from that which exists during his time; this is why he (Plato) made the search for this other nation. He began by discussing justice and what true justice is; he discussed conventional justice, practiced in the cities; and after having discussed it, he acknowledged that this was true injustice and extreme wickedness [*malice*], and that these evils would endure for as long as there are cities. This is why he had to organize another city in which true justice and the goods that are goods in truth would be found, and in which nothing of the things necessary to attain happiness would be lacking, of which the philosophers would be the principal part . . ."[82] Now, the search

---

81. *Guide* 1.36 (p. 44a). [See *Guide*, trans. Pines, 1.36, p. 84.] Cf. *Musterstaat*, p. 70, 1–3, and 70, 23 [*Perfect State*, trans. Walzer, para. 2, pp. 278–79, and para. 4, pp. 282–83]. Cf. also Averroes, *In Rempubl. Plat.* (fol. 182b, col. 1, I. 50–54). The condition that the philosopher-king be eloquent is not mentioned by Plato. The *falasifa* attach a greater importance to rhetoric than did Plato; according to them, the prophet is at once a philosopher and orator (cf. in particular Averroes, *Fasl al-Maqal* [*Decisive Treatise*] passim, and n. 80 above). As a result, one finds some interesting remarks concerning the revealed law in the discourses of the *falasifa* on rhetoric (cf., e.g., Farabi, *Ihsa al-ulum*, p. 26, and Averroes, *Paraphrase de la Rhétorique d'Aristote*. Paris manuscript, Hebrew cod. 1008, fol. 92bff.), and on dialectic [*la topique*]. Let us recall, moreover, the original relation between rhetoric and political science. [For Averroes, *Paraphrase de la Rhétorique d'Aristote*, see Averroes, *Three Short Commentaries on Aristotle's "Topics," "Rhetoric," and "Poetics*,*"* ed. and trans. Charles E. Butterworth (Albany: SUNY Press, 1977); for Averroes, *Fasl al-Maqal*, see *Decisive Treatise*, ed. and trans. Charles E. Butterworth (Provo: Brigham Young University Press, 2001).]

82. Falaquera, *Reshit Ḥokhmah*, ed. [Moritz] David, p. 76. [Cf. *Plato and Aristotle*, trans. Mahdi, para. 30, pp. 63–65.]

for the perfect city has been rendered superfluous by the divine legislation; and as the divine law has not been given to a city but a nation, it was above all the idea of the perfect city that had to fall into desuetude,[83] to become a symbol. One finds the perfect city, the city of God, as the subject of a parable in *Guide* 3.51. Munk remarked in one of his notes to this chapter: "It seems evident to me that here, as in many other passages of these last chapters, Maimonides has taken as his model the citizen of the ideal state, whose depiction Farabi has given us in his treatise, *Principles of the Beings* . . . and the philosopher presented by Ibn Bajja, in his *Governance of the Solitary* . . . In the two works we just indicated, many features [*traits*] are borrowed from Plato's *Republic* and Aristotle's *Ethics*."[84] Farabi had said in the treatise indicated by Munk: "Naturally bestial men are not city dwellers, and by no means do they gather together in a city-dwelling (political) way; but they resemble in part domestic animals, in part wild animals . . . (There are some who) are found in the extremities of the inhabited earth, either in the extreme North or the extreme South. These must be treated as beasts. Those among them who are more human and who can be more useful in the cities, are to be spared and employed as beasts are employed. Those among them who cannot be useful or who are harmful are treated like the other harmful animals. One must proceed in the same manner if it happens that someone bestial is born among the inhabitants of the cities."[85] Maimonides takes this description up again; he also speaks of men living "outside the city" like "the most distant of the Turks who live in the far North and the Negroes who live in the far South, and those who resemble them in our climate; these are to be considered as irrational animals; I do not place them among the ranks of man, for they occupy among the beings a rank inferior to that of man and superior to that of

---

83. Cf., however the prediction concerning the "faithful city" in Isaiah 1:21–26.

84. See Munk, *Le Guide des égarés*, 3.51, p. 438 n. 4. [Munk: "It appears evident to me that here, as in many other passages of these last chapters (3.51–54), Maimonides has taken as his model the citizen of the ideal state which Farabi has described in his *The Principles of the Beings* (*The Political Regime*) . . . , and the philosopher as presented by Ibn Bajja in his *Regimen of the Solitary*. . . . Ibn Bajja says, among other things, of his philosopher: 'The solitary will remain pure in his contact with his fellow men; for it is his duty not to become intimate with *material* men, nor even with those whose end is only the *spiritually* absolute, but on the contrary his duty is only to become intimate with the men of science. Now, as the men of science are many in certain localities, but few in number in certain other localities, it is the duty of the solitary in those certain other localities to withdraw completely from men, inasmuch as is possible, and only to mix with them for the sake of the necessary things, and only in the measure which is necessary.' In the two works that we have mentioned, many ideas (*traits*) are borrowed from Plato's *Republic* and Aristotle's *Ethics*. Maimonides, as was his practice, applied to these descriptions verses of Holy Scripture and passages borrowed from the ancient rabbis."]

85. *Kitab al-siyasat*, pp. 57–58. [See "The Political Regime," trans. Najjar, in *Medieval Political Philosophy*, ed. Lerner and Mahdi, pp. 41–42.]

the ape . . ."[86] But Maimonides characterizes these men as nonpolitical men, living "outside the city" only in a metaphorical sense: these barbaric men, devoid and even incapable of all intellectual culture, live "outside the city" because they do not have the least knowledge [*connaissance*] of the sovereign of the "city," i.e., of God.

However, the search for the perfect city—the problem of Plato solved by the divine legislation—could not be forgotten by the Jew. The Jewish nation, which is the perfect nation inasmuch as it is constituted by the perfect law and on the condition that it obeys that law, did not obey it. Thus the prophets themselves had run the same risks in Jerusalem as Socrates in Athens. They had shown by their actions or by their speeches [*paroles*] that the man who loves perfection and justice must leave the cities inhabited exclusively by the wicked [*méchant*], to search for a city inhabited by good men, and that he must prefer, if he does not know of such a city or if he is prevented from bringing one about, wandering in the desert or in caves to the association with evil men. This manner of acting is obligatory for the Jew, as Maimonides explains it, basing himself on the teaching of the Jewish tradition and relying on a verse of Jeremiah (9:1).[87] And it is this same passage that Falaquera has in mind when translating the passage of the Farabian summary of the *Republic*, which describes the fate of Socrates and all those who, living in an unjust city, search for perfection.[88]

---

86. *Guide* 3.51 (p. 123b). [See *Guide*, trans. Pines, 3.51, p. 618.]

87. See "Hilkhot De'ot" VI, 1. Cf. also *Shemoneh Perakim*, ed. Wolff (Leiden: Brill, 1903): IV, pp. 10–11, where the same verse is cited. Cf. Farabi, *Kitab al-siyasat*, p. 50. [See Maimonides, "Hilkhot De'ot," trans. Hyamson, p. 54b; "Laws Concerning Character Traits," in *Ethical Writings*, trans. Weiss and Butterworth, chap. 6, para. 1, pp. 46–47; "Eight Chapters," in *Ethical Writings*, trans. Weiss and Butterworth, 4th chap., pp. 69–70. Cf. "The Political Regime," trans. Najjar, in *Medieval Political Philosophy*, ed. Lerner and Mahdi, p. 37. Though not relying on Jeremiah 9:1, cf. also Maimonides, "Epistle to Yemen," trans. Kraemer, pp. 111.]

88. *Reshit Ḥokhmah*, p. 77. Cf. above [in the present essay, twelfth paragraph of section II]. [In what seems to have been a "supplement" to the text associated with this note, among Strauss's marginal handwritten additional comments (date unknown) that have been transcribed by Heinrich Meier, the following appears: "One eternal *shari'a*—but infinite repetition of messianic ages. For: the messianic age comes to an end, and yet mankind lives on. Thus the difficulty can be solved that RMbM (=Maimonides) insists in an unusual way on the sacrificial laws and yet depreciates them as necessary only for combating idolatry (Sabianism): paganism has disappeared; in the messianic age, true knowledge of God will be universal: hence the need of sacrificial laws is zero, and God does not do, nor command, anything superfluous. The solution: *return* of Sabianism at the end of the messianic age. But: *Moreh* 2.29 (Weiss 187). (See *Guide*, trans. Pines, 2.29, pp. 519, 521.) Cf. Cohen in MbM 130. (MbM = Hermann Cohen, "Characteristik der Ethik Maimunis," in *Moses ben Maimon: Sein Leben, seine Werke, und sein Einfluss*, ed. W. Bacher, M. Brann, D. Simonsen, and J. Guttmann, 2 vols. (Leipzig: G. Fock, 1908–14; reprint, Hildesheim: Olms, 1971), I, 63–134.) Paganism an *eternal* danger: the counterpoison must be *always* disposable [i.e., at one's disposal]. The counterpoison has not only its *specific* virtue (against Sabianism), but also a general one (against paganism as such). Connection between paganism and the specific charms of normal political life:

But it is not only for the city inhabited by good men that the Jew must look. Through the loss of its political freedom, the Jewish nation equally lost the means of practicing the law to the full extent. The members of the perfect nation being dispersed among pagan, idolatrous, "ignorant" nations, the question of Plato surfaced anew. The answer was furnished there by the hope for the Messiah. The Messiah is king; this means that his rank is inferior to that of the legislator-prophet: while the latter has proclaimed the divine law, the king compels men to obey the law.[89] The king-messiah will thus change nothing of the law of Moses, but, devoting his life to the study of the Torah, attending to the commandments according to the written and oral Torah, and compelling Israel to follow it, he will reestablish the carrying out [*l'exécution*] of all the prescriptions that cannot be practiced during captivity.[90] The days of the Messiah, then, will be situated in this world, the natural course of which will not be changed.[91] Not that the goal of the messianic regime is the welfare [*bien-être*] of the body or earthly happiness. To the contrary: the Messiah is not only king, [but] he is at the same time wiser than

---

no need for that counterpoison in exile (cf. *Republic* (s.v. Theages) on the advantages of exile). *Guide* 1.36 (56, 21): on the possibility of *'ayin zayin* [i.e., *'avodah zarah* = idolatry] in the *future*." See *Philosophie und Gesetz: Frühe Schriften*, vol. 2 of *Gesammelte Schriften*, p. 163. For *Guide*, trans. Pines, 1.36, p. 83: "In fact, no human being of the past has ever imagined on any day, *and no human being of the future will ever imagine* [emphasis added by present editor], that the form that he fashions from cast metal or from stone and wood has created and governs the heavens and the earth. Rather it is worshiped in respect of its being an image of a thing that is an intermediary between ourselves and God." For *Republic* ("Theages"), Book VI, 496a–d, p. 176, trans. Allan Bloom (New York: Basic Books, 1968): "'Then it's a very small group, Adeimantus,' I said, 'which remains to keep company with philosophy in a way that's worthy; perhaps either a noble and well-reared disposition, held in check by exile, remains by her side consistent with nature, for want of corruptors; or when a great soul grows up in a little city, despises the business of the city and looks out beyond; and, perhaps, a very few men from another art, who justly despise it because they have good natures, might come to her. And the bridle of our comrade Theages might be such as to restrain him. For in Theages' case all the other conditions for an exile from philosophy were present, but the sickliness of his body, shutting him out of politics, restrained him. My case—the demonic (*daimonion*) sign—isn't worth mentioning, for it has perhaps occurred in some one other man, or no other, before. Now the men who have become members of this small band have tasted how sweet and blessed a possession it is. At the same time, they have seen sufficiently the madness of the many, and that no one who minds the business of the cities does anything healthy, to say it in a word, and that there is no ally with whom one could go to the aid of justice and be preserved.'"]

89. Cf. "Hilkhot Melakhim" XI, 4, with *Guide* 2.40 (p. 85b). [Cf. "Laws Concerning Kings and Wars," trans. Hershman, pp. 240, with xxiii–xxiv; "Laws of Kings and Their Wars," trans. Weiss and Butterworth, pp. 173–74, with *Guide*, trans. Pines, 2.40, p. 382.]

90. "Hilkhot Melakhim" XI, 1 and 4 ["Laws Concerning Kings and Wars," trans. Hershman, pp. 238–39, 240, with xxiii–xxiv; "Laws of Kings and Their Wars," trans. Weiss and Butterworth, pp. 171–72, 173–74].

91. Cf. "Hilkhot Teshuvah" IX, 2, and "Hilkhot Melakhim" XII, 1 ["Laws of Repentance," trans. Hyamson, p. 92a; "Laws Concerning Repentance," trans. Weiss and Butterworth, pp. 170–71; "Laws Concerning Kings and Wars," trans. Hershman, p. 240; "Laws of Kings and Their Wars," trans. Weiss and Butterworth, p. 174].

Solomon, indeed, a prophet almost equal to Moses;[92] uniting in his person the qualities of the king and the sage, he will establish peace for all time [*toujours*] so that men can at last find the repose, the leisure to apply themselves to wisdom and the law without being troubled by sickness, war, and famine.[93] Thus, "the earth will be filled with the knowledge of God" (Isaiah 11:9), without the difference between the knowers and the vulgar being abolished:[94] much better, it is only then that the privileges of the philosophers will be fully recognized. The Messiah is distinguished from all the other prophets because he does not perform [*accomplit*] the signs and it is not asked of him to do so.[95] And is the eternal peace, realized by the Messiah, anything other than the necessary consequence of knowledge, of the knowledge of God?[96] The Messiah, being a king-philosopher, will establish for all time [*toujours*] the "perfect city," whose inhabitants will apply themselves, according to their respective faculties, to the knowledge of God, and he will thereby bring to an end the evils that today trouble the cities.[97]

III

The perfect law, the divine law, is distinguished from the human laws in that it aims not only at the welfare [*bien-être*] of the body, but also and above all at the welfare [*bien-être*] of the soul. This consists in man's having sound opinions, above all concerning God and the angels. To guide man toward the welfare [*bien-être*] of the soul, the divine law has therefore indicated the most important of these opinions, but only in a manner that does not surpass the understanding of the vulgar. This is the reason it was necessary that the prophets have at their disposal the supreme perfection of the imaginative

---

92. "Hilkhot Teshuvah" IX, 2 ["Laws of Repentance," trans. Hyamson, p. 92a; "Laws Concerning Repentance," trans. Weiss and Butterworth, pp. 170–71].

93. "Hilkhot Teshuvah" IX, 1–2, and "Hilkhot Melakhim" XII, 3–4 ["Laws of Repentance," trans. Hyamson, pp. 91a–92a; "Laws Concerning Repentance," trans. Weiss and Butterworth, pp. 169–71; "Laws Concerning Kings and Wars," trans. Hershman, pp. 241–42; "Laws of Kings and Their Wars," trans. Weiss and Butterworth, pp. 175–76].

94. Cf. the interpretation of Joel 11:28 in *Guide* 2.32 (p. 74a). [See *Guide*, trans. Pines, 2.32, p. 363.]

95. Cf. "Hilkhot Melakhim" XI, 3 with "Hilkhot Yesodei ha-Torah" X, 1–2 ["Laws Concerning Kings and Wars," trans. Hershman, pp. 239–40; "Laws of Kings and Their Wars," trans. Weiss and Butterworth, pp. 172–73, with Maimonides, "Hilkhot Yesodei ha-Torah," trans. Hyamson, p. 45b].

96. *Guide* 3.11. [See *Guide*, trans. Pines, 3.11, pp. 440–41.]

97. We do not take up in the present article the important question concerning the relation between the explication of the Mosaic laws given by Maimonides, and political philosophy. We only point out [*signalons*] here the fact that Maimonides twice cites passages from the *Nicomachean Ethics* in order to explain biblical commandments (*Guide* 3.43, p. 96a, and 3.49 beginning). [See *Guide*, trans. Pines, 3.43, pp. 571–72, with the translator's note, and 3.49, p. 601.]

faculty:[98] imagination makes possible the metaphorical exoteric representation of the truths whose proper, esoteric meaning must be concealed from the vulgar. For one neither can nor ought to speak of the principles except in an enigmatic manner; this is what not only the "peoples of the Law" ["*les 'gens de la loi'*"] but also the philosophers say. Maimonides names only one of these esoteric philosophers: Plato.[99]

To communicate to the vulgar a certain knowledge of the principles, which are incorporeal and intellectual things, they must be represented by corporeal and sensible things. Not by just any corporeal things, but by those that occupy, in the sensible domain, a place analogous to that occupied, in the intellectual domain, by the principle in question. God and His attributes, then, will be represented by the most noble sensible things.[100] It is for this reason that the prophets represent, for example, divine perception by hearing and sight, i.e., by the most noble sensations, and that they do not attribute to God, even metaphorically, the sense of touch, which is the basest of our senses.[101] But the external meaning of the prophets' speeches is sometimes more than a means to indicate the esoteric truths; there are cases in which the exterior meaning has a value in itself: it may be that the prophet pronounces some speeches which communicate by their esoteric sense a speculative truth, while their exoteric sense indicates "a wisdom useful for many

---

98. For prophecy is essentially related to legislation, and the "legislative virtue is man's art of representing those speculative concepts which are difficult to comprehend for the vulgar, by means of the imaginative faculty, and the ability to produce political actions which are useful for attaining happiness, and the amphibolous discourse concerning speculative and practical matters that the vulgar know (only) in an amphibolous manner." This is what Falaquera says in a passage of the *Reshit Ḥokhmah* (ed. M. David, p. 30, ll. 25-27), which is probably founded on a writing not yet identified as Farabi's. [Brague, in *Maïmonide*, corrects, as "in fact 28," either the page or the lines on which Falaquera's words, quoted by Strauss, appear in the edition of M. David. But at least in the copy of M. David's edition to which I had access, both the page and the lines cited by Strauss seem correct. Brague very helpfully comments (p. 175, n. 98) that the original of this passage, unknown in the period during which Strauss wrote his article, has since been rediscovered. It was indeed something which Alfarabi wrote, as Strauss had surmised: Farabi, *Book of Letters (Kitab al-Huruf): Commentary on Aristotle's Metaphysics*, Arabic text, ed. Mushin Mahdi (Beirut: Darel-Mashreq, 1969), para. 144, p. 152, ll. 9-13.]

99. *Guide* 1.17. Cf. a similar remark of Avicenna, cited in my study *Philosophie und Gesetz*, p. 114, n. 2. [See *Philosophy and Law*, p. 152, n. 65; see chap. 4 above, n. **[65]**. For the remark on Plato, see *Guide*, trans. Pines, 1.17, p. 43. For what has been translated as "'peoples of the Law'" (with Strauss's original following Munk's translation: "*les 'gens de la loi'*"), Pines renders it as "people adhering to Law" (1.17, p. 43). Pines also renders a similar Maimonidean phrase as "nations adhering to (religious) law."]

100. Farabi, *Musterstaat*, p. 50, 9-15 [*Perfect State*, trans. Walzer, para. 6, pp. 218-19].

101. *Guide* 1.47. [See *Guide*, trans. Pines, 1.47, pp. 104-6. For something closer to the precise words which Strauss ascribes to Maimonides, although as attributed to Aristotle (*Nicomachean Ethics* and *De Anima*) rather than to the prophets, see *Guide*, trans. Pines, 2.36, p. 371; 2.40, p. 384; 3.8, pp. 432-33; 3.49, p. 608; 3.51, p. 620. But for Aristotle's fuller view based on an alternate passage, which contrasts with the one Maimonides (although it is most likely he also knew of this passage—whatever that may mean) seems most often to attribute to him, cf. *De Anima* 29.421b3-4.]

things, and among others for the improvement [*amelioration*] of the state of human societies."[102] There is then among corporeal things, worthy of being employed for the representation of the principles, a class which particularly lends itself to this use, namely, political matters.[103] The political hierarchy is an adequately faithful counterpart to the cosmic hierarchy. This is why the comparison of God to a king is so common.[104] It goes without saying that such comparisons must not be taken literally: they contain an esoteric meaning, while their exoteric meaning is one of great utility for political life. The divine law attaches so great a value to the representations, useful for political life, of divine matters that it invites men to believe not only in the most important speculative truths, but also in certain things which are "necessary for the good order of political conditions"; it is in this way that it invites the belief in divine anger and mercy.[105] The most illustrious example of this are the "thirteen *middot*" [characteristics or attributes] of God, revealed to Moses: they do not signify the attributes of God but the most perfect manner of acting which the most perfect statesman, i.e., "the governor of the city who is a prophet," must take as his model; they are the essential conditions of the "governance of the (most perfect) cities."[106] However, the unity and the scope of the dogmatic politics inserted [*insérée*] into the *Guide* are highlighted in no part more than in the theory of providence, which forms one of the principal parts of this work.

According to Maimonides, the teaching of the divine law concerning providence is summarized in the thesis that God rewards or punishes men according to their merits or faults so well that all that happens to an individual human being is in perfect accord with the moral value of his actions. This

---

102. *Guide* 1.Intro. (p. 7a). A remarkable example of this is found in *Guide* 2.31 (cf. *Rasa'il Ikhwan al'Safa* IV, 190). [See *Guide*, trans. Pines, 1.Intro., p. 12; 2.31, pp. 359–60.]

[Know that the divine books contain [both] manifest revelations, namely, writings to be read and heard, as well as interpretations hidden and internal, namely, meanings which are the object of intellectual comprehension; thus, for those who established the religious Law, there are fundamental theses on which [basis] they established the religious Law; those [theses] contain [both] manifest and evident statutes, and internal and hidden secrets. In the fulfillment of the manifest statutes there is found the welfare [*salut*] of those who avail themselves of this lower world, while in the knowledge of the hidden and internal secrets there is found the welfare [*salut*] of those who concern themselves with their resurrection and their future life.

I translate from Rémi Brague's French translation of *Rasa'il Ikhwan al'Safa* in *Maïmonide*, p. 176, n. 2.]

103. Cf. Farabi, *Kitab tahsil*, p. 41 [*Plato and Aristotle*, trans. Mahdi, para. 55, p. 45].

104. *Guide* 1.46 (p. 52b). Cf. 1.9, and 3.51 beginning. [See *Guide*, trans. Pines, 1.46, pp. 102–3; cf. 1.9, pp. 34–35; and 3.51, pp. 618–20.]

105. *Guide* 3.28. [See *Guide*, trans. Pines, 3.28, p. 514.]

106. *Guide* 1.54. [See *Guide*, trans. Pines, 1.54, pp. 125, 126, 128.]

doctrine is diametrically opposed to the doctrine of the "philosophers," i.e., of Aristotle, who denies divine omniscience and, as a result, particular providence. However, "there have been some philosophers who believed what we believe, namely, that God knows everything and that nothing is in any way hidden from him; these are certain great men prior to Aristotle, whom Alexander (of Aphrodisias) also mentions in his treatise (*De Providentia*), but whose opinion he rejects."[107] There would be a certain interest in knowing who the philosophers are, prior to Aristotle, whose doctrine concerning providence is in accord with the biblical doctrine according to Maimonides. As Alexander's treatise *De Providentia* is lost, one is confined to the succinct summary of this writing given by Maimonides. Here are Alexander's theses: the philosophers were led to deny divine omniscience and providence first and foremost by the observation of the lack of order in human matters, by the observation of the misfortune of the just and the good fortune of the unjust.[108] They then came to pose the following disjunctions: either God knows nothing of the circumstances [*conditions*] of individual human beings, or He knows them; if He knows them, one of these three cases must necessarily be admitted: either that God orders [*règle*] them and there establishes the most perfect order, or that He is impotent or, while knowing them and being able to introduce order there He neglects to do so, either through disdain and contempt [*mepris*], or because of jealousy [*envie*]. Now of these three cases two are impossible with respect to God, namely, that God is impotent or that He neglects the things He knows; only the first case then remains, namely, that God orders [*règle*] the individual circumstances [*conditions*] in the most perfect manner. Now, we find such circumstances completely disordered [*déréglées*]; as a result, the presupposition that God knows individual beings [*les choses individuelles*] is false, and the other part of the first disjunction,

107. *Guide* 3.16 (p. 31a). [See *Guide*, trans. Pines, 3.16, p. 463.]
108. Cf. *Guide* 3.16 (p.31a) where this reasoning is expressly attributed to Alexander, *De Providentia*. [See *Guide*, trans. Pines, 3.16, pp. 463–64. The shorter passage discussed by Strauss is translated by Pines as follows:

> There are also some philosophers who believe, as we do, that He, may He be exalted, knows everything, and that nothing secret is hidden from him. These are great men, prior in time to Aristotle, who are also mentioned by Alexander in that treatise. But he (Alexander) rejects their opinion (i.e., of the "great men" prior to Aristotle), saying that it is principally refuted by the fact that we see good men are attained by evils and evil men obtain the good things.

For the impact made by the thought and the works Alexander of Aphrodisias on Maimonides, see Pines, "Translator's Introduction," in *Guide*, pp. lxiv–lxxiv. For *De providentia* (concerning the view of Plato), see Alexandre d'Aphrodise, *Traité de la providence [Peri pronoias]*, Arabic version of Abu Bisr Matta ibn Yunus, edited and introduced, with a French translation, by Pierre Thillet (Lagrasse: Verdier, 2003), pp. 101–2, with the editor's comment, p. 17.]

namely that God knows nothing of individual beings [*des choses individuelles*], is true.[109] This argument against particular providence was certainly not invented by Alexander. A trace of it is found in the comparable argument of the Academician against the Stoic in Cicero.[110] But, what is more interesting, Chrysippus and the Stoics themselves had posed similar disjunctions to those cited by Maimonides with the intention (opposed to that of the Academicians and Alexander) of proving that there is a divine providence concerning human matters.[111] It seems then that the reasoning, summarized by Maimonides, was first employed to affirm providence. It must even be said that it was invented for this end. In the tenth book of the *Laws* Plato addresses an "exhortation" to him who, while admitting the existence of the gods, believes that they "contemn [*méprisent*] and neglect human affairs." He begins by noting [*constater*] that the good fortune of the unjust is the reason that leads men to this impious belief.[112] He then proves that God is no less concerned with the small (human) matters than with the great (cosmic) ones, starting with the following premises: (1) God knows all things; (2) He is able to concern Himself with the small matters as well as the great; (3) being perfectly virtuous, He chooses to be so concerned.[113] It is this distinction between divine knowledge, power, and will, made for proving particular providence, which is at the basis of the disjunctions posed by Alexander with a view to refuting this belief and, before him, by Chrysippus to confirm it; and one finds in Plato some indications of these very disjunctions.[114] Moreover, Alexander had begun his reasoning by noting [*en constatant*], in the

---

109. *Guide* 3.16 (p. 30a-b). [See *Guide*, trans. Pines, 3.16, pp. 461–62. For the word "*envie*" translated as "jealousy" (following Pines) rather than "envy" (following Munk), see 3.16 (p. 462). The longer passage discussed by Strauss is translated by Pines as follows:

> One of two things must be true: God either knows nothing about these individual circumstances and does not comprehend them, or he knows and apprehends them. This is a necessary division. Thereupon they said: If he apprehends them and knows them, one of three things must be true: either He orders them, settling them according to the best, the most perfect, and the most accomplished order; or He is incapable of establishing order in them and has no power over them; or again He knows and is able to establish excellent order and governance, but neglects to do it in consequence of His disdain and contempt or in consequence of His jealousy.]

110. *De natura deorum* [*On the Nature of the Gods*] III, 39, 92. [See Cicero, *De Natura Deorum*, trans. Harris Rackham (Cambridge, MA: Harvard University Press, 1933), pp. 322–23, 378–79.]

111. Cf. Cicero, *De divinatione* [*On Divination*] I, 38, 82–39, 84, with *De natura deorum* [*On the Nature of the Gods*] II, 30, 77. [See Cicero, *On Divination*, bk. 1, trans. David Wardle (Oxford: Clarendon Press, 2006), pp. 72–75; *De Natura Deorum*, trans. Harris Rackham (Cambridge, MA: Harvard University Press, 1933), pp. 150–53, 196–99.]

112. *Laws* [bk. X], 899dff.
113. *Laws* [bk. X], 902e and 901d–e.
114. *Laws* [bk. X], 901b–c and 902a.

same manner as Plato, that the reason that brings men to deny particular providence is the good fortune of the unjust, which Maimonides repeats in his own account of providence.[115] Since Alexander had spoken expressly of philosophers prior to Aristotle who believed in divine omniscience, we do not hesitate to conclude that Maimonides knew, if only through other texts, [and] at least through Alexander's treatise *De Providentia*, the doctrine of the *Laws* on providence. And if Alexander did not cite Plato's text, one would have to say that Maimonides, without his knowing it, reestablished this text: it was certainly not Alexander who had characterized the negation of particular providence as a "bad and absurd opinion."[116] But Maimonides not only knew of the doctrine of the *Laws* on providence, he even approved of it: according to him, the doctrine of certain "great men prior to Aristotle" concerning providence is in accord with the doctrine of the divine law. And can one judge otherwise, since Plato speaks of God's retributive justice in almost the same terms as Scripture?[117] It will be objected that the agreement [*concordance*] between Plato and the prophets is specious, it being a given that Plato affirms the dogma of particular providence only because of its political utility: a city governed by laws, and not by philosophers, cannot be perfect unless the belief that God rewards or punishes men according to their actions, is there established.[118] We do not dispute this. But it is precisely in this sense that Maimonides accepts the biblical doctrine: while in his discussion of both creation and prophecy he identifies his own opinion with that of the law, he clearly distinguishes, in his discussion of providence, his own opinion from that of the law.[119] Maimonides is thus, here again, in accord with Plato.[120]

---

115. *Guide* 3.19 beginning. [See *Guide*, trans. Pines, 3.19, pp. 477–78.]

116. *Guide* 3.16. [See *Guide*, trans. Pines, 3.16, p. 461: Maimonides speaks about "their evil and incongruous opinions." The similar French words used by Strauss, as Alexander's words, are "opinion mauvaise et absurde."] Cf. *Laws* [bk. X], 903a.

117. Cf. *Laws* [bk. X], 905a–b with Amos 9:1–3.

118. Cf. *Laws* [bk. II], 663d–e.

119. Cf. above all *Guide* 3.17 (p. 34b), and 3.23 (p. 49b). [See *Guide*, trans. Pines, 3.17, p. 469; and 3.23, p. 494.]

120. There is, moreover, direct testimony of this; after having set out his doctrine on providence, in opposition to Aristotle's doctrine, Maimonides declares:

> The philosophers have equally spoken in this sense (i.e., that providence watches over individual human beings in accord with the extent of their perfection). Abu-Nasr [al-Farabi], in the introduction to his commentary on Aristotle's *Nicomachean Ethics*, expresses himself in these terms: those who possess the faculty of causing their souls to pass from one moral quality to another are those of whom Plato has said God's providence watches over them most.

Having arrived at this point, one cannot avoid posing the questions, decisive for the understanding of Maimonides, concerning the relation between the theology of the *Guide* and the Platonic doctrine of the One, and the relation between the cosmology of the *Guide* (i.e., the discussion of the creation of the world) and the doctrine of the *Timaeus*. The analysis of these relations must be reserved for a subsequent study.

Guide 3.18 (pp. 38b–39a). [See *Guide*, trans. Pines, 3.18, p. 476.] Maimonides could have found similar texts in Aristotle; there is no doubt that he knew this; why then did he not cite Aristotle, but Plato and Farabi?

6

The Place of the Doctrine of Providence according to Maimonides

EDITOR'S NOTE

"The Place of the Doctrine of Providence according to Maimonides" basically reproduces the translation made by Gabriel Bartlett and Svetozar Minkov, which appeared in *Review of Metaphysics* 57 (March 2004): 537–49. The original German version by Strauss from which it was translated, "Der Ort der Vorsehungslehre nach der Ansicht Maimunis," first appeared in print in *Monatsschrift für Geschichte und Wissenschaft des Judentums* 81, no. 1 (January–February 1937): 93–105. Bartlett and Minkov added a version of the following note to their English translation: "We are grateful to the publisher J. B. Metzler (Stuttgart, Germany) for the permission to publish our translation of the German text as it appeared, with marginalia, in *Philosophie und Gesetz—Frühe Schriften, vol. 2, Gesammelte Schriften*, pp. 179–90. We are grateful to Professors Kenneth Hart Green, Joel L. Kraemer, Ralph Lerner, Heinrich Meier, and Thomas L. Pangle for their assistance." The present editor has made some slight changes to the original translation and also to the notes. Further, the number (amounting to 35) and division of Strauss's notes are rearranged from the original English translation, in order to make them conform to how they appeared in the original German version. Also, parallel page numbers in the Pines English translation of the *Guide* are provided in square brackets following Strauss's references to the *Guide*. So as to simplify the reading of Strauss's text and not complicate it by undue editorial pedantry, the differences between the original translators' comments and those of the present editor will be designated only in cases of absolute necessity, the present edition regarding it as sufficient to put all editorial notes in the same square brackets. This is to acknowledge the debt that the present editor owes to the translators, Bartlett and Minkov, although of course I alone assume full responsibility for any differences between the two versions. See also *Philosophie und*

Gesetz: Frühe Schriften, vol. 2 of *Gesammelte Schriften*, pp. 191–94, for marginal handwritten comments subsequently added by Strauss to his own copy of the essay, which have been helpfully transcribed by Heinrich Meier. These are eminently and even imperatively worthy of consulting for Strauss's additional thought and research on numerous topics treated in his own article.

IN *THE GUIDE OF THE PERPLEXED*, MAIMONIDES DOES NOT TREAT the doctrine of divine omniscience and divine providence in a strictly theological context. He only comes to speak of this subject in the third part of the *Guide*, after he has concluded the thematic treatment of at least the following subjects: (1) the names and attributes of God (1.1–70); (2) the proof of the existence, unity, and incorporeality of God (1.71–2.1); (3) the separate intelligences and the order of the world (2.2–12); (4) the creation of the world (2.13¹–31); and (5) prophecy (2.32–48). The consideration of prophecy is immediately followed by the thematic interpretation of *ma'aseh merkavah* [account of the chariot]—Ezekiel 1 and 10—(3.1–7). This interpretation concludes with the remark that while *all* of the preceding "up to this chapter"—i.e., 1.1 through 3.7—is indispensable for the understanding of *ma'aseh merkavah*, the matters to be spoken about "after this chapter," i.e., from 3.8 to the end, will in no way—neither in an explicit manner, nor by way of hints—address "this subject," namely, *ma'aseh merkavah*. Accordingly, Maimonides turns directly to "other subjects."[2] Now, for Maimonides *ma'aseh merkavah* is identical with metaphysics (theology as a philosophic discipline).[3] Therefore, the closing remark at the end of *Guide* 3.7 means that while all preceding discussions (1.1–3.7) are of a metaphysical character, the following discussions will not belong to metaphysics. The subjects of the

---

1. See 2.11 end [*Guide*, trans. Pines, 2.11, p. 276].
2. 3.7 end. Compare 1.70 end [*Guide*, trans. Pines, 3.7, p. 430; cf. 1.70, p. 175].
3. *ma'aseh bereshit hu 'al-'ilm 'al-tabi'i wa ma'aseh merkavah hu 'al-'ilm 'al'ilahi* "The Account of the Beginning is identical with natural science and the Account of the Chariot with divine science." I, Intro., *Le Guide des égarés*, 3 vols. (Paris, 1870), ed. Salomon Munk, p. 3b [*Guide*, trans. Pines, 1.Intro. (p. 6)]. The restrictions to which this identification is subject (see 2.2 end) [*Guide*, trans. Pines, 2.2, p. 254] can only be treated adequately within the framework of an examination of the structure and the secret teaching of the *Guide*. We content ourselves with saying that these restrictions may be neglected in an introductory consideration, since Maimonides himself sets forth the unconditional identification of *ma'aseh merkavah* with metaphysics in *Sefer ha-Madda* (*The Book of Knowledge*). I refer provisionally to what the hidden structure of the *Guide* involves in footnote 35. [For Maimonides' discussion of the two secret topics in the first four chapters of *Sefer ha-Madda*, see "Book of Knowledge," trans. Lerner, pp. 141–53, and especially 2.11, and 4.10–13; "Laws of the Basic Principles of the Torah," trans. Hyamson, pp. 36b and 39b–40a. For Strauss's fuller treatment of the structure and the secret teaching of the *Guide*, see "Literary Character," chap. 8 below; "Introduction to Maimonides' *Guide*," chap. 10, below; and "How to Begin," chap. 11 below.]

main nonmetaphysical section of the *Guide* are: (1) divine providence (and the questions which belong most closely to the question of providence, [i.e.,] those concerning the origin and kinds of evil as well as divine omniscience) (3.8–24); and (2) the end of the Torah in general and of its arrangements in particular (3.25–50). Whatever else may be the case with regard to the plan of the *Guide*, there is no doubt that Maimonides, through precisely this plan, excludes the question of divine omniscience and of divine providence from the thematic realm of metaphysics.[4]

This determination requires four supplements in order to be precise. (1) The main first section of the *Guide* (1.1–3.7), which we have provisionally characterized as metaphysical, treats not only themes of metaphysics such as *theologia naturalis* [natural theology], but also such themes as one would have to—in the sense of Maimonides, or at any rate in the sense of his exoteric teaching—attribute to *theologia revelata* [revealed theology] (especially the doctrine of the creation of the world). The division of the subjects of the *Guide* into metaphysical and nonmetaphysical therefore in no way follows from the distinction between natural and revealed theology.[5] Consequently, the exclusion of the doctrine of providence from the realm of metaphysics is not identical with an attribution of this doctrine to a *theologia revelata*. (2) Physics finds its proper place within the first main section of the *Guide*. The discussion of physics—through the thematic interpretation of *ma'aseh bereshit* [the account of creation]—is concluded in a similar manner[6] to that

---

4. A further piece of evidence for this is supplied by the remark in 3.23 (50b) that the sublunar things and *"nothing else"* are to be taken into account in proving the true doctrine of providence in the Book of Job, and that, therefore, this proof, i.e., the only possible proof, is not of a metaphysical character. See also the beginning words in 3.8 [*Guide*, trans. Pines, 3.23, p. 496: "the description of natural matters . . . but of nothing else"; 3.8 (p. 430)].

5. Cf. 3.21 end, with 2.16ff. [*Guide*, trans. Pines, 3.21, p. 485, with 2.16–18, pp. 293–302]. [In the judgment of the present editor, I cannot discern any evident reason, based on the contents, to treat this paragraph in the text as of "a supplementary character," as did the English translators in the original version. They so judged this paragraph because of the use of a smaller font in it. But it seems to me that this is an accidental feature, and I can only speculate that it may have been due to an error or a necessity in the typographic production of the journal. In any case, I am in accord with the opinion of Rémi Brague, conveyed *ad oculos*, who in his French edition—*Maïmonide*, pp. 184–87—also did not suggest its difference from the rest of the article. Similarly, Heinrich Meier, *Philosophie und Gesetz: Frühe Schriften*, vol. 2 of *Gesammelte Schriften*, seems to have been of the same opinion: he signals his accord with that view by showing no distinction between this paragraph and the rest of the article (pp. 180–82). Therefore, unlike the original version that was presented by the English translators, the second paragraph will not be separated by parentheses in the present version.]

6. In 2.30. Compare 2.29 (65b) [*Guide*, trans. Pines, 2.30, pp. 348–59; cf. 2.29, pp. 346–47] and footnote 3. [Cf. Munk, same chapter, p. 228: "An allusion to a passage in Proverbs 25:2 ('It is the glory of God to conceal a thing, But the glory of kings is to search out a matter'), which the ancient rabbis applied to the mysteries of the first chapter of Genesis. See Bereshit Rabba, sect. 9, toward the beginning."]

in which the comprehensive metaphysical discussion is later concluded through the thematic interpretation of *ma'aseh merkavah*. Therefore, the subjects of the main second nonmetaphysical section of the *Guide* belong just as little to physics as they do to metaphysics. Physics and metaphysics form together with mathematics the whole of theoretical philosophy.[7] Since the subjects of the main nonmetaphysical section of the *Guide* are clearly not of a mathematical character, Maimonides—insofar as he treats these subjects only after the formal conclusion of both physics and metaphysics—expresses the view that these same subjects should be altogether excluded from the realm of theoretical philosophy. (3) Maimonides already treats providence within the main theoretical section of the *Guide* (above all in 2.10).[8] The discussion that appears in this context admittedly concerns general providence alone, i.e., the intelligent and artful governance of the world as a whole. Therefore, Maimonides withdraws only the question of particular providence from theoretical philosophy.[9] Accordingly, Maimonides already treats divine knowledge within the main theoretical section, namely, in order to show that the attribution of knowledge to God does not contradict the absolute unity of God; it is the question of divine omniscience alone, which is comprehensible and necessary only on the basis of the question of particular providence, that belongs to the main nontheoretical section. (4) Philosophy as a whole is divided—if one abstracts from logic, which is merely a tool [*Organon*]—into

---

7. Maimonides, *Millot ha-Higgayon* [*Treatise on Logic*], Ch. 14. [See "Logic," in *Ethical Writings*, trans. Weiss and Butterworth, chap. 14 (complete), pp. 158–61. The section with the discussion of political science alone is available as "Chapter XIV, Political Science," trans. Mahdi, in *Medieval Political Philosophy*, ed. Lerner and Mahdi, pp. 189–90.]

8. I of course leave out here the numerous, occasional mentions of providence.

9. Maimonides designates the providence of which he speaks in the first section of the *Guide* as *tadbir* (*hanhagah*) [governance], the providence of which he speaks in the second section as *'inayah* (*hashgaḥah*) [supervision]; compare especially the indication of the respective themes at the beginning of 2.10 on the one hand, and at the end of 3.16 and the beginning of 3.17 on the other [*Guide*, trans. Pines, 2.10, p. 269; cf. 3.16–17, p. 464]. Even though he in no way pedantically adheres to this terminological distinction—he mostly uses both expressions synonymously—it is nevertheless striking that in the relevant chapters of the main, first section (1.72 and 2.4–11), he prefers to speak of *tadbir* [governance], whereas in the relevant chapters of the main, second major division (3.16–24) he prefers to speak of *'inayah* [supervision]. One should refer also to 1.35 (42a) where he says: *wafi safah tadbiruhu lil'alam wakayf 'inayatuhu bima siwahu* "the character of His governance of the world, the 'how' of His providence with respect to what is other than He" [*Guide*, trans. Pines, 1.35, p. 80]. The origin of this distinction would require an investigation. Munk perhaps furnishes a pointer (*Le Guide des égarés* III, 111 n. 2), with which one should compare Julius Guttmann, "Das Problem der Willensfreiheit [bei Hasdai Crescas und den islamischen Aristotelikern]," in *Jewish Studies in Memory of George A. Kohut* (New York: Alexander Kohut Memorial Foundation, 1935), pp. 346–49. The distinction mentioned agrees in part in its result, though in no way in its intention, with the distinction between *'inayah naw'iyah* (general providence) and *'inayah shakhsiyah* (particular providence), which occurs in 3.17 (36b and 37a) and 3.18 (39a). [See *Guide*, trans. Pines, 3.17, pp. 472–73, and 3.18, p. 476.]

theoretical philosophy, on the one hand, and practical or human or political philosophy, on the other.[10] This is to say that the exclusion of the doctrine of divine omniscience and of divine (particular) providence from theoretical philosophy amounts to the attribution of this doctrine to practical or political philosophy. What seems to speak against this is that Maimonides remarks on one occasion—in the context of a presentation that is certainly meant to prepare the treatment of the question of providence—that the treatment of "ethical subjects" does not belong to the scope [*Aufgabenbereich*] of the *Guide*.[11] For it is precisely in this manner that he especially appears to rule out that the main, second section of the *Guide* (3.8 to the end) belongs to practical philosophy. Against this objection, one must note that ethics is in Maimonides' view only a part, and indeed in no way the central part, of practical or political philosophy: the understanding of the essence of happiness and what leads to it is not the business of ethics, but of politics in the true sense (the doctrine of the governance of the city).[12] What follows from this is that Maimonides can very well deny that the main, second section of the *Guide* belongs to ethics, without thereby in the least having to deny that this main section belongs to practical or political philosophy in general.

Maimonides thus excludes, through the plan of the *Guide*, the question of particular providence (and the question of divine omniscience, which essentially belongs to it) from the realm of theoretical philosophy, and does so in such a way that this exclusion amounts in no way to the attribution of this question to revealed theology [*theologia revelata*], but rather to politics. The implied characterization of the above-mentioned question would appear strange to the historian of philosophy. Indeed, in the Western, Latin tradition, from which the history of philosophy is derived, the view that prevailed at any rate was that precisely this question was a theme of natural theology, and thus of theoretical philosophy.[13]

10. *Millot ha-Higgayon* [*Treatise on Logic*], chap. 14.
11. *Guide* 3.8 end. [Strauss renders Maimonides' phrase as "ethischer Gegenstände," but Pines translates it as "moral . . . matters" (p. 436). Staying closer to Strauss's German, it has been rendered in English as "ethical subjects." However, it should be clear to readers that this refers to the same phrase as occurs in Maimonides, *Guide*, trans. Pines, 3.8, p. 436. Similarly, Strauss's "scope" [*Aufgabenbereich*] in *Guide*, trans. Pines, is "purpose."]
12. *Millot ha-Higgayon* [*Treatise on Logic*], chap. 14. For an interpretation, compare ["Quelques Remarques sur la Science Politique de Maïmonide et de Farabi,"] *Revue des Études Juives* 100 (1936), 7–12 and 15. [See "Some Remarks on the Political Science of Maimonides and Farabi," chap. 5 above.]
13. It should not therefore be contested that this view is also encountered within Islamic-Jewish philosophy. I refer to Avicenna's *Great Metaphysics* and to his *Compendium of Metaphysics*, to Averroes' *Compendium of Metaphysics*, to Gersonides' *Milḥamot ha-Shem* [*The Wars of the Lord*], and to Crescas' *Or ha-Shem* [*The Light of the Lord*]. Albo follows the older tradition, represented by Saadia and Mai-

In order to understand Maimonides' at first strange view, one must distinguish two moments in it. It is characteristic of this view that: (1) the doctrine of providence is treated at a much later point, namely, after the doctrines of God's unity, of creation, and of prophecy; and (2) this late treatment implies the attribution of the doctrine of providence to politics.

As regards the late treatment of the question of providence as such, one encounters it in the beginnings of medieval Jewish philosophy with Saadia [ben Yosef ha-Gaon]. In his *[Sefer] Emunot ve-Deot [Book of Beliefs and Opinions]*, the question of providence only comes up for discussion from the fifth treatise on, or after creation, the unity of God, law and prophecy, and the freedom of the will have been treated in the preceding treatises. While Saadia begins to discuss the doctrine of the Law (third treatise: *Of Commandments and Prohibitions*) before the doctrine of providence—and with a sharpness that Maimonides lacks in the *Guide*, at least at first glance—he lets the original reason for the late treatment of the doctrine of providence be known, which is also significant for Maimonides: Providence means justice in reward and punishment, and it thereby presupposes precisely a law, the fulfillment of which is rewarded and the violation of which is punished.[14] Now, since the doctrine of the Law presupposes the doctrine of prophecy, which in turn presupposes the doctrine of the angels (the separate intelligences), and which itself finally presupposes the doctrine of God,[15] there arises the necessity (which Maimonides has especially taken into account in the *Guide* as well) to

---

monides, even though the leading idea [*Leitgedanke*] of this tradition has become incomprehensible to him. (See *[Sefer ha-]Ikkarim [Book of Roots]* III beginning.) ["Treating of the second principle, which is revelation of the Torah. Inasmuch as the derivative dogmas depending upon this principle are, as we said in the First Book, the knowledge of God, prophecy, and the genuineness of the messenger, and since God's knowledge of the existing things of the lower world necessarily comes before all other dogmas—for if God does not know the existing things of the lower world, neither prophecy nor message can come from him—[it] would be appropriate to speak first of the knowledge of God. But inasmuch as God's knowledge of the lower existences must be compatible with the nature of the contingent, which depends upon freedom of choice, we found it proper to postpone treatment of God's knowledge until the Fourth Book, when we shall discuss the problem of freedom. We will therefore first speak of the principle of revelation of the Torah, and then we will explain the dogmas depending upon it, prophecy and the genuineness of the messenger." Albo, *Ikkarim* (*Roots*), trans. Husik, vol. 3, p. 1.]

14. Compare *Guide* 3.17 (34b–35a) [*Guide*, trans. Pines, 3.17, p. 469] with the 11th Article of Faith in the *Commentary on the Mishnah* (Sanhedrin X). ["The eleventh fundamental principle is that the Exalted One rewards the one who observes the commandments of the Torah, and punishes the one who transgresses its admonitions. The greatest reward is the world to come and the greatest punishment is extinction. We have already spoken sufficiently about this matter. The scriptural verse that alludes to this fundamental principle is: '*If Thou wilt forgive their sin—and if not, blot me out, I pray Thee, of Thy book.*' And God replied: '*Whosoever hath sinned against Me (him will I blot out of My book).*' This is proof that God knows both the one who serves Him and the transgressor, and rewards the one and punishes the other." Maimonides, *Commentary on the Mishnah (Sanhedrin)*, trans. Rosner, pp. 156–57.]

15. *Guide* 3.45 (98b–99a) [*Guide*, trans. Pines, 3.45, pp. 576–77].

present the doctrine of providence only after the treatment of each of the four preceding doctrines. Saadia, for his part, follows the Muʿtazilite *kalam* in the structure of his above-mentioned work. The Islamic-Jewish *kalam* tradition, however, prescribed not only the late treatment of the doctrine of providence, but also, and at the same time, the formal division of the entire matter of discussion into two parts (doctrine of the unity of God, and doctrine of the justice of God), in accordance with which the doctrine of providence—just as already the doctrine of law and prophecy earlier—belonged to the second part.[16] Thus, the arrangement deriving from this tradition is always, within certain limits, acknowledged by Maimonides,[17] even in his philosophical presentations. That is to say, this arrangement is for him a reliable foundation on which he can build, or rather the exoteric foreground which requires and at the same time veils an esoteric background. For the attribution of the doctrine of providence to the doctrine of the justice of God is one thing, the attribution of that doctrine to political science is another. In other words, the conception of the doctrine of providence as a theme of politics does not go back to the Islamic-Jewish *kalam* tradition, but to a genuinely philosophic tradition.

The doctrine of providence becomes, then, a theme of politics when the preceding doctrines of prophecy and law are attributed to politics. This

---

16. See Jacob Guttmann, *Die Religionsphilosophie des Saadia* (Göttingen 1882), p. 131, and Shlomo Pines ["Review of M. Ventura, *La philosophie de Saadia Gaon*"], *Orientalistische Literaturzeitung* (*OLZ*) 38 (1935): col. 623.

17. How much Maimonides is indebted to this tradition, one recognizes if one (radicalizing the suggestion of Pines, *OLZ*, 1935, col. 623) compares the structure of the *[Sefer] Emunot ve-Deot* [*Book of Beliefs and Opinions*, by Saadia ben Yosef al-Fayumi ha-Gaon: see trans. Samuel Rosenblatt (New Haven: Yale University Press, 1948); *Doctrines and Beliefs*, trans. Alexander Altmann, in *Three Jewish Philosophers* (New York: Atheneum, 1969)], with the corresponding arrangements in Maimonides: (1) The enumeration of the "Articles of Faith" in the *Commentary on the Mishnah*; (2) the parallels (which are also in agreement with Sanhedrin X) in "Hilkhot Teshuvah" ["Laws of Repentance"] III, 6-8; (3) the structure of the *Sefer ha-Madda* [*The Book of Knowledge*], and of the *Mishneh Torah* as a whole; (4) the structure of the *Guide*. It must be stressed in our context that in all four arrangements Maimonides brings up the acknowledgment of providence *after* he brings up the acknowledgment of prophecy in general and the prophecy of Moses in particular. The comparison teaches above all that the "Articles of Faith" concerning the Law (the 8th and 9th) find their counterpart in *Guide* 2.39-40, not in 3.25-50—as I had mistakenly assumed in *RÉJ* 100 (1936), 15 [see "Some Remarks on the Political Science of Maimonides and Farabi," chap. 5 above, third paragraph of section II]—and that therefore in the *Guide* also the doctrine of the Law (2.39-40) precedes the doctrine of providence (3.8-24) [*Guide*, trans. Pines, 2.39-40, pp. 378-85]. Compare especially the references to Deuteronomy 29:28 and 30:12 on the duration of the Torah provided in 2.39 (84b) with "Yesodei ha-Torah" IX, 1. [For "Hilkhot Teshuvah" III, 6-8, see "Laws of Repentance," trans. Hyamson, p. 83a; for "Yesodei ha-Torah" IX, 1, "Laws of the Basic Principles of the Torah," trans. Hyamson, p. 44b; for the "enumeration of the 'Articles of Faith' in the *Commentary on the Mishnah*," especially as concerns Sanhedrin X, see *Commentary on the Mishnah (Sanhedrin)*, trans. Rosner. See *Guide*, trans. Pines, 2.39, p. 380.]

last attribution is found from the beginning in the *falasifa*, the so-called Islamic Aristotelians: they understand the prophet, the prophetic lawgiver, as a philosopher-king in Plato's sense, as a founder of an ideal, Platonic city[18] (either in the sense of the *Republic* or in the sense of the *Laws*). That the doctrine of providence is also and at the same time handed over to politics[19] does not follow, then, merely from the adherence to a traditional arrangement ("providence after law and prophecy"), but also directly from the transformation, or reformation, of the doctrine of providence itself, which necessarily takes place with the turn to philosophy. Maimonides carries out this transformation in the *Guide* in the manner by which he explicitly distinguishes between the doctrine of providence "of our Law," and the correct doctrine of providence, which he himself follows.[20] Through this dis-

---

18. Averroes states this in his paraphrase of the *Republic*: "Quae omnia, ut a Platone de ... optima Republica, deque optimo ... viro dicta sunt, videre est in antiqua illa Arabum Reipublicae administratione, quae haud dubie optimam Platonis Rempublicam imitari putabat ... " *Opera Aristotelis* (Venice 1550), III, fol. 188a, col. 2, 1. 33–50. [Cf. Averroes, *On Plato's "Republic,"* trans. Lerner, p. 121: "You may understand what Plato says concerning ... the virtuous governance ... and ... the virtuous individual ... from the case of the governance of the Arabs in early times, for they were used to imitate the virtuous governance."] The Platonic-political origin of Maimonides' prophetology is usually not appreciated. One is led to the origin of this failure of appreciation if one considers the way in which that prophetology was received in Christian Scholasticism: Thomas Aquinas completely separates the doctrine of prophecy from the doctrine of divine Law; he treats the divine Law in the general section on morality (*Summa Theologica*, II 1, q. 91ff.); prophecy, however, in the specific section, namely, in the discussion of those *virtutes, quae specialiter ad aliquos homines pertinent* (II 2, q. 171 in the beginning) ["virtues, which apply in particular to certain men"].

19. That this handing-over is not carried out everywhere by the later *falasifa*, has been made clear in footnote 13.

20. Cf. 3.23 (49b) with 3.17 (34b and 35b) [*Guide*, trans. Pines, 3.23, p. 494, with 3.17, pp. 469, 471]. In order to assess the meaning and the importance of this distinction, one must consider that Maimonides: (1) does not make such a distinction in the two other enumerations that occur in the *Guide* (the opinions on creation and on prophecy); and (2) that he elaborates that distinction in a covert manner. In order merely to "hint at" his view, he enumerates twice the different opinions on providence (of which there are five): in 3.17, i.e., the chapter with which the doctrine of providence formally begins, and in 3.23, i.e., in the interpretation of the Book of Job, with which the teaching on providence formally ends. In 3.17: the opinions of Epicurus, Aristotle, the Asharites, the Mu'tazilites, and of "our Law"; in 3.23: the opinions of Aristotle, "our Law," the Mu'tazilites, the Asharites, and the right opinion (Elihu's opinion in the Book of Job, or Job's own opinion after the final revelation). The two enumerations are distinguished by two seemingly minor, but in truth decisive, moments: (1) Whereas in the first enumeration[, which is] initial and provisional, the traditional Jewish opinion and the right opinion (Maimonides' own opinion) seem to be subordinate to the opinion of "our Law," in the second enumeration, [which is] concluding and authoritative, the opinion of "our Law" is explicitly distinguished from the right opinion. (Notice also the sharp break after the discussion of the traditional Jewish opinion in the first enumeration: 3.17; 35a–b [*Guide*, trans. Pines, 3.17, p. 469]. (2) The opinion of Epicurus is explicitly mentioned in the first enumeration, but shortly thereafter (3.17; 34a and 35b [*Guide*, trans. Pines, 3.17, pp. 468 and 469] it is silently dropped as not worth mentioning, whereas in the enumerations of the opinions on creation and prophecy Epicurus' opinion was explicitly dropped as not worth mentioning (2.13; 29a, and 2.32; 72b) [*Guide*, trans. Pines, 3.17, pp. 464, 468, 470–71; 2.13, p. 285, and 2.32, p. 360]. Epicurus' opinion is not mentioned at all in the second enumeration of the opinions on providence: in the first enumeration it was mentioned only so that the external correspondence between the two enumerations (they both concern five opinions) can

tinction, as goes without saying, he does not give expression to a rebellion against the Law—rather, he finds also his own doctrine of providence in the Law[21]—but merely to the view according to which the doctrine found in the foreground of the Law, and which characterizes the Law as such, is simply of an exoteric character. The Law teaches that everything good (bad) that befalls men is reward (punishment) for their good (bad) *actions*.[22] Maimonides' own teaching, which thus coincides with the esoteric teaching of the Law, states that "providence is consequent upon the *intellect*."[23] The decisive difference between the two teachings consists in the following: the exoteric teaching asserts that moral virtue and external happiness are *coordinated to one another* [*Zugeordnetheit*]; the esoteric teaching, on the other hand, asserts the *identity* of true happiness with knowledge of God. Accordingly, the esoteric doctrine of providence coincides with the understanding of the essence of happiness, with the fundamental and logically consistent distinction between true and merely supposed happiness.[24] Now, the teaching on happiness belongs essentially to political science, as Maimonides[25] contends in unison with Farabi.[26] On the other hand, what concerns the exoteric doc-

---

conceal their internal discrepancy. Maimonides himself finds the principle of repeating the vulgar (initial) view with apparently minor, but in truth decisive, deviations to be at work in the procedure of Elihu, the representative of the right view (3.23; 50a); this remark on Elihu's way of presentation conveys an authentic indication of Maimonides' own way of presentation [*Guide*, trans. Pines, 3.23, p. 494]. To be explained in a corresponding way, is the fact that Maimonides asserts at first (3.17; 35b) in a most sharply defined manner [*in aller Schärfe*] that the right view is based primarily not on the insight of understanding but on Scripture, whereas at the end (in 3.23; 48b) Job's conversion to the right opinion is traced back to the fact that Job, who initially has at his disposal only traditional, i.e., vulgar, knowledge of God, is at the end led to true (i.e., philosophical) knowledge of God: Maimonides lets his reader repeat Job's path. The decisive rationalism of Maimonides thus shows itself only *at the end*—which, as may be parenthetically remarked, distinguishes him from modern rationalism—and it is in fact not shown openly in Maimonides' presentation of his own teaching (in 3.17), but only in his interpretation of the Book of Job [*Guide*, trans. Pines, 3.17, pp. 469–70; 3.23, pp. 492–93]. [One of the anonymous reviewers of the University of Chicago Press has observed that in this note, Strauss fluctuates between two key terms: "opinion" (*Meinung*) and "view" (*Ansicht*). It anticipates a perplexing peculiarity in his subsequent plan of the *Guide*, in which the book is divided between "views" and "actions" rather than "opinions" and "actions." This, according to the reviewer, is a significant difference of or choice in terminology ("views" vs. "opinions") that is in need of serious reflection. See "How To Begin," chap. 11 below.]

21. 3.17 (36a and 37b) [*Guide*, trans. Pines, 3.17, pp. 471 and 474].
22. 3.17 (34a–35b), and 3.23 (49a). That the emphasis is on "actions," is shown by the passages given in note 24 below [*Guide*, trans. Pines, 3.17, pp. 469–70, and 3.23, p. 492].
23. 3.17 (37b) [*Guide*, trans. Pines, 3.17, p. 474].
24. Cf. 3.23 (48b) with 3.22 (45b) [*Guide*, trans. Pines, 3.23, pp. 492–93, with 3.22, pp. 487–88].
25. See above [second and third paragraphs from the beginning].
26. Cf. the so-to-speak programmatic definitions in *Ihsa al-ulum*, chap. 5 ["The Enumeration of the Sciences," chap. 5, trans. Najjar, in *Medieval Political Philosophy*, ed. Lerner and Mahdi, pp. 24–30; "The Enumeration of the Sciences," chap. 5, trans. Butterworth, in *Political Writings*, ed. Butterworth, pp. 76–84], and *Kitab tahsil al-sa'ada* [*The Attainment of Happiness*] (Hyderabad, 1345), 16 ["The Attainment of Happiness," in *Plato and Aristotle*, trans. Mahdi, pp. 13–50], with the structure of *The Political*

trine of providence—the doctrine of divine reward and punishment—also belongs, and as exoteric doctrine indeed precisely as such, to politics. For what are exoteric doctrines other than such doctrines of faith as are not true, but "whose acknowledgment is necessary for the welfare [*Heil*] of the affairs of the city"?[27] And in conceiving the doctrine of divine reward and punishment as an exoteric doctrine, Maimonides is also in agreement with Farabi.[28]

Regime (*Haṭhalot ha-nimẓa'ot*) [which is one of the other titles (in Hebrew) by which *The Political Regime* is known, i.e., "The Principles of the Beings"], and the so-called *Musterstaat* ["The Ideal City" or "The Perfect State"]. [For sections of "The Political Regime," trans. Najjar, see *Medieval Political Philosophy*, ed. Lerner and Mahdi, pp. 32–56; for the *Musterstaat*, see *Perfect State*, trans. Walzer.] In the *Musterstaat* the doctrine of happiness is treated only *after* the doctrine of the "first leader" and of the "perfect city." The doctrine of "providence," which is found in the theoretical sections of both of Farabi's theological-political works, coincides with the doctrine of general providence, which occurs in the theoretical section of the *Guide*; compare above [second and third paragraphs from the beginning].

27. 3.28 (61a). Cf. 1.Intro. (7a) [*Guide*, trans. Pines, 3.28, p. 512: "the Law also makes a call to adopt certain beliefs, belief in which is necessary for the sake of political welfare"; 1.Intro., p. 12].

28. That Farabi regards this teaching as exoteric is already shown by the fact that it occurs in neither of his two main theological-political works. It is found, however, in his "Harmonization of the Opinions of Plato and Aristotle" (*Philosophische Abhandlungen*, ed. F. Dieterici, 32f.), an exoteric work that is dedicated to the defense of philosophy (i.e., Platonic-Aristotelian philosophy), especially against an orthodox attacker. [See "The Harmonization of the Two Opinions of the Two Sages: Plato the Divine and Aristotle," in *Political Writings*, trans. Butterworth, pp. 115–67, and especially pp. 164–67.] According to Ibn Sina, the teaching of reward and punishment after death, and especially of bodily resurrection, belongs not to the "roots," but to the "branches" of metaphysics (compare *Avicennae de anima etc., ab A. Alpago . . . in latinum versa* (Venice 1546), fol. 144, or Falaquera, *Reshit Ḥokhmah*, ed. Moritz David, p. 55). What is meant by that is shown by Maimonides' remark in the *Ma'amar Teḥiyat ha-Metim* [*Treatise on Resurrection*]: his opponent cites passages from Ibn Sina's treatise on retribution and regards them as philosophical statements! [*Moses Maimonides' Treatise on Resurrection (Ma'amar Teḥiyat ha-Metim): Original Arabic and Hebrew Translation of Samuel ibn Tibbon*, ed. Joshua Finkel (New York: American Academy for Jewish Research, 1939); the passage on Avicenna to which Strauss refers is on p. 13, ll. 8–9. It has appeared subsequently in the following editions: see "Ma'amar Teḥiyat ha-Metim," in *Igrot ha-Rambam*, ed. Kafah; and most recently in the critical edition of *Igrot ha-Rambam*, ed. Shailat, I, pp. 315–74, and especially pp. 366–67. For English translations, see "Essay on Resurrection," trans. Halkin, pp. 211–45; and especially "Treatise on Resurrection," trans. Fradkin, in Lerner, *Maimonides' Empire of Light*, pp. 154–77. The mention of Avicenna is in Halkin, pp. 213 and 218, and especially Fradkin, pp. 156 and 161.] In the third chapter of his *Kitab al-ma'ad* (Alpagues, fol. 48f.) [Avicenna (Ibn Sina), *Kitab al-Mabda' wa-l-ma'ad* (*Book of the Beginning and the Return*), ed. A. Nurani (Tehran: Institute of Islamic Studies, McGill University–Tehran University, 1984); *Livre de la genèse et du retour*, trans. Yahya J. Michot (Oxford: Centre for Islamic Studies, 2002)] Ibn Sina says that the doctrine of resurrection is not actually true, but is necessary for the essential, practical accomplishment of the goals which the Law intends [*des Gesetzes willen*]. [Brague (*Maïmonide*, p. 192, n. 28) comments that this affirmation of Avicenna's is undoubtedly rather diffuse or vague; however, he contends that the "precise reference" to which this affirmation must relate is actually to fol. 48a, which I reproduce as he presents it in its Latin translated version: "Dixit enim Maumethus in libro suo Alchorano ubi loquitur de *mahad* ('resurrection') iam declaratum esse, quod melior et dignior intentio legum divinarum est pars practica quae est de operationibus hominis, ita, ut unusquisque operetur bonum in seipso, et in eis quae communicant secum, in specie, et genere." For the Latin version, see Avicennae, *Philosophi Praeclarissimi Ac Medicorum Principis: Compendium de anima, De mahad, etc.* (Venice, 1546; republished, Gregg International Publishers: Westmead, England, 1969), p. 48a. For a translation: "For Muhammad said in his book the Qur'an, where it says that the Resurrection [of the body] has been laid down, that a better and worthier intention of divine laws is the practical application that concerns the deeds of man, thus [the Resurrection has been declared] in order that each and every man may produce good in himself and especially in those practical obligations that [men] share

This conception is an essential component of Platonic politics: inasmuch as Maimonides, just like Farabi and the other *falasifa*, adopts Platonic politics, he at the same time makes his own the doctrine of providence of the *Laws* in the sense of the *Laws*.[29]

---

among themselves individually and generally." My thanks to Sara Kathleen Alvis for her translation. She says that this is probable, rather than accurate in an absolute sense, because of the unusual nature of the original medieval Latin.]

29. The doctrine of providence in the *Laws* was perhaps known to Maimonides through Alexander of Aphrodisias, *De Providentia* (compare "Quelques Remarques sur la Science Politique de Maïmonide et de Farabi," in *Revue des Études Juives* 100 (1936), pp. 32ff. [See "Some Remarks on the Political Science of Maimonides and Farabi," chap. 5 above, third paragraph of section III. For *De providentia*, see Alexandre d'Aphrodise, *Traité de la providence [Peri pronoias]*, Arabic version of Abu Bisr Matta ibn Yunus, edited and with a French translation by Pierre Thillet (Lagrasse: Verdier, 2003).] Otherwise, the fact that the doctrine of providence belongs to politics could be understood from Galen, who explicitly relies on Plato for his overall view. He asserts: the question of providence is actually in opposition to the genuine metaphysical questions (concerning the nature of the gods and of the soul, the having-come-into-being [i.e., creation] and the not-having-come-into-being [i.e., eternity] of the universe, the immortality of the soul, and so on), while it is of decisive importance for "ethical and political philosophy" *and* soluble by scientific means. Compare in particular, *De Placitis Hippocratis et Platonis* IX (V, 780f. and 791ff. Kühn) [see Galen, *On the Doctrines of Hippocrates and Plato*, 2nd pt., bks. VI–IX, ed. Phillip de Lacy (Berlin: Akademie Verlag, 1980), pp. 588–89, and 596–601], and *De Substantia Facultatis Naturae* (IV 764 Kühn). [See Galen, *On (the Substance of) the Natural Faculties*, ed. and trans. Arthur John Brock (Cambridge, MA: Harvard University Press, 1963), especially pp. 42–49. Strauss's references to Galen are to *Claudii Galeni Opera Omnia*, ed. C. G. Kühn (Leipzig: C. Cnobloch, 1821–33; reprint, Hildesheim: Olms, 1964–65; Greek texts edited, with Latin translations).] That Maimonides had Galen's statements of this kind in front of him as he wrote the *Guide* is shown by 2.15 (33b) [*Guide*, trans. Pines, 2.15, p. 292]. The fact that, in "middle Platonism," the genuine Platonic view concerning the place of the doctrine of providence is not fully superseded by the Stoic view, according to which the doctrine of providence belongs to physics or theology (cf. Cicero, *De natura deorum* [*On the Nature of the Gods*], II 1, 3 and 65, 164ff., as well as Diogenes Laertius [*Lives, Teachings, and Sayings of the Eminent Philosophers*], VII 149 and 151), is shown also by Diogenes Laertius' account of the Platonic teaching (III 67–80). In that account, which is structured according to the scheme physics (theology)-ethics-dialectics, divine supervision of the human things is not spoken of in the presentation of physics and theology ([paras.] 67–77), but only in the presentation of ethics ([para.] 78), and divine retributive justice is mentioned only after dialectics (in [paras.] 79–80), i.e., at the very end, and indeed with the clear indication of the exoteric character of that teaching. Above all, however, one should recall Cicero, who, perhaps under the influence of his Platonizing teacher, took a similar position, as a comparison of *De republica* [*The Republic*] and *De legibus* [*The Laws*], on the one hand, and of *De natura deorum* [*On the Nature of the Gods*] and *De divinatione* [*On Divination*], on the other, brings out. [Galen, *On the Doctrines of Hippocrates and Plato*, p. 780f. Kühn (ed. de Lacy, pp. 588–89):

> To inquire also into matters that are not useful for ethics and political action is appropriate only for those philosophers who have chosen speculative philosophy; thus they also raise the question whether there is anything after this universe, and if there is, what its character is, and whether this universe is self-contained, whether there is more than one universe, whether the number of universes is very large, and similarly whether this universe is generated or ungenerated, and if it had a beginning, whether some god was the artisan of it, or whether it was no god but some irrational and artless cause that by chance made it as beautiful as if a god supreme in wisdom and power had supervised its construction. But such inquiries as these contribute nothing to managing one's own household well or caring properly for the public interest or acting with justice and friendliness toward kinsmen, citizens, and foreigners. But some who hold that the end (of philosophy) is practical have arrived at the investigation of these matters by a gradual passage from useful inquiries, supposing that they were passing to inquiries of a similar kind. The truth is that while it

The preceding presentation is confirmed by the structure of the *Sefer ha-Madda* [*Book of Knowledge*], the first and most philosophic part of the *Mishneh Torah*. There Maimonides first treats metaphysics ("Hilkhot Yesodei ha-Torah" ["Laws of the Basic Principles of the Torah"] I–II), and physics (ibid., III–IV), and then—only after the formal conclusion of metaphysics and physics, i.e., after the formal conclusion of theoretical philosophy—prophecy and the Law (ibid., VII–X). Prophecy and law are themes, not of theoretical philosophy, but of politics. The discussion of the scientific foun-

---

is useless to ask whether the universe had a beginning or not, this is not the case with an inquiry about divine providence. It is better for all of us to examine the statement that there is something in the universe superior to men in power and wisdom; but it is not necessary to consider the question what sort of substance the gods have, whether they are entirely bodiless or whether they have bodies too, as we do. These matters and many others are completely useless for those virtues and actions that we call ethical and political, and no less for the cure of the soul's ills. Xenophon's statement about them is best, not only did he condemn them as useless himself, but he said that Socrates also held this view. The other companions of Socrates agree, among them Plato himself; for when he adds to his philosophy a theory of nature he gives the exposition of it to Timaeus, not to Socrates, just as he gives the more extended dialectic to Parmenides and his pupil Zeno.

As with the bearing of the previous passage for reading Maimonides, Strauss points also for the treatment of providence in the *Guide* to the following passage in Galen, *On the Doctrines of Hippocrates and Plato*, 791ff. ed. Kühn (ed. de Lacy, pp. 596–601):

But Plato declared that the cause that made us, the god who is the craftsman of the universe, commanded his children by speech to fashion the human race, receiving from him the substance of the immortal soul and inserting it in the part that is generated. But we must recognize this fact, that there is no similarity in kind between proving and positing that we were made in accordance with the providence of some god or gods, and knowing the substance of the maker, or even of our own soul. My earlier remarks make it clear that the fashioning of our bodies is a work of the highest wisdom and power; but the statements of the most divine Plato about the substance of the soul and of the gods who formed us, and still more all that he says about our whole body, extend only to the point of being plausible and reasonable, as he himself pointed out in the *Timaeus* when first he was about to enter upon an account of the natural world, and again when he inserted the statement in the middle of the account. Accordingly, as Timaeus was about to begin it—for (Plato) presented this man as expounding in detail an account of the nature of the whole universe—he spoke as follows: "If there are many items, Socrates, concerning many matters—the gods and the origin of the universe—about which we should prove unable to give an entirely accurate and self-consistent explanation, do not be surprised; rather, if the accounts we provide are no less reasonable than another's, you and the rest must be content, remembering that (I) the speaker and you the jury are human; about this subject, therefore, we must accept the likely story and look no further." And in the same way he says that what he has written about the soul is a matter of plausibility and reasonableness, in these words: "Now as to this account of the soul, how much is mortal and how much is divine, and where, and in what company, and for what reasons its parts were given separate dwellings, we could assert its truth with confidence only if a god joined in the assertion; but even now, as we reflect still more on the matter, we must venture to claim that our account is plausible, and let this claim be made." Therefore, just as he said our knowledge of these earlier statements about the soul extends to what is plausible and reasonable, I too for this reason am not so bold as to make rash assertions about them; but on the other hand I claim to have proofs that the forms of the soul are more than one, that they are located in three different places, that one of them is divine, by which we reason, and the other two have to do with the feelings—with the one we are angry; and with the other, which plants have too, we desire the pleasures that come through the body.]

dations of the Torah, of the four fundamental doctrines susceptible of proof ([*ara usuliyya*]), concludes thus: God, angels, prophecy, and Law.[30] Only after this, that is, more particularly, after politics, does Maimonides treat ethics ("Hilkhot De'ot" ["Laws Concerning Character Traits"]),[31] which is of a lower scientific dignity.[32] The doctrine of providence is found in full only at the conclusion of the *Sefer ha-Madda*: Maimonides discusses the compatibility of divine omniscience and omnipotence with human free will in the fifth and sixth chapter of "Hilkhot Teshuvah" ["Laws of Repentance"]; reward and punishment in the world to come in the eighth chapter; reward and punishment in this world or the messianic age in the ninth chapter; the true happiness in the tenth chapter, with which the *Sefer ha-Madda* concludes. Maimonides, in bringing forward the doctrine of providence in the context of an explanation of the commandment to conversion, i.e., in an edifying context and not in a discussion of the (philosophic) foundations of the Torah, shows that he is guided by the view that this teaching is a necessary supplement to politics. For edification is nothing other than didactic politics, and there is no politics, for Maimonides, whose end is not primarily didactic, [and] which would be primarily "*Realpolitik*" ["realist" politics].

The structure of the *Guide* is less transparent because in fact in this work the political doctrine of prophecy and Law appears to be classified under metaphysics. This deviation from the most obvious arrangement is not explained solely by the fact that prophetology is indispensable for the interpretation of the *ma'aseh merkavah*,[33] but also and above all by the fundamental character of the *Guide*. This work intends, as Maimonides explains at the beginning, to offer nothing other than the "science of the Law."[34] The Law (which, according to both the commonly-held [*gewöhnlichen*] view, and the

---

30. Cf. 3.35 beginning, and 3.36 beginning, with 3.45 (98b–99a) [*Guide*, trans. Pines, 3.35, p. 535, and 3.36, p. 539, with 3.45, pp. 576–77].

31. The [sequential] arrangement politics-ethics(-economics) is commonly found in the time of Maimonides; see *RÉJ* 100 (1936), p. 11, n. 5. [See "Some Remarks on the Political Science of Maimonides and Farabi," chap. 5 above, fifth paragraph of section I, n. 29. In a marginal comment, added by Strauss at some unknown date, he declared of what he had written in this note: "that is wrong!" ("das ist verkehrt!"). He offers no further elucidation of the point. See *Philosophie und Gesetz: Frühe Schriften*, vol. 2 of *Gesammelte Schriften*, p. 193.]

32. 1.2 (14a). Cf. above [second and third paragraphs from the beginning] [*Guide*, trans. Pines, 1.2, pp. 24–25].

33. See, for example, 2.43 end [*Guide*, trans. Pines, 2.43, p. 393].

34. 1.Intro. (3a). It is no doubt with a view to this passage that, in his autobiography (Berlin 1793), II, 15, Salomon Maimon has entitled the first chapter of his review of the *Guide* as follows: "*Moreh Nevukhim* [*The Guide of the Perplexed*], its plan, goal, and method is *Theologia politica* [political theology]." Maimon renders the above-mentioned passage from the Introduction to the *Guide* in the following words: the

one accepted by Maimonides, is only one among many philosophic themes, [and] a theme of only one philosophic discipline among others, namely, political science) is the unique theme in the *Guide*: it is because and only because the *Guide* is not less "political" but rather more "political" than, for example, Ibn Sina's *Metaphysics*, that Maimonides can treat prophecy in the *Guide* apparently within the framework of metaphysics, whereas Ibn Sina treats it within the framework of politics. For it is because the *Guide* is entirely devoted to the science of the Law that its structure is not arranged according to the order of the philosophic disciplines, but according to the articulation [*Gliederung*] of the Law itself.[35] According to this articulation,

---

Guide "is solely aimed [*soll bloss*] to lay the foundation for the science of lawgiving (the wisdom of the Laws)" (ibid., 20) [*Guide*, trans. Pines, 1.Intro., p. 5].

35. The Law serves two purposes: the welfare [*Heil*] of the soul and the welfare [*Heil*] of the body; the welfare of the soul is attained through true *opinions*, the welfare of the body through the political order, which is based on the rightness of *actions* [*Guide*, trans. Pines, 3.27, pp. 510–11]. The true opinions, whose goal is the *love* of God, lead back to the four fundamental doctrines susceptible of proof (concerning God, angels, prophecy, and Law); those are explained by Maimonides in the *Mishneh Torah* in the "Hilkhot Yesodei ha-Torah," [and] in the main, first section of the *Guide* (1.1–3.7). That the deepest break within the *Guide* is found at the end of 3.7 [*Guide*, trans. Pines, 3.7, p. 430], has been shown at the beginning of the present essay. The right actions, which as such lead to the *fear* of God, are called forth: (1) through opinions which are not true but are necessary for the sake of the political order (to these opinions belongs above all the opinion that one must *fear* God, along with the corollary that He has pity [*erbarme*]); and (2) through the totality [*Gesamtheit*] of the commandments and prohibitions. Accordingly, the main, second section of the *Guide* is divided into two subsections: (1) an explanation of the "necessary" opinions (i.e., the most important of these opinions, the doctrine of divine reward and punishment) = 3.8–24; and (2) an explanation of the totality of the commandments and prohibitions = 3.25–50. Maimonides' explicit articulation of the Law is found in 3.27–28 and 3.52 (130a bottom [of the page] until the end [of the chapter]) [*Guide*, trans. Pines, 3.27–28, pp. 510–14, and 3.52, pp. 629–30]. For the division of "religion" into opinions and actions, compare Farabi, *Ihsa al-ulum* ["The Enumeration of the Sciences"], ch. 5 (or Falaquera, *Reshit Ḥokhmah*, 59, 9). Note the first word of *Guide* 3.25 [i.e., "the actions"]. [For "The Enumeration of the Sciences," chap. 5, see the translations mentioned in n. 26 above. In it Farabi says the following of political science:

> This science is divided into two parts: (A) One part comprises making known what happiness is; distinguishing between true and presumed happiness; enumerating the general voluntary actions, ways of life, morals, and states of character that are to be distributed in the cities and nations; and distinguishing between the ones that are virtuous and the ones that are not. (B) Another part comprises the way of ordering the virtuous states of character and ways of life in the cities and nations; and making known the royal functions by which the virtuous ways of life and actions are established and ordered among the citizens of the cities, and the activities by which to preserve what has been ordered and established among them. It then enumerates the various kinds of the nonvirtuous royal crafts—how many they are, and what each one of them is; and it enumerates the functions each one of them performs, and the ways of life and the positive dispositions that each seeks to establish in the cities and nations under its rulerships. (These things are to be found in the *Politics*, the book on the regime by Aristotle. They are to be found also in Plato's *Republic* and in [other] books by Plato and others.)

See also the very first line of Alfarabi, "Book of Religion," in *Political Writings*, trans. Butterworth, p. 93: "Religion is opinions and actions, determined and restricted with stipulations and prescribed for a com-the doctrine of prophecy and law as a true and demonstrable fundamental doctrine belongs to the main first part, which is devoted to the explanation of those fundamental doctrines, whereas the doctrine of providence as an edifying doctrine belongs to the first subdivision of the main second part, which treats the "necessary" doctrines.

---

munity by their first ruler, who seeks to obtain through their practicing it a specific purpose with respect to them or by means of them." See *Guide*, trans. Pines, 3.25, p. 502.]

7

Review of *The Mishneh Torah,* Book 1, by Moses Maimonides, Edited according to the Bodleian Codex with Introduction, Biblical and Talmudical References, Notes, and English Translation by Moses Hyamson

EDITOR'S NOTE

Leo Strauss's review of Moses Hyamson's Hebrew edition and English translation of Maimonides' *Sefer ha-Madda* (*Book of Knowledge*) originally appeared in *Review of Religion 3*, no. 4 (May 1937): 448–56. *Sefer ha-Madda* is the first of fourteen volumes of the *Mishneh Torah* (literally, *Repetition of the Torah*), also known as Maimonides' *Code of Law*. Hyamson's edition of the Hebrew text is based on the Bodleian manuscript, which not only bears Maimonides' own Hebrew signature on it, rendering the version "authorized" as authentic, but also contains his attestation that this copy was corrected according to his own master copy. However, the editor's English translation was not done according to the Bodleian manuscript, but followed instead the previous printed versions, which makes it not as dependable or correct as it could have been. Square brackets in the text are used by Strauss to convey the printed versions, which he contrasts with the Bodleian version (although not as it is translated by Hyamson). Parentheses in the text connected with his translations are used by Strauss to further explain what Maimonides intended or how the versions differ. Strauss's references have been moved from the text to the notes, although no notes of any sort actually appeared in the original review. Otherwise, the notes are entirely the work of the present editor. To signal the difference, the editor's comments have been set in square brackets. For those who wish to study for themselves the Bodleian manuscript of portions of the *Mishneh Torah* (MS. Huntington 80), on which version Maimonides' put his own signature, it is a great good fortune that this has recently (2010) been put online by Oxford University. Henceforth we can view it complete on our computer screens with a click of the mouse (http://harambam.org/), while in the past it was not readily accessible to even the most serious students of Maimonides, save for those scholars who were able to travel to the Bodleian Library.

PROFESSOR HYAMSON HAS MADE A VERY IMPORTANT CONTRIBUTION TO our knowledge of Maimonides, by making accessible to the public for the first time the most authentic version which has come down to us of the *Sefer ha-Madda*, i.e., the first "book" of the *Mishneh Torah*. "The text in this edition closely follows, line by line, a unique manuscript in the Bodleian Library of the Oxford University"; that "manuscript has the unique distinction that it contains Maimonides' autograph at the end of Book II," i.e., practically at the end of the manuscript; and the subscription in Maimonides' hand is "a certification by Maimonides that the manuscript had been revised and corrected by comparison with the author's original copy." How necessary is the work, the first half of which has now been achieved by Professor Hyamson, was eloquently pointed out by Professor Alexander Marx some years ago.[1] The

---

1. See *Jewish Quarterly Review*, New Series, 25/4 (April 1935): pp. 371f. [Alexander Marx was professor at the Jewish Theological Seminary of America, and also perhaps the dean of Maimonides scholars during the period in which Strauss wrote his review. The "eloquent" remarks to which Strauss refers appeared in the article "Texts By and About Maimonides," edited and introduced by Marx; it appeared on pp. 371–428. The article itself appeared in the number of the journal issued "In Commemoration of the Eight Hundredth Anniversary of the Birth of Maimonides," edited by Cyrus Adler, with essays contributed by Boaz Cohen, Israel Davidson, Louis Finkelstein, Sabato Morais, and Harry Wolfson. The "eloquent" remarks by Marx to which Strauss makes reference run as follows:

> It seems incredible that the Ms. of the first two books of the *Mishneh Torah* with the author's autograph attestation that it was corrected according to his own copy, is still unpublished and that we are still satisfied with unreliable reproductions of the early editions without any recourse to the numberless Mss. And yet even a few years after the author's death many mistakes had crept into the Mss. of his works. For this, curiously, we have authentic evidence from the pen of Maimonides' great antagonist, R. Meir ha-Levi Abulafia. In a letter to Burgos he declares that he had compared several Mss. of the *Code* for the list of open and closed *parashas* of the Torah contained in chapter eight of the laws of Sefer Torah and found them all contradictory and incorrect. Finally he appealed to R. Samuel ibn Tibbon at Marseilles for his copy which bore an autograph attestation by Maimonides similar to the one in the Oxford Ms. 577. This authentic list agreed with all the views of Abulafia. This fact alone should be sufficient to indicate the necessity of a critical edition of the *Code*. It is to be hoped that the planned edition of the Oxford Ms. will appear soon.

best way of appreciating the editor's achievement is to make a survey (which cannot but be somewhat arbitrary) of some of the most striking differences between the text of the new edition and that of the current editions.

It is hardly necessary to point out that the text of the new edition is much superior in grammatical correctness to the text of the current editions. It is no more surprising, if somewhat more interesting, to observe, by comparing the two texts, how much the original has been adulterated under the direct or indirect influence of Christian censorship. I shall briefly indicate, by putting the readings of the current editions into angular brackets, the typical adulterations caused by that factor.[2]

(1) *goyyim* <*'ac"um*>

(2) *ha-komerim, ha-kemarim* <*kohaneihem*>

(3) *komerei 'edom* <*kohanei 'ac"um*>

(4) *min* <*'epiqoros*>

(5) *nokheri* <*'ac"um* or *goy*>

(6) *'avodah zarah* <*'ac"um*>

(7) *malkhuyyot ha-rasha'h* <*malkhut 'ac"um* or *malkhuyyot*>

(8) *shemad* <*gezerah*>

(9) *meshummad* <*mumar*>

(10) *talmud* <*gemara'*>

"The planned edition of the Oxford Ms." is the book produced by Hyamson, which Strauss reviewed. As for Meir ben Todros HaLevi Abulafia (c. 1170–1244), he was a major Spanish Talmudist and legal authority, roughly contemporary with Maimonides. He launched the first phase in the "Maimonidean Controversy" by his criticism of *The Guide of the Perplexed* and his opposition to the study of philosophy in Jewish society.]

2. [For the benefit of readers with no Hebrew, the terms will be rendered in English (while repeating the transliterated Hebrew), to convey at least a sense of the difference between Maimonides' own original terms as they appear in the Bodleian manuscript and the terms imposed by medieval Christian censors, which unwittingly entered Jewish use through the standard printed editions. As Strauss notes, the Bodleian manuscript is a uniquely authoritative version of *Sefer ha-Madda* because it is one of the rare documents with Maimonides' actual signature on it, which authorizes it as checked by him. Doctored versions of the Maimonidean text employing the terms which Strauss chooses to highlight (as well as others not discussed by Strauss) had been printed in most texts prior to the appearance of Hyamson's edition of the Bodleian manuscript. Since the appearance in print of the Bodleian Hebrew text as edited by Hyamson, Yosef Kafah (also in English as both Kafih and Kapach) in Israel has edited Yemenite Jewish printed texts or manuscripts of the *Mishneh Torah* in general and of the *Sefer ha-Madda* specifically, which claim equal authority with the Bodleian text. These have certainly added much helpful material for scholarly use. However, the scholarly debate on the definitive Maimonidean text is not yet settled, especially on several highly controversial items, since a true critical edition of the *Sefer ha-Madda* (never mind of the entire *Mishneh Torah*) has not yet been produced. Strauss's original journal review of Hyamson's edition conveys a list of contrasting Hebrew terms (Bodleian manuscript versus the printed editions), seemingly produced in Strauss's own handwritten style (with the words in the form of printed letters), rather than in Hebrew typed letters. Strauss's list of divergent Hebrew terms is to be presented in the following format:

first, in quotation marks and angle brackets, a term (or its occasional alternate) is translated, showing how it appears in the Bodleian-manuscript Hebrew version of the text of Maimonides' *Sefer ha-Madda* (ed. Hyamson); second, in curly brackets and italicized, the same term (or its occasional alternate) is shown as transliterated from the original Hebrew; third, in parentheses, I attempt to highlight what these terminological differences might seem to imply, in terms of how Strauss will bring these implications to light; fourth (and shifting to the next line), in quotation marks and angle brackets, the parallel term (or its occasional alternate) is translated, showing how it appears in most printed (i.e., censored) Hebrew versions of the text of Maimonides' *Sefer ha-Madda*, hitherto the only ones available; fifth, in curly brackets and italicized, the same parallel term (or terms) from the printed versions is shown as transliterated from the original Hebrew; sixth, in parentheses, I attempt to highlight what these terminological differences might seem to imply, in terms of how Strauss will bring these implications to light. Prior to his detailed, categorized explanations of the differences between the Bodleian manuscript and previous printed editions, Strauss suggests by this contrasting list itself that the printed versions often seriously mislead about the original language of Maimonides, and hence about the original intentions of Maimonidean thought in this crucial text that contains some of the most significant theological and political dimensions of his law code in their philosophic grounding.

1. <"nations"> or <"Gentiles"> {*goyyim*} (foreign nations; but implying: religious unbelievers)
   <"idolators"> {*'ac"um = 'ovedei kokhavim u-mazzalot*} (literally: worshipers of stars or planets and constellations; it is a standard Hebrew contraction of those three key words, in which a novel word has been formed as an acronym)
2. <"the priests"> {*ha-komerim, ha-kemarim*} (implying: the idolatrous priests)
   <"their priests"> {*kohaneihem*} (implying: not as differentiated, because it uses the same word for Israelite-monotheistic and for idolatrous priests)
3. <"Edomite priests"> {*komerei 'edom*} (figuratively: "priests of Rome"; and hence implying: Christian priests)
   <"priests of idolatry"> {*kohanei 'ac"um*}> (implying: priests of the worship of stars or planets and constellations)
4. <"heretic">, <"sectarian">, or <"apostate"> {*min*}
   <"Epicurean"> {*'epiqoros*} (literally: Epicurean; implying: atheist, skeptic, or unbeliever)
5. <"foreigner"> or <"Gentile"> {*nokheri*}
   either <"idolator"> {*'ac"um = 'oved kokhavim u-mazzalot*} (worshiper of stars or planets and constellations)
   or <"Gentile"> {*goi*} (literally: a member of a foreign nation; implying: a religious unbeliever)
6. <"idolatry"> {*'avodah zarah*} (literally: strange, foreign, or alien worship; implying: non-monotheistic, usually non-Israelite, worship, and with a stronger note of censure)
   <"idolatry"> {*'ac"um = 'avodat kokhavim u-mazzalot*} (worship of stars or planets and constellations, and with a weaker note of censure)
7. <"kingdoms of wickedness or evil"> {*malkhuyyot ha-rasha'h*} (evil kingdoms, or kingdoms steeped in wickedness; Brague, *Maïmonide*, p. 198, prefers to read the vowels of the phrase in the Bodleian manuscript as {*malkhuyot ha-risha'h*}; however, it in no sense alters the meaning of the phrase)
   either <"idolatrous kingdom"> {*malkhut 'ac"um*}
   or <"kingdoms"> {*malkhuyyot*}
8. <"religious persecution"> or <"forced apostasy"> {*shemad*}
   <"decree"> or <"edict"> {*gezerah*} (implying: an evil decree or edict; Brague, *Maïmonide*, p. 198, prefers to read Strauss's handwritten Hebrew as saying {*sakhar*}, "wages," "payment," "remuneration," or "recompense"; I differ with Brague as to how to most accurately read the letters of the word in Strauss's handwritten Hebrew printing; I judge the last two letters to be a *mem* and a *dalet*, rather than a *kaf* and a *resh*; for the word differently used by the Bodleian manuscript and the printed texts, see "Hilkhot Yesodei ha-Torah," chap. V, para. 3: Hyamson, p. 40a, l. 18, for {*shemad*} as opposed to {*gezerah*}; cf. also *Mishneh Torah, Sefer ha-Madda* [in Hebrew], ed. Shmuel Tanhum Rubenstein (Jerusalem: Mosad ha-Rav Kook, 1983), p. 25, which follows the printed texts {*gezerah*}; *Mishneh Torah, Sefer*

To the same connection belongs the omission in the current editions of the name of Jesus, which occurs in "Hilkhot Avodah Zarah" X, 1, in "Hilkhot Teshuvah" III, 10 (end), and IV, 2 (4). The most important group of the variants, for which we are indebted to Professor Hyamson's edition, consists of such readings as have, or may have, some bearing on the understanding of Maimonides' thought. For the convenience of the reader, I shall indicate some examples of those variants by arranging them according to subject matter.

I. *The character of the Mishneh Torah and its plan.* The *Mishneh Torah* begins with the motto (omitted in the current editions) "In the name of the Lord, the everlasting God" (Gen. 21:33), i.e., with the same motto with which each part of *The Guide of the Perplexed* opens. That motto is explained in the *Mishneh Torah* ("Avodah Zarah" I, 3) in the same way as it is in the *Guide* (2.13 and 2.30; 3.29), namely as indicating, first, God's existence, and then, His governing the sphere as well as His creating the world. In "Teshuvah" IV, 5, we now read "we have compiled in the 'Hilkhot De'ot' . . . ," instead of the usual reading "we have explained in the 'Hilkhot De'ot.' . . ." It is important to note that, when quoting in the *Sefer ha-Madda* (and, indeed, the entire *Mishneh Torah*) an earlier chapter, Maimonides usually says: "we have explained (in this or that chapter)" (see "Teshuvah" V, 5, VIII, 3, and X, 6); on the other hand, the *Mishneh Torah* as such is called by him a "compi-

---

ha-Madda [in Hebrew], ed. Yohai Makbili, Yehiel Kara, and Hillel Gershuni (Haifa: Or Vishua, 2009), p. 39, which follows the Yemenite manuscripts {*shemad*})

9. <"apostate"> or <"convert to another religion"> {*meshummad*} (implying: betrayal or treason)

<"apostate"> or <"convert to another religion"> {*mumar*} (implying: a renegade or rebel, and thus carrying a slightly milder tone; vis-à-vis the term Strauss records as used by Maimonides according to the Bodleian manuscript, it should be noted that in this case Brague, *Maïmonide*, p. 198, prefers to read the former as {*meshumar*} and the latter as {*munar*}; i.e., in the former case he reads the last letter of the word to be a *resh*, while I judge it to be a *dalet* instead; in the latter case he reads the middle letter of the word to be a *nun*, while I judge it to be a *mem* instead; thus, again I differ with Brague as to how to most accurately read the letters of the words in Strauss's handwritten Hebrew printing; however, in the present case, we curiously arrive at similar results with regard to the sense of those words: he defines {*meshumar*} as "apostat," and he defines {*munar*} as "renégat"; for the word differently used by the Bodleian manuscript and the printed texts, see "Hilkhot Avodah Zarah," chap. II, para. 5: Hyamson, p. 68a, l. 6 (cf. also l. 7), for {*meshumad*}; for its contrast with {*mumar*}, see also p. XI, the tenth variant which is dealt with on the same page; cf. also *Mishneh Torah, Sefer ha-Madda*, ed. Rubenstein, p. 135, which follows the printed texts {*mumar*}; *Mishneh Torah, Sefer ha-Madda*, ed. Makbili, Kara, and Gershuni, p. 64, which follows the Yemenite manuscripts {*meshumad*})

10. <"Talmud"> {*talmud*} (generally, the entire oral law and its study; specifically *the* Talmud, i.e., Mishnah and Gemara, which encompasses a law code as well as elaborate legal discussion and amplification, theological lore, midrash on scripture, and much else besides)

<"Gemara"> {*gemara*} (implying, even if it is not terminologically required to do so: the legally focused half of the Talmud only)

lation" (of traditional materials). By occasionally using the expression "we have compiled" (instead of "we have explained") when expressly quoting the "Hilkhot De'ot" (the laws concerning morals and hygiene), Maimonides possibly alludes to the peculiar character of that section of the *Sefer ha-Madda*, as indicated in the *Guide* 3.35 (394, 5–6 Joel) and 3.38, if not to the peculiar character of all parts of the *Mishneh Torah* other than its first four chapters.[3] At the beginning of "Hilkhot Yesodei ha-Torah" III, we now read: "And the spheres" ["The spheres"]. The new reading makes clear the inseparability of physics (= "Yesodei" III–IV) from metaphysics (= "Yesodei" I–II), and vice versa; it is explained in the *Guide* 1.Intro. (5, 6), where Maimonides says: "Physics are contiguous to metaphysics." Our insisting on apparently slight variations of expression is justified by another variant, which, indeed, was already known from other sources. In "Yesodei" IV, 8, Maimonides says: "Therefore, one must be careful as regards names (terms) [as regards their names (sc., the terms mentioned immediately before which designate soul or spirit)], in order that you (singular number!) will not err [in order that nobody will err with regard to them] and each individual term has to be understood (sc., in each individual case) from its context." (The statement quoted refers not only to biblical terms, but likewise to terms as used by Maimonides himself; this is shown by the parallel to "Yesodei" IV, 8 in "Teshuvah" VIII, 3; cf. also *Guide* 1.Intro. [9, 26ff.].) The new reading conveys a much more general warning (a warning with regard to an unlimited number of words, and not only with regard to the two words mentioned immediately before), and it conveys at the same time a much more specified warning: it is addressed, not to all men, but to one man only. For the secret teaching which is transmitted, especially by words of manifold meanings, is addressed to "one man" only.

II. *Theology*. "One says [He says (sc., the Scripture says)] 'By the life of Pharaoh' and 'By the life of thy soul,' and one does not say [and he does not say] 'By the life of the Eternal,' but 'The Eternal lives'" ("Hilkhot Yesodei ha-Torah" II, 10). The authentic reading is confirmed by the parallel passage in the *Guide* (1.68 [112, 18]). In the enumeration of the names of God in "Yesodei" VI, 2, we now read *Eheyeh* instead of *Elohai*. Cf. *Kesef Mishneh* on the passage,[4] and *Guide* 1.62 (105, 4) and 1.63 (106, 14ff.). Speaking of man's

---

3. [See chaps. 8 and 12 below.]

4. [Joseph Caro (1488–1575) is better known as the author of the *Shulḥan Arukh*, his still authoritative code of Jewish law, which was based on, but superseded, the *Mishneh Torah* as the accepted first source used by almost all jurists and legalists. Previously he had composed the *Kesef Mishneh* as his commentary

imitation of God's moral attributes, Maimonides in one case says: "to assimilate himself [to assimilate himself to Him]" ("De'ot" I, 6). The omission of the object is perfectly understandable on the basis of the *Guide* 1.54. "If the divinities were many [If there were many divinities]" ("Yesodei" I, 7). "The worship of him whose name is Molech [The worship (sc., the idol) the name of which is Molech]" ("Avodah Zarah" VI, 3). The scriptural proof of God's incorporeality is introduced by the words: "It is clearly set forth in the Pentateuch and in the prophet [prophets]" ("Yesodei" I, 8). As a matter of fact, Maimonides mentions in that context one prophet only. "If He were living by life and knowing by knowledge, there would be many divinities: He, His life, and His knowledge" ("Yesodei" II, 10). The current editions read: "and knowing by knowledge external to Himself." One line before, Dr. Hyamson's text, as well as the text of the current editions, reads: "He does not know by a knowledge which is external to Himself." But there, *de'ah* (knowledge) means intelligence, strictly speaking, whereas one line further on, that term is used in a sense similar to that in which it occurs in the heading "Hilkhot De'ot" ("Laws Concerning Moral Qualities"). The passage "We do not find that God ever revoked anything good (which He had promised) except at the destruction of the First Temple, when He had promised to the just that they would not die together with the wicked, and He revoked His words; this is clearly set forth in the talmudic treatise Shabbat" ("Yesodei" X, 4) does not occur in the text of the new edition.

III. *Angelology.* Maimonides indicates the problem of the relation between the biblical angelology and the philosophic doctrine of separate intelligences by the following irregular expression: "the rank of those forms [that form] which *is* called Ḥayot)" ("Yesodei" II, 7). Compare one line further on the statement: "the rank of the form which is called *Ishim*, and they are the angels who speak with the prophets."

IV. *Ethics.* "Man ought to direct all his actions [his heart and all his actions] to the knowledge of God alone" ("De'ot" III, 2). "Their hearts (sc., the hearts of men) are left to them (sc., to their discretion)." The current editions read: "All is left to them" ("Teshuvah" V, 3). "So also what he (David) said, 'Let a noble spirit uphold me,' that is to say, 'Suffer my spirit to accomplish its desire [Thy desires]'" ("Teshuvah" VI, 4). The question of the limits of human liberty is the secret topic of "Teshuvah" V, as is indicated by the be-

---

on Maimonides' *Mishneh Torah*. Most of the book was first printed in Venice in 1574 (together with the *Mishneh Torah*), during Caro's life.]

ginning of that chapter: "The freedom of every man is given to him [Freedom is given to every man]." (Cf. *Migdal Oz* on the passage,[5] and "Teshuvah" V, 2 and VII, 1.) For the interpretation of the passage, compare *Guide* 3.17 (cf. 337, 24–28 and 338, 21–30 with 340, 10ff.), and 19 (345, 10). In the enumeration of (faulty) extremes in "De'ot" I, we observe the following two interesting variants: "extremely [particularly] humble"; and "particularly pure as regards his body (sc., his bodily appetites)" instead of "of a very pure heart" (I, 1). The second variant is illustrated by another variant which occurs somewhat later on (I, 4): "that he will be perfect [as regards his body]" (i.e., an addition). (Cf. *Shinuyei nushaot* [= variant readings], ad loc.)[6] "Every man whose moral dispositions are all of them in the middle (sc., between the two faulty extremes) is called wise" ("De'ot" I, 4). "All of them" has been omitted by the current editions, perhaps in order to avoid the apparent contradiction to "De'ot" II, 3, where Maimonides shows that the extremes of humility and meekness were recommended by Jewish tradition. "It is impossible to understand or to know [something belonging to the knowledge of the Creator] (i.e., an addition), while one is sick" ("De'ot" IV, 1).

V. *The Law*. Rabbi Judah the Saint "compiled from all (those materials) the Mishnah, which was taught in public [to the wise]" (i.e., an addition) (Intro., 2b10 Hyamson). "These were the great ones [the greatest of the wise] ... and together with them were thousands and tens of thousands [and tens of thousands] (i.e., an omission) of other wise (men)" (ibid., 2b19f.). "The great Bet-Din of seventy [seventy-one]" (ibid., 3b25). "Forty men [Forty generations]" (ibid., 3a8. Cf. also 4a12f.). "... Elijah at Mount Carmel, who offered up burnt offerings outside (the Temple), and Jerusalem was chosen [had

---

5. [Shem-Tov ben Abraham ibn Gaon (1283–1330) was a Spanish rabbinic scholar and author of *Migdal Oz*. The *Migdal Oz* is a commentary on Maimonides' *Mishneh Torah*, in which he defends the work against its critics, and especially against the strictures of Abraham ben David. As a careful scholar, he also corrected textual errors in the manuscripts of the *Mishneh Torah* as these had been transmitted by scribes. But he likewise noted changes in the work made by Maimonides himself during the course of his own life, regarding which consider most recently Herbert A. Davidson, *Moses Maimonides: The Man and His Works* (Oxford: Oxford University Press, 2005), pp. 221, 269–70. The *Migdal Oz* was first printed (although not completely) together with the *Mishneh Torah* in Constantinople in 1509, and in Venice in 1524.]

6. [See for variant readings of the *Mishneh Torah*, and especially of the *Sefer ha-Madda*, besides the edition of Hyamson, two recent Hebrew editions of the entire *Mishneh Torah*, which both appeared subsequent to Strauss's demise. Both are helpful in certain respects; but the editions of neither Shabtai Frankel nor Yosef Kafah constitutes in any sense of the word a critical edition properly speaking. (Thus, neither Frankel nor Kafah contains variants obtained from the Genizah texts.) See Moshe bar Maimon, *Sefer Mishneh Torah, hu ha-yad ha-ḥazaḳah*, ed. Shabtai Frankel et al. anon. (New York: Kehilat Bene Yosef, 1975). See also his *Yalqut shinuyei nushaot* (*Collected Textual Variants*, i.e., in the *Mishneh Torah*). Moshe ben Maimon, *Sefer Mishneh Torah*, ed. Yosef Kafah (Ḳiryat Ono: Mekhon Mishnat ha-Rambam, 1984).]

been chosen for that purpose], and anyone who offered them up outside, incurred the penalty of excision" ("Yesodei" IX, 3).

VI. *Eschatology.* To the statement "he who commits idolatry under compulsion, does not incur the penalty of excision and, needless to say, the judicial penalty of death," the current editions add the following remark, which does not occur in Dr. Hyamson's edition: "But if he is able to save himself and to escape from the power of the wicked king and does not do so, he is like a dog that returns to its vomit, and he is called a willful idolater, and he is excluded from the world to come, and he descends to the lowest rank of *gehinnom*" ("Yesodei" V, 4). Cf. *Shinuyei nushaot*, ad loc. To the expression "the intelligences that are devoid of matter" ("Yesodei" IV, 8), the current editions add the explanation: "such as the angels that are form without matter." The addition creates the impression, contradictory to what had been indicated in "Yesodei" II, 3, that there are immaterial creatures apart from the angels. In "Yesodei" IV, 4, the current editions substitute the unambiguous term *nifsad* (perishable) for the ambiguous term *nifrad*, which may mean "separate, sc., from matter" as well as "susceptible of disintegration." (For the first meaning, see "Teshuvah" VIII, 3, and for the second meaning see "Yesodei" IV, 3. The term occurs in yet another meaning in "Yesodei" I, 10 and II, 3.) Compare for this and the preceding variant *Shinuyei nushaot*, ad loc.

VII. *Words of particular significance.* In "De'ot" II, 3, the current editions substitute in one case *middah* for *de'ah*. Maimonides prefers the latter because of its specific ambiguity. "In discussing Torah and discussing wisdom, the words of the wise [the words of a man] should be few, and their meanings (or contents) should be many" ("De'ot" II, 4). In "De'ot" IV, 21, the current editions substitute in one case *hanhagot* for *minhagot*. Maimonides seems to wish to avoid, in this context, the word *hanhagah*, which, according to him, is the "translation" of *merkavah*, i.e., of the term designating the most secret topic. He prefers *minhag* (custom), which he sometimes uses as a synonym of *nature*. In "Avodah Zarah" I, 3 and II, 1, we now read in a number of cases "people" or "peoples" instead of "world."

There is one point of no small importance with regard to which Dr. Hyamson's edition seems not to be quite satisfactory. One cannot see from his edition to what extent the division of chapters into numbered paragraphs is based on the manuscript, and to what extent that division is due to the editor's discretion. The indication which he gives in his Introduction (p. iv) is difficult to reconcile with his note at the bottom of page 34a.

As regards the English translation, it is in most cases correct, and in many cases even excellent. It certainly will be most helpful to the general reader. Its most obvious shortcoming is that very often it is based, not on the manuscript text, together with which it is printed, but on the text of the current editions. But, apart from this, the question may be raised whether a translation meeting all the conditions which excellent translations of most philosophic or halakhic books have to fulfill, would be an adequate translation of a work of Maimonides. The answer to that question naturally depends on which view we hold of the character of Maimonides' writings. As far as the *Sefer ha-Madda* is concerned, we could learn from the author's own statements what kind of a book it is. Being a part of the *Mishneh Torah*, it is addressed to "all men" (*Guide* 2.35 in the beginning; cf. 1.Intro. [3, 7] with "Yesodei" IV, 13), i.e., it is not addressed to philosophers in particular; it is, therefore, less scientific and more exoteric than the *Guide*. The most striking proof of this is the fact that Maimonides, as it were, hesitates to use within the *Mishneh Torah* the word *nature*: he speaks, to begin with, not of the *nature* of the elements, but of their *custom* or their *way*. ("Yesodei" III, 11 and IV, 2. Professor Hyamson wrongly renders the two words in question by "governing principle" and "nature.") Now, an exoteric book, if it is the work of an unexoteric or initiated mind, is, by its very nature, more difficult to decipher than is an esoteric book. For in an exoteric book, the author can explain his views only in a rather haphazard and vague way. (Compare *Guide* 1.Intro. [6, 8–9], and 1.71 [125, 24].) One may venture to say that an exoteric work such as the *Sefer ha-Madda* (or the *Mishneh Torah* as a whole) is much more esoteric than are most esoteric works. Or, to avoid that paradox, we shall simply say that the *Sefer ha-Madda* is a book full of mystery. To see this, one only has to consider what secret teaching, according to Maimonides' principles, means. It means teaching the truth to those who are able to understand by themselves, while at the same time hiding it from the vulgar. The most important method, used by him, of thus teaching the truth, is to make contradictory statements about those exalted subjects with regard to which the truth shall flash up for one moment and then disappear again. Now, it is obvious to anyone who reads the *Sefer ha-Madda* with a reasonable degree of care, that Maimonides uses the method of "contradictions" in that work not less than he does in the *Guide*. The most famous examples are the contradictory statements about piety which occur in the first two chapters of the "Hilkhot De'ot." From the translator's point of view, however, contradictions are of minor importance, as they do not, by themselves, present a serious difficulty of translation. But it is of decisive importance for the translator of the *Sefer ha-Madda* to be aware of the fact that Maimonides, in a number of instances, reveals what he considers to be the truth by the use of ambiguous as well as unambiguous words of secret meanings, and that he does this in the *Sefer ha-Madda* not less than in the *Guide*. This being the case, a translation of the *Sefer ha-Madda* ought to be as literal as possible: the same Hebrew word has, if possible, always to be rendered by the same English word, if the allusions intended by Maimonides are to be noticed by the reader who cannot understand the original. In a translation of a work of Maimonides, the principle of literalness has to overrule all other considerations, to the same, or even to a greater, extent than in the medieval translations of the works of Aristotle and Averroes.

In "Yesodei" I, 6, Professor Hyamson translates *benei 'adam* by "majority of mankind," one line further on by "men." At the beginning of "Avodah Zarah," he translates the same expression by "the people." Towards the end of "Yesodei" III, he translates it more literally by "children of men." It might be worth considering whether one ought not to translate it in all cases by "sons of man," since the translation "men" would not remind us of the fact that the expression in question sometimes does not designate mankind as such, but only the great majority of mankind. Besides, the translation suggested would bring out the connection of that expression with the expressions "sons of the prophets" and "sons of the wise." (As regards the ambiguity of "son," see *Guide* 1.7.) One might even raise the question whether in some cases Hebrew proper names ought not to be accompanied by a translation, e.g., in the case of Enosh ("Avodah Zarah," at the beginning), where an adequate translation might solve the difficulty presented by Maimonides' statement about that person. In "Yesodei" II, 3, Professor Hyamson translates two Hebrew words of very different meanings by the same English words "such are," and thus renders unrecognizable an important hint given by Maimonides. In "Yesodei" IV, 2, he translates both *'afar* (dust) and *'erez* (earth) by "earth." He translates *ḥakhamim* by "sages," "our sages," "wise," "wise men," and "Chachamim." The translator is not to blame for his failure to find a single English rendering for that most important word *de'ah*. He translates it by "intelligence," "knowledge," "moral disposition," "moral principle," "mind," "passion," "sentiment," and "idealistic being." It may very well be that there is not a single English word which could be used for designating separate intelligences as well as knowledge, moral qualities, and mind. But it can safely be said that, until such an English word has been found, or coined, the reader of even the best English translation of the *Sefer ha-Madda* will miss important points of Maimonides' teaching. For Maimonides did not use the ambiguous word in question without good reason.

The biblical and talmudical references given by Professor Hyamson are doubtless very useful, although they are less complete than they could easily have been made. But, by omitting to add references to the non-Jewish sources of the *Sefer ha-Madda*, the editor unintentionally creates a somewhat misleading impression of that work. It would have been interesting, and even important for some readers, to know that the titles, both of the whole work and of its first section, are practically identical with the titles of the first two books of Ghazali's *Ihyâ*, not to mention other parallels which are perhaps less obvious.[7] The editor has also omitted to give cross-references to other passages of the *Mishneh Torah* or to the other works of Maimonides. Such cross-references are indispensable in order to enable the great majority of readers to notice the contradictions which both hide and reveal Maimonides' secret teaching.

---

7. Cf. Boaz Cohen, "The Classification of the Law in the *Mishneh Torah*," in *Jewish Quarterly Review*, New Series, 25/4 (April 1935): 519–40, and especially pp. 529ff. [See now also, on the parallels to and differences from Ghazali, Steven Harvey, "Alghazali and Maimonides on Their Books of Knowledge," in *Be'erot Yitzhak: Studies in Memory of Isadore Twersky*, ed. Jay M. Harris (Cambridge, MA: Harvard University Press, 2005), pp. 99–117, especially for what Strauss mentions as perhaps the leading "non-Jewish source of the *Sefer ha-Madda*."]

8

The Literary Character of
The Guide of the Perplexed

EDITOR'S NOTE

"The Literary Character of *The Guide of the Perplexed*" essentially reproduces the study which appeared in Leo Strauss, *Persecution and the Art of Writing* (New York: Free Press, 1952; Chicago: University of Chicago Press, 1988), pp. 38–94. The article first appeared in *Essays on Maimonides*, ed. Salo W. Baron (New York: Columbia University Press, 1941): 37–91. The present editor has made some additions to the notes, with occasional references directly to the text and to Strauss's notes. These aim to be helpful to readers in searching Strauss's sources, comprehending his references by offering reliable English translations, or clarifying certain difficult aspects of the text. To differentiate them from Strauss's own work, all such editorial additions to the notes are set in square brackets. Strauss's epigraph to his essay is from Aristotle's *Metaphysics*, bk. 3, chap. 1 (B1.995a27–30): "Now those who wish to succeed in arriving at answers will find it profitable to go over the difficulties well; for answers successfully arrived at are solutions to difficulties previously discussed, and one cannot untie a knot if he is ignorant of it." See Aristotle, *Metaphysics*, trans. Hippocrates G. Apostle (Bloomington: Indiana University Press, 1966), p. 39. The only change made by the present editor that might seem substantial to some is a slight alteration in the title of Maimonides' book as used in the title of Strauss's essay and once also at the beginning of the first section: "The Guide *of* the Perplexed" rather than "The Guide *for* the Perplexed." This was done both for the sake of consistency with the other essays in the volume, and also because it seems to have been Strauss's preferred usage in most of his English-language works. Consider especially "Review of *The Mishneh Torah*, Book 1, . . . Edited . . . by Moses Hyamson," chap. 7 above (which preceded the present essay, and which used Strauss's preferred title), but also "Plan of a Book Tentatively Entitled *Philosophy and the Law: Historical Essays*" (1946), in *Jewish Philosophy and the Crisis of Modernity*, p. 469, for how he refers to the title of Maimonides' book in his essay referring to a chapter heading of his proposed book; and also "Maimonides' Statement on Political Science," chap. 9 below. However, no doubt he was not always able to determine such matters in common scholarly enterprises (perhaps especially at the starting point of his academic career in America), such as the volume edited by the eminent Salo W. Baron, in which a contributor might well have had to conform with the choice of titles preferred by the editor or by the publisher. In fact, the "for" was still fairly conventional and even commonly accepted in much English-language scholarship about Maimonides around the date of his essay's original publication and of its reprinting in *Persecution*. However, I believe Strauss definitely preferred "The Guide *of* the Perplexed," and this seems to have been because it is closer to the literal meaning that must be assigned to both the original Judeo-Arabic title chosen by Maimonides himself and to the Hebrew title chosen by his contemporary translator, Samuel ibn Tibbon, who (although Maimonides may not have ever actually checked the finished Hebrew version in detail) was as close as it is possible to be to an "authorized" translator. In general, Ibn Tibbon strove to closely imitate the Judeo-Arabic in his Hebrew translation, sticking as faithfully as possible to the language and even syntax of Maimonides' original text, and the title would certainly have been a paradigmatic case. I do not as yet know of a written statement by Strauss in which this preference is definitively enunciated (although cf. "Plan of a Book"), but I believe that everything else he wrote even during the 1930s, 1940s, and 1950s, i.e., insofar as he was able to control such matters, makes it evident. Indeed, I would venture to suggest that the general (even if not unanimous) acceptance of this form of the title—with the "of"—among English-speaking scholars since the 1950s is in substantial measure due to Strauss's insistence that this is a much better expression of what Maimonides intended. No doubt its general acceptance was also greatly expedited by the choice made by translator Shlomo Pines, who decided (undoubtedly together with Strauss) to use the possessive "of" in the title of his remarkable English translation. The present editor has also decided, for the sake of consistency, to make the further change (which some might not regard as similarly required) of joining the second of three definite articles in the title of Strauss's essay to the title of Maimonides' book, although it is not in Strauss's original essay or in its reprinted version in *Persecution and the Art of Writing*: "The Literary Character of '*The* Guide of the Perplexed.'" It is the form which Strauss most often (even if not always) chooses to use in formal references to the full title of the *Guide*. However, as helping to justify the further slight change made by the editor (besides the need for consistency), Strauss especially makes a point of it in his perhaps most prominent study, i.e., in the title of his introduction which precedes Pines's English translation of the *Guide*, i.e., "How To Begin To Study *The Guide of the Perplexed*." See chap. 11 below. It is on the basis of this same reasoning that the title of Strauss's lecture (see chap. 10 below) was designated "Introduction to Maimonides' *The Guide of the Perplexed*," although accepted English style might dispose one to remove the definite article.

ἡ γὰρ ὕστερον εὐπορία λύσις τῶν πρότερον ἀπορουμένων ἐστί,
λύειν δ' οὐκ ἔστιν ἀγνοοῦντας τὸν δεσμόν
ARISTOTLE

AMONG THE MANY HISTORIANS WHO HAVE INTERPRETED MAIMONIDES' TEACHing, or who are making efforts to interpret it, there is scarcely one who would not agree to the principle that that teaching, being essentially medieval, cannot be understood by starting from modern presuppositions. The differences of view between students of Maimonides have thus to be traced back, not necessarily to a disagreement concerning the principle itself, but rather to its different interpretation, or to a difference of attitude in its application. The present essay is based on the assumption that only through its most thoroughgoing application can we arrive at our goal, the true and exact understanding of Maimonides' teaching.[1]

---

1. In the footnotes Roman and Arabic figures before the parentheses indicate the part and chapter of the *Guide*, respectively. The figures in the parentheses before the semicolon indicate the page in [Salomon] Munk's edition [*Le Guide des égarés* (Paris: A. Franck, 1870)], and figures following the semicolon indicate pages and lines in [Issachar] Joel's edition [*Dalalat al-ha'irin* (Jerusalem: J. Junovitch, 1931)]. For the first book of the *Mishneh Torah*, I have used [Moses] Hyamson's edition [(New York: Feldheim, 1937)]. [For Strauss's book review of *Mishneh Torah*, Book 1, ed. and trans. Moses Hyamson, see chap. 7 above. It is imperative for readers to note that in this edition, both in the text and in the notes, Arabic figures rather than Roman figures are used prior to the parentheses in order to designate the part of the *Guide*. That is followed next by a period rather than a comma. This has been done for the sake of consistency with the rest of Strauss's essays as they are reproduced in the present volume, and in order to conform with contemporary usage as has become customary in the scholarly study of the *Guide*. This method of reference to the part of the *Guide* is next followed by chapters referred to in Arabic figures, but that is unchanged from the method of reference used by Strauss in the original edition and its reprinting, e.g., 2.48 rather than II, 48.]

I. THE SUBJECT MATTER

The interpreter of *The Guide of the Perplexed* ought to raise, to begin with, the following question: To which science or sciences does the subject matter of the work belong? Maimonides answers it almost at the very beginning of his work by saying that it is devoted to the true science of the law.

The true science of the law is distinguished from the science of the law in the usual sense, i.e., the *fiqh*.[2] While the term *fiqh* naturally occurs in the *Guide* on more than one occasion, the explanation of its meaning has been reserved for almost the very end of the work. *Fiqh* is the exact determination, by way of "deduction" from the authoritative statements of the law, of those actions by means of which man's life becomes noble, and especially of the actions of worship.[3] Its most scientific treatment would consist in a coherent and lucid codification of the law, such as achieved by Maimonides in his *Mishneh Torah*, which he calls "our great work on the *fiqh*." In contradistinction to the legalistic study of the law, which is concerned with what man ought to do, the true science of the law is concerned with what man ought to think and to believe.[4] One may say that the science of the law in general is divided into two parts: a practical part which is treated in the *Mishneh Torah*, and a theoretical part which is treated in the *Guide*. This view is confirmed by the fact that the former work deals with beliefs and opinions only insofar as they are implied in prohibitions and commands, whereas the *Guide* deals with commands and prohibitions only in order to explain their reasons.

The relation between the two parts, or kinds, of the science of the law, may be described in a somewhat different way by saying that, whereas science of the law in the usual sense is the study of the *halakha*, the true science of the law corresponds to the *agada*. As a matter of fact, the *Guide* is a substitute for two books, planned by Maimonides, on the nonlegal sections of the Bible and the Talmud. But, above all, its most important feature, which distinguishes it from all philosophic as well as halakhic books, is also characteristic of a part of the agadic literature.[5]

Since Maimonides, however, uses an Islamic term to designate the ordinary science of the law, it may be worth while to consider what Islamic term would supply the most proper designation for that science of the law which

---

2. 1.Intro. (3a; 2, 14f., 26f.).
3. 3.54 (132b; 467, 20–25); cf. 3.27 (59b; 371, 29); 3.51 (123b; 455, 21–22).
4. 2.10 (22b; 190, 14); 1.Intro. (11a–b; 13, 3–5). Cf. the passages quoted in note 3.
5. 1.Intro. (5b and 11b; 5, 18ff. and 13, 12–15). Cf. 1.70 (92b; 120, 4–8); 1.71 (94a; 121, 25–28).

is the subject of the *Guide*. Students of the *fiqh* deal with the actions prescribed by the law, but do not deal with the "roots of religion," i.e., they do not attempt to prove the opinions or beliefs taught by the law. There seems to be little doubt that the science dealing with those roots is identical with the true science of the law.[6] Since the students of the roots are identified by Maimonides with the *Mutakallimun*, the students of the *kalam*, we shall say that the true science of the law is the *kalam*.[7] It is true that Maimonides vigorously attacks the *kalam*; yet in spite of his ruthless opposition to the assumptions and methods of the *Mutakallimun*, he professes to be in perfect harmony with their intention.[8] The intention of the science of *kalam* is to defend the law, especially against the opinions of philosophers.[9] And the central section of the *Guide* is admittedly devoted to the defense of the principal root of the law, the belief in creation, against the contention of the philosophers that the visible world is eternal.[10] What distinguishes Maimonides' *kalam* from the *kalam* proper is his insistence on the fundamental difference between intelligence and imagination, whereas, as he asserts, the *Mutakallimun* mistake imagination for intelligence. In other words, Maimonides insists on the necessity of starting from evident presuppositions, which are in accordance with the nature of things, whereas the *kalam* proper starts from

6. 3.51 (123b–124a; 455, 21–23). Cf. 3.54 (132a–b; 467, 7–9) with 1.Intro. (3a; 2, 12–14).

7. 1.71 (96b–97a; 125, 12). Cf. 1.73 (105b; 136, 2). Maimonides was called a *sharashi* ["one who speculates on the roots," i.e., a *mutakallim*] by [R. David ben Judah] Messer Leon [(1470–1526)]; see [Moritz] Steinschneider, *Jewish Literature [from the Eighth to the Eighteenth Century*, trans. William Spottiswoode (London: Longman, Brown, Green, 1857; reprint, Hildesheim: Georg Olms, 1967), p.], 310[, n. 7]. ["The expression *shoreshei 'emuna* and the like abound in the *Cusari* . . . , and the book *Cusari* itself . . . is thus much earlier than Maimonides, who is considered the first important authority . . . for the doctrine of the *mutakallimun*. . . . *shorashim* is even used for tradition against the Karaites . . . Joshua ben Jehuda (Jeshua ben Judah, a distinguished Karaite theologian) . . . says distinctly that he is following a method different from that of the *medabberim* or *al-mutakallimun*, without referring especially to the Karaites. The designation subsequently became more general; according to Joseph ben Shemtob, Saadja (Saadia ben Joseph ha-Gaon) and Bechai (Baḥya ben Joseph ibn Paquda) 'incline' towards the *mutakallimun* . . . , and David ben Jehuda (Messer) Leon calls Maimonides himself a *sharashi* . . ."]

8. 2.19 (40a; 211, 24–25); 1.71 (97b; 126, 4–5). Cf. also 1.73 (111b; 143, 6).

9. Farabi, *Ihsa al-'ulum* [(Cairo, 1931)], chap. 5. (See the Hebrew translation in [Shem-Tov ben Joseph ibn] Falaquera's *Reshit Ḥokhmah*, ed. [Moritz] David [(Berlin, 1902; reprint, Jerusalem: Mekorot, 1970)], 59ff.) Farabi's discussion of the *kalam*, and the framework of that discussion, are of decisive importance for the understanding of the *Guide*. Cf. also Plato's *Laws* [bk.] X, 887b8 and 890d4–6. 1.71 (94b, 95a; 122, 19–22; 123, 2–3). [The *Ihsa* has been partially translated by Fauzi M. Najjar, in *Medieval Political Philosophy*, ed. Lerner and Mahdi, pp. 24–30; he translated a section of chap. V, "On Political Science, Jurisprudence, and Dialectical Theology." For a new and complete version of the same chap. V by Charles E. Butterworth ("more literal and . . . more faithful to Alfarabi's own prose style"), see Alfarabi, *Political Writings*, trans. Butterworth, pp. 76–84. In the present context, it is helpful and indeed almost essential to consult Strauss's "Farabi's *Plato*": see *Louis Ginzberg Jubilee Volume*, ed. Saul Lieberman et al. (New York: American Academy for Jewish Research, 1945), pp. 357–93.]

10. 1.71 (96a; 124, 18–19); 2.17 (37a; 207, 27–28).

arbitrary presuppositions, which are chosen not because they are true but because they make it easy to prove the beliefs taught by the law. Maimonides' true science of the law and the *kalam* thus belong to the same genus,[11] the specific difference between them being that the *kalam* proper is imaginative, whereas that of Maimonides is an intelligent, or enlightened *kalam*.

The tentative descriptions of the true science of the law which have been set forth thus far are useful, and even indispensable, for the purpose of counteracting certain views more commonly held of the character of the *Guide*. In order to arrive at a more definitive description of the subject matter of that work, we have to make a fresh start by reminding ourselves again of the authoritative statements with which it opens.

Maimonides states that the intention of his work is to explain the meaning of biblical words of various kinds, as well as of biblical parables. Such an explanation is necessary, because the external meaning of both lends itself to grave misunderstanding. Since the internal meaning, being hidden, is a secret, the explanation of each such word or parable is the revelation of a secret. The *Guide* as a whole is thus devoted to the revelation of the secrets of the Bible.[12] *Secret*, however, has manifold meanings. It may refer to the secret hidden by a parable or word, but it also may mean the parable or word itself which hides a secret. With reference to the second meaning, the *Guide* may more conveniently be said to be devoted to the explanation of the secrets of the Bible. Thus the true science of the law is nothing other than the explanation of the secrets of the Bible, and in particular of the Torah.

There are as many secrets of the Torah as there are passages in it requiring explanation.[13] Nevertheless, it is possible to enumerate at least the most momentous secret topics. According to one enumeration, these topics are: divine attributes, creation, providence, divine will and knowledge, prophecy, names of God. Another enumeration, which seems to be more lucid, presents the following order: *ma'aseh bereshit* (the account of creation), *ma'aseh merkavah* (the account of the chariot, Ezekiel 1 and 10), prophecy, and the

---

11. Cf. Aristotle, *Nicomachean Ethics*, 1098a8–10. ["Now if the function of man is an activity of soul in accordance with, or not without, rational principle, and if we say a so-and-so and a good so-and-so have a function which is the same in kind, e.g., a lyre-player and a good lyre-player, and so without qualification in all cases, eminence in respect of function being added to the function ... if this is the case, human good turns out to be an activity of the soul in conformity with excellence, and if there are more than one excellence, in conformity with the best and most complete." *Nicomachean Ethics*, trans. W. D. Ross, rev. J. O. Urmson, in *The Complete Works of Aristotle*, ed. Jonathan Barnes (Princeton: Princeton University Press, 1984), vol. 2, p. 1735.]

12. 1.Intro. (2b–3b, 6a, 6b–7a; 2, 6–29; 6, 12–19; 7, 10–8, 3). Cf. ibid. (2a, 8a; 1, 14; 9, 6).

13. See in particular 3.50, beginning.

knowledge of God.[14] However those two enumerations may be related to each other, it is certain that *ma'aseh bereshit* and *ma'aseh merkavah* occupy the highest rank among the secrets of the Bible. Therefore, Maimonides can say that the first intention, or the chief intention of the *Guide* is the explanation of *ma'aseh bereshit* and *ma'aseh merkavah*. The true science of the law is concerned with the explanation of the secrets of the Bible, and especially with the explanation of *ma'aseh bereshit* and of *ma'aseh merkavah*.[15]

II. A PHILOSOPHIC WORK?

The finding that the *Guide* is devoted to the explanation of the secret teaching of the Bible seems to be a truism. Yet it is pregnant with the consequence that the *Guide* is not a philosophic book.

The fact that we are inclined to call it a philosophic book is derived from the circumstance that we use the word "philosophy" in a rather broad sense. We commonly do not hesitate, for example, to count the Greek sophists among the philosophers and we even speak of philosophies underlying mass movements. The present usage may be traced back to the separation of philosophy from science—a separation which has taken place during the modern centuries. For Maimonides, who knew nothing of "systems of philosophy" and consequently nothing of the emancipation of sober science from those lofty systems, philosophy has a much narrower, or a much more exact meaning than it has at the present time. It is not an exaggeration to say that for him philosophy is practically identical with the teaching as well as the methods of Aristotle, "the prince of the philosophers," and of the Aristotelians.[16] And he is an adversary of philosophy thus understood. It is against the opinions of "*the* philosophers"[17] that he defends the Jewish creed. And what he opposes

---

14. 1.35 (42a; 54, 20–26); 2.2 (11a–b; 176, 18–23).

15. 2.29 (65b; 243, 17–19); 3.Intro. (2a; 297, 5–7). Cf. the distinction between *fiqh* and secrets of the Torah in 1.71 (93b; 121, 20–22) with the distinction between *fiqh* and the true science of the law at the beginning of the work. For an interpretation, see A[lexander] Altmann, "Das Verhältnis Maimunis zur jüdischen Mystik," in *Monatsschrift für Geschichte und Wissenschaft des Judentums* 80 (1936): 305–30. [See now "Maimonides' Attitude toward Jewish Mysticism," in *Studies in Jewish Thought: An Anthology of German Jewish Scholarship*, ed. Alfred L. Jospe (Detroit: Wayne State University Press, 1981), pp. 200–219.]

16. 1.5, beginning; 2.23 (51a; 225, 4). I[saac] Heinemann goes too far, however, in stating (*Die Lehre von der Zweckbestimmung des Menschen im griechisch-römischen Altertum und im jüdischen Mittelalter* [Breslau: M. & H. Marcus, 1926], 99, n. 1) that "*Failasûf* heisst nicht Philosoph, sondern steht fur Aristoteles oder Aristoteliker." ["*Failasuf* does not mean 'philosopher,' but rather is equivalent to 'Aristotle' or 'Aristotelian.'"] Cf. 1.17; 1.71 (94b; 122, 26–28); 2.21 (47b; 220, 20); 3.16 (31a; 334, 22–24), where *falsafa* or *falasifa* other than Aristotelian are mentioned.

17. Cf., for instance, 3.16, beginning.

to the wrong opinions of *the* philosophers is not a true philosophy, and in particular not a religious philosophy, or a philosophy of religion, but "our opinion, i.e., the opinion of our law," or the opinion of "us, the community of the adherents of the law," or the opinion of the "followers of the law of our teacher Moses."[18] He obviously assumes that the philosophers form a group[19] distinguished from the group of adherents of the law and that both groups are mutually exclusive. Since he himself is an adherent of the law, he cannot possibly be a philosopher, and consequently a book of his in which he explains his views concerning all important topics cannot possibly be a philosophic book. This is not to deny that he acknowledges, and even stresses, the accordance which exists between the philosophers and the adherents of the law in every respect except as regards the question (which, however, is the decisive question) of the creation of the world. For certainly such an accordance between two groups proves their nonidentity.

There is, perhaps, no greater service that the historian can render to the philosopher of our time than to supply the latter with the materials necessary for the reconstruction of an adequate terminology. Consequently, the historian is likely to deprive himself of the greatest benefit which he can grant both to others and to himself, if he is ashamed to be a micrologist. We shall, then, not hesitate to refrain from calling the *Guide* a philosophic book. To justify fully our procedure we only have to consider Maimonides' division of philosophy. According to him, philosophy consists of two parts, theoretical philosophy and practical philosophy; theoretical philosophy in its turn is subdivided into mathematics, physics, and metaphysics; and practical philosophy consists of ethics, economics, "government of the city," and "government of the great nation or of the nations."[20] It is obvious that the *Guide* is not a work on mathematics or economics; and there is practically complete

---

18. Cf., for instance, 2.21 (47a; 220, 17f.); 2.26 (56a; 230, 30); 3.17 (34b; 338, 21); 3.21 (44b; 351, 17–18).

19. That kind of group, one individual case of which is the group of the philosophers, is called by Maimonides *firkah* [in Judeo-Arabic] or *farik* (Ibn Tibbon [in Hebrew]: *cath* ["group" or "sect"]). The Greek equivalent is *airesis* ["group," "school," "sect," "party," "faction," or (in the wake of the New Testament) "heresy"]; cf. C. Bergsträsser, *Hunain ibn Isḥâq über die syrischen und arabischen Galen-Übersetzungen* [Leipzig, 1925], p. 3 of the Arabic text); cf. 2.15 (33a; 203, 17f.); 3.20 (42a; 348, 16).

20. *Millot ha-Higgayon*, ch. 14. Cf. H. A. Wolfson, "The Classification of the Sciences in Mediaeval Jewish Philosophy," in *Hebrew Union College Jubilee Volume, 1875–1925* (Cincinnati: Hebrew Union College, 1925), pp. 263–315. [For the *Treatise on the Art of Logic*, chap. 14, see "Logic," in *Ethical Writings*, trans. Weiss and Butterworth, pp. 158–61. The section with the discussion of political science alone is available in *Medieval Political Philosophy*, ed. Lerner and Mahdi, pp. 189–90. "Classification" has been reprinted: see Wolfson, *Studies in History*, vol. 1, pp. 493–545.]

agreement among the students of Maimonides that it is not devoted to political science of either kind. Nor is it an ethical treatise, since Maimonides expressly excludes ethical topics from the *Guide*.[21] The only sciences, then, to which that work could possibly be devoted are physics and metaphysics, which occupy the highest rank among the sciences.[22] This view seems to be confirmed by Maimonides' professions (1) that the chief intention of the *Guide* is to explain *ma'aseh bereshit* and *ma'aseh merkavah*, and (2) that *ma'aseh bereshit* is identical with physics, and *ma'aseh merkavah* with metaphysics.[23] For these two statements seem to lead to the inference that the chief intention of the *Guide* is to treat of physics and metaphysics. This inference is contradicted, however, by another express statement of Maimonides, according to which all physics and an unlimited number of metaphysical topics are excluded from the *Guide*. He mentions in this connection particularly the doctrine of separate intelligences.[24] Thus the only philosophic subject treated, as such, in the *Guide* seems to be the doctrine of God.[25] But Maimonides excludes further all subjects proved, or otherwise satisfactorily treated by the philosophers and leaves no doubt that the philosophers succeeded in proving the existence of God as well as His unity and incorporeity.[26] In accordance with this, Maimonides clearly states that these three doctrines do not belong to the secrets of the Torah,[27] and hence neither to *ma'aseh bereshit* nor to *ma'aseh merkavah*, the principal subjects of the *Guide*. Thus we are led to the conclusion that no philosophic topic of any kind is, as such, the subject matter of the *Guide*.

We are then confronted with the perplexing contradiction that Maimonides, on the one hand, identifies the main subjects of the *Guide* with physics and metaphysics, the most exalted topics of philosophy, while on the other hand he excludes from the field of his investigation every subject satisfactorily treated by the philosophers. To solve that contradiction one might suggest that the *Guide* is devoted to the discussion of such "physical" and "metaphysical" topics as are not satisfactorily treated by the philosophers.

21. 3.8, end. Cf. 1.Intro. (11a–b; 13, 3–5).
22. 3.51 (124a; 456, 1–4).
23. 1.Intro. (3b; 3, 8–9). Cf. n. 15.
24. 2.2 (11a–12a; 176, 3–27). Cf. also 1.71 (97b; 126, 13–15). As regards the philosophic doctrine of the sublunary world, cf. 2.22 (49b–50a; 223, 15–17); for that of the soul, cf. 1.68, beginning.
25. Notice the identification of *ma'aseh merkavah*, or metaphysics, with the doctrine of God in 1.34 (40b; 52, 24–25).
26. 1.71 (96b; 124, 29–125, 6); 2.2 (11a–12a; 176, 3–27). Cf. 2.33 (75a; 256, 21–25).
27. 1.35.

This would amount to saying that the subjects of the *Guide* are "physics" and "metaphysics," insofar as these transcend philosophy, and consequently that the *Guide* is not a philosophic book.

Yet the objection may be raised that this suggestion disregards Maimonides' explicit and unqualified identification of *ma'aseh bereshit* with physics and of *ma'aseh merkavah* with metaphysics. If we assume for the time being that this objection is sound, we seem to have no choice but to admit that the question of the subject matter of the *Guide* does not allow of any answer whatsoever. But, as a matter of fact, the very obviousness of the only possible answer[28] is the reason why that answer could escape our notice. The apparently contradictory facts that (1) the subject matter of the *Guide* are *ma'aseh bereshit and ma'aseh merkavah* and that (2) Maimonides, in spite of his identifying *ma'aseh bereshit* with physics and *ma'aseh merkavah* with metaphysics, excludes physics and metaphysics from the *Guide*, may be reconciled by the formula that the intention of the *Guide* is to prove the identity, which to begin with was asserted only, of *ma'aseh bereshit* with physics and of *ma'aseh merkavah* with metaphysics. Physics and metaphysics are indeed philosophic disciplines, and a book devoted to them is indeed a philosophic book. But Maimonides does not intend to treat physics and metaphysics; his intention is to show that the teaching of these philosophic disciplines, which is presupposed, is identical with the secret teaching of the Bible.[29] The demonstration of such identity is no longer the duty of the philosopher, but is incumbent upon the student of the true science of the law. The *Guide* is then under no circumstances a philosophic book.[30]

As a corollary we have to add that the *Guide* cannot be called a theological work, for Maimonides does not know of theology as a discipline distinct from metaphysics. Nor is it a book of religion, for he expressly excludes religious, together with ethical topics from the subject matter of his work.[31] Until we shall have rediscovered a body of terms which are flexible enough to fit Maimonides' thought, the safest course will be to limit the description of the

---

28. That is to say, the only answer which could be given if the suggestion made in the foregoing paragraph is ruled out. Cf., however, [the third through sixth paragraphs of section III above].

29. As regards the identification of the teaching of revelation with the teaching of reason in medieval Jewish philosophy, cf. Julius Guttmann, *Die Philosophie des Judentums* (Munich: E. Reinhardt, 1933), 71f. [See *Philosophy of Judaism*, trans. David W. Silverman (Northvale, NJ: Jason Aronson, 1988), pp. 62–65.]

30. Cf. also above, the second and third paragraphs of section I (and n. 5), and below, the eleventh paragraph of section III (and n. 60), and the fifth paragraph of section IV (and n. 64).

31. 3.8, end.

Guide to the statement that it is a book devoted to the explanation of the secret teaching of the Bible.

III. THE CONFLICT BETWEEN LAW AND NECESSITY

When Maimonides embarked upon the explanation of the secrets of the Torah, he was confronted with the apparently overwhelming difficulty created by the "legal prohibition"[32] against explaining those secrets. The very same law, the secrets of which Maimonides attempted to explain, forbids their explanation. According to the ordinance of the talmudic sages, *ma'aseh merkavah* ought not to be taught even to one man, except if he be wise and able to understand by himself, and even to such a one only the "chapter headings" may be transmitted. As regards the other secrets of the Bible, their revelation to many people met with scarcely less definite disapproval in the Talmud.[33] Explaining secrets in a book is tantamount to transmitting those secrets to thousands of men. Consequently, the talmudic prohibition mentioned implies the prohibition against writing a book devoted to their explanation.[34]

This prohibition was accepted by Maimonides not only as legally binding, but also as evidently wise; it was in full accordance with his own considered judgment that oral teaching in general is superior to teaching by writing. This view may be traced back to an old philosophic tradition.[35] The works of Aristotle, which were known to Maimonides, are "acroamatic" and not "exoteric," and his method of expounding things betrays more often than not its provenance from Platonic or Socratic dialectics. Even *the* classical statement about the danger inherent in all writing may have been known to Maimonides, for the famous doctrine of Plato's *Phaedrus* had been summarized by Farabi in his treatise on Plato's philosophy.[36] Be this as it may, not the ambiguous advice of the philosophers but the unequivocal command of the law was of primary importance to Maimonides.[37]

If a book devoted to the explanation of the secrets of the Bible is prohib-

---

32. 3.Intro. (2a and b; 297, 16 and 25).
33. 1.Intro. (3b–4a; 3, 9–19); 1.33 (36a; 48, 19–21); 1.34 (40b; 52, 24–53, 3); 3.Intro.
34. 1.Intro. (4a; 3, 19–20); 3.Intro. (2a; 297, 15–16).
35. 1.71 (93b; 121, 14–24); 3.Intro. (2b; 297, 25–26). Cf. 1.17 and 1.Intro. (4a; 3, 19–20).
36. Cf. Falaquera's Hebrew translation of Farabi's treatise in *Reshit Ḥokhmah*, ed. [Moritz] David, p. 75 bottom. [Cf.: Alfarabius, *De Platonis Philosophia*, ed. Franz Rosenthal and Richard Walzer (London: Warburg Institute, 1943), chap. VI, para. 28, p. 16; Alfarabi, *Plato and Aristotle*, trans. Mahdi, p. 62.]
37. The inferiority of writing is also indicated by the designation of those biblical works which had not been composed by prophets proper as "writings." Cf. 2.45 (94a, 95b; 283, 1–5; 284, 21–285, 3).

ited by law, how then can the *Guide*, being the work of an observant Jew, be a book? It is noteworthy that Maimonides himself in the *Guide* never calls it a book, but consistently refers to it as a *maqala* (*ma'amar*).[38] *Maqala* (just as *ma'amar*) has several meanings. It may mean a treatise; it is used in that sense when Maimonides speaks, for instance, of the *Treatise on Government* by Alexander of Aphrodisias. But it may also mean—and this is its original connotation—a speech. Maimonides, by refraining from calling the *Guide* a book and by calling it a *maqala*, hints at the essentially oral character of its teaching. Since, in a book such as the *Guide*, hints are more important than explicit statements, Maimonides' contentions concerning the superiority of oral teaching very probably have to be taken quite literally.

If the *Guide* is, in a sense, not a book at all, if it is merely a substitute for conversations or speeches, then it cannot be read in the way we may read, for instance, Ibn Sina's *Al-Shifa*, or Thomas Aquinas's *Summa Theologica*. To begin with, we may assume rather that the proper way of studying it is somehow similar to the way in which traditional Judaism studies the law.[39] This would mean that if we wish to know what Maimonides thinks, say, about the prophecy of Moses, it would not be sufficient to look up that chapter of his work which is explicitly devoted to that subject, and in which we might find perfectly clear and apparently final statements about it; nor would it be

---

38. This fact is pointed out by Abravanel in his *Ma'amar Katzer be-Bi'ur Sod ha-Moreh*. ["Short Treatise in Elucidation of the Secret Meaning of the *Guide*." See *Sefer Moreh ha-Nevukhim*, trans. Shmuel even Tibbon, with the commentaries of Efodi (i.e., Profiat Duran), Shem Tov ben Joseph, Asher Crescas, and Isaac Abravanel, pp. 73a–74b in the pagination of pt. 3 (Warsaw, 1872; reprint, Jerusalem, 1960): p. 73b, 1st col., l. 34.] Ibn Tibbon, in his preface to his translation of the *Guide*, calls it *ha-sefer ha-nikhbad ha-ze ma'amar Moreh Nevukhim* ["this eminent book, the treatise *Guide of the Perplexed*": p. 1a, l. 22].

39. Cf. H. A. Wolfson, *Crescas' Critique of Aristotle* (Cambridge, MA: Harvard University Press, 1929), 22ff. Maimonides indicates the similarity between the prohibition against writing down the oral law and that against writing down the secret teaching of the law; see 1.7, beginning. [The decisive passage in Wolfson's book of which Strauss seems to have been thinking is perhaps the following (p. 24):

> But there is even something more than this in Crescas' method of literary composition. He not only re-echoes the ideas of his predecessors but he collocates torn bits of their texts. The expository part of his work is a variegated texture into which are woven many different strands. Mosaic in its structure, it is studded with garbled phrases and expressions torn out of their context and strung together in what would seem to be a haphazard fashion. At times the text is entirely unintelligible and at times it is still worse—misleading. We read it, and think we understand it. If we do happen to come across some ambiguity, some abrupt transition, some change of point of view, or some unevenness of style, we are apt to attribute it to an inadequacy of expression on the part of the author and try our best, by whatever general information we may happen to possess or may be able to gather, to force some meaning upon it—and trying, think we succeed. But sometimes by a stroke of good luck, we may happen to stumble upon the immediate source of Crescas' utterances and at once our eyes are opened wide with surprise and astonishment, ambiguities are cleared up, certainties call for revision and what has previously seemed to us meaningless or insignificant assumes an importance undreamed of.]

sufficient to contrast the latter with divergent statements unexpectedly occurring in other chapters. We would also have to take into account analogous "decisions" given by Maimonides with regard to entirely different "cases," and to make ourselves familiar with the general rules of analogy which obtain in oral discussions of that kind. Producing a clear statement of the author, in the case of a book like the *Guide*, is tantamount to raising a question; his answer can be ascertained only by a lengthy discussion, the result of which may again be open, and intended to be open, to new "difficulties." If it is true that the *Mishneh Torah* is but the greatest post-talmudic contribution to the oral discussions of the *halakha*, then it may be asserted with equal right that Maimonides, while writing the *Guide*, continued the agadic discussions of the Talmud. And just as the *Mishneh Torah*, far from terminating the halakhic discussions, actually served as a new starting point for them, in the same way the *Guide*, far from offering a final interpretation of the secret teaching of the Bible,[40] may actually have been an attempt to revive the oral discussion thereof by raising difficulties which intentionally were left unsolved.

But although the method employed by Maimonides in the *Guide* may come as near as is humanly possible to the method of oral teaching, the *Guide* does not for that reason cease to be a book. Consequently the very existence of the *Guide* implies a conscious transgression of an unambiguous prohibition. It seems that Maimonides for a while intended to steer a middle course between oral and confidential teaching, which is permitted, and teaching in writing, which is forbidden. That kind of writing which comes nearest to confidential conversation is private correspondence with a close friend. As a matter of fact, the *Guide* is written in the form of letters addressed to a friend and favorite pupil, Joseph.[41] By addressing his book to one man, Maimonides made sure that he did not transgress the prohibition against explaining *ma'aseh merkavah* to more than one man. Moreover, in the *Epistula dedicatoria* addressed to Joseph, he mentions, as it were in passing and quite unintentionally, that Joseph possessed all the qualities required of a student of the secret lore and explains the necessity of written communication by his pupil's departure.[42] This justification would have held good if Maimonides had refrained from making public these private "letters to a friend." In spite

---

40. Cf., for instance, 3.Intro. (2b; 298, 1–2); 1.21 (26b; 34, 10–12).
41. Cf. in particular 2.24.
42. These observations on the "Epistle Dedicatory" cannot furnish a sufficient interpretation of that remarkable piece of literature, but deal merely with its more superficial meaning. Maimonides mentions Joseph's poems in order to show that the latter possessed the indispensable ability of expressing himself beautifully; cf. 1.34 (41a; 53, 14) with 1.Intro. (7a–b; 8, 7–8). As regards the other qualities of Joseph,

of this inconsistency and in spite of his evident determination to write the *Guide* even if he had never met Joseph, or if Joseph had never left him,[43] it would be a mistake to assume that the dedicatory epistle is wholly ironical. For we need only ask ourselves: what was the ultimate reason for Joseph's premature departure, and we are going over from the sphere of private and playful things to the sphere of public and serious matters. Joseph's departure, we may say, was the consequence of his being a Jew in the Diaspora. Not a private need but only an urgent necessity of nation-wide bearing can have driven Maimonides to transgressing an explicit prohibition. Only the necessity of saving the law can have caused him to break the law.[44]

The necessity of taking such an extraordinary measure was a consequence of the long duration of the Diaspora. The secrets of the Torah, "the fountainhead of ancient Greek, and, consequently, also of Arabian wisdom,"[45] had been handed down from time immemorial by oral tradition. Even when the oral law, which likewise ought not to have been written down, was finally compiled in written form, the talmudic sages wisely insisted on the secret teaching being transmitted to posterity only by word of mouth from one scholar to another. Their command was obeyed; there is not a single book extant which contains the secret teaching in whole or in part. What had come down to Maimonides were only slight intimations and allusions in Talmud

---

see Shem Tov's commentary on the "Epistle Dedicatory." [See *Sefer Moreh ha-Nevukhim*, trans. Even Tibbon, p. 3a.]

43. It is controversial whether Maimonides finished the *Guide* before he made the acquaintance of Joseph or thereafter. According to Z. Diesendruck, "On the Date of the Completion of the *Moreh Nebukim*," *Hebrew Union College Annual* 12–13 (1937–38)[: 461–97, and especially p.], 496, the *Guide* was finished in 1185, i.e., at about the time when Joseph's sojourn with Maimonides began. Even if the *Guide* was not finished before the year 1190, which is the latest possible date (see ibid., pp. 461, 470), it certainly had been conceived and partly elaborated before Joseph's arrival.

44. 1.Intro. (9b; 10, 28–29) in the interpretation of [Raphaël] Fürstenthal[, ed., *Guide*, German translation of pt. I, with Hebrew commentary (Krotoschin, 1839), p. 16, n. 225,] and [Salomon] Munk[, *Le Guide des égarés*, p. 25, n. 3]. [For the consideration of readers, I translate the rendering in French by Rémi Brague (*Maïmonide*, p. 223, n. 44) of what he isolates as the relevant comment by Fürstenthal to which Strauss points: "with reference to the Mishnah, Berakhot 9, end (54a): R. Nathan would have added to the text of a prayer in order to avoid a heretical interpretation." To compare with Munk, consider his comment: "It is known that the rabbis ascribe to Psalm 119:126 the meaning given as follows: 'When it is time to act for the Lord, it is at the same time permitted to transgress the Law,' that is to say, one is permitted to violate some of the secondary precepts (of the Law) when one is acting to secure the religious constitution (*l'édifice religieux*) in general." Cf. also *Guide*, trans. Pines, p. 16.]

45. [Salo W.] Baron, "[The Historical] Outlook [of Maimonides]," *Proceedings of the American Academy for Jewish Research* 6 (1934–35): 5–113], 105, with reference to 1.71, beginning. Cf. also 2.11 (24a–b; 192, 17–29). [See also "The Historical Outlook of Maimonides," in Salo W. Baron, *History and Jewish Historians: Essays and Addresses*, ed. Arthur Hertzberg and Leon A. Feldman (Philadelphia: Jewish Publication Society of America, 1964), pp. 109–63, 348–404.]

and Midrash.[46] However, continuity of oral tradition presupposes a certain normality of political conditions. That is why the secrets of the Torah were perfectly understood only as long as Israel lived in its own country in freedom, not subjugated by the ignorant nations of the world.[47] Particularly happy was the period when the supreme political authority rested in the hands of King Solomon who had an almost complete understanding of the secret reasons of the commandments.[48] After Solomon, wisdom and political power were no longer united; decline and finally loss of freedom followed. When the nation was led into captivity, it sustained further loss in the perfect knowledge of the secrets. Whereas Isaiah's contemporaries understood his brief hints, the contemporaries of Ezekiel required many more details in order to grasp the sacred doctrine. The decline of knowledge became even more marked with the discontinuation of prophecy itself.[49] Still more disastrous was the victory of the Romans, since the new Diaspora was to last so much longer than the first.[50] As time went on, the external conditions for oral communication of the secrets of the Torah became increasingly precarious. The moment seemed imminent when it would become altogether impossible. Confronted with that prospect, Maimonides decided to write down the secret teaching.

The question naturally arises as to how Maimonides came into its possession. Once, in suggesting a date for the coming of the Messiah (in *Iggeret Teiman*), he refers to a tradition, obviously oral, which he had received from his father, who in turn had received it from his father and grandfather, and which in that way went back to the very beginning of the Diaspora. If we were to generalize from this remark, we would have to assume that he owed his entire knowledge of the secrets of the Torah to an uninterrupted oral tradition going back to the time of the Second Temple. We would then not only have to accept the legend of his conversion to the Kabbalah in his old age, but we would be forced to admit that he was a Kabbalist throughout his mature life, since the content of the *Guide* would be nothing but a secret teaching based

---

46. 1.Intro. (9b; 10, 26–27); 1.71 (93b–94a; 121, 9–26) (the words *tanbihat yasira wa-isharat* [Pines: "slight indications and pointers"] recall the title of Ibn Sina's book [*Kitab*] *Isharat wa-tanbihat* [*Book of Directives and Admonitions*]; cf. also 2.29 (46a; 244, 8)); 3.Intro. (2a–b; 297, 15–20). Maimonides here tacitly denies any authenticity or value to books such as the *Sefer ha-Yetzirah* [*The Book of Formation*] or *Shi'ur Komah* [*Measurement of the (Divine) Body*]; cf. Baron, "Outlook," 89.

47. 1.71 (93b; 121, 10–11).

48. 3.26 (58a; 369, 14–16). Cf. Baron, "Outlook," 51–54.

49. 3.6 (9b; 307, 12–15); 2.32 (73b; 254, 23–24); 2.36 (80a; 263, 19–26).

50. Cf. 1.71 (93b; 121, 10). Cf. also *Mishneh Torah*, Intro. ["Introduction" to the *Misnheh Torah*, trans. Lerner, pp. 135–36].

on (oral) tradition. Indeed, as it seems that there had existed no Kabbalah, strictly speaking before the completion of the *Guide*,[51] one might suggest that Maimonides was the first Kabbalist.

Such venturesome hypotheses are, however, ruled out by his express statements. He not only disclaims the privilege of having had a special revelation about the hidden meaning of *ma'aseh merkavah*, but also disavows his indebtedness to any (human) teacher for his knowledge of the secret doctrine.[52] He apparently believed that the oral tradition of the secret teaching had been interrupted long before his time. That is also why he could not find any traces of a genuine Jewish secret tradition in the Gaonic literature, whereas he claims to have found such traces in the Talmud and in the Midrash. Neither was he able to detect any remnant of the holy doctrine still living in the nation.[53] He was, then, not the last heir of an age-old tradition, but rather its first rediscoverer after it had been lost for a long time. He rediscovered the secret teaching by following the indications which are met with in the Bible and in the words of the sages but also by making use of speculative premises.[54] Since the Bible and the Talmud had been studied no less thoroughly by his predecessors than by him, his rediscovery must have been due to a particularly deep understanding of the "speculative premises," i.e., of philosophy. He did not feel conscious of thereby introducing a foreign element into Judaism, for long before his time the "Andalusian" Jews had accepted the teachings of the philosophers as far as these were consonant with the basis of the Torah.[55] Philosophic teachings thus belonged, in a sense, to the tradition of Maimonides' family. Perhaps he even believed that the resurgence of philosophic studies in the Middle Ages more or less coincided with the disappearance of the secret teaching of Judaism and that thus the chain of tradition never was interrupted. After all, the defensible part of the

---

51. "Zur Bezeichnung der Mystik wurde der Terminus [Kabbala] erst sehr spät verwandt, und ist zuerst bei Isaak dem Blinden (ca. 1200) nachweisbar." G[ershom] Scholem, *Encyclopedia Judaica*, IX, 632. ["The term (Kabbalah) is used to designate mysticism only very late, and it is first demonstrable in the case of Isaac the Blind (circa 1200)." Scholem was to confirm and reiterate his youthful historical judgment: "The new, precise usage" of "the word 'kabbalah' to denote a mystical or esoteric tradition" only "originated in the circle of Isaac the Blind (1200) and was adopted by all his disciples." See his "Kabbalah," in *Encyclopedia Judaica* (Jerusalem: Keter, 1972), vol. 10, p. 494, as well as his "Terms Used for Kabbalah," in *Kabbalah* (New York: Meridian, 1978), p. 6. The Hebrew title mentioned toward the beginning of the paragraph, *Iggeret Teiman*, is Maimonides' "Letter to [the Jews of] Yemen."]

52. 3.Intro. (2b; 297, 27–28). Cf., however, 3.22 (46a; 353, 21–22). Cf. also the allusion to a spurious "mystical" tradition in 1.62 (80b; 104, 26).

53. 1.71 (94a; 121, 25–122, 3); 3.Intro. (2b; 297, 17–18).

54. 3.Intro. (2b; 297, 28–29).

55. 1.71 (94a; 122, 9–10).

philosophic teaching appeared to him as but a last residue of Israel's own lost inheritance.[56]

The philosophic tradition of enlightened Andalusia thus gave Maimonides the first impulse to search the Bible for its secrets. Owing to his exertions during the greater part of his life, he succeeded in detecting a great many of them. At the same time he clearly realized that his achievement was not likely to be repeated by many others, if by any. For the age of philosophy in Muslim countries was drawing to its close. Fearing, therefore, that the precious doctrine might again be lost for centuries, he decided to commit it to writing, notwithstanding the talmudic prohibition. But he did not act imprudently. He insisted on taking a middle course[57] between impossible obedience and flagrant transgression. He thought it his duty to give such a written explanation of the biblical secrets as would meet all the conditions required from an oral explanation. In other words, he had to become a master of the art of revealing by not revealing and of not revealing by revealing.

The law requires that only the "chapter headings" be transmitted. Maimonides decided to abide by that precept. But the law goes further: it requires that even those "chapter headings" be not transmitted even to one, except he be wise and able to understand by himself. As long as the secret teaching was transmitted by oral instruction, that requirement was easily complied with: if the teacher had not known the pupil for a long time beforehand, as probably was almost always the case, he could test the pupil's intellectual capacities by having a talk with him on indifferent subjects before he started to explain to him some of the secrets of the Bible. But how can the author of a book examine his readers, by far the greater part of whom may not yet be born when the book is published? Or does there exist some sort of examination by proxy which would allow the author to prevent incompetent readers not only from understanding his book—this does not require any human effort—but even from finding out the very formulation of the "chapter headings"? To see that such a device does exist, we have only to remind ourselves of how a superior man proceeds if he wishes to impart a truth, which he thinks not to be fit for everybody's use, to another man who may or may not be able to become reconciled to it. He will give him a hint by casting some doubt on a remote and apparently insignificant consequence or premise of the accepted opinion. If

---

56. See above, the sixth paragraph of section III. Cf. Altmann, op. cit., 315ff. [For a discussion of whether Maimonides actually believed in the ancient Jewish origins of Greek philosophic wisdom, see especially "Introduction to Maimonides' *The Guide of the Perplexed*," chap. 10 below, with n. 26.]

57. Cf. 3.Intro. (3a; 298, 8–9).

the listener understands the hint, the teacher may explain his doubts more fully and thus gradually lead him to a view which is of necessity nearer the truth (since it presupposes a certain reflection) than is the current opinion. But how does he proceed, if the pupil fails to understand the hint? He will simply stop. This does not mean that he will stop talking. On the contrary, since by suddenly becoming silent he would only perplex the pupil without being of any help to him, he will continue talking by giving the first, rather revealing sentence a more conventional meaning and thus gradually lead him back to the safe region of accepted views. Now this method of stopping can be practiced in writing as well as in speech, the only difference being that the writer must stop in any case since certainly the majority of readers must be prevented from finding out the "chapter headings." That is to say, the writer has to interrupt his short hints by long stretches of silence, i.e., of insignificant talk. But a good author will never submit to the ordeal of indulging in insignificant talk. Consequently, after having given a hint which refers to a certain chapter of the secret teaching, he will write some sentences which at first glance seem to be conventional, but which on closer examination prove to contain a new hint, referring to another chapter of the secret teaching. By thus proceeding, he will prevent the secret teaching being prematurely perceived and therefore inadequately understood; even those readers who not only noticed but even understood the first hint and might understand further hints directly connected with it, would experience considerable difficulty even in suspecting the second hint, which refers to a different section of the argument. It is hardly necessary to add that there are as many groups of hints as there are chapters, or subdivisions of chapters, of the secret teaching, and that in consequence an ingenious author has at his disposal almost infinite possibilities of alternatively using hints of different groups.

We are now in a position to appreciate the bearing of the following statement of Maimonides: "You will not demand from me here [in the *Guide*] anything except chapter headings; and even those headings are, in this treatise, not arranged according to their intrinsic order or according to any sequence whatsoever, but they are scattered and intermingled with other subjects, the explanation of which is intended."[58] It is true Maimonides makes this statement with regard to his explanation of *ma'aseh merkavah* only. But there

---

58. 1.Intro. (3b; 3, 11–14). [For Strauss's own attempt at instruction as to how this form of communication might still be relevant to modern readers, one may refer to his example of how a free-minded writer in a modern "totalitarian country" might proceed: see *Persecution and the Art of Writing*, pp. 24–25.]

can be no doubt that he has followed the same method in his explanation of *ma'aseh bereshit* and, indeed, of all the secrets of the Torah.[59] It is for this reason that the whole work has to be read with particular care, with a care, that is, which would not be required for the understanding of a scientific book.[60] Since the whole teaching characteristic of the *Guide* is of a secret nature, we are not surprised to observe Maimonides entreating the reader in the most emphatic manner not to explain any part of it to others, unless the particular doctrine had already been clearly elucidated by famous teachers of the law,[61] i.e., unless it is a popular topic, a topic only occasionally mentioned in the *Guide*.

The *Guide* is devoted to the explanation of an esoteric doctrine. But this explanation is itself of an esoteric character. The *Guide* is, then, devoted to the esoteric explanation of an esoteric doctrine. Consequently it is a book with seven seals. How can we unseal it?

IV. A MORAL DILEMMA

No historian who has a sense of decency and therefore a sense of respect for a superior man such as Maimonides will disregard light-heartedly the latter's emphatic entreaty not to explain the secret teaching of the *Guide*. It may fairly be said that an interpreter who does not feel pangs of conscience when attempting to explain that secret teaching and perhaps when perceiving for the first time its existence and bearing lacks that closeness to the subject which is indispensable for the true understanding of any book. Thus the question of adequate interpretation of the *Guide* is primarily a moral question.

We are, however, entitled to object to raising that moral question because the historical situation in which we find ourselves is fundamentally different from that of the twelfth century, and therefore we ought to be justified in not taking too personally, so to speak, Maimonides' will. It is true, at first glance, that objection seems to beg the question: it is based on the assumption that it is possible to have a sufficient knowledge of the historical situation of the twelfth century without having a true and adequate knowledge of the secret teaching of Maimonides. Yet, if one looks more closely, one sees that by the historical situation no historian understands the secret thoughts of an indi-

---

59. 2.29 (46a; 244, 10f.). Cf. 1.Intro. (3b–4b; 3, 17–4, 22); 1.17; 1.35 (42a; 54, 20–28). See also 3.41 (88b; 409, 16).
60. 1.Intro. (8b; 9, 26–10, 2), ibid. (3b; 3, 11–14); ibid. (4b; 4, 12–15).
61. 1.Intro. (9a; 10, 4–8).

vidual, but rather the obvious facts or opinions which, being common to a period, give that period its specific coloring. We happen to be excellently informed by competent historians about the opinions prevalent in the twelfth century, and each of us can see that they are fundamentally different from those prevalent in our time. Public opinion was then ruled by the belief in the revealed character of the Torah or the existence of an eternal and unchangeable law, whereas public opinion today is ruled by historic consciousness. Maimonides himself justifies his transgression of the talmudic injunction against writing on the esoteric teaching of the Bible by the necessity of saving the law. In the same way we may justify our disregard of Maimonides' entreaty not to explain the esoteric teaching of the *Guide* by appealing to the requirements of historic research. For both the history of Judaism and the history of medieval philosophy remain deplorably incomplete, as long as the secret teaching of Maimonides has not been brought to light. The force of this argument will become even stronger if we take into consideration that basic condition of historic research, namely, freedom of thought. Freedom of thought, too, seems to be incomplete as long as we recognize the validity of any prohibition to explain any teaching whatsoever. Freedom of thought being menaced in our time more than for several centuries, we have not only the right but even the duty to explain the teaching of Maimonides, in order to contribute to a better understanding of what freedom of thought means, i.e., what attitude it presupposes and what sacrifices it requires.

The position of Maimonides' interpreter is, then, to some extent, identical with that of Maimonides himself. Both are confronted with a prohibition against explaining a secret teaching and with the necessity of explaining it. Consequently, one might think it advisable for the interpreter to imitate Maimonides also with regard to the solution of the dilemma, i.e., to steer a middle course between impossible obedience and flagrant transgression by attempting an esoteric interpretation of the esoteric teaching of the *Guide*. Since the *Guide* contains an esoteric interpretation of an esoteric teaching, an adequate interpretation of the *Guide* would thus have to take the form of an esoteric interpretation of an esoteric interpretation of an esoteric teaching.

This suggestion may sound paradoxical and even ridiculous. Yet it would not have appeared absurd to such a competent reader of the *Guide* as Joseph ibn Kaspi, who did write an esoteric commentary on it. Above all, an esoteric interpretation of the *Guide* seems to be not only advisable, but even necessary.

When Maimonides, through his work, exposed the secret teaching of the

Bible to a larger number of men, some of whom might not be as obedient to the talmudic ordinance nor as wise as he was, he did not rely entirely on those readers' compliance with the law or with his own emphatic entreaty. For the explanation of secrets is, as he asserts, not only forbidden by law but also impossible by nature:[62] the very nature of the secrets prevents their being divulged. We are then confronted with a third meaning of the word "secret": secret may mean not only the biblical word or parable which has an inner meaning, and the hidden meaning itself, but also, and perhaps primarily, the thing to which that hidden meaning refers.[63] The things spoken of by the prophets are secret, since they are not constantly accessible, as are the things described by the ordinary sciences,[64] but only during more or less short and rare intervals of spiritual daylight which interrupt an almost continuous spiritual darkness; indeed they are accessible not to natural reason, but only to prophetic vision. Consequently, ordinary language is utterly insufficient for their description; the only possible way of describing them is by parabolic and enigmatic speech.[65] Even the interpretation of prophetic teaching cannot but be parabolic and enigmatic, which is equally true of the interpretation of such an interpretation, since both the secondary and the primary interpretation deal with the same secret subject matter. Hence the interpretation of the *Guide* cannot be given in ordinary language, but only in parabolic and enigmatic speech. That is why, according to Maimonides, the student of those secrets is required not only to be of mature age, to have a sagacious and subtle mind, to possess perfect command of the art of political government and the speculative sciences, and to be able to understand the allusive speech of others, but also to be capable of presenting things allusively himself.[66]

---

62. 1.Intro. (3b; 3, 15). Cf. 1.31, beginning.

63. "Secrets of the being and secrets of the Torah," 2.26 (56b, 232, 5). For the distinction between various meanings of "secret," cf. Bacon, *Advancement of Learning*, ed. G. W. Kitchin, 205. ["Concerning Government, it is a part of knowledge secret and retired, in both these respects in which things are deemed secret; for some things are secret because they are hard to know, and some because they are not fit to utter."]

64. 1.Intro. (4b; 4, 15). This passage implies a fundamental distinction between esoteric and exoteric sciences. As regards such distinctions, cf. I[gnaz] Goldziher, *Kitab ma'ani al-nafs* (Berlin: Weidmannsche, 1907) ["Book on the Essence of the Soul," also subtitled by the editor *Buch vom Wesen der Seele*, an edition of an original Arabic manuscript of an anonymous treatise once attributed to pseudo-Baḥya], pp. 28–31. According to a usual distinction, "the exterior science" (*al-'ilm al-barrani*) is identical with Aristotelian philosophy and also with the *kalam*; "the interior philosophy" (*al-falsafa al-dahila* or *al-falsafa al-hassa*), treated by the *muhakkikun*, deals with "the secrets of nature." The teaching of esoteric science is the knowledge of *al-madnun bihi*. Cf. 1.17, beginning; 1.35 (41b; 54, 4); 171 (93b; 121, 20).

65. 1.Intro. (4a, 4, 4–7). See the commentaries of Efodi and Shem Tov on the passage. 1.Intro. (4a–b; 3, 23–4, 20).

66. 1.34 (41a; 53, 12–19); 1.33 (37b; 48, 22–25).

If each student actually had to meet all these conditions, we should have to admit at once, i.e., before any serious attempt has been made to elucidate the esoteric teaching of the *Guide*, that the interpretation of that work is wholly impossible for the modern historian. The very intention of interpreting the *Guide* would imply an unbearable degree of presumption on the part of the would-be interpreter; for he would implicitly claim to be endowed with all the qualities of a Platonic philosopher-king. Yet, while a modest man, confronted with the requirements which we have indicated, will be inclined to give up the attempt to understand the whole *Guide*, he may hope to make some contribution to its understanding by becoming a subservient part of the community of scholars who devote themselves to the interpretation of the *Guide*. If that book cannot be understood by the exertions of one man, it may be understood by the collaboration of many, in particular of Arabists, Judaists, and students of the history of philosophy. It is true that when speaking of the conditions to be fulfilled by students of the secret teaching, Maimonides does not mention disciplines such as those just alluded to; as a matter of fact, he thought very slightly of history in general.[67] But in all justice it may be said that he did not know, and could not know history in the modern sense of the word, a discipline which, in a sense, provides the synthesis, indispensable for the adequate understanding of the secret doctrine, of philosophy and politics. Yet, however greatly we may think of the qualities of the modern historian, he certainly is neither per se able to understand esoteric texts nor is he an esoteric writer. Indeed the rise of modern historic consciousness came simultaneously with the interruption of the tradition of esotericism. Hence all present-day students of Maimonides necessarily lack the specific training required for understanding, to say nothing of writing, an esoteric book or commentary. Is, then, an interpretation of the *Guide* altogether impossible under the present circumstances?

Let us examine somewhat more closely the basic assumption underlying the conclusion at which we have just arrived, or rather upon which we have just come to grief. Maimonides, it is true, states in unambiguous terms that direct and plain communication of the secrets of the things, or of the secrets of the Torah, is impossible by nature. But he also asserts in no less unambiguous terms that such a communication is forbidden by law. Now a rational

---

67. Cf. Baron, "Outlook," 3–4. [The pages to which Strauss wished to refer seem to have been unwittingly misnumbered; Baron's article only begins on p. 5. (See n. 45 above.) However, as I might suggest, it is not entirely impossible that this reference was aimed at Baron's nn. 3 and 4, if one compares their contents with what is being discussed by Strauss.]

law does not forbid things which are impossible in themselves and which therefore are not subject to human deliberation or action; and the Torah is the rational law par excellence.[68] Consequently the two statements appear to be contradictory. Since we are not yet in a position to decide which of them is to be discarded as merely exoteric, it will be wise to leave the question open for the time being and not to go beyond briefly discussing the possibilities of an answer. There are three possible solutions: (1) Maimonides may actually have believed in the unavoidable necessity of speaking enigmatically of secrets; (2) he may have conceded the possibility of plainly discussing them; (3) he may have approved some unknown intermediary position. There is, then, certainly a prima facie probability in the ratio of two to three that the first solution, which is wholly incompatible with our desire to understand the *Guide*, has to be ruled out. But even if the first solution had to be ultimately accepted, we need not be altogether despondent, since we may very well reject that view as erroneous. Esotericism, one might say, is based on the assumption that there is a rigid division of mankind into an inspired or intelligent minority and an uninspired or foolish majority. But are there no transitions of various kinds between the two groups? Has not each man been given freedom of will, so that he may become wise or foolish according to his exertions?[69] However important may be the natural faculty of understanding, is not the use of this faculty or, in other words, method, equally important? And method, almost by its very definition, bridges the gulf which separates the two unequal groups. Indeed, the methods of modern historical research, which have proved to be sufficient for the deciphering of hieroglyphs and cuneiforms, ought certainly to be sufficient also for the deciphering of a book such as the *Guide*, to which access could be had in an excellent translation into a modern language. Our problem reduces itself, therefore, to detecting the specific method which will enable us to decipher the *Guide*. What are, then, the general rules and the most important special rules according to which this book is to be read?

V. SECRETS AND CONTRADICTIONS

The clue to the true understanding of the *Guide* is provided by the very feature of that book which, at first glance, seems to make it for all modern

---

68. 3.26. Cf. 3.17 (33a–b; 337, 8–15).
69. *Mishneh Torah*, "Teshuvah" V, 2. [See "Laws of Repentance," trans. Hyamson, pp. 86b–87a.]

generations a book sealed with seven seals. I am referring to the fact that it is devoted to the esoteric explanation of an esoteric text. For it is merely a popular fallacy to assume that such an explanation is an esoteric work of the second power, or at least twice as esoteric, and consequently twice as difficult to understand as is the esoteric text itself. Actually, any explanation, however esoteric, of a text is intended to be helpful for its understanding; and, provided the author is not a man of exceptional inability, the explanation is bound to be helpful. Now, if by the help of Maimonides, we understand the esoteric teaching of the Bible, we understand at the same time the esoteric teaching of the *Guide*, since Maimonides must have accepted the esoteric teaching of the law as the true teaching. Or, to put it somewhat differently, we may say that, thanks to Maimonides, the secret teaching is accessible to us in two different versions: in the original biblical version, and in the derivative version of the *Guide*. Each version by itself might be wholly incomprehensible; but we become able to decipher both by using the light which one sheds on the other. Our position resembles then that of an archaeologist confronted with an inscription in an unknown language, who subsequently discovers another inscription reproducing the translation of that text into another unknown language. It matters little whether or not we accept Maimonides' two assumptions, rejected by modern criticism, that the Bible is an esoteric text, and that its esoteric teaching is closely akin to that of Aristotle. As far as Maimonides is concerned, the Bible is an esoteric book, and even the most perfect esoteric book ever written. Consequently, when setting out to write an esoteric book himself, he had no choice but to take the Bible as his model. That is to say, he wrote the *Guide* according to the rules which he was wont to follow in reading the Bible. Therefore, if we wish to understand the *Guide*, we must read it according to the rules which Maimonides applies in that work to the explanation of the Bible.

How did Maimonides read the Bible, or rather the Torah? He read it as the work of a single author, that author being not so much Moses as God Himself. Consequently, the Torah was for him the most perfect book ever written as regards both content and form. In particular, he did not believe (as we are told to believe by modern biblical criticism) that its formal deficiencies—for instance, the abrupt changes of subject matter, or repetitions with greater or slighter variations—were due to its having been compiled by unknown redactors from divergent sources. These deficiencies were for him purposeful irregularities, intended to hide and betray a deeper order, a deep, nay, divine meaning. It was precisely this intentional disorder which he took as his model when writing the *Guide*. Or, if we accept the thesis of modern biblical criticism, we have to say that he took as his model a book which unintentionally lacks order and that by so doing he wrote a book which intentionally lacks order. At any rate the *Guide* certainly and admittedly is a book which intentionally lacks order. The "chapter headings" of the secret teaching which it transmits "are not arranged according to their intrinsic order or according to any sequence whatsoever, but they are scattered and intermingled with other subjects."[70] Instances of apparently bad composition are so numerous in the *Guide* and so familiar to its students that we need not mention here more than one example. Maimonides interrupts his explanation of biblical expressions attributing to God place, local movement, and so on (1.8–26) by an exposition of the meaning of *man* (1.14) and by a discussion of the necessity of teaching *ma'aseh bereshit* esoterically (1.17), just as the Bible itself interrupts the story of Joseph by inserting into it the story of Judah and Tamar. Consequently, whenever we are confronted in the *Guide* with an abrupt change of subject matter, we have to follow the same rule of interpretation which Maimonides was wont to follow whenever he had to face a similar apparent deficiency of the Bible: we have to find out, by guessing, the hidden reason of the apparent deficiency. For it is precisely that hidden reason, accessible only to guesswork, which furnishes a link between the scattered "chapter headings," if not a "chapter heading" itself. Certainly the chains of reasoning connecting the scattered "chapter headings," and possibly even some "chapter headings" themselves, are not stated within the chapters, but are written with invisible ink in the empty spaces between the chapters, between the sentences, or between the parts of the *Guide*.

Another kind of irregularity occurs, for example, in his explanation of the various groups of biblical commandments (3.36–49). At the beginning of each chapter reference is made to the book or books of the *Mishneh Torah* in which the laws under review had been codified. Maimonides deviates from that rule in the case of one chapter only (chapter 41). That this is not a matter of chance can easily be seen from the context. There he points out with unusual clarity the difference between the text of the biblical commands and their traditional interpretation; his intention is, as he expressly states, to explain the "texts," and not the *fiqh*.[71] The *Mishneh Torah* is devoted to the *fiqh*. Consequently, it would have been most misleading if he had referred, at

---

70. 1.Intro. (3b; 3, 11–14).
71. 3.41 (88b; 409. 15–16).

the beginning of that chapter, to the corresponding "book" of the *Mishneh Torah*, i.e., to the "Book of Judges." It may be added in passing that a full discussion of this irregularity, which space does not here permit, would help explain the scarcely less perplexing difficulty of the inclusion in the "Book of Judges" of the laws concerning mourning.

As a last instance of those devices, which may be called intentional perplexities, suggested to Maimonides by his model, we may mention here repetitions of the same subject with apparently no, or only insignificant variations. He observes that Ezekiel had twice the same vision of the celestial chariot, the most secret subject, and that both visions, in their turn, were but repetitions of the corresponding vision of Isaiah.[72] Hardly less important was for him the realization that in the Book of Job all interlocutors apparently repeat continually one another's statements; in particular Elihu, supposedly superior in wisdom to Job, Eliphaz, Bildad, and Zophar, does not seem to add anything of weight to what the others had said before him.[73] Maimonides naturally asserts that these repetitions are apparent rather than real, and that closer examination will reveal that the opinions of Job, Eliphaz, Bildad, and Zophar, as well as Elihu, differ materially from one another, and that the report of Ezekiel's second vision makes important additions to that of the first.[74] This method of repeating the same thing with apparently insignificant, but actually highly important variations was extremely helpful for Maimonides' purposes. An outstanding example may be found in his repeating in the *Guide*, with certain variations, the division of the biblical laws into 14 groups, an arrangement which had determined the whole plan of the *Mishneh Torah*.[75] He thus created the impression of merely repeating the

---

72. 3.3, beginning; 3.6.

73. 3.23 (50a; 359, 4–9 and 14–15). Cf. also 3.24 (52b; 362, 22–23).

74. 3.23 (50a; 359, 9–15); 3.1 (3a; 298, 23–24); 3.3 (6b and 7a; 303, 5, 19; 304, 4–5). Cf. *Mishneh Torah*, Intro., 186th and 187th prohibitions. ["186. Not to boil flesh-meat with milk, as it is said, 'Thou shalt not seethe a kid in its mother's milk' (Exod. 23:19). 187. Not to eat flesh with milk, as it is said, a second time, 'Thou shalt not seethe a kid in its mother's milk' (Exod. 34:26). It is learnt by tradition that one of these texts (Exod. 23:19) refers to the prohibition of boiling, the other (Exod. 34:26) refers to the prohibition of eating." See "List of Precepts ... Negative Precepts," in *Mishneh Torah*, vol. 1, *The Book of Knowledge (Sefer ha-Madda)*, ed. and trans. Moses Hyamson (New York: Feldheim, 1981) p. 13b.]

75. Cf. also the fourteen principles in *Sefer ha-Mitzvot* [*Book of the Commandments*]. ["When a knowledge of the enumeration (of the commandments) will be attained in accordance with the proofs in this treatise, then I shall list them briefly at the head of that general work (i.e., the *Mishneh Torah*), as we have mentioned.... Now I shall begin to mention the principles—fourteen in number—which are to guide us in the enumeration of the commandments." For the fourteen principles listed only, see "Book of Commandments" in *Reader*, ed. Twersky, pp. 424–36, and especially pp. 429–32. Twersky's book only reproduces the summary statement of the fourteen principles in the beginning. For both the summary statement and their complete elaboration, see *The Commandments*, trans. Chavel, vol. 2, pp. 361–425. However, Chavel's edition itself rearranges Maimonides' own presentation; what should appear first in

division made in the code, whereas actually the two divisions greatly differ from each other. As further obvious examples of the application of the same method, one may cite the differences between the arrangement of the 248 affirmative precepts in the enumeration at the beginning of *Mishneh Torah* (or in *Sefer ha-Mitzvot*) on the one hand, and that in the body of that code on the other; the differences between the enumeration of the 5 opinions concerning providence in the *Guide* 3.17, on the one hand, and that in the same work, 3.23, on the other;[76] and the differences between the enumeration of the 3 opinions concerning creation in the *Guide* 2.13, on the one hand, and that in the same work, 2.32, on the other. In all these cases Maimonides apparently merely repeats himself by speaking twice of the same number, but actually he introduces in the repetitions new points of view which had not even been hinted at in the first statements. His aim in so doing is clearly revealed by his explanation of the method employed by the first 4 interlocutors in the Book of Job (Job, Eliphaz, Bildad, and Zophar): "Each one of them repeats the subject of which the other had spoken . . . in order to hide the subject peculiar to the opinion of each, so that it should appear to the vulgar that the opinion of all of them is one opinion generally agreed upon."[77] That is to say, the purpose of repeating conventional statements is to hide the disclosure, in the repetition, of unconventional views. What matters is, then, not the conventional view, constantly repeated, which may or may not be true, but the slight additions to, or omissions from the conventional view which occur in the repetition and which transmit "chapter headings" of the secret and true teaching. This is what Maimonides rather clearly intimates by saying that closer examination of Elihu's repetitious speech brings to light "the additional subject which he introduced, and this subject was the intention."[78] The question as to whether and to what extent Maimonides has generally employed this method of making hardly discernible additions to the "first statement" par excellence, i.e., to the biblical text itself, must remain unanswered in the present discussion.[79]

---

the first volume—i.e., "Introduction" and "The Principles"—is instead put last in the second volume. For the proper arrangement, the Arabic original, and a modern Hebrew translation, see *Sefer ha-Mitzvot*, ed. and trans. Joseph Kafah (Jerusalem: Mosad ha-Rav Kook, 1971/5731), pp. 1–57. The passage translated above appears on p. 7.]

76. Notice also the three opinions on providence indicated in 3.17 (37b; 342, 20f.), as well as the two opinions indicated in 3.21 (44b; 351, 17–18).

77. 3.23 (50a; 359, 11–14).

78. 3.23 (50a; 359, 9–10).

79. Cf. 3.Intro. (2b–3a; 298, 3–9). The method of "repetition" was certainly not invented by Maimonides; it was applied before him on a large scale by Farabi who "repeated" the same teaching by making

Since these rules of interpretation seem to confer excessive importance on every word used by Maimonides, we must have recourse again to our initial assumption that the *Guide* is an imitation of the Bible, and in particular of the Torah. Maimonides read the Torah as a book, every word of which was of divine origin and, consequently, of the greatest importance.[80] How conscientiously he strove to detect the full significance of each biblical term, however indifferent it might seem to be in its context, is known to every reader of the *Guide*, the first intention of which was to explain certain groups of biblical words.[81] He expressly applied the same principle of reading, or writing, to his own work:

> if you wish to grasp the totality of what this treatise contains, so that nothing of it will escape you, then you must connect its chapters one with another;[82] and

---

additions to it or omissions from it, in *Al-siyâsât al-madaniyya* [*The Political Regime*], in *Al-madîna al-fâdila* [*The Virtuous City*], and in *Al-milla al-fâdila* [*The Virtuous Religion*]. And let us not forget Plato who (to mention only two examples) "repeated" the teachings of the *Republic* in the *Laws*, and in the *Apology* "reiterated" the defense of Socrates as well as the charge brought against him three times. [What Strauss refers to as *Al-milla al-fâdila*, *The Virtuous Religion*, may well have been *Kitab al-milla*, *The Book of Religion*, of which Muhsin Mahdi has produced a critical Arabic edition (Beirut: Dar al-Mashriq, 1968), and which has appeared in Alfarabi, *Political Writings*, trans. Butterworth, pp. 87–113.]

80. *Mishneh Torah*, "Teshuvah," III, 17. [See "Laws of Repentance," trans. Hyamson, pp. 84b–85a. The paragraph cited by Strauss is perplexing, for the following reason. The Bodleian manuscript (with Maimonides' signature on it, which makes it the most authentic known manuscript) has numbered paragraphs only in "Hilkhot Teshuvah," or "Laws of Repentance." But these do not match the paragraph numbering in the previous printed editions, which were obviously added by scribes or printers in subsequent centuries. Hyamson provides both numberings, at least in the English translation: the Bodleian manuscript's paragraphs are put in Roman numerals, and the printed versions' paragraphs in Arabic numerals. In chapter III, there are only fourteen numbered paragraphs of the printed versions (Arabic numerals in Hyamson), but the Bodleian manuscript has twenty-seven numbered paragraphs (Roman numerals in Hyamson). The trouble is that Strauss refers to "III, 17," i.e., this is a paragraph in Arabic numerals that is not known. Was he, as seems likely, actually thinking of paragraph XVII (Roman numeral) of the Bodleian? If so, he would then have had in mind a substantial part of III, 8 (about the last two-thirds) in Hyamson's text. (In fact, Rémi Brague, *Maïmonide*, p. 240, n. 80, suggests "peut-être III, 8" as a whole.) On the assumption that Strauss was instead thinking of chap. III, (Bodleian) para. *XVII*—which is certainly reasonable, considering the contents and the point which Strauss wished to make ("Maimonides read the Torah as a book, every word of which was of divine origin and, consequently, of the greatest importance.")—I shall reproduce this complete paragraph (Hyamson, pp. 84b–85a): "Three classes are deniers of the Torah: he who says that the Torah is not of divine origin—even if he says of one verse, or of a single word, that Moses said it, of himself—is a denier of the Torah; likewise, he who denies its interpretation, that is, the Oral Law, and repudiates its reporters, as Zadok and Boethius did; he who says that the Creator changed one commandment for another, and that this Torah, although of divine origin, is now obsolete, as the Nazarenes (Christians) and Hagarites (Muslims) assert. Everyone belonging to any of these classes is a denier of the Torah."]

81. 1.Intro. (2b; 2, 6ff.).

82. That is to say, you must do with the chapters of the *Guide* what Solomon did with the words and parables of the Bible; just as Solomon found out the secret teaching of the Bible by connecting word with word, and parable with parable, in the same way we may find out the secret teaching of the *Guide* by connecting chapter with chapter, and, indeed, secret word with secret word. Cf. 1.Intro. (6b; 6, 26–7, 2).

when reading a given chapter, your intention must be not only to understand the totality of the subject of that chapter, but also to grasp each word which occurs in it in the course of the speech, even if that word does not belong to the intention of the chapter. For the diction of this treatise has not been chosen by haphazard, but with great exactness and exceeding precision.[83]

Maimonides naturally read the Torah as a book which is in no way frivolous. Since he considered histories and poems to be frivolous writings, he was compelled to conceive of the biblical stories as of "secrets of the Torah."[84] As he had such a contempt for stories, it is most unlikely that the few stories which he inserted into the *Guide* have to be accepted at their face value: some necessity must have driven him to tell those stories in order to instill either some true opinion or some good moral habit into the minds of his readers.[85] In one case he tells us the story of how, "many years ago," a scientist had put to him a certain question, and how he had answered it.[86] Since the *Guide* is written "with great exactness and exceeding precision," it is safe to say that the framework of the story conveys some teaching which is not transmitted by the content of the discussion with the scientist. We find in the *Guide* more stories of things which happened "many years ago," such as the history of the science of *kalam* and the story of the two books which Maimonides had begun to write on the parables of the prophets and of the Midrashim.[87] We do not hesitate to call also the "dedicatory epistle" a story, i.e., to assume that it, too, is one of the "secrets" of the *Guide*. Quotations from Maimonides' *Commentary on the Mishnah* and his code, indeed all quotations in the *Guide*, belong to the same class of hints.

After these preliminary remarks, we must try to place the method of reading the *Guide* on a firmer basis. In order to arrive at rules which would relieve us of the burdensome necessity of guessing Maimonides' secret thoughts, we must make a fresh start by discussing more exactly the relation between the model, the Bible, and its imitation or repetition, the *Guide*. What is the literary genus including the Bible and the *Guide*, and what is the specific difference giving the *Guide* its peculiar character?

Both the Bible, as Maimonides was wont to understand it, and the *Guide*

---

83. 1.Intro. (8b; 9, 26–30).
84. 1.2 (13b; 16, 9–11); 3.50. Cf. Baron, "Outlook," 8, n. 4.
85. Cf. 3.50 (120a; 451, 1–3).
86. 1.2.
87. 1.71. 1.Intro. (5b; 5, 17ff.); 3.19 (40a; 346, 3ff.). Cf. 3.32 (70a–b; 385, 13–20).

are esoteric books. To cite but one other assertion of the author, his intention in writing the *Guide* was that the truths should flash up and then disappear again.[88] The purpose of the *Guide* is, then, not only to reveal the truth, but also to hide it. Or, to express the same thing in terms of quantity, a considerable number of statements are made in order to hide the truth rather than to teach it.

But what is the difference between the esoteric method of the Bible and that of the *Guide*? The authors of the Bible chose, in order to reveal the truth by not revealing it, and not to reveal it by revealing it, the use of words of certain kinds and of parables and enigmas.[89] Parables seem to be the more important vehicle, for Maimonides speaks of them much more fully than he does of the kinds of words in question.[90] Thus the suspicion arises that the species of esoteric books to which the Bible belongs is parabolic literature. That suspicion leads us to raise the question whether parables and enigmas are indispensable for esoteric teaching. As a matter of fact, that question is raised by Maimonides himself. After asserting that nobody is capable of completely explaining the secrets and that therefore every teacher speaks of them by using parables and enigmas, he goes on to say that, if someone wishes to teach the secrets without using parables and enigmas, he cannot help substituting for them obscurity and briefness of speech.[91] This remark may refer to an extreme case which is not likely to occur, but it also may suggest a possible innovation. Whether or not that case is likely and whether Maimonides is willing to make the innovation,[92] the substitution indicated by him is certainly possible. Thus his remark implies the admission that there exists a species of unparabolic esoteric literature and, consequently, that the species of esoteric books to which the Bible belongs may rightly be described as parabolic literature.

The question of how to avoid parables and enigmas when speaking of the secrets is taken up again by Maimonides a little further on in the general introduction to his work, in his discussion of the explanation of parables. He discusses that question by telling us a story. He narrates that once upon a time he had intended to write two books in order to explain the parables of the Bible and those of the Midrashim, but that when attempting to write

88. 1.Intro. (3b; 3, 14).
89. 1.Intro. (5a; 5, 11 and 16).
90. Cf. the index to Munk's *Guide*, see under "allégories" and "noms." [*Le Guide des égarés*: on "allegories," p. 483; on "noms" (both "noms, en grammaire et en logique," and "noms de Dieu"), p. 502.]
91. 1.Intro. (4b–5a; 4, 11–13, 17–19, 26–28).
92. 1.Intro. (9b; 10, 24–28).

these books he was faced by a dilemma. Either he could give the explanation in the form of parables, which procedure would merely exchange one individual for another of the same species, or he could explain the parables in unparabolic speech, in which case the explanation would not be suitable for the vulgar. Since the explanations given in the *Guide* are not addressed to the vulgar, but to scholars,[93] we may expect from the outset that they would be of an unparabolic character. Moreover, we know from Maimonides' earlier statement that parabolic and enigmatic representation of the secret teaching can be avoided: it can be replaced by obscurity and briefness of speech, i.e., by ways of expression which are suitable exclusively to scholars who, besides, are able to understand of themselves. Above all, in the case of an explanation of parabolic texts, it is not only possible, but even necessary to avoid parabolic speech: a parabolic explanation would be open to the objection so aptly made by Maimonides himself, that it merely replaces one individual by another individual of the same species, or, in other words, that it is no explanation at all. What is then, the species of speech, different from that of parabolic speech, the use of which Maimonides had to learn after he had decided to write the *Guide* instead of the two popular books? What is the species, of which all expositions of the truth, given in the *Guide*, are individuals? To answer this question, we must first raise the more general question as to what is the genus which includes the species, hitherto unknown, of the expositions of the truth characteristic of the *Guide*, as well as of the species of parabolic expositions? The answer to this question, which no careful student of the *Guide* can help raising, is given by Maimonides in the last section of the general introduction to his work, where he quite abruptly and unexpectedly introduces a new subject: the various reasons for contradictions occurring in various kinds of books. We already know the hidden motive underlying this sudden change of subject matter; that hidden motive is the somewhat disguised question of the method characteristic of the *Guide* or, to speak more generally and vaguely, the question of the genus including the esoteric methods of both the Bible and the *Guide*. To the latter question, Maimonides gives here the rather undisguised answer that the genus looked for is contradictory speech. To the former question, he answers with equal daring that the contradictions met with in the *Guide* are to traced back to two reasons: to the requirements of teaching obscure matters, i.e., of making them understood, and to the requirements of speaking, or writing, of such

---

93. Cf. 1.Intro. (5b; 5, 18−25) with ibid. (3a and 4b; 2, 11ff. and 4, 8−12).

matters. The contradictions caused by the former are bound to be known to the teacher (provided he did not make them deliberately), and they escape the pupil until he has reached an advanced stage of training; that is to say, they certainly escape the vulgar. But as regards the contradictions caused by the latter requirements, they always are deliberately made, and the author must take the utmost care to hide them completely from the vulgar.[94] Those disclosures of Maimonides enable us to describe the form of the esoteric teaching of the *Guide*: Maimonides teaches the truth not by inventing parables (or by using contradictions between parabolic statements), but by using conscious and intentional contradictions, hidden from the vulgar, between unparabolic and unenigmatic statements.[95]

From this result the inference must be drawn that no interpreter of the *Guide* is entitled to attempt a "personal" explanation of its contradictions. For example, he must not try to trace them back to the fact, or assumption, that the two traditions which Maimonides intended to reconcile, i.e., the biblical tradition and the philosophic tradition, are actually irreconcilable; or, more philosophically but scarcely more adequately, to explain them by assuming that Maimonides was on the track of philosophic problems transcending the horizon of the philosophic tradition, but was unable to free himself sufficiently from its shackles. Such attempts would serve a useful purpose if meant to explain highly complicated and artificial reconciliations of contradictions. They are both erroneous and superfluous if they are destined to explain contradictions which, if unintentional, would betray not the failure of a superior intellect in the face of problems either insoluble or very difficult to solve, but rather scandalous incompetence.[96] All these attempts would tacitly or expressly presuppose that the contradictions had escaped Maimonides' notice, an assumption which is refuted by his unequivocal statements. Therefore, until the contrary has been proved, it must be maintained that he was fully aware of every contradiction in the *Guide*, at the very time of writing the contradictory sentences. And if the objection is made that we ought to allow for the possibility that unconscious and unintentional contradictions have crept into the *Guide*, since philosophers hardly inferior to Maimonides have been found guilty of such contradictions, we answer by referring to Maimonides' emphatic declaration concerning the extreme care with which he

---

94. 1.Intro. (10a, 10b, 11b; 11, 19–26 and 12, 7–12 and 13, 13–15).
95. Cf. 1.Intro. (10a; 11, 13–16). Cf. the somewhat different interpretation followed by Altmann, op. cit., 310f.
96. Cf. 1.Intro. (10b; 12, 4–7).

had written every single word of his book and by asking the objectors to produce similar declarations from those books of other philosophers which they may have in mind. Therefore the duty of the interpreter is not to explain the contradictions, but to find out in each case which of the two statements was considered by Maimonides to be true and which he merely used as a means of hiding the truth.

Maimonides has raised the question whether contradictions caused by the requirements of speaking, or writing, of obscure matters are also to be found in the Bible: he demands that this question be very carefully studied.[97] In fact, it reveals itself as being the decisive question, once one has looked beneath the surface of the teaching of the *Guide*. Since he does not answer it explicitly, it must here be left open. Neither can we discuss here the related questions as to whether the Maimonidean method of teaching the truth was influenced by a philosophic tradition; whether it is characteristic of a particular kind of philosophic literature; and whether, in accordance with the terminology of the philosophic tradition, the *Guide* ought not to be described rather as an exoteric work. If this description should ultimately prove correct, the meaning of the term "addition" would have to undergo a profound change: it would not mean the decisively important secret teaching which is added to the conventional view, but rather the imaginative representation which is added to the undisguised truth.[98]

Since the contradictions in the *Guide* are concealed, we must briefly consider at least some of the ways of hiding contradictions. (1) The most obvious method is to speak of the same subject in a contradictory manner on pages far apart from each other. The symbol of this method is: a = b (page 15) − a ≠ b (page 379). Considering, however, the carelessness with which we usually read, one may reduce the distance between the pages to any positive number. (2) A variation of this method is to make one of the two contradictory statements in passing, as it were. A good example is Maimonides' incidental

---

97. 1.Intro. (11b; 13, 6−8).
98. For the two meanings of *addition*, cf. 1.Intro. (7a−b; 8, 6, 15), on the one hand, and ibid. (8a; 9, 8), on the other. Cf. also in the *Treatise on Resurrection* the beginning of the treatise proper. The importance of the term "addition," for instance, for the doctrine of attributes may be indicated here in passing. [For "the beginning of the treatise proper," see "Treatise on Resurrection," trans. Fradkin, p. 162: "Know, O thou man of speculation, that our aim in this treatise is the clarification of what we ourselves believe concerning this foundation about which the speech occurred among the students, namely, Resurrection of the Dead. There is nothing at all in this treatise in addition to what we said in the *Commentary on the Mishnah* or the *Compilation* (i.e., *Mishneh Torah*); there is in it nothing but a repetition of matters and a popular (lit., vulgar) elaboration, and an additional explanation that the women and the ignorant will understand, nothing more."]

denial of the obligatory character of the entire sacrificial legislation.[99] (3) A third method is to contradict the first statement not directly, but by contradicting its implications. The symbol of this method is: $a = b - b = c - [a = c] - a \neq c - [a \neq b]$, the brackets indicating propositions which are not to be pronounced. It may be illustrated by the contradiction between the statements that "one of the main subjects of the *Guide* is *ma'aseh bereshit*" and that "*ma'aseh bereshit* is physics" on the one hand, and that "physics is not a subject of the *Guide*" on the other; or by the contradiction between the contentions that "explanation of the secrets is impossible by nature" and that "explanation of the secrets is forbidden by the law." (4) Another method is to contradict the first statement not directly, but by seemingly repeating it while actually adding to it, or omitting from it, an apparently negligible expression. The symbol of that method is: $a = b - [b = \beta + \varepsilon] - a = \beta - [a \neq b]$. (5) Another method is to introduce between the two contradictory statements an intermediary assertion, which, by itself not contradictory to the first statement, becomes contradictory to it by the addition, or the omission, of an apparently negligible expression; the contradictory statement creeps in as a repetition of the intermediary statement. The symbol of this method is: $a = b - a \neq \beta - [b = \beta + \varepsilon] - a \neq b$. (6) To use ambiguous words. The symbol is: $a = c - \left[c \genfrac{}{}{0pt}{}{=}{\neq} b < \genfrac{}{}{0pt}{}{a = b}{a \neq b} \right]$. For example, the sentence, "a certain statement is an addition," may mean a true addition to an untruth, or an untrue addition to the truth.

While on the subject of ambiguous words, we may indicate their great importance for the reader of the *Guide*. According to Maimonides, the Bible teaches the truth by using certain kinds of words, as well as by parables. While excluding the latter from his own work, he nowhere indicates his intention of avoiding the former, and in particular ambiguous words. The expression "ambiguous word" is itself ambiguous. Used as a technical term, it means a word which is applied to "two objects between which there is a similarity with regard to some thing which is accidental to both and which does

---

99. 3.46 (102a–b; 427, 14–16). Cf. Munk, *Guide* [*Le Guide des égarés*], III, 364, n. 5. An allusion to this statement is implied in Joseph ibn Kaspi's commentaries on Deut. 17:14f. and I Sam. 8:6. [*Guide*, trans. Pines, 3.46, p. 582: "All this was addressed to those who wished to offer sacrifices. Then (Scripture) explains to us that in regard to this kind of divine service, I mean sacrifices, no sin whatever will fall upon us if we do not perform it at all. For it says: 'But if thou shalt forbear to vow, it shall be no sin in thee.' (Deut. 23:23)." Munk: "The text expresses itself in a most concise manner: 'All this is for those who wished.' The author wants to say that the legislator, with respect to all of these prescriptions, only wishes to regulate sacrifices for those who voluntarily practice this form of worship; for, as the author has elucidated above (III, 32), the sacrificial cult was only an accommodation to the customs of the times, and was more tolerated than intended (*ordonné*)."]

not constitute the essence of either of them."[100] In another less technical, but scarcely less important sense, it means "a word fitly spoken" (Proverbs 25:11). For, according to Maimonides, this biblical expression describes "a speech spoken according to its two faces," or "a speech which has two faces, i.e., which has an exterior and an inner" face; an exterior useful, for instance, for the proper condition of human societies, and an inner useful for the knowledge of the truth.[101] An ambiguous speech in the second sense would, then, be a speech with one face toward the vulgar, and with another face toward the man who understands by himself. Not only speeches, or sentences, but also words with two faces were indispensable to Maimonides, when he attempted to reveal the truth to the latter while hiding it from the former. For a secret is much less perfectly concealed by a sentence than by a word, since a word is much smaller in extent, and consequently *ceteris paribus* a much better hiding place than a whole sentence. This is especially true of common words, placed unobtrusively within an unobtrusive sentence. It is just such common words of hidden ambiguity which Maimonides has primarily in mind when he asks the reader to pay very close attention to every word which he happens (or rather seems to happen) to use; and when he emphatically entreats him not to explain anything in the *Guide*, not even a single word, unless it expressed something which had already been accepted and openly taught by earlier Jewish authorities.[102] Evidently the explanation of a single word cannot be so grave a matter unless that word is filled with high explosive which can destroy all beliefs not firmly grounded in reason; i.e., unless its actual and hidden meaning lends to some important statement a sense totally different from, or even diametrically opposed to the sense which it would have, if this particular word were to be accepted in its apparent or conventional meaning. Is such a word not to be called an ambiguous word, "a word fitly spoken"? Apart from all general considerations, one may cite a number of individual examples of ambiguous terms intentionally used by Maimonides. Such terms are: "the wise" or "the learned," "the men of speculation,"[103] "the virtuous," "the community of the believers in [God's]

---

100. 1.56 (68b; 89, 18—20). Cf. H. A. Wolfson, "The Amphibolous Terms in Aristotle, Arabic Philosophy and Maimonides," *Harvard Theological Review* 31 (1938): 164. [See also Wolfson, *Studies in History*, vol. 1, p. 468.]

101. 1.Intro. (6b—7a; 7, 15—8, 3). The fact that the whole passage (6a—8b; 6, 19—9, 25), which apparently deals with parables only, actually has still another meaning, is indicated by the seeming clumsiness with which the apparent subject is introduced.

102. 1.Intro. (9a; 10, 4—7). [Strauss's Latin phrase, *ceteris paribus*, may be translated as "all other things being equal."]

103. Cf., for instance, 1.Intro. (9b; 10, 21); 3.15 (28b; 331, 27—29).

unity," "government," and "providence," "addition," "secret," "belief," "action," "possible."

Returning to Maimonides' use of contradictions, one may assume that all important contradictions in the *Guide* may be reduced to the single fundamental contradiction between the true teaching, based on reason, and the untrue teaching, emanating from imagination. But whether this be the case or not, we are certainly in need of a general answer to the general question: which of the two contradictory statements is in each instance considered by Maimonides as the true statement? That answer would be *the* guide for the understanding of Maimonides' work. It is provided by his identification of the true teaching with some secret teaching. Consequently, of two contradictory statements made by him, that statement which is most secret must have been considered by him to be true. Secrecy is to a certain extent identical with rarity; what all people say all the time is the opposite of a secret. We may therefore establish the rule that of two contradictory statements in the *Guide* or in any other work of Maimonides that statement which occurs least frequently, or even which occurs only once, was considered by him to be true. He himself alludes to this rule in his *Treatise on Resurrection*, the most authentic commentary on the *Guide*, when he stresses the fact that resurrection, though a basic principle of the law, is contradicted by many scriptural passages, and asserted only in two verses of the Book of Daniel. He almost pronounces that rule by declaring, in the treatise mentioned, that the truth of a statement is not increased by repetition nor is it diminished by the author's failure to repeat it: "you know that the mention of the basic principle of unity, i.e., His word 'The Lord is one,' is not repeated in the Torah."

To sum up: Maimonides teaches the truth not plainly, but secretly; i.e., he reveals the truth to those learned men who are able to understand by themselves and at the same time he hides it from the vulgar. There probably is no better way of hiding the truth than to contradict it. Consequently, Maimonides makes contradictory statements about all important subjects; he reveals the truth by stating it, and hides it by contradicting it. Now the truth must be stated in a more hidden way than it is contradicted, or else it would become accessible to the vulgar; and those who are able to understand by themselves are in a position to find out the concealed statement of the truth. That is why Maimonides repeats as frequently as possible the conventional views which are suitable to, or accepted by the vulgar, but pronounces as rarely as possible contradictory unconventional views. Now a statement contradictory to another statement is, in a sense, its repetition, agreeing with it in almost every respect and differing only by some addition or omission. Therefore we are able to recognize the contradiction only by a very close scrutiny of every single word, however small, in the two statements.

Contradictions are the axis of the *Guide*. They show in the most convincing manner that the actual teaching of that book is sealed and at the same time reveal the way of unsealing it. While the other devices used by Maimonides compel the reader to guess the true teaching, the contradictions offer him the true teaching quite openly in either of the two contradictory statements. Moreover, while the other devices do not by themselves force readers to look beneath the surface—for instance, an inappropriate expression or a clumsy transition, if noticed at all, may be considered to be merely an inappropriate expression or a clumsy transition, and not a stumbling block—the contradictions, once they are discovered, compel them to take pains to find out the actual teaching. To discover the contradictions or to find out which contradictory statement is considered by Maimonides to be true, we sometimes need the help of hints. Recognizing the meaning of hints requires a higher degree of understanding by oneself than does the recognition of an obvious contradiction. Hints are supplied by the application of the other Maimonidean devices.

To make our enumeration of those devices somewhat more complete, and not to mention intentional sophisms and ironical remarks, we shall first briefly clarify our foregoing remark on Maimonides' extensive use of words of certain kinds. We may call those words secret words. His secret terminology requires a special study, based upon a complete index of words which have, or may have, secret meaning. These words are partly ambiguous, as in the instances mentioned above, and partly unambiguous, such as *adamiyyun, fiqh, dunya*. In the second place we may mention various kinds of apostrophes to the reader and mottoes prefixed to the whole work or to individual parts. Another device consists in silence, i.e., the omission of something which only the learned, or the learned who are able to understand of themselves, would miss. Let us take the following example. Maimonides quotes in the *Guide* four times, if I am not mistaken, expressly as an utterance of Aristotle, and with express or tacit approval, the statement that the sense of touch is a disgrace to us.[104] Such fourfold repetition of an express quotation in a book so carefully worded as the *Guide* proves that the quotation is something like

---

104. 2.36 (79a; 262, 11–12); 2.40 (86b; 272, 4–5); 3.8 (12b; 311, 9–10); 3.49 (117a; 447, 1–2). Cf. also 3.8 (14a; 313, 18–19).

a leitmotif. Now, that quotation is incomplete. Maimonides omits two words which profoundly alter its meaning. Aristotle says: δόξειεν ἄν δικαίως (ᾗ ἁφῇ) ἐπονείδιστος εἶναι [*doxeien an dikaiōs (ē haphē) eponeidistos einai*].[105] Maimonides omits, then, those two words which characterize the utterance as an ἔνδοξον [*endoxon*]. Readers of the *Guide*, cognizant of the teachings of the "prince of philosophers," naturally noticed the omission and realized that the passages into which the quotation is inserted are of a merely popular, or exoteric character. If one examines the four quotations more closely, one notices that while in the second and third citation Maimonides mentions the name of Aristotle, but not the work from which it is taken, he expressly cites the *Ethics* in the first passage, thus intimating that its source is a book based mainly on ἔνδοξα [*endoxa*]. In the last quotation Maimonides adds the remark that the quotation is literal, but two or three lines further on, while speaking of the same subject, he refers to the *Ethics* and the *Rhetoric*, i.e., to books devoted to the analysis of ἔνδοξα [*endoxa*]. There can be no doubt that Maimonides was fully aware of the fact that his citation from Aristotle actually reflected popular rather than philosophic opinion. It is still less doubtful that Maimonides, while agreeing with the complete statement of Aristotle, viz., that the sense of touch is popularly considered disgraceful, by no means believed in the soundness of this popular judgment. As a matter of fact, he contradicted it quite openly by denying any difference in dignity between the senses and by ascribing to the imagination of the vulgar the distinction between senses which are supposed to be perfections and those believed to be imperfections.[106] The reader of the *Guide*, familiar with the main controversial topics of the Middle Ages, will at once realize the bearing

---

105. *Nicomachean Ethics* 1118b2. ["Thus the sense with which self-indulgence is connected is the most widely shared of the senses; and self-indulgence would seem to be justly a matter of reproach, because it attaches to us not as men but as animals. To delight in such things, then, and to love them above all others, is brutish." *Nicomachean Ethics*, trans. W. D. Ross, rev. J. O. Urmson, in *The Complete Works of Aristotle*, ed. Jonathan Barnes (Princeton: Princeton University Press, 1984), vol. 2, p. 1765.] I am naturally following that interpretation of the passage cited, on which is based the Arabic translation as quoted by Maimonides. Cf. Averroes ad loc.: "et iustum est nos opinari a nobis [sic] quod sensus iste opprobriosus est nobis." ["and it is just for us to suppose on our own [sic] that this sense is disgraceful to us." Latin translated by Martin D. Yaffe.] Cf. [Aristotle,] *De anima* 421a19–26. ["Taste is with us more discriminating because it is itself a form of touch, and this sense (i.e., touch) in man is highly discriminating; in the other senses he is behind many kinds of animal, but in touch he is much more discriminating than the other animals. This is why he is of all living creatures the most intelligent. Proof of this lies in the fact that among the human race men are well or poorly endowed with intelligence in proportion to their sense of touch, and no other sense; for men of hard skin and flesh are poorly, and men of soft flesh well endowed, with intelligence." *On the Soul, Parva Naturalia, On Breath*, trans. W. S. Hett (Cambridge, MA: Harvard University Press, 1957), pp. 118–21.]

106. 1.47; 1.46 (51b–52a; 68, 16–21); 1.2 (14a; 16, 22–17, 3).

of Maimonides' misquotation: the statement of Aristotle, as cited by Maimonides, would afford an excellent justification of ascetic morality—for what Maimonides would call "exaggeration"—and in particular for an ascetic attitude toward sexuality.[107] And the reader who looks up the passages in question in the *Guide* will notice that one of these misquotations is inserted into what Munk calls the "définition générale de la prophétie." Another characteristic omission is Maimonides' failure to mention the immortality of the soul or the resurrection of the body, when he attempts explicitly to answer the question of Divine Providence.[108] He begins his discussion (3.16–24) by reproducing the philosophic argument against individual providence, mainly based on the observation that the virtuous are stricken with misery, while the wicked enjoy apparent happiness. It is therefore all the more perplexing that he pays no attention to what Leibniz has called[109] "le remède [qui] est tout prêt dans l'autre vie." Neither does he mention that remedy in his express recapitulation of the view of providence characteristic of the literal sense of the Torah.[110] On the other hand, he elsewhere explains in the same context the "good at thy latter end" alluded to in Deuteronomy 8:16 as the fortitude acquired by the privations from which Israel had suffered while wandering through the desert.[111]

The fourth and last kind of hints to be indicated here are the *ra'shei peraqim*. This expression, which we have hitherto rendered as "chapter headings," may also mean "beginnings of chapters." In some cases, indeed, Maimonides gives us important hints by the initial word or words of a chapter. The opening word of the section devoted to the rational explanation of biblical commandments (3.25–49) is the noun, *al-af'al* ("the actions"). The

---

107. Cf., in this connection, 3.8 (14a–b; 313, 22–314, 14).

108. This is not to deny that Maimonides mentions here the "other world," in connection with such views of Providence as he rejects or the truth of which he neither discusses nor asserts. The phrase in 3.22 (46a; 354, 3–4), "the thing which remains of man after death," is naturally noncommittal with respect to the immortality of the individual soul. Cf. 1.74 (121b; 155, 9–10).

109. *Théodicée*, para. 17. [The standard English translation is G. W. Leibniz, *Theodicy*, trans. E. M. Huggard, ed. Austin Farrer (London: Routledge and Kegan Paul, 1951). See p. 132 for the line quoted by Strauss. However, one should notice that this French line is not translated literally; or at least, the English version points to quite another meaning than the one which Strauss derives from Leibniz's actual words. Strauss construes Leibniz ("le remède [qui] est tout prêt dans l'autre vie") as saying, "the remedy which is always ready-made (in the sense of "ready at hand"), the other life." Huggard (ed. Farrer) instead translates it rather too "literally" (i.e., so as to misconsture its significance) as: "the remedy is all prepared in the other life."]

110. 3.17 (34b–37b; 338, 21–343, 5).

111. 3.24 (52b–53a; 362, 10–363, 4). Cf. *Mishneh Torah*, "Teshuvah," VIII, 1–2. [See "Laws of Repentance," trans. Hyamson, pp. 90a–90b. This reference assumes that Strauss deliberately used the Arabic numerals. If vis-à-vis these paragraphs, he is instead thinking of the (Bodleian) Roman numerals I–II, then there is only material referred to on p. 90a.]

af'al, synonymously used with *a'mal*, constitute the second half of the law, the first half consisting of *ara'*[112] ("opinions"). Thus this opening gives us a hint that all the preceding chapters of the *Guide* (1.1–3.24) are devoted to the "opinions," as distinguished from "actions," which are taught or prescribed by the law. The initial words in the first chapter (3.8) devoted to theodicy, or the question of providence, is the expression "All bodies which come into existence and perish." These words indicate that this whole group of chapters (3.8–24) deals exclusively with bodies which come into existence and perish, and not with bodies or souls which do not come into existence or perish. That this guess is correct is shown by other remarks of Maimonides.[113] From this opening, moreover, we must draw the inference that all preceding chapters (1.1–3.7) are devoted to things which do not come into existence and perish, and in particular to souls or intelligences which do not come into existence and perish, i.e., to *ma'aseh merkavah*. This inference is confirmed by Maimonides' statement, made at the end of Book 3, Chapter 7, that all the preceding chapters are indispensable for the right understanding of *ma'aseh merkavah*, whereas in the following chapters not a word will be said, either explicitly or allusively, about that most exalted topic. Equally important are the beginnings of Book 3, Chapter 24, which opens with the ambiguous word *'amr*, which may mean "thing" as well as "command,"[114] and the beginning of the very first chapter of the whole work.

Necessity has led us to make such incoherent and fragmentary remarks about Maimonides' methods of presenting the truth that it will not be amiss if we conclude this chapter with a simile which may drive home its main content to those readers who are more interested in the literary than in the philosophic question. There are books the sentences of which resemble highways, or even motor roads. But there are also books the sentences of which resemble rather winding paths which lead along precipices concealed by thickets and sometimes even along well-hidden and spacious caves. These depths and caves are not noticed by the busy workmen hurrying to their fields, but they gradually become known and familiar to the leisured and attentive wayfarer. For is not every sentence rich in potential recesses? May not every noun be

---

112. Cf. in particular 3.52 (130b; 464, 26–465, 5) with Farabi, *Ihsa al-'ulum*, chap. 5 (or the Hebrew translation by Falaquera, in *Reshit Ḥokhmah*, ed. [Moritz] David, p. 59). For the two Arabic words for "actions," cf., for instance, 3.25 (57a; 368, 8 and 10). [For Farabi's *Ihsa* ("Enumeration of the Sciences"), chap. 5, see *Medieval Political Philosophy*, ed. Lerner and Mahdi, pp. 24–30; Alfarabi, *Political Writings*, trans. Butterworth, pp. 76–84.]

113. 3.23 (50b–51a; 360, 1–14); 3.54 (135a; 470, 21–26).

114. Cf. 3.24 (54a; 364, 16 and 20f.)

explained by a relative clause which may profoundly affect the meaning of the principal sentence and which, even if omitted by a careful writer, will be read by the careful reader?[115] Cannot miracles be wrought by such little words as "almost,"[116] "perhaps," "seemingly"? May not a statement assume a different shade of meaning by being cast in the form of a conditional sentence? And is it not possible to hide the conditional nature of such a sentence by turning it into a very long sentence and, in particular, by inserting into it a parenthesis of some length? It is to a conditional sentence of this kind that Maimonides confides his general definition of prophecy.[117]

VI. THE *GUIDE* AND THE CODE

As we have seen, the *Guide* is devoted to the true science of the law, as distinguished from the science of the law in the usual sense, the *fiqh*. It remains to be considered whether, according to Maimonides, the two kinds, or parts, of the science of the law are of equal dignity or whether one of them is superior to the other.

Several arguments tend to show that Maimonides attached a higher importance to the *fiqh*, or to use the Hebrew term, to the *talmud*,[118] than he did

---

115. Cf. in this connection 1.21 (26a; 33, 11–17); 1.27, toward the end.
116. Cf. 3.19 (39a; 345, 6).
117. 2.36 (78b–79b; 262, 2–263, 1). Cf. Munk, *Guide*, II, 284, n. 1. [Munk translates the text to be saying: "it must be known that this concerns the case of a human individual." (*Guide*, trans. Pines, p. 371, translates it as: "you should know that the case to be taken into consideration is that of a human individual.") Munk's note reads: "Literally, 'that there is a human individual, etc.' In our translation, we have been compelled to modify slightly the first words of this phrase, which begins a long hypothetical sentence that enumerates all the physical and moral qualities requisite for prophetic inspiration.... If there is a human individual, the author says, who possesses all of the qualities just enumerated, this individual, drawn by the action of a perfect imaginative faculty, and summoned by his perfection to speculative inspiration from the active intellect, will undoubtedly perceive divine and extraordinary things, etc.... It was much more necessary, for the sake of clearness, that the author break this sentence up, but he himself loses the thread and even interrupts himself with a short digression on a passage from Aristotle's *Ethics*." I venture my impression that Strauss refers readers to this note by Munk, not because he accedes to Munk's analysis of Maimonides' literary deficiencies, but rather because he wishes to show how a competent scholar can completely misapprehend Maimonides' intentions and their stylistic expressions.] Other examples of the same method occur in 3.51 (127b; 460, 27–461, 1) [cf. Munk, *Guide*, III, 445, n. 2] and 3.18 (39a; 344, 22). [The above reference to Munk in square brackets is Strauss's own (perhaps a supplementary addition?), not that of the present editor. This note by Munk (*Guide*, III, 445, n. 2) reads as follows: "Ibn Tibbon translates: '*Ve-aḥar she-ha-'inyan ken*,' '*since* it is thus.' Ibn Falaquera rightly points out that it should have been translated, '*ve-im haya ha-davar ken*,' '*if the matter is thus*'; for the author affirms nothing, and it is a matter of a mere hypothesis." *Guide*, trans. Pines, 3.51, p. 625, renders it as "If this is so."]
118. Cf. 3.54 (132b; 467, 19–22) with *Mishneh Torah*, "Talmud Torah," I, 11. [See "Laws Concerning the Study of the Torah," trans. Hyamson, p. 58a: "11. The time allotted to study should be divided into three parts. A third should be devoted to the Written Law; a third to the Oral Law; and the last third should be spent in reflection, deducing conclusions from premises, developing implications of state-

to the subject of the *Guide*: (1) He calls his talmudic code "our great work," whereas he describes the *Guide* as "my treatise." (2) The former exercised a great influence on traditional Judaism, in which respect the *Guide*, already two or three centuries after its publication far surpassed by the Zohar[119] in deep and popular appeal, cannot possibly compete. (3) Even under the profoundly changed circumstances of the present time, the *Mishneh Torah* is able to elicit strong and deep emotions in modern readers, whereas the *Guide* is of hardly any interest to people who do not happen to be historians. (4) Whereas the subject matter of the *Mishneh Torah* is easily ascertainable, the question of the field to which the subjects of the *Guide* belong is highly perplexing; it is not a philosophic nor a theological work, nor a book of religion.[120] (5) The code is styled a "repetition of the Torah," whereas the "treatise" is a mere "guide of the perplexed." (6) The *fiqh*'s precedence to the subject matter of the *Guide* (the *maʿaseh bereshit* and *maʿaseh merkavah*) is expressly stated by Maimonides when he says, as it were in defense of the *talmud* against the sages of the Talmud, that "although those things [the explanation of the precepts of the Torah] were called by the sages a small thing—for the sages have said 'a great thing is *maʿaseh merkavah*, and a small thing is the discussion of Abbaye and Raba'—yet they ought to have precedence."[121] (7) Having gone so far, one might be tempted to go even farther and assert that the subject of the *Guide* is subservient to and implied in the *talmud*. For Maimonides

---

ments, comparing dicta, studying the hermeneutical principles by which the Torah is interpreted, till one knows the essence of these principles, and how to deduce what is permitted and what is forbidden from what one has learned traditionally. This is termed Talmud."]

119. Cf. G[ershom] Scholem, *Die Geheimnisse der Schöpfung: Ein Kapitel aus dem Sohar* [*The Secrets of Creation: A Chapter from the Zohar*] (Berlin: Schocken, 1935[; reprint, Frankfurt on Main, 1971, 1992)], 6f. ["Very slowly but surely did the Zohar work its effect: the Zohar achieved in later—although extremely intensive—aftereffects [Nachleben], the powerful historical function of a holy text complementary to the Bible and Talmud on a new level of religious consciousness, as the level on which it won its authority, proving itself in its turn as the bearer in the storms of Jewish history of a new religious tendency [Haltung], for which it laid claim to and in fact obtained authority. This inspired character [of the book] was recognized by many Jewish circles in eastern Europe and the Orient well into our own era, and they in no sense shrunk back from gradually drawing the final conclusion from the recognition of [it as] a holy text: namely, that in the final analysis its effect on the soul depends on its being in no sense understood. Only with the breakdown of those circles of life and faith in which the Kabbalah was able to constitute itself as a historical force, dimming even the luster of the Zohar—which now in its Enlightenment revaluation was turned into that 'book of lies' ['Lügenbuch']—that the pure light of authentic [echten] Judaism has had to be eclipsed." Translated by the present editor. Scholem's remark about the Zohar characterized as a "book of lies" refers to a polemical statement made by the great 19th-century German Jewish historian Heinrich Graetz.]

120. See above, sixth paragraph of section II.

121. *Mishneh Torah*, "Yesodei ha-Torah," IV, 13. [See "Laws of the Basic Principles of the Torah" ("Hilkhot Yesodei ha-Torah"), trans. Hyamson, pp. 39b–40a; "Book of Knowledge," trans. Lerner, pp. 152–53.]

explicitly says that *pardes* (i.e., *ma'aseh merkavah* and *ma'aseh bereshit*) is included in the *talmud*.¹²² This argument might be reinforced by (8) a hint which, as such, in a book such as the *Guide*, is incomparably more significant than an explicit statement. Maimonides explains the true science of the law at the very beginning of his work, whereas he explains the meaning of *fiqh* in the very last chapter. To understand this hint, we must make use of another hint contained in the "chapter headings" of the first and the last chapters. The first chapter begins with the word "Image," while the last chapter opens with the term "Wisdom." This indicates that readers of the *Guide* are to be led from "Image," the sphere of imagination, to "Wisdom," the realm of intelligence: the way which readers of the *Guide* go is an ascent from the lower to the higher, indeed, from the lowest to the highest knowledge. Now the last of the themes treated in the *Guide* is law proper, i.e., the commands and prohibitions of the Torah, and not *ma'aseh bereshit* and *ma'aseh merkavah*, which are dealt with in the preceding sections. Consequently, the precepts of the law, far from being "a small thing," are actually the highest subject, indeed, the end and purpose of the true science of the law. (9) This conclusion is confirmed by an express statement by Maimonides, which establishes the following ascending order of dignity: (a) knowledge of the truth, based on tradition only; (b) such knowledge, based on demonstration; (c) *fiqh*.¹²³ (10) This hierarchy is also in accordance with the saying of the sages that not study, but action is most important, and it is actions which are determined by the *fiqh*. That hierarchy is imitated by the whole plan of the *Guide*, inasmuch as Maimonides assigns the explanation of the laws to the last group of chapters of that work, and as he explains the meaning of *fiqh* in the last chapter of it: the end is the best.

We have marshaled here all the evidence in favor of the view that Maimonides attached greater importance to the *Mishneh Torah* than to the *Guide*, and hope not to have missed a single argument which has been or could plausibly be adduced in its support. Impressive as they may seem at first sight, however, these arguments possess no validity whatsoever. The second and third arguments are wholly immaterial, for they do not reflect Maimonides' own conviction, but deal exclusively with what other people thought,

---

122. *Mishneh Torah*, "Talmud Torah," I, 12. [See "Laws Concerning the Study of the Torah," trans. Hyamson, p. 58a: "The subjects styled *Pardes* (Esoteric Studies), are included in Talmud. This plan applies to the period when one begins learning. But after one has become proficient . . . (one) should devote all his days exclusively to the study of Talmud, according to the breadth of his mind and maturity of intellect."]

123. 3.54 (132b; 467, 18–25).

or think of the matter. Neither can the fourth argument claim serious consideration, for it, too, is neither based on a Maimonidean statement, nor does, in itself, the perplexing nature of the subject matter of a book necessarily prove its lower rank; the example of Aristotle's *Metaphysics* might be to the point. We shall, then, turn to the remaining seven arguments which are at least apparently based on explicit or implicit statements of Maimonides.

The inference drawn from the description of the *Mishneh Torah* as "our great work" and of the *Guide* as "my treatise" is of little weight. For it is based on a hint, and no evidence has thus far been forthcoming to prove the fact that, or to show the reason why, Maimonides was prevented from stating quite openly that the *halakha* is of higher dignity than the subject of the *Guide*. The description of the *Mishneh Torah* as a "great" work may very well refer to its length rather than to its dignity, for it is quite natural that a code should be lengthier than the discussion of "roots." Or are we to believe that Maimonides attached a higher value to the "great book" of the Sabian Ishaq "on the laws of the Sabians and the details of their religion and their feasts and their sacrifices and their prayers and the other subjects of their religion" than he did to the "book" of the same unknown author "on the defense of the religion of the Sabians"?[124] Moreover, it is doubtful whether Maimonides actually called the *Guide* a "treatise," rather than a "speech," and whether he called the *Mishneh Torah* a "work." "Work" would be a synonym for "book."[125] While Maimonides, for the most part, uses the two terms interchangeably, yet in one instance at least he hints at a distinction between *kitab* (*sefer*, "book") and *ta'lif* (*ḥibbur*, usually translated by "work"). He does this when speaking of the contradictions which are to be found "in any book or in any *ta'lif*."[126] Abravanel, in his commentary on this passage, suggests that Maimonides means by "books" the books par excellence, i.e.,

---

124. Cf. 3.29 (66b; 380, 13–15).
125. See Louis Ginzberg's note, see under *ḥibbur*, in his appendix to I[srael] Efros's *Philosophical Terms in the Moreh Nebukim* (New York: Columbia University Press, 1924). [Efros discusses *ḥibbur* on p. 46. A condensed version of what Ginzberg writes (p. 133) is offered in what follows: "*ḥibbur*, work. Compare the very instructive remarks of (Leopold) Zunz (*Gesammelte Schriften* II, 56–58) on the history of this word to which I would like to add as follows. In Geonic literature *ḥibbur* is composition, diction, or style; compare Sherira Gaon in his *Letter*, ed. Lewin. . . . In some of these passages *ḥibbur* is used almost in the sense of work, book; it is, however, Albarceloni who was the first to employ it as a synonym for *sefer* (book). . . . R. Nissim Gaon speaks of *al ḥibbur ha-Talmud*, which means 'following the order of the Talmud,' and of the Mishnah as *ḥibbur nimraẓ*, which is to be translated as 'a composition of excellent style,' and not as Zunz has it, 'an excellent work.' Interesting is the *eḥad min ha-miḥabbrim* for 'an author' in Albarceloni."] Cf. above, third paragraph of section III.
126. 1.Intro. (9b; 11, 7–8).

the Bible, while he means by *tawalif* (or, rather, *ḥibburim*) the talmudic and philosophic literature. However grateful we ought to be to Abravanel for his indicating the problem, we certainly cannot accept his solution. For in the same section of the *Guide* Maimonides mentions also the "books" of the philosophers.[127] On the other hand, two lines below this distinction, Maimonides applies the word *ta'lif* to such works as the Mishnah, the Baraitot, and the Gemara.[128] We shall then suggest that by occasionally distinguishing between "books" and *tawalif*, Maimonides intended to point out once for all the distinction between such writings as the Bible and the works of philosophers on the one hand, and other literature, as exemplified by the talmudic compilation on the other hand. In fact, "compilation" would be a more literal translation of *ta'lif* or *ḥibbur* than is "work" or "book." We know from the example of *maqala* that Maimonides, when using a word emphatically, uses it in its original sense, which, as such, is often more hidden, rather than in its derivative and more conventional meaning. Thus we ought to render *ta'lif* or *ḥibbur*, when emphatically used by Maimonides, by "compilation," rather than by "work." Since he doubtless uses it emphatically when he regularly calls the *Mishneh Torah* a *ta'lif* or a *ḥibbur*, we ought to substitute the translation "our great compilation," for the usual translation "our great work."[129]

127. 1.Intro. (11b; 13, 8). Abravanel's comment may have been suggested by a mistake of Ibn Tibbon (or of a copyist or printer), since we find, in our editions of Ibn Tibbon's translation, the words "the books of the philosophers" rendered by "the words of the philosophers." But it is also possible that that suggestion was caused by 1.8 (18b; 22, 26—27), where a distinction is drawn between the "books" of the prophets and the *tawalif* (or *ḥibburim*) ["compilations"] of the "men of science."

128. Cf 1.Intro. (10a; 11, 10) with ibid. (10b—11a; 12, 12—19).

129. The correctness of this translation becomes fully apparent when one examines the way in which Maimonides employs, in his introduction to *Mishneh Torah*, the terms *ḥibber* ["composition"] and *ḥibbur* ["compilation"] as against *ketav* ["writing"] and *sefer* ["book"]. The *Mishneh Torah* is a *ḥibbur* ["compilation"], because he has composed it *le-ḥabber devarim ha-mitbarerim mi-kol 'elu ha- ḥibburin* ["to compile clarifying words from all of these compilations"] (i.e., from the talmudic and gaonic literatures). Cf. *Mishneh Torah*, "Teshuvah" IV, 7 (86b 11 Hyamson). ["Laws of Repentance," trans. Hyamson, p. 86b, l. 11; the English and the Hebrew are disparately numbered by Hyamson, which is sure to confuse readers; Strauss refers to a word used by Maimonides in the last line of para. 7 (Hebrew), which is para. 5 as well as VI (English).] For the original meaning of *ḥibbur* ["compilation"], see also *Mishneh Torah*, "Yesodei ha-Torah," I, 11 ["composition"]; III, 7 ["conjunction"]. [See "Laws of the Basic Principles of the Torah," trans. Hyamson, pp. 35a (English: para. 11; Hebrew: para. 8, l. 14) and 37a (English: para. VIII or 7; Hebrew: para. 8, l. 24); cf. "Book of Knowledge," trans. Lerner, para. 8, p. 143 and para. 8, p. 148.] L[udwig] Blau's suggestion ["Das Gesetzbuch des Maimonides historisch betractet,"] (in *Moses ben Maimon: Sein Leben, seine Werke, und sein Einfluss*, ed. W. Bacher, M. Brann, D. Simonsen, and J. Guttmann (Leipzig: G. Fock, 1908—14; reprint, Hildesheim: Olms, 1971), vol. II, [pp. 331—44, and especially] p. 339f.) that *ḥibbur* ["compilation"] corresponds to *summa*, as distinguished from *commentatio*, is ruled out by the fact that both *Mishneh Torah* and *Commentary on the Mishnah* are called by Maimonides *ḥibburim* (or *tawalif*) ["compilations"]. See, for example, 1.71 (93b; 121, 19).

Maimonides does not, then, distinguish between the *Guide* and the *Mishneh Torah* as between a treatise and a sublime work, but rather as between a confidential communication and an extensive compilation.

It is likewise but a popular fallacy to assume that Maimonides attributes a higher dignity to the *Mishneh Torah* than to the *Guide*, because he calls the former "*our* great composition," whereas he calls the latter "*my* treatise." For the plural is not necessarily a *pluralis majestatis*. The significance of the singular and the plural in Maimonidean usage comes out most clearly in the discussion of providence. There, he distinguishes, with an unequivocalness which could hardly be surpassed, between "*our* opinion" and "*my* opinion." He introduces "what I believe" as one interpretation of "our opinion, i.e., the opinion of our law," and contrasts it with the interpretation accepted by "the general run of our scholars." Somewhat later he distinguishes the opinion of "our religious community" about divine knowledge from "my discourse" upon that subject.[130] Even more explicitly he demarcates "what we say, viz., we, the community of the adherents of the law" and "our belief" from the opinion of the philosophers and "what I say." Finally, he distinguishes between "the opinion of our law," which he had identified before with "our opinion," and the correct, or "my" opinion.[131] One may explain this distinction in the following way: "our opinion" is based on the literal sense of the Bible, whereas "my opinion" is in accordance with the intention of the Bible, i.e., with its hidden or secret meaning. For "my opinion" brings into harmony the intelligible view with the literal sense of the Bible.[132] "My opinion" is distinguished from "our opinion" by including some additional idea which reveals itself only after a careful examination and which alone really matters. "Our opinion," on the other hand, is the opinion to which all consent and which all repeat and which does not contain any idea peculiar to any individual, and especially not to "my opinion."[133] Although the identity of the correct opinion with "my opinion" is yet to be proved, and although in the present stage of research it would be rash to exclude the possibility that "my opinion," too, is an exoteric opinion, it is most important in the present connection to realize that the distinction between "our opinion" and "my opinion" is characteristic not only of Maimonides' discussion of Provi-

---

130. 3.17 (34b; 338, 21–24). Cf. ibid. (35b; 340, 10ff.). 3.18, end. [Strauss's Latin phrase, *pluralis majestatis*, is literally the "plural of majesty"; but colloquially, it is the "royal 'we.'"]

131. 3.20 (41a–42a; 347, 21–348, 16); 3.23 (49b; 358, 26–359, 1).

132. 3.17 (34b–35b; 338, 22; 339, 16; 340, 13f.). Cf. ibid. (37b; 342, 26–27).

133. Cf. 3.23 (50a; 359, 4–15).

dence, but also of the whole *Guide*. This is, indeed, the considered view of a medieval commentator, who sees in the distinction here made between the opinion of "the general run of our scholars" and "my opinion" merely the application of a general principle which Maimonides pronounces at the beginning of his book by quoting Proverbs 22:17.[134] He understands this verse to signify "Bow down thine ear, and hearken to the words of the sages,[135] *but* apply thine heart unto mine opinion." This verse, then, establishes from the outset the principle of the *Guide* to reveal "my opinion" as an "addition" to "our opinion." Therefore the work is called "my speech." This conclusion is confirmed, rather than refuted, by Maimonides' immediately preceding quotation from Proverbs 8:4, "Unto you, O men, I call; and my voice is to the sons of man," which, in Maimonides interpretation, means to say that his call is addressed to the few elect individuals partaking of the angelic nature, while his articulate speech is addressed to the vulgar.[136] For, as has been shown, "my speech" is far from being identical with "my articulate speech"; "my speech" or perhaps "my opinion" is much more likely to be identical with "my call." Thus, we repeat, the *Guide* is "my speech" revealing "my opinion," as distinguished from "our opinion," expressed in "our compilation," the *Mishneh Torah*, where generally speaking, Maimonides appears as the mouthpiece of the Jewish community or of the Jewish tradition. Since Maimonides doubt-

134. Shem Tov on 3.7 (34b; 338, 21–24): *ve-'al ze ve-'al ke-yoẓe bo ne'emar*: *'huṭ oznekha u-shema' diverei ḥakhamim ve-libekha taẓit le-da'ati* ["It is about this and similar subjects that it is said, 'Give ear and listen to the words of the sages, and—"*and*" in the sense of "*but*"—apply your heart to my thought'"]. See also idem on 3.18, end. Cf. also W[ilhelm] Bacher, ["Die Agada in Maimunis Werken," in] *Moses ben Maimon*, ed. Bacher, Brann, Simonsen, and Guttmann, op. cit., vol. II, [pp. 131–97, and especially] p. 180.

135. Cf. 2.33 (76a; 257, 26–258, 1); *Mishneh Torah*, "Yesodei ha-Torah," IV, 13. Cf. also *Commentary on the Mishnah* on Sanhedrin X (Holzer, p. 9, or Pococke, p. 147). [See "Laws of the Basic Principles of the Torah," trans. Hyamson, pp. 39b–40a; "Book of Knowledge," trans. Lerner, pp. 152–53. Rémi Brague believes (*Maïmonide*, p. 264, n. 135; and see also p. 294, n. 25) that in this reference to Pococke, *Porta Mosis*, Strauss was undoubtedly thinking of the following lines in the *Commentary on the Mishneh*, Sanhedrin X, which I translate from his French rendering of the Arabic original: "If they would have applied themselves to the sciences, so that they would have known how to properly speak on divine (i.e., metaphysical or theological) matters and things which resemble them, to the vulgar and to the elite, and if they would have mastered the practical part of philosophy, it would have been clear (to them) on this subject whether the sages were scientists [*savants*] or not." For a tolerable rendering to English of the same passage, done—more or less—from the Kafah Hebrew translation of the Arabic original, consider the following (which has been corrected to bring it closer to Kafah's own Hebrew version): "If only they would apply themselves to the sciences, so that they would know how to write both for the masses and for the educated on matters dealing with theology and the like, and if they would understand the practical portion of philosophy, then they would clearly see whether or not the sages were really men of science, and the real meaning of the words (of the sages) would become comprehensible to them." See Maimonides, *Commentary on the Mishnah (Sanhedrin)*, trans. Rosner, p. 141. Cf. also Maimonides, *Commentary on the Mishnah*, trans. Kafah.]

136. 1.14; *Mishneh Torah*, "Yesodei ha-Torah," II, 7. [See "Laws of the Basic Principles of the Torah," trans. Hyamson, p. 36a; "Book of Knowledge," trans. Lerner, p. 145.]

less subordinated his own views to those of the Jewish tradition, one may object, his hint of calling the *Guide* "my" book and the *Mishneh Torah* "our" book would still prove that he attached a higher dignity to the latter work. We must therefore discuss the remaining six arguments.

The fifth argument is based on the hints supplied by the titles of the two books; a "repetition of the Torah" must be of a much higher order than a mere "guide of the perplexed." We shall not raise the objection that the former title ought not to be translated by "repetition of the Torah," but rather by "the second [book] after the Torah." It is true that the latter translation is based on the only explicit statement by which Maimonides justifies the title of his code.[137] But a book which is second to another book and which restates its only authentic interpretation may also rightly be called a repetition thereof.[138] The *Mishneh Torah* certainly is a repetition of the oral law, which, according to Maimonides, is the only authentic interpretation of the (written) Torah. It is hardly necessary to add that the allusion to Deuteronomy, is anything but unintentional. It should not be forgotten, however, that, some time before Maimonides, Abraham bar Hiyya had drawn the inference from the traditional designation of the fifth book of Moses as "Mishneh Torah" that a distinction is to be made between the Torah, i.e., the second, third, and fourth books of Moses, and the Mishneh Torah, i.e., the fifth book. According to Abraham, who, as it were, anticipated the most important result of modern biblical criticism, the Torah regulates the "order of service" (i.e., of worship) to be followed by the "holy congregation," which cares little for earthly things and in particular not for national defense. This "order of service" is the rule of life which Israel followed while wandering through the desert, when it was protected in a miraculous way against any external menace, and which is also to be followed by Israel whenever it lives in exile and, unable to defend itself against its enemies, must place its reliance exclusively upon God's mercy. The Mishneh Torah, on the other hand, adds to the "order of service," which it presupposes or repeats, "the order of service to the kingdom"; it is addressed to the "just kingdom," a community undetached

---

137. See [Ludwig] Blau, *Moses ben Maimon*, op. cit., vol. II, p. 338. From this fact, pointed out by him, Blau draws the inference that "das Wesen des Buches ist im Worte ḥibbur ausgedrückt" ["the essence of the book is expressed in the word ḥibbur"], i.e., it is not expressed by the words *Mishneh Torah*. And he adds in italics: "Der Name *Mischne Torah* findet sich tatsächlich kein zweitesmal bei Maimuni" ["The name 'Mishneh Torah' is not in fact found anywhere else in (the works of) Maimonides"]. If this remark were correct, it certainly would deserve to be italicized, since it would show that Maimonides attached an extremely high and secret importance to the name *Mishneh Torah*. But as a matter of fact, that name occurs, I believe, ten times in the *Guide*.

138. Cf. S[olomon] Zeitlin, *Maimonides[: A Biography]* (New York: Bloch, 1935), p. 86.

from earthly things and concerned about national defense. Mainly devoted to matters of jurisdiction, especially in agricultural life, and to laws concerning kings and wars, it establishes a rule of life which Israel followed as long as it lived in its own land.[139] I venture to suggest that Maimonides remembered Abraham bar Hiyya's interpretation when he selected the name *Mishneh Torah* for his code, which contained not only the laws of exile but also those of the land; and that a certain reason, implied in Abraham's interpretation, led Maimonides to conclude his code so impressively with the laws regarding kings and their wars. In translating the title by "repetition of the Torah," we are also mindful of the peculiar significance with which the word *repetition* is used by Maimonides. But does the fact that the *Mishneh Torah* is a repetition of the Torah entitle us to assume that Maimonides judged that work, or its subject, to be more important than the *Guide* or its subject? "Repetition of the Torah" is an ambiguous expression: it may mean a repetition, reproducing the Torah in accordance with its external proportions, or one reproducing it with regard to the hidden and true proportions of its various subjects. There can be no doubt that the code reproduces the Torah according to its external proportions only. For the Torah consists of true "opinions" and

---

139. *Hegyon ha-Nefesh*, ed. [Eisek] Freimann (Leipzig, 1860; reprinted, Jerusalem, 1966), pp. 38a–39b. [See also: Abraham bar Hiyya (1065–1136), *Hegyon ha-Nefesh ha-'Azuvah*, ed. Geoffrey Wigoder (Jerusalem: Mosad Bialik, 1971); Abraham bar Hiyya, *The Meditation of the Sad Soul*, trans. Geoffrey Wigoder (New York: Schocken, 1969), pp. 136–39. To offer some highlights of the discovery made by Strauss about Abraham bar Hiyya, insofar as he already "anticipated the most important result of modern biblical criticism," consider the following passages: "It will also be clear that the commandments in the rest of the three books of the Pentateuch—Exodus, Leviticus, and Numbers—are the statutes and judgments intended for the separate community.... After the explanation of the second of our three divisions—the holy community—we must consider the worship of the just kingdom, which has to take external events into consideration and guard against those who provoke them. This division requires additional commandments and statutes and these are set forth in the Book of Deuteronomy. The only distinction between the second and the third division is that the latter has to take into account external events and has to interest itself in affairs of this world, and so requires fences and limits, not required by the second category." It is unfortunate that what the English translation has as the "the Book of Deuteronomy," Bar Hiyya has in his original Hebrew (famed for its elegant precision) as "Mishneh Torah." To be sure, it is the case that this is the most ancient Hebrew name for the Book of Deuteronomy ("Mishneh Torah"), and so such a use could have been accidental or a mere matter of style. However, by considering its use in the context of the rest of what is made to appear in this passage, Strauss seems to take Bar Hiyya to have used it in order to give a significant hint. With regard to Strauss's reference to Maimonides' purposes in constructing the *Mishneh Torah*, i.e., as aimed to both remember and to reconstitute the "just kingdom," consider Maimonides' remarks on the "worldly" or natural, political reasons why ancient Israel lost its kingdom, which as it were determined its theological errors: Maimonides, "Letter on Astrology," trans. Lerner, pp. 179–80; cf. Machiavelli, *Discourses on Livy*, trans. Harvey Mansfield and Nathan Tarcov (Chicago: University of Chicago Press, 1996), bk. II, chap. 2, pp. 131–32: "The world appears to be made effeminate and the world disarmed." For a concerted effort to compare Maimonides and Machiavelli precisely along the lines which seems to have been suggested by Strauss, see Steven Lenzner, "Author as Educator: Strauss's Twofold Treatment of Maimonides and Machiavelli," a paper posted on The Claremont Institute website, http://www.claremont.org./publications/pubid.255/pub_detail.asp.]

of "actions," and whereas the "actions" are determined by it in great detail and with extreme precision, the true "opinions" are indicated only in bare outline. This proportion was preserved intact by the Talmud, since the sages of the Talmud spoke for the most part of precepts and manners, and not of opinions and beliefs.[140] In exactly the same way, the *Mishneh Torah* deals in the most detailed fashion with "actions," but speaks of the basic truths only briefly and allusively (though by allusions approximating clear pronouncements) and by haphazard.[141] The *Guide*, on the other hand, is devoted mainly, if not exclusively, to "opinions," as distinguished from "actions." Now "opinions" are as much superior in dignity to "actions" as is the perfection of the soul to that of the body. Therefore, the highest aim of the Torah is the regulation of our opinions, to which the order, prescribed by the Torah, of our actions is subservient.[142] Thus the true proportions of the subjects of the Torah are imitated not by the *Mishneh Torah*, which is devoted to the science of the law in its usual sense, but by the *Guide*, which is devoted to the true science of the law. We conclude, then, that whereas the *Mishneh Torah* is the "repetition of the Torah" *simpliciter* the *Guide* is the "repetition of the Torah" *par excellence*.[143] Should the objection be raised that the title of the *Guide* does not indicate its being a repetition of the Torah, we need only refer to the affinity between *guide* and *guidance* (*torah*).[144] The *Guide* is a repetition or imitation of the Torah particularly suitable to "perplexed" people, while the *Mishneh Torah* is such a repetition addressed primarily to people who are not "perplexed."

The sixth argument, referring to the explicit statement of Maimonides concerning the precedence of the *fiqh*, ignores his failure to contradict the talmudic saying that "the discussion of Abbaye and Raba is a small thing" as

---

140. 3.27 (59b and 60a; 371, 29f.; 372, 9f.); 3.28 (60b–61a; 373, 7–17); 1.Intro. (11a–b; 13, 2–5).
141. 1.Intro. (3b and 6a; 3, 7; 6, 8–9); 1.71 (97a; 125, 14).
142. 3.27.
143. An allusion to that relation may be found in the fact that the *Mishneh Torah* consists of 14 (= 2 × 7) books, and that the precepts of the law are divided in the *Guide*, too, into 14 groups, whereas the explanation of the highest secret of the Torah, i.e., of *ma'aseh merkavah*, is given in 7 chapters of the *Guide*. Compare also the 49 (= 7 × 7) chapters which lead up from "Image" to "Angels," i.e., to a subject which is second to one subject only; and the 70 (= 10 × 7) chapters which lead up from "Image" to *rakhav*, i e., to the grammatical root of *merkavah*. To understand the number 70, one has to bear in mind that the word *addamiyyun* [human beings] occurs, if I am not mistaken, 10 times in the *Guide*, and that the Torah speaks according to the language of *benei 'adam* [the sons of man]. The word *'adam* is explained in the fourteenth chapter of the *Guide*; the number of the chapter explaining the various meanings of man is the same as the number of books of the *Mishneh Torah* or of parts of the law. See also above, n. 137.
144. Compare the explanation of *torah* as *hidaya* ["guidance"] in 3.13 (25a; 327, 10f.); 1.2 (13b; 16, 9) with the synonymous use of *hada* ["to guide"] and *dalla* ["to direct"] in 2.12 (26b; 195, 27). See also 3.45 (101a; 425, 17).

compared with *ma'aseh merkavah*. He merely explains that saying by adding to it the remark that knowledge of the precepts ought to precede concern with the secret topics. For knowledge of the precepts is indispensable for their execution, and their execution is indispensable for one's composure of mind, as well as for the establishment of peace and order; these, in turn, are indispensable for acquiring "the life of the coming world" or for acquiring true opinions.[145] That is to say, knowledge of the precepts is merely a means to an end, which, in its turn, is only a means to another, the ultimate end, i.e., to the understanding of *ma'aseh bereshit* and *ma'aseh merkavah*. Knowledge of the precepts precedes, then, knowledge of the secrets, as the means precedes the end. Maimonides adds yet another reason: the precepts can be known to everybody, to young and old, to unintelligent as well as intelligent, whereas the secret teaching, which is clear and manifest to the "men of speculation" only, was not fully grasped even by some of the greatest sages of the Talmud.[146] We conclude, therefore, that the precedence attributed by Maimonides to knowledge of the precepts is merely a priority in time, and not at all a superior dignity.

The seventh argument is based on Maimonides' statement that *ma'aseh bereshit* and *ma'aseh merkavah* belong to the *talmud*. Maimonides makes this statement in connection with his division of the study of the Torah into three parts: the study of the written Torah, that of the oral Torah, and the Talmud. The study of the prophetic writings and hagiographa belongs to that of the written Torah; the study of explanations thereof is part of the oral Torah; and the study of secret subjects is included in the *talmud*.[147] In order to understand this statement correctly, we must first bear in mind that *talmud* may be used ambiguously for a certain group of writings (the Babylonian and Jerusalem Talmuds), as well as for a peculiar kind of study. In the former sense, the statement that secret topics belong to the *talmud*, and not to the written or oral Torah, would mean that they are to be found in the Talmud rather

---

145. *Mishneh Torah*, "Yesodei ha-Torah," IV, 13. Cf. *Mishneh Torah*, "Teshuvah," VIII, 5–6, 14; *Moreh Nevukhim* [*Guide of the Perplexed*—Strauss uses the Hebrew title devised by Samuel ibn Tibbon presumably because he wishes to direct careful readers to the Hebrew translation of 3.27 specifically] 3.27 (59b; 371, 25–28). [See "Laws of the Basic Principles of the Torah," trans. Hyamson, pp. 39b–40a; "Book of Knowledge," trans. Lerner, pp. 152–53; "Laws of Repentance," trans. Hyamson, paras. 5–6 or VI (English) and paras. 7–8 (Hebrew), p. 86b, especially l. 14.]

146. 3.Intro. (2a; 297, 6–8, 9–10). Cf. also 1.17. *Mishneh Torah*, "Yesodei ha-Torah," IV, 13. [See "Laws of the Basic Principles of the Torah," trans. Hyamson, pp. 39b–40a; "Book of Knowledge," trans. Lerner, pp. 152–53.]

147. *Mishneh Torah*, "Talmud Torah," I, 12. [See "Laws Concerning the Study of the Torah," trans. Hyamson, p. 58a. See also n. 122 above.]

than in the Bible,[148] but it would have no bearing upon the subordination of the secret teaching to the *fiqh*. If we take *talmud*, as we probably should, in its second meaning, it would indeed seem at first sight that Maimonides subordinates the study of the secret topics to the *fiqh*, just as he certainly subordinates the study of the prophetic writings and the hagiographa to that of the Pentateuch. But what does he actually say? Starting from the implicit assumption that all studies which are of any value are comprised within the study of the Torah, he raises the question: to which part of that study does the study of that "great thing" (i.e., of the secret teaching) belong? And he answers: since the secret topics are the most difficult topics,[149] their study must belong to the most advanced part of the all-comprising study of the Torah, i.e., to the *talmud*. He does not preclude the possibility that this most advanced study be subdivided into two distinct parts, the *fiqh* and the true science of the law.[150] In fact, he alludes to this possibility when he says that men, after having reached a more advanced stage of wisdom, ought to devote their time almost exclusively to the *talmud*, according to the level of their intelligence.

The tenth argument is based on the saying of R. Simeon ben Gamaliel that not study, but action is most important, and on the assumption that Maimonides must have accepted this saying in its apparent meaning. But, according to his explanation,[151] it merely refers to speeches about laws and virtues and merely demands that man's actions be in accordance with his speeches expressing obedient and virtuous thoughts. Otherwise, he expressly recognizes in the *Mishneh Torah* that study of the Torah is superior in dignity to all other actions.[152] Above all, in the last chapter of the *Guide* he asserts that most precepts of the law are merely a means for the acquisition of moral virtue, which,

---

148. Cf. 1.71 (93b and 94a; 121, 11f., 25f.) and the parallel passage in 3.Intro. (2b; 297, 17f.).

149. *Mishneh Torah*, "Yesodei ha-Torah," II, 12; IV, 11, 13. [See "Laws of the Basic Principles of the Torah," trans. Hyamson, pp. 36b and 39b—40a; "Book of Knowledge," trans. Lerner, pp. 146—47 and 152—53.]

150. 1.Intro. (3a; 2, 12—14); 3.54 (132a—b; 467, 2—22).

151. *Commentary on the Mishnah* on Avot I, 17. [See Maimonides, *The Commentary to Mishnah Aboth*, trans. Arthur David (New York: Bloch, 1968), pp. 16—24. The key passage to which Strauss would seem to refer reads as follows (p. 20): "However, one needs to be cautious of two things. The first of them—that his deeds be consistent with his words, as they said (Tosefta Yevamot 8:4, ed. Zuckermandel, p. 250): 'Pleasant are the words that emanate from the mouth of one who practices them'; and it was to this subject that he (Simeon ben Gamaliel) referred when he said, 'The expounding is not the fundamental point, but the practice' (Avot I, 17). The sages say to the righteous that he should teach the virtues, as they said: 'Expound, because it becomes you to expound'; and the prophet said (Psalm 33:1), 'Rejoice in the Lord, you who are righteous; praise is comely for the upright.'"]

152. *Mishneh Torah*, "Talmud Torah," I, 3; III, 3—5. [See "Laws Concerning the Study of the Torah," trans. Hyamson, pp. 57b; 59a.]

in turn, is merely a means subservient to the true end, namely, speculative virtue, or the true knowledge of things divine.[153]

In the light of this Maimonidean assertion and of the place where it is found, the eighth argument cannot possibly be sound. If, indeed, the first "chapter heading" of the *Guide*, "Image," were contrasted with a last "chapter heading," "Wisdom," we certainly would have to conclude that all readers of the *Guide* are meant to ascend from the lowest to the highest knowledge. But, as it happens, the last "chapter heading" is not "Wisdom," but "The word wisdom." Now "The word wisdom" is not necessarily superior to "Image," as is shown by the fact, constantly present in Maimonides' mind, that many learned people living in a world of imaginary and imaginative ideas call their possession and use of these ideas "wisdom" or "speculation." On the other hand, "wisdom," if rightly understood, indicates something absolutely superior to "image"; a man who understands the word wisdom according to its true meaning has overcome, or is on the way to overcoming, his imaginary views. The equivocal last "chapter heading," when contrasted with the unequivocal first "chapter heading," indicates the ambiguity inherent in the reading of the *Guide*. Its reader may ascend from imaginary views to true wisdom, but he also may not leave the world of imagination for a single moment, so that he finally arrives at the mere word "wisdom," which is but a shadow or image of wisdom itself. But let us apply to such readers the Maimonidean dictum that there is no reason for mentioning them in this place in this treatise.[154] Let us think of that reader only to whom the *Guide* is addressed and who, after having undergone training by the *Guide*, will certainly have substituted intelligent views for imaginary ones. For such a reader the study of the *Guide* is an ascent from the lowest to the highest knowledge. This is only tantamount to saying that by understanding the last chapter, or the last group of chapters, he will have attained to a knowledge more complete than that which he had acquired before reading these chapters. But it obviously does not of necessity indicate the superior dignity of the subjects treated in the last group of chapters.

In order to grasp the principle underlying the arrangement of the various subjects in the *Guide*, we must remind ourselves of its original purpose to repeat the Torah with regard to the hidden proportions of its subjects. The Torah having been given to man by an intermediary prophet, we may be per-

---

153. 3.54 (133b–134b; 468, 22–470, 11).
154. 1.Intro. (4b; 4, 11–12).

mitted for a little while to replace Torah by prophecy. Maimonides asserts that the prophet's ascent to the highest knowledge is followed by his descent to the "people of the earth," i.e., to their government and instruction.[155] The prophet is, then, a man who not only has attained the greatest knowledge, indeed a degree of knowledge which is not attained by mere philosophers, but who is able also to perform the highest political functions.[156] A similar combination of theoretical and political excellence is required for the understanding of the secret teaching of the prophets.[157] Since the *Guide* is devoted to the

155. 1.15 (22b; 28, 4−7). Cf. Plato, *Republic*, VII, 519c8−520a4 (also 514a, 517d5).

156. That Maimonides conceived of the prophets as statesmen is shown also by the main division of the affirmative precepts in *Sefer ha-Mitzvot* [*Book of the Commandments*] (or in the enumeration of the 613 commandments at the beginning of *Mishneh Torah*). There he lists first the precepts regulating the relations between man and God, and then those which order the relations among men. (See the remarks of [Moritz] Peritz[, "Das Buch der Gesetze,"] in *Moses ben Maimon*, ed. Bacher, Brann, Simonsen, and Guttmann, op. cit., vol. I, [pp. 439−74, and especially] p. 445ff.). The second class of these precepts (nos. 172−248) opens with the commandments regarding the prophet, the king, and the high court; the prophet evidently is the head of the political organization. Cf. 2.40 (85b−86a; 270, 24−27). The question of the relation between king and priest is touched upon in 3.45 (98b; 422, 9−13). How far Maimonides accepted the teaching of the *falasifa*, according to which a "priestly city" is one of the bad regimes, must here remain an open question. See Ibn Bajja, *Kitab Tadbir al-Mutawahhid* [*The Book of the Governance of the Solitary*], chap. 1, in the Hebrew extraction by Moses Narboni, ed. D. Herzog, p. 8; and Averroes, *Paraphrasis in Rempublicam Platonis*, tr. 3, in *Opera Aristotelis* (Venice, 1550), III, 187c19−24. [See *The Commandments*, trans. Chavel, vol. 1, pp. xvii−xxiv, for the positive commandments listed; precepts 1 through 171 would seem to constitute those which regulate relations between man and God, and precepts 172 through 248 would seem to constitute those which order relations among human beings. Notice that this transition is brought about by first commanding human beings to "heed the prophets" (172), which is immediately followed by the commandment to "appoint a king" (173). See also, in the enumeration of the 613 commandments at the beginning of Maimonides, *Mishneh Torah*, vol. 1, *The Book of Knowledge*, trans. Hyamson, pp. 5a−17a, and especially p. 8b, the same transition from those between man and God to those among human beings is repeated: "heeding the prophets" (172), and next "appointing a king" (173). See Avempace (Ibn Bajja), *The Governance of the Solitary*, trans. Lawrence Berman, in *Medieval Political Philosophy*, ed. Lerner and Mahdi, chap. 1, pp. 123−29. I did not have access to Narboni's Hebrew paraphrase, and hence I am not able to convey what his version might suggest about Ibn Bajja's work. See also *Averroes' Commentary on Plato's "Republic,"* ed. and trans. E. I. J. Rosenthal (Cambridge: Cambridge University Press, 1969), Hebrew version (V, 6), p. 86, ll. 8−11, and English translation, para. 6, pp. 216−17: "But this is not the case in the tyrannical State, for in it the masters seek no other aim in respect of the masses but their own. Therefore the similarity between the 'priestly' and the tyrannical States often leads the 'priestly' parts that exist in these States to be transformed into tyrannical ones, thus bringing into disrepute him whose aim is 'priestly,' as is the case with the 'priestly' parts that exist in the States to be found in our time." Compare with Averroes, *On Plato's "Republic,"* trans. Lerner, "Third Treatise," pp. 104−49, and especially pp. 114−15, ll. 8−11: "Such is not the case in the tyrannical city, for in it and as regards the multitude, the lords seek no intention other than their private intention. Therein is the similarity between aristocratic cities and tyrannical cities. The aristocratic parts existing in these cities often turn into tyrannical ones, and give the lie to the aristocratic intention—as is the case with the aristocratic parts found in cities existing in this time of ours." Between Rosenthal and Lerner a division thus shows itself concerning the purport of this section and whether it is about "priestly" or "aristocratic" factions that tend toward the tyrannical. Besides Strauss's reference to Ibn Bajja, his apparent further dependence on the Latin translation of Averroes' commentary on Plato's *Republic* in order to help establish his point about "the teaching of the *falasifa*" on the "priestly city" as "one of the bad regimes," needs to at least be reviewed in light of the difference that is seen to have emerged on how best to translate this passage.]

157. See above, fifth and sixth paragraphs of section IV.

interpretation of that secret teaching, Maimonides will also have imitated, in some manner or other, the way of the prophets. To be sure, the prophet is enabled to perform his political function of governing the "people of the earth" and of teaching them by the power of his imagination, i.e., by his capacity of representing the truth to the vulgar by means of images or parables, as Maimonides clearly intimates in the general definition of prophecy and in the chapter following it.[158] He himself, however, attempts to replace the parables by another method of representing the truth. Yet the fundamental similarity between the prophet, the bringer of the secret teaching, and the interpreter of the secret teaching remains unaltered by that change in the method. Therefore, we are from the outset entitled to expect that the sequence of topics in the *Guide* would imitate the way of the prophets, which is ascent, followed by descent. This expectation is proved to be correct by the actual structure of the *Guide*. Maimonides, or his reader, gradually and slowly climbs up from the depth of "image" to *maʿaseh merkavah*, the highest subject, which is fully treated in Book 3, Chapters 1–7 only. At the end of this exposition, Maimonides declares that he will say no more about that subject. Accordingly, he begins the next chapter with the heading, "All bodies which come into existence and perish." Finally, he descends one more step, from "opinion" to "actions." The same prophetic way of ascent, followed by descent, is evidently used as a model in his recommended order of studies for unprophetic men, referred to in the ninth argument, namely, (1) knowledge of the truth, based on tradition only; (2) such knowledge based on demonstration; (3) *fiqh*. For the demonstrative knowledge of truth is the highest degree attainable to unprophetic men.[159]

To sum up, according to Maimonides the *Mishneh Torah* is devoted to *fiqh*, the essence of which is to deal with actions; while the *Guide* deals with the secrets of the Torah, i.e., primarily opinions or beliefs, which it treats demonstratively, or at least as demonstratively as possible. Demonstrated opinions or beliefs are, according to Maimonides, absolutely superior in dignity to good actions or to their exact determination. In other words, the chief subject of the *Guide* is *maʿaseh merkavah*, which is "a great thing," while the chief subject of the *Mishneh Torah* is the precepts, which are "a small thing." Consequently, the subject of the *Guide* is, according to Maimonides, absolutely superior in dignity to the subject of the *Mishneh Torah*. Since the

---

158. See also Falaquera, *Reshit Ḥokhmah*, ed. [Moritz] David, p. 30.
159. 3.54 (132b; 467, 18–27). Cf. 1.33 (36b; 47, 25–26).

dignity of a book, *ceteris paribus*, corresponds to the dignity of its subject, and since, as is shown by a comparison of Maimonides' own introductory remarks to the two books, he wrote the *Guide* with no less skill and care than his code, we must conclude that he considered the *Guide* as absolutely superior in dignity.

This conclusion, based on the general principle underlying his entire work and nowhere contradicted by him, that knowledge of the truth is absolutely superior in dignity to any action, is reinforced by some further statements or hints. We have started from the distinction made by him at the very beginning of the *Guide* between the true science of the law and the *fiqh*: the former deals chiefly with the secrets of the Bible or, more generally, with opinions and beliefs both secret and public;[160] in other words, it demonstrates the beliefs taught by the law. Maimonides repeats this distinction in the last chapter, in a somewhat modified manner; he there distinguishes three sciences: the science of the Torah, wisdom, and *fiqh*.[161] The science of the law, or the science of the Torah, does not demonstrate the basic principles taught by the law, since the law itself does not demonstrate them.[162] The *fiqh*, which at the beginning of the *Guide* had been identified with the science of the law, is now clearly distinguished from it or from the science of the Torah, as well as from wisdom.[163] Wisdom is the demonstration of the opinions taught by the law. Now the *Guide* is devoted to such demonstration; hence the true science of the law, mentioned at the beginning as the subject of the work, is identical with wisdom, as distinguished from both the science of the law and from the *fiqh*. Maimonides repeats, then, the distinction between the true science of the law and the science of the law; yet he no longer calls the former a science of the law, but wisdom, and no longer identifies the (ordinary) science of the law (or of the Torah) with the *fiqh*. The relation of wisdom to the *fiqh* is explained by a simile: the students of the *fiqh*, arriving at the divine palace, merely walk around it, whereas only speculation on the "roots," i.e., demonstration of the basic truths taught by the law, leads one unto the presence of God.[164]

Though Maimonides discloses his view at the end of his work only, he

---

160. Cf., for example, 1.1 (12a; 14, 14); 1.18 (24a; 30, 7) with 1.35.
161. 3.54 (132b; 467, 18–20).
162. 3.54 (132a–b; 467, 2–9, 13–14).
163. 3.54 (132a–b; 467, 18–23 and 7 and 13–14). Cf. 3.41 (88b; 409, 15–16); *Mishneh Torah*, "Talmud Torah," I, 11–12. [See "Laws Concerning the Study of the Torah," trans. Hyamson, p. 58a.]
164. 3.51 (123b–124a; 455, 21–28). In his commentary on this chapter, Shem Tov relates that "many talmudic scholars have asserted that Maimonides had not written this chapter, and that, if he did write it, it ought to be suppressed, or rather, it would deserve to be burned."

does not fail to give hints of it on previous suitable occasions. When he tells the story of his abandoned plan to write two books on the parables of the prophets and the Midrashim, he states that he had intended those books for the vulgar, but later realized that such an explanation would neither be suitable for, nor fill a need felt by the vulgar. That is why he has limited himself to that brief and allusive discussion of the basic truths of the law, which is to be found in his code. In the *Guide*, however, he goes on to say, he addresses himself to a man who has studied philosophy and who, while believing in the teachings of the law, is perplexed in regard to them.[165] Those sentences, enigmatic and elusive as they are, show clearly that the *Guide* was not addressed to the vulgar, nor the *Mishneh Torah* to the perplexed. Are we, then, to believe that the latter was written for students of philosophy who had not become perplexed as regards the teachings of the law? Hardly, since Maimonides does not tire of repeating that the code is devoted to the *fiqh* and consequently is addressed to students of *fiqh*, who may or may not be familiar with philosophy. This is also shown by his failure to discuss in the *Mishneh Torah* the basic truths of the law, according to his primary and main intention and only, as it were, incidentally or haphazardly.[166] Evidently the *Mishneh Torah* was written also for people who had not studied philosophy at all and therefore were not perplexed; in other words, it was addressed to "all men."[167] This is quite clearly the meaning of the following passage in the *Guide*: "I have already explained to all men the four differences by which the prophecy of our teacher Moses is distinguished from the prophecy of the other prophets, and I have proved it and made it manifest in the *Commentary on the Mishnah* and in the *Mishneh Torah*." The meaning of "all men" (*al-nas kaffa*) is incidentally explained in connection with a synonymous phrase (*jami' al-nas*): "all men, i.e., the vulgar."[168] This allusion to the exoteric char-

165. 1.Intro. (5b–6a; 5, 18–6, 11).
166. 1.Intro. (3a; 2, 13–16); 1.71 (97a; 125, 23–24).
167. Cf. *Mishneh Torah*, "Yesodei ha-Torah," IV, 13. [See "Laws of the Basic Principles of the Torah," trans. Hyamson, pp. 39b–40a; "Book of Knowledge," trans. Lerner, pp. 152–53.]
168. 2.35, beginning; 3.22 (45b; 353, 10). Cf. also *Mishneh Torah*, Intro., 4b, 4–19 (Hyamson), and *Kovetz*, II, 15b. [Strauss seems to refer to Maimonides' "Letter to Joseph ibn Jabir of Baghdad," which was written in Arabic, the original of which survives only in a truncated version, but which circulated mostly in a complete medieval Hebrew translation. If I am correct that it is a passage in this letter to which he points, it seems to occur on p. 16b (*Kovetz*). In the most recent critical edition of Maimonides' letters, *Igrot ha-Rambam*, ed. Shailat, it appears as I, pp. 402–18. For an English translation (not based on Shailat), see "The Response of Maimonides to Joseph ibn Gabir," in *Letters*, trans. Stitskin, pp. 86–94. In what I believe is the passage that Strauss aimed to highlight, this may be translated (not quite conforming with the version of Stitskin) as follows: "We do not pay attention to the reproaches of the multitude" (*'anaḥnu lo nashgiah' bi-genut he-hamon*). See Shailat, p. 416 (Hebrew); the original Arabic of the passage highlighted

acter of the code and the commentary naturally has to be taken into account, not only in the interpretation of these two works but also for the adequate understanding of all quotations from them in the *Guide*.

We conclude: The *Mishneh Torah* is primarily addressed to the general run of men, while the *Guide* is addressed to the small number of people who are able to understand by themselves.

---

by Strauss (which, in a complete version, should appear approximately on p. 407) has not survived. See also *Letters*, trans. Stitskin, p. 93.]

9

Maimonides' Statement on Political Science

EDITOR'S NOTE

"Maimonides' Statement on Political Science" essentially reproduces the study which appeared in Leo Strauss, *What Is Political Philosophy? And Other Studies* (New York: Free Press, 1959; Chicago: University of Chicago Press, 1988), pp. 155–69. The article first appeared in *Proceedings of the American Academy for Jewish Research* 22 (1953): 115–30. The present editor has made some additions to the notes, with occasional references directly to the text. These aim to be helpful to readers in searching Strauss's sources, comprehending his references by offering reliable English translations, or clarifying certain difficult aspects of the text. To differentiate them from Strauss's own work, all such editorial additions to the notes are set in square brackets. The epigraph to the essay—drawn from Cicero's dialogue, *On Divination* (*De divinatione*), bk. I, chap. XXVI, l. 55—may be translated as follows: "But what have I to do with the Greeks? Though I am not sure why, things which are my own bring me greater pleasure." It is a line spoken by the character Quintus Tullius Cicero, who in actual life was the name of Cicero's younger brother, and whose point of view as a character is mostly articulated in the first book of the dialogue. For different translations, one may consult: (a) *On Divination*, ed. and trans. W. A. Falconer (Cambridge, MA: Harvard University Press {Loeb Classical Library}, 1923), which also contains the original Latin; (b) *On Divination*, trans. C. D. Yonge, in Cicero, *Opera Philosophica* (London: G. Bell, 1892); (c) Cicero, *On Divination*, bk. 1, trans. David Wardle (Oxford: Clarendon Press, 2006), para. 55, p. 63, rendered by Wardle as "Why am I speaking of Greek examples? Somehow our own give me more pleasure."

Sed quid ego Graecorum? Nescio quo modo me magis nostra delectant.
CICERO, DE DIVINATIONE, I

MAIMONIDES DISCUSSES THE SUBJECT MATTER AS WELL AS THE FUNCTION OF political science at the end of the last chapter (chap. 14) of his *Treatise on the Art of Logic* (*Millot ha-Higgayon*). Philosophy or science, he says, consists of two parts: theoretical philosophy and practical philosophy, the latter also being called human philosophy, political philosophy, or political science. Theoretical philosophy consists of three parts: mathematics, physics, and theology. Practical philosophy consists of four parts: man's governance of himself, governance of the household, governance of the city, and governance of the great [numerous] nation or of the nations. The first part of political science deals with the virtues and the vices, or with good and bad habits. "There are many books by the philosophers on the habits." Ethics does not deal with "commands," i.e., with that form of guidance by which a man guides other men, whereas the three other parts of practical philosophy do deal with them. Governance of the household supplies knowledge of how its members can help each other, and of what is sufficient for the best possible ordering of their affairs with due regard to time and place. Governance of the city is the science that supplies knowledge of human happiness and of the way toward its acquisition, as well as of the opposites of both those things; "furthermore, it lays down the rules of justice through which human associations are ordered properly; furthermore, the wise men belonging to the perfect [ancient][1] nations, each of them according to his perfection, lay down rules

---

1. Could the original have read *al-umam al-madiyuna*? The expression *al-umam al-madiyuna* in Farabi's *Siyasat* 51, 6 (Hyderabad, 1346) is rendered by Samuel ibn Tibbon *ha-ummot he'ovrot* (42, 7 Filipowski). The adjective does not necessarily mean "ancient" or "past." It might also mean "piercing" or "penetrating." That Maimonides could have applied a term of praise of this kind to the Greeks, the Persians, and so on, in contradistinction to the Chaldeans, the Egyptians, and so on, appears from *Iggeret Teman* 8, 15 (Halkin), the *Letter on Astrology* 351, 17-18 (Marx), and *Guide* 3.29 (63a Munk). ["Epistle to Yemen," trans. Kraemer, pp. 99-132, and especially p. 103; "Epistle to Yemen," trans. Halkin, pp. 93-131, and especially p. 97; "Letter on Astrology," trans. Lerner, pp. 178-87, and especially p. 180; "Letter to the Jews of Marseilles in 1194," trans. Stitskin, pp. 118-29, and especially pp. 120-21. See also *Igrot ha-Rambam*, ed. Shailat, I, pp. 82-168 ("Epistle to Yemen"); III, pp. 478-90 ("Letter to the Rabbis of Montpelier on Astrology"). For the edition of Maimonides' *Logic* to which Strauss refers, see Israel Efros, "Maimonides' *Treatise on Logic* (*Makalah Fi-Sina'at Al-Mantik*): The Original Arabic and Three Hebrew Translations," *Proceedings of the American Academy for Jewish Research* 8 (1937-38): 1-136. A fuller and better text of the Arabic original has since been edited by Mubahat Türker (based on two manuscripts rediscovered in Turkey). See *Revue de la Faculté de Langues, d'Histoire, et de Geographie de l'Université d'Ankara* 18 (1960): 9-64. For the same rediscovered text of the Arabic original in Hebrew letters, see Israel Efros, "Maimonides' Arabic 'Treatise on Logic,'" *Proceedings of the American Academy for Jewish Research* 34 (1966): 6-34. Farabi's *Siyasat al-Madaniyyah* refers to *The Political Regime*. The Arabic text of *Kitab al-siyasat al-madaniyya* has been edited: *Al-Farabi's The Political Regime*, ed. Fauzi M. Naj-

of governance through which their subjects are governed [through which their kings govern their multitude]; they called [call] them [i.e., those rules of governance] *nomoi*; the nations were governed by those *nomoi*. On all these subjects, the philosophers have many books which have already been translated into Arabic, but perhaps more which have not been translated. But we have no need in these times for all this, viz. for [the commands], the laws, the *nomoi*, the governance by [of] [these] human beings in divine things [for the laws and the *nomoi*; the governance of human beings is now through divine things]."

The meaning of this statement is not entirely clear. The obscurities are partly due to the facts that the Arabic original of about the second half of the *Logic* is lost, and that the differences between the three Hebrew translations, or even between the various manuscripts of these translations, are sufficiently great as to make doubtful the reconstruction of the original in every important point. In the preceding paragraph, the bracketed expressions correspond to alternative translations or readings which seem to be as defensible as the preferred versions.

Three difficulties strike us at first sight: Maimonides rejects the books of the philosophers on politics proper as useless for "us" "in these times." Also, he divides politics proper in an unusual manner. And finally, while assigning the study of the virtues to ethics, he assigns the understanding of happiness,

---

jar (Beyrouth: Imprimerie Catholique, 1964). A translation of the whole work has not yet been made. For a partial translation, see: Alfarabi, "Political Regime," trans. Najjar, in *Medieval Political Philosophy*, ed. Lerner and Mahdi, pp. 31–57. The translated passage to which Strauss refers occurs on p. 37 Najjar (in Lerner and Mahdi). The phrase at issue is rendered "past imams" (cf. Brague, *Maïmonide*, p. 278, n. 1); this shows that Najjar did not follow Strauss's suggestion for how to translate the phrase, based on the Hebrew version. The medieval Hebrew translation, attributed to Moses ben Samuel ibn Tibbon, was titled *Sefer ha-Hathalot ha-Nimzaot ha-Tiviyim*, and edited by Zvi Hershel Filipowski (Leipzig, 1849/5610); based on its Hebrew title, it may be translated as *The Book of First Natural Existents*; based on its other Arabic title, *The Principles of the Beings*. For a first critical examination of Strauss's interpretation of chap. 14 of the *Logic*, as seen in light of the rediscovered, fuller text, see Lawrence V. Berman, "A Re-examination of Maimonides' 'Statement on Political Science,'" *Journal of the American Oriental Society* 89 (1969): 106–11. A subsequent critical review of the present essay by Strauss was made by Joel L. Kraemer as contained in his "Maimonides on the Philosophic Sciences in his *Treatise on the Art of Logic*," in *Perspectives on Maimonides: Philosophical and Historical Studies*, ed. Joel Kraemer (Oxford: Oxford Unversity Press, 1991), pp. 77–104. For an elaborate attempt to disprove Maimonidean authorship of the *Treatise on the Art of Logic*—a "higher criticism" based largely on circumstantial evidence related to aspects of the contents and form of the *Treatise*, and in a certain measure also supported by some editorial features which emerged from the rediscovery in the 1950s of two versions of the original Arabic text in two Turkish libraries—see Herbert Davidson, *Moses Maimonides: The Man and His Works* (New York: Oxford University Press, 2004), pp. 313–22. In my opinion and to say the very least, it is not a definitive disproof, although I leave the last word to specialized scholars of Maimonides' works, who have not yet spoken. In one of Davidson's notes, he makes a critical remark on Strauss's present essay which is not related to the issue of Maimonidean authorship: see p. 314 n. 30.]

not to ethics, the first part of practical philosophy, but to politics proper, the last part of practical philosophy.

To begin with the first difficulty, we are naturally inclined to believe that "we" means "we Jews": we Jews do not need the political teaching, nor perhaps the economic teaching, of the philosophers, since we have the Torah which guides us perfectly in every respect, and especially in respect of the divine things.[2] Yet this is not precise enough. In the first place, whereas Maimonides says in regard to politics proper, or a part of it, that we do not need the books of the philosophers on this subject, he says in regard to ethics merely that the philosophers have many books on ethics: he does not say that we do not need the books of the philosophers on ethics.[3] He says nothing whatever in this context about the books of the philosophers on theoretical subjects. There is no need to prove that Maimonides knew of the existence of such books and that he was very far from regarding them as useless for "us": the statement under discussion occurs in a summary of logic which is based upon the philosophers' books on logic and on theoretical philosophy. What he suggests then is that of all genuinely philosophic books, only the books on politics proper (and perhaps on economics) have been rendered superfluous by the Torah. This implies that the function of the Torah is emphatically political. This interpretation is confirmed by *The Guide of the Perplexed*. In that work, Maimonides says that the Torah gives only summary indications con-

---

2. Cf. Comtino and Mendelssohn ad loc. [Strauss refers to two commentaries on Maimonides' *Treatise on the Art of Logic*: Mordechai ben Eliezer Comtino (1420–87), and Moses Mendelssohn (1729–86). For Comtino, see *Be'ur Millot ha-Higgayon*, by Moses Maimonides, with commentaries by Moses Mendelssohn, Mordecai ben Eliezer Comtino, Moses ibn Tibbon, and Isaac Satnow (Warsaw: Baumritter, 1865), or Maimonides, *Millot ha-Higgayon (On Logic)*, ed. Y. Satnov (Berlin: B. Cohen, 1927). See *Be'ur Millot ha-Higgayon*, in *Moses Mendelssohn Gesammelte Schriften Jubiläumsausgabe* (Frommann-Holzboog, 1938, 1972), vol. 14, *Hebräische Schriften*, ed. Haim Borodianski (Bar-Dayan), p. 117 (bottom five lines on the page). The commentaries of Comtino and Mendelssohn have recently been edited in Hebrew in a comprehensive version of Maimonides' *Treatise on Logic*, containing a critical edition of the Arabic original, a Hebrew translation, and the major commentaries. See *Be'ur melekhet ha-Higayon*, ed. Kafah. Based on the Hebrew versions in the commentary edition of Kafah, and the French translation of Rémi Brague in *Maïmonide*, the relevant passages are rendered in English as follows. Comtino (Kafah, p. 195, end of section; Brague, p. 279, n. 2): "This is to say that it is the Torah which guides to their perfection, of body and of soul, as it says, 'the law of the Lord is perfect, restoring the soul, ... rejoicing the heart' (Psalm 19: 8-9)." Mendelssohn (Kafah, p. 193, toward the bottom of the page; Brague, p. 279, n. 2): "It is because the Torah, which was commanded to us by Moses, makes straight our ways in the eyes of God, and the ways of justice between man and his neighbor, that we only have to meditate on it and to learn from it the actions which man must do in order to live. But then with regard to the government of the city, this (i.e., the Torah) is likewise neither of help nor of use to us, so long as the lamb of Israel is dispersed among the nations, and so long as there is no one among us who leads the nation, no one who is a ruler (Hebrew: *moshel*; French: *chef*) in the city."]

3. Cf. *Eight Chapters (Shemonah Perakim)*, Introduction. [See "Eight Chapters," in *Ethical Writings*, trans. Weiss and Butterworth, pp. 59–104, and especially "Introduction," pp. 60–61.]

cerning theoretical subjects, whereas regarding the governance of the city, everything has been done to make it precise in all its details.[4]

Still, Maimonides adds an important qualification to his statement that we do not need the books of the philosophers on politics proper: he says that we do not need those books "in these times." The Torah antedates philosophy, or Greek wisdom, by centuries. If it were the Torah which rendered superfluous the political books of the philosophers, those books would not have been needed by the Jewish people at any time. Hence we would seem to be compelled to understand Maimonides' statement as follows: not the Jews as such, but the Jews in exile, the Jews who lack a political existence, do not need the political books of the philosophers. The Torah is not sufficient for the guidance of a political community.[5] This would imply that the political books of the philosophers will again be needed after the coming of the Messiah, as they were needed prior to the exile.

These strange consequences force us to reconsider the assumption that Maimonides means by "we" "we Jews," or that his *Logic* is a Jewish book, i.e., a book written by a Jew as a Jew for Jews as Jews. The author describes himself as a student of logic, and he describes the immediate addressee as an

---

4. *Guide* 3.27 (59b–60a). Cf. 1.Intro. (5a [cf. *Treatise on Resurrection* 32 Finkel], 11a); 1.33 (37a); 1.71 (93b–94a); 3.Intro. (2b); 3.28 (60b–61a); 3.54 (132a). Cf. Albo, *Ikkarim*, I, 3 (63, 13–19 Husik), 11 (100, 18), and 15 (133, 9–134, 1). [See *Moses Maimonides' Treatise on Resurrection*, ed. Joshua Finkel (New York: American Academy for Jewish Research, 1939); "Treatise on Resurrection" in *Igrot ha-Rambam*, ed. Shailat, I, pp. 319–64, and especially pp. 368–69; "Treatise on Resurrection," trans. Fradkin, pp. 154–77, and especially p. 173; "Essay on Resurrection," trans. Halkin, pp. 211–33, and especially pp. 229–30. The Albo passages (with some slight adjustments) are as follows: I, 3: "And a more serious difficulty is that we find no clear pronouncement upon this matter in the discussions of the talmudic Rabbis. And yet they should have treated of those principles which are the bases and foundations of divine law, seeing that human happiness and spiritual reward are based upon them, as they have treated of damages and contracts which have to do with material interests merely, and are the basis of political and social order." I, 11: "The reason they are laid down in the section 'Bereshit' (Gen. 1:1–6:8) is to indicate that they are principles of divine law." I, 15: "For although we have already assumed God's knowledge, viz., that He knows the deeds of men and orders their affairs by means of a divine law (Torah from heaven) so that their social life may be permanent and well conditioned, it might still be said that by reason of man's inferiority and little esteem in the eyes of God, the individual is ignored and not recompensed for his specific conduct in relation to his Maker, and that he is taken account of merely as part of the whole, and not as an individual. For this reason we regard providence as a principle that is prior to reward and punishment, in order to call attention to the fact that divine providence extends to every individual, and recompenses him for his individual relations to God, as we are told that God 'did not have respect unto Cain and his offering.'"]

5. Cf. Mendelssohn ad loc. Cf. the reference to the military art (which belongs to politics proper and is certainly not a part of the Torah) in Maimonides' *Letter on Astrology* with "Hilkhot Melakhim" XI 4 and XII 2–5 as well as *Resurrection* 21, 11–23, 12. Cf. also *Eight Chapters* VIII (28, 13–20 Wolff) with ibid. (28, 2–3 and 27, 19–20). [See "Letter on Astrology," trans. Lerner, pp. 179–80; "Treatise on Resurrection," trans. Fradkin, pp. 166–68; "Hilkhot Melakhim," ed. Rubenstein, pp. 415–20; "Laws of Kings and Their Wars," trans. Weiss and Butterworth, pp. 173–76, and "Laws Concerning Kings and Wars," trans. Hershman, pp. 240–42; "Eight Chapters," in *Ethical Writings*, trans. Weiss and Butterworth, 8th chap., pp. 83–95.]

authority on the sciences based upon divinely revealed law, as well as on Arabic eloquence: he does not describe himself and the addressee as Jews. When using the first person plural in his *Logic*, he normally means "we logicians," although he also speaks of "the logicians" in the third person. Yet on some occasions he speaks of subjects which belong to philosophy proper as distinguished from logic. Therefore, "we" might mean in some cases "we philosophers," although Maimonides normally speaks of "the philosophers" in the third person and even seems to indicate that he does not belong to them.[6] We are tempted to say that the *Logic* is the only philosophic book which Maimonides ever wrote. One would not commit a grievous error if he understood by "we" "we men of theory," which term is more inclusive than "we philosophers" and almost approaches in comprehensiveness the present-day term "we intellectuals." Accordingly, Maimonides must be understood to say that the men who speculate about principles or roots do not "in these times" need the books of the philosophers which are devoted to politics proper because of the dominance of divinely revealed laws.[7] Since Maimonides' statement as a whole implies that the need for the books of the philosophers on ethics and, especially, on theoretical philosophy has not been affected by the rise to dominance of revealed religions, he in effect suggests that the function of revealed religion is emphatically political. Moreover, he regards as useless "in these times" only the books of the philosophers on "the laws, the *nomoi*, the governance by human beings in divine things." He does not deny the validity of the basic part of the political teaching of the philosophers:[8] the philosophers do distinguish adequately between true and imaginary happiness and the means appropriate to both, and they have an adequate knowledge of the

---

6. *Logic*, Preface; ch. 9 (43, 11–14 Efros), 10 (46, 16–18), and 14 (61, 12–14).—The first person plural is used with unusual frequency in a section of *Eight Chapters* IV (9, 6–10, 16). There "we" occurs in the following four different meanings: 1) the author (3 times); 2) we human beings (3 times); 3) we physicians (4 times); 4) we physicians of the soul (i.e., we men of science; see ibid. III [7, 6]) (17 times). It goes without saying that in *Eight Chapters* IV "we" frequently means "we Jews"; it occurs there in the meaning "we Jews," I believe, 14 times; see especially ibid. (12, 23) where Maimonides says that he is speaking only of "our law" or "the adherents of our law." For the interpretation, consider *Guide* 1.71 (97a).—A kindred subtlety (*nukta*) is the emphatic use of "we" (e.g., *anachnu nirah*) [i.e., "we ourselves see"], in contradistinction to its non-emphatic use, of which one finds good examples in Albo's *Ikkarim* II, 4 (27, 9), 5 (48, 3–6), etc. [See "Eight Chapters," in *Ethical Writings*, trans. Weiss and Butterworth, 4th chap., pp. 67–74. For Albo, *Ikkarim*, II, 4: "We see things which are potential and then become actual"—which is literally "We ourselves see," although it must be considered how it is not a stylistic choice, but rather an emphatic use; similarly, II, 5: "We see that 'in His light we see light'" (Psalm 36:10)—again, it is literally "We ourselves see," although it too must be considered how it is not a stylistic choice, but rather an emphatic use.]

7. Cf. H. A. Wolfson, "Notes on Maimonides' Classification of the Sciences," in *Jewish Quarterly Review*, New Series 26 (1936): 377n. [See also Wolfson, *Studies in History*, vol. 1, p. 559, n. 22.]

8. Note the transition from the perfect tense to the past tense in Maimonides' statement.

rules of justice. Furthermore, if only the most practical part of the political teaching of the philosophers is superfluous "in these times" because its function is at present fulfilled by revealed religions; if, therefore, the function of revealed religion is emphatically political, political philosophy is as necessary "in these times" as in all other times for the theoretical understanding of revealed religion.

The normal division of politics proper may be said to be that which distinguishes governance of the city, governance of the nation, and governance of many or of all nations (i.e., governance of the political union, as distinguished from a mere alliance, of many or of all nations)."[9] At first glance, Maimonides seems to replace "city—nation—many [all] nations" by "city—great nation—the nations." He therefore seems to replace the nation by the great nation, which leaves us wondering why the small nation is not a subject of politics. Yet it seems to be equally possible that he uses "the great nation" as equivalent to "the nations" or "many or all nations," in which case he would have dropped the nation altogether, leaving us to wonder why the nation is not a subject of politics. However this may be, he certainly does not substitute a new tripartition of politics proper for the normal one, but rather replaces the tripartition by a bipartition: he assigns the governance of the city to one branch of political philosophy, and the governance of the great nation or of the nations to another branch. The principle underlying the tripartition was consideration of the difference of size between political communities (small, medium, and large). It is reasonable to assume that the bipartition is based upon consideration of another important difference between political communities.

Maimonides' references to the nations are framed partly in the past tense. It is possible that he even spoke explicitly of "the ancient nations." Furthermore, he calls the governance of the nations *nomoi*. Finally, in the same context, he speaks of a governance by human beings in divine things such as belongs to the past. With a view to these facts and to certain parallels in the *Guide*, Professor H. A. Wolfson has suggested that "the nations" stands for the ancient pagan nations, and "the great nation" stands for Israel, and therefore that Maimonides tacitly goes over from the distinction between political communities in regard to size to their distinction in regard to religion: the

---

9. Farabi, *Siyasat* (Hyderabad 1346) 39 and 50; *Al-madina al-fadila* 53, 17-19 and 54, 5-10 Dieterici. [For *Siyasat*, see "Political Regime," trans. Najjar, in *Medieval Political Philosophy*, ed. Lerner and Mahdi, pp. 32-57, and especially pp. 32, and 36-37. For *Al-madina al-fadila*, see Alfarabi, *Perfect State*, trans. Walzer, and especially pp. 228-31.]

city stands for the "civil state," and the pagan nations and Israel stand for different forms of the "religious state."[10] This suggestion necessarily implies that the governance, or guidance, of Israel, i.e., the Torah, is a subject of political philosophy. More precisely, Wolfson's suggestion necessarily implies that the governance of the great nation, i.e., the Torah, and the governance of the nations, i.e., the *nomoi*, are the subjects of one and the same branch of political philosophy. This should not be surprising: the same science deals with opposites. Accordingly, the chapters of the *Guide* which deal with the difference between the Torah and the *nomoi* of the pagans would belong to political science. Since one of these chapters (2.40) is the central chapter of the part devoted to prophecy, one would be justified in suggesting that Maimonides' prophetology as a whole is a branch of political science. This suggestion is confirmed by considerations which are in no way based on the teaching of the *Logic*. These inferences are in perfect agreement with Maimonides' concluding remark, which is to the effect that we have no need in these times for the books of the philosophers on the laws, the *nomoi*, the governance by human beings in divine things: the practical use of books meant only for practical use is one thing; an entirely different thing is the use for purely theoretical purposes of books which are at least partly theoretical.

Wolfson's suggestion is partly confirmed by Avicenna's division of political philosophy. Avicenna makes use of a bipartition which is based upon exactly the same principle that Wolfson discerned in Maimonides' statement. According to Avicenna, one branch of political philosophy deals with kingship; the classic texts on this subject are the books of Plato and Aristotle on government. The other branch deals with prophecy and divine law; the classic texts on this subject are the books of Plato and Aristotle on *nomoi*. This second branch considers the existence of prophecy and the need of the human race for divine law; it considers the characteristics common to all divine codes as well as those which are peculiar to individual divine codes; it deals with the difference between genuine and spurious prophecy.[11]

There is then one point in Wolfson's suggestion which must be changed. There is no reason for identifying the great nation with Israel. If Maimonides had spoken of "the nation" or of "the virtuous nation," one might say that

---

10. Wolfson, loc. cit., pp. 372–376. [See also Wolfson, *Studies in History*, pp. 554–58.]

11. *Tis' Rasa'il*, Istanbul 1298, 73–74. Cf. Falaquera, *Reshit Ḥokhmah* 58–59 David. See Wolfson, "Additional Notes," in *Hebrew Union College Annual* 3 (1926): 374. [For the *Tis' Rasa'il* passages to which Strauss refers, see Avicenna, "On the Division of the Rational Sciences," trans. Mahdi. For the "Additional Notes," see also Wolfson, *Studies in History*, vol. 1, pp. 554–58.]

he might have meant Israel. But he speaks of "the great nation." He is fond of quoting Deuteronomy 4:6, where Israel is called "a great nation." As he indicates, the biblical verse implies that Israel is not the only great nation. It is then impossible in precise speech to call Israel "the great nation" simply. On the contrary, since "great" here means "numerous," the term would apply to Islam (and to Christianity) rather than to Israel. Indeed, it would be more appropriate to call Israel the small nation: Jacob "is small" (Amos 7:5).[12] One might for a moment imagine that Maimonides speaks of the great nation precisely in order to exclude the small nation, i.e., Israel, and hence the Torah, from the scope of political philosophy. But this possibility is contradicted by all the considerations which have been set forth here, and in particular by the fact that the *Logic* is not a Jewish book. We suggest then that Maimonides means by "the nations" the ancient pagan nations, and by "the great nation" any group constituted by a universalistic religion. In speaking of the great nation in the singular, he refers to the universalistic and hence exclusive claim raised by each of the three great monotheistic religions: on the premises of each, there can be only one legitimate religious community. In speaking of the nations in the plural, he refers to the national character of the religions of the pagans: that national character explains the coexistence of many equally legitimate religious communities.[13]

It is true that after having divided politics proper into governance of the city and governance of the great nations at the beginning of his statement on political science, Maimonides does not make explicit use of the bipartition in the sequel: when discussing the function and the scope of politics proper, he identifies the whole of politics proper with governance of the city. This does not mean however that he drops the original bipartition as unimportant. On the contrary, it means that that bipartition is a hint which is addressed to the attentive reader and which may safely be lost on the others. To understand Maimonides' thought means to understand his hints. It is possible to explain

---

12. *Iggeret Teman* 4, 8–10; 8, 3–6; 38, 1–2; 40, 4–6 (cf. Ibn Tibbon's translation); 40, 11 ff. Halkin. Cf. *Guide* 2.11 toward the end, and 3.31. Cf. the use of "the great nations" which as such are distinguished from Israel, in "Ibn Aknin's Commentary on the Song of Songs," ed. and trans. Abraham S. Halkin in *Alexander Marx Jubilee Volume*, ed. Saul Lieberman, English section (New York: Jewish Theological Seminary of America, 1950), pp. 389–424, and especially p. 421. [For *Iggeret Teman*, see "Epistle to Yemen," trans. Kraemer, pp. 101–2, 103, 111–12; "Epistle to Yemen," trans. Halkin, pp. 95–96, 97, 123–24.]

13. Cf. *Guide* 1.71 (94b): "the Christian nation embraced these nations." As regards the universalistic intention of the Torah, cf., e.g., "Hilkhot Teshuvah" IX, 9 and *Resurrection* 32, 4–6. [For the *Resurrection*, see "Treatise on Resurrection," trans. Fradkin, p. 173; "Essay on Resurrection," trans. Halkin, p. 229. See also "Hilkhot Teshuvah," trans. Hyamson, p. 92a.]

a particular hint with utmost explicitness, but the nature of the subject matter compels the interpreter to have recourse, sooner or later, to other hints.

These remarks do not suffice to clarify the obscurities of Maimonides' statement. As a rule, he enumerates at the end of each chapter of the *Logic* the terms which he has explained in the body of the chapter. In the enumeration at the end of Chapter 14, he does not mention the terms designating the four parts of practical or political philosophy, whereas he does mention the terms designating the three parts of theoretical philosophy. Thus he does not even claim to have explained the meaning of "governance of the great nation or of the nations" in particular. We have seen how appropriate this silent declaration is. There are only two terms pertaining to politics proper and to economics which he mentions as having been explained in the chapter: "commands"[14] and *nomoi*. He did define "command": command is that guidance by which a man guides other men. But he did not define *nomos*. Yet the remark at the end of the chapter shows that the definition of *nomos* is implicitly conveyed through the statement on economics and on politics proper. It is obvious that *nomos* must be a species of the genus "command." Discussing the governance of the household, he says that that governance takes due account of time and place. He does not mention the consideration of time and place when discussing politics proper. We suggest that *nomos* is that species of command which is general in the sense that it does not regard time and place, or that it does not consider the individual in his individuality. The other species of command is that of particular commands, commands which change in accordance with changing circumstances, and especially in accordance with differences among the individuals to be guided.[15]

Does this mean that all political governance, or all sound political governance, is government by law? According to Farabi, whom Maimonides re-

---

14. Ibn Tibbon: *ha-ḥuqqim* [customs]; Vives: *ha-ḥoq* [custom]; Aḥitub: *ha-hanhagah* [government]. Could the original have read *hukm* ["authority"]? [As Rémi Brague notes (*Maïmonide*, p. 287, n. 14), the original as it has since become known reads "*as-siyasah*," i.e., "government" or "regime": see Israel Efros, "Maimonides' Arabic Treatise on Logic," *Proceedings of the American Academy for Jewish Research* 34 (1966): p. 33, l. 25. It seems to me, if I may venture a comment, that this term, properly translated as "regime" rather than "command," only confirms Strauss's main thesis. His main thesis is that Maimonides' primary concern as a logician in the fourteenth chapter, although he may not shout this from the rooftops, is with the natural forms of political life, i.e., with regimes and with their *nomoi*, even if he will also say something by hints about derivative "religious" regimes, defined or guided by divine law.]

15. Cf. *Guide* 3.34 with 2.40 (85b), where Maimonides speaks about the conventional character of the agreement produced by law between individuals of different and opposite temperaments. Consider the implications of the distinction between those psychically ill people who, being men of science, can heal themselves and those who are in need of being treated by others in *Eight Chapters* III–IV. [See "Eight Chapters," in *Ethical Writings*, trans. Weiss and Butterworth, chaps. 3 and 4, pp. 65–74.]

garded as the philosophic authority second only to Aristotle, the unchangeable divine law (*shari'a*) is only a substitute for the government of a perfect ruler who governs without written laws and who changes his ordinances in accordance with the change of times as he sees fit.[16] The rule of living intelligence appears to be superior to the rule of law. There is then a form of sound political governance which is akin to the governance of the household, or to paternal rule, in that it pays due regard to time and place as well as to what is good for each individual—the form of political governance which Plato and Aristotle had praised most highly. Maimonides mentions the rule of living intelligence in the household and the rule of law in the city; he does not mention the rule of living intelligence in the city. He omits the central possibility. One of our first impressions was that he might have omitted from the normal enumeration of the kinds of political governance the governance of the nation, i.e., the central item. We see now that this impression was not entirely wrong: he did omit a central item. But whereas it remained uncertain whether he had omitted the nation or only the small nation, it is quite certain that he omitted the rule of living intelligence in the city or nation.

If *nomos* is essentially a general command in the sense indicated, it is not, as we have previously assumed, essentially a religious order. Perhaps Maimonides even made an explicit distinction between *nomos* and "governance by human beings in divine things" at the end of his statement. However this may be, in his thematic discussion of *nomos* in the *Guide*, he suggests that the *nomos*, in contradistinction to the divinely revealed law, is directed only toward the well-being of the body and is unconcerned with divine things.[17] The *nomos* is, then, to use Wolfson's expression, essentially the order of a "civil state" as distinguished from a "religious state." One might think that the philosophers did not admit the possibility of a "civil state": according to them, divine worship is an essential function, and in a sense the primary function, of civil society. But this objection overlooks the fact that while the *nomos* must indeed be strengthened by myth or by a "governmental religion," that religion is not part of the primary intention of the *nomos* and of the association which is ordered by it.[18]

---

16. *Siyasat* 50–51; *Al-madina al-fadila* 60, 15ff. [See "Political Regime," trans. Najjar, in *Medieval Political Philosophy*, ed. Lerner and Mahdi, p. 37. For *Al-madina al-fadila*, see Alfarabi, *Perfect State*, trans. Walzer, pp. 248–51.]

17. Cf. 2.39 end with 2.40 (86a–b).

18. Cf. Aristotle, *Politics* 1299a18–19, 1322b16–22, 1328b11, and *Metaphysics* 1074b1ff. Cf. Yehuda Halevi, *Kuzari* I, 13; Maimonides' *Commentary on the Mishnah*, "Avodah Zarah" IV, 7 (27 Wiener). [Rémi Brague (in *Maïmonide*, p. 289, n. 18) translates from Arabic to French what he says is "probably the

Whereas the *nomos* entails a religion that is in the service of government, the divinely revealed law which is a subject of the same branch of political philosophy as the *nomos* puts government in the service of religion, of the true religion, of the truth. The divinely revealed law is therefore necessarily free from the relativity of the *nomos*, i.e., it is universal as regards place and perpetual as regards time. It is then a much loftier social order than the *nomos*. Hence it is exposed to dangers which did not threaten the pagan *nomoi*. For instance, the public discussion of "the account of creation," i.e., of physics, did not harm the pagans in the way in which it might harm the adherents of revealed laws. The divinely revealed laws also create dangers which did not exist among the Greeks: they open up a new source of disagreement among men.[19]

To summarize, Maimonides directs our attention first to the differences between political societies in regard to size. He then directs our attention to their differences in regard to religion. He finally directs our attention to their differences in regard to the presence or absence of laws. He thus forces us to consider the effects produced upon the character of laws by the change from paganism to revealed religion.

Maimonides' unusual division of practical or human philosophy has the result that philosophy or science consists of 7 parts. An uncommon chain of reasoning leads to a common result.[20] We cannot in the present case ac-

---

designated passage" in the *Commentary on the Mishnah*; what follows is my English rendering of his translation: "All of these things (i.e., idolatrous, and especially astrological, practices) came into being because of the needs [*nécessités*] (of the situation). Indeed, in primitive times during which cities were formed, the common people [*la masse du vulgaire*] were made to believe in these things, and were told that the well-being [*salut*] of their country and their (private) concerns rested on these images, which had been assembled in their temples and venerated by the ancients who knew the secrets. The royalty counted themselves fortunate, and persuaded themselves that there was something of the truth in it. They said: 'This is what one such star says, and this is what another such star says,' and they venerated them and they followed them. They believed in these things as we ourselves believe with respect to the prophets, peace be on them, in their excellence and in their virtue. Does one not see how Scripture refers to them: 'prophets of Baal and prophets of Ashtarte'? Then next weak-minded people [*gens faible d'esprit*] came along who found these books and these teachings, and who imagined that they were true and that they contained useful things; however, they did not know that they were lies, fabricated during a certain era in order to profit from the circumstances."]

19. *Guide* 1.17; 1.31 (34b); 3.29 (65b). Cf. the variant reading of 2.39 (85a Munk; 269, 27 Jonovitz) and *Eight Chapters* IV (15, 13–20). [See "Eight Chapters," in *Ethical Writings*, trans. Weiss and Butterworth, 4th chap., pp. 67–74. It seems that the most palpable statement of this point is made in *Guide* 1.31 (p. 67): "However, in our times there is a fourth cause (of disagreement about things) that he (i.e., Alexander of Aphrodisias) did not mention because it did not exist among them. It is habit and upbringing.... All this is due to people being habituated to, and brought up on, texts that it is an established usage to think highly of and to regard as true."]

20. Cf. H. A. Wolfson, "The Classification of the Sciences in Mediaeval Jewish Philosophy," in *Hebrew Union College Jubilee Volume, 1875–1925* (Cincinnati: Hebrew Union College, 1925), 277–79 and 283–85. [See also Wolfson, *Studies in History*, vol. 1, pp. 507–9, 513–15.]

count for the result by its commonness, precisely because it is arrived at in so uncommon a manner. We must consider the significance of the number 7 in Maimonides' own thought. Considerations of this kind are necessarily somewhat playful. But they are not so playful as to be incompatible with the seriousness of scholarship. The *Logic* itself consists of 14 (= 7 × 2) chapters; the number of terms explained in the work is 175 (= 7 × 25); in Chapter 7, Maimonides discusses the 14 moods of valid syllogism. His *Mishneh Torah* consists of 14 books. In the *Guide*, he divides the biblical commandments into groups in a manner which differs considerably from the division underlying the *Mishneh Torah*, yet the number of groups of commandments is again 14. In *Guide* 3.51 (123b–124a), which happens to be the 175th chapter of that work, he assigns, in the first interpretation of a simile, the same place to law which he assigns, in the second interpretation, to logic: there seems to be a certain correspondence between law and logic. Could there be a connection between the number 14 on the one hand, and logic and law on the other? In the 14th chapter of the *Guide*, he explains the meaning of "man." We suggest this explanation: Man, being the animal which possesses speech, is at the same time the rational animal which is perfected by the art of reasoning, and the political animal which is perfected by law. Man is a compound of form and matter; he has a dual nature. The number 7 itself, as distinguished from its double, would then seem to refer to beings of a simple nature, to pure intelligences, i.e., to God and the angels which are the subjects of philosophic theology or of "the account of the chariot." The *Guide*, the highest and central theme of which is precisely "the account of the chariot," consists of 7 sections: 1/ the names and attributes of God (1.1–70); 2/ demonstration of God's existence, etc., on the presupposition of the eternity of the world and discussion of that presupposition (i.e., defense of the belief in creation out of nothing) (1.71–2.31); 3/ prophecy (2.32–48); 4/ "the account of the chariot" (3.1–7); 5/ providence (3.8–24); 6/ the Torah (3.25–50); 7/ conclusion (3.51–54). The central section of Maimonides' *Heptameres*, the thematic discussion of "the account of the chariot," the secret of secrets, consists of 7 chapters. It would be premature to attempt a discussion of the question why the number 7 is preeminent. We must limit ourselves to noting that the section devoted to "the account of the chariot" is surrounded by two sections of 17 chapters each, and to referring the reader to the 17th chapter of the *Guide*.

It is of the essence of devices of this kind that, while they are helpful up to a certain point, they are never sufficient and are never meant to be sufficient: they are merely hints. But there are no isolated hints: the deficiency of one hint is supplied by other hints. The suggestion stated in the preceding paragraph suffers from an obvious flaw. The same strange division of practical philosophy which leads to the result that philosophy or science consists of 7 parts leads to the further result that ethics occupies the central place in the order of the sciences. And, as Maimonides intimates in his statement on political science, ethics does not deserve the central place.

Ethics is the study of the virtues, which means primarily of the moral virtues; it is not the study of happiness or man's true end; the study of man's end belongs to politics proper. This means in the first place that the moral virtues and their exercise are not man's end. It means furthermore that the moral virtues can only be understood with a view to their political function. This does not mean of course that the true end of man is political or, more radically, the well-being of his body. But it does mean that the true end of man or man's final perfection can only be understood in contradistinction to his first perfection, the well-being of his body, and hence in contradistinction to man's political life at its best. In other words, morality in the common sense of the term belongs to the realm of generally accepted opinions, of the *endoxa*. The theoretical understanding of morality traces morality in the common sense to two different roots: to the requirements of society and the requirements of man's final perfection, i.e., theoretical understanding. Common-sense morality belongs to the realm of generally accepted opinion because the requirements of society and the requirements of theoretical understanding are not completely identical but are in a certain tension with each other. Common-sense morality is essentially unaware of its being a mixture of heterogeneous elements which has no clear or exact principle, and yet it is sufficiently consistent for almost all practical purposes: it is *doxa*. It is the most impressive expression of man's dual nature.[21]

---

21. *Logic*, ch. 8; *Eight Chapters* IV (12, 19–21), VI; *Guide* 1.2; 2.33 (75a); 2.36 (79a–b); 2.40 (86b); 3.22 (45b); 3.27; 3.28 (61b); 3.46 (106a). Cf. the distinction between justice and the virtues in Farabi's *Plato* sect. 30 Rosenthal-Walzer with the enumeration of the virtues in *Eight Chapters* II on the one hand, and with their enumeration in ibid. IV on the other: justice is replaced by wit, liberality, and sense of shame. Cf. *Guide* 3.23 (47b) and 1.34 (39b). [See "Logic," in *Ethical Writings*, trans. Weiss and Butterworth, chap. 8, pp. 156–58. See also "Eight Chapters," in *Ethical Writings*, trans. Weiss and Butterworth, 4th chap., pp. 67–74; 6th chap., pp. 78–80. With regard to Strauss's reference to "Farabi's *Plato* sect. 30 Rosenthal-Walzer," Rémi Brague notes (*Maïmonide*, p. 292, n. 21) what appears to have been an error, and instead refers readers (as the passage of which Strauss may have been thinking) to section (or paragraph) 36, which is also Alfarabi, *Plato and Aristotle*, trans. Mahdi, p. 66. In the previous paragraph, Strauss refers to what he dubs Maimonides' "*Heptameres*": he defines the *Guide* as a sevenfold work.]

Let us then look once more at Maimonides' division of the sciences. His division of theoretical philosophy into 3 parts and practical philosophy into 4 parts is not final. There is a further subdivision of two of the parts of theoretical philosophy: of mathematics into 4 parts (arithmetic, geometry, astronomy, music) and theology into 2 parts (speech about God and the angels, metaphysics). This might appear strange at first sight, but there is no mention of any subdivision of physics. We are justified in regarding the subdivisions of practical philosophy as no more important than the subdivisions of mathematics: neither of them is mentioned at the end of the chapter in the enumeration of the terms explained in the body of the chapter. We arrive then at a division of philosophy or science into 11 parts (arithmetic, geometry, astronomy, music, physics, speech about God and the angels, metaphysics, ethics, economics, governance of the city, governance of the great nation or of the nations). The central part in this second division, which is slightly less noticeable than the first, is occupied by speech about God and the angels, i.e., by a science which obviously deserves the central place.[22] Yet the very plausibility of this consequence of the second division renders questionable the first division and therewith the significance of the number 7 and the implications thereof.[23] We are therefore forced to wonder whether "the account of the chariot" is identical with the science of God and the angels. By merely raising this question, we recognize the error of those who hold that Maimonides' allusive treatment of "the account of the chariot" is unreasonable because the secret toward which that treatment points is familiar to

22. In *Hebrew Union College Annual* 3 (1926): 373, Wolfson reports a division of science into 7 parts which is composed in Arabic, and also its Hebrew translation which, while deviating from the original in regard to the sciences mentioned, preserves the division of science into 7 parts: in both the original and the translation the central place is occupied by metaphysics. [See also Wolfson, *Studies in History*, p. 548.]

23. On the basis of the second division, theoretical philosophy consists of 7 parts, with music in the center. The underlying view is that the theoretical sciences by themselves complete philosophy or science, or that only the theoretical sciences are philosophic. But this view is the view of "the ancients" (60, 11–14 and 61, 16–17): it is not the true view. It is a pre-Aristotelian and even pre-Socratic view. (Cf. Farabi's *Plato*, loc. cit.) Cf. the report on "the ancient opinion" of the Pythagoreans and their "musical" philosophy in *Guide* 2.8. It was the Pythagorean doctrine which offered a solid justification for arithmology. After the refutation of Pythagoreanism by the discovery of the irrational numbers, arithmology ceased to be unqualifiedly serious and became serious play. Maimonides obviously does not share "the ancient opinions." Cf. *Guide* 3.23 (49b). In his first enumeration of moral virtues in the *Eight Chapters* (II), Maimonides mentions 7 moral virtues; the section of his Code dealing with ethics ("Hilkhot De'ot") consists of 7 chapters. [See Alfarabi, *Plato and Aristotle*, trans. Mahdi, p. 66. See also "Eight Chapters," in *Ethical Writings*, trans. Weiss and Butterworth, 2nd chapter, pp. 64–65. For "Hilkhot De'ot," see "Laws Relating to Moral Dispositions," trans. Hyamson, pp. 47a–57a; "Laws Concerning Character Traits," in *Ethical Writings*, trans. Weiss and Butterworth, pp. 27–52.]

the scholars of all religions.[24] And to recognize that a scholarly criticism of Maimonides is unreasonable is equivalent to progressing in the understanding of his thought. The section of the *Guide* which is devoted to "the account of the chariot" is most reasonably the most mysterious section of the book.

The study of Maimonides' statement on practical philosophy or political science thus leads directly into the center of the fundamental problem. This is no accident. The recovery of what we are in the habit of calling classical political philosophy and of what Maimonides called simply political science or practical philosophy is, to say the least, an indispensable condition for understanding his thought. Only those, he says, are able to answer the question of whether the talmudic Sages were men of science or not, who have trained themselves in the sciences to the point of knowing how to address the multi-

---

24. Cf. Munk, *Le Guide des égarés*, III, p. 8, n. 1. See also the statement on theology in *Logic*, ch. 14. [See "Logic," in *Ethical Writings*, trans. Weiss and Butterworth, chap. 14, pp. 158–61. The portion of Maimonides' "Logic," chap. 14, which is focused on in Strauss's essay has also been translated by Muhsin Mahdi: *Medieval Political Philosophy*, ed. Lerner and Mahdi, pp. 189–90. And the entire chapter has also been translated by Joel Kraemer, dispersed by paragraphs through his "Maimonides on the Philosophic Sciences in his *Treatise on the Art of Logic*," section II, pp. 80–97. (See the editor's note above for full reference.) The "statement on theology" to which Strauss refers is translated as follows by Weiss and Butterworth (pp. 159–60): "Divine science is divided into two parts. One (part) is the investigation of every being which is neither a body nor a power in a body. It is the discourse about what pertains to the deity, may His name be magnified. According to the opinion (of the ancients) it is also a discourse about the angels, for they do not believe that the angels are separate from matter. The second part of divine science investigates the very remote causes for everything which all the other sciences encompass. They call this part both divine science and metaphysics. These, in sum, are the sciences of the first things." The same "statement" is rendered by Kraemer as follows (p. 88): "The divine science is divided into two parts. One of them is the investigation of every entity that is neither a body nor a force in a body. It is the discourse concerning what pertains to the deity—may His name be exalted—and the angels as well, according to the opinion (of the ancients); for they do not believe the angels to be bodies, but call them instead separate intellects, by which they mean that they are separate from matter. The second part of the divine science investigates the ultimate causes of everything that all the other sciences include. And they call the divine science also metaphysics. These are the sciences of the ancients." As for that to which Strauss points by his reference to "Munk, *Le Guide des égarés*, III, p. 8, n. 1," this must have been meant, I surmise, as a reference instead to p. 7, n. 1 as it continues on p. 8, rather than to n. 1 as it appears entirely on p. 8. (If for no other reason, the phrase "familiar to the scholars of all religions" occurs in it.) If I am correct in my surmise, I believe that it is the last paragraph of this note which is most relevant to his discussion, and which I shall translate. Munk: "Moreover, the complete interpretation that Maimonides offers here of the vision of Ezekiel, in obscure (*couvert*) words, is based, as we have said, on the Peripatetic (or Aristotelian) cosmology. But if the prophet, as is probable, avails himself of astronomical symbolism, he only has the power to borrow from the astronomy of his time, and it is (thus) necessary to direct oneself to Chaldean (or Babylonian) science in order to find the explanation (of the symbols) in it. Isaac Abravanel overturns totally the interpretation of Maimonides by rightly remarking that if this is the meaning of the vision of Ezekiel, then there is no place in it for much of a mystery, since what it consists of is a science which is taught in all schools of philosophy, and which is familiar to the scholars of all religions (*communions*). See the second preface to Abravanel's commentary on the Book of Ezekiel, and also (his comments) on chapter 1 of the same book; cf. also Abravanel's commentary on various parts of *The Guide of the Perplexed*, part II, fol. 48ff."]

tude on the one hand and the elite on the other concerning divine things and things similar to the divine, and to the point of knowing the practical part of philosophy.[25] The question of whether the talmudic Sages were men of science or not is identical with the question of the relation of "the account of the chariot" to metaphysics: the mystical meaning of "the account of the chariot" was vouched for by the talmudic Sages.[26]

Maimonides' one-page statement on political science is a masterful epitome of the problem of revelation as it presents itself from the point of view of the philosophers, i.e., from the most sublime point of view to which pagans could rise. Once we realize this, we are on our way toward solving the other riddles of the *Logic*—for instance, the strange reference to the Sabian Abu Ishaq in chapter 4 and the related strange definition of substance in chapter 10. Maimonides pursued the philosophic approach up to its end because he was "the great eagle" who, far from fearing the light of the sun, "by virtue of the strength of his sense of sight, enjoys the light and longs to fly high in order to get near to it,"[27] or because he was animated by that intrepid piety

---

25. Introduction to the *Commentary on the Mishnah* (E. Pococke, *Porta Mosis*, Oxford 1655, p. 147). Cf. *Commentary on Berakhot* IX, 5 and *Guide* 3.22 (46b). [Brague believes (*Maïmonide*, p. 264, n. 135, and p. 294, n. 25) that in this reference to Pococke, *Porta Mosis*, Strauss was undoubtedly thinking of the following lines in the *Commentary on the Mishnah*, Sanhedrin X, which I translate from his French rendering of the Arabic original: "If they would have applied themselves to the sciences, so that they would have known how to properly speak on divine (i.e., metaphysical or theological) matters and things which resemble them, to the vulgar and to the elite, and if they would have mastered the practical part of philosophy, it would have been clear (to them) on this subject whether the sages were scientists [*savants*] or not." For a rendering into English of the same passage, done—more or less—from the Kafah Hebrew translation of the Arabic original, consider the following (which has been corrected to bring it closer to Kafah's Hebrew version): "If only they would apply themselves to the sciences, so that they would know how to write both for the masses and for the educated on matters dealing with theology and the like, and if they would understand the practical portion of philosophy, then they would clearly see whether or not the Sages were really men of science, and the real meaning of the words (of the Sages) would become comprehensible to them." See Maimonides, *Commentary on the Mishnah (Sanhedrin)*, trans. Rosner, p. 141. Cf. Maimonides, *Commentary on the Mishnah*, trans. Kafah. Brague also maintains ("sans doute") that the reference by Strauss at the end of his n. 25 is not so much concerned with *Guide* 3.22 (46b) in general, but specifically concerns a comment made by Munk, *Le Guide des égarés*, p. 167, l. 2f. On the assumption that this is correct (as a reference to Munk, p. 167, n. 1), I shall translate the seemingly most relevant portion of Munk's note: "See Babylonian Talmud, Baba Batra, 16a. It is to this passage that the author alludes in previously saying: 'I shall mention the words of the Sages who have drawn my attention to everything that I understand in this momentous (*importante*) parable.'" Cf. also *Guide*, trans. Pines, pp. 486, 488–89.]

26. Cf. *Guide* 3.5.

27. Cf. Albo, *Ikkarim* II, 29 (190, 5–6) and *Guide* 3.6 end. [No one seems to know when, where, or with whom "the great eagle" originated as an epithet bestowed on Maimonides. Some prefer to trace it to a passage in Ezekiel 17:3 (cf. also 17:7): "Thus saith the Lord God: The great eagle with the great wings and long pinions, full of feathers with brilliant colors, . . ." However, no doubt this epithet is not derived unqualifiedly from that passage (which refers to the king of Babylon!), but rather it might serve for some as a sort of proof-text because of its poetic force. Albo's complete statement on the eagle (which, if it is not

which does not shrink from the performance of any duty laid upon us in the prayer "Purify our heart so that we can serve Thee in truth." If he had not brought the greatest sacrifice, he could not have defended the Torah against the philosophers as admirably as he did in his Jewish books.

---

the passage in which the epithet originated, certainly suggests an endorsement of it as a fitting metaphor to use about Maimonides) is as follows. This passage begins by contrasting it with the bat that is

> unlike the eagle which, by reason of its intense power of vision, takes pleasure in light and flies high by reason of its desire to get near to it. All these qualities of light bear a greater similarity to the things which are free from matter than to anything else to which the things may be compared.

Albo, *Ikkarim* (*Roots*), trans. Husik, vol. II, chap. 29, p. 190; see also chap. 30, p. 197. For *Guide* 3.6 end (which makes no mention of "eagles," but which contrasts the detailed images of Ezekiel with those of Isaiah): "I refer to their [i.e., the Sages'] dictum in Hagigah: 'All that was seen by Ezekiel was [likewise] seen by Isaiah. Isaiah is like unto a city man who saw the king; whereas Ezekiel is like unto a villager who saw the king.'... It is also possible that the author of this remark believed that Isaiah was more perfect than Ezekiel, and that the apprehension that amazed Ezekiel and was regarded by him as terrible was known by Isaiah through a knowledge the exposition of which did not require extraordinary language, the subject being well known to those who are perfect." Strauss refers at the end to a well-known line from a Jewish prayer: "*taher libenu le-'avdekha be-'emet*," "purify our hearts to serve You in truth." It occurs in the fourth (or middle) of seven blessings, which constitute the "Amida" (i.e., "standing") prayer as it is formulated for Sabbaths and festivals, and for Rosh ha-Shanah and Yom Kippur, as it is read during Shaḥarit, Musaf, Minḥa, and Maariv worship services on these holy days (as well as in the Musaf of the New Moon prayers). It is a constituent of the special prayer known as "*Kedushat ha-Yom*" ("The Holiness of the Day"), which is made essential in the prayer services on these days of added sanctity. This line probably originated with that prayer (whose author is unknown), since no other source for it is known. Some variation occurs in the first portion of the prayer during the different services, but this line occurs in the second portion of the prayer that is constant and unchanged. The line has been reproduced as it is translated in the *Koren Siddur* of Chief Rabbi Lord Jonathan Sacks (Jerusalem: Koren, 2009), pp. 486–87, 546–47, 614–15, and 780–81. What is perhaps most significant to note is that Strauss translates this term with strict literalness as a singular term, "our heart," while almost all prayerbooks translate it loosely as a plural term, "our hearts." So far as I have been able to determine, it is not actually deployed by Maimonides in any of his works (other than in repeating the content of the prayer), whether as a proof-text or as suggesting a further point. Consequently, I have not been able to discover any greater "Maimonidean" point made in a different context that Strauss may have been hinting at as relevant to the present context, in the sense of a reason for his choice (beyond its poetic power) to finish the present essay with the mention of just this one line. Yet it is possible that *Guide* 1.39, trans. Pines, p. 89 (i.e., the chapter dealing with "heart" as a biblical term which, in applying it to God, one has to be careful about), has some relevance to why Strauss chose to employ just this liturgical phrase to conclude his essay. Maimonides says: "[Heart] is also a term denoting the intellect. ... It is in this sense—I mean that indicative of the intellect—that the term is applied figuratively to God in all the passages in question, save certain exceptional ones where it sometimes is used to indicate the will. Every passage should therefore be understood according to its context.... Accordingly the intended meaning is ... that you should make His apprehension the end of all your actions."]

10

Introduction to Maimonides' *The Guide of the Perplexed*[1]

EDITOR'S NOTE

"Introduction to Maimonides' *The Guide of the Perplexed*" is a lecture by Leo Strauss which was delivered at the Hillel House of the University of Chicago in two sessions: on Sunday, February 7, and Sunday, February 14, 1960. It survives in tape recordings and is preserved in five separate tapes. Those five tapes were technically remastered by the Leo Strauss Center at the University Chicago, and reduced to three CD-ROM files. The present editor transcribed the lecture employing the complete set of both versions. And further, I would like to thank Dr. Yehuda Halper (Tulane University) for his willingness to make available to me an alternate set of the tapes of Strauss's Maimonides lecture, which had been in the possession of the late Professor Aryeh Motzkin, and which had some very slight differences in the amount of material preserved. These were used as a sort of "control" for comparative purposes, and did help to clarify certain obscure words and passages in the previously mentioned taped versions. The lecture brings together, summarizes, and advances the results of Strauss's mature study of Maimonides and his *Guide*, which he presented in several essays reproduced in the present volume. However, beyond any all-purpose summary or even condensed version which this tape-recorded lecture might seem to present, one of the great advantages which accrues to students of Strauss on Maimonides from its being made available in transcribed form (however imperfect and lacking certain words or passages) is that it offers a more accessible and less "technical" approach to the major themes and topics treated in one of Strauss's

---

1. This title of Strauss's lecture is approximate. The precise form in which the original lecture was advertised is unknown to the present editor. It is also unknown whether, in whatever form it appeared, the title was Strauss's own choice or that of the University of Chicago Hillel House. The title is not mentioned on the tapes. Hence it is not clear whether the title mentioned the full name of *The Guide of the Perplexed*, or whether it only appeared in the form of "Introduction to Maimonides."

most difficult and yet deepest essays, "How To Begin To Study *The Guide of the Perplexed*" (henceforth, "How To Begin"). The editor-transcriber would like to thank Dr. Nathan Tarcov and his associates at the Leo Strauss Center at the University of Chicago for their much-appreciated technical assistance in helping to make available to me copies of the tapes on which the transcription is based, and for readying the remastered versions that were much clearer than the tapes themselves. However, as readers will observe by following the notes, this has not made the lecture free of a certain ambiguity, not due to any fault or any lack of effort in the technical remastering process, but rather due to the limits of the original, antiquated recordings themselves. I am also very grateful to Dr. Tarcov, Erik Dreff of the University of Chicago, and Jessica Radin of the University of Toronto for their great assistance in trying to discern some of the most difficult words or passages in the tape. Of course, the final decisions were mine, so I bear sole responsibility if any errors may have been made. For those who would like to hear the lecture itself, the Leo Strauss Center of the University of Chicago plans to make the remastered version available on its website (http://leostrausscenter.uchicago.edu/). That, it is hoped, will be coordinated with the publication of this book. The notes below to this lecture are entirely the work of the present editor. Nothing that appears in them should be attributed to Leo Strauss.

PART 1

LADIES AND GENTLEMAN, THE OCCASION FOR THIS LECTURE IS A KIND of celebration, a premature celebration to be sure. We have been preparing a new translation, a new English translation, of Maimonides' *Guide of the Perplexed* for a number of years now. And it will not be *the* perfect translation for which I [had] originally hoped; but it will be the best translation into any modern language, and it may even be the best translation ever made. Chiefly responsible for the translation is Professor Salomon Pines, whom some of you may have heard last year, who is a great Arabist and Hebraist; furthermore Professor Ralph Lerner, of this university; and also myself. I think that [this] is a proper occasion to express my thanks to the University of Chicago: not only to the University of Chicago Press, but also to the central administration, which[2] has been sponsoring this work from the very beginning. The

---

2. Strauss actually says "who." Since it in no sense changes the meaning, it has been corrected to "which."

attention of that august body was directed toward Maimonides by a friend of mine, to whom we ultimately all are obliged for this matter, Mr. Robert Goldwin.[3]

Now the purpose of this lecture is to show the *way* toward Maimonides' *Guide of the Perplexed*, and of course not to go it. "To go it" would mean to study the *Guide*, and this could be done only in common readings of many years. Lectures, even lectures for a whole year, would be wholly inadequate. We must first trace the question: Why should we be interested in Maimonides? There is a well-known answer: Maimonides was the greatest intellect, the greatest mind, whom the Jewish people have brought forth since the completion of the Talmud, if not since the cessation of prophecy. It is important to remember human greatness at all times, but especially in ours, in a time of excessive *speed*, where we have no time to look back and to remember, and where the first question is, What next?, rather than questions regarding the past. We need concrete standards of human greatness, standards supplied by the works of great men, lest we be deceived by the rush and the noise of those who advertise ephemeral figures, to say nothing of the self-advertisers.

But this duty may come into conflict with higher or more pressing duties. No human being, however great, can be our ultimate concern; his very greatness depends on the greatness of the cause which he serves, or the greatness of his concern. Maimonides' concern was to reconcile Judaism, the Torah, with reason, or intellect, or *theoria*. His greatness consists in the way in which he achieved this reconciliation, or if you wish, in the way in which he worked towards this reconciliation. Very simply stated, Maimonides does not admit of any shortcuts; he gives a full presentation of the magnitude, of the enormity, of the difficulties. He *faces* these difficulties; and what enables him to do so was what would formerly have been called "love of truth," and which in a more modern fashion is called "intellectual probity." It goes without saying that he had the highest competence in both fields. Yet however admirable his work, his achievement may have been, it seems to be obsolete. In a general way, his problem was the same as ours. But the specific terms of the problem

---

3. Robert A. Goldwin (1922–2010) was a student of Strauss's, who received his Ph.D. in 1963 at the University of Chicago and then taught there for several years. He served as dean at St. John's College in Annapolis, Maryland, worked for his friend Donald Rumsfeld in his capacity as U.S. ambassador to NATO, and ultimately acted as consultant to the White House during the administration of Gerald Ford. Subsequently he was for several decades a Resident Scholar at the American Enterprise Institute. His main area of scholarly study concentrated on the U.S. Constitution. For whatever reason, his name is not mentioned in the finished version of the *Guide* (1963), so it is perhaps fitting that with the appearance in print of this lecture, Strauss at last gets to properly acknowledge the role played by his friend and student Goldwin.

were for him very different than they are for us. In the first place, reason, one term, meant for him, for all practical purposes, Aristotle; and Aristotle, as you know, is obsolete; he has been replaced by modern science. And that means that on this new basis no philosophic or natural theology is possible. And as for revelation, the second term, Maimonides understood by it the Bible and the Talmud, the written and the oral Torah, understood as verbally inspired at least as far as the written Torah was concerned, and inspired to Moses. The implication: there was no development of law and doctrine. We, however, are confronted with biblical criticism, which teaches that there was an evolution of Jewish thought, an evolution even of biblical thought. According to that teaching, there is no unchangeable Jewish dogma. Maimonides, on the other hand, was *the* dogmatist of Judaism; he was the one who formulated the dogmas of Judaism, or more strictly, the "roots" of Judaism—the thirteen "roots" of Judaism.[4] And I mention two of them to indicate the difference. The first is the resurrection of the dead; the second (I mean, not in the order of Maimonides) is the belief in the Messiah. The Messiah means the descendant of David, who restores or will restore the Temple, the sacrifices, and all the other things. A very small minority of Jews today still believes in these dogmas. At that time the Jewish community was united by an all-comprehensive *law*, and by agreement regarding the roots, closed off from the peoples of the world. We on the other hand live in modern society, which is a secular society. The social bond is not Judaism nor Christianity. Judaism is *only* a religion, a denomination, something very partial. And in addition, there is no longer any agreement among Jews regarding law and doctrine.

Now let us grant for argument's sake that these profound differences justify the conclusion that Maimonides' teaching is obsolete. Nevertheless, fundamentally our problem is still the same as his. To see how we can live as *thinking* Jews, how we can reconcile reason or science with the Jewish faith, which we affirm in one way or another by the very fact that we are Jews. Granted, then, that Maimonides' "what" is obsolete; his "how," the manner in which he approached this same problem which we have to approach, could still remain a model for us. This "how" is, so to speak, entirely separable from the content of his teaching. But it finds its unambiguous expression in his style. Maimonides is most famous for the Hebrew of his great code, the *Mishneh*

---

4. For the thirteen "roots," dogmas, or principles of Judaism according to Maimonides, see further discussion in "How To Begin," chap. 11 below, n. 7.

Torah; he did not write this work in the language of transcendent sublimity of the Bible, of Deuteronomy in particular. He adopted the Hebrew of the Mishnah,[5] judiciously using, especially at the beginnings and the ends of sections, biblical quotations. He chose a postbiblical Hebrew because he knew the difference between the bringer of the divine law, and the human codifier of the divine law.[6] And we may add: the noncommissioned, the self-appointed codifier of the divine law. One may describe Maimonides' style in his code as follows: elevation suffusing legal precision, elevation culminating in legal precision; unfathomable mystery tending toward transparent order, unfathomable mystery culminating in transparent order; and therefore also, transparent order dissolving itself into unfathomable mystery, but into a mystery which is not alien to man, to the Jew, but rather the mystery of the whole, of the origin.

In trying to speak only of the "how" as distinguished from the "what," I could not help speaking of the "what." For this relation of mystery and transparent order is the substance of Maimonides' thought. Let me explain this by reference to the 114th psalm, which I will read:

> When Israel came forth out of Egypt, the House of Jacob from a people of strange language, Judah became His sanctuary, Israel His dominion. The sea saw it, and fled; the Jordan turned backward. The mountains skipped like

---

5. The title "Mishneh Torah" is borrowed from the most ancient Jewish name for the Book of Deuteronomy in the Torah, although in recent centuries the book has been known in Hebrew by the name of "Devarim." The main constituents of the "oral Torah" are the twofold Talmuds: the Babylonian Talmud, completed circa 500 C.E.; and the Jerusalem (also known as the Palestinian) Talmud, completed circa 400 C.E. Both Talmuds consist of a whole of two parts; the second part is "Gemara" (in Aramaic); these are the "Babylonian" versus "Jerusalem" components. The first part, which they both happen to share, is "Mishnah" (in Hebrew), completed circa 200 C.E. According to tradition, "Mishnah" was the work of a single man, or rather was edited by a single man, Judah ha-Nasi ("the Prince"), who dwelled in Judea or the Land of Israel. Judea or the Land of Israel had fairly recently been renamed Palestine by the victorious Roman empire ruled by Hadrian, in wake of the lost "Bar Kokhba War" of the Jews (132–35 C.E.). They had been trying (again) to free themselves of imperial domination by Rome. Judah ha-Nasi got along very well with the Roman governing authorities and was a virtual governor who ruled the remaining, still very substantial Jewish population of Judea (or Palestine). Judah ha-Nasi chose to compose his "Mishnah" in Hebrew (whether for religious or for nationalist reasons is unclear), for which it is distinctive and famous. Indeed, his Hebrew language style set a virtually "classical" standard in written Hebrew for both medieval and modern Jews, at least prior to and until the revival of modern Hebrew during the 1870s and 1880s which derived from the modern Zionist movement. See also n. 238 below.

6. Consider "Literary Character," chap. 8 above, for a key passage about Maimonides' self-consciousness: "the fundamental similarity between the prophet, [who is] the bringer of the secret teaching, and the interpreter of the secret teaching."

rams, the hills like lambs. What ails thee, O thou sea that thou fleest? Thou Jordan that thou turnest backward? The mountains that ye skip like rams, the hills like lambs? Tremble thou earth at the presence of the Lord, at the presence of the God of Jacob, Who turneth the rock into a pool of water, the flint into a fountain of water.

I can articulate the message of this psalm here only very partly. But I will speak of that part which, I believe, is closest to what Maimonides means. The psalm speaks of the transformation of the lifeless, of the dead—sea, Jordan, mountains, little hills, earth—into living beings; of the massive and rugged into the dancing and graceful; of the old into the young; of the ugly into the beautiful; of the transformation which is spontaneous, not imposed. Dormant beauty awakens. It awakens to joyous, if trembling, worship. The psalm lets us see what a miracle is, not the miracle of beauty but the miracle as beauty: it is a visible link between the visible order and the mystery hidden beneath it. The visible world is not a world of always visible beauty, nor is the order of the visible world transparent without a mysterious background. But its beauty is mostly dormant, and it awakens only when it awakens to the invisible, mysterious God, the God of Jacob.

To return to the question of Maimonides' style, I give two brief specimens, which are taken from the "Introduction" to *The Guide of the Perplexed*. I must warn you that these translations are, because they are supposed to be as literal as possible, a bit awkward. But I hope you can see through the slight awkwardness the movement of the original.

> I am the man who when the concern pressed him and his way was straitened and he could find no other device by which to teach a demonstrated truth other than by giving satisfaction to a single virtuous man while displeasing ten thousand ignoramuses—I am he who prefers to address that single man by himself, and I do not heed the blame of those many creatures. For I claim to liberate that virtuous one from that into which he has sunk, and I shall guide him in his perplexity until he becomes perfect and until he finds rest.

And at the end of the "Introduction":

> I shall begin now to mention the terms whose true meaning, as indicated in every passage according to its context, must be indicated. This, then, will be a key permitting one to enter places the gates to which were locked. And when

these gates are opened and these places are entered into, the souls will find rest therein, the eyes will be delighted, and the bodies will be eased of their toil and of their labor.

Hitherto I have taken it for granted that Maimonides' doctrine has been rendered obsolete by the emergence of modern science, modern biblical criticism, modern society, i.e., by the emergence of the modern premises. In doing so I have assumed that the modern premises are true. But are they? Only if they are questionable can we become seriously interested in Maimonides. To see that they are questionable, we must first give them the fullest benefit of the doubt. I seem to have made an unwarranted assumption by assuming that our problem is the reconciliation of Jewish faith and reason, for this statement presupposes the truth of Judaism on the one hand, and the soundness or competence of reason on the other. But these presuppositions are questioned by many of our contemporaries, of our Jewish contemporaries. The only authority which today is universally and unquestionably recognized is the authority of *science*. I am aware of the fact that the expression "the authority of science" is incongruous, but the expression cannot be avoided. That incongruity is a part of the fact, it is the core of the most fundamental fact, of modern life. The rejection of prejudice—science—has itself become a prejudice, an authority. This is not merely the unintended result of the modern development, but was from the outset the meaning of what we might well call the modern project, a project which arose with clarity in the minds of some great men of the 16th and 17th centuries. Reason was to replace authority; that is to say, no authority except that which for everyone was knowable as derivative from reason was to be recognized. Hence, a purely rational society, a purely secular society, was demanded. And this led eventually but inevitably to the conclusion that all men should be united in one society, in *the* world society,[7] through the actualization of reason in all through universal enlightenment, the city of man on the ruins of the city of God. Or as it has been called, "the universal and homogeneous state,"[8] a state in which there would be no castes or classes based on ancestry or race, but the stratification

---

7. The word occurring between "in" and "society" cannot be precisely determined. It is a reasonable surmise that this word is "world," as in "*the* world society."

8. The conception of "the universal and homogeneous state" as what will necessarily be actualized in the progress of history, indeed as the goal of History and its end, was devised by Strauss's philosophic friend Alexandre Kojève, perhaps the greatest Hegelian philosopher in the 20th century. Concerning the conception and whether it is *philosophically* sustainable or sufficient, see the powerful philosophic debate focused around the issue between Strauss and Kojève in *On Tyranny*.

strictly corresponding to function, that is to say, to qualification, to the merit of the individual. To prepare its emergence, the forces dividing men had to be weakened, and the mind [animating such forces had to be] annihilated.[9] Religion, positive religion, is divisive, whereas commerce, technology, science, reason [are] not. This much about the [modern] project.

Now let us consider the difficulties to which it has proved to be exposed. Now we Jews know these difficulties unusually well; we know them in our bones. Modern secular liberal society has abolished persecution of the Jews, and for this we are grateful to modern liberal society. But a certain inequality of the Jews, a certain "discrimination" against Jews, persists, and necessarily so.[10] For liberal society as liberal society cannot stamp out hatred of Jews or dislike of Jews, because as liberal society it must recognize the sanctity of a private sphere: everyone is free to think, to feel, to like and dislike, to choose his friends and associates as he pleases. Liberal society demands limited power of government, limited power of legal regulation. Some people, and even some Jews, sometimes get impatient with this state of things, and wish government and law to interfere more drastically with privacy. They thus unwittingly open the door to unlimited power of government, the indispensable condition for governmental actions like stamping out such things

---

9. The words in square brackets had to be added so as not to create a misunderstanding, which may not have been so forcefully suggested during speaking. As I believe Strauss wished to suggest, the forces in favor of "the universal and homogeneous state" did not aim to immediately "annihilate the mind" pure and simple, but rather they aimed to "annihilate the mind" only of those forces which animate "reactionary" actions against the achievement of "the universal and homogeneous state." It is the overturning of every type of faith-based "reasoning" which concerned the forces in favor of "the universal and homogeneous state," claiming they alone were not faith-based, being purely rational. Strauss certainly suggests that "the annihilation of the mind" may be the ultimate unpremeditated consequence of this goal as the only proper goal to be pursued by humanity. Whether even for Strauss this is something that can actually be discussed only in the past tense (as Strauss's language suggests), or is not rather still immediately relevant for the future based on current Western beliefs, is worthy of serious reflection. But in case I may be wrong about the narrower reading which I believe makes best sense in the context of the lecture, and so as to honestly consider the possibility that Strauss may have intended this phrase ("annihilate the mind") just as he expressed it even in the spontaneity of speech and thus also the broader reading that this seems to imply, one may juxtapose it with the following sentence by Strauss. In it, he makes a future projection of what will be in store for those thinkers who anticipate the "universal and homogenous state" as a blessing for humanity instead of the absolute tyranny which, as he maintains, it is sure to be: "Thanks to the conquest of nature and to the completely unabashed substitution of suspicion and terror for law, the Universal and Final Tyrant has at his disposal practically unlimited means for ferreting out, and for extinguishing, the most modest efforts in the direction of thought." See *On Tyranny*, p. 211.

10. For Strauss's detailed argument on the limits of liberalism in its ability to provide a complete solution to the "Jewish problem," and for Strauss's resistance to the use of the word "discrimination" as a morally deficient euphemism constructed in the social sciences to avoid calling hatred of Jews or dislike of Jews what they are, see respectively "Preface to *Spinoza's Critique of Religion*," and "Why We Remain Jews," in *Jewish Philosophy and the Crisis of Modernity*, pp. 143–44, 314–18.

as dislike of Jews. But how do they know that the unlimited power will be used for this purpose, that it will not be in fact tyrannical government? And tyrants are proverbially as such indifferent to considerations of decency, humanity, or right, and care only for expediency. We have a good example in the Communist policy toward Jews. The Soviet government knows that the Jews, just as the Pope, do not have many divisions, or even battalions, and is aware that the Jews are a very unpopular minority in Russia. In utter indifference to principle, it follows the primrose path of convenience by showing some respect for the Russian Orthodox Church and utter contempt for the Synagogue. It reduces the Jews to the status of hewers of wood and drawers of water. The "Jewish problem," that is to say, the problem of how to establish equality for the Jews, could be solved only in a country in which the Jews form the majority, in a Jewish state. But I choose this seemingly trite expression advisedly: only God knows why the threads of the Jewish faith are so finely woven that there cannot be a Jewish state which gathers in all Jews, and even the majority of Jews. There were once in the remote past people who thought that the Jewish problem could be solved if the Jews were to disappear through complete assimilation. They forgot that the forces which make for hatred of the Jews also make for resistance to their assimilation; and above all, that the very demand for assimilation, the demand that we deny our past, our origin, is not only an insult, but a particularly impudent insult. What kind of people do they think we are?

Now the Jewish problem may be said to be only an illustration, although perhaps the clearest illustration, of a universal phenomenon, obstructing the emergence of the universal, homogeneous state or society. For the foreseeable future, the power of the past, of divisions originating in the past, is by far stronger than that of any futuristic hope. One may say, this may change in the course of a few generations, but it may also not. We do not know and we cannot know. What we can know is whether that change would be desirable, whether it would be a change for the better. *Can* all men be united in and by reason? *Can* all men become wise and, on this basis, decent? If not, what will unite all men will be some form of unreason, which will be quite unbearable for many men, and they will be quite unfairly deprived of the right or possibility to build their society according to their form of unreason, according to their prejudice. The union of all men is not possible on the level of reason or of wisdom. The union of all men would be possible only by reducing human thought to the lowest common denominator, the satisfaction of the lowest desires, bread and circuses. The divisions which have caused so much misery have also kept men on their toes. All mental life has its roots in the things which divide men, and is at any rate connected with those things.

Maimonides has given much thought to this question. He thought that universal society, which is not a universal datum,[11] is possible only by union in the highest, knowledge of God. But such a society could come into being only by divine intervention, by the miracle of redemption. Judaism is the faith of a particular people, of the chosen people. It is essentially particularistic prior to the messianic age. Christianity and Islam claim to be, of right, all-inclusive; but in fact too they are exclusive, as is shown by their antagonism to each other as well as to Judaism. Men cannot be united by reason, for very few people are by nature able, and still fewer are willing, to cultivate their reason properly. Hence, societies can be united only by faiths, be it the true faith or untrue faith. Hence society is essentially particularistic or closed.

But can there not be a faith different from positive faith, a universal faith of which all men are by nature capable: the faith in God as love, as the basis of all men's love for one another, of universal brotherhood. This universal faith or universal religion is not Judaism or Christianity, but Judaism or Christianity "upon one leg," if I may use this expression of Hillel.[12] But above all, it is not indeed itself universal,[13] as is shown most simply by Buddhism, which does not admit or require God as love, a personal god. The universal religion in question does not rest on any *natural* religious experience, an experience

---

11. Strauss uses the plural word "data." However, it seems evident to me that the correct use for what he intends in this context has to be the singular. In order not to confuse readers for no good reason to which I am able to ascribe significance, I have accordingly changed it to express the singular.

12. Strauss refers to perhaps the most famous story told about the ancient Rabbi Hillel the Elder (circa 80 BCE–circa 10 CE). It concerns the pagan who was willing to be converted to Judaism if the good rabbi could summarize the essence of Judaism during the time he was able to stand in place "upon one leg" or "on one foot" ["*al regel aḥat*"]. The phrase has become an idiom in modern Hebrew. The statement made by Hillel in response (Shabbat 31a) is a negative formulation of the "golden rule": "What is hateful to you, do not do to your neighbor." Jesus in the New Testament offers a positive formulation (Matthew 7:12). Much energy of religious debate has been spent in polemics on the never-resolved issue of which version is the wiser or the truer. Most often ignored, although I venture to suggest that Strauss may have had this "supplement" in mind, are the two sentences uttered by Hillel which immediately follow the famous statement: "The rest is commentary. Now go and study." See Joseph Telushkin, *Hillel: If Not Now, When?* (New York: Nextbook, 2010), pp. 18–23; Nahum N. Glatzer, *Hillel the Elder: The Emergence of Classical Judaism* (Washington: B'nai B'rith Hillel, 1956), pp. 74–75; Judah Goldin, "Hillel the Elder," *Journal of Religion* 26, no. 4 (1946): 263–77, and especially pp. 273–74.

13. The two words between "not" and "universal" cannot be precisely determined. It is a reasonable surmise that these words are "indeed itself." However, as is also quite possible, this phrase might be "in itself." The ambiguity occurs because Strauss may have merely hesitated and repeated himself, in which case the "in" repeated might sound as if he is saying "indeed."

equally accessible to all men. For a religious experience, which is equally accessible to all men, is literally speechless, inarticulate. It needs articulation, interpretation. Whereas the experience in itself, the experience of the presence or the call, is self-evident, every interpretation of the experience is in need of argument.[14] That argument may be either rational—then it leads to rational or natural theology, with which Maimonides was concerned, and which as such is not fit for all men, but only for an elite—[or], if it is to become effective for the large majority, it needs transrational arguments, and the transrational arguments are necessarily divisive. The universal society as a society fit for human beings is impossible because of the recalcitrance of men to reason. But it is impossible not only because of the weakness of men. It is impossible also because of the weakness of reason, at least as that which reason has come to mean. According to the view which prevails today, the highest perfection of reason is modern science; and modern science cannot validate any value judgments. Science can teach us which means are conducive to which ends, but it is utterly incompetent to discriminate between good and bad, noble and base ends. Before the tribunal of human reason, the case for universal society is as strong or as weak as the case for preliterate cannibalism. Science can do no more than to establish causal relations, or to predict, but it cannot account for *the* premise of all quest for causal relations, or for prediction, namely, the principle of causality itself. The principle has here the status of a mere assumption. There is no evident necessity that the world will not disappear through nothing into nothing, or that it has not come into being out of nothing through nothing.

However this may be, science as science presupposes that the world is essentially intelligent, or that being is rational. *Modern* science regards itself as essentially progressive; it can never be completed; its process is essentially infinite. This, however, means that the object of modern science, the world, will always remain a mystery, that being is radically elusive or mysterious. This mystery, tacitly admitted by science as essentially progressive, makes science itself radically mysterious.[15] Science cannot answer the question,

---

14. For Strauss's argument that religious experience, once it is humanly processed and communicated, is always in need of interpretation, see "Preface to *Spinoza's Critique of Religion*," in *Jewish Philosophy and the Crisis of Modernity*, pp. 149–50. At the point at which it becomes articulated in terms of a language or interpreted in terms of a tradition, this experience ceases to be universal and instead becomes unavoidably particular.

15. For Strauss on modern science as it culminates in being as a mystery, see his subsequent Hillel lecture, "Why We Remain Jews" (1962), in *Jewish Philosophy and the Crisis of Modernity*, pp. 328–29.

Why science? Is science good? Science rests then ultimately on a nonevident, mysterious choice. Only by virtue of this choice could science come into being. The fundamental phenomenon is not science or any object of science, but an abysmal freedom—one may say, not reason, but will. The victory of modern science over the science of Aristotle which Maimonides to some extent accepted, culminates in the self-destruction of that victorious science as an attempt . . .

[*A break in the tape apparently occurred.*][16]

. . . and is also a matter of faith. Now for philosophy it is fatal if its very basis proves to be faith and not self-evident. Hence by proving that the teaching of faith of the Torah is possible, one proves in effect that the alternative, the teaching of philosophy taken as a whole, is impossible, and thus that the teaching of the Torah is not only possibly true, but simply true. Maimonides alludes to this by saying that while he does not possess a demonstration of the creation [of the world] out of nothing, someone else may have such a demonstration.[17] Still this does not mean more than that we may know *that*

Several themes mentioned in passing by Strauss in this earlier lecture, such as the treatment of the Jews by the Soviet Union, are also dealt with in the later lecture.

16. As a result of the break in the tape which apparently occurred, a portion of the lecture material is undoubtedly missing. It is not known from anything in the tape precisely how much material this may be. However, it is obvious that he has made a major transition to a direct focus on Maimonides' *Guide*.

17. In *Guide* 2.13, pp. 281–82, Maimonides refers to creation as "one of the [three] opinions"—to be sure, it is "the opinion of all who believe in the Law of Moses our Master." In 2.16, pp. 293–94, he maintains that creation is an opinion which is "not impossible"; insofar as the eternity of the world has also not been demonstrated, this makes the problem of the origin or permanence of the world an "open question." In 2.23, pp. 321–22, once he has traced the substantial flaws in Aristotelian celestial physics or natural science, and in Ptolemaic astronomy (2.17–22, 24), he rejects the notion of a demonstration for eternity being available; as he even suggests, this is absent "in nature," or somehow in principle, due to the nature of things or the limits of human perception. This is the case, he admits, even if he has had to support his case for creation by the use of "the rhetorical mode of speech," since he shows that Aristotle did the same thing for eternity. He also significantly refers to the conflict between Aristotelian celestial physics or natural science and Ptolemaic astronomy as "the true perplexity," which for the moment prevents human beings from knowing the truth about the origin of the universe (2.24). In 1.74 (pp. 215–22), he presents one by one the supposed *kalam* (dialectical theology) proofs for creation, which he reduces to "seven methods"; in this very process of distinguishing and presenting their "methods" of argument, he elucidates that (and how) not a single one of those proofs is valid in any logical sense or of worth in any scientific sense. However, in 2.24 (p. 327), he refuses to close the door on the possibility of someone in the future discovering a valid demonstration of either creation or eternity, based on adequate knowledge of the movements of the heavens; it is to this comment that Strauss seems to allude. ("It is possible that someone else may find a demonstration by means of which the true reality of what is obscure for me will become clear to him.") As Strauss seems to suggest, if "it is possible" for "someone else" to discover a demonstration which might settle once and for all the great debate about creation versus eternity, this very possibility that "what is obscure [to him] . . . will become clear [to someone else]" shows an astonishing open-mindedness toward what is (or appears to be) *the* fundamental issue. In 2.25 (pp. 327–28), Maimonides says it was in his power to offer a figurative reading of Genesis 1, so as to prove it teaches eternity; he makes this comment merely in order to clarify that he did not reject eternity because of "a text figuring in the Torah," i.e., on the basis

the world was created out of nothing, it does not mean that we can know *why* it was created.

I illustrate this by a parallel. According to Maimonides, the laws given by the Torah are perfectly rational,[18] but this does not mean that God had to give these laws. He could have created men who would do by nature and unvaryingly the right things, and not through obedience to laws, which they can transgress. We do not know why God preferred the one alternative to the other. The ultimate reason is that we do not know and cannot know why God created man or anything else. Since God is the most perfect Being, the highest and complete Good, creation does not increase goodness. God as the good God is under no obligation to create man and the world because this would increase goodness.[19] Creation is an absolutely free or gratuitous act, and absolutely mysterious.[20]

The coherent expression of this view is Maimonides' doctrine of the divine attributes. The eleven chapters devoted to the doctrine are probably that part of the *Guide* which in the nineteenth and twentieth centuries is most famous.[21] According to that doctrine, God is absolutely one, absolutely simple; strictly speaking, He does not possess *any* attributes. Hence we cannot speak

---

of mere authority grounded in Scripture. Precisely this admission by Maimonides, proffered in a spirit of intellectual honesty, is seized on by Spinoza as perfectly exemplary of the fact that Maimonides refused to follow the "proper" notion of literal reading of the Torah (as opposed to the allegory of the philosophers, in which they supposedly ground their unwarranted claim to authority), which he elaborates in his book: see *Theologico-Political Treatise*, trans. Yaffe, chap. 7, pp. 97–100. References to the *Guide* in the notes of the present chapter will be to the *Guide*, trans. Pines.

18. See *Guide* 3.31, pp. 523–24.

19. Strauss starts to say "create," but halts quickly in the middle of saying the word and corrects it to "increase."

20. With regard to the question which Strauss has Maimonides ask, Why did God not "put the accomplishment of the commandments and the nontransgression of the prohibitions into our nature?" see *Guide* 2.25, p. 329. Cf. also "How To Begin," chap. 11 below. The proper answer parallels the mere fact of creation: His will wanted it or His wisdom required it. But it is also dealt with in 3.32, pp. 528–29, which contains the discussion of the deity's "wily graciousness" and "gracious ruses." For the "cunning" or "stratagems" of God in both nature and history, see also Shlomo Pines, "Translator's Introduction," in *Guide*, pp. lxxii–lxxiv.

21. See *Guide* 1.50–60, pp. 111–47. Perhaps still the most impressive 19th-century scholarly statement of this view was presented by David Kaufmann, *Geschichte der Attributenlehre in der jüdischen Religionsphilosophie des Mittelalters von Saadja bis Maimûni* (Gotha: F. A. Perthes, 1877; reprint, Hildesheim: Georg Olms, 1982). It has been much elaborated and deepened in the 20th century by Harry A. Wolfson, who maintained that in the doctrine of attributes is contained the high point of Maimonides' originality as a thinker: see especially Wolfson, *Studies in History*, vol. 2, "The Aristotelian Predicables and Maimonides' Division of Attributes," "Maimonides on Negative Attributes," and "Maimonides and Gersonides on Divine Attributes as Ambiguous Terms." See also "How To Begin," chap. 11 below. In terms of 20th-century Jewish philosophers, Hermann Cohen claimed to discern in the doctrine of attributes the cornerstone of Maimonides' teaching, which "most decisively" makes him "a classic of rationalism in the monotheistic tradition": see *Religion of Reason out of the Sources of Judaism*, trans. Simon Kaplan (Atlanta: Scholars Press, 1995), pp. 39, 61–64, 94–95. See also n. 79 below.

of God, all speech presupposing the distinction, the difference between subject and predicate. God is simply beyond speech, beyond *logos*, pure mystery. But we could not pray, for example, if we did not speak about God or ascribe attributes to God. But these attributes, according to Maimonides, are only homonyms with the *corresponding* attributes we ascribe to man: wise, willing, just, merciful, etc. We cannot help speaking of God as knowing and of God as willing; insofar as something is intelligent, we trace it to God's wisdom; insofar as it is not intelligent, but merely factual, merely given, we trace it to God's will. Strictly understood, God's intellect and God's will are identical. But it is slightly less misleading to trace the world as a whole to God's unfathomable will than to His inscrutable knowledge.

This doctrine of attributes is set forth in the *Guide* on the basis of the *assumption* that God is one or absolutely simple. The proof of the assumption is given later on in the book. That proof, however, is identical with the proof that the world has been created out of nothing. Creation by God as the most perfect being presupposes that God is absolutely mysterious, beyond *logos*, absolutely simple.[22] In other words, philosophy as the attempt to replace opinion about the whole by knowledge of the whole presupposes that the whole is intelligible. But the whole is not intelligible. Only a small part of the whole, the earth and the earthly beings, can be understood by man.[23] Yet the earth and earthly beings are conditioned by the nonearthly, and the nonearthly can only very imperfectly be understood by man. Philosophy or science is then decisively insufficient; philosophy must be supplemented, completed, or crowned by revelation, and revelation is necessarily a particular revelation, the Torah, and revelation to chosen human beings. The[24] choice, while related to Abraham's meritorious faith, cannot be explained by that faith. The content of the revelation is necessarily mysterious, but not ir-

---

22. See *Guide* 1.50, pp. 111–12.

23. Cf. *Guide* 2.19, pp. 306–7; 22, pp. 319–20; 24, pp. 326–27. Perhaps the most clear and distinct statement which Maimonides makes, vis-à-vis man's *certain* knowledge being limited to "earthly" things, is contained in the following passage of the *Guide*: "Everything that Aristotle has said about all that exists from beneath the sphere of the moon to the center of the earth is indubitably correct, and no one will deviate from it unless he does not understand it or unless he has preconceived opinions that he wishes to defend or that lead him to a denial of the thing that is manifest. On the other hand, everything that Aristotle expounds with regard to the sphere of the moon and that which is above it is, except for certain things, something analogous to guessing and conjecturing. All the more does this apply to what he says about the order of the intellects and to some of the opinions regarding the divine that he believes."

24. The word "the" is a reasonable surmise. However, the word is not entirely distinguishable; it is fully possible that this might just as well also be "that."

rational. If the letter of the Bible is against reason, we are under an obligation to explain the passage as a figure of speech.[25] The *Guide* is then opposed to both the philosophers and the literalists. Also it makes use of philosophy, but this use is not more than the recovery of our own. All wisdom of the Greeks ultimately stems from the Torah.[26]

    25. See, e.g., *Guide* 2.25, p. 328.
    26. See *Guide* 1.Intro., p. 16; 71, pp. 175–76; and 2.11, p. 276. As it is only accurate to acknowledge, in none of these passages is Maimonides actually laying claim to the common medieval legend (often traced to Philo Judaeus of Alexandria) of the ancient Jewish origins of the philosophy and science of the classical Greeks, who according to the legend were taught what they knew by Moses or by subsequent Jews. Instead, Maimonides merely speaks of an autonomously generated philosophic and scientific wisdom known and cultivated in ancient Israel, which was lost among the Jews due to the centuries of their being oppressed in exile. (Cf. Pines, "Translator's Introduction," in *Guide*, p. cxx.) Avraham Melamed, in his recently issued book, *Rakaḥot ve-Tabaḥot: ha-Mitos 'al Mekor ha-Ḥokhmot* (*The Myth of the Jewish Origins of Science and Philosophy*) [in Hebrew] (Haifa: Haifa University Press; Jerusalem: Magnes Press, 2010), traces the "myth" to Artapanus, a 3rd- to 2nd-century-BCE Jewish scholar in Alexandria, who wrote the lost apologetic work "On the Jews," fragments of which are preserved in two Church Fathers: in Eusebius's *Praeparatio Evangelica* and in Clement of Alexandria's *Stromata*. He was himself building on the Hellenistic Greek fascination with the ancient wisdom of the East, which embraced the Jewish sages in Jerusalem or Judea. Borrowing the motif from pagan Greeks, Jewish authors like Artapanus proceeded to make it their own, and (as Melamed puts it) "the rest is history." Thus, Philo and Josephus, who rehearsed the point, based themselves on an already well-established tradition. As for Maimonides, he held what Melamed calls a "weak" version of the myth, especially as compared with Yehuda Halevi's "strong" version, which achieved much greater popularity. My thanks to Professor Melamed for offering me a condensed summary of the results fully and properly elaborated in his book. See also Norman Roth, "The Theft of Philosophy by the Greeks from the Jews," in *Classical Folia* 33, no. 1 (1978): pp. 53–67. For Halevi, see *Kuzari* 1.63, but especially 2.66. Contrast with Strauss's comment in a letter to Jacob Klein, of 20 January 1938: he thinks Maimonides knew that this was a myth, and unconditionally rejected it in his own mind, as hints conveyed by Maimonides seemed to show him. See Strauss, *Hobbes Politische Wissenschaft und zugehörige Schriften—Briefe*, vol. 3 of *Gesammelte Schriften*, p. 545. With respect to drawing far-reaching conclusions about Strauss's thought derived from the correspondence, it is to be noted that—besides its being a comment made in a private letter sent to a specific friend at a certain moment in Strauss's life, and not designed as a completed public statement—this comment and those like it in the letters to Klein were made only at the very beginning of Strauss's discovering hidden depths in Maimonides' books, and of his knowing how to deal with and absorb his great discovery in general. How much he would have been willing in later days to publicly stand by these earlier statements made in his private letters cannot be known. (If it were the case that he was not willing subsequently to patently declare his views even in letters to friends, this is not proof of his merely getting better at the concealment of his views, or of his greater reticence as a matter of principle; he may well have merely changed his mind on some of these issues, as his thought advanced and deepened!) Such an unanswerable question should at least be grounds for a certain reticence in the drawing of far-reaching conclusions from the letters, although it has so far not been much of a deterrent to some scholars. Much has recently been written which shows the wish to see the later public statements of Strauss the thinker and scholar (i.e., his essays, lectures, and books) in light of, and as merely reflecting, these earlier experimental postulations and investigative hypotheses played with in private, as if they were purely revelatory of his hidden mind, which henceforth never again changed or reached greater subtlety and depth. This is not even to broach the matter of whether it is so simple to offer a definitive interpretation of the meaning of those epistolary expressions, for it cannot be assumed that they contain an unambiguous content evident in themselves, since he often writes to his friend in the mode of irony and high playfulness, never mind their being abbreviated epistolary thoughts. With regard to the fact that "the Torah antedates philosophy, or Greek wisdom, by centuries," Strauss mentions this fact as bearing consequences for how Maimonides has to be read: see "Maimonides' Statement on Political Science,"

This may suffice as a very rough sketch of the surface of the *Guide*. To prepare a somewhat better understanding of Maimonides' work, let us have a somewhat closer look at Maimonides' discussion of the biblical commandments. Prior to him, the view seems to have prevailed that these commandments are partly rational, say, the prohibition against murder, and partly merely positive, say, the prohibition against eating meat and milk together. But the merely positive commandments are nonetheless of high dignity, if not of higher dignity than the rational ones. Moreover, the examination of the grounds of the commandments was discouraged, not to say forbidden. This view agrees perfectly with Maimonides' tendency to find the ground of everything ultimately in God's unfathomable will.[27] But, very surprising, Maimonides attempts to lay bare the grounds of *all* commandments, the rational as well as the nonrational ones; he claims that he has virtually explained *all* biblical commandments; he refers to the warning against explaining the commandments, but he disregards that warning by deed.[28] He explains these commandments, which at first glance are wholly unintelligible, for example, the details of the sacrificial legislation, as measures taken to combat idolatry, and therewith as not necessary in themselves, but only negative, and therewith, given the disappearance of idolatry proper, as useless now.[29] Nor is this all. His assertion that he has explained virtually all biblical commandments, is matched by the assertion that he has not explained more than a few of the

---

chap. 9 above; see also "Literary Character," chap. 8 above. Maimonides himself stresses the originality of Abraham as an autonomous thinker of profundity who utilized fundamental philosophic principles, who as it were "discovered" the one God by proceeding from rational grounds and from empirical evidence, and who began to teach others the truth about God and the error of idolatry, much prior to the Greeks. See *Guide* 3.29, pp. 514-18, and "Hilkhot Avodah Zarah" 1.1-4. Of course, Alfarabi too recognized the fact that "philosophy" preceded the Greeks; he traced this to the "Chaldeans," i.e., the people from whom Abraham emerged. As he puts it: "It is said that this science [i.e., philosophy as the highest wisdom] existed anciently among the Chaldeans, who are the people of al-Iraq, subsequently reaching the people of Egypt." See Alfarabi, "The Attainment of Happiness," in *Plato and Aristotle*, trans. Mahdi, section 53, pp. 42-43. And even Aristotle, in his account of philosophical theology, acknowledges "the ancients" (as also "the opinion of our forefathers," and "the first thinkers") as the source of true rational knowledge of God, albeit "bequeathed to posterity in the form of a myth." In ancient myth the essential truth about the divine may be perceived, although (similar to the history provided by Maimonides) as with "every art and every philosophy," reaching "a stage of development" as far as was there possible and then perishing due to extraneous causes. Their doctrines about the divine, preserved in myths and so "saved like relics," are capable of showing those who know how to read them how much profundity of thought was contained in them. See Aristotle, *Metaphysics*, trans. Hippocrates G. Apostle (Bloomington: Indiana University Press, 1966), bk. 12 (Lambda), chap. 8, 1074b1-14, pp. 208-9.

27. Consider, e.g., *Guide* 3.24, pp. 500-501.
28. See *Guide* 3.26, pp. 506-10; and 31, pp. 523-24; cf. also 3.49, p. 612.
29. See *Guide* 3.29, pp. 514-22; and 32, pp. 525-31.

biblical commandments. He very conspicuously contradicts himself regarding a matter of the greatest importance.³⁰ What does this mean?

Before I begin to answer this question, I must cast a glance at the common understanding of Maimonides. There is a long history of interpretation of Maimonides; that history began in his lifetime and continued in an unbroken tradition until the end of the eighteenth century. In the nineteenth century, historical understanding took over; a break in the continuity occurred. Students of Maimonides in the nineteenth century were men brought up in modern Western philosophy, i.e., in a philosophy of Christian origin. Furthermore, it was thought that the modern historian has a better understanding of Maimonides' background than Maimonides himself. For instance, the modern historians all could read Aristotle in Greek, and Maimonides had access to Aristotle only in Arabic translation, not to say only in Arabic commentaries on the Arabic translation of Aristotle. The modern historians saw that Maimonides' Aristotle was not the true Aristotle, but a mixture of Aristotle and neo-Platonism; a part of Plotinus' *Enneads* had been accepted in this period as the *Theology of Aristotle*.³¹

A more adequate understanding of Maimonides may be said to have started when people began to take seriously what Maimonides said himself

---

30. Cf., e.g., *Guide* 3.26, pp. 507, 509; 3.28, p. 513; 3.29, p. 518; 3.31, pp. 523-24; and 3.49, p. 613 versus 3.26, p. 510; 3.35, p. 538; 3.45, p. 578; and 3.49, p. 612. Perhaps Maimonides' boldest statement of his ability to account for the reasons concealed beneath *every single* commandment occurs in 3.28, p. 513: "However, you will hear my explanation for all of them [i.e., the commandments] and my exposition of the correct and demonstrated causes for all of them." Perhaps the most blatant admission by Maimonides that he is unable to account for at the very least one of the 613 commandments is in 3.45, p. 578: "As for the table and the bread that was always upon it, I do not know the reason for this and I have not found up to now something to which I might ascribe this practice." Cf. 3.46, p. 591: "As for the offering of wine, I am up to now perplexed with regard to it. . . . [But] someone else gave the following reason . . ." He also says (3.26, p. 578): "so that only very few commandments will remain whose cause has not been clear to me up to now." This is to be contrasted, of course, with the ultimately impenetrable reasons for specific details, such as why offer a lamb rather than a ram, or why sacrifice a definite number of animals. According to Maimonides' repeated iterations, such matters are necessarily arbitrary or chance, as elucidated most clearly in 3.26, p. 509: "This resembles the nature of the possible, for it is certain that one of the possibilities will come to pass." Indeed, "those who imagine that a cause may be found for suchlike things are as far from the truth as those who imagine that the generalities of a commandment are not designed with a view to some real utility." Previously he notes: "In my opinion, all those who occupy themselves with finding causes for something of these particulars are stricken with a prolonged madness."

31. See Plotinus, *The Enneads*, trans. A. H. Armstrong, 7 vols. (Cambridge, MA: Harvard University Press, 1966-88); trans. Stephen MacKenna, 4th edition revised by B. S. Page (London: Faber, 1969); *The Theology of Aristotle*, English translation by Geoffrey Lewis, in vol. 2 of *Plotini Opera*, ed. and trans. Paul Henry and Hans-Rudolf Schwyzer, 3 vols. (Paris: Desclée de Brouwer, 1951-73); Peter Adamson, *The Arabic Plotinus: A Philosophical Study of the "Theology of Aristotle"* (London: Duckworth, 2002). Maimonides treated critically books ascribed to Aristotle and certainly did not accept them merely because the ascription was allegedly venerable or seemingly ancient. Cf. *Guide* 3.29, pp. 520-21, with 1.31, p. 67.

about his background. Maimonides regarded as the highest philosophic authority after Aristotle, Farabi, Abu Nasr al-Farabi.[32] One of Farabi's most important writings is devoted to *the* two philosophies, that is to say, the philosophy of Plato and the philosophy of Aristotle.[33] There is not the slightest trace of neo-Platonism in his presentation of Plato on the one hand, and of Aristotle on the other. More particularly, Farabi puts an emphasis, wholly alien to the Christian Middle Ages, on Plato's political work; he understands Plato's whole philosophy as political philosophy.[34] He even uses Plato's political philosophy for understanding Islam, the revealed law of Islam. This lets us see that Plato's doctrine of the philosopher-king supplies the basis for Maimonides' doctrine of revelation or prophecy;[35] it then lets us see some other things of importance connected with this.

It compels us to make an entirely new beginning, which is in fact identical with Maimonides' own beginning. That beginning consists in not taking philosophy for granted, as all the historians of the nineteenth century have done; that beginning consists in not presupposing philosophy, i.e., the legitimacy of philosophy. Philosophy must be understood as in need of justifying[36] itself before a higher or a prephilosophic tribunal. That tribunal is the Torah, or [is] constituted by the Torah. In a word, the beginning of any understanding of Maimonides' work is to realize that the *Guide* is not a philosophic book; it is a Jewish book, written by a Jew for Jews.[37] The *Guide* is based on the old Jewish premise that to be a Jew and to be a philosopher is mutually exclusive. In the talmudic accounts of conversations between rabbis and the philosopher, the philosopher is as a matter of course a pagan. Accordingly in the

32. See Maimonides' letter to Samuel ibn Tibbon, his contemporary and the virtually authorized Hebrew translator of the *Guide: Igrot ha-Rambam*, ed. Shailat, II, pp. 511–24; Alexander Marx, "Texts by and about Maimonides," *Jewish Quarterly Review*, N.S., 25 (1935): 374–81; *Letters*, trans. Stitskin, pp. 130–36. See also "Some Remarks on the Political Science of Maimonides and Farabi," chap. 5 above. Cf. "Farabi's *Plato*," in *Louis Ginzberg Jubilee Volume*, ed. Saul Lieberman et al. (New York: American Academy for Jewish Research, 1945), pp. 357–58. Maimonides speaks of Farabi (in his letter to Ibn Tibbon) only in superlative terms, with nary a hint of criticism: "I tell you: as for works on logic, one should only study the writings of Abu Nasr al-Farabi. All his writings are faultlessly excellent. For he is a great man." The most relevant passages of Strauss's article "Farabi's *Plato*" as it bears on Maimonides may be read in "Editor's Preface" above, n. 4.

33. See Alfarabi, *Plato and Aristotle*, trans. Mahdi.

34. See "Some Remarks on the Political Science of Maimonides and Farabi," chap. 5 above. Cf. Strauss, "Farabi's *Plato*," pp. 372–77.

35. See "Maimonides' Doctrine of Prophecy," chap. 4 above.

36. Strauss's actual words are "to justify"; in accord with proper grammar, it has been changed to "of justifying."

37. See "Spinoza's Critique of Maimonides," chap. 2 above; "Literary Character," chap. 5 above; "Maimonides' Statement on Political Science," chap. 9 above; "How To Begin," chap. 11 below.

Guide, the philosophers are always distinguished from the Jews, and sometimes opposed to them. Philosophers are men who try to give an account of the whole by starting from what is accessible to men as men. Maimonides, however, starts from accepting the Torah; the *Guide* is explicitly devoted to the science of the Torah.[38] The three books of Maimonides are all of them Jewish books. Almost all his other writings are Jewish writings.[39] Nor would it be correct to call his books theological; "theology" is not a Jewish term. The Jewish tradition distinguishes between "*halakha*," the law, and "*agada*," which I may circumscribe as follows: musings or meditations on the Torah, which do not lead up to legal decisions. The *Guide* continues the Jewish tradition of *agada*.[40]

Some centuries before Maimonides the Gaon Saadia had introduced into Judaism the Islamic art of *kalam*, which is the defense of the roots of the law, or the demonstration of the roots of the law.[41] The *Guide* can also be described as a defense of the roots of the Torah. But Maimonides' thematic declarations at the beginning of the work induce us to prefer the former characterization. We must then begin from this simple and obvious point: the *Guide* is devoted to the true science of the Torah, of the Law. Its primary subjects are biblical terms and biblical similes; all those terms and those similes have a literal or

38. See *Guide* 1.Intro., p. 5.

39. By "the three books of Maimonides," Strauss seems to think of his three big books: *Commentary on the Mishnah, Mishneh Torah*, and *The Guide of the Perplexed*. (Besides his correspondence, and his medical works, Strauss seems to neglect to consider or to count Maimonides' *Book of the Commandments/ Sefer ha-Mitzvot*, which enumerates the 613 commandments of the Torah in their proper order. However, perhaps this is because he judged that it is not a "book" in the same sense?) As he adds: "Almost all his other writings [besides the three big books] are Jewish writings." With regard to the reason for the "almost," cf. the remark in "Note on Maimonides' *Treatise on the Art of Logic*," chap. 13 below. He begins the "Note" by commenting on the fact that this "is not a Jewish book," which at least seems to imply that this is perhaps the *only* such book. See also "Maimonides' Statement on Political Science," chap. 9 above.

40. See "Literary Character," chap. 8 above.

41. Saadia ben Yosef al-Fayyumi (882–942) was originally an Egyptian Jew, the first to become the head (*Gaon*, a formal title suggesting a scholarly luminary, but literally "majesty" or "pride") of one of the great Babylonian academies of Jewish learning, specifically the academy (*yeshiva*) in Sura. (It was in the country known, since the Arab conquest, as "Iraq," but still called by the Jews "Bavel," i.e., "Babylon" or "Babylonia.") He was a sort of polymath and genius, and besides his legal, grammatical, polemical, translational, poetical, and scientific works, he wrote in Arabic (*Kitab al-Amamat wa-al-Itiqadat*) what is conventionally known as the *Book of Beliefs and Opinions* (according to its Hebrew translated title, *Sefer Emunot ve-Deot*), i.e., the first work of systematic *kalam* by a (Rabbinite) Jewish thinker, in the style of the Mutazilite school. Maimonides may not have thought very highly of *kalam*, but he did think highly of Saadia, at least as a leader and legalist. At one point in the "Epistle to Yemen," Rambam says about him (in its Hebrew version): "If not for our master Saadia Gaon, Torah would have been forgotten in Israel." Or as Joel Kraemer translates from the original Judeo-Arabic the even tougher-minded statement: "the religion of God ... might have vanished if not for him," i.e., if not for "our master Saadia." See Maimonides, "Epistle to Yemen," trans. Kraemer, p. 119.

external meaning, and an inner or hidden meaning. The latter is the most important meaning, and in important cases, the only true meaning. The inner meaning is as such a secret meaning. The primary subject of the *Guide* is therefore "the secrets of the Torah," which is a traditional expression.[42] The most important of these secrets are the *ma'aseh bereshit* and *ma'aseh merkavah*. *Ma'aseh bereshit* is the story or the work of the beginning, i.e., the account of creation. And *ma'aseh merkavah* [is] the work or the account of the divine chariot, i.e., the vision of Ezekiel, Ezekiel chapters 1 and 10 especially. Being devoted to the interpretation of the biblical terms and biblical similes, the *Guide* is an exegetic work.[43]

Now according to the legal injunction, the secrets of the Torah are[44] to be taught only secretly. Maimonides abides by that injunction. The *Guide* is therefore devoted to the secret interpretation of the secret teaching of the Bible. Now what does this mean? The Hebrew expression for "the secrets of the Torah," *siterei torah*,[45] means also, because of a certain ambiguity of the Hebrew term, "the contradictions of the Torah."[46] To teach secretly means to teach through contradictions, through the conscious use of contradictions, and it is easy to understand how.[47] If you teach that A is B, and that A is non-B, you keep your teaching secret. [*Audience laughter.*] (But it is no laughing thing, I think.)[48] The mysteriousness of God and His creation is

42. The traditional formula is "*siterei torah*," i.e., the secrets, but also the mysterious contradictions, of the Torah. See "Literary Character," chap. 8 above. See also nn. 45, 46, and 48 below.

43. *Guide* 1.Intro., pp. 5–9. See "How To Begin," chap. 11 below. The term which Strauss renders as "similes" (i.e., "biblical similes"), is translated by Pines as "parables" (i.e., "biblical parables"). Note, for whatever it might signify, that Strauss continues to use this term ("similes") even in his "Introductory Essay" to the *Guide* as appears with Pines's translation, i.e., "How To Begin," chap. 11 below. See also n. 62 below. As should of course also be noted, the two passages from Maimonides' "Introduction" to the *Guide*, which Strauss reads toward the beginning of the lecture, are also his own rendering, and differ slightly from the version in the Pines translation: see *Guide*, pp. 16–17 and 20.

44. The word "are" is the most reasonable surmise. However, it is not clearly audible; hence, it is not impossible that this might also be "ought."

45. For purposes of clarity, and due to a certain awkwardness in the way Strauss spoke these two phrases, the order of the Hebrew phrase (*siterei torah*) and the English phrase ("the secrets of the Torah") have been reversed from the way in which Strauss uttered them. See also nn. 42 above and 46 and 48 below.

46. See "Literary Character," chap. 8 above. See also nn. 42 and 45 above, and n. 48 below.

47. See "Literary Character," chap. 8 above.

48. The audience seems to laugh because of the way in which Strauss states it: as he at least suggests, those who simultaneously teach *both* A is B *and* A is non-B do so not because they want to keep their teaching secret, but rather because they do not know what they are doing, and necessarily keep their teaching "secret" from themselves as well. But Maimonides definitely knew of the type that provoked this audience laughter: he refers to it as the sixth cause of contradictions in books. Cf. *Guide* 1.Intro., p. 18. The author of books containing such contradictions in them (whether due to lack of sufficient attention or due to forgetfulness) "should not be reckoned among those whose speeches deserve consideration."

expressed in this revelation, and hence reflected in any interpretation of that revelation. To teach secretly, we can also say, means to observe the economy of the truth. To practice thrift, only chapter headings of the secret teachings are to be transmitted.[49] Furthermore, even these chapter headings are transmitted by Maimonides only in a very irregular way, interspersed with other subjects. The chapter headings of the secret teaching are "scattered." How can one discover the secret teaching? Answer: through the observation of the contradictions, because ultimately Maimonides must have preferred either A is B or A is non-B. And further, as Maimonides emphasizes very strongly in a passage from his "Introduction," every word of the *Guide* is chosen with *exceeding* care.[50] By reading the *Guide* with *exceeding* care, one can discover its secret teaching.

But the *Guide* contains also a public teaching, for example, the incorporeality of God. This teaching is demonstrated, and therefore openly presented. The *Guide* is then not only an exegetic work, it is also a work of speculation. The relation between the exegetic element and the speculative element in the *Guide* is not immediately clear. But one can say that the exegetic element is predominant.

A few conclusions from these remarks. Since every word is chosen in the *Guide* with *exceeding* care, we can assume that the order of the work is also not simply haphazard.[51] We can assume that the *Guide* possesses a secret order. More precisely, its public teaching is likely to possess a manifest order, and its secret teaching to possess a secret order. The order of the *Guide* as a whole would then be a combination of manifest and secret order. And as a matter of fact, the plan of the *Guide* is partly clear and partly obscure. The work is divided into three parts, and each part is divided into chapters. But there is no uniformly clear division of the work into sections, i.e., groups

---

Strauss speaks to the same point, but draws a slightly different result from it, with regard to keeping a teaching secret, in "How To Begin," chap. 11 below.

49. In the lecture as the tape recording preserves it, Strauss suddenly shifts to the plural, i.e., "secret teaching*s*." It is difficult to know whether this is entirely deliberate, or merely a function of the spontaneity of speech. In most cases, he uses the singular word, "teaching." In this case, I have chosen *not* to change the plural to the singular (unlike the text referred to in n. 65 below), since he makes no audible effort to correct himself by repeating the singular of the phrase, so as to make it conform to that which precedes and follows. But the reader should know that it is uncertain to the editor precisely which form Strauss intends to express (plural or singular). See also n. 65 below.

50. *Guide* 1.Intro., p. 15: "For the diction of this Treatise has not been chosen at haphazard, but with great exactness and exceeding precision, and with care to avoid failing to explain any obscure point." It is to be noted that Strauss has already read this passage to his hearers at the beginning of the lecture. See also n. 206 below.

51. Ibid.

of chapters. The plan is obscure in the beginning, that is to say, in that part which is to the highest degree exegetic and to the least degree speculative, and it becomes clearer as one approaches the end.[52]

Now the problem to which I would like to turn next time, and which I must prepare by a brief remark now, is (because it is the clue to the understanding of the work): what is the order, the plan of that work which at first glance does not have a clear plan of the whole at all? To discover the principle underlying the plan of the *Guide*, I must take a step back. The *Guide* consists, I said, of a public teaching and a secret teaching; the public teaching is addressed to every Jew, the secret teaching is addressed to the elite. I conclude that to the extent to which the *Guide* is a whole, a unity, it is not addressed to every Jew nor to the elite. That the *Guide* is not addressed to every Jew is very simply shown by the fact that it is written in Arabic. The book is a bilingual work, abounding with Hebrew and Aramaic quotations, but basically written in Arabic, and not all Jews could read Arabic. Who then is its addressee? Maimonides answers this question at the beginning of the book, at the beginning of the "Introduction," as well as in the "Epistle Dedicatory." He is a religious and virtuous Jew who has studied philosophy, with the effect that he is perplexed by the contradictions between the Torah and philosophy. This contradiction will be resolved at least partly by the distinction between the external or literal meaning and the inner or hidden meaning of the Torah. More generally, [it will be resolved] by the understanding of the secret teaching of the Torah. As a secret teaching, it ought to be an oral teaching, according to the traditional Jewish demand. But for urgent reasons, Maimonides had to disregard the prohibition against setting down the secret teaching in writing. He chose a middle course between impossible obedience and flagrant transgression.[53] He set forth the secret teaching in private letters to a young friend, Yosef. Yosef is a primary addressee and, as we will find out, the typical addressee of the *Guide*.

Now what kind of man is he? In the "Epistle Dedicatory,"[54] addressed to Yosef, Maimonides describes the virtues of Joseph and indicates his limitations.[55] Joseph had a passionate love for speculation, and a wonderfully

---

52. See "How To Begin," chap. 11 above. Strauss's is the first attempt ever made to decipher and to map the plan of the *Guide*. His thoughts on the matter, insofar as they represent a genuine discovery, are not based on any known predecessor, medieval commentator, modern scholar, or "tradition."
53. See "Literary Character," chap. 8 above.
54. See *Guide*, "Epistle Dedicatory," pp. 3–4.
55. Strauss shifts in the same sentence from the Hebrew to the English version of the first name of the main addressee of the *Guide*: Yosef versus Joseph. Whatever Strauss may have meant by this shift, it is

quick grasp, but he was somewhat impatient. Maimonides was compelled to recommend that he[56] proceed in an orderly, methodical fashion. He was passionately interested in divine science, but while he had studied astronomy and the other mathematical sciences as well as logic, it does not appear that he had studied natural science. In fact, from the ninety-first chapter of the *Guide* we learn that while Joseph knew Aristotle's *Topics*, he did not know the *Physics* and the *De Caelo* [*On the Heavens*].[57] Now according to the proper order,

---

imperative for the reader of the lecture to know that he is referring to the same person (or rather, character) in Maimonides' book, its formal addressee.

56. Strauss's actual words are "recommend him to"; in accord with better English grammar, it has been changed to "recommend that he."

57. Strictly speaking at least in terms of numbered chapters, there is no "ninety-first chapter of the *Guide*": part 1 contains 76 chapters, part 2 contains 48 chapters, and part 3 contains 54 chapters (which makes for a total of 178 chapters in the *Guide*). But loosely speaking, if one starts to count from the very beginning (while disregarding the "Epistle Dedicatory" and the two introductions, i.e., to part 1, and to part 2), then the ninety-first chapter of the *Guide* will be 2.15, pp. 289–93. In support of this result is a similar comment that Strauss makes in "How To Begin." Cf. chap. 11 below: "From the ninety-first chapter (2.15), it appears that while he knows Aristotle's *Topics* and Farabi's commentary on that work, he does not know the *Physics* and *On the Heaven* (cf. 2.8)." In favor of disregarding the "Epistle Dedicatory" and the three introductions in the counting of the chapters, see "Maimonides' Statement on Political Science," chap. 9 above. As an additional matter, serious doubts have been raised as to whether the system of assigning numbers to the chapters in the *Guide* is Maimonides' own, but is not rather his Hebrew translator Samuel ibn Tibbon's: see Raphael Jospe, "'The Garden of Eden': On the Chapter Divisions and Literary Structure of the *Guide of the Perplexed*," in *Jewish Philosophy: Foundations and Extensions*, vol. 2, *On Philosophers and Their Thought* (Lanham, MD: University Press of America, 2008), pp. 65–78. The numbering of the chapters in the standard Judeo-Arabic (ed. Munk and Joel) and Hebrew versions (Ibn Tibbon, Kafah, and Schwarz) amounts to a total of 178 chapters, following the traditional numbering. However, Jospe notes that this is different for Abraham Abulafia, as well as for Joseph ibn Kaspi and Isaac Abravanel, who reach instead a total of 177 chapters, if for apparently divergent reasons. It issues in a very different numerological (or even mystical) result, i.e., *gan 'eden* or the mystical "Garden of Eden." For Abulafia, see Moshe Idel, "Maimonides' *Guide of the Perplexed* and the Kabbalah," *Jewish History* 18, no. 2–3 (2004): 197–226, and especially p. 214. In any case, if this is the chapter to which Strauss refers as the ninety-first, then Maimonides never actually states in 2.15 that Joseph "did not know the *Physics* and the *De Caelo* [*On the Heavens*]"; it is a surmise of Strauss's about a hint provided by Maimonides. How did he uncover it or reach his surmise? First things first: the three specific books of Aristotle—*Physics*, *On the Heavens* (or *De Caelo*), and the *Topics*—are discussed (or at least touched on) in this chapter, which is itself a rare occurrence of Aristotle passages concentrated in a single chapter of the book; indeed, I believe it is the only such case. But beyond that, the basis for Strauss's uncovering of the hint seems to have been that in this chapter Maimonides quotes from both the *Physics* and *On the Heavens* (or *De Caelo*), but in both cases he did not do so quite precisely. (This is not to mention that Maimonides also draws on a passage from the *Topics*, although in the words of Pines, it is only "by and large accurate." See *Guide*, p. 292, n. 12.) Maimonides also did not indicate that this was not precisely how Aristotle expressed himself; he seems to assume that his student Joseph (or the typical addressee like him) will not notice his divergence, although he is supposed to do so, or at least to check all of Maimonides' sources and references, accepting nothing on trust or authority, since his highest point is to teach Joseph to know and to think for himself. This, Strauss seems to suggest, is a hint, pointing careful readers toward something about the books cited, as texts to verify for the purpose at hand, and simultaneously as reflections on Joseph. But prior to reaching such firm results, it must be asked whether Strauss is actually referring to chapter 2.15? To support this numerical designation of 2.15 as "the ninety-first chapter of the *Guide*" (and it seems that this is a hint of Strauss's own, for him to have emphasized it as such, whatever its significance was for him), is the fact that it is the only chapter of the *Guide* in which these three works of Aristotle are discussed together, even if it

lacks any apparent statement of Joseph's general ignorance of those two specific books by Aristotle. The reader will have to judge for himself both why Strauss was disposed not just to refer to 2.15, but also to highlight "the ninety-first chapter of the *Guide*"; and he will also have to judge whether it is to 2.15 that Strauss actually refers, although as noted this seems most likely to have been the one to which he was pointing. However, the reader may want to consider another perplexity, to which the present editor is unable to conjecture any resolution, related to his phrase "the ninety-first chapter of the *Guide*." It might prompt the reader to begin to speculate on thoughts hinted at by Strauss himself about Maimonides' literary purposes, as evident in the arrangement, if not the numbering, of the chapters. Strauss's pointing to "the ninety-first chapter of the *Guide*" may bear a greater significance than at first appears to be the case if the counting is done differently. For if one also counts the three introductions to the three separate parts of the *Guide* as "chapters," but refrains from adding the "Epistle Dedicatory" to the total as not a separate "chapter," since as a sort of "cover letter" it precedes the book proper, then there are a total of 181 chapters in the book (77 + 49 + 55 = 181), rather than the most obvious total of 178 (76 + 48 + 54 = 178) previously calculated. This leads to the fact—in the spirit of Strauss's emphasis on Maimonides' numerology as a mode of concealment in the *Guide*—that the ninety-first chapter is *the* central or middle chapter of the entire book, once the total reached is 181 (i.e., by counting the introductions as chapters even if not numbered as such), with the added "advantage" of being an odd number. However, with such a result, "the ninety-first chapter of the *Guide*" is no longer 2.15, but is instead 2.13. This is the chapter that happens to deal with the three opinions on creation, which might make for a pertinent, but still obscure, hint. However, such a method of counting the chapters in the *Guide* has the definite disadvantage of nullifying the previous point, i.e., regarding 2.15 as the ninety-first chapter inasmuch as it may say something significant about what Joseph did not know with regard to Aristotle's *Physics* and *On the Heavens* (or *De Caelo*). Perhaps one might suggest that some things about this subject (i.e., knowledge of Aristotle's physics in its connection with his astronomy) are discussed in 2.13: the *Physics* (or *Akroasis*) is at least mentioned in general by name; and a specific passage is also referred to (on p. 283). However, *On the Heavens* (or *De Caelo*) is certainly not the object of any explicit discussion, although it might perhaps be construed to have been implicitly mentioned by hints: cf. pp. 281–82, for a "notion . . . not belonging to the purpose pursued"; and p. 284, for whether the heavens are susceptible of being generated and corrupted (or whether they can come to be and pass away). Consequently, these remain obscure points in the argument of Strauss's lecture, which he chose not to clarify, but at best to hint at. (This of course assumes that he was aware of some careful listeners and knowledgeable students of the *Guide* being in his audience, or of some listeners who he assumed would make careful notes, or of this lecture being taped as would eventually lead to its being transcribed—in which three cases he could hope for someone to catch the gist of his hint and to embark on a search for its bearing.) Thus, in the end one cannot achieve absolute certainty of why Strauss makes a highlighted point of referring just to "the ninety-first chapter of the *Guide*": whether, on the one hand, it is perhaps to suggest *the* central or middle chapter of the book (*if* the total is 181 chapters), which however turns the focus to 2.13; or whether, on the other hand, it is—as still seems to me most likely—a reference to 2.15, insofar as it might be construed to allude very obliquely to a specific deficiency of knowledge in Joseph as representing "the typical addressee" with regard to Aristotle, physics, and astronomy. How to reconcile these two possibilities, which still seem somehow connected, is not known to the present editor. As should also be noted, Aryeh Tepper, in his *Theories of Progress in Leo Strauss's Later Writings on Maimonides* (Albany: State University of New York Press, forthcoming [2013]), attains a very different and very pertinent result with regard to the center of the *Guide* (based precisely on what Strauss himself writes), and what is purposefully contained in it. Focusing on "How To Begin," he notes that Strauss ends his detailed introductory essay with a discussion of *Guide* 2.24, and he naturally wonders why. As is undoubtedly significant, this chapter deals with what Maimonides himself refers to as "the true perplexity," i.e., a philosophic-scientific perplexity on which an adequate demonstration for the existence of God depends. According to Tepper, it is also highly significant that this is the chapter with which Strauss chooses to conclude his "Introductory Essay" to studying the *Guide*. To be sure, it is to be counted as the center of the *Guide* only if one disregards the number of chapters in the book as a totality, and instead deems the middle chapter (irrespective of the subsequent chapter numbering) of the middle part as deliberately put in the center, i.e., the 24th chapter of the 48 chapters in part 2, surrounded by 24 chapters on each side; this assumes as self-evident only that the introduction to part 2 is to be counted as a separate chapter, which consequently allows it to be used to determine both the completed order and the middle-

natural science precedes the divine science.[58] The fact that the addressee of the *Guide* is a man lacking competence in natural science is *the* root of the lack of order, or rather of the apparent disorder, of the work. Since the divine science needs a preparation or basis, Maimonides needs a substitute for natural science as a demonstrative science, and he finds that substitute in the traditional Jewish beliefs, ultimately in biblical texts correctly interpreted. The preparation for the divine science in the *Guide* is primarily not speculation, but exegesis.

Now we would naturally raise this question: Why did Maimonides choose in the first place such an addressee? What is the virtue of *not* being sufficiently trained in natural science?[59] That is surely the very first question we will have to take up next time.

[*The lecture ends on the tape with loud and prolonged audience applause.*]

Joseph Cropsey, Chairman: I've been asked to make some announcements. The first is that the second lecture on Maimonides by Dr. Strauss will be next week, on Sunday, February 14th at the same hour, here [in Hillel House]. On Tuesday, February 9th at 8:00 p.m. there will be a discussion of Herman Wouk's book, *This Is My God*, by Rabbi H. G. Perlmutter and Rabbi S. Rabinowitz. On Friday, February 12th, at 8:30 p.m., the program will be: "An Evening of Isaac Loeb Peretz," by Herbert Lamm, associate professor of philosophy in the Department of Philosophy here at the university. Sabbath services will be at 7:45 p.m. on Friday. I believe that the custom is at this time to interrupt the proceedings with a brief refreshment of coffee and accessories. And after that, if I'm not mistaken, Dr. Strauss has consented to answer questions or comment on the remarks of anybody who wants to engage his attention. So there will be a brief recess.

[*The tape ends. The discussion period of part 1 of the lecture seems not to have survived, or perhaps it was never taped. If notes were made by any audience member of the discussion period of part 1 and if they survive, they are not known to the present editor. A transcription of the discussion period of part 2 of the lecture follows the lecture proper.*]

---

most chapter. In support of counting only the numbered chapters, see "How To Begin," chap. 11 below, in which he refers to "the 169th chapter," which is 3.45; at least from this it would follow that the total number of chapters is 178, and hence the ninety-first chapter would (again) have to be 2.15. Cf. also his reference to "the one hundred and two chapters of the Second and Third Parts."

58. *Guide* 1.33, pp. 70–72. See also "How To Begin," chap. 11 below.
59. See "How To Begin," chap. 11 below.

PART 2

... You remember perhaps the end of the "Introduction" [to the *Guide*], which I read to you, where Maimonides says: once one enters these gates, the eyes will be delighted indeed, for the tree of knowledge is a delight to the eyes.[60]

I repeat the main points which I made last time, trying to clarify one point which has been left very unclear. The *Guide*, I said, is a Jewish book, a book written by a Jew for Jews, not a philosophic book. It is devoted to the true science of the Torah, that is to say, to the explanation of the secrets of the Torah,[61] and therefore in particular to biblical terms and biblical similes.[62] These secrets of the Bible are to be interpreted in a secret manner. From this point of view the *Guide* is an exegetic work. But the *Guide* contains also a public teaching, a teaching in which Maimonides demonstrates or defends the roots of the Torah. From this point of view, the *Guide* is a speculative work.

The question was raised in the discussion whether these are mutually exclusive, speculation and exegesis.[63] I think they are, because speculation as

---

60. *Guide* 1.Intro., p. 20. Compare and contrast with "How To Begin," chap. 11 below. With regard to "How To Begin," one must carefully consider the significance of several anomalies occurring in Strauss's use of this passage that have been noted by Marvin Fox:

> Strauss begins his discussion by quoting the last sentence of Maimonides' own Introduction to the *Guide* and ends his essay with the same quotation. But the two versions are not identical. In the second version the order of the last two clauses is reversed, and a phrase is omitted. The first version is an accurate translation of the original; the second is not. Moreover, neither is absolutely identical with the reading in Pines' translation. . . . Are these careless errors, or do they contain clues planted deliberately to test readers and lead them to the inner secrets of Strauss's interpretation?

See *Interpreting Maimonides: Studies in Methodology, Metaphysics, and Moral Philosophy* (Chicago: University of Chicago Press, 1990), p. 57. Cf. also "How To Begin," chap. 11 below, p. 495, for what else may be called "a delight to the eyes."

61. The four sentences at the beginning of part 2 of the lecture are derived solely from the Motzkin tapes, which contain a very slightly different version of the same lecture. Other than this rare case, the Motzkin version is the same as the University of Chicago remastered version that has served as the basis on which most of the lecture, parts 1 and 2, has been transcribed.

62. See n. 43 above for "similes" versus "parables." It represents Strauss's own slight divergence from the Pines translation, or rather, it is his own translation which is not in full accord with what Pines thought the best translation of the term.

63. Strauss begins the sentence with "Speculation," but quickly corrects himself. Because no tape or transcription survives of the discussion period that occurred in the first lecture, it is unknown how Strauss originally answered this question, or even precisely what the original questioner might have asked. In the spontaneity of speech, Strauss actually said: "this is mutually exclusive"; it seems to me that it is grammatically better if these two terms which might exclude one another are not treated as if they were a single thing which includes both; hence, the grammar has been corrected. Similarly, Strauss actually said: "speculative or exegesis." But it seems to me that this is a spontaneously uttered discrepancy, and not a deliberate (or

meant here is in no way based on biblical texts. Either it is a philosophic truth of certain realities, or it is a defense by argument of the teaching of the Torah against the teaching of the philosophers. Or else it is an argument starting from the concept of a divine law and raising the question: What are the conditions of a divine law (of course: God, revelation, and so on)? And these roots are then established by inference from the notion of a divine law, without any necessary reference to texts.

Now from the fact that the *Guide* combines a secret teaching and a public teaching, it follows that the plan of the *Guide* cannot be clear, because insofar as it transmits a secret teaching, it must present that in a *scattered* manner. The "chapter headings," as Maimonides puts it using a traditional Hebrew phrase,[64] the "chapter headings" of the secret teaching[65] are "scattered." But as a public teaching, it has a clear plan. So by combining these two elements, the secret and the public, the *Guide* must have a plan which is not clear, which is more or less obscure.

There is one way in which one might think one could solve the problem

---

rather, a significant) one. Thus, this has been corrected; the editor has made them two nouns that are to be equivalently compared, rather than an adjective and a noun. These changes have been made to the transcribed lecture by the editor in the wake of judgments based on listening to the tape from which the lecture was transcribed, and do not reflect any written text of Strauss's in which they are so designated. However, so readers may judge for themselves, the unedited transcribed version of the sentence at issue is as follows: "The question was raised in the discussion whether this is mutually exclusive, speculative and exegesis."

64. With regard to the "traditional Hebrew phrase," the "chapter headings" [*ra'shei peraqim*] originally referred to the names of the weekly liturgical readings from the Torah elaborated in the tradition and thus not provided by the Torah itself, which in Maimonides' view offered significant hints about concealed truths of great profundity. They are uniformly based on a word or a phrase occurring in the first sentence of the weekly liturgical Torah readings (i.e., sing.: *parasha*; pl.: *parshiyyot*). Tradition, and especially post-Maimonidean tradition, considered these "chapter headings" to contain in themselves concealed depths of the Torah, hints pointing to hidden secrets. Cf. also "Literary Character," chap. 8 above. For Maimonides' discussion of the ancient Jewish tradition of "scattering" truths in books, which he praises for its wisdom and which he chooses to imitate, see *Guide* 1.Intro., pp. 6–8, 15, 17–19. He also speaks about truths "entangled" with other matters; it is not evident whether his main purpose is to clarify these truths, or to obscure them from view for the unsuited and unprepared. For a similar method of "scattering" also followed by Plato as well as "the [ancient] philosophers and learned men of various communities," see Maimonides' comments in *Guide* 1.17, pp. 42–43, and 1.33, pp. 70–71. Compare with "Literary Character," chap. 8 above; and "How To Begin," chap. 11 above.

65. In the lecture as preserved on the tape recording, Strauss utters the plural of the phrase, i.e., "secret teachings"; however, almost immediately he corrects himself and repeats the word in the singular: "teaching." Thus, in the present case this is apparently not a deliberate shift to the use of the plural, but merely a function of misspeaking in the spontaneity of speech. Of course, it is difficult to assert in a completely confident sense that this is the use of Strauss in every case, i.e., the singular of "teaching." I have made it singular in the present case since it conforms to his own seeming correction, as well as with what is done by him in most cases that precede and follow. However, the reader should know that it is not possible to know for certain whether Strauss intended to express this in every case. See also n. 49 above.

of the relation between the speculative [element] and the exegetic element of the *Guide* very simply. The highest secrets,[66] according to the traditional Jewish teaching accepted by Maimonides, are *ma'aseh bereshit*, the work of the beginning,[67] the story of creation, and the other is *ma'aseh merkavah*, the work or the story of the divine chariot, [in] Ezekiel 1 and 10. Now Maimonides says, *ma'aseh bereshit* is identical with natural science, and *ma'aseh merkavah* is identical with the divine science.[68] Now if this were so, [then] it would follow that natural science and divine science are of course *sciences*, which as such can be publicly transmitted (it would seem), and that [these sciences] are[69] speculative. What is secret and exegetic is the *relation* between natural science and the story of creation, and the *relation* of divine science to the story of the divine chariot. That [i.e., the relation between science and biblical text] would be exegetic and secret, and this [i.e., the status of natural science (also *ma'aseh bereshit*) and of divine science (also *ma'aseh merkavah*) as sciences] would be speculative and public.

But there is one obvious difficulty there, because if [the] account of creation—these equations, I think, are Maimonides' [own equations], they are not traditional—because now if this is so, if *ma'aseh bereshit* (account of creation) is natural science, [then] natural science does not deal with creation proper. Nor does the story of the chariot deal with it, as you could see immediately when reading chapters 1 and 10 of Ezekiel, where there is no possible basis for a teaching of creation. In other words, *the* problem, the central problem of the book—creation of the world versus eternity of the world—would be evaded if these equations were the last word of Maimonides. Therefore, we [shall] forget about it and leave it as an open problem for the time being.

66. Based on the sounds accompanying the lecture, Strauss seems to have turned around in order to write the two terms on a chalkboard for the benefit of his listeners; hence he was turning away from the recording device, which caused his speech to be muffled. Strauss starts "Maimonides is . . ." but halts himself, and apparently turned toward the chalkboard. As a result, the phrase he spoke while turning away, "and I have to write these words here," is barely audible on the tape recording. Hence it is only tentative.

67. On the tape Strauss first says "of" (as he normally translates the phrase), but very quickly he changes his speech by saying "at": "the work of . . . at the beginning." Is he supplementing in some sense, or is he correcting himself? He may merely have wished to add the nuance that this is an account of things at the beginning, or it is a text at the beginning of the Torah. In any case, it is difficult to know with how much intention this slightly changed expression is uttered, or whether it is an error that occurred in the spontaneity of speech. I leave it as is in the first form with which he says it, because it is his normal choice; but I cannot be certain that this is preferred.

68. See *Guide* 1.Intro., pp. 6-7. Cf. also *Mishneh Torah*, *Sefer ha-Madda*, "Hilkhot Yesodei ha-Torah," chaps. 1-4. For specific references, "Laws of the Basic Principles of the Torah," trans. Hyamson, p. 36b, chap. II, paras. 11-12, and pp. 39b-40a, chap. IV, paras. 10-13; "Book of Knowledge," trans. Lerner, pp. 146-47, chap. 2, paras. 11-12, and pp. 152-53, chap. 4, paras. 10-13.

69. In his actual speech, he uses the singular "is"; but since he clearly seems to be referring to two sciences, which are both of a speculative nature, it has been changed to "are."

In order to understand the unity of the exegetic and the speculative elements, in order to understand the unity of the *Guide*, I propose that we start from the unity presented by the addressee of the book. The book as a whole is addressed to a single individual *and his like*:[70] here we have a unity. And let us try to start from that unity represented by the addressee. The main point I made at the end of last week's discussion, or [rather] lecture, [is that] the addressee is characterized by the fact—[and this the] most important characteristic—that he is not competent in natural science. So that I concluded last time with a question: Why did Maimonides choose such an addressee of the *Guide*? What is the virtue of *not* being sufficiently trained in natural science? Now we learn from the seventeenth chapter of [part 1 of] the *Guide*[71] that natural science was treated as a secret teaching already by the pagan philosophers, "upon whom the charge of corruption could not be laid if they had exposed natural science clearly." All the more are we, the community of the adherents of the Law, obliged to treat natural science as a secret science.[72]

This remark has a certain external basis in the fact that Aristotle's *Physics* was known as the "*Akroasis*" in Greek, with the corresponding Arabic and Hebrew terms [known] to Maimonides. Now "*akroasis*" means "a thing listened to," and therefore a lecture paradoxically, because "lecture" is really "something to read"; but in the original, lectures should not be read, as I do it, but should be simply spoken. So "*akroasis*" is a thing listened to; and in pre-Aristotelian usage, in the so-called Pythagorean tradition, an "*akroamatic*" teaching was a teaching designed for *hearing only*, i.e., an esoteric teaching. And[73] only Aristotle's *Physics*, and no other work of Aristotle's, was called in the Middle Ages, the "*akroasis*," the oral teaching simply.

70. See *Guide*, "Epistle Dedicatory," p. 4.
71. See *Guide* 1.17, pp. 42–43. Cf. especially "How To Begin," chap. 11 below.
72. See "How To Begin," chap. 11 below. The following paragraph from "How To Begin," chap. 11 below, closely resembles the words used in the lecture. Compare Strauss's version with how the same passage of the *Guide* is translated by Shlomo Pines:

> Now as even those upon whom the charge of corruption would not be laid in the event of clear exposition used terms figuratively and resorted to teaching in similes, how much all the more is it incumbent upon us, the community of those adhering to Law, not to state explicitly a matter that is either remote from the understanding of the multitude or the truth of which as it appears to the imagination of these people is different from what is intended by us.

Thus, the second sentence (as opposed to the first) is a paraphrase of the passage in the *Guide*, rather than the precise words of Maimonides himself.

73. Strauss hesitantly begins the sentence with the word "natural," immediately following "And," but he seems to withdraw the word and continue on a different note. It is not impossible that in this sentence perhaps Strauss meant to say: "And naturally only Aristotle's *Physics*, and no other work of Aristotle's, was called in the Middle Ages, the '*Akroasis*,' the oral teaching simply." But it seems to me likelier that Strauss did not deliberately speak this word, but rather had as his intent to express the title of Aristotle's *Physics*,

The reason why natural science is dangerous is not that it contributes to undermining the Law. Only fools believe that, says Maimonides,[74] and his whole life, as well as the life of his successors,[75] refutes this suspicion. But natural science affects the understanding of the *meaning* of the Law, of the grounds on which it is to be obeyed, and of the weight which is to be attached to its different parts. Think only of one really obvious thing: the Torah speaks all the time of God "speaking" to Moses. The simple, commonsensical observation—that speaking proper presupposes vocal organs and so on—belongs, technically developed of course, to natural science. And this means that one has to understand God's "speaking" in a figurative manner, which has certain consequences. In a word, natural science has to be treated as a secret because it upsets habits. Hence, Maimonides has to begin with subjects, the understanding of which does not upset habits, or at least does this to the smallest possible degree. He himself tells us what habit is in particular need of being changed. He reports the opinion of an ancient philosopher on the obstacles to speculation, and then he adds a remark that there exists now an obstacle which the ancient philosopher had not mentioned because it did not exist in his society, namely, the habit of relying on revered *texts*, i.e., on their literal meaning.[76]

---

perhaps as his "natural science." Thus, it seems to me that he withdrew this word immediately following his uttering of it because neither is *"Akroasis"* "natural" as the title of Aristotle's book nor is *Natural Science* the proper title of his book. As an aside, it is evident to me from careful and repeated hearings of the tapes that Strauss improvised, even while he mostly read, this lecture; he did not stick rigidly to his written text. This, it seems to me, is just such a word improvised in passing that he immediately recognized as wrong and withdrew just as quickly.

74. See *Guide* 1.33, p. 71. This passage in the lecture closely resembles the passage in "How To Begin," chap. 11 below, that runs as follows: "The reason why natural science is dangerous and is kept secret 'with all kinds of artifices' is not that it undermines the Law—only the ignorant believe that (1.33), and Maimonides' whole life as well as the life of his successors refutes this suspicion."

75. Strauss did actually say: "the life of his successors." I have resisted the temptation to correct this to "the lives of his successors" inasmuch as that would have been grammatically better or stylistically preferable, i.e., since his successors did not have a single "life." However, speaking against this correction is that Strauss uses the precise phrase, "the life of his successors," in "How To Begin": see chap. 11 below (cf. also previous note), which he had the chance to revise and correct himself and seems to have decided not to do so. Insofar as he chose this form and it was not merely a slip of the pen, was his aim perhaps to suggest that the "successors" of Maimonides, however individual, form a sort of single collective tradition (or "life"), descending from him? Strauss did not specify by name any "successors" of Maimonides which he may have had in mind. At least one received article-length treatment by him, which is reprinted in the present book: see "Abravanel's Philosophic Tendency," chap. 15 below. In the middle of part 2 of the lecture, he will also refer to Joseph Albo. Thus, in the course of these essays and lectures Strauss refers to such assorted "successors" of Maimonides as Ibn Tibbon, Gersonides, al-Ḥarizi, Efodi, Ibn Kaspi, Narboni, Falaquera, Albo, Ibn Zarza, Asher Crescas, and Abravanel. In spite of this great diversity, they might be said to form a unity in proof of the thesis that the study of natural science did not destroy their adherence to the Law.

76. These sentences closely resemble the passage in "How To Begin," chap. 11 below, which deals with a novel or "modern" obstacle to speculation, not mentioned by an "ancient philosopher." See *Guide* 1.31, pp. 66–67. The "ancient philosopher" about whom Maimonides speaks in the aforementioned

This is the reason why Maimonides had to open his work with exegesis, with the interpretation of biblical terms and biblical similes, but more particularly of biblical terms, for terms are the elements of similes. He cures this vicious habit of superstitiously adhering to the literal meaning of texts, by making use of another *habit* of his pupil. The pupil was accustomed not only to rely on the literal meaning of biblical texts, but also to understand such texts according to traditional interpretations, which differed from the literal meaning. Just one example: "an eye for an eye" means, according to the traditional interpretation, not what it literally means, but only the monetary value of an eye for an eye. Now being accustomed to listen to authoritative interpretations of the biblical texts, the reader will listen to Maimonides' interpretation as an *authoritative* interpretation.

But we must not forget here that we have three types of addressees: the typical addressee, and the two kinds of atypical addressees. First the vulgar, meaning: the wholly unlearned people. And regarding the vulgar, I can only repeat Maimonides himself: there is no reason for mentioning them here in this place.[77] Now the other one is the man trained in all fields, and especially natural science.[78] The latter will of course not accept Maimonides' hidden authority. He will examine Maimonides' interpretation in the light of the principles stated by Maimonides himself, that we cannot establish the mean-

---

chapter referred to by Strauss is Alexander of Aphrodisias (3rd century C.E.), the philosophic thinker and commentator in the Aristotelian tradition whom Maimonides regarded as most excellent (besides Aristotle and Farabi). Maimonides' "personal point of view and his conception of Aristotelianism were decisively influenced by Alexander. Moreover it would seem that he was aware of this fact." See Shlomo Pines, "Translator's Introduction," in *Guide*, pp. lxiv–lxxv. Alexander's three theses about the (natural?) obstacles to speculation Maimonides has to supplement with a fourth thesis about the (historical?) obstacle related to the present era, which is as Strauss characterizes it: a blockage to speculation based on undue reverence for texts, which is based as Maimonides puts it on "people being habituated to . . . texts" which it has been made "an established usage to think highly of and to regard as true." As Strauss stresses, it is "the habit of relying on . . . their literal meaning" which is the chief difficulty produced by such reverence for texts.

77. See *Guide* 1.Intro., pp. 7–8; cf. also 1.31, p. 66. Strauss's actual speech says: "mentioning of them"; but the grammar has been corrected by doing away with the "of" as superfluous. Maimonides puts it as follows: "They are the vulgar among the people. There is then no occasion to mention them here in this Treatise," i.e., the *Guide*. He claims he is not interested in explaining anything—at least in this book—in a way that will be graspable by or satisfying to the vulgar. However, he knows that members of this class of human beings may get hold of his book, and so he never forgets about them completely, which is a fundamental element of the reasons why he wrote the book as he did.

78. Strauss shifts quickly from plural to singular forms, apparently on a spontaneous basis: in the first sentence, it is "the *men*" (who "*are*" trained); in the next and following sentences, it is "he." It has been decided to change the first sentence (concerning the nonvulgar, atypical addressee) to singular "man," so as to make the related sentences consistent and so as not to confuse readers about their direct relatedness. To justify the seemingly unconditional favoring or praise of singular, excellent individuals ("the single virtuous man") in Maimonides, which Strauss might seem to imitate, see *Guide* 1.Intro., pp. 16–17; and for the same, the first passage read by Strauss toward the beginning of part 1 of the lecture.

ing of biblical terms if we do not consider the *contexts* in which the terms occur, or that while grammar is not a sufficient condition, it surely is a necessary condition of interpretation. These requirements are completely disregarded by Maimonides in the first, say, fifty chapters of his book.[79] The critical student of the *Guide* will also notice contradictions occurring in the *Guide* and [he will] ponder over them.

Now to return to the typical reader of the *Guide*, the opening of the work is determined by the right answer to the question: which subject is least upsetting and at the same time of the greatest importance? That subject will in its turn determine which biblical terms will be discussed first, and in which order they will be discussed. Now the first subject of the *Guide* is God's "incorporeality." The first biblical terms discussed are those which seem to suggest that God is a corporeal Being. Why is incorporeality both the safest and the most important subject? According to Maimonides, incorporeality is the third of the three most fundamental truths, the preceding ones being the existence of God, and His unity. Now when I am going to speak of incorporeality in the following, I mean always the incorporeality of God.

Now the existence of God and the unity of God were universally admitted by all Jews. We can say, all Jews *know* that God exists and that He is one, through the biblical narratives they know them,[80] but as regards God's incorporeality there existed a certain confusion. When Maimonides declared in his legal work that he who denies incorporeality denies a fundamental principle of the Torah, he was attacked by one of the most famous teachers of the law at that time, Rabbi Abraham ben David from Posquières, who said: "Greater and better men than he accepted the corporeality of God."[81] Now incorpore-

---

79. If Strauss did not pick an arbitrary number ("say, fifty"), then there may be special significance in the fact that Strauss highlights part 1, chapter 50: it brings to an end the densely lexicographic first forty-nine chapters of the book; but this also begins the consideration of the famous "negative theology" (or "doctrine of attributes"). Its supposedly supreme status in Maimonides' thought, at least according to some of the most distinguished modern Maimonidean scholars, has already been commented on by Strauss, who clearly regards it as a deficient view: see n. 21 above, and the text to which it relates, as well as *Guide* 1.50–60, pp. 111–47; see also "How To Begin," chap. 11 below. With regard to two of Maimonides' principles of reading (i.e., context and grammar), in which Strauss locates the key to the atypical addressee, see *Guide* 2.29, pp. 336–37, as well as "How To Begin," chap. 11 below.
80. Strauss actually says, "he knows them"; but since the prior subject to which he refers is the plural "all Jews," so the subsequent passage has been changed to "they know them." The object addressed in the plural "them" is of course the existence *and* the unity of God.
81. *Mishneh Torah*, *Sefer ha-Madda*, "Hilkhot Teshuvah" 3.7, with the gloss on it of Rabbi Abraham ben David (Rabad), in the standard printed version. Cf. Isadore Twersky, *Rabad of Posquières: A Twelfth-Century Talmudist* (Cambridge, MA: Harvard University Press, 1962; rev. ed.: Philadelphia: Jewish Publication Society of America, 1980), pp. 282–86. For a much sharper comment by Maimonides (which is

ality, however, is according to Maimonides not only demonstrably true, [but] it is also the necessary consequence of unity.[82] The belief in God's unity is therefore endangered if it is not followed up by the belief in incorporeality. Furthermore, the belief in corporeality is one of the major reasons for the conflict between [the] Bible and philosophy. Furthermore [again], to teach the incorporeality [of God] was not a shocking deviation from the traditional teaching, to say the least. Above all, the gravest of all things is idolatry, the worship of images. This evil can be eradicated only if it is believed that God has no visible shape whatever, that God is incorporeal. Maimonides goes so far as to say that the original sin (if I may use now this un-Jewish expression), the basic sin, is not idolatry, but belief in corporeality. These are then the reasons why the first theme of the *Guide* is the biblical terms apparently implying that God is corporeal, such terms as "the hand of God," "the arm of God," and so on.

Now it is necessary that we should understand as clearly as possible the situation in which Maimonides and his addressee find themselves at the beginning. Maimonides *knows* that God is incorporeal, he knows this by demonstration, and the demonstration is based on physics, natural science. The addressee who has not studied physics properly does not *know* that God is incorporeal, nor does he learn yet from Maimonides a demonstration; that is given much later. He accepts God's incorporeality on Maimonides' authority. Both Maimonides and the addressee *know* that the Torah is true, but that its true meaning is not always its literal meaning. Only Maimonides *knows* that the corporealistic passages cannot be literally true, but must be taken as figurative. The addressee does not *know*, and *cannot know*, that Maimonides' figurative interpretation of these expressions is true. After all, Maimonides does not advance *any* argument based on grammar. The addressee accepts,

---

quite shocking, at least according to its surface meaning) in a completely nonlegal context on belief in divine corporeality as not just equivalent to, but rather as much worse than, idolatry (although it was not the direct target of Abraham ben David's barb), see *Guide* 1.36, pp. 84–85. Further along in this lecture, Strauss with rather greater gentleness will make the comment that for Maimonides, "corporealism ... [is] a hidden premise of idolatry": see the twenty-fifth paragraph of part 2. However, consider "How To Begin," chap. 11 below, for perhaps his most sophisticated reflection on this theme: he contends that while God's unity and incorporeality are "dictates of reason" for Maimonides, the same thing is not true for the rejection of idolatry; "the true ground of the rejection of 'forbidden worship' [i.e., idolatry, or the worship of God in images] is the belief in creation out of nothing." Or as Strauss restates his view on the logic concealed beneath the obscure beginning of the *Guide*: "it conceals the difference in cognitive status between the belief in God's unity and incorporeality on the one hand and the belief in creation on the other; it is in accordance with the opinion of the *kalam*."

82. See *Guide* 1.1, p. 21; 35, p. 81; 57, p. 132.

then, or is expected to accept, Maimonides' interpretation just as he is in the habit of accepting,[83] say, the Aramaic translation of the Torah as a correct translation or interpretation.[84] Maimonides, in other words, enters the rank of the traditional authorities: he simply tells the addressee what to believe. Maimonides introduces reason in the guise of authority.[85] We can even say, for a moment, [that] he usurps an authority. He *dictates* to the addressee to believe in incorporeality because—as he *dictates* to him, contrary to the appearance[86]—the Torah does not teach corporeality.

Now one of the biblical terms designating idols or images is *ẓelem*, "image."[87] In the most conspicuous passage the Torah says, God created man "in His *ẓelem*," "in His image."[88] This passage seems to imply that just as man has a visible shape, God has a visible shape, and even the visible shape of a human being. This gives rise to or supports the vulgar view according to which God looks like a large human being, but lacks flesh and blood, and hence is not in need of food and drink. No wonder then that Maimonides devotes the first chapter primarily to this word, *ẓelem*. He tells his addressee that *ẓelem* means, if not exactly never, at any rate not in the present case, a visible shape, but means here at any rate the natural form, the essence, of a being. The passage means: God created man in His image, God created man as a being endowed with intellect. Now this interpretation seems to be contradicted by the fact that the Torah speaks shortly afterward of the divine prohibition addressed to man against eating of the fruit of the tree of knowledge. If man was created as an intellectual being, and hence *for* the life of the intellect, his Creator could not well have forbidden him to strive for knowl-

---

83. Strauss actually says "the habit to accept"; in accord with better English grammar, it has been changed to "the habit of accepting."

84. The chief Aramaic translation of the Torah, known as "Targum Onkelos," was done by or attributed to Onkelos (or Onqelos) usually know as "the Proselyte." It is to be dated to the period between the destruction of the Second Jerusalem Temple (70 C.E.) and the Bar Kokhba Revolt (132–35 C.E.) of Judea against Rome. He was designated this unusual honorific because his conversion to Judaism (not to mention his Roman origins) is surrounded with legends. The translation was assigned great authority in the ancient Jewish tradition, especially during the period of Aramaic as still a significant spoken language of the Jews. It also plays a major role in the *Guide*, which shows that Maimonides held a high opinion of it in general, insofar as it mediated a noncorporeal view of God by virtue of how it translated key terms about divinity, angels, revelation, etc. See also n. 140 below.

85. See "How To Begin," chap. 11 below.

86. Although Strauss says "contrary to the appearance," and although it is actually better English grammar to remove the "the," the "the" was retained since to remove it as a correction might well change Strauss's meaning slightly.

87. Strauss repeated the terms "*ẓelem*" and "image" as he apparently wrote them on the chalkboard.

88. See Genesis 1:26–27; *Guide* 1.1, pp. 21–23. See also "How To Begin," chap. 11 below.

edge. Maimonides tells, therefore, his addressee (in the second chapter of the *Guide*)[89] that the knowledge which was originally forbidden to man was a low kind of knowledge, knowledge of good and evil, i.e., of the noble and base, and that the noble and base are objects not of the intellect, but of opinion. Strictly speaking, they are not objects of knowledge at all. This surely disposes of one perplexity, but it may give rise to other perplexities.

Then Maimonides turns to the second most important passage of the Torah which seems to support the view that God is corporeal—Numbers 12:8—"He (Moses) beholds the figure of the Lord," "*temunat ha-Shem yabbit*."[90] In the next three chapters Maimonides tells the addressee that the Hebrew words for "figure" and "form," as well as for "seeing" and "beholding," do not mean sense perception of something sensible if they are applied to God. But then he does something strange: he turns to discussing the Hebrew words for "man" and "woman" in chapter six, and the Hebrew word for "generating" (*yalad*) in chapter seven.[91] This change ceases to be strange once one considers the fact that chapter seven . . .[92] (I will rather be concerned to make here some notes; I have explained why he begins chapter 1 the way he does, why chapter 2, chapters 3 through 5, and now I'm concerned with chapters 6 and 7. The unity will be perfectly clear in five minutes.)

Now the question is then: why does he discuss "man" and "woman," the words "man" and "woman" (*'ish* and *'isha*), and "to generate" (*yalad*), here? This chapter seven deals again with "*ẓelem*," "image." Maimonides returns to the theme of [chapters] one and two here [in chapter seven], that is to say, [to] Genesis 1:27, or rather the *context*, namely, [to] the preceding verse too [i.e., 1:26]. I read it to you in the ordinary translation, but I emphasize crucial words: "And God said, Let *us* make man in *our* image, after *our* likeness. So God created man in His image, in the image of God created He him, *male* and *female* created He them." Now literally and stupidly understood, the passage might seem to suggest, not only that God has a visible shape, "*ẓelem*," "likeness," "image," but also that He is not absolutely simple,

89. See *Guide* 1.2, pp. 23–26. See also "How To Begin," chap. 11 below.
90. See *Guide* 1.3–5, pp. 26–31. See also "How To Begin," chap. 11 below.
91. See *Guide* 1.6–7, pp. 31–33. See also "How To Begin," chap. 11 below.
92. Strauss apparently interrupted himself in the midst of explaining the strangeness of Maimonides' procedure at the very beginning of the *Guide* (and especially at 1.7), and turned away from the recording device in order to write the previously discussed chapter numbers on the chalkboard, so as to show a certain pattern of the chapters in their arrangement. What he said while doing so is difficult to hear, but it seems as if, while he wrote those chapter numbers on the board, he said something like what follows in the text.

[i.e., notice] the plural, but contains in Himself different beings, at least one male and one female element. Maimonides does not go into this difficulty explicitly, since this difficulty would belong to the secrets of the Torah, but he alludes to it by this arrangement.[93] What he tells the addressee regarding "man" and "woman," and "to generate," is useful for the addressee, to say nothing of [its usefulness for] us, but [it is] not exhaustive. He alludes to a kind of corporealism, which is much more shocking than the one explicitly discussed by him. In the fourteenth chapter he refers to the words of the Torah (Genesis 6:2), which says, literally translated: "the sons of the gods saw the daughters of men."[94] At any rate, [in] this chapter seven, the last word of that chapter is again the word "*ẓelem*," the main theme of the first chapter.[95] Chapters six and seven, they conclude the discussion which has been begun in chapter one; in other words, chapters one through six and seven deal with the one key verse (Genesis 1:26–27), and they surround the discussion of the other key verse (Numbers 12:8), "he beholds the figure of the Lord." The discussion of the two most important passages of the Torah regarding God's corporeality is the fittest subject of the first subsection of the *Guide*. I think you have now understood the beginning of the *Guide*, what I call the first subsection, [i.e.,] the first seven chapters.

Now a new subsection begins here in chapter eight, and this goes to chapter twenty-eight. And the meaning of that subsection can much more easily be recognized, because there is *clearly* a theme indicated not by biblical

---

93. A recent book has both praised and criticized Strauss for his supposed contention that this passage in Genesis might seem to imply, for the thought of Maimonides, a sexual element in the esoteric teaching about God. First they praise him as follows: "Strauss rightly recognized the concern of Maimonides' secrets with sexuality." However, the authors also fault him for carrying his recognition too far, allowing Maimonides (according to the view attributed to Strauss by the authors) to "secretly attribute sexual dualism to God." May I suggest with all due respect that the authors of this otherwise very original and thought-provoking book have not read Strauss carefully enough, perhaps due to their resolute commitment to the uncovering of an anticipatory Freudianism in Maimonides. In any case, they fault Strauss for purportedly diminishing Maimonides' emphasis on divine incorporeality because he supposedly "secretly attributes sexual dualism to God," and they instead attribute the sexual dualism (seemingly suggested by Maimonides, but based of course on the biblical text) to a dualism pertaining to angels. To consider how they conceive Maimonides to have defined "angels," it is requisite to recur to their book. See David Bakan, Dan Merkur, and David S. Weiss, *Maimonides' Cure of Souls: Medieval Precursor of Psychoanalysis* (Albany: State University of New York Press, 2009), pp. 106–7. May I call attention to a remark in which the authentically biblical view is discussed by Strauss, although admittedly it is not directly addressed to his view of Maimonides: "On the Interpretation of Genesis" (1957), in *Jewish Philosophy and the Crisis of Modernity*, pp. 366–67: "The dualism chosen by the Bible, the dualism as distinguished from the dualism of male and female, is not sensual but intellectual, noetic."
94. See *Guide* 1.14, p. 40.
95. See *Guide* 1.7, p. 33.

verses, but by subject matter. Now what is that theme? The Hebrew terms designating "place" [*maqom*], as well as certain outstanding places, furthermore occupying place, changing place, and in the last chapter the human organ for changing place or for locomotion, I mean "foot" [*regel*]. Seventeen out of these twenty-one chapters are manifestly devoted to this theme. There are certain perplexing irregularities here, although the meaning of the whole is perfectly clear.[96] Chapter fourteen deals suddenly with "man," now not man as a male, as we had it before, but "human being," "'*adam*." Chapter seventeen deals with the fact that natural science must be treated secretly. And chapter twenty-six deals with the universal principle of interpreting the Torah, namely, according to an old Jewish saying: "The Torah speaks according to the language of human beings."[97] These chapters are subtly connected with those immediately preceding and following them, but to begin with, they clearly interrupt the continuity. This irregularity, these strange insertions, I believe are meant to draw our attention to a certain numerical symbolism, which I can here only state dogmatically, '*al derekh sippur*, [i.e., by] just telling you: fourteen stands for man; seventeen stands for nature; twenty-six stands originally (as all people who know Hebrew know) for the Lord,[98] and derivatively for the Torah.[99] Now there is a thing which, I mentioned, puzzles: the Hebrew numeral for fourteen is "*yad*" [i.e., "*yod*" (10) and "*dalet*" (4)], which [besides being a chapter number, also] means "hand," the Hebrew consonants all having a numerical value. Now strangely enough, the double of fourteen—twenty-eight—is the chapter devoted to "foot" [*regel*]. That is by no means meaningless. We note the fact that there is

---

96. This sentence might seem to require a supplement, even though Strauss makes a point which I do not challenge on the ground of what is audible: he obviously decided not to clarify for his hearers *how* "the whole is perfectly clear"; instead, one can only observe that as he proceeds through the paragraph, he tends to stress the "perplexing irregularities" of the parts.

97. See *Guide* 1.26, p. 56: "'The Torah speaks according to the language of the sons of man.'" The reference is to two passages, which make use of the same sentence, in the Babylonian Talmud: Yevamot 71a and Baba Metzia 31b. See also *Guide* 1.29, p. 62; 1.33, p. 71; 1.46, p. 100; 1.47, p. 105; 1.53, p. 120; 1.57, p. 133; 1.59, p. 140; 3.13, p. 453. And cf. also the middle of three scriptural verses (Proverbs 8:4), which are used as Maimonides' epigraph to the "Introduction," p. 5. See also n. 145 below.

98. This is based on the numerical value of the Tetragrammaton, the holiest name of God in the Torah and all subsequent Judaism, i.e., the four-letter Hebrew name of God (*yod, he, vav, he*), which is knowable, or rather available, only in consonants. It is a name that cannot be properly pronounced, and as a result no definite "meaning" can be ascribed to it, because we do not know the correct vowels, which have been lost and hence which remain a mystery. However, its numerical worth derives from the four consonants standing on their own, which amount to 26 ($yod = 10 + he = 5 + vav = 6 + he = 5$). See also *Guide* 1.61–62, pp. 147–52; and nn. 173, 174, and 175 below.

99. Cf. also "How To Begin," chap. 11 below.

no chapter in the *Guide* on "hand" as applied to God, although the term "the hand of God" ("*yad ha-Shem*") is very common in the Bible. The hand is a specifically human organ, as distinguished from the foot. Maimonides' quasi silence on "hand" draws our attention to the secret that the Bible does not speak of the "head" of God.[100] But these are already subtleties which should be postponed.

Now I come to the more obvious things.[101] The first chapter of this subsection deals with the Hebrew word for "place" ("*maqom*"), which appears to be God's place: His throne, be it the temple, or heaven, or mountain [*Guide* 1.8]. If God's place is heaven or some other high place, and since man's place is the earth, the meeting of God and man seems to require God's descending, and therefore also to require God's return to His place, by ascending. "Descending" and "ascending" are therefore the theme of the third chapter of this subsection [*Guide* 1.10]. Now on the basis of these primitive notions, this vulgar imagination, as Maimonides says, the natural state of God would be sitting on His throne, hence the following subject [i.e., "sitting" in *Guide* 1.11, linked with "throne" in 1.9].[102] "Sitting" leads naturally to its opposite, "standing up" or "rising," subjects of chapters twelve[103] and thirteen. But at this point the order of the chapters ceases to be intelligible, unless one makes a fresh start.

---

100. Language pertaining to the "head of God" was always controversial among medieval Jewish thinkers; the mystics (and subsequently Kabbalists) embraced what the rationalists (and subsequently Maimonideans) rejected. But then again, there was some precedent in the Hebrew Bible and Jewish tradition for legitimate use of the term: God seems possessed of a "face," apparently on a head, even if this cannot be seen by man (Exodus 33:20); His face can shine on you (Numbers 6:25); He can hide His face (Deuteronomy 32:20 or Psalm 102:3). Ancient language allowing that God wears a crown also seems to require a "head" to put it on (Isaiah 62:3 and Zechariah 9:16); the Song of Songs, once it is to be read as an allegory for God and man or Israel, mentions frequently the lover's head (4:1–4; 5:2, 10–13), which suggests *something* about God; and the famous Sabbath prayer, "Shir ha-Kavod," also known as "Anim Zemirot" (attributed to Yehuda ha-Hasid, the 12th-century German mystic) also raises still-contentious issues pertaining to imagery suggesting "God's head." That Strauss wished to suggest something about Maimonides' thought on this point is evident; what it may have been cannot be readily discerned from his brief and allusive comments but requires serious and prolonged reflection as well as research. To begin with: Why is Maimonides in the *Guide* silent on "the head of God"? Why is no chapter in the *Guide* dedicated to "hand," especially as applied to God? For "hand" of God, see "How To Begin," chap. 11 below. Cf. also *Guide* 1.46, pp. 100–101. See also n. 222 below.

101. The word "things" is uncertain. Strauss's voice fades away at the end of this sentence, so that it is difficult to know whether he swallowed the word "things" quietly spoken (which it sounds like to my ear), or whether he allowed the word "obvious" to dangle.

102. The tape is not entirely audible. The phrase "hence the following subject" is only tentative.

103. Strauss actually says "eleven" on the tape, but he must have misspoken, and it has been corrected accordingly to "twelve": he had just finished with the comments he wished to make on chapter 11 ("sitting"), and continued by mentioning the specific themes of chapters 12 ("rising") and 13 ("standing up"). As a subsidiary note, the theme of locomotion resumes in chapter 15 ("to stand erect"), and continues again with verbal forms of locomotion in chapters 18–24.

The first chapter of this subsection[104] is devoted to the Hebrew word for "place." Now this is very strange. This word, "*maqom*," is used in postbiblical Hebrew for *God*, one of the many names for God. Maimonides is completely silent about this postbiblical meaning, [this] theological meaning, of the term "place." In other words, when he speaks at the beginning that he is concerned with biblical terms, that has to be taken *very* literally: he means *biblical* terms, [and] not terms used in the Jewish tradition postbiblically. There are very few references to postbiblical Hebrew literature, Jewish literature, in this part of the *Guide*. Maimonides is emphatically *biblicistic* here, meaning: concerned with the text of the Bible as distinguished from the talmudic and other later Jewish literature. In order to understand the meaning of this biblicism, which is to begin with very strange, we must discuss another irregularity which is, I'm afraid, rather complicated.

Now ordinarily these chapters begin with the Hebrew term which is to be explained in the chapter, so they look like chapters of a dictionary, although they don't have alphabetical order, of course. Now two subsequent chapters begin with the Hebrew terms to be explained, but the Hebrew terms are supplied with the Arabic article.[105] (Well, if you want an example,[106] the Arabic

---

104. Strauss begins by hesitantly saying "section," corrects himself by saying "subject," and then quickly moves on. Judged in context, I believe there is the greatest probability that he meant to say "subsection," which makes most sense, but dwelling on the larger thought, he did not tarry long enough to catch himself on this smaller point. Hence I have substituted "subsection" for either "section" or "subject." As in the rest of these notes, I have assumed (even if this is not yet established with absolute certainty) that Strauss's plan of the *Guide* (see "How To Begin," chap. 11 below) was already fully elaborated by him in 1960 as the lecture was being delivered. The Shlomo Pines English translation of the *Guide* has 1963 as its original date of publication; but the introductory essay which Strauss wrote for it, and which contains the plan, was composed much in advance of the appearance in print of the *Guide* translation. Heinrich Meier explains that in the original manuscript of this essay, Strauss indicates that it was composed between May and August of 1960. See *Philosophie und Gesetz: Frühe Schriften*, vol. 2 of *Gesammelte Schriften*, p. XXII, n. 26. However, as this lecture of 7 and 14 February 1960 shows, Strauss must undoubtedly have been working it on much prior to May–August of the same year. It was during this period that he presumably only finalized it. If this celebratory lecture, occurring three years in advance of the *Guide*'s appearance in print, is not regarded as sufficient supporting evidence for the date of composition of "How To Begin," consider as further circumstantial evidence the letters between Strauss and Gershom Scholem in Jerusalem, in which Strauss implores Scholem to ask Pines how things are proceeding (perhaps applying gentle pressure) with his introduction, since the translation (and presumably also Strauss's introductory essay) was already with the printer by 15 March 1962, as if most of the work may already have been completed for quite a while. In reply, Scholem demurs, saying that Pines bristles if asked about this sort of thing. See *Hobbes Politische Wissenschaft und zugehörige Schriften—Briefe*, vol. 3 of *Gesammelte Schriften*, pp. 744–45. In any case, I especially bring the manuscript evidence uncovered by Meier (but also these letters) to suggest that, if Strauss had finalized his essay by 1960, never mind that almost this entire translation project was already at the printers by 1962, besides Pines's "Translator's Introduction," this entitles me to utilize "How To Begin" to illuminate some of the obscurities and allusions in the lecture.

105. Strauss turned to write terms on the chalkboard and to indicate the difference in these two chapters, which he will also explain in the following passage.

106. The tape is not entirely audible. The words "want an example" are only tentative.

is written in Hebrew like this, *al-yez'ia*—which in Hebrew would mean *ha-yez'ia*, [and] that means "going out"—[and] that's [with] the Arabic article.)[107] There are two such chapters immediately following one another.[108] Now this is prepared and emphasized by the beginning of the immediately preceding chapter, chapter twenty-two.[109] At the beginning of that [chapter], Maimonides does this: he gives first just the simple, ordinary Hebrew form for the verb, "*ba*," "he came" [or just] "came," and then he begins his sentence with a substantivated verb, [i.e.,] the verb is substantive in Hebrew, [but] supplied with the Arabic article; and then the next two chapters begin simply with the [Hebrew] verbal noun supplied with the Arabic article.[110] Now one expects therefore, since he went over from the simple Hebrew verb to the Hebrew verbal noun supplied with the Arabic article, that this will go on, but then we get a surprise. In chapter twenty-five, he begins again with the simple Hebrew verb. The word in Hebrew is "*shakhan*," "he dwelled." And those of you who know a bit of Hebrew know already what is happening: one expects that the next sentence would begin with "*al-shekhinah*"; instead, he begins with "*shakhan*." Now "*shekhinah*" is the "Indwelling," the "divine Indwelling"; it is another of these postbiblical theological terms which Maimonides, as he thus emphasizes, wishes to avoid. The form in which he does it in this case is a bit different, because he uses in that chapter the Arabic translation of the Hebrew word "*shekhinah*."[111] But I hope the main point has become clear. By these strange irregularities, Maimonides draws our attention to the fact that he is going to be emphatically biblicistic, disregarding the postbiblical usage. I could give additional evidence for that, but I can't bore you with the details.

I suggested [that] in the second subsection[112] Maimonides draws our at-

---

107. The Arabic definite article, ordinarily put at the beginning of a noun, is *al-*. The Hebrew definite article, also ordinarily put at the beginning of a noun, is *ha-*. It is conventional for Maimonides—who wishes to discuss *only* the key biblical terms, as Strauss has just so emphatically stressed—to use only original biblical Hebrew words. But suddenly, according to Strauss, he is adding a nonbiblical and a "modern" element (i.e., the Arabic definite article) entirely foreign to the ancient source with which he is supposed to be categorically concerned.

108. See *Guide* 1.23, p. 52, and 1.24, p. 53.

109. See *Guide* 1.22, p. 51. At several points in the discussion which the present paragraph represents, Strauss turned to write the terms of which he spoke on the chalkboard.

110. See "How To Begin," chap. 11 below, for further discussion on Maimonides' deliberate use in the *Guide* of the Arabic article, *al-*.

111. See *Guide* 1.25, p. 55. See also "How To Begin," chap. 11 below. The Arabic form of the similar Hebrew word "*shekhinah*" is "*sakina*," although they carry a different range of meanings in the two languages.

112. In fact, Karaism has not yet been mentioned by Strauss vis-à-vis the second subsection. However, he may well have been thinking of his own "How To Begin," and certainly its approximate first half, "On

tention to the problem posed by Karaitism.[113] Now Karaitism can very loosely be compared to Protestantism in Christianity: not the traditions, only the Bible; or more probably with the Shia in Islam: only the Qur'an, and not the tradition, not the Sunna. Maimonides poses here the problem of Karaitism, of those Jews—at that time, numerically very many—who said: only the biblical text is authoritative, and the Talmud has no authority whatever. He also indicates, however, in this section that he solves [or rather] how he solves the problem posed by Karaitism. He solves it naturally in the direction of Rabbinitism (Rabbinitism being the word for the opposite, for the Jews who accept the rabbinical tradition). But this creates certain problems, as you will see.

I mentioned that the first seven chapters lean on two or three verses of the Torah, which I identified. Now we can discern in the second subsec-

---

the Plan of *The Guide of the Perplexed*." It had likely already been finished, and he may well have based the present lecture on its manuscript. It is in this work that he suggests a definite relation between Karaism and the second subsection. Cf. "How To Begin," chap. 11 below, and n. 113 below.

113. I have not changed Strauss's usage, although it is conventional (in contemporary English-language scholarly discussion especially) that this religious movement is usually referred to by the name of "Karaism," not "Karaitism." However, the followers of the movement are usually known as "Karaites." Karaism was a medieval Jewish religious movement, which started in 8th-century Iraq (still known to Jews as Babylonia), and which continued as an impressive force for several centuries, during which this movement was both very popular among the Jews and exercised a powerful, creative, and lasting influence on Judaism as an entirety. It was based on the principle that Judaism consists solely of the religion, teachings, and laws of the Hebrew Bible. Hence their name "Karaites," which might be idiomatically translated as "biblicists." The movement rejected (as a corruption and a divergence) the dependence of the Jews, in the post–70 C.E. era, on the Talmuds (Babylonian and Jerusalem) and Midrashim, i.e., on "oral Torah" as an idea, and on rabbinical tradition as it had subsequently unfolded generally speaking. Hence their opponents are usually known as "Rabbinites," i.e., followers of rabbinical tradition in addition to biblical tradition. (Strauss calls the movement "Rabbinitism," but again the conventional scholarly name is "Rabbinism.") Maimonides' dialectical (often even contradictory) attitude toward the Karaites—definitely not *merely* critical and rejecting—is a fascinating topic in itself, which (so far as I am aware) has not yet been the focus of a full-length study. For some preliminary approaches, see Daniel J. Lasker, "The Influence of Karaism on Maimonides" [in Hebrew], *Sefunot* 5 (1991): 145–61; Gerald J. Blidstein, "The 'Other' in Maimonidean Law," *Jewish History* 18, no. 2-3 (May 2004): 173–95, and especially pp. 184–89. Strauss obviously gave careful consideration to how seriously Maimonides took the challenge of the Karaites: it was an acute and critical stimulant of thought not containable in the "mere" category of heresy. Though Strauss's comment is apparently only of a passing nature, in context he is implying much about Maimonides' thought: "He is alive to the question raised by the Karaites." (See "How To Begin," chap. 11 below.) Strauss seems to suggest the following greater point: Maimonides was alive to *all* the most significant and vital intellectual arguments which engaged contemporary Judaism, and he addressed them as serious challenges, rather than merely dismissing them or vilifying them. He believed they eminently deserve consideration and debate on the highest level, or in terms of their most excellent arguments. Further, it is not fair or honest to reduce them to their most debased, destitute, or demeaned level, since this is not to meet the true and genuine challenge (both theoretical and practical) that they legitimately represent. Their criticism reveals a frailty or debility in rabbinical Judaism, which is in need of being addressed and undoubtedly also corrected. Maimonides zestfully (if quietly and calmly) wrestles with their challenges and their criticism, tacitly suggests a cure, treatment, or remedy for his side, and so shows how by doing so Judaism attains a deeper cognitive profundity and moral integrity.

tion a corresponding use of two verses from the Torah. In this case they are taken from Exodus 33. I mention it only for those who have any knowledge of Hebrew: "... *hinne maqom 'itti v-nizzavta 'al-ha-zur. Ve-haya ba-'avor* ..." ["... behold, there is a place by Me, and thou {Moses} shall stand erect upon the rock. And it shall come to pass while {My Glory}[114] passes by..."][115] Of these words, *maqom* [place][116] is discussed in this subsection,[117] *nazav* [to stand erect],[118] *zur* [rock],[119] and *'avar* [to pass by].[120] But we see also the use of some entirely different biblical terms,[121] not from the Torah, but from Isaiah, chapter 6, the famous chapter of Isaiah's vocation.[122] The terms *kise'* [throne],[123] *yashav* [to sit],[124] *'amad* [to stand],[125] *naga'* [to touch],[126] *male'* [to fill],[127] *ram ve-nisa'* [high and raised up],[128] *regel* [foot][129]—which all occur in chapter six of Isaiah's speech[130]—are all discussed in this subsection.[131]

114. The two words in curly brackets, "Moses" and "My Glory," do not occur in the passage as Strauss offers it, although of course the former is implicitly and the latter is explicitly present in the original biblical verses themselves. These two words have been added so that this passage will make greater sense in reading, better conveying the biblical context in which the passage, of which Strauss makes selective use, originally appears.

115. See Exodus 33:21-22. Compare, e.g., with *Guide* 1.8, p. 34; 1.15, p. 41; and 1.21, p. 50.

116. See *Guide* 1.8, pp. 33-34.

117. Although Strauss plainly says "chapter" in the tape of the lecture, undoubtedly he means "subsection," since all of these words are not discussed in any single chapter of the *Guide*; hence the word "subsection" has been substituted for "chapter." One must see these issues in light of Strauss's treatment in "How To Begin," chap. 11 below, especially considering how he delineates the previously concealed "plan" of the *Guide*, which he magisterially uncovered, or rather reconstructed.

118. See *Guide* 1.15, pp. 40-41.

119. See *Guide* 1.16, p. 42.

120. See *Guide* 1.21, pp. 47-51.

121. Strauss's voice is not entirely audible on the tape; he swallows two words in this sentence. The words that are most probable, but not certain, are "entirely" and "terms."

122. "The famous chapter of Isaiah's vocation" refers of course to his "calling" as a prophet, in which he is allowed to receive a vision of the celestial court; he witnesses both angels singing God's praises and God sitting on His throne. During his vision, he responds to God's call; he is chosen and sent, once his "lips" to speak prophetically with have been "cleansed."

123. Isaiah 6:1; *Guide* 1.9, pp. 34-35. The passage from Isaiah 6 is not actually cited or quoted by Maimonides in this chapter, but "throne" is the theme that the chapter focuses on.

124. Isaiah 6:1; *Guide* 1.11, pp. 37-38. The passage from Isaiah 6 is not actually quoted or cited by Maimonides in this chapter, but "sitting" is the theme that the chapter focuses on.

125. Isaiah 6:2; *Guide* 1.13, pp. 39-40. The passage from Isaiah 6 is not actually quoted or cited by Maimonides in this chapter, but "standing" is the theme that the chapter focuses on.

126. Isaiah 6:7; *Guide* 1.18, pp. 43-45.

127. Isaiah 6:3; *Guide* 1.19, pp. 45-46.

128. Isaiah 6:1; *Guide* 1.20, pp. 46-47. The passage from Isaiah 6 is not actually quoted or cited by Maimonides in this chapter, but "high" and "raised up" are the themes that the chapter focuses on.

129. Isaiah 6:2; *Guide* 1.28, pp. 59-61. The passage from Isaiah 6 is not actually quoted or cited by Maimonides in this chapter, but "foot" is the theme that the chapter focuses on.

130. The tape is not entirely audible. The word "speech" is only tentative. It is also possible that in this phrase, he repeats the word "six."

131. Strauss undoubtedly meant to say "subsection," and not "section"; hence the word "subsection" has been substituted for "section."

Now what does this mean? Isaiah says here, in chapter six: "My eyes have seen the King, the Lord *ẓibaot*."[132] Isaiah does not say, as Moses said, or as is said of Moses: "My eyes have seen the *figure* of the Lord."[133] Still less does he say, as is said in the Torah: "Man cannot see Me and live," "*ve-lo yir'ani ha-'adam va-ḥai*."[134] Now if we believe in the Torah, in the Bible, we seem to be compelled to say on the basis of the text that Isaiah reached a higher stage in the knowledge of God than Moses—"my eyes have seen the King,"[135] [and] not "figure" of the King—that there was, in other words, a *progress* from Moses to Isaiah. At first glance, this suggestion would have justly to be rejected as preposterous for anyone who knows anything of Maimonides: the supremacy of Moses is one of the roots of the Torah, and so on and so on. But that this is not entirely wrong I could show you by referring to a discussion of this subject in Yosef Albo's work on the *Roots*, early fifteenth century.[136] And Albo was a very respectable man, not as he is . . .

---

132. Isaiah 6:5. The name of God, "the Lord *ẓibaot*," the last Hebrew word of which Strauss leaves untranslated, is ordinarily translated in English as "the Lord of hosts." It might be rendered more literally as "the Lord of armies," or less concisely as "the Lord with assembled multitudes [at His command]."

133. Numbers 12:8. The verse itself employs the third person, and not the first person. In this verse it is apparently God saying that he (Moses) has seen the figure of the Lord; it is not Moses himself claiming, I have seen the figure of the Lord.

134. Exodus 33:20. The passage which Strauss recites from memory in Hebrew (one may presume), he begins with "*va*"—usually, but not always, "and" in Hebrew. However, the actual passage itself begins with "*ki*," usually, but not always, "for" in Hebrew: *ki lo yirani ha-'adam va-ḥai*." It has not been corrected in the text, but remains as Strauss recited it. The tape breaks in the middle of Strauss's declaiming this verse, which I must assume that he finished uttering, so I complete the verse beyond what the tape preserves.

135. Isaiah 6:5.

136. Joseph Albo (c. 1380–1444) was a major Jewish thinker in Christian Spain in the fifteenth century, for whom Strauss had great respect. His magnum opus was *Sefer ha-Ikkarim* [literally, *Book of Roots*, or figuratively, *Book of Principles*], which Strauss seems to regard as a book directly inspired by the *Guide*, if not almost a sort of commentary, expressing certain corrections, qualifications, or "advances," as well as a supposed progress in clarity of presentation. Certainly Albo almost constantly refers to Maimonides, even if only for the purpose of differing from him. For what may perhaps have been the specific discussion in Albo on the prophecy of Moses vis-à-vis the prophecy of Isaiah, to which Strauss was referring or had in his mind, see Albo, *Ikkarim* (*Roots*), trans. Husik, vol. 3, chap. 17, especially pp. 151–54. His general consideration of subsequent prophets relative to Moses concludes with the following words:

> From all this it is clear that an inferior prophet must not oppose the words of a prophet who is superior to him, but that his words must be so interpreted that they should not conflict with the words of the superior. . . . Whether, however, any prophet may interpret the words of Moses and say that though they are stated without qualification, they are conditional in their meaning, or that a time limitation should be attached to them, though no such limitation is explicitly stated—this will be discussed in the sequel with the help of God.

The "sequel," i.e., the chapters that follow in volume 3, address numerous aspects of this issue. Strauss frequently made reference to Albo. See "How To Begin," chap. 11 below: "Albo was a favorite companion living at the court of a great king." See also "Maimonides' Statement on Political Science," chap. 9 above. For recent reconsiderations of Albo seen in light of Strauss's suggestions and high estimate of him as a thinker, consider Ralph Lerner, "Natural Law in Albo's 'Book of Roots,'" in *Ancients and Moderns: Essays*

[A break in the tape apparently occurred.][137]

... not in the Torah. He gives there three.[138] Our ancestors were brought up in the belief of the Sabians, i.e., of pagans, and therefore denied the possibility of miracles. Hence they needed a very long education and habituation until they could be brought to believe in that greatest of miracles, the miracle of resurrection. Now this does not mean that Moses did not *know* this root, this principle, [i.e.,] resurrection, but he surely did not teach it. Similarly, it

---

on the Tradition of Political Philosophy in Honor of Leo Strauss, ed. Joseph Cropsey (New York: Basic Books, 1964), pp. 132–147; "The Politic Art of Joseph Albo," in *Averroismus im Mittelalter und in der Renaissance*, ed. Friedrich Niewöhner and Loris Sturlese (Zurich: Spur, 1994), pp. 251–68; "Postscript: Survival Training—Albo's 'Book of Roots,'" in *Maimonides' Empire of Light: Popular Enlightenment in the Age of Belief* (Chicago: University of Chicago Press, 2000), pp. 89–95; David Novak, "Albo's Theory of Noahide Law," in *The Image of the Non-Jew in Judaism: The Idea of Noahide Laws*, ed. Matthew LaGrone, 2nd ed. (Oxford: Littman Library of Jewish Civilization, 2011), pp. 176–94; Dror Ehrlich, "A Reassessment of Natural Law in Rabbi Joseph Albo's 'Book of Principles,'" *Hebraic Political Studies* 1, no. 4 (Summer 2006): 413–39; *The Thought of R. Joseph Albo: Esoteric Writing in the Late Middle Ages* [in Hebrew] (Ramat Gan, Israel: Bar-Ilan University Press, 2009).

137. As a result of the break in the tape which apparently occurred, a portion of the lecture material is undoubtedly missing. It is not known from anything in the tape precisely how much material this may be. It is obvious that it continues on a very slightly different topic. However, inasmuch as Strauss's lecture at this point is roughly in accord with the argument of "How To Begin," chap. 11 below, it follows that the missing material may well have made the transition from the question of the specific relation, according to Maimonides, between the prophecy of Moses and the prophecy of Isaiah to the general problem of progress in the tradition, as Maimonides attempted to resolve the genuine but unavoidable dilemma that this raises. Strauss seems to assume that Maimonides (a) was honest with himself about this issue, and (b) was capable of thinking it through prior to modern notions of progress. This led him to that dilemma to which Strauss will turn next, as the taped lecture resumes. It begins "... not in the Torah," which resembles the sentence in "How To Begin," chap. 11 below: "In his *Treatise on Resurrection*, Maimonides teaches that resurrection, one of the thirteen roots of the Law, is clearly taught within the Bible only in the book of Daniel, but certainly not in the Torah." Thus he asks: Is it possible for Maimonides that Moses did not know this fundamental principle or root of the Torah? Compare with the next note.

138. If I may venture a hypothetical reconstruction of the strange sentence in the text to which n. 138 is affixed, according to what has been discussed in the previous note about what of Strauss's material may be missing between the break in the tape, I suggest something like the following: "He," i.e., Maimonides, "gives there," i.e., in the *Treatise on Resurrection* together with the *Guide*, "three," i.e., examples of instruction in the Jewish tradition which *seem* to progress beyond the teaching of the Torah of Moses: (1) the fundamental teaching of resurrection first attributed to Daniel, (2) the true teaching of providence first evident in Job, and (3) the supreme story of the divine chariot as told by Ezekiel, or as perfected by Isaiah. See Maimonides, "Treatise on Resurrection," trans. Fradkin, pp. 169–77; *Guide* 3.Intro., pp. 415–16; 3.1–7, pp. 417–30; 3.17, pp. 464–74; 3.19, pp. 477–80; 3.22–23, pp. 486–97. In line with the point made in the previous note about the advantages which accrue to the reader from seeing the lecture in light of "How To Begin," chap. 11 below, the argument in the start of the sentence which is missing, "... not in the Torah," may well have been something like the following. The teaching of resurrection is not evident in the Torah, at least as Maimonides seems to have honestly viewed the matter. However, as Strauss will directly present it, Maimonides also believed, or at least wished to suggest, that this fundamental teaching was even so *known* to Moses. (In the logic of Maimonides, Moses must have taught it secretly and passed it on through an oral teaching to his closest students, because his people were not yet ready to receive it.) According to Maimonides, as Strauss will continue, Moses decided not to *teach* resurrection (although he knew it) for a particular reason which was very wise, i.e., due to his judgment both about the spiritual-historical situation, and about the state of mind dominant in his people, i.e., the well-nigh universal rule of "Sabianism."

is the Book of Job, a nonprophetic book dealing with non-Jewish prophets (of which Job was one), and not the psalms and the prophets, which solves the problem of providence. But above all, the highest of all themes, according to Maimonides, is *ma'aseh merkavah*, the story of the divine chariot. It is a higher theme than the story of creation. The story of creation is told by Moses, but the story of the chariot is told by Ezekiel. But as Maimonides makes clear, Ezekiel's presentation of the divine chariot is inferior in dignity to Isaiah's presentation, and Isaiah's presentation is precisely that given in chapter six to which I have referred before.[139] So the highest presentation in the Bible of the highest teaching is found in chapter six of Isaiah, which I think proves my point.

Once the possibility of an intrabiblical progress, meaning a progress beyond the teaching of Moses, is granted, there is no fundamental difficulty in granting also a postbiblical progress. I mention only one point. The prophets are distinguished from the nonprophetic wise men by the fact that the prophets have *intuitive* knowledge of the highest truth, or that they can recognize those truths without the use of reasoning. The prophets do teach their disciples, but this teaching probably serves the purpose of guiding the disciples toward *intuitive* knowledge. Teaching proper, a teaching which does not presuppose on the part of teacher and pupil prophetic illumination, was the discovery of the wise men of Greece. The introduction of Greek science into Judaism, in due subordination to Judaism, can therefore be regarded as a further progress. It enables nonprophets truly to *know* that God exists, that He is one, and that He is incorporeal. It is perhaps not an accident that the authoritative translator of the Torah into Aramaic, who did so much to counteract the corporealistic tendencies of the text, was Onkelos the *Proselyte*.[140]

---

139. Maimonides ranks the prophecy of Isaiah higher than the prophecy of Ezekiel in *Guide* 3.6, p. 427. For Maimonides' view on the error of Ezekiel in science, see the discussion by Warren Zev Harvey, "How to Begin to Study *The Guide of the Perplexed*, I, 1" [in Hebrew], *Daat: A Journal of Jewish Philosophy and Kabbalah* 21 (1988): 5–23, and especially pp. 21–23.

140. Cf., e.g., *Guide* 1.2, p. 23; 1.27, p. 57; and 1.48, p. 106. At least in these three passages, Maimonides refers to him by the full name of "Onkelos the Proselyte," which for Strauss conforms to the suggestion that this full name may be an honorific title or a form of praise in Maimonides, as well as a pointer or hint. If this is correct, it would have to be significant that in at least one passage in which he raises doubts about the correctness of Onkelos' translation, i.e., *Guide* 1.48, pp. 107–8, he disregards the full name, although he also defends him by pointing to the possibility of scribal errors. By way of contrast, for his criticism of Onkelos consider and compare, e.g., 1.5, p. 31, with 1.28, p. 60. And cf. "How To Begin," chap. 11 below. In that essay, this name is translated as "Onkelos the Stranger." This is closer to the original (i.e., literal biblical) meaning of the Hebrew term "*ger*," which was used for a stranger or foreigner who sojourned with the ancient Israelites and who accepted, or at least willingly followed, certain fundamental laws. It was only in subsequent, i.e., talmudic (which is perhaps to say: post-70 C.E.) Jewish history that the term acquired the meaning of formal "convert" or "proselyte." By so rendering it, Strauss seems to

Last but not least, there is Maimonides himself, the first Jew who attempted completely to eradicate corporealism from the Jewish community as a whole as a hidden premise of idolatry. What Maimonides did was not only superfluous at the beginning, in the golden times of the revelation, biblical times, but it was also impossible at that time.

There is a certain link—I indicate the argument for those who have any interest in the text; for the others, I could well omit it:[141] now [with regard to] these two chapters which begin with the Hebrew word supplied with the Arabic article, [i.e.,] 1.23 and 24, there is something similar [which] occurs in a very different part of the *Guide*, 3.36–49, each of the chapters [of which] begins with an expression, "*al-miẓvot*," [meaning] the "*miẓvot*," i.e., the commandments, [but notice:] Arabic article, Hebrew word—there is a certain connection between these two sections, which we can state as follows. The theme of this section[142] is the biblical ritual, especially the sacrifices. And Maimonides makes the point that these sacrifices were meant to eradicate the idolatrous sacrificial cults of the pagans. There is a similar polemical reference to prebiblical paganism underlying the first section of the work. In both cases Maimonides brings out a certain *adaptation* to Sabianism, a certain concession to Sabianism.[143] This concession, the half-corporealistic language [of the Torah], can be retracted only now, after the very last vestiges of paganism have been destroyed, thanks to the ever-deepened influence of the Torah directly on the Jews, and indirectly through Christianity and Islam. The time has come when the last relics of paganism can be removed, now, in Maimonides' time.

This observation solves the great difficulty inherent in Maimonides' discussion of incorporeality in the Bible. The Bible teaches incorporeality of God [metaphorically],[144] i.e., the literal meaning of the expressions (say, "the hand of God") is *figurative*; in other words, it was not meant for one moment that God has a hand; it was used from the beginning metaphorically. But Mai-

---

stick closely to what he considers to have been the "originalist" emphasis of Maimonides in the *Guide*. See also n. 84 above.

141. At this point, Strauss apparently turned again toward the chalkboard and wrote on it the relevant chapters and terms that he was discussing.

142. This refers to section VI, according to the plan of the *Guide* that Strauss delineates in "How To Begin," chap. 11 below.

143. For further discussion of Sabianism in the *Guide*, see the discussion period, and also nn. 235 and 237 below. Cf. also "How To Begin," chap. 11 below.

144. Strauss did not finish this phase of the sentence; the word in square brackets is an attempt to suggest what it is that he seems to have been getting at, borrowing a word from how he will eventually finish the sentence.

monides also says in other passages that the literal meaning *is* corporealistic, for the Torah speaks according to the language of human beings,[145] that is to say, of the vulgar, and the vulgar does not conceive of anything incorporeal. The Bible teaches incorporeality of God, but it speaks constantly of God in corporealistic terms—while opposing the belief in corporeal gods, the Bible fosters the belief in [God's] corporeality. That is called a paradoxical fact. This, according to Maimonides, will be explained as follows. The Bible is primarily addressed to the vulgar, and the vulgar can be brought to believe in God only by being induced to believe that God is a body. For according to the vulgar mind, to be is the same as to be a body or to be in a body.[146] The only way to bring the vulgar, and especially a vulgar brought up in paganism, to believe in the Lord, the one God, is through ascribing to Him body, and towards the vulgar that God is perfection. The most powerful Being whose place is in heaven, but who descends from heaven and again ascends to it, with utmost speed, and whose place is also in the Temple, that is the only way in which the vulgar could understand it.

Now if I may again use an expression which will not be intelligible to everyone: if "*rabbenu Moshe*" marks then, in a way, a progress beyond "*Moshe rabbenu*";[147] or if the "Torah of the Perplexed," [i.e.,] the "Guide of the Perplexed"—["*moreh*"] is the same as "*torah*," by the way[148]—marks a prog-

---

145. See n. 97 above.

146. See *Guide* 1.46, p. 98.

147. The phrase "*Moshe rabbenu*" means literally "Moses our teacher," i.e., Moses the prophet as the bringer of the Torah, who taught it to Israel. This traditional title for Moses stresses not only that he was known as a teacher, but it also highlights reverence and affection for him as "our teacher." The phrase "*rabbenu Moshe*" means literally "our teacher Moses" (but it also suggests "our rabbi Moses"): it is the title by which Maimonides was traditionally known, especially among the commentators on the *Guide*. Of course it stretches the affection and reverence for "Moses" to cover Maimonides, even while not diminishing the traditional title for Moses. It also at least suggests the traditional saying, "from Moses to Moses, there is none like Moses." But then is Strauss somehow implying that Maimonides himself subtly suggested this continuity from Moses to Moses, as if he even consciously prepared the traditional saying? If Strauss is correct that Maimonides viewed his own teaching as a sort of progress "beyond" Moses, even so simultaneously this was also undoubtedly aimed to be continuous with Moses. At least as tacitly claimed by Maimonides about his own teaching, he merely brings to light the essential, even if hidden, teaching of the original Moses, based on a more auspicious and less archaic historical situation. But as Strauss presents Maimonides, he had in no sense turned aside from the original intention of Moses. For even with his claim of progress, it is still the same tradition from which his transformation derives, but moved to a different historical time and place such as legitimates progress as needed by changes of condition in life and mind. According to Strauss, Maimonides was able to achieve this lawful feat because he had mastered the art of properly reading the mode of expression by which Moses had conveyed his original prophecy, for its true thought had been concealed in a teaching that had to be pedagogically determined by time, place, and people.

148. This would seem to imply that, for Strauss, the conventional Hebrew title of Maimonides' book, "*Moreh* ha-Nevukhim," "The *Guide* of the Perplexed," is based on the same Hebrew root as "Torah": although slightly different grammatical forms, the latter ("*torah*") may be translated as "teaching," and the

ress beyond the "Torah for the Unperplexed," i.e., for the Torah proper,[149] it was necessary for Maimonides at a fairly early stage in his argument to draw the attention of his reader to the difference between the biblical and the postbiblical Jewish teaching, and therefore the strange goings-on regarding the Hebrew word for "place" ("*maqom*"), as well as "*shekhinah*." In that early stage, that difference was the only difference of importance, the only distinction of importance. Hence, Maimonides treats to begin with in the first, say, forty-eight chapters,[150] the Bible as a unity, and the postbiblical literature, the Talmud in the widest sense, also as a unity. And when he quotes from the Bible, he generally says, "He says" ([i.e.,] He [with a] capital ["H"]), "He says"; and when he quotes the Talmud, he says, "they say"—without making any distinction of individuals. Only very gradually does he bring in the distinction of individuals, by quoting from some of the individual prophets by name, say, Isaiah or Zechariah maybe, or individual talmudic teachers by name. That is a part of this slowly developing argument.

If I may summarize this point: Maimonides' link with the Torah is, to begin with, an iron bond; it gradually turns [and] becomes a fine thread. But

---

former ("*moreh*") may be translated as "teacher" (or "guide"). For those with knowledge of Hebrew, the three-letter Hebrew root of both words (*moreh* and *torah*) is *yod-resh-he* (*yrh*). It covers a range of words which in verbal form may be summarized as "to point," "to shoot [an arrow]," "to throw [a stone]," "to direct," "to teach," "to guide," "to instruct," and "to explain." For its original biblical forms, see *A Hebrew and English Lexicon of the Old Testament, Based on William Genesius*, trans. Edward Robinson, ed. Francis Brown, S. R. Driver, and Charles A. Briggs (Oxford: Clarendon Press, 1906; reprint, 1953), pp. 434–36. Strauss at least suggests that in this similarity of terms is manifest the deliberate expression of the intention of Maimonides to draw a link between the two books, Torah and *Moreh* (even though Strauss of course knew that calling it by this Hebrew title, by which it was known to most medieval and modern Jews, was the decision of Maimonides' Hebrew translator, Samuel ibn Tibbon).

149. As recorded on the tape, Strauss says "for the Torah proper." Compare also with "How To Begin," chap. 11 below. Strauss seems to suggest the following, somewhat paradoxical, result about what Maimonides was thinking: the surpassing of elements in the original Torah is for the good of the Torah itself. Or to restate it again: a certain sort of progress beyond the "original" Torah is a progress for that Torah itself, and is actually continuous with it as grounded in it, inasmuch as during the post-Sabian era the *original intention*, i.e., the fundamental principles, of this holy book may receive better or truer expression precisely in the "Torah of the Perplexed." Thus, Maimonidean progress beyond the Torah proper also "marks a progress ... for the Torah proper" insofar as what he brings to clearer and purer light are the original Torah's fundamental principles, its true teachings concealed beneath a historical surface which a distorting literalism will falsify.

150. One might well wonder why Strauss called a halt at chapter forty-eight, keeping in mind that 1.50–60 is concerned with the doctrine of attributes and so begins something quite different: why did he seemingly disallow chapter forty-nine from a connection to the bigger issue, i.e., the issue being whether either the Bible or the Talmud can be treated as a simple unity? (Of course, it might also be somehow significant, according to Strauss's scheme, that the next chapter's number is seven squared, sevens playing such a great role for this approach to the *Guide*.) It seems appropriate to ask: is this mention of "forty-eight chapters" merely accidental, or is it deliberate? Further along he defines the specific difference characteristic of chapter forty-nine, perhaps implying why something in it may be key: "Chapter forty-nine is in a class by itself; it deals not with God but with the angels."

however far the conscious spiritualization of the Torah may go, that spiritualization always remains a spiritualization of the Torah.[151]

Now the second subsection (if we can, we will try to go a bit faster)[152] has dealt chiefly with the terms ascribing to God [His] occupying place, change of place, and so on. Occupying place and changing place belong to bodies as such, regardless of whether they are animate or inanimate. In chapter twenty-nine, where a new subsection begins,[153] Maimonides turns to terms which ascribe to God characteristics of *animate* beings. He discusses there the Hebrew word, "*'azav*," "to suffer pain," and in the following chapter, thirty, "*'akhal*," [which is] the Hebrew word for "eating." The next six chapters are speculative rather than exegetic[, i.e., chapters thirty-one through thirty-six].[154] That is[, this makes for] a new unity, a new subsection: [chapters] twenty-nine to thirty-six. Chapters thirty-one and thirty-five are the first chapters without any Jewish quotation, and that later on becomes more frequent. In chapter thirty-seven, he turns again to the discussion of biblical terms, primarily terms designating parts of the living being, and terms designating sense perception: that begins here, in [chapter] thirty-seven.[155] But we may first try to understand this subsection, which I called the third subsection.

Now what is the connection between these [terms]? There are only two

---

151. These sentences in the lecture closely resemble the sentences of "How To Begin," chap. 11 below, which deal with "Maimonides' link with the Torah" even as he seems to "progress" beyond it. Both versions speak of an "iron bond" and a "fine thread," but the lecture prefers "the spiritualization of the Torah," while the essay prefers "the intellectualization of the Torah." For persuasive evidence that Maimonides definitely believed in the progress of science, even beyond his own era, which reflects the provisional character of the science presented by him as law in "Hilkhot Yesodei ha-Torah," chaps. I–IV, of *Sefer ha-Madda* in the *Mishneh Torah*, see Menachem Kellner, "Maimonides on the Science of the *Mishneh Torah*: Provisional or Permanent?," in *Science in the Bet Midrash: Studies in Maimonides* (Brighton, MA: Academic Studies Press, 2009), pp. 193–215. It originally appeared in *AJS Review* 18, no. 2 (1993): 169–94. This, of course, is the discrete unit of chapters ("Hilkhot Yesodei ha-Torah," I–IV) that Strauss detects Maimonides to have deliberately highlighted as *the* "book of knowledge": see "Notes on Maimonides' *Book of Knowledge*," chap. 12 below. Though it was apparently not Kellner's intention, even so his article is an expression of the thesis presented in Strauss's lecture, i.e., Maimonides believed in the genuine possibility of progress. However, in Strauss's thesis, it is not limited to science: the belief in progress for Maimonides cannot be disconnected from certain essential and comprehensive teachings of the Torah as apply on every level.

152. The tape is not entirely audible. The words "if we can" are only tentative.

153. He said "a new section" begins," but he must have meant to say "a new subsection begins," as accords with his presentation in "How To Begin" of how the plan is divided: the third subsection is *Guide* 1.29–36. See "How To Begin," chap. 11 below. The change has been made by the editor.

154. Strauss next apparently turned away from the recording device in order to write the chapters of the third subsection on the chalkboard, and he repeated their numbers while doing so.

155. Strauss apparently again turned to write the chapter numbers, or related points, on the chalkboard.

lexicographic or exegetic chapters here: the terms for "pain," and the terms for "food," let me say. In the context of divine science, [as] Maimonides makes clear, "knowledge" means,[156] [or rather] "to eat" means, first[157]—it is used in such expressions as "God's consuming fire," in Hebrew "*'esh 'okhelet*": "eating fire" [is literally how one says] "consuming fire" [in Hebrew,] i.e., God's anger—that anger is directed chiefly or exclusively against idolatry.[158] Secondly, "eating" means the taking in of spiritual food, i.e., of the highest knowledge, knowledge of God.[159] Now this word "*aẓav*" ["to suffer pain"] also denotes anger and rebellion, and idolatry is the rebellion per excellence against God. Hence this subsection deals with two themes: knowledge of God, on the one hand, and idolatry, on the other. More precisely, as would appear if you were to read the chapters, this subsection deals with the difficulties obstructing knowledge or the dangers attending knowledge on the one hand, and with idolatry on the other. In the whole subsection, the discussion of "anger," i.e., of idolatry, surrounds the discussion of the dangers attending knowledge.[160] This is then the third subsection. We note in passing that whereas there are two exegetic chapters devoted to God's anger, there is none devoted to God's joy and laughing, also terms applied to God in the Bible.[161]

The fourth subsection, [chapters] thirty-seven to forty-nine, deals primar-

---

156. It is not entirely clear whether he intended to withdraw this phrase—"knowledge means"—because he seems to hesitate and start again, in order to explain, for Maimonides, what the biblical significance of "eating" is in divine science. Strauss is just starting to establish the connection between "eating" and knowledge for Maimonides, which will have great relevance, although one cannot be certain what precisely he had in mind just in this current sentence, since he has not yet discussed that connection. Because it is not entirely clear what he is thinking at this point, I have decided to leave that phrase as is, even though it may be a little bewildering for readers. To show what he was likely thinking, i.e., that he meant to withdraw this phrase (which is not quite wrong, but it is premature), I have removed the "um" sound which he uttered, and instead I have added the words "or rather" in square brackets, so as to show his evident reconsideration.

157. I have substituted "first" for "(a)" as what he actually spoke. He started to enumerate by letter, and next quickly changed, proceeding to enumerate by number. For the sake of clarity in reading, I have made it a consistent numbering of items.

158. Cf. *Guide* 1.29, pp. 62–63, with 1.36, pp. 82–85. To generalize Strauss's point about the significance of divine "anger" (and, relatedly, what idolatry is) in Maimonides, consider *Guide* 2.47, p. 409: "For only truth pleases Him, may He be exalted, and only that which is false angers Him."

159. See *Guide* 1.30, pp. 63–64, and 1.32, p. 69.

160. Strauss has not yet had the chance to explain fully what he intends by referring to chapters on "anger," i.e., idolatry, surrounding the discussion of knowledge and its difficulties: although 1.36 is a "speculative" rather than an exegetic (or rather lexicographic) chapter strictly speaking, its main theme is precisely "anger" and idolatry. Thus, he is not just speaking loosely in saying that the third subsection begins and end on this theme.

161. With respect to the two exegetical chapters "devoted to God's anger," Strauss seems to be referring to *Guide* 1.29 (less emphatically), and to 1.36 (more emphatically).

ily with the parts of the body, and then with the sense perceptions ascribed to God. The last subject in this subsection in regard to God is again "seeing," just as the first action of God discussed in the work was "seeing" in chapter four. Chapter forty-nine is in a class by itself; it deals not with God but with the angels, with the fact that the angels too are incorporeal.

In contradistinction to the third subsection, the fourth subsection is again predominantly exegetic; and the fifth subsection, which will come later, is again predominantly speculative.[162] So you have this: [an] almost entirely exegetic [subsection, i.e., the second]; [then] this is predominantly speculative [i.e., the third subsection]; [then] exegetic [i.e., the fourth subsection]; [then] speculative [i.e., the fifth subsection].[163] Maimonides did not want to have a great density of speculative chapters in the early parts of the work.

Now the fourth subsection ends with the theme, the incorporeality of angels, that is to say, the incorporeality of something which is in a plurality, which is many[, i.e.,] many angels. Not unity but incorporeality was the theme of this whole section up to this point. Unity (of God) was only the presupposition. Now Maimonides turns to this presupposition in chapter fifty.[164] (Let me make some order here. So, the fifth subsection is chapters fifty to sixty.)[165] I will explain that immediately.

---

162. Strauss apparently turned to the chalkboard, and to the diagram of sections, subsections, and chapters that he had presumably written on the board; next he knocked on the board with his chalk to show the main characteristic of each subsection in terms of mode of presentation. What he said while doing this is what follows in the text.

163. Obviously I cannot observe, on the tape, what Strauss actually did, but it sounds like him banging on the chalkboard and pointing to his itemized list, on which list he charted the subsections with which he has so far dealt or has at least mentioned. I have designated (in square brackets) the subsections in the order which I have suggested, because I am following the order of how it is stated by "How To Begin," chap. 11 below: "The majority of chapters of the first subsection [are] nonlexicographic and the majority of chapters of the second subsection [are] lexicographic." If one may assume that this statement makes the first subsection not mainly exegetical but rather mainly speculative, and since he begins his list with an exegetical subsection, and since he has referred to the fifth subsection as speculative (although he has not yet discussed it in detail), then there is good reason to think that he commenced this listing with the second subsection and concluded it with the fifth subsection, as exegesis and speculation alternate by subsection. (However, to what he was actually pointing on the board while banging with his chalk obviously cannot be definitely known.) If readers peruse these subsections for themselves, I believe they will confirm what has been suggested, i.e., subsections two through five alternate by exegesis and speculation. To be sure, I am unable to ascertain with certainty, but can only hypothesize about, why he chose to remain silent on the first subsection (although he dealt with it in some detail during his lecture), and why he began his list with the highlighting of the second subsection. My hypothesis is that the first subsection is not typical, being neither predominantly exegetical nor predominantly speculative, whatever this may signify.

164. Strauss next apparently turned to the chalkboard in order to write, adding some details about the fifth subsection, which cannot be determined from the tape.

165. Some of the words which Strauss spoke as he turned to the chalkboard are barely audible; they cannot be discerned with any certainty or confidence. He also makes a couple of trivial errors in speech, which he himself quickly corrects; I have decided not to preserve the details of these in the text. However,

Up to this point unity was presupposed, and on the basis of the belief in unity of God, incorporeality was taught. Now Maimonides turns to unity. The belief in unity,[166] as he is going to show, must be strictly understood, and not as the Christians do so that the unity of God is compatible with His trinity. In eleven chapters, Maimonides effects a radical transformation of the common, not to say traditional, conception of God's unity, in accordance with the requirements of speculation or of demonstration. But unity is not *demonstrated* here; that is to say, the demonstration is still postponed. The argument is based on the *premise* that God is one, in *every* respect. Maimonides indicates the gravity of the change which he effects in the ordinary understanding of God's unity by not quoting a single time, in the whole context devoted to God's unity, *the* biblical passage on unity, the *shema*.[167] The famous words [are]: "Hear Israel, the Lord is our God, the Lord is one."[168] He only indicates that the "one" in this verse means: God has no equal, which is not the same as absolute unity and absolute simplicity. Here there are no longer lexicographic chapters. And in this whole, long section, or series of subsections [as has previously been considered], there was only one chapter without *any* Jewish expression, to say nothing of [Jewish] quotation.[169] In these eleven chapters, there are five such chapters.[170] So, in other words, the alien element of philosophy comes in to a much higher degree.[171] And there is also a relatively clear distinction between the speculative discussion of unity

---

for those readers who want to know everything that is to be heard, even while these additions were being made to the list of subsections and chapters on the chalkboard, I will provide what has not been written, insofar as this is discernible by me: "Let me make some order here. So. The sixth subsection is, no, no, five, fifth, is chapters fifty to sixty-one—I will explain that later—no! fifty to sixty, I'm sorry."

166. The "which" occurring in spontaneous speech at this juncture in the sentence has been removed, since with it the rest of the sentence is forced to be a subordinate clause; if retained, there is no longer a proper sentence, and then the point that he aims to make becomes confused. He himself seems to have shifted strategy for uttering his thought in the middle of the sentence.

167. Curiously it is only mentioned once in the *Guide*, toward the end and almost in passing, or at least for a purpose seemingly not of the essence with regard to God's unity, i.e., to establish "the validity of the opinion affirming the existence of angels," which in spite of being many do not contradict the oneness of God: see *Guide* 3.45, p. 577.

168. Deuteronomy 6:4. The *shema* (or *sh'ma*) in its simpler form is usually regarded as the most ancient Jewish confession of faith or doxology. As a formal liturgical phrase, it is repeated at least twice daily, once each in the morning and evening Jewish worship services in its full form associated with a panoply of related verses, i.e., as the centerpiece of a bigger series and structure of scriptural passages, prayers, and blessings built around it, especially but not only Deuteronomy 6:4–9, 11:13–21; and Numbers 15:37–41.

169. See *Guide* 1.31, pp. 65–67. Cf. also "How To Begin," chap. 11 below. Whatever it may mean, previously Strauss says: "Chapters thirty-one and thirty-five are the first chapters without any Jewish quotation." However, he is obviously speaking precisely: 1.35 contains not any "Jewish quotations," but certainly several "Jewish expressions."

170. See *Guide* 1.51, 52, 56, 58, 60.

171. Strauss's voice on the tape is not entirely audible. The word "degree" is likely, but not certain.

INTRODUCTION TO *THE GUIDE OF THE PERPLEXED* / 469

in these chapters, and in the next subsection, [chapters] sixty-one to sixty-seven, which are exegetic. I [shall] explain that briefly.

According to Maimonides, the unity of God means absolute simplicity in every respect. God does not possess, strictly speaking, a multiplicity of attributes: living, wise, being, and so on. We know only *that* God is, but not *what* He is. But when we ascribe "being" to God and to creatures, being has only the name in common. We do not know what we mean when ascribing any attribute to God. We know only the name, so to speak. [Chapters] sixty-one to sixty-seven deal with the names of God, the Hebrew names.[172] This subsection is altogether exegetic, although no longer lexicographic. (Forgive me that word, but I hope it is intelligible; it does not look like a dictionary any more.) We note again a remarkable silence. *The* key passage regarding God's name—Exodus 6:2–3—is never mentioned in the whole *Guide*.[173] I mean the passage: "And God said to Moses: I am the Lord. And I appeared unto Abraham, and to Isaac, and to Jacob by the name of El-Shaddai, but by My name Ha-Shem, was I not known unto them," I mean, the Name, [the] Sacred Name.[174] This word[, i.e., verse] is never quoted [by Maimonides]. This is obviously one of the greatest secrets of the Torah. Name is connected, the name of God, with the honor of God: "*shem ha-Shem kevod ha-Shem*."[175] The audible, holy

---

172. According to Strauss's plan, *Guide* 1.61–67 constitutes the sixth subsection of the first section.

173. I am not quite sure what to make of this statement, or just what Strauss had in mind by it. In any case, it seems to me that it is of a certainty not quite accurate: see *Guide* 2.35, p. 367. Perhaps one might think Strauss wished to make readers aware of the fact that, of the two continuous verses which he cited, only a portion of this unit is actually quoted by Maimonides in the just-designated chapter, and not the complete divine utterance? Or that this verse is "never mentioned" or dealt with in the chapters dedicated to the divine name (1.61–67)? Or one might perhaps also think by this "never mentioned" that Strauss means to say: only the mysterious four-letter Name of God is not discussed. But this too is not accurate, as one may be confident that he knew: both 1.61, pp. 147–50, and 1.64, pp. 156–57, deal with the four-letter name of God, although to be sure not in the same context in which Exodus 6:2–3 is raised, and as might seem to call for a separate discussion of the name of God as raised in those verses. See also nn. 98 above, and 174 and 175 below. Similarly I assume that the sentence occurring in a moment ("This word[, i.e., verse] is never quoted [by Maimonides]."), reiterates the same point; but it is no answer to the question raised in this note.

174. "Ha-Shem," "the Name," or "the Sacred Name," i.e., the Tetragrammaton, is the mysterious four-letter, consonantal Hebrew name of God, which *cannot* be properly pronounced because the correct vowels are not known, or rather are no longer known since the destruction of the Jerusalem Temple in 70 C.E. Subsequent Judaism employs assorted euphemisms ("the Lord," "God," "the Name" [i.e., "Ha-Shem"], the four consonants, "Yod-He-Vav-He" but instead with the substitute letters "Yod-Qe-Vav-Qe," etc.) in order to be able to both "pronounce" and yet not pronounce the true name of God. See also nn. 98 and 173 above, and 175 below.

175. "The name of God is the honor (or glory) of God." Strauss seems to suggest that he is referring by this sentence to a well-known Jewish saying, as if from a classical Jewish source; but I do not know this saying, nor have I been able to locate it in the sources that I have attempted to search. The Bar-Ilan University Global Jewish Database also did not know of this sentence, either in the precise form used by Strauss or in any form that closely resembles it, at least which I have been able to trace. Maimonides deals

names take the place of the visible, holy images or shapes.[176] God is named not by Himself, but by man. This brings up the question of God's speaking. The whole subsection here deals somehow with God's not being a speaking Being, a rational Being in the literal sense of the word, *logikon*,[177] just as this whole subsection, or [rather] this series of subsections, dealt with the fact that God is not a body nor a living being proper, an animal, and so on.

Now with 1.68[178] a new subsection [i.e., the seventh] begins, and which goes as a matter of fact up to chapter seventy. This subsection is very clearly again based on philosophy, perhaps more clearly than any previous subsection.[179] What do we see is its subject?[180] Chapter sixty-eight takes up the teaching of chapters fifty to sixty, according to which God's life is identical

---

most thoroughly with the themes of *the* one true Name of God, with the other divine names, as well as with what they signify separately and together, in what Strauss calls the sixth subsection (*Guide* 1.61–67); in 1.64 especially, he deals with *the* Name of God, i.e., the Tetragrammaton, as an equivocal term. So far as I have been able to determine, Maimonides never uses this phrase "the name of God is the honor (or glory) of God," and definitely not in the sixth subsection. It is certainly possible that Strauss has invented this sentence himself, in order to express (in an original phrase) an idea which he presents as representative of Maimonides' thought. It also seemed to me not impossible, based on ideas the Jewish mystics are known to have taught, that this saying may have originated with one of them, or may have derived from a Jewish mystical source not yet uncovered. (Gershom Scholem speaks about a certain Jewish attitude of mind which may be summarized in the saying "In the beginning was the Name.") However, it is the opinion of Professor Elliot R. Wolfson that this is Strauss's own formulation, and is not derived from any mystical source at least that is known to him. My thanks to Professor Wolfson for his generous advice and assistance on this matter. It should at least be parenthetically noted that the word "glory" (*kavod*), as in the "glory of God" (*kevod Elohim*), is occasionally used in the Hebrew Bible for "the hidden things," as in "It is the glory of God to conceal a thing, but the glory of kings is to search out a matter" (Proverbs 25:2). Curiously in the *Guide* Maimonides never actually refers directly to this verse (and it is missing from Pines's index at the end of "Biblical Passages Appearing in the Text"); but he uses it obliquely, or at least he alludes to it, through its midrashic treatment (Bereshit Rabba IX) in *Guide* 2.29, p. 347.

176. See "How To Begin," chap. 11 below.

177. What is usually translated by Aristotle's definition of the human being, "*zoon logikon*," i.e., "rational animal" or "rational living being," can just as literally be translated as "speaking animal" or "speaking living being." See *Guide* 1.1, pp. 21–23, as well as "Logic," in *Ethical Writings*, trans. Weiss and Butterworth, p. 158: similar to Aristotle's phrase, the Arabic word he uses for man's "rational power" (in the sense of logic) can just as correctly be translated as his power of speech.

178. Strauss must have misspoken. He clearly said 1.61 on the tape; however, according to his own plan of the *Guide* (see "How To Begin," chap. 11 below), the next, i.e., seventh, subsection distinctly begins with 1.68 and ends with 1.70. Also, the contents that he is about to discuss evidently derive from what is manifestly contained in 1.68, and not in 1.61. Thus, in the text of the transcribed lecture, this chapter reference has been corrected.

179. For the sake of clarity and consistency, the two references in this sentence to "section" have been corrected so as to make them references to "subsection." It is especially urgent to make clear distinctions, in that Strauss's plan of the *Guide* depends substantially on the significance of divisions between sections and subsections.

180. The tape is barely audible on some of the words in this sentence. It is especially the middle words of "What do we see is its subject?" that are only tentative. Strauss either swallowed his words, or the tape ran them together. It is also possible that in this sentence he could also have been saying, "What is it, is its subject?"

with His self-apprehension. The chapter deals with God as mind, *nous*, intellect. Now the word "intellect" if applied to God and man is univocal, and not merely homonymous, as all other terms are. It means that God is the intellect, the act of intellect[ion], and the intellected thing in one. That is the point which he makes here. A similar triad is the subject of the next chapter: God is the final, the formal, and the efficient cause of the world. He is the efficient cause especially by being the first Mover.[181] . . .

[*A break in the tape apparently occurred.*][182]

. . . first glance, the God of Abraham, Isaac, and Jacob, the God Whose existence is proven by the miracles[183] of survival. Now as Maimonides says, people who are not perfect, are corrupted in their beliefs when they are brought to realize that things are different than they had imagined them. *Now* it has become necessary to demonstrate God's existence, unity, and incorporeality. This is the theme of the second section,[184] which begins here, and which has a clear overall plan; the details are also understood:[185] chapter seventy-one in the first part through chapter thirty-one in the second part. By the way, the first chapter of this section, [chapter] seventy-one, is a most readable chapter of the *Guide*. It is a very clear summary of the history of theology as far as it was known and relevant to Maimonides, and states the issues with mag-

---

181. See *Guide* 1.69, pp. 166–70.
182. As a result of the break in the tape which apparently occurred, a portion of the lecture material is undoubtedly missing. It is not known from anything in the tape precisely how much material this may be. However, he has moved from the first section (seventh subsection) to the second section of Maimonides' *Guide*. The topic that Strauss merely broaches—God as *nous*, and as final, formal, and efficient cause of the world (discussed in 1.68)—constitutes one of the famous contradictions in the *Guide*, especially if contrasted with 1.50–60.
183. The word is less than perfectly audible: it is not entirely clear whether Strauss says the singular "miracle," or the plural "miracles." However, to my hearing, the plural seems definitely more probable.
184. Strauss next apparently turned to the chalkboard in order to write, presumably adding the chapter numbers of the second section. Strauss actually says "subsection" in the spontaneity of his speech, but it is evident that this is a reference, according to his own plan of the *Guide*, to "the second section," and not to "the second subsection." The second section covers *Guide* 1.71–2.31. His title for it is "Demonstrations of the existence, unity, and incorporeality of God."
185. The words which follow "the details are" are only barely audible. Thus, what I have recorded Strauss as saying is only very tentative: "The details are also understood." It is also quite possible that this might actually be "The details are up on the board." He spoke from a distance while he wrote on the chalkboard, which is why it is difficult to hear, presumably listing the chapters contained in the second section. But the former seems to me to make better sense in context than the latter, which is why I preferred it: both the "overall plan" and "the details" of the second section are "clear" or "understood"; this makes sense in terms of that which he will proceed to say about the structure of the second section; it is readily comprehended. However, "the details are up on the board" is also possible because he may be referring to what the specific chapters ("the details") of the second section are, as he writes them on the chalkboard.

nificent clarity. So if anyone would like to have a specimen of Maimonides, which can be digested in a purely historical manner, I advise the individual in question to read it.

Now, I have to explain now something which is of very great importance. Maimonides is confronted here with this problem: he has to prove now the basic principles—existence, unity, and incorporeality of God. There was one well-known way of doing that, the way of *kalam*. This was originally an Islamic, later a Jewish, way of thinking, which Maimonides rejects. The *kalam* proves the existence of God by *assuming* creation, creation of the world, and concludes from the fact of creation, the existence of a Creator—which sounds to be almost an analytical thing.[186] But in greater fairness I would have to say, they tried first to *prove* the fact of creation. But these proofs were, according to Maimonides, entirely spurious proofs. Starting from imaginary premises, such as atomism—they took over[187] Greek atomism in certain variations—and on this basis they tried to prove that the world has been created, and then of course it must have a Creator. The first problem of Maimonides is to refute *kalam*, and that he does in chapters seventy-three through seventy-six. And then he begins with the true premises, the premises supplied by the world as it is;[188] as we say, he begins as the philosophers begin. Therefore the second part begins with twenty-six premises, and they are all taken from Aristotle. And so then he has a philosophic argument, a philosophic cosmology, in a subsection which goes roughly—no, which goes exactly—from chapters two to twelve.[189] And then he has the next . . . I will explain immediately. One

---

186. It is difficult to know for certain why Strauss asserts about the *kalam* approach that it is "almost an analytical thing." Most likely Strauss uses "analytical" in (to speak anachronistically) the Kantian sense of an "analytic judgment" (as opposed to a "synthetic judgment"), i.e., a judgment based on an analysis of the term, and not referring to anything empirical. But this may also have been an allusion to the "Analytical" (also known as the "Anglo-American") school of philosophy, which was quite popular in the 1950s and 1960s, especially in the English-speaking academic world? If so, one might be helped by considering Stanley Rosen, *The Limits of Analysis* (New York: Basic Books, 1980). As is perhaps noteworthy, at a certain point Rosen uses Maimonides' critique of the *kalam* to illustrate a fundamental flaw in the premises on which "analysis" is based.

187. Just prior to this phrase "they took over," Strauss started to say "they wanted"; but he seems to withdraw that word and to restate the thought as it is.

188. See *Guide* 1.71, pp. 178–79: "All the first Mutakallimun from among the Greeks who adopted Christianity and from among the Muslims did not conform in their premises to the appearance of that which exists, but considered how being ought to be in order that it should furnish a proof for correctness of a particular opinion or at least should not refute it." Or as he lucidly continues: "I shall say to you that the matter is as Themistius puts it: that which exists does not conform to the various opinions, but rather the correct opinions conform to that which exists."

189. Strauss next apparently turned to the chalkboard in order to write, adding the chapter numbers presumably in the subsection of the second section with which he was presently concerned. He was closer to the mark, at least according to the finished version of his own plan, by saying in the lecture "roughly"

point is clear about it even now. [To understand] this new part, the second part, now let us look at the first part: we have this discussion first of incorporeality, and then of unity, i.e., exegetic discussion[190] generally speaking, based on authoritative traditional religion.[191] Here he refutes a spurious theology; the true principles, the true basis comes to sight only at the beginning of the second part.

Now there is this difficulty: the proof of the existence, unity, and incorporeality of God as given by Aristotle is based on the premise that the visible universe is eternal, and that of course is unacceptable to any Jew. Therefore Maimonides is concerned then, after having proven existence, unity, and incorporeality of God on the basis of Aristotle, [that] he must then take issue with Aristotle, with a view to Aristotle's premise, namely, that the world is eternal, and establish the creation of the world. And that he does in chapters thirteen to thirty-one. So there is, I say, a roughly tripartite argument: critique of *kalam*; the philosophic argument; critique of philosophy, i.e., of Aristotle. The first part, we can say with a permissible exaggeration, is fundamentally unphilosophic, prephilosophic if you will. The part based on philosophy begins in the second part.

Now I must say a few words at any rate about the rest of the plan. Yeah, I'm thinking [it's] almost [a matter of] compassion for you, because what I began I must finish.[192] [*Audience laughter.*] That was the second section. Now we come to the third section, and that is easy and no one has ever doubted that this is a clear section, it is obvious: 2.32–48.[193] This is the end of the second part, dealing with prophecy. It is equally clear that the beginning of the third part is a unity [i.e., *Guide* 3.1–7, which forms section IV], seven chapters

---

rather than "exactly": section II, subsection 4, in his plan consists of *Guide* 2.2 *only* (i.e., "Maimonides' demonstration"), while section II, subsection 5, in his plan consists of Guide 2.3-12 (i.e., "the angels"). But these small "errors" in remembering his own plan do not alter the flow of his larger point.

190. Strauss seems to have corrected what he was starting to say: he started with "exegetic doctrine," but substituted for it "exegetic discussion."

191. Strauss seems to say "authoritative traditional religion," which is most probable. However, speaking quickly, he slurs the words together; it is also not impossible that this phrase is "authoritative rabbinical tradition," or even "authoritative exegetical tradition."

192. Strauss made a joke while speaking very quietly, which is barely audible on tape, and which aroused loud audience laughter as he was talking. Unfortunately that joke is followed by a phrase submerged by the laughter, so several further words also cannot be discerned. I have attempted to reconstruct what this previous joke may have been, although it is mostly a guess.

193. Strauss while speaking gives the chapters on prophecy as 2.33-41. I assume he misspoke in the spontaneity of speaking while on a break from the formal lecture and his notes, and while he walked away recounting what he had just written on the chalkboard. Neither in his plan nor in any of his other works are these chapters named as what constitutes the section on prophecy. As he himself was wont to emphasize, "no one has ever doubted" that this is clearly a separate section, "it is [so] obvious": *Guide* 2.32-48. As a result, a certain liberty has had to be taken by the editor in order to correct what he misspoke.

devoted to the secret interpretation of the *ma'aseh merkavah*, [i.e.,] Ezekiel chapters one and ten.[194] At the end of chapter seven there is a most important remark about the plan of the book, [perhaps one of the most important] which is ever made.[195] Maimonides says here, he will not say any further word about the "chariot," about the divine science proper, in this sequel. Everything going before was required for that, so that it's really very complete, a unity. Everything was required; and nothing in this sequel has anything to do with it[, i.e., with the "chariot"]. So that's the greatest incision, you can say, which exists in the book.[196]

The next section, [i.e.,] the next chapter, begins with the words: "Bodies which come into being and perish."[197] The preceding parts dealt with God and angels, with nonbodily beings,[198] which as such do not come into being. One little conclusion for us: there is missing a discussion of the bodies which do not come into being and perish;[199] that means to say, the celestial bodies. That [missing discussion] is connected with an omission of physics to which I have referred before.[200]

So, that this [next section] is [part] three, [chapters] eight through twenty-four[, it] is the section dealing with the problem of providence. Providence meanwhile is about human beings, i.e., beings living in bodies, which come

---

194. Strauss apparently turned in order to write the words *ma'aseh merkavah* on the chalkboard, and perhaps also presumably the chapter numbers and the section number, adding these things to the record he has kept for his listeners on the board. For the benefit of those readers who are following these things with some care, I have added the same data in square brackets. According to Strauss's plan, this is the middle section of the book, and that makes it somehow perhaps the most significant section in terms of its contents: "the account of the chariot."

195. A phrase is added because of the way in which Strauss uttered the sentence. In my judgment, this shows he intended two thoughts that were imperfectly expressed by being combined in the spontaneity of speech. As spoken, it was "At the end of chapter seven there is a most important remark about the plan of the book ever made."

196. Strauss's words have been reordered slightly for the sake of greater syntactical correctness in English. The way the sentence was spoken is as follows: "So that's the greatest incision, you can say, in the book, which exists." The "which exists" was added at the end to clarify the prior phrase; but it belongs prior to the last three words, which is as I have rearranged it.

197. *Guide*, 3.8 (trans. Pines), p. 430, renders it: "All bodies subject to generation and corruption."

198. At the end of this phrase Strauss seems to swallow a word that could be either "beings" or "being." It seems to me most probable that this is "beings."

199. Strauss's point is not made with the greatest clarity in this context. It seems that he refers to the heavenly bodies, i.e., the planets, stars, constellations, and spheres. Consider especially "How To Begin," chap. 11 below: "It suffices to mention that no section or subsection of the *Guide* is devoted to the bodies that do not come into being and perish . . . , i.e., to the heavenly bodies, which according to Maimonides possess life and knowledge, or to 'the holy bodies,' to use the bold expression used by him in his Code."

200. See above, the last two paragraphs at the end of part 1 of the lecture. The word in the previous sentence, "celestial," is very uncertain; it is only a guess, based on its quite garbled or muffled sound, combined with a reasonable surmise about he is saying.

into being and perish. Maimonides is absolutely silent about the immortality of the soul, and therefore the discussion of providence becomes identical with the discussion of certain bodies which come into being and perish.[201] [Part] three, [chapters] twenty-five through fifty deals with the Torah in the stricter sense, with the commandments of the Torah as well as with the stories told in the Torah. And [part] three, [chapters] fifty-one through fifty-four is the conclusion of the whole work. So you have altogether seven sections. The central one is [part] three, [chapters] one through seven: seven chapters devoted to the most sacred and most secret things. And this, one could say, is as it should be. I cannot show it here, in detail, that all these sections, with the exception of the last one, are all divided into seven subsections, so that seven is in a way—but not completely—the key number for this mysterious work.

I believe, though I have some more material, that there is a limit to everything. Thank you for your patience.

[*The lecture ends with loud audience applause.*]

DISCUSSION PERIOD FOLLOWING THE LECTURE PART 2[202]

Strauss: [spoken quietly] Have the discussion now.

Joseph Cropsey, Chairman: We're deeply indebted to Dr. Strauss. Normally at this point there would be a break for refreshments, but I think that the ingestion of food would be unduly reminiscent of the corporeality [*audience laughter*], which ought not to be intruded on the intention at this point. And so there has been a change proposed, and Dr. Strauss has consented to accept the questions directly.

Strauss: Yeah, or the objections. All right. Perhaps we can do it this way, that we [can] have a subsection. Prior to the food . . .

---

201. Strauss swallows his words, so that a phrase at the end of this sentence is barely audible; it is probable that this is "which come into being and perish."

202. The only discussion period that survives, as preserved on the tape recordings, is of the second part of Strauss's lecture, which was like the first part also called "Introduction to Maimonides' *The Guide of the Perplexed*," and which continues directly from the lecture, part 1, delivered at the Hillel House of the University of Chicago on 14 February 1960. A transcribed version of this discussion period following part 2 of the lecture is preserved on a tape recording and is what ensues. In a remark expressed at the end of the first part of the lecture by the chairman, Professor Joseph Cropsey, and in a passing comment made by Strauss during the second part of the lecture (both preserved on tape), it is indicated that a discussion period did also follow the part 1 of the lecture, but (unlike part 2) this was either not recorded, or the tape has been lost.

Audience member: Because we mature during the . . .

Strauss: . . . prior to the food and water . . . No, three: one, while we're eating, and one, not . . . [*Audience laughter.*] Now, all right: do you have any questions. . . . There are so many objections possible![203] For example: why did I speak so much about the mere *experience* of the book, and not about the substance?

Questioner: That is not a question.

Strauss: It is an objection. But I said "objection." And that is in order.[204]

Questioner: Would you like then to explain why you [spoke mostly about the plan of the *Guide*, which does not actually appear in the *Guide*?][205]

[*Audience laughter.*]

Strauss: Because it is also part of the book. And if the author says that this book was written with *exceeding* care,[206] one has also to consider the externals. Furthermore, when one goes into the substantive issues, one gets into very great difficulties, which cannot be solved except by considering these things. But I give you a similar point. When I was much younger, I was about your age or a bit older, I tried to understand Maimonides' doctrine of providence. I was not [so] innocent at this point; [knowing his book, I had some access to it].[207] And it seemed too clear that when I read a few and more lines, I had to revise the sentence I had put down already. And then I revised it. And then after a few [more] lines I began again to revise it. So there was this strange elusiveness about it. And then I observed that he uses two terms for providence, in Hebrew *hashgaḥah* and *hanhagah*, and which we can translate, the one as "providence" and the other as "governance." And I found he used them synonymously. But somehow it didn't seem [quite so]; [on repeated readings] they appeared [to be] completely

---

203. If I may surmise, what seems to have happened is that a long silence ensued in which no one immediately raised a hand. This caused Strauss to suggest objections of his own to his approach, in order to embolden the audience members, and perhaps also to allow them a chance to gather their thoughts.

204. Strauss's voice becomes muted. This sentence is difficult to decipher, and it is only a reasonable guess that he says: "And that is in order."

205. The questioner starts to speak clearly, but by the end grows so faint that his voice is not distinct. My attempt to reconstruct this question is in the square brackets; it is derivative of Strauss's answer.

206. Strauss refers to the *Guide*, 1.Intro., p. 15. See n. 50 above, with the text of Strauss's lecture to which it refers.

207. The end of this sentence, even if the words are quasi-audible on the tape, is barely discernible. It seems that either Strauss ran these words together or the original tape garbled them; even the remastered version is of little help to unscramble them. Hence, what is offered in the present sentence is my best guess at what he is saying. It is put in square brackets, even though Strauss did say something; but I cannot be certain that this is truly what he says.

different.²⁰⁸ So I was compelled to make revisions through [my reading of] the book. And then I saw that there are large sections in which only "governance" occurs, and then there are other sections in which only "providence" occurs, and then [there] are others in which both occur promiscuously. Furthermore (and then this became decisive for that), I saw that a reference to the chapters on *hanhagah*, on governance, [occurs] somewhere around 1.40 or so,²⁰⁹ which is ordinarily understood to refer to the section on providence, the fifth section.²¹⁰ Now, as you [can] see, if *maʿaseh merkavah* is the most important thing, [and] if that means translated, "governance," then it is, you know, incredibly important. I mean, after all, that you can follow without any understanding from the mere verbal expression: if the greatest thing is the *merkavah*, the "chariot"—and you can find a technical term (I mean a technical term for "governance") as the translation of that—that is or must be of terrible importance for understanding the text.²¹¹ And so I saw that such things like, for example, the specificities²¹² of words, are meant, have to be meant. Now [if] in fact you cannot know [at first] which [word is] extra, [that] may not be [so] important.²¹³ I mean,

---

208. Strauss slurred together certain words in this sentence while speaking quickly, so that they are not all clearly distinguishable; my attempt at a reconstruction is more or less speculative. Hence the words in square brackets, although they represent Strauss saying something, are too garbled or muted to declare for certain as his own words.

209. See *Guide* 1.40, p. 90, on "air" (*ruaḥ*), one of whose uses in Hebrew is "purpose or will." Maimonides says he will explain this sixth use of the term "in the chapters that will deal with His governance." According to Strauss's plan, the formal treatment of providence occurs in the fifth section, *Guide* 3.8–24. However, the discussion promised in 1.40 curiously begins to resume not in the section on providence, or even in the formally designated subsection on "the views regarding providence," i.e., 3.17–18, but rather in the middle portion of the book, which is the fourth section, and which is dedicated to interpreting *maʿaseh merkavah*: *Guide* 3.2, p. 419. It is known to be the resumption because of a direct reference by Maimonides himself in the aforementioned passage. As Strauss makes readers of the *Guide* aware, it is hence unclear what the chapters dealing with governance are. Or to restate this point more precisely although not less perplexingly: he compels readers to acknowledge that the "chapters on governance" cannot automatically be associated, never mind equated, with the "chapters on providence." Cf. also Strauss's statement in n. 211 below.

210. I am not absolutely certain that the phrase uttered by Strauss is "the fifth section," although this is most probable.

211. "How To Begin," chap. 11 below: "'governance' being as it were the translation of *Merkavah* ("Chariot"), as appears from 1.70." For the passage in *Guide* 1.70 to which he seems to be referring, see pp. 174–75. Strauss utters a phrase at the end of this sentence that is very quietly spoken, and almost too difficult to discern the words. The phrase "for understanding the text" is highly speculative, and closer to an educated guess.

212. The word "specificity" is certain. However, it is uncertain whether this is spoken as a plural, although that seems most probable.

213. I have added so many words in square brackets because I have had to surmise what this condensed sentence aims to communicate, based on relatively few words that have not been swallowed or garbled.

then one has simply to [continue thinking about it].[214] And I think the plan [is central,[215] and yet] I believe I have never found this plan at least in any writings. And I think it is . . . I believe if you read these studies [of mine], you will find it [i.e., this plan] helpful [for understanding the *Guide*].[216] And it is an absolute condition, it seems to me, for understanding the substantive issues.

Questioner: I would appreciate a word about your distinction between the "secret" and the "nonsecret" teaching. Is "secret" in terms of some area of ideas or knowledge? Or is "secret" that which represents a dimension of all the knowledge? [Of course,] I don't know[, even if Maimonides did assign "secret" to an area of ideas or knowledge, whether this is clearly demarcated in his book].[217]

Strauss: No, no, there is a clear division of subject matter. Well, clear in principle. But there are so many overlapping subjects that you get into real troubles. I advise you to read chapter thirty-five of the first part of the *Guide*,[218]

---

214. I have added the words "[continue to think about it]," because it seems obvious to me Strauss did not finish the sentence. As it further seems to me, it is not much of a stretch to maintain that this is what he was implying. However, readers can judge for themselves and dismiss what I have done if they wish, since whatever is in square brackets is the surmise of the editor. I can only defend my decision by saying that I reached this result, as likewise in similar cases, by repeated hearings and through much reflection on what Strauss actually says. The choice was either to leave the sentence unfinished and hence potentially misleading, or try to surmise what I believe he was trying to say. Obviously a much higher than average occurrence of unfinished phrases or sentences is manifest in the present reply.

215. I have added the words in square brackets, "the plan [is central, and yet]," because it seems to me that he starts this thought or something like it, but changes course briefly. He will return to a similar thought in a moment; but as it seems to me in the context of the rest of this sentence, it is not fitting to merely repeat that word which he will say ("helpful").

216. As has been noted, this series of sentences has had to be reconstructed, since Strauss often changes course and breaks his own continuity. It seems he is trying to compress or abbreviate several thoughts, so much so that he leaves phrases to dangle unfinished. But for those readers who are sure to want to know how it actually sounds, so as to judge for themselves, I shall reproduce these sentences as I hear them on the tape: "Now if that you cannot know which extra, may not be important. I mean, then one has simply to . . . and I think the plan, . . . I believe that I have never found it at least in any writings, this plan, and I think it is . . . I believe if you read these studies, you will find it helpful." I have obviously assumed that by "these studies," he presumably means his own studies of Maimonides, i.e., those gathered together in the present book. This must especially refer to "How To Begin," which focuses on the plan of the *Guide*, although it had not yet appeared in print as of 1960.

217. The questioner is unusually clear and audible at first—until his last sentence, which completely fades away. The rest of the sentence is my guess about what he is getting at, based again on Strauss's reply.

218. *Guide* 1.35, pp. 79–81, announces his absolute requirement: everyone in society (even the children) must know, or rather must be taught to believe, that God is incorporeal. This belief, as he unconditionally states, must in no sense whatsoever be kept secret. Strauss adds the existence and unity of God; but of course in Maimonides' era he had no reason to state these two additional points as things to teach about God. They constituted self-evident truths, as it were.

if I am not mistaken [but] I am almost sure, where Maimonides tries to draw a line. But one can say this: the existence, unity, and incorporeality of God cannot be secret teachings. But the precise meaning of providence, for example, it belongs to the secret teaching. One can also say, the peculiar status of Moses, the highest of the prophets, is a secret, as is indicated by the following massive contradiction: on the one hand, Maimonides says Moses[219] is the only prophet who did not use his imagination, imagination being regarded as a lower faculty.[220] And then one can prove it from *n* pages in the *Guide* that Moses did use his imagination. It's never cleared up. Let me put it this way: where, in any subject, regarding which there is a contradiction, there is a safe assumption that it is secret.

Questioner: How do you harmonize the "image of God" with corporeality, and His using human bodies, our [visible] shape?[221]

Strauss: No, I mean, well, what Maimonides says is that God is incorporeal, and that the passage[222] ["man created in the image of God"] must not be taken literally. But still, if you have no knowledge and are suddenly confronted with this sentence, you might think God is a corporeal being. If God created man in His image or likeness, there would seem to be also an inverse relation, and hence that God would also be in the image or likeness of man, and therefore looks like man. After all, there were quite a few nations in the world who believed that the gods have human shape, I mean, the pagans. And therefore Maimonides is compelled to go into this whole question of corporeality. And [yet] there were also certain mystical doctrines in Judaism which, in a mystical way, spoke of "the body of God."

---

219. Strauss begins this sentence with a phrase that I cannot discern clearly. I only surmise that this is "on the one hand." Strauss also misspeaks by saying "Maimonides is the only prophet"; it has been corrected to "Moses," which is undoubtedly what he meant.

220. See *Guide* 2.35, pp. 367–68; 2.36, p. 373; and 2.45, p. 403: the prophecy of Moses is unique in that it is completely free of the imagination. (To be sure, other things also make it unique, such as his alone being a lawgiving prophet, his miracles, etc.) Maimonides puts an even greater emphasis on this notion in the *Commentary on the Mishnah* and the *Mishneh Torah* (to which he refers his readers in *Guide* 2.35). Cf. also "How To Begin," chap. 11 below.

221. A phrase at the end of this question is not clear enough to discern definitely. I only speculate that the questioner says "our shape" (with "[visible]" obviously added by the editor). It is also remotely possible that this questioner may be saying "our Savior"; in this case, it is reasonable to assume that he is asking the question from a Christian perspective. It is to be noted that Strauss employs the word "shape" in his answer, but this is not a proof of what is said in the question. Some also hear the word "our form" following "our shape"; if so, obviously the questioner refers to bodily form.

222. That this word is "passage" is quite probable, but not absolutely certain. By "passage" I believe Strauss means to say "biblical passage," in the sense of either a whole biblical verse or part of a biblical verse. Hence I have added in square brackets the "passage" to which I presume he refers in Genesis 1:26–27. See also n. 100 above.

Somehow they did not simply reject the notion that God is corporeal,[223] although they did not mean that in a crude way.[224]

Questioner: I have two questions, one of which concerns the remark you made at one point that one concept which was applied to man and to God is not merely used homonymously . . .

Strauss: Yeah, it is used for that. Yeah, that is the teaching.

Questioner: There was one term [which was so used], I think it was mind, intellect?

Strauss: Yeah.

Questioner: I would like a clarification of this issue. I mean, in what sense is this one not used, and in what sense are the others used?

Strauss: Yeah, well, I can only say that it's a fact.

Questioner: Well, Maimonides explains this, does he?

Strauss: No. No, no.

Questioner: Does he see this?

Strauss: No. Maimonides says . . . See, eleven[225] chapters, which are generally known as the chapters on the doctrine of attributes, [*Guide*] 1.50–60, they come up with this final suggestion, that all terms applied to God have only the *name* in common, terms corresponding to [living beings],[226] man or any other beast. And then in fact when you read this chapter, [*Guide*] 1.68, dealing with the mind, you see here [that there] is no homonymity, but he has cut it [out].[227] And especially if one takes the minor trouble of looking

---

223. Strauss started to formulate this thought positively as "simply say," but corrects himself to "simply reject," obviously considering that the thought is better formulated negatively. His self-correction has been deleted from the text (and added to the notes), so as not to confuse readers about Strauss's meaning in the rest of sentence.

224. For Strauss's point about "the body of God" (i.e., God as corporeal) as a notion not rejected by the Jewish mystics, even if they did not affirm it "in a crude way," perhaps the best starting point for any further study is the essay by Gershom Scholem "The Mystical Shape of the Godhead," in *On the Mystical Shape of the Godhead: Basic Concepts in the Kabbalah*, trans. Joachim Neugroschel, and ed. and rev. Jonathan Chipman (New York: Schocken, 1991), pp. 15–55. See also n. 100 above.

225. In spontaneous speech Strauss says "ten chapters." However, the chapters of the *Guide* in which Maimonides elaborates what is known as "the doctrine of attributes" actually consist of eleven chapters (i.e., *Guide* 1.50–60), what even in Strauss's plan is designated as the fifth subsection. In fact, at three points in the lecture he has already spoken of the "eleven chapters" on the doctrine of attributes. ("The eleven chapters devoted to the doctrine"; "In eleven chapters, Maimonides effects a radical transformation"; "In these eleven chapters.") I have corrected it in the text accordingly.

226. The phrase "living beings" is an educated guess. I base it only on what it makes sense for him to have been saying. Strauss, or the tape recording, slurs his words together so that this phrase cannot be discerned with any certainty.

227. The phrase "he has cut it [out]" is probable at best. Others hear the future tense: "he will cut it [out]." Strauss, or the tape recording, slurs his words together so that this phrase almost cannot be discerned. But the sounds I hear uttered roughly correspond to these words. In my opinion, whether it is in the past or in the future tense is a smaller point because it in no sense changes the meaning. Strauss speaks

up the source of Maimonides' statement, that the intellect, and the act of intellection, intelligizing if one can say that, and the *intellectum*, [i.e.,] the intellected thing, are identical. Because that apparently is Aristotle's point to show, where he says of man, that he becomes filled with the *noumena*.[228] So that is so. I mean, that leads to great questions. And one wants to read and reread it to understand it.

Questioner: That was one question. The second question concerns a reference to what you said, that Maimonides says that the people to whom the Torah was given were previously (I think he uses the word) "Sabians," or "S'bians"?[229]

Strauss: Sabians, yes. I don't know how you pronounce it properly. I can write it.

Questioner: Well that word is definitely, it seems to me, of Islamic origin . . .

Strauss: True, it's from the Qur'an.

Questioner: . . . I mean the use of this term. Now I would like to know, if you can just say a few words, whether this is merely a passing allusion, or whether Islamic theology has a large amount of place in this?

Strauss: I think, I don't believe [it's quite as you put it, i.e., either a passing allusion or filling a large amount]. There are certain Islamic terms, for example, the term which he uses for [divine] "unity," *tawhid*, distinct, is a term that you know;[230] and there are other terms he uses, *du'a*,[231] and this kind [of thing] occurs. But I think . . . And of course, he uses Islamic philosophers; but whether the Islamic philosophers were such models of Muslims is a very moot question, you know. And therefore that doesn't quite fall under this setting. But I would say, no. I mean, the only point

---

colloquially as if the reader were studying Maimonides's book in order, and so he will first encounter the doctrine of attributes (1.50–60). If, as it were, standing at this point he looks from what is to what is yet to be, he sees that Maimonides "will cut [out]" intellect from homonymity in the "future" section, 1.68. Strauss's larger point is that rather than explain why homonymity has been dropped in the case of intellect, Maimonides just proceeds as if it is something obvious, and he never indicates any reason why he has suddenly changed course on the supposedly absolute impossibility of assigning common attributes to God and man, ergo, a contradiction.

228. The sentence is not entirely audible, but I believe it is most probable that this is what he is saying. Others hear "we" instead of "he"; however, I do not believe that this changes the meaning. The discussion by Aristotle to which Strauss refers, and which Maimonides bases himself on, is *Metaphysics* book Lambda, especially 1072b14–31. Cf. also the brief but enlightening discussion in Pines, "Translator's Introduction," in *Guide*, pp. xcvii–xcviii.

229. The voice of the speaker who asks two linked questions is obviously the same questioner: he asks first about the one concept not used homonymously about God and man, and presently he asks about the Sabians.

230. Immediately following "*tawhid*," the word "distinct" is clearly spoken. However, I am not able to account for why he speaks it.

231. *du'a*, the Islamic term for supplication in prayer.

for certain, [is that] he has some expressions [borrowed from Islamic terminology]. For example, this is [one] that I learned of only a short while ago: he calls Moses "*said il-alimun*" in Arabic, which means: "the master of those who know"—like Dante, only Dante calls Aristotle that.[232] But then I asked my friend Mahdi,[233] whom you know (he is a professor of Arabic here), and he told me what I didn't know, [about how Maimonides' phrase is] a modification [of an Islamic term], that in the Qur'an it doesn't appear[234] quite as *alimun*, but as *alamun*; that is said of Muhammad, and [it] means a master of the *worlds*, of men and angels. Now that, I'm sure, cannot be interpreted, [i.e.,] this expression [in Maimonides], but by taking into account [the fact] that it is a *modification* of a Qur'an expression. These things occur. But I think one . . . And also when you read even in his "Jewish" works, the code [*Mishneh Torah*], the last section [of *Book of Judges*, the fourteenth book] deals with "Kings and Their Wars": the description of the "law of war" reminds you of the "holy war." I mean, that is somehow surely from the Gemara; but there is a certain warlike element in it which is not so obvious in the Gemara or in any other place except the Bible, and which is naturally at home in Islam. So these things, there are some influences of this kind there. But I don't believe that they affect the fundamental point.

Questioner: My question was specifically for the following reason. If I remember correctly, the question was raised in Islam: were the Sabians—specifically the Sabians, that is to say, people who believed in the planets as gods . . .

Strauss: Yeah, yeah.

Questioner: . . . were or were [they] not [among the] "peoples of the book," that is to say, to be treated like Jews and Christians? Is there any connection between the specific use of this term [in Maimonides], and the specific kind of pagans, so to speak, which the Qur'an sees in the Sabians?

232. For Moses as "the master of those who know" in the *Guide*, see the following four passages: 1.54, p. 123; 2.28, p. 336; 3.12, p. 448; 3.54, p. 637. See also Pines, "Translator's Introduction," in *Guide*, pp. lxi (n. 8) and cv. Cf. Dante, *Divine Comedy*, *Inferno* IV, 131.

233. Muhsin Mahdi (1926–2007) was the great contemporary authority in the study of medieval Islamic philosophy. He made an especially careful and deep study of Farabi, which culminated in *Alfarabi and the Foundation of Islamic Political Philosophy* (Chicago: University of Chicago Press, 2001). He also edited and translated several of Farabi's most significant works. Together with Ralph Lerner, he edited *Medieval Political Philosophy: A Sourcebook* (Glencoe, IL: Free Press, 1963; reprint, Ithaca: Cornell University Press, 1972). He was, of course, originally a student of Strauss's, from whom he received his Ph.D. at the University of Chicago in 1954.

234. Strauss actually says "means"; but this use confuses the point that he makes, which is about how the phrase appears in the Qur'an. Hence I have changed the word to "appears."

Strauss: I can answer this question. For Maimonides, the Sabians certainly did not belong to the "*Ahl al-Kitab*" ["people of the book"]; I mean, [for him] they did not recognize any revelation. This Maimonides emphasizes. They were pagans. And now Maimonides relied . . . Well, what Maimonides does is really quite extraordinary: Maimonides claims that he has understood all biblical laws—virtually. . . . And out of this grew a tremendous code, as you know. And now, how did he[235] . . . And that leads to a very grave question, because Sabians in the end disappeared: what is the use of these laws now? I don't want to go into that [now]; that is major; we discussed [it] when Dr. Pines gave his lecture a year ago.[236] But how did Maimonides know [about the Sabians]? Of course, the remarks of the Qur'an, but they were in no way authoritative for him. But there was a certain literature which pretended to be Sabian. These were [books written by] Arabic-writing people, and Maimonides refers to them, and he says he has read them.[237] And Maimonides somehow claims—but that is a bit unclear—that he takes this for granted, that this [is] an old literature, say, going back to the oldest [times]. But there is also yet of course a source of knowledge of "idola-

---

235. This section is confused and rather choppy; Strauss starts several sentences that he never finishes. I can only offer to speculatively complete them, based on what Strauss says in other essays and lectures, as might be enlightening for some readers: "And now Maimonides relied [on reading Sabian and other pagan sources in order to make sense of the Torah, of the Mosaic law]. Well, what Maimonides does is really quite extraordinary: Maimonides claims that he has understood all biblical laws—virtually[—on the belief that this law consisted of modifying Sabian law in order to move people in a monotheistic direction. But it still means to say, most of the laws are derived from Sabian customs. He also made an enormous effort to systematize the development of Jewish law in its various stages since the Torah was revealed, yet at least based in certain measure on what he had derived from his study of the Sabians, and about the anti-Sabian origins of the law,] and out of this grew a tremendous code, as you know. And now how did he [*not* in the end make much of Jewish law paradoxically dependent on Sabianism?]" I repeat: these are entirely speculative efforts to complete Strauss's sentences. I could also be completely wrong about what I think he may have been about to say, but never finished saying.

236. The last sentence has been slightly rearranged, so as to make it grammatically (or at least rhetorically) correct. As he spoke it, it is heard as follows: "I don't want to go into that; that is major; which we discussed when Dr. Pines gave his lecture a year ago."

237. This sentence begins rather haltingly, and Strauss obviously decided that he wanted to state it differently. He began with the following words but withdrew them immediately: "and which . . . eh, . . . brought up . . . eh, . . ." These halting phrases have been removed from the text. Maimonides lets his readers know that he was well acquainted with this "ancient" Sabian literature; but the one that he most draws on is *The Nabatean Agriculture*, by Abu Bakr Ahmad ibn Wahshiyya. This well-known medieval book made its first appearance in 904 C.E. Maimonides highlights this book, and mentions others that are connected with it, in *Guide* 3.29 and 3.32. See the translator's notes, as well as his discussion, pp. cxxiii–cxxiv. These books seem to have been written in order to counteract biblical religion, and to show a different, often unflattering, perspective on Abraham (not to mention related biblical figures) and how he became a monotheist. See also Paul Fenton, "Maïmonide et *L'Agriculture nabatéeanne*," in *Maïmonide: Philosophe et Savant (1138–1204)*, ed. Tony Lévy and Roshdi Rashed (Leuven: Éditions Peeters, 2004), pp. 303–27. See also nn. 235 and 143 above.

try" in the talmudic discussion,[238] by the way [not to mention] in much of the biblical text. But there is one other source which we must never forget, and that was that he had studied Aristotle. Now Aristotle doesn't give many details of Greek mythology and ritual, but enough to give him an idea. And there are at least two passages from Aristotle's *Ethics*, which he quotes, in discussing the biblical commandments.[239] So the interesting problem is not that, although that should also be treated confidently and properly. The interesting problems are this: Maimonides had two independent sources of paganism, or regarding idolatry (you can use "*'avodah zarah*," the Jewish term): one is the Jewish tradition, Bible and Talmud; the other was the Greeks,[240] you know. He knew it from both angles, as it were. And that leads to very interesting studies, if one were to pursue that. The Sabians appear in two entirely different lights. There are passages in which they are presented as the seven Canaanite tribes, as presented in the Bible and the Jewish tradition; and there are also passages in which they are presented as philosophers, I mean, at least their leading men. And

---

238. See n. 5 above. The talmudic discussion is properly divided in three, based on the historical and literary differences between the three parts of the "Talmud," whose unity in fact forms two wholes: the one same Mishnah (second century C.E.) followed by two different Gemaras ("Jerusalem," 4th century C.E., and "Babylonian," 5th century C.E.). Each presents debates, legends, thoughts, and deliberations on idolatry, derived from their different locales and different eras; and each is contained in a tractate with the apt name of "Avodah Zarah" ("Idolatrous Worship"), i.e., literally, "alien, strange, or foreign worship." In these books we witness the multifarious confrontations of the ancient rabbis with the issue of whether, and just how much, Greco-Roman or Persian paganism is continuous with the "idolatry" of the ancient Near East, known to us from the biblical accounts in the Torah and the prophets, and hence whether and how it is still "idolatry." Maimonides wrote a *Commentary on the Mishnah*, in which he addressed himself to some of these issues; and in his *Mishneh Torah*, he drew (somewhat unconventionally) on disparate material derived from both the Jerusalem Talmud and the Babylonian Talmud.

239. For Aristotle's *Ethics* mentioned in the discussion of the laws, see *Guide* 3.43, pp. 571–72, and 3.49, pp. 601 and 608. For the reference to Aristotle's *Ethics* in 3.49, p. 608; compare with 2.36, p. 371, and 40, p. 384; 3.8, pp. 432–33, and 3.51, p. 620. For the contraposition to that which Maimonides *seems* to stress by repeating his remark about the sense of touch, even if we disregard how he slants Aristotle's words in a certain direction ("it is a disgrace to us, as Aristotle stated in his *Ethics*"), one should consider *De Anima (On the Soul)*, bk. 2, chap. 9, 421b3–4: "In most cases of the other senses, man is inferior to many animals, but in discriminations of touch he is far superior to the others. For this reason man is the most intelligent animal. A proof of this is the fact that within the human race the good and bad native endowment of individuals depends upon this sense organ, and no other. Men who have hard flesh are poorly endowed intellectually, men who have soft flesh are gifted." I employ *Aristotle's Psychology*, trans. William Alexander Hammond (New York: Macmillan, 1902), pp. 82–83. This repetition about the shameful or disgraceful sense of touch, together with Strauss's likely being convinced of Maimonides' knowledge of this passage in *De Anima*, led Strauss to suggest that Maimonides cannot be read as merely favoring asceticism (even with the "authority" of Aristotle, and even with his frequent repetitions), as it might appear, but was conveying a different message, and perhaps even a subtle and pointed criticism between the lines, for reasons pertaining to his philosophic education of the addressee of his book, i.e., Rabbi Joseph and those like him: see "Literary Character," chap. 8 above.

240. Strauss's use of the plural "were" has been changed to the singular "was" as grammatically better.

that of course corresponds to the truth to a certain extent, because there were pagans and pagans, you know. I mean, [it depends on] the currency of definitions: [there is] Ishtar, and Baal, and so forth, and that was something very different from the Greek current. Maimonides was somehow aware of that [difference]. I do not know whether I answered your question. It is an important subject, that's quite true, because what is obvious, and what everyone knows, is that there is a long discussion of Sabianism as the target of the Torah legislation, that part which the Christians call the "ceremonial law," and which Maimonides calls the "*ḥuqqim*," and that is anti-Sabian.[241] That is very well known. But one must not forget that Maimonides also discerned a kind of concession[242] [in the sacrifices, etc., to the native Sabianism of the ancient Israelites]; and therefore a kind of premise[243] of Sabianism was in the text of the Bible.

Questioner: I mean, this would be an adequate answer at least to the question if instead of using the terms "Sabians," the term "pagans" or "unbelievers" had been used. But I was concerned with the specific use of this term ["Sabians"], which in the Qur'an certainly does not refer to all kinds of pagans, but only to a very specific [kind].[244]

Strauss: Well, Maimonides means pagans.[245]

---

241. For the Sabians, see *Guide* 1.63, pp. 153–54; 1.70, p. 172; 3.29, pp. 514–16, 520–22; 3.30, pp. 522–23; 3.37, pp. 540–50; 3.47, pp. 594–95; 3.48, p. 599; for "the ravings of the Sabians" see 2.23, p. 322; 2.39, p. 381; 3.29, p. 520. For further comments by Strauss on Maimonides' Sabians, see "How To Begin," chap. 11 below. For discussion of the Sabians in Maimonides' thought, see the brief remarks by Shlomo Pines, "Translator's Introduction," in *Guide*, pp. cxxiii–cxxiv; Mark R. Sunwall, "Maimonides on the Sabians: A Case of Constructive Disapproval," in *College of Nursing Art and Science Hyogo Bulletin* 6 (1999): 63–83 (http://www.friesian.com/sunwall.htm); Jonathan Elukin, "Maimonides and the Rise and Fall of the Sabians: Explaining Mosaic Laws and the Limits of Scholarship," *Journal of the History of Ideas* 63, no. 4 (October 2002): 619–37; Sarah Stroumsa, "La Longue Durée: Maimonides as a Phenomenologist of Religion," in *Maimonides in His World: Portrait of a Mediterranean Thinker* (Princeton: Princeton University Press, 2009), chap. 4, pp. 84–124. For the "ravings of the Sabians" versus science, see J. I. Gellman, "Maimonides' 'Ravings,'" *Review of Metaphysics* 45 (1991): 309–28; Sarah Stroumsa, "'Ravings': Maimonides' Concept of Pseudo-science," *Aleph* 1 (2001): 141–63.

242. This word, "concessions," is plural as Strauss spontaneously uttered it; since that is not compatible with the rest of the sentence, I have reduced it to the singular. However, it is possible that in this context, he had in mind several specific concessions made to Sabianism, rather than just a general, comprehensive concession. Yet previously in the lecture he had used twice the singular of "concession" (refer to the text at note marker 143), which action by the lawgiver one may apply to the Sabian relics, or rather to the anti-Sabian measures, in the Torah.

243. The tape is not entirely audible. However, the word "premise" is most likely.

244. This question would seem to have been asked by the same person who previously asked at least two questions about the Sabians.

245. Perhaps the clearest effort to identify the Sabians with what Maimonides defines as the essential teaching of paganism (i.e., worship of the heavens as God or the gods, or God as "the spirit of the sphere") is in *Guide* 3.29, p. 514. The origins of paganism are also dealt with in *Mishneh Torah, Sefer ha-Madda*, "Hilkhot Avodah Zarah," I, 1–3, although curiously with no mention of the name "Sabianism." In

Questioner: Oh, he uses that term?

Strauss: There's no question that it has this meaning. He also used from time to time the term *jahiliyya*, the "ignorant," which the Qur'an comes with it. But no, there cannot be any question. He has of course also breakdowns of the pagans. For example, there are the Chasdeans, the Chaldeans, and the Egyptians, and the Persians, and the Hindus, and the Greeks. And he makes a distinction between the more civilized among them: the Greeks, the Persians, and—which is the third? I don't know, [beyond] the Persians?[246] [Is it] the Egyptians perhaps too? I don't know[247]—and the others, [i.e., those

---

this chapter is contained a far-reaching discussion (for a law code) of how man had descended from his original or primeval monotheism to astral worship, to be rescued from such benightedness by the mind of Abraham, who was in search of the genuinely divine to guide his life by. He was the only man who had thought to dissent (based on speculation) from the well-nigh globalized consensus that had attained the status of a generally accepted opinion, seemingly beyond the possibility of being doubted.

246. Strauss said "perhaps the Persians," although he has just mentioned them as definite. Hence it has been changed slightly, to avoid the redundancy, by adding in square brackets "[beyond] the Persians."

247. Strauss says on the tape "I don't know," but in the sense of "I can't recall the texts at the moment." Strauss's memory momentarily lapsed on the details, but the numbers and the essential scheme are both quite accurate. This is not so much dealt with by Maimonides in the *Guide* as it is in two other works: see Maimonides, "Epistle to Yemen," trans. Kraemer, pp. 103-4; and Maimonides, "Letter on Astrology," trans. Lerner, pp. 180-81. (In *Mishneh Torah*, "Hilkhot Tefilah," toward the beginning, he also mentions the Greeks and the Persians, but it is only in the context of the languages to which the Jews first assimilated themselves during their exiles.) He argues that the wise pagans were concerned with genuine science, which is to be fully respected and even commended. But this cleverness of the "civilized" pagans was abused with respect to the Jews, for they also attempted to persuade them by argument to abandon their Judaism. Maimonides contrasted this sophisticated and almost cultured procedure with the "uncivilized" or barbaric pagans (not to mention their monotheistic heirs), who often used violence in trying to force the Jews by compulsion, persecution, and privation to abandon their Judaism. (To be sure, Maimonides undoubtedly affirms that the procedure of the "civilized" pagans, if regrettable, was still much better, i.e., it was better for the pagans to try to persuade the Jews, however vehemently or cunningly, than to use violence against them.) Yet curiously Strauss's momentary lapse of memory on those whom Maimonides designated as "civilized" pagans, may well have been due to an ambiguity, or at least to a noticeable divergence, in Maimonides' thought itself about which pagans he considered "civilized," for good and for bad. On the one hand, the three peoples—as the number which Strauss focuses on—who rightly concerned themselves with genuine science were the Greeks, the Persians, *and the Indians*; on the other hand, those three which concerned themselves with swaying the Jews by argument to abandon their Judaism were the Greeks, the Persians, and the *Syrians*. The "Syrians" likely refers to those Christians who first developed the dialectical theology which flourished among medieval Jews, Christians, and Muslims, and which Maimonides with possible irony refers to as the "science of *kalam*": see *Guide* 1.71, pp. 177-78. It is not utterly impossible, although highly unlikely, that this reference to the "Syrians" may also stand for those who were missionaries of Hellenism during the reign of the Seleucid king Antiochus IV Epiphanes, who was militarily defeated by the Jews in the period of the Maccabees. Those "Syrians" ruled the Hellenized, Greek-speaking Seleucid empire established from the eastern half of the imperial conquests made by Alexander the Great, and in which Judea remained captive until the Maccabeean (or Hasmonean) state rose to power. The Seleucids seem to have made the enforced spread of Hellenism imperial policy during a certain period of their rule. However, since the main mode used to dissuade the Jews from adherence to their Judaism during this specific period (i.e., in Antiochus's reign) was persecutory violence, by which the king's edicts against Judaism were brutally and cruelly enforced, it seems most unlikely that Maimonides was thinking of them in mentioning "civilized" Syrians who had used arguments against the Jews

pagans,] you know, [who practice] the horrible sacrifice of their children and so on. So that is very interesting. One of the greatest follies, which we ordinarily commit, is to believe that a historical perspective, and a historical sense, is in a position of the mind to know every century. Maimonides has an amazingly clear notion of the past; the more one understands, the more one sees that. And I mean, he didn't have access to many things to which we have access today; but on the basis of material [which he did have], he was an amazingly careful and sober student of the past. And that was a very pertinent part[248] of his work.

Questioner: You speak of the use of homonyms, that is, [for interpreting how] the Bible refers to God or names His attributes, and yet the names indicate nothing about God, because the only thing in common between the things ordinarily referred to and the attributes are the names. And this seems quite meaningless, to apply, to name an attribute with a word that already has meaning, when there is nothing shared between them.

Strauss: Yeah, well, I can answer that question, if you give me about five minutes, because that is what I would need. Now Maimonides' doctrine of attributes, to reduce [it] to the simplest formula, is this: all attributes are either negative [attributes], or attributes of action. Negative attributes: for example, if we say "God is wise," what we understand of that is only that He is not ignorant, that the character of His wisdom could [not] be this case [as in any sense ignorant];[249] it has nothing in common with what we understand of this.[250] Attributes of action: say, God is the creator, and governor of the world. Now, so the negative attributes are really only denials of imperfection, not more. The implication is, and the presupposition is, God's perfection is unfathomable; anything we say about it is really mere words. God is the absolutely perfect Being, the absolutely good

---

to dissuade them from their Judaism. See "Maimonides' Statement on Political Science," chap. 9 above, n. 1; "Note on Maimonides' *Letter on Astrology*," chap. 14 below. Cf. also Shlomo Pines, "Translator's Introduction," in *Guide*, pp. cxxiv–cxxxi.

248. Strauss actually said: "And that was very pertinent a part of his work." It has been corrected as "And that was a very pertinent part of his work."

249. The tape is barely audible at this point, so that the phrase "could be this case" is highly tentative, if not virtually a guess, based on what seems to follow. Either Strauss speaks quickly and slurs his words together, or the tape did not manage to capture his words clearly. So as not to allow the uncertain phrase to mislead readers, Strauss's point in this sentence concerns Maimonides' view that God's wisdom and knowledge cannot in any respect be deficient, i.e., it is impossible to think of God as ignorant in any sense.

250. The tape is barely audible. Either Strauss speaks quickly and slurs his words together, or the tape did not manage to capture his words clearly. The phrase "what we understand of this" is highly tentative. If this is what Strauss is saying, he means that phrase for Maimonides in the sense of "His understanding has nothing in common with our understanding."

Being. Being absolutely good, being *the* good, there is no possible reason for creation, because the amount of goodness is not increased by creation. Now but God, this absolutely perfect Being, absolutely good Being, has created the world. "[He] has created the world" is the comprehensive formula for all [the attributes of] action. The absolutely good Being is the formula for negative attributes, because we do not understand [His absolute goodness or perfection]; it is unfathomable.[251] A groundless action, an abyss, an abyss so to speak for that which came to be here,[252] an abyss by virtue of His absolute goodness. And that means of course that the crucial implication of the doctrine of attributes is this, that if you want to apply attributes to God, to the extent that we cannot avoid it, "will" is somehow a bit better than this, because "will" points more directly to the mere fact, the fact which is derived from coming into being [as creation].[253] So from this point of view one can say that Maimonides' doctrine of the attributes, so far from being a so-called derivation from neo-Platonism or whatever they say, is a very sophisticated expression for what the Bible may mean.[254] Therefore, he can sometimes use the verse:[255] God has created things "*le-ma'anehu*," "for His own sake."[256] We can't understand, we can only see

---

251. Regarding what is audible on the tape, Strauss begins with "because we do not understand," halts, hesitates for a brief moment, and continues with "it is unfathomable." The words in square brackets have been added by the editor and are speculative, as an attempt to reconstruct the apparent thought of his sentence in its logical continuity, as well as of his break in it.

252. Several words following his uttering of "an abyss, an abyss so to speak," cannot in good conscience be declared with any certainty: they are so muffled or garbled as to make it almost completely impossible to discern them with any definiteness. What I am suggesting, "for that which came to be here," amounts merely to an educated guess. However, others might regard these words as too speculative and instead either to be put in square brackets or to be omitted entirely. The decision to preserve them in the text is of course the responsibility of the editor.

253. Several words, following his uttering of "derived from," cannot in good conscience be declared with any certainty: they are so muffled or garbled as to make it almost completely impossible to discern them with any definiteness. What I am suggesting, "coming into being," amounts merely to an educated guess. However, others interpret this as "creation"; as a result, I have decided to add "[as creation]" in square brackets, as if he were explaining himself. My working hypothesis is that both versions are possible hearings of what Strauss says, although obviously I still favor "coming into being" as likelier.

254. The tape is not entirely audible. The word "mean" is only tentative.

255. On the tape Strauss first says "quotation," but seems to correct himself; this is shown by the fact that he makes a quick change of the word he wanted to say to "verse."

256. Proverbs 16:4. In fact, Maimonides uses this verse only once, in *Guide* 3.13, pp. 452–53. It occurs in his consideration of the end or final cause of all that exists. Grounded in an ambiguity, he suggests "*le-ma'anehu*" bears the double significance of "for His sake," and "for its own sake." (This is an ambiguity that is possible on the basis of the original Hebrew.) It is also the chapter in which Maimonides raises the question of whether any unifying purpose of *everything* is evident; in his answer, he declares it best to think that God has made everything in this world for the sake of His will (pp. 451–56). However, as he significantly adds, this is the same thing as saying that He created it also for the sake of His wisdom: "God has wished it so, or His wisdom has required it to be so" (p. 452). With respect to "*le-ma'anehu*," might Strauss also have had in mind Isaiah 43:25 or 48:11? But Maimonides never uses these verses; and in both

that—looking at things, trying to understand them—we cannot find any other ground which makes us intelligible except this unintelligible abyss of goodness. That's what I think the whole doctrine is about.

Questioner: But in particular, for example, . . .

Strauss: But Maimonides says something, you know, well, [these are] the famous difficulties, when you speak of the problem of divine providence and the future contingents, a famous story, yeah?: God knows in advance everything; hence He knows in advance that X will commit this sin; is X not then determined by this foreknowledge? You know, it's an abyss of a problem. What will you do? I mean, no distinctions will help you. Because the distinctions are only rather poor means for admitting, I think, an unsolvable [thing].

Questioner: Well in particular, say, with God is good—how can you understand this in terms of negative attributes?

Strauss: I mean, "good" means He is the absolute perfection, absolute perfection. I mean, this is then, . . . Maimonides did not argue that out except very accidentally when he takes issue with the Epicureans, [and] lets them argue from the alternative, say, the last sum of the world is evil—and then you arrive at absolute absurdity.[257] Because the very fact that you can realize that, proves that you can free yourself from that. To recognize something as evil is already incipient[258] goodness. So no one's got rid of this, and [of] this kind of thing.[259] But the point which is getting you involved in our discussion on this issue,[260] I do not believe that this is [the same thing as] the doctrine of attributes. Of course, a Jew brought up only in the biblical-talmudic tradition will be greatly surprised [by Maimonides' doctrine], that

---

of them, while the point Strauss makes is roughly the same as the point of Isaiah, God through the prophet speaks in first person, and not in third person, as with the words of Strauss.

257. See *Guide* 3.17, p. 464 for Maimonides' rejection of the view of Epicurus on providence. Maimonides derives support from Aristotle in 2.20, pp. 312–14, since he demonstrates the absurdity of a universe generated by chance. The view that the universe is, on balance, evil, is attributed to Razi, not to Epicurus, in 3.12, pp. 441–48, although this may (if Strauss is pointing to what he is suggesting Maimonides thinks) put Razi, or those who hold his view, in the camp of the Epicureans. Indeed, as one of the anonymous reviewers of the University of Chicago Press has added, is not Razi—perhaps precisely as an opponent of revelation—highly similar to Epicurus, if not in just this sense derived from him?

258. The word Strauss has uttered on the tape is discernible to me as the word "incipient." It is most probable, even if it is not certain.

259. The beginning of the prior clause of the sentence spoken by Strauss on the tape (which finishes clearly with "and this kind of thing") is almost completely impossible to discern with any definiteness, at least as a distinct series of words. Thus, "So no one's got rid of this," is closer to being merely an educated guess. Others hear "So perhaps other people in the world insist on this kind of thing."

260. What Strauss is fully trying to express in the phrase "But the point which is getting you involved in our discussion on this issue" is difficult to be certain about. Some of the words in the middle of the phrase may well have been garbled by the tape or slurred together by the speaker.

goes without saying. But that does not yet mean that the doctrine may not bring out in a new medium—in a new medium which was made possible by the influence of Greek philosophy surely—what the Bible fundamentally means. But that [Maimonidean doctrine of attributes as an interpretation of the biblical teaching][261] is surely not an Aristotelian teaching. And it is not even, in the way in which Maimonides presents it at any rate, what one could ascribe to neo-Platonism. In the end one must realize, I think, that it is so crucial to distinguish it from these Greek teachings.

[*Joseph Cropsey, Chairman*: Let's bring it to a close, shall we?][262]

Strauss: Yeah, you mean the second subsection?

Cropsey: I think so.

Strauss: Yeah.

[*The discussion period ends with loud audience applause. The tape ends.*]

261. The editor has added this phrase in square brackets in order to make sense of what the word "that" spoken by Strauss refers to. The effort has been made to do this by attempting to employ the same words, or similar notions, as those used previously by Strauss himself to bring to the light the theme that he is addressing.

262. Strauss spoke a last sentence on the tape, which he made in response to a remark whispered to him by the man who was chairing this second lecture and who presumably thought that the event should be brought to a close. (The voice on the tape belonging to the chairman of this event appears again to have been that of Strauss's colleague and friend Joseph Cropsey, who, though it was much clearer in the tape of the first lecture, was apparently also chairing the second lecture.) On the tape the content of the chairman's whispered comment to Strauss is barely audible, but not discernible. I guessed (as put in square brackets) at what might have been the gist of his comment, just in order to set the stage for Strauss's last remark. If Strauss recognized the close of the discussion period, he also made a joke about it as ending "the second subsection." He seems to refer to a joke he made at the beginning of the discussion period on how they might justly divide the discussion and the refreshments so as to produce "subsections."

11

How To Begin To Study
The Guide of the Perplexed

EDITOR'S NOTE

"How To Begin To Study *The Guide of the Perplexed*" basically reproduces Strauss's "Introductory Essay" to Moses Maimonides, *The Guide of the Perplexed*, trans. Shlomo Pines (Chicago: University of Chicago Press, 1963), pp. xi–lvi. It subsequently apeared in print again in *Liberalism Ancient and Modern* (New York: Basic Books, 1968; reprint: Ithaca: Cornell University Press, 1989; Chicago: University of Chicago Press, 1995), pp. 140–84, with some slight if noteworthy changes made by the author, but with the same title: "How To Begin To Study *The Guide of the Perplexed*." Note that in both versions of this essay (however significant one may wish to consider a rather picayune typographic point), Strauss chose to capitalize the first letters of the prepositions ("To" and "To," but neither the preposition "of" nor the definite article "the" in Maimonides' own title, or in any other title of his numerous works), although it is not conventional to do so in most contemporary English-speaking publishing styles. Thus, the peculiar typography of the title seems to have been deliberately maintained in both versions. It is closest to a newspaper headline style; did he do so in order to make a point that he wanted to make most emphatic? Was he perhaps saying, this and only this is "How To Begin To Study": use it as a model for beginning the serious study of any truly great work that repays most careful and repeated study? For the significance of the word "study"—as opposed especially to "read"—in Strauss's title, see Aryeh Tepper, *Theories of Progress in Leo Strauss's Later Writings on Maimonides* (Albany: State University of New York Press, forthcoming [2013]). Cf. also "How to *Study* Medieval Philosophy," chap. 1 above (which has been italicized to emphasize another use of the word in the present book, although it is not set in a "how to *begin* to study" context). The first portion of the essay also appeared in print as "On the Plan of *The Guide of the Perplexed*," in *Harry Austryn Wolfson Jubilee*

Volume, ed. Saul Lieberman et al. (Jerusalem: American Academy for Jewish Research, 1965), vol. 2, pp. 775–91. All of Strauss's parenthetical references in which there is an Arabic numeral, next a period, which is then followed by an Arabic numeral are to, respectively, part and chapter of the *Guide*. Readers should note (as per "The Literary Character," chap. 8 above, n. 1) that in this edition, both in the text and in the notes, Arabic figures rather than Roman figures have been used in order to designate the part of the *Guide*. That is followed next by a period rather than a comma. This has been done for the sake of consistency with the rest of Strauss's essays as they are reproduced in the present volume, and in order to conform to contemporary usage as has become customary in the scholarly study of the *Guide*. This method of reference to the part of the *Guide* is next followed by the chapter number referred to in Arabic figures, but that is unchanged from the method of reference used by Strauss in the original edition and its reprinting, e.g., 2.48 rather than II, 48. Since Strauss seems to have deliberately chosen to put all of his references in parentheses (rather than in notes), even if they might occasionally seem to break the flow of the argument and of the reader's progress through the "Introductory Essay," it was decided that this should not be changed, and Strauss's references should remain in parentheses. For those who might wish to refer to the original version, the page numbers of Strauss's essay in the Shlomo Pines translation of the *Guide* have been provided, set in curly brackets, and with the page numbers (Roman numerals) in bold. Readers should also be aware that Strauss has made some changes in this essay from how it appeared in the *Guide* translation to how it appeared as reprinted in *Liberalism Ancient and Modern*. Besides certain slight changes in the design features of Strauss's plan of the *Guide* (i.e., the use of Hebrew letters to mark the titles by which the two halves of the first section are divided, which in the reprinted version are instead italicized and lack the Hebrew letters), the number of paragraphs—not counting the plan itself—has been changed, from 43 in the former to 58 in the latter. The differences have been marked by adding the paragraph mark [¶] at the points at which further paragraph breaks were added to the text of the reprinted version. See also nn. 28 and 33 below, for further slight differences between the two versions. For manuscript evidence uncovered by Heinrich Meier about the precise period during which Strauss may have written—or at least completed—the essay, see the discussion in n. 104 of "Introduction to Maimonides' *Guide*," chap. 10 above. Other than the change from Roman to Arabic numerals for references to the part of the

Guide, the one significant change made by the editor is to add some supplementary notes, which attempt to provide additional scholarly data useful for some readers in studying the contents of Strauss's own parenthetical references. Thus, the notes are entirely the work of the present editor, who is alone responsible for offering the additional data about Strauss's references and sources.

{XI} I BELIEVE THAT IT WILL NOT BE AMISS IF I SIMPLY PRESENT THE plan of the *Guide* as it has become clear to me in the course of about twenty-five years of frequently interrupted but never abandoned study. In the following scheme Roman (and Arabic) numerals at the beginning of a line indicate the sections (and subsections) of the *Guide* while the numbers given in parentheses indicate the Parts and the chapters of the book.

A. Views (1.1–3.24)
A'. Views regarding God and the angels (1.1–3.7)
I. BIBLICAL TERMS APPLIED TO GOD (1.1–70)
א. Terms suggesting the corporeality of God (and the angels) (1.1–49)

1. The two most important passages of the Torah that seem to suggest that God is corporeal (1.1–7)
2. Terms designating place, change of place, the organs of human locomotion, etc. (1.8–28)
3. Terms designating wrath and consuming (or taking food) that if applied to divine things refer to idolatry on the one hand and to human knowledge on the other (1.29–36)
4. Terms designating parts and actions of animals (1.37–49)

ב. Terms suggesting multiplicity in God (1.50–70)

5. Given that God is absolutely one and incomparable, what is the meaning of the terms applied to God in nonfigurative speech? (1.50–60)
6. The names of God and the utterances of God (1.61–67) {xii}
7. The apparent multiplicity in God consequent upon His knowledge, His causality, and His governance (1.68–70)

II. DEMONSTRATIONS OF THE EXISTENCE, UNITY, AND INCORPOREALITY OF GOD (1.71–2.31)

1. Introductory (1.71–73)
2. Refutation of the *kalam* demonstrations (1.74–76)
3. The philosophic demonstrations (2.1)

4. Maimonides' demonstration (2.2)

5. The angels (2.3-12)

6. Creation of the world, i.e., defense of the belief in creation out of nothing against the philosophers (2.13-24)

7. Creation and the Law (2.25-31)

III. Prophecy (2.32-48)

1. Natural endowment and training the prerequisites of prophecy (2.32-34)

2. The difference between the prophecy of Moses and that of the other prophets (2.35)

3. The essence of prophecy (2.36-38)

4. The legislative prophecy (of Moses) and the Law (2.39-40)

5. Legal study of the prophecy of the prophets other than Moses (2.41-44)

6. The degrees of prophecy (2.45)

7. How to understand the divine actions and works and the divinely commanded actions and works as presented by the prophets (2.46-48)

IV. The Account of the Chariot (3.1-7)

A". Views regarding bodily beings that come into being and perish, and in particular regarding man (3.8-54)

V. Providence (3.8-24)

1. Statement of the problem: matter is the ground of all evils and yet matter is created by the absolutely good God (3.8-14)

2. The nature of the impossible or the meaning of omnipotence (3.15)

3. The philosophic arguments against omniscience (3.16)

4. The views regarding providence (3.17-18) {xiii}

5. Jewish views on omniscience and Maimonides' discourse on this subject (3.19-21)

6. The book of Job as the authoritative treatment of providence (3.22-23)

7. The teaching of the Torah on omniscience (3.24)

B. Actions (3.25-54)

VI. The actions commanded by God and done by God (3.25-50)

1. The rationality of God's actions in general and of His legislation in particular (3.25-26)

2. The manifestly rational part of the commandments of the Torah (3.27-28)

3. The rationale of the apparently irrational part of the commandments of the Torah (3.29-33)

4. The inevitable limit to the rationality of the commandments of the Torah (3.34)

    5. Division of the commandments into classes and explanation of the usefulness of each class (3.35)
    6. Explanation of all or almost all commandments (3.36–49)
    7. The narratives in the Torah (3.50)

VII. Man's perfection and God's providence (3.51-54)
    1. True knowledge of God Himself is the prerequisite of providence (3.51–52)
    2. True knowledge of what constitutes the human individual himself is the prerequisite of knowledge of the workings of providence (3.53–54)

The *Guide* consists then of seven sections or of thirty-eight subsections. Wherever feasible, each section is divided into seven subsections; the only section that does not permit of being divided into subsections is divided into seven chapters.

The simple statement of the plan of the *Guide* suffices to show that the book is sealed with many seals. At the end of its Introduction Maimonides describes the preceding passage as follows: "It is a key permitting one to enter places the gates to which were locked. When those gates are opened and those places are entered, the souls will find rest therein, the eyes will be delighted, and the bodies will be eased of their toil and of their labor."[1] The *Guide* as a whole is not merely a key to {xiv} a forest but is itself a forest, an enchanted forest, and hence also an enchanting forest: it is a delight to the eyes. For the tree of life is a delight to the eyes.

The enchanting character of the *Guide* does not appear immediately. At first glance the book appears merely to be strange and in particular to lack order and consistency. But progress in understanding it is a progress in becoming enchanted by it. Enchanting understanding is perhaps the highest form of edification. One begins to understand the *Guide*, once one sees that it is not a philosophic book—a book written by a philosopher for philosophers—but a Jewish book, a book written by a Jew for Jews. Its first premise is the old Jewish premise that being a Jew and being a philosopher are two incompatible things. Philosophers are men who try to give an account of the whole by starting from what is always accessible to man as man; Maimonides starts from the acceptance of the Torah. A Jew may make use of philosophy and

---

    1. Cf. *Guide*, 1.Intro., p. 20, which Strauss's version pretty much matches. However, contrast with the last paragraph of the present chapter for several significant differences. Note especially the relative position of "eyes" and of "bodies," and what the "bodies" will be eased of. These differences are also compared in detail in n. 36 below.

Maimonides makes the most ample use of it; but as a Jew he gives his assent where as a philosopher he would suspend his assent (cf. *Guide* 2.16).

Accordingly, the *Guide* is devoted to the Torah or more precisely to the true science of the Torah, of the Law. Its first purpose is to explain biblical terms and its second purpose is to explain biblical similes. The *Guide* is then devoted above all to biblical exegesis, although to biblical exegesis of a particular kind. That kind of exegesis is required because many biblical terms and all biblical similes have an apparent or outer and a hidden or inner meaning; the gravest errors as well as the most tormenting perplexities arise from men's understanding the Bible always according to its apparent or literal meaning. The *Guide* is then devoted to "the difficulties of the Law" or to "the secrets of the Law." The most important of those secrets are the Account of the Beginning (the beginning of the Bible)[2] and the Account of the Chariot (Ezekiel 1 and 10). The *Guide* is then devoted primarily and chiefly to the explanation of the Account of the Beginning and the Account of the Chariot.

Yet the Law whose secrets Maimonides intends to explain forbids that they be explained in public, or to the public; they may only be explained in private and only to such individuals as possess both theoretical and political wisdom as well as the capacity of both understanding and using allusive speech; for only "the chapter headings" of the secret teaching may be transmitted even to those who belong to the natural elite. Since every explanation given in writing, at any rate in a book, is a public explanation, Maimonides seems to be compelled by his intention to transgress the Law. There were other cases in which he was under such a compulsion. The Law also forbids one to study the books of idolators on idolatry, for the first intention of the Law as a whole is to destroy every vestige of idolatry; and yet Maimonides, as he openly admits and even emphasizes, has studied all the {**xv**} available idolatrous books of this kind with the utmost thoroughness. Nor is this all. He goes so far as to encourage the reader of the *Guide* to study those books by himself (3.29–30, 32, 37; *Mishneh Torah*, "Hilkhot Avodah Zarah" II, 2

---

2. In the present case Strauss refrains (with seeming deliberateness) from mentioning the specific biblical chapters in the book of Genesis that the Account of the Beginning encompasses, i.e., he only speaks generally of "the beginning of the Bible." However, it seems deliberate because in every other case something similar to this one also occurs: he *never* names the chapter numbers in Genesis. See "Literary Character," chap. 8 above, in which he merely translates the phrase as "the account of creation"; "Introduction to Maimonides' *Guide*," chap. 10 above, in which he refers only to "the work of the beginning, the story of creation." Contrast with *ma'aseh merkavah*, which Strauss consistently refers to as Ezekiel 1 and 10. For Maimonides' own delimiting in the chapter of the *Guide* specifically devoted to discussing *ma'aseh bereshit* (2.30, pp. 348–59), his version seems to encompass Genesis 1–4, from which four chapters he elucidates or makes use of only selected verses.

and III, 2).³ The Law also forbids one to speculate about the date of the coming of the Messiah, yet Maimonides presents such a speculation or at least its equivalent in order to comfort his contemporaries (*Epistle to Yemen*, 62, 16ff., and 80, 17ff., ed. Halkin; cf. Halkin's Introduction, pp. xii–xiii; *Mishneh Torah*, "Hilkhot Melakhim" XII, 2).⁴ Above all, the Law forbids one to seek for the reasons of the commandments, yet Maimonides devotes almost twenty-six chapters of the *Guide* to such seeking (3.26; cf. 2.25).⁵ All these irregularities have one and the same justification. Maimonides transgresses the Law "for the sake of heaven," i.e., in order to uphold or to fulfill the Law (1.Intro., and 3.Intro.). Still, in the most important case he does not, strictly speaking, transgress the Law, for his written explanation of the secrets of the Law is not a public but a secret explanation. The secrecy is achieved in three ways. First, every word of the *Guide* is chosen with exceeding care; since very few men are able or willing to read with exceeding care, most men will fail to perceive the secret teaching. Second, Maimonides deliberately contradicts himself, and if a man declares both that *a* is *b* and that *a* is not *b*, he cannot be said to declare anything.⁶ Lastly, the "chapter headings" of the secret teach-

---

3. For *Mishneh Torah*, "Hilkhot Avodah Zarah" II, 2 and III, 2, see Maimonides, "Laws Concerning Idolatry," trans. Hyamson, II, 2, and III, 2 (pp. 67b and 68b). In II, 2, especially, the law is enunciated which forbids the reading of idolatrous books. But in *Guide* 3.29, pp. 518 and 521, Maimonides says: "The meaning of many of the laws became clear to me and their causes became known to me through my study of the doctrines, opinions, practices, and cult of the Sabians. . . . I shall mention to you the books from which all that I know about the doctrines and opinions of the Sabians will become clear to you. . . . All the books that I have mentioned to you are books of idolatry that have been translated into Arabic. . . . The knowledge of these opinions and practices is a very important chapter in the exposition of the reasons for the commandments." In *Guide* 3.37, pp. 540 and 542, he specifically urges his student to read "all the books I have mentioned" which pertain to idolatry. Similarly, according to Maimonides in the last book of the *Mishneh Torah*, *Sefer Shoftim*, "Hilkhot Sanhedrin," the Law requires members of the Sanhedrin to study and know thoroughly the books of idolatry: see Maimonides, "Laws of the Sanhedrin," trans. Hershman, II, 1, p. 7; Maimonides, "Hilkhot Sanhedrin," ed. Rubenstein, II, 1, pp. 8–9.

4. *Epistle to Yemen*, ed. Halkin, refers to *Moses Maimonides' Epistle to Yemen: Arabic Original and Three Hebrew Versions*, ed. Abraham S. Halkin, with English trans. Boaz Cohen (New York: American Academy for Jewish Research, 1952). For improved English translations, see especially "Epistle to Yemen," trans. Kraemer, pp. 99–132; and also "Epistle to Yemen," trans. Halkin, pp. 93–149. The most recent critical edition (Arabic and Hebrew) of the "Epistle to Yemen" ("Iggeret Teiman") appears in *Igrot ha-Rambam*, ed. Shailat, I, pp. 77–168. For *Mishneh Torah*, "Hilkhot Melakhim" XII, 2, see especially Maimonides, "Laws of Kings and Their Wars," trans. Weiss and Butterworth, pp. 174–75; and see also "Laws Concerning Kings and Wars," trans. Hershman, pp. 240–41.

5. For the notion that the search for the reasons of the commandments was actually forbidden by God, see the end of the *Sefer ha-Mitzvot*, negative commandment 365; see also *Guide* 3.26, pp. 507–8. Strauss did not relate this point to what Maimonides says in *Guide* 3.31, pp. 523–24: a group of human beings regard it as "a grievous thing" to provide reasons for *any* laws or commandments. Maimonides refers to such human beings as suffering from a discernible "sickness" in their "souls." Perhaps the difference is in a certain respect obvious, which is why Strauss did not relate the two chapters: the latter (3.31) characterizes a group of human beings, while the former (3.26) is attributed to God.

6. Cf. "Introduction to Maimonides' *Guide*," chap. 10 above.

ing are not presented in an orderly fashion but are scattered throughout the book. This permits us to understand why the plan of the *Guide* is so obscure. Maimonides succeeds immediately in obscuring the plan by failing to divide the book explicitly into sections and subsections or by dividing it explicitly only into three Parts and each Part into chapters without supplying the Parts and the chapters with headings indicating the subject matter of the Parts or of the chapters.

The plan of the *Guide* is not entirely obscure. No one can reasonably doubt for instance that 2.32-48, 3.1-7, and 3.25-50 form sections. The plan is most obscure at the beginning and it becomes clearer as one proceeds; generally speaking, it is clearer in the second half (2.13-end) than in the first half. The *Guide* is then not entirely devoted to secretly transmitting chapter headings of the secret teaching. This does not mean that the book is not in its entirety devoted to the true science of the Law. It means that the true science of the Law is partly public. This is not surprising, for the teaching of the Law itself is of necessity partly public. According to one statement, the core of the public teaching consists of the assertions that God is one, that He alone is to be worshiped, that He is incorporeal, that He is incomparable to any of His creatures, and that He suffers from no defect and no passion (1.35). From other statements it would appear that the acceptance of the Law on every level of comprehension presupposes belief in God, in angels, and in prophecy (3.45) or that the basic beliefs are those in God's unity and in Creation {xvi} (2.13). In brief one may say that the public teaching of the Law in so far as it refers to beliefs or to "views," can be reduced to the thirteen "roots" (or dogmas) which Maimonides had put together in his *Commentary on the Mishnah*.[7] That part of the true science of the Law which is devoted to the public teaching of the Law or which is itself public has the task of demonstrating the roots to the extent to which this is possible or of establishing the roots by means of speculation (3.51 and 54). Being speculative, that part of the true science of the Law

---

7. These were first articulated by Maimonides in his *Commentary on the Mishnah*, Tractate Sanhedrin, "Introduction" to chap. 10. See *Hakdamot ha-Rambam le-Mishnah*, ed. Shailat, pp. 129-46; *Commentary on the Mishnah (Sanhedrin)*, trans. Rosner, pp. 151-58; *Commentary on the Mishnah*, Sanhedrin X, in *Reader*, ed. Twersky, pp. 401-23. Among the attempts to resolve the puzzle of the relation of the thirteen principles to the *Guide*, an effort still worth consulting, even if the resolution offered may not be quite definitive, is Menachem Kellner, "Maimonides' Thirteen Principles and the Structure of the *Guide of the Perplexed*," *Journal of the History of Philosophy* 20, no. 1 (January 1982): 76-84. It is reprinted in his *Science in the Bet Midrash: Studies in Maimonides* (Brighton, MA: Academic Studies Press, 2009), pp. 123-31. Maimonides' thirteen principles were formulated as a poem or song in the Middle Ages, known as "*Yigdal*." They are recited every day by religious Jews in the preliminary section of the Morning Prayer Service (*Shaḥarit*), as well as sung at the end of other holy day prayer services in the religious calendar.

is not exegetic; it is not necessarily in need of support by biblical or talmudic texts (cf. 2.45 beginning). Accordingly, about 20 per cent of the chapters of the *Guide* contain no biblical quotations and about 9 per cent of them contain no Hebrew or Aramaic expressions whatever. It is not very difficult to see (especially on the basis of 3.7 end, 23, and 28) that the *Guide* as devoted to speculation on the roots of the Law or to the public teaching consists of sections II–III and V–VI as indicated in our scheme and that the sequence of these sections is rational; but one cannot understand in this manner why the book is divided into three Parts, or what sections I, IV, and VII and most, not to say all, subsections mean. The teaching of the *Guide* is then neither entirely public or speculative nor is it entirely secret or exegetic. For this reason the plan of the *Guide* is neither entirely obscure nor entirely clear.

Yet the *Guide* is a single whole. What then is the bond uniting its exegetic and its speculative ingredients? One might imagine that while speculation demonstrates the roots of the Law, exegesis proves that those roots as demonstrated by speculation are in fact taught by the Law. But in that case the *Guide* would open with chapters devoted to speculation, yet the opposite is manifestly true. In addition, if the exegesis dealt with the same subject matter as that speculation which demonstrates the public teaching par excellence, namely, the roots of the Law, there would be no reason why the exegesis should be secret. Maimonides does say that the Account of the Beginning is the same as natural science and the Account of the Chariot is the same as divine science (i.e., the science of the incorporeal beings or of God and the angels). This might lead one to think that the public teaching is identical with what the philosophers teach, while the secret teaching makes one understand the identity of the teaching of the philosophers with the secret teaching of the Law. One can safely say that this thought proves to be untenable on almost every level of one's comprehending the *Guide*: the nonidentity of the teaching of the philosophers as a whole and the thirteen roots of the Law as a whole is the first word and the last word of Maimonides. What he means by identifying the core of philosophy (natural science and divine science) with the highest secrets of the Law (the Account of the Beginning and the Account of the Chariot) and therewith by somehow identifying the subject matter of {xvii} speculation with the subject matter of exegesis may be said to be the secret par excellence of the *Guide*.[8]

---

8. "Literary Character," chap. 8 above, contains the following passage: Maimonides' "intention is to show that the teaching of these philosophic disciplines [i.e., physics and metaphysics], which is presupposed, is identical with the secret teaching of the Bible." This passage at least appears to suggest just what

Let us then retrace our steps. The *Guide* contains a public teaching and a secret teaching. The public teaching is addressed to every Jew including the vulgar; the secret teaching is addressed to the elite. The secret teaching is of no use to the vulgar and the elite does not need the *Guide* for being apprised of the public teaching. To the extent to which the *Guide* is a whole, or one work, it is addressed neither to the vulgar nor to the elite. To whom then is it addressed? How legitimate and important this question is appears from Maimonides' remark that the chief purpose of the *Guide* is to explain as far as possible the Account of the Beginning and the Account of the Chariot "with a view to him for whom (the book) has been composed" (3.[Intro.], beginning). Maimonides answers our question both explicitly and implicitly. He answers it explicitly in two ways; he says on the one hand that the *Guide* is addressed to believing Jews who are perfect in their religion and in their character, have studied the sciences of the philosophers, and are perplexed by the literal meaning of the Law; he says on the other hand that the book is addressed to such perfect human beings as are Law students and perplexed. He answers our question more simply by dedicating the book to his disciple Joseph and by stating that it has been composed for Joseph and his like. Joseph had come to him "from the ends of the earth" and had studied under him for a while; the interruption of the oral instruction through Joseph's departure, which "God had decreed," induced Maimonides to write the *Guide* for Joseph and his like. In the Epistle Dedicatory addressed to Joseph, Maimonides extols Joseph's virtues and indicates his limitation. Joseph had a passionate desire for things speculative and especially for mathematics. When he studied astronomy, mathematics, and logic under Maimonides, the teacher saw that Joseph had an excellent mind and a quick grasp; he thought him therefore fit to have revealed to him allusively the secrets of the books of the prophets and he began to make such revelations. This stimulated Joseph's interest in things divine as well as in an appraisal of the *kalam*; his desire for knowledge about these subjects became so great that Maimonides was compelled to warn him unceasingly to proceed in an orderly manner. It appears that Joseph was inclined to proceed impatiently or unmethodically in his study and that this defect had not been cured when he left Maimonides. The most important consequence of Joseph's defect is the fact, brought out

---

it is that, by a surface resemblance, Strauss says "proves to be untenable on almost every level of one's comprehending the *Guide*." Is he correcting himself? Or do these two passages not actually say the same thing? Of course, he also continues by saying Maimonides' "identifying [of] the subject matter of speculation with the subject matter of exegesis may be said to be the secret par excellence of the *Guide*."

by Maimonides' silence, that Joseph turned to divine science without having studied natural science under Maimonides or before, although natural science necessarily precedes divine science in the order of study.

The impression derived from the Epistle Dedicatory is confirmed by the book itself. Maimonides frequently addresses the reader by using expressions like "know" {**xviii**} or "you know already." Expressions of the latter kind indicate what the typical addressee knows and expressions of the former kind indicate what he does not know. One thus learns that Joseph has some knowledge of both the content and the character of divine science. He knows for example that divine science in contradistinction to mathematics and medicine requires an extreme of rectitude and moral perfection, and in particular of humility, but he apparently does not yet know how ascetic Judaism is in matters of sex (1.34, 3.52). He had learned from Maimonides' "speech" that the orthodox "views" do not last in a man if he does not confirm them by the corresponding "actions" (2.31). It goes without saying that while his knowledge of the Jewish sources is extensive, it is not comparable in extent and thoroughness to Maimonides' (2.26, 33). At the beginning of the book he does not know that according to the Jewish view and according to demonstration, angels have no bodies (1.43, 49) and he certainly does not know, strictly speaking, that God has no body (1.9). In this respect as well as in other respects his understanding necessarily progresses while he advances in his study of the *Guide* (cf. 1.65 beginning). As for natural science, he has studied astronomy but is not aware of the conflict between the astronomical principles and the principles of natural science (2.24), because he has not studied natural science. He knows a number of things that are made clear in natural science, but this does not mean that he knows them through having studied natural science (cf. 1.17, 28; 3.10). From the ninety-first chapter (2.15) it appears that while he knows Aristotle's *Topics* and Farabi's commentary on that work, he does not know the *Physics* and *On the Heaven* (cf. 2.8). Nor will he acquire the science of nature as he acquires the science of God and the angels while he advances in the study of the *Guide*. For the *Guide*, which is addressed to a reader not conversant with natural science, does not itself transmit natural science (1.2). The following remark occurring in the twenty-sixth chapter is particularly revealing: "It has been demonstrated that everything moved undoubtedly possesses a magnitude and is divisible; and it will be demonstrated that God possesses no magnitude and hence possesses no motion." What "has been demonstrated" has been demonstrated in the *Physics* and is simply presupposed in the *Guide*; what "will be demonstrated" belongs to divine science and not to natural science; but that which "will be demonstrated" is built on what "has been demonstrated." The student of the *Guide* acquires knowledge of divine science but not of natural science. The author of the *Guide* in contradistinction to its addressee is thoroughly versed in natural science. Still, the addressee needs some awareness of the whole in order to be able to ascend from the whole to God, for there is no way to knowledge of God except through such ascent (1.71, toward the end); he acquires that awareness through a report of some kind (1.70) that Maimonides has inserted into the *Guide*. It is characteristic of that report {**xix**} that it does not contain a single mention of philosophy in general and of natural science in particular. The serious student cannot rest satisfied with that report; he must turn from it to natural science itself, which demonstrates what the report merely asserts. Maimonides cannot but leave it to his reader whether he will turn to genuine speculation or whether he will be satisfied with accepting the report on the authority of Maimonides and with building on that report theological conclusions. The addressee of the *Guide* is a man regarding whom it is still undecided whether he will become a genuine man of speculation or whether he will remain a follower of authority, if of Maimonides' authority (cf. 1.72 end). He stands at the point of the road where speculation branches off from acceptance of authority.

Why did Maimonides choose an addressee of this description? What is the virtue of not being trained in natural science? We learn from the seventeenth chapter that natural science had already been treated as a secret doctrine by the pagan philosophers "upon whom the charge of corruption would not be laid if they exposed natural science clearly": all the more is the community of the Law-adherents obliged to treat natural science as a secret science. The reason why natural science is dangerous and is kept secret "with all kinds of artifices" is not that it undermines the Law—only the ignorant believe that (1.33), and Maimonides' whole life as well as the life of his successors refutes this suspicion. Yet it is also true that natural science has this corrupting effect on all men who are not perfect (cf. 1.62). For natural science surely affects the understanding of the meaning of the Law, of the grounds on which it is to be obeyed, and of the weight that is to be attached to its different parts. In a word, natural science upsets habits. By addressing a reader who is not conversant with natural science, Maimonides is compelled to proceed in a manner that does not upset habits or does so to the smallest possible degree. He acts as a moderate or conservative man.

But we must not forget that the *Guide* is written also for atypical addressees. In the first place, certain chapters of the *Guide* are explicitly said to be useful also for those who are simply beginners. Since the whole book is somehow accessible to the vulgar, it must have been written in such a way as not to be harmful to the vulgar (1.Introduction; 3.29). Besides, the book is also meant to be useful to such men of great intelligence as have been trained fully in all philosophic sciences and as are not in the habit of bowing to any authority—in other words, to men not inferior to Maimonides in their critical faculty. Readers of this kind will be unable to bow to Maimonides' authority; they will examine all his assertions, speculative or exegetic, with all reasonable severity; and they will derive great pleasure from all chapters of the *Guide* (1.Introduction; 1.55, 68 end, 73, tenth premise).

How much Maimonides' choice of his typical addressee affects the plan of his book will be seen by the judicious reader glancing at our scheme. It suffices to {xx} mention that no section or subsection of the *Guide* is devoted to the bodies that do not come into being and perish (cf. 3.8 beginning, and 1.11), i.e., to the heavenly bodies, which according to Maimonides possess life and knowledge, or to "the holy bodies," to use the bold expression used by him in his Code (*Mishneh Torah*, "Hilkhot Yesodei ha-Torah" IV, 12).[9] In other words, no section or subsection of the *Guide* is devoted to the Account of the Beginning in the manner in which a section is devoted to the Account of the Chariot. More important, Maimonides' choice of his typical addressee is the key to the whole plan of the *Guide*, to the apparent lack of order or to the obscurity of the plan. The plan of the *Guide* appears to be obscure only so long as one does not consider the kind of reader for which the book is written or so long as one seeks for an order agreeing with the essential order of subject matter. We recall the order of the sciences: logic precedes mathematics, mathematics precedes natural science, and natural science precedes divine science;[10] and we recall that while Joseph was sufficiently trained in logic and mathematics, he is supposed to be introduced into divine science without having been trained properly in natural science. Maimonides must therefore seek for a substitute for natural science. He finds that substitute in the traditional Jewish beliefs and ultimately in the biblical texts correctly interpreted: the immediate preparation for divine science in the *Guide* is exegetic rather than speculative. Furthermore, Maimonides wishes to proceed in a manner that changes habits to the smallest possible degree. He himself tells

---

9. For *Mishneh Torah*, "Hilkhot Yesodei ha-Torah" IV, 12, see especially "Book of Knowledge," trans. Lerner, p. 152; and also "Laws of the Basic Principles of the Torah," trans. Hyamson, p. 39b.

10. See *Guide* 1.34, p. 75. But for a different order, cf. "Epistle Dedicatory," p. 3.

us which habit is in particular need of being changed. After having reported the opinion of a pagan philosopher on the obstacles to speculation, he adds the remark that there exists now an obstacle that the ancient philosopher had not mentioned because it did not exist in his society: the habit of relying on revered "texts," i.e., on their literal meaning (1.31). It is for this reason that he opens his book with the explanation of biblical terms, i.e., with showing that their true meaning is not always their literal meaning. He cures the vicious habit in question by having recourse to another habit of his addressee. The addressee was accustomed not only to accept the literally understood biblical texts as true but also in many cases to understand biblical texts according to traditional interpretations that differed considerably from the literal meaning. Being accustomed to listen to authoritative interpretations of biblical texts, he is prepared to listen to Maimonides' interpretations as authoritative interpretations. The explanation of biblical terms that is given by Maimonides authoritatively is in the circumstances the natural substitute for natural science.

But which biblical terms deserve primary consideration? In other words, what is the initial theme of the *Guide*? The choice of the initial theme is dictated by the right answer to the question of which theme is the most urgent for the typical addressee and at the same time the least upsetting to him. The first theme of the {**xxi**} *Guide* is God's incorporeality. God's incorporeality is the third of the three most fundamental truths, the preceding ones being the existence of God and His unity. The existence of God and His unity were admitted as unquestionable by all Jews; all Jews as Jews know that God exists and that He is one, and they know this through the biblical revelation or the biblical miracles. One can say that because belief in the biblical revelation precedes speculation, and the discovery of the true meaning of revelation is the task of exegesis, exegesis precedes speculation. But regarding God's incorporeality there existed a certain confusion. The biblical texts suggest that God is corporeal and the interpretation of these texts is not a very easy task (2.25, 31, 3.28). God's incorporeality is indeed a demonstrable truth but, to say nothing of others, the addressee of the *Guide* does not come into the possession of the demonstration until he has advanced into the Second Part (cf. 1.1, 9, 18). The necessity to refute "corporealism" (the belief that God is corporeal) does not merely arise from the fact that corporealism is demonstrably untrue: corporealism is dangerous because it endangers the belief shared by all Jews in God's unity (1.35). On the other hand, by teaching that God is incorporeal, one does not do more than to give expression to what the talmudic Sages believed (1.46). However, the Jewish authority who had given the most consistent and the most popularly effective expression to the belief in God's incorporeality was Onkelos the Stranger,[11] for the primary preoccupation of his translation of the Torah into Aramaic, which Joseph knew as a matter of course, was precisely to dispose of the corporealistic suggestions of the original (1.21, 27, 28, 36 end). Maimonides' innovation is then limited to his deviation from Onkelos' procedure: he does explicitly what Onkelos did implicitly; whereas Onkelos tacitly substituted noncorporealistic terms for the corporealistic terms occurring in the original, Maimonides explicitly discusses each of the terms in question by itself in an order that has no correspondence to the accidental sequence of their occurrence in the Bible. As a consequence, the discussion of corporealism in the *Guide* consists chiefly of a discussion of the various biblical terms suggesting corporealism, and, vice versa, the chief subject of what Maimonides declares to be the primary purpose of the *Guide*, namely, the explanation of biblical terms, is the explanation of biblical terms suggesting corporealism. This is not surprising. There are no biblical terms that suggest that God is not one, whereas there are many biblical terms that suggest that God is corporeal: the apparent difficulty created by the plural *Elohim* can be disposed of by a single sentence or by a single reference to Onkelos (1.2).

The chief reason why it is so urgent to establish the belief in God's incorporeality, however, is supplied by the fact that that belief is destructive of idolatry. It was of course universally known that idolatry is a very grave sin, nay, that the Law has, so to speak, no other purpose than to destroy idolatry (1.35, 3.29 end). {xxii} But this evil can be completely eradicated only if everyone is brought to know that God has no visible shape whatever or that He is incorporeal. Only if God is incorporeal is it absurd to make images of God and to worship such images. Only under this condition can it become manifest to everyone that the only image of God is man, living and thinking man, and that man acts as the image of God only through worshiping the invisible

---

11. Cf. also "Introduction to Maimonides' *Guide*," chap. 10 above. In the present essay, Strauss translates the honorific title of Onkelos as "the Stranger" (while in the previous lecture, he rendered it as "the Proselyte"). This is closer to the original (i.e., biblical) meaning of the Hebrew term "*ger*," which was used for a stranger or foreigner who sojourned with the ancient Israelites and who accepted, or at least willingly followed, certain fundamental laws. It was only in subsequent (i.e., talmudic, which is perhaps to say post–70 C.E.) Jewish history that the term acquired the meaning of "convert" or "proselyte." By so rendering it in the present context, Strauss seems to imitate or at least to stick closely to what he considers to have been the "originalist" emphasis of Maimonides in the *Guide*. In the present chapter, several further significant references to Onkelos help to clarify the role he plays in Strauss's conception of Maimonides' purpose and literary strategy as author of the *Guide*.

or hidden God alone. Not idolatry but the belief in God's corporeality is a fundamental sin. Hence the sin of idolatry is less grave than the sin of believing that God is corporeal (1.36). This being the case, it becomes indispensable that God's incorporeality be believed in by everyone whether or not he knows by demonstration that God is incorporeal. With regard to the majority of men it is sufficient and necessary that they believe in this truth on the basis of authority or tradition, i.e., on a basis that the first subsections of the *Guide* are meant to supply. The teaching of God's incorporeality by means of authoritative exegesis, i.e., the most public teaching of God's incorporeality, is indispensable for destroying the last relics of paganism: the immediate source of paganism is less the ignorance of God's unity than the ignorance of His radical incorporeality (cf. 1.36 with *Mishneh Torah*, "Hilkhot Avodah Zarah" I, 1).[12]

It is necessary that we understand the character of the reasoning that Maimonides uses when he determines the initial theme of the *Guide*. We limit ourselves to a consideration of the second reason demanding the teaching of Incorporeality. While the belief in Unity leads immediately to the rejection of the worship of "other gods" but not to the rejection of the worship of images of the one God, the belief in Incorporeality leads immediately only to the rejection of the worship of images or of other bodies but not to the rejection of the worship of other gods: all gods may be incorporeal. Only if the belief in God's incorporeality is based on the belief in His unity, as Maimonides' argument indeed assumes, does the belief in God's incorporeality appear to be the necessary and sufficient ground for rejecting "forbidden worship" in every form, i.e., the worship of other gods as well as the worship of both natural things and artificial things. This would mean that the prohibition against idolatry in the widest sense is as much a dictate of reason as the belief in God's unity and incorporeality. Yet Maimonides indicates that only the theoretical truths pronounced in the Decalogue (God's existence and His unity), in contradistinction to the rest of the Decalogue, are rational. This is in agreement with his denying the existence of rational commandments or prohibitions as such (2.33; cf. 1.54, 2.31 beginning, 3.28; *Eight Chapters* VI).[13]

---

12. For *Mishneh Torah*, "Hilkhot Avodah Zarah" I, 1, see "Laws Concerning Idolatry," trans. Hyamson, p. 66a.

13. For *Eight Chapters* VI, see "Eight Chapters," in *Ethical Writings*, trans. Weiss and Butterworth, chap. 6, pp. 78–80, and especially the key passage, p. 80. For its most recent critical edition with a modern Hebrew translation, see *Hakdamot ha-Rambam le-Mishnah*, ed. Shailat, pp. 227–56, chap. VI, pp. 244–46, and especially the key passage, p. 245. A further modern Hebrew translation has just recently appeared, but I have not yet been able to obtain a copy to peruse it: Maimonides, *Shemonah Perakim*, ed. and

Given the fact that Aristotle believed in God's unity and incorporeality and yet was an idolator (1.71, 3.29), Maimonides' admiration for him would be incomprehensible if the rejection of idolatry were the simple consequence of that belief. According to Maimonides, the Law agrees with Aristotle in {xxiii} holding that the heavenly bodies are endowed with life and intelligence and that they are superior to man in dignity; one could say that he agrees with Aristotle in implying that those holy bodies deserve more than man to be called images of God. But unlike the philosophers he does not go so far as to call those bodies "divine bodies" (2.4–6; cf. Letter to Ibn Tibbon).[14] The true ground of the rejection of "forbidden worship" is the belief in creation out of nothing, which implies that creation is an absolutely free act of God or that God alone is the complete good that is in no way increased by creation. But creation is according to Maimonides not demonstrable, whereas God's unity and incorporeality are demonstrable. The reasoning underlying the determination of the initial theme of the *Guide* can then be described as follows: it conceals the difference of cognitive status between the belief in God's unity and incorporeality on the one hand and the belief in creation on the other; it is in accordance with the opinion of the *kalam*. In accordance with this, Maimonides brings his disagreement with the *kalam* into the open only after he has concluded his thematic discussion of God's incorporeality; in that discussion he does not even mention the *kalam*.

It is necessary that we understand as clearly as possible the situation in which Maimonides and his addressee find themselves at the beginning of the book, if not throughout the book. Maimonides knows that God is incorporeal; he knows this by a demonstration that is at least partly based on natural

---

trans. Michael Schwarz (Jerusalem: Ben Zvi Institute, 2011). Maimonides' generally dim view of dialectical theologians (i.e., those who embrace the specific notion of "rational moral laws") is presented by him in chap. I. Cf. also *The Eight Chapters of Maimonides on Ethics (Shemonah Perakim): A Psychological and Ethical Treatise*, ed. and trans. Joseph I. Gorfinkle (New York: Columbia University Press, 1912; reprint, New York: AMS, 1966); and *Traité d'éthique*, ed. Brague.

14. For a critical edition of two versions of Maimonides' "Letter to Samuel Ibn Tibbon," see Alexander Marx, "Texts By and About Maimonides," *Jewish Quarterly Review*, n.s., 25 (1935): 371–428, and especially pp. 374–81. For a critical edition of the Arabic original (although much of the Arabic original has been lost), and with an original Hebrew translation, see *Igrot ha-Rambam*, ed. Shailat, II, pp. 525–54. For an abridged English translation, see *Letters*, trans. Stitskin, pp. 130–36. An adequate and complete (and as much as possible critical) English translation of Maimonides' letter to Ibn Tibbon (not to mention his entire oeuvre of letters) has not yet been produced, and is a scholarly desideratum. But very competent translations, at least of those portions of the letter to Ibn Tibbon in which philosophy is discussed, appear in the following: Shlomo Pines, "Translator's Introduction," in *Guide*, pp. lix–lx; Joel Kraemer, "Maimonides and the Spanish Aristotelian Tradition," in M. M. Meyerson and E. D. English, eds., *Christians, Muslims, and Jews in Medieval and Early Modern Spain: Interaction and Cultural Change* (Notre Dame: Notre Dame University Press, 1999), pp. 40–68, and especially pp. 43–44.

science. The addressee does not know that God is incorporeal; nor does he learn it yet from Maimonides: he accepts the fact that God's incorporeality is demonstrated, on Maimonides' authority. Both Maimonides and the addressee know that the Law is a source of knowledge of God; only the Law can establish God's incorporeality for the addressee in a manner that does not depend on Maimonides' authority. But both know that the literal meaning of the Law is not always its true meaning and that the literal meaning is certainly not the true meaning when it contradicts reason, for otherwise the Law could not be "your wisdom and your understanding in the sight of the nations" (Deut. 4:6). Both know in other words that exegesis does not simply precede speculation. Yet only Maimonides knows that the corporealistic expressions of the Law are against reason and must therefore be taken as figurative. The addressee does not know and cannot know that Maimonides' figurative interpretations of those expressions are true: Maimonides does not adduce arguments based on grammar. The addressee accepts Maimonides' interpretations just as he is in the habit of accepting the Aramaic translations as correct translations or interpretations. Maimonides enters the ranks of the traditional Jewish authorities: he simply tells the addressee what to believe regarding the meaning of the biblical terms. Maimonides introduces Reason in the guise of Authority. He takes on the garb of authority. He tells the addressee to believe in {xxiv} God's incorporeality because, as he tells him, contrary to appearance, the Law does not teach corporeality, because, as he tells him, corporeality is a demonstrably wrong belief.

But we must not forget the most important atypical addressee, the reader who is critical and competent. He knows the demonstration of God's incorporeality and the problems connected with it as well as Maimonides does. Therefore the exegetic discussion of God's incorporeality which is presented in the first forty-nine chapters of the *Guide*, and which is prespeculative and hence simply public as far as the typical addressee is concerned, is postspeculative and hence secret from the point of view of the critical and competent reader. The latter will examine Maimonides' explanations of biblical terms in the light of the principle that one cannot establish the meanings of a term if one does not consider the contexts in which they occur (2.29; cf. *Epistle to Yemen* 46, 7ff.),[15] or that while grammar is not a sufficient condition, it is surely the necessary condition of interpretation. For while the competent reader

---

15. For Maimonides, *Epistle to Yemen* 46, 7ff., see "Epistle to Yemen," trans. Kraemer, p. 114; "Epistle to Yemen," trans. Halkin, p. 109; "Igeret Teman," in *Igrot ha-Rambam*, ed. Shailat, I, p. 135. Kraemer translates the passage as follows: "All this is something that happened before the revelation of the Torah.

will appreciate the advantages attendant upon a coherent discussion of the biblical terms in question as distinguished from a translation of the Bible, he will realize that such a discussion may make one oblivious of the contexts in which the terms occur. He will also notice contradictions occurring in the *Guide*, remember always that they are intentional, and ponder over them.

The readers of the *Guide* were told at the beginning that the first purpose of the book is the explanation of biblical terms. They will then in no way be surprised to find that the book opens with the explanation of biblical terms in such a way that, roughly speaking, each chapter is devoted to the explanation of one or several biblical terms. They will soon become habituated to this procedure: they become engrossed by the subject matter, the What, and will not observe the How. The critical reader, however, will find many reasons for becoming amazed. To say nothing of other considerations, he will wonder why almost the only terms explained are those suggesting corporeality. It is perhaps not a matter of surprise that one chapter is devoted to the explanation of "place" and another to the explanation of "to dwell." But why is there no chapter devoted to "one," none to "merciful," none to "good," none to "intelligence," none to "eternity"? Why is there a chapter devoted to "grief" and none to "laughter"? Why is there a chapter devoted to "foot" and another to "wing" but none to "hand" nor to "arm"? Assuming that one has understood Maimonides' selection of terms, one still has to understand the order in which he discusses them. To what extent the explanation of terms is limited to terms suggesting corporeality, appears with particular clarity when one considers especially those chapters that are most visibly devoted to the explanation of terms, the lexicographic chapters. By a lexicographic chapter I understand a chapter that opens with the Hebrew term or terms to be explained {**xxv**} in the chapter regardless of whether these terms precede the first sentence or form the beginning of the first sentence, and regardless of whether these terms are supplied with the Arabic article *al-* or not. The lexicographic chapter may be said to be the normal or typical chapter in the discussion of God's incorporeality (1.1–49); thirty out of the forty-nine chapters in question are lexicographic whereas in the whole rest of the book there occur at most two such chapters (1.66 and 70). All these thirty chapters occur in 1.1–45: two thirds of the chapters in 1.1–45 are lexicographic. Thus the question arises why nineteen chapters of the discussion of God's

---

Hence, verbs in the past tense were used: *He came*, *He shone*, *He appeared*. They are not prefigurations of what will happen."

incorporeality—and just the nineteen chapters having both the subject matters and the places that they do—are not lexicographic. Why do ten of these thirty lexicographic chapters begin with Hebrew terms preceding the first sentence and twenty of them begin with Hebrew terms forming part of the first sentence? Thirteen of the terms in question are nouns, twelve are verbs, and five are verbal nouns: why does Maimonides in some cases use the verbs and in other cases the verbal nouns? Within the chapters, generally speaking, he discusses the term that is the subject of the chapter in question, first in regard to the various meanings it has when it is not applied to God and then in regard to the various meanings it has when applied to God; he proves the existence of each of these meanings in most cases by quoting one or more biblical passages; those quotations are sometimes explicitly incomplete (ending in "and so on") and more frequently not; the quotations used to illustrate a particular meaning of a particular term do not always follow the biblical order; they are frequently introduced by "he said" but sometimes they are ascribed to individual biblical authors or speakers; in most cases he does not add to the name of the biblical author or speaker the formula "may he rest in peace," but in some cases he does; sometimes "the Hebrew language" or "the language" is referred to. In a book as carefully worded as is the *Guide* according to Maimonides' emphatic declaration, all these varieties, and others that we forgo mentioning, deserve careful consideration. It goes without saying that there is not necessarily only one answer to each of the questions implied in each of these varieties; the same device—e.g., the distinction between lexicographic and nonlexicographic chapters or the tracing of a biblical quotation to an individual biblical author—may fulfill different functions in different contexts. In order to understand the *Guide*, one must be fully awake and as it were take nothing for granted. In order to become enabled to raise the proper questions, one does well to consider the possibility that there exists the typical chapter or else to construct the typical chapter, i.e., to find out which of the varieties indicated are most in accordance with the primary function of the chapters devoted to the explanation of biblical terms: only the other varieties are in need of a special reason. {**xxvi**}

The first chapter of the *Guide* is devoted to "image and likeness." The selection of these terms was necessitated by a single biblical passage: "And God said, Let us make man in our image, after our likeness. . . . So God created man in his image, in the image of God created he him, male and female created he them" (Gen. 1:26-27). The selection of these terms for explanation in the first chapter is due to the unique significance of the passage quoted. That passage suggests to the vulgar mind more strongly than any other biblical passage that God is corporeal in the crudest sense: God has the shape of a human being, has a face, lips, and hands, but is bigger and more resplendent than man since He does not consist of flesh and blood, and is therefore in need, not of food and drink, but of odors; His place is in Heaven from which He descends to the earth, especially to high mountains, in order to guide men and to find out what they do, and to which He ascends again with incredible swiftness; He is moved, as men are, by passions, especially by anger, jealousy, and hate, and thus makes men frightened and sad; His essence is Will rather than Intellect. (Cf. 1.10, 20, 36–37, 39, 43, 46, 47, 68.) Maimonides tells his addressee that *ẓelem* (the Hebrew term which is rendered by "image") does not mean, if not exactly in any case, but certainly in the present case, a visible shape; it means the natural form, the specific form, the essence of a being: "God created man in his image" means that God created man as a being endowed with intellect or that the divine intellect links itself with man. [¶] Similar considerations apply to the Hebrew term rendered by "likeness." The Hebrew term designating form in the sense of visible shape is *to'ar*, which is never applied to God. After having dispelled the confusion regarding "image" Maimonides says: "We have explained to thee the difference between *ẓelem* and *to'ar* and we have explained the meaning of *ẓelem*." He thus alludes to the twofold character of his explanation here as well as elsewhere: one explanation is given to "thee," i.e., to the typical addressee, and another is given to indeterminate readers; the latter explanation comes to sight only when one considers, among other things, the context of all biblical passages quoted. To mention only one example, the second of the three quotations illustrating the meaning of *to'ar* is "What form is he of?" (I Sam. 28:14). The quotation is taken from the account of King Saul's conversation with the witch of Endor, whom the king had asked to bring up to him the dead prophet Samuel; when the woman saw Samuel and became frightened and the king asked her what she saw, she said: "I saw gods (*elohim*) ascending out of the earth." The account continues as follows: "And he said unto her, What form is he of? And she said: an old man cometh up; and he is covered with a mantle." Maimonides himself tells us in the next chapter that *elohim* is an equivocal term that may mean angels and rulers of cities as well as God; but this does not explain why that term is also applied to the shades of the venerable departed—beings {xxvii} without flesh and blood— which frighten men either because those shades do not wish to be "disquieted," i.e., they wish to rest in peace, or for other reasons. To say nothing of other reasons, the rational beings inhabiting the lower depth are in truth not men who have died, but all living men, the Adamites, i.e., the descendants of Adam, who lack Adam's pristine intellectuality (cf. 1.2 with 1.10). It looks as if Maimonides wished to draw our attention to the fact that the Bible contains idolatrous, pagan, or "Sabian" relics. If this suspicion should prove to be justified, we would have to assume that his fight against "forbidden worship" and hence against corporealism is more radical than one would be inclined to believe, or that the recovery of Sabian relics in the Bible with the help of Sabian literature is one of the tasks of his secret teaching. [¶] However this may be, his interpretation of Genesis 1:26 seems to be contradicted by the fact that the Torah speaks shortly afterward of the divine prohibition addressed to Man against eating of the fruit of the tree of knowledge: if Man was created as an intellectual being and hence destined for the life of the intellect, his Creator could not well have forbidden him to strive for knowledge. In other words, the biblical account implies that man's intellectuality is not identical with man's being created in the image of God but is a consequence of his disobedience to God or of God's punishing him for that sin. As we are told in the second chapter, this objection was raised not by the addressee of the *Guide* but by another acquaintance of Maimonides, a nameless scientist of whom we do not even know whether he was of Jewish extraction and who was apparently not very temperate in regard to drink and to sex. (Compare the parallel in 3.19.) Maimonides tells his addressee that he replied to his objector as follows: the knowledge that was forbidden to Man was the knowledge of "good and evil," i.e., of the noble and base, and the noble and base are objects not of the intellect but of opinion; strictly speaking they are not objects of knowledge at all. To mention only the most important example, in Man's perfect state, in which he was unaware of the noble and base, although he was aware of the naturally good and bad, i.e., of the pleasant and painful, he did not regard the uncovering of one's nakedness as disgraceful. [¶] After having thus disposed of the most powerful objection to his interpretation of Genesis 1:26, or after having thus taught that the intellectual life is beyond the noble and base, Maimonides turns to the second most important passage of the Torah that seems to suggest that God is corporeal. More precisely, he turns both to the terms applied in that passage to God and to kindred terms. The passage, which occurs in Numbers 12:8, reads as follows: "he (Moses) beholds the figure of the Lord." He devotes to this subject three chapters (1.3–5); in 1.3 he discusses explicitly the three meanings of "figure" and in 1.4 he discusses explicitly the three meanings of the three terms designating "beholding" or "seeing"; in one of the biblical passages partly quoted, the Lord is {**xxviii**} presented as having appeared to Abraham in the guise of three men who yet were one. Maimonides tells the addressee that the Hebrew terms designating "figure" and "beholding" (or its equivalents) mean, when they are applied to God, intellectual truth and intellectual grasp. The relation of 1.5 to 1.3–4 resembles the relation of 1.2 and 1.1. The view that man was created for the life of the intellect was contradicted by the apparent prohibition against acquiring knowledge. Similarly, "the prince of the philosophers" (i.e., Aristotle) apparently contradicts his view that man exists for the life of the intellect by apologizing for his engaging in the investigation of very obscure matters: Aristotle apologizes to his readers for his apparent temerity; in fact, he is prompted only by his desire to know the truth. This restatement of an Aristotelian utterance affords an easy transition to the Jewish view according to which Moses was rewarded with beholding the figure of the Lord because he had previously "hid his face; for he was afraid to look upon God" (Exod. 3:6). The pursuit of knowledge of God must be preceded by fear of looking upon God or, to use the expression that Aristotle had used in the passage in question (*On the Heaven* 291b21ff.) and that does not occur in Maimonides' summary, by sense of shame: the intellectual perfection is necessarily preceded by moral perfection—by one's having acquired the habit of doing the noble and avoiding the base—as well as by other preparations. Maimonides' emphasis here on moral perfection, especially on temperance, as a prerequisite of intellectual perfection is matched by his silence here on natural science as such a prerequisite. The weeding-out of corporealism proceeds *pari passu* with the watering of asceticism.[16] [¶] Having arrived at this point, Maimonides does something strange: he abruptly turns to the explanation of the terms "man and woman" (1.6) and "to generate" (1.7). The strangeness, however, immediately disappears once one observes that 1.6–7 are the first lexicographic chapters after 1.1 and one remembers that 1.2 is merely a corollary of 1.1: the explanation of "man and woman" and of "to generate" forms part of the explanation of Genesis 1:26–27. There it is said that "in the image of God created (God man); male and female created he them." Literally understood, that saying might be thought to mean that man is the image of God because he is bisexual or that the Godhead contains a male and a female element that generate "children of God" and the like. Accordingly, the last word of 1.7 is the same as the first word of 1.1: "image." Maimonides does

---

16. *pari passu* = "hand-in-hand," "in step with," or "at an equal pace with."

not discuss the implication which was stated, for it is one of the secrets of the Torah and we are only at the beginning of our training. The explanation of the key terms (or their equivalents) occurring in Genesis 1:26–27 surrounds then the explanation of the key terms (or their equivalents) occurring in Numbers 12:8. The discussion of the most important passages of the Torah regarding Incorporeality forms the fitting subject of the first subsection of the *Guide*. That subsection seems to be devoted to {xxix} five unconnected groups of terms; closer inspection shows that it is devoted to two biblical passages: Maimonides seems to hesitate to sever the umbilical cord connecting his exegesis with Onkelos'.

At first glance the theme of the second subsection is much easier to recognize than that of the first. This seems to be due to the fact that that theme is not two or more biblical passages but biblical terms designating phenomena all of which belong essentially together: place as well as certain outstanding places, occupying place, changing place, and the organs for changing place. Nineteen of the twenty-one chapters of the second subsection are manifestly devoted to this theme. The discussion begins with "place" (1.8), turns to "throne" (1.9), a most exalted place that if ascribed to God designates not only the temple but also and above all the heaven, and then turns to "descending and ascending" (1.10). While this sequence is perfectly lucid, we are amazed to find that, whereas 1.8 and 1.9 are lexicographic chapters, 1.10 is not a lexicographic chapter. This irregularity can be provisionally explained as follows: when Maimonides treats thematically several verbs in one lexicographic chapter, those verbs are explicitly said to have the same or nearly the same meaning (1.16, 18); when he treats thematically verbs that primarily designate opposites but do not designate opposites if applied to God, he treats them in separate chapters (1.11, 12, 22, 23); but "descending" and "ascending" designate opposites both in their primary meaning and if applied to God: God's descending means both His revealing Himself and His punitive action, and His ascending means the cessation of His revelation or punitive action (cf. the silence on "returning" at the beginning of 1.23). Maimonides indicates the unique character of the subject "descent and ascent" by treating it in a nonlexicographic chapter surrounded on the one side by four and on the other side by three lexicographic chapters. On the basis of "the vulgar imagination" God's natural state would be sitting on His throne and sitting is the opposite of rising. "Sitting" and "rising" (1.11 and 12) designate opposites but do not designate opposites if applied to God: although God's "sitting" refers to His unchangeability, His "rising" refers to His keeping His promises or threats, it being understood that His promises to Israel may very well be threats to Israel's enemies. A talmudic passage that confirms Maimonides' public explanation and in which "sitting" is mentioned together, not with "rising," but with "standing up" naturally leads to the discussion of "standing up" (1.13), which term, according to Maimonides, means if applied to God His unchangeability, an unchangeability not contradicted, as he indicates, by God's threats to destroy Israel.

Having arrived at this point, Maimonides interrupts his discussion of verbs or of other terms that refer to place and turns to the explanation of "man" (1.14). A similar interruption occurs shortly afterwards when he turns from "standing" and "rock" (1.15 and 16) to an explanation of the prohibition against {xxx} the public teaching of natural science (1.17). Although these chapters are subtly interwoven with the chapters preceding and following them, at first glance they strikingly interrupt the continuity of the argument. By this irregularity our attention is drawn to a certain numerical symbolism that is of assistance to the serious reader of the *Guide*: 14 stands for man or the human things and 17 stands for nature.[17] The connection between "nature" and "change of place" (or, more generally, motion), and therewith the connection between the theme of 1.17 and the subsection to which that chapter belongs, has been indicated before. The connection between "14" and the context cannot become clear before we have reached a better understanding of the relation between nature and convention; at present it must suffice to say that 1.7 deals with "to generate." Although 1.26 obviously deals with terms referring to place, it also fulfills a numerological function: the immediate theme of that chapter is the universal principle governing the interpretation of the Torah ("the Torah speaks according to the language of human beings"); 26 is the numerical equivalent of the secret name of the Lord, the God of Israel; 26 may therefore also stand for His Torah. Incidentally, it may be remarked that 14 is the numerical equivalent of the Hebrew for "hand"; 1.28 is devoted to "foot": no chapter of the *Guide* is devoted to "hand," the characteristically human organ, whereas Maimonides devotes a chapter, the central chapter of the fourth subsection, to "wing," the organ used for swift descent and ascent. In all these matters one can derive great help from studying Joseph Albo's *Roots*. Albo was a favorite companion living at the court of a great king.[18]

17. Cf. "Introduction to Maimonides' *Guide*," chap. 10 above, and also what follows.
18. For Albo, *Roots*, see Albo, *Ikkarim* (*Roots*), trans. Husik. Strauss seems to suggest by this remark that, as a key to deciphering Albo's *Roots*, it is to be read as a certain sort of critical commentary on the *Guide*. With regard to specific points: for "hand," see vol. II, chap. 14, p. 84, and vol. III, chap. 10, p. 92;

Of the twenty-one chapters of the second subsection sixteen are lexicographic and five (1.10, 14, 17, 26, 27) are not. Of these sixteen chapters two begin with Hebrew terms supplied with the Arabic article (1.23 and 24). Thus only seven of the twenty-one chapters may be said to vary from the norm. In seven of the fourteen chapters beginning with a pure Hebrew term, that term precedes the first sentence and in the seven others the Hebrew term forms part of the first sentence. Seven of these chapters begin with a verb and seven with a noun or a verbal noun. It is one thing to observe these regularities and another thing to understand them. The distinction between the verbs and the verbal nouns is particularly striking, since lexicographic chapters beginning with verbal nouns occur only in our subsection. Furthermore, of the three lexicographic chapters of the first subsection, one opens with nouns preceding the first sentence, one with nouns forming part of the first sentence, and one with a verb preceding the first sentence; orderliness would seem to require that there be a chapter opening with a verb that forms part of the first sentence. One of the chapters of the second subsection (1.22) begins with a verb preceding the first sentence but the first sentence opens with the verbal noun (supplied with the Arabic article) of the same verb; there occurs no other {xxxi} case of this kind in the whole book. If we count this ambiguous

---

for "sitting," see vol. II, chap. 14, pp. 89–90; for "the Torah speaks according to the language of human beings," see vol. II, chap. 14, p. 90, and chap. 17, p. 108; for "wing," see vol. II, chap. 15, p. 95; for "place," see vol. II, chap. 17, pp. 101–8. For Albo's "Maimonidean" literary procedure, see the "Observation" with which vol. II begins, pp. 1–4. If Strauss was thinking of a definite passage (rather than just employing a metaphor) concerned with "a great king" and "a favorite companion," I was not able to locate it. (Yet for the requisite qualities of kings, see vol. IV, chap. 26, pp. 245–48.) However, I did encounter a passage in Albo's book which speaks of "love between friends," which he represents as follows (vol. III, chap. 37, p. 339):

> First, there is the love of equality or similarity, the kind that obtains between friends who are equal in a certain respect in a virtue, in an accomplishment, or in beneficence, i.e., if each derives a benefit from the other or finds pleasure in the other, or they are both equal in goodness. That one of the two who receives more benefit than he gives must love his friend more than his friend loves him because of the greater benefit or pleasure he receives from the other or because of his friend's superior goodness. If they are equal in beneficence, pleasure, or goodness, their love is without doubt more complete.

(The editor's note helpfully refers to Aristotle's *Nicomachean Ethics* VIII, 6, 1158b [1–12]; however, perhaps rather than the passage mentioned—insofar as Albo is addressing "friendship between equals"—it might be closer to Albo's point to consider VIII, 3, 1156b6–25.) For Strauss on Albo, see also "Maimonides' Doctrine of Prophecy," chap. 4 above, n. 55; "The Place of the Doctrine of Providence," chap. 6 above, n. 13; "Maimonides' Statement on Political Science," chap. 9 above, nn. 4, 6, and 27; "Notes on Maimonides' *Book of Knowledge*," chap. 12 below, nn. 17, 18, 19, and 28; and the forthcoming *Leo Strauss and the Rediscovery of Maimonides* (University of Chicago Press) by the present writer. Insofar as a passage by Maimonides is on Strauss's mind vis-à-vis his remark about "a favorite companion living at the court of a great king," consider of course the great parable in *Guide* 3.51.

chapter among the chapters beginning with a verbal noun forming part of the first sentence, we reach this conclusion: the second subsection contains four chapters beginning with verbs or verbal nouns preceding the first sentence and eight chapters beginning with verbs or verbal nouns forming part of the first sentence. Furthermore, the second subsection contains six chapters beginning with verbs and six chapters beginning with verbal nouns; of the latter six chapters three begin with pure verbal nouns and three begin with verbal nouns supplied with the Arabic article. The second subsection surpasses the first subsection in regularity especially if 1.22 is properly subsumed. From all this we are led to regard it as possible that 1.22 somehow holds the key to the mystery of the second subsection.

The first chapter of the second subsection (1.8) is devoted to "place," a term that in postbiblical Hebrew is used for designating God Himself. To our great amazement Maimonides is completely silent about this meaning of "place." His silence is all the more eloquent since he quotes in this very chapter postbiblical Hebrew expressions containing "place," since he admonishes the readers in this very chapter to consult regarding his explanation of any term not only "the books of prophecy" but also other "compilations of men of science"—Talmud and Midrash are such compilations—and since he had concluded the preceding chapter with a quotation from the Midrash. In the only other lexicographic chapter devoted to a term used for designating God Himself—in 1.16, which is devoted to "rock"—he does not hesitate to say that that term is also used for designating God, for that meaning of "rock" is biblical. We see then how literally he meant his declaration that the first intention of the *Guide* is to explain terms occurring in "the books of prophecy," i.e., primarily in the Bible: he is primarily concerned with the theology of the Bible in contradistinction to postbiblical Jewish theology. He is alive to the question raised by the Karaites. As he puts it, not only does criticism of the talmudic Sages do no harm to them—it does not even do any harm to the critic or rather to the foundations of belief (1.Intro., 5 end, 19 end, 46 end; cf. *Resurrection* 29, 10–30, 15 Finkel).[19] This observation enables us to solve the difficulty presented by 1.22.

19. Strauss's reference, "*Resurrection* 29, 10–30, 15 Finkel," is to *Moses Maimonides' Treatise on Resurrection (Ma'amar Tehiyat ha-Metim): Original Arabic and Hebrew Translation of Samuel ibn Tibbon*, ed. Joshua Finkel (New York: American Academy for Jewish Research, 1939), p. 29, l. 10 through p. 30, l. 15. It has appeared subsequently in the following editions: *Igrot ha-Rambam* (Arabic original with fresh Hebrew translation), ed. Kafah, pp. 69–101; and *Igrot ha-Rambam* (Arabic original with Hebrew translation of Samuel ibn Tibbon), ed. Shailat, I, pp. 315–74 (the passage of special concern to Strauss occurs,

1.18–21 opened with verbs; 1.22 marks the transition from chapters opening with verbs to chapters opening with verbal nouns supplied with the Arabic article; 1.23–24 open with verbal nouns supplied with the Arabic article. 1.25 opens again with a verb. That verb is "to dwell." The transition made in 1.22 and the procedure in 1.23–24 make us expect that 1.25 should open with the verbal noun "the dwelling," the *Shekhinah*, the postbiblical term particularly used for God's Indwelling on earth, but this expectation is disappointed. Maimonides makes all these preparations in order to let us see that he is anxious to avoid as a {**xxxii**} chapter heading the term *Shekhinah*, which does not occur in the Bible in any sense, and to avoid the Hebrew term *Shekhinah* in its theological sense within the most appropriate chapter itself: when speaking there of the *Shekhinah* theologically, he uses the Arabic translation of *Shekhinah* but never that Hebrew term itself. He does use the Hebrew term *Shekhinah* in a theological meaning in a number of other chapters, but *Shekhinah* never becomes a theme of the *Guide*: there are no "chapters on the *Shekhinah*" as there are "chapters on providence" or "chapters on governance" (1.40 and 1.44). It should also be noted that the chapter devoted to "wing" does not contain a single reference to the *Shekhinah* (cf. particularly Maimonides' and Ibn Janaḥ's explanation of Isaiah 30:20 with the Targum

---

in the Hebrew, on pp. 366–67, and the Arabic, p. 334). For English translations, see "Essay on Resurrection," trans. Halkin, pp. 211–45, and especially p. 228; and "Treatise on Resurrection," trans. Fradkin, pp. 154–77, and especially pp. 171–72. The long passage to which Strauss refers is translated by Fradkin as follows:

> Know that the return of the soul to the body is denied for either one of two causes: (1) It is denied because it is an unnatural thing. Then it follows, in accord with this cause, that all the miracles must be denied because they are unnatural. (2) It is denied because it is not mentioned in the text and there are no truthful reports concerning it as there are concerning the (other) miracles. But we have already explained that texts do exist, even if they are few, that point to the return of the dead. If someone should say, "Let us ourselves interpret those texts just as we have interpreted others," we will speak to him (as follows): "What is it that summons you to interpret them? (Perhaps) it is that the return of the dead is unnatural. Then you yourself interpret the texts for it until you make it congruent with natural matters. You are similarly obliged to interpret the staff's turning back into a snake and the raining down of the *manna* and *the Gathering at Mount Sinai* and *the pillar of fire and smoke*. You must interpret all of this until you make it congruent with the natural things." But we have already explained in the 'Guide,' in our speech concerning the Creation of the world, that with belief in the Creation of the world it follows necessarily that all the miracles are possible, and therefore *Resurrection of the Dead* is also possible. And whenever there is a report of the prophet about any possible thing, we consider it truthful; and we do not resort to any interpretation concerning it, nor do we wrench it from its literal meaning.

For any doubts which some may entertain concerning the number of references to the (popular) "Treatise on Resurrection" in Strauss's Introductory Essay to the (philosophic) *Guide*, it is well to keep in mind his rather unconventional and even astonishing statement that this work is "the most authentic commentary on the *Guide*." See "Literary Character," chap. 8 above.

ad loc.).[20] In the chapter implicitly devoted to the *Shekhinah*, which is the central chapter of the part devoted to Incorporeality (1.1–49), Maimonides had mentioned the *Shekhinah* together with providence, but *Shekhinah* and providence are certainly not identical (cf. 1.10 and 23). One should pay particular attention to the treatment of the *Shekhinah* in the chapters obviously devoted to providence strictly understood (3.17–18 and 22–23). With some exaggeration one may say that whereas the *Shekhinah* follows Israel, providence follows the intellect. In other words, it is characteristic of the *Guide* that in it *Shekhinah* as a theological theme is replaced by "providence," and "providence" in its turn to some extent by "governance," "governance" being as it were the translation of *Merkavah* ("Chariot"), as appears from 1.70. Needless to say, it is not in vain that Maimonides uses the Arabic article at the beginning of 1.23 and 24. He thus connects 1.23 and 24 and the context of these chapters with the only other group of chapters all of which begin with a Hebrew term supplied with the Arabic article: 3.36–49. That group of chapters deals with the individual biblical commandments, i.e., with their literal meaning rather than their extrabiblical interpretation, as is indicated in the chapter (3.41) that stands out from the rest of the group for more than one reason and that is devoted to the penal law. One reason why that chapter stands out is that it is the only chapter whose summary, in 3.35, is adorned

20. "Ibn Janaḥ" is Jonah ibn Janaḥ (985–1050), a Spanish Jew who wrote his works in Arabic. He was undoubtedly the most distinguished medieval Hebrew grammarian, philologist, lexicographer, and comparative linguist. His major work is the *Kitab at-tanqiḥ* (*Book of Minute Research*). Those who followed him were provided with vastly deeper knowledge of the Hebrew language than had previously been available, and they were especially able to fruitfully apply it in commenting on the Hebrew Bible. (This is scarcely to say that he did not have his critics.) Maimonides refers with respect to Ibn Janaḥ in the *Guide*; that puts him in the very select company of those Jewish authors to whom he refers by name in this book. (For his attitude in the *Guide* toward his Jewish predecessors on matters of speculative consequence, see Shlomo Pines, "Translator's Introduction," in *Guide*, p. cxxxiii, n. 123.) The passage from the Targum of Isaiah, with regard to Isaiah 30:20, may be translated as follows: God "will no longer raise His Shekhinah from the sanctuary." See also Rémi Brague, in *Maïmonide*, p. 327, n. 13. Is Strauss suggesting by this Targum passage that "discovering" references to the Shekhinah in the Hebrew Bible is almost the default position of the postbiblical Jewish tradition—which contrasts strikingly with what Maimonides himself did? Regarding Strauss's mention of the "chapter devoted to 'wing'" in the *Guide* (which for some reason he neglects to identify, i.e., 1.43), the translator adds the following note (p. 93, n. 10): "See *The Book of Hebrew Roots*, by Abu 'l-Walid Marwan ibn Janaḥ, ed. A. Neubauer (Oxford, 1875), p. 325." As for the treatment of Isaiah 30:20 in the same chapter to which Strauss points (pp. 93–94), Maimonides refers to Ibn Janaḥ's rendering of the key word, with which he is fully in accord. He writes the following: "Ibn Janaḥ says that the term [i.e., 'wing,' Hebrew '*kanaph*'] also occurs with the signification of concealing, as it is akin to the Arabic, in which one may say, '*kanaftu*' a thing, meaning: I have concealed it. He accordingly interprets the verse, '*Yet shall not thy Teacher be winged*' [*yikaneph*], as meaning: thy Enlightener shall not be concealed and hidden away from thee; and this is a good explanation." Cf. also n. 9 above, for Albo, *Ikkarim* (*Roots*), trans. Husik, on "wing."

with a biblical quotation, 3.35 being the chapter that serves as the immediate introduction to 3.36–49. To repeat, the second subsection of the *Guide* draws our attention to the difference between the biblical and the postbiblical Jewish teaching or to the question raised by the Karaites. Maimonides, it need hardly be said, answered that question in favor of the Rabbanites, although not necessarily in their spirit. It suffices to remember that not only *Shekhinah* but also "providence" and "governance" are not biblical terms.

Like the first subsection, the second subsection is based on two biblical passages, although not as visibly and as clearly as the first. The passages are Exodus 33:20–23 and Isaiah 6. In the former passage the Lord says to Moses: {xxxiii} "Thou canst not see my face; for there shall no man see me, and live: . . . thou shalt see my back parts: but my face shall not be seen." Accordingly, Moses sees only the Lord's "glory pass by." In the latter passage Isaiah says: "I saw the Lord sitting upon a throne, high and lifted up. . . . Mine eyes have seen the king, the Lord of hosts." Isaiah does not speak, as Moses did, of "the figure of the Lord" or of "the image of God." Nor is it said of Isaiah, as it is said of Moses, Aaron, Nadav, Avihu, and seventy of the elders of Israel: "they saw the God of Israel: *and there was under his feet etc.* . . . And the nobles of the children of Israel . . . saw God, *and did eat and drink*" and thus suggested that the vision was imperfect (cf. 1.5 with Albo's *Roots* III, 17).[21] We are thus induced to believe that Isaiah reached a higher stage in the knowledge of God than Moses, or that Isaiah's vision marks a progress beyond Moses'. At first hearing, this belief is justly rejected as preposterous, not to say blasphemous: the denial of the supremacy of Moses' prophecy seems to lead to the denial of the ultimacy of Moses' Law, and therefore Maimonides does not tire of asserting the supremacy of Moses' prophecy. But the belief in the ultimacy of Moses' Law and even in the supremacy of Moses' prophecy in no way contradicts the belief in a certain superiority of Isaiah's speeches to Moses' speeches—to say nothing of the fact that Maimonides never denied that he deliberately contradicts himself. The following example may prove to

---

21. See Albo, *Ikkarim (Roots)*, trans. Husik, vol. III, chap. 17, pp. 149–54. Based on the context, may Strauss perhaps especially point to Albo's comment on p. 154: "Whether, however, any prophet may interpret the words of Moses and say that though they are stated without qualification, they are conditional in their meaning, or that a time limitation should be attached to them, though no such limitation is explicitly stated—this will be discussed in the sequel with the help of God." However, he may also have been thinking of the thought in Isaiah's mind attributed to him by Albo (pp. 152–53): "Isaiah, on the other hand, made use also of the power of imagination . . . and hence was misled by it into thinking that he saw God. He was not unaware that his perception was an error due to the imagination, and said so, explaining that his matter was not as pure as that of Moses, 'Because I am a man of unclean lips,' . . . This is why he complained, 'Woe is me! For I am affected by imagination.'"

be helpful. In his *Treatise on Resurrection*, Maimonides teaches that resurrection, one of the thirteen roots of the Law, is clearly taught within the Bible only in the book of Daniel, but certainly not in the Torah. He explains this apparently strange fact as follows: at the time when the Torah was given, all men, and hence also our ancestors, were Sabians, believing in the eternity of the world, for they believed that God is the spirit of the sphere, and denying the possibility of revelation and of miracles; hence a very long period of education and habituation was needed until our ancestors could be brought even to consider believing in that greatest of all miracles, the resurrection of the dead (26, 18–27, 15 and 31, 1–33, 14 Finkel).[22] This does not necessarily mean that Moses himself did not know this root of the Law but he certainly did not teach it. At least in this respect the book of Daniel, of a late prophet of very low rank (2.45), marks a great progress beyond the Torah of Moses. All the easier is it to understand that Isaiah should have made some progress beyond Moses.

The reason why progress beyond the teaching of the Torah is possible or even necessary is twofold. In the first place, the Torah is the law par excellence. The supremacy of Moses' prophecy—the superiority of Moses' knowledge even to that of the Patriarchs—is connected with its being the only legislative prophecy (1.63, 2.13, 39). But precisely because his prophecy culminates in the Law, it rejects the limitations of law. Law is more concerned with actions than with thoughts {xxxiv} (3.27–28; 1.Intro.). Mosaic theology reflects this orientation. According to the opinion of many of our contemporaries, Maimonides' theological doctrine proper is his doctrine of the divine attributes (1.50–60). In that subsection he quotes passages from the Torah only in that single chapter (1.54) in which he discusses the thirteen divine attributes revealed to Moses (Exod. 34: 5–7); those attributes—all of them moral qualities—constitute the Mosaic theology; they express positively what in negative expression is called in the same context "God's back parts." Although God's goodness had been revealed to Moses in its entirety, the thirteen attributes articulate only that part of God's goodness which is relevant for the ruler of a city who is a prophet. Such a ruler must imitate the divine attributes of wrath and mercy not as passions—for the incorporeal God is above all passion—but because actions of mercy or wrath are appropriate in the circumstances, and he must imitate God's mercy and wrath in

---

22. For 26, 18–27, 15 and 31, 1–33, 14 Finkel: see *Igrot ha-Rambam*, ed. Shailat, I, pp. 364–65, and 368–370; for English translations, see "Essay on Resurrection," trans. Halkin, pp. 226 and 229–30; but see especially "Treatise on Resurrection," trans. Fradkin, pp. 170 and 172–74.

due proportion. The ruler of a city on the other hand must be more merciful than full of anger, for extreme punitiveness is required only because of the necessity, based on "human opinion," to exterminate the idolators by fire and sword (1.54). Following another suggestion of Maimonides (1.61-63) one could say that the adequate statement of Mosaic theology is contained in the divine name YHVH—a name by which God revealed Himself for the first time to Moses as distinguished from the Patriarchs: "I appeared unto Abraham, unto Isaac, and unto Jacob, by the name of God Almighty, but by my name YHVH was I not known to them" (Exod. 6:3). Maimonides recognizes that this verse asserts or establishes the superiority of Moses' prophecy to that of the Patriarchs (2.35) but he does not explain that verse: he does not explain, at least not clearly, which theological verities other than the thirteen attributes were revealed to Moses but were unknown to the Patriarchs. Only this much may be said to emerge: Abraham was a man of speculation who instructed his subjects or followers rather than a prophet who convinced by miracles and ruled by means of promises and threats, and this is somehow connected with the fact that he called "on the name of YHVH, the God of the world" (Gen. 21:33) (1.63, 2.13), i.e., the God of the transmoral whole rather than the lawgiving God. It is this Abrahamitic expression that opens each Part of the *Guide* as well as other writings of Maimonides. Considering all these things, one will find it wise to limit oneself to saying that the Mosaic theology par excellence is the doctrine of the thirteen moral attributes.

Second, the Mosaic legislation was contemporary with the yet unbroken and universal rule of Sabianism. Therefore the situation in the time of Moses was not different from the situation in the time of Abraham, who disagreed with all men, all men having the same Sabian religion or belonging to the same religious community. The innovation was naturally resisted, even with violence, although {xxxv} it was not a principle of Sabianism to exterminate unbelievers. Yet the Torah has only one purpose: to destroy Sabianism or idolatry. But the resistance by the Sabians proper was less important than the inner Sabianism of the early adherents of the Torah. It was primarily for this reason that Sabianism could be overcome only gradually: human nature does not permit the direct transition from one opposite to the other. To mention only the most obvious example, our ancestors had been habituated to sacrifice to natural or artificial creatures. The sacrificial laws of the Torah are a concession to that habit. Since the simple prohibition or cessation of sacrifices would have been as unintelligible or distasteful to our ancestors as the prohibition or cessation of prayer would be now, God provided that henceforth all sacrifices be transferred to Him and no longer be brought to any false gods or idols. The sacrificial laws constitute a step in the gradual transition, in the progress from Sabianism to pure worship, i.e., pure knowledge, of God (cf. 1.54, 64); the sacrificial laws were necessary only "at that time." The Sabians believed that success in agriculture depends on worship of the heavenly bodies. In order to eradicate that belief, God teaches in the Torah that worship of the heavenly bodies leads to disaster in agriculture whereas worship of God leads to prosperity. For the reason given, the open depreciation of sacrifices as such occurs not yet in the Torah but in the prophets and in the Psalms. Conversely, the Torah is less explicit than the later documents regarding the duty of prayer (3.29, 30, 32, 35–37). [¶] No less important an adaptation to Sabian habits is the corporealism of the Bible. For Sabianism is a form of corporealism; according to the Sabians, the gods are the heavenly bodies or the heavenly bodies are the body of which God is the spirit (3.29). As for the Bible, Maimonides' teaching on this subject is not free from ambiguity. The first impression we receive from his teaching is that according to it the corporealistic understanding of the Bible is a mere misunderstanding. For instance, *zelem* simply does not mean visible shape but only natural form, and even if it should sometimes mean visible shape, the term must be considered to be homonymous, and it certainly does not mean visible shape but natural form in Genesis 1:26–27 (1.1; cf. 1.49). In other cases, perhaps in most cases, the primary meaning of the term—say, "sitting"—is corporealistic but when it is applied to God, it is used in a derivative or metaphoric sense; in those cases the meaning of the text, the literal meaning, is metaphoric. Generally stated, the literal meaning of the Bible is not corporealistic. But there are also cases in which the literal meaning is corporealistic, for instance in the many cases in which the Bible speaks of God's anger (cf. 1.29). One must go beyond this and say that generally speaking the literal meaning of the Bible is corporealistic because "the Torah speaks in accordance with the language of the children of Man,"[23] i.e., in accordance with "the imagination of the vul-

---

23. Compare with how Strauss thrice differently translates one of Maimonides' key sentences (e.g., *Guide* 1.26): "the Torah speaks according to the language of human beings" vs. "the Torah speaks in accordance with the language of the children of Man" vs. "He (i.e., God) 'speaks in accordance with the language of the children of man.'" According to *Guide*, trans. Pines, the same original Hebrew sentence is to be translated literally and consistently as "The Torah speaketh in the language of the sons of man." (In the original *Guide*, trans. Pines, it is italicized as a sign of the fact that this is a Hebrew sentence put by Maimonides in the midst of his mostly Judeo-Arabic text.) Are these slight differences for Strauss significant and deliberate in any sense? Are they due to the different contexts in which he uses the sentence, so as to prove a certain point? For Strauss on discussions which "may make one oblivious of the contexts in which the terms occur," for "one cannot establish the meanings of a term if one does not consider the

gar," and the vulgar mind does not admit, at {xxxvi} least to begin with, the existence of any being that is not bodily; the Torah therefore describes God in corporealistic terms in order to indicate that He is (1.26, 47, 51 end). The Bible contains indeed innumerable passages directed against idolatry (1.36), but, as we have seen, idolatry is one thing and corporealism is another. The corporealistic meaning is not the only meaning, it is not the deepest meaning, it is not the true meaning, but it is as much intended as the true meaning; it is intended because of the need to educate and to guide the vulgar and, we may add, a vulgar that originally was altogether under the spell of Sabianism. What is true of the biblical similes is true also of the metaphoric biblical terms. According to the talmudic Sages, the outer of the similes is nothing while the inner is a pearl; according to King Solomon, who was "wiser than all men" (I Kings 5:11), the outer is like silver, i.e., it is useful for the ordering of human society, and the inner is like gold, i.e., it conveys true beliefs (1.Intro.). Hence it is not without danger to the vulgar that one explains the similes or indicates the metaphoric character of expressions (1.33). For such biblical teachings as the assertions that God is angry, compassionate, or in other ways changeable, while not true, yet serve a political purpose or are necessary beliefs (3.28).

[¶] A third possibility emerges through Maimonides' thematic discussion of providence. There he makes a distinction between the view of the Law regarding providence and the true view (3.17, 23). He could well have said that the true view is the secret teaching of the Law. Instead he says that the true view is conveyed through the book of Job, thus implying that the book of Job, a nonprophetic book whose characters are not Jews and that is composed by an unknown author (2.45; *Epistle to Yemen* 50, 19–52, 1 Halkin)[24]

---

contexts in which they occur": see the eighteenth paragraph above (not counting the plan). But why vary even slightly such a key sentence? Is this one of those "hints" that Strauss suggests he might be offering at certain points? (See the thirty-second paragraph.) For the key sentence with its slight differences, see above the twenty-second paragraph, the twenty-eighth paragraph, and the twenty-ninth paragraph. This is to be attributed significance in terms of what Strauss has written if it can be assumed that to read "with the proper care" his introduction to the *Guide*, "all its windings" must also be considered, on the model of the *Guide* itself. (See the beginning of the forty-second paragraph.) "If the *Torah for the Perplexed* thus marks a progress beyond the Torah for the Unperplexed," hence Strauss's introduction also "marks a progress" by being a contemporary commentary on the *Torah for the Perplexed*, seeing it in light of contemporary thought while searching for what endures, guides, and still challenges beyond its historical origins. (See the thirty-first paragraph.)

24. For *Epistle to Yemen* 50, 19–52, 1 Halkin: see "Epistle to Yemen," trans. Halkin, p. 111; "Epistle to Yemen," trans. Kraemer, p. 115; "Igeret Teman," in *Igrot ha-Rambam*, trans. Shailat, I, pp. 135–36. Kraemer translates the passage as follows:

> It has been explained and made clear that the prophet who is promised is not a prophet who will bring a Law or make a religion. He is rather an individual who will enable us to dispense with divination and astrology. And we shall ask him about all that may befall us, just as the (general)

marks a progress beyond the Torah and even beyond the prophets (cf. 3.19). We recall that the simple co-ordination, taught by the Torah, of the worship of the Lord with agricultural and other prosperity was merely a restatement of the corresponding Sabian doctrine. As Maimonides indicates when explaining the account of the revelation on Mount Sinai, the beautiful consideration of the texts is the consideration of their outer meaning (2.36 end, 37). This remark occurs within the section on prophecy in which he makes for the first time an explicit distinction between the legal (or exegetic) and the speculative discussion of the same subject (cf. 2.45 beginning). Accordingly, he speaks in his explanation of the Account of the Chariot, at any rate apparently, only of the literal meaning of this most secret text (3.Intro.). Or to state the matter as succinctly as Maimonides does in the last chapter, the science of the Law is something essentially different, not only from the postbiblical or at any rate extrabiblical legal interpretation of the Law, but from wisdom, i.e., the demonstration of the views transmitted by the Law, as well.

Undoubtedly Maimonides contradicts himself regarding Moses' prophecy. He declares that he will not speak in the *Guide* explicitly or allusively about the {xxxvii} characteristics of Moses' prophecy because or although he had spoken most explicitly about the differences between the prophecy of Moses and that of the other prophets in his more popular writings. And yet he teaches explicitly in the *Guide* that Moses' prophecy, in contradistinction to that of the other prophets, was entirely independent of the imagination or was purely intellectual (2.35, 36, 45 end). His refusal to speak of Moses' prophecy has indeed a partial justification. At least one whole subsection of the section on prophecy (2.41–44) is devoted to the prophecy of the prophets other than Moses, as is indicated by the frequent quotation in that subsection of this passage: "If there be a prophet among you, I the Lord will make myself known unto him in a vision, and will speak unto him in a dream"; for the Bible continues as follows: "My servant Moses is not so, who is faithful in all my house" (Num. 12:6–7). Still the assertion that Moses' prophecy was entirely independent of the imagination leads to a great difficulty if one consid-

---

nations consult *soothsayers* and *diviners*. Thus we find *Saul* asking *Samuel* about something he lost, as it says: "*For the prophet of today was formerly called a seer*." (1 Sam. 9:9) That we do not believe in the prophecy of Umar and Zayd is not because they are not of *Israel*, as the common folk suppose, so that we must have recourse to (reasoning from Scripture's) statement, *from your midst, of your brethren*. For *Job, Zophar, Bildad, Eliphaz, and Elihu* are all prophets according to us although they are not of *Israel*. Likewise, *Hananiah son of Azzur* was a cursed *false prophet* though an *Israelite*. We only believe or disbelieve in a prophet because of his claim, not because of his descent.

ers the fact, pointed out by Maimonides in the same context (2.36; cf. 2.47 beginning), that it is the imagination that brings forth similes and, we may add, metaphors, as well as the fact that the Torah abounds if not with similes, at any rate with metaphors. To mention only one example, Moses' saying that Eve was taken from one of Adam's ribs or that Woman was taken out of Man (Gen. 2:21–23) or derived from man reflects the fact that the word *'ishah* (woman) is derived from the word *'ish* (man) and such substitutions of the relation of words for the relation of things are the world of the imagination (cf. 2.30 and 43; 1.28; and *Mishneh Torah*, "Hilkhot Yesodei ha-Torah" I).[25]

[¶] In order to understand the contradiction regarding Moses' prophecy, we must return once more to the beginning. Maimonides starts from accepting the Law as seen through the traditional Jewish interpretation. The Law thus understood is essentially different from "demonstration" (2.3), i.e., the views of the Law are not as such based on demonstration. Nor do they become evident through "religious experience" or through faith. For, according to Maimonides, there is no religious experience, i.e., specifically religious cognition; all cognition or true belief stems from the human intellect, sense perception, opinion, or tradition; the cognitive status even of the Ten Commandments was not affected by or during the revelation on Mount Sinai: some of these utterances are and always remained matters of "human speculation," while the others are and always remained matters of opinion or matters of tradition (1.51 beginning and 2.33; *Letter on Astrology* §§ 4–5 Marx; and *Logic* chap. 8).[26] As for faith, it is, according to Maimonides, only one of the moral virtues, which as such do not belong to man's ultimate perfection, the perfection of his intellect (3.53–54). The views of the Law are based on a kind of "speculative perception" that human speculation is unable to understand and that grasps the truth without the use of speculative premises or without reasoning; through this kind of perception peculiar {xxxviii} to prophets, the prophet sees and hears nothing except God and angels (2.38, 36, 34). Some of the things perceived by prophets can be known with cer-

---

25. For *Mishneh Torah*, "Hilkhot Yesodei ha-Torah" I, see "Laws of the Basic Principles of the Torah," trans. Hyamson, pp. 34a–35b; but see especially "Book of Knowledge," trans. Lerner, pp. 141–44.

26. *Letter on Astrology* §§ 4–5 Marx refers to the Hebrew text critically established by Alexander Marx, "The Correspondence between the Rabbis of Southern France and Maimonides about Astrology," *Hebrew Union College Annual* 3 (1926): 349–58. The establishment of a critical Hebrew text has been further advanced: see *Igrot ha-Rambam*, ed. Shailat, II, pp. 478–90, and especially pp. 479–80. For an English translation, see especially "Letter on Astrology," trans. Lerner, pp. 178–87. Marx's paragraph numbers are not retained by Lerner; paras. 4 and 5 occur in Lerner, pp. 179–80 (which are his actual fourth and fifth paragraphs, even if unnumbered). For *Logic* chap. 8, see "Logic," in *Ethical Writings*, trans. Weiss and Butterworth, chap. 8, pp. 156–58.

tainty also through demonstration. While for instruction in these things nonprophetic men are not absolutely in need of prophets, they depend entirely on prophets regarding those divine things that are not accessible to human speculation or demonstration. Yet the nonrational element in the prophetic speeches is to some extent imaginary, i.e., infrarational. It is therefore a question how nonprophetic men can be certain of the suprarational teaching of the prophets, i.e., of its truth. The general answer is that the suprarational character of the prophetic speeches is confirmed by the supranatural testimony of the miracles (2.25, 3.29). In this way the authority of the Law as wholly independent of speculation is established wholly independently of speculation. Accordingly the understanding or exegesis of the Law can be wholly independent of speculation and in particular of natural science; and considering the higher dignity of revelation, exegesis will be of higher rank than natural science in particular; the explanations given by God Himself are infinitely superior to merely human explanations or traditions. This view easily leads to the strictest biblicism. "The difficulty of the Law" may be said to arise from the fact that the miracles do not merely confirm the truth of the belief in revelation but also presuppose the truth of that belief; only if one holds in advance the indemonstrable belief that the visible universe is not eternal can one believe that a given extraordinary event is a miracle (2.25). It is this difficulty that Maimonides provisionally solves by suggesting that Moses' prophecy is unique because it is wholly independent of the imagination, for if this suggestion is accepted, the difficulty caused by the presence of an infrarational element in prophetic speeches does not arise. Yet if Moses' prophecy alone is wholly independent of the imagination, the Torah alone will be simply true, i.e., literally true, and this necessarily leads to extreme corporealism. Since corporealism is demonstrably wrong, we are compelled to admit that the Torah is not always literally true and hence, as matters stand, that the teaching of the other prophets may be superior in some points to that of Moses. [¶] The fundamental difficulty of how one can distinguish the suprarational, which must be believed, from the infrarational, which ought not to be believed, cannot be solved by recourse to the fact that we hear through the Bible, and in particular through the Torah, "God's book" par excellence (3.12), not human beings but God Himself. It is indeed true in a sense that God's speech gives the greatest certainty of His existence, and His declaring His attributes sets these attributes beyond doubt (cf. 1.9 and 11, 2.11), but God Himself cannot explain clearly the deepest secrets of the Torah to flesh and blood (1.Intro., 31 beginning), He "speaks in accordance with the language of the children of man" (1.26), things that might have been made clear in the Torah are not made clear in it {**xxxix**} (1.39), God makes use of ruses and of silence for only "a fool will reveal all his purpose and his will" (1.40; cf. 3.32, 45 and 54) and, last but not least, as Maimonides explains in the *Guide*, God does not use speech in any sense (1.23) and this fact entails infinite consequences. One is therefore tempted to say that the infrarational in the Bible is distinguished from the suprarational by the fact that the former is impossible whereas the latter is possible: biblical utterances that contradict what has been demonstrated by natural science or by reason in any other form cannot be literally true but must have an inner meaning; on the other hand, one must not reject views the contrary of which has not been demonstrated, i.e., which are possible—for instance, creation out of nothing—lest one become thoroughly indecent (1.32, 2.25). [¶] Yet this solution does not satisfy Maimonides. Whereas he had originally declared that the human faculty that distinguishes between the possible and the impossible is the intellect and not the imagination, he is compelled, especially in his chapters on providence, to question this verdict and to leave it open whether it is not rather the imagination that ought to have the last word (1.49, 73, 3.15). He is therefore induced to say that the certainty of belief is one's awareness of the impossibility of the alternative or that the very existence of God is doubtful if it is not demonstrated or that man's intellect can understand what any intelligent being understands (1.50 and 51 beginning, 71, 3.17). This is acceptable if the Account of the Beginning and the Account of the Chariot are indeed identical with natural science and divine science and if these sciences are demonstrative. But this enigmatic equation leaves obscure the place or the status of the fact of God's free creation of the world out of nothing: does this fact belong to the Account of the Beginning or to the Account of the Chariot or to both or to neither? (Cf. *Commentary on the Mishnah*, Hagigah II, 1.)[27] According to the *Guide*, the Account of the Chariot deals with God's governance of the world, in contradistinction not only to His providence (cf. 1.44 on the one hand, and on the other 1.40, where Maimonides refers to 3.2 and not, as most commentators believe, to the chapters on providence, just as in 3.2 he refers back to 1.40), but also to His creation. By considering the relation of the Account of

---

27. *Commentary on the Mishnah*, Hagigah II, 1: it is in this section that he comments on the law with regard to the teaching of "*ma'aseh bereshit*" and "*ma'aseh merkavah*." It very closely resembles the discussion of the same matters in *Guide* 1.Intro., pp. 6–7 (3b–4a); and in "Laws of the Basic Principles of the Torah," trans. Hyamson, II, 11–12; IV, 10–13 (pp. 36b and 39b); "Book of Knowledge," trans. Lerner, pp. 146–47 (chap. 2, paras. 11–12), and 152–53 (chap. 4, paras. 10–13).

the Beginning and the Account of the Chariot, one is enabled also to answer completely the question that has led us to the present difficulty, the question concerning the order of rank between the Mosaic theophany and the Isaian theophany. The Account of the Beginning occurs in the Torah of Moses but the Account of the Chariot, which is identical with the divine science or the apprehension of God (1.34), occurs in the book of Ezekiel and in its highest form precisely in the sixth chapter of Isaiah (3.6; cf. also the quotations from the Torah on the one hand and from other biblical books on the other in 3.54).

Once one has granted that there is an intrabiblical progress[28] beyond the {xl} teaching of Moses, one will not be compelled to deny the possibility of a postbiblical progress of this description. The fact of such a progress can only be proven if there are characteristic differences between the Bible and the postbiblical authoritative books. We could not help referring for instance to Maimonides' tacit confrontation of the talmudic view according to which the outer of the similes is "nothing" and of Solomon's view according to which it is "silver," i.e., politically useful; taken by itself this confrontation suggests that Solomon appreciated the political to a higher degree than did the talmudic Sages. The differences in question are to some extent concealed, since the postbiblical view ordinarily appears in the guise of an explanation of a biblical text. Maimonides discusses this difficulty in regard to homiletic rather than legal explanations; he rejects both the opinion that these explanations are genuine explanations of biblical texts and the opinion that since they are not genuine explanations, they ought not to be taken seriously; in fact the talmudic Sages used a poetic or a charming device, playing as it were with the text of the Bible, in order to introduce moral lessons not found in the Bible (3.43). He indicates that he will not stress his critique of the talmudic Sages (3.14 end). Since the emphasis on serious differences between the Bible and the Talmud could appear in the eyes of the vulgar as a criticism of the talmudic Sages, he has spoken on this subject with considerable, although not extraordinary, restraint. Whenever he presents a view as a view of the

---

28. In the version of "How To Begin To Study *The Guide of the Perplexed*" as it was reprinted in *Liberalism Ancient and Modern*, p. 168, the word "progress" has been changed to "process." In my considered judgment, this is a simple printing error that was not caught by Strauss or the copyeditor. As it seems to me, the proper sense of this sentence requires that it be "progress" and not "process," especially because the main point being made by Strauss is a marked contrast between "intrabiblical *progress*" and "postbiblical *progress*" (emphasis added). Hence, in the present edition the word appears according to the version of the *Guide*, trans. Pines (1963), i.e., "progress"—rather than as it was printed in the aforementioned version (1968), i.e., "process"—since I am persuaded that this represents a printing error, and not a significant revision in the thought of Strauss.

Law, one must consider whether he supports his thesis at all by biblical passages, and if he does so, whether the support is sufficient according to his standards as distinguished from traditional Jewish standards. In other words, in studying a given chapter or group of chapters one must observe whether he uses therein any postbiblical Jewish quotations at all and what is the proportion in both number and weight of postbiblical to biblical quotations. [¶] In the first chapter explicitly dealing with providence (3.17), he speaks of an "addition" to the text of the Torah that occurs "in the discourse of the Sages"; as one would expect, he disapproves of this particular "addition." This statement is prepared by an immediately preceding cluster of talmudic quotations that are in manifest agreement with the teaching of the Torah and that strike us with particular force because of the almost complete absence of talmudic quotations after the end of 3.10. In this twofold way he prepares his silence on the future life in his presentation of the Torah view on providence: the solution of the problem of providence by recourse to the future life is more characteristic of the postbiblical teaching than of the Bible. According to the talmudic Sages, "in the future life there is no eating, nor drinking" and this means that the future life is incorporeal (*Mishneh Torah*, "Hilkhot Teshuvah" VIII, 3).[29] It follows that the Talmud is freer from corporealism than the Bible (1.46, 47, 49, 70, 2.3). Accordingly certain talmudic thoughts resemble Platonic thoughts and are expressed with the help of terms of {xli} Greek origin (2.6). Similarly it was Onkelos the Stranger who more than anyone else made corporealism inexcusable within Judaism and may well have thought that it would be improper to speak in Syriac (i.e., Aramaic), as distinguished from Hebrew, of God's perceiving an irrational animal (1.21, 27, 28, 36, 48; cf. 2.33). The progress of incorporealism is accompanied by a progress of asceticism. To mention only one example, the Talmud is to say the least much clearer than the Bible about the fact that Abraham had never looked at his beautiful wife until sheer self-preservation compelled him to do so (3.8, 47, 49). There is a corresponding progress in gentleness (1.30 and 54). Finally, the Talmud is more explicit than the Bible regarding the value of the intellectual life and of learning for men in general and for prophets in particular (2.32, 33, 41, 3.14, 25, 37, 54). [¶] But even the Talmud and Onkelos do not contain the last word regarding the fundamentals as Maimonides indicates by a number of remarks (1.21, 41, 2.8–9, 26, 47, 3.4–5, 14, 23). One

---

29. For an English translation (with Hebrew text) of *Mishneh Torah*, "Hilkhot Teshuvah" VIII, 3, see "Laws of Repentance," trans. Hyamson, p. 90a (chap. VIII, para. Roman numeral III).

example for each case must suffice. The talmudic Sages follow at least partly the opinion according to which the Law has no other ground than mere Will, whereas "we," says Maimonides, follow the opposite opinion (3.48). "We" is an ambiguous term. As Maimonides has indicated by as it were opening only two chapters (1.62 and 63) with "we," the most important meanings are "we Jews" and "Maimonides." As for Onkelos, he removes through his translation the corporealistic suggestions of the original but he does not make clear what incorporeal things the prophets perceived or what the meaning of a given simile is; this is in accordance with the fact that he translated for the vulgar; but Maimonides explains the similes and he is enabled to do so because of his knowledge of natural science (1.28). Progress beyond Onkelos and the Talmud became possible chiefly for two reasons. In the first place, the ever more deepened effect of the Torah on the Jewish people as well as the rise and political victory of Christianity and Islam have brought it about that the Sabian disease has completely disappeared (3.49, 29). Second, the fundamental verities regarding God are genuinely believed in by nonprophetic men only when they are believed in on the basis of demonstration, but this requires for its perfection that one possess the art of demonstration, and the art of demonstration was discovered by the wise men of Greece or the philosophers, or more precisely by Aristotle (2.15). Even *kalam*, i.e., what one may call theology or more precisely the science of demonstrating or defending the roots of the Law, which is directly of Christian origin, owes its origin indirectly to the effect of philosophy on the Law. In spite of its defects, the *kalam* is very far from being entirely worthless; and properly understood, as prior to Maimonides it was not, it is even indispensable for the defense of the Law. *Kalam* entered Judaism long after the talmudic period, in the Gaonic period (1.71, 1.73). All the more must the introduction of philosophy into Judaism {**xlii**} be regarded as a great progress, if it is introduced in due subordination to the Law or in the proper manner (i.e., as Maimonides introduced it to begin with in his legal works). One must also consider the considerable scientific progress that was made by both Greeks and Muslims after Aristotle's time (2.4, 19). All this does not mean, however, that Maimonides regarded his age as the peak of wisdom. He never forgot the power of what one may call the inverted Sabianism that perpetuates corporealism through unqualified submission to the literal meaning of the Bible and thus even outdoes Sabianism proper (1.31); nor did he forget the disastrous effect of the exile (1.71, 2.11): "If the belief in the existence of God were not as generally accepted as it is now in the religions [i.e., Judaism, Christianity, and Islam], the darkness of our times would even be greater than the darkness of the times of the sages of Babylon" (3.29). This is to say nothing of the fact that Sabianism proper was not completely eradicated and could be expected to have a future (cf. 1.36). It goes without saying that Maimonides also never forgot the messianic future, a future that may or may not be followed by the end of the world (cf. 1.61 with 2.27). In spite of this, one is entitled to say that Maimonides regarded the step that he took in the *Guide* as the ultimate step in the decisive respect, namely, in the overcoming of Sabianism. As he modestly put it, no Jew had written an extant book on the secrets of the Law "in these times of the exile" (1.Intro.). At the beginning, the power of Sabianism was broken only in a limited part of the world through bloody wars and through concessions to Sabian habits; those concessions were retracted almost completely by the post-Mosaic prophets, by the Aramaic translators, and by the Talmud, to say nothing of the cessation through violence of the sacrificial service, and the conversion of many pagans, which was assisted by military victories, to Christianity or Islam. Now the time has come when even the vulgar must be taught most explicitly that God is incorporeal. Since the Bible suggests corporealism, the vulgar will thus become perplexed. The remedy for this perplexity is the allegoric explanation of the corporealistic utterances or terms that restores the faith in the truth of the Bible (1.35), i.e., precisely what Maimonides is doing in the *Guide*. But the progress in overcoming Sabianism was accompanied by an ever increasing oblivion of Sabianism and thus by an ever increasing inability to remove the last, as it were, fossilized concessions to Sabianism or relics of Sabianism. Maimonides marks a progress even beyond the post-Mosaic prophets in so far as he combines the open depreciation of the sacrifices with a justification of the sacrificial laws of the Torah, for his depreciation of the sacrifices does not as such mean a denial of the obligatory character of the sacrificial laws. He is the man who finally eradicates Sabianism, i.e., corporealism as the hidden premise of idolatry, through the knowledge of Sabianism recovered by him. He recovered that knowledge {xliii} also through his study of Aristotle, who after all belonged to a Sabian society (2.23).

If the *Torah for the Perplexed* thus marks a progress beyond the Torah for the Unperplexed, Maimonides was compelled to draw the reader's attention at an early stage to the difference between the biblical and the postbiblical teaching. In that stage that difference alone was important. Hence to begin with he treats the Bible on the one hand and the postbiblical writings on the other as unities. Generally speaking, he introduces biblical passages by "he says" (or "his saying is") and talmudic passages by "they say" (or "their saying is"). He thus suggests that in the Bible we hear only a single speaker while in the Talmud we hear indeed many speakers who, however, all agree at least in the important respects. Yet in the first chapter of the *Guide* "he" who speaks is in fact first God, then the narrator, then God, and then "the poor one"; in the second chapter "he" who speaks is the narrator, the serpent, God, and so on; God "says" something and the narrator "makes clear and says." But the *Guide* as a whole constitutes an ascent from the common view, or an imitation of the common view, to a discerning view. Accordingly, Maimonides gradually brings out the differences concealed by the stereotyped, not to say ritual, expressions. For instance, in 1.32 he introduces each of four biblical quotations by the expression "he indicated by his speech"; only in the last case does he give the name of the speaker, namely, David; the saying of David is somewhat more akin in spirit than the preceding three sayings (of Solomon) to a saying of the talmudic Sages quoted immediately afterward; the talmudic Sages had noted that Solomon contradicted his father David (1.Intro. toward the end). In 1.34 he introduces by the expression "they say" the saying of a talmudic Sage who tells what "I have seen." The unnamed "he" who, according to 1.44, spoke as Jeremiah's providence was Nebuchadnezzar. In 1.49 he quotes five biblical passages; in two cases he gives the names of the biblical authors, in one of the two cases adding "may he rest in peace" to the name. In 1.70 he introduces a talmudic passage with the expression "They said," while he says at the end of the quotation, "This is literally what he said." Names of biblical teachers occur with unusual frequency in some chapters, the first of which is 2.19 and the last of which is 3.32. Near the beginning of 2.29 Maimonides notes that every prophet had a diction peculiar to him and that this peculiarity was preserved in what God said to the individual prophet or through him. The prophet singled out for extensive discussion from this point of view is Isaiah; thereafter six of the other prophets are briefly discussed in a sequence that agrees with the sequence of their writings in the canon; only in the case of the prophet who occupies the central place (Joel) is the name of the prophet's father added to the name of the prophet. One must also not neglect the references to the difference between the Torah proper and the {xliv} Mishneh Torah, i.e., Deuteronomy (cf. 2.34–35 and 3.24). Maimonides' link with the Torah is, to begin with, an iron bond; it gradually becomes a fine thread. But however far what one may call his intellectualization may go, it always remains the intellectualization of the Torah.

Our desire to give the readers some hints for the better understanding of the second subsection compelled us to look beyond the immediate context. Returning to that context we observe that after Maimonides has concluded the second subsection, he again does something perplexing. The last chapter of the second subsection dealt with "foot"; that passage of the Torah on which the second subsection is based speaks emphatically of God's "face" and His "back"; nothing would have been simpler for Maimonides than to devote the third subsection to terms designating parts of the animate body or of the animal. Instead he devotes the fourth subsection to this subject; the first two chapters of the fourth subsection are devoted precisely to "face" and to "back" (1.37 and 38). The third subsection, which deals with an altogether different subject, thus seems to be out of place or to be a disconcerting insertion. Furthermore, the third subsection is the least exegetic or the most speculative among the subsections devoted to Incorporeality; six of its eight chapters are not lexicographic; five of them are in no obvious sense devoted to the explanation of biblical terms and do not contain a single quotation from the Torah; one of these chapters (1.31) is the first chapter of the *Guide* that does not contain a single Jewish (Hebrew or Aramaic) expression, and another (1.35) does not contain a single quotation of Jewish (biblical or talmudic) passages. One is tempted to believe that it would have been more in accordance with the spirit of the book if the most speculative among the subsections devoted to Incorporeality had formed the end of the part devoted to that subject. [¶] In order to understand these apparent irregularities, it is best to start from the consideration that, for the general reason indicated, Maimonides desired to divide each of the seven sections of the *Guide* into seven subsections and that for a more particular reason he decided to treat Unity in three subsections; hence Incorporeality had to be treated in four subsections. Furthermore, it was necessary to place almost all lexicographic chapters within the part treating Incorporeality or conversely it was necessary that the majority of chapters dealing with Incorporeality should be lexicographic. For the reasons given where they had to be given, it proved convenient that the majority of chapters of the first subsection should be nonlexicographic and the majority of chapters of the second subsection should be lexicographic. It is this proportion of the first two subsections that Maimonides decided to imitate in the last two subsections devoted to Incorporeality: the majority of chapters of the third subsection became nonlexicographic and the majority of chapters of the fourth subsection became lexicographic, but—for a reason to be indicated presently—in such a way {xlv} that the third subsection is more predominantly nonlexicographic than the first, and the fourth subsection is more predominantly lexicographic than the second. It is reasonable to expect that the distribution of lexicographic and nonlexicographic chapters among the four subsections has some correspondence to the subject matter of those subsections. If one defines their subject matter by reference to the subject matter of their lexicographic chapters, one arrives at this result: the first subsection deals with the specific form, the sexual difference, and generating, while the third subsection deals with sorrow and eating; the second subsection deals chiefly with acts of local motion or rest, while the fourth subsection deals chiefly with the parts of the animate body and sense-perception. To understand this arrangement it suffices both to observe that the first quotation regarding sorrow is "in sorrow thou shalt bring forth children" (Gen. 3:16) and to read Maimonides' explanation (in 1.46) of the relation that links the parts of the animal and its acts to the ends of preservation. Furthermore, it would be a great mistake to believe that the emphasis on sorrow and eating is weakened because these two themes are the only lexicographic themes of the subsection in which they are discussed. Finally, Maimonides used in the most appropriate manner the lexicographic chapters devoted to sorrow and to eating as an introduction to the first series of speculative chapters occurring in the *Guide* and thus brought it about that the third subsection (in contradistinction to the first and the second) ends with nonlexicographic chapters (1.31–36); he thus prepared a similar ending of the fourth subsection (1.46–49); this enabled him to indicate by the position of the next lexicographic chapter (1.70), which is the last lexicographic chapter, as clearly as possible the end of the first section or the fact that 1.1–70 form the first section.

The term ʿaẓav, which we thought convenient in our context to render by "sorrow," as well as the term "eating," may refer to God's wrath with those who rebel against Him or to His enmity to them. Since His wrath is directed exclusively against idolatry and since His enemies are exclusively the idolators (1.36), the two terms refer indirectly to idolatry. But "eating" is used also for the acquisition of knowledge. With a view to this second metaphoric meaning of "eating," Maimonides devotes to the subject of human knowledge the five speculative chapters immediately following the explanation of "eating" (1.30). In the last chapter of the subsection (1.36) he reconsiders the prohibition against idolatry on the basis of what had emerged in the five speculative chapters. The third subsection deals then with both idolatry and knowledge in such a way that the discussion of idolatry surrounds the discussion of knowledge. This arrangement affects the discussion of knowledge: Maimonides discusses knowledge with a view to its limitations, to the harm that may come from it, and to the dangers attending it. {**xlvi**} One can say that the first series of speculative chapters occurring in the *Guide* deals with forbidden knowledge (cf. particularly 1.32)—forbidden to all or to most men—within the context of forbidden worship.

The third subsection throws light on the relation between the Bible and the Talmud. Since we have treated this subject before, we limit ourselves to the following remark. In the chapter dealing with "eating," Maimonides explicitly refuses to give an example of the use of the word in its primary meaning: the derivative meaning according to which the word designates the taking of noncorporeal food has become so widespread as to become as it were the primary meaning (cf. the quotation from Isa. 1:20 with Isa. 1:19). Regarding the meaning of "eating" as consuming or destroying, which he illustrates by four quotations from the Torah and two quotations from the prophets, he says that it occurs frequently, namely, in the Bible; regarding the meaning of "eating" as acquiring knowledge, which he illustrates by two quotations from Isaiah and two from the Proverbs, he says that it occurs frequently also in the discourse of the talmudic Sages and he proves this by two quotations. No talmudic quotation had illustrated the meanings of *'azav*. The talmudic Sages compared the acquisition of knowledge of the divine things to the eating of honey and applied to that knowledge the saying of Solomon: "Hast thou found honey? Eat so much as is sufficient for thee, lest thou be filled therewith, and vomit it." They thus taught that in seeking knowledge one must not go beyond certain limits: one must not reflect on what is above, what is below, what was before, and what will be hereafter—which Maimonides takes to refer to "vain imaginings" (1.32): Maimonides, who explains what is meant by the fact that man has a natural desire for knowledge (1.34), warns not against the desire for comprehensive knowledge, but against seeming knowledge.

With regard to the fourth subsection, we must limit ourselves to the observation that it is the first subsection that lacks any reference to philosophy or philosophers. On the other hand the expression "in my opinion" (*'indī*), which indicates the difference between Maimonides' opinion and traditional opinions, occurs about twice as frequently in the fourth subsection as in the first three subsections taken together. Another substitute is the references to grammarians in 1.41 and 43—references that ought to be contrasted with the parallels in 1.8 and 10—as well as the rather frequent references to the Arabic language. One grammarian is mentioned by name: Ibn Janaḥ, i.e., the Son of Wing who with the help of Arabic correctly interpreted the Hebrew term for "wing" as sometimes meaning "veil" and who may therefore be said to have uncovered "Wing." Another substitute is the reference (in 1.42) to an Andalusian interpreter who, in agreement with Greek medicine, had explained as a natural event the apparent {xlvii} resurrection of the son of a widow by the prophet Elijah. Through his quotations from the Bible in the same chapter Maimonides refers among other things to a severe illness caused by the circumcision of adults as well as to the biblical treatment of leprosy. The chapter in question deals with the Hebrew term for "living"; that term is the only one occurring in the lexicographic chapters of this subsection that is not said to be homonymous; this silence is pregnant with grave implications regarding "the living God" (cf. 1.30 and 41).

The last chapter of the fourth subsection is the only chapter of the *Guide* that opens with the expression "The angels." This chapter sets forth the assertion that the angels are incorporeal, i.e., it deals with the incorporeality of something of which there is a plurality. Maimonides thus makes clear that Incorporeality and not Unity is still the theme as it had been from the beginning. The next chapter opens the discussion of Unity. Incorporeality had presented itself as a consequence of Unity; Unity had been the presupposition, an unquestioned presupposition. Unity now becomes the theme. We are told at the beginning that Unity must be understood clearly, not, as it is understood by the Christians, to be compatible with God's trinity, or, more generally stated, with a multiplicity in God (1.50). In the fifth subsection Maimonides effects the transformation of the common, not to say traditional, understanding of Unity, which allowed a multiplicity of positive attributes describing God Himself, into such an understanding as is in accordance with the requirements of speculation. The fifth subsection is the first subsection of the *Guide* that may be said to be entirely speculative. Hence the discussion of Unity, in contradistinction to the discussion of Incorporeality, is characterized by a clear, if implicit, distinction between the speculative and the exegetic discussion of the subject. In the first four subsections there occurred only one chapter without any Jewish expression; in the fifth subsection five such chapters occur. In the first forty-nine chapters there occurred only nine chapters without any quotation from the Torah; in the eleven chapters of the fifth subsection ten such chapters occur. In spite of its speculative character the fifth subsection does not demonstrate that God is one; it continues the practice of the preceding subsections by presupposing that God is one (1.53, 58, 68). Yet from this presupposition it draws all conclusions and not merely the conclusion that God is incorporeal: if God is one, one in every possible respect, absolutely simple, there cannot be any positive attribute of God except attributes describing His actions.

Maimonides knows by demonstration that God is one. The addressee, being insufficiently trained in natural science (cf. 1.55 with 1.52), does not know Unity by demonstration but through the Jewish tradition and ultimately through the Bible. The most important biblical text is "Hear, O Israel, the Lord is our God, the Lord is one" (Deut. 6:4; cf. *Mishneh Torah*, "Hilkhot Yesodei ha-Torah" I, 7).[30] To our very great {**xlviii**} amazement, Maimonides does not quote this verse a single time in any of the chapters devoted to Unity. He quotes it a single time in the *Guide*, imitating the Torah, which, as he says, mentions the principle of Unity, namely, this verse, only once (*Resurrection* 20, 1–2).[31] He quotes the verse in 3.45, i.e., the 169th chapter, thus perhaps alluding to the thirteen divine attributes ("merciful, gracious . . .") proclaimed by God to Moses. Whatever else that silence may mean, it certainly indicates the gravity of the change effected by Maimonides in the understanding of Unity. The demonstrated teaching that positive attributes of God are impossible stems from the philosophers (1.59, 3.20); it clearly contradicts the teaching of the Law in so far as the Law does not limit itself to teaching that the only true praise of God is silence but it also prescribes that we call God "great, mighty, and terrible" in our prayers. Hence the full doctrine of attributes may not be revealed to the vulgar (1.59) or is a secret teaching. But since that doctrine (which includes the provision that certain points that are made fully clear in the *Guide* are not to be divulged), is set forth with utmost explicitness and orderliness in that book, it is also an exoteric teaching (1.35), if a philosophic exoteric teaching.

30. For *Mishneh Torah*, "Hilkhot Yesodei ha-Torah" I, 7, see "Laws of the Basic Principles of the Torah," trans. Hyamson, p. 35a (which appears as I, 10, although it follows as such in sequence of the Roman numerals—for which see Hymamson, pp. III–IV); and especially "Book of Knowledge," trans. Lerner, p. 143, chap. 1, para. 7.

31. For *Resurrection* 20, 1–2, see "Treatise on Resurrection," in *Igrot ha-Rambam*, ed. Shailat, I, p. 367; for English translations, see "Essay on Resurrection," trans. Halkin, p. 221; and see especially "Treatise on Resurrection," trans. Fradkin, p. 165, who translates it as follows:

> There is no need for us, in accord with the aim of this treatise, to describe this in detail because the truth of things is not added to by repeated expression nor does truth diminish by not being repeated. You yourself know that the mention of the foundation of unity—it being its saying, '*The Lord is one*' (Deut. 6:4)—is not repeated in the *Torah* at all.

As Maimonides indicates, the meaning of "the Lord is one" is primarily that there is no one or nothing similar or equal to Him and only derivatively that He is absolutely simple (cf. 1.57 end with 1.58). He develops the notion of God's incomparability, of there being no likeness whatsoever between Him and any other being on the basis of quotations from Isaiah and Jeremiah as distinguished from the Torah (cf. 1.55 with 1.54). He is silent here on Deuteronomy 4:35 ("the Lord he is God; there is none else beside him"), on a verse that he quotes in a kindred context in his Code ("Hilkhot Yesodei ha-Torah" I, 4)[32] and in different contexts in the *Guide* (2.33, 3.32 and 51). Yet absolute dissimilarity or incomparability to everything else is characteristic of nothing as well as of God. What is meant by God's absolute dissimilarity or incomparability is His perfection: it is because He is of incomparable perfection that He is incomparable; it is because He is of unspeakable perfection that nothing positive can be said of Him in strict speech and that everything positive said of Him is in fact (if it does not indicate His actions rather than Himself) only the denial of some imperfection. The meaning of the doctrine of attributes is that God is the absolute perfect being, the complete and perfectly self-sufficient good, the being of absolute beauty or nobility (1.35, 53, 58, 59, 60 end, 2.22). If this were not so, Maimonides' doctrine of attributes would be entirely negative and even subversive. For that doctrine culminates in the assertion that we grasp of God only that He is and not what He is in such a manner that every positive predication made of Him, including that He "is," has only the name in common with what we mean when we apply such predications to any being (1.56, {xlix} 58, 59, 60). If we did not know that God is absolutely perfect, we would ascribe we know not what to what we do not know, in ascribing to Him "being," or we would ascribe nothing to nothing; we certainly would not know what we were talking about. What is true of "being" is true of "one," i.e., of the immediate presupposition of the whole argument of the first section of the *Guide*. Let no one say that Maimonides admits attributes of action as distinguished from the negative attributes; for, not to enter into the question whether this distinction is ultimately tenable (cf. 1.59), through the attributes of action God is understood as the cause of certain effects, and it is difficult to see how "cause," if applied to God, can have more than the name in common with "cause" as an intelligible

---

32. For "Hilkhot Yesodei ha-Torah" I, 4, see "Laws of the Basic Principles of the Torah," trans. Hyamson, p. 34a (which is also I, 4); and especially "Book of Knowledge," trans. Lerner, p. 141, chap. 1, para. 1. (In the present context, Strauss's paragraph numbering seems to follow the printed editions, while Lerner consistently follows the paragraph numbering of the Bodleian manuscript.)

expression. But since we understand by God the absolutely perfect being, we mean the goodness of His creation or governance when we say that He is the "cause" of something (cf. 1.46). By his doctrine of attributes Maimonides not only overcomes all possible anthropomorphisms, but also answers the question whether the different perfections that God is said to possess in the highest degree are compatible with one another or whether certain perfections known to us as human perfections—for instance, justice—can be understood to constitute in their absolute form divine perfection: God's perfection is an unfathomable abyss. Thus we understand why the doctrine in question in spite of its philosophic origin can be regarded as the indeed unbiblical but nevertheless appropriate expression of the biblical principle, namely, of the biblical teaching regarding the hidden God who created the world out of nothing, not in order to increase the good—for since He is the complete good, the good cannot be increased by His actions—but without any ground, in absolute freedom, and whose essence is therefore indicated by "Will" rather than by "Wisdom" (3.13).

From the speculative discussion of the divine attributes, which as positive predications about God Himself proved to be mere names, Maimonides turns in the second of the three subsections dealing with Unity to the purely exegetic discussion of the divine names; the exegetic discussion still deals with "the denial of attributes" (1.62 and 65 beginning). It seems that the audible holy names have taken the place of the visible holy images, and it is certain that "name" is connected with "honor" and everything related to honor. The difficulty is caused less by the multiplicity of divine names—for, as the prophet says, in the day of the Lord "the Lord shall be one and his name shall be one" (Zech. 14:9)—than by the fact that this most sacred name, the only divine name antedating creation (1.61), is communicated to men by God (Exod. 6:2-3) and not coined or created by human beings. Since God does not speak, Maimonides must therefore open the whole question of God's speaking, writing, and ceasing to speak or to act (1.65-67). Furthermore, the most sacred name, which is the only name indicating God's essence and which thus {l} might be thought to lead us beyond the confines of human speculation, is certainly no longer intelligible, since we know very little of Hebrew today (1.61-62). Therefore in the last subsection devoted to Unity (1.68-70), which is the last subsection of the first section, Maimonides returns to speculation. It would be more accurate to say that he now turns to philosophy. In the three chapters in question he refers to philosophy, I believe, more frequently than in the whole discussion of Incorporeality (1.1-49) and certainly more frequently than in the speculative discussion of the attributes (1.50-60); in the exegetic discussion of the divine names (1.61-67), if I am not mistaken, he does not refer to philosophy at all. He now with the support of the philosophers takes up the subject that we cannot help calling the divine attribute of intellect as distinguished from the divine attribute of speech in particular (cf. 1.65 beginning). We learn that in God the triad "intellect, intellecting, and the intellected" are one and the same thing in which there is no multiplicity, just as they are one in us when we actually think (1.68). Maimonides does not even allude here to the possibility that "intellect" when applied to God has only the name in common with "intellect" when applied to us. It may be true that God thinks only Himself so that His intellection is only self-intellection and is therefore one and simple in a way in which our intellection cannot be one and simple, but this does not contradict the univocity of "intellect" in its application to God and to us. Self-intellection is what we mean when we speak of God as "living" (cf. 1.53). It follows that even "life" is not merely homonymous when applied to God and to us. It likewise follows that what is true of the intellect is not true of the will: the act of willing and the thing willed as willed are not the same as the act of thinking and the thing thought as thought are the same. The reader of the next chapter (1.69) may find this observation useful for understanding Maimonides' acceptance of the philosophic view according to which God is not only the efficient or moving and the final cause of the world but also the form of the world or, in the expression of the Jewish tradition, "the life of the worlds," which he says means "the life of the world."

This must suffice toward making clear the perplexing and upsetting character of Maimonides' teaching regarding Unity. The true state of things is somewhat obscured, to say nothing of other matters, by a certain kind of learning that some readers of the *Guide* can at all times be presumed to possess: the doctrine of attributes restates the neo-Platonic teaching, and neo-Platonism had affected Jewish thinkers long before Maimonides; those thinkers had already succeeded somehow in reconciling neo-Platonism with Judaism. But when different men do the same thing, it is not necessarily the same thing, and Maimonides surely did not do exactly the same thing as the pagan, Islamic, or Jewish neo-Platonists who preceded him. Every open minded and discerning reader must be struck by the {li} difference between the hidden God of Maimonides' doctrine of attributes and the hidden God who spoke to the Patriarchs and to Moses or, to employ Maimonides' manner of expression, by the difference between the true understanding of God as it was possessed by the Patriarchs and by Moses and the understanding of God on the part of the uninitiated Jews. The result of his doctrine of the divine attributes is that the notion of God that gives life and light to the ordinary believers is not only inadequate or misleading but is the notion of something that simply does not exist—of a merely imaginary being, the theme of deceived and deceiving men (1.60). What is true of the ordinary believer is true at least to some extent of the addressee of the *Guide*. The destruction of the old foundation forces him to seek for a new foundation: he is now compelled to be passionately concerned with demonstration, with the demonstration not only of God's unity but of His very being in a sense of "being" that cannot be entirely homonymous. For now he knows that the being of God is doubtful as long as it is not established by demonstration (1.71). Now he has been brought to the point where he must make up his mind whether or not he will turn altogether to the way of demonstration. Maimonides shows him three ways of demonstrating God's being, unity, and incorporeality: the way of the *kalam*, the way of the philosophers, and Maimonides' own way (1.71 end, 76 end, 2.1 end). While Maimonides cannot simply accept the philosophers' way, he prefers it to that of the *kalam* for the following reason. The *kalam* begins, not from the world as we know it through our senses or from the fact that things have determinate natures, but from asserting that what the philosophers call the nature, say, of air is only custom and hence of no inherent necessity: everything could be entirely different from what it is. The *kalam* cannot live without reference to what we know through our senses, for in contradistinction to simple belief whose first premise is the absolute will of God, it attempts to demonstrate that God is and hence it must start from the given, and at the same time it must deny the authoritative character of the given. The philosophers on the other hand start from what is given or manifest to the senses (1.71, 1.73). [¶] Maimonides turns first to the analysis and critique of the *kalam* demonstrations.[33] He presents the premises of the *kalam* (1.73) and then the *kalam* demonstrations that are based on those premises (1.74–76). Maimonides' critique does not limit itself to the technical *kalam* reasoning. For instance, the first proof of the createdness of the

---

33. It should be noted that (in *Liberalism Ancient and Modern*, p. 179) a very slight grammatical correction has been made by Strauss to this sentence: the hyphen between "*kalam*" and "demonstrations" has been removed.

world and therewith of the being of the Creator assumes that the bodies that we see around us have come into being through an artificer and infers from this that the world as a whole is the work of an artificer. This proof, which does not make any use of the premises peculiar to the *kalam*, is based on inability, or at any rate failure, to distinguish between the artificial and the natural. The second proof is based on the premise that no infinite whatever is possible; it {lii} therefore first traces men to a first man, Adam, who came out of dust, which in turn came out of water, and then traces water itself to unqualified nothing out of which water could not have been brought into being except by the act of the Creator (1.74; cf. *Logic* chaps. 7, 8, 11).[34] It is not difficult to recognize in this proof elements of biblical origin. Since the *kalam* premises as stated by Maimonides are necessary for the *kalam* proofs (1.73 beginning and toward the end) and the *kalam* proofs do not in all cases follow from those premises, those premises while necessary are not sufficient. After all, the *kalam* selected its premises with a view to proving the roots of the Law: the premise of its premises is those roots. While the First Part ends with the critique of the *kalam*, the Second Part opens with "The premises required for establishing the being of God and for demonstrating that He is not a body nor a force in a body and that He is one," i.e., with the premises established by the philosophers. Maimonides thus indicates that the seventy-six chapters of the First Part, which lead up to philosophy through a critique of the popular notions of God as well as of theology, are negative and prephilosophic, whereas the one hundred and two chapters of the Second and Third Parts are positive or edifying. In other words, the First Part is chiefly devoted to biblical exegesis and to the *kalam*, i.e., to the two translogical and transmathematical subjects mentioned even in the very Epistle Dedicatory.

The *kalam* proves that God as the Creator is, is one, and is incorporeal by proving first that the world has been created; but it proves that premise only by dialectical or sophistical arguments. The philosophers prove that God is, is one, and is incorporeal by assuming that the world is eternal, but they

---

34. For *Logic* chap. 8, see especially "Logic," in *Ethical Writings*, trans. Weiss and Butterworth, "Chapter Eight," pp. 156–58. Weiss and Butterworth did not translate the entire "Logic"; for chaps. 7 and 11, see Israel Efros, "Maimonides' *Treatise on Logic (Makalah Fi-Sina'at Al-Mantik)*: The Original Arabic and Three Hebrew Translations," *Proceedings of the American Academy for Jewish Research* 8 (1937–38): 1–136, especially pp. 41–47 and 54–57. The remainder of the Arabic original has since been rediscovered and edited: see Israel Efros, "Maimonides' Arabic 'Treatise on Logic,'" *Proceedings of the American Academy for Jewish Research* 34 (1966): 6–34.

cannot demonstrate that assumption. Hence both ways are defective. Maimonides' way consists in a combination of these two defective ways. For, he argues, "the world is eternal—the world is created" is a complete disjunction; since God's being, unity, and incorporeality necessarily follow from either of the only two possible assumptions, the basic verities have been demonstrated by this very fact (1.71, 2.2). Yet the results from opposed premises cannot be simply identical. For instance, someone might have said prior to the Second World War that Germany would be prosperous regardless of whether she won or lost the war; if she won, her prosperity would follow immediately; if she lost, her prosperity would be assured by the United States of America who would need her as an ally against Soviet Russia; but the predictor would have abstracted from the difference between Germany as the greatest power which ruled tyrannically and was ruled tyrannically, and Germany as a second-rank power ruled democratically. The God whose being is proved on the assumption of eternity is the unmoved mover, thought that thinks only itself and that as such is the form or the life of the world. The God whose being is proved on the assumption of creation is the biblical God who is characterized by Will {liii} and whose knowledge has only the name in common with our knowledge. If we consider the situation as outlined by Maimonides, we see that what is demonstrated by his way is only what is common to the two different notions of God or what is neutral to the difference between God as pure Intellect and God as Will or what is beyond that difference or what has only the name in common with either Intellect or Will. But God thus understood is precisely God as presented in the doctrine of attributes: Maimonides' demonstration of God's being illumines retroactively his merely assertoric doctrine of attributes. God thus understood can be said to be more extramundane not only than the philosophers' God but even than the biblical God; this understanding of God lays the foundation for the most radical asceticism both theoretical and practical (3.51). In other words, both opposite assumptions lead indeed to God as the most perfect being; yet even the Sabians regard their god, i.e., the sphere and its stars, as the most perfect being (3.45); generally stated, everyone understands by God the most perfect being in the sense of the most perfect possible being; the doctrine of attributes understood in the light of its subsequent demonstration leads to God as the most perfect being whose perfection is characterized by the fact that in Him Intelligence and Will are indistinguishable because they are both identical with His essence (cf. 1.69). Yet, since the world is of necessity either created or eternal, it becomes necessary to restore the distinction between Intellect and Will. Generally speaking, the *Guide* moves between the view that Intellect and Will are indistinguishable and the view that they must be distinguished (and hence that one must understand God as Intelligence rather than as Will) in accordance with the requirements of the different subjects under discussion (cf. 2.25 and 3.25). For instance, in his discussion of Omniscience—in the same context in which he reopens the question regarding the relative rank of imagination and intellect—Maimonides solves the difficulty caused by the apparent incompatibility of Omniscience and human freedom (3.17) by appealing to the identity of Intellect and Will, whereas in his discussion of the reasons for the biblical commandments he prefers the view that the commandments stem from God's intellect to the view that they stem from His will.

The reader of the *Guide* must consider with the proper care not only the outline of Maimonides' way but also all its windings. In doing this he must never forget that the demonstration of the basic verities and the discussion of that demonstration is immediately preceded by the discussion of Unity or that the discussion of Unity constitutes the transition from exegesis to speculation. If the world or more precisely the sphere is created, it is indeed self-evident that it was created by some agent but it does not necessarily follow that the creator is one, let alone absolutely simple, and that he is incorporeal. On the other hand, if the sphere is eternal, it follows, as Aristotle has shown, that God is and is incorporeal; but on this {liv} assumption the angels or separate intelligences, each of which is the mover of one of the many spheres, are as eternal as God (cf. 1.71, 2.2 and 6). It is therefore a question whether monotheism strictly understood is demonstrable. Maimonides does say that Unity and also Incorporeality follow from certain philosophic proofs that do not presuppose either the eternity of the world or its creation, but it is, to say the least, not quite clear whether the proofs in question do not in fact presuppose the eternity of the world (cf. 2.2 with 2.1). Besides, if there were such proofs, one is tempted to say that there is no need whatever for provisionally granting the eternity of the world in order to demonstrate God's being, unity, and incorporeality, yet Maimonides asserts most emphatically that there is such a need. None of these or similar difficulties is, however, by any means the most serious difficulty. For while the belief in God's unity, being, and incorporeality is required by the Law, that belief, being compatible with the belief in the eternity of the world, is compatible with the unqualified rejection of the Law:

the Law stands or falls by the belief in the creation of the world. It is therefore incumbent on Maimonides to show that Aristotle or Aristotelianism is wrong in holding that the eternity of the world has been demonstrated: the eternity of the world which was the basis of the demonstration of God's being, unity, and incorporeality is a dubious assumption. Yet it is not sufficient to refute the claims of Aristotelianism in order to establish the possibility of creation as the Law understands creation, for if the world is not necessarily eternal it may still have been created out of eternal matter. Maimonides is then compelled to abandon or at any rate to refine the disjunction on which his original argument was based. The original disjunction (the world is either eternal or created) is incomplete at least to the extent that it blurs the difference between creation out of matter and creation out of nothing. It brings out the opposition between Aristotle and the Law but it conceals the intermediate possibility presented in Plato's *Timaeus*. Plato's version of the doctrine of eternity is not inimical to the Law, for while Aristotle's version excludes the possibility of any miracle, the Platonic version does not exclude all miracles as necessarily impossible. [¶] Maimonides does not say which miracles are excluded by the Platonic teaching. Two possible answers suggest themselves immediately. It is according to nature that what has come into being will perish; but according to the Law both Israel and the souls of the virtuous have come into being and will not perish; hence their eternity *a parte post* is a miracle, a miracle that is more in accordance with creation out of nothing than with creation out of eternal matter. Second, God's special providence for Israel, according to which Israel prospers if it obeys and is miserable if it disobeys, is a miracle not likely to be admitted by Plato, whose teaching on providence seems to have been identical with that presented in the book of Job: providence follows naturally the intelligence of the individual {lv} human being. In accordance with his judgment on the relation between the Aristotelian doctrine and the doctrine of the Law, Maimonides proves by an extensive argument that the Aristotelian doctrine is not demonstrated and is in addition not probable. As for the Platonic doctrine, he explicitly refuses to pay any attention to it on the additional ground that it has not been demonstrated (2.13, 25–27, 29, 3.18; *Yemen* 24, 7–10; *Resurrection* 33, 16–36, 17; *Letter on Astrology* § 19ff. Marx).[35] That ground is somewhat strange because

---

35. For *Yemen* 24, 7–10, see "Epistle to Yemen," trans. Kraemer, pp. 107–8. For *Resurrection* 33, 16–36, 17, see "Essay on Resurrection," trans. Halkin, pp. 230–32; and especially "Treatise on Resurrection," trans. Fradkin, pp. 174–76. For *Letter on Astrology* § 19ff. Marx, see "Letter on Astrology," trans. Lerner,

according to Maimonides the Aristotelian and the biblical alternatives have not been demonstrated either. In his critique of the Aristotelian doctrine he makes use of the *kalam* argument based on a premise that so defines the possible that it might be either the imaginable or the non-self-contradictory or that regarding which we cannot make any definite assertions because of our lack of knowledge; the premise in question excludes the view according to which the possible is what is capable of being or what is in accordance with the nature of the thing in question or with what possesses an available specific substratum (cf. 1.75, 2.14, 3.15). The reader must find out what the premises of the preferred premise are, how Maimonides judges of those premises, and whether the argument based on the premise in question renders improbable not only the eternity of the visible universe but the eternity of matter as well. [¶] At any rate, being compelled to question the Aristotelian doctrine, Maimonides is compelled to question the adequacy of Aristotle's account of heaven. That questioning culminates in the assertions that Aristotle had indeed perfect knowledge of the sublunar things but hardly any knowledge of the things of heaven, and ultimately that man as man has no such knowledge: man has knowledge only of the earth and the earthly things, i.e., of beings that are bodies or in bodies. In the words of the Psalmist (115:16): "The heavens, even the heavens, are the Lord's; but the earth hath he given to the children of Man." Accordingly, Maimonides suggests that the truth regarding providence, i.e., that theological truth which is of vital importance to human life, comes to sight by the observation of the sublunar phenomena alone. Even the proof of the First Mover of heaven, i.e., the philosophic proof of God's being, unity, and incorporeality, to say nothing of the being of the other separate intelligences, becomes a subject of perplexity (2.22, 24; cf. 2.3, 19, 3.23). And yet it was knowledge of heaven that was said to supply the best proof, not to say the only proof, of the being of God (2.18). Maimonides had said earlier that very little demonstration is possible regarding divine matters and much of it regarding natural matters (1.31). Now he seems to suggest that the only genuine science of beings is natural science or a part of it. It is obvious that one cannot leave it at this apparent suggestion. The least that one would have to add is that the strange remarks referred to occur within the context in which Maimonides questions Aristotle's account of heaven in the

---

pp. 183–84. For Hebrew translations (with Arabic originals), see *Igrot ha-Rambam*, ed. Shailat: "Epistle to Yemen," I, p. 125; "Treatise on Resurrection," I, pp. 369–71; "Letter on Astrology," II, pp. 485–86.

name of astronomy or, more precisely, {lvi} in which he sets forth the conflict between philosophic cosmology and mathematical astronomy—that conflict which he calls "the true perplexity": the hypotheses on which astronomy rests cannot be true and yet they alone enable one to give an account of the heavenly phenomena in terms of circular and uniform motions. Astronomy shows the necessity of recurring for the purpose of calculation and prediction to what is possible in a philosophically inadmissible sense (2.24).[36]

We have been compelled to put a greater emphasis on Maimonides' perplexities than on his certainties, and in particular on his vigorous and skillful defense of the Law, because the latter are more easily accessible than the former. Besides, what at first glance seems to be merely negative is negative only in the sense in which every liberation, being a liberation not only to something but also from something, contains a negative ingredient. So we may conclude with the words of Maimonides with which we began: The *Guide* is "a key permitting one to enter places the gates to which were locked. When those

---

36. Herbert Davidson quotes twice in the same book the words that Strauss uses in this paragraph, as if they constituted something strange. He focuses on Strauss's sentence that runs as follows: "Now [Maimonides] seems to suggest that the only genuine science of beings is natural science or a part of it." Davidson writes as if it is obvious that no contradiction could be involved in this seeming suggestion, which Strauss claims was made by Maimonides, because he apparently expressed himself with complete clarity and with no ambiguity on the matter against which this is supposedly to be juxtaposed: for Maimonides, probative scientific demonstrations of God's existence are knowable. Strauss, by way of contrast and "in his typically allusive style," transports his readers to "the land of irony," in which Maimonides presumably never dwelled or even visited. What, according to Davidson, did Strauss wrongly observe about Maimonides so as to concoct a contradiction with apparently no textual basis? Strauss contends—according to Davidson's restatement, which is not precisely as Strauss originally states it—that Maimonides may have believed that "natural science is indeed 'the only genuine science.'" As Davidson continues, this contention (which Strauss surrounds with gratuitous hints) is badly misleading, if not unreasonable. Yet Davidson proceeds as if Maimonides never wrote what he did in *Guide* 2.24 (this being the chapter which Strauss indeed cites): "All that Aristotle states about that which is beneath the sphere of the moon [i.e., natural science] is in accordance with reasoning. . . . However, regarding all that is in the heavens, man grasps nothing but a small measure of what is mathematical." In a previous chapter (2.22), Maimonides had made the same point with even greater bluntness: "Everything that Aristotle expounds with regard to the sphere of the moon and that which is above it [i.e., astronomy and celestial physics] is, except for certain things, something analogous to guessing and conjecturing." Put side by side with Maimonides' radically divergent assertions about readily available scientific demonstrations which are able to point with absolute definiteness to God's existence based on evident knowledge derived from soundly observed movements of the heavens, this and similar skeptical statements about astronomy and celestial physics certainly should make one wonder whether one is not confronting an obvious contradiction which needs to be addressed rather than dismissed. Besides Davidson's dubious criticism, only if it were prima facie *impossible* that deliberate contradictions were used by Maimonides as a literary device (which he in fact declares he will use) would Strauss's equitable question be rendered unreasonable or even misleading. Strauss might instead be credited with awakening thoughtful readers to wonder how one is supposed to deal with this most serious of problems in Maimonides' text. See Herbert Davidson, *Maimonides the Rationalist* (Oxford: Littman Library of Jewish Civilization, 2011), pp. 174–75 and 220–21.

gates are opened and those places are entered, the souls will find rest therein, the bodies will be eased of their toil, and the eyes will be delighted."[37]

> 37. Readers should consider whether Strauss ended with precisely the same words as those with which he began, or indeed with precisely the same words as those with which Maimonides himself ended his own introduction to *The Guide of the Perplexed*.
> At the beginning Strauss makes the following statement:
>> "It is a key permitting one to enter places the gates to which were locked. When those gates are opened and those places are entered, the souls will find rest therein, the eyes will be delighted, and the bodies will be eased of their toil and of their labor."
>
> But at the end, Strauss puts it as follows:
>> "The *Guide* is 'a key permitting one to enter places the gates to which were locked. When those gates are opened and those places are entered, the souls will find rest therein, the bodies will be eased of their toil, and the eyes will be delighted.'"
>
> One may contrast these with what Maimonides says at the end of own introduction to the *Guide*:
>> This, then, will be a key permitting one to enter places the gates to which were locked. And when these gates are opened and these places are entered into, the souls will find rest therein, the eyes will be delighted, and the bodies will be eased of their toil and of their labor.
>
> If these are not precisely the same words, it is of course another matter entirely why Strauss may have chosen to conclude by differing from his own original words as well as from Maimonides' own words; why he did so with just these divergences; whether these divergences are in any ultimate sense significant; and if so, what they might signal. For one of the first readers of Strauss's "Introductory Essay" who both noticed these (and other) irregularities and who appeared in print with them, see Marvin Fox, *Interpreting Maimonides: Studies in Methodology, Metaphysics, and Moral Philosophy* (Chicago: University of Chicago Press, 1990), especially pp. 54–62. Fox also reflected seriously on *the* big issue that still needs to be confronted, i.e., just how precisely and deliberately did Strauss compose this essay. But see now also Aryeh Tepper, *Theories of Progress in Leo Strauss's Later Writings on Maimonides* (Albany: State Universy of New York Press, forthcoming [2013]), for a serious, detailed study of how Strauss composed his introductory essay to the *Guide*, "How To Begin."

12
Notes on Maimonides'
Book of Knowledge

EDITOR'S NOTE

"Notes on Maimonides' *Book of Knowledge*" basically reproduces Strauss's study which first appeared in *Studies in Mysticism and Religion Presented to Gershom G. Scholem*, ed. Efraim E. Urbach, R. J. Zwi Werblowsky, and Chaim Wirszubski (Jerusalem: Magnes Press, 1967), pp. 269–83. It was reprinted in the last book of Strauss's own design, whose contents he assembled and arranged himself: *Studies in Platonic Political Philosophy*, pp. 192–204. No differences between the two versions are evident. The supplementary reference material set in square brackets in the notes is entirely the work of the present editor; it attempts to provide additional scholarly data useful for some readers who may wish to study the contents of Strauss's own notes or to search Strauss's sources, to comprehend his references by offering reliable English translations, or to clarify certain difficult aspects of the text.

IF IT IS TRUE THAT *THE GUIDE OF THE PERPLEXED* IS NOT A PHILOSOPHIC book but a Jewish book, it surely is not a Jewish book in the same manner in which the *Mishneh Torah* is a Jewish book. Maimonides has made clear the difference between these two kinds of Jewish books by saying that the *Guide* is devoted to the science of the Law in the true sense: the *Mishneh Torah* as well as the *Commentary on the Mishnah* belong to the science of the Law in the ordinary sense, i.e., the *fiqh* or *talmud*. The most obvious difference between these two kinds of Jewish books corresponds to the most obvious difference between the two kinds of science of the Law: the foundations of the Law are treated in the *Mishneh Torah* with much greater brevity than in the *Guide*, although they are alluded to in the former work in a manner that approaches clear exposition. Consequently, in the *Guide* Maimonides discusses as fully as possible the fundamental question at issue between the adherents of the Law and the philosophers—the question whether the world is eternal or has a beginning in time—whereas in his *fiqh* books he establishes the existence of God on the basis of the view, which he rejects in the *Guide*, that the world is eternal.[1] This would seem to mean that in an important respect Maimonides' *fiqh* books are more "philosophic" than the *Guide*.

Within the *Mishneh Torah* philosophy seems to be most powerfully present in the First Book, the Book of Knowledge. That Book is the only one in which the term indicating the theme is supplied with the article. More precisely, it is the only Book of the *Mishneh Torah* in which the noun indicating the theme is supplied with the article both in the Introduction to the whole work and in the heading of the Book. For in the case of the Book of Sacrifices the noun indicating the theme is supplied with the article in the heading of the Book but not in the Introduction.[2] On the basis of the *Guide* this seeming irregularity could easily be understood as a hint: the Book of Knowledge deals first and above all with the foundations of the Torah; the first intention of the whole Torah is the elimination of idolatry, or the foundation of

---

1. *Guide of the Perplexed* 1.Intro. (6a Munk) and 1.71 (97a). [See *Guide*, trans. Pines, 1.Intro., pp. 9–10; 1.71, pp. 180–81.]

2. Cf., besides, *Mishneh Torah, Book 1*, ed. M. Hyamson, 28a22 with 19a3. [See Maimonides, *Mishneh Torah*, vol. 1, *The Book of Knowledge (Sefer ha-Madda)*, ed. and trans. Moses Hyamson (New York: Feldheim, 1981), p. 28a, l. 22, and p. 19a, l. 3. These are Maimonides' own titles and contents of the books in *Mishneh Torah*. The noun, as the title which defines the theme of the book, is assigned the definite article in both the "Introduction" to the entire work, and in the heading of the book itself: in both it is called "Sefer *ha*-Madda," "*The* Book of Knowledge." In the case of the one other book in which a definite article is also used, the noun as the title which defines the theme of the book is provided with the definite article only in the heading of the book itself: it is called "Sefer *ha*-Korbanot," "*The* Book of Sacrifices" (also capable of being translated as "The Book of the Sacrifices"). But it is not so fashioned in the "Introduction" to the entire code, which briefly characterizes what each book contains, and which styles it only "Sefer Korbanot," "Book of Sacrifices." However, with regard to the additional reference that Strauss provides in his note (contrasting p. 28a22 with p. 19a3), this points those who wish to read as carefully as Strauss to a peculiar feature of the Bodleian manuscript in the Hyamson edition (with Maimonides' signature sanctioning it as authentic), which Strauss employs for studying the "Introduction" and "The Book of Knowledge" ("Sefer ha-Madda"). Maimonides' "Introduction" is followed by his list of the commandments (what Hyamson styles "precepts"), positive and negative respectively, each separately listed. This is followed by the "Division of Books of the Code and the Topics Treated in Each of Them" (according to the title assigned to it by Hyamson), a general and brief listing of the titles and topics of each book. In this general and brief listing (p. 19a3), the Hebrew title of the ninth book is formulated as "Sefer Korbanot," or "Book of Sacrifices," thus lacking the definite Hebrew article. However, in the section that follows, in which Maimonides sketches in greater detail the contents of each book (a section that Hyamson styles "Detailed Account of the Contents of Each Book"), the heading of the ninth book (p. 28a22) is also "Sefer *ha*-Korbanot," or "*The* Book of Sacrifices," possessing the definite Hebrew article—the same as the title of the book itself. If one compares these same sections with the *Mishneh Torah*, 3rd ed. (Jerusalem: Mosad ha-Rav Kook, 1965), one notices that the definite article only appears in the heading of the book itself; this only is titled "Sefer *ha*-Korbanot," "*The* Book of Sacrifices," while in both sections of the "Introduction" to the entire code, no definite article is used. Hence, Strauss notes that this is a discrepancy, but he leaves it unaccounted for—other than perhaps as a sort of hint not further elaborated? Is this to suggest that the Torah has two roots, one being genuine knowledge, and the other being (educative or corrective) "sacrifices" of one sort or another?]

our Torah as a whole and the pivot around which it turns consists in the elimination of the opinions that support idolatry, and the primary instrument for uprooting idolatry is the Mosaic legislation regarding sacrifices.[3] On the basis of the *Mishneh Torah* alone that hint could hardly be said to approach clear exposition.

Maimonides could easily have given to the First Book of the *Mishneh Torah* the title *Sefer Madda*. In the 70th chapter of the *Guide* he refers to what he had said on the equivocity of "soul" and "spirit" at the end of the *Sefer Madda*. One could think for a moment that he thus refers to "Teshuvah" VIII, 3; but apart from the fact that that passage could not properly be called the end of the Book of Knowledge, Maimonides does not speak there of "spirit" nor of the difficulties attending the meaning of the term "soul." He refers in *Guide* 1.70 to "Yesodei ha-Torah" IV, 8. By this reference he suggests that there is a difference between the *Sefer ha-Madda* and the *Sefer Madda*, the latter consisting only of the "Yesodei ha-Torah" I–IV. By this hint he underlines the obvious and radical difference between those four chapters and the rest of the Book of Knowledge, to say nothing of the 13 other books of the *Mishneh Torah*. One may say that those four chapters are the Book of Knowledge par excellence, for they are devoted to the Account of the Chariot and

---

3. *Guide* 3.29 and 3.32; cf. *Mishneh Torah, Book 1*, 18a3–4, and "Avodah Zarah" II, 4. [See *Guide*, trans. Pines, 3.29, pp. 514–24, and 3.32, pp. 525–31. Strauss points to Maimonides' brief and general statement of the purpose of "The Book of Knowledge" in the section Hyamson styles "Division of Books of the Code and the Topics Treated in Each of Them," p. 18a3–4. One may translate these lines as follows:

> The first book, containing all of the commandments which constitute the fundamental principle of the religion (or law) of Moses our teacher, and which man must know at the start, such as the unity of God, and the prohibition against idolatry, I have called the book, The Book of Knowledge.

This immediate mention of God's unity together with the ban on idolatry might seem to confirm Strauss's summary expression of "the first intention" of the Torah and "the pivot around which it turns" for Maimonides, that being to eliminate the opinions supporting idolatry, first through the medium of "the Mosaic legislation regarding sacrifices." With regard to "Avodah Zarah" II, 4 ("Laws Concerning Idolatry," trans. Hyamson, pp. 67b–68a), it is also worth presenting the entire paragraph (translated to stay as close as possible to Maimonides' Hebrew):

> The commandment concerning idolatry is equal in significance to all the other commandments put together, as it says (Num. 15:22–23) "Lest you err and not observe these commandments which the Lord spoke to Moses, all those which the Lord commanded you by the hand of Moses, from the day . . . , etc." Tradition teaches that this (verse) refers to idolatry. Thus is it taught that everyone who acknowledges idolatry denies the entire Torah as a totality, and all the prophets, and everything commanded by the prophets, from Adam until the end of the world [or: forever on], as the verse continues, "from the day which the Lord commanded you and onward through your (future) generations." And likewise, anyone who denies idolatry acknowledges the entire Torah in its totality. This (denial of idolatry) is the fundamental principle of all the commandments.]

the Account of the Beginning, which are identical, according to the *Guide*, with the divine science and the natural science respectively.[4]

The four chapters indicated, and only these four chapters, are devoted to the Account of the Chariot and the Account of the Beginning. These two Accounts and especially the first are a great thing, whereas the halakhic discussions are a small thing ("Yesodei ha-Torah" IV, 13). Yet the *halakha* proper is not the only subject excluded from the two Accounts. Also excluded from the Account of the Chariot and the Account of the Beginning are the following subjects taken up in the Book of Knowledge after "Yesodei ha-Torah" IV: the names of God (VI, 2), prophecy (VII–X), the unchangeable and absolute character of the Torah of Moses (IX, 1), ethics ("De'ot"), man's free will ("Teshuvah" V), particular providence (ibid., IX, 1–8), the life to come (ibid., VIII), and the messianic age (ibid., IX, 9–10).

In the *Mishneh Torah* the Account of the Chariot precedes the Account of the Beginning. This order is in accordance with the order of rank of the two Accounts, but it is not in accord with the fact that the Account of the Beginning (natural science) supplies the premises from which the Account of the Chariot (divine science) starts.[5] What then is the foundation of the Account of the Chariot in the *Mishneh Torah*? We note a kindred difficulty. According to Maimonides the Account of the Chariot is the doctrine of God and the angels while the Account of the Beginning is the doctrine of the creatures lower than the angels. Hence his distinction between the two Accounts blurs the fundamental difference between the Creator and the creatures. He overcomes the second difficulty to some extent by his division of the five commandments that he explains in the first four chapters; he devotes the first chapter (the chapter devoted to the doctrine of God) to the explanation of the first three commandments, and the three following chapters (the chapters devoted to the doctrine of the creatures) to the explanation of the two remaining commandments. This implies that the foundation of the doctrine of God is supplied in the Book of Knowledge, not by natural science, but by the most fundamental commandments. For instance, the first commandment—the commandment to acknowledge the existence of God—takes the place of the proof of His existence.

This must be taken with a grain of salt. Maimonides opens the body of

---

4. *Guide* 1.Intro. (3b). [See *Guide*, trans. Pines, 1.Intro., p. 6.]
5. *Guide* 1.Intro. (5a) and 1.71 (98a). [See *Guide*, trans. Pines, 1.Intro., p. 8, and 1.71, p. 182.]

the Book of Knowledge with the assertion that knowledge of the existence of God is the foundation of the foundations and the pillar of the sciences: he does not call it the pillar, or a pillar, of the Law, while he calls the knowledge of God's inspiring human beings with prophecy a pillar of the Law ("Yesodei ha-Torah" VII, beginning). Accordingly he hints at the demonstration of the existence of God that starts from the sempiternal, never-beginning and never-ending, revolution of the sphere; he also refers a few times to what is "impossible." (Cf. also "Yesodei ha-Torah" I, 11, beginning.) Furthermore, according to Maimonides, knowledge of the existence of God is commanded by the words "I am the Lord, thy God"; this commandment is immediately followed by the commandment that forbids thinking or imagining that "there is another God besides this one." It is not as clear as it might be whether the words that follow immediately—namely, "this is the great root on which everything depends"—refer to both commandments or only to the prohibition (cf. "Avodah Zarah" II, 4), nor whether the first commandment obliges us to recognize the absolute uniqueness and incomparability of God rather than His existence. At any rate, the first chapter of the *Mishneh Torah*, the theological chapter par excellence of the *Mishneh Torah*, sets forth that God exists, is one, and is incorporeal. God's incorporeality is not presented as the subject of a commandment; that God is incorporeal is inferred partly from His being one and partly from biblical passages.[6]

In the first chapter Maimonides had avoided the term "to create" (*bara'*) and derivatives from it. He begins to use that term when he comes to speak of the creatures. The treatment of the creatures as creatures ("Yesodei ha-Torah" II–IV) serves the purpose of explaining the commandments to love God and to fear Him. The doctrine of the creatures is emphatically Maimonides' own,[7] at least to the extent that it does not go back to Jewish sources. Knowledge of the creatures is the way toward love of God and fear of Him because that knowledge makes us realize God's wisdom; it is not said to be required for knowing God's existence or His unity and incorporeality. Maimonides enumerates the three classes of creatures (the earthly beings, the heavenly bodies, and the angels) initially in the ascending order ("Yesodei ha-Torah" II, 3) while he discusses them in the descending order. This change makes no difference at least in so far as in both cases the heavenly bodies occupy the central place. In his discussion of the heavenly bodies he

---

6. Cf. *Guide* 3.28, beginning. [See *Guide*, trans. Pines, 3.28, p. 512.]
7. Cf. the "I" in "Yesodei ha-Torah" II, 2. [See "Laws of the Basic Principles of the Torah," trans. Hyamson, p. 35b; "Book of Knowledge," trans. Lerner, p. 144.]

does not speak of "creating," nor does he quote the Bible; he refers, however, to the Sages of Greece (III, 6). It is not surprising that he speaks of God's knowledge and in particular of His omniscience, not in the theological chapter proper, but when speaking of the creatures, for the problem concerns precisely His knowledge of the creatures. His knowledge of all His creatures is implied in His self-knowledge (II, 9–10). Accordingly, the angels knew God much less adequately than He knows Himself, and the heavenly bodies are aware of God still less adequately than are the angels; but as they are aware of God, so are they aware of themselves and of the angels (II, 8; III, 10). Maimonides is here silent on whether the angels and the heavenly bodies know the beings inferior to them. This is not contradicted by the fact that the angels of the lowest degree "speak with the prophets and appear to them in prophetic vision," for Maimonides speaks here "according to the language of human beings"; it suffices to say that in fact there is only one angel of the lowest degree (cf. II, 7 with IV, 6).

The Account of the Beginning is more accessible to men in general than the Account of the Chariot. The most accessible part of the Account of the Beginning is the one dealing with the sublunar creatures.[8] When discussing the characteristics of the four elements, Maimonides speaks first of the "way" of each element, then of its "custom," and only after this preparation, of its "nature" (IV, 2). He thus lets us see that "nature"—a notion pointing back to the Sages of Greece—cannot be used in the context without some preparation.[9] Maimonides calls air "spirit"; this enables him to throw light on the relation between spirit and water as stated in Gen. 1:2 and on the relation between spirit and dust as stated in Eccles. 12:7.[10]

Knowledge of the creatures leads to love of God and to fear of Him because it leads to knowledge of His infinite wisdom and therewith to thirst and longing for knowledge of the Great Name. Yet when man considers His marvelous and great creatures themselves, he recoils and becomes afraid and re-

---

8. "Yesodei ha-Torah" IV, 11; III, end; cf. *Guide* 2.24 (54a) and 3.23 (50b). [See "Laws of the Basic Principles of the Torah," trans. Hyamson, pp. 39b and 38a; "Book of Knowledge," trans. Lerner, pp. 152 and 149; *Guide*, trans. Pines, 2.24, p. 326, and 3.23, p. 496.]

9. Cf. Strauss, *Natural Right and History* (Chicago: University of Chicago Press, 1953), pp. 81–83.

10. "Yesodei ha-Torah" IV, 2 and 9; cf. the mention of *'avir* in III, 3 (*Mishneh Torah, Book 1*, 37a9); cf. *Guide* 1.40 and 2.30 (68a). [See "Laws of the Basic Principles of the Torah," trans. Hyamson, pp. 38a–b and 39a–b; "Book of Knowledge," trans. Lerner, pp. 149–50 and 152. For "the mention of *'avir*," see "Book of Knowledge," trans. Lerner, p. 147, chap. 3, para. 4; Hyamson, p. 37a9, is of course correct, but what Strauss points to as appearing in "III, 3" (as it is in the Hebrew), is actually chap. III, para. IV.3. in the English. As Lerner translates it: "That we see them (i.e., the spheres in the sky) as having a blue color is only an appearance to the eye owing to the height of the air (*'avir*)." See *Guide*, trans. Pines, 1.40, pp. 90–91, and 2.30, p. 351.]

alizes his littleness and lowliness and the poverty of his knowledge compared with that of God. Although knowledge of the creatures is to lead to both love and fear of God, Maimonides introduces his account of the angels as the way to love of God (II, 2). At the end of his account of the creatures other than the angels, i.e., of the bodily beings, he says that through knowledge of all creatures, man's love of God is increased; and by comparing himself with any of the great and holy bodies (i.e., the heavenly bodies) and still more with any of the pure immaterial forms (i.e., the angels) man comes into a state of fear and realizes his utter lowliness (IV, 12). This seems to imply that love of God, as distinguished from fear of Him, does not altogether depend on knowledge of the creatures. This agrees with the well-known teaching of the *Guide*[11] only

---

11. 3.52. Cf. 3.27–28 and 3.51 (125a). Cf. above all the explanation of the commandments to love God and to fear Him in the *Sefer ha-Mitzvot*. [See *The Commandments*, trans. Chavel, pp. 3–6:

3rd [commandment]: *Love of God.* By this injunction we are commanded to love God (exalted be He); that is to say, to dwell upon and contemplate His commandments, His injunctions, and His works, so that we may obtain a conception of Him, and in conceiving Him absolute joy. This constitutes the love of God, and is obligatory. As the Sifré says: "Since it is said, 'And thou shalt love the Lord thy God,' the question arises, how is one to manifest his love for the Lord? Scripture therefore says: 'And these words which I command thee this day, shall be upon thy heart'; for through this (i.e., contemplation of God's words) you will learn to discern Him whose word called the universe into existence."

We have thus made it clear to you that through this act of contemplation you will attain a conception of God and reach that stage of joy in which love of Him will follow of necessity.

The Sages say that this commandment also includes an obligation to call upon all mankind to serve Him (exalted be He), and to have faith in Him. For just as you praise and extol anybody whom you love, and call upon others to love him, so, if you love the Lord to the extent of the conception of His true nature to which you have attained, you will undoubtedly call upon the foolish and ignorant to seek knowledge of the Truth which you have already acquired.

As the Sifré says: "And thou shalt love the Lord thy God: this means that you should make Him beloved of man as Abraham your father did, as it is said, 'And the souls they had gotten in Haran.'" That is to say, just as Abraham, being a lover of the Lord—as Scripture testifies, "Abraham My friend"—by the power of his conception of God, and out of great love for Him, summoned mankind to believe, you too must so love Him as to summon mankind unto Him.

4th [commandment]: *Fear of God.* By this injunction we are commanded to believe in the fear and awe of God (exalted be He), and not to be at ease and self-confident but to expect His punishment at all times. This injunction is contained in His words, "Thou shalt fear the Lord thy God."

The Gemara in Tractate Sanhedrin discusses the verse, "he that blasphemeth (*nokev*) the name of the Lord, he shall surely be put to death": "Perhaps the word *nokev* should be taken to mean, 'pronounceth' (rather than 'blasphemeth'), as we find elsewhere, 'The men that were pronounced (*nikevu*) by name,' the (requisite) admonition being derived from the verse, 'Thou shalt fear the Lord thy God'?" That is to say, the verse, "he that blasphemeth (*nokev*) the name of the Lord," etc., might be understood as meaning one who merely mentions the Name of the Lord, without committing blasphemy; and if you ask, "What sin is there in that?," we reply that such a one abandons fear of the Lord, for it is part of the fear of the Lord not to pronounce His Name in vain.

The Sages answer this question, and refute the view involved in it, as follows: "First, in order to constitute blasphemy the Name must be used (in such a way that it might be represented as both the agent and the object of blasphemy), and in this instance (of merely pronouncing the

in so far as both teachings ascribe a higher rank to the love of God than to the fear of Him.

The highest theme of the first four chapters is God and His attributes. From God's attributes one is easily led to His names,[12] which are in a sense the theme of the next two chapters, i.e., of the central chapters of the "Yesodei ha-Torah." Maimonides' treatment of the names or rather of the name of God serves the purpose of explaining the three commandments to sanctify His name, not to profane it, and not to destroy things bearing His name. The opening of these two chapters makes it clear that these three commandments, in contradistinction to the study of the Accounts of the Chariot and of the Beginning (II, 12; IV, 11), are obligatory on every Jew. The discussion of the commandments regarding the sanctification and the profanation of the Name includes the discussion of the question of which prohibitions may not be transgressed under any circumstances or are in the strictest sense universally valid;[13] the strictest of those prohibitions are those against idolatry, unchastity (incest), and murder. In the seventh chapter Maimonides returns to "the foundations" by taking up the subject of prophecy to which he devotes the last four chapters of the "Yesodei ha-Torah." While prophecy belongs to "the foundations of the Law," it does not belong, as is indicated by the

---

Name) the condition is absent"; that is to say, (the accused) must be guilty of blaspheming the Name (of the Lord) in (His own) Name, just as (the Sages) say (by substituting) "Let José smite José."

"Moreover, the admonition you cite is in the form of a positive commandment, and it is an accepted principle that such an admonition is invalid." That is to say, your suggestion that a prohibition against the mere pronouncing of the Name of God can be derived from the verse, "Thou shalt fear the Lord thy God," is inadmissible, because that verse is a positive commandment, and a prohibition cannot be based on a positive commandment.

Thus it has been made clear to you that the words, "Thou shalt fear the Lord thy God," lay down a positive commandment.

For a critical version of the original Arabic and a fresh translation in modern Hebrew (i.e., not the medieval Hebrew translation of Moses ibn Tibbon, on which Chavel based his English translation), see *Sefer ha-Mitzvot*, ed. and trans. Joseph Kafah (Jerusalem: Mosad ha-Rav Kook, 1971/5731), pp. 59–60. For related comments by Maimonides on especially love but also fear of God, see "Book of Knowledge," trans. Lerner, chap. 2, paras. 1 and 2; "Laws of the Basic Principles of the Torah," trans. Hyamson, II, 1–2; "Eight Chapters," chap. 5, in *Ethical Writings*, trans. Weiss and Butterworth, pp. 75–78; "Laws Concerning Character Traits," chap. 3, para. 2, in *Ethical Writings*, trans. Weiss and Butterworth, p. 34 ("Man needs to direct every single one of his deeds solely toward attaining knowledge of the Name, blessed be He."). See *Guide*, trans. Pines, 3.52, pp. 629–30; cf. 3.27–28, pp. 510–14, and 3.51, pp. 621. In general, for a very different approach by Maimonides in the *Guide* to the love and fear of God as opposed to his other works, in which both terms receive several, clearly different senses, and in which subtle distinctions between those senses are highlighted, cf. *Guide*, trans. Pines, 3.24 (pp. 500–502); 3.28 (pp. 512–14); 3.51 (pp. 625–26); 3.52 (pp. 629–30); 3.53 (pp. 630–31).]

12. Cf. *Guide* 1.61ff. with 1.50–60. [Cf. *Guide*, trans. Pines, 1.61–64, pp. 147–57, with 1.50–60, pp. 111–47.]

13. Cf. "Hilkhot Melakhim" X, 2. [See "Laws Concerning Kings and Wars," trans. Hershman, p. 235.]

place where it is discussed, to the Accounts of the Chariot and of the Beginning. Maimonides did speak of prophecy when treating the Account of the Chariot, but only in order to reject such views of God and the angels as are based on ignorance of the character of prophetic utterances. The sole positive commandment regarding prophecy opens Maimonides' enumeration of the positive commandments regulating man's conduct toward man, as distinguished from his conduct toward God; it is there immediately followed by the commandment to appoint a king.[14] One is tempted to say that prophecy is a subject, not of theoretical, but of practical wisdom. As for the sole negative commandment regarding prophecy—the prohibition against excessive testing of claimants to prophecy—it is identical with the prohibition against testing or trying God.[15]

The plan of the *Mishneh Torah* and all of its parts must be presumed to be as rational as possible. This does not mean that that plan is always evident. That this is the case would seem to be shown sufficiently by the mere fact that Maimonides could divide all the commandments into fourteen classes in so different ways in the *Mishneh Torah* and in the *Guide* (3.35). The plan of the first chapter devoted to prophecy (VII) is very lucid. Maimonides states first that if a man fulfills all requirements for becoming a prophet, the Holy Spirit immediately rests on him (1). As we learn from the *Guide* (2.32), this is the view of the philosophers; it differs from the view of the Torah, according to which God may miraculously withhold prophecy from a man who is perfectly fit for becoming a prophet. Maimonides next states the characteristics of all prophets (2–4); he speaks here emphatically of "all" prophets. He then qualifies his first statement: if a man is properly prepared for prophecy, he will not necessarily become a prophet (5). While in the first statement he had stated, or almost stated, the philosophic view, he states in the repetition the view of the Torah. In the first statement he has spoken of "the Holy Spirit," which he had used synonymously with "the spirit,"[16] whereas in the repetition he speaks of the *Shekhinah*. One may compare this change with the avoidance of "creation" in chapter I and its use in the sequel. To begin with philosophy (although not *eo nomine*) and to turn almost at once to the Torah may be said to be the law governing the *Mishneh Torah* as a whole. He then

---

14. Nos. 172–73. [Consider: Positive commandment no. 172: Heeding the prophets; Positive commandment no. 173: Appointing a king.]

15. Negative commandment no. 64. [Consider: Negative commandment no. 64: Not testing His promises and warnings.]

16. Cf. his use or interpretation of Gen. 1:2 in IV, 2.

qualifies his second statement: everything said about the nature, or rather the way, of prophecy is true of all prophets with the exception of Moses. Both second or qualifying statements have the same character: both introduce, or make explicit, the miraculous or supernatural. Moses' knowledge is more radically supernatural than that of the other prophets since it is angelic rather than human (6). Finally, Maimonides makes clear that signs and wonders are necessary but not sufficient for accrediting a prophet; the signs and wonders, together with the claimant's possession of wisdom and holiness, do not make certain that he is a prophet although they establish a binding legal presumption in his favor. In accordance with this Maimonides speaks rather frequently of "believing," i.e., of believing in a prophet, when discussing prophecy, while he had not spoken at all of "believing" when discussing the Accounts of the Chariot and of the Beginning.[17] The difficulty caused by the difference between binding legal presumption and indubitable truth is solved in the next chapter in which Maimonides shows—on the basis of the premise established in chapter VII that the prophecy of Moses is absolutely superior to that of the other prophets—that Israel believed in Moses because they were eye- and ear-witnesses of the Sinaitic revelation.[18] The authority of the other prophets is therefore derivative from the authority of the Torah.

As is sufficiently indicated by the title "Hilkhot Yesodei ha-Torah," the *Mishneh Torah* stands or falls by the distinction between what is a foundation or a root and what is not. Yet the fact that all commandments of the Torah are equally of divine origin and meant to be valid for ever and ever, deprives that distinction of much of its importance.[19] Therefore one ought not to expect

---

17. Cf. Albo, *Roots* I, 14 (128, 4–5 Husik). [Albo, *Ikkarim* (*Roots*), trans. Husik, p. 128, ll. 3–5: "Maimonides . . . includes specific commandments among his principles, counting in his list the first of the ten commandments, 'I am the Lord thy God,' which he interprets as a command to believe that there is a necessarily existent Being." For Albo's discussion of "belief," see chaps. 19–22, pp. 165–81.]

18. Cf. the thorough discussion of this subject in Albo's *Roots* I. [See Albo, *Ikkarim* (*Roots*), trans. Husik, especially the chapters mentioned in the previous note. For connections between Albo and Maimonides, see the first line in bk. 1, chap. 1, p. 43: "The investigation of the fundamental principles is extremely dangerous." In spite of his criticism of Maimonides, consider also chap. 4, p. 69: "It may be that Maimonides has the same idea concerning the number of fundamental principles as the one we have just indicated, and that his list consists of the three chief principles that we have just mentioned, plus the derivative dogmas issuing from them, being all called by him principles."]

19. Cf. Abravanel, *Rosh Amanah*, chs. 23–24; cf. Albo, *Roots* I, 2, end. [See Isaac Abravanel, *Principles of Faith* (*Rosh Amanah*), trans. and ed. Menachem M. Kellner (Rutherford, NJ: Fairleigh Dickinson University Press, 1981), pp. 194–209. Consider, e.g., the following (pp. 194–95):

> That which I believe to be "true, certain, and established" in this matter is that these men, Maimonides and those who follow after him, . . . were brought to postulate principles in the divine Torah only because they were drawn after the custom of gentile scholars as described in their books. For they saw in every science, whether natural or mathematical, roots or principles which ought not to

that the fundamental distinction made by Maimonides should be entirely lucid. The foundations of the Torah in the strict sense consist of (1) what one must know regarding God, His attributes, and His names, and (2) what one must know or believe regarding the "absoluteness" of the Torah of Moses. We have seen that already the first part of these foundations consists of heterogeneous ingredients. The first four chapters of the "Yesodei ha-Torah" (and perhaps most obviously the paragraph devoted to the bodily creatures), in contradistinction to the last six chapters, introduce philosophy into the Holy of Holies by as it were rediscovering it there. Since philosophy requires the greatest possible awareness of what one is doing, Maimonides cannot effect that fundamental change without being aware that it is a fundamental change, i.e., without a conscious, although not necessarily explicit, criticism of the way in which the Torah was commonly understood. The two parts of the "Yesodei ha-Torah" are linked to each other by the fact that the God whose knowledge is commanded is "this God," the God of Israel.[20] Accord-

> be denied or argued against. . . . These first principles in turn would be explained by a different, more general science, or they would be self-evident, like the primary intelligibles. God, however, understands the way of the divine Torah. . . . Nor is there any other Torah, or any other science or divine understanding more general than or prior to our Torah, such that we could derive first principles for the Torah from it, or explain or validate them from it.

Consider, e.g., the attempt by Abravanel to escape the facts standing against his position evident in the tradition (pp. 201, 209):

> Someone might object to this contention and say that the Sages (themselves) laid down principles for the divine Torah in the first mishnah in *Perek Ḥelek*. . . . It would appear that there are principles and foundations in the Torah about which they said that he who denies them has no portion in the world to come. Maimonides, in his commentary to that mishnah, presented his thirteen principles of faith, saying that he found that an appropriate place in which to discuss them. . . . It is thus made clear that these things were not mentioned because they are principles and foundations in religion, but because they are serious transgressions and reprehensible actions.

Compare with Albo, *Ikkarim (Roots)*, trans. Husik, p. 55:

> I had to write all this because I have seen insignificant men, who think they are wise, open their mouths wide in lengthy and unintelligent discourses against great men. It is clear now that every intelligent person is permitted to investigate the fundamental principles of religion and to interpret the biblical texts in accordance with the truth as it seems to him. And though he believe concerning certain things which the ancients regarded as principles, like the dogma of the Messiah and of the creation, that they are not fundamental principles, but merely true doctrines, which the believer in the Torah is obliged to believe in the same way as he believes in the earth's opening its mouth on the occasion of Korah's rebellion, or the coming down of fire from heaven, and similar miracles and promises mentioned in the Torah, which are true without being fundamental principles of the Torah—he is not a denier of the Torah or of its principles. For if he were, it would follow that there are as many fundamental principles in the Law of Moses as there are miracles and promises in the Torah, an idea which has never occurred to any one.]

20. *Mishneh Torah*, Book 1, 34b5 and 15. ["Laws of the Basic Principles of the Torah," trans. Hyamson, p. 34b5, para. III.7.; as for l. 15, it is not clear if Strauss points to the last line of para. IV. or the first line of para. V.8. See also "Book of Knowledge," trans. Lerner, p. 141, para. 3: "This God is one. He is neither

ingly, the first section of the *Mishneh Torah* teaches that only "this God" is to be acknowledged, loved, and feared and that only His Torah is true.

On the basis of what Maimonides says in the *Guide* (3.38) on the "De'ot," one is inclined to suggest that with an obvious qualification the "De'ot" are devoted to man's fundamental duties toward his fellows, just as the "Yesodei ha-Torah" are devoted to man's fundamental duties toward God. In fact all commandments discussed in the "Yesodei ha-Torah" explicitly speak of God; yet the same seems to be true of the first two of the eleven commandments discussed in the "De'ot." However, the second of these commandments ("to Him shalt thou cleave")[21] means, according to the interpretation which Maimonides follows, "to those who know Him (i.e., the Sages and their disciples) shalt thou cleave" (VI, 2). Accordingly one must wonder whether the first of the two commandments in question (the commandment to assimilate oneself to His ways or to walk in His ways) has an immediate theological reference. To walk in God's ways means to be gracious, merciful, just, mighty, powerful, and so on (I, 6). In order to understand the meaning of the "De'ot," one must understand the plan of this section. The first three chapters are devoted to the explanation of the commandment to walk in the ways of God, whereas the last two chapters (VI–VII) are devoted to the explanation of the ten other commandments whose explanation Maimonides assigned to the "De'ot." The central chapter is an appendix to the first three; it is medical rather than halakhic. The fifth chapter is another appendix to the first three, but its purport is not obvious. To understand its purport, one must first consider the chief point made in the first three chapters.

Maimonides makes there a distinction between two kinds of human goodness, which he calls wisdom and piety. Wisdom comprises all character traits that are the mean between the corresponding two faulty extremes. Piety, on the other hand, consists in deviating somewhat from the middle toward one or the other extreme, for instance in being not merely humble but very humble. One may say that what Maimonides calls wisdom is moral virtue in Aristotle's sense and that by juxtaposing wisdom and piety he in fact juxtaposes philosophic morality and the morality of the Torah. Accordingly the tension between philosophy and the Torah would here become thematic to

---

two or more than two, but one." See also p. 142, paras. 4 and 5: "4. . . . Knowledge of this thing is a positive commandment, as it is said, 'The Lord our God, the Lord is one' (Deut. 6:4). 5. It is clearly set forth in the Torah and in the prophet that the Holy One (blessed by He) is not a corporeal body, as it is said: 'For the Lord your God, He is the God in heaven above and upon the earth beneath,'" which Lerner notes is "a conflation of Josh. 2:11 and Deut. 4:39."]

21. Deut. 10:20; the passage is not quoted in the *Guide*.

a higher degree than in "Yesodei ha-Torah."²² The tension proves on closer inspection to be a contradiction. Just as in "Yesodei ha-Torah" VII he said in effect, first, that all prophets prophesy by means of the imagination, and then that the prophet Moses did not prophesy by means of the imagination; he says now, first, that in the case of all character traits the middle way is the right way, and then that in the case of some character traits the pious man deviates from the middle way toward one or the other extreme. More precisely, according to Maimonides the right way, the way in which we are commanded to walk, is in every case the middle way that is the way of the Lord ("De'ot" I, 3-5, 7; II, 2, 7); yet in the case of anger and pride, man is forbidden to walk in the middle way (II, 3). One obviously does not solve this difficulty by saying that Maimonides explicitly identifies the ways of the Lord only with wisdom as distinguished from piety; this act of Maimonides could be compared with his leaning toward the doctrine of the eternity of the world in "Yesodei ha-Torah" I. The difficulty is solved somehow in the fifth chapter of the "De'ot." That chapter is apparently devoted to "actions" of the wise man as distinguished from his character traits (and his wisdom). But the "actions" of which he speaks here cannot be dealt with separately from character traits.²³ In fact the fifth chapter differs from the chapters preceding it in that Maimonides therein moves from the theme of the wise man in the strict or narrow sense as defined above to the "disciple of the wise," i.e., the Jewish sage who is both wise and pious or in some respects wise and in others pious (cf. especially V, 5 and 9). The transition is illustrated by Maimonides' interpreting the commandment to love one's neighbor as meaning that everyone is obliged to love every Jew (VI, 3-5, 8; VII, 1, 8), as well as by his here qualifying the duty to be truthful by the requirements of peace (V, 7; cf. II, 10); furthermore, he limits, with a view to the practice of all prophets in Israel, the prohibition against publicly humiliating a Jew by the duty to proclaim his sins toward God, as distinguished from his sins toward other men (VI, 8-9). His hesitation to identify unqualifiedly the right way with

---

22. Consider the relative frequency of "nature" in "De'ot" I, 2-3. [See "Laws Relating to Moral Dispositions," trans. Hyamson, pp. 47a-b; but for "nature" consistently translated from the Hebrew to the English, see especially "Laws Concerning Character Traits," chap. 1, paras. 2-3, in *Ethical Writings*, trans. Weiss and Butterworth, pp. 28-29.]

23. Cf. "De'ot" VI, 5 and "Sanhedrin" XVIII, 1 with "De'ot" I, 7. [See "Laws Relating to Moral Dispositions," trans. Hyamson, p. 55a; and "Laws Concerning Character Traits," in *Ethical Writings*, trans. Weiss and Butterworth, chap. 6, para. 5, p. 48. For "Hilkhot Sanhedrin," XVIII, 1, see "Laws of the Sanhedrin," trans. Hershman, p. 50, with "Laws Relating to Moral Dispositions," trans. Hyamson, p. 48a; and "Laws Concerning Character Traits," in *Ethical Writings*, trans. Weiss and Butterworth, chap. 1, para. 7, p. 30.]

the middle way may be explained by an ambiguity occurring in his source (*Pirkei Avot* V, 13-14). There it is said that he who says "what is mine is thine and what is thine is thine" is pious, but that he who says "what is mine is mine and what is thine is thine" possesses the middle character or, according to some, the character of Sodom.

The "Talmud Torah" reasonably follows immediately on the "De'ot" and thus forms the center of the Book of Knowledge. If God's demands on man—on his conduct both towards God and towards his fellow men—are delivered in the most perfect manner in the Torah and only in the Torah, knowledge of the Torah, study of the Torah is the first of all duties; for even the Accounts of the Chariot and of the Beginning form part of the study of the Torah (I, 11-12). The central section makes clear that the extreme humility demanded by the Torah does not preclude the sage's concern with being honored and enjoying other privileges, for that concern only reflects his concern with the Torah being honored (V, 1; VI, 11-12).

The commandments explained in the "Avodah Zarah" are mostly the immediate specifications of the first and most fundamental prohibition, namely, the prohibition against thinking that there is any other god but the Lord. Accordingly, 49 of the 51 commandments discussed there are prohibitions; even the two commandments that are positive in form are in fact also negative. In order to see why the laws regarding forbidden worship form part of the Book of Knowledge, we start from the most obvious peculiarity of this section. That peculiarity is that the section is opened by an introductory chapter preceding the explanation of any of the 51 commandments in question. That chapter sets forth the relation in time of forbidden worship to the true or right worship. True worship preceded forbidden worship. This, we may say, follows necessarily from man's having been created by God in His image. Man originally knew that all beings other than God are God's creatures. This knowledge was gradually lost, with the result that the great majority of men became worshipers of idols while the wise men among them knew no other god but the stars and the spheres; the truth was preserved only by solitary individuals like Noah. The truth was recovered by the efforts of Abraham, who realized that the sphere cannot possibly move itself and that its mover is the creator of the whole, the only God. He fought the worship of idols as well as of the heavenly bodies by deed and by speech, his speech consisting of demonstrations. He was therefore persecuted, but saved by a miracle. This miracle is all the more remarkable since it is the only divine intervention in Abraham's recovery and propagation of the truth that is mentioned by Maimonides here. At any rate, forbidden worship—the worship of any creatures (II, 1)—is based on the most fundamental error, a demonstrably wrong view, the alternative to "the foundation of the foundations and the pillar of the sciences."[24] It is for this reason that forbidden worship is a proper theme of the Book of Knowledge.

It could seem that the teaching of "Avodah Zarah" I is at variance with the teaching of the *Guide*, according to which the creation of the world is not demonstrable and the prohibition against idolatry is not accessible to reason or the intellect.[25] This would cause no difficulty since the purposes of the *Guide* and the *Mishneh Torah* differ so greatly. The case would be different if this particular difference between the two works flatly contradicted what Maimonides says in the *Guide* about the most important substantive difference between them.[26] Nor are we perplexed by his stressing the defects of the minds of most men and the ensuing necessity of establishing certainty and unanimity by means of revelation even regarding the existence of God, for what is true of most minds is not true of all ("Avodah Zarah" II, 3). A difficulty is caused by what he says toward the end of this section (XI, 16), at the end of his discussion of the prohibitions against divination, astrology, the use of charms, and similar things: everyone who "believes" in such things and thinks that they are true and words of wisdom but to be forgone only because they are forbidden by the Torah, is a fool. One wonders whether this statement is meant to apply retroactively to idolatry proper or whether Maimonides is here suggesting a distinction between idolatry and what we would call superstition.

The last section of the Book of Knowledge is devoted to the explanation of a single commandment—the commandment that the sinner repent his sins before the Lord and make confession—as well as of the roots, or dogmas, that are "connected with [that commandment] for its sake." The dogmas in question do not belong, then, to the Accounts of the Chariot and of the Beginning.

---

24. "Yesodei ha-Torah," beginning, and "Avodah Zarah" II, 4. [See "Laws of the Basic Principles of the Torah," trans. Hyamson, chap. I, para. 1, p. 34a; "Book of Knowledge," trans. Lerner, chap. 1, para. 1, p. 141. For "Avodah Zarah" II, 4, see "Laws Concerning Idolatry," trans. Hyamson, pp. 67b–68a; compare with n. 3 above. Abraham's being miraculously saved by God from Nimrod, who consigned him to a fiery furnace, is not in the Hebrew Bible, but in the Midrash: see Midrash Rabba, "Bereshit: Parshat Noaḥ," 38.13 (various editions).]

25. *Guide* 2.33 (75a). [See *Guide*, trans. Pines, 2.33, p. 364. Strauss elaborates the consequences of what he believes is tacitly present in Maimonides' treatment of what is revealed in the Ten Commandments: "For these two principles [i.e., God's existence and unity] are knowable by human speculation alone.... As for the other commandments, they belong to the class of generally accepted opinions and those adopted in virtue of tradition, not to the class of the intellecta."]

26. Cf. the beginning of this article. [See the first paragraph above.]

Their rationale is solely that without their acceptance repentance would be impossible; they are purely practical, i.e., they are more practical than the dogmas concerning prophecy and the Torah of Moses, for revelation also discloses theoretical truths; or, to use a distinction made by Maimonides in the *Guide* (3.28), they are opinions that ought to be believed not so much on account of themselves as because they are necessary for the improvement of human living together. Besides, the heading of the last section of the Book of Knowledge implies that none of the 613 commandments of the Torah explicitly commands acceptance of the opinions in question.

The question arises, why are dogmas of this kind connected with repentance and required for the sake of repentance, as distinguished from other commanded actions, such as prayer; and which are the dogmas in question? Maimonides' codification of the particulars of the law on repentance prepares the answers to these questions. The distinction between perfect repentance and repentance as such seems to be of decisive importance. Perfect repentance requires that the sinner not again commit the repented sin although the relevant circumstances have not changed or although he is exposed to the same temptation to which he earlier succumbed: an old man cannot perfectly repent the sins he committed in his youth by virtue of his youth. From this it follows that there cannot be any perfect repentance on one's deathbed. Hence if there were not repentance pure and simple, men could not repent many of their sins. Yet they are commanded to repent all their sins. Hence repentance pure and simple requires only that man deplore his sins, confess them with his lips before the Lord, and resolve in his heart not to commit them again. Even if a man has perfectly repented a given sin, he is not for this reason free from sin, for he will commit other sins. Repentance pure and simple, as distinguished from perfect repentance, is sufficient for his sins being forgiven him (II, 1-3; cf. III, 1). Forgiveness of sins is needed because sinfulness, i.e., preponderance of one's sins over his meritorious deeds, is literally deadly, and only God knows the true weight of the various kinds of sins and meritorious deeds (III, 2). When Maimonides mentions in this context (III, 4) the fact that the sounding of the Shofar on Rosh ha-Shanah is a decision of Scripture, i.e., not explicable, he gives us a hint to the effect that the commandment to repent has a reason accessible to man; that reason is the one that has just been restated. Repentance is then not possible if there is not particular providence, which in turn requires that God be omniscient. Furthermore, the crucial importance of deathbed repentance is connected with the prospect of the life to come. Accordingly Maimonides enumerates in the immediate sequel (III, 6ff.) the kinds of men who do not have a share in the world to come; among those kinds we find him who says that the Creator does not know what men do and those who deny the resurrection of the dead and the coming of the Redeemer.

Maimonides does not explicitly introduce these three dogmas in the "Teshuvah" as dogmas or roots. He speaks in the "Teshuvah" of roots in the sense of dogmas only in chapters V-VI, i.e., in the central chapters of that section. "The great root," without which repentance is impossible, is man's freedom. Man is free in the sense that it depends entirely on him whether he will choose the good or the bad; it is in every man's power to be as just as Moses or as wicked as Jeroboam, to be wise or to be foolish. No other being in the world possesses this privilege. One must go beyond what Maimonides says and say that no other being possesses that privilege: God cannot be unjust or unwise. Man would not be truly free to choose good and evil, truth or error, if he did not by his own power know good or evil or truth and error. Neither God nor anyone else nor anything[27] compels man to act well or badly or draws him to either justice and wisdom or injustice and folly. Maimonides thus implicitly denies what he had asserted in the "De'ot" (I, 2) that different human beings have from their birth, by nature, inclinations to different vices; in fact, he now refrains from speaking of "nature" (*teva'*) altogether. Since the difficulty is not disposed of by silence, he replaces the statement "freedom is given to everyman" by the statement "the freedom of everyman is given to him."[28]

---

27. *Mishneh Torah*, Book 1, 87a18. [See "Laws of Repentance," trans. Hyamson, chap. V, para. 6 (in English, para, 4.VI.):

> If God had decreed that the human being be either righteous or wicked, or if there were some force inherent in his nature which irresistibly drew him to a particular course, or to a special branch of knowledge, to special views or activities, as the foolish astrologers, out of their own fancy, pretend, how would the Almighty have charged us, through the prophets: "Do this and do not do that, improve your ways, do not follow your wicked impulses," when, from the beginning of his existence, his destiny had already been decreed, or his innate constitution irresistibly drew him to that from which he could not set himself free?]

28. Cf. "Teshuvah" V, beginning with VII, beginning. The latter formulation may be the correct reading also of V, beginning; cf. Hyamson's edition, and Albo, *Roots* I, 3 (59, 17–18). Cf. Pines' Introduction to his English translation of the *Guide* (Chicago: University of Chicago Press, 1963), p. xcv, n. 63. [See "Laws of Repentance," trans. Hyamson, chap. V, para. 1, p. 86b: "Free will is bestowed on every human being." See also "Laws of Repentance," trans. Hyamson, chap. VII, para. 1, p. 89a: "Since free will is bestowed on every human being, . . ." (Contrary to Hyamson's own translation, the Hebrew of the key words in V, 1, and VII, 1, is identical; hence, the second sentence has been translated so as to make it express the same thought as the first, as was clearly intended. The same correction has to be made to Albo, *Ikkarim* (*Roots*), I, 3 (p. 59, ll. 17–18), as translated by Husik: "(Maimonides) himself writes, in *The Book of Knowledge*, chapter 5 of 'Laws of Repentance': 'Free will is bestowed on every human being' . . ." The

Man's freedom is a pillar of the whole Torah: he could not reasonably be told "do this" or "do not do that" if he were not able to do in each case the opposite of what he is told. In particular, if he lacked freedom he could not reasonably be punished for his transgressions or rewarded for his obedience. Man can avoid the punishment he deserves by repenting his evil deeds; because man is free to do evil, he is also free to repent his evil deeds. Man's freedom extends even to his knowledge or science and to his emotions. Man's freedom seems to be incompatible with God's omniscience, with His knowledge of all future things. The solution of this difficulty requires profound thought—thought that is not at the disposal of all men—and "many great roots" depend on that solution. The solution is supplied by the insight that God's knowledge differs radically from human knowledge, so much so, that God's knowledge is as unfathomable to man as His essence. But while we cannot know how God knows all creatures and their actions, we know without any doubt that man is free. This knowledge derives not merely from the acceptance of the Law but from clear demonstrations taken from the words of wisdom, i.e., from science. There remains another difficulty to the solution of which Maimonides devotes the whole sixth chapter. This difficulty is caused by many scriptural passages that seem to contradict the dogma of human freedom; in those passages God seems to be said to decree men's doing evil or good. To solve this difficulty, Maimonides explains in his own name "a great root." The explanation starts from the fact that every unrepented sin of an individual or community requires a fitting punishment—

---

comment of Pines (made as a note to *Guide*, p. xcv, n. 63), which Strauss says should be compared with the previous discussion in his text and his notes, reads as follows: "It may be apposite to remark in this connection that in my opinion the commonly held view that Maimonides qua philosopher believed in the freedom of man's will and action is mistaken, if one accepts the current definitions of such freedom. See the preliminary observation made in S. Pines, 'Abu'l Barakat's Poetics and Metaphysics,' in *Scripta Hierosolymitana* VI, 'Studies in Philosophy' (Jerusalem, 1960), Excursus, pp. 195-98." The three-page excursus is entitled "Notes on Maimonides' Views concerning Human Will." Discussing mainly two key chapters of the *Guide* in which the issue of freedom is addressed more or less directly—3.17 and 2.48 (Pines accidentally refers to it erroneously as 2.47)—he concludes with the following statement:

> This statement [in 2.48] to which the rest of the chapter serves as an illustration proves, as I believe, conclusively that in Maimonides' opinion volition and choice are no less subject to causation than natural phenomena and do not form in this respect a domain governed by different laws or by no laws at all. Q.E.D. The further question may of course be asked as to whether natural phenomena are ruled in Maimonides' view by a stricter determinism than the one admitted by Aristotle; in other words, it may be asked whether Maimonides followed Avicenna rather than the Greek philosopher. But this is a different problem and cannot be discussed here.

With respect to Strauss's statement made two paragraphs previously about "opinions . . . to be believed not so much on account of themselves" as because of the needs of human life in common and of its improvement, see *Guide*, trans. Pines, 3.28, pp. 513-14.]

God alone knowing which punishment is fit—in this life or in the life to come or in both lives. If the individual or the community has committed a great sin or many sins, justice requires that the sinner not escape punishment through his repentance and hence that repentance, i.e., the freedom to return from his wickedness, be withheld from him. This is what is meant by God's hardening the heart of Pharaoh and similar expressions.

Maimonides concludes the thematic discussion of repentance in the seventh chapter, in which he speaks more emphatically than before of the exalted rank of repentance: the rank of those who repent is higher than that of those who never sin; Israel will not be redeemed except through repentance; repentance brings man near to the Presence. Particularly remarkable is the suddenness with which a man through his repentance is transformed from an enemy of God into a friend of God. Those who repent have the characteristics of the pious as distinguished from the wise.

The next two chapters deal with the world to come and the messianic age; the connection of these two themes with repentance has become clear from the thematic discussion of repentance. The life to come is the highest reward for the fulfillment of the commandments and the acquisition of wisdom. Yet, as Maimonides points out in the last chapter, as long as we fulfill the commandments of the Torah and concern ourselves with the wisdom of the Torah in order to receive any reward, we do not yet serve God properly, for we serve Him only from fear, not from love. But one can love God only to the extent to which one knows Him. Therefore one must dedicate oneself to the study of the sciences and insights that enable him to know God to the extent to which this is possible for man, "as we have made clear in the *Yesodei ha-Torah*." With these words the Book of Knowledge ends. The reference to the *Sefer Madda* makes it unnecessary for Maimonides to state explicitly what the required sciences or insights are.

13

Note on Maimonides' *Treatise on the Art of Logic*

EDITOR'S NOTE

"Note on Maimonides' *Treatise on the Art of Logic*" basically reproduces Strauss's work which first appeared in his last book whose contents he assembled and arranged himself, although it was edited by Joseph Cropsey: *Studies in Platonic Political Philosophy*, pp. 208-9. As for the matter of the period in which Strauss composed the present work, Stephen Gregory of the University of Chicago has discovered (among the files generated during Joseph Cropsey's period as administrator of the Leo Strauss Literary Estate) the manuscript and the typescript of the "Note on Maimonides' *Treatise on the Art of Logic*." The date of composition, at least according to what is written on the manuscript in Strauss's own handwriting, was 11–19 July 1968. My sincere thanks to Nathan Tarcov for his help in establishing the date of composition of the "Note." The only significant change made by the editor is to add supplementary notes, which attempt to provide additional scholarly data useful for some readers in studying the contents of Strauss's own references and sources in the "Note." Thus, the following notes are entirely the work of the present editor, and are not to be attributed to Strauss himself.

MAIMONIDES' *TREATISE ON THE ART OF LOGIC* IS NOT A JEWISH BOOK. He wrote it in his capacity as a student of logic at the request of a master of the legal (religious) sciences, of a man of high education in the Arabic tongue who wished to have explained to him as briefly as possible the meaning of the terms frequently occurring in the art of logic.[1] One ought therefore not to ex-

---

1. Maimonides, "Logic," trans. Efros, p. 34. For the edition of Maimonides' *Logic* to which Strauss refers, see Israel Efros, "Maimonides' *Treatise on Logic* (*Makalah Fi-Sina'at Al-Mantik*): Original Arabic and Three Hebrew Translations," *Proceedings of the American Academy for Jewish Research* 8 (1937-38): pp. 1-136. The remainder of the Arabic original has since been rediscovered and edited: see, e.g., Israel Efros, "Maimonides' Arabic 'Treatise on Logic,'" *Proceedings of the American Academy for Jewish Research* 34 (1966): pp. 6-34. A complete and critical English translation based on the recent discovery

pect that Maimonides' *Logic* is an ordinary scholastic compendium, original or unoriginal. It is natural in the circumstances that he should introduce in the first chapter the terms which "we" (i.e., we logicians) use, as equivalents of the terms used by "the Arabic grammarians."[2] In chapter 3, he mentions not only the possible, the impossible, and the necessary but also the obligatory, the base and noble, and the like among the modes of the proposition: is this due to an adaptation to a way of thinking to be expected from a master of the legal sciences?[3] When he takes up in the next chapter the necessary, the possible, and the impossible, he makes clear that the truly possible can only be said with a view to the future (e.g., it is truly possible that a newborn normal child will write); as soon as the truly possible is actualized, it resembles the necessary. One of the examples used in this connection deals with Abu Ishaq the Sabian.[4] This example is not strange if one considers that the *Logic* is not a Jewish book and that Sabianism is an alternative to Judaism. (An author, Ishaq the Sabian, is mentioned in the *Guide* 3.29.) In chapter 7, he refers without discussing them to "the legal syllogisms."[5] He discusses there, when treating "analogical syllogism" and "inductive syllogism," syllogisms proving that heaven is created; the syllogisms in question are based on a disregard of the difference between natural and artificial things.

In chapter 8 however we learn that it is the art of rhetoric as distinguished from the art of demonstration that uses analogical syllogisms.[6] In chapter 9 it is made clear that the philosophers—here mentioned for the first time—admit God to be only the remote cause in particular also of what befalls human beings and seek in each case for a proximate cause.[7] In the center of chapter 10 we read that "body simply" comprises everything or is the highest

---

and edition of the original Arabic text has not been made but is a desideratum in the scholarly study of Maimonides' thought. The major Hebrew commentaries on Maimonides' *Logic* have recently been edited in Hebrew in a comprehensive version of Maimonides' *Treatise on Logic*, containing a critical edition of the Arabic original, a Hebrew translation, and the major commentaries. See *Be'ur melekhet ha-Higayon*, ed. Kafah. Full details about the recent scholarly editions and translations of Maimonides' *Treatise on the Art of Logic* are mentioned above in the "Editor's Note" to "Maimonides' Statement on Political Science," chap. 9 above.

2. "Logic," trans. Efros, pp. 34–35.
3. Ibid., p. 37.
4. Ibid., p. 39. See "Maimonides' Statement on Political Science," chap. 9 above. For *Guide* 3.29, p. 521: "Among these books [of idolatry] there is also . . . the book written by Ishaq al-Sabi [i.e., the Sabian] on the defense of the religious community of the Sabians, and the big book of this same author concerning the laws of the Sabians, the details of their religion, their festivals, their sacrifices, their prayers, and other matters belonging to their religion."
5. "Logic," trans. Efros, p. 47.
6. Ibid., p. 49; "Logic," in *Ethical Writings*, trans. Weiss and Butterworth, p. 158.
7. "Logic," trans. Efros, p. 50.

genus of beings: the Sabians knew no gods but the stars.[8] We are reminded at the end of the chapter that the *Logic* is written for beginners.[9] In chapter 11 Maimonides quotes the saying of a philosopher according to which "everyone who does not distinguish between the potential and the actual, the essential and the accidental, the conventional things and the natural things, and the universal and the particular, is unable to discourse."[10]

Toward the end of chapter 11 and in chapter 13, Maimonides begins to refer again to the Arabic grammarian.[11] In chapter 14, the concluding chapter, he speaks above all of the division of the sciences and at greatest length of political science. According to him, political science consists of four parts: self-government of the individual, government of the household, government of the city, government of the great nation or of the nations. The silence on government of a nation remains strange; perhaps Maimonides wished to exclude the government of a small nation. The expression "the great nation or the nations," as distinguished from "the great nation or all nations," may indicate that there cannot be a great nation comprising all nations.[12] This "Averroist" view is best known to us from Marsilius of Padua's *Defensor Pacis* (I 17.10).[13]

---

8. Ibid., p. 52. What Strauss renders as "body simply," Efros translates as "absolute matter."

9. Ibid., p. 54.

10. Ibid., p. 55: Efros translates it as "unfit to reason." I have not been able to trace the source of this sentence, highlighted by Strauss, that Maimonides attributes to what "philosophers say." But may I suggest considering Aristotle, *Metaphysics*, bk. Gamma, chap. 4 (1005b35–1009a6)? My thanks to Professor Deborah L. Black of the University of Toronto for the suggestion.

11. Ibid., pp. 56 and 58.

12. Ibid., pp. 63–65; "Logic," in *Ethical Writings*, trans. Weiss and Butterworth, pp. 158–61.

13. See "Maimonides' Statement on Political Science," chap. 9 above. For Latin Averroism and *Defensor Pacis*, see Strauss's essay "Marsilius of Padua," in *History of Political Philosophy*, 3rd ed., ed. Leo Strauss and Joseph Cropsey (Chicago: University of Chicago Press, 1963, 1972, 1987), pp. 276–95, and especially pp. 291–94. It is reprinted in *Liberalism Ancient and Modern*, pp. 185–202, and especially pp. 199–201. For Machiavelli's modernized "Averroism," see Leo Strauss, *Thoughts on Machiavelli* (Glencoe, IL: Free Press, 1958; reprint, Chicago: University of Chicago Press, 1995), pp. 175, 202–3, 207–8, 333–34, n. 68. See also, for a brief comment, *Studies in Platonic Political Philosophy*, p. 226, or *History of Political Philosophy*, p. 314: "The substance of Machiavelli's religious teaching is not original, but his manner of setting it forth is very ingenious." This is the passage that Strauss refers to from Marsilius of Padua, *Defensor Pacis*, trans. Alan Gewirth (New York: Columbia University Press, 1956; reprint, 2001), pp. 84–85:

> As to whether it is advantageous to have one supreme government in number for all those who live a civil life in the whole world, or whether on the contrary it is at a certain time advantageous to have different such governments in different regions of the world which are almost necessarily separate from one another in place, and especially for men who use different languages and who differ widely in morals and customs—this question merits a reasoned study, but it is distinct from our present concern. The heavenly cause moves perhaps toward the latter alternative, in order that the procreation of men may not become excessive. For one might perhaps think that nature, by means of war and epidemics, has moderated the procreation of men and other animals in order that the earth may suffice for their nurture; wherein those who say that there is eternal generation would be very strongly upheld.

14

Note on Maimonides' *Letter on Astrology*

EDITOR'S NOTE

"Note on Maimonides' *Letter on Astrology*" basically reproduces Strauss's work which first appeared in his last book, whose contents he assembled and arranged himself, although it was edited by Joseph Cropsey: *Studies in Platonic Political Philosophy*, pp. 205–7. As for the matter of the period in which Strauss composed the present work, Stephen Gregory of the University of Chicago has discovered (among the files generated during Joseph Cropsey's period as administrator of the Leo Strauss Literary Estate) the manuscript and the typescript of the "Note on the *Letter on Astrology*." The date of composition, at least according to what is written on the manuscript in Strauss's own handwriting, was 21–23 July 1968. The only significant change made by the present editor is to add the supplementary notes, which attempt to provide additional scholarly data useful for some readers in studying the contents of Strauss's own references and sources in the "Note." Thus, the following notes are entirely the work of the present editor and are not to be attributed to Strauss himself. However, a single note by Strauss in typescript has been uncovered by Yiftach Ofek (whom I thank for his discovery) in the Leo Strauss Archive of the Library of the University of Chicago. The note was on a single typed sheet alongside the original manuscript, but not necessarily belonging to it. It is not clear not only whether the uncovered note belongs to this essay, but also, if it did, at what point in the text it is to be ascribed as a note. At the top of the page it says "p. 5, n. 2"; but it is to be observed that the original typed manuscript is only four pages long, and contains no notes by Strauss. It is a very tentative suggestion that these figures at the top of the page may reflect an aim of appending an additional page with further notes, but Strauss never got around to finishing the work, other than this "note 2." Thus, it is merely an educated guess by the present editor to suggest (based mainly, although not solely, on their proximity of preservation in the Archive) that this note may perhaps have been assigned by Strauss to the present essay. Likewise its assignment to note eight in the present edition of Strauss's essay is not based on anything known distinctly from Strauss's own hand. As a result, I put the text of the note in square brackets, to express the uncertainty about its location, although also to indicate that this is a note composed by Strauss himself, even if not sufficiently known whether it was designed for the present essay. My sincere thanks to Nathan Tarcov for transmitting the aforementioned note to me, for his help in deciphering one of the words appended in Strauss's own handwriting, and for his help in establishing the date of composition of the "Note."

THE ADDRESSEES OF THIS LETTER HAD ASKED MAIMONIDES FOR HIS view about astrology. After having praised their question, he says that if they had known his *Mishneh Torah*, they would have known his opinion on the subject.[1] He uses the first person plural when speaking of himself as the author of the *Mishneh Torah*, while when speaking of his opinion or of his *Guide* he uses the first person singular.[2] He begins by speaking of the sources of knowledge: knowledge stems from reason (*de'ah*), sense, and tradition from the prophets and the just. He tacitly excludes the *endoxa* either because they deal chiefly with what one ought to do or forbear, as distinguished from what one ought to believe or not, or because they can be understood to be parts of the traditional lore. Sense occupies the central place, and among the senses the sense of touch. Maimonides exhorts his addressees to a critical posture toward anything they might be inclined to believe and especially toward opinions supported by many old books.[3] This is not to deny the immense usefulness of the astrological literature or, since astrology is the root of idolatry, of the idolatrous literature: by studying the whole available idolatrous literature Maimonides has succeeded in explaining all commandments which otherwise seemed inexplicable and thus in explaining all commandments (see the *Guide* 3.26 [end], and 3.49 [end]).

In Maimonides' view astrology is not a science at all but sheer nonsense;

1. See "Letter on Astrology," trans. Lerner, pp. 178–79. See also "Letter to the Jews of Marseilles in 1194," trans. Stitskin, pp. 118–29. For a critical edition of the Hebrew original, see *Igrot ha-Rambam*, ed. Shailat, III, pp. 478–90 ("Letter to the Rabbis of Montpelier on Astrology").
2. See "Letter on Astrology," trans. Lerner, pp. 178 and 180: "the compilation we have made . . . which we titled 'Mishneh Torah'" versus "you would have known my opinion" and "I already have a great compilation on this subject in the Arabic language (i.e., the 'Guide of the Perplexed') with lucid proofs for every single commandment."
3. Ibid., p. 179. Cf. also *Guide*, trans. Pines, 1.31, pp. 66–67.

none of the wise men of the nations who are truly wise has ever written an astrological book; those books go back to the Chasdeans, Chaldeans, Canaanites, and Egyptians to whose religion astrology belonged.[4] Maimonides is silent here, as distinguished from the *Guide* (3.37 [beginning]), on the Sabians.[5] But the wise men of Greece, the philosophers, held up to ridicule those four nations and refuted their tenets thoroughly. The wise men of Persia and even of India also realized the absurdity of astrology. Maimonides mentions here altogether seven nations. The reminder of the seven nations whose destruction is commanded in the Bible may not be accidental: all those nations were idolators, regardless [of] whether their wise men were astrologers or not; this fact, I believe, was for Maimonides of greater importance than is commonly thought; the relation of astrology and idolatry is more complex than appears from the few words devoted to it in the *Letter on Astrology*. The true science of the stars is astronomy whose scope is set forth by Maimonides at considerable length.

Maimonides next puts the whole question on the broadest basis by speaking of the relation of the philosophers and the Torah.[6] The great philosophers agree that the world has a governor, namely, the mover of the sphere. Most of them say that the world is eternal while some of them say that only its matter is eternal and others say what the prophets said that God as the only uncreated being created all creatures out of nothing. Maimonides refers to his "great compilation in Arabic" (i.e., the *Guide*) in which he had refuted the alleged proofs of the philosophers against creation and in particular creation out of nothing.[7] By speaking of philosophers who teach creation out of nothing Maimonides reduces the difference, as stated in the *Guide*, between philosophy and the Torah.[8] As appears from the context, his purpose in doing this is to present as it were a unitary front of philosophy and the Torah against astrology.[9] For, as he goes on, all three groups of thinkers agree that

4. "Letter on Astrology," trans. Lerner, p. 180.
5. *Guide* 3.37, pp. 540–41. For the Sabians, see also above, "Introduction to Maimonides' *Guide*," chap. 10 , and "How To Begin," chap. 11.
6. "Letter on Astrology," trans. Lerner, p. 181.
7. Ibid., p. 182.
8. Ibid., p. 183.
9. [*Note composed by Leo Strauss*: Maimonides distinguishes prophets and philosophers from those men who, endowed with a vigorous imagination but lacking understanding, become governors of cities, lawgivers, diviners, and sorcerers (*Guide* 2.37 [Munk pp. 80b–81a]). This description of one class of men recalls Plato's observation on one class of atheists who, having, a strong memory and seeming to be very clever, become diviners and sorcerers and tyrants and demagogues (*Laws* 908c2–d7). As "imagination" is used by Maimonides in a rather wide sense, it may well be that this word represents what Plato called "memory." Compare *Guide* 2.38, toward the end.]

this nether world is governed by God by means of the sphere and the stars. "Just as we say that God performs signs and miracles through the angels, so these philosophers say that all the things are always done by the nature of the world by means of the sphere and the stars, and they say that the sphere and the stars are animate and intelligent."[10] Maimonides claims to have proved (in the *Guide*) that there is no disagreement whatever between the Sages of Israel and the philosophers regarding the general government of the world.[11]

All the greater is the disagreement between all philosophers and the Torah regarding particular providence. According to the philosophers what happens to individual human beings or individual societies is altogether a matter of chance and has no cause in the stars. As against this the true religion, the religion of Moses, believes that what happens to human individuals happens to them in accordance with justice. Whereas according to the *Guide* the dividing line between the Torah and philosophy is their teaching regarding the eternity or non-eternity of the world or at least of matter, according to the *Letter on Astrology*, they are divided by what they teach regarding providence: even the philosophers, who teach creation out of nothing, deny particular providence. The Torah and all philosophers also agree as to men's actions not being subject to compulsion. Yet from this fact Maimonides draws the conclusion that what happens to human beings is not what happens to the beasts, as the philosophers have said.[12]

Just as there are three opinions regarding the world as a whole, there are three opinions regarding the fate of men: the opinion of the philosophers that it is a matter of mere chance, the opinion of the astrologers that it is fully determined by the stars, and the opinion of the Torah. The opinion of the philosophers is to be rejected on account of the acceptance of the Torah. There is no visible connection between the two tripartitions.

In the *Guide* Maimonides had considerably mitigated the opposition between philosophy and Judaism in regard to particular providence especially

---

10. "Letter on Astrology," trans. Lerner, pp. 182–83.

11. Ibid., p. 183. See perhaps *Guide* 3.17, pp. 471–74. The complete accord which Maimonides "claims" to have achieved is between his reading of the Torah's view and the philosophers' (i.e., the Aristotelians') view concerning governance: "But regarding all the other animals [beside man] and, all the more, the plants and other things, my opinion is that of Aristotle.... For all this is in my opinion due to pure chance, just as Aristotle holds." Yet by way of contrast in the very same chapter, "the opinion of our Law" seems to have been something quite different for him. If I am not misled, Strauss voices a skeptical note: "Maimonides claims to have proved (in the *Guide*) ... " It seems as if Strauss wants readers to wonder why Maimonides in this context needs to overstate his total reconciliation of the Torah's (as opposed to his own) understanding of governance with that of the philosophers.

12. "Letter on Astrology," trans. Lerner, pp. 183–84.

by his interpretation of the Book of Job. One may find a trace of this intention in a rather casual remark that he makes in the *Letter on Astrology* long before he comes to speak on particular providence. We lost our kingdom since our fathers sinned by turning to astrology, i.e., to idolatry, and neglected the art of war and conquest. This would seem to be an illustration of the view according to which the philosophers trace events to their proximate, not to their remote, cause. The remark referred to is at the same time a beautiful commentary on the grand conclusion of the *Mishneh Torah*: the restoration of Jewish freedom in the messianic age is not to be understood as a miracle.[13]

13. Cf. ibid., pp. 179–80, with "Laws Concerning Kings and Wars," trans. Hershman, chap. XI, paras. 3–4, pp. 239–40, and chap. XII, paras. 1–2, pp. 240–41; "Laws of Kings and Their Wars," trans. Weiss and Butterworth, chap. 11, paras. 3–4, pp. 172–73, and chap. 12, paras. 1–2, pp. 174–75.

III

On Isaac Abravanel, the Last Medieval Maimonidean

15
On Abravanel's Philosophical Tendency and Political Teaching[1]

EDITOR'S NOTE

Leo Strauss's essay "On Abravanel's Philosophical Tendency and Political Teaching" originally appeared in *Isaac Abravanel: Six Lectures*, ed. J. B. Trend and H. Loewe (Cambridge: Cambridge University Press, 1937), pp. 95–129. See also Strauss, *Philosophie und Gesetz: Frühe Schriften*, vol. 2 of *Gesammelte Schriften*, pp. 195–227 (with Strauss's marginal handwritten additional comments transcribed, pp. 229–31). A French translation has also been produced, appearing in print as "Sur l'orientation philosophique et l'enseignement politique d'Abravanel," trans. Adrien Barrot, *Revue de Métaphysique et de Morale*, no. 4 (1998): 559–84. Readers should note that in this present version (as follows both Meier's edition of the original English, and Barrot's French translation), Strauss's notes are numbered consecutively, i.e., from 1 to 80, as was not the case in the original, which numbered the notes of Strauss's essay separately on each page. I would venture to suggest that this was likely the convention of the publisher of the book in which the essay originally appeared, rather than the choice of the author, which has been assumed in renumbering them consecutively. The supplementary reference material set in square brackets in the notes is entirely the work of the present editor; it attempts to provide additional scholarly data useful for some readers in studying the contents of Strauss's own notes.

ABRAVANEL MAY BE CALLED THE LAST OF THE JEWISH PHILOSOPHERS of the Middle Ages. He belongs to the Middle Ages as far as the framework and the main content of his doctrine are concerned. It is true that there are features of his thought which distinguish it from that of all or of most other Jewish

---

1. I wish to express my thanks to the Board of the Faculty of History (at the University of Cambridge) for a grant enabling this essay to be written, and to Mrs. M. C. Blackman for kindly revising the English.

medieval philosophers; but most of those features are probably of medieval Christian origin. Yet Abravanel is a son of the humanist age, and thus we shall not be surprised if he expresses in his writings opinions or tendencies which are, to say the least, not characteristic of the Middle Ages. Generally speaking, however, Abravanel is a medieval thinker, a Jewish medieval thinker.

The central figure in the history of Jewish medieval philosophy is Maimonides. Thus it will be advisable to define the character of Abravanel's philosophical tendency by contrasting it with that of Maimonides. One is all the more justified in proceeding thus, since there is scarcely any other philosopher whom Abravanel admired so much, or whom he followed as much, as he did Maimonides.

What was then the general tendency of Maimonides? The answer to this question seems to be obvious: Maimonides attempted to harmonize the teachings of Jewish tradition with the teachings of philosophical tradition, i.e., of the Aristotelian tradition. This answer is certainly not altogether wrong, but it is quite insufficient, since it fails to explain which ultimate assumptions enabled Maimonides to harmonize Judaism and Aristotle. Now those truly decisive assumptions are neither of Jewish nor of Aristotelian origin: they are borrowed from Plato, from Plato's political philosophy.

At a first glance, the philosophical tradition from which Maimonides starts seems to be identical with that which is the determining factor of Christian scholasticism. Indeed, to Maimonides as well as to Thomas Aquinas, Aristotle is *the* philosopher. There is, however, one striking and at the same time highly important difference between Maimonides and the Christian scholastic as regards the philosophical tradition on which they build. For Thomas Aquinas, Aristotle is the highest authority, not only in other branches of philosophy, but also in political philosophy. Maimonides, on the other hand, could not use Aristotle's *Politics*, since it had not been translated into Arabic or Hebrew; but he could start, and he did start, from Plato's political philosophy.[2] For the *Republic* and the *Laws*, which were inaccessible to the Latin Middle Ages,[3] had been translated into Arabic in the ninth century, and com-

---

2. For details I must refer the reader for the time being to my book *Philosophie und Gesetz* (Berlin: Schocken, 1935); and to my article "Quelques Remarques sur la Science Politique de Maïmonide et de Farabi," in *Revue des Études Juives* 100 (1936): 1–37. [See *Philosophy and Law*, and "Some Remarks on the Political Science of Maimonides and Farabi," chap. 5 above. For the fate and fortune of Aristole's *Politics* in the medieval Arabic-speaking world, see Shlomo Pines, "Aristotle's *Politics* in Arabic Philosophy," *Israel Oriental Studies* 5 (1975): 150–60; reprinted in *The Collected Works of Shlomo Pines* (Leiden: E. J. Brill, 1989), vo. 2, pp. 146–56.]

3. Cf. Ernest Barker, *Plato and his Predecessors* (London: Methuen, 1918), p. 383 [also named *Greek Political Theory: Plato and His Predecessors* (London: Methuen, 1960), p. 445]: "For a thousand years the

mentaries on them had been written by two of the most outstanding Islamic philosophers.[4] By considering these facts we gain, I believe, a clear impression of the philosophical difference which exists between the philosophy of Maimonides (and of his Islamic predecessors) on the one hand, and that of Christian scholasticism on the other: the place occupied in the latter by Aristotle's *Politics* is occupied in the former by Plato's *Republic* and *Laws*. I have read that in some Italian pictures Plato is represented holding in his hand the *Timaeus* and Aristotle his *Ethics*. If a pupil of Maimonides or of the Islamic philosophers[5] had found pleasure in representations of this kind, he might have chosen rather the inverse order: Aristotle with his *Physics* or *Metaphysics* and Plato with his *Republic* or *Laws*.

For what is the meaning of the fact that Maimonides and the Islamic philosophers whom he followed start from Platonic political philosophy, and not from Aristotle's *Politics*? One cannot avoid raising this question, especially since the circumstance that the *Politics* was not translated into Arabic may well be, not a mere matter of chance, but the result of a deliberate choice, made in the beginning of this medieval development. Now, in order to answer that question, we must remind ourselves of the general character of the medieval world, and of the particular character of the Islamic philosophy adopted by Maimonides. The medieval world is distinguished both from the classical and from the modern world by the fact that its thought was fundamentally determined by the belief in revelation. Revelation was the deter-

---

Republic has no history, for a thousand years it simply disappeared. From the days of Proclus, the neo-Platonist of the fifth century, almost until the days of Marsilio Ficino and Pico della Mirandola, at the end of the fifteenth, the *Republic* was practically a lost book." The same holds true, as far as the Latin Middle Ages are concerned, of the *Laws*.

4. Farabi's paraphrase of the *Laws* will be edited in the near future by Dr. Paul Kraus. [See now Paul Kraus, "Le sommaire du livre des *Lois* de Platon par Abu Nasr al-Farabi," ed. Thérèse-Anne Druart, *Bulletin d'Études Orientales* 50 (1998): 109–55; Muhsin Mahdi, "The Editio princeps of Farabi's *Compendium Legum Platonis*," *Journal of Near Eastern Studies* 20 (1961): 1–24; Alfarabius, *Compendium Legum Platonis/Talkhis nawanis Aflatun*, ed. Franciscus Gabrieli (London: Warburg Institute, 1952). See now also Leo Strauss, "How Farabi Read Plato's *Laws*," in *What Is Political Philosophy?*, pp. 134–54.] The original of Averroes' paraphrase of the *Republic* seems to be lost, but this paraphrase is accessible in an often-printed Latin translation. The more reliable Hebrew translation is being edited by Dr. Erwin Rosenthal; see the *Journal of the Royal Asiatic Society* (October 1934), pp. 737ff. [See now *Averroes' Commentary on Plato's "Republic*," ed. E. I. J. Rosenthal (Cambridge: Cambridge University Press, 1969), which contains a critical edition of the Hebrew translation and an English translation. But see especially for the English translation Averroes, *On Plato's "Republic*," trans. Lerner. This version is based on an additional and often better manuscript of the Hebrew translation; different principles of translation which offer a version closer to Averroes' language (as presented, of course, by the Hebrew translator); and a different view of the intention of Averroes that receives expression in his work.]

5. When speaking of Islamic philosophers, I am limiting myself strictly to the *falasifa*, the so-called Aristotelians.

mining factor with the Islamic philosophers as well as with the Jewish and Christian philosophers. But as was clearly recognized by such contemporary and competent observers as Ghazali, Maimonides, and Thomas Aquinas, the Islamic philosophers did not believe in revelation properly speaking. They were philosophers in the classical sense of the word: men who would hearken to reason, and to reason only. Consequently, they were compelled to give an account of the revelation which they had to accept, and which they did accept, in terms of human reason. Their task was facilitated by the fact that revelation, as understood by Jews or Muslims, had the form of law. Revelation, thus understood, lent itself to being interpreted by loyal philosophers as a perfect, ideal law, as an ideal political order. Moreover, the Islamic philosophers were compelled, and so was Maimonides, to justify their pursuit of philosophy before the law to which they were subject; they had, therefore, to prove that the law did not only entitle them, but even oblige them, to devote themselves to philosophy. Consequently, they were driven to interpret revelation more precisely as an ideal political order, the ideal character of which consists in the very fact that it lays upon all men endowed with the necessary qualities the duty of devoting their lives to philosophy, that it awakens them to philosophy, that it holds out for their guidance at least the most important tenets of philosophy. For this purpose they had to assume that the founder of the ideal political order, the prophetic lawgiver, was not merely a statesman, but that he was, at the same time, a philosopher of the highest authority: they had to conceive, and they did conceive, of Moses or Muhammad as philosopher-kings. Philosopher-kings and a political community governed by philosopher-kings were, however, the theme not of Aristotelian but of Platonic political philosophy. Thus we may say: Maimonides and his Islamic predecessors start from Platonic political philosophy because they had to conceive of the revelation to which they were subject as of an ideal political order, the specific purpose of which was guidance to philosophy. And we may add that their belief in the authority of Moses or Muhammad was perhaps not greatly different from what would have been the belief of a later Greek Platonist in the authority of Plato, if that Platonist had been the citizen of a commonwealth governed by Plato's *Laws*.

Judaism on the one hand, Aristotelianism on the other, certainly supplied the greatest part of the matter of Maimonides' teaching. But Platonic political philosophy provided at any rate the framework for the two achievements by which Maimonides made an epoch in the history of Judaism: for his codification of the Jewish law, and for his philosophical defense of the Jewish law. It is open to question which of Plato's political works was the most important for Maimonides and the Islamic philosophers. But it is safe to say that the best clue to the understanding of their teaching is supplied by the *Laws*.[6] I cannot discuss here the true meaning of this most ironical of Plato's works, although I believe that only the full understanding of its true meaning would enable us to understand adequately the medieval philosophy of which I am speaking. For our present purpose, it is sufficient to state that the *Laws* are certainly the primary source of the opinions which Maimonides and his teachers held concerning the relation between philosophy and revelation, or more exactly between philosophy and law. Those opinions may be summarized in the following ways: (1) Law is based on certain fundamental beliefs or dogmas of a strictly philosophical character, and those beliefs are, as it were, the prelude to the whole law. The beliefs of this kind were called by Farabi, who was, according to Maimonides, the highest philosophical authority of his period, "opinions of the people of the excellent city." (2) Law contains, apart from those rational beliefs, a number of other beliefs which, while being not properly true but representing the truth in a disguised way, are necessary or useful in the interest of the political community. The beliefs of this type may be called, as they were by Spinoza, who was perhaps the latest exponent of that medieval tradition, *pia dogmata*, in contradistinction to the *vera dogmata* of the first group.[7] (3) Necessary beliefs, i.e., the beliefs which are not common to philosophy and law but peculiar to law as such, are to be defended (either by themselves or together with the whole law) by probable, persuasive, rhetorical arguments, not recognizable as such to the vulgar; a special science is to be devoted to that "defense of the law" or "assistance to the law."

We are now in a position to define more precisely the character of Maimonides' attempt to harmonize the Jewish tradition with the philosophical

---

6. Ernest Barker, loc. cit., p. 351, says with regard to the Latin Middle Ages: "The end of the *Laws* is the beginning of the Middle Ages." [See *Greek Political Theory*, p. 409.] This statement is all the more true of the Islamic and Jewish Middle Ages. Compare, for example, the quotations from Avicenna in *Philosophie und Gesetz*, p. 111, and from R. Sheshet in *Revue des Études Juives* 100 (1936), p.2, n. 1. [For the Avicenna passage, see "Maimonides' Doctrine of Prophecy," the fourth paragraph of section IV, chap. 4 above; and for the R. Sheshet passage, see "Some Remarks on the Political Science of Maimonides and Farabi," chap. 5 above, n. 2.]

7. *Tractatus theologico-politicus*, ch. 14 (§20, Bruder).

["It follows, finally, that faith does not require true dogmas so much as pious ones, that is, such as move the spirit toward obedience—even though among them there may be very many that do not have even a shadow of truth, yet so long as he who embraces them is ignorant of their being false. Otherwise he would necessarily be rebellious. For how could it happen that someone who loves Justice and is eager to follow God will adore as divine what he knows to be alien to the divine nature." See Spinoza, *Theologico-Political Treatise*, trans. Yaffe, p. 164.]

tradition. He effects the harmony between those two traditions by starting from the conception of a perfect law, perfect in the sense of Plato's *Laws*, i.e., of a law leading to the study of philosophy and based on philosophical truth, and by thus proving that Judaism is a law of this character. To prove this, he shows that the fundamental beliefs of Judaism are identical with the fundamental tenets of philosophy, i.e., with those tenets on which an ideal law ought to be based. By showing this, he shows at the same time that those Jewish beliefs which are of an unphilosophical nature are meant by the Jewish legislator himself, by *the* philosopher legislator, to be necessary beliefs, i.e., beliefs necessary for political reasons. The assumption underlying this proof of the ideal character of the Jewish law is the opinion that the law has two different meanings: an exterior, literal meaning, addressed to the vulgar, which expresses both the philosophical and the necessary beliefs, and a secret meaning of a purely philosophical nature. Now this property of law had to be imitated by Maimonides in his philosophic interpretation of the law. For if he had distinguished explicitly between true and necessary beliefs, he would have endangered the acceptance of the necessary beliefs on which the authority of the law with the vulgar, i.e., with the great majority, rests. Consequently, he could make this essential distinction only in a disguised way, partly by allusions, partly by the composition of his whole work, but mainly by the rhetorical character, recognizable only to philosophers, of the arguments by which he defends the necessary beliefs. As a consequence, Maimonides' philosophical work, the *Guide of the Perplexed*, is a most ingenious combination of "opinions of the people of the excellent city," i.e., of a strictly demonstrative discussion of the beliefs which are common to philosophy and law, with "defense of the law," i.e., with a rhetorical discussion of the unphilosophical beliefs peculiar to the law. Thus not only the law itself, but also Maimonides' philosophical interpretation of the law, has two different meanings: a literal meaning, addressed to the more unphilosophic reader of philosophic education, which is very near to the traditional Jewish beliefs, and a secret meaning, addressed to true philosophers, which is purely philosophical. This amounts to saying that Maimonides' philosophical work was liable to, and was intended to be liable to, two fundamentally different interpretations: to a "radical" interpretation which did honor to the consistency of his thought, and to a "moderate" interpretation which did honor rather to the fervor of his belief.

The ambiguous nature of Maimonides' philosophical work must be recognized if one wants to judge properly of the general tendency of Abravanel.

For Abravanel has to be characterized to begin with as a strict, even passionate, adherent of the literal interpretation of the *Guide of the Perplexed*. The more philosophic interpretation of this work had appealed to some earlier commentators. Those commentators, who were under the spell of Islamic philosophy rather than of Christian scholasticism, are vehemently attacked by Abravanel,[8] who finds words of the highest praise for the Christian scholastics.[9] But Abravanel accepts the literal teaching of the *Guide* not only as the true expression of Maimonides' thought: that literal teaching is at the same time, if not identical with, at least the framework of, Abravanel's own philosophy.

The beliefs peculiar to the law are founded upon and, as it were, derived from one fundamental conviction: the belief in *creatio ex nihilo*.[10] That belief had been defended by Maimonides in his *Guide* with great care and vigor. The discussion of the creation of the world, or, in other words, the criticism of the contention of the philosophers that the visible world is eternal, forms literally the central part of the *Guide*. It is the central part of this work also because of the fact that the interpretation of the whole work depends on the interpretation of this very part. Indeed, this is the crucial question for the

---

8. Cf. his judgments on Ibn Kaspi and others, quoted by Jacob Guttmann, *Die religionsphilosophischen Lehren des Isaak Abravanel* (Breslau: M. & H. Marcus, 1916), pp. 34–6 and 71. [For a different perspective on Abravanel's attitude toward Maimonides and such philosophic commentators as Ibn Kaspi, see Eric Lawee, "'The Good We Accept and the Bad We Do Not': Aspects of Isaac Abarbanel's Stance towards Maimonides," in *Be'erot Yitzhak: Studies in Memory of Isadore Twersky*, ed. Jay M. Harris (Cambridge, MA: Harvard University Press, 2005), pp. 119–60.]

9. See his commentary on Joshua 10:12 (fol. 21, col. 2). I have used Abravanel's commentary on Joshua, Judges, Samuel, and Kings in the Frankfort edition of 1736.

10. Cf. Abravanel, *Rosh Amanah*, ch. 22, with Maimonides' *Guide* 2.25, beginning, and 3.25, end. [For an English translation, see: Isaac Abravanel, *Principles of Faith (Rosh Amanah)*, trans. and ed. Menachem M. Kellner (Rutherford, NJ: Fairleigh Dickinson University Press, 1982), chap. 22, pp. 190–93. The conventional reading makes Abravanel's defense of Maimonides' "entire project of creed formulation" halt sharply at chap. 22. Kellner asserts (pp. 31–36) to the contrary that "far from turning around to attack Maimonides, [beginning in chap. 23] . . . Abravanel continues to defend him." This especially concerns Strauss's main point about *creatio ex nihilo*, as it had been the focus of Maimonides on the difference between philosophy and the Torah. For Abravanel, it is absolutely prior, as he states unambiguously in the following (pp. 192–93):

> Were I to choose principles to posit for the divine Torah I would only lay down one, the creation of the world. It is the root and foundation around which the divine Torah, its cornerstones, and its beliefs revolve and includes creation at the beginning, the narratives about the Patriarchs, and the miracles and wonders which cannot be believed without belief in creation. So, too, with belief in God's knowledge and providence, and reward and punishment according to (one's observance of) the commandments, none of which can one perfectly believe without believing in the volitional creation of the whole world. . . . So, too, Maimonides, at *Guide* 2.13 wrote that belief in the creation of the world 'is undoubtedly a basis of the Torah of Moses our Master. . . . Nothing other than this should come to your mind.' . . . It is thus shown to you from the words of these rabbis that belief in the creation of the world is a great principle of our Torah.]

interpretation of Maimonides' philosophical work: whether the discussion of the question of creation expresses Maimonides' own opinion in a direct way, or whether it is in the service of the "defense of the law." However one may answer this question, the very question itself implies the recognition of the fact that the literal teaching of the *Guide* is most decidedly in favor of the belief in creation. Now while Maimonides carefully maintains this belief, on which all other beliefs peculiar to the law depend, he takes a rather hesitating, if not self-contradictory position, as regards those other beliefs, i.e., as regards belief in the miracles, in revelation, in the immortality of the soul, in individual providence, in resurrection. If he actually believed in *creatio ex nihilo*, he was as little under a stringent necessity to depreciate those beliefs, or to restrict their bearing, as were the Christian scholastics, who also had combined Aristotelianism with the belief in creation, and who accepted the Christian dogma as a whole. Abravanel accepted Maimonides' explicit doctrine of the creation as true—he defended it in a special treatise (*Shamayim Ḥadashim*), and he knew Christian scholasticism. It was, therefore, only natural that he should have defended, and that he did defend, on the very basis of Maimonides' doctrine of creation and against his authority, all the other beliefs which are dependent on the belief in creation and which Maimonides had endangered. Thus, his criticism of Maimonides' dangerous doctrines is, in principle, not more than an immanent criticism of the literal teaching of the *Guide*; it is not more than a subsequent correction of that teaching in the sense of the Jewish traditional beliefs. It would not be much of an exaggeration to say that Abravanel's philosophical exertions as a whole are a defense of the Jewish creed, as drawn up by Maimonides in his *Commentary on the Mishnah*, against the implications, dangerous to this creed, of the teaching of the *Guide*.

The creed compiled by Maimonides was defended expressly by Abravanel in a special treatise (*Rosh 'Amanah*). This treatise, by itself perhaps the most striking evidence of the admiration which Abravanel felt for Maimonides, gives us a clear idea both of Abravanel's own tendency and of his interpretation of Maimonides. Maimonides' arrangement of the Jewish beliefs, the so-called "Thirteen Articles of Faith," had been attacked by some later Jewish writers for philosophical as well as for religious reasons. Abravanel defends Maimonides against those critics by showing that Jewish orthodoxy is perfectly defined by the recognition of just those thirteen articles which Maimonides had selected, and that the order of those articles is completely lucid. As regards the latter point, Abravanel asserts that the former part of those articles indicates the beliefs common to philosophy and law, while the latter part is concerned with those beliefs which either are not accepted, or which are even contested, by the philosophers.[11] It is not necessary for our purpose to dwell on the detail of Abravanel's arguments. One point only must be stressed. After having devoted twenty-two chapters to defending Maimonides' compilation, Abravanel rather abruptly explains, in the two concluding chapters of his treatise, that a creed as such is incompatible with the character of Judaism as a divinely given law. For since any and every proposition of the law, any and every story, belief, or command contained in the law, immediately proceeds from revelation, all those propositions are of equal value, and none of them ought to be thought of as more fundamental than any other. Abravanel does not think that by holding this opinion he is in conflict with the teaching of Maimonides; strangely enough, he asserts that that opinion was shared by Maimonides himself. According to Abravanel, Maimonides selected the thirteen more general articles of belief for the use of the vulgar only, who are unable to grasp the whole doctrine of faith. To prove this statement, he contends that Maimonides mentioned those articles only in his *Commentary on the Mishnah*, i.e., in an elementary work which he wrote in his youth, but not in the *Guide*, in which he treats the philosophy of the Jewish law in a scientific way. Now this contention is not only wrong, but it is contradicted by Abravanel himself. He asserts, in the same treatise,[12] that the articles of belief—the first eleven out of the thirteen explicitly, the last two implicitly—occur as such in the philosophical first part of Maimonides' codification of the Jewish law (in the "Hilkhot Yesodei ha-Torah"); and in another writing of his,[13] he explains the decisive influence exercised by the articles of belief on the whole composition of the *Guide*. But however this may be, it is certain that Abravanel, by denying the possibility of distinguishing between fundamental and nonfundamental beliefs, actually undermines

---

11. *Rosh Amanah*, ch. 10. [See *Principles of Faith*, trans. Kellner, chap. 10, pp. 98–105, and especially pp. 100–102.]

12. Ibid., ch. 19. [See *Principles of Faith*, trans. Kellner, chap. 19, pp. 166–72, and especially p. 168: "By careful study of those chapters in 'Hilkhot Yesodei ha-Torah,' you will find references to all the principles and foundations. They are not presented here, however, in the same order in which they are presented in the *Commentary on the Mishnah*, according to the intention of each place, as I have indicated."]

13. *Ma'amar Katzer be-Bi'ur Sod ha-Moreh*. [See Isaac Abravanel, "Short Treatise in Elucidation of the Secret Meaning of the *Guide*" (in Hebrew). It is printed at the end of the standard traditional edition, with numerous printings, of *Sefer Moreh ha-Nevukhim*, trans. Samuel ibn Tibbon, with the commentaries of Efodi (i.e., Profiat Duran), Shem Tov ben Joseph, Asher Crescas, and Isaac Abravanel, pp. 73a–74b in the standard edition pagination of part 3 (Warsaw, 1872; reprint, Jerusalem, 1960).]

the whole structure of the philosophy of the Jewish law which was built up by Maimonides.[14] Abravanel has sometimes been blamed for the inconsistency of his thought. I cannot praise him as a very consistent thinker. But a certain consistency ought not to be denied him. Accepting the literal teaching of Maimonides' *Guide* and trying to correct that teaching in the sense of the traditional Jewish beliefs, he was consistent enough to draw the final conclusion from his premises: he contested, if only occasionally, the foundation on which every philosophy of the law divine ultimately rests. However deeply he may have been influenced by the philosophical tradition in general and by the philosophical teaching of Maimonides in particular, his thought was decisively determined, not by philosophy, but by Judaism as a tradition based on a verbally inspired revelation.

The unphilosophic, to some extent even antiphilosophic, traditionalism of Abravanel accounts for the fact that for him political philosophy loses the central importance which it had for Maimonides. From what has been said about Maimonides' philosophy of Judaism, it will have appeared that the significance which he actually attaches to political philosophy is in exact proportion to his rationalism: identifying the fundamental beliefs of Judaism with the fundamental tenets of philosophy means at the same time interpreting the beliefs peculiar to Judaism in terms of political philosophy; and it means, in principle, interpreting Judaism as a whole as a perfect law in the Platonic sense. Accordingly, a follower of Maimonides, who rejected the thoroughgoing rationalism of the latter, as did Abravanel, deprived by this very fact political philosophy of all its dignity. One cannot raise the objection against this assertion that the Christian scholastics, while far from being radical rationalists, did indeed cultivate political philosophy. For the case of those scholastics who were citizens of existing states was obviously quite different from the case of the Jewish medieval thinkers. For a medieval Jew, political philosophy could have no other field of application than the Jewish law. Consequently, the value which political philosophy could have for him was entirely dependent on how far he would accept philosophy in general

---

14. Cf. in this connection, [i.e.,] Abravanel's criticism of Maimonides' explanation of the Mosaic laws, see his commentary on I Kings 3:14 (fol. 210, col. 2) and his commentary on Deut. 12:28 (fol. 286, col. 4). (I have used Abravanel's commentary on the Pentateuch in the Hanau edition of 1710.) Cf. also his criticism of Gersonides' method of drawing maxims out of the biblical narratives in the introduction to the commentary on Joshua (fol. 5, col. 2). [For Abravanel's criticism of Gersonides' method of reading which issues in maxims, see Eric Lawee, "Isaac Abarbanel: From Medieval to Renaissance Jewish Biblical Scholarship," in *Hebrew Bible/Old Testament: The History of Its Interpretation*, vol. II, *From the Renaissance to the Enlightenment*, ed. Magne Saebo (Göttingen: Vandenhoeck & Ruprecht, 2008), pp. 190–214.]

and political philosophy in particular as a clue to the understanding of the Jewish law. Now according to Maimonides, the prophet who brought the law is a philosopher statesman, and at least the greater part of the Mosaic law is concerned with the "government of the city."[15] Abravanel, on the other hand, denies that philosophy in general is of the essence of prophecy. As regards political philosophy in particular, he declares that the prophet does not stoop to such "low" things as politics and economics. He stresses in this connection the fact that the originator of the biblical organization of jurisdiction was not Moses, but Jethro.[16] In making these statements, Abravanel does not contest that Moses, as well as the other prophets, exercised a kind of government. As we shall see later, he even asserts this expressly. But he obviously does not accept the view, presupposed by Maimonides, that prophetic government is a legitimate subject of political philosophy. Political philosophy, as he understands it, has a much more restricted field than it had for Maimonides; it is much more of the Aristotelian than of the Platonic type.[17] Abravanel's depreciation of political philosophy, which is a consequence of his critical attitude towards Maimonides' rationalism, thus implies a decisive limitation of the content of political philosophy.

Political philosophy, as outlined by Maimonides, had dealt with three main topics: the prophet, the king, and the Messiah. According to Maimonides, the prophet as such is a philosopher statesman, and the highest prophet, Moses, was that philosopher statesman who was able to give the perfect, and consequently eternal, unchangeable law.[18] As regards kingship, Maimonides teaches that the institution of a king is indispensable, and expressly commanded by the Mosaic law. The king is subordinate to the lawgiver; his func-

---

15. *Guide* 3.27-28. [See *Guide*, trans. Pines, 3.27-28, pp. 510-14.]

16. Commentary on I Kings 3:14 (fol. 211, col. 1). Cf. however the commentary on Exodus 18:13-27 (fol. 134, col. 2-3). [For Abravanel's comments on Jethro (Exodus 18:13-27), see *Medieval Political Philosophy*, ed. Lerner and Mahdi, pp. 259-61. For further discussion on the theme of Jethro in Abravanel, see also Avraham Melamed, "Jethro's Advice in Medieval and Early Modern Jewish and Christian Political Thought," *Jewish Political Studies Review* 2, no. 1-2 (Spring 5750/1990): 3-41.]

17. As regards Abravanel's knowledge of Aristotle's *Politics*, see J. F. Baer, "Don Yitzchak Abravanel[: His Relation to Problems of History and Politics]," in *Tarbiz* vol. 8, nos. 3-4 (June 1937): [241-59, and especially pp.] 241f., 245 n. 11, and 248. See also below, n. 47. [See now Avraham Melamed, "Isaac Abravanel and Aristotle's *Politics*: A Drama of Errors," *Jewish Political Studies Review* 5, nos. 3-4 (Fall 1993): 55-75. Melamed arrives at the firm result, through careful research, which Strauss offers only as a surmise: Abravanel did not know the *Politics* at firsthand, but made contact with it only through secondary sources, such as the commentary by Thomas Aquinas. See also below in the present chapter.] In his commentary on Genesis 10:1ff. (fol. 40, col. 1), Abravanel seems occasionally to adopt the Aristotelian doctrine of natural masters and servants.

18. Cf. *Guide* 1.54 with 2.39-40. [See *Guide*, trans. Pines, 1.54, pp. 123-28, with 2.39-40, pp. 378-85.]

tion is to force men to obedience to the law, to establish justice, and to be the military leader. He himself is bound by the law, and therefore subject both to punishment in case of transgression of the law and to instruction by the supreme court, the guardians of the law. The king has extraordinary powers in case of urgent necessity, and his claims both to honor and to glory are acknowledged by the law.[19] The Messiah, as Maimonides conceives of him, is in the first instance a king, obedient to the law, and a successful military leader, who will rescue Israel from servitude, restore the kingdom of David in the country of Israel, establish universal peace, and thus create, for the first time in history, the ideal earthly condition for a life devoted to knowledge. But the Messiah is not only a king; he is at the same time a prophet of a rank not much inferior to that of the lawgiver Moses: the Messiah, too, is a philosopher king. Even according to the literal teaching of Maimonides, the Messiah does not work miracles, and the messianic age in general does not witness any alteration of the ordinary course of nature. It goes almost without saying that that age is not the prelude to the end of the visible world: the present world will remain in existence forever.[20] Thus we may define the distinctive features of Maimonides' messianology by saying that messianism, as he accepts it, is a rational hope rather than a superrational belief.[21] Maimonides' rationalism accounts in particular for the fact that he stresses so strongly the character of the Messiah as a successful military leader—he does this most definitely by inserting his thematic treatment of messianology within that section of his great legal work which deals with "the kings and their wars." For military ability or deficiency seems to be the decisive natural reason for the rise or decline of states. Maimonides, at any rate, thinks that the reason for the destruction of the Jewish state in the past was the neglect of the arts of war and

19. See *Guide* 2.40; 3.41 (Munk, p. 91a) and 3.45 (Munk, p. 98b), as well as "Hilkhot Melakhim" I, 3 and 8; III, passim; IV, 10, and V, 2. [For "Hilkhot Melakhim," see "Laws Concerning Kings and Wars," trans. Hershman, pp. 207 (I, 3), 209 (I, 8), 212–14 (III, passim), 216 (IV, 10), and 217 (V, 2). See *Guide*, trans. Pines, 2.40, pp. 381–85; 3.41, p. 562, and 3.45, p. 576.]
20. "Hilkhot Melakhim" XI–XII; "Hilkhot Teshuvah" IX; *Guide* 2.29. ["Laws Concerning Kings and Wars," trans. Hershman, pp. 238–42 (XI–XII). For "Hilkhot Teshuvah," see "Laws of Repentance," trans. Hyamson, pp. 91a–92a (IX). See also *Guide*, trans. Pines, 2.29, pp. 344–46.]
21. Notice the distinction between "belief" and "hope" in "Hilkhot Melakhim" XI, 1. ["Laws Concerning Kings and Wars," trans. Hershman, pp. 238–39 (XI, 1). In the key sentence, neither Maimonides' original Hebrew nor Hershman's English translation can be read quite precisely to contain the literal word "hope," to which Strauss points as a significant Maimonidean distinction. (It no doubt contains the word "belief.") However, one may say that this is a possible implication drawn from Maimonides' words. To bring such a possible implication to light with greater clarity, one might translate the sentence (unlike Hershman) as follows: "Anyone who does not believe in it (i.e., those matters previously stated which pertain to the King Messiah), or who does not wait (i.e., hope) for his coming, denies not only the teachings of the prophets, but also the Torah of Moses our teacher."]

conquest.[22] Accordingly, he expects that military virtue and military ability will play a decisive part in the future restoration of the Jewish state.[23]

It is a necessary consequence of Abravanel's antirationalist premises that he must exclude the two most exalted topics of Maimonides' political philosophy from the field of political philosophy properly speaking altogether. As regards the prophets, the prophetic lawgiver, and the law divine, he takes away their treatment from political philosophy by contesting the assertions of Maimonides that prophecy is a natural phenomenon,[24] and that philosophy belongs to the essence of prophecy.[25] For by denying this, he destroys the foundation of Maimonides' conception of the prophet as a philosopher statesman. The leadership of the prophet, as Abravanel sees it, is, just as prophecy itself is, of an essentially supernatural, and thus of an essentially superpolitical character. As regards the Messiah, Abravanel devoted to this theme a much more detailed and a much more passionate treatment than Maimonides had done.[26] Indeed, as we are informed by a most competent historian, Abravanel stressed in his writings the messianic hopes more than any other Jewish medieval author, and he was the first to give the messianic beliefs of Israel a systematic form.[27] This increase of the interest in eschatological speculation is explained by the fact that Abravanel was a contempo-

---

22. See his letter to the community at Marseilles. [See "Letter on Astrology," trans. Lerner, pp. 178–87, and especially pp. 179–80. See also "Note on Maimonides' *Letter on Astrology*," chap. 14 above.]

23. I am not competent to judge whether Maimonides' legal treatment of kings and wars is influenced by the Islamic conception of the "holy war." But it is certain that his stressing the importance of military virtue in his philosophic prophetology was influenced by the prophetology of the Islamic philosophers, who attach a much higher value to war and to the virtue of courage than Plato and Aristotle had done. Cf. *Revue des Études Juives* 100 (1936), pp. 19f. and 35f. [See "Some Remarks on the Political Science of Maimonides and Farabi," chap. 5 below, sixth paragraph of section II, and n. 59. See also, for related and pertinent discussion, Joel L. Kraemer, "The *Jihad* of the *Falasifa*," *Jerusalem Studies in Arabic and Islam* 10 (1987): 288–324. Consider also *Jihad in Medieval and Modern Islam: The Chapter on Jihad from Averroes' Legal Handbook "Bidayat al-Mudjtahid,"* ed. and trans. Rudolph Peters (Leiden: E. J. Brill, 1977).]

24. See Abravanel's commentary on *Guide* 2.32. [For translations of Abravanel's discussion and criticism of Maimonides' definition of prophecy as it appears in his commentary on *Guide* 2.32, see Alvin J. Reines, *Maimonides and Abrabanel on Prophecy* (Cincinnati: Hebrew Union College Press, 1970), pp. 1–27.]

25. See, for example, commentary on I Kings 3:14 (fol. 210, col. 4).

26. In this connection, the fact has to be mentioned that some prophecies which, according to Maimonides, were fulfilled in the past, i.e., at a time comparatively near to their announcement, are interpreted by Abravanel as messianic prophecies. Cf. the interpretation given in *Guide* 2.29, of Isaiah 24:17ff. and Joel 3:3–5, with Abravanel's explanations of those passages in his commentary on the later prophets.

27. Baer, loc. cit., pp. 257–59. [This is a historical judgment that has been confirmed by Gershom Scholem: see n. 29 below. For a very different approach than Strauss's to Abravanel's messianism, see Eric Lawee, "The Messianism of Isaac Abarbanel, 'Father of the [Jewish] Messianic Movements of the Sixteenth and Seventeenth Centuries,'" in *Millenarianism and Messianism in Early Modern European Culture*, vol. 1, *Jewish Messianism in the Early Modern World*, ed. Matthew Goldish and Richard H. Popkin (Dordrecht: Kluwer, 2001), pp. 1–39.]

rary of the greatest revolutions in the history of the Jewish diaspora, and of that great revolution of European civilization which is called the end of the Middle Ages and the beginning of the modern period. Abravanel expected the coming of the Messiah in the near future. He saw signs of its imminence in all the characteristic features of his time, from the increase of heresies and unbelief down to the appearance of the "French disease."[28] Reflections of this kind show that his messianistic view was not, as was at least to some extent that of Maimonides, of an evolutionist, but of a catastrophic character. It is hardly necessary to add that the messianic age is for Abravanel a period rich in miracles, the most impressive of them being the resurrection of the dead. That age, which is the age of universal peace, even among the animals, as predicted by Isaiah, lasts only for a limited time; it is followed by the end of the present world.[29] It is preceded by a most terrible war, the final war. That war is, however, not so much a war of liberation, fought and won by Israel as Maimonides had taught; it is rather an event like the capture of Jericho, as told in the book of Joshua: Israel is a looker-on at the victory rather than the

---

28. That disease is, according to Abravanel, probably meant in Zechariah 14:12 (see his commentary on that passage). [For Zechariah 14:12,

But this shall be the plague wherewith the Lord will smite all the peoples that have warred against Jerusalem: their flesh shall consume away while they stand upon their feet, and their eyes shall consume away in their sockets, and their tongue shall consume away in their mouth.

It is what the Italians of the sixteenth century called "the French disease," and what the French of the sixteenth century called "the Italian disease," i.e., syphilis.]

29. See Gershom Scholem's remark in *Encyclopedia Judaica* vol. IX, col. 688. [Strauss was obviously not referring to the well-known English language *Encyclopedia Judaica* (Jerusalem: Keter, 1972), since the appearance of Strauss's article on Abravanel much preceded it. Instead he refers to the unfinished German-language *Encyclopedia Judaica* (Berlin: Eshkol, 1928–34), ed. Jakob Klatzkin and Ismar Elbogen. Its first ten volumes appeared in print (from Aach to Lyra), but work on the project was halted because of the persecution of the Jews in Nazi Germany. Gershom Scholem did not write the equivalent entry for the English-language *Encyclopedia Judaica*. The present editor was unfortunately not able to obtain access to a copy of the original *Encyclopedia Judaica* in order to check the German-language passage to which Strauss refers. But in his article, "Toward an Understanding of the Messianic Idea in Judaism," Scholem makes the following comment, the last phrase of which addresses the point being made by Strauss (as well as further confirming the point Strauss made in n. 27):

The most important codifications of the messianic idea in later Judaism are the writings of Isaac Abravanel (circa 1500) and *The Victory of Israel* [or *The Eternity of Israel*, i.e., *Netzah Yisrael*] by the "High Rabbi Loew," Judah Loew ben Bezalel of Prague (1599). The authors are not visionaries but writers who endeavor to embrace as a whole the legacy of ideas which has been transmitted in such contradictory traditions. Despite their otherwise reticent manner, they richly avail themselves of the apocalyptic traditions.

See *The Messianic Idea in Judaism and Other Essays in Jewish Spirituality* (New York: Schocken, 1971), p. 33.]

victor.³⁰ Accordingly in Abravanel's description of the Messiah,³¹ the military abilities and virtues are, to say the least, not predominant.³² To him, the Messiah is certainly much more a worker of miracles than a military leader: the Messiah, not less than the prophets, belongs to the sphere of miracles, not of politics. Abravanel's messianology as well as his prophetology are essentially unpolitical doctrines.³³

Now these unpolitical doctrines belong, as it were, to the framework of what Abravanel himself would have called his political teaching, i.e., of his discussion of the best form of human government as distinguished from divine government. Since the unpolitical framework was to Abravanel doubtless incomparably more important than its political content, and since, besides, the understanding of the former is indispensable for the right appreciation of the latter, it will be proper for us to describe the background of his political teaching somewhat more exactly than we have done up to now. That background is not only of an unpolitical, but even of an antipolitical character. As has been shown recently by Professor [Yizḥak] Baer,³⁴ Abravanel takes over

---

30. The "realistic" element of Abravanel's conception of the final war, i.e., his identification of the final war with the war which he thought to be imminent between the Christian nations of Europe and the Turks for Palestine, does not change the character of his conception as a whole. [For further discussion of Abravanel's messianic "realism," see Eric Lawee, "'Israel Has No Messiah' in Late Medieval Spain," *Journal of Jewish Thought and Philosophy* 5 (1995): 245–79, and especially pp. 275–76.]

31. See his commentary on Isaiah 11.

32. Those qualities, I venture to suggest, are ascribed by Abravanel not so much to *the* Messiah (i.e., the Messiah ben David) as to the Messiah ben Joseph, a midrashic figure, not mentioned by Maimonides.

33. Restating the genuine teaching of the Bible against Maimonides' rationalistic and therefore political teaching, Abravanel goes sometimes farther in the opposite direction than does the Bible itself. The most striking example of this which occurs to me is his interpretation of Judges 1:19—Judah "could not drive out the inhabitants of the valley, because they had chariots of iron." Abravanel explains this passage in the following way: "Judah could not drive out the inhabitants of the valley, *not* because they had chariots of iron."

As regards the difference between Maimonides' political teaching and Abravanel's unpolitical teaching, I have to emphasize the following example. According to Maimonides, the main reason for the fact (told in Exodus 13:17f.) that God did not lead Israel on the direct way, through Philistia, to Palestine, was His intention of educating them in courage (*Guide* 3.24, p. 53a, and 3.32, pp. 70b–71a). According to Abravanel, on the other hand, the main reason was His intention to divide the sea for Israel and to drown the Egyptians (and there was no sea on the way through Philistia); see commentary on the passage (fol. 125, cols. 1–2). [See *Guide*, trans. Pines, 3.24, pp. 499–500, and 3.32, pp. 527–28.]

34. Loc. cit., pp. 248–53. I have to make only some slight additions to the ample evidence adduced by Baer: (a) Abravanel's description of the innocent life in the first period as a life "in the field" (Baer, p. 252) is literally taken over from Seneca, *Epistle* 90, § 42 (*agreste domicilium*). [See Seneca, *Epistles*, trans. Richard M. Gummere (Cambridge, MA: Harvard University Press, 1920), pp. 394–430, letter 90, "On the Role Played by Philosophy in the Progress of Man": *agreste domicilium* or "rude homes" (pp. 426–27).] (b) Abravanel uses in his commentary on Genesis 11:1ff. (fol. 42, col. 2) the doctrine of Posidonius, discussed by Seneca, of the government of the best and wisest men in the Golden Age, in a modified form;

from Seneca's 90th letter the criticism there developed of human civilization in general (of the "artificial" and "superfluous" things) and of the city in particular. Following Josephus and the Christian Fathers, he combines that Hellenistic teaching with the teaching, in important respects similar, of the first chapters of Genesis. He conceives of urban life and of coercive government, as well as of private property, as productions of human rebellion against the natural order instituted by God: the only life in accordance with nature is a state of liberty and equality of all men, and the possession in common of the natural goods, or, as he seems to suggest at another place,[35] the life "in the field," of independent families. This criticism of all political, "artificial" life does not mean that Abravanel intends to replace the conception of the city as of something "artificial" by the conception of the nation as of something "natural"; for, according to Abravanel, the existence of nations, i.e., the disruption of the one human race into a plurality of nations, is not less "artificial," not less a result of sin, than is the existence of cities.[36] Thus, his criticism of political organization is truly all-comprehensive. And the ultimate reason of this antipolitical view is Abravanel's antirationalism, the predominance in his thought of the belief in miracles. It is true he accepts the classical teaching

---

he says that in the first period of the world, divine providence extended itself without any intermediary over mankind, and that, therefore, there were then always wise men, versed in theology. Cf. also Seneca, *Epistle* 90, § 44. [See letter 90, trans. Gummere, para. 44, pp. 428–29: "But no matter how excellent and guileless was the life of the men of that age, they were not wise men; for that title is reserved for the highest achievement. Still, I would not deny that they were men of lofty spirit and—if I may use the phrase—fresh from the gods. For there is no doubt that the world produced a better progeny before it was yet worn out. However, not all were endowed with mental faculties of highest perfection, though in all cases their native powers were more sturdy than ours and more fitted for toil. For nature does not bestow virtue; it is an art to become good." (44. Sed quamvis egregia illis vita fuerit et carens fraude, non fuere sapientes, quando hoc iam in opere maximo nomen est. Non tamen negaverim fuisse alti spiritus viros et, ut ita dicam, a dis recentes; neque enim dubium est quin meliora mundus nondum effetus ediderit. Quemadmodum autem omnibus indoles fortior fuit et ad labores paratior, ita non erant ingenia omnibus consummata. Non enim dat natura virtutem: ars est bonum fieri.)] (c) The criticism of Cain as the first founder of the city (Baer, p. 251) is to be found also in Josephus, *Jewish Antiquities* I, § 62. [See Josephus, *Jewish Antiquities*, books I–IV, trans. Henry St. J. Thackeray (Cambridge, MA: Harvard University Press, 1965), Volume IV of the *Loeb Complete Works of Josephus*, pp. 28–29.] (d) Abravanel uses the general criticism of civilization most properly in his interpretation of Exodus 20:25 (fol. 143, col. 1). (e) The distinction between the three ways of life (the bestial, the political, and the theoretical life) (Baer, p. 251) is obviously taken from Aristotle, *Nicomachean Ethics* 1095b17ff. That distinction had been applied to the three sons of Adam, in the same way as it is by Abravanel, by Maimonides; see *Guide* 2.30 and Efodi's commentary. [Efodi: "For there are, we may say, three prominent types of life—the (vulgar), the political, and thirdly the contemplative life. Now the mass of mankind are evidently quite slavish in their tastes, preferring a life suitable to beasts." See Aristotle, *Nicomachean Ethics*, trans. David Ross (London: Oxford University Press, 1925), 1095b17ff. The passage of Efodi in the standard editions is on pp. 62b–63b. See *Guide* 2.30, p. 357.]

35. Commentary on Gen. 11:1ff. (fol. 41, col. 1–2).

36. Ibid. (fol. 42, cols. 1–2). According to Abravanel's usage, "nation" often has the meaning of "religious community"; he speaks, for example, of the "Christian nation." See, e.g., *Ma'yenei ha-Yeshu'ah* xi, 8, and commentary on I Kings 15:6 (fol. 250, col. 3).

of man's "natural" way of life in the beginning, in the Golden Age. But that "natural" state is understood by Abravanel to be of an essentially miraculous character.[37] It is highly significant that he finds an analogy of man's "natural" state in the life led by Israel in the desert,[38] where Israel had to rely entirely for everything on miraculous providence. Abravanel, as it were, interprets the "life in the fields," praised by Seneca and the Bucolics, in the spirit of Jeremiah's words (2:2): "I remember for thee the kindness of thy youth, the love of thine espousals; how thou wentest after me in the wilderness, in a land that was not sown." The "natural" state of mankind is in principle not less miraculous than the messianic age in which that natural state is to be restored. Maimonides, who held, to say the least, a rather hesitating attitude towards miracles, had adopted, without making any reservation apart from those made by Aristotle himself, the Aristotelian principle that man is naturally a political being; Abravanel, on the other hand, who unhesitatingly accepts all the miracles of the past and of the future, judges of man's political existence as being sinful in its origin, and not instituted, but only, as it were, reluctantly conceded to man, by God.[39] And, [as] he goes on to say, it is with the political and urban life as with the king.[40] That is to say, Abravanel's political teaching, his discussion of the value of monarchy, or more generally of the best form of human government, to which I am turning now, is only an application, if the most interesting application, of his fundamental conception, which is strictly antipolitical.

Abravanel deals with the question of the best form of human government in his commentaries both on Deut. 17:14f., i.e., on the law which seems to command to Israel the institution of a king, and to I Sam. 8:6f., i.e., on the narration that God and the prophet Samuel were offended by the fact that Israel did ask Samuel for a king.[41] The question is for Abravanel thus primarily

37. Cf. above n. 34, point (b), with commentary on Joshua 10:12 (fol. 21, col. 3).
38. Commentary on Genesis 11:1ff. (fol. 41, col. 3). Cf. also commentary on Exodus 18:13-27 (fol. 134, col. 2) on the connection between the absence of slavery among the Israelites while they were wandering through the desert (i.e., between their being then in a state of "natural" equality) and their miraculous maintenance by the manna.
39. Bound by Genesis 2:18, however, he occasionally adopts that Aristotelian proposition. See Baer, loc. cit., pp. 249f.
40. Commentary on Genesis 11:1ff. (fol. 41, col. 3).
41. The treatment of the question is in both versions (in the earlier version in the commentary on I Samuel 8:6f. [fol. 91, col. 2; fol. 93, col. 4], and in the later version in the commentary on Deuteronomy 17:14f. [fol. 295, col. 2; fol. 296, col. 2]) identical as regards the tendency, and even, to a large extent, literally identical. The earlier version is the more important as regards the details of the criticism of kingship; but only the later version provides us with an insight into Abravanel's conception of the ideal government as a whole: his explanation of Deuteronomy 17:14f. is only the continuation of his statements concerning the government of the Jewish nation in general, which are to be found in his interpretation of Deuter-

an exegetical one: how are the two apparently opposed passages of the Bible to be reconciled? Proceeding in the scholastic way, Abravanel begins with surveying and criticizing the earlier attempts, made by Jews and Christians,[42] to solve that exegetical problem. He shows that all those attempts, in spite of their divergencies, and apart from the individual deficiencies of each of them, are based on one and the same decisive assumption. All the earlier commentators mentioned by Abravanel assumed that Israel's asking for a king was a sin, not as such, but only because of the manner or circumstances of their demand. In other words, those commentators presupposed that Deut. 17:14f. expresses a divine command to institute a king. This, however, includes the further presupposition that monarchy is a good, nay, that it is the best form of human government; for God would not have given His nation any political constitution but the best. Consequently, Abravanel has to discuss first whether monarchy is indeed the best form of human government, and secondly whether the meaning of Deut. 17:14f. is that Israel is commanded to institute a king.

The first discussion is a criticism, based on reason only, of the monarchist teaching of *the* philosophers, i.e., of Aristotle[43] and his medieval followers. That discussion is, unfortunately, far from being of scholastic orderliness and precision.[44] But the main argument is quite clear. The philosophers who are criticized by Abravanel asserted the necessity of monarchic government by comparing the relation of the king to the political community with the relation of the heart to the human body, and with the relation of the First Cause to the universe.[45] Against such kinds of proof Abravanel objects that

---

onomy 16:18ff. These statements have not been taken into account by Baer, nor by Ephraim E. Urbach, "Die Staatsauffassung des Don Isaak Abrabanel," in *Monatsschrift für Geschichte und Wissenschaft des Judentums* 81 (1937): 257–70, who come, therefore, to conclusions more or less different from those set forth in the present article. [For an English translation of Abravanel's commentary on Deut. 17:14–20, see "On Kingship," in *Abravanel on the Torah: Selected Themes*, ed. and trans. Avner Tomaschoff (Jerusalem: Jewish Agency for Israel, 2007), pp. 421–40. For some of what Abravanel writes on kingship in his commentary on I Samuel 8, see *Medieval Political Philosophy*, ed. Lerner and Mahdi, pp. 265–68; for some of his comments on Deuteronomy 17, see in the same book, pp. 261–64.]

42. The three opinions of Christian commentators, which are dealt with in the earlier version, are not, however, discussed in the later version.

43. See commentary on I Samuel 8:6f. (fol. 92, col. 1).

44. It has been made somewhat more lucid in the later version.

45. Those comparisons were known to Abravanel not only from Christian sources, but also and primarily from Jewish and Islamic ones. In his commentary on Exodus 18:13–27 (fol. 134, col. 2) he expressly refers to Farabi's *Principles of the Beings* (i.e., to the Hebrew translation of *k. al-siyyasat al-madaniyya*) as proving the necessity of hierarchy leading up to one chief, and in the sentence immediately following that reference, he mentions the examples of the hierarchy in the human body, and of the universal hierarchy which leads up to the First Cause. (Cf. Farabi, loc. cit., ed. Hyderabad, 1346 A.H., p. 54, and *Musterstaat*, ed. F. Dieterici, pp. 54ff. See also Maimonides, *Guide* 1.72.) In the passage mentioned, Abravanel accepts

they are based on a *metabasis eis allos genos* [shifting from one genus to another], on a *metabasis* from things natural and necessary to things merely possible and subject to the human will. Those philosophers tried further to prove the necessity of monarchic government by contending that the three indispensable conditions of well-ordered government are fulfilled only in a monarchy. Those conditions are: unity, continuity, and absolute power. As regards unity, Abravanel states that it may well be achieved by the consent of many governors.[46] As regards continuity, he doubts whether the annual change of governors, who have to answer for their conduct of public affairs after the expiration of their office, and who are, therefore, restrained by "fear of flesh and blood" (*mora' basar va-dam*) and by their being ashamed of their crimes becoming publicly denounced and punished, is not much to be preferred to the irresponsible, though continuous, government of one. As regards absolute power, Abravanel denies altogether that it is indispensable or desirable: the power of the governors ought to be limited by the laws. He adduces further in favor of the government of many, the principle of majority, as accepted by the Jewish law in matters of the interpretation of the law, and the statement made by Aristotle "in the beginning of the *Metaphysics*" that the truth is more easily reached by the collaboration of many than by the exertions of one.[47] After having thus disposed of the philosophic arguments in

---

those examples and the monarchist consequence derived from them, while he rejects them in his commentary on Deuteronomy 17:14f. and on I Samuel 8:6f. [See Farabi, "The Political Regime," trans. Najjar, in *Medieval Political Philosophy*, ed. Lerner and Mahdi, pp. 39–40; *Perfect State*, trans. Walzer, pp. 230–33. In the sentence to follow, Strauss speaks of Abravanel's use of a logical argument to refute the philosophers among his exegetical opponents in biblical interpretation with regard to anointing a king: he claims they commit a *metabasis eis allos genos* by allowing themselves to compare a king in the city to the First Cause of the universe. This is the error in logic of an unacknowledged shift from one genus to another, that being a most serious error if one is trying to genuinely demonstrate a truth. See Aristotle, *Posterior Analytics*, bk. 1, chap. 7, 75a38–75b20.]

46. Cf. Marsilius of Padua, *Defensor pacis*, lib. I, cap. 15, § 2. [See Marsilius of Padua, *Defensor pacis*, trans. Alan Gewirth (New York: Columbia University Press, 1956, 2001), discourse 1, chap. XV, § 2, pp. 61–62.]

47. The passage which Abravanel has in mind is the beginning of *Metaphysics* α or II (993a30–993b19). I wonder why he did not quote such more suitable passages as *Politics* III, 16 (1287b), and VII, 14 (1332b–1333a). It may be that he knew the *Politics* only from quotations. [For whether Abravanel knew the *Politics*, see Melamed, "Isaac Abravanel and Aristotle's *Politics*" (n. 17 above).]

[The investigation of the truth is in one way hard, in another easy. An indication of this is found in the fact that no one is able to attain the truth adequately, while, on the other hand, no one fails entirely, but every one says something true about the nature of things, and while individually they contribute little or nothing to the truth, by the union of all a considerable amount is amassed. Therefore, since the truth seems to be like the proverbial door, which no one can fail to hit, in this way it is easy, but the fact that we can have a whole truth and not the particular part we aim at shows the difficulty of it. Perhaps, as difficulties are of two kinds, the cause of the present difficulty is not in the facts but in us. For as the eyes of bats are to the blaze of day, so is the reason in our

favor of monarchy, Abravanel turns to the teaching of experience; for as Aristotle "has taught us," "experience prevails over the syllogism." Now the experience of the present shows that such states as Venice, Florence,[48] Genoa, Lucca, Siena, Bologna and others, which are governed, not by monarchs, but by "judges" elected for limited periods of office, are much superior to the monarchies, as regards both administration of justice and military achievements. And the experience of the past teaches that Rome, when governed by consuls, conquered the world, while it declined under the emperors. In eloquent sentences which betray a deep hatred of kings and their ways, Abravanel contrasts the admirable character of classical or modern republics with the horrors of monarchies. He arrives at the conclusion that the existence of a king is not only not necessary for a political community, but that it is even

---

soul to the things which are by nature most evident of all. It is just that we should be grateful, not only to those whose opinion we may share, but also to those who have expressed more superficial views; for these also contributed something, by developing before us the powers of thought. It is true that if there had been no Timotheus we should have been without much of our lyric poetry; but if there had been no Phrynis there would have been no Timotheus. The same holds good of those who have expressed views about the truth; for from the better thinkers we have inherited certain opinions, while the others have been responsible for the appearance of the better thinkers. (See *Metaphysics*, trans. W. D. Ross, in *The Complete Works of Aristotle*, ed. Jonathan Barnes [Princeton: Princeton University Press, 1984], α or II 993a30–993b19, vol. 2, pp. 1569–70.)]

48. Cf. Leonardo Bruni, *Oratio in funere Nannis Strozae* (in Baluzius, *Miscellanea*, III, pp. 230ff.): "Forma reipublicae gubernandae utimur ad libertatem paritatemque civium maxime omnium directa: quae quia aequalissima in omnibus est, popularis nuncupatur. Neminem unum quasi dominum horremus, non paucorum potentiae inservimus.... Monarchiae laus veluti ficta quaedam et umbratilis (est), non autem expressa et solida.... Nec multum secus accidit in dominatu paucorum. Ita popularis una relinquitur legitima reipublicae gubernandae forma, in qua libertas vera sit, in qua aequitas juris cunctis pariter civibus, in qua virtutum studia vigere absque suspicione possint.... Ingeniis vero ac intelligentia sic valent cives nostri ut in ea quidem laude pares non multi, qui vero anteponendi sint, nulli reperiantur. Acritas quidem inest atque industria, et in rebus agendis celeritas et agilitas, animique magnitudo rebus sufficiens. Nec in moderata republica solum nec in domestica tantum disciplina ... valemus, sed etiam bellica gloria insignes sumus. Nam majores quidem nostri ... finitimos omnes populos virtute bellica superarunt.... Nostra semper civitas ... scientissimos rei militaris duces procreavit." ["The constitution we use for the government of the republic is designed for the liberty and equality of indeed all the citizens. Since it is egalitarian in all respects, it is called a 'popular' constitution. We do not tremble beneath the rule of one man who would lord it over us, nor are we slaves to the rule of the few.... This is why praise of monarchy has something fictitious and shadowy about it, and lacks precision and solidity.... Nor is it very different under the rule of the few. Thus the only legitimate constitution left is the popular one, in which liberty is real, in which legal equity is the same for all citizens, in which pursuit of the virtues may flourish without suspicion.... In talent and intelligence our citizens are so capable that they have few equals, and no superiors. They possess shrewdness and industry, and an ability to do things with speed and agility, and sufficient breadth of conception for the proper conduct of affairs.... We also have a reputation for military glory.... For our ancestors ... with their warlike virtue conquered all their neighbors. ... Our city has moreover ... produced the leaders best versed in military science." See "Oration for the Funeral of Nanni Strozzi," in *The Humanism of Leonardi Bruni: Selected Texts*, trans. Gordon Griffiths, James Hankin, and David Thompson (Binghamton, NY: Medieval and Renaissance Texts and Studies, 1987), pp. 124–26.]

an enormous danger and a great harm to it, and that the origin of kingdoms is not the free election of the king by the people, but force and violence.[49]

In spite of his strong indictment of monarchic government, Abravanel no less strongly contends that, if in a country a monarchy exists, the subjects are bound to strict obedience to the king. He informs us that he has not seen in the writings of Jews a discussion of the question whether the people has the right to rebel against the king, or to depose him in case the king becomes a tyrant, and that the Christian scholars who did discuss that question, decided that the people had such a right, according to the classical precedent of the defection of the ten tribes from Rehoboam. Abravanel, who had spoken about this subject "before kings with their wise men," judges that the people has no right to rebellion or deposition, even if the king commits every crime. For the people has, when crowning the king, made a covenant with him by which it promised to him obedience; "and that covenant and oath was not conditional, but absolute; and therefore he who rebels against the king is guilty of death, whether the king is righteous or wicked; for it is not the people that inquires into the king's righteousness or wickedness." Besides, the king represents God; he is an image of God as regards both absolute power (the extralegal actions of the king correspond to the miracles) and unity (the king is unique in his kingdom, as God is unique in His universe). The king is therefore entitled to a kind of honor which has something in common with

---

49. Cf. John of Salisbury, *Policraticus*, lib. IV, cap. 11: "Regum scrutare historiam, ad hoc petitum regem a Deo invenies, ut praecederet faciem populi. . . . Qui tamen non fuerat necessarius, nisi et Israel praevaricatus esset in similitudinem gentium, ut Deo rege sibi non videretur esse contentus. . . . Hospitem meum Placentinum dixisse recolo . . . hoc in civitatibus Italiae usu frequenti celeberrimum esse, quod dum pacem diligunt, et iustitiam colunt, et periuriis abstinent, tantae libertatis et pacis gaudio perfruuntur, quod nihil est omnino, quod vel in minimo quietem eorum concutiat. . . . Adiiciebat etiam quod merita populi omnem evacuant principatum, aut eum faciunt esse mitissimum. . . ." ["Scrutinize the history of kings, you will find that a king was sought from God for the reason that he might lead in the sight of the people. . . . Still he was not necessary, except that Israel was a transgressor in the manner of the Gentiles, insofar as it did not seem to be content with God for its king. . . . I recall that my host at Placentia, . . . had said that it was famous from the recurrent experiences of the Italian cities that so long as they cherished peace and cultivated justice and refrained from perjury, they enjoyed fully and rejoiced in such liberty and peace that there was nothing at all, or very little, which disturbed their calm. . . . He had also added that the merits of the people cancel all princely regimes or they are administered with the greatest mildness . . ."] See John of Salisbury, *Policraticus: Of the Frivolity of Courtiers and the Footprints of Philosophers*, trans. Cary J. Nederman (New York: Cambridge University Press, 1990), bk. IV, chap. 11 ("What utility princes may acquire from the cultivation of justice"), p. 60.] Ibid., lib. VIII, cap. 17: "Nisi enim iniquitas, et iniustitia . . . tyrannidem procurasset, omnino regna non essent, quae . . . iniquitas aut per se praesumpsit, aut extorsit a domino." ["For unless iniquity and injustice had advanced tyranny, . . . there would be absolutely no kingdoms, for . . . these were iniquitous in themselves; they either encroached upon or were extorted from God." See John of Salisbury, *Policraticus*, trans. Nederman, bk. VIII, chap. 17 ("In what way the tyrant differs from the prince; and of the tyranny of priests; and in what way a shepherd, a thief, and an employee differ from one another"), p. 191.]

the honor owed by man to God. Consequently, any attempt on the side of the people to depose or to punish their king, is in a sense sacrilegious.[50] It is obvious that the second argument is contradictory to the assertions made by Abravanel two or three pages earlier, in his discussion of the value of monarchy. It would, however, be unfair perhaps to so prolific a writer as Abravanel to attach too much stress to his inconsistencies; and in particular to the present inconsistency.[51] For if the second argument used by him in support of his thesis, that the people has no right to depose or punish a tyrannous king, is inconsistent with his denial of the value of monarchy, the thesis itself is perfectly consistent with his main contention, that monarchy as such is an enormous danger and a great evil.

Was, then, the political ideal of Abravanel the republic? He does not use a word which could be translated by "republic"; the kind of government which he praises is called by him government of "many." This is very vague indeed. The statements occurring in his criticism of monarchy might convey the impression that his ideal was democracy. But, as we shall see later, he accepted the doctrine of the necessity of a "mixed" constitution. Thus, his ideal cannot have been a "pure" constitution of any kind. I believe we would not be wide of the mark if we defined his political ideal by saying that it was, like that of Calvin[52] one or two generations later, an "aristocracy near to democracy."[53] But in order to avoid any hypothesis, we shall do best to confine ourselves to the statement that Abravanel's political ideal was the republic. For "republic" is a term of a polemic and negative character; it does not say more than "not

---

50. Commentary on Deuteronomy 17:16-20 (fol. 296, col. 4; fol. 297, col. 1). [For an English translation of Abravanel's commentary on Deut. 17:14-20, see "On Kingship," in *Abravanel on the Torah*, trans. Tomaschoff, pp. 421-40.] Abravanel further adduces a third argument which, however, applies to Jewish kings only. Cf. also his commentaries on Judges 4:9 (fol. 46, col. 1); on I Kings 2:37 (fol. 202, col. 3); on I Kings 13:2 (fol. 246, col. 1); and on I Kings 12 passim.

51. Cf. also above n. 45. Another example of this kind of inconsistency may be mentioned in passing. In his commentary on I Samuel 8:7 (fol. 93, col. 4), i.e., only two or three pages after he had finished the proof that the existence of a king is not necessary in any nation, Abravanel says: "the king is necessary for the other nations" (for all nations except Israel).

52. *Institutio*, lib. IV, cap. 20, § 8 (with regard to the Jewish commonwealth). [See John Calvin, *Institutes of the Christian Religion*, trans. Henry Beveridge (Edinburgh: T. and T. Clark, 1875; reprint, Grand Rapids, MI: Wm. B. Eerdmans, 1981), vol. II, bk. fourth, chap. XX, "Of Civil Government," para. 8, pp. 656-57. See also Baer, loc. cit., p. 259, and Lawee, "'Israel Has No Messiah,'" loc. cit., p. 257, n. 127.]

53. The aristocratic element in the ideal constitution, as conceived by Abravanel, i.e., of the Jewish constitution, is the *Synhedrion* [i.e., Sanhedrin] of 70. Cf. also commentary on Exodus 18:13-27 (fol. 134, col. 3). Abravanel's ideal is characterized as "*status aristocraticus*" [an aristocratic government] by Menasseh ben Israel, *Conciliator*, qu. 6, ad Deut. [17: 14, 5] (Frankfort, 1633, p. 227). [See Menasseh ben Israel, *The Conciliator: A Reconcilement of the Apparent Contradictions in Holy Scripture*, trans. Elias Hiam Lindo (London: Duncan and Malcolm, 1842; reprint, New York: Hermon Press, 1972), vol. I, pp. 285-89, and especially p. 288.]

monarchy," without defining whether that nonmonarchical government desired is democratic, aristocratic, oligarchic, and so on.[54] And what Abravanel says of the best form of human government is hardly more than just this: that it is unmonarchical.

But was the political ideal of Abravanel really the republican city-state? That this was the case is most unlikely from the outset. If it were the case, it would betray not only inconsistency—inconsistent Abravanel admittedly was—but even an almost insane looseness of thought. Indeed, it is inconceivable that the very man who, in accordance with his deepest theological convictions, judged the city to be the work of human wickedness, should have been at the same time a genuine and unreserved admirer of the worldly greatness of Rome and Venice. One cannot explain the contradiction by supposing that Abravanel was merely a humanist orator who was able to devote eloquent sentences to any subject. For, eloquent though he could be, he certainly was no sophist: he had a strong and sincere belief in the one truth. The only possible explanation is that Abravanel's admiration for the classical and modern city-states was not more than a tribute which he paid to the fashion of his time; that it was a sidetrack into which he was guided occasionally, if on more than one occasion, by the influence of humanism, but primarily by his disgust at kings and their worldly splendor, which had a deeper root than the humanist influence.

Before beginning to define the true character of Abravanel's political ideal, let us emphasize the fact that the exaltation of the republican city-state belongs to the discussion, based on reason only, of the best form of human government, i.e., to a mere prelude to the central discussion of it, which is based on the Scripture only. After what has been said about Abravanel's philosophical tendency, there is no need for a further proof of the assertion that only his interpretation of the teaching of the Scripture can provide us with his authentic conception of the ideal form of human government. What, then, does the Scripture teach concerning the human government of Israel?

This question is answered by Abravanel both precisely and lucidly. He begins by stating his thesis, which runs as follows: even if he granted that the king is useful and necessary in all other nations for the ordering of the

---

54. Cf. Montesquieu's definition in *De l'esprit des lois*, livre II, ch. 1. [See Montesquieu, *The Spirit of the Laws*, trans. Thomas Nugent (New York: Hafner Press, 1949), bk. II, chap. 1, p. 8: "There are three species of government: republican, monarchical, and despotic. . . . A republican government is that in which the body, or only a part of the people, is possessed of supreme power; monarchy, that in which a single person governs by fixed and established laws; a despotic government, that in which a single person directs everything by his own will and caprice. This is what I call the nature of each government."]

political community and for its protection—which, however, he does not grant, but even vigorously denies—even in that case the king would certainly not be necessary for the Jewish nation. For their king is God, and therefore they need, even incomparably less than the other nations, a king of flesh and blood. A king could be necessary for three purposes: for military leadership, for legislation, and for extraordinary power to punish the wicked. All those purposes are achieved in Israel in the most perfect way by God, who vouchsafes His particular providence to His elected nation. Thus, a king is not necessary in Israel. He is even most dangerous in Israel. Experience has shown that all the kings of Israel and most of the kings of Judah led Israel and Judah into idolatry, while the judges and the prophets were, all of them, God-fearing men. This proves that the leadership of "judges" is good, while that of kings is bad. The result, at which the discussion based on reason only had arrived, is confirmed by the scrutiny of the Scripture, and particularly of the biblical narratives. More exactly, that result has undergone, as a consequence of the scrutiny of the Bible, an important precision, which is at the same time an important correction: the ideal form of human government is not the republic as such, but a "republican" government, instituted and guided by God.[55]

Arrived at this point, Abravanel has yet to overcome the greatest difficulty. The earlier Jewish commentators, whose views he had criticized to begin with, were no less familiar with the innumerable passages of the Bible which attribute the kingship to God than he himself was. They also remembered, no less well than he did, the evil which Israel and Judah had experienced under their wicked kings. But they remembered also the deeds and words of such God-fearing kings as David, the author of many Psalms, as Solomon, the author of the Song of Songs, and as Jotham, Hezekiah, and Josiah, who were "saints of the Highest."[56] And even more important than this, the Messiah for whose speedy coming they prayed, was conceived of by them as a king. Now, as regards the last point, Abravanel was consistent enough to deny that the Messiah is a king properly speaking: the Messiah too is, according to him, not a king, but a prophet and a judge.[57] But this conception of the leadership of the Messiah is already based on the truly decisive assumption that the institution of a king in Israel was not expressly commanded by God. The earlier commentators were convinced that Deut. 17:14f. did express such a command. As long as the difficulty offered by that passage was not overcome,

---

55. See also Urbach, loc. cit., pp. 263f.
56. Cf. Abravanel's Introduction to his commentary on the Books of the Kings (fol. 188, col. 3).
57. See Baer, loc. cit., p. 259.

all other passages of the Bible which Abravanel might adduce in support of his thesis were of little weight. For none of those other passages contained a definite law concerning the institution of kingship in Israel.

Abravanel denies that Deut. 17:14f. expresses a command to institute a king in Israel. According to him, that passage merely gives permission to do this. We need not examine whether his interpretation is right or not. What matters for us is that the interpretation rejected by Abravanel was accepted as legally binding by Jewish tradition, which was as a rule decidedly in favor of monarchy. The traditional interpretation had been accepted in particular by Maimonides, who had embodied it in his great legal work [*Mishneh Torah*] as well as in his *Sefer ha-Mitzvot* [*Book of the Commandments*].[58]

[58]. It was accepted also, for example, by Naḥmanides, Moses of Coucy, Gersonides, and Baḥya ben Asher. (This is not to deny that Gersonides' and Baḥya's statements in their commentaries on Deuteronomy 17:14f. are almost as much antimonarchistic as those of Abravanel—there are a number of important literal concords between the statements of Abravanel and those of both Gersonides and Baḥya—but still, both of them interpret the passage in question as conveying a command to institute a king.) As far as I know, the only Jewish medieval commentator who, in his commentary on Deuteronomy 17:14ff., expressly understands that passage as conveying a permission is Ibn Ezra. The exceptional character of Abravanel's interpretation is implicitly recognized by Moses Hayyim Alsheikh (*Mar'ot ha-Tzove'ot*, on I Samuel 8:6f.), who vigorously rejects that interpretation by referring himself to the Jewish tradition, and expressly by Menasseh ben Israel (*Conciliator*, ed. cit., p. 228), who says "*Haec opinio* (i.e., *Abravanelis*) *quamvis satis congrua verbis S. Scripturae, a multis tamen accepta non est, quia adversatur sententiae ac traditioni antiquorum.*" ["This opinion (i.e., Abravanel's) is highly consistent with the words of Scripture, but it is not accepted by many because it is opposed to the beliefs and the tradition of the ancients." See also *Conciliator*, trans. Lindo, vol. I, p. 289, which version allows Menasseh to comment that "this opinion, although it is very conformable to the text, as it is at variance with the tradition and the decisions of the ancients, is not generally received" (p. 289).] Abravanel's interpretation was tacitly accepted by Moses Mendelssohn, *Jerusalem* (Berlin, 1783), II, pp. 117ff. ["The people persisted in their resolution . . . and (they) experienced what the prophet had threatened them with. Now the constitution was undermined. . . . State and religion were no longer the same." See *Jerusalem*, trans. Allan Arkush (Hanover, NH: University Press of New England, 1983), pp. 132–33; *Jerusalem*, in *Moses Mendelssohn Gesammelte Schriften Jubiläumsausgabe*, vol. 8, *Schriften zum Judentum*, ed. Alexander Altmann (Frommann-Holzboog, 1983), pp. 197-98], and rejected by S. R. Hirsch and by Buber-Rosenzweig. Cf. also Isaak (Yiẓḥak) Heinemann, *Philons griechische und jüdische Bildung: kulturvergleichende Untersuchungen zu Philons Darstellung der jüdischen Gesetze* (Breslau: Marcus, 1932; reprint, Hildesheim: Georg Olms, 1973), pp. 185f., and Urbach, loc. cit., p. 269. (The essay of Heinrich Heinemann in the *Jahrbuch der Jüdisch-literarischen Gesellschaft*, 1916, was not accessible to me.) [For a sustained critique of Strauss's argument about Abravanel, see David Polish, "Isaac Abravanel (1427–1509)," in *Give Us a King: Legal-Religious Sources of Jewish Sovereignty* (Hoboken, NJ: Ktav, 1989), chap. IX, pp. 119–49, and especially pp. 122, 129–38. Polish treats Abravanel as a representative medieval exponent of the classical Jewish sources and as a sound interpreter of Maimonides. He also rejects the view articulated by Strauss that the classical Jewish tradition is, generally speaking, staunchly and almost uniformly in favor of monarchy as a political regime, or at least monarchy in its righteous form. Based on a closer adherence to the view advanced by Abravanel, Polish raises numerous doubts about whether this leaning toward monarchy is so consistently or unambiguously maintained by the Jewish tradition, although it may well have been maintained consistently and unambiguously by Maimonides. For two recent treatments of the same topic, in which the discussion is further advanced, see Amos Funkenstein, "Political Theory," in *Perceptions of Jewish History* (Berkeley: University of California Press, 1993), pp. 159–65; with the response by Aviezer Ravitzky, "Political Philosophy: Nissim of Gerona and Isaac Abrabanel," in *History and Faith: Studies in Jewish Philosophy* (Amsterdam:

According to the interpretation accepted by the Jewish tradition, Deut. 17:14f. would have to be translated as follows:

> When thou art come unto the land which the Lord thy God giveth thee, and shalt possess it, and shalt dwell therein; and shalt say (or:[59] *then thou shalt say*), I will set a king over me, like as all the nations that are round about me; *Thou shalt in any wise set a king over thee*. Thou shalt set him king over thee, whom the Lord thy God shall choose: one from among thy brethren shalt thou set over thee: thou mayest not put a foreigner over thee, which is not thy brother.

According to Abravanel's interpretation, the passage in question would read as follows:

> When thou art come unto the land which the Lord thy God giveth thee, and shalt possess it, and shalt dwell therein; and shalt say, I will set a king over me, like as all the nations that are round about me; *then thou shalt set him king over thee whom the Lord thy God shall choose*: one from among thy brethren shalt thou set king over thee: thou mayest not put a foreigner over thee, which is not thy brother.

According to the traditional interpretation, the purport of the law, contained in the passage, is that Israel is commanded to institute a king. According to Abravanel's interpretation, its purport is that, *if* Israel wishes to institute a king—and to do this, Israel is by the law implicitly permitted, but permitted only—then Israel may do it only in such and such a manner. Now Abravanel's interpretation, which is directly opposed to that of the Jewish tradition, is in substance identical with that implied in the Vulgate.[60] Abra-

---

J. C. Gieben, 1996), pp. 46–72. For Maimonides' *Mishneh Torah*, see "Laws Concerning Kings and Wars," trans. Hershman, chap. 1, paras. 1–2, p. 207. As for his *Book of the Commandments*, the 591st law is to appoint a king of Israel; hence, it is enumerated as a divine commandment in the Torah; it is counted among the positive commandments.]

59. According to Naḥmanides.

60. "Cum ingressus fueris terram, quam Dominus Deus tuus dabit tibi, et possederis eam, habitaverisque in illa, et dixeris: Constituam super me regem, sicut habent omnes per curcuitum nationes; *eum constitues, quem Dominus tuus elegerit de numero fratrum tuorum.* . . ." ["When you will have entered the land that the Lord your God will give you and you will have possessed it and you will have dwelled in it and you will have said: I shall establish a king over myself just as have all the nations roundabout; *you will establish him whom your Lord will have chosen from the number of your brothers.* . . ." Latin translated by Sara Kathleen Alvis.] Cf. also the English translation: ". . . Thou shalt in any wise set him king over thee, whom the Lord thy God shall choose. . . ."

vanel is, of course, much more explicit than the Vulgate can be.[61] And, apart from this, he goes much further than the Latin translation does. He says, explaining the passage in question more precisely:

(When thou shalt wish to do this), in spite of its not being proper, (thou mayest not do it but in such and such a manner). This is similar to the section of the law which runs as follows: When thou goest forth to battle against thine enemies, and the Lord thy God deliverest them into thine hands ... and seest among the captives a beautiful woman, and thou hast a desire unto her. ... For there the precept is not that he shall desire her, and not that he shall take her to him to wife ..., since this is permitted only, and an effect of the wicked inclination. But the precept is that, after the first cohabitation, thou shalt bring her home into thine house. ... Israel was not commanded in the Torah to ask for a king ..., and the king was not necessary and indispensable for the government of their gatherings ..., for God was their king truly. ... Therefore, when Israel asked for a king ..., the anger of the Lord was kindled against them, and He said: they have not rejected thee, but they have rejected me, that I should not be king over them; and Samuel said: ye said unto me, Nay, but a king shall reign over us; when the Lord your God was your king. This shows that the sin consisted in their "kicking" at God's kingship and their choosing a human kingship. For this reason, neither Joshua nor the other Judges instituted a king.

The final expression of Abravanel's interpretation is that Deut. 17:14f. contains a permission given "with regard to the wicked inclination" (*yezer ha-ra'*). Now this more precise expression, too, is in substance borrowed from a Christian source. That source is the *Postilla* of Nicholas of Lyra.[62]

61. It will be proper to give a more complete (if partially free) rendering of Abravanel's interpretation by putting his explanatory remarks on the biblical words into brackets. He explains: "When thou art come unto the land which the Lord thy God giveth thee, and shalt possess it, and shalt dwell therein (i.e., it will be foolish that in the time of the wars, during the conquest of the land you will not ask for a king; for this would be the most proper time for the need for a king; but after you will possess the land, and you will have divided it, and you will dwell in it in safety, and this will have happened by the providence of God, without there being then a king—then, without any necessity and need whatsoever) thou shalt say, I will set a king over me(, namely,) like as all the nations that are round about me (i.e., for no other necessity and purpose [but to assimilate yourselves to the nations of the world]; when this will happen), thou shalt (not) set (him) king over thee (whom you wish, but him) whom the Lord thy God shall choose...." Commentary on I Samuel 8:6 f. (fol. 93, col. 2).

62. Nicholas says on Deuteronomy 17:14f.: "non est praeceptum, nec simplex concessio, quia sic non peccasset populus Israel petendo regem, cujus contrarium dicitur I Reg. 12: sed est permissio quae est de malo. Bonum enim populi consistebat in hoc, quod solus Deus regnaret super eum, eo quod erat populus peculiaris Dei; veruntamen si importune regem habere vellent, permittebatur eis, sub conditionibus

tamen. . . ." ["It is not a precept nor a simple concession since the people of Israel would not have sinned thus by seeking a king, of which the contrary is said in 1 Kings 12: but it is a permission that is concerning evil. For the good of the nation was consisting in this, that God alone should rule over it in that this was a nation belonging to God; nevertheless if they were wishing to have a king persistently, it was permitted to them, though under conditions. . . ." Latin translated by Sara Kathleen Alvis.] This is explained more fully in the *Postilla* on I Kings 8: "illud quod dicitur Deut. 17 de constitutione regis . . . non fuit concessio proprie dicta, sed magis permissio, sicut repudium uxoris fuit permissum ad duritiam cordis eorum. . . ." ["That which is said in Deut. 17 about the establishment of a king . . . was not a concession properly stated, but rather a permission, just as the repudiation of a wife was permitted in accord with the hardness of their heart. . . ." Latin translated by Sara Kathleen Alvis.] The comparison shows that Abravanel has merely replaced Nicholas' example by the example of the "beautiful woman." But the point of view of Abravanel is identical with that of Nicholas. There is one important difference between the Jewish and the Christian commentator: while Abravanel thinks that monarchy is intrinsically bad, Nicholas is of the opinion that monarchy is in principle the best form of government. Nicholas only contests that that which holds true of all other nations, holds equally true of Israel, the nation governed by God. Only this part of Nicholas' argument has been taken over by Abravanel. (Cf. the beginning of Abravanel's discussion concerning monarchy in Israel: "Even if we grant, that the king is most necessary in the nation for the ordering of the political community . . . he is not necessary in the nation of Israel. . . .") Nicholas says on I Kings 8: "Ad maiorem praedictorum evidentiam quaeritur, utrum filii Israel peccaverint petendo super se regem. Et arguitur quod non, quia petere illud quod est bonum simpliciter, et de dictamine rationis rectae, non est peccatum; gubernatio autem populi per regem est optima, ut dicit Philosophus 3. Politicorum. et per consequens est de dictamine rationis rectae. . . . Item illud quod conceditur lege divina licitum est, quia nullum peccatum concedit, sed Deut. 17. c. concedit lex divina filiis Israel constitutionem regis. . . ." ["For the greater proof of the argument, it is asked whether the sons of Israel sinned in seeking a king over themselves and it is argued not so since to seek that which is good simply and according to the dictate of right reason is not sin; moreover, the governance of a nation by a king is best, as the Philosopher says in book 3 of the *Politics* and consequently is in accord with the dictate of right reason. . . . Also, that which is granted by divine law is allowed since it grants no sin but in Deut. chap. 17 divine law grants to the sons of Israel the establishment of a king. . . ." Latin translated by Sara Kathleen Alvis.] (Notice that even in this "monarchist" objection, Deuteronomy 17:14f. is understood to contain a *concessio* only.) "Contra infra 12. c. dicitur: Scietis et videbitis. . . . Ad hoc dicendum quod, cum regnum sit optima politia, caeterae gentes a filiis Israel petendo vel constituendo super se regem non peccaverunt, sed magis bonum egerunt. Filii autem Israel hoc faciendo peccaverunt. . . . Cuius ratio est, quia Deus populum Israel elegit sibi specialem et peculiarem prae caeteris populis . . . et idem voluit esse rex immediatus illius populi . . . propter quod voluit homines gubernatores illius populi ab ipso immediate institui, tanquam eius vicarii essent, et non reges vel domini: ut patet in Moyse et Josue, et de iudicibus sequentibus. . . ." ["On the contrary subsequently in I Samuel chapter 12 (verse 17) it is said: 'You will know and you will see. . . .' In this regard it must be said that since kingship is the best polity the other nations have not sinned by seeking a king from the sons of Israel or by establishing a king over themselves, but rather they have accomplished a good thing. However, the sons of Israel did sin by doing this. . . . The reason for this is that God chose the people of Israel as special to Himself and preferred before other peoples . . . and He wished likewise to be the direct king of that nation . . . because He wished men to be established by Himself directly as governors of that nation such that they would be His representatives and not kings or rulers as it is made plain in Moses and Joshua and from the judges following after. . . ." Latin translated by Sara Kathleen Alvis.] (That Abravanel knew the *Postilla*, is shown by his express quotations from it—see Guttmann, loc. cit., p. 46. But, apart from that, that interpretation given by earlier commentators of Deuteronomy 17:14f. (or I Samuel 8:6f.), which he esteems most highly and which he discusses most fully, is the interpretation given by Paulus of Burgos, and this interpretation is to be found in Paulus' *Additiones* to the *Postilla*.) [See Nicolaus de Lyra, *Postilla super totam Bibliam* (Strassburg 1492; facsimile reprint, Frankfurt am Main: Minerva, 1971).] Cf. further Thomas Aquinas, *Summa theologiae* II, 1, qu. 105, art. 1: "regnum est optimum regimen populi, si non corrumpatur. Sed . . . de facili regnum degenerat in tyrannidem . . . ideo *Dominus a principio* (Judaeis) *regem non instituit* cum plena potestate, sed judicem et gubernatorem in eorum custodiam; sed postea regem ad petitionem populi *quasi indignatus concessit*, ut patet per hoc quod dixit ad Samuel I Reg. 8:7. . . . Instituit tamen a principio circa regem instituendum, primo quidem modum

Thus we are entitled to say that Abravanel's interpretation of Deut. 17:14f., i.e., of the chief biblical passage, or, in other words, that his opinion concerning the incompatibility of monarchy with the constitution of Israel, goes immediately back to Christian, not to Jewish sources.

Generally speaking, both the Jewish and the Christian tradition, and in particular both the Jewish and the Christian Middle Ages, were in favor of monarchy. Antimonarchist statements are, in both traditions, exceptional up to the humanist age. Thus one is at a loss to state which of the two traditions shows a comparatively stronger monarchist (or antimonarchist) trend than the other. One could, however, dare to make such a statement if it were based on a comparison of comparable magnitudes, i.e., of a Jewish source which is at the same time authoritative and popular, with the corresponding Christian source. Now if we compare the manner in which the Jewish Bible on the one hand (i.e., the Targum Onkelos, the Targum Jonathan, and the commentaries of Rashi, Ibn Ezra, and Naḥmanides), and the Christian (Latin) Bible on the other (i.e., the *Glossa interlinearis*, the *Glossa ordinaria*, the *Postilla* of

---

eligendi. . . . Secundo ordinavit circa reges institutos. . . ." [See Thomas Aquinas, *Summa Theologica*, trans. Fathers of the English Dominican Province (Cambridge: Blackfriars, 1976): "A kingdom is the best form of government of the people, so long as it is not corrupt. But . . . it easily degenerates into tyranny. . . . Hence *from the very first the Lord did not set up (for the Jews) the kingly authority* with full power, but gave them judges and governors to rule them. But afterwards when the people asked Him to do so, *being indignant with them, so to speak, He granted them a king*, as is clear from His words to Samuel (1 Samuel 8:7). . . . Nevertheless, as regards the appointment of a king, He did establish the manner of election from the very beginning. . . . He prescribed how the king after his appointment should behave. . . ."] The fact that the kings had absolute power, while the power of the judges was more limited, is stressed by Abravanel in the introduction to his commentary on Judges (fol. 40, col. 1). Cf. also John of Salisbury, *Policraticus*, lib. VIII, cap. 18: " . . . primi patres et patriarchae vivendi ducem optimum naturam secuti sunt. Successerunt duces a Moyses sequentes legem, et iudices qui legis auctoritate regebant populum; et eosdem fuisse legimus sacerdotes. Tandem in furore Domini dati sunt reges, alii quidem boni, alii vero mali . . . populus . . . a Deo, quem contempserat, sibi regem extorsit . . . (Saul) tamen christus Domini dictus est, et tirannidem exercens regium non amisit honorem. . . ." ["The first fathers and the patriarchs were in obedience to nature, the best guide to living. They were succeeded by leaders following the laws of Moses and by judges who ruled the people according to the authority of the law; and we read that these were priests. Finally, against the wrath of God, they were given kings, some good, yet others bad. . . . The people . . . had extorted a king for themselves from God, whose will was disregarded. . . . Yet the same man (Saul) was called the anointed of the Lord, and exercising tyranny, he did not lose the honor of kingship. . . ." See John of Salisbury, *Policraticus*, trans. Nederman, bk. VIII, chap. 18 ("Tyrants are the ministers of God; and what a tyrant is; and of the moral characters of Gaius Caligula and his nephew Nero and each of their ends"), pp. 201–2.] With this passage, the whole of Abravanel's political teaching should be compared. As regards the later development, I would refer the reader particularly to Milton, *Pro populo Anglicano defensio contra Salmasii Defensionem Regiam*, cap. 2. It is interesting in our connection to observe that, while Salmasius (*Defensio Regia*, cap. 2) makes ample use of the rabbinic interpretations of Deuteronomy 17:14f. (and of I Samuel 8) for the proof of his royalist thesis, Milton much prefers Josephus to the "tenebrionibus Rabbinis" [rabbinical obscurities] (cf. on Josephus below, third paragraph from the end of the chapter). [See "Defence of the People of England Against Anonymous, Alias Salmasius (and) His 'Defence of the King,'" in John Milton, *Areopagitica and Other Political Witings*, ed. John Alvis (Indianapolis: Liberty Fund, 1999), chap. II, pp. 125–54, and especially p. 128.]

Nicholas of Lyra, and the *Additiones* of Paulus Burgensis) deal with the chief passage, i.e., with the law concerning the institution of a king, we find that the Jewish Bible shows not the slightest sign of an antimonarchist tendency,[63] while the Christian Bible exhibits a definite antimonarchist trend, based on theocratic assumptions.[64] The only exception to this rule in the Christian Bible is the explanation of the passage in question given by Paulus of Burgos, i.e., by a baptized Jew. The result of this comparison confirms our impression that the immediate origin of Abravanel's antimonarchist conclusions from his theocratic premises has to be sought for not in Jewish, but in Christian, sources.

Of Christian origin is above all Abravanel's general conception of the government of the Jewish nation. According to him, that government consists of two kinds of governments, of a government human and of a government spiritual or divine. This distinction is simply the Christian distinction between the authority spiritual and the authority temporal. Abravanel further divides each of these two governments into three degrees. As regards the government human, the lowest degree is the "little *bet din*," i.e., the court of justice of every town. The members of those courts are elected by the people. The second degree of the government human is the "great *bet din*," i.e., the *Synhedrion* in Jerusalem. The members of the *Synhedrion* are not elected by

---

63. The Targum Onkelos renders the passage literally. The Targum Jonathan renders the words "Thou shalt in any wise set a king over thee, whom the Lord thy God shall choose: one from among thy brethren shalt thou set king over thee," in the following way: "You shall inquire for instruction before the Lord, and afterwards appoint the king over you." Rashi does not say anything on the passage. Ibn Ezra simply says that the passage expresses a permission; Naḥmanides conceives of it as containing a command to ask for a king and to institute a king.

64. The *Glossa interlinearis* remarks on "et dixeris": "Tu non ego," and on "Constituam super me regem": "Non Deum sed hominem." ["'And you will have said': 'You, not I,' and on 'I shall establish a king over myself': 'Not God but man.'" Latin translated by Sara Kathleen Alvis.] The *Glossa ordinaria* (Augustinus, qu. 26) says: "Quaeri potest cur displicuit populus Deo, cum regem desideravit, cum hic inveniatur esse permissus? Sed intelligendum est merito non fuisse secundum voluntatem Dei, quia hoc fieri non praecepit sed desiderantibus permisit." ["It can be asked why the nation was displeasing to God when the people desired a king, since it is found here to be permitted? But it must be understood that deservedly the will of God was not favorable, since He did not command this to be done but He permitted it to those desiring a king." Latin translated by Sara Kathleen Alvis.] As regards the *Postilla*, see above [n. 62]. Paulus Burgensis says: "Praeceptum istud de constitutione regis non est permissive intelligendum . . . sed est simplex concessio cum conditionibus in litera scriptis. Nec sequitur quod si sit concessio simplex, tunc non pecasset populus Israel petendo regem. Nam petierunt regem aliter quam fuit sibi concessum." ["That precept concerning the establishment of a king must not be understood as a permission . . . but it is a simple concession with conditions written out to the letter. Nor does it follow that if it were a simple concession, then the nation of Israel would not have sinned in seeking a king. For they sought a king otherwise than it was granted to them." Latin translated by Sara Kathleen Alvis. See, in various editions and printings, *Biblia Latina*, with the *Glossa Ordinaria* of Walafrid Strabo, the *Glossa Interlineari* of Anselm of Laon, the *Postilla* of Nicholas of Lyra, and the *Additions* of Paulus Burgensis.]

the people, but nominated either by the king, or, if there is no king, by the president of the *Synhedrion*, after consultation with the other members; the president himself is chosen by the members of the *Synhedrion*. This body, being an image of the seventy elders led by Moses, consists of seventy-one persons. The highest place in human government is occupied by the king. The king is chosen by God, not by the people, who have therefore no right whatsoever to rebel against the king or to depose him. The office of the king is not the administration of justice, but, in the first instance, military leadership, and then the extrajudicial punishment of the wicked in cases of urgency. His claim to obedience and honor is stressed by Abravanel scarcely less than it is by Maimonides; in this respect both alike are simply following Jewish tradition.[65] If one takes into account Abravanel's criticism of monarchy in general and of monarchy in Israel in particular, one has to define his view concerning the highest degree of human government in the Jewish nation more exactly by saying that the chief of that government is, according to the original intention of the legislator, not a king properly speaking, but a leader of the kind that Moses and the Judges were. As a matter of fact, Abravanel expressly states that "the first king who reigned over Israel" was Moses.[66] At any rate, the human government of the Jewish nation, as Abravanel sees it, consists of a monarchic element (Moses and his successors), of an aristocratic element (the Sanhedrin), and of a democratic element (the local judges elected by the people). It is a "mixed" government, in full accordance with the classical doctrine. The immediate source of this view of Abravanel is again a Christian one: Thomas Aquinas's description of the Jewish constitution in the *Summa theologiae*,[67] which has been altered by Abravanel only in detail. So

---

65. Commentary on Deuteronomy 16:18–17:1, and on 17:8–15 (fol. 293, cols. 1–2; fol. 294, col. 1; fol. 296, cols. 2–3). Cf. commentary on I Kings 1 (fol. 196, col. 4) and Introduction to commentary on Judges (fol. 39, col. 3; fol. 40, col. 1). In the commentary on Deuteronomy 16:18–17:13 (fol. 293, col. 2 and fol. 294, col. 2), Abravanel says, however, that the extraordinary power of jurisdiction belongs, not to the king, but to the *Synhedrion*. Following the ruling of the Jewish tradition, he points out that all appointments in Israel are for life, and, in principle, hereditary (loc. cit., fol. 293, col. 2). In his "rational" discussion of the best form of human government, he showed a definite preference for short periods of office.

66. Commentary on I Kings 1 (fol. 196, col. 4). See also commentary on Exodus 18:13–27 (fol. 134, col. 1).

67. *Summa theologiae* II, 1, qu. 105, art. 1. Thomas defines the character of the government instituted by the *lex vetus* [the Old Law] by calling that government a "politia bene commixta ex regno, inquantum unus praeest, ex aristocratia, inquantum multi principantur secundum virtutem, et ex democratia, id est, potestate populi, inquantum ex popularibus possunt eligi principes, et ad populum pertinet electio principum. Et hoc fuit institutum secundum legem divinam; nam Moyses et ejus successores (i.e., Josua, Judices, et reges) gubernabant populum, quasi singulariter omnibus principantes, quod est *quaedam specie regni*. Eligebantur autem septuaginta duo seniores secundum virtutem ... et hoc erat aristocraticum. Sed democraticum erat quod isti de omni populo eligebantur. ..." ["For this is the best form of polity, being partly kingdom, since there is one at the head of all; partly aristocracy, in so far as a number of persons

much about Abravanel's conception of the government human. As regards the government spiritual, he again distinguishes three degrees: the prophet, who is the chief; the priests; and, in the lowest category, the Levites.[68] This distinction implies that the hierarchy spiritual, not less than the hierarchy human, leads up to a monarchical head. In this again Abravanel is following the teaching of the Christian Middle Ages, according to which the government of the whole church must be monarchical: he merely replaces Petrus [i.e., Peter] (or his successors) by the prophet.[69] The government spiritual, as conceived by Abravanel, is of course not purely monarchical; it contains also an aristocratic and, perhaps, a democratic element. This view of the spiritual hierarchy is also borrowed from Christians.[70] And it is for Abravanel no less a matter of course than it is for the papalist writers among the Christians, that human government, and in particular government by kings, which was not instituted by, but extorted from God, is much inferior in dignity to the government spiritual. And besides, the aristocratic element of the human government of the Jewish nation, the *Synhedrion*, consists as Abravanel points out mainly of priests and Levites.[71] The ideal commonwealth, as understood by Abravanel, is governed mainly by prophets and priests; and the ideal leader is for him not, as for Maimonides, a philosopher king, but a priest king.[72] His political ideal is of a strictly hierocratic character. He was, as far

---

according to virtue are set in authority; partly democracy, i.e., government by the people, in so far as the rulers can be chosen from the people, and the people have the right to choose their rulers. Such was the form of government established by the Divine Law. For Moses and his successors (i.e., Joshua, the judges, and the kings) governed the people in such a way that each of them was ruler over all; so that there was *a kind of kingdom*. Moreover, seventy-two men were chosen, who were elders in virtue ... so that there was an element of aristocracy. But it was a democratic government in so far as the rulers were chosen from all the people...."] Cf. also the passage from the same article [of the *Summa theologiae*] quoted above, n. 62 [in the present chapter].

68. Commentary on Deuteronomy 16:18–17:1 (fol. 293, col. 1), and on 18:1–8 (fol. 297, cols. 1–2).

69. Cf. Thomas Aquinas, *Summa contra Gentiles*, lib. IV, cap. 76. [Strauss may have had in mind especially bk. 4, chap. 76, para. 3: "3. None can doubt that the government of the Church is excellently well arranged, arranged as it is by Him through whom 'kings reign and lawgivers enact just things' (Prov. 8:15). But the best form of government for a multitude is to be governed by one; for the end of government is the peace and unity of its subjects, and one man is a more apt source of unity than many together." See *Summa Contra Gentiles*, trans. Joseph Rickaby (London: Burns and Oates, 1905).]

70. [See Robert] Bellarmine, *De Romano Pontifice*, lib. I, cap. 5: "Jam vero doctores catholici conveniunt omnes, ut regimen ecclesiasticum hominibus a Deo commissum, sit illud quidem monarchicum, sed temperatum ... ex aristocratia et dimocratia." ["Now in truth all learned Catholics agree that the ecclesiastical rule granted by God to men is indeed that monarchic one, but moderated ... by aristocracy and democracy." Latin translated by Sara Kathleen Alvis.]

71. Commentary on Deuteronomy 17:8–13 (fol. 294, cols. 2–3). [See *Medieval Political Philosophy*, ed. Lerner and Mahdi, pp. 261–64.]

72. Commentary on I Kings 1 (fol. 196, col. 4), and on Exodus 18:13–27 (fol. 134, cols. 1–2). Cf. John of Salisbury, *Policraticus*, lib. VIII, cap. 18 (quoted above, n. 62 [in the present chapter,] and Augustinus [de Ancona] Triumphus, *Summa de potestate ecclesiastica*, Pt. I, qu. 1, art. 7–8.

as I know, the first Jew who became deeply influenced by Christian political thought. It deserves to be stressed that he adopted the views of the extreme papalists. He had preferred Christian scholasticism to the philosophy of the Jewish rationalists, and he arrived at a political ideal which was nearer to the ideal of Gregory VII[73] and Innocent III than to that of Maimonides. He had undermined Maimonides' political philosophy of the law by contesting its ultimate assumption that the city is "natural," and by conceiving of the city as a product of human sin, i.e., he had started from unpolitical, and even antipolitical premises, and he arrived at the political creed of clericalism.

But however great the influence of Christian medieval thought on Abravanel's political teaching may have been, that influence scarcely accounts for his so-called republicanism. This part of his political creed is not of Christian medieval, but of humanist origin. Humanism means going back from the tradition to the sources of the tradition. *The* sources, however, are for Abravanel, not so much the historians, poets, and orators of classical antiquity, but the literal sense of the Bible—and Josephus.[74] Josephus understood Deut. 17:14f. as permitting only, not commanding, the institution of a king. And he unequivocally states that the government instituted by Moses was an aristocracy as opposed to a monarchy.[75] Above all, the *aristoi*, who govern the Jewish state, are identified by him with the priests, whose chief is the high priest.[76] Thus we conclude that Abravanel's view of the Jewish government as a whole is taken over from Josephus. And by taking into account the result of our previous analysis, we shall sum up by saying that Abravanel restates the aristocratic and antimonarchist view of Josephus in terms of the Christian distinction between the authority spiritual and the authority temporal.

When speaking of the influence of humanism on Abravanel's political teaching, we have, then, to think not primarily of his "republicanism"—of

---

73. Cf. with Abravanel's statements those of Gregory VII and others, quoted by Robert Warrant Carlyle and Alexander James Carlyle, *A History of Mediaeval Political Theory in the West*, III (2nd ed., Edinburgh: William Blackwood, 1936), pp. 94 and 99.

74. As regards Abravanel's knowledge of Josephus, see Baer, loc. cit., p. 246. [See also Eric Lawee, *Isaac Abarbanel's Stance toward Tradition: Defense, Dissent, and Dialogue* (Albany: State University of New York Press, 2001), p. 199.]

75. *Antiquitates Judaicae*, lib. IV, § 223, and lib. VI, § 35. [See Josephus, *Jewish Antiquities*, bks. I–IV, trans. Henry St. J. Thackeray, vol. IV of *Loeb Complete Works of Josephus* (Cambridge, MA: Harvard University Press, 1930), pp. 582–83; *Jewish Antiquities*, bks. V–VIII, trans. Henry St. J. Thackeray and Ralph Marcus, vol. V of *Loeb Complete Works of Josephus* (Cambridge, MA: Harvard University Press, 1934), pp. 182–83.]

76. See in particular *Contra Apion*, lib. II, 185–88 and 193–94, but also *Antiquitates Judaicae*, lib. IV, §§ 218 ("high priest, prophet, and *Synhedrion*") and 224. [See Josephus, *Against Apion*, trans. Henry St. J. Thackeray, volume I of *Loeb Complete Works of Josephus* (Cambridge, MA: Harvard University Press, 1926), bk. II, pp. 366–69; *Jewish Antiquities*, bks. I–IV, pp. 580–81, and 582–83.]

his admiration for the greatness of republican Rome and for the patriotism of its citizens—which is rather on the surface of his thought. His humanism has indeed hardly anything in common with the "heathenish" humanism of men like Leonardo Bruni. Abravanel is a humanist of the kind represented by Coluccio Salutati, who might be said to have served as his model.[77] That is to say, he is a humanist who uses his classical learning to confirm his thoroughly medieval conceptions rather than to free himself from them. He is distinguished from the medieval writers rather by the method which he uses than by the views which he expresses. This method may be called historical.[78] Abravanel tends to pay more attention to the sources of the tradition than to the tradition itself. He often urges the difference between the literal sense of the Bible and the midrashic interpretations; in doing this, he is guided, not as a medieval rationalist might have been, by an opposition to the "mythical" or "mystical" tendencies of the Midrash—for these tendencies are in full accordance with his own deepest inclinations—but by an interest in establishing the pure, undistorted meaning of the divinely inspired text, by an interest not so much in proving that a certain favored doctrine is revealed, and therefore true, but to know exactly what Revelation teaches, in order to be able to adopt that teaching, whatever it may be. By preferring in this spirit the sources of the tradition to the tradition itself, he can scarcely avoid the danger of coming into conflict with the teaching of tradition. An important example of that criticism of traditional views, which is based on the return to the sources (both the literal sense of the Bible and Josephus), has attracted our attention in the foregoing pages. To the same connection belongs Abravanel's criticism of certain traditional opinions concerning the authorship of some biblical books, a criticism by which he paved the way for the much more thoroughgoing biblical criticism of Spinoza.[79] When considering these

77. Cf. Alfred von Martin, *Mittelalterliche Welt- und Lebensanschauung im Spiegel der Schriften Coluccio Salutatis* (Munich and Berlin, 1913), pp. 22, 61ff., 82ff., and 97ff., and the same author's *Coluccio Salutati's Traktat Vom Tyrannen* (Berlin and Leipzig, 1913), pp. 75ff. [Coluccio Salutati (1331–1406) was an Italian humanist of the fourteenth century: he was the author of numerous works on philosophic and literary matters (e.g., *On the Labors of Hercules*), and on textual and historical criticism; a cultural and political leader in Renaissance Florence; a gatherer of ancient and medieval manuscripts in an impressive library; and a student of Petrarch's in helping to rediscover ancient arts and texts, and to recover their wisdom.]

78. With due caution.

79. Cf. Leo Strauss, *Die Religionskritik Spinozas* (Berlin: Akademie-Verlag, 1930), pp. 279ff. [See Leo Strauss, *Spinoza's Critique of Religion*, pp. 318–21, which lists passages in medieval Jewish biblical commentaries which likely served as Spinoza's sources; of the seventeen passages in Spinoza, seven of the sources are located in Abravanel. For Abravanel's scriptural commentary and its method as a precursor to Spinoza, see Lawee, "Isaac Abarbanel: From Medieval to Renaissance Jewish Biblical Scholarship," in *Hebrew Bible/Old Testament*, op. cit.]

and similar facts, we may be inclined to complete our earlier statement that Abravanel's thought was fundamentally determined by the Jewish tradition by adding that his teaching tends to be more of a biblicist than of a traditionalist character. But after having granted this, we must stress all the more that the assumptions of the premedieval world to which Abravanel turns back, sometimes by criticizing medieval opinions, are not fundamentally different from the medieval assumptions from which he started. He goes back, it is true, from the monarchist ideal of the Middle Ages to the aristocratic ideal of antiquity. But, as matters stand, this does not mean more than that he goes back from the moderate hierocratic ideal of the Middle Ages to the much more intransigent hierocratic ideal of the period of the Second Temple, as expounded by Josephus. He is distinguished from the Jewish medieval writers by the fact that he is much more clerical than they are.

His descent was, as he believed, royal. His soul was the soul of a priest—of a priest who had not forgotten that the Temple, built by King Solomon in the holy city, was "infinitely inferior in sanctity" to the tabernacle erected by Moses in the desert.[80] Whatever he may have had to learn from the Cynics or from the Bucolics of antiquity as regards the dubious merits of human arts and city life, his knowledge of the sinful origin of cities, and of towers, and of kingdoms, and of the punishment following the eating of the fruit of the tree of knowledge was not borrowed from any foreign source: it was the inheritance of his own race which was commanded to be a kingdom of priests.

80. Commentary on I Kings 6:1 (fol. 217, col. 3).

Appendix

THE SECRET TEACHING OF MAIMONIDES[1]

EDITOR'S NOTE

"The Secret Teaching of Maimonides" is a previously unpublished fragment by Strauss. It was uncovered by Yiftach Ofek in the Leo Strauss Archive in the library of the University of Chicago. It is published with the permission of the Leo Strauss Literary Estate and its administrator, Professor Nathan Tarcov. The fragment, originally a one-page typescript, offers no clue to its date of composition. However, it is obviously a proposal made to spend an academic year on a research project concerned with the study of Maimonides and with uncovering his "secret teaching." Strauss was already starting to recognize this notion as fundamental in "On Abravanel" (1937), but he did not yet perceive that it had very far-reaching implications. See chap. 15 above. Thus, he mentions in passing the "two different meanings" of Maimonides' approach to the law: "a literal meaning" and "a secret meaning." In the opinion of the present editor, the proposal preceded the publication of, and perhaps also the research done for, "The Literary Character of *The Guide of the Perplexed*," while previewing some of its themes in a rudimentary form. "Literary Character" first appeared in print, i.e., prior to *Persecution and the Art of Writing*, in *Essays on Maimonides*, ed. Salo W. Baron (New York: Columbia University Press, 1941). See chap. 8 above. If the editor may be permitted an educated guess, this fragment is likely to have been originally composed between 1937 and 1940, based on its literary style and on its contents, never mind the fact that this is written in English. (Indeed, it is the first work in this language that Strauss wrote specifically dedicated to Maimonides, not counting the essay on Abravanel: see chap. 15 above.) Strauss makes no reference to his work on "Literary Character," and yet he indicates his planned exploration of themes that were put in clearer focus, and became quite differently formulated, once he had actually researched and written the aforementioned

---

1. The title is Strauss's own and appears on the top of the typed page.

article. A possible clue to the date is also provided by the language of the very first line of this proposal: in the wake of "Literary Character," and for reasons pertaining to the main argument contained in that article, Strauss as a rule refrained from speaking unequivocally of "the *philosophical* teaching of Maimonides." (Cf. Strauss's comment in "Editor's Introduction" above, n. 7.) If this was produced subsequent to 1941, he may perhaps have decided *not* to refrain from the use of such language in an academic proposal because he did not want those whom he was addressing to misconceive his purpose, until his novel thesis about and original approach to Maimonides was better known. But it seems most likely that he would have made reference to his major article of 1941 on Maimonides in order to at the very least establish his scholarly bona fides in the field. Thus, the proposal is likely to have been submitted either to the Department of History at Columbia University, at which Strauss had a visiting one-year appointment (1937-38) on his first arrival in the United States, or to the Department of Philosophy of the New School for Social Research in New York, at which he received an appointment as visiting researcher beginning in 1938, made more or less permanent shortly thereafter (since he remained at the New School until 1949). If the fragment shows no evidence of the results that he reached in "Literary Character" and elaborated subsequently (see chaps. 8-14 above), the progress toward it is in a certain measure reflected in his letters of this period to his friend Jacob Klein, which progress also is not echoed in the language of the proposal: see *Hobbes Politische Wissenschaft und zugehörige Schriften—Briefe*, vol. 3 of *Gesammelte Schriften*, pp. 544-87. The notes to "The Secret Teaching of Maimonides" are entirely the work of the present editor and are not to be attributed to Strauss himself.

BEFORE TRYING TO INTERPRET THE PHILOSOPHICAL TEACHING OF Maimonides, one must know exactly what this teaching is. The intention of the study which I propose to make during the academic year now beginning, is to establish the essential content of Maimonides' philosophical teaching.

The specific difficulty which the student of Maimonides has to overcome to begin with, is a consequence of the fact that Maimonides' main work, *The Guide of the Perplexed*, cannot be read and understood as either a modern system of philosophy, or a medieval summa of theology, or a handbook of philosophy in the style of Avicenna's or Averroes' metaphysics. For *The Guide of the Perplexed* is consciously and intentionally an enigmatic work: its teaching is set forth not in plain language, but by allusions and hints. It would perhaps be impossible to solve its enigmas, if it were not itself devoted to the purpose of solving the enigmas of another enigmatic work. That other enigmatic work is the Bible.[2] Consequently, we shall be able to understand the teaching of the *Guide* by reading that work in the same way as Maimonides himself has read the Bible. When reading the Bible, Maimonides makes a distinction between its literal and its interior meaning. In the same way, the interpreter of the *Guide* has to distinguish between the literal and the interior meaning of the *Guide*. Only its interior meaning can be accepted as its true meaning.

More than one rule for the interpretation of the *Guide* can be gained by the observation of Maimonides' methods of biblical interpretation. But that rule which has the widest field of application is the following one. Maimonides begins his work with discussing the meanings of a number of biblical words which have, according to him, a secret meaning. Following this procedure, I shall discuss, to begin with, the secret words used by Maimonides in the *Guide*.

What I am proposing to make is then a kind of a dictionary of Maimonides' secret terminology.[3] That secret terminology has nothing to do with the terminology of the Aristotelian tradition, for the terminology of that tradition is not secret. It is also not a mystical terminology, for Maimonides was not a mystic. It is rather a group of expressions which are concerned with the relationship between philosophy and religious law.

These expressions have to be collected and properly arranged; the meaning attached to them in the *Guide* and elsewhere has to be established; the chapters or the larger parts of the work in which they occur or in which they do not occur, have to be noted. For not less significant than the absolute meaning of those expressions is the place in which they are to be found: it is exactly by using or not using the one or other of the secret words in the different parts of his work that Maimonides marks the distinction between the philosophic and the nonphilosophic parts of the *Guide*. Consequently, by using those words as signposts, we shall be able to recognize the line of

---

2. This is a theme that is probed and elucidated with great subtlety in "Literary Character," chap. 8 above.

3. In none of Strauss's works did he ever actually produce the promised "dictionary of Maimonides' secret terminology." However, his discussion in "How To Begin," as also in "Introduction to Maimonides' *Guide*," acutely concentrates on, and most carefully elaborates, what he will eventually call the "lexicographic" chapters of the *Guide*, mainly but not solely in 1.1–49. In these two works Strauss discusses the biblical Hebrew terms which each such lexicographic chapter of Maimonides' *Guide* deals with as his keys to unlocking the deepest secrets of the Hebrew Bible. See especially chaps. 10 and 11 above.

demarcation which separates those two parts, i.e., the hidden composition of the whole work. When we can clearly distinguish between the philosophic and the nonphilosophic part of the *Guide*, we have discovered Maimonides' secret teaching: for that teaching is identical with the teaching of the philosophical part of the *Guide*, while that of the nonphilosophic part is merely of an exoteric nature.

Abbreviations

Editions to which Leo Strauss frequently refers, or recent editions and translated versions of works to which the editor frequently refers:

GENERAL WORKS

Albo, *Ikkarim* (*Roots*), trans. Husik
    Joseph Albo, *Sefer ha-Ikkarim* (*Book of Roots or Book of Principles*), ed. and trans. Isaac Husik (Philadelphia: Jewish Publication Society of America, 1930).
Alfarabi, *Perfect State*, trans. Walzer
    Al-Farabi on the Perfect State, a revised text with introduction, translation, and commentary by Richard Walzer (Oxford: Clarendon Press, 1985).
Alfarabi, *Plato and Aristotle*, trans. Mahdi
    Alfarabi, *The Philosophy of Plato and Aristotle*, trans. Muhsin Mahdi (Ithaca: Cornell University Press, 1969; reprint, 2002).
Alfarabi, "Political Regime," trans. Najjar
    Alfarabi, "The Political Regime," trans. Fauzi M. Najjar, in *Medieval Political Philosophy: A Sourcebook*, ed. Ralph Lerner and Muhsin Mahdi (Ithaca: Cornell University Press, 1972), pp. 31–57.
Alfarabi, *Political Writings*, trans. Butterworth
    Alfarabi, *The Political Writings: "Selected Aphorisms" and Other Texts*, ed. and trans. Charles E. Butterworth (Ithaca: Cornell University Press, 2001).
Averroes, *Decisive Treatise*, trans. Butterworth
    Averroes, *Decisive Treatise and Epistle Dedicatory*, trans. and ed. Charles E. Butterworth (Provo: Brigham Young University Press, 2001).
Averroes, *On Plato's "Republic,"* trans. Lerner
    Averroes on Plato's "Republic," trans. Ralph Lerner (Ithaca: Cornell University Press, 1974; reprint, 2005).
Avicenna, *The Metaphysics*, trans. Marmura
    Avicenna, *The Metaphysics of "The Healing": A Parallel English-Arabic Text = al-Ilahīyāt min al Shifā*, ed. and trans. Michael E. Marmura (Provo: Brigham Young University Press, 2005).
Avicenna, "On the Division of the Rational Sciences," trans. Mahdi
    Avicenna, "On the Division of the Rational Sciences," trans. Muhsin Mahdi, in *Medieval Political Philosophy: A Sourcebook*, ed. Ralph Lerner and Muhsin Mahdi (Ithaca: Cornell University Press, 1972), pp. 95–97.

Avicenna, "On the Proof of Prophecies," trans. Marmura
    Avicenna, "On the Proof of Prophecies and the Interpretation of the Prophets' Symbols and Metaphors," trans. Michael E. Marmura, in *Medieval Political Philosophy: A Sourcebook*, ed. Ralph Lerner and Muhsin Mahdi (Ithaca: Cornell University Press, 1972), pp. 112–21.

Cambridge Companion to Leo Strauss
    The Cambridge Companion to Leo Strauss, ed. Steven B. Smith (New York: Cambridge University Press, 2009).

Falaquera, "Epistle of the Debate"
    Shem-Ṭov ben Joseph Ibn Falaquera, "Epistle of the Debate," trans. Steven Harvey, in *Maimonides' Empire of Light: Popular Enlightenment in an Age of Belief*, by Ralph Lerner (Chicago: University of Chicago Press, 2000), pp. 188–208.

Green, *Jew and Philosopher*
    Kenneth Hart Green, *Jew and Philosopher: The Return to Maimonides in the Jewish Thought of Leo Strauss* (Albany: State University of New York Press, 1993).

History of Political Philosophy, ed. Strauss and Cropsey
    History of Political Philosophy, ed. Leo Strauss and Joseph Cropsey, 2nd ed. (Chicago: Rand McNally, 1972); 3rd ed. (Chicago: University of Chicago Press, 1987).

Lerner, *Maimonides' Empire of Light*
    Ralph Lerner, *Maimonides' Empire of Light: Popular Enlightenment in an Age of Belief* (Chicago: University of Chicago Press, 2000).

Medieval Political Philosophy, ed. Lerner and Mahdi
    Medieval Political Philosophy: A Sourcebook, ed. Ralph Lerner and Muhsin Mahdi (Glencoe, IL, 1963; reprint, Ithaca: Cornell University Press, 1972).

Munk, *Le Guide des égarés*. See *Le Guide des égarés* under "Works by Maimonides."

Spinoza, *Theologico-Political Treatise*, trans. Yaffe
    Benedict Spinoza, *Theologico-Political Treatise*, trans. Martin D. Yaffe (Newburyport, MA: Focus, 2004).

Wolfson, *Studies in History*
    Harry Austryn Wolfson, *Studies in the History of Philosophy and Religion*, ed. Isadore Twersky and George H. Williams (Cambridge, MA: Harvard University Press, 1973), vol. 1 and vol. 2.

Yaffe
    Benedict Spinoza, *Theologico-Political Treatise*, trans. Martin D. Yaffe (Newburyport, MA: Focus, 2004).

WORKS BY MAIMONIDES

"Avodah Zarah." *See* "Hilkhot Avodah Zarah."

Be'ur Melekhet ha-Higayon, ed. Kafah
    Be'ur Melekhet ha-Higayon (Maqālah fī ṣinā'at al-manṭiq) le-Rabbeinu Moshe ben Maimon: Maḵor ve-Tirgum im Haḵdamoteihem u-Ferusheihem shel R. Moshe mi-Dessau (Mendelssohn), et al., ed. and trans. Joseph Kafah (Kiryat Ono: Mekhon Mishnat ha-Rambam, 5757/1997).

"Book of Knowledge," trans. Lerner
    "Book of Knowledge," in *Mishneh Torah*, trans. Ralph Lerner, in *Maimonides' Empire of Light: Popular Enlightenment in an Age of Belief*, by Ralph Lerner (Chicago: University of Chicago Press, 2000), pp. 141–53.

The Commandments, trans. Chavel
> *The Commandments (Sefer ha-Mitzvot)*, trans. and ed. Charles B. Chavel (London: Soncino, 1967).

Commentary on the Mishnah, trans. Kafah
> *Commentary on the Mishnah* [Judeo-Arabic original with facing Hebrew translation], ed. and trans. Joseph D. Kafah (Jerusalem: Mosad ha-Rav Kook, 1963–68).

Commentary on the Mishnah (Sanhedrin), trans. Rosner
> *Commentary on the Mishnah, Tractate Sanhedrin*, trans. Fred Rosner (New York: Sepher-Hermon, 1981).

Commentary on the Mishnah, Sanhedrin X, ed. Twersky
> "Ḥelek: Sanhedrin, Chapter Ten," in *Commentary on the Mishnah*, Sanhedrin X, in *A Maimonides Reader*, ed. Isadore Twersky (New York: Behrman House, 1972), pp. 401–21.

Crisis and Leadership
> *Crisis and Leadership: Epistles of Maimonides*, trans. Abraham Halkin, ed. David Hartman (Philadelphia: Jewish Publication Society of America, 1985).

"De'ot." *See* "Hilkhot De'ot."

"Eight Chapters," in *Ethical Writings*, trans. Weiss and Butterworth
> "Eight Chapters," in *Ethical Writings of Maimonides*, ed. and trans. Raymond L. Weiss and Charles E. Butterworth (New York: New York University Press, 1975), pp. 60–104.

"Epistle to Yemen," trans. Halkin
> "The Epistle to Yemen," in *Crisis and Leadership: Epistles of Maimonides*, trans. Abraham Halkin, ed. David Hartman (Philadelphia: Jewish Publication Society of America, 1985), pp. 91–149.

"Epistle to Yemen," trans. Kraemer
> "Epistle to Yemen," trans. Joel L. Kraemer, in *Maimonides' Empire of Light: Popular Enlightenment in an Age of Belief*, by Ralph Lerner (Chicago: University of Chicago Press, 2000), pp. 99–132.

"Essay on Resurrection," trans. Halkin
> "The Essay on Resurrection," in *Crisis and Leadership: Epistles of Maimonides*, trans. Abraham Halkin, ed. David Hartman (Philadelphia: Jewish Publication Society of America, 1985), pp. 211–33.

Guide, trans. Pines
> *The Guide of the Perplexed*, trans. Shlomo Pines, with an introductory essay by Leo Strauss (Chicago: University of Chicago Press, 1963).

Le Guide des égarés
> *Le Guide des égarés*, trans. Salomon Munk (Paris: A. Franck, 1870); nouv. éd. rev. Charles Mopsik (Paris: Verdier, 1980). (*Note*: the 1980 "revised edition" lacks the valuable notes of Munk, contained only in the original edition. However, the complete 1870 edition is available online through several portals.)

Hakdamot ha-Rambam le-Mishnah, ed. Shailat
> *Hakdamot ha-Rambam le-Mishnah: The Introductions of Maimonides in the "Commentary on the Mishnah"* [in Hebrew], ed. Isaac Shailat (Jerusalem: Ma'aleh Adumim, 5756/1996).

"Hilkhot Avodah Zarah" (also just "Avodah Zarah"), trans. Hyamson
> "Hilkhot Avodah Zarah" ("Laws of Idolatry"), in *Mishneh Torah*, vol. 1, *The Book of Knowledge* (*Sefer ha-Madda*), ed. and trans. Moses Hyamson (New York: Feldheim, 1981).

"Hilkhot De'ot" (also just "De'ot"), trans. Hyamson
"Hilkhot De'ot" ("Laws Relating to Moral Dispositions"), in *Mishneh Torah*, vol. 1, *The Book of Knowledge* (*Sefer ha-Madda*), ed. and trans. Moses Hyamson (New York: Feldheim, 1981).

"Hilkhot Melakhim" (also just "Melakhim"), ed. Rubenstein
"Hilkhot Melakhim," in *Sefer Shoftim*, in *Mishneh Torah*, bk. 14, ed. Shmuel Tanhum Rubenstein (Jerusalem: Mosad ha-Rav Kook, 5145/1985).

"Hilkhot Sanhedrin" (also just "Sanhedrin"), ed. Rubenstein
"Hilkhot Sanhedrin," in *Sefer Shoftim*, in *Mishneh Torah*, bk. 14, ed. Shmuel Tanhum Rubenstein (Jerusalem: Mosad ha-Rav Kook, 5145/1985).

"Hilkhot Talmud Torah" (also just "Talmud Torah"), trans. Hyamson
"Hilkhot Talmud Torah" ("Laws Concerning the Study of the Torah"), in *Mishneh Torah*, vol. 1, *The Book of Knowledge* (*Sefer ha-Madda*), ed. and trans. Moses Hyamson (New York: Feldheim, 1981).

"Hilkhot Teshuvah" (also just "Teshuvah"), trans. Hyamson
"Hilkhot Teshuvah" ("Laws of Repentance"), in *Mishneh Torah*, vol. 1, *The Book of Knowledge* (*Sefer ha-Madda*), ed. and trans. Moses Hyamson (New York: Feldheim, 1981).

"Hilkhot Yesodei ha-Torah" (also just "Yesodei ha-Torah"), trans. Hyamson
"Hilkhot Yesodei ha-Torah" ("Laws of the Basic Principles of the Torah"), in *Mishneh Torah*, vol. 1, *The Book of Knowledge* (*Sefer ha-Madda*), ed. and trans. Moses Hyamson (New York: Feldheim, 1981).

"Idolatry." *See* "Laws Concerning Idolatry."

Igrot ha-Rambam, ed. Kafah
Igrot ha-Rambam, ed. and trans. Joseph Kafah (Jerusalem: Mosad ha-Rav Kook, 5732/1972).

Igrot ha-Rambam, ed. Shailat
Igrot ha-Rambam: Letters and Essays of Maimonides, ed. Isaac Shailat, 3rd ed. (Jerusalem: Ma'aleh Adumim, 5755/1995).

"Introduction" to the *Mishneh Torah*, trans. Lerner
"Introduction," in *Mishneh Torah*, trans. Ralph Lerner, in *Maimonides' Empire of Light: Popular Enlightenment in an Age of Belief*, by Ralph Lerner (Chicago: University of Chicago Press, 2000), pp. 133–41.

"Kings." *See* "Laws Concerning Kings and Wars."

Kovetz
Kovetz Teshuvot ha-Rambam ve-Igrotav (*Collected Responsa and Letters of Maimonides*), ed. Abraham Lichtenberg (Leipzig, 1859; reprinted, Westmead, UK: Gregg International, 1969).

"Laws Concerning Character Traits," in *Ethical Writings*, trans. Weiss and Butterworth
"Laws Concerning Character Traits," in *Ethical Writings of Maimonides*, ed. and trans. Raymond L. Weiss and Charles E. Butterworth (New York: New York University Press, 1975), pp. 28–52.

"Laws Concerning Idolatry" (also just "Idolatry"), trans. Hyamson
"Laws Concerning Idolatry" ("Hilkhot Avodah Zarah"), in *Mishneh Torah*, vol. 1, *The Book of Knowledge* (*Sefer ha-Madda*), ed. and trans. Moses Hyamson (New York: Feldheim, 1981).

"Laws Concerning Kings and Wars" (also just "Kings"), trans. Hershman
"Laws Concerning Kings and Wars," in *The Book of Judges*, bk. 14 of *The Code of Maimo-*

nides (Mishneh Torah), trans. Abraham M. Hershman (New Haven: Yale University Press, 1949), pp. 205–42.
"Laws Concerning Repentance," trans. Weiss and Butterworth
"Laws Concerning Repentance," chap. 9, in *Ethical Writings of Maimonides*, ed. and trans. Raymond L. Weiss and Charles E. Butterworth (New York: New York University Press, 1975), pp. 169–71.
"Laws Concerning the Study of the Torah," trans. Hyamson
"Laws Concerning the Study of the Torah" ("Hilkhot Talmud Torah"), in *Mishneh Torah*, vol. 1, *The Book of Knowledge (Sefer ha-Madda)*, ed. and trans. Moses Hyamson (New York: Feldheim, 1981).
"Laws of Kings and Their Wars," trans. Weiss and Butterworth
"Laws of Kings and Their Wars," chaps. 11 and 12, in *Ethical Writings of Maimonides*, ed. and trans. Raymond L. Weiss and Charles E. Butterworth (New York: New York University Press, 1975), pp. 171–76.
"Laws of Repentance" (also just "Repentance"), trans. Hyamson
"Laws of Repentance" ("Hilkhot Teshuvah"), in *Mishneh Torah*, vol. 1, *The Book of Knowledge (Sefer ha-Madda)*, ed. and trans. Moses Hyamson (New York: Feldheim, 1981).
"Laws of the Basic Principles of the Torah," trans. Hyamson
"Laws of the Basic Principles of the Torah" ("Hilkhot Yesodei ha-Torah"), in *Mishneh Torah*, vol. 1, *The Book of Knowledge (Sefer ha-Madda)*, ed. and trans. Moses Hyamson (New York: Feldheim, 1981).
"Laws of the Sanhedrin," trans. Hershman
"Laws of the Sanhedrin" ("Hilkhot Sanhedrin"), in *The Book of Judges*, bk. 14 of *The Code of Maimonides (Mishneh Torah)*, trans. Abraham M. Hershman (New Haven: Yale University Press, 1949), pp. 3–80.
"Laws Relating to Moral Dispositions," trans. Hyamson
"Laws Relating to Moral Dispositions" ("Hilkhot De'ot"), in *Mishneh Torah*, vol. 1, *The Book of Knowledge (Sefer ha-Madda)*, ed. and trans. Moses Hyamson (New York: Feldheim, 1981).
"Letter on Astrology," trans. Lerner
"Letter on Astrology," trans. Ralph Lerner, in *Maimonides' Empire of Light: Popular Enlightenment in an Age of Belief*, by Ralph Lerner (Chicago: University of Chicago Press, 2000), pp. 178–87.
Letters, trans. Stitskin
Letters of Maimonides, ed. and trans. Leon D. Stitskin (New York: Feldheim, 1977).
"Letter to the Jews of Marseilles in 1194," trans. Stitskin
"Letter to the Jews of Marseilles in 1194," in *Letters of Maimonides* ed. and trans. Leon D. Stitskin (New York, Feldheim, 1977), pp. 118–29.
"Logic," in *Ethical Writings*, trans. Weiss and Butterworth
"Treatise on the Art of Logic," in *Ethical Writings of Maimonides*, ed. and trans. Raymond L. Weiss and Charles E. Butterworth (New York: New York University Press, 1975), 155–63.
"Logic," trans. Efros
"'Treatise on Logic' (*Makalah fi-Sina'at al-Mantik*): The Arabic Original and Three Hebrew Translations," ed. and trans. Israel Efros, *Proceedings of the American Academy for Jewish Research* 8 (1937–38): 1–136.
Logic = "Treatise on the Art of Logic." See "Logic," trans. Efros.
"Melakhim." *See* "Hilkhot Melakhim."

Mishneh Torah
   Code of Law, 14 vols. (several editions: Frankel; Kafah; Rabinovitch; Shailat; Or Vishua; Mechon Mamare).
Reader, ed. Twersky
   A Maimonides Reader, ed. Isadore Twersky (New York: Behrman House, 1972).
"Repentance." *See* "Laws of Repentance" and "Laws Concerning Repentance."
"Sanhedrin." *See* "Hilkhot Sanhedrin" (also just "Sanhedrin"), ed. Rubenstein, and "Laws of the Sanhedrin," trans. Hershman
"Talmud Torah." *See* "Hilkhot Talmud Torah."
"Teshuvah." *See* "Hilkhot Teshuvah."
Traité d'éthique, ed. Brague
   Traité d'éthique—"Huite chapitres," ed. and trans. Rémi Brague (Paris: Desclée de Brouwer, 2001).
Traité de logique, ed. Brague
   Traité de logique, ed. and trans. Rémi Brague (Paris: Desclée de Brouwer, 1996).
"Treatise on Resurrection," trans. Fradkin
   "Treatise on Resurrection," trans. Hillel Fradkin, in *Maimonides' Empire of Light: Popular Enlightenment in an Age of Belief*, by Ralph Lerner (Chicago: University of Chicago Press, 2000), pp. 154–77.
"Yesodei ha-Torah." *See* "Hilkhot Yesodei ha-Torah."

WORKS BY LEO STRAUSS

Brague. See *Maïmonide*.
Early Writings
   The Early Writings: 1921–32, ed. and trans. Michael Zank (Albany: State University of New York Press, 2002).
Hobbes Politische Wissenschaft und zugehörige Schriften—Briefe, vol. 3 of *Gesammelte Schriften*
   Hobbes Politische Wissenschaft und zugehörige Schriften—Briefe, vol. 3 of *Gesammelte Schriften*, ed. Heinrich Meier (Stuttgart: J. B. Metzler, 2001).
Jewish Philosophy and the Crisis of Modernity
   Jewish Philosophy and the Crisis of Modernity: Essays and Lectures in Modern Jewish Thought, ed. Kenneth Hart Green (Albany: State University of New York Press, 1997).
Liberalism Ancient and Modern
   Liberalism Ancient and Modern (New York: Basic Books, 1968; reprint, Chicago: University of Chicago Press, 1995).
Maïmonide
   Maïmonide, trans. and ed. Rémi Brague (Paris: Presses Universitaires de France, 1988; 2nd ed., 2012).
On Tyranny
   On Tyranny, ed. Victor Gourevitch and Michael S. Roth (Chicago: University of Chicago Press, 2000).
Persecution and the Art of Writing
   Persecution and the Art of Writing (Glencoe, IL: Free Press, 1952; reprint, Chicago: University of Chicago Press, 1988).
Philosophie und Gesetz: Frühe Schriften, vol. 2 of *Gesammelte Schriften*
   Philosophie und Gesetz: Frühe Schriften, vol. 2 of *Gesammelte Schriften*, ed. Heinrich Meier (Stuttgart: J. B. Metzler, 1997).

Philosophy and Law
  Philosophy and Law: Contributions to the Understanding of Maimonides and His Predecessors, trans. Eve Adler (Albany: State University of New York Press, 1995).
Rebirth of Classical Political Rationalism
  The Rebirth of Classical Political Rationalism: An Introduction to the Thought of Leo Strauss; Essays and Lectures by Leo Strauss, ed. Thomas L. Pangle (Chicago: University of Chicago Press, 1989).
Die Religionskritik Spinozas und zugehörige Schriften, vol. 1 of *Gesammelte Schriften*
  Die Religionskritik Spinozas und zugehörige Schriften, vol. 1 of *Gesammelte Schriften*, ed. Heinrich Meier (Stuttgart: J. B. Metzler, 1996; rev. ed., 2001).
Spinoza's Critique of Religion
  Spinoza's Critique of Religion, trans. Elsa Sinclair (New York: Schocken, 1965; reprint, Chicago: University of Chicago Press, 1997).
Studies in Platonic Political Philosophy
  Studies in Platonic Political Philosophy, ed. Joseph Cropsey, with an introduction by Thomas L. Pangle (Chicago: University of Chicago Press, 1983).
What Is Political Philosophy?
  What Is Political Philosophy? And Other Studies (New York: Free Press, 1959; reprint, Chicago: University of Chicago Press, 1988).

Sources and History of the Texts

All essays and lectures of Leo Strauss that appear in the present volume are the sole possession of the Literary Estate of Leo Strauss. It preserves and asserts all legal rights with respect to ownership of the materials in this volume.

"How to Study Medieval Philosophy" was first delivered as a lecture at the Fourth Institute of Biblical and Post-biblical Studies, 16 May 1944. It has been previously edited and published twice. First, it appeared in print as "How to Begin to Study Medieval Philosophy," in Leo Strauss, *The Rebirth of Classical Political Rationalism*, ed. Thomas L. Pangle (Chicago: University of Chicago Press, 1989), pp. 207–26. Second, it appeared in print as "How to Study Medieval Philosophy," ed. David Bolotin, Christopher Bruell, and Thomas L. Pangle, *Interpretation: A Journal of Political Philosophy* 23, no. 3 (Spring 1996): 321–38.

"Spinoza's Critique of Maimonides" first appeared in print as a chapter, "Die Kritik an Maimuni," of Leo Strauss, *Die Religionskritik Spinozas als Grundlage seiner Bibelwissenschaft* (Berlin: Akademie-Verlag, 1930; reprinted, Hildesheim: Georg Olms Verlag, 1981), chapter B, pp. 129–81. It first appeared in English translation as a chapter, "The Critique of Maimonides," of Leo Strauss, *Spinoza's Critique of Religion*, translated by Elsa M. Sinclair (New York: Schocken, 1965; reprinted with corrections, Chicago: University of Chicago Press, 1989), chapter VI, pp. 147–92, with the notes appearing on pp. 293–98. The German original has since been reedited and republished in Leo Strauss, *Die Religionskritik Spinozas und zugehörige Schriften*, vol. 1 of *Gesammelte Schriften*, ed. Heinrich Meier (Stuttgart: J. B. Metzler, 1996; 3rd rev. ed. 2008), pp. 195–247.

"Cohen and Maimonides" first appeared in print as "Cohen und Maimuni," in Leo Strauss, *Philosophie und Gesetz: Frühe Schriften*, vol. 2 of *Gesammelte Schriften*, ed. Heinrich Meier (Stuttgart: J. B. Metzler, 1997, rev. ed., 1998), pp. 393–436. The editor of the German version deciphered the handwritten original text from notebooks in which Strauss had first composed it, as well as changes made by Strauss in the margins. It is assumed that these notebooks were used by Strauss as the basis of a lecture, "Cohen und Maimuni," which he was to deliver in the auditorium of the Academy for the Science of Judaism in Berlin on 4 May 1931. It is first appearing in English translation in the present volume, as translated by Martin D. Yaffe and Ian A. Moore, in consultation with the present editor. The notes to "Cohen and Maimonides" in this volume are mainly the work of the translators and of the present editor, although they would also like to acknowledge that in this present version they have greatly benefited from the editorial notes of Heinrich Meier.

"The Philosophic Foundation of the Law: Maimonides' Doctrine of Prophecy and Its Sources" first appeared in German as "Maimunis Lehre von der Prophetie und ihre Quellen," *Le Monde Oriental* (Uppsala) 28 (1934): 99-139. It was reproduced (with slight revisions) as chapter 3, with the addition to the title of "Die philosophische Begründung des Gesetzes," in Leo Strauss, *Philosophie und Gesetz: Beiträge zum Verständnis Maimunis und Seiner Vorlaüfer* (Berlin: Schocken Verlag, 1935), pp. 87-122. It first appeared in English translation as chapter 3 of *Philosophy and Law: Essays toward the Understanding of Maimonides and His Predecessors*, trans. Fred Baumann (Philadelphia: Jewish Publication Society, 1987), pp. 81-110, with the notes appearing on pp. 125-34. It next appeared in English translation as chapter 3 of *Philosophy and Law: Contributions to the Understanding of Maimonides and His Predecessors*, trans. Eve Adler (Albany: State University of New York Press, 1995), pp. 101-33, with the notes appearing on pp. 145-54. It is the translation of the late Eve Adler which is reprinted in the present volume. The German original has since been reedited and republished in Leo Strauss, *Philosophie und Gesetz: Frühe Schriften*, vol. 2 of *Gesammelte Schriften*, ed. Heinrich Meier, pp. 87-123.

Appendix A to the fourth essay, i.e., the first two paragraphs and the last three paragraphs of the "'Introduction' to *Philosophy and Law*," originally appeared as the same paragraphs (first two and last three) in the German "Einleitung" to Leo Strauss, *Philosophie und Gesetz: Beiträge zum Verständnis Maimunis und Seiner Vorlaüfer* (Berlin: Schocken Verlag, 1935), pp. 9-10 and 28-29. These paragraphs first appeared in English translation in the "Introduction" of *Philosophy and Law: Essays toward the Understanding of Maimonides and His Predecessors*, trans. Fred Baumann (Philadelphia: Jewish Publication Society, 1987), pp. 3-4, 19-20. They next appeared in English translation in the "Introduction" of *Philosophy and Law: Contributions to the Understanding of Maimonides and His Predecessors*, trans. Eve Adler (Albany: State University of New York Press, 1995), pp. 21-22, 38-39. It is the translation of the late Eve Adler which is reprinted in the present volume. These same paragraphs in the original German have since been reedited and republished in Leo Strauss, *Philosophie und Gesetz: Frühe Schriften*, vol. 2 of *Gesammelte Schriften*, ed. Heinrich Meier, pp. 9-10, 26-27.

Appendix B to the fourth essay, the introductory section and section B, "Maimonides," of "The Legal Foundation of Philosophy," originally formed sections in chapter 2 of the original German, "Die gesetzliche Begründung der Philosophie: Das Gebot des Philosophieren und die Freiheit des Philosophierens," in Leo Strauss, *Philosophie und Gesetz: Beiträge zum Verständnis Maimunis und Seiner Vorlaüfer* (Berlin: Schocken Verlag, 1935), pp. 68-69, 76-79. They first appeared in English translation as the same sections in chapter 2 of *Philosophy and Law: Essays toward the Understanding of Maimonides and His Predecessors*, trans. Fred Baumann (Philadelphia: Jewish Publication Society, 1987), pp. 61-62, 68-71. They next appeared in English translation as the same sections in chapter 2 of *Philosophy and Law: Contributions to the Understanding of Maimonides and His Predecessors*, trans. Eve Adler (Albany: State University of New York Press, 1995), pp. 81-82, 89-92. It is the translation of the late Eve Adler which is reprinted in the present volume. These same sections in the original German have since been reedited and republished in Leo Strauss, *Philosophie und Gesetz: Frühe Schriften*, vol. 2 of *Gesammelte Schriften*, ed. Heinrich Meier, pp. 67-68, 75-78.

"Some Remarks on the Political Science of Maimonides and Farabi" first appeared in print in the original French as "Quelques Remarques sur la Science Politique de Maïmonide et de Farabi," *Revue des Études Juives* 100 (1936): 1-37. It first appeared in English translation as "Some Remarks on the Political Science of Maimonides and Farabi," trans. Robert Bartlett, *Interpretation: A Journal of Political Philosophy* 18, no. 1 (Fall 1990): 3-30. The translation of Robert Bartlett has been essentially reprinted in the present volume; however, some revisions, corrections, and alterations have been made by the translator in consultation with the present editor. The French original has since been reedited and republished in Leo Strauss, *Philosophie und Gesetz: Frühe Schriften*, vol. 2 of *Gesammelte Schriften*, ed. Heinrich Meier, pp. 125-58.

"The Place of the Doctrine of Providence according to Maimonides" first appeared in print in the original German as "Der Ort der Vorsehungslehre nach der Ansicht Maimunis," in *Monatsschrift für Geschichte und Wissen-*

schaft des Judentums 81, no. 1 (January–February 1937): 93–105. It first appeared in English translation as "The Place of the Doctrine of Providence according to Maimonides," trans. Gabriel Bartlett and Svetozar Minkov, *Review of Metaphysics* 57 (March 2004): 537–49. It is the translation of Gabriel Bartlett and Svetozar Minkov which is reprinted in the present volume. The German original has since been reedited and republished in Leo Strauss, *Philosophie und Gesetz: Frühe Schriften*, vol. 2 of *Gesammelte Schriften*, ed. Heinrich Meier, pp. 179–90.

"Review of *The Mishneh Torah*, Book 1, by Moses Maimonides, Edited according to the Bodleian Codex with Introduction, Biblical and Talmudical References, Notes, and English Translation by Moses Hyamson" originally appeared in *Review of Religion* 3, no. 4 (May 1937): 448–56.

"The Literary Character of *The Guide of the Perplexed*" first appeared in *Essays on Maimonides*, ed. Salo W. Baron (New York: Columbia University Press, 1941), pp. 37–91. It was reprinted by the author in Leo Strauss, *Persecution and the Art of Writing* (New York: Free Press, 1952; reprint, Chicago: University of Chicago Press, 1988), pp. 38–94. In the present edition, it appears essentially unchanged, although the title has been very slightly altered from how it appeared in the original and the reprinted versions ("The Literary Character of the *Guide for the Perplexed*"). This title form makes it conform with the translated title of Maimonides' book in the version of Shlomo Pines (*The Guide of the Perplexed*). It also happens to be the case that this title form was usually preferred by Strauss. And it is the title form that is used consistently in the present book.

"Maimonides' Statement on Political Science" first appeared in *Proceedings of the American Academy for Jewish Research* 22 (1953): 115–30. It was reprinted by the author in Leo Strauss, *What Is Political Philosophy? And Other Studies* (New York: Free Press, 1959; reprint, Chicago: University of Chicago Press, 1988), pp. 155–69.

"Introduction to Maimonides' *The Guide of the Perplexed*" was a lecture delivered by Leo Strauss at the Hillel House, University of Chicago, on 7 and 14 February 1960. It is preserved solely on tape, with the original written manuscript apparently lost, or at least unknown to the present editor. The lecture appears as it has been transcribed from the tape recordings by the present editor. It has not previously appeared in print in any form.

"How To Begin To Study *The Guide of the Perplexed*" first appeared in print as the introductory essay to Moses Maimonides, *The Guide of the Perplexed*, trans. Shlomo Pines (Chicago: University of Chicago Press, 1963), pp. xi–lvi. The first portion of the essay also appeared in print as "On the Plan of *The Guide of the Perplexed*," in *Harry Austryn Wolfson Jubilee Volume*, ed. Saul Lieberman et al. (Jerusalem: American Academy for Jewish Research, 1965), vol. 2, pp. 775–91. It was reprinted, with some slight changes, by the author in Leo Strauss, *Liberalism Ancient and Modern* (New York: Basic Books, 1968; reprint, Chicago: University of Chicago Press, 1995), pp. 140–84.

"Notes on Maimonides' *Book of Knowledge*" first appeared in print in *Studies in Mysticism and Religion Presented to Gershom G. Scholem*, ed. Efraim E. Urbach, R. J. Zwi Werblowsky, and Chaim Wirszubski (Jerusalem: Magnes Press, 1967), pp. 269–83. It was reprinted by the author in Leo Strauss, *Studies in Platonic Political Philosophy* (Chicago: University of Chicago Press, 1983), pp. 192–204.

"Note on Maimonides' *Treatise on the Art of Logic*" first appeared in print in Leo Strauss, *Studies in Platonic Political Philosophy* (Chicago: University of Chicago Press, 1983), pp. 208–9. Its date of composition is recorded in Strauss's handwriting on the original manuscript as July 11–19, 1968.

"Note on Maimonides' *Letter on Astrology*" first appeared in print in Leo Strauss, *Studies in Platonic Political Philosophy* (Chicago: University of Chicago Press, 1983), pp. 205–7. Its date of composition is recorded in Strauss's handwriting on the original manuscript as July 21–23, 1968.

"On Abravanel's Philosophical Tendency and Political Teaching" first appeared in print in *Isaac Abravanel: Six Lectures*, ed. J. B. Trend and H. Loewe (Cambridge: Cambridge University Press, 1937), pp. 95–129. The English original has since been reedited and republished in Leo Strauss, *Philosophie und Gesetz: Frühe Schriften*, vol. 2 of *Gesammelte Schriften*, ed. Heinrich Meier, pp. 195–227. The version in the present book is based on the 1937 version, while also referring to the *Gesammelte Schriften* version, and with some further editing done by the present editor.

"The Secret Teaching of Maimonides" is a one-page typescript, which records no date of composition. It was uncovered by Yiftach Ofek in the Leo Strauss Archive in the library of the University of Chicago. It has not previously appeared in print in any form.

Bibliography

Selected works on Leo Strauss and medieval thought related to Maimonides:

Abbas, Makram. "Leo Strauss and Arab Philosophy." *Diogenes* 226 (2010): 101–19.
Adler, Eve. "Translator's Introduction." In *Philosophy and Law: Contributions to the Understanding of Maimonides and His Predecessors*, by Leo Strauss, 1–19. Albany: State University of New York Press, 1995.
———. "Leo Strauss's *Philosophie und Gesetz*." In *Leo Strauss's Thought: Toward a Critical Engagement*, ed. A. Udoff, 183–226. Boulder, CO: Lynne Rienner, 1991.
Adorisio, Chiara. "Philosophy of Religion or Political Philosophy? The Debate between Leo Strauss and Julius Guttmann." *European Journal of Jewish Studies* 1, no. 1 (2007): 135–55.
Alfarabi. *The Philosophy of Plato and Aristotle*. Trans. Muhsin Mahdi. Ithaca: Cornell University Press, 1969; reprint, 2002.
———. *The Political Writings: "Selected Aphorisms" and Other Texts*. Ed. and trans. Charles E. Butterworth. Ithaca: Cornell University Press, 2001.
Altman, William. "Exotericism after Lessing: The Enduring Influence of F. H. Jacobi on Leo Strauss." *Journal of Jewish Thought and Philosophy* 15, no. 1 (2007): 59–83.
———. "Leo Strauss on 'German Nihilism': Learning the Art of Writing." *Journal of the History of Ideas* 68, no. 4 (October 2007): 587–612.
Altmann, Alexander. "Maimonides on the Intellect and the Scope of Metaphysics." In *Von der mittelalterlichen zur modernen Aufklärung*, 60–129. Tübingen: J. C. B. Mohr (Paul Siebeck), 1987.
———. "Review of *The Guide of the Perplexed*, by Moses Maimonides, translated with an introduction and notes by Shlomo Pines, and with an introductory essay by Leo Strauss." *Journal of Religion* 44 (1964): 260–61.
Anastaplo, George. "Maimonides on Revelation and Reason." In *The American Moralist: On Law, Ethics, and Government*, 58–79. Athens: Ohio University Press, 1992.
Batnitzky, Leora. *Leo Strauss and Emmanuel Levinas: Philosophy and the Politics of Revelation*. New York: Cambridge University Press, 2006.
Becker, Jacob. *The Secret of "The Guide of the Perplexed": A Reevaluation of the World View of the Rambam* [in Hebrew]. Tel Aviv: J. Shimoni, 1955.
Belaval, Yvon. "Pour une sociologie de la philosophie." *Critique* 9 (1953): 852–66.
Ben-Asher, Mordechai. "Religion and Reason in Maimonides: Contribution to an Explanation of the Views of Julius Guttmann and Leo Strauss" [in Hebrew]. *Bash-Sha'ar* 4 (1961): 78–87.

Berman, Lawrence V. "Maimonides on the Fall of Man." *AJS Review* 5 (1980): 1–15.

———. "The Structure of *The Guide*: Reflections Occasioned by L. Strauss and S. Rawidowicz." In *Proceedings of the Sixth World Congress of Jewish Studies*, vol. 3, ed. Avigdor Shinan, 7–13. Jerusalem: World Union of Jewish Studies, 1977.

———. "Maimonides, the Disciple of Alfarabi." *Israel Oriental Studies* 4 (1974): 154–78.

———. "A Re-examination of Maimonides' 'Statement on Political Science.'" *Journal of the American Oriental Society* 89 (1969): 106–11.

Berns, Laurence. "The Relation between Religion and Philosophy: Reflections on Leo Strauss's Suggestion Concerning the Source and Sources of Modern Philosophy." *Interpretation* 19, no. 1 (1991): 43–60.

Bernstein, Jeffrey A. "Leo Strauss's Re-origination of the Athens/Jerusalem Opposition: Reflections on 'What Is Political Philosophy?'" Unpublished manuscript, 2011.

Botwinick, Aryeh. "Skeptical Motifs Linking Together Maimonides' *Guide* and His *Mishneh Torah*." In *The Trias of Maimonides: Jewish, Arabic, and Ancient Culture of Knowledge*, ed. Georges Tamer, 151–74. Berlin: Walter de Gruyter, 2005.

Bouretz, Pierre. "The Legacy of Leo Strauss (1899–1973)." In *Witnesses for the Future: Philosophy and Messianism*, trans. Michael B. Smith, 477–585, 865–908. Baltimore: Johns Hopkins University Press, 2010.

Brague, Rémi. "Leo Strauss and Maimonides." In *Leo Strauss's Thought: Toward a Critical Engagement*, ed. A. Udoff, 93–114. Boulder, CO: Lynne Rienner, 1991. For a French version, see "Leo Strauss et Maïmonide," in *Maimonides and Philosophy*, ed. S. Pines and Y. Yovel (Dordrecht: Martinus Nijhoff, 1986), 246–68.

———. "Athènes, Jérusalem, La Mecque: L'interprétation 'musulmane' de la philosophie grecque chez Leo Strauss." *Revue de Metaphysique et de Morale* 94, no. 3 (1989): 309–36. For an English version, see "Athens, Jerusalem, and Mecca: Leo Strauss's 'Muslim' Interpretation of Greek Philosophy," *Poetics Today* 19, no. 2 (Summer 1998): 235–59.

Brumlick, Micha. "Der Kronzeuge: Hegels Maimonides zwischen Philo und Spinoza." In *Moses Maimonides (1138–1204): His Religious, Scientific, and Philosophical 'Wirkungsgeschichte' in Different Cultural Contexts*, ed. G. K. Hasselhoff and O. Fraisse, 385–95. Würzburg: Ergon Verlag, 2004.

Buijs, Joseph A. "The Philosophical Character of Maimonides' *Guide*: A Critique of Strauss's Interpretation." *Judaism* 27 (1978): 448–57. Also in *Maimonides: A Collection of Critical Essays*, ed. J. A. Buijs (Notre Dame: University of Notre Dame Press, 1988), 59–70.

Butterworth, Charles E., ed. *The Political Aspects of Islamic Philosophy: Essays in Honor of Muhsin Mahdi*. Cambridge, MA: Harvard University Press, 1992.

Carpino, Joseph J. "Review of *Christianity and Political Philosophy*, by Frederick D. Wilhelmsen." *Interpretation* 8 (1979–80): 204–22.

Chalier, Catherine. *Spinoza, lecteur de Maïmonide: La question théologico-politique*. Paris: Les Éditions du Cerf, 2006.

———. "Les lumières médiévales." *Les cahiers de philosophie* 18 (1994): 246–60.

———. "Léo Strauss: Entre le théologique et le politique." *Les temps modernes* 48, no. 551 (1992): 123–44.

Cohen, Jonathan. *Philosophers and Scholars: Wolfson, Guttmann, and Strauss on the History of Jewish Philosophy*. Trans. Rachel Yarden. Lanham, MD: Lexington Books, 2007. Originally published as *Reason and Change: Perspectives on the Study of Jewish Philosophy and Its History* [in Hebrew] (Jerusalem: Mosad Bialik, 1997).

———. "Jew and Philosopher: The Return to Maimonides in Leo Strauss; Review Essay." *Modern Judaism* 16, no. 1 (1996): 81–91.

Cohen, Mordechai Z. *Opening the Gates of Interpretation: Maimonides' Biblical Hermeneutic.* Leiden: Brill, 2011.

Colmo, Christopher A. *Breaking with Athens: Alfarabi as Founder.* Lanham, MD: Lexington Press, 2005.

———. "Alfarabi on the Prudence of Founders." *Review of Politics* 60, no. 4 (1998): 719–41.

———. "Theory and Practice: Alfarabi's *Plato* Revisited." *American Political Science Review* 86, no. 4 (1992): 966–76.

———. "Reason and Revelation in the Thought of Leo Strauss." *Interpretation* 18, no. 1 (1990): 145–60.

Daiber, Hans. "Das Farabi-Bild des Maimonides: Ideentransfer als hermeneutischer Weg zu Maimonides' Philosophie." In *The Trias of Maimonides: Jewish, Arabic, and Ancient Culture of Knowledge*, ed. Georges Tamer, 199–209. Berlin: Walter de Gruyter, 2005.

Dannhauser, Werner J. "Leo Strauss in His Letters." In *Enlightening Revolutions: Essays in Honor of Ralph Lerner*, ed. Svetozar Minkov, 355–61. Lanham, MD: Lexington Books, 2006.

———. "Leo Strauss as Jew and Citizen." *Interpretation* 17 (1990): 433–47.

———. "Leo Strauss: Becoming Naïve Again." *American Scholar* 44 (1974–75): 636–42.

Davidson, Herbert A. *Maimonides the Rationalist.* Oxford: Littman Library of Jewish Civilization, 2011.

———. *Moses Maimonides: The Man and His Works.* Oxford: Oxford University Press, 2005.

———. *Alfarabi, Avicenna, amd Averroes on Intellect: Their Cosmologies, Theories of the Active Intellect, and Theories of Human Intellect.* Oxford: Oxford University Press, 1992.

———. "Maimonides' Secret Position on Creation." In *Studies in Medieval Jewish History and Literature*, ed. I. Twersky, 16–40. Cambridge, MA: Harvard University Press, 1979.

Davies, Daniel. *Method and Metaphysics in Maimonides' "Guide for the Perplexed."* New York: Oxford University Press, 2011.

Dethier, Hubert. "Some Remarks on the Political Philosophy of Maimonides and Al-Farabi with Regard to Their Conception of Astral Determinism and in the Light of German Idealism." In *Sobre la Vida y Obra de Maimónides: I Congreso Internacional (Córdoba, 1985)*, ed. J. Peláez del Rosal, 95–115. Córdoba: Ediciones El Almendro, 1985.

Diamond, James A. *Maimonides and the Hermeneutics of Concealment: Deciphering Scriptures and Midrash in "The Guide of the Perplexed."* Albany: State University of New York Press, 2002.

Dienstag, Jacob I. "Rambam or Maimonides—Unity or Duality: A Bibliographical Survey." In *Hazon Nahum: Studies in Jewish Law, Thought, and History, Presented to Dr. Norman Lamm*, ed. Y. Elman and J. S. Gurock, 129–48. New York: Yeshiva University Press, 1997.

Druart, Thérèse-Anne. "Al-Farabi, Emanation, and Metaphysics." In *Neoplatonism and Islamic Thought*, ed. P. Morewedge, 127–48. Albany: State University of New York Press, 1992.

Drury, Shadia B. *Leo Strauss and the Political Right.* New York: St. Martin's Press, 1997.

———. *The Political Ideas of Leo Strauss.* New York: St. Martin's Press, 1988.

Fackenheim, Emil L. "Leo Strauss and Judaism." In *Jewish Philosophers and Jewish Philosophy*, ed. Michael L. Morgan, 7–20. Bloomington: Indiana University Press, 1996. Originally appearing in *Claremont Review of Books* 4, no. 4 (Winter 1985): 21–23.

———. "The Possibility of the Universe in Alfarabi, Ibn Sina, and Maimonides." *Proceedings of the American Academy for Jewish Research* 16 (1946–47): 39–70. Also reprinted in *Jewish Philosophers and Jewish Philosophy*, ed. Michael L. Morgan (Bloomington: Indiana University Press, 1996), 97–105.

Fakhry, Majid. *Al-Farabi, Founder of Islamic Neoplatonism: His Life, Works, and Influence.* Oxford: Oneworld, 2002.

Fortin, Ernest L. "Faith and Reason in Contemporary Perspective: Apropos of a Recent Book." *Interpretation* 14 (1986): 371–87. Also in *Classical Christianity and the Political Order: Reflections on the Theologico-Political Problem*, ed. J. B. Benestad (Lanham, MD: Rowman and Littlefield, 1996), 297–316.

———. "Rational Theologians and Irrational Philosophers: A Straussian Perspective." *Interpretation* 12 (1984): 349–56. Also in *Classical Christianity and the Political Order: Reflections on the Theologico-Political Problem*, ed. J. B. Benestad (Lanham, MD: Rowman and Littlefield, 1996), 287–96.

———. "Christian Political Theory." *Review of Politics* 41 (1979): 578–82. Also in *Classical Christianity and the Political Order: Reflections on the Theologico-Political Problem*, ed. J. B. Benestad (Lanham, MD: Rowman and Littlefield, 1996), 355–59.

Fox, Marvin. *Interpreting Maimonides: Studies in Methodology, Metaphysics, and Moral Philosophy.* Chicago: University of Chicago Press, 1990.

———. "Review of *The Guide of the Perplexed*, by Moses Maimonides, translated with an introduction and notes by Shlomo Pines, and with an introductory essay by Leo Strauss." *Journal of the History of Philosophy* 3 (1965): 265–74.

Fradkin, Hillel. "A Word Fitly Spoken: The Interpretation of Maimonides and the Legacy of Leo Strauss." In *Leo Strauss and Judaism: Jerusalem and Athens Revisited*, ed. D. Novak, 55–86. Lanham, MD: Rowman and Littlefield, 1996.

———. "Philosophy and Law: Leo Strauss as a Student of Medieval Jewish Thought." In *Leo Strauss: Political Philosopher and Jewish Thinker*, ed. K. L. Deutsch and W. Nicgorski, 129–41. Lanham, MD: Rowman and Littlefield, 1994.

Fraisse, Otfried. "Die Abwesenheit des Maimonides im Denken Franz Rosenzweig oder: Zwischen Erfahrung und Interpretation." In *Moses Maimonides (1138–1204): His Religious, Scientific, and Philosophical 'Wirkungsgeschichte' in Different Cultural Contexts*, ed. G. K. Hasselhoff and O. Fraisse, 525–47. Würzburg: Ergon Verlag, 2004.

Frank, Daniel H. "Maimonides and Medieval Jewish Aristotelianism." In *The Cambridge Companion to Medieval Jewish Philosophy*, ed. D. H. Frank and O. Leaman, 136–56. Cambridge: Cambridge University Press, 2003.

———. "Reason in Action: The Practicality of Maimonides' *Guide*." In *Commandment and Community: New Essays in Jewish Legal and Political Philosophy*, ed. D. H. Frank, 69–84. Albany: State University of New York Press, 1995.

Frazer, Michael L. "A Critical Re-evaluation of the Esoteric Character of Maimonides' *Guide of the Perplexed*." In *Children of Athena*, ed. Douglas W. Schrader, 179–209. Oneonta: Oneonta Philosophy Studies, 1999.

Galston, Miriam. *Politics and Excellence: The Political Philosophy of Alfarabi.* Princeton: Princeton University Press, 1990.

———. "Philosopher-King vs. Prophet." *Israel Oriental Studies* 8 (1978): 204–18.

Goodman, Micha. *Sodotav shel "Moreh ha-Nevukhim"* [The secrets of *The Guide of the Perplexed*]. Or Yehuda, Israel: Dvir, 2010.

Green, Kenneth Hart. "Leo Strauss and Jewish Philosophy." In *Routledge History of Jewish Philosophy*, ed. D. Frank and O. Leaman. London: Routledge, 1996.

———. *Jew and Philosopher: The Return to Maimonides in the Jewish Thought of Leo Strauss.* Albany: State University of New York Press, 1993.

———. "Religion, Philosophy, and Morality: How Leo Strauss Read Judah Halevi's *Kuzari*." *Journal of the American Academy of Religion* 61, no. 2 (1993): 225–73.

———. "'In the Grip of the Theological-Political Predicament': The Turn to Maimonides in the Jewish Thought of Leo Strauss." In *Leo Strauss's Thought: Toward a Critical Engagement*, ed. A. Udoff, 41–74. Boulder, CO: Lynne Rienner, 1991.

Guidi, Angela. "L'obscurité intentionelle du philosophe: Thèmes néoplatoniciens et Farabiens chez Maïmonide." *Revue des études juives* 166 (2007): 129–45.

Gutas, Dimitri. "The Study of Arabic Philosophy in the Twentieth Century: An Essay on the Historiography of Arabic Philosophy." *British Journal of Middle Eastern Studies* 29, no. 1 (May 2002): 5–25.

Guttmann, Julius. "Philosophie der Religion oder Philosophie des Gesetzes?" *Proceedings of the Israel Academy of Sciences and Humanities* 5 (1976): 146–73 (in Hebrew translation, pp. 188–207).

Harris, Jay M. *Maimonides after 800 Years: Essays on Maimonides and His Influence*. Cambridge, MA: Harvard University Press, 2007.

Hartman, David. *Maimonides: Torah and the Philosophic Quest*. Philadelphia: Jewish Publication Society, 1976; 2nd augmented ed., 2009.

Harvey, Steven. "The Value of Julius Guttmann's *Die Philosophie des Judentums* for Understanding Medieval Jewish Philosophy Today." In *Studies in Hebrew Literature and Jewish Culture*, ed. Martin F. J. Baasten and Reinier Munk, 297–308. Dordrecht: Springer, 2007.

———. "Falaquera's Alfarabi: An Example of the Judaization of the Islamic Falâsifah." *Trumah* 12 (2002): 97–112.

———. "Did Maimonides' Letter to Samuel Ibn Tibbon Determine Which Philosophers Would Be Studied by Later Jewish Philosophers?" *Jewish Quarterly Review* 83, no. 1–2 (July–October, 1992): 51–70.

———. "Maimonides in the Sultan's Palace." In *Perspectives on Maimonides: Philosophical and Historical Studies*, ed. J. L. Kraemer, 47–75. Oxford: Oxford University Press, 1991.

———. *Falaquera's "Epistle of the Debate": An Introduction to Jewish Philosophy*. Cambridge, MA: Harvard University Press, 1987.

Harvey, Warren Zev. "How Leo Strauss Paralyzed Scholarship on the *Guide of the Perplexed* in the 20th Century" [in Hebrew]. *Iyyun* 50 (2001): 387–96.

———. "The *Mishneh Torah* as a Key to the Secrets of the *Guide*." In *Me'ah She'arim: Studies in Medieval Jewish Spiritual Life in Memory of Isadore Twersky*, ed. E. Fleischer, G. Blidstein, C. Horowitz, and B. Septimus, 11–28. Jerusalem: Magnes Press, 2001.

———. "Maimonides' First Commandment, Physics, and Doubt." In *Hazon Nahum: Studies in Jewish Law, Thought, and History, Presented to Dr. Norman Lamm*, ed. Y. Elman and J. S. Gurock, 149–62. New York: Yeshiva University Press, 1997.

———. "Political Philosophy and Halakhah in Maimonides." In *Binah: Studies in Jewish Thought*, vol. 3, ed. J. Dan, 47–64. Westport, CT: Praeger, 1994.

———. "Why Maimonides Was not a *Mutakallim*." In *Perspectives on Maimonides: Philosophical and Historical Studies*, ed. J. L. Kraemer, 105–14. Oxford: Oxford University Press, 1991.

———. "How to Begin to Study *The Guide of the Perplexed* I, 1" [in Hebrew]. *Daat: A Journal of Jewish Philosophy and Kabbalah* 21 (Summer 1988): 5–23.

———. "A Portrait of Spinoza as a Maimonidean." *Journal of the History of Philosophy* 19 (1981): 151–72.

———. "The Return of Maimonideanism." *Jewish Social Studies* 42 (1980): 249–68.

Hyman, Arthur. "Interpreting Maimonides." *Gesher* 5 (1976): 46–59. Also reprinted in *Maimonides: A Collection of Critical Essays*, ed. J. A. Buijs (Notre Dame: Notre Dame University Press, 1988), 19–29.

Idel, Moshe. "Maimonides' *Guide of the Perplexed* and the Kabbalah." *Jewish History* 18, no. 2-3 (2004): 197-226.
———. *Maimonïde et la mystique juive*. Paris: Les Éditions du Cerf, 1991.
———. "Maimonides and Kabbalah." In *Studies in Maimonides*, ed. I. Twersky, 31-82. Cambridge, MA: Harvard University Press, 1990.
Ivry, Alfred L. "Hermann Cohen, Leo Strauss, Alexander Altmann: Maimonides in Germany." In *The Trias of Maimonides: Jewish, Arabic, and Ancient Culture of Knowledge*, ed. Georges Tamer, 175-83. Berlin: Walter de Gruyter, 2005.
———. "Strategies of Interpretation in Maimonides' *Guide of the Perplexed*." *Jewish History* 6, no. 1-2 (1992): 113-30.
———. "Leo Strauss on Maimonides." In *Leo Strauss's Thought: Toward a Critical Engagement*, ed. A. Udoff, 75-91. Boulder, CO: Lynne Rienner, 1991.
Janssens, David. *Between Athens and Jerusalem: Philosophy, Prophecy, and Politics in Leo Strauss's Early Thought*. Albany: State University of New York Press, 2008.
———. "The Problem of Enlightenment: Strauss, Jacobi, and the Pantheism Controversy." *Review of Metaphysics* 56, no. 3 (March 2003): 605-31.
———. "Weimar Revisited: Judaism, Zionism, and Enlightenment in Leo Strauss's Early Thought" [in Hebrew]. *Iyyun* 50 (2001): 407-18.
———. "Questions and Caves: Philosophy, Politics, and History in Leo Strauss's Early Work." *Journal of Jewish Thought and Philosophy* 10 (2000): 111-44.
Jospe, Raphael. *Jewish Philosophy in the Middle Ages*. Boston: Academic Studies Press, 2009.
———. "'The Garden of Eden': On the Chapter Divisions and Literary Structure of the *Guide of the Perplexed*." In *Jewish Philosophy: Foundations and Extensions*, vol. 2, *On Philosophers and Their Thought*, 65-78. Lanham, MD: University Press of America, 2008. Originally published as "The Number and Division of Chapters in *The Guide of the Perplexed*" [in Hebrew]. *Jerusalem Studies in Jewish Thought* 6 (1988): 387-97.
Kaplan, Lawrence. "Monotonically Decreasing Esotericism and the Purpose of *The Guide of the Perplexed*." In *Maimonides after 800 Years: Essays on Maimonides and His Influence*, ed. Jay M. Harris, 135-50. Cambridge, MA: Harvard University Press, 2007.
Kasher, Hannah. "Maimonides: Halakhic Philosopher or Philosophical Halakhist; On Skeptical Epistemology and Its Implications." In *Moses Maimonides (1138-1204): His Religious, Scientific, and Philosophical 'Wirkungsgeschichte' in Different Cultural Contexts*, ed. G. K. Hasselhoff and O. Fraisse, 51-64. Würzburg: Ergon Verlag, 2004.
———. "The Art of Writing in *The Guide of the Perplexed*: A Close Reading of Chapter 26 in Part 3" [in Hebrew]. *Daat: A Journal of Jewish Philosophy and Kabbalah* 37 (Summer 1996): 63-106.
———. "*The Guide*: Masterpiece or Holy Writ?" [in Hebrew]. *Daat: A Journal of Jewish Philosophy and Kabbalah* 32-33 (1994): 73-84.
Kellner, Menachem. "The Literary Character of the *Mishneh Torah*: On the Art of Writing in Maimonides' Halakhic Works." In *Me'ah She'arim: Studies in Medieval Jewish Spiritual Life in Memory of Isadore Twersky*, ed. E. Fleischer, G. Blidstein, C. Horowitz, and B. Septimus, 29-45. Jerusalem: Magnes Press, 2001. Also in *Science in the Bet Midrash: Studies in Maimonides* (Brighton, MA: Academic Studies Press, 2009), 45-61.
———. "Strauss's Maimonides vs. Maimonides' Maimonides." *Le'ela* 50 (December 2000): 29-36. Also in *Science in the Bet Midrash: Studies in Maimonides* (Brighton, MA: Academic Studies Press, 2009), 33-44.
———. "Reading Rambam: Approaches to the Interpretation of Maimonides." *Jewish His-*

tory 5 (1991): 73–93. Also in *Science in the Bet Midrash: Studies in Maimonides* (Brighton, MA: Academic Studies Press, 2009), 19–32.

Klein-Braslavy, Sara. "Maimonides' Exoteric and Esoteric Biblical Interpretations in the *Guide of the Perplexed*." In *Study and Knowledge in Jewish Thought*, ed. Howard Haim Kreisel, 137–64. Jerusalem: Bialik Institute, 2010.

———. *King Solomon and Philosophic Esotericism in the Teaching of the Rambam* [in Hebrew]. Jerusalem: Magnes Press, 1996.

Kleven, Terence J. "A Study of Part I, Chapters 1–7 of Maimonides' *The Guide of the Perplexed*." *Interpretation* 20, no. 1 (1992): 3–16.

Kochin, Michael S. "Morality, Nature, and Esotericism in Leo Strauss's *Persecution and the Art of Writing*." *Review of Politics* 64, no. 2 (2002): 261–83.

Kraemer, Joel L. "The Medieval Arabic Enlightenment." In *The Cambridge Companion to Leo Strauss*, ed. Steven B. Smith, 137–70. New York: Cambridge University Press, 2009.

———. *Maimonides: The Life and World of One of Civilization's Greatest Minds*. New York: Doubleday, 2008.

———. "Moses Maimonides: An Intellectual Portrait." In *The Cambridge Companion to Maimonides*, ed. Kenneth Seeskin, 10–57. New York: Cambridge University Press, 2005.

———. "The Islamic Context of Medieval Jewish Philosophy." In *The Cambridge Companion to Medieval Jewish Philosophy*, ed. Daniel H. Frank and Oliver Leaman, 38–68. Cambridge: Cambridge University Press, 2003.

———. "Naturalism and Universalism in Maimonides' Political and Religious Thought." In *Me'ah She'arim: Studies in Medieval Jewish Spiritual Life in Memory of Isadore Twersky*, ed. E. Fleischer, G. Blidstein, C. Horowitz, and B. Septimus, 47–81. Jerusalem: Magnes Press, 2001.

———. "Maimonides on the Philosophic Sciences in his *Treatise on the Art of Logic*." In *Perspectives on Maimonides: Philosophical and Historical Studies*, ed. J. L. Kraemer, 77–104. Oxford: Oxford University Press, 1991.

———. "Alfarabi's *Opinions of the Virtuous City* and Maimonides' *Foundations of the Law*." In *Studia Orientalia, memoriae D. H. Baneth dedicata*, ed. J. Blau, S. Pines, M. J. Kister, and S. Shaked, 107–53. Jerusalem: Magnes Press, 1979.

Kraemer, Joel L., and Josef Stern. "Shlomo Pines on the Translation of Maimonides' *Guide of the Perplexed*." *Journal of Jewish Thought and Philosophy* 8 (1998): 13–24.

Kravitz, Leonard. *The Hidden Doctrine of Maimonides' "Guide for the Perplexed": Philosophical and Religious God-Language in Tension*. Lewiston, NY: Edwin Mellen Press, 1988.

Kreisel, Howard. *Maimonides' Political Thought: Studies in Ethics, Law, and the Human Ideal*. Albany: State University of New York Press, 1999.

Lampert, Laurence. "Strauss's Recovery of Esotericism." In *The Cambridge Companion to Leo Strauss*, ed. Steven B. Smith, 63–92. New York: Cambridge University Press, 2009.

Langermann, Tzvi. "The 'True Perplexity': *The Guide of the Perplexed*, Part II, Chapter 24." In *Perspectives on Maimonides: Philosophical and Historical Studies*, ed. J. L. Kraemer, 159–74. Oxford: Oxford University Press, 1991.

Leaman, Oliver. "Orientalism and Islamic Philosophy." In *Routledge History of Islamic Philosophy*, ed. S. H. Nasr and O. Leaman, 1143–48. London: Routledge, 2001.

Lenzner, Steven J. "Leo Strauss and the Problem of Freedom of Thought: The Rediscovery of the Philosophic Arts of Reading and Writing." Ph.D. dissertation, Harvard University, 2003.

———. "A Literary Exercise in Self-Knowledge: Strauss's Twofold Interpretation of Maimonides." *Perspectives on Political Science* 31, no. 4 (2002): 225–34.

———. "Strauss's Farabi, Scholarly Prejudice, and Philosophic Politics." *Perspectives on Political Science* 18, no. 4 (Fall 1999): 194–202.

Lerner, Ralph. "Dispersal by Design: The Author's Choice." In *Reason, Faith, and Politics: Essays in Honor of Werner J. Dannhauser*, ed. A. M. Melzer and R. P. Kraynak, 29–41. Lanham, MD: Lexington Books, 2008.

———. "Averroes and Maimonides in Defense of Philosophizing." In *The Trias of Maimonides: Jewish, Arabic, and Ancient Culture of Knowledge*, ed. Georges Tamer, 223–36. Berlin: Walter de Gruyter, 2005.

———. *Maimonides' Empire of Light: Popular Enlightenment in an Age of Belief*. Chicago: University of Chicago Press, 2000.

———. "Foreword." In *Philosophy and Law*, by Leo Strauss, trans. Fred Baumann, ix–xiii. Philadelphia: Jewish Publication Society, 1987.

———. "Moses Maimonides." In *History of Political Philosophy*, ed. L. Strauss and J. Cropsey, 203–22. Chicago: University of Chicago Press, 1972.

Lerner, Ralph, and Muhsin Mahdi, eds. *Medieval Political Philosophy: A Sourcebook*. Ithaca: Cornell University Press, 1972.

Levy, Ze'ev. "On the Motives of Spinoza's and Maimonides' Esoteric Writing." In *Moses Maimonides (1138–1204): His Religious, Scientific, and Philosophical 'Wirkungsgeschichte' in Different Cultural Contexts*, ed. G. K. Hasselhoff and O. Fraisse, 271–88. Würzburg: Ergon Verlag, 2004.

Lorberbaum, Menachem. "Medieval Jewish Political Thought." In *The Cambridge Companion to Medieval Jewish Philosophy*, ed. D. H. Frank and O. Leaman, 176–200. Cambridge: Cambridge University Press, 2003.

———. *Politics and the Limits of Law: Secularizing the Political in Medieval Jewish Thought*. Stanford: Stanford University Press, 2001.

Lorberbaum, Yair. "On Contradictions, Rationality, Dialectics, and Esotericism in Maimonides' *Guide of the Perplexed*." *Review of Metaphysics* 55, no. 4 (2002): 711–50. For a Hebrew version, see "The 'Seventh Cause': On Contradictions in Maimonides' *Guide of the Perplexed*." *Tarbiz* 69, no. 2 (1999–2000): 211–37.

Luz, Ehud. "Leo Strauss as a Jewish Thinker." In *Leo Strauss, Jerusalem and Athens: Selected Writings* [in Hebrew], ed. E. Luz, 1–86. Jerusalem: Leo Baeck Institute/Bialik Institute, 2001.

Mahdi, Muhsin S. *Alfarabi and the Foundations of Islamic Political Philosophy*. Chicago: University of Chicago Press, 2001.

———. "Al-Farabi." In *History of Political Philosophy*, ed. L. Strauss and J. Cropsey, 182–202. Chicago: University of Chicago Press, 1972.

Manekin, Charles H. *On Maimonides*. Belmont, CA: Thomson Wadsworth, 2005.

McCallum, Donald. *Maimonides' "Guide for the Perplexed": Silence and Salvation*. New York: Routledge, 2007.

Meier, Heinrich. "How Strauss Became Strauss." In *Enlightening Revolutions: Essays in Honor of Ralph Lerner*, ed. Svetozar Minkov, 363–82. Lanham, MD: Lexington Books, 2006.

———. *Leo Strauss and the Theologico-Political Problem*. Trans. Marcus Brainard. New York: Cambridge University Press, 2006.

———. "Vorwort des Herausgebers." In *Hobbes Politische Wissenschaft und zugehörige Schriften—Briefe*, vol. 3 of *Gesammelte Schriften*, by Leo Strauss, ed. Heinrich Meier, pp. VII–XXXVIII. Stuttgart: J. B. Metzler, 2001.

———. "Vorwort des Herausgebers." In *Philosophie und Gesetz: Frühe Schriften*, vol. 2 of *Gesammelte Schriften*, by Leo Strauss, ed. Heinrich Meier, pp. IX–XXXIV. Stuttgart: J. B. Metzler, 1997.

Melamed, Abraham. "Is There a Jewish Political Thought? The Medieval Case Reconsidered." *Hebraic Political Studies* 1, no. 1 (Fall, 2005): 24–56.

———. *The Philosopher-King in Medieval and Renaissance Jewish Political Thought*. Albany: State University of New York Press, 2003.

Melzer, Arthur. "Esotericism and the Critique of Historicism." *American Political Science Review* 100 (2006): 279–95.

Momigliano, Arnaldo. "Hermeneutics and Classical Political Thought in Leo Strauss." In *Essays on Ancient and Modern Judaism*, ed. S. Berti, 178–89. Chicago: University of Chicago Press, 1994.

Motzkin, Aryeh Leo. "On Halevi's *Kuzari* as a Platonic Dialogue." *Interpretation* 9 (1980–81): 111–24. Also in *Philosophy and the Jewish Tradition: Lectures and Essays by Aryeh Leo Motzkin*, ed. Yehuda Halper (Leiden: Brill, 2012), 19–35.

———. "On the Interpretation of Maimonides." *Independent Journal of Philosophy* 2 (1978): 39–46. Also in *Philosophy and the Jewish Tradition: Lectures and Essays by Aryeh Leo Motzkin*, ed. Yehuda Halper (Leiden: Brill, 2012), 125–41.

Nicgorski, Walter. "Reason, Politics, and Christian Belief: Review of *The God of Faith and Reason*, by Robert Sokolowski." *Claremont Review of Books* 4, no. 2 (Summer 1985): 18–21.

Novak, David. "The Mind of Maimonides." In *The Second One Thousand Years: Ten People Who Defined a Millennium*, ed. R. J. Neuhaus, 15–27. Grand Rapids, MI: Eerdmans, 2001.

———. "Philosophy and the Possibility of Revelation: A Theological Response to the Challenge of Leo Strauss." In *Leo Strauss and Judaism: Jerusalem and Athens Revisited*, ed. D. Novak, 173–92. Lanham, MD: Rowman and Littlefield, 1996.

———. "Responding to Leo Strauss: Four Recent Maimonidean Studies." *Conservative Judaism* 54 (1992): 80–86.

Nuriel, Avraham. *Revealed and Hidden in Medieval Jewish Philosophy* [in Hebrew]. Jerusalem: Magnes Press, 2000.

Orr, Susan. "Review of *Jew and Philosopher: The Return to Maimonides in the Jewish Thought of Leo Strauss*, by K. H. Green." *Interpretation* 23, no. 2 (1996): 307–16.

Pangle, Thomas L. *Political Philosophy and the God of Abraham*. Baltimore: Johns Hopkins University Press, 2003.

———. "Introduction." In *Studies in Platonic Political Philosophy*, by Leo Strauss, 1–26. Chicago: University of Chicago Press, 1983.

Parens, Joshua. "Escaping the Scholastic Paradigm: The Dispute between Strauss and His Contemporaries about How to Approach Islamic and Jewish Medieval Philosophy." In *Encountering the Medieval in Modern Jewish Thought*, ed. James A. Diamond and Aaron W. Hughes, 203–27. Leiden: Brill, 2012.

———. *Maimonides and Spinoza: Their Conflicting Views of Human Nature*. Chicago: University of Chicago Press, 2012.

———. "Strauss on Maimonides' Secretive Political Science." *Perspectives on Political Science* 39, no. 2 (April–June 2010): 82–86.

———. *An Islamic Philosophy of Virtuous Religions: Introducing Alfarabi*. Albany: State University of New York Press, 2006.

―――. *Metaphysics as Rhetoric: Alfarabi's Summary of Plato's "Laws."* Albany: State University of New York Press, 1995.
Parens, Joshua, and Joseph C. MacFarland, eds. *Medieval Political Philosophy: A Sourcebook.* 2nd ed. Ithaca: Cornell University Press, 2011.
Patch, Andrew. "Leo Strauss on Maimonides' Prophetology." *Review of Politics* 66, no. 1 (2004): 83–104.
Pines, Shlomo. "Truth and Falsehood versus Good and Evil: A Study in Jewish and General Philosophy in Connection with *The Guide of the Perplexed* I, 2." In *Studies in Maimonides*, ed. I. Twersky, 95–157. Cambridge, MA: Harvard University Press, 1990.
―――. "On Leo Strauss." Trans. Aryeh Leo Motzkin. *Independent Journal of Philosophy* 5, no. 6 (1988): 169–71. For a Hebrew version, see *Molad* 30, no. 247–48, or n.s., 7, no. 37–38 (1976): 455–57.
―――. "The Limitations of Human Knowledge according to Al-Farabi, ibn Bajja, and Maimonides." In *Studies in Medieval Jewish History and Literature*, ed. I. Twersky, 82–109. Cambridge, MA: Harvard University Press, 1979.
―――. "Spinoza's *Tractatus Theologico-Politicus*, Maimonides, and Kant." *Scripta Hierosolymitana* 20 (1968): 3–54.
―――. "Translator's Introduction: The Philosophic Sources of *The Guide of the Perplexed*." In *The Guide of the Perplexed*, by Moses Maimonides, trans. S. Pines, lvii–cxxxiv. Chicago: University of Chicago Press, 1963.
Prufer, Thomas. "Juxtapositions: Aristotle, Aquinas, Strauss." In *Leo Strauss's Thought: Toward a Critical Engagement*, ed. A. Udoff, 115–21. Boulder, CO: Lynne Rienner, 1991.
Rashkover, Randi L. "Justifying Philosophy and Restoring Revelation: Assessing Strauss's Medieval Return." In *Encountering the Medieval in Modern Jewish Thought*, ed. James A. Diamond and Aaron W. Hughes, 229–57. Leiden: Brill, 2012.
Ravitzky, Aviezer. "Maimonides: Esotericism and Educational Philosophy." In *The Cambridge Companion to Maimonides*, ed. K. Seeskin, 300–23. Cambridge: Cambridge University Press, 2005.
―――. "The Secrets of *The Guide of the Perplexed*: Between the Thirteenth and Twentieth Centuries." In *Studies in Maimonides*, ed. I. Twersky, 159–207. Cambridge, MA: Harvard University Press, 1991. Also in Aviezer Ravitzky, *History and Faith: Studies in Jewish Philosophy* (Amsterdam: J. C. Gieben, 1996), 246–303.
―――. "Samuel Ibn Tibbon and the Esoteric Character of the *Guide of the Perplexed*." *AJS Review* 6 (1981): 87–123. Also in Aviezer Ravitzky, *History and Faith: Studies in Jewish Philosophy* (Amsterdam: J. C. Gieben, 1996), 205–46.
Rechnitzer, Haim O. *Prophecy and the Perfect Political Order: The Political Theology of Leo Strauss* [in Hebrew]. Jerusalem: Mosad Bialik, 2012.
Rethelyi, Mari. "Guttmann's Critique of Strauss's Modernist Approach to Medieval Philosophy: Some Arguments toward a Counter-critique." *Journal of Textual Reasoning* 3, no. 1 (June 2004). http://etext.virginia.edu/journals/volume3/rethelyi.html.
Rosen, Stanley. "Wittgenstein, Strauss, and the Possibility of Philosophy." In *The Elusiveness of the Ordinary*, 135–58. New Haven: Yale University Press, 2002.
―――. "The Golden Apple." In *Metaphysics in Ordinary Language*, 62–80. New Haven: Yale University Press, 1999.
Sabine, George H. "Review of *Persecution and the Art of Writing*, by Leo Strauss." *Ethics* 63 (1953): 220–22.
Samuelson, Norbert M. "Maimonidean Scholarship at the End of the Century: Review Essay." *AJS Review* 26, no. 1 (2002): 93–107.

Sandoz, Ellis. "Medieval Rationalism or Mystic Philosophy? Reflections on the Strauss-Voegelin Correspondence." In *Faith and Political Philosophy: The Correspondence between Leo Strauss and Eric Voegelin*, ed. P. Emberley and B. Cooper, 297–319. University Park: Pennsylvania State University Press, 1993.
Schall, James V. "A Latitude for Statesmanship? Strauss on St. Thomas." In *Leo Strauss: Political Philosopher and Jewish Thinker*, ed. K. L. Deutsch and W. Nicgorski, 211–30. Lanham, MD: Rowman and Littlefield, 1994.
———. "Revelation, Reason and Politics: Catholic Reflexions on Strauss." *Gregorianum* 62 (1981): 349–65, 467–97.
Schwartz, Dov. "Polemical and Esoterical Writing in *The Guide of the Perplexed*: Creation and the Teleological Issue." In *Moses Maimonides (1138–1204): His Religious, Scientific, and Philosophical 'Wirkungsgeschichte' in Different Cultural Contexts*, ed. G. K. Hasselhoff and O. Fraisse, 29–50. Würzburg: Ergon Verlag, 2004.
———. *Contradiction and Concealment in Medieval Jewish Thought* [in Hebrew]. Ramat-Gan, Israel: Bar-Ilan University Press, 2002.
Schweid, Eliezer. "Religion and Philosophy: The Scholarly-Theological Debate between Julius Guttmann and Leo Strauss." *Maimonidean Studies* 1 (1990): 163–95.
Seeskin, Kenneth, ed. *The Cambridge Companion to Maimonides*. Cambridge: Cambridge University Press, 2005.
———. "Appendix: Esotericism and the Limits of Knowledge; A Critique of Leo Strauss." In *Searching for a Distant God: The Legacy of Maimonides*, 177–88. New York: Oxford University Press, 2000.
———. "Maimonides' Conception of Philosophy." In *Leo Strauss and Judaism: Jerusalem and Athens Revisited*, ed. D. Novak, 87–110. Lanham, MD: Rowman and Littlefield, 1996.
Septimus, Bernard. "What Did Maimonides Mean by *Madda*?" In *Me'ah She'arim: Studies in Medieval Jewish Spiritual Life in Memory of Isadore Twersky*, ed. E. Fleischer, G. Blidstein, C. Horowitz, and B. Septimus, 83–110. Jerusalem: Magnes Press, 2001.
Sfez, Gérald. "Maïmonide: L'adresse contre le système." In *Léo Strauss, lecteur de Machiavel: La modernité du mal*, 50–66. Paris: Ellipses, 2003.
Sharpe, Matthew J. "'In the Court of a Great King': Some Remarks on Leo Strauss's Introduction to the *Guide of the Perplexed*." *Sophia* 50 (2011): 141–58.
Sheppard, Eugene R. *Leo Strauss and the Politics of Exile: The Making of a Political Philosopher*. Waltham, MA: Brandeis University Press, 2006.
Smith, Steven B., ed. *The Cambridge Companion to Leo Strauss*. New York: Cambridge University Press, 2009.
———. *Reading Leo Strauss: Politics, Philosophy, Judaism*. Chicago: University of Chicago Press, 2006.
Stern, Josef. "Maimonides' Demonstrations: Principles and Practice." *Medieval Philosophy and Theology* 10 (2001): 47–84.
Strauss, Leo. *Maïmonide*. Ed. and trans. Rémi Brague. Paris: Presses Universitaires de France, 1988; 2nd ed., 2012.
Stroumsa, Sarah. "'From Moses to Moses': Maimonides' Vision of Perfection." In *Maimonides in His World: Portrait of a Mediterranean Thinker*, pp. 153–88. Princeton: Princeton University Press, 2009.
———. "The Political-Religious Context of Maimonides." In *The Trias of Maimonides: Jewish, Arabic, and Ancient Culture of Knowledge*, ed. Georges Tamer, 257–65. Berlin: Walter de Gruyter, 2005.

Tamer, Georges. "The Influence of Medieval Islamic Philosophy on Leo Strauss." Unpublished manuscript, 2004.

———. *Islamische Philosophie und die Krise der Moderne: Das Verhältnis von Leo Strauss zu Alfarabi, Avicenna, und Averroes.* Leiden: E. J. Brill, 2001.

Tanguay, Daniel. *Leo Strauss: An Intellectual Biography.* Trans. Christopher Nadon. New Haven: Yale University Press, 2007.

Tepper, Aryeh. *Theories of Progress in Leo Strauss's Later Writings on Maimonides.* Albany: State University of New York Press, forthcoming [2013].

Twersky, Isadore. "Aspects of Maimonidean Epistemology: Halakhah and Science." In *From Ancient Israel to Modern Judaism: Intellect in Quest of Understanding; Essays in Honor of Marvin Fox,* ed. J. Neusner, E. S. Frerichs, and N. M. Sarna, 3–23. Atlanta: Scholars Press, 1989.

———. *Introduction to the Code of Maimonides (Mishneh Torah).* New Haven: Yale University Press, 1980.

Umar, Yusuf K. "Strauss and Farabi: Persecution, Esotericism, and Political Philosophy." Ph.D. dissertation, University of Calgary, 1987.

Vajda, Georges. "La pensée religieuse de Moïse Maïmonide: Unité ou dualité?" *Cahiers de civilization médiévale* 9 (1966): 29–49.

———. "Review of *The Guide of the Perplexed,* by Moses Maimonides, translated with an introduction and notes by Shlomo Pines, with an introductory essay by Leo Strauss." *Revue des études juives* 123 (1964): 209–16.

Verskin, Alan. "Reading Strauss on Maimonides: A New Approach." *Journal of Textual Reasoning* 3, no. 1 (June 2004). http://etext.virginia.edu/journals/tr/volume3/verskin.html.

Urban, Martina. "Persecution and the Art of Representation: Schocken's Maimonides Anthologies of the 1930s." In *Maimonides and His Heritage,* ed. Idit Dobbs-Weinstein, Lenn E. Goodman, and James Allen Grady, 153–79. Albany: State University of New York Press, 2009.

Weiss, Raymond L. *Maimonides' Ethics: The Encounter of Philosophic and Religious Morality.* Chicago: University of Chicago Press, 1991.

———. "The Adaptation of Philosophic Ethics to a Religious Community: Maimonides' Eight Chapters." *Proceedings of the American Academy for Jewish Research* 54 (1987): 261–87.

Wolfson, Elliot R. "Beneath the Wings of the Great Eagle: Maimonides and Thirteenth-Century Kabbalah." In *Moses Maimonides (1138–1204): His Religious, Scientific, and Philosophical 'Wirkungsgeschichte' in Different Cultural Contexts,* ed. G. K. Hasselhoff and O. Fraisse, 209–38. Würzburg: Ergon Verlag, 2004.

———. *Abraham Abulafia—Kabbalist and Prophet: Hermeneutics, Theosophy, and Theurgy.* Los Angeles: Cherub Press, 2000.

Yaffe, Martin D. "On Leo Strauss's *Philosophy and Law*—Review Essay." *Modern Judaism* 9 (1989): 213–25.

Wurgaft, Benjamin Aldes. "How to Read Maimonides after Heidegger: The Cases of Strauss and Levinas." In *The Cultures of Maimonideanism: New Approaches to the History of Jewish Thought,* ed. James T. Robinson, chap. 15, 353–83. Leiden: Brill, 2009.

Zank, Michael. "Review of Eugene Sheppard, *Leo Strauss and the Politics of Exile: The Making of a Political Philosopher* (Waltham, MA: Brandeis University Press, 2006)." *AJS Review* 22, no. 2 (November 2008): 437–41.

———. "Arousing Suspicion against a Prejudice: Leo Strauss and the Study of Maimonides'

Guide of the Perplexed." In *Moses Maimonides (1138–1204): His Religious, Scientific, and Philosophical 'Wirkungsgeschichte' in Different Cultural Contexts*, ed. G. K. Hasselhoff and O. Fraisse, 549–72. Würzburg: Ergon Verlag, 2004.

Zuckert, Catherine, and Michael Zuckert. *The Truth about Leo Strauss: Political Philosophy and American Democracy*. Chicago: University of Chicago Press, 2006.

Index

Aaron, 83, 520
Abbaye and Raba, 382, 390
Abd-ul-alim, Mr., 245
Abraham, 156–57, 157n49, 213, 298n64, 430, 431n26, 469, 471, 483n237, 485n245, 513, 522, 530, 556n11, 563, 564n24. *See also* Patriarchs
Abraham bar Hiyya, 388–89, 389n139
Abraham ben David of Posquières (Rabad), 336n5, 448, 448n81
Abraham ibn Daud. *See* Ibn Daud, Abraham
Abravanel, Isaac (Abarbanel, Abrabanel), xv, 2, 55, 79–84, 244n142, 352n38, 384–85, 385n127, 414n24, 439n57, 446n75, 559n19, 579–613, 585nn8–10, 587n13, 588n14, 589nn16–17, 591n24, 591nn26–27, 592nn28–29, 593n30, 593nn32–34, 594n36, 595n41, 596n45, 597n47, 600nn50–51, 600n53, 602n56, 603n58, 605nn61–62, 609nn65–66, 611nn73–74, 612n79, 615
Abulafia, Abraham, 439n57
Abulafia, Meir ben Todros ha-Levi, 330n1
Academicians, 311
Adam, 512, 526, 543, 552n3, 593n34
Adler, Eve, 223, 224, 225n10, 226n21, 227n27, 231n57, 239n112, 242n126, 248n152, 257nn207–8, 269
Albarceloni (Isaac ben Reuven), 384n125
Albo, Joseph (Yosef), 251nn171, 318n13, 403n4, 404n6, 415n27, 446n75, 459, 459n136, 515, 515n18, 519n20, 520, 520n21, 559nn17–19, 566n28
Alexander of Aphrodisias, 34, 34n27, 78, 310–12, 310n108, 312n116, 324n29, 352, 410n19, 446n76
Alexander the Great, 486n247
Alfarabi (Abu Nasr al-Farabi). *See* Farabi
Alghazali. *See* Ghazali
Al-Ḥarizi, Judah (Yehuda), 174n2, 233n73, 446n75
Al-Mawardi, Ali ibn Muhammad, 244n142
Alpagus, Andreas, 251n175
Alsheikh, Moses Hayyim, 603n58
Altmann, Alexander, 347n15, 357n56, 372n95
Alvis, Sara Kathleen, 109n38, 323n28, 604n60, 605n62, 608n64, 610n70
Anderson, Fulton B., 110n39
Andrae, Tor, 259n222
Aquinas. *See* Thomas Aquinas (Thomist, Thomism)
Aristotle (Aristotelian, Aristotelianism), xiv, xv n4, xxvii–xxviii, 2–3, 16, 17n14, 18, 20–21, 23–24, 26, 28, 31, 34–36, 62, 65, 80, 83, 94, 98, 103, 109, 113–14, 115n57, 123, 125–26, 132, 135–36, 151, 158, 160, 162n55, 162n55, 164, 167, 179–80, 183, 186, 186n55, 189–91, 189n90, 191n103, 192–94, 196–98, 197n147, 198n150, 202–4, 202nn168–71, 203nn173–74, 207n98, 209–12, 212n222, 217–19, 218nn256–57, 221, 227, 229, 229n41, 230, 233, 249n163, 251, 254, 260–64, 261n232, 264n240, 264n243, 266, 268, 270, 278–79, 278n5, 279n6, 281, 284n20, 284, 286, 286nn28–29, 295n59, 303–4, 304n84, 308n101, 310, 310n108, 312, 312n120, 321n20, 323n28, 327n35,

647

Aristotle (*continued*)
339, 341, 343, 346n11, 347, 347n16, 351, 364, 377–79, 378n105, 381n117, 384, 406, 408–9, 409n18, 414n24, 420, 428, 428n17, 430n23, 431n26, 433, 433n31, 434, 439, 439n57, 445, 445n73, 446n76, 470n177, 472–73, 481, 481n228, 482, 484, 484n239, 489n257, 490, 501, 507, 513, 515n18, 531, 532, 545–47, 548n36, 561, 566n28, 571n10, 575n11, 580–82, 589, 589n17, 591n23, 593n34, 595–98, 595n39, 596n45, 617. See also *falasifa*
Asharites, 321n20
Ashwell, George, 106n30
Atiyeh, George, 106n29
At-Tabari, Ali ibn Rabban (Al-Tabari), 244n142
Avempace. *See* Ibn Bajja, Abu Bakr
Averroes (Ibn Rushd), xv n4, xxvii, 35n29, 111–12, 111n46, 114, 126, 162n55, 164n57, 218, 221, 221n269, 243n134, 244n142, 265n258, 269, 271–74, 271n2, 273n9, 276n1, 278–79, 278n5, 279n6, 285n24, 292, 295n59, 303n81, 318n13, 321n18, 339, 378n105, 394n156, 581n4, 616
Avicenna (Ibn Sina), xv, xv n4, xxvii, 6n7, 24, 27, 31–33, 33n24, 34, 80–81, 107, 113, 216–17, 216nn244–47, 217nn248–49, 217n253, 218n256, 220–21, 225, 225n10, 227n27, 239, 243–44, 243nn130–31, 243nn133–35, 244n137, 244nn141–42, 246, 251–55, 251n172, 251nn174–75, 252n177, 253n187, 254n188, 254n190, 254nn193, 277, 280, 291–92, 291n49, 294, 308n99, 318n13, 323n28, 327, 352, 355n46, 406, 406n11, 566n28, 583n6, 616
Avihu, 520

Bacon, Francis, 110, 110n39, 361n63
Baer, Yiẓḥak (J. F.), 589n17, 591n27, 593, 593n34, 595n39, 595n41, 600n52, 602n57, 611n74
Baḥya ben Asher (Bechai), 603n58
Baḥya ben Joseph ibn Paquda, 345n7; pseudo-Baḥya, 361n64
Bakan, David, Dan Merkur, and David S. Weiss, 287n30, 452n93
Balling, Peter, 162n55

Barker, Ernest, 580n3, 583n6
Baron, Salo W., 341–42, 354n45, 355n46, 355n48, 362n67, 369n84, 615
Bartlett, Gabriel, and Svetozar Minkov, 314, 630
Bartlett, Robert, 275, 629
Bellarmine, Robert, 610n70
Ben David, Abraham. *See* Ibn Daud, Abraham
Berman, Lawrence V., 400n1
Bildad, 366–67, 524n24
Birkenhead, Lord (Frederick Smith, 2nd Earl), xxiv n18
Black, Deborah L., 571n10
Blackman, Mrs. M. C., 579n1
Blau, Ludwig, 385n129, 388n137
Blidstein, Gerald, 457n113
Boethius, 368n80
Bolotin, David, 91
Börne, Ludwig, 193n124
Brague, Rémi, 249n164, 255n194, 275–76, 276n1, 282n13, 286n25, 308n98, 309n102, 316n5, 323n28, 331n2, 354n44, 368n80, 387n135, 400n1, 402n2, 408n14, 409n18, 412n21, 415n25, 519n20
Brandes, Georg, 193n124
Bruell, Christopher, 91, 275
Bruni, Leonardo, 598n48, 612
Buber, Martin, xx n14, 603n58
Bucolics, 595, 613
Burgh, Albert, 132
Bush, George W., xxiii
Butterworth, Charles E., 287n32, 345n9
Buxtorf, Johannes, the Younger, 174n2

Calvin, John, 108n35, 143n33, 144, 163n66, 172, 172n71, 600, 600n52
Caro, Joseph, 122n1, 334n4
Cassirer, Ernst, 23n17
Chisdai ha-Levi, 273n11
Chrysippus, 311
Churchill, Winston, xxiv, xxiv n18
Cicero, Marcus Tullius, 33, 114, 220, 220n267, 259n218, 311, 311nn110–11, 324n129, 399
Clement of Alexandria, 431n26
Cohen, Boaz, 330n1, 340n7
Cohen, Hermann, xi n1, xiii, xxi–xxii,

xxii n16, 1n1, 2–3, 12, 17–24, 17n14,
23n17, 26, 28–29, 39, 93, 93nn4–5,
97, 101, 101n22, 122n1, 173–222, 175n4,
177n11, 178nn18–19, 178n23, 179n28,
180n29, 184n53, 184n58, 185n60,
187n70, 188n82, 188n84, 189n87,
189n90, 190n94, 190n100, 191nn102–5,
192n107, 193n122, 193n126, 195n136,
197n147, 201n165, 202n168, 202n171,
203nn175–76, 204nn180–81, 205n187,
205n189, 207n198, 209n206, 210n207,
211n215, 219n263, 221n272, 222n274,
260, 260nn225–27, 260n229, 261n232,
262–63, 262n234, 263n237, 264n240,
266, 267, 305n88, 429n21
Cohen, Jonathan, 101n20
Comtino, Mordechai ben Eliezer, 402n2
Cremona. *See* Gerard of Cremona
Crescas, Asher, 352n38, 446n75, 587n13
Crescas, Hasdai, 115n57, 318n13, 352n39
Cropsey, Joseph, xi n1, 441, 475, 475n202,
490, 490n262, 569, 572
Cynics, 613

Dafoe, Daniel, 106n29
Daniel, 376, 460nn137–38, 521
Dante Alighieri, 482, 482n232
David (King), 335, 420, 533, 590, 602
David ben Jehuda (Messer) Leon. *See*
Messer Leon, David ben Judah
Davidson, Herbert A., 336n5, 400n1, 548n36
Davidson, Israel, 330n1
de Boer, T. J., 164n57
Descartes, René, 98, 149, 158–64, 159n50,
160n51, 161nn53–54, 164n57
Diesendruck, Zevi, 223n1, 224n3, 244n141,
354n43
Dieterici, Friedrich Heinrich, 239n112,
284n20, 286n25
Diogenes Laertius, 324n29

Efodi (Profiat Duran), 244n142, 352n38,
361n65, 446n75, 587n13, 593n34
Efros, Israel, 281n12, 282n13, 384n125,
400n1, 408n14, 543n34, 569n1, 571n8,
571n10
Ehrlich, Dror, 459n136
Eisen, Robert, 226n21

Elihu, 321n20, 366–67, 524n24
Elijah, 336, 537
Eliphaz, 366–67, 524n24
Elukin, Jonathan, 485n241
Ennius the Vestal, 259n218
Epicurus (Epicurean, Epicureanism),
124–25, 299, 321n20, 331n2, 489, 489n257
Eusebius, 431n26
Eve, 526
Ezekiel, 65, 315, 346, 355, 366, 414n24,
415n27, 436, 444, 460n138, 461, 461n139,
474, 496, 496n2, 529

Falaquera, Shem Tov ben Joseph ibn, 216,
216n244, 233n73, 251, 251n175, 256–57,
257n207, 279n6, 289n45, 297n60,
303n82, 305, 305n88, 308n98, 323n28,
327n35, 345n9, 345n36, 352n38, 353n42,
361n65, 380n112, 381n117, 387n134,
395n158, 396n164, 408n11, 446n75,
587n13
falasifa, 80, 215n241, 229–30, 238–39,
239n110, 243, 244n142, 246–47, 247n147,
256–60, 259n223, 261n232, , 262–64,
263n237, 266–78, 266n271, 281, 292,
295n59, 303n81, 321, 321n19, 324, 347n16,
394n156, 581n5. *See also* Aristotle (Aristotelian, Aristotelianism)
Farabi (Abu Nasr al-Farabi, Alfarabi, al-
Farabi), xiv, xv n4, xix n19, xxvii, 24–25,
27, 31–39, 34n26, 35n29, 52, 80–81, 83,
92n2, 107, 113, 220n266, 221, 225, 227n27,
239, 239nn111–12, 240n113, 241–44,
241n125, 243n130, 244n141, 247, 249,
255, 255nn194–95, 257, 275–313, 278n5,
279nn6–7, 280nn8–9, 281n11, 284n20,
285nn21–24, 286nn25–29, 288n35,
291n47, 292n54, 293n56, 295n59,
298n66, 302n80, 303n81, 304n84,
305n87, 308n98, 308n100, 309n103,
312n120, 322–24, 322n26, 323n28,
327n35, 345n9, 351, 351n36, 367n79,
380n112, 400n1, 405n9, 408, 409n16,
412n21, 413n23, 431n26, 434, 434nn32–33,
439n57, 446n76, 482n233, 501, 581n4,
583, 596n45
Fenton, Paul, 483n237
Fichte, Johann Gottlieb, 177, 177n12

Ficino, Marsilio, 580n3
Forbes, Hugh Donald, 120
Fox, Marvin, 27n21, 442n60, 549n37
Fradkin, Hillel, 91, 102n23, 275, 517n19
Frankel, Shabtai, 336n6
Freudenthal, Jacob, 144n35, 172n71
Funkenstein, Amos, 603n58
Fürstenthal, Raphael, 123n2, 354n44

Gadamer, Hans-Georg, 300n71
Galen, of Pergamon, 324n29
Galileo Galilei, 98
Gauthier, Leon, 35n29, 274n13
Gebhardt, Carl, 119–20, 144n34
Gellman, J. I., 485n241
Gerard of Cremona, 301n74
Gersonides (Levi ben Gershom), xxvii, 166n61, 226n21, 251n171, 269, 271, 318n13, 446n75, 588n14, 603n58
Ghazali (Al-Ghazali, Alghazali), 243n134, 340, 340n7, 582
Ginzberg, Louis, 384n125
Glatzer, Nahum N., xx, xx n14, xxi, xxi n15, 426n12
Gogarten, Friedrich, 155n48
Goldin, Judah, 426n12
Goldwin, Robert A., 419, 419n3
Goldziher, Ignaz, 361n64
Gottheil, Richard, 282n14, 286n29
Gottschalk, Dr., 17n14
Graetz, Heinrich, 382n119
Green, Kenneth Hart xi n1, xiv n3, xvii n7, xix n11, xxii n16, 26n18, 155n48, 209n206, 216n244, 244n142, 276n1, 314, 316n5, 341–42, 382n119, 439n57, 515n18, 592n29, 615
Guttmann, Jacob, 320n16, 585n8, 605n62
Guttmann, Julius, xxi n15, 101, 101n20, 103, 317n9, 320n16, 350n29
Guttmann, Moritz M., 298n63

Halevi, Judah (Yehuda), xxvii, 102, 112, 115n57, 409n18, 431n26
Halkin, Abraham S., 497
Halper, Yehuda, 417
Hananiah, son of Azzur, 524n24
Harvey, Steven, 101n20, 288n35, 340n7
Harvey, Warren Zev, 461n139

Hegel, G.W.F., 5, 110, 191
Heidegger, Martin, xxi–xxii, xxv–xxvi, 22, 23n17, 25, 29
Heine, Heinrich, 193n124
Heinemann, Heinrich, 603n58
Heinemann, Isaac (Yizḥak), 115, 115n57, 347n16, 603n58
Hezekiah, 167n62, 602
Hillel the Elder, 426, 426n12
Himmelfarb, Gertrude, 6, 7n8
Hirsch, Samson Raphael, 184n58, 603n58
Hitler, Adolf, xx n14, 25, 104. *See also* Nazis
Hobbes, Thomas, xv n4
Huggard, E. M., 379n109
Hyamson, Moses, 41–43, 69, 329–40, 330n1, 331n2 341, 343n1, 368n80, 385n129, 551n2, 552n3, 566n28

Ibn Bajja, Abu Bakr (Avempace), xv n4, 113n49, 244n142, 304, 304n84, 394n156
Ibn Daud, Abraham, 156, 157n49, 282n14
Ibn Ezra, Abraham, 131, 166n61, 603n58, 607, 608n63
Ibn Falaquera, Shem Tov ben Joseph. *See* Falaquera, Shem Tov ben Joseph ibn
Ibn Janāḥ, Jonah (Abu 'l Walid Marwan), 518, 519n20, 537
Ibn Kaspi, Joseph, 233n73, 360, 374n99, 439n57, 446n75, 585n8
Ibn Khaldun, 246n145
Ibn Rushd. *See* Averroes
Ibn Sina. *See* Avicenna
Ibn Tibbon, Moses, 288n35, 402n2, 556n11
Ibn Tibbon, Samuel, xv n4, 35, 35n29, 123n2, 174n2, 233n73, 272n6, 280, 280n8, 282n13, 330n1, 342, 348n19, 352n38, 381n117, 385n127, 391n145, 400n1, 407n12, 408n14, 434n32, 439n57, 446n75, 463n148, 507, 507n14, 517n19, 587n13
Ibn Tufayl, Abu Bakr Muhammad, 106, 106nn29–30, 113n49, 243n130, 244n142
Ibn Wahshiyya, Abu Bakr Ahmad, 483n237
Ibn Yunus, Abu Bisr Matta, 310n108, 324n29
Idel, Moshe, 439n57
Isaiah, 304n83, 307, 355, 366, 415n27, 458–61, 458nn122–29, 459n132,

459nn135–36, 460nn137–38, 461n139, 464, 488n256, 518, 519n20, 520–21, 520n21, 529, 533, 536, 539, 591n26, 592, 593n31
Ishaq, Abu, the Sabian, 74, 384, 415, 570, 570n4

Jaffa, Harry V., 33n24
Jesus, 169n67, 333, 426n12
Jethro, 83, 589, 589n16
Jewish mystics. *See* Kabbalah (Kabbalists, Jewish mystics)
Job, 168, 316n4, 321n20, 366–67, 460n138, 461, 494, 524, 524n24, 546, 576
Joel, 533, 591n26
Joel, Issachar, 123n2, 174n2, 343n1, 439n57, 591n26
Joel, Manuel, 120, 122n1, 126n7, 141n25, 164n57, 165n59
John of Salisbury, 599n49, 605n62, 610n72
Joseph (Yosef) ben Judah ibn Shamun of Centa, 66, 353–54, 438–39, 439n57, 484n239, 500–501, 505
Joseph (Yosef) ibn Gabir, 289n45, 397n168
Josephus, 431n26, 593n34, 594, 605n62, 611–13, 611nn74–76
Joshua, 166n61, 585n9, 588n14, 592, 595n37, 605, 605n62, 609n67
Joshua ben Judah (Jeshua ben Jehuda), 345n7
Josiah, 602
Jospe, Raphael, 439n57
Jotham, 602
Judah, 365, 421, 593n33, 602
Judah ha-Nasi (Rabbi), 336, 421n5
Justinianus, Augustinus, 174n2

Kabbalah (Kabbalists, Jewish mystics), xiii, xviii, 4–5, 79, 99, 100, 103, 103n24, 355–56, 382n119, 439n57, 454n100, 469n175, 479–80, 480n224
Kafah (Kafih, Kapach), Yosef (Joseph), 174n2, 331n2, 387n135, 402n2, 439n57, 569n1
Kafka, Franz, xx n14
kalam, 123–25, 164n57, 167, 215n241, 246, 289, 320, 345–46, 345n9, 361n64, 369, 428n17, 435, 435n41, 449n81, 472, 472n186, 473, 486n247, 493, 500, 507, 531, 542, 542n33, 547. See also *mutakallimun*
Kant, Immanuel, 2, 17n14, 18, 23n17, 93–94, 93n3, 154, 184n58, 185, 185n59, 189–92, 189n90, 227, 472n186
Karaites (Karaism), 345n7, 456n112, 457, 457n113, 517, 520
Kaufmann, David, 101, 429n21
Kellner, Menachem, 227n21, 465n151, 498n7, 585n10
Kimchi, David, 166n61
Klatzkin, Jacob, 288n35
Klein, Jacob, xvii n6, xx n13, xxi n15, 6n7, 431n26, 616
Kojève, Alexandre, 423n8
Kraemer, Joel, 400n1, 414n24, 435n41, 507n14, 508n15, 524n24, 591n23
Kramer, Jacob, 165n59
Kraus, Paul, 35n29, 255n194, 279n7, 280n10, 581n4
Kristol, Irving, 6–7, 7n8

Lamm, Herbert, 441
Lampert, Laurence, xvii n6
Landauer, Samuel, 243n133
Lasker, Daniel J., 457n113
Lawee, Eric, 585n8, 588n14, 591n27, 593n30, 600n52, 611n74, 612n79
Leibniz, Gottfried Wilhelm, 2, 18, 379, 379n109
Lenzner, Steven, 389n139
Lerner, Ralph, 272n6, 285n24, 292nn53–54, 322n26, 394n156, 418, 459n136, 526n26, 539n32, 555n10, 560n20
Levi ben Gershom. *See* Gersonides
Lewy, Hans, 259n233
Loew, Judah ben Bezalel, of Prague, 592n29
Lorberbaum, Menachem, 288n35
Lucas, Jean Maximilian, 144n35
Lucretius, 124, 125n5
Luther, Martin, 111, 184

Mahdi, Muhsin, 285n24, 288n35, 367n79, 482, 482n233, 581n4
Maimon, Salomon, 2, 18, 67, 326n34
Maimonides, Moses, *passim*
Manser, G. M., 274n13

Mantino, Jacob, 174n2
Maresius, Samuel, 163n56
Marmura, Michael, 217n249, 218n256
Marsilius of Padua, xxvii, 76, 114, 571, 571n13, 597n46
Martin, Alfred von, 612n77
Marx, Alexander, 277n2, 280n8, 330, 330n1, 434n32, 507n14, 526n26
Meier, Heinrich, xi n1, xv–xvii, xix n11, xxviii, xxi n15, xxviii, 91, 173–74, 173n1, 224, 276, 305n88, 314–15, 316n5, 455n104, 492
Melamed, Avraham, 431n26, 589nn16–17, 597n47
Menasseh ben Israel, 600n53, 603n58
Mendelssohn, Moses, 74n41, 103, 106, 106n31, 111, 122n1, 271n1, 282n14, 288n35, 402n2, 403n5
Merkur, Dan. *See* Bakan, David, Dan Merkur, and David S. Weiss
Messer Leon, David ben Judah, 345n7
Meyerhof, Max, 279n6
Milton, John, 605n62
Minkov, Svetozar. *See* Bartlett, Gabriel, and Svetozar Minkov
Montesquieu, 601n54
Moore, Ian Alexander. *See* Yaffe, Martin D., and Ian Alexander Moore
Morais, Sabato, 330n1
Moses, 33, 66, 68–69, 77, 83, 130–32, 130n12, 134, 144–45, 148n43, 155, 167, 184, 209, 213–14, 232–35, 233n69, 233n73, 244n142, 291, 292n54, 293, 295, 297–98, 298n64, 298n66, 299, 306–7, 309, 320n17, 348, 352, 364, 368n80, 388, 397, 402n2, 420, 428n17, 431n26, 446, 451, 458, 458n114, 459, 459n133, 459n136, 460, 460nn137–38, 461, 463n147, 469, 479, 479nn219–20, 482, 482n232, 494, 512–13, 520–22, 520n21, 525–27, 529, 538, 542, 552n3, 553, 559–60, 559n19, 562, 565–66, 575, 582, 585n10, 589–90, 590n21, 605n62, 609, 609n67, 611, 613
Moses of Burgos, 103, 103n24, 330n1
Moses of Coucy, 603n58
Motzkin, Aryeh Leo, 275, 417, 442n6
mutakallimun, 114, 345, 345n7, 472n188. *See also kalam*

Muʿtazilites, 292n54, 320, 321n20
Munk, Salomon, 31, 55, 101, 109n37, 120, 123n2, 174n2, 221, 221n268, 229n44, 233n73, 244n142, 278, 278n4, 293n56, 300nn69–70, 304, 304n84, 316n6, 317n9, 354n44, 370n90, 374n99, 379, 381n117, 414n24, 415n25

Nadav, 520
Nagy, A., 279n6
Naḥmanides, 603n58, 604n59, 608n63
Nahon, Gérard, 275
Najjar, Fauzi M., 288n35, 400n1
Narboni, Moses, 234n75, 244n142, 394n156, 446n75
Nazis, xxiv, 25, 224, 592n29. *See also* Hitler, Adolf
Nebuchadnezzar, 533
Neo-Kantianism (neo-Kantian), xi n1, xiii, xxi–xxii, 17n14, 24
neo-Platonism (neo-Platonic, neo-Platonist), xv n4, 62, 260, 278, 281, 433–34, 488, 490, 541
Neo-Pythagoreanism, 259
Neo-Thomism, 104
Newton, Isaac, 98, 103n24, 191, 191n105
Nicholas of Lyra (Nicolaus de Lyra), 605, 605n62, 608
Nicolai, Friedrich, 177, 177n12
Nietzsche, Friedrich, xxv–xxvi, 29, 33, 36, 64, 194n127
Nissim Gaon, 384n125
Novak, David, 459n136

Ockley, Simon, 106n30
Ofek, Yiftach, 572, 615, 631
Onkelos (Onqelos) the Proselyte (the Stranger), 450n84, 461, 461n140, 505, 505n11, 514, 530–31

Pangle, Thomas L., 314
Parens, Joshua, 217n249
Patriarchs, 297–98, 298n64, 521–22, 542, 585n10, 605n62
Paul (Apostle), 221
Paulus of Burgos (Paulus Burgensis), 605n62, 608, 608n64
Peritz, Moritz, 394n156

Perlmutter, H.G., and S. Rabinowitz (rabbis), 441
Pharisees, 132
Philo Judaeus of Alexandria, 259, 259n223, 431n26
Pico della Mirandola, 580n3
Pines, Shlomo (Salomon), xix n10, 34n26, 63, 113n49, 146n39, 174n2, 229n43, 233n73, 249n164, 278n5, 292n54, 300nn69–70, 307n97, 308n99, 310n108, 311n109, 314, 318n11, 320nn16–17, 342–43, 381n117, 418, 429n20, 431n26, 436n43, 439n57, 442n60, 442n62, 445n72, 446n76, 455n104, 481n228, 482n232, 483, 483n236, 485n241, 486n247, 507n14, 519n20, 523n23, 566n28, 580n2
Plato (Platonic, Platonism), xiv, xvii n6, xix, xix n10, xxviii, 5, 6n7, 17n14, 18, 19n15, 20–26, 28, 31–33, 33n24, 35–37, 35n28, 39–41, 45, 62, 80–81, 83, 104, 109, 113, 115, 137, 178n23, 179–80, 179n27, 180n29, 190, 190n94, 191–205, 191n101, 199nn153–55, 201n162, 209, 209n206, 211, 217–22, 218n256, 219n262, 251, 251n175, 254–66, 254n193, 255nn194–95, 256n204, 257n207, 257n209, 261n232, 263n237, 264nn240–43, 265n264, 270, 277, 279–81, 277n2, 278n5, 279n6, 286n28, 287, 289–90, 295n59, 298, 300–306, 303n81, 304n84, 308, 308n99, 310n108, 311–13, 312n120, 321, 321n18, 323n28, 324, 324n29, 327n35, 345n9, 351, 362, 367n79, 394nn155–56, 406, 409, 434, 443n64, 530, 546, 574n9, 580–84, 580n3, 588–89, 591n23
Plotinus, 281, 433, 433n31. *See also* neo-Platonism (neo-Platonic, neo-Platonist)
Pocock, Edward, 106n30, 387n135, 415n25
Polish, David, 603n58
Poseidonius, 259n218
Psalmist, 166n61, 547, 602
Pythagoras (Pythagorean), 254n193, 413n23, 445

Raba. *See* Abbaye and Raba
Rabbanites (Rabbinites, Rabbinism), 457, 457n113, 520

Rabinowitz, S. *See* Perlmutter, H.G., and S. Rabinowitz (rabbis)
Rahman, Fazlur, 216n245, 243n134
Rambam (Rabbi Moshe ben Maimon, RMbM), xv n4, 1n1, 174–222 *passim*, 305n88, 435n41. *See also* Maimonides, Moses
Ranke, Leopold von, 96n12
Ravitsky, Aviezer, 603n58
Rashi, 607, 608n63
Razi, Abu Bakr Muhammad ibn Zakariya, 280n10, 489n257
Reagan, Ronald, xiii, 46
Reines, Alvin J., 591n24
Reinhardt, Karl, 220n266, 259n218
Renan, Ernest, 35n29
Rosen, Stanley, 472n186
Rosenthal, Erwin I. J., 278n3, 280n8, 394n156, 412n21, 581n4
Rosenzweig, Franz, xx n14, xxii, 12, 15, 101, 101n22, 103, 139n23, 194, 197, 197n143, 603n58
Roth, Leon, 164n57
Roth, Norman, 431n26
Rumsfeld, Donald, 419n3

Saadia ben Joseph (Yosef) al-Fayyumi ha-Gaon, 292n54, 318n13, 319–20, 320n17, 345n7, 435, 435n41
Sabians (Sabianism), 74, 75, 77, 202n171, 305n88, 384, 415, 460, 460n138, 462, 462n143, 464n149, 481, 481n229, 482–85, 483n235, 483n237, 485nn241–42, 485nn244–45, 497n3, 512, 521, 522–25, 531–32, 544, 570–71, 570n4, 574, 574n5. *See also* Ishaq, Abu, the Sabian
Sacks, Jonathan (Chief Rabbi), 415n27
Sadducees, 132
Sages (talmudic), 146n39, 259n223, 307, 339, 351, 354, 356, 382–83, 387, 387nn134–35, 390–91, 392n151, 414–15, 415n25, 415n27, 431n26, 505, 517, 524, 529–31, 533, 536, 556n11, 559n19, 561–63, 575
Salutati, Coluccio, 612, 612n77
Samuel, 96, 511, 524n24, 595, 605, 605n62
Satnow, Isaac (Satnov, Yiẓḥak), 402n2
Saul, 96, 511, 524n24, 605n62

Scheyer, S., 123n2
Schiller, Friedrich, 192, 192nn10–11
Scholem, Gershom, xiii, xv n4, xviii 70, 99–102, 99n14, 100nn15–19, 103n24, 356n51, 382n119, 455n104, 469n175, 480n224, 591n27, 592n29
Schwarz, Michael, 174n2, 439n57, 506n13
Schwarzschild, Steven, 122n1
Seneca, 593n34, 594–95
Shahrastani, Muhammad ibn Abd al-Karim al-, 244n141
Shem-Tov. *See* Falaquera, Shem Tov ben Joseph ibn
Shem-Tov ben Abraham ibn Gaon, 336n5
Sherira Gaon, 384n125
Sheshet ha-Nasi, 277n2, 583n6
Shi'ites (Shia), 279, 457
Simeon (Shimon) ben Gamaliel, 392, 392n151
Smith, Steven B., 99n14
Socrates (Socratic), 17n14, 18, 21, 23, 28, 46, 46n33 57, 57n35, 59, 62, 190n94, 198–202, 254n193, 261n232, 262, 280–81, 305, 324n29, 351, 367n79, 413n23
Solomon (King), 307, 355, 368n82, 524, 529, 533, 536, 602, 613
Spengler, Oswald, 23n17
Spinoza, Benedict, xi n1, xix n10, 1n1, 2, 11–16, 18, 24, 26, 28, 39, 85 ,107, 115n57, 119–72 *passim*, 122n1, 129n11, 141nn26–27, 143n32, 144n34, 148n43, 150n46, 159n50, 160n51, 162n55, 164nn57–58, 165n59, 166n61, 169n67, 170n69, 172n71, 181, 184, 232, 232n65, 428n17, 583, 583n7, 612, 612n79
Steinschneider, Moritz, 35n29, 218n257, 244n142, 254n191, 255n195, 278n5, 281n12, 345n7
Stern, M., 123n2
Stoics, 311, 324n29. *See also* Chrysippus
Strauss, Leo, *passim*
Strauss, Leo, on Maimonides, supplementary material, xv n4, 6n7
Sunnis, 457
Sunwall, Mark R., 485n241
Swift, Jonathan, 94n8

Tamar, 365
Tamer, Georges, xix n8
Tanguay, Daniel, xix n9, 80n42
Tarcov, Nathan, xvii n7, xxvi n19, 418, 569, 573, 615
Teicher, J. L., 281n11
Telushkin, Joseph, 426n12
Tepper, Aryeh, 439n57, 491, 549n37
Thomas Aquinas (Thomist, Thomism), xviii, 108n35, 111, 143n33, 158, 163n56, 167n62, 321n18, 352, 580, 582, 589n17, 605n62, 609, 609n67, 610n69
Tryneski, John, xvii n7
Tschirnhaus, Ehrenfried Walter von, 287n30
Turker, Mubahat, 281n12, 400n1
Twersky, Isadore, 366n75, 448n81

Udoff, Alan, 17n14
Urbach, Efraim E., 595n41, 602n55, 603n58

Voltaire, 169n67, 177, 186n67, 226, 226n21

Walzer, Richard, 239n112, 412n21
Weiss, David S. *See* Bakan, David, Dan Merkur, and David S. Weiss
Wolff, Christian, 288n35
Wolfson, Elliot R., 469n175
Wolfson, Harry A., 101, 115, 115n57, 330n1, 348n20, 352n39, 375n100, 404n7, 405–6, 406n10, 406n11, 409, 410n20, 413n22, 429n21
Wouk, Herman, 441
Wurgaft, Benjamin Aldes, 209n206

Yaffe, Martin D., 19n15, 74n41, 106n31, 120, 378n105
Yaffe, Martin D., and Ian Alexander Moore, xxxiii, 174

Zadok, 368n80
Zarza, Samuel (Ibn Zarza), 233n73, 446n75
Zeitlin, Solomon, 388n138
Zhou Enlai, xxii
Zophar, 366–67, 524n24
Zuckert, Michael, xxiii n17
Zunz, Leopold, 384n125